THE WORLD BANK

VOLUME ONE
History

THE WORLD BANK
Its First Half Century

DEVESH KAPUR

JOHN P. LEWIS

RICHARD WEBB

BROOKINGS INSTITUTION PRESS
Washington, D.C.

Library of Congress Cataloging-in-Publication data:

Kapur, Devesh, 1959–
The World Bank : its first half century / Devesh Kapur, John P. Lewis, and Richard Webb.
p.   cm.
Includes bibliographical references and index.
ISBN 0-8157-5230-X (set). — ISBN 0-8157-5234-2 (v. 1). — ISBN 0-8157-5236-9 (v. 2)
1. World Bank—History. I. Lewis, John Prior. II. Webb, Richard Charles, 1937–   .
HG3881.5.W57L49   1997
332.1′532′05—dc21   97-21093
                                                                               CIP

9 8 7 6 5 4 3 2 1

The paper used in this publication meets the minimum requirements of the
American National Standard for Information Sciences—Permanence of Paper for
Printed Library Materials, ANSI Z39.48-1984.

Composition by Princeton Editorial Associates
Scottsdale, Arizona, and Roosevelt, New Jersey

Printed by R. R. Donnelley and Sons Co.
Crawfordsville, Indiana

Foreword

IN 1973, in connection with the World Bank's first twenty-five years, Edward Mason and Robert Asher wrote *The World Bank since Bretton Woods,* the first major authorized but independent history of the institution. Some years later, the Bank's retired senior executive, William Diamond, proposed that an overall history of the Bank's first half century be prepared by authors who, like Mason and Asher, would have full access to the Bank's people and papers but would write free of institutional control. It was decided the study should be seated administratively at an external organization, and, as a matter of fresh choice, not tradition, the Bank and the Brookings Institution agreed that, like the study by Mason and Asher, the new project would be based at Brookings.

Again there were to be two authors, but this time one should come from the North, the other from the South. In 1989 John Lewis of Princeton University in the United States and Richard Webb of Peru were recruited. Both had long known the Bank but neither had worked for it at great length. Webb had been on the research staff for five years in the 1970s before returning to Peru as governor of its central bank; Lewis, a veteran of USAID and OECD/DAC, had worked for and with the Bank in various consulting capacities. As research associate to the project, Brookings employed Devesh Kapur, an Indian national then pursuing a Ph.D. in public and international affairs at Princeton's Woodrow Wilson School. By mid-1993 Kapur had become so indispensable and so engaged in the writing that, by common consent, he was graduated to coauthorship.

For two components of this project the authors sought and gratefully accepted reenforcement. The record of the Bank's subsidiary, the International Finance

Corporation, was important but substantially separate from that of the mother institution. Jonas Haralz of Iceland, a World Bank economist earlier in his career and the Nordic executive director on the Bank board in the late 1980s, was well qualified to address the IFC. Robert Wade, originally of New Zealand, later of the Institute of Development Studies in the United Kingdom, and currently of Brown University in the United States, wrote the chapter on the Bank's relationship with the environment.

From the beginning all parties to the project—the authors, the Bank, Brookings, and the international advisory committee recruited to help guide the venture— agreed that along with the main volume of history for which the authors themselves would be responsible, the work should include a second volume (edited by the authors of the first volume) consisting of views of the Bank from various external perspectives. The perspectives—a dozen in number—are those of close observers of the Bank's work and relations with its major shareholders, its interaction with financial markets and its Bretton Woods sister institution, the International Monetary Fund, its standing with the profession of development economics, and country and regional experiences with borrowers.

Brookings extends its thanks to the World Bank for the freedom and accessibility it has afforded the authors and adds its gratitude to all those whose help the authors acknowledge in the preface.

Brookings gratefully acknowledges funding for the project, which was provided in part by The Ford Foundation, The World Bank, The John D. and Catherine T. MacArthur Foundation, Deutsche Bank AG, The Japan Foundation, Japan Center for International Finance, The Life Insurance Association of Japan, The Federation of Bankers Association of Japan, Nikko Securities Company, Ltd., Nomura Securities Company, Ltd., Yamaichi Securities Company, Ltd., Daiwa Securities Company, Ltd., F. L. Smidth & Company A/S (Denmark), Haldor Topsoe A/S (Denmark), Landsvirkjun, The National Power Company (Iceland), Reykjavik Hot Water System (Iceland), Swedish Bankers Association, A/S Veidekke (Norway), Central Bank of Norway, Statkraft SF (Norway), Asea Brown Boveri AS, and Robert S. McNamara.

The views expressed in this book are those of the authors and should not be ascribed to the organizations acknowledged above or to the trustees, officers, or staff members of the Brookings Institution or the World Bank.

MICHAEL H. ARMACOST
President

July 1997
Washington, D.C.

Preface

THE FOREWORD has outlined the general development of the World Bank history project and the focus and organization of the two volumes. We wish here to elaborate a bit. It may be useful to know the division of labor in volume 1. John Lewis was the principal drafter of chapters 8–10, 17, and 18; Richard Webb of chapters 2–7; and Devesh Kapur of chapters 11, 12, and 14–16. Kapur and Lewis collaborated on chapter 1. Robert Wade was chosen to write a chapter on the subject of the bank and environmental protection, not only because of his record as a policy analyst but also because he undertook the assignment without having a position on the issues. He wrote well and covered the subject thoroughly, but the chapter was long and the physical balance of the two volumes was better if we included it in volume 2. Its location there satisfies the concept of volume 2 well enough, but it should be read as an integral component of volume 1, analogous to the chapters on agriculture, poverty, and the social sectors.

Half the contributed chapters of volume 2 focus on the World Bank's relations with particular member countries. Volume 1 grapples even more with these relations. It was clear as we progressed that the Bank's overall experience and performance had to be illustrated by its transactions with individual borrowing countries. We could not possibly discuss the relations with each of them, but neither could we convey the texture of the experience without digging into country cases. We have done so fairly widely, selecting countries arbitrarily if not randomly. The result is a richer view of the record, but a lumpy one. In volume 1, along with fairly intensive discussions of Bank relations with fifteen or so borrowing countries during various portions of the fifty years covered in the story, we have one long chapter on the most challenging geographic region (sub-Saharan Africa) and another on a region (Latin America) that was involved in a particularly traumatic episode (the debt crisis). As a result, treatment of other areas—China is a major example—is thinner than we would have preferred.

We must record one particular regret. The biggest hole in the study's coverage is the Bank's experience since 1990 in eastern Europe and the former Soviet Union. That we would face a problem in this regard was evident when the subject surged into prominence well after our plan for these volumes, and related allocations of time and assignments, had become firm. Although we recruited a highly qualified author to write a chapter on the subject for volume 2, the deadline for submission was not met. By then it was altogether too late to contrive any substitute for the missing material. We apologize to our readers.

We acknowledge some of the volume 2 authors—among them S. Guhan, Catherine Gwin, Jacques Polak, and Nicholas Stern—whose final drafts were completed long before volume 1 was finished.

The principal authors are most grateful to the World Bank for the combination of access and independence they have been afforded. It is hard to think of another instance in which a public or private institution has made its personnel, present and past, as well as its documents and files (recent as well as earlier, most of them nonpublic, many still explicitly confidential) so freely accessible to a group of outsiders and then exercised virtually no control over the conclusions of the research and the resulting publication.

This is by no means to say that Bank people approved our work in all instances. Many objected to the drafts we presented and wrote dissenting commentaries that were enlightening. But there was no instance in which the Bank sought to overrule one of our interpretations.

From the beginning the Brookings Institution also afforded us a very large measure of autonomy. What it and the Bank regretted was the length of time the study consumed. Like our two principal sponsors, we started out expecting the entire exercise to occupy four or five years instead of the more than seven that it finally consumed, and there were extra costs, opportunity and otherwise, to seeing it through. But there was no good way to anticipate how long a thorough job would take. Although not disagreeing much with the conclusions of Edward Mason and Robert Asher's *The World Bank since Bretton Woods*, which was published in 1973, we needed to address various issues that had their roots at the Bank's inception. That meant twice as much time to cover. And in its second quarter century the Bank had become more complex: its emphases had changed, and its membership, clientele, and staff and the variety of its portfolio, as well as the span of its external relations, had grown exponentially. Moreover, a researcher needed to be careful. As we pursued the rare opportunity to look into the recesses of the institution, it often took several trial drafts to get our narrative straight.

In one respect our exceptional access to internal Bank sources skewed the selection of subject matter and references. Historians of the Bank are bound to deal in some measure with the political, economic, geographic, and cultural contexts in which the institution has operated. Some senior Bank personnel urged more attention to these aspects, and some academic readers would have preferred further citation of the nonofficial studies that bear upon many facets of the present work. As members of the nonofficial research community ourselves, we sympathized with such views. Yet if one really respects these studies, it is clear that no history of the World Bank can pretend to be an adequate review of issues involving general development and development policy. Besides, our comparative advantage was to tell outsiders some of the content of internal Bank thinking and debate that they cannot readily obtain elsewhere.

Our research method has been commonplace: we conducted hundreds of interviews; read countless memoranda, minutes, reports, and other materials; traveled to developing countries to investigate Bank operations on site; and cross-referenced readers' seminars and comments. Bank staff members' support for the project was uneven. Some did not welcome intrusions on their work or thought the time was inappropriate for investigative reporting or simply lacked interest. Some forgot the research was under way. But these were far outnumbered by the many who were curious and responsive and volunteered their help.

We do have some complaints. Although we benefited greatly from the Bank's extensive and admirably managed archives, we suffered, as will other researchers, from the institution's lack of a clear policy about ownership of officers' personal files. Some senior executives of the Bank have, upon retirement, taken with them large quantities of papers that by rights, it seems to us, should remain with the institution. We were fortunate (and grateful) to gain access to some of these files. But the policy should be clarified. In addition, in its internal correspondence the Bank uses the classification "confidential" rather freely. This is understandable for facilitating operations, although greater restraint would be appropriate. What is less excusable is that there has been no regular regime for declassifying papers after a specified time has passed or some other marker has been reached.

In our work we have been counseled by two worthy committees. The first was a formal advisory committee formed at the start of the project that had three meetings and continued to comment on drafts and correspond with the authors. It consisted of Abdlatif Al-Hamad, Rodrigo Botero, Robert Cassen, William Diamond, Crauford Goodwin, Catherine Gwin, Gerald Helleiner, Takashi Hosomi, the late Philip Ndegwa, Widjojo Nitisastro, I. G. Patel, Helga Steeg, and John Williamson. The second ("guidance and closure") group was formed by Brookings to assist us in the final stages. It met quarterly during the later years of the project and consisted of William Diamond and Gerald Helleiner together with Jonas Haralz and Mervyn Weiner. We extend many thanks to the members of both committees.

At Brookings, we are grateful to former president Bruce MacLaury and former Foreign Policy Studies director John Steinbruner. For editorial work, we thank the staff of the Brookings Institution Press, Sam Allen, and Princeton Editorial Associates, and for verification, Christopher Dall, Maya Dragicevic, Gary Gordon, and Alexander Ratz. The volumes were typeset and indexed by Princeton Editorial Associates. In and around the Bank we are indebted to Jochen Kraske, before and after he became Bank historian, and to the godfather of the project, William Diamond, who has never lost concerned interest in it. The regional and joint Bank-Fund libraries, the Offices of the Secretary and General Counsel, the Operations Evaluation Department, and the Bank's archives under Charles Ziegler are among the units to which we owe particular thanks.

We would especially like to thank the staff at the Executive Director's Library (now renamed the Board Resources Center) under Kenlee Ray: Michael Dompas, Andrea Nash, and Herve Tien-Sing Young. We are also most grateful to Charles McCaskill for his help in steering us through the maze of data on the Bank's operations and William Silverman on personnel data. Concetta DeNaro and William Katzenstein (both in the Planning and Budget Department) also assisted our access to data.

We much appreciate the counsel of our predecessor, Robert Asher. It is impossible to name all the people of the Bank, of various vintages, who have helped. But we must list those who were exceptionally generous with their time and attention: Warren Baum, Robert Calderisi, Barber Conable, Richard Demuth, Stephen Eccles, Nicholas Hope, S. Shahid Husain, Benjamin King, Burke Knapp, David Knox, Robert McNamara, Barbara Opper, Guy Pierre Pfeffermann, Eugene Rotberg, Ibrahim Shihata, Ernest Stern, Willi Wapenhans, Christopher Willoughby, and Peter Wright.

We also gratefully acknowledge the help of these other past or present Bank personnel and executive directors: Yoshiaki Abe, James Adams, Bilsel Alisbah, Gerald Alter, Robert Ayres, Jean Baneth, Bernard Bell, Munir Benjenk, Hans Binswanger, Nancy Birdsall, Shirley Boskey, Pieter Bottelier, Mark Bowyer, Aron Broches, Shahid Javed Burki, Sven Burmester, Elkyn Chaparro, Roger Chaufournier, Russell Cheetham, S.H. Choi, Armeane Choksi, Lief Christoffersen, Anthony Churchill, A.W. Clausen, Kevin Cleaver, Roberto Cuca, P. N. Damry, Stephen Denning, Kemal Dervis, Dennis De Tray, Shantayanan Devarajan, Ashok Dhareshwar, Graham Donaldson, Robert Drysdale, Stanley Fischer, Edward Fried, Marie Gallup, Michael Gillette, Joseph Goldberg, Melvin Goldman, Mohan Gopalan Gopal, Julian Grenfell, Enzo Grilli, Ann Hamilton, Marianne Hang, Randolph Harris, James Harrison, John Holsen, David Hopper, Ishrat Husain, Gregory Ingram, Paul Isenman, Ruth Jacoby, Bimal Jalan, Frederick Jasperson, Edward V. K. Jaycox, William Jones, Charlotte Jones-Carroll, Andrew Kamarck, Ravi Kanbur, Robert Kaplan, Shiv Kapur, Martin Karcher, Gautam Kasi, Basil Kavalsky, James Kearns, Timothy King, Ciao Koch-Weser, K. P. Krishnan, Anne

Krueger, Olivier Lafourcade, Luis Landau, Kenneth Lay, Mark Leiserson, Enrique Lerdau, Robert Liebenthal, Johannes Linn, Richard Lynn, Dirk Mattheisen, Oey Meesook, Paul Meo, Marisela Montoliu, Ricardo Moran, Gobind Nankani, Binod Nayak, Julio Nogues, Lester Nurick, Michel Petit, Robert Picciotto, Lewis Preston, V. S. Raghavan, V. Rajagopalan, Luis Ramirez, D. C. Rao, Martin Ravallion, Christopher Redford, Helena Ribe, Peter Richardson, Ronald Ridker, Andres Rigo, William Ryrie, Francisco Sagasti, Joanne Salop, Hugh Scott, Marcelo Selowsky, Alexander Shakow, John Shilling, Gerardo Sicat, Richard Skolnik, Parita Soebsaeng, Davidson Sommers, Rainer Steckhan, Ashok Subramanian, Sachi Takeda, Wilfred Thalwitz, Rene Vandendries, Adriaan Verspoor, Paulo Vicira Da Cunha, Frank Vogl, Harry Walters, Dennis Whittle, D. Joseph Wood, Ngaire Woods, Hans Wyss, Lorene Yap, Montague Yudelman, and Manuel Zymelman.

Among the non-Bank people consulted, we acknowledge, in particular, Edward Bernstein, David Cole, Vijay Jagannadakan, Alexander Kafka, Gustav Papanek, Judith Tendler, and Paul Volcker.

The project has had a very small staff to whom the authors are greatly indebted and who have served mostly in series: as secretary–office manager–research assistant: Polly Buechel, Laura Powell, Deborah Jaffe, Alison Bishop, Seiko Kyan, and Kurt Lindblom; as research assistants: Karen Semkow, Chris Watkins, David Brindley, Esther Benjamin, and Sachiko Kataoka.

Despite all the help, final responsibility for the outcome lies with the authors.

Contents of Volume One

Contents of Volume Two

ONE

Introduction

SOME SEE the twentieth century as roughly divided in the middle. They see the first half as an era of imperialism, economic fluctuation and collapse, and massive global violence; the second half as a period of less trauma. Although the latter has been replete with searing regional wars and harsh rivalry between the cold war's Western and Eastern blocs, broad-scale peace has been preserved. Vast nations have become independent, and, despite gross, sometimes worsening, inequalities, average real incomes, health, life spans, and levels of schooling have risen in much of the world, including many of the poor countries of Latin America, Asia, and Africa, collectively referred to as "the third world," during the decades of East-West rivalry. It is in this world that governments have tried to engineer development. Those intervening have included not only governments of the areas themselves but also external states acting through their own bilateral agencies and various multilateral institutions that governments have jointly sponsored and partly owned. The formation of such multilaterals surged after World War II, and many of those created, whether or not beleaguered, have endured.

The present work is about one of the postwar multilaterals that started quietly but that by the 1990s (whatever its future) had become one of the strongest of the group: the International Bank for Reconstruction and Development, commonly known as the World Bank. To facilitate the telling of the Bank's story, it is useful to identify the defining characteristics that would resonate during the Bank's first half century, shaping the experience throughout and in some instances changing it considerably.

Abiding Traits of the First Multilateral Development Bank

The new IBRD, the first "Multilateral Development Bank," was born in 1944 and opened its doors in 1946. It was a *public sector* institution. Then as now public affairs tended to be more highlighted in social discourse than private affairs. But this public institution was peculiarly linked to the private sector and private resources. Moreover (a distinguishable point, we shall be saying), the public sector World Bank would always appreciate the efficiency of self-adjusting markets for much of society's detailed economic decisionmaking.

In a world dominated by nation-states, the new Bank was indeed a multilateral: it was owned and governed by national governments, and its clients were governments, but it was not formally or legally the creature of any one of them. Its owners did not like the thought of the Bank being "above" them. They were the principals, and it was their agent. But, like a variety of post–World War II constructs, including its sister, the International Monetary Fund, the Bank was an intergovernmental cooperative.

As to governance, the Bretton Woods multilaterals were rooted in political realism. The national representatives who drew up the Bank and the Fund, unlike their counterparts who formulated the United Nations General Assembly at San Francisco a year later, did not follow the juridical theory that all states, large and small, rich and poor, were equal. The founders vested predominant ownership and control in the economically more powerful countries, which, it appeared, would have been unwilling to delegate as much voice and as many resources to the Bretton Woods institutions had the case been otherwise.

Although the World Bank received less attention than its IMF "sister" at Bretton Woods, it became, for many, the world's premier economic multilateral. From the outset, the Bank's subject matter covered a broader span than that of the Fund, and over the decades, it expanded. Early on, events bumped the Bank aside from the first of its two mandates ("reconstruction") and prompted a determined commitment to development. Geographically speaking, this was a commitment across the totality of those economically developing countries that joined the Bank and was in contrast, for example, to the limited spatial terrain of the regional development banks that would begin to appear about 1960. At the same time, the Bank had characteristics that outstripped those of such a universal multilateral as the United Nations Development Program (UNDP). The Bank brought to its client countries not only intellectual products—ideas, information, institutional assistance, and policy influence—but also substantial flows of financial resources. Furthermore, the Bank could get such resources through channels that were fairly accessible politically. In the first place, with the wealthier-country governments contributing more in the way of national guarantees than direct finance, the Bank got most of the resources for its IBRD loans from private financial markets content to invest in IBRD bonds. Such operations inflicted minimal pain on taxpayers in the "donor" countries. In the second place, the Bank's concessional transfers—that is, the International Development Association (IDA) credits (begun in 1960) that *did* have to be funded out of member governments' national budgets—were, in the eyes of reluctant foreign-aid givers, still a safer bet than multilateral programs subject to one-flag, one-vote governance.

In the first fifty years, the Bank did not begin to escape the charge that the United States had not only the heaviest weight but, compared with the legalities, a disproportionate one in the governance of the institution. At the outset, especially after the second hegemon—the Soviet Union— withdrew itself from consideration for Bank membership, the weighting could not have been otherwise.[1] As the world emerged from World War II, when the new practice of national income accounting was just beginning, the United States was estimated to be earning an extraordinary fraction of global real income, and its exports dominated trade. Against a very mixed history on the matter, the United States projected international economic leadership that inclined toward trade openness. Its currency was the only major one yet convertible, and to repair the breakdown of private capital flows in the 1930s, it initiated an era of government-arranged transfers. Substantial fractions of these tranfers (as the 1960s approached) were meant to be concessional, for less creditworthy countries and less self-liquidating activities.

In the World Bank specifically, these circumstances created competing tensions about and involving the United States. From 1960 onward, American governments of whatever party and presidency would have a "burden-sharing" bias, seeking, when feasible, to scale down relative U.S. financial inputs to Bank activities, without diminishing the U.S. voice. Partisans of the United States sometimes argued that the country, as quasi boss of the Bank, was not a bad hegemon, as hegemons go. But the same partisans were unlikely to emphasize the windfall of low-cost influence that Bank dominance gave the United States, especially when the Bank's lead carried along other, including bilateral, donors with it. Within the Bank, however, the inside track that the United States enjoyed would be recognized as distinctive. Thus in 1985 a senior vice president would remark in a note to President A. W. Clausen, "The Bank is an influential element in the international system. U.S. influence in UN organizations is weak; the ADB [Asian Development Bank] is dominated by Japan; the IDB [Inter-American Development Bank] by the borrowers. The U.S. does not control the Bank but, as the largest shareholder and in association with other like-minded OECD [Organization for Economic Co-

1. Although representatives of the Soviet Union participated in the Bretton Woods Conference, the USSR failed to ratify the Articles of the Bank, or of the International Monetary Fund, arguing at a 1947 meeting of the UN General Assembly that the Bretton Woods institutions were merely "branches of Wall Street" and that the Bank was "subordinated to political purposes which make it one instrument of one great owner." Edward S. Mason and Robert E. Asher, *The World Bank since Bretton Woods* (Brookings, 1973), p. 29, quoting a 1948 article by Klaus Knorr.

operation and Development] countries, [it] exercises an influence unmatched elsewhere."[2]

The Americans had a secure enough lead in the Bank throughout the half century to help it avoid the clutter of country quotas in its hiring, to recruit personnel on merit from the developed and developing countries alike, and to build a work force that some saw as comparatively denationalized and homogenous (although others, to be sure, perceived a set of nationality cliques). One unmistakable factor that contributed to this homogenizing and that grew stronger over time was economics. As this work demonstrates, economics would become the Bank's hallmark scholarly discipline, and the economists who heavily shaped Bank operations as well as its research were recruited from a wide array of countries. To a large degree, however, they were the product of the graduate economics departments of English-speaking, but especially American, universities. This fact, as it played into the Bank's consulting, research, technical assistance, and agenda setting, would enhance the U.S. role in the institution beyond the apparatus of formal governance.

The full-time leader of a multilateral agency—president, managing director, director-general, or whatever—tends to be powerful vis à vis the representative component of agency government. Members of the agency board, even if full-time residents, as in the case of the World Bank, are unlikely to be deeply schooled or experienced in the substance of the program. But the pro-management tilt of power within the Bank was accentuated when, in 1947, the second president, John McCloy, imposed an agreement on the Executive Board that blocked it from taking operational initiatives. Henceforth, all loan proposals would have to come from the staff, that is, management.

Under the Bank's constitution, the institution's headquarters was to be located in the capital city of the largest shareholder, but by convention this shareholder, which was the United States, also chose the president. The latter was a powerful prerogative; yet, as widely perceived, the United States, in using it, did not always try hard to serve the collective interests of the Bank's constituents.[3] Principally, this was because the Bank, albeit a "good deal" for the United States, was not as important to that country as it was to many others.[4]

2. Ernest Stern to A. W. Clausen, March 29, 1985.

3. The prerogative as to IMF leadership was traded off to West Europeans, collectively, and Fund executive directors, allowed more initiatives than the Bank's, have generally been perceived, compared with Bank executive directors, to identify more with the institution and less with the governments they represent.

4. On Sunday, June 9, 1996, U.S. National Public Radio, as one of its one-liners for the day, remarked from Washington, D.C.: "Today is the 80th birthday of Robert McNamara, former secretary of defense." On both plus and minus grounds, McNamara was clearly a memorable U.S. defense chief, a position he held for seven years. But he was arguably the most memorable leader of the World Bank, which he served for nearly twice as long. Yet even McNamara himself dealt solely with Vietnam in his memoirs. Robert McNamara with Brian Van De Mark, *In Retrospect: The Tragedy and Lessons of Vietnam* (Times Books, 1995).

The fact that the World Bank enjoyed, for the most part, good presidential leadership was more serendipitous than by design. Thus if one had asked the international development community what credentials a World Bank president should have, Robert McNamara would have been one of the least qualified. Other nominations, if more substantively relevant, were delayed by dissension within the United States, and, in particular, in the cases of George Woods (1963), A. W. Clausen (1981), Barber Conable (1986), and Lewis Preston (1991), were indifferent to the importance of choosing presidents clearly young enough to serve more than single five-year terms.

Autonomy has been a desire of every World Bank president, and, for the most part, the degree of freedom that management has sought has been freedom from control by the United States, both from the executive branch personified by the U.S. Treasury and, in particular, from micromanagement by the U.S. Congress, which, in contrast to the Westminster model, has an unusually independent voice in the American constitutional scheme. The autonomy that Bank managers extracted from their owners was never more than partial, of course. But quasi autonomy grew significantly and steadily until the launching of IDA, with its taxpayer funding, gave the institution's owners an added stake in the oversight of lending decisions. Momentum together with the pro-autonomy political skills and energy of McNamara kept the squeeze-down on management discretion largely at bay through the 1970s. But diminished autonomy, albeit resisted, was the trend from 1981.

One of the continuing challenges for the institution over the years has been to find and sustain a proper balance between the Bank's intellectual products and its resource transfers. During the 1970s, transfer volumes rose strikingly (see table 1-1), arguably in a way and to an extent that (along with changes in global conditions outside the Bank) inhibited the effective delivery of certain intellectual wares, notably influences on recipient policies. As the 1970s passed into the 1980s, powerful shifts took place in events both in the Bank and in the world surrounding it. Internally, the Bank had begun placing much more emphasis on policy-based lending of a "structural adjustment" kind that involved an explicit bracketing of dollar transfers and conditioned policy reforms. Viewed in retrospect, structural adjustment lending overreached itself, partly because of its unexpectedly heavy use in connection with the 1980s debt crisis and partly because of the development crisis in Sub-Saharan Africa. In so doing, it encountered procedural pitfalls.

Furthermore, the volume of both IDA and IBRD lending plateaued, raising the question of whether, and how well, the mix of the institution's joint product could be shifted away from resource flows toward ideational stimulus, transfers, and interaction. Put differently, if the Bank could no longer buy itself a "seat at the policy table" in the old-fashioned way, would it tend to fall out of not only the policy game but the development game more generally? This remains a live question.

The most defining characteristic of the World Bank as viewed in this history is that, from the beginning, whether the institution knew it or not, its pivotal issue was

Table 1-1. *World Bank Lending, 1946–95*

Lending	1946–49	1950–59	1960–69	1970–79	1980–89	1990–95
Commitments (annual averages)						
Nominal (billions of U.S. dollars)	0.22	0.39	1.05	5.36	15.69	22.03
Real (billions of 1995 U.S. dollars)	1.19	2.37	5.52	12.09	22.24	23.66
By regions (percent)						
Africa	0	15	12	14	15	15
Asia	0	38	40	38	43	37
Europe	81	20	12	12	9	16
Latin America	19	22	28	24	26	25
Middle East/North Africa	0	5	7	11	7	7
By sectors (percent)						
Agriculture	0	4	13	28	24	16
Finance and industry	2	13	12	16	18	11
Infrastructure[a]	21	61	64	36	29	24
Social[b]	0	0	4	13	15	26
Other[c]	76	22	8	8	15	24
By lending instruments (percent)						
Program and adjustment[d]	76	21	6	5	18	20
Specific investment	2	53	67	56	46	60
Other[e]	0	2	11	17	16	10

Source: World Bank lending (LCI).

a. Telecommunications, transportation, electric power, and other energy.

b. Education, environment, population, urban development, water supply, and sanitation.

c. Oil and gas, mining and other extractives, public sector management, tourism, multisector, and sector unclassified.

d. Includes reconstruction, sector adjustment, structural adjustment, and other program loans.

e. Debt reduction, emergency recovery, financial intermediation, and technical assistance.

that of coping with poverty, both between countries and within developing countries. Nearly the whole Bank experience can be interpreted under this proposition, as explained in chapters 2 through 7.

During the years in which this work has been in preparation, the World Bank has been under a heavy cross fire of criticism and debunking. A common claim is that the Bank's importance has been exaggerated because its operations, whether measured by the amount of Bank lending or the numbers of its staff or other factors, have not been of world-class size. The dollar volume of Bank activity is said to have been far smaller than that of private capital markets, or particular commercial lending institutions, or bilateral official lenders, or even (as to current net lending) one or another of the regional development banks.

Such commentary may encourage World Bank humility. But it compares apples and oranges. The World Bank has been important because of its strategic role in the development promotion process. The Bank has been the one public sector, resource-weighted, multilateral that intervened throughout the developing world into a broad array of developmental and development-related issues. The scale of the Bank's resources has lent weight to the intervention. But the sheer size of other nonstrategically placed players has little relevance.

To explore the Bank's role in the promotion of development, we have grouped the chapters in this volume of our history along thematic and sectoral lines. Within this framework, each chapter is organized chronologically. The present chapter, also a chronological treatment, draws from across the set. Before the discussion can go forward, however, a word is in order about one other defining Bank characteristic.

The Project Focus

In the 1950s one of the Bank's more central characteristics came to full bloom: its mandated commitment to "project" lending. This would remain a defining feature of the institution in succeeding decades.

One might wonder why, in fact, projects came to have so dominating a position at the Bank. Before 1944–46, "project" was a noun in common usage with a variety of meanings: such large civil engineering ventures as the Suez Canal and the Hoover Dam often were called "projects"; and commercial banks did a good deal of project lending. Indeed, mortgage financing of new construction could be called project lending. But the term was seldom associated with the varieties of lending done by public financial institutions. Therefore, it might have surprised some participants when, at Bretton Woods, the British urged that the new Bank should be confined to funding "specific projects" (whether by loan or by guarantee). In preparatory drafts for the conference, the United Kingdom had taken this position, while the United States had envisioned loans for "programs and projects."[5] And at Bretton Woods itself, the Americans insisted on the provision that other loans could be made under "special circumstances."[6] Thus at the outset—with the institution's leading owner tending to relax the project formula, and in the absence, even, of an agreed definition of what a project was—one might have guessed that the Articles' commitment to specific projects would prove largely cosmetic.

What the country conferees, the United States included, sought to forestall, however, was a replay of the financial looseness of the 1930s. They did not want this new (multilateral) public sector lender to fall into the pattern of nonaccountability

5. Mason and Asher, *World Bank since Bretton Woods*, p. 24.

6. Warren C. Baum and Stokes M. Tolbert, *Investing in Development* (Oxford University Press, 1985), p. 7, which cites testimony by Harry Dexter White to the House Committee on Banking and Currency, Hearings on H.R. 2211, 79th Cong., 1st sess. (1945), p. 78. This, White told the U.S. Congress, would give the Bank "wider discretion."

that had become the norm in the years before the war. As soon as the Bank was launched, its American leadership had reason to embrace the project formula. It needed to demonstrate institutional creditworthiness to private lenders in New York, and, as noted in chapters 3 and 9, that demonstration had parallel requirements. The financial community had to be persuaded that the Bank's sovereign borrowers were adopting competent policies. But once the context into which the Bank was lending passed muster, the New York lenders were reassured to have the institution do its own lending in concrete project packages that were identifiable and assessable.

As the term took on technical meaning in the Bank's early years, "project loans" were seen as investments, mainly in physical assets that consisted primarily (in the early years) of infrastructure of one kind or another. In the 1940s and 1950s, the assets in which the Bank's borrowers invested were intended to generate income that the project entity would recover; thus the project could become self-liquidating. The most distinctive thing about projects, however, was their finiteness. They concerned limited, bounded pieces of the sector of activity—hydroelectric energy, rail transport, or whatever—to which they belonged.

This boundedness of projects was politically important. It tended to make project loans less intrusive on the sovereign sensibilities of borrowing countries. At least as a matter of appearances, the project could be quarantined against the general meddling in national policies of which balance of payments loans commonly were accused.

To become a project specialist, the Bank needed to have—and needed to give the impression of—technical expertise. Proposed project loans had to be carefully vetted by sectoral specialists. At the very beginning the Bank thought it could hire the needed expertise from short-term consultants. But this did not suit the operation it was building. As a matter of imagery as well as efficiency, the expertise needed to be in-house, and by the start of the 1950s the Bank began hiring technical specialists at a much higher rate than overall staff. Moreover, such expansion was not just a demand-driven phenomenon. It was facilitated by the growing availability of field-seasoned sector specialists previously employed by the colonial regimes of Asia and Africa.

To be a brainy project lender also was politically circumspect. The Bank was mandated to be apolitical. The advantage that project lending offered in this regard became plainer as the cold war intensified. The conflict was for higher financial stakes than the Bank could table; in dollars and cents, the Marshall Plan was out of the Bank's class. But geopolitics also was taking a much harsher, more strident shape. For all its pro-West partisanship, the Bank as a multilateral institution thought it safer and more seemly to operate as a seasoned technocrat standing above the political fray.

For these various reasons, by the end of the 1950s the culture of the Bank had become project-led. The Bank was admired as the most distinguished practitioner of accomplished, appropriately deliberate project lending. Its cachet in the field was not sophisticated project analysis per se (in the 1960s, the latter made a back-door, never fully complete, entrance into Bank operations) but rather rested on an already entrenched reputation for high-quality project work performed by specialists of good professional pedigree. This project culture has had a marked effect on the Bank's history.

Origins: 1942–47

In 1942 both the American and British governments were planning innovations that would prevent the international economy from sinking back into the morass of the 1930s once World War II was over. In the United States, the leading planner was Assistant Secretary of the Treasury Harry Dexter White, although lively discussion also was going on in the State Department. In Britain, planning was dominated by John Maynard Keynes, the most influential economist of his generation, who had been made adviser to the Treasury and was just being elevated to the peerage. Both White and Keynes were mainly concerned with forming an institution that would maintain a system of fixed international exchange rates. But both also had a secondary interest in establishing an international bank to supplement financing that depression- and war-shocked private financial markets would provide toward the reconstruction of war damage and toward the development of less economically advanced countries (which was being urged by Latin Americans, in particular, at that time).

In a remarkably efficient conference in July 1944 representatives of forty-four countries met in a New Hampshire resort hotel to implement the White-Keynes scenario. Although the IMF remained the focal subject, the founders built fateful features into the fledgling Bank. It was to obtain most of its money from the private money markets (initially, New York) making use of member government guarantees. The institution was given an endowment: at the outset, the equity consisted solely of paid-in capital, but it was gradually bolstered by growing reserves (in turn augmented by transfers from net income) and modest infusions of paid-in capital. These actions had two consequences. First, in its early years the Bank had to be preoccupied with winning a high credit rating in the New York financial market; those who would sell its bonds were its most critical constituency. Second, from the beginning the Bank faced a soft budget constraint. As we say in chapter 18, "The Bank made money; it more than could pay its own way. It could go first class, and hire and develop the quality to justify doing so." The young Bank took pains not to be profligate, but per million dollars lent, compared with most other public interveners, it "could employ more staff at higher average salaries, hire more consultants, commission more country studies, hold more seminars, issue more publications, and provide its functionaries better creature comforts" (chapter 18).

The (U.S.) Truman administration had trouble finding a president for the new institution. Finally, it settled on seventy-year-old Eugene Meyer, former investment banker and U.S. government official and currently president of the *Washington Post*. The Bank opened in June 1946, and immediately Meyer, a partisan of cautious beginnings, fell into dispute with Emilio Collado, the young State Department official who had been appointed the executive director for the United States. They differed over the size and speed of operations but also over the balance of power between the Bank's management and its Executive Board. Collado favored an activist Board, with the president implementing the Board's policy initiatives. Meyer resisted bitterly, then decided the game was not worth the candle. He resigned barely six months into his term, leaving the White House to face an even bigger appointment problem.

The McCloy Imprint

John J. McCloy, the Bank's second president, held the job only two years and three months, but he left a heavy imprint on the institution. McCloy had been a senior Washington official but now was a New York lawyer. With his accession, New York took over the Bank. For vice president, McCloy brought in Robert Garner, former commercial banker and now vice president of General Foods. And Collado was replaced by Eugene Black from Chase Bank. Most important, McCloy extracted an agreement from a reluctant Executive Board that henceforth it would be only a reactive body: a ratifier, occasionally a naysayer. But all lending proposals and other operational initiatives would come from management. By common consent, with the Board so circumscribed, its average quality diminished during the next two decades.

McCloy presided over a major shift in institutional focus that was driven more by circumstances than by choice. The Bank's first loans were non–project reconstruction loans to France, the Netherlands, Denmark, and Luxembourg in 1947, and there followed a trickle of such loans to economically developed countries. However, as cold war psychology became entrenched in 1947–48, the Western rationale for third-world development was powerfully reinforced. At the same time, the scale of the reconstruction need in Western Europe and Japan was quickly recognized to be far beyond the financial capacity of the young Bank. Reconstruction was taken on bilaterally by the United States in the Marshall Plan program launched in June 1947. President McCloy testified in the U.S. Congress in support of that program, but simultaneously he was urging his colleagues to recognize that the institution needed to turn to its second designated mission, development, rather sooner and more fully than had been expected. They all, he concluded, had much studying and traveling to do as they took up this relatively unfamiliar cause.

John McCloy and his U.S. executive director, Eugene Black, worked as a team. McCloy, despite the strong lead he had quickly given the World Bank, wanted to get on with other things, and he accepted an offer to become the U.S. high commissioner in Germany. One reason he could leave so quickly was that both the Truman White House and the Bank Board agreed that Black could take over without breaking stride.

Mr. Black's Bank: 1949–59

Eugene Black's incumbency extended into the 1960s, but toward the end it changed character. The period running through 1959, in part building on starts under McCloy and focusing on IBRD proper, contained the vintage Black years.

Black was a charming autocrat. McCloy having tamed the executive directors, Black coddled them. Relying heavily for administrative management on his lieutenant, Robert Garner (and then, when Garner became president of the new International Finance Corporation in 1956, on Burke Knapp), Black hired an able, loyal, generally congenial staff. He recognized that the U.S. government had mastery of the Bank in the 1950s but insisted on dignity for the multilateral and fought a spirited turf war with the U.S. Export-Import Bank.

At this time, the World Bank was heavily into physical infrastructure (see table 1–1). Agriculture, except for the great Indus and Aswan projects (discussed later in this section) had so far received little attention in the Bank. Meanwhile, industry was at the center of a heated debate: many borrowing countries wanted it in the public sector, whereas Black, Garner, and their Board wanted it to be private. In any event, the significant programmatic development of the decade was procedural: the Black Bank carried the craft of project lending to a new level.

But there were costs as well to the Bank's deliberate operating style. In 1951 Eugene Black was visited by a panel of UN experts that included the future Nobel laureates Arthur Lewis and Theodore Schultz. Black brushed aside their proposal that the Bank quickly expand its rate of development lending to $1 billion annually. Four hundred million, he said, would do nicely. Moreover, the rapid buildup of the institution's project process and mystique left some of those working on the regional, country-by-country, and country-policies side of the lending program feeling they had been upstaged. They noted the contrast with the bilateral aid agencies beginning to emerge, and, indeed, with external affairs ministries and (for that matter) militaries, in which the "lines" of organizations, in contrast with their staffs, all ran through the geographically defined components. A Bank reorganization in 1952 establishing regional subdivisions was expected to put the projects-versus-policies issue to rest. But the matter would remain a sore point for decades to come.

Aside from this one tension, Mr. Black's Bank plotted a comparatively serene, intelligent, self-contained course in the 1950s. Its greatest challenge, namely, to win AAA rating for the Bank's bonds in Wall Street, was essentially won by the mid-1950s but remained elusive until 1959, in part because of the U.S. market's lingering bias against foreign lending and in part because the Bank's outstanding obligations were approaching the U.S. share of the Bank's callable capital. In 1959, however, there was a General Capital Increase (GCI) that doubled the Bank's capital, albeit without any increase in paid-in capital. The AAA rating was bestowed shortly thereafter, and the great credit-standing battle had been won.

The Bank was also active intellectually. The effort on this front had begun under McCloy, with a push to learn about development through a series of searching one-off country studies manned partly by Bank staff, partly by specialists recruited for the purpose. Under Black, the studies proceeded vigorously, especially during the first half of the 1950s. In 1956 the Bank established the Economic Development Institute in Washington for developing-country officials and gave it a broader curriculum than the Bank's own lending program had yet attained. But in terms of the Bank's later research activities, those of Black's Bank were minor. And the economics mainly practiced and favored was of the workaday kind that was integral to country and project analysis.

The Black Bank also took on three high-profile ventures of a mediational type that were almost out of character. The first was to reconcile differences over oil issues between the British and the 1951 Mossadegh government of Iran. The second was to mediate the Indus water dispute between India and Pakistan. The third was to secure Western (British, U.S., and Bank) funding for Egypt's Aswan High Dam. The first and third failed but in ways that brought little discredit to the Bank. The second was a resounding success that reflected dogged and imaginative work on the part of Black and his colleague William Iliff, and, in the end, considerable flexibility on the part of the parties involved.[7] Together they added some dash to the Bank's rather circumspect progress under Black.

For all of its soundness (some would emphasize, self-satisfaction), Black's Bank became discontented on two counts. The president, vice president, and others were unhappy with the way the Articles inhibited the promotion of the private sector in developing countries: they could not lend directly to private enterprises without obtaining politically hard-to-get and encumbering guarantees from host governments.

Second, and more threatening to IBRD's future, the Bank was rapidly running out of the capacity to serve those developing countries that were exhausting—or had never yet achieved—creditworthiness. The most conspicuous examples in the late 1950s were India and Pakistan. At the start of the decade Eugene Black had been dead set against the idea of multilateral programs that would make concessional capital transfers (grants or loans at softer than market terms) to poor countries. By the end of the 1950s Black had come to the view that, if there was going to be such concessional multilateral lending, it would be better for it to be done under the work habits and style of the Bank than of some New York–based UN agency.

7. All three have been described by Harold Graves in Mason and Asher, chapter 18.

But second, there was the strong positive appeal of widening the clientele for the Bank's constructive operations.

Well before the end of the Black period, the Bank had acquired a habit that was seldom mentioned in polite official discourse. Project lending seemed to assume that an external lender could be selective, picking and choosing among activities to be supported, with the chosen ones being segregated from the rest of the recipient's affairs. The pretense was that, when the Bank lent for a capital asset, say, a piece of infrastructure, that was the particular item the loan would help add to the borrower's capital stock. Yet it seemed self-evident that if, in the absence of the loan for item A, the recipient would have acquired A anyway, the loan's effect was to enable the acquisition of something else.

The point did not escape policymakers in the early Bank. In fact, sometimes they spelled it out. The institution's Annual Report for 1949–50 addressed the issue head-on. Noting that Bank investment needed to be addressed to priority uses, the report remarked: "The Bank recognizes, of course, that by financing one particular investment project, it may be releasing resources already available to the borrower for some other investment activity" (or, the report could have added, for extra consumption).[8] Indeed, Paul Rosenstein-Rodan, the Bank's star professional economist from 1947 to 1952, reflected that he could never understand why bankers took the link between particular loans and particular assets so seriously.[9]

But in the eyes of the institution's management—and, most development promoters of the period—simple acceptance of unadorned fungibility as a doctrine would have proved too much; it would have undermined the importance of the transfers of information, technical skills, and institutional tutelage that lenders linked to their particularized loans; it would have denied that the particularized resource transfers added thrust to the cognitive elements that accompanied them. Further, many of the Bank's stakeholders—lending and borrowing governments, private financial institutions, and other members of the development community— shared the same view. It was their own practice to join the Bank in coupling specific funds with specific uses of funds. Fungibility became almost an unmentionable. The 1949–50 Annual Report's candor on the subject was seldom repeated.

IDA and Black's Last Years

Beginning in 1956 the Bank acquired various affiliates that came to be known as the "World Bank Group" in the 1960s (later the term was less widely used). Among the lesser ones were the International Center for the Settlement of International Disputes (ICSID), established in 1966 to institutionalize the positive aspects of the 1950s mediation experiences, and the Multinational Investment Guarantee Agency

8. The passage was drafted by Richard Demuth and Benjamin King.
9. Paul Rosenstein-Rodan, interview, World Bank Oral History Program, 1961, p. 7.

(MIGA), established in 1988. But the two overwhelmingly important members of the Group were the International Finance Corporation (IFC, 1956) and IDA (1960). And of these, IDA was the affiliate that changed the whole history of the World Bank.[10]

IDA's birth was one of those phenomena that underscore the role of happenstance in history. The scheme was strongly resisted by Eugene Black as well as by the first Eisenhower administration, although it had some keen American advocates, including Nelson Rockefeller. But the idea of IDA caught the eye of a determined U.S. senator, Mike Monroney of Oklahoma, who was able to sell the second Eisenhower administration and, for the reasons indicated, the latter-day Eugene Black, on the IDA scheme as a kind of fall-back strategy.

The scheme changed the Bank as nothing up to that time had. It radically increased the Bank's roll of clients (that is, IDA clients) and its potential resources. As a consequence, the new IDA protected the Bank from impairing IBRD creditworthiness by making unserviceable loans to poor countries that needed credit but could not afford it on market terms.

IDA quickly broadened Bank lending's substantive scope to include agriculture, water, and education. The newly accessible borrowers had these needs, and loans no longer had to be directly self-liquidating. Eugene Black in his last two years began to press such changes. He also began to urge higher rates of IDA financing than member countries had contemplated. The $1 billion figure for the agency's initial resources to which members notionally had agreed was extremely modest compared with the scales of multilateral concessional transfers that had been bruited about during the 1950s. Even so, when it came to putting up the money, the OECD-affiliated Bank members thought $750 of their convertible currencies was enough. When these initial funds were being drawn down over the space of three years, the same members, led by the United States, provided a first replenishment of only a sustaining amount, that is, $250 million annually, for a further three years. The members agreed to this quite readily, but with a deaf ear to Bank management's effort to raise the size of the effort. Nevertheless, when the next president arrived in January 1963, it was widely sensed that IDA was off to a fairly promising start.

George Woods: Reforms and Ill Temper

Although George Woods and Eugene Black were both New York bankers, they had different styles. Woods was unpolished, criticized staff harshly and publicly, and argued with, rather than pacified, his Executive Board. His demeanor may

10. As chapter 13 explains, however, the IFC experienced wide swings in its agenda (promoting private investment) and effectiveness during its first four decades. Only recently has it regained a position of considerable salience.

have been aggravated by ill health; in his first year he suffered a life-threatening aneurism.

Moreover, most of the Woods term was blighted by the Bank's first major experience with what became a recurring trauma for the institution: having to conduct an IDA replenishment exercise every three, or if the particular effort stalled, every four years. As indicated, the first two rounds of IDA money raising while Black was still president of the Bank, although rather disappointing in their yields, had been quiet. But then there was a change of leadership in the U.S. government. As secretary of the Treasury, Douglas Dillon, friend of development and of the Bank, was succeeded by Henry H. ("Joe") Fowler, much less of an enthusiast. Fowler told George Woods that henceforth the Bank could expect no pro-IDA fund-raising leadership from the United States; it would have to do its own money raising. The middle 1960s were an awkward time for the exercise; the United States was having to cope, in the first instance postwar, with a foreign exchange shortage, and other donors did not like Woods's tactics in, as they saw it, playing favorites with the United States. The favoritism was scaled back to timing "IDA 2" inputs (as the new terminology had it) so that the United States was put at the back end of the queue. The whole replenishment episode was so protracted that the negotiation of IDA 2 did not finish until almost a year after the end of George Woods's term.

Given his stylistic problems and preoccupations, it is remarkable that Woods did as much as he did in his five and a quarter years at the Bank. He sought radically to build up the strength of macroeconomic analysis, although in many eyes his importation of Irving Friedman from the IMF for this purpose was ill-considered. Woods was prepared to have the Bank become an active influencer of recipient government policies: in Latin America, during Gerald Alter's directorship, the Bank brought "programs of projects" to bear on the need for macroeconomic reforms, and, in India, the Bernard Bell mission chalked out an extensive reform program. Moreover, Woods, unintimidated by the letter of the Bank's Charter, was prepared to use nonproject loans as well as loans for local currency expenditures as vehicles for transferring both resources and influence.

Woods nurtured the IFC as a promoter of private investment and, signaling the Bank's private sector preference, transferred to the Corporation the Bank's industrial promotion activities. Woods's post-IDA focus on agriculture was far more serious than Black's; the growth rate of lending to agriculture under Woods (admittedly it started from a low base) was higher than any the Bank has since seen. Also Woods was not ideologically nervous about agricultural promotion; he was prepared to have the Bank favor serious land reform and do supportive lending around the edges of such an effort. He was also keen on educational support, and, instead of shunning the specialized United Nations agencies in these fields, he reached out to them with cooperative operational agreements with the Food and Agriculture Organization (FAO) and the United Nations Educational, Scientific, and Cultural

Organization (UNESCO). Woods went out of his way to make a supportive speech to the first meeting of the UN Conference on Trade and Development (UNCTAD) in Geneva in 1964. He started the Bank thinking about the need for more active agricultural research. And he left for his successor the idea for a grand assize reviewing the world community's development promotion effort, which became the Pearson Commission of 1968–69.

McNamara-I: 1968–73

Robert McNamara "hit the ground" on April 1, 1968, in a way that accelerated the pulse of the Bank and rewrote its priorities to a degree not previously experienced. But development pundits quickly found themselves arguing over how original the McNamara revolution was. Only a few months earlier, the man had been fighting a war, and before that he built automobiles. Meanwhile, in early 1968 the development policy world—in Washington, various European capitals, such developing-country capitals as New Delhi, and such United Nations centers as New York, Geneva, and Rome—was beginning an intellectual upheaval, the gist of which was that, although development had almost achieved the growth targets set for the "First Development Decade," the averages were not good enough. Performance had sloughed over too many distributional and equity problems.

McNamara obviously was not the first author of these ideas, but he arrived articulating some of them, and he was a quick study. He crowded in a group of field visits to developing countries and was authoritatively verbalizing more quality-of-life concerns such as education, nutrition, and population restraint by the time of his first annual meetings speech in September (the series would become a major podium for the McNamara administration).

Substantively, McNamara's range of sectoral concerns went beyond poverty as usually conceived. To be sure some concerns were more apparent in rhetoric than in operations. Environment, for example, was ostensibly added, at the time of the global environment conference in 1972, but its impact on Bank operations was quite minimal during most of the 1970s. But the overriding concern, along with poverty itself, was growth. McNamara was adamant that no trade-off was necessary between the goals of output growth and equity for poor countries. Within this broad advocacy of equitable growth, the new Bank president was doubly insistent about Bank growth: the institution had an almost unparalleled opportunity to do good, and it was obligated, while maintaining the high quality of its project lending, to get on with it.

The scale of the McNamara expansion was formidable. Over the last four years of McNamara's presidency (fiscal 1978–81), compared with the five years before his arrival (1964–68), Bank lending expanded more than 3 times in real terms (IBRD lending, 2.8 times, IDA lending, 3.7 times); professional staff rose fourfold. The administrative budget increased 3.5 times in real terms.

Personally, Robert McNamara was as engaged with the financing of his program as he was with its contents. On the IDA side, he and his top executives lavished thought and time on maneuvering the politics of members' concessional funding. With respect to raising IBRD money in private markets, the president led a growing penetration of non-U.S. markets. The very first bond offering (in Switzerland, following his radical speech at the annual meetings) failed. Stung, McNamara dropped the Treasurer and hired as his replacement Eugene Rotberg, a U.S. government lawyer who had caught McNamara's eye despite his limited relevant experience. It was a brilliant appointment: by the time Rotberg left the Bank in 1987, he would be something of a legend for having placed about $100 billion in IBRD security offerings.

McNamara did indeed bring originality to his office, both in his energy and in the comprehensiveness of his personal grasp of Bank affairs. He took two key organizational steps: instituting Country Program Papers (CPPs) and vastly extending the scope of the Programming and Budgeting Department. Yet dissatisfied with the institution's response to his guidance, especially on the poverty front, he launched the first major reorganization in two decades. This encouraged a further move toward country programming and a region-by-region deployment of most sectoral project work—but, as had been the case in 1952, the tensions between project and area (that is, technical and regional) interests continued.

One of Robert McNamara's lasting and strongest personal legacies to the Bank was a massive increase in the financial support and status of research. A foretaste of this had been McNamara's immediate recognition of the importance of Bank sponsorship of the Consultative Group on International Agricultural Research (CGIAR). But the decisive move was the recruitment of the distinguished development economist, Hollis Chenery, to run the Bank's research activity and to be its chief economist. Chenery was encouraged to build a research establishment that, as strong globally as any in the development economics field, would appropriately engage in basic research as well as feed analytical guidance to the institution's regional and country-policy economic staffs. The Chenery complex sustained a level of intellectual authority for the Bank that was higher than it otherwise would have had.

Chenery was a leading example of particular hirings with which McNamara refreshed the organization. Not much of this needed to be self-conscious when the whole staff was expanding so rapidly, but yeast was indeed sought and provided, among others, by Mahbub ul Haq, who had come to doubt the thrust of orthodox import-substitution industrial planning in Pakistan; by Ernest Stern, brought from USAID after serving as the deputy staff director of George Woods's "grand assize," which Robert McNamara organized and which became the commission led by Lester Pearson; and by Montague Yudelman, who, coming from a stint at OECD, impressed McNamara with the potency of a development strategy focused on the small farmer. Yudelman arrived in time to take over the rump central agricultural and rural development staff that emerged from the 1972 reorganization when the bulk of the Bank's agricultural specialists had been dispersed to the institution's regional cadres, still residing in Washington.

For a dynamic leader who had singled out poverty alleviation as at least one of his primary goals for the institution, McNamara had, by 1973, taken a remarkably long time to come up with a focused antipoverty program. Part of the difficulty was that, with such a preponderance of poor developing country populations still in the countryside, a focused program, it seemed, needed to be heavily rural and agricultural. And, as discussed in chapter 8, many rural development specialists felt that policy was failing to tackle the main problem in many rural developing areas if it did not plump for thoroughgoing, ownership-changing land reform. But some supporters of the Bank felt this was too radical a venture for the institution, and (more to the point) few developing country governments were inclined to welcome such interventions.

What the small-farmer focus, picked up in McNamara's 1973 annual speech at Nairobi, pressed was that the largest fraction of rural householders already were landowners, of small, viable, potentially progressive farms. Antipoverty reforms could focus on their outputs and incomes and thereby quite explicitly marry growth with poverty reduction for a large class of the poor.

McNamara-II: October 1973 to May 1979

The 1973 Nairobi speech marking the rhetorical culmination of McNamara's antipoverty, smallholder doctrine, was overshadowed in less than a month by the Yom Kippur War, which in turn launched events that triggered the oil shock issuing from the Organization of Petroleum Exporting Countries (OPEC) at the end of the year. The shock was severe: the price of crude oil rose fourfold in the space of three months. But what made it historic was the way the effects ramified. The OPEC countries received windfalls of political power as well as earnings. For the ones lightly populated and richest in oil, the dollar windfall was much larger than they quickly could spend; they put it in Western bank accounts.

To developing countries of some creditworthiness—middle-income oil importers and, indeed, such newly expanding oil exporters as Indonesia, Mexico, and Nigeria —these banked earnings of the oil-rich exporters became windfalls for hire if the borrowers could pay the fees. The fees (real interest rates) were kept low by the hike in the supply of loanable funds and the oil shock's dampening of the credit demands of the OECD countries. The OPEC governments themselves set up new development assistance programs. These became additional financial sources for selected developing countries.

The shock also had political dimensions. Just as some of OECD's members, in particular, the U.S. government of the day, were put off by the sudden outbreak of

OPEC affluence, the members of OPEC were determined to maintain solidarity with the majority of developing countries for whom the main initial effect of the oil shock was a rise in the cost of oil imports. Those now wielding oil power rallied their less fortunate colleagues into a new North-South dialogue in behalf of a (South-favoring) "New International Economic Order" (NIEO) under UN auspices. With intermittent changes of venue, the dialogue would extend from 1974 to 1981 with few results.

The World Bank could not stand clear of all this oil-triggered turbulence. It *did* avoid most of the rhetoric; it took care to avoid routinely joining either the North's or the South's debating positions. But there were practical effects. First, the Bank's immediate concern in 1974 was to provide and promote offsets to the losses of foreign exchange that higher oil prices were imposing on oil-importing developing countries. Second, the Bank quickly began to interest itself in investments in the exploration and development of energy—not only renewable kinds but also hydrocarbon energy—in developing countries seeking to escape oil's current scarcity pricing. The idea was frowned on by "Part I" members, especially the United States, who argued that ample private capital was available for these purposes.

The oil shock's third impact on the Bank was the greatest. The shock generated relatively low-cost alternatives to Bank and IDA loans for many Bank borrowers. This occurred just when President McNamara was driving the institution to expand its lending. With great effort, the Bank maintained the expansion. But its customers (some of them also were experiencing more rewarding commodity sales) were less receptive to the Bank's policy coaching and reform guidance than otherwise would have been the case. (The alternatives to Bank loans not only were affordable but came without lectures.) This, as is spelled out in various country cases in this volume and volume 2, diminished Bank leverage.

Nevertheless, the story of the latter 1970s is that within this weakened context, the growing Bank, under McNamara's leadership, carried on a lively, diverse, and on average productive program. The interventionist development community, if it had force-fed the president at the start of his tenure, had accepted his leadership by the middle of the decade. Having pushed redistributive, pro-employment, population, nutritional, and other reforms, the development-focused side of the community (in contrast to the contentious NIEO school) achieved a measure of North-South consensus in the "basic needs" conference of the International Labor Organization (ILO) in 1976. The Bank had difficulty signing onto the basic-needs nomenclature. But in fact the proposition that such needs were to be met mainly by raising the productivity of the poor accorded with the thrust of the late 1970s Bank.

As for the matter of agriculture and rural development, from McNamara's first years in the Bank, agriculture had been seen as a growth, not just an equity, activity. In the 1970s water management gains of different limited kinds were achieved in South Asian agriculture. Although agriculture faced a tougher slog in Africa, there were some single, including commercial, crop successes there. The Bank extolled and propagated an improved mode of agricultural extension that had good results in several regions and countries. By analytic and informational interventions, the Bank helped smooth violent investment cycles in the global fertilizer industry.

The institution's least successful rural initiatives (it scarcely acted at all in such other fields as land reform and rural public works) were the integrated rural development projects that appeared to be the conceptual progeny of the Nairobi speech. These new-style projects, taken up also by a variety of other donors, were particularly popular and notably unsuccessful in Africa. Recognizing that the real world was complex, they sought to tackle many dimensions of rural underdevelopment simultaneously. They placed excessive demands on newly building national administrations, or, weakening the local bureaucracy, they hived off personnel and resources into project authorities that were donor-dependent enclaves. By the end of the 1970s it was widely agreed that donors, including the Bank, needed to retreat into simpler partial ventures. They would need to rely on—and, as feasible, help—the development of institutional capacities that would allow countries to do their own assembly of the various pieces of altered societal systems.

In the middle and later 1970s, the Bank made a run at assisting borrowing countries with urban development. As several parts of this volume and also volume 2 attest, the 1970s' approach to industrial development reflected the president's view that government ownership of manufacturing and financial establishments, and (in Africa) parastatal conduct of processing and marketing activities, were less objectionable than the Black Bank had thought. What mattered more were the quality and independence of management. Bank research, as the decade wore on, produced growing support for the salience of export promotion as a growth strategy. As a considerable variety of country cases in both volumes 1 and 2 make clear, distinctive country-by-country analysis was characteristic of and valued by the 1970s Bank. Indonesia, the South Asian countries, Mexico, the Philippines, and Turkey are among the cases we examine. Indeed, for all its vigor, complexity, and president-driven goals, McNamara's Bank exhibited a good deal of intellectual pluralism. The institutional ear was tuned to fresh research and unanswered questions.

This last does not square easily with the complaint of many observers that the Bank buckled too easily to out-of-channels pressures from its country owners, especially the largest. The Bank's attitude to Allende's Chile became a cause célèbre in this regard (see chapter 15). Late in the decade a U.S. congressional committee, threatening to kick over an IDA replenishment appropriation, pressured McNamara into forswearing early lending to Vietnam in a move that was at least procedurally flawed. He made a commitment that, rightfully, was only the Executive Board's to make. Management occasionally accepted similar interferences from France with respect to Francophone Africa.

Such improprieties were in fact rare, perhaps because of a McNamara house rule. He was, for a servant of owners, aggressive in pressing the economic needs, indeed, the economic "rights" of his underprivileged clients. But he was quite serious about insulating himself from both recipient and donor politics.

One financial point belongs in this sketch of the later but not the last McNamara years. The commercial banks, recycling Arab oil earnings and pressed by competition to charge their borrowers very low real interest rates, defended themselves against the risk of future rate increases by persuading their clients to accept variable (that is, indexed) rates. The World Bank, out of concern for its borrowers, did not do likewise. Hence the Bank was due for trouble—and belatedly it shifted to variable rates—after market rates started exploding in late 1979.

The Great Bend in Events: May 1979 to October 1981

Nineteen hundred seventy-nine was a jarring year for the world. It started with the Iranian revolution in January, which, with a lag of a few months, led to the second oil shock. That shock, though not as extreme as its predecessor, saw the price of crude rise 160 percent in twelve months. Although the upward lurch in petroleum prices would subside sooner than most experts expected, in mid-1979 it triggered violent fiscal-monetary policy reactions in the OECD countries that caused the so-called Volcker Shock to interest rates. U.S. rates (with the rise reaching other currencies in different degrees) quickly outstripped oil prices in their claims on the foreign exchange budgets of developing countries.[11] More was in store. In November came the taking of U.S. hostages in Iran, which helped not only Ronald Reagan's nomination but also his election in 1980. And in December the Soviet Union invaded Afghanistan. By prompting Jimmy Carter to lift the U.S. defense budget, this raised the defense budgetary bar that Reagan, once elected, would have to clear to demonstrate that he was a more robust nation defender than his predecessor. This, of course, aggravated the deep (government) deficit-generating problem of the Reagan presidency.

In retrospect, the combination of Margaret Thatcher and Ronald Reagan would symbolize a sea change in economic ideology attributed to the period. Changes going on in the World Bank itself were sui generis but afterward blended with a swing in global fashions. The first internal change was that by 1979 Robert McNamara had decided—although he had scarcely yet told anyone—that he would retire in June 1981 when he reached age sixty-five. Meanwhile he would not rest on his oars; he would keep pace with new operational thinking. But he also was not a personal participant in the conservative surge that later would be perceived to have been under way.

Ernest Stern, McNamara's new operations chief after the retirement of Burke Knapp, also was not an ideologue. But he, with McNamara agreeing, albeit less

11. After assuming the chair of the U.S. Federal Reserve Board, Paul Volcker in October 1979 shifted the board's anti-inflationary regime from interest rate monitoring to control of the monetary stock—which sent rates sky-high.

vehemently, was quite dissatisfied with the way the Bank's project lending and its limited, ad hoc, weakly conditioned, nonproject lending were failing to motivate borrowing governments to undertake needed macropolicy reforms, especially to close unsustainable balance of payments gaps. McNamara included in a speech he gave to the UNCTAD conference in Manila in May 1979 the thought that the Bank should undertake some "structural adjustment lending" to facilitate and cushion developing-country reforms to promote exports. A few days later Stern produced a memorandum that became a kind of charter for structural adjustment loans (SALs); he was careful to point out sensitivities and pitfalls, as well as advantages.

The SAL scheme was inherently double valued. It would use program loans to induce reforms, but it also would deliver to a borrower significant negotiable resources. The second (transfers) function took on increased importance during the middle of 1979 as the impact of the oil shock heightened country appetites for quick-disbursing foreign exchange. On the one hand, this prompted Bank members to become more favorably disposed toward the kind of lending innovation McNamara and Stern were recommending (the former put another statement about it in his September speech to the annual meetings, this time in Belgrade). But the stepped-up interest in nonproject transfers clashed with one of the prime ingredients of the original SAL design: these new loans were to be made very carefully only to governments, mostly of middle-income countries, that were conspicuously ready and willing politically to institute major reforms and that had the bureaucratic capacity to do so. From the beginning of SALs, therefore, the Bank had to grapple with a tug-of-war between doing SA lending carefully and very well, on the one hand, and doing a lot of it, on the other. (The push toward quantity would be greatly aggravated by the onset of Latin America's debt crisis in 1982 and then by the urgency of Sub-Saharan Africa's need for financial rescue during the 1980s.)

The SAL innovation, which quickly became the fashion in-house, was enough to stir up the Bank. But there also were enough personnel changes to agitate any organization. Most important was the president himself. Not only was McNamara an inherently hard act to follow, but the need of two U.S. administrations, those of Carter and Reagan, to agree on a replacement narrowed the field. They chose A. W. Clausen, an experienced, evidently successful commercial banker. But he knew very little about development and less about Washington. It was a chancy choice, especially when in the new U.S. administration senior White House and Treasury staffers would arrive with an a priori hostility to the Bank. Several of McNamara's leading lieutenants left with him: William Clark, his public affairs chief; Mahbub ul Haq, his most visible and articulate progressive; and, in particular, Hollis Chenery.

Given the new wave of neoclassical economic orthodoxy that was building in the intellectual communities around the Bank, Chenery's replacement was especially significant. Clausen chose Anne Krueger, an able, unflinching neoclassical trade economist, and she, in turn, replaced large fractions of the Bank's central economics establishment until she had a highly compatible staff.

Representing the spirit of all this and yet semidetached from it was the so-called Berg Report of September 1981. As chapter 12 discusses, economic development in Sub-Saharan Africa (SSA) and the World Bank's interventions in its behalf were in disarray in much of the continent as the 1970s drew toward a close. The Bank accepted the request of its African governors to make a special study of the problem. Elliot Berg, an academic market-oriented development economist, was recruited to lead a team of four Bank staff and himself. In their opinion, the problem they detailed was attributable in part (as official African views of the time had it) to adverse external factors. But the principal fault, said the Berg group, lay with flawed domestic policies. Thus, by implication, SAL was on the right track: it was right for the Bank to lever policy reform. But it was wrong to delay such reforms in Africa; they were needed now. The report had another facet with Bank-wide ramifications. It found African government-owned parastatals so hopelessly corrupt and inefficient that it argued in effect for privatization. This marked the institution's de facto desertion of the McNamara doctrine that strengthening the market and the quality of management, not private versus public ownership, was the dominant industrial policy consideration for the Bank. The latter reverted to a Black-Garner view of the ownership issue.

The renewed emphasis on the comparative advantage of the private sector would have obvious implications for the IFC. However, circumstances delayed their development. In 1977 McNamara had recruited Moeen Qureshi from the IMF to be executive vice president (that is, working head) of the IFC. Qureshi shared McNamara's view that, for purposes of industrial development, ownership was less important than the quality and independence of management as well as market flexibility. But then McNamara was so taken with Qureshi that he not only brought him over to the Bank proper in mid-1979 to succeed Peter Cargill in one of the two senior vice presidencies, that for finance, but, reflecting a limited regard for the IFC, the president did not replace Qureshi there. In other words, until the beginning of 1981 Qureshi wore two hats but spent most of his time at the Bank. The new appointee to head the IFC, Hans A. Wuttke, did not work out to his own satisfaction or that of others, and by the time President Clausen had found a successor, Sir William Ryrie, the latter was not able to take over until October 1984. Thus, partly for lack of leadership, the IFC was slow in giving its full attention to the private sector opportunities the 1980s offered.

The Clausen Presidency and the First Phase of the Debt Crisis: 1981–86

The early post-McNamara years were a complex period for the Bank. This was the running-in time for structural adjustment lending, soon to be supplemented by a sectoral look-alike, sector adjustment lending programs (SECALs), which used conditioned program loans in support of less than macropolicy agendas. But a more telling point is that, procedurally, both SALs and SECALs were advertised to use comparatively specific ex-ante policy conditioning: recipients would not get follow-on transfers unless they had done what they had contracted to do when the loan in question was given. One reason for the procedural choice was that this kind of rigorous, verifiable conditioning was the type popularly associated with the International Monetary Fund, and of the two Bretton Woods sisters, the Fund was the favorite of the larger Part I governments. Relations with the IMF would remain a preoccupation of the Bank. The former would get the jump on responding to the 1982 triggering of the (mainly Latin American) debt crisis, but this was not simply because the Fund had quicker reflexes. The wishful but almost universal estimate was that the crisis posed a "liquidity" not a "solvency" problem, and the division of labor between the two agencies allocated such short-run matters mainly to the IMF.

In the early 1980s, the Bank's foray into adjustment lending demonstrated a caution that steadily loosened as the decade wore on, and the balance of payments crisis of many borrowers worsened. With some exceptions, adjustment loans in Asia were few and far between. The Bank's standard, shelf-model, SAL procedures became most apparent in Africa and, later in the decade, in Latin America, where adjustment lending was most pronounced. SALs to larger, more assertive borrowers, generally had the strongest borrower "ownership," with the countries typically insisting on making agreed policy changes before loan approval, in order to avoid the domestic stigma of overt conditionality.

The most promising client—in retrospect recording one of the most successful interactions of the World Bank with a borrower—was China. The accession of China into the World Bank had occurred toward the end of McNamara's tenure at the Bank. As the world's largest nation sought to reintegrate itself into the world community after three decades, the Bank became an important facility for the Chinese leadership for understanding the outside world. In the first few years the Bank's role was primarily a didactic one of educating a cadre of senior Chinese officials in new economic ideas and technical systems, putting together comprehensive reports on the Chinese economy,[12] and using its early loans to rebuild a higher education system still suffering from the aftermath of the havoc wrecked by the Cultural Revolution.

At the aggregate level, the sectoral composition of the Bank's lending to China in the 1980s was similar to the rest of the Bank (about half for transportation and energy, a quarter for agriculture, a sixth for industry and finance, and ten percent for education). In agriculture, the Bank played an important role in accentuating reforms that had been well under way in the late 1970s before the Bank appeared on the scene. Using a half billion dollar investment loan for grain production, for

12. The Bank's first comprehensive report on the Chinese economy, *China: Socialist Economic Development,* released in 1981, became a primer for senior Chinese officials and went a long way in establishing the Bank's credibility in that country.

example, it helped elicit a decision to change urban grain price subsidies. Its credibility and quiet low-key approach meant that its many nonlending decisions were taken seriously by the Chinese authorities in the formulation of the country's public investment decisions. Whereas almost all private foreign investment was concentrated in the coastal provinces, the Bank's lending focused on poorer inland and deep interior provinces. At the behest of the central authorities, much of the Bank's lending was at the provincial level, which (unlike the situation in other large countries) was also responsible for repayment. This decentralized approach appears to have played an important role in ensuring the high success of Bank operations in China.

To be sure, nurturing the relationship required all of the Bank's diplomatic skills. China's acute sensitivity regarding Taiwan was a continuous headache, whether over how it could be mentioned in Bank documents or the hiring of nationals from that jurisdiction. China demanded that any reference to Taiwan in any Bank document be deleted or state clearly, "Taiwan Province, China." The Bank, however, recognized that the issue was so salient to the Chinese authorities that it had little choice in the matter, unless it was prepared to sacrifice the entire relationship.[13] Boundary disputes between the two giants, China and India, spilled over into strong exchanges on cartographic issues in Bank documents. Operationally, IDA allocation became a contentious issue. With overall IDA volumes stagnating and Africa's predicament worsening, China's IDA claims could only be accommodated at the expense of another poor giant, India. The Bank gradually reduced India's share over the decade, but even then, until the mid-1980s, China's insistence that its IBRD borrowing should not exceed its IDA allocation meant that the volume of lending to China did not grow as rapidly as anticipated. Still, the quite steady and substantial progress with China for most of the decade would be one of the Bank's prouder achievements in the 1980s. With very few exceptions, the intimacy and rapport between the Bank's Beijing resident mission and the Chinese authorities were unmatched in the Bank's history.

The Clausen administration clearly did not accord the same overt priority to poverty and its several ramifications that McNamara had.[14] Clausen's admirers, however, valued the new president as a manager. He was far more careful, evidently, with

13. The minutes of a Managing Committee meeting, referring to a letter received from Minister Wang Bingqian, record that "The letter . . . is somewhat threatening to the Bank. It is also a threat to the Bank's independence in publishing." "Minutes of the January 25, 1982 Meeting of the Managing Committee," February 9, 1982.

14. At an informal Board seminar on a major internal exercise on the future of the Bank, Joseph Wood (who was leading the team), in pointing to the issues the task forces would not be looking at, referred to poverty alleviation as one example. The reason he gave was that "we are building on the consensus of the 1970's with regard to the development objectives of the institution. We are deliberately taking some things for granted. . . . [W]e do not see [this planning exercise] as involving questions about our fundamental purpose and objectives." Board seminar, June 8, 1984.

small-scale, lowercase housekeeping processes and administration. Furthermore, his formal decisionmaking style was consensual. Under Clausen, McNamara's weekly "President's Council" of seniors meeting to discuss the Bank's business at the upper management level became, instead of a committee to advise the president, a "Management Committee" with prepared papers and recorded votes that shared the president's decisions. Some of the players found the system cumbersome. More important, there was little easy consensus. The two senior vice presidents, Stern and Qureshi, headed two factions that managed to generate pervasive tension in the organization, which kept many, including the president, on edge.

Under Clausen, the tone and substance of the Bank's message began to emphasize the virtues of liberalization. Although the often ideological tones in which the Bank was transmitting its new gospel undermined the effectiveness with which it was perceived, there could be little doubt that in the areas where its message was most strident—trade liberalization and the importance of market forces—it anticipated the revolution that was sweeping much of the developing world. Another initiative launched by Clausen, and carried to fruition by the Bank's new general counsel, was the creation of a new Bank affiliate: the Multilateral Insurance Guarantee Authority (MIGA). It would, however, only become a force in the next decade.

The new U.S. administration, which took its place in Washington a few months before President Clausen, arrived with a hostility to the Bank that their nominee had little early success in quelling. Internally, even though the Bank had several staff units already studying the dangers of excessive developing-country debt, the Bank was taken by surprise by the Mexico collapse. The definition of the "debt crisis" as one threatening the global financial system rather than the well-being of borrowing countries determined its handling. The Bank did not seriously challenge the view. Thereafter the Bank was kept in its place by the severe uncertainty and risks posed to the global financial system. The principal actors in the G-7 (central banks, treasuries, and academia) quickly agreed on the liquidity diagnosis and on the consequent need—in both Mexico and other borrowing countries to which the crisis spread, as well as in the U.S.-centered global financial system—for a one-shot stabilization adjustment. This, once successful (conventional wisdom held), would allow developing countries and their supporters to get back to growth promotion. Policymakers were intent on maintaining reliable debtor performance and therefore the system of trust on which the whole global credit system (and, indeed, the creditworthiness of such lenders as the World Bank) depended. The Bank's principal contribution was to keep a focus on those structural features of borrowing country policies that needed to adjust to changing exogenous circumstances.

The steep economic decline in the borrowing countries led to a revision in the debt strategy. Officially admitting that sensible debt and adjustment policy no longer could keep growth resumption on hold, James Baker, the new U.S. Treasury secretary, signaled a shift at Seoul in October 1985. The Bank, along with the Fund, would have a major role to play in a formula that would use multilateral lending to nudge the private international banks back into fresh lending to highly indebted middle-income countries that were prepared to undertake further reforms to narrow their foreign and domestic deficits. Although the Bank welcomed "the Baker Plan," it was bruised by the way the United States issued the plan in Seoul as a kind of diktat, especially when at the same meetings Clausen was informed that the United States would not support his reelection the following year.

Within the Bank, serious misgivings about the Baker Plan mounted as it became apparent that private commercial bank lending was not going to resume to anywhere near the extent the plan contemplated. Although Bank analysts were beginning to entertain the need for debt reduction and forgiveness by the middle 1980s, it was taboo to say so in public. But the leash had been loosened enough for the institution to begin gearing up its Latin American programs. Relations with Mexico, in particular, became quite intimate.

In the same vein, SSA countries had been forced by impending insolvencies into short-term borrowing, especially from the IMF. Although the Bank had initially regarded the instrument as unsuited for most countries in the region, the depth of the financial crisis—and repayments due to the IMF—led it increasingly into quick-disbursing adjustment lending from 1983 onward. The weakness of most countries in the region would mean that as conditionalities swelled, their enforcement was necessarily weak.

Barber Conable's Term: 1986–91

Barber Conable, erstwhile Republican member of the U.S. House of Representatives and taxation expert from upstate New York, was, during the first fifty years of the World Bank, the only professional politician the United States nominated for the Bank presidency. He says he was the single nominee on whom James Baker, secretary of the Treasury, George Shultz, secretary of state, and Donald Regan, chief of staff to President Ronald Reagan, could agree. Wooed by Baker and a personal friend of Vice President George Bush, Conable expected to have friendly support from his government. Instead the United States voted with those Bank members who refused to approve President Clausen's administrative budget just before his departure. Conable deduced from James Baker's explanation that Conable would need to commission a major reorganizational study of the World Bank (and then implement its findings) to regain the support of his Part I members. He hired a somewhat obscure consulting firm and, at the consultants' suggestion, put the in-house aspects of the study in the hands of a group of cerebral, fast-track young Turks in the Bank staff. The last deserve much of the blame for a misjudgment for which, in their innocence, neither Conable nor the consultants were fully responsible.[15]

The reorganization effort advertised that the Bank payroll was going to be significantly reduced.[16] At the same time, in what looked like a romantic simulation of a free labor market, the exercise reorganized Bank staff from the top down. All jobs short of the president were theoretically vacated. Conable chose his top executives, four senior vice presidents, the principal result of which was to remove Ernest Stern as the powerful head of the operations complex and exchange his position with Moeen Qureshi as head of finance. Then the executives were able to bid competitively for whichever subordinates they wished, and the selectees for their subordinates, and so on. One effect was that the regional vice presidencies (likes choosing likes) wound up being somewhat more differentiated. But the whole exercise was also a game of musical chairs: a staff that had been enjoying privileged job security and, in some cases, were earning multiples of what they would at home, found themselves locked into heavy financial commitments while they faced a possible loss of jobs as well as their U.S. visas. Many panicked.

The substance of the reorganization—in part a further entrenchment of country programming—had some merit. But the process followed was highly disruptive. Against this background, Bank morale during the balance of the Conable term gained surprisingly. The president, although careful to avoid formal ventures out of channels, was persuasive in winning pro-Bank funding from the U.S. Congress. In addition to IDA, obtaining agreement on a general capital increase (GCI) of the IBRD in 1988—the largest ever in the Bank's history—was a singular achievement, providing the institution with enough headroom to forestall the seeking of another capital increase for the foreseeable future. Given the strong pressures from the U.S. Treasury on the Bank to become more market and private sector oriented, the 1991 capital increase of the IFC should have faced easy sailing. But here again, as recorded in chapter 13, there was considerable acrimony. Still, when the dust settled, the financial capacity of the Bank Group was significantly augmented in these years.

Conable's affable style was effective with his shareholders, both borrowing and non-borrowing (the sole exception being the government that nominated him). There was a sense that under him the Bank reexhibited some of the heart that recently had been obscured. Poverty, culminating in the *World Development Re-*

15. At the same time, the president was more aware of the reorganizational issues than other folklore has suggested. Edward Kim Jaycox, chairman of the exercise's steering group and in-house task force, interview, World Bank Oral History Program. A key problem, Jaycox thought in retrospect, was that Conable was not prepared to take charge of the institution— genuinely and hands on—to the extent required by the management model that the president, the consultants, and the in-house team all chose.

16. "There was no numerical objective, but there was the idea that we were going to clear out a lot of people in the process. We were going to cut a lot of costs of doing business and costs equal people." Ibid., p. 12.

port 1990, was once again "in." The adjustment umbrella with which the institution had been so preoccupied since 1980 was stretched in two ways—one, to protect the poor against adjustment shocks to their jobs and incomes, and two, to add to the macro adjustment targets an assortment of related matters that spelled out the quality of life for the poor and disadvantaged, among others.

The Bank was pushed from outside on both kinds of amendments to its adjustment agenda. UNICEF, the United Nations Children's Fund, was vocal and persuasive on the first (safety-net) count. Of the add-on subjects, Conable himself was very keen on environmental protection. But the challenge facing the Bank was the continuous expansion of the "environment" agenda beyond its earlier concerns with the health of the natural environment. Thus, because of particular interests both inside and outside the Bank, issues relating to resettlement and the protection of indigenous peoples, which could have been part of a poverty agenda, were instead subsumed in the environmental set. By the mid-1990s, "environment" had virtually become code language for groups frustrated with the prevailing development paradigm, and therefore with the Bank as the flag bearer of the paradigm.

As chapter 13 in volume 2 describes, the issue was pressed by first-world nongovernmental organizations (NGOs), who took on the Bank as an adversary. Within the Bank there was ambivalence; some, especially some of the economists, thought the environmental case was exaggerated. But the decision in 1987 was to go with pro-environmental reforms—whereupon implementation was impaired by problems in the formation of a new environment department. It also led to a decision by the Bank in 1988 to expand its work with NGOs.

In addition to the programs of special emphasis identified by Conable—environment, protections and improvements for women in development, the private sector—the Bank furthered its involvement in the social sectors (education, health, population, and nutrition). Meanwhile the continued poor performance of African countries led the Bank, at the urging of African intellectuals, to take the covers off and address more forthrightly the political roots of Africa's problems. Hemmed in by the Bank's Articles that mandated the institution to remain apolitical, the new "governance" agenda was initially a cautious attempt to address the political realities in many borrowing countries while remaining within the bounds of the Articles. However, this period coincided with the end of the cold war; it proved increasingly difficult to hold the line on sharp, narrow boundaries. As in the case of "environment," "governance" soon became a code word for quite varied agendas ranging from defense expenditures by borrowing countries to human rights and political and administrative reform.

All these policy targets had informed, motivated advocates in the Bank staff and Board. As more and more IDA deputies began taking a leaf out of the U.S. book, goal proliferation was not simply psychically rewarding, it was the grease that lubricated replenishments. For practically all subjects a good case could be made that the issue was important for development. But the steady expansion sidestepped the thorny issue of institutional comparative advantage and the trade-offs involved: in budgets, institutional and borrower attention, and skills.

Meanwhile, trying to enforce multiple preconditioned policy targets was sapping the seriousness of the Bank's adjustment lending. It was a kind of Catch-22. Targets had been added to adjustment exercises because they were good causes and it was administratively easy to do so. But procedurally the choice had been for preconditioning: borrowers entered into fairly precise contracts to do or not do things that were sufficiently measurable for nonperformance to be conspicuous. Review after review of adjustment lending wrung its hands over the proliferation of borrowers' agreed undertakings. In the second (1990) Review of Adjustment Lending (RAL), the last under Conable, the average number of undertakings per adjustment loan was up to fifty-six, and it continued to rise. There was no way so many simultaneous agreements could be monitored, let alone enforced. The procedure was committed to revealed ineffectiveness. It also was psychologically off-putting. By the mid-1980s Bank operatives were discovering the essentiality of persuading borrowers to make induced reforms their own, to take "ownership" of them. The growing judgment was that, procedurally, interactive dialogues between borrowers and lenders had a better chance of achieving reform ownership than did the imposition of ex-ante conditions.

Even when stretched widest in the late 1980s, in the aggregate "adjustment" covered no more than a minority of the World Bank's lending. There still was a large agricultural program, for example, despite the decline in the volume and quality of agriculture in the Bank's portfolio. Several factors seemed to be at work: the declining role of agriculture as some borrowers progressed into postagricultural phases of development; the poor performance of the agriculture portfolio and, relatedly, a weakening of the Bank's technical agricultural expertise; shifts to less micro-interventionist, more macro-market, freeing, modes of pro-agricultural policies; and finally, reflecting the pressures on the Bank, a shift in budgetary resources from agriculture into environment-related activities.

The shifts in approaches in this large and troubled portfolio in the 1980s epitomized broader shifts in thinking and lending. There was more inclination to link agriculture issues and policies to central macroeconomic matters. It was increasingly argued that, in many countries, "urban bias" was alive and well: the system of tariffs, other trade restrictions, and overvalued exchange rates imposed hidden taxes on agriculture that, together with direct taxes, placed formidable drags on farming. Similarly, doubt was cast on the treatment of what had been the segregated realm of agricultural credit. Reformers who gained voice within the Bank in the later 1980s advocated raising farm interest rates to general credit market levels, eliminating subsidies, using rural financial institutions to mobilize deposits as well as lend resources, and reducing the insulation of such institutions from the rest of the credit market. Third, and especially by the end of the decade, the Bank also began to backtrack on its earlier support for parastatals, calling first for their reform and later for their elimination. Signaling a more eclectic approach, it began to be more overt in its support of land reform. And finally, by the early 1990s it was pushing its borrowers to adopt more decentralized approaches to rural development.

The markets and private sector shift that began under Clausen continued under Conable. With the accent of structural adjustment continuing to be on economic liberalization, the Bank's role was in a broad sense to improve the "enabling environment" for the private sector, although not at a pace that satisfied the U.S. Treasury. The period marked a major rethinking within the Bank of its principal lending instrument for the private sector: development finance companies (DFCs). Once the IFC was back on track under Ryrie, the Corporation again became a lively force both for direct lending and in support of capital market development.

In this sketch of highlights, we revert to the unfinished debt crisis. Conable arrived to find the institution getting deep into lending of the Baker Plan type. But the plan was not working. The private banks had little appetite for fresh lending. Indeed, the Baker effect was to transfer major fractions of the commercial bank debt to the multilateral institutions. Pundits—whether academic, congressional, or journalistic—recognized the insolvency problem: they argued for debt reduction, as did the Bank's Treasurer, Rotberg, who had recently resigned.

Within the Bank there was little doubt that debt forgiveness was unavoidable (although there was still unease about how to structure and denominate action so as to do as little damage as possible to the institution's own credit). Until the U.S. government provided a changed signal, however, the Bank had good reason to keep its head down. Nicholas Brady, Bush's secretary of the Treasury, seemed to have an embedded disinterest in the Bank. He left the whole matter to his undersecretary, David Mulford, who, although presumably with broader goals, seemed to enjoy harassing the institution.

Thus matters remained in quasi suspension until Secretary Brady in March 1989 delivered the plan, far more realistic than Baker's, that bears his name, its draft (ironically) being the product of Secretary Mulford and his colleagues. In fact the plan had been largely anticipated during the preceding year by both the French and the Japanese. But the Americans accepted the credit, and while the implementation of this scheme did not follow its script very well, the crisis, as our debt chapter says, finally seemed to subside out of sheer weariness, as well as to be dampened by external events, in particular, a sharp decline in interest rates. For Mexico, at least, problems would be resurrected following the crisis of 1994–95.

Alongside the debt issue, President Conable faced the perennial problem of the nature of interaction with the IMF. The book engages this matter in a number of places and contexts. Sibling rivalry was sometimes less than sororal, especially in Latin America and Africa, and relations came to a head over the stance toward Argentina in 1988 and 1989. One version of what happened is provided in volume 2 of this work by former IMF staffer, Jacques Polak, who sees the Bank as ill-advised in an attempt to supersede the Fund's macropolicy conditioning of Argentina. Chapter 10 gives another version of the story.

The hiatus in Bank lending to China following the Tiananmen Square repression of 1989—at the behest of the G-7—and the broad issue of "governance" that bubbled up in Africa, exemplified a gradual move by the Bank into its borrowers' politics. The changing political climate and pressures, as well as the reality of its borrowers' governments, meant that as aspects of the matter became subjects of Bank influence and loan conditioning, it would henceforth have to be somewhat acrobatic to maintain the consistency of its actions with the parameters of the Articles.

After his rocky start, Barber Conable gave the impression of having gotten more or less on top of a complex job in a complex period. By the end of his tenure it appeared that the institution was back on track. Like a good politician, however, Conable had staved off pressures by various compromises that often added to the Bank's goals and commitments. That legacy would prove costly in the long term. Still, Conable had regained the confidence of shareholders and staff, as well as external pressure groups. His retirement, when in 1991 he probably could have won renomination by the Bush administration if he had so wanted, was therefore surprising. There were various factors, including other interests, but principally he was weary of the lack of support he and his Bank had received from the American administration, despite his hitherto close political and personal ties with it.

The Preston Presidency: 1991–95

Lewis Preston's term as Bank president, cut short by his death in May 1995, was a troubled, stressful time for the World Bank. More than anything, the end of the cold war changed the global environment and with it the political support the Bank had enjoyed in its major shareholders. Preston was widely viewed as the most distinguished commercial banker to head the institution. His work of steering J. P. Morgan around the shoals of the debt crisis of the 1980s was much admired. He was a renowned manager. But Preston did not bring a substantive agenda with him. He picked up what he found. Programmatically and administratively, he was a fine tuner. He was distracted by personal tragedy and bad health. The troubles with which he had to grapple were less currently generated from within the institution than accumulations from the past and external pressures and matters of psychology and perception.

One of Preston's first acts, in what had become a habit of all new chief executives at the Bank, was to turn his managerial talents to making various limited adjustments in the organizational structure. The most conspicuous and controversial was the installation of the same top structure he had used at Morgan, namely, a trio of "managing directors" just short of himself who ostensibly had no "line" responsibilities but collectively, subject to his decision, had all of them. Managing directors could, as needed, act for each other but all had areas of sectoral and regional specialization. This structure cut sharply into the fiefdoms that had formed around the senior vice presidencies following the 1987 reorganization. But the creation of new thematic vice presidencies reflecting institutional priorities (poverty, environment, and the private sector) led to its own set of problems, not least being their preoccupation with their own public relations.

A key issue confronting the Bank was to gear up for operations in East Europe, while limiting the diversion of institutional energies from its traditional borrowers. Despite substantial pressures from its major shareholders, the Bank skillfully reconciled these competing interests. An increase in staff and budgetary resources ensured that, for the most part, the interests of old borrowers were not compromised. In acceding to G-7 pressures for major lending to Russia, the Bank included clauses in its loans that curbed risks to the rest of its portfolio.

In terms of program, Preston emphatically reiterated, and in terms of institutional priorities, extended, Conable's renewal of poverty reduction as a central mission of the Bank. The institution was in an active mode with respect to environmental protection. It became the key multilateral cooperator in the formation of the Global Environmental Facility. In addition the Bank was more forthcoming to NGOs, a process begun by Conable.

For this presidency it is not wrong to put matters of image high on the topical agenda. The Bank continued to be battered by the (mainly rich-country, particularly U.S.) environmental NGOs. Bank bashing became an easy blood sport for many media. There were disgruntled employees to quote and always disgruntled legislators put off by the (tax-free) personnel costs the Bank incurred; its budget constraint was still soft.

A set of random factors converged in the early 1990s. Chief, in fact, was the same chronological fact that gave birth to the present work. The approach of the Bank's fiftieth anniversary raised its profile rather awkwardly. Any number of memorial exercises were launched, not all benign. "Fifty years is enough" became a rather shrill theme. There was some spillover from inaugural excesses of the *European* Bank for Reconstruction and Development in London. And the World Bank picked a bad time to be revealed in some serious construction miscalculations and cost overruns in the construction of its new headquarters building. Retrospectively, management controls and Board supervision had been weak. This plainly was a problem Preston inherited. Yet he also looked too expedient in the way one vice president, with a long record of intelligent and worthy service, was sacrificed in institutional penance.

The Preston Bank was given little credit for self-criticism. The press lionized the negative findings of the report of the task group on portfolio management in 1993 (named for its chairman, the recently retired vice president Willi Wapenhans). The group concluded that the procedures and incentives of the institution tended to reward project and program design—and, indeed, lending—at the expense of implementation and follow-up. But external critics were slow to note that all of this useful (and, in fact, familiar) criticism of shortfalls was self-analyzed and self-revealed, not something thrown at the Bank from outside. Similarly, an independent 1994 study by a team chaired by Bradford Morse, former head of the UNDP, was critical of the Bank, the government of India, and the governments of three Indian states for their insufficient attention to the environmental and population-displacement aspects of a set of dam projects on India's Narmada River. The whole study, although insistently promoted from outside (see the environment chapter in volume 2), was done at Bank behest. This was the first time the institution had brought in outside evaluators to make a major assessment of one of "its" infrastructure projects. One consequence was the setting up of a continuing inspection panel.

The Narmada reactions deserve some elaboration. Critics charged that the problems stemmed from the "secretive" nature of the institution: more openness would have allowed stronger external scrutiny and, with it, better quality control. A new disclosure policy was now put in place and public information centers were opened. Yet it was also clear that the way these decisions were arrived at distorted outcomes. Bank staff and management discussed drafts of the disclosure policy with Washington-based NGOs before most executive directors saw the drafts; indeed, some executive directors first received the drafts from the NGOs. It was not surprising that the first center for information dissemination opened in Washington, D.C., not in borrowing countries.

The establishment of an inspection panel also was a step to pacify vocal critics.[17] It was evident at the time to both senior management and many members of the Bank's Executive Board that creating a new bureaucratic entity was not a real answer. The need was better accountability, both of staff and managers. More bureaucratic baggage was not what an institution already overburdened by a surfeit of rules and procedures required. Any new administrative mechanism would be inclined to assert its jurisdiction and inaugurate an inspection at any prompting by complainants. The Bank was now operating in a supercharged atmosphere, where appearance and moral posturing were all-important.

The United States, pressed by a self-righteous Congress to link IDA to the creation of such an entity, was the principal force behind the panel. In the Board, the vote on the panel was a close one, sealed only after the United Kingdom reluctantly went along, trading its vote for U.S. support for the British drive to secure the 1997 Annual General Meeting in Hong Kong. In fact, nearly all the Narmada-related changes reflected unilateral pressure by the U.S. Congress, which used the leverage of IDA to force its preferences—and then retreated in its IDA contributions. Accountability was a one-way street.

17. Ibrahim Shihata, *The World Bank Inspection Panel* (Oxford University Press, 1994).

For the first time in many years, the state of Bank finances, in particular those of the IBRD and the IFC, was robust. The financial capacities of both institutions had been increased tremendously by the recently concluded capital increases. Profits were ample. And the IBRD had emerged as one of the cheapest borrowers, bar the G-3 treasuries. With the abatement of the debt crisis and the entry of East Europe, a strong demand for IBRD lending seemed likely. But instead such lending stagnated, and loan repayments became as big a source of the institution's cash flows as market borrowings. The Bank's capital intermediation role waned even as its financial capacity and potential effectiveness flowered.

Although booming private capital transfers and a reduced role of states (the Bank's principal customers) in economic activities contributed to the diminishing demand for Bank funds, it was still puzzling that demand was so weak for loans from an institution whose loans were still unmatched in financial cost and maturity. Part of the reason undoubtedly lay in the increased transaction costs of Bank loans that had been bartered over time with donors being persuaded to contribute to IDA.

IDA replenishment exercises had lost whatever spirit of cooperation had motivated participants to reach for good collective results in the past. In December 1992, Ernest Stern, the Bank's representative at the IDA 10 negotiation, told the Board that the final agreement of the negotiation reflected the disintegration of the whole system of collective multilateralism. Burden-sharing had become the opposite of collaboration.

Projects and Project Quality

In 1992 the Wapenhans Report called into question the effectiveness of project lending, the very signature activity of the World Bank. Perspectives on the activity—and on the quality of project performance—shifted during the 1970s, 1980s, and 1990s.

Evolving Project Operations

The Bank developed a standard set of loan-processing procedures that became known as the "project cycle." In the course of identification, preparation, appraisal, and supervision phases, Bank loans, to varying degrees, analyzed the economic, technical, institutional, financial, commercial, environmental, and sociological impacts of its projects. The relative weight and quality of the analyses addressed to these several criteria differed by project type, but also over the institution's own life cycle. Thus although commercial and technical criteria were prominent in the early years of the Bank, environmental and sociological criteria became more important in later years. Whereas the borrower and the Bank exercised joint responsibility during the project cycle, the relative responsibilities among borrowers and at different stages of the cycle differed markedly.

The Bank's clearest responsibility—and involvement—was at the appraisal stage, which undertook to "examine and evaluate the economic and social objectives that a project is designed to meet, to assess whether the proposed project is likely to meet these objectives efficiently, and to recommend conditions that should be met to ensure that the purpose of the project will be achieved."[18] Appraisal normally covered seven broad areas, although their relative weight varied significantly with the sector and over time.[19] Weaker borrowers called for a greater degree of Bank involvement, and in more extreme cases the projects literally were "Bank" projects. The institution's direct involvement in project identification and preparation was particularly marked in Africa, where, more often than not, the project ideas governments advanced were only peripherally represented in their official public investment programs. The formulation of a full project concept was in most cases the product of Bank identification and preparation missions and work done by Bank-financed or Bank-supervised consultants, owing to the limited capacity of local public administration.[20] Similarly, during the implementation period (that is, while the investment was being physically made and shaped), technical assistance supplied by the Bank and Bank supervision missions were integral parts of the average project. The downside was that the institution's heavy involvement in the project cycle (and the concomitant light involvement by the local authorities) meant that the locals in many cases had little interest in the project's fate. All too often in weaker countries, projects were associated with their main external sponsor; they lost their identification with the national agency that should have been primarily responsible for their success or failure.

The Bank's project work encompassed many issues. While the factors underlying the decision to finance a specific project were the most intellectually engaging, other matters—ranging from technical and financial questions to procurement—were also important. The financial issues included the share of total project cost to be financed by the Bank Group. Normally the shares were higher in poorer countries with severe domestic resource constraints. The Bank, however, felt that ceilings on its share helped ensure country "ownership." In addition, the lower the Bank's share, the more projects it could assist in a country. A related issue was the degree of financing of local costs. The scarcity of domestic saving often was as

18. Operational Manual Statement 2.20, January 1984.

19. These were: economics (project benefits, economic return); technical (engineering design and project costs); institutional (management, organization); financial (implementing agency and direct beneficiaries); commercial (procurement, marketing arrangements); environmental assessment; and sociological aspects (for example, sociocultural factors, target groups, involuntary resettlement).

20. The staff intensity of the Bank's project cycle translated into higher administrative costs. By the mid-1980s the administrative expenses of the operations departments for processing new loans amounted to about 1 percent of loan commitments (about 0.3 percent of average total project costs). Supervision costs were about 0.16 percent of the outstanding portfolio.

serious a constraint on investment as the shortage of foreign exchange. Yet the Bank's Articles, based on the hard lessons of the 1930s, had focused the institution's role on foreign exchange financing to deter countries from piling up foreign debt for purposes to which local resources could be deployed. Similarly, the financing of recurrent costs was severely restricted; they usually involved goods and services susceptible to local financing. The Bank's prevailing policies in these areas had been quite restrictive. During the 1980s, as the institution ventured increasingly into social sectors and many of its borrowers faced acute budgetary problems, it loosened its practice.

Another object of attention was procurement. Activity involving expenditures also concerned contracts. Since Bank lending was largely to public entities, procurement issues on Bank contracts always entailed intense scrutiny. Although in its very early years the Bank did not have a system of international competitive bidding (ICB), this feature soon became integral to its loans. The ICB process became a prerequisite of Bank loans as borrowers learned how to employ processes for preparing bidding documents and evaluating bids. Borrowers often complained that the bidding procedures tended to steer contracts in particular directions. The Bank did indeed use ICB as a means for selling the institution to important developed-country constituencies: participating in the Bank was good not just for the soul, but also for the pocket. Many prominent executive director offices in developed countries kept a close tab on Bank projects and contracts therein, to help domestic firms in their constituencies. While close scrutiny maintained a certain discipline in the process, over time countries learned how to nudge outcomes to favor constituency firms. One such mechanism was the use of trust funds. Since the choice of consultants often affects ex ante the design and technical criteria that a project adopts, it was hoped trust funds would enhance the competitiveness of constituency firms and steer project procurement in their direction.

Nevertheless, the large equipment and construction entailed in most Bank projects—especially in infrastructure—meant that established procedures preserved a certain integrity in the awarding of public contracts.[21] Indeed, it was not infrequent for a worried public official to try to secure Bank funding simply to shield himself from political pressures. In larger countries, however, since Bank loans usually funded only small fractions of public investments, governments commonly could steer the Bank away from sectors where particular interests were paramount. Furthermore, in recent years, with the Bank's infrastructural financing role waning, the benefits of its contractual integrity were diminished.

The choice of projects was always guided by a mix of tangible and intangible factors. One view was to direct Bank projects into areas and sectors faced with the most critical "bottlenecks": ports where importers and exporters were paying high

21. This could not always be maintained. In the 1970s Bank officials grew suspicious at the inordinately high percentage of contracts on projects in Romania subject to ICB won by Romanian firms relative to their quite limited success outside Romania.

demurrage, power plants if there were severe power shortages, a highway connecter, and so on. A variant of this view held that the Bank should engage those institutions that were the worst run. This variant of the approach could offer high returns, as in the case of the Spanish railways in the 1950s. Yet, according to a contrary argument, to attempt to reform such institutions—PEMEX in Mexico, the Argentina railways—was to throw good money after bad. Instead, the institution should involve itself with those institutions and ministries that offered the greatest opportunity for a constructive relationship. The question of whether to concentrate on where the need was greatest or where projects had the best chance of succeeding was not confined to projects. It extended to regions within a country as well as to choices between countries. From the late 1970s onward the Bank was more likely to justify its involvement on the ground that a bad situation would be even worse without the institution. One consequence, as the Bank took up more difficult cases, was a worsening of the average performance of the Bank's portfolio.

The rate of return was never the basis for choosing a project. It was an important element of discipline—a reality check—although in practice its principal purpose was either to ratify a choice or to reject unwise projects suggested by borrowers. The Bank was always aware that as a practical matter a rate of return could be, simply, one indicator. The benefits of dams plainly consisted in good part of externalities: effects on regional development. The psychological benefits—what it meant to a government to support a major development project while achieving at least a minimum rate of return—had other advantages. As it turned out, if positive externalities were overplayed in benefit-cost calculus, negative externalities usually were underplayed. Dams were a classic example. George Woods, himself an investment banker, leaned toward broader assessments. "Little people," he said, "only think in rates of return."[22]

The analytical role of rates of return had been both strengthened and weakened in the 1970s. On the one hand, the techniques of cost-benefit analysis were becoming more refined, and by the mid-1970s the Bank's poverty thrust resulted in major efforts to develop and operationalize the techniques of social cost-benefit analysis. Such techniques, using poverty weights, were tried in a very few cases in the 1970s but almost never since. In the 1980s even shadow prices were used only sporadically.[23]

As a practical matter, it could not have been otherwise.[24] A cost-benefit analysis of social cost-benefit analysis would yield low returns. The conviction grew that it

22. Roger Chaufournier, interview, World Bank Oral History Program, July 22, 1986.

23. A report in the mid-1990s on the quality of economic analysis in Bank project appraisals found that, with the exception of projects in China, there was little systematic use of opportunity cost estimates to reflect the value of nontraded items or foreign exchange.

24. For a contrary viewpoint, see I. M. D. Little and J. A. Mirrlees, "Project Appraisal and Planning Twenty Years On," in Stanley Fischer, Dennis de Tray, and Shekhar Shah, eds., *Proceedings of the World Bank Annual Conference on Development Economics, 1990* (World

was better to grapple with broader economy-wide distortions at their conceptual roots instead of trying to piece together the effects through individual projects. Rules of thumb such as spatially situating a project in a poor region went a long way, especially in countries where poverty was pervasive. There were technical difficulties in capturing the benefits of projects (or components of projects, as in rural development cases) that did not involve direct production. The problem became more apparent as the Bank moved into social sectors. Although the point was rarely made explicitly, there were those who felt "that some things had to be considered as absolutes although there was still very much the mystique of the rate of return."[25]

The traditional project emphasis of the Bank was considerably downplayed in the 1980s, as institutional focus shifted to adjustment lending. Another, more modest, modification of the project emphasis was the sector approach. To a considerable degree, Bank projects were linked to broader sector investments and policies. Thus in telecommunication and railway projects, a sector investment program usually was called a project; the Bank would establish broad sector conditions but at the same time make a technical appraisal of the proposed investments that composed the project.

Following the first oil shock, sector lending began to receive greater attention. In a note to the operations managers in 1974, Burke Knapp called attention to it as a suitable lending technique in those "situations when the Bank could use its staff more effectively and make a greater contribution to the development of the borrowing countries if it were to focus more on the achievement of over-all sector objectives, the improvement of sector policies and the development of appropriate institutions, and relatively less on the merits of specific investment projects."[26] Requiring both a large investment program and an experienced and sophisticated borrower, sector loans were not a general-purpose tool. Knapp's note acknowledged that the Bank had made "very few sector loans" that included all the desired elements. Examples of those few included power loans to Mexico, Indian railway loans, and water supply loans to Brazil. Although DFC loans appeared to have some of the elements of sector loans, they were not based on Bank analysis of specific projects; they were not predicated on reviews of sector programs; nor were sector conditions attached to them.

But, noted the vice president, sector lending also was a convenient means for accelerating the disbursement of loans "in cases where a rapid transfer of resources is essential," considerations that took on an added significance in the light of the energy crisis and the expanded lending targets. Nevertheless, sector lending remained relatively modest. The Bank found few institutions capable of carrying out investment programs in accordance with the criteria established for invest-

---

Bank, 1991), pp. 351–82. Further observations are offered by Glenn P. Jenkins, "Project Analysis and the World Bank," AEA Papers and Proceedings, May 1997, pp. 38–42.

25. Chaufournier, Oral History, July 22, 1986.

26. Memorandum, J. Burke Knapp to regional vice presidents, "Sector Lending," June 10, 1974.

ment, procurement, and disbursement by sector-lending standards. Moreover, countries that did have the capability—in Latin America, for instance—were unwilling to adhere to the Bank's sector loan conditions, given the easy availability of commercial funds in the middle 1970s.

After going into abeyance in the 1980s (although elements of the approach were to be found in SECALs) sector loans resurfaced in the 1990s, the logic being that it was the sector, rather than the more particular activities ostensibly financed, that really constituted the project. In their more recent rendition, sector loans have begun to pay greater attention to sectorwide expenditures (and not just investments), as well as donor coordination in countries that depend greatly on aid.

Process changes took the Bank along yet another new path: the Bank now put more emphasis on participatory approaches, which encouraged relevant groups to become involved early in lending operations.[27] Although the issue had seeped in as part of the poverty agenda of the 1970s, its effects on project design and execution had been limited. Borrowing countries were rarely eager to embrace the concept. Issues of participation were closely linked to those of decentralization, and in turn to the distribution of political power.

Over the 1980s the issues of participation, NGOs, and decentralization all came to the fore and were soon joined by their cousins, "civil society" and "stakeholders." At the rhetorical level, the terminology became integral to the "environmental" agenda that gradually expanded beyond concerns for the physical biosphere to a broader emerging critique of the dominant development paradigm.

Although some enterprising Bank staff seized on these new fashions to advance terminology (and themselves), other staff sought to use issues of participation and decentralization to address long-simmering problems facing Bank projects, particularly those affecting large numbers of poor people. Bank projects in agriculture, population, health and nutrition, low-income housing and urban upgrading, and water and sanitation were particularly affected by this shift. Equity considerations apart, painful experience had shown that there were sound reasons in these fields to expand the participation of beneficiaries if project effectiveness was to be improved, especially with regard to better cost recovery, expenditure patterns, and monitoring and maintenance of operations.

Project Quality, Then and Now

The high quality attributed to Bank project lending in its early decades rested on several factors. Borrowers were relatively capable technically, the choices of tech-

27. These changes were codified in a series of memoranda: OP10.00 (6/94), "Investment Lending"; ODs 4.00 (10/89), 4.01 (10/91), and OP/BP 4.02 (10/94), "Environmental Assessment"; OD4.20 (6/90), "Resettlement"; and "World Bank and Participation," Operations Policy Department, September 1994.

nique were clearly defined, and measures of project performance were comparatively unambiguous. Over time Bank lending moved into countries and sectors
where all these factors were less favorable. Even as project goals and designs
required more sophisticated administrative capabilities, these were lacking in-
digenously. This discrepancy and its impact were most evident in rural development projects in Africa in the 1970s. Animated by desirable goals, the projects
outreached prevailing local capacity. In the 1990s new goals, similarly worthy,
posed similar questions. Thus although poverty targeting had much intellectual
merit, borrowers rarely had the implementation capacity.

For two decades (1952–72), quality standards in Bank projects were maintained
by the Central Projects Staff. This group ruled the roost with an iron hand. The
1972 reorganization dispersed much of its staff and weakened its bureaucratic
hegemony. As an institutional characteristic, the "quality" trait did, however, have
trade-offs: it incurred a quantity cost and imparted a reluctance to experiment.
Many have criticized the McNamara era for an emphasis on quantity. But such
complaints fail to acknowledge that conceptualizing quality versus quantity as a
zero-sum trade-off is false. One could always do a single project in a country and
make it nearly perfect. But would that make a dent?

The rapid expansion of project lending meant that current resources devoted to
appraisal increased in relation to those going to supervision. Per se, the shift to the
upstream part of the project cycle had merit. Repeatedly (most recently in the
mid-1990s), internal analysis pointed out that quality at entry was a crucial determinant of project outcomes. Intensive supervision of projects poorly conceived was
akin to locking the stable doors after the horses had bolted. Still, by the mid-1970s
staff were asking whether quality was being sacrificed in behalf of quantity. The
Bank's senior management insisted there were no such trade-offs: no one was ever
forced to bring for funding a project that he or she felt was not ready. Indeed, the
authors have found little documentation of such behavior. However, the lending
targets set for staff clearly placed them under pressure to deliver; even more, this
was strongly *perceived* to be the case.

Questions about the quality of its projects were central to the Bank's psyche—
and indeed those of its critics. Debates about the quality of Bank projects invariably
drew upon the Bank's own internal analysis and evaluations, in particular, project
evaluations of the Operations Evaluation Department (OED). In 1983, a decade
after it was formed, the OED evaluated more than a thousand projects implemented
over a ten-year period and involving more than $22 billion in Bank loans and about $67
billion in total investments. That review found that 86 percent of all projects (and 90
percent by value) appeared to have achieved their major objectives and were judged to
have been worthwhile. For projects for which an economic rate of return was calculated, the reestimated rate of return averaged about 18 percent.

Over the next decade, however, evaluations of Bank projects, as determined by
periodic OED findings, declined (table 1-2) and became a subject of much analysis,

Table 1-2. *Assessments of Project Performance*[a]

Sector and region	Percentage satisfactory		
	1974–80	*1981–89*	*1990–94*
Sector			
Agriculture	75	58	65
Energy	86	85	75
Finance	83	72	49
Human resources	86	74	85
Industry	83	61	69
Power	93	77	74
Program and policy	100	64	69
Technical assistance	100	56	43
Telecommunication	97	83	80
Transport	87	73	76
Urban	100	80	75
Water and sanitation	100	71	60
Region			
Sub-Saharan Africa	79	58	56
East Asia and Pacific	92	78	86
Europe and Central Asia	86	77	72
Latin America and Caribbean	85	62	66
Middle East and North Africa	89	78	72
South Asia	89	73	75
Bank-wide	85	68	69

Source: OED data.

a. The time periods refer to the closing year of the project, that is, when all disbursements are completed.

both inside and outside the Bank. In addition to a string of embarrassing setbacks in projects that earned the institution indictment by environmental groups (see volume 2, chapter 13), the issue was the subject of intense scrutiny, thanks to the 1992 report of a "portfolio management task force" (PMTF). The review had been prompted by the new president, Lewis Preston, who had been struck by the institution's preoccupation with preparing new projects, relative to managing its large portfolio of already approved projects in various stages of completion. The task force, headed by recently retired Senior Vice President Willi Wapenhans, produced a report whose analysis and conclusions were a landmark in the institution's history, as much due to the external attention as any new revelations, since much of its findings had been documented by a series of internal reports during the 1980s.[28]

28. World Bank, Portfolio Management Task Force, "Effective Implementation: Key to Development Success," September 22, 1992. In turn its findings were based on an analysis by the country operations staff, "The Relationship of Loan Processing to Project Quality," March 27, 1992, which in turn drew upon sundry OED reports and the Annual Review of Implementation and Supervision (ARIS).

Although the PMTF noted weaknesses in the appraisal process, it put the onus of weaknesses in project quality on supervision. That analysis had played well with the many who were by now convinced that institutional incentives had generated a strong "approval" culture, that is, one preoccupied with getting projects approved by the Board, while giving limited attention to their implementation.

Yet matters were not as simple as the PMTF made out. With reviews showing that the quality of appraisal was an important determinant in the success or failure of projects, perhaps the problem was still at the appraisal end of the process.[29] Another study covering projects approved in calendar year 1993 found that the quality of economic analysis was poor in 13 percent and barely acceptable in 25 percent of the projects subject to cost-benefit analysis. This finding suggested that rapid progress had not been made in following the PMTF's recommendations.[30]

For the Bank, the major embarrassment was provided by results in areas that constituted its core of infrastructural lending: power, transport, major irrigation systems, water and sewage, and telecommunications. These were the areas on which the Bank had built its reputation. Most of the enterprises in them were state-owned monopolies, natural monopolies with economies of scale. Severe capital market limitations and foreign exchange intensity had made these sectors natural channels for Bank lending.

The key factors underlying success in earlier years had included the borrowing governments' strong commitment to maintain institutional autonomy and enforce financial covenants, Bank staff and managers whose technical and managerial competence was widely acknowledged, and favorable macroeconomic environments. During the 1970s and 1980s all these factors had eroded, as was repeatedly documented in internal reports.[31] Foremost was the inability of the project entities and the Bank to enforce capital structure covenants (typically debt-to-equity ratios and debt-service coverage) as well as revenue covenants (concerning rate of return and internal cash generation). This inability was both cause and consequence of the enterprises' declining autonomy from government pressures. The

29. In the 1995 evaluation cohort, 85 percent of projects with satisfactory (or better) outcomes had satisfactory (or better) appraisals, while 57 percent of those with unsatisfactory (or highly unsatisfactory) outcomes had deficient appraisals.

30. World Bank, "A Review of the Quality of Economic Analysis in Staff Appraisal Reports for Projects Approved in 1993," Operations Evaluation Department and Operations Policy Department report, May 5, 1995.

31. Examples include "The Bank's Role in the Electric Power Sector," Industry and Energy Department, 1992; "The Bank's Evolving Policy toward Railway Lending," Infrastructure and Urban Development Department, 1991. Relevant OED reports include, "A Review of World Bank Lending for Natural Gas," 1992; "Water Supply and Sanitation Projects: The Bank's Experience, 1967–89"; "The Bank's Experience in Telecommunications Lending: An OED Review," 1993; "A Review of World Bank Lending for Irrigation," 1994; "Lending for Electric Power in Sub-Saharan Africa," 1995.

Bank itself, especially in its managerial cadre, was increasingly staffed by generalists who were poorly equipped to manage these issues credibly. Moreover, sector needs had shifted away from investments toward maintenance expenditures, matters that were more difficult to manage from outside. Though the Bank time and again pressed governments to follow good practice, they did so only sporadically.

The institution's unwillingness to enforce project covenants over long periods of time reflected a dilemma: whether to endanger broad country relations over issues in particular sectors, especially when the country was reeling under external shocks (1970s) or delicate macroeconomic matters were under negotiation (1980s). Timidity, however, ill-served either the borrowers or the institution over the long run.

A different problem arose from the complex institutional aspects underlying many project problems. Despite its mounting incantations of "institution building," the Bank had limited internal expertise in what admittedly always had been a most difficult area. Solutions invariably included large (and expensive) doses of technical assistance, studies, and analysis, despite widespread acknowledgment of the severe limitations of such inputs. Technical assistance required special skills not always easily available in the Bank or to the Bank, especially in the difficult environments in poor countries where it was most needed.

Another factor that contributed to perceptions of declining project quality was unrealism in initial estimates of economic rates of return. Optimism biased various aspects of project estimation, running from price projections of specific project outputs to borrowers' administrative capacity to implement ambitious goals. Time and again, the unrealism was signaled in various internal analyses and OED reports, with little effect. At the end of the 1980s, in fact, an analysis showed that the difference between ex-ante and ex-post rates of return had widened almost continuously during that decade. The PMTF also singled out high-side bias as a matter needing improvement in the Bank's economic analysis.[32] At the behest of the Board, another study examined the issue.[33] Recent OED reviews of evaluation results indicate that while the declining trend of past years seems to be stabilizing, about a third of

32. The postappraisal review of economic analysis, begun in early 1990 by the Working Group on Economic Analysis (ECON), was integrated into the Portfolio Management Task Force Report. It concluded, among other things, that substantial improvement in economic analysis was required, given the findings that in only 55 percent of the reviewed projects was the economic analysis rated acceptable or better, and in the remainder it was deemed to be barely acceptable or poor.

33. World Bank, "Project Appraisal: A Process Study—Approach Paper," p. 1 The study found that for projects subject to cost-benefit analysis, the quality of the economic analysis was rated good or better in 20 percent of project SARs, average or acceptable in 42 percent, barely acceptable or marginal in 25 percent, and poor in 13 percent. This was similar to the overall project ratings referred to in the PMTF Report. The rating criteria were specially adapted for projects normally not subject to cost-benefit analysis, those in the education and population, health, and nutrition sector where the results showed that economic analysis was acceptable or better in 74 percent, and poor in 2 percent.

projects reviewed at the end of the investment phase still had unsatisfactory outcomes.[34] There was some evidence that the Bank in its haste to genuflect to environmental and social pressure groups was paying less attention to economic and technical aspects, thereby casting another stone at measured project quality.

For all the hand-wringing over project deterioration, few questioned the fitting-ness of the standards being applied. Projects designed to first-world standards might be showcases radiating best design and best practice. But they, including those in the social sectors, also could be overengineered. They could stick out as high-cost cases soon to be overwhelmed. Projects that kept only a few steps ahead of—and thereby led—good borrowing country practice often were fundable and had better chances of replication. But in the Bank, the high-cost showcase projects were often pushed by interests in the Part I countries that were harshest concerning the Bank and could hold it to ransom. Borrowers with options began to exit. In a few others, notably China, which had both the domestic capacity and the size always to come up with mutually agreeable projects, projects flourished. But in the smaller poorer countries, the steady escalation of conditions and social standards meant that the dice were heavily loaded against project success.

Three points stand out in these debates on the quality of Bank projects. First, they are based on the Bank's own assessments, whose limitations render simple judgments nearly impossible. The judgments are not based on a project's performance during its working life, but at a point in time when the Bank's financial disbursements ceased, typically at the beginning of the artifact's working life. Even trends are difficult to interpret: was it due to poor inputs, the Bank's venturing into more risky terrain (whether by country or sector), changed value judgments, or a more volatile global environment?

Second, and this has been little emphasized, the Bank's lending effort was really the equivalent of venture capital in economic development. This meant risks, and with it, the risks of failure. For a venture capitalist, a record of two out of three is admirable. The problem of project failures was most manifest in those projects that not only did not deliver the benefits expected but did substantial harm, clearly violating a sort of Hippocratic code of development: above all, do no harm. On the other hand, in many cases the worst consequence of a low-return project was debt without development. In the IDA countries, where the Bank had greater responsibility, the debt itself was not financially very onerous. In the IBRD case where it was, the clients were more sophisticated and had to bear a greater burden of responsibility for their projects. All of this said, however, the Bank did not act like a venture capitalist, since it was little disposed to share risks with its clients in the event of project failure.

Issues of accountability and discipline were also complicated by the actions of the Board. Although management held the initiative for bringing projects to the Board and the Board never turned down any management proposal, it had in-

34. World Bank, "Annual Review of Evaluation Results, 1993," OED report, December 1994.

fluence before projects arrived and in collective discussion of future projects. If major shareholders held strong views about particular projects, these were discussed quietly ahead of time. In more recent years, such backroom dealing became more intensive, especially as Washington-based NGOs used the mechanism to influence Bank projects. During Board discussions that body gave management a sense of direction, in particular regarding sectors and types of projects. More recently there has been so much partly conflicting guidance as to be enervating.

We have dwelled on the complexities of project lending for the Bank because it has been the institution's prototypical activity. But in fact the same complexities inhered in most of the World Bank's first half century of operations, many of them designated as sectoral or other categories of project lending, some of them called differently. The project issues just discussed will reverberate through the rest of the book.

A Half-Century Crisis

The World Bank's fiftieth anniversary created a stir about whether the institution should survive or not. Arguably, the fifty-years-is-enough concern simply was contrived by the calendar. The Bank long since had become a robust organization with an identity of its own; it was not about to expire quickly. As the institution crossed its half-century mark, however, it seemed to face a middle-age crisis of confidence with the entry of East Europe, the sharply contrasting fortunes of East Asia and Africa, and the multiplication of small borrowers whose circumstances and needs were highly differentiated.

The institution's predicament reflected, in part, the angst of its progenitors: nation-states—more particularly, the flagging power of central governments. Buffeted by pressures for international cooperation and conformity on both economic and political matters, central governments were faced with difficult times, and disillusionment with them, almost inevitably, spilled over to their international creations: multilateral institutions.

The formal levers of the Bank's governance—its Board of Governors, executive directors, and the president—have been increasingly undermined by a plethora of interest groups ("stakeholders" in more recent parlance): NGOs, financial markets, international business, bilateral foreign aid bureaucracies, and multilateral "do-gooders," the broader "intellectual" community (academics, think tanks, and the media), and, not least, the interests of the Bank's own staff and management.

In contrast, formal Bank decisionmaking continues to be driven by the financial and political structure of the past, especially by a dominant U.S. voice and over-weighted Europeans. Japan has managed to gain some influence, by overtly flexing its financial muscle in IDA as well as through the G-7. But other rising economic powers in East Asia, as well as the borrowers whose reflows in practice fund much of IBRD and an increasing fraction of IDA, have little voice. The result has been a gradual erosion of activity through a retreat of both creditors and borrowers.

Shareholders frustrated by their lack of influence on the Bank began to adopt one or another of two alternatives. One was partial withdrawal. Following a time-honored tradition begun with the IDB, in more recent years European governments have been shifting their allegiances to the European Union and to the new EBRD. The "Tiger" economies of Asia simply inclined toward a policy of benign apathy. The other option, adopted by the Nordic countries, for instance, was to influence the Bank's agenda by supplementing its administrative budget by providing, outside the regular budget process, "trust funds" that targeted particular activities and consultants.

By the half-century mark the link between the Bank's funding and its governance had weakened. From the early 1980s, the core of the resources-governance tie shifted to IDA and by the mid-1990s the nexus was in dire straits, squeezed between rising aid niggardliness, growing conditionality on IDA funding, and a more competitive relationship with other multilateral seekers of concessional funds. Quite apart from the financial needs of the poorest countries, the institutional impact on IBRD—pressures on its administrative budget and a weakening of an important financial buffer—was likely to be challenging. At the same time, there could be little doubt that, having made access to concessional funds an indispensable issue, the Bank had itself been a willing accomplice to the steady undermining of its institutional autonomy and effectiveness. An unwillingness to walk away from the triennial wheedling and the inevitable compromises and Faustian bargains the Bank had been making to retain access to concessional funds had become increasingly damaging.

More diffuse "ownership" was creating increasingly confusing expectations of the Bank. This was leading the institution to pursue public relations as a substitute for performance and to imbue its lending with more regulations. Furthermore, competition from other sources of finance—particularly flows with stronger risk-sharing characteristics (such nondebt finance as foreign direct investment (FDI) and portfolio flows) as well as (to a lesser extent) regional development banks and other official lenders—began eroding the Bank's portion of external financing, and therefore also its external leverage. The results were a reduction in the demand for Bank lending, exit by stronger borrowers, and perverse selectivity in the institution's portfolio.

At the same time, when the Bank's comfortable reserves and ample annual net income are coupled with the difficult fiscal atmosphere that major shareholders face, the distribution of the Bank's net income has emerged as the new battleground among its shareholders. The institution's net income looks like a convenient source for funding foreign policy objectives, such as those posed by the emergencies in Bosnia, Mexico, Palestine, and the former Soviet Union.[35] Even as

35. A "global public good" case could indeed be made in all the examples cited. Yet, there was no analysis whether alternatives—such as funding tropical disease research—would better serve global welfare.

late as the mid-1980s, during discussions surrounding the establishment of MIGA, the United States argued that "decision-making should be based on a voting system which relates member voting power to financial contributions."[36] Indeed, that was the principle that distinguished the Bretton Woods system of governance from that of the United Nations. By the mid-1990s, however, as discussions on a capital increase for MIGA were in progress, several G-7 shareholders, citing legislative helplessness, insisted that IBRD net income should become the principal source of paid-in capital. The influence that came with ownership had become less expensive, indeed almost costless, and therefore more attractive.

A silver lining for the Bank, however, was the way the global demand for transnational problem-solving institutions grew. The Bank was better positioned than most suppliers to meet the demand; it promised to maintain a strong niche in the financial markets through its capacity to borrow at low rates and lend for the medium and long term. A common perception, moreover, was that the Bank had no near competitor as a purveyor of development wisdom. It was a reasonably disinterested, practical, well-informed, accessible, and generally respected source of economic development advice to governments. History, its Charter, its accumulated expertise, and its mind-set all pointed to a continuing, principal role as a lender cum adviser to central governments. Although political fashion as well as developmental needs justified a greater involvement with other entities, the Bank's real strengths lay in its government-related relationships.

The record, to be sure, did indicate severe limits on the institution's effectiveness as a social engineer. When it tried to enhance its antipoverty impact through social assessments and associated conditionality, it seemed, still, to overestimate its ability to achieve good outcomes. Yet in these very difficult areas, the Bank *had* served a worthy role by being a moral gadfly from its "bully pulpit." It was continuing to put the hard issues on many borrowing countries' agendas.

Concluding Remarks

One of the authors of the World Bank's first authorized history was preoccupied with whether the Bank would be able to "change its spots" from being mostly a bank to mostly a development agency.[37] That question no longer is widely contested; the Bank, without abandoning some of its bankerly attributes, is generally

36. Letter, Bruce Thompson, Jr., assistant secretary, Legislative Affairs, U.S. Treasury, to U.S. Congress, June 11, 1985.

37. "Can the leopard change its spots? Can an agency that at first closely resembled a bank and until fairly recently has continued to make noises like a bank, be transformed into an institution that could more accurately be termed a development agency?" Robert E. Asher, in J. P. Lewis and I. Kapur, eds., *The World Bank Group, Multilateral Aid, and the 1970s* (Lexington, Mass.: D.C. Heath, 1973), p. 21.

credited with having become, not just *a* but *the* leading development agency of its time. Now that the institution has reached the half-century mark, another spot-changing question has arisen. The Bank is a multilateral; but could it—indeed, should it—change from one kind of multilateral to another?

The Bank's owners are nation-states. They inevitably have large arrays of varied, theoretically unlimited, partially conflicted, purposes. The Bank is not like a private firm, which could be conceived in theory to be oriented to a single (profit-seeking) objective. The Bank has several goals, of which the pivotal, according to the present interpretation, is poverty alleviation. But the total number of basic, animating institutional goals, while several, is small. Thus, the Bank has been a specialized institution over its first fifty years; it has been a *functional* multilateral; like the ILO, FAO, UNESCO, and, indeed, IMF, it has dealt with one slice of the array of issues that multilaterals compositely address. The Bank's strength lies in the depth of its specialized expertise.

That has been the theory. But throughout much of its history and especially from the 1980s onward, the Bank has been under several internal and external pressures to proliferate its subjects and broaden its mission. Internally, the staff has consisted of able, energetic, highly purposed people who are inclined, in a changing problem environment, to take on important new subjects. Broadening the Bank's work agenda seems to be a function of its emergence as the leader of the development cause. Moreover, the soft-budget constraint has made it easier to play the proliferation game.

Externally, from time to time, a number of the institution's owners together with many of its NGO and other civil society contemporaries have added to the call for new subjects. And both inside and outside it is sometimes said that the Bank needs to fill a partial vacuum left by other multilaterals.

The UN set of agencies includes some generalist components—the Secretariat, UNDP, ECOSOC, the General Assembly itself—with assigned attention spans and responsibility almost as varied as those of a nation-state. But as the century moves toward a close, the reputation of the generalist units has been sinking. This is partly unfair; it is the result, among other things, of delinquent support by the larger industrialized countries, especially the United States. Partly it is owed to the intransigence of developing countries in their insistence on hiring quotas. And partly the slide may be a matter more of perception than of fact.

But the perception has been pulling the Bank toward substantive proliferation. It encountered a similar temptation in the 1970s, but the attraction then was weaker, and the institution's response was more circumspect than the slightly frantic rate at which the institution took up new causes in the 1980s and 1990s. By the mid-1990s, substantive scatteration was posing a major threat to the quality of Bank interventions.

POVERTY AND THE WORLD BANK'S EVOLVING PURPOSE

CHAPTERS 2–7

ON DECEMBER 31, 1991, Lewis Preston, president of the World Bank, issued an instruction to be inserted into each staff member's Operational Manual: "Sustainable poverty reduction is the Bank's overarching objective."[1] Poverty reduction, his cover note added, would be the benchmark by which the Bank's performance as a development institution would be measured. Preston appeared to be announcing a new policy and, to some, even "serving notice of a cultural revolution," the most audacious aspect of which was a new form of conditionality.[2] Both the International Development Association and the International Bank for Reconstruction and Development would henceforth link loan approvals to a country's commitment to poverty reduction.

The 1991 directive and the expectations that it created raise several questions about the Bank's objectives. Does the Bank see poverty reduction and development as distinct objectives? How much of a change in policy did Preston propose? What is the Bank's mandate for this policy? If there is such a mandate, and if Preston was indeed launching a "revolution" in 1992, why had the Bank waited forty-six years to instigate it?

Preston's directive provides a partial answer to these questions. "In the 1960s," it read, "the Bank focused on economic growth as the key to poverty reduction.

---

1. World Bank, Operational Directive 4.15: Poverty Reduction, *The World Bank Operational Manual* (December 1992), p. 2.

2. Michael Prowse, "World Bank Links Loan Volume to Poverty Relief," *Financial Times* (London), May 11, 1992, p. 4.

During the 1970s, attention shifted first to *redistribution with growth* and later to satisfaction of *basic human needs.* In the early 1980s policy-based adjustment lending overshadowed the Bank's poverty reduction objectives." However, this phase of the Bank's operations "eventually enabled the Bank to address more effectively the relationship between poverty and the policy environment. In 1987 and 1988, the primacy of the Bank's poverty reduction objective was reemphasized in task force reports," and subsequent reports "contributed to a further reaffirmation of the Bank's commitment to poverty reduction as its fundamental objective."[3]

These words suggest that the Bank made almost steady progress in learning about and addressing poverty. Yet they make no mention of the years 1946–59, which account for almost one-third of the Bank's life. If the Bank was trying to reduce poverty through growth during the 1960s (and presumably the 1950s), why were the poor, the very target of those growth efforts, seldom mentioned? After so much experimentation, "reemphasis," and "reaffirmation," why, in 1992, was the Bank compelled to introduce operational measures of such great import that outside observers took them for a cultural revolution?[4] Was there any connection between Preston's initiative and the war on poverty waged by the Bank under Robert McNamara's leadership during the 1970s, a time when much of the world came to see the Bank as the standard bearer and champion of aid to the world's poorest populations? Should Preston's directive be understood as a recommitment to McNamara's priorities, or as an admission that new strategies were required to meet those goals? Over the decades, did Bank operations keep pace with these evolving battle strategies and managerial guidelines?

The Bank's Articles of Agreement contain no references to poverty or to related notions such as social welfare or equity, and, to judge by the almost two thousand pages of published documents and proceedings of the Bretton Woods meetings, the conference debates paid only passing attention to the concept of relative need. The first twenty-six annual reports of the Bank barely touch on the subject of poverty, and the Bank's twenty-fifth anniversary history almost ignores the concept: its index lists "poverty" only three times (in each case, "rural poverty").[5] That long silence on the subject is a startling contrast to the latter-day, ringing affirmations of social commitment and concern, such as the opening remarks of Armeane Choksi, Bank vice president, to a meeting at the United Nations in 1993: "Poverty reduction is now at the top of the World Bank's agenda."

Language has its fashions. Diffidence, even prudishness, about the embarrassing subject of poverty was more customary fifty years ago, certainly when bankers,

3. World Bank, Operational Directive 4.15.

4. Press releases and articles in the *Bank's World* during 1992 and 1993 reinforced the image of significant change in policy toward poverty.

5. Edward S. Mason and Robert E. Asher, *The World Bank since Bretton Woods* (Brookings, 1973). In contrast to poverty, "Income distribution" makes a few more appearances in the index.

government officials, and economists were addressing one another. Writing in 1946, the Brazilian Josue de Castro spoke of "the taboo of hunger," a subject that "could not safely be discussed in public" because of "its explosive political and social implications."[6] During the Great Depression and World War II, poverty, and even hunger, were visible throughout the world, certainly in Europe, but even in the United States and Britain. Its very nearness may explain the circumlocution. Expressions such as "economic growth" and "development" served as adequate reminders, in polite company, of social realities that today are discussed more explicitly and graphically. The audience, too, has changed. To an increasing extent, what the Bank says no longer takes the form of discreet conversation with a few experts and public officials but is treated as a public announcement and is listened to attentively by a congeries of elected and self-appointed representatives of countries and groups around the world.

Two additional factors have contributed to the elasticity of the Bank's statements about poverty. One is the rhetorical function of internal management's key words. Rhetoric is a whip to spur the troops; and the bigger the beast, the stronger the rhetoric needed to instill the organization with values, a sense of purpose, and meaning. Statements about poverty and other goals legitimize and reinforce the institution while affirming their objective, functional content. The other factor is the way the Bank handles its external image. The Bank's message about itself to the outside world has changed over the decades, from one emphasizing financial respectability to one concerned with social issues, in response to the winds of political change in the donor community, but also in accord with the Bank's own life cycle. Image adjustment may explain in part the radical change in the Bank's expressed stance regarding poverty.

Or, could it simply be that the Bank has been a slow learner? And that the eventual, and rather sudden, emergence of the poverty objective on the Bank's agenda was the result of a prolonged learning process, involving both reflection and field experimentation, during which the Bank came to a clearer perception of the mechanisms that cause growth and help reduce poverty? Or perhaps the learning occurred in the legal sphere, as the Bank gradually gained a clearer understanding of its own constitutional mandate? Learning surely did occur, as the Bank grew, as

---

6. Josue de Castro, *The Geopolitics of Hunger* (New York: Monthly Review Press, 1977; originally published in Portuguese in 1946 under the title *The Geography of Hunger: Hunger in Brazil*), p. 49. De Castro served as the first director of the Food and Agriculture Organization, established in 1945. David Knox, who would retire as Bank vice president for Latin America in 1987, was lecturing at the London School of Economics in the early 1950s. Although the subject matter was the poor countries, he was required to call the course "Economic Problems of the Tropics and Sub-Tropics." "[It was] not only [the] Bank; most people [had a] problem with calling a spade a spade [when it came] to poverty. We always tried to hide the true facts by the use of words that were less offensive to the poor." Conversation with the authors, September 24, 1996.

economists around the world turned their attention to the developing countries, and as the development problem itself evolved, making it necessary continually to reevaluate the diagnosis. From its earliest days, the Bank has had a highly professional staff, in terms of both education and experience, and has supported a large, information-gathering research effort. In the Bank's first decade, many of its staff members were former colonial administrators, wartime planners, and postwar relief managers. The Bank's slow arrival at the poverty objective was hardly due to protracted intellectual obtuseness. What the Bank has been prone to is intellectualizing. The dramatic turns in its agenda partly reflect the freedom with which staff have explored the realm of ideas and opinions, whereas lending operations have in practice been subject to a number of constraints.

The account of the Bank's evolving poverty and social mission in chapters 2 to 7 begins with a puzzle: the apparent discontinuity between Bank rhetoric, on the one hand, and the constancy of the Bank's Charter and uninterrupted growth of its financial position and international reputation, on the other. As mentioned earlier, part of the explanation may lie in the fact that the Bank's day-to-day business has followed a steadier course than its rhetoric. Much of what appears to be a change in ends has perhaps been a change in the choice of instruments.

If rhetoric is put aside, the Bank for the most part and throughout its history has seen the promotion of economic growth as its principal means of bringing about poverty reduction. The Bank has encouraged such growth as much by financing the expansion of productive capacity as by seeking to improve the way in which capacity is used. Underlying these activities is the unwavering assumption that a rising tide lifts all boats. That is to say, growth in output eventually benefits a majority of the population or, at least, increases a nation's capacity to reduce poverty within its borders.

Over much of its lifetime, however, the Bank has thought that it should and could do better than rely on economic growth and "trickle-down" to help the poor. Growth, it came to believe, could be made more poor-friendly by redesigning the geographical, sectoral, factor-mix, and other aspects of production so that additional output might accrue more directly to the poor. A combination of internal and external factors pushed the Bank in that direction during the 1960s. It was during the 1970s, however, that the institution set out in earnest on an ambitious path of poverty-oriented social engineering, seeking to improve on the economic and political processes that, in many developing countries, appeared to be shortchanging the poor when it came to the distribution of benefits from growing production. Those efforts to help the poor, over and above the promotion of growth, came to be understood, in a stricter sense, as "poverty alleviation," a distinction that is the simplest explanation for the discontinuity in Bank rhetoric. Whereas poverty reduction through growth has been the Bank's constant, if mostly implicit, pursuit, "poverty alleviation" in the more ambitious sense—of doing better than trickle-down—has followed a more eventful course in the Bank's history.

This and the remaining chapters in part 1 provide an account of the Bank's changing and overlapping approaches to poverty alleviation and of the effort to relate those changes to ideas and rhetoric concerning the Bank's goals.

TWO

The Bank for Reconstruction, 1944–1948

HARRY WHITE'S first draft of a proposal for an international bank, written in early 1942, made no mention of development. This original proposal referred simply to a Bank for Reconstruction, designed "chiefly to supply the huge volume of capital . . . that will be needed for reconstruction, for relief, and for economic recovery."[1] An April 1942 draft called for a "Bank for Reconstruction of the United and Associated Nations" and did include, at the end of a long list of other objectives, a reference to development, stating that the Bank would also "raise the productivity and hence the standard of living of the peoples of the member countries," but this draft failed to mention specifically the poorer or less developed countries.[2] When Edward Bernstein, White's deputy at the U.S. Treasury, asked what they would do with the bank once reconstruction was over, White threw the question back: "What do you suggest?" "Let's have it there for after," Bernstein said. It could lend to other areas that needed development. The draft, when it was subsequently circulated to other governments in November 1943, arrived with the words "and Development" appended to the institution's name.[3]

---

1. First draft of the Bank plan. Richard N. Gardner, *Sterling-Dollar Diplomacy: The Origins and the Prospects of Our International Economic Order* (McGraw-Hill, 1969), pp. 74, 84–85.

2. U.S. Department of State, *Foreign Relations of the United States Diplomatic Papers 1942*, vol. 1, *General, The British Commonwealth, The Far East* (Washington, D.C.: U.S. Government Printing Office), p. 184.

3. Personal conversation with Edward Bernstein, July 1993. White's August 2, 1943, draft already stated in its introduction: "Asia, Europe, Africa and South America can for many

Bretton Woods, 1942–46

"Development" barely made it on board. In fact, it almost found itself on the wrong boat. The proposal for an international bank was in doubt until the last minute.[4] When the U.S. secretary of state in May 1944 invited forty-four governments to send representatives to a conference at Bretton Woods, he said the meeting was "for the purpose of formulating definite proposals for an International Monetary Fund, and *possibly* a Bank for Reconstruction and Development."[5] The British, however, had expressed no interest in what thus far was an entirely American idea. John Maynard Keynes's initial proposal envisaged a stabilization fund able to provide substantial overdraft facilities. Ansel Luxford, a member of the small U.S. Treasury team headed by Harry White, has suggested that the British delegation's sudden interest in such a bank at the conference was related to the larger Bretton Woods negotiations between the U.S and British teams, which, in essence, traded British sovereignty over domestic economic policy for U.S. funding. Both sides were also conscious of the need for formulas that would minimize expected U.S. congressional resistance to postwar foreign aid. The multilateral nature of the proposed bank and its perceived role as a guarantor rather than lender seemed to favor its chances of ratification. According to Luxford,

> In the early days, as long as Keynes had his $30 million where he thought it might be accepted . . . the British delegation by and large manifested no interest in the Bank. . . . When the British finally realized that they were not going to get this . . . at that very point Keynes reversed himself and became a very strong proponent of the Bank. The logic of it is perfectly natural. He realized that he was not going to get an open check on the monetary side, that he was going to need reconstruction funds.[6]

Roy Harrod, who assisted Keynes during the negotiations, says that the White plan "was conceived on a niggardly scale," but he defends the British from selfish motivations: "Keynes wanted a Fund so large as to give governments the confidence necessary to relax unneighborly restrictions."[7] At the same time, he concedes that

> the British, painfully and correctly aware of their enormous prospective balance of trade difficulties, may have tended to stress them too much, and thus have given the impression that plans, which they had really designed for wider purposes, had been thought of

years profitably use for the creation of capital goods $5 to $10 billion of foreign capital each year provided they can get it on reasonable terms." Quoted in Robert Oliver, *Early Plans for a World Bank*, Princeton Studies in International Finance 29 (September 1971), pp. 37–38.

4. Edward S. Mason and Robert E. Asher, *The World Bank since Bretton Woods* (Brookings, 1973), p. 12.

5. Ibid., p. 12. Emphasis added.

6. Ansel Luxford, interview, World Bank Oral History Program, July 1961, p. 7. Luxford joined the Bank's Legal Department as assistant general counsel in 1946.

7. R. F. Harrod, *The Life of John Maynard Keynes* (Harcourt, Brace, 1951), p. 549.

in the first instance primarily as means for helping Britain in her immediate post-war difficulties. The Americans, on their side, tended to think of any assets they might contribute to or acquire in the Fund, as a charitable "hand-out" to help their poor, benighted neighbours. . . . [I]t was wrong to mix the two streams of thought.[8]

In the event, Keynes took up the question of the Bank with colleagues from the British delegation and representatives from other countries while crossing the Atlantic on the Queen Mary to attend the Bretton Woods Conference. At the conference, he chaired the commission charged with drafting the Bank's Articles of Agreement.

Burke Knapp has remarked on "how little attention was paid to the Bank in the pre–Bretton Woods planning or in the Bretton Woods Conference itself. I suppose if one measured the time spent during those fourteen days of work at the Bretton Woods Conference, the Bank probably didn't take more than a day and a half."[9] Doubts about the Bank's prospects continued even after Bretton Woods. The inauspicious birth was prolonged by difficulties over appointments and disagreements over the respective roles of the Executive Board and management. Clearly "an afterthought" at Bretton Woods, the Bank was by early 1947 "at its lowest ebb, its reputation considerably tarnished, its accomplishments nil, and its problems mounting."[10] When a plaque was placed outside the Mount Washington Hotel in Bretton Woods some years later to commemorate the conference, the text recorded the birth of the International Monetary Fund but failed to mention the Bank.

There was some debate at the conference on the relative priority of the Bank's twin purposes, reconstruction and development. In his opening remarks to the first meeting of the Bretton Woods Commission on the Bank, Keynes stated: "It is likely, in my judgment, that the field of reconstruction from the consequences of war will mainly occupy the proposed Bank in its early days. But, as soon as possible, and with increasing emphasis as time goes on, there is a second primary duty laid upon it, namely, to develop the resources and productive capacity of the world, with

8. Ibid., p. 552.

9. Burke Knapp, interview, World Bank Oral History Program, July 24 and 30, 1975, pp. 40–41. Knapp, who had worked on the pre–Bretton Woods planning for the Federal Reserve System, attended both planning meetings and the conference. He joined the Bank in 1949, becoming vice president and chairman of the Loan Committee in 1956, a position he held until his retirement in 1978. Aron Broches, who was a member of the Dutch delegation and later the Bank's general counsel, reported to his government on the Bretton Woods meeting. Explaining the limited time given the Bank in comparison with that given to the Fund, he argued that it did not imply a lesser valuation, because the Bank and Fund were complementary institutions, for it was understood that the Bank's existence would protect the Fund from pressure for long-term financing, and setting up the Bank's Charter had been a much easier technical task. Communication from Jacques Polak, based on his translation of Broches's report.

10. Mason and Asher, World Bank since Bretton Woods, p. 49.

special attention to the less developed countries."[11] In private, at the British Embassy in Washington, he put it more bluntly. While expounding on his vision that, with proper economic management, governments could have "a boom that would raise the standard of living of all Europe to the levels of America today," he was asked, "Does that apply also to India and the rest of the Empire?" Keynes replied: "That must wait until the reconstruction of Europe is much further advanced."[12]

The underdeveloped countries at the meeting, however, urged participants to give development greater priority. Both Venezuela and Mexico submitted amendments that would have put development first or, at least "on the same footing," in Mexico's words. Mexico argued that the Bank was meant to outlive reconstruction, and that European reconstruction needed the output of raw material and the markets that would be created by the development of other nations. If anything, the Mexican delegates suggested, priorities should be reversed: "What we ask is only that . . . in the event that countries requesting loans for development purposes do not use up the resources and facilities made available to them, countries requiring loans for reconstruction projects could have a claim on the unused funds."[13] Surprisingly, the most forceful effort on behalf of the developing countries arose not in Commission II, which was charged with drafting the Bank's Charter, but in the debates on the Fund. Speaking for the Indian delegation, Sir Shanmukham Chetty stated that the Fund's Charter should "mention specifically the needs of economically backward countries." Contrary to past practice, he said, international organizations should begin to "give due consideration to the economic problems of countries like India."[14] Although the proposal was not accepted, Chetty's shot appears to have caromed into the Bank's Charter, which originally stated that the Bank was "To assist . . . member countries" without distinction but now included a direct reference to "less developed countries."

When the commission on the Bank reported to the Executive Plenary, the phrasing was more diplomatic than that used by Keynes: "As for the purpose of the Bank, it should be noted that the Bank is established both for the reconstruction and for the development of the member countries, and these two objectives are to be pursued on a footing of equality."[15] The final wording of Article I was a tactful

11. Opening remarks of Lord Keynes at the First Meeting of the Second Commission on the Bank for Reconstruction and Development, U.S. Department of State, *Proceedings and Documents of United Nations Monetary and Financial Conference, Bretton Woods, N.H., July 1–22, 1944*, vol. 1 (GPO, 1948), doc. 47, p. 84.

12. William Clark, *From Three Worlds: Memoirs* (Sidgwick and Jackson, 1986), p. xi.

13. *Proceedings and Documents of United Nations Monetary and Financial Conference*, vol. 2, p. 1177.

14. Ibid., p. 1181.

15. Georges Theunis (Belgium), reporting delegate, *Proceedings and Documents of United Nations Monetary and Financial Conference*, vol. 1, p. 1103. Dean Acheson recalls a more sympathetic position by Keynes toward the developing countries in this debate, saying that he and Keynes favored an equitable consideration of both the reconstruction and development claims, against White's disagreement. Dean Acheson, *Present at the Creation: My Years in the State Department* (W. W. Norton, 1969), p. 84.

compromise. It stated that the purpose of the Bank was "to assist in the reconstruction and development of territories of members." Perhaps more to the point, the letter of the agreement left a comfortably wide margin for the Bank's management to exercise administrative discretion in lending decisions. As delegates generally understood, that discretion was to be exercised by an Executive Board and staff dominated by the United States, the only country with the capacity to guarantee or fund the institution's loans.

Despite the diplomatic nod to the representatives of less developed countries and the broader political recognition of the development cause provided by the United Nations Charter, which called for "economic and social progress and development," the special claims of poorer areas of the world were far from the collective mind of the conference.[16] Delegates focused firmly on the "wider purposes" of the meeting. They strongly felt that they all stood to gain from cooperation, and that their overriding priority should be to agree on a system that would ensure international monetary order, open trade, and capital flows. Many details of the proposal were abstruse and would normally have been the province of seminar room speculation. But it was not intellectual persuasion or the calculations of immediate self-interest that spurred the delegates. The energy that drove the Bretton Woods delegates to seize the moment and carry the plans through to final approval had its source in the palpable and shared experience of the Great Depression and the world war still in progress, horrors that were widely associated with the collapse of international economic arrangements. Delegates feared, with good reason, that failure at Bretton Woods would result in a nightmare of postwar depression and a new cycle of nationalism and war.

When the conference did, for brief moments, descend from the higher spheres of global arrangements to consider particular countries, it was to discuss the reconstruction needs of those in Europe and the Far East. Pressing for reconstruction capital and the creation of the Bank, Harry White said, "There is nothing that will serve to drive these countries into some kind of ism—communism or something else—faster than having inadequate capital."[17] But in 1944 White was thinking about countries that were being destroyed by the war; what he had in mind was the reconstruction not the development function of the Bank. "Except in the most general terms, neither White nor his assistants had given much attention to the long-term implications of an international bank."[18] The same could be said of Keynes, who forcefully disputed U.S. expectations that private international investment would recover after the war. Since the Bank was originally to be a guarantor rather than a lender, Keynes's pessimism on postwar private capital flows meant

16. Roosevelt's 1941 proclamation of four freedoms, including "freedom from want . . . everywhere in the world," was perhaps a more significant pointer.

17. John Morton Blum, *The Morgenthau Diaries: Years of War 1941–1945* (Houghton Mifflin, 1967), vol. 3, 1967, p. 272.

18. Alfred Eckes, *A Search for Solvency: Bretton Woods and the International Monetary System 1941–1971* (Austin: University of Texas Press, 1975), p. 131.

that he envisioned a limited role for a postreconstruction bank. Keynes was in effect undercutting the raison d'être for the Bank's proposed development purpose: "He had long held the doctrine that nations which invest their savings abroad are never likely to recoup them in total; they are only able to keep the borrowing nations in play by always re-lending."[19]

Keynes's attitude toward the conference seemed to combine a single-minded pursuit of the broader monetary and stabilization arrangements with an imperial distaste for the democratic charade of an international agreement. Meeting privately with White in 1942, he had argued against a conference and for direct negotiations between the United States and the United Kingdom alone, but White had insisted on the broader meeting.[20] In a later dispatch to the British Treasury, Keynes expressly objected to the participation of less developed countries.

> Twenty-one countries have been invited which clearly have nothing to contribute and will merely encumber the ground, namely, Colombia, Costa Rica, Dominica, Ecuador, Salvador, Guatemala, Haiti, Honduras, Liberia, Nicaragua, Panama, Paraguay, Philippines, Venezuela, Peru, Uruguay, Ethiopia, Iceland, Iran, Iraq, Luxembourg. The most monstrous monkey-house assembled for years. To these might perhaps be added: Egypt, Chile and (in present circumstances) Yugo-Slavia.[21]

Opening the first session of the conference commission on the Bank, after referring to the Bank's development purpose, he went on to make development appear to be a means for international stabilization, rather than its end. The Bank's second duty, he said, "is to develop the resources and productive capacity of the world, with special attention to the less developed countries, to raise the standard of life and the conditions of labour everywhere, to make the resources of the world more fully available to all mankind, *and so to order its operations as to promote and maintain equilibrium in the international balances of payments of all member countries.*"[22]

Perhaps what both White and Keynes were striving for was best expressed in a personal anecdote told by Roy Harrod in which he describes his elation on receiving a draft of the U.S. plan in early 1943. The proposed "scarce currency" clause confirmed that "the Americans were admitting the principle of joint [deficit and surplus country] responsibility for disequilibrium" and that American and British planners shared the same internationalist vision. He read the draft sitting in a dark railway carriage crowded with soldiers.

19. Harrod, *The Life of John Maynard Keynes*, p. 566.

20. Oliver, *Early Plans for a World Bank*, p. 44.

21. Donald Moggridge, ed., *The Collected Writings of John Maynard Keynes*, vol. 26 (Macmillan, 1980), p. 42. Cited by Gerald M. Meier and Dudley Seers, *Pioneers in Development* (Oxford University Press, 1984), p. 9. Keynes could not foresee that, by March 31, 1994, IBRD membership would total 177 countries.

22. *Proceedings and Documents of United Nations Monetary and Financial Conference*, vol. 1, p. 85. Emphasis added.

I felt an exhilaration such as only comes once or twice in a lifetime. There were the dishevelled soldiers sprawling over one another in sleep; and here was I, tightly pressed into my corner, holding these flimsy sheets. One had the urge to wake them all up. "Here, boys, is great news. Here is an offer, which can make things very different for you when the war is over; your lords and masters do not seem to have realised it yet; but they soon will . . . I know that you set great store by the Beveridge [Welfare State] scheme; but that is only written on a bit of paper; it will all fall to pieces, if this country has a bad slump and trade difficulties. Here is the real thing, because it will save us from a slump and make all those Beveridge plans lastingly possible."[23]

Harrod's "message" to the soldiers, that world order and recovery had to precede plans for social welfare and redistribution, was the implicit message of the entire Bretton Woods Conference to the less developed world.

During 1943–44, an unusually severe famine killed several million people in Bengal.[24] Hunger and epidemics of cholera and malaria kept the death rate high through the first months of 1944, just prior to the conference. On April 15, 1944, the *Economist* painted a picture of "pauperism, disease, extortionate landlords, streets strewn with corpses and garbage, persistent muddle and chronic ignorance of the facts among officials."[25] Dramatic as the Bengal famine was, mass starvation was not uncommon at the time. Major famines were often in the news, but the greater tragedy was chronic hunger, or in today's parlance, absolute poverty. At the time of Bretton Woods, probably 50 to 60 percent of the population in the under-developed countries lived in absolute poverty as defined today.[26] Life expectancy for the poor was twenty-five years in India and about forty years in Colombia and Mexico. In India 90 percent of the population aged ten or older was illiterate, and in Mexico the figure was 50 percent.[27] The absolute poor were almost entirely

23. Harrod, *The Life of John Maynard Keynes*, p. 545.

24. The estimate is by the official Famine Inquiry Commission, presided over by Sir John Woodhead, cited in Jawaharlal Nehru, *The Discovery of India* (New York: John Day, 1946), p. 496, but refers only to Bengal. Nehru called it the "biggest and most devastating famine in 170 years of British Dominion." The Department of Anthropology of Calcutta University, using sample survey techniques, estimated 3.4 million deaths by famine in Bengal. Though the famine was centered in Bengal, other areas in eastern and southern India were also affected.

25. During the final stages of the famine, in April 1944, a young American army major, Robert S. McNamara, was assigned to a British base in Kharagpur, seventy miles west of Calcutta. His assignment: to carry out a statistical analysis of the logistics of airlift operations over the "Hump" to China.

26. Authors' rough estimates, based on backward extrapolation of World Bank figures for 1970–90 and other sources on poverty incidence and levels and on GDP trends. The poverty line was defined as the 1990 purchasing power of $1 per person per day.

27. *United Nations Statistical Yearbook, 1948;* International Bank for Reconstruction and Development, *The Basis of a Development Program for Colombia* (Johns Hopkins University Press, 1950), p. 171; Angus Maddison and Associates, *The Political Economy of Poverty, Equity, and Growth: Brazil and Mexico* (Oxford University Press, 1992), p. 185.

dependent on agriculture, were vulnerable to continually recurring natural disasters and plagues, and were locked into poverty by technological backwardness, illiteracy, systematic coercion and extraction practiced by layers of political overlords, and the inability of institutions to deal with disasters such as famines.[28]

In the 1940s the economically less developed areas of the world were entering a period of unprecedented change and dislocation caused by population growth, urbanization, new technology, and, in most areas, political revolution. Many such areas, especially in Latin America and Africa, had been in the early stages of these changes for decades. In the 1930s gross domestic product had grown at the rate of 4.8 percent a year in Chile, 4.2 percent in Colombia, and 3.6 percent in Brazil.[29] By the mid–twentieth century centralized government, taxation, export crops and mines, railroads, and urban growth had appeared in Sub-Saharan Africa and had transformed much of the region; over the same period Latin America experienced a spurt in industrialization, large-scale settlement of new farmlands, and substantial expansion in primary production. The rate of change accelerated following the war, primed by high prices for raw material, rising levels of investment, and a decline in mortality. These upheavals were only in small part a direct consequence of economic growth. New political regimes, medical breakthroughs, advances in communication, and urbanization were thrust on nations independently of their individual economic advances. One result was that the poor came to be a moving target in several respects: their number began to increase, they migrated (especially to towns and cities), and their needs changed. In addition, governments were transformed by independence, granted by or wrested from imperial powers, and by communism, war, a revolution in transport and communications, and the gradual spread of democracy. These upheavals would add to the burden of development but also create opportunities for progress.

Peasant society—the modus vivendi of almost all the poor at the time—was, in essence, a culture, a complex and sophisticated web of economic, social, and political life that had developed as an accommodation to particular circumstances over centuries, even millennia. Despite the variety of peasant societies across continents, valleys, and even neighboring villages, each was a construct of production techniques, religious beliefs, social obligations, and political rules, all woven into one cloth or particular culture. The separate threads that might correspond to the theoretical categories recognized by a neoclassical economist were barely discernible to outside observers. The economy was opaque: implicit prices in barter, rights over factors of production, and obligations to the needy, to the

28. Jean Dreze and Amartya Sen, *Hunger and Public Action* (Oxford: Clarendon Press, 1989). Josue de Castro, a Brazilian medical doctor, made the same point with considerable descriptive force and empirical references in *The Geopolitics of Hunger* (New York: Monthly Review Press, 1977).

29. Vittorio Corbo, "Development in Latin America," Occasional Paper 22, International Center for Economic Growth, San Francisco.

powerful, and to collective tasks were all melded in with, and hard to distinguish from, the religious, social, and political aspects of family and communal life.[30] "Attacks on rural poverty" were destined to be carried out with little understanding of the very society that was to be transformed. That ignorance was shared by elites in the poorer countries and by foreign economists and officials who would eventually design foreign aid efforts.

Because the social life of the poor was complex, it was also easily disrupted. A fifty-year program for poverty alleviation designed in 1946 might have attached as much importance to the survival of human cultures as some of today's social programs place on the survival of biological species and the physical environment. In addition to having intrinsic worth, human cultures played a vital economic role. Consequently even small changes, or "developmental improvements," posed a threat to the survival mechanisms of interrelated villages. As it happened, the next half century brought unplanned change on the scale of an avalanche. Although deliberate interventions formed only a fraction of the upheaval, the planning and design of those interventions appear to have been as blind as the much more powerful social, technological, and market forces at play. Peasant societies were reduced to sociological and statistical abstractions—"village society," "the rural poor," "the bottom 40 percent"—and became quantitative "targets" for the delivery of ditches, seeds, visiting experts, and health clinics. By the 1990s, Western civilization had by and large completed its onslaught. Today, most of the social and economic effects of rural transformation have already been incurred, and the need for policymakers to understand them is no longer as urgent as it was, or should have been, fifty years ago. At the same time, the human costs and benefits of those changes raise questions about past attitudes toward poverty alleviation.[31]

If the Bretton Woods delegates seemingly gave little attention to mass poverty in the world, it was not because their monetary and trade agenda precluded the subject. It was less the subject and more the timing. Had the agenda been drawn up five years later, development would have had a seat at the table. In his opening remarks to the conference, Franklin Roosevelt had said: "Economic diseases are highly communicable. It follows, therefore, that the economic health of every

30. Yet faith pierces the dark. Jose Carlos Mariategui, an influential Peruvian socialist, writing in 1930, described Andean peasant society as being based on "collective" values that should be protected from capitalism, in *Siete Ensayos sobre la Realidad Peruana* (Santiago de Chile: Editorial Universitaria, 1955). Others, such as Sol Tax, who studied a Guatemalan village in 1950, saw "penny capitalism." By the 1970s economists were applying the X-ray powers of multivariate statistical analysis to discover "market response" in the behavior of villagers.

31. "Mopping-up" operations continue. Decades of colonial efforts to end Masai communal land ownership are being continued by the current Kenyan government. George Monbiot, "The Last Warriors, Betrayed, Defeated, Dispossessed," *Financial Times* (London), November 19–20, 1994, sec. 2, p. 1.

country is a proper matter of concern to all its neighbors, near and distant." Roosevelt was ahead of his audience and of the political mood in 1944. But by 1950 it was becoming clearer that the stability and development of poorer countries were necessary parts of the larger security and economic picture. With the onset of the cold war during 1946–47, attention began turning to the poorer areas of Europe, and then to other regions, as national security moved beyond a reliance on the atom bomb immediately after the war to a policy of containment, and subsequently to a competition for allegiances among political philosophies.

What had delayed the emergence of this awareness of poverty was that in the early 1940s the poor countries did not yet exist as a category. In 1942 the greater part of what is now called the third world consisted of colonies or "dependent territories." This covered practically all of Africa, the Indian subcontinent, most of the Caribbean, and much of East Asia.[32] The main exceptions were China, Central and South America, Thailand, and parts of the Middle East. Colonies were commonly referred to as territories rather than countries. Despite some indigenous entrepreneurship (including a well-developed industrial sector in India), development policy in concept and practice consisted principally of colonial administration. At Bretton Woods, colonies were the backyards of member countries, not a subject for diplomatic commentary. Furthermore, some areas that are now part of the developing world were then perceived, correctly, as being highly developed. Most notable among these were Argentina, Uruguay, and Venezuela, which had higher per capita incomes than much of Europe.[33] Even the Belgian Congo—later Zaire—was at times referred to as "an advanced country," in view of its small population, rich mineral resources, and paternalistic social welfare system, at least in urban areas, which included high levels of primary school enrollment.[34] Before

32. In that year, Liberia was the only truly independent nation in Africa. Italy lost control of Ethiopia in 1941, but Allied military control continued through the war. Libya became independent in 1951. India, governed under the British Colonial Administration and Welfare Act, was represented at Bretton Woods.

33. United Nations statistics cited in Harold Wilson, *The War on World Poverty: An Appeal to the Conscience of Mankind* (London: Victor Gollancz, 1953), pp. 11–13.

34. John Gunther wrote in 1955 that the Congo "is indeed highly advanced in some respects, but even today no road exists between Leopoldville [now Kinshasa], the capital, and Stanleyville, the third most important town in the country." And, "This is a rich country in almost all senses of the word. Its exports come close to being worth three billion dollars a year (as compared to less than $60,000,000 for Kenya, as an example) and the trade balance is fat and favorable. One should also mention, I daresay, such facts as that [the] Congo has fewer than five hundred doctors of medicine for more than 12,000,000 Africans, and that its university . . . has at the moment exactly twenty-eight students." *Inside Africa* (Harper and Brothers, 1955), p. 647. As late as 1962 Barbara Ward wrote: "For centuries, for millennia, the East had been the region of known and admired wealth. . . . Today, for instance, Indonesia seems obviously better endowed . . . than are some European countries—one might perhaps pick Norway." *The Rich Nations and the Poor Nations* (Norton, 1962), p. 39.

television, cheap air travel, roads within the poor countries, and the mass production of census, health, and other statistics, Europeans and North Americans knew little about these regions except for factual tidbits remembered from school, occasional newspaper reports of natural disasters, and romantic accounts in travel books and magazines. The war provided an unprecedented geography lesson for the general public, especially in the United States.

This state of affairs is clearly reflected in the League of Nations' *World Economic Survey* for 1938, which reported on the state of business activity in the world. The document devoted twenty-six pages to the United States, Europe, and Japan; one paragraph to a set of nine "primary producing countries" (Australia, Canada, New Zealand, Argentina, Brazil, Chile, Hungary, Rumania, Yugoslavia); one paragraph to the rest of South America; and one sentence each to the Balkans and the Dutch East Indies. Africa, the USSR, and the rest of Asia were not mentioned.[35]

There was a corresponding gap in economic science when it came to development and growth. When Hans Singer was persuaded in 1947 to take a job at the United Nations, he was assigned to what had been his last choice for a research topic: the underdeveloped countries. Arriving in the United States, he visited his former professor, Joseph Schumpeter at Harvard University, to share the news of his appointment. Singer recalls, "When I told him that my work in the U.N. was to be on the problems of the underdeveloped countries his surprised—and surprising—response was: 'but I thought you were an economist!'"[36] Paul Samuelson's first edition of his classic introductory textbook, *Economics,* published in 1948, contained less than three sentences on development.

This lack of scientific attention dated from the middle of the nineteenth century when, with British industrialization well on its way, mainstream economics turned from broader questions of development over the long run to economic fine-tuning. With Marshallian microeconomics bestriding the profession, Anglo-Saxon academia focused on allocative efficiency and business cycles, unaware of or indifferent to the contemporary growth-starting concerns of Japan and much of Europe. Even as economists in British and American universities between 1850 and 1940 busied themselves with refinements to allocative and business cycle theory, Japan, Russia, Germany, and the Nordic countries were intensely involved in the struggle for economic development, debating and experimenting with institutional reforms, industrial protection, five-year plans, mass education, vocational training, credit allocation, and state-financed acquisition of technology. Yet, when one of the authors of this volume chanced to meet Evsey Domar at Harvard University in 1947 and asked him what he was working on, he was astonished and perplexed by

35. H. W. Arndt, *Economic Development: The History of an Idea* (University of Chicago Press, 1987), p. 33.

36. Hans Singer, "Early Years, 1910–1983," in Alec Cairncross and Mohinder Puri, eds., *Employment, Income Distribution and Development Strategy: Problems of the Developing Countries, Essays in Honour of H. W. Singer* (Holmes and Meier, 1976), p. 6.

Domar's answer, "economic growth." At that time, growth and development were rarely mentioned in mainstream economics.[37]

Paradoxically, in the 1940s poverty and basic needs were high on the academic and political agendas of the industrialized countries. Great Britain was caught up in debates and proposals, including the Beveridge Plan—slighted by Harrod in his railway carriage story—that would soon produce the welfare state. British scholars and politicians could look back to several centuries of Poor Law debate and experiment, and Sweden was already a role model for modern welfare legislation.[38] The president of the United States in 1933 had proclaimed a New Deal, and Secretary of the Treasury Henry Morgenthau, in planning for the Bretton Woods Conference, "envisaged a kind of New Deal for a new world."[39] In Europe, Christian Democrats and Social Democrats were preparing postwar political programs that would go a long way toward meeting and thus undercutting leftist demands. In the industrialized world, social needs were being studied, new institutions were being proposed, and basic human needs were on the way to being accepted as rights. This activity created both an intellectual precedent and potential inspiration for a future response to poverty and social problems in the underdeveloped world. Indeed, social welfare goals figured large in the agenda of the International Labor Organization and other international organizations soon to be born. During the 1950s and 1960s, however, meeting the social needs of underdeveloped countries was seen as "consumption," to be attended to where political emergency required, but for the most part to be postponed. Aid efforts were designed to bring about overall economic growth in national economies, rather than to provide a more immediate response to poverty or social needs.

Development arrived almost by accident and played a bit role at Bretton Woods, but it got on the books, becoming part of the Bank's name and official purpose. The strength, meaning, and direction given to this objective would be determined by a host of factors in the following decades. Meanwhile, several themes of the Bretton Woods conference served, from the beginning, to nurture and shape the still embryonic development mission of the Bank.

One of those themes was internationalism, in the sense of international participation in decisionmaking. Despite Keynes's preference for a summit, Bretton

---

37. One factor that prompted David Knox to move from the London School of Economics to the World Bank in 1963 was the school's refusal to allow him to include development, along with allocation, as course subject matter. He was told by Lionel Robbins that development "was not a respectable topic." Personal conversation, September 24, 1996.

38. Gosta Esping-Andersen, *Politics against Markets: The Social Democratic Road to Power* (Princeton University Press, 1985); and Peter Mathias and Sidney Pollard, eds., *The Industrial Economies: The Development of Economic and Social Policies, the Cambridge Economic History of Europe*, vol. 8 (Cambridge University Press, 1990).

39. According to his biographer, John Morton Blum. Cited in David Rees, *Harry Dexter White: A Study in Paradox* (New York: Coward, McCann and Geoghegan, 1973), p. 138.

Woods was organized as a "United Nations Monetary and Financial Conference." Key rules and institutions that would govern the postwar world economy thus came to be decided by an international agreement signed by forty-four small and large nations. This was White's contribution. From the beginning, he had insisted that the Bank must be truly international and that "it must not be a rich man's club."[40] Admittedly, there was an element of charade in all these remarks, of token respect to internationalism, and also an element of politics; the United States sought Latin American participation as a source of support on key issues against the United Kingdom. The hard fact is that the agreement was negotiated by the British and Americans, and it was their idea. Nonetheless, the international character of the Bank, part real and part appearance, imbued the organization with a degree of legitimacy and authority that, over the decades, has contributed in an important degree to its fund-raising capacity and to the influence that it has exercised over development policy.

A closely related theme at Bretton Woods was that of international interdependence, in the economic sense. This idea was best expressed by President Roosevelt in his remarks about the importance of the "economic health" of one's neighbors, a phrase that had both a practical and a moral dimension.[41] The two concepts, international decisionmaking and economic interdependence, worked to legitimize the development objective. As Secretary Morgenthau pointed out, "Prosperity, like peace, is indivisible," and "poverty, wherever it exists, is menacing to us all."[42] The idea of economic interdependence, firmly imprinted on everyone's mind by the depression and the war, was of course the driving force for the entire Bretton Woods project, a mantra repeated constantly up to the final ratification of the agreement. But no one went on to state its corollary with regard to aid, namely, that development assistance was in the self-interest of the giver. There were allusions to the importance of developing the resources available in undeveloped areas, by which delegates meant, principally, raw materials. The Mexican delegate, when arguing the case for development lending, reminded his colleagues that raw materials were needed for reconstruction. In the middle of a war, he was playing an ace. And Morgenthau's formulation of the interdependence argument—"Poverty . . . is menacing to us all"—would be echoed later in the cold war argument for development assistance.

A third notion needs to be mentioned mostly because of its absence at Bretton Woods: moral obligation. Roosevelt's opening message to the conference, justifying "concern to all its neighbors near and distant," was glossed over at Bretton Woods. The collective commitment to reconstruction was certainly an expression of soli-

40. Oliver, *Early Plans for a World Bank,* p. 5.

41. *Proceedings and Documents of United Nations Monetary and Financial Conference,* vol. 1, p. 71.

42. Ibid., p. 81.

darity, especially since this was decided well before the cold war. But even reconstruction was justified by reference to economic interdependence and the need to recreate a dynamic world economy. Morgenthau mentioned China only to point out the export potential of its 450 million people, noting in passing that "good customers are prosperous customers."[43] To reiterate, the case for development lending by the Bank was argued more on grounds of general world recovery and interdependence than human solidarity. This appeal to business, rather than moral obligation, was probably good, indeed necessary, politics and, over the long run, has probably been the best stance for the Bank.[44] Moral obligation would not have sold the Bank's bonds. Even public purses, which funded the Bank's capital and most of the IDA's annual lending, have been more responsive to a businesslike Bank than they would have been to an institution strongly motivated by charity or notions of economic justice. At the time, the opportunity to borrow at Wall Street interest rates and long repayment periods, all eventually augmented with technical assistance, amounted to a substantial benefit.

The appeal to economics rather than ethics at Bretton Woods has colored the Bank's development efforts. But it is also true that the arrival of the IDA in the 1960s and the concern with "basic needs" in the 1970s, followed by an emphasis on social safety nets, women in development, disaster relief, and other objectives that are debatably "noneconomic," if not frankly welfare or ethical goals, have gradually worn down the Bank's strictly business facade and increased the weight of ethical considerations in Bank decisionmaking. Moreover, because it transfers funds and expertise from the rich to the poor, the Bank can be said to exist for a moral purpose, though it has chosen to operate as a business. But throughout the Bank's history, the necessary and predominant justification for its specific operations has been economic rather than ethical. When it did finally venture into education, health, women-in-development, and social emergency programs, it had in each case first persuaded itself and the development community that it had found another highly productive investment opportunity.

From Reconstruction to Development, 1946–48

Close to three years slipped by after the conclusion of the Bretton Woods Conference while signatory countries ratified the agreement, president and staff were appointed, and policies, procedures, and organization were decided. It was

43. Ibid., pp. 80–81.

44. Public and congressional opinion in the United States was running against additional foreign expenditures, and Roosevelt faced elections in 1944. Truman's haste in 1945 to accommodate opinion probably caused his cancellation of the Lend-Lease blunder. In 1946 efforts to approve a postwar loan to Britain almost failed, and the 1947 Marshall Plan proposal to Congress was stuck until the February 1948 communist coup in Czechoslovakia.

not until May 1947, a year after its official opening, that the Bank made its first loan, a $250 million reconstruction credit to France. In the ensuing year and a half, lending was almost entirely for reconstruction: loans were approved for the Netherlands, Luxembourg, and Denmark. Similar financing for Poland and Czechoslovakia was discussed, though loans did not result. By late 1948 the Bank had lent $497 million (approximately $2.0 billion in 1993 prices) for reconstruction purposes and appeared to be fully engaged in what Keynes had defined, implicitly, as its primary duty, that of assisting countries in the task of reconstruction made necessary by the war. The Bank's first two annual reports, dated September 1946 and September 1947, reflect that purpose, commenting principally on the progress, and lack of progress, recorded on the reconstruction front.

Despite the Bank's continuing emphasis on reconstruction, it did take some early steps to promote development. For one thing, it accepted loan applications from Chile, Mexico, and Iran, the first such requests from underdeveloped countries. For another, it began reflecting on the nature of the development problem, and on the contribution that the Bank could make to finding a solution. The 1980s resonate with those reflections: the need to settle debt arrears, establish sound monetary and fiscal policies, and rely on private investment.

What the authors of the 1947 annual report could not foresee was that the Bank's reconstruction role, barely launched, was about to end, even though Bank officials had become involved in formulating alternative funding plans for Europe. The 1947 report does express some unease, admitting that an unexpected gap had arisen between the supply of and need for financial assistance in Europe, in part because of the delays in launching the Bank, and in part because of the underestimation of reconstruction needs. As the report saw it, "When the Bank's charter was drafted at Bretton Woods in the summer of 1944, high hopes were held that the Bank would prove to be the principal instrument for restoring the war-torn nations of the world to economic life. . . . We now know that the problem is deeper and more difficult than was envisaged at Bretton Woods."[45] American-funded relief efforts, especially through the United Nations Relief and Rehabilitation Administration (UNRRA), were being used to help fill that gap. Furthermore, a speech on June 6 by Secretary of State George Marshall had implicitly raised questions about the Bank's role, questions that were expressed in the same report. "Because the requirements are greater than anticipated, because the scope of activity and loanable resources of the Bank are limited, it is manifest that the Bank can provide only a part of the answer to the problems which confront the world today."[46] Nevertheless, these glimpses of a changing world had not yet developed into a realization that the Bank's original and "primary" reconstruction purpose was about to be cut short. If

45. International Bank for Reconstruction and Development, *Second Annual Report to the Board of Governors for the Year Ended June 30, 1947*, p. 7.
    46. Ibid., p. 7.

the Bank was to be only "a part of the answer," it still expected to be a major, even the principal, part. The Bank admitted to a performance gap in its reconstruction efforts caused by administrative delays and statistical underestimates, but, understandably, by September 1947 it had not yet come to realize that a new world war was beginning.

A turning point had occurred six months earlier, in March 1947, when President Harry S Truman, responding to rapidly escalating distrust and friction between the Soviet Union and its wartime allies, and more immediately, to a British pullout from the civil war in Greece, where a communist victory looked possible, announced the U.S. government's commitment to intervene in support of "free peoples." Against the grain of traditional U.S. foreign policy, which advocated neutrality until provoked, Truman was engaging the country in a plan of active resistance to, or "containment" of, perceived communist aggression; in effect, he was announcing the start of the cold war.[47] An almost immediate consequence would be a drastic change in the purpose, size, and mode of foreign aid.

This foreign policy about-turn occurred less than two years after Truman's sudden cancellation of Lend-Lease, on the eve of Japan's surrender. The undiplomatic abruptness of that act was a measure of America's wartime opposition to foreign aid. In fact, as chairman of the Congressional War Investigating Committee in 1942, Truman had himself taken a hard line on assistance, insisting that Britain repay Lend-Lease aid in raw materials after the war.[48] He partly reversed his July 1945 order, authorizing the continuation of Lend-Lease to China, and later called the cancellation the "worst decision" of his presidency, but American sentiment approved the move at the time.[49] The anti–foreign aid mood in the United States was even more apparent when Truman endorsed Britain's July 1945 request for a loan, though not before extending negotiations over six months and cutting the amount from $6 billion to $3.75 billion. The request was submitted to Congress in January 1946. After a hostile debate, Congress finally voted in favor, but not until July 1946, a full year after the original "emergency" request by Britain. Its final approval was due as much to the rapid deterioration of relations with the Soviet Union, which had issued threats in Iran and Europe, as to the emergency postwar needs of America's closest wartime ally. The American people, says Richard Gardner, felt that they "had provided their allies with huge sums to aid in winning the war; they had given additional sums to aid in winning the peace. In their view, it was

47. Walter LaFeber, *America, Russia and the Cold War, 1945–1992* (McGraw-Hill, 1992), pp. 38–39, argues that Josef Stalin's February 9, 1946, election speech, stating that war was inevitable as long as capitalism existed, and Winston Churchill's Iron Curtain speech in Fulton, Missouri, one month later, may be considered the "two declarations" of the cold war.

48. Gardner, *Sterling-Dollar Diplomacy*, p. 172.

49. Gregory A. Fossedal, *Our Finest Hour: Will Clayton, the Marshall Plan, and the Triumph of Democracy* (Hoover Institution Press, 1993), p. 182; Gardner, *Sterling-Dollar Diplomacy*, p. 186.

high time to end controls, reduce taxes, and return to 'normalcy.' . . . Surely the rest of the world, with the assistance the United States had already given, would now be able to look after itself."[50] Foreign aid was not the only, nor the principal victim of this citizen rebellion against continuing sacrifice. Between January and June 1945, while the U.K. loan was being debated, the American economy was hit by strikes in various quarters, including the steel and automobile industries and dockyards.

The "Truman Doctrine" was thus announced against a background of strong opposition to further domestic sacrifice, foreign aid, and foreign involvement. In his policy statement, Truman asked Congress for $400 million in aid for Greece and Turkey. This request was the tip of the iceberg. Two months later, Dean Acheson hinted publicly that "the facts of international life . . . mean that the United States is going to have to undertake further emergency financing" of foreign countries, whose needs "may be of a type which existing national and international institutions are not equipped to handle."[51] A few weeks later, in June 1947, Secretary of State George Marshall used an address at Harvard University to expand on this message: "The truth of the matter is that Europe's requirements for the next three years for foreign food and other essential products—principally from America—are so much greater than her present ability to pay that she must have substantial additional help." A week later he estimated that "the Marshall Plan" might cost $5 billion to $6 billion a year ($21 billion to $25 billion in 1993 prices) for several years. These figures, which would have been mere fantasy only months earlier (as Truman's $400 million request suggests), were now an admissible point of departure for debate. Public opposition to Truman's policy continued during 1947, even after the August communist takeover in Hungary. In September, Marshall insisted on the need for assistance to Europe to reduce hunger and cold during the coming winter, and he drew attention to the distress already caused by serious droughts, a severe winter, and restrictive financial measures.[52] With presidential elections scheduled for 1948, a hostile Congress continued to block a plan described as an "international W.P.A." and a "bold Socialist blue-print."[53] Public and congressional resistance ended, however, with the communist coup in Czechoslovakia in February 1948, and on April 13 the government passed the Economic Cooperation Act, authorizing an initial $5 billion ($21 billion in 1993 dollars) for financial assistance to Europe.

Although the IBRD had been conceived as a tool for peacetime economic rebuilding and development, in 1947 it and other instruments of foreign aid became a potential weapon. As originally conceived, European reconstruction was

50. Gardner, *Sterling-Dollar Diplomacy*, p. 188.

51. Ibid., p. 302.

52. Charles L. Mee, *The Marshall Plan: The Launching of the Pax Americana* (Simon and Schuster, 1984), pp. 200–201.

53. Stephen E. Ambrose, *Rise to Globalism: American Foreign Policy since 1938* (Penguin Books, 1985), p. 92. The WPA (Works Progress Administration) was a New Deal "make-work" program.

to be a humanitarian act that also made long-term economic sense for the United States. And, in keeping with those low-key objectives, the rebuilding was to have been financed almost painlessly through credits on commercial terms issued by the World Bank. But almost overnight, between March 1947 and March 1948, European reconstruction became the most urgent objective of American national security. Economic disruption, shortages, and hunger throughout Europe came to be associated with communist-led strikes and riots, and with threats of communist takeovers or electoral victories in France, Italy, Greece, and other countries. In short, "political health in Europe depended on economic medicine."[54] The Bretton Woods vision—a world of open trade, capital flows, and monetary stability anchored on the Fund and encouraged by World Bank credits and guarantees—was put aside and subordinated to the requirements of an intensive program to rehabilitate and integrate Europe under the Marshall Plan. As Richard Gardner has pointed out,

> The new measures devised to deal with the post-war disequilibrium soon overshadowed the financial institutions designed in the war. The normal objectives of the International Monetary Fund were gradually subordinated to the immediate requirements of European recovery. In the year beginning 1 July 1947 the Fund abandoned its conservative lending policy and extended $610 million in aid to member countries. Many of these loans could hardly be considered for short-term stabilization purposes, but they did serve to fill the gap until the new measures of European aid were passed by the American Congress.
>
> The operations of the International Bank also yielded priority to the new programme of reconstruction aid, [but], [i]n practice, the Western European countries preferred Marshall Aid to assistance from the Bank, since the former came as grants or loans on easier credit terms than the Bank could make available. Therefore, as the Marshall Plan gained momentum, the Bank moved out of the reconstruction field. It turned instead, somewhat modestly at first, to the job of helping underdeveloped countries.[55]

In fact, all four reconstruction credits, negotiated in previous months, were signed after Marshall's June 5 speech, beginning with a $250 million loan to France on June 7. The fourth and last reconstruction loan, for $12 million to Luxembourg, was approved on August 28, 1947, almost three months after the announcement of the Marshall Plan. But this three-month spate of reconstruction lending ended in August, pending a resolution of the continuing debate on the Marshall Plan. As the September 1948 annual report explained, "So far as European reconstruction is concerned, substantial loans by the Bank have been precluded primarily because of the uncertainties which have existed, first with respect to the shape and content of the European Recovery Program and later with respect to the manner in which loans by the Bank could best be brought into harmony with that program."[56]

54. Robert A. Packenham, *Liberal America and the Third World: Political Development Ideas in Foreign Aid and Social Science* (Princeton University Press, 1973), pp. 33, 34.

55. Gardner, *Sterling-Dollar Diplomacy*, pp. 303–4.

56. IBRD, *Third Annual Report to Board of Governors, 1947–1948*, p. 5.

A virtual lending pause of seventeen months followed the Luxembourg operation.[57] In that period the Bank made only three small loans, for a total of $28 million: two in March 1948 to Chile totaling $16 million, the first Bank loan to a less developed country; and one in August to the Netherlands in the amount of $12 million, for imports. This was a difficult time of waiting, outside criticism, and defensive explanations. Though observers saw indecision and inactivity, it was, in fact, a decisive period, during which, by saying no, the Bank protected its financial respectability.

From the day it opened, the Bank had been besieged by European governments and some members of the American administration who pressed it to relieve urgent European needs for foreign exchange, raw materials, and food. Speaking at the Bank's inaugural meeting in 1946, U.S. Secretary of the Treasury John Snyder had said that "if there were any keynote that he wished to make it was speed to get the Bank and the Fund in operation at the earliest moment."[58] In part, the pressure was a consequence of the ambitious claims that had been made for the Bretton Woods institutions by members of the U.S. administration, as they strove to obtain congressional approval for ratification, and later, for the postwar loan to Britain. When the loan was questioned on the grounds that the United States could soon be faced with additional requests for reconstruction aid, the administration replied that the Bretton Woods institutions would make available "some fifteen billion dollars."[59] The pressure increased during 1947, as approval of the Marshall Plan was delayed and conditions in Europe worsened. Before he resigned, in December 1946, the Bank's first president, Eugene Meyer had been moved to state that "the Bank was not a relief agency."[60] Nine months later President John McCloy thought it necessary to state publicly that the Bank was not in the stopgap business.[61] At a Board meeting on October 15, 1947, Vice President Robert Garner commented that "responsible" members of the American government understood that the Bank did not exist for relief operations, implying that other officials were being irresponsible in urging the Bank to move in this direction.[62] Pressure for quick lending also came from the less powerful but nonetheless audible voices of repre-

57. From August 1947 to January 1949. John McCloy was president through this period, from March 17, 1947, through May 18, 1949.

58. August Maffry, interview, World Bank Oral History Program, January 19, 1973, p. 14. Maffry worked for the Department of Commerce and attended Bretton Woods as an adviser.

59. Gardner, *Sterling-Dollar Diplomacy*, p. 292. The United Nations Assembly had also been encouraged to believe that ample postwar financial assistance would be forthcoming from the Fund and the Bank, with an explicit reference to the $15 billion figure. Press release no. 78 by the U.S. delegation, November 14, 1946.

60. Kai Bird, *The Chairman: John J. McCloy, The Making of the American Establishment* (Simon and Schuster, 1992), p. 283.

61. Ibid., p. 293. Originally cited in the *Washington Post*, September 11, 1947.

62. Meeting of Executive Directors, October 15, 1947.

sentatives of underdeveloped countries both in the Bank and in the United Nations. Victor Moller, the Chilean executive director on the Bank's Board, protested that large-scale lending to Europe threatened its future capacity to make development loans.[63]

The Bank did not succumb to these urgings and criticisms by becoming, as the *Financial Times* had speculated, a universal soup kitchen.[64] Both the first, brief administration, under President Meyer, and more particularly the second, under McCloy, Garner, and U.S. Executive Director Eugene Black, were of one mind on the need to preserve the Bretton Woods design for a multilateral and respectable financial institution capable of self-financing in the market. McCloy's determination was most likely hardened by a weakening in the market for World Bank bonds during the summer and fall of 1947, prompted by speculation that the Bank would be forced into a relief role in Europe. At a Board meeting on November 19, 1947, at the peak of uncertainty and speculation regarding the Bank's future, McCloy asked what position the Board would take if the United States were to offer more funding in return for the Bank's active participation in the European assistance program. Such possibilities had in fact been raised in discussions between the Bank and the U.S. government and included a proposal that the Bank use all of its borrowing capacity to lend $3.1 billion exclusively in Europe, which had been reported by McCloy to the Board two weeks earlier.[65] In McCloy's opinion, any such offer would mean turning the Bank more and more into an American organization: "The real sixty-four dollar question is do we lose our character as an international organization and do we lose the chance of accomplishing *what we were formed for, as an international banking agency,* if we accept a substantial amount of additional aid from one member?" The British director, Sir Gordon Munro, seconded McCloy's concern: "Unless we are very careful we definitely may lose our international character as an international bank."[66] For McCloy, however, multilateralism was in all likelihood more of a device for gaining institutional—and personal—autonomy than a concession to non-U.S. authority. When he reaffirmed the Charter provision that there would be no "political loans," he defined these as "loans inconsistent with American foreign policy."[67]

63. Meeting of Executive Directors, August 22, 1947.

64. Bird, *The Chairman,* p. 283. Originally cited in the *Financial Times* (London), December 9, 1946.

65. Meeting of Executive Directors, November 5, 1947. At an earlier, August 1947, Board meeting, McCloy said that he refused to throw the Bank out like a baby into the snow from the back of a sled.

66. Meeting of Executive Directors, November 19, 1947. Emphasis added. By contrast, the Indian delegate, Mr. Sundaresan, insisted that greater U.S. influence should not inhibit the Bank from accepting more funds. "I don't think we should attach importance to that. In this world, only a country like the United States can come forward to help. We must accept."

67. Quoted by Thomas Alan Schwartz, *America's Germany: John J. McCloy and the Federal Republic of Germany* (Harvard University Press, 1991), p. 27. McCloy was con-

It was above all the insistence on being a bank, as the Charter had intended, that determined the character of the institution. By depending on the market, McCloy and Munro went a long way toward preserving the Bank's international character. At the same time, market discipline, which was first imposed, later served management as a whipping boy for the Bank's exacting project standards and country policies.

If a bank's first building block is a hard cash investment, all further additions to the structure are made out of a less substantial material: confidence. It was the World Bank's challenge to win financial trust, beginning with that of U.S. investors, and to do so despite its odd character as an international, public sector institution, and, what was an even greater challenge, to do so despite its mandate to make overseas sovereign loans. Sovereign lending had ended with the depression. By 1933, as Karin Lissakers has written,

> countries were in default on more than $20 billion [approximately $180 billion in 1993 dollars], and interest arrears exceeded $12 billion. Eighty-two percent of Latin America's dollar bonds were in default, as were 40 percent of U.S. loans to Europe. . . . This . . . debt debacle was followed by a hiatus in private foreign lending of more than twenty years during which few countries had access to commercial financing outside their own borders.[68]

It is hardly surprising, then, that the Bank proceeded gingerly. Nor that its first three presidents were men with close Wall Street connections. Eugene Meyer had been the head of a successful investment banking house as well as chairman of a Federal Reserve bank; McCloy had been a lawyer in New York who worked closely with banks; and Black, for most of his life, had been engaged in banking and in the marketing of securities. Vice President Garner had also spent more than twenty years at Guaranty Trust. And many of the first officers had worked in government treasury departments or central banks. Even the Bank's first chief economist, Leonard Rist, was a banker with little training in economics. When approached by Meyer in 1946 to become the Bank's treasurer, he asked instead to be appointed head of the Economic Department, though admitting that his command of economics was limited to banking matters. According to Rist, Meyer accepted, saying "that was exactly what he wanted."[69] Robert Cavanaugh, who joined the Bank in March 1947 to head the Finance Division, which dealt with the borrowing of funds, recalls the difficulties that the Bank faced in placing bonds:

---

tinuously involved in U.S. foreign policy before, during, and after his term at the Bank. He is the only Bank president who has testified before a congressional committee. During his term he participated in the planning for what became the Central Intelligence Agency and for the Marshall Plan and left the Bank to become U.S. high commissioner in Germany.

68. Foreign Bondholders Protective Council, *Annual Report of 1934* (New York: Foreign Bondholders Protective Council, 1935). Cited by Karin Lissakers, *Banks, Borrowers, and the Establishment* (Basic Books, 1991), p. 15.

69. Leonard Rist, interview, World Bank Oral History Program, July 1961, p. 4.

Many people said that . . . American institutions and public would not buy World Bank bonds because the World Bank was a foreign organization. . . . Nobody knew how the Bank was going to be operated and whether it was going to be a soundly run organization or not, but they did trust McCloy and Black and the people who were together in the World Bank at that time.[70]

Another witness, Richard Demuth, remembers Meyer's first meeting with investment bankers in New York. "They were thoroughly unenthusiastic. . . . [The Bank] smacked of having to do with foreign lending, which at that time was in very bad repute." The Bank was seen as a "do-good institution, a wild idea."[71] And when Garner consulted a banker friend about the offer he had just received from McCloy to join the Bank, in 1947, the banker said he thought the institution could be useful, but "I wouldn't touch your bonds with a ten-foot pole."[72]

As Mason and Asher put it, the task of making bonds eligible and attractive to the most conservative U.S. investors, "reinforced pressures toward caution. . . . Procedural safeguards that delayed the granting of loans, or limited the purposes for which they could be granted, or required ancillary modification of the borrower's policies as the price for their approval could all be justified as essential in order to gain and hold the confidence of private investors."[73]

Chile was the first developing country borrower to experience those "safeguards" in the flesh. Chile's $40 million loan application for a package of industrial and power projects had been filed shortly after the Bank opened in 1946.[74] In those first months of operation, a power struggle was being waged between the Board of Executive Directors, led by the U.S. representative Emilio Collado, and President Eugene Meyer. Collado had worked closely with Harry Dexter White in Treasury and then in the State Department and shared White's vision of a Bank that would rapidly play a large role in postwar reconstruction and development. At the State

70. Robert Cavanaugh, interview, World Bank Oral History Program, June 1961, pp. 66, 67.

71. Demuth accompanied Meyer on his first trip to New York as Bank president to meet investment bankers. He remembers that the bankers were "thoroughly unenthusiastic about giving any financial support for the Bank" and that "there was an amazing discrepancy between the attitude of the bankers and the expectations of Bretton Woods, where it was believed that the Bank could easily borrow up to the total amount of its subscribed capital, reserves and surplus." Richard H. Demuth, interview, World Bank Oral History Program, August 1961, p. 12.

72. Robert L. Garner, interview, World Bank Oral History Program, December 1972, p. 206.

73. Mason And Asher, *World Bank since Bretton Woods*, p. 54.

74. The Chileans had applied first to the Export-Import Bank, where they were established customers and which was lending at an interest rate below that of the Bank. But the National Advisory Council, a U.S. government coordinating agency, had decided that, at the next application from Chile, the newly created World Bank should be put to work. When Vergara, the Chilean representative arrived at the Export-Import Bank in September 1946, the president, Bill Martin, said, "You have to take your application over to the World Bank."

Department he had worked many years on Latin American affairs. Collado pushed the Bank to go out and issue bonds on the market quickly and disagreed with Meyer that a great deal of educational work should be done first. Demuth recalls that, when the Chilean request arrived,

> Collado told Mr. Meyer that the Bank was darned well going to make this loan by December 1946 or he'd know the reason why. Meyer pointed out that we knew nothing about Chile's economy or anything about the projects. Collado said he knew Chile, he'd known them for a long time, and they were good for $40 million and the Bank was darned well going to make the loan.[75]

Collado, who dominated the Board and had close connections with U.S. government officials, might have forced through the loan, but Meyer resigned in December without approving the application. His successor, John McCloy, put a firm end to Collado's influence and liberal ambitions for the World Bank: he accepted the presidency—after first refusing—on the understanding that Collado would be replaced by Eugene Black, and he obtained from the Board of Directors an understanding that, henceforth, only "management" (a term that McCloy introduced into the Bank's jargon) would present loans for approval to the Board. He also brought in Robert Garner to be his vice president. McCloy's coup was a positive signal to Wall Street, where former colleagues had seen his rumored appointment as an opportunity to wrest control of the World Bank "from the New Deal crowd." *The American Banker,* a mouthpiece of the investment-banking community, applauded Collado's removal as a sign that the Bank would now . . . minimize political considerations and maximize economic factors in making its loans."[76] That view was shared by Richard Demuth, who had joined the Bank in July 1946 as Meyer's assistant and saw the issue as one of "whether the Bank was just going to be an institution to hand out money to governments or whether it was going to be a real investment banking institution."[77]

McCloy promptly turned his attention to the preparation of the Bank's bond issues, delegating lending policy to Garner, but joined Garner in the negotiation of the Bank's first reconstruction loan, to France. The new Bank team took a tough stance with the French, cutting the proposal from $500 million to $250 million, insisting on fiscal and monetary discipline, demanding a "negative pledge" that France would not offer collateral without securing the Bank equally, and imposing

---

Vergara said, "Why do we have to be the guinea pigs?" Martin replied, "Well you're such experienced borrowers it would make it easier for them." The Chilean representative then drove over to Meyer's office at 1818 H Street, in Washington, D.C., and presented his application. Half an hour later Meyer called Martin to say, "We just got a loan application. What do we do now?" Bernard Bell, interview, World Bank Oral History Program, November 13, 1990, p. 3.

75. Demuth, Oral History, August 1961, p. 5.
76. Cited in Bird, *The Chairman,* p. 289.
77. Demuth, Oral History, August 1961, p. 5.

elaborate procedures to control the end use of Bank-financed imports. The last condition led the French to accuse the Bank of infringing upon their sovereignty. The French minister asked, indignantly, "Mr. Garner, you expect me to identify every lump of coal as to which boiler it's going into?" Garner replied, "No. I just want to be sure it is not being diverted to Paris nightclubs. I want it to be used in French industrial activity."[78] Though it was first applied in the French loan and in the subsequent three reconstruction loans, Garner made end-use supervision a key feature of what would later be the Bank's dominant mode of lending, the investment project. "We would have control of disbursements against specific requests for specific purposes. That pattern has been followed by the Bank throughout its history, and I think has been one of the things that has given people confidence in the Bank."[79]

Testifying before the Senate Committee on Foreign Relations during hearings on the Marshall Plan, on January 16, 1948, McCloy explained that the reconstruction loans had, at the same time, a "productive" purpose.[80] Thus the loans to France, the Netherlands, and Denmark had been earmarked for locomotives, steel rails, steel for the building of bridges, stocks of raw materials, and agricultural equipment, while disbursement of the Luxembourg loan was tied to improvements in a steel mill, "a very key spot in that area of the European economy."

> Mr. McCloy. [The Luxembourg loan] is a very productive loan. We must have productive loans or we can not stay in business. . . .
> Senator Connally. You will probably get that money back.
> Mr. McCloy. I believe we are going to get all our money back.
> Senator Connally. That is a very frugal country. They will pay you back.
> Mr. McCloy. We must by our charter, as well as by the necessity of appealing to hard-headed people who are responsible for the savings in this country, convince them that their money will be paid back.

McCloy added that repayment was assured not only by the productive purpose of loans, but by the Bank's system of supervision.

> Mr. McCloy. There is one other aspect . . . the emphasis that we place upon following the proceeds of our loans . . . to see that the proceeds are dispensed in the manner in which they were approved . . . if there is any diversion they must have our consent. . . . I think this a very beneficial provision . . . to avoid, if possible, the unfortunate consequences of the English loan. . . . [P]eople got the feeling that that was an ineffective loan largely because they did not know what it was being used for.
> The Chairman. . . . Is that process you now describe the result of any statutory language in your Charter or in the law?

78. Robert Garner, interview by Robert Oliver, July 19, 1961, p. 10.
79. Ibid., pp. 10–11.
80. Bank staff members assisted United States government officials in preparations for the Marshall Plan. This cooperation became the one occasion on which a Bank president has testified before any national legislature.

Mr. McCloy. No, it is a matter of policy that we have adopted. It is an implication, I think, of the fact that our loans must be productive, which is a statutory requirement. . . .

Chairman [of Senate Committee]. That one single protective device put into ERP [European Recovery Program] would do more, I think, to satisfy American public opinion than any other single thing I know of.[81]

Neither McCloy nor the senators raised the question of substitutability or fungibility of funds within the budgets of borrowing countries, that is, of the difficulty, indeed perhaps the impossibility, of determining the true or ultimate use of additional aid funds. It was a question that troubled Averell Harriman, the Marshall Plan's special representative in Europe. That year Harriman cabled Dean Acheson: "French spending in Vietnam was about as much as we are giving them in Paris." Acheson rebuked Harriman for not minding his own business.[82] McCloy and the senators had no such misapprehension about their respective "businesses": their schemes for tracking the use of funds had less to do with an ultimate accounting than with satisfying American public opinion, on the one hand, and with reassuring buyers of World Bank bonds, on the other. McCloy was well aware that his European reconstruction loans were risky.[83] Waxing confident about end-use control and productive investments, he was putting the best face on the situation.

By the time Chile's application was taken up again, a year later, and despite the reconstruction and program loan character of its lending thus far, the Bank had established many of the procedures and precedents that would shape its future development lending: close scrutiny and discussion of proposals; conditionality related to monetary, fiscal, and balance of payments policies that would bear on a country's capacity to repay; supervision of the use of funds; and a negative pledge.[84] All of these procedures came to bear on Chile's application, along with a significant additional condition: that Chile settle with the holders of $150 million in Chilean government bonds in default since the 1930s.

After the initial discussions of Chile's proposal in 1946, and Collado's failure to push it through the Board, the request had been set aside on grounds of financial instability. In May 1947 the Bank informed Chile that its "unbalanced budgets and deficit financing, its need to limit non-essential imports and build up foreign exchange reserves . . . unsatisfactory system of multiple foreign exchange rates . . .

81. Memorandum from Secretary to Board, no. 335, January 20, 1948, pp. 14–16. Attached statement by President John McCloy to the U.S. Senate, Committee on Foreign Relations, Washington, D.C., Friday, January 16, 1948.

82. Averell Harriman memo, June 28, 1971, Harriman Oral History Truman Era, cited by Bird, *The Chairman*, p. 296. France had agreed to NATO on the condition that the United States accept French rule in Indochina.

83. Demuth, Oral History, August 1961, p. 14.

84. Until much later, the Bank preferred de facto conditioning of lending on macroeconomic policies that the institution considered adequate. In the 1980s it adopted the International Monetary Fund's practice of contractual, or de jure, conditionality for some of its lending.

unsatisfactory tax and exchange relationships with foreign enterprises . . . [and] unsettled defaults [were] cause for grave concern."[85] It was only in November 1947, over a year after the original submission, that management reported to the Board that, in its view, the improvement in the financial and budgetary situation of Chile was sufficient to "feel that maybe progress can be made."[86] Before the loans were made, Chile had reached an agreement with the International Monetary Fund. In the course of the negotiations, several missions visited Chile; the Bank made suggestions about the financial plan, contributed to the economic analysis of the proposed projects, suggested engineering changes, and helped study measures for improving the organization of the company that was to carry out the projects. End-use supervision was made easier by rejecting the semi-program nature of Chile's request, a package that included power generation, forest development, port equipment, railway modernization, and urban transport. In the end, the $40 million request was cut down to a $13.5 million loan for a hydroelectric plant and transmission lines and $2.5 million for agricultural machinery. At the same time, in keeping with what would come to be standard practice, the Board was told that the remaining items in the loan application had not been rejected but rather were being investigated for future consideration, that independent engineers were in Chile studying the railway electrification project, and that the Bank was collaborating in sending engineers on the forest industries projects.[87]

The principal sting in the conditions was the requirement that Chile reach a settlement with the holders of defaulted prewar bonds, the Bank arguing that it "does not see how [it] can make loans in the face of widespread dissatisfaction in financial and investment circles to whom the Bank must sell its own bonds."[88] The Chileans were "very annoyed," as Black later put it, but finally agreed, and the two loans were announced on the day after the settlement with the foreign bond-holders.[89]

The Bank's 1947–48 lending pause became a step toward its development purpose in a second and more direct way: during this period the institution set out to discover the less developed world. Davidson Sommers came to the World Bank from the U.S. Defense Department in 1946 and served the institution, in the Legal Department and then as vice president, until 1959. He remembers that "when the Bank started, people in the West didn't know much about the developing world

85. World Bank, Memorandum from Secretary to Board, no. 379, April 6, 1948, pp. 1–2.

86. Meeting of Executive Directors, November 18–19, 1947.

87. Memorandum from Secretary to Board, no. 379, April 6, 1948, p. 2.

88. Mason and Asher, *World Bank since Bretton Woods*, p. 157. Originally cited in notes in Bank files on meeting of May 21, 1947, of Garner and Burland (for the Bank) with Pedregal, Santa Cruz, and Levine (for Chile).

89. Eugene R. Black, interview, World Bank Oral History Program, August 6, 1961, p. 6.

except as colonies. They didn't know much about development lending, didn't know much about development economics."[90]

Yet the notion that its mission was about to change was dawning on the Bank. At the November 5, 1947, Board meeting, McCloy stated, "I think we are going to be driven into a very different field sooner than I thought, into the development field."[91] McCloy went on two two-month trips, first to South America and then to Central America; senior officials were dispatched to visit foreign lands; consultants were engaged to help man large survey missions to several countries; and data collection and research were begun. The Bank multiplied its contacts with potential borrowers, exploring possible projects, and it began to coordinate with other international organizations. By September 1948 it could report that active project discussions were under way with twenty member countries, and that its travel and contacts had produced "a much clearer understanding" of its development role. For the first time, it published income estimates for different parts of the world, indicating that whereas income per capita in the more highly developed countries of North America and Europe was in excess of $1,300, in the bulk of the underdeveloped countries it was only about $100. The report went on to discuss underdevelopment and the potential role of the Bank in development.

A year later, at the Bank's fourth Annual Meeting in September 1949, the first section of its annual report was titled, as in previous reports, "Role of the Bank," but it now carried a subtitle, "Economic Development," drawing attention to its changing role: "An outstanding feature of the year under review has been the increased attention given to the problem of economic development."[92] The report analyzed the causes of underdevelopment and of "the general conditions of poverty in the underdeveloped areas," including, with surprising candor,

> the difficulties arising from the social structure of many of the underdeveloped nations where there are wide extremes of wealth and poverty. In such cases, strong vested interests often resist any changes which would alter their position. In particular, the maintenance in a number of countries of inefficient and oppressive systems of land tenure militates against increase in agricultural output and improvement in the general standard of living.[93]

This analysis was followed by an impressive account of loan approvals, project discussions, and visits by senior Bank officials to eighteen countries in Latin America, to eight in other underdeveloped regions, and to the United Kingdom

90. Davidson Sommers, interview, California Institute for Technology Oral History, July 18, 1985, pp. 1, 10–11.

91. Meeting of Executive Directors, November 5, 1947.

92. International Bank for Reconstruction and Development, *Fourth Annual Report 1948–1949*, p. 47.

93. Ibid., pp. 8–9.

and France for talks regarding assistance to their colonies. Finally, attention was given to the Bank's first steps in the field of technical assistance, mostly to its poorer member countries. Those steps were said to be a response to "a substantial number of requests . . . from member countries,"[94] and they were linked to the January 1949 announcement of the Point Four program.[95] As the report pointed out,

> The increasing importance of this aspect of the Bank's activities has resulted in part from a growing recognition by the Bank that, *if its loans are to be sound and productive,* it must aid its underdeveloped member countries to analyze their development problems and potentialities, to formulate practical investment programs adapted to their particular needs and to mobilize their resources and otherwise strengthen their financial position.[96]

By 1949 the Bank was aware that technical assistance—which it took to mean a range of guidance, from project specifics to wider investment programs to policies that bore on national creditworthiness—was an integral part of the business of being a development bank.

Over the brief "lending pause" period, between the middle of 1947 and the end of 1948, the Bank readjusted its objective from reconstruction—principally in Europe—to economic development across the world. Knowing little about the less developed world, it went a considerable distance to educate itself about those countries and to formulate a working model for its future role as a development bank. At the same time, it set out on a course of financial respectability, ignoring what it saw as the unrealistic expectations of the Bretton Woods delegates and turning a deaf ear to pressures for quicker, large-scale financial assistance. Buttressed on one side by a multilateral shield against the political whims of any one owner and on the other by an operational discipline that established the practice of well-studied, conservative lending for visibly productive investments in creditworthy countries, the Bank began to acquire a reputation for hard-headed banking and disinterested expertise. Over subsequent decades, that reputation was to unlock an unprecedented flow of development lending.

94. Ibid., p. 10.

95. Most readers of the *Fourth Annual Report*'s reference to the Bank's "response" to the Point Four initiative were probably unaware that McCloy had opposed the Point Four proposal to provide bilateral loans and grants to underdeveloped countries, a position shared by Garner, who wrote in his private diary that Truman's speech was "another indication of impulsive bungling." Ironically, the authorship of Truman's proposal was at first attributed to McCloy. Bird, *The Chairman,* p. 299.

96. IBRD, *Fourth Annual Report,* p. 10. Emphasis added.

THREE

The Bank of the 1950s

FROM THE resumption of lending in January 1949 to the approval of the first International Development Association credit in April 1961, the World Bank operated as a development bank, lending $5.1 billion in 280 loans to fifty-six countries, all, officially, for development purposes. But the meaning of "development bank" vis-à-vis sovereign lending was defined along the way. Neither history nor economics nor the Charter provided a blueprint for this role, though all helped to shape the character of the Bank's objectives and operations. For the most part, a succession of managerial responses to financial and political circumstances defined the particular character of the Bank's role. Those circumstances evolved continuously during this twelve-year period, and, as in the making of common law, the Bank's rulemakers practiced gradual adaptation, relatively unencumbered by formal terms of reference or by the operational oversight of a higher authority.

The eventual drift of that adaptation was a cautious change in emphasis in the phrase "development bank," as the accent shifted from "bank" to "development." Nonetheless, the Bank of the 1950s did have a consistency that was partly a reflection of the popular wisdom about development but was mostly the result of the institution's dependence on market funding. The need to project creditworthiness to a skeptical postdepression and postwar Wall Street was a major constraint on the Bank's operations and rhetoric. This need was acute in the first years and lessened rapidly early in the decade; still, the exclusive dependence on private savings lasted the decade and, in any case, by the early 1950s the Bank's operations and development thinking had been set into a banker's mold. Though the mold began to dissolve almost immediately, the process was barely perceptible until the

Table 3-1. *World Bank Development Lending before IDA*
Billions of U.S. dollars

Recipient	Gross commitments		Net lending
	1948–61[a]	1956–61[b]	1948–61[c]
Total development loans	5.1	2.8	3.9
More developed countries[d]	1.7	0.9	1.1
Colonies[e]	0.5	0.3	0.4
Less developed countries[f]	2.9	1.7	2.3
Power and transportation	2.4	1.4	2.0
Agriculture and irrigation	0.1	0.1	0.1

Source: World Bank, *Annual Report 1961*. All figures exclude reconstruction loans. Sums may not total because of rounding.

a. Commitments from March 1, 1948, through April 30, 1961.

b. Commitments from July 1, 1956, through April 30, 1961.

c. Gross commitments from March 1, 1948, through April 30, 1961, less repayment of principal, cancellations, and participations and sales from portfolio to other investors.

d. Australia, Austria, Belgium, Denmark, Finland, Iceland, Israel, Italy, Japan, Netherlands, Norway, and South Africa.

e. Algeria, Belgian Congo (Zaire), Côte d'Ivoire, Gabon, Kenya, Mauritania, Nyasaland (Malawi), Nigeria, Northern Rhodesia (Zambia), Ruanda-Urundi (Burundi), Southern Rhodesia (Zimbabwe), Tanganyika (Tanzania), and Uganda.

f. Brazil, Burma (Myanmar), Ceylon (Sri Lanka), Chile, Colombia, Costa Rica, Ecuador, El Salvador, Ethiopia, Guatemala, Haiti, Honduras, India, Iran, Iraq, Lebanon, Malaya (Malaysia), Mexico, Nicaragua, Pakistan, Panama, Paraguay, Peru, Philippines, Sudan (after independence in 1956), Thailand, Turkey, United Arab Republic (Egypt), Uruguay, and Yugoslavia.

1961 appearance of a powerful solvent, in the form of IDA tax money. Periodic fiscal grants to replenish the IDA fund reduced the Bank's subjection to balance sheet criteria, making room for the political objectives of donor governments, and for the experimental and ethical leanings of the Bank's own management.[1]

When the Bank first sought to define itself as more than a bank, it found an answer in the postulated catalytic effect of public utility investments. Chosen properly, Bank investments would act as multipliers, an idea that was loosely justified by concepts such as "development priorities," "bottlenecks," and "preconditions." Investment planning and engineering expertise became key tools in the search for investment opportunities, and, as it happened, the resulting list of potential projects consisted mainly of public utility projects, such as electric power, transportation, and other economic infrastructure. An additional reason was that such investments were conventionally expected to be in the public sector; borrowing governments were reluctant to guarantee loans to the private sector, while private firms were equally reluctant to accept government guarantees. Power and transportation projects came to dominate the loan portfolio, accounting for more than half of lending during this period, and the proportion rose to 78 percent in poorer countries (table 3-1). The Bank's size and credit terms were favorable for

1. The Bank invariably jibed at the term "ethical." The more acceptable term was "socially oriented."

the financing of large-scale and long-lived capital facilities: interest rates, including commission, averaged 5.3 percent, and twenty- to twenty-five-year terms, with two years of grace period, were standard for infrastructure.

More important, the development role came to be associated with technical assistance in the broadest sense, extending to project supervision and conditionality. The Bank settled quickly into the role of a heavily interventionist lender, assisting with project preparation and implementation, dispensing economic and technical advice, and conditioning its lending on specific behavior by borrowers. There was a strong link between the Bank's advisory role and its concentration on infrastructure: because of the potential for waste in large, capital-intensive projects, there were few areas of activity in which Bank expertise and persuasion could produce so high a return.

President Eugene Black, endeavoring to explain the Bank to a group of Canadian investment dealers in 1950, described it as a new departure for an international financing institution, but one that was analogous to the U.S. government's program of supervised credits to poor farmers during the depression. Recounting the many precautions taken by the U.S. program to ensure repayment, he appeared anxious to convince his listeners that tough standards and hands-on lending could reconcile doing good with good business:[2]

> As a result of this close combination of financial and technical assistance, practically all the loans were repaid, the fertility of millions of acres was restored, and many thousands of people were transformed from a drag on the economy into self-respecting and self-supporting producers.
>
> What the International Bank is trying to do is quite similar. . . . Technical advice alone is not sufficient . . . nor is financial assistance. What is needed is a combination of the two.[3]

The rationale for the Bank's tutelary role and interventionist style of lending was developed in successive speeches and annual reports. The 1954 report devoted a major chapter to "collaboration in project preparation and execution" with borrowers. By 1956, speaking at the Annual General Meeting, Black had shifted the

---

2. "If the land was too poor, or on too steep a slope, or too remote, or too small in area, the loan was refused on the ground that it would simply saddle the farmer with a debt he could never pay and which could only leave him worse off in the long run. [The supervisor] might conclude that with certain types of agricultural tools, seed or fertilizer, some livestock or perhaps some canning equipment, it would be possible for the farmer to live better and at the same time obtain the wherewithal to repay the loan. The supervisor would then approve a loan earmarked for these specific purposes. He would also instruct the farmer in the use of the new equipment and in better farm practices, and would pay periodic visits to check on his progress." Eugene R. Black, address before the Investment Dealers' Association of Canada, Eastern District, Montreal, Canada, February 23, 1950, IBRD Press Release 173, pp. 12–13.

3. Ibid., p. 12.

emphasis by calling the Bank a *development agency*. Though "originally conceived solely as a financial institution," he said, the Bank "has evolved into a development agency which uses its financial resources as but one means of helping its members."[4]

Observers in later decades would not be impressed. Looking back in 1981, Burke Knapp described the Bank of the 1950s as "merely a bank" and "a fairly conventional financial institution." It was a period, he said, in which "there was a great deal of emphasis upon the formulation of individual projects and even the formulation of self-liquidating projects." By contrast, in the 1960s major infrastructure projects came to be seen "not [as] an end in themselves, but simply a means toward promotion of development." It was only in the 1960s that "we came to feel that, as the banker to a country, we ought to evolve into the role also of a development adviser."[5] To some extent, such judgments reflect later standards; at the time, many saw the Bank as "the most successful of the international bodies concerned with economic development," measured not only by its funding achievements but also by respect gained from the underdeveloped countries.[6] Nevertheless, Black's rhetoric does seem to have run ahead of the conservative character of Bank operations during this period. How much of that overreach was deliberate image management and how much managerial underachievement is less clear. Certainly "the circumstances" of the period placed narrow constraints on the Bank's operations.[7]

The Wall Street Bank

By the time of Black's first Annual General Meeting in September 1949 the Bank was no longer the unfamiliar, do-good institution that Wall Street had perceived when the institution opened for business under Eugene Meyer in June 1946, an institution that "smacked of having to do with foreign lending."[8] The annual report cited the satisfactory record of Bank bonds and even claimed "a

4. Eugene R. Black, "Address to the Board of Governors," in IBRD, *Summary Proceedings, Eleventh Annual Meeting of the Board of Governors* (November 15, 1956), p. 11.

5. J. Burke Knapp, interview, World Bank Oral History Program, October 16 and 29, 1981, pp. 2–4. Knapp had expressed a similar opinion much earlier, in the course of an interview with Robert Oliver, World Bank Oral History Program, July 1961.

6. Andrew Shonfield, *The Attack on World Poverty* (Random House, 1960), p. 116. Shonfield was the economic columnist for the *London Observer.* Paul Rosenstein-Rodan criticized the Bank of the 1950s but came to the same conclusion, that it was "perhaps the most successful international organization." Rosenstein-Rodan, interview, World Bank Oral History Program, 1973, p. 40.

7. Edward S. Mason and Robert E. Asher, *The World Bank since Bretton Woods* (Brookings, 1973), pp. 189–90.

8. Richard H. Demuth, interview, World Bank Oral History Program, August 1961, p. 12.

substantial unsatisfied demand for the bonds."[9] The appointment of John McCloy, Black, and Robert Garner and the earlier presence of Wall Street lawyer Chester McLain as general legal counsel had gone a long way to change that image. The Bank backed up its intensive lobbying among investors and regulators by taking a hard line on prior settlement of debt arrears with bondholders and by cautiously scrutinizing loan requests and borrower financial policies. In July 1947 it success- fully placed $250 million in IBRD bonds. New, smaller issues were made in 1950 and 1951 and received improved ratings.

This initial success was not followed by a relaxation in lending discipline or in the effort to present an image of creditworthiness. On the contrary, success seemed to confirm and reinforce the conservative inclinations of Black and Garner, who chose to insist on the main ingredients of the lending model that had been taking shape as the Bank responded to the first loan applications from underdeveloped countries.[10] There was ample justification for sticking to a cautious approach to foreign lending: at the turn of the decade, most potential borrowers, even in Europe, were tainted by unsettled defaults; the dollar shortage made repayment prospects uncertain; underdeveloped areas were little known in the United States investor community and many were embroiled in nationalist and leftist rebellions; communists even seemed to threaten Brazil and Chile; and investors were still trying to grasp the nature of the U.S. government guarantee on Bank obligations. That guarantee was based mostly on the American unpaid, callable capital sub- scription, but the institution was naturally extremely reluctant to call on that commitment.

At the same time it was evident that future lending would be contingent on continuous borrowing, which, for the foreseeable future, would be restricted to the U.S. financial market. By June 1949 net loan disbursements had amounted to $622 million, almost the full amount of the $746 million in usable capital paid in up to that date. The Bank could look forward to a likely, though uncertain, inflow of loanable funds, first, as members complied with unpaid capital subscriptions com- mitted under the Charter, and second, from net income generated by ongoing operations. Loanable funds would also include cash in hand. The cash position in 1950 was highlighted by the annual report for that year, which reported funds available for lending at $267 million, roughly equal to the $250 million that had been raised thus far through bond sales.[11] These amounts, however, were too small to sustain the lending volumes already achieved between 1947 and 1949, or to finance the scale of commitments that were being built up by the rapid expansion of contacts and negotiations with potential borrowers during 1949 and 1950. The

9. IBRD, *Fourth Annual Report, 1948–1949,* p. 5.

10. Some of these lending procedures and conditions were described in the account of the first loan to Chile in this chapter.

11. IBRD, *Fifth Annual Report, 1949–1950,* p. 39.

Bank would in fact disburse an additional $2.8 billion during the following decade, lending that was necessarily financed largely by new borrowings of $2.2 billion.[12] It is no surprise, then, that the annual report for 1948–49 describes an energetic marketing effort, including "an extensive program of information to acquaint investors [with the Bank]," "periodic information conferences held at the Bank's headquarters," "close contact with the investment community," and "visits to financial and investment centers throughout the United States."[13] For this purpose, the Bank established a Marketing Department, which had its headquarters in New York and which existed until 1963. The market for Bank obligations was an obligatory and constant topic of discussion at Board meetings throughout 1950.

The Volume of Lending

The most visible and, at the time, controversial feature of the Black-Garner Bank was the relatively modest level and slow expansion of lending. Over the first eight years of this period, between 1949 and 1957, annual commitments averaged $307 million and showed almost no tendency to rise. The rate increased sharply in 1958, reaching between $600 and $700 million per year through 1961, but the average for the twelve-year period was $428 million. These figures were far below those suggested at Bretton Woods and repeated after the war; as mentioned in chapter 2, the U.S. delegation to the United Nations had made a vague reference to $15 billion when speaking of potential assistance by the Bretton Woods institutions.[14] Aid to Europe did in fact reach $18 billion over four years under the Marshall Plan, rapidly quelling the sharpest of the criticisms that were directed at the Bank between 1946 and 1948. Bilateral assistance to underdeveloped countries also climbed into the billions: from 1949 to 1961, U.S. aid to those countries, not including military assistance, averaged $1.8 billion per year, some four to five times

12. Over the full period between July 1, 1949, and June 30, 1961, funding included $3,034 million in net borrowing, $905 million in additional payments of capital subscription, and $2,072 million in net income. Cash on hand, kept to meet forthcoming disbursements on earlier loan commitments, rose from $390 million to $543 million. See Mason and Asher, *World Bank since Bretton Woods*, p. 857, and World Bank annual reports.

13. World Bank, *Annual Report, 1948*, pp. 36–37, and summaries of Board meetings during 1950.

14. Richard N. Gardner, *Sterling-Dollar Diplomacy in Current Perspective: The Origins and the Prospects of Our International Economic Order* (Columbia University Press, 1980), p. 292. Gardner adds that William Clayton, assistant secretary of state for economic affairs, "in an attempt to justify the termination of U.N.R.R.A., went even further. He declared not only that 'fifteen billion dollars' had been made available by the Bank and the Fund but that measures had been taken 'for the provision of a total of nearly 30 billion dollars of foreign exchange to countries which needed it.'"

the level of Bank lending over the same period, with the additional feature of carrying soft terms.[15]

World Bank lending was also seen as modest in relation to estimates of need and demands for assistance that were being put forward by advocates for the developing countries. A 1951 United Nations report argued that underdeveloped areas of the world needed about $10 billion a year in external capital to sustain a 2 percent annual growth in per capita national income.[16] A year earlier, Walter Reuther, president of the United Automobile Workers of America, had proposed that the United States spend $13 billion a year in international assistance, which he argued would amount to less than 5 percent of annual output.[17] In 1953 Harold Wilson, British member of Parliament and future prime minister, published *The War on World Poverty: An Appeal to the Conscience of Mankind,* calling for large-scale aid. If the call went unheeded by other nations, said Wilson, "the war on world poverty . . . must be Britain's historic mission in what remains of the twentieth century."[18] By the late 1950s, aid advocates were producing more sober estimates of aid needs, rationalized in part, perhaps, by the fact that domestic savings and economic growth in developing areas over the decade had greatly exceeded expectations. In 1961 Paul Rosenstein-Rodan, who had moved from the Bank to the Massachusetts Institute of Technology, calculated a more modest but still large capital inflow "need" of $5.7 billion per year during the 1960s.[19] A decade before, as a member of the Bank's Economic Department, he had criticized from within, saying that it was "partly mistaken and partly intellectually dishonest" for the Bank to argue that it could not lend more for the lack of well-prepared projects.[20]

15. Data from Ruth Logue, *History of U.S. Foreign Aid since the Second World War* (Washington, D.C.: Board of Governors of the Federal Reserve System, 1961); and Robert E. Wood, *From Marshall Plan to Debt Crisis: Foreign Aid and Development Choices in the World Economy* (University of California Press, 1986).

16. United Nations, *Measures for the Economic Development of Underdeveloped Countries,* Report by a Group of Experts (New York, May 1951), pp. 75–80. The report was drafted by Arthur Lewis. The authors argue that the $10 billion figure is not unrealistic, since 2 percent of the national income of Western Europe, Australasia, the United States, and Canada would amount to $7 billion. Also, they say, "We wish only to emphasize that the order of magnitude involved is well in excess of what is now generally believed. When members of the United Nations speak about rapidly increasing the standards of living of the underdeveloped world, they should realize that what they are talking about involves a transfer of several billions every year."

17. Harold Wilson, *The War on World Poverty: An Appeal to the Conscience of Mankind* (London: Victor Gollancz, 1953), p. 94.

18. Ibid., p. 203.

19. Paul Rosenstein-Rodan, "International Aid for Underdeveloped Countries," *Review of Economics and Statistics,* vol. 43, no. 2 (May 1961), pp. 107–38.

20. Rosenstein-Rodan, Oral History, 1973, p. 5. According to William Bennett, Rosenstein-Rodan would say to Garner, who opposed large-scale lending to India, "If you don't do it in

In any case, the Bank was on the defensive throughout the 1950s. Garner was unapologetic: "In the early days there was a very strong criticism of the Bank for not doing enough," but our "slow start was a sound start."[21] Black never stopped arguing for less emphasis on large-scale external assistance, and more on domestic policies and effort: "The theory that backwardness can be overcome with billions of dollars is based on the assumption that most countries . . . are backward solely because they lack financial resources. It ignores the fact that the insufficiency of financial and other resources . . . is itself the product of political and social evils within the countries themselves; and these evils . . . can be eradicated."[22] In 1961 he found himself repeating this argument with some vehemence in the course of an interview: "It doesn't make any difference how much you pour in. Money doesn't do any good on earth, no matter how much it is, unless that money is well spent."[23] Black was generally supported by the Executive Board in this view. Shortly after the outbreak of the Korean War, a Board member asked whether the Bank should accelerate lending as a response to the hostilities. Another disagreed, saying that the Bank should ignore the war and continue to develop slowly.[24]

To those who insisted that poor countries needed more money as well as better management, Black went on to say, "That's why I think that if all the emphasis were put on the quality of the money and not the quantity, that the quantity would be forthcoming."[25] Here is the keystone of Black's philosophy for the Bank, the banker's justification for what others saw as an exaggerated caution and concern for quality: quality, he was saying, was the door, and the only door, to those billions. As a relatively small lender, Black was perhaps making a virtue of necessity, but the belief came naturally to a banker and was certainly affirmed with energy and consistency through the decade.

But the pressure to lend increased over the period, fueled by a succession of authoritative reports that argued the need for economic assistance to the under-developed nations, and by the spreading cold war. Bank lending did increase sharply, between 1957 and 1958, precipitated in part by India's balance of payments crisis and the creation of the India Aid Consortium, the first of a series of consortia and consultative groups.

---

a big way, don't do it at all. You can't lend to an economy with a population the size of India in little dribs and drabs." Bennett, interview, World Bank Oral History Program, January 20, 1988, p. 9.

21. Robert Garner, interview, World Bank Oral History Program, July 19, 1961, pp. 43–44.

22. Eugene R. Black, "Some Considerations Affecting Foreign Aid," address to the Economic Club of New York, January 14, 1953, p. 5.

23. Eugene R. Black, interview, World Bank Oral History Program, August 6, 1961, p. 37.

24. Meeting of Executive Directors, July 11, 1950.

25. Black, Oral History, August 6, 1961, p. 37.

Country Allocation

If Black was on strong ground on the volume of lending, he found it harder to rebut academic and political criticisms on the issue of allocation—who he was lending to, and what for. The issue raised a question of ethical and political norms—Who *should* the Bank lend to?—and of economic theory—What is the best use of resources to raise living standards for the majority? Neither Black nor his critics had a text to refer to in either argument. Beyond general expressions, such as "reconstruction and development" and "productive purposes," the Charter was silent on allocation; and there was scant guidance from the fledgling discipline of development economics, or from a body of widely accepted and publicly stated norms. When it came to allocation, contemporary critics had little to hold on to and simply reiterated the demand for more assistance to the underdeveloped areas. The more biting critique—that the Bank bypassed the poor by lending for large-scale economic infrastructure rather than agriculture and social sectors—was to come in later decades. This subsequent, revisionist criticism evolved out of shifting political norms, more experience regarding the mechanics of growth and the distribution of wealth, and disregard for the Bank's early circumstances, especially the need to create and sustain its own creditworthiness. In this way the prism rotated and cast a less favorable light on the Bank of the 1950s.

The two principal features of lending allocation over this period, shown in table 3-1, were the high share received by richer economies, and a concentration on public utilities. Of the $5.1 billion in total lending commitments for development purposes, one-third ($1.7 billion) went to European or other more developed countries, such as Australia, Japan, and South Africa. Large areas within the borrowing countries of Western Europe were indeed poverty-stricken, notably in the Mediterranean nations. Conversely, South American countries such as Uruguay and Chile were well-off by the standards of the 1950s. It is nonetheless striking that so large a share of what the Bank recorded as "postreconstruction" lending was granted to countries with a relatively high income per person, such as Australia ($317 million by June 1961), Japan ($447 million), Norway ($120 million), Austria ($101 million), Finland ($102 million), France ($168 million), and Italy ($299 million). By contrast, it was only in 1958 that India caught up with Australia to become, and remain, the largest borrower. Indeed, loans to Australia and Japan together still exceeded those to India by 1961.[26]

Did loans to Europe, Japan, and Australia mean fewer loans to poorer countries? One consideration is that, during this period, the Bank financed itself partly by selling loans and participations in loans to other investors, a strategy that proved somewhat easier in the case of richer borrowers. The effect was to reduce the immediate opportunity cost, in terms of the use of available funds, on potential

26. IBRD, *Annual Report, 1960–1961.*

poorer borrowers. As shown in table 3-1, the proportion of net lending to the more developed countries, 28.2 percent, was slightly lower than that of gross credit, 33.3 percent. From a longer perspective, however, what may have mattered most was that in lending to Europe, Japan, and Australia the Bank was improving its portfolio in Wall Street eyes and so increasing and cheapening its access to market funding.

In lending to better-off nations, the Bank was doing no violence to its mandate. The Articles direct the Bank to assist in the reconstruction and development of "members," without distinction, with no suggestion of an income criterion for allocation. The Charter does speak of "less developed countries" and "standard of living," terms that could be understood as approximations to the idea of "poverty alleviation." The words appear in two sections of Article I, which sets out the Bank's purposes, but in both cases the references seem to be a long way from the Bank's present-day definition of its mission as poverty reduction, especially since the reference to standard of living is applied to "members" of the Bank in general, rather than to poor countries, while "less developed countries" are mentioned at the end of a list of lending options. The single reference to relative poverty appears in a list of suggestions for bringing about reconstruction and development, one of which is "the encouragement of the development of productive facilities and resources in less developed countries."[27]

There was nothing incongruous, therefore, in the statement by the second annual report (1946–47) that a number of European countries were underdeveloped, and further that there were areas in Latin America, Asia, Africa, and the Middle East with "well developed industrial and agricultural economies."[28] When Black proposed a $100 million loan to Australia in August 1950, the largest "development" loan proposed thus far, negotiated in a record three weeks, Burke Knapp argued in favor of the loan by pointing to the country's high income. Australia, he said, already enjoyed one of the highest per capita national incomes in the world. He also pointed out that Australia had been very successful in building up its external assets.[29] None of the representatives of poorer countries on the Board questioned the operation, nor, indeed, any of the five subsequent loans to

27. IBRD, *Articles of Agreement,* art. I (i): "To assist in the reconstruction and development of territories of members by facilitating the investment of capital for productive purposes, including the restoration of economies destroyed or disrupted by war, the reconversion of productive facilities to peacetime needs and the encouragement of the development of productive facilities and resources *in less developed countries.*" Emphasis added.

Art. I (iii): "To promote the long-range balanced growth of international trade and the maintenance of equilibrium in balances of payments by encouraging international investment for the development of the productive resources of members, thereby, assisting in raising productivity, *the standard of living and conditions of labor* in their territories." Emphasis added.

28. IBRD, *Second Annual Report, 1946–1947,* p. 9.

29. 13th Meeting of Executive Directors, August 22, 1950.

Australia over 1952 to 1956. As late as 1959, Alec Cairncross, the founding director of the Bank's Economic Development Institute, could write that "the Bank's international role need not consist in raising capital in developed countries in order to lend it to underdeveloped countries. It may borrow from either group to lend to either group."[30]

Moreover, the meaning of "development" was changing. At Bretton Woods it more often meant physical output than human betterment, economic opportunity rather than social justice. The word still evoked an age of discovery and settlement of "underdeveloped territories," when overseas economic development could be cheerfully described as "the hacking down of the forest or the sheep rearing or the gold mining which made Canada, Australia, and South Africa into world factors," an age when, for the most part, it was the land, not the people, that was to be developed.[31] If there was a sense of duty, it was that expressed by Joseph Chamberlain on the eve of his becoming colonial secretary in 1895: "[It is] not enough to occupy certain great spaces of the world's surface unless you are willing to develop them. We are the landlords of a great estate; it is the duty of the landlord to develop his estate."[32] Through World War II, colonial "development" in French colonies was not thought inconsistent with the use of forced labor, a practice that persisted in Portuguese colonies through the 1960s.[33] It is true that by the 1940s colonial administrators were often preoccupied by efforts to improve native welfare, though hampered by small budgets. The concern for welfare, particularly urban wages, schooling, health, and housing, had grown during the interwar period in proportion to the strength of political opposition in the colonies, but it remained a secondary and separate objective. In its name, Britain's 1939 Colonial Development and Welfare Act was explicit about the distinction; the separate terms in the title addressed separate foreign policy objectives, "development" to extract raw materials, and "welfare" to maintain political control and, to some degree, fulfill a humanitarian duty.[34] The distinction was being blurred as urbanization and political

30. Sir Alec Cairncross, *The International Bank for Reconstruction and Development,* Essays in International Finance, no. 33 (Princeton University, March 1959), pp. 5–6. According to Cairncross, the Bank "has always been willing to make loans to countries that would not normally be regarded as backward, or even under-developed" (p. 5).

31. C. A. Knowles, *The Economic Development of the British Overseas Empire,* 2d ed. (London: Routledge, 1928), p. vii.

32. Cited in Michael Cowen and Robert Shenton, "The Origin and Course of Fabian Colonialism in Africa," *Journal of Sociology,* vol. 4, no. 2 (June 1991), p. 145.

33. Cited in Frederick Cooper, "Modernizing Bureaucrats, Backward Africans, and Dualistic Development Theory," paper prepared for the workshop "Historicizing Development," Emory University, December 10–12, 1993 (draft), p. 11. On the association between development, raw material needs, and postwar shortages, see Paul Johnson, *Modern Times: The World from the Twenties to the Nineties* (Harper Perennial, 1991), p. 519.

34. H. W. Arndt, *Economic Development: The History of an Idea* (University of Chicago Press, 1987), pp. 27–29. "The objective of native welfare . . . was throughout this period regarded as quite distinct from that of economic progress or development" (p. 27).

mobilization in the colonies increased the frequency and effectiveness of strikes and other "disturbances," threatening imperial dominance but also hampering production. Welfare spending was becoming, more and more, a necessary input to sustain production. British and French colonial bureaucrats used this convergence to argue for larger colonial budgets, for health and schools as well as productive investments, with their reluctant finance ministers.[35]

The convergence of welfare and output goals in colonial administration was hastened by the dilemma of Britain's postwar Labor government. In 1945 Britain elected its first anticolonial government just as the country's need for colonial resources reached a peak; postwar shortages of food, fuel, and materials became major obstacles to recovery. Stafford Cripps, British minister for economic affairs, said in November 1947 that "the whole future of the sterling group and its ability to survive depends in my view upon a quick and extensive development of our African resources."[36] Ernest Bevin, the foreign secretary, had visions of "great mountains of manganese" and other raw materials and said, "If only we pushed on and developed Africa, we could have [the] U.S. dependent on us, and eating out of our hand in four or five years."[37]

The government looked to its remaining colonies but was acutely embarrassed by the fear that investments to raise raw material production could be construed as colonial exploitation. In January 1948 Norman Brook, the Cabinet secretary, reported to Clement Attlee:

> At recent meetings there has been general support for the view that the development of Africa's economic resources should be pushed forward rapidly in order to support the political and economic position of the United Kingdom. . . . [This policy] could, I suppose, be said to fall within the ordinary definition of "Imperialism." And, at the level of a political broadcast it might be represented as a policy of exploiting native peoples in order to support the standards of living of the workers in this country.
>
>   This policy is doubtless inevitable—there are compelling reasons. . . . But if it is disclosed incautiously or incidentally, without proper justification and explanation, may it not be something of a shock to Government supporters—and indeed, to enlightened public opinion generally? . . . It can, of course, be argued that the more rapid development of Africa's resources will bring social and economic advantages to the native peoples in addition to buttressing the political and economic influence of the United Kingdom.[38]

35. Speaking in 1937, a colonial governor signaled the coming change. He referred to the view of the colonies as "a vast estate which it is our duty to develop," as "an improvement on the old view of Africa, as a sort of mine from which the contents, mineral, vegetable and in old times human, should be extracted as quickly and as cheaply as possible. The exploitation theory . . . is dead and the development theory has taken its place." Bernard Bourdillon, "The African Producer in Nigeria," *West Africa*, January 30, 1937, p. 75.

36. Cited in Cooper, "Modernizing Bureaucrats," p. 14.

37. Quoted in ibid.

38. Mike Cowen, "Early Years of the Colonial Development Corporation: British State Enterprise Overseas during Late Colonialism," *African Affairs*, vol. 83 (1984), pp. 67–68.

The solution, suggested by Brook, was to finesse the prickly distinction between economic and social objectives, and that between imperial self-interest and colonial welfare, by playing the "development" card.[39] "Development," the government claimed, would bring complementary and harmonious progress in both output and living standards, to the gain of both Britain and the colonial peoples.[40] There would be no conflicts nor trade-offs under the umbrella of "development." In the name of development, Britain's Laborites proceeded to address the immediate raw materials emergency. But the ambiguity in "development" stuck. In succeeding years, much of the inevitable, indeed, necessary, debate over economic and social priorities has been muddied by a struggle over linguistic turf, over the "true" meaning of development. Worse, by suggesting that every step forward in the name of development is an advance on all fronts, the term has hobbled economic advisers in carrying out their principal role, which is to bear the bad news of opportunity cost.

Politics influenced the meaning of development in the early postwar years in another way. Poor countries began to emerge out of the mist, their numbers increased by decolonization and their voice amplified by the United Nations, and to coalesce into what a French demographer would baptize "le tiers monde."[41] Poverty as a national characteristic, defined as low average national income rather than a lack of natural resources, became a conceptual and political category. The common feature, poverty, lent itself to a common demand, economic assistance, and the term "development" was quickly appropriated to the job. In their opening paragraphs to a 1951 United Nations report, *Measures for the Economic Development of Under-Developed Countries,* the authors admit to some difficulty regarding the interpretation of the term "underdeveloped countries" but quickly go on to set out their own definition—and tool for advocacy—of low income per capita.[42] Academic critics of the report objected that relative poverty was not a fruitful analytical category for the study of either economic growth or welfare, but no one was listening.[43] The concept of development defined as poverty reduction among countries (not, as yet, within countries) had moral and political potency even as the 1950s opened, and its political clout was soon multiplied by the cold war.

Though the meaning of development was changing rapidly, so that by the mid-1950s "underdevelopment" was generally understood to signify poverty, and

39. Cooper, "Modernizing Bureaucrats," pp. 14–15.

40. Ibid., p. 23.

41. Attributed to French economist and demographer Alfred Sauvy, writing in a 1952 article, by the Penguin *Dictionary of Third World Terms,* comp. Kofi Buenor Hadjor (London: I. B. Tauris, 1992), p. 3.

42. United Nations, *Measures for the Economic Development of Under-Developed Countries* (New York, May 1951), p. 3.

43. A. Herbert Frankel, "United Nations Primer for Development," *Quarterly Journal of Economics,* vol. 66, no. 3 (August 1952), pp. 301–26. See also, Peter T. Bauer, "The United Nations Report on the Economic Development of Under-Developed Countries," *Economic Journal,* vol. 63 (March 1953), pp. 210–22.

though the number of poor borrowing countries rose from eight in 1950 to thirty in 1960, the Bank continued to assign a large fraction of its lending volume to Europe, Australia, and Japan. Twenty-nine percent of lending commitments made during the last two years of the decade were for more developed countries. This figure does not include loans for colonial development, which, to some degree, were a means of balance of payments and fiscal support for the mother countries. Looking at the 1949–60 period as a whole, loans for colonial development accounted for 10 percent of total commitments (table 3-1).

The first of the Bank's colonial loans was made to Belgium. Beyond a small $16 million loan in 1949, lending to that nation had been frustrated by the objections of other Europeans.[44] This coincided with a growing conviction in the Bank that it should begin to associate with dependent territories, "with an eye to independence," as expressed by S. Raymond Cope, who thought the idea was reinforced by "a certain distaste for colonialism on the part of some in the Bank."[45] When Garner returned from a trip in early 1950 to Rhodesia and South Africa, however, his report to the Board discussed mineral and transport projects but made scant reference to the native economy or living standards. "There is nothing much in Northern Rhodesia except the mines," he said, though the area held as many people as Southern Rhodesia, a territory that he described with much more interest. He expressed particular enthusiasm for the agricultural prospects of a valley in Southern Rhodesia.[46]

A year later, in a stroke of inspiration, the desire to lend in Africa came together with the impasse in lending to Belgium. Management proposed a two-part loan for the development of the Belgian Congo, one part to go to the Belgian Congo Development Authority, the other to the Belgian central bank to finance the indirect impact of colonial spending on Belgium's balance of payments. According to Cope, "The Belgians were not enthusiastic about this for the simple reason that they wanted to get the foreign exchange themselves."[47] At the Board meeting, however, Beyen commented that it seemed like a good solution to a sensitive issue.[48] What had not been foreseen was that, as loan negotiations proceeded and

44. Davidson Sommers, interview, World Bank Oral History Program, August 2, 1961. According to Sommers, "All of the Europeans felt kind of peeved about the Belgians, because in the first place they felt the Belgians had got out of the war relatively cheaply, and there was a lot of feeling in the US Marshall Plan people that the Belgians were getting away too easy." Belgium shouldered even more of the blame because of its postwar monetary policy, described as "too conservative," and "a policy of deliberate deflation" (pp. 21–22).

45. S. R. Cope, interview, World Bank Oral History Program, August 9, 1961, p. 24.

46. Meeting of Executive Directors, April 11, 1950.

47. Cope, Oral History, August 9, 1961, p. 24.

48. Meeting of the Executive Directors, May 9, 1951.

Bank economists, making field trips to the Belgian Congo, became more familiar with the colonial administration and its projects, Bank staff would come to be increasingly attracted by what they saw as a well-formulated development plan. Belgium was pressed into accepting a tighter link between future loan disbursements and development spending. In the end, the two-part $70 million loan ($30 million to the Central Bank of Belgium, $40 million to the Belgian Congo Development Authority) helped both Belgium and the Congo. Belgium received dollars and fiscal relief, and, for a time, revenues from higher production in its colony. The cause of development was served by having the power and transportation facilities available in the Congo, and by engaging the Bank in African development. Moreover, the unexpectedly early independence of the colony in 1960 transferred the full benefit of the revenues from new investments to the former colony.

Other loans were made for the development of Belgian, French, and British colonies in Africa, providing some degree of indirect financial support to their mother countries. The colonial projects financed by the Bank—such as those for Algerian gas, Belgian Congo minerals, Mauritanian iron, and Northern Rhodesian ores—were initially drawn up to meet the raw material needs of European powers. But these intentions were largely frustrated by the combination of slow bureaucratic implementation of these projects and rapid political evolution toward independence. In the end, close to 60 percent of these loans were committed after 1956, toward the end of the colonial period, with the result that the major part of project output came onstream after independence. However, the extent to which project benefits were in effect "nationalized" is generally a difficult matter of interpretation. Most French colonies, for instance, when offered the choice by Charles de Gaulle, chose "interdependence" rather than separation, and French interests have continued to participate in the governmental and business activities of those nations.[49]

The expansion of lending to independent poor nations had the uncertain and erratic character of a voyage of discovery. The large number of visits and missions sent out by the Bank to reconnoitre and establish relations with potential borrowers has already been mentioned. Lending relationships developed somewhat fitfully, the result of inexperience, occasional clumsiness, and the different winds that were driving the ship. The number of poor borrower countries rose more steadily than the volume of lending, as shown in table 3-2. After the early, 1948 loan to Chile, the Bank added new countries to its clientele of poor borrowers almost every year over the period, reaching thirty by 1960. The volume of lending rose, instead, in

49. See Jacques Pégatiénan and Bakary Ouayogode, "Relations between the World Bank and Côte d'Ivoire," *The World Bank: Its First Half Century,* vol. 2, *Perspectives* (Brookings, 1997).

Table 3-2. *World Bank Commitments before IDA*[a]
Millions of U.S. dollars

| | Commitments to less developed countries[b] | | | |
Fiscal year	Total	India	Latin American countries	Cumulative number of borrowers
1948	16	0	16	1
1949	109	0	109	3
1950	137	63	59	8
1951	145	0	85	13
1952	163	0	79	16
1953	110	51	29	16
1954	144	0	99	19
1955	163	26	123	19
1956	227	75	75	24
1957	179	35	50	26
1958	423	166	121	27
1959	426	135	137	29
1960	339	60	134	30
1961	332	90	71	30
Total	2,913	701	1,187	30

Source: World Bank annual reports, 1948–61.

a. Commitments from March 1, 1948, through April 30, 1961.

b. See table 3-1 for a list of less developed countries.

stepwise fashion, after stagnating at about $140 million per year between 1949 and 1955, to about $200 million between 1956 and 1957, and then doubling to $380 million between 1958 and 1961. A small number of countries became regular borrowers, most prominently India (24 loans), Colombia (16), Pakistan (13), Peru (11), Nicaragua (10), and Chile and Mexico (8 each). The lending relationship, however, was less stable in others. Thus Brazil was also a major client (11 loans), but lending was interrupted for four years between 1954 and 1958, and then again for four years after 1959. It bears noticing that Korea, both Chinas, Indonesia, Morocco (which became independent in 1956), and Venezuela were not borrowers, while the Philippines, Egypt, and Malaya each borrowed only once, and that most African nations did not share in the colonial loans.[50]

With its first loan to India, in 1949, the Bank was at grips with extreme poverty. In the non-communist world, India accounted for a large proportion, perhaps one-third, of the poor (see table 3-1). The Bank's reach toward the poor increased

50. Loans to present-day Taiwan began in 1962, ended in 1971, and were recorded as loans to China, or the Republic of China. Lending to mainland China, or the People's Republic of China, began in 1981.

with the beginning of lending to Pakistan in 1952, and to several steady borrowers in Latin America with large impoverished populations.[51] From the earliest years of the decade, the Bank found itself lending, on a continuing basis, to countries that were the home of more than half of the world's absolute poor. And the coverage was larger if more occasional borrowers are included. On the other hand, loans to India and Pakistan were relatively small before 1958, averaging only $31 million together per year, and accounting for 11 percent of the Bank's development lending up to that year. Annual lending to those two countries then jumped to $154 million between 1958 and 1961.[52]

Several obstacles and distractions delayed the extension of Bank credit and advice to poor countries. The Bank's regard for creditworthiness was the more visible obstacle. Less visibly, lending was influenced by political priorities of the Bank's major shareholders, above all, the United States, France, and Great Britain. Finally, the Bank's efforts to develop lending relationships with individual countries were at times unsuccessful.

Two of the earliest loans to extremely poor countries, India in 1949 and Ethiopia in 1951, had strikingly different outcomes. Both were encouraged by political priority, India as a bastion to contain communism in Asia and Ethiopia, targeted as an African client-state by the United States.[53] India was to become the Bank's steadiest and largest borrower. Impressed by the moral and intellectual qualities of India's leaders and civil service, the Bank developed an unusually respectful and constructive relationship with that country. Though most lending to India has taken the form of project loans, the Bank's supportive and respectful attitude to the Indian government meant that, in effect, lending to India took on characteristics of program lending. Furthermore, the fact that Indian policies and public expenditures contained many elements favorable to the poor meant that Bank lending, whether interpreted at face value as transport and power loans or as general foreign exchange and budgetary assistance, was in practice supporting poverty reduction in a more direct way, and at an earlier moment than was true of most of Bank lending.

Ethiopia was visited by a Bank mission early in 1950, and it appears that a decision to lend had been taken even before projects were prepared. The mission

51. Bangladesh, formerly East Pakistan, declared itself independent in 1971.

52. Garner's dislike for India was well known in the Bank. His departure to the IFC in 1956 was followed by an increase in lending to that country. His candid views on India are described in a memoir written after retirement for his grandchildren: Robert Garner, *This Is the Way It Was* (Chevy Chase, Md.: Chevy Chase Printing, 1972).

53. Describing the postwar situation, Dean Acheson recalled "the overshadowing fear of the Soviet Union no longer contained by the stoppers on the east, west, and south—Japan, Germany, and British India," causing him, on one occasion, to put up with a "prickly" and "difficult" Jawaharlal Nehru, because, "he was so important to India and India's survival so important to all of us that if he did not exist—as Voltaire said of God—he would have to be invented." Acheson, *Present at the Creation: My Years in the State Department* (W. W. Norton, 1969), pp. 336, 728.

found a wretchedly poor country governed by an autocrat, a public administration with virtually no technical capacity or authority to formulate or execute public works, and public services severely damaged by war and administrative neglect. Returning to report to the Board, the mission resorted to a slide show to introduce directors to what one staff member explained was "rather a different animal from any other situations that we have hitherto dealt with." Viewing the slides, an awed director commented that Ethiopia was "an underdeveloped country in the pure state."[54] Yet Garner confessed that he had already agreed to certain projects before the government program was "all laid out," telling a surprised Board, "Otherwise we don't think anything would happen."[55] Breaking his own rule, Garner had authorized the Bank to step in to do most of the project preparation for Ethiopia. Three loans were prepared and approved in this way. Each included an "institution-building" component in the form of newly created, Bank-designed, autonomous administrative authorities, and the Bank assisted in the recruitment of foreign managers for an industrial development finance company. Yet all of these "autonomous authorities" suffered from regal interference, resignations of foreign managers, and poor implementation, and until 1962 the Bank found it impossible to make further loans, with the exception of one in 1957.[56]

Lending decisions were frequently influenced by political priorities. Black and Garner understandably denied this fact, since, from their perspective, they were indeed continuously and successfully parrying and staving off political pressures, principally from the American, British, and French governments. Moreover, politics and "creditworthiness" would often coincide, as when a reformist or leftist regime expropriated foreign assets, for instance, or when countries dragged their feet in settling previous loan defaults.[57] Also, political priorities were common

54. 10th Meeting of the Executive Directors, July 25, 1950.

55. Ibid., pp. 22–23.

56. For a lively and perceptive account of Black's Bank, including a chapter on its involvement in Ethiopia, see James Morris, *The Road to Huddersfield: A Journey to Five Continents* (Pantheon Books, 1963), pp. 77–108.

57. According to Mason and Asher, the policy of not lending to countries in default on outstanding (mostly prewar) loans emerged as part of the Bank's response to Chile's application for a loan in 1947. The policy was agreed to by McCloy and Garner and seconded by Black on becoming president. Garner wrote: "The most difficult policy problem facing the Bank is where borrowers are in default on previous debt. . . . The present management does not see how the Bank can make loans in the face of widespread dissatisfaction in financial and investment circles to whom the Bank must sell its own bonds." As quoted in Mason and Asher, *World Bank since Bretton Woods*, pp. 156–57. Mason and Asher state that the policy "was applied even-handedly throughout the world (Greece, Yugoslavia, and elsewhere), but the initial victims were mostly in Latin America (Brazil, Peru, Bolivia, Ecuador, Costa Rica)" (p. 157). According to Black, the burden of this policy was softened in practice, requiring only "a reasonable offer by the defaulting country to settle." Black, Oral History, August 6, 1961, p. 5.

knowledge and inevitably exerted an influence on lending decisions. In any case, the meeting of minds was helped along by routine meetings with State Department officials, in which the Bank was often urged by State to "support" specific countries.

Thus one of the largest developing country borrowers, in number of loans, was Nicaragua, a nation with one million inhabitants, controlled by the Somoza family.[58] "Washington and the Somozas found their relationship highly convenient. The United States supported the Somozas and the Somozas supported the United States—in votes at the United Nations, in regional councils, and by offering Nicaragua as a base for training and launching the Cuban exile forces that met disaster at the Bay of Pigs in 1961."[59] Between 1951 and 1956 Nicaragua received nine World Bank loans, and one in 1960. An American military base was established in 1953 from which was launched the successful overthrow, by the U.S. Central Intelligence Agency (CIA), of Guatemalan President Jacobo Arbenz, who had legalized the Communist Party and threatened to expropriate the assets of the United Fruit Company. Guatemala itself, with three times the population of Nicaragua, and though it was one of the first countries to receive a survey mission (published in 1951), did not obtain a loan until 1955, after the overthrow of its "communist" regime.

The Bank lent to Yugoslavia soon after its break from the Soviet bloc in 1948. George Kennan had recommended "discreet and unostentatious support" by the West, fearing Russian reaction, and aware that Congress would be unwilling to assist a Communist country.[60] The "International Bank" was an appropriate vehicle for such a role, and a mission traveled to Belgrade the following year. Yugoslavia wanted $400 million in aid, but refused to disclose key information. Black traveled to negotiate with Marshal Tito himself. In his account to the Board, Black said that Tito had banged the table with his fist but had eventually agreed to the Bank's conditions. "Selfishly and from the standpoint of the Bank," Black preferred that Tito reject the conditions, "because it would be a very difficult loan to explain to the market," but, "it's also very important that Titoism succeeds." In fact, Black waived the condition that a borrower first settle arrears. On his side, Tito seemed more interested in the Bank's endorsement than in the funds, which he expected to obtain from the United States as bilateral aid.[61]

58. The Somozas ruled Nicaragua from 1935 through 1978.

59. Anthony Lake, *Somoza Falling* (Houghton Mifflin, 1989), p. 18. Though Truman had made a show of democratic principle when Somoza deposed elected president Arguello in 1949, the U.S. position rapidly came to be dominated by cold war priorities. Lake cites a 1950 speech by George Kennan at a meeting of Latin American ambassadors: "It is better to have a strong regime in power than a liberal government if it is indulgent and relaxed and penetrated by Communists" (p. 16). Quoted from James Chace, *Endless War: How We Got Involved in Central America—And What Can Be Done* (New York: Vintage Books, 1984), p. 54.

60. Acheson, *Present at the Creation*, p. 332.

61. Meeting of Executive Directors, October 12, 1950.

Middle Eastern oil priorities also came into play. One month before the Bretton Woods Conference, an article in *Oil Weekly* published one of the first hints that U.S. domestic oil might run out, forecasting supplies for only fourteen years.[62] European dependence on Middle East oil was rising even more rapidly, from 13 percent of consumption in 1938 to 50 percent in 1949, and would surpass 80 percent by 1955. The State Department saw larger oil production and revenues in that area as necessary to quiet the nationalists and communists who threatened to open Middle East doors to Russia.[63]

A loan to Iraq was rushed through the Board in 1950. One director requested a two-day postponement to review the unorthodox nature of the proposed guarantees, though acknowledging that "great importance is given to the time of this approval because of some political reason." Black explained immediate approval was needed "because of the interest of the British government." Black pushed the loan through, earning the congratulation of the Iraqi executive director "for such a fine and quick work. . . . From last March up to now it is only a matter of a few months."[64] British relations with Iraq, and access to its oil, were at stake.

The American embassy in Tehran wrote the Bank in early 1947 to support a forthcoming application by Iran for a loan of $250 million—an extraordinary sum—arguing that "Iran is in desperate need of economic development and the political situation is such that in the absence of constructive progress, eventual absorption of the country into the Soviet sphere is a probability."[65] This concern prompted a visit by Garner, who wrote McCloy to say that "in view of the Russian menace, prompt and positive steps must be taken to improve the conditions of the masses or Iran may blow up."[66] At a June 15 meeting, State Department officials reported that the Shah was anxious to obtain the moral and tangible support that foreign loans would provide, and that they "would . . . like to be in a position to say that the IBRD is definitely interested in the possibility of making a loan to Iran at this time."[67] One month later, William Iliff, the director of the Loan Department, was informed that "Iran has come to life as a potential borrower."[68] But political turmoil in Iran, and its demand for larger oil royalties, led to a postponement of the loan. The proposal was revived in 1954, after Mossadegh's overthrow, at a meeting in which Secretary of the Treasury George M. Humphrey again referred to the urgency of the political situation and proposed that the Bank and the Eximbank

62. Johnson, *Modern Times*, pp. 480–81.

63. Daniel Yergin, *The Prize: The Epic Quest for Oil, Money, and Power* (Simon and Schuster, 1991), pp. 470–72.

64. Meeting of Executive Directors, June 14, 1950.

65. "Preliminary Analysis of Proposed Iranian Application for a World Bank Loan," Report prepared by Attaché Randall S. Williams, 1947, p. 1.

66. Letter, Robert L. Garner to John J. McCloy, March 15, 1949, Iran files, p. 1.

67. Memorandum, F. Dorsey Stephens to files, June 15, 1949.

68. Memorandum, F. Dorsey Stephens to W. A. B. Iliff, July 13, 1949.

open a joint line of credit to Iran for $70 million. Black said that "the World Bank had never extended a line of credit of this kind and was not prepared to do so in this case."[69] Black did not rule out a project loan, but, as in the case of other recipients of large-scale, unconditioned, grant aid from the United States, such as the Philippines and Korea, he thought it inappropriate for the Bank to lend. In 1956, however, Black gave in. Despite the Bank's policy against program lending to underdeveloped countries, it approved a $75 million loan "to support the Second Seven-Year Plan," the first such general-purpose loan to an underdeveloped nation.[70] Black's change of mind coincided with an American diplomatic offensive in the Middle East that was, at once, protective and proprietary. Reacting to setbacks in Hungary and Suez, the Eisenhower Doctrine announced that the United States would intervene in the Middle East against communist threats. In 1956 Black was also urged by Undersecretary Hoover to "go as far as it reasonably can in being concretely helpful to Iceland." But, said Hoover, "the foregoing is based on the assumption that a Communist influenced Government will not be formed in Iceland as result of the recent elections."[71] As it happened, after making four loans to that country between 1951 and 1954, the Bank did not resume lending until 1962.

If politics often pushed the Bank forward into the underdeveloped world, the tight rules to ensure both country creditworthiness and project quality, together with the erratic chemistry between Bank representatives and government officials, sometimes had the opposite effect, delaying the Bank's lending in other countries. After an energetic six loans between 1950 and 1954, the relationship with Turkey broke down in a cloud of confrontational meetings between prickly government officials and exigent Bank officers, including the Bank's representative in Ankara, Pieter Lieftinck, a former Dutch minister of finance. The relationship with Brazil followed a parallel course, also breaking down in 1954 after several loans, though it sputtered in 1958–59 before finally reviving in 1964. The impasse centered on inflationary policies, administrative reform of the railway system, and the introduction of controls on foreign exchange remittances. In 1953 Knapp, recently returned from a year's leave to direct a joint Brazil–United States Economic Development Commission, drafted a sympathetic and perceptive account of the troubled Bank–Brazil relationship, which, he said, was "more unhappy and strained than [with] any other member," a situation in which both parties were "guilty of unwise actions."[72] References to Brazil by staff members often expressed impatience, even exaspera-

69. Memorandum, A. Kruithof to files, October 19, 1954.
70. The loan to the Belgian Congo Development Authority had been guaranteed by Belgium.
71. Letter, Herbert Hoover, Jr., undersecretary of state, to Eugene Black, July 13, 1956.
72. Memorandum, Burke Knapp to files, January 11, 1953.

tion, and a tendency to characterize Brazil as the archetype of Latin unreliability and undiscipline, suggesting a degree of cultural prejudice by some.[73] Just as Italy, vulnerable to similar criticisms from a Northern European perspective, especially in the 1950s, achieved the second highest OECD postwar growth rate in per capita GDP (after Japan), so a distressingly untidy Brazilian society, turned down by the Bank, was beginning a development process that would produce the highest growth rate in per capita GDP (3.1 percent) in Latin America over the same four decades.[74]

There were other obstacles to lending relationships. The Bank's condition that earlier debt defaults be settled was one cause of the failure to lend to Bolivia during the 1950s. Guatemala's unwillingness to settle until 1966 was an obstacle to borrowing, though the Bank broke its own rule by making one loan in 1955, a year after the anti-Arbenz coup. Borrowing by Costa Rica and Ecuador was also delayed by unsettled defaults. A similar problem arose with expropriations of foreign assets, most notably by Indonesia. Indonesia's failure to compensate its former Dutch colonial masters became a sticking point for Bank lending, though it surely coincided with a political unwillingness to support Sukarno.

The Bank's rivalry with the Export-Import Bank was yet another factor that delayed or excluded Bank lending. Black went to great lengths to avoid lending to countries that were also Eximbank clients. One of the conditions that he placed on Tito's desk was that Yugoslavia choose between Eximbank and the World Bank; as he told the Board, "They either would do business with us alone or not at all; one or the other."[75] Black gave Mexico the same message in 1951. Mexico had already borrowed from the Bank, in 1949 and 1950, but had since transgressed by flirting with the Eximbank. Mexico agreed to Black's condition, opening the door to one of the Bank's closest lending relationships. Lending to Paraguay was dropped after that country accepted an Eximbank loan in 1953. Rivalry extended to other development agencies. At a Board meeting in May 1951, Black objected that the

---

73. Chile, by contrast, though also suffering from a lack of fiscal discipline and inflation, was put into a different cultural category. Reporting to the Board, Larsen noted Chile's macroeconomic problems but said that these were "compensated by psychological factors. . . . The Chilean people . . . are energetic . . . [and] apply themselves." Admittedly, they suffer "difficulties common to democratic countries . . . but one does not regard Chile in the same light as one would some other, even Latin-American, countries." Meeting of Executive Directors, October 9, 1951.

74. Growth rates are from Angus Maddison, *Dynamic Forces in Capitalist Development: A Long-Run Comparative View* (Oxford University Press, 1991), pp. 6–7; World Bank, *World Development Report*, several years; Angus Maddison, *Economic Progress and Policy in Developing Countries* (Norton, 1970). The average OECD growth rate in per capita GDP from 1950 to 1989 was 2.9 percent; the United Kingdom grew at 2.3 percent, the United States at 2.0 percent. In Latin America, Mexico grew at 2.3 percent, Colombia at 2.1 percent, Chile at 1.0 percent.

75. Meeting of Executive Directors, October 12, 1950.

United Nations was planning a mission to El Salvador shortly after that country had received a large power loan from the Bank. The Canadian director defended the mission, pointing out that the United Nations "is able to provide services . . . that the Bank can't do [such as] technical assistance [in] public health and various fields which are more or less closed to us." But Black exploded, accusing the United Nations of "looking for business," and saying, "I plan to get the whole story on this."[76]

Black's message, repeated also to Iran, Japan, and other countries, was that the World Bank was offering to be not *a* banker to their country, but *the* banker.[77] Mexico accepted, but countries that were receiving large U.S. economic and military assistance, including Eximbank loans, such as the Philippines and Korea, had less demand for market-based loans and did not become World Bank borrowers during the decade. The Bank's unwillingness to lend to Turkey and Brazil, after 1954, was also, in part, due to their continuing use of Eximbank funds. Conversely, the rivalry with the Eximbank motivated the Bank's substantial lending to Australia; Black's rapid accession to Australia's first loan request, in 1950, was, in part, a decision to capture an important and previously steady Eximbank client.[78] But if there was an element of turf rivalry in Black's either-or demand to clients, the position also made sense from the perspective of the larger development objectives that were already being pursued by the Bank, since the Eximbank's easy lending policy undercut the Bank's efforts to require policy and administrative improvements by borrowers.

The problems with Turkey and Brazil were in contrast to the strong relationships that developed with other countries, the most notable being India and Pakistan. Particularly close ties developed with Colombia, Peru, Mexico, and Chile, involving frequent missions, some of long duration, and numerous loans. One test of those relationships was the Bank's positive response to the foreign exchange difficulties of many underdeveloped countries during the 1957–59 recession in world trade. Those difficulties were highlighted in the Bank's 1958 and 1959 annual reports. An economic mission sent to India in 1958 opened its report with the words, "India is in the grips of a foreign exchange crisis."[79] In the spirit of a

76. Meeting of Executive Directors, May 24, 1951.

77. Mason and Asher, *World Bank since Bretton Woods*, p. 535.

78. Sommers, Oral History, August 2, 1961. The Australians first approached the American government to borrow from the Export-Import Bank but were asked to speak to the World Bank first. "So the Australians came to us, hoping and expecting to be turned down, and making some impossible conditions." Black asked Sommers to receive them, saying, "I want you to go in and chair this meeting with them at which you hear their demands, and you do what you want but I would like to make this loan. I don't want them to go back to the Export-Import Bank" (pp. 30–31).

79. IBRD, "Current Economic Position and Prospects of India," Report AS-68A, July 28, 1958, p. iii.

Table 3-3. *World Bank Disbursements to Less Developed Countries before IDA*[a]
Millions of U.S. dollars

	Disbursements[b]		
Fiscal year	Total	India	Latin American countries
1948	0	0	0
1949	19	0	19
1950	72	31	38
1951	57	12	42
1952	89	3	65
1953	102	6	57
1954	117	4	62
1955	115	3	71
1956	143	19	86
1957[c]	67	10	22
1958[c]	275	149	54
1959	449	192	154
1960	243	73	74
1961	226	57	76
Total	1,974	559	820

Source: World Bank annual reports, 1948–61.

a. Disbursements on loans committed from March 1, 1948, through April 30, 1961.

b. See table 3-1 for a list of less developed countries.

c. Data from Summary Statement of Loans; disbursed portion of effective loans held by Bank.

committed banker, the Bank sharply increased both new loans and disbursements
to the underdeveloped countries as a whole, as may be seen in tables 3-2 and 3-3.
In effect, the Bank responded with balance of payments relief, though all of it took
the form of project loans, including both new loans that were disbursed over one to
two years, and an acceleration in the rate of disbursement of previously approved
project loans. This assistance was extended on a large scale to India, but disbursements to other major borrowers also rose significantly. The acceleration was made
possible, in part, by the fruition of earlier project preparation, and the Bank's 1958
annual report, wanting to avoid the image of a balance of payments lender, attributes the increased lending to this reason.[80] At the same time, by 1959 borrower
creditworthiness was being reinforced by soft funding from the recently created

80. World Bank, *Annual Report, 1957*. After noting the recent worsening in the terms of
trade and increased pressure on the balance of payments of the underdeveloped countries,
the report says: "It would be a mistake, however, to relate the large increase in the Bank's
lending over the year to this immediate background. The main explanation lay in longer term
factors which are operating to make a larger number of development projects ready and
eligible for financing" (p. 5). Yet this argument would not explain the acceleration in
disbursements, as distinct from commitments, nor the fact that three project loans made to
India in 1958 and 1959 were each disbursed in less than two years.

Development Loan Fund.[81] And as the Bank then knew, borrowing capacity would soon be further increased by IDA.

If the Bank was drawn into balance of payments support in 1957 by its nascent partnership role with underdeveloped countries, the logic of the balance of payments rationale for lending sometimes worked in the opposite direction. Because the Charter discouraged local cost funding, and, in its "lender of last resort" provision required that a borrower not have a "reasonable" alternative, a strong balance of payments could become an obstacle to lending.[82] This happened in the case of countries that had built up large foreign exchange reserves during the war. India's requests for increased lending before 1957 were turned down because, among other reasons, in those years it had not significantly reduced its high levels of reserves. Large holdings of foreign exchange were also an argument for postponing or reducing loans to Thailand, Southern Rhodesia, and Nigeria during the 1950s.[83] The Philippines' first loan request, in 1947, for a shipyard reconstruction project was turned down on that basis.[84] But the rules for poorer countries were at times reversed for the rich: as noted above, possession of "tremendous" foreign exchange reserves had been used to justify the first loan to Australia.

Sector Allocation

Even more than who was getting Bank loans—rich or poor countries—it was the type of activity financed that has come to characterize the Bank of the 1950s, and to be used as a criterion for judging the institution's goals. As indicated in table 3-1, 83 percent of pre-IDA development lending to poorer countries was for power and transportation projects. Furthermore, when it came to poorer borrowers, the Bank was relentless in this policy of concentration on power and transport. Measured by the volume of lending, there was no move toward a more diversified sectoral pattern of lending as the decade advanced: the share of lending to these two sectors was as high (in excess of 80 percent) in the second half of the period (1956–61) as in the first half. And most of the balance was lent for other forms of economic overhead, such as industry and telecommunications. Only a small fraction was

81. A U.S. aid program created in August 1957 to lend for economic development purposes at low interest rates and long repayment periods.

82. Art. IV, sect. 3(b), and art. III, sect. 4 (ii).

83. On the decision to lend to Nigeria during the 1950s, Kamarck said, "It took quite some justification for us to make a loan to Nigeria at all, because they were so well off in terms of their existing [foreign exchange] reserves." Andrew M. Kamarck, interview, World Bank Oral History Program, August 10, 1961, p. 22. Postwar lending to Italy was held up on the grounds that Italian economic policy was overly conservative. On Southern Rhodesia, see Benjamin King, interview, World Bank Oral History Program, July 24, 1986, p. 8.

84. Meeting of Executive Directors, July 11, 1950; Mason and Asher, *World Bank since Bretton Woods*, p. 173.

made available for agriculture, and none for education, health, or other social sector needs.

The Bank's investment philosophy during most of its first quarter century has been explained as follows:

> The Bank recognized that investments of many kinds were needed for development but frequently implied that one kind was more essential than any other. The relative ease with which it could finance electric power, transportation, and economic infrastructure projects . . . made it an exponent of the thesis that public utility projects, accompanied by financial stability and the encouragement of private investment, could do more than almost anything else to trigger development.

> Projects to develop electric power and transport facilities were accordingly considered especially appropriate for Bank financing. At the same time the Bank was led to eschew certain fields traditionally open to public investment, even in the highly developed free-enterprise economies: namely, sanitation, education, and health facilities. Investments in these so-called "social overhead" fields were widely considered to be as fundamental to development as are investments in hydroelectric sites, railroads, highways, and "economic overhead" programs. The contribution of social overhead projects to increased production, however, is less measurable and direct than that of power plants, and they can be completed without large outlays of scarce foreign exchange. Financing them, moreover, might open the door to vastly increased demands for loans and raise hackles anew in Wall Street about the "soundness" of the Bank's management. It therefore seemed prudent to the management during the first postwar decade to consider as unsuitable in normal circumstances World Bank financing of projects for eliminating malaria, reducing illiteracy, building vocational schools, or establishing clinics. . . . The Bank became the leading proponent of the view that investment in transportation and communication facilities, port developments, power projects, and other public utilities was a precondition for the development of the rest of the economy.[85]

Not all staff members agreed on the necessity or desirability of that policy. According to Davidson Sommers, the Bank's general counsel through the decade, "the Bank would not finance city water supplies although it would finance irrigation, because water supplies were not 'productive' and irrigation water was. I thought this was ridiculous."[86] But, for the most part, the Bank seemed to have few doubts with regard to the soundness of its choice of sectors to fund. Garner, especially, imposed a flinty, unquestioning tone: "Why should such and such a country have a water supply system in its town? When I was brought up in

85. Mason and Asher, *World Bank since Bretton Woods,* pp. 189–90, 151–52. When lending for city water supplies did begin in the early 1960s, staff members sometimes referred to these services as "amenities" and "consumption," language not entirely consistent with the explanation given by Mason and Asher.

86. Davidson Sommers, interview, World Bank Oral History Program, July 18, 1985, p. 11. According to a personal recollection by Mervyn Weiner, Sommers's view was shared by the Bank's major shareholders.

Mississippi . . . we didn't have any water in our house."[87] When Paraguay accepted a $7 million Eximbank loan in 1954 for a water supply system in Asunción, the Bank, arguing that the project was an unproductive amenity, and moved as well by its rivalry with the Eximbank, dropped plans for lending to that country, an interruption that lasted until 1962.[88] In 1949 Lauchlin Currie, a former special adviser to Franklin Roosevelt, headed a general survey mission to Colombia, preparatory to lending. After completing the study, Currie remained in Bogotá to help Colombians formulate a set of project proposals based on the study and then persuaded Robert Garner to visit the country to discuss Bank support. Garner was presented with a program of wide-ranging reforms and balanced economic and social infrastructure: roads and energy, of course, but schools and public health as well. Lauchlin Currie recalled: "One fateful day, however, Garner suddenly realized where I was leading him, and drew back, saying 'Damn it, Lauch. We can't go messing around with education and health. We're a *bank*!' . . . The Bank retreated to . . . financing the foreign exchange costs of transport and power projects."[89]

The Bank also ignored the even more emphatic recommendations of its 1952 Survey Mission Report on Nicaragua. The report stated:

> Expenditures to improve sanitation, education and public health should, without question, be given first priority in any program to increase the long-range growth and development of the Nicaraguan economy.
>
> Without exception the mission found that in every sector of the economy high disease rates, low standards of nutrition, and low education and training standards are the major factors inhibiting the growth of productivity. . . .
>
> The mission [members] feel more strongly on [the provision of pure water and sanitation facilities] than on any other [recommendation] presented in the report . . . pure water and sanitary facilities should take overriding priority.[90]

These urgings, addressed to the Nicaraguan government, were not considered an argument for changing the Bank's established lending policy. Of the eleven loans to Nicaragua between 1951 and 1960, however, not one was for water, sanitation, health, or education, though three loans (9 percent of total lending) were for agriculture.

Agriculture received little funding from the Bank during its first years of development lending, though more attention than might be concluded by the lending figures (table 3-1). Almost one in five loans to poorer countries between 1949 and 1955 was for agriculture, reflecting an early recognition of the importance of the sector and a significant administrative effort to provide support. Five of the eleven loans received by Peru through the decade were for agricultural development. But,

87. Sommers, Oral History, July 18, 1985, p. 8.

88. Mason and Asher, *World Bank since Bretton Woods*, p. 502.

89. Lauchlin Currie, *The Role of Economic Advisors in Developing Countries* (Greenwood Press, 1981), p. 61.

90. World Bank, *The Economic Development of Nicaragua* (Johns Hopkins University Press, 1953), pp. 22–23. The mission chief was E. Harrison Clark.

because agricultural loans tended to be small by comparison with those for power and transport, the amount of total lending for this sector was a small fraction—3 percent—of all development lending to poorer countries through 1961. Also, the specific purposes of these loans, mostly to finance tractors and other machinery and for irrigation works, point to a concern for aggregate farm productivity, not, in any direct way, for the productivity and living standards of peasants and smallholders. The numbers of agricultural loans, moreover, diminished over the decade.

In sidelining the social sectors through the entire period, and agriculture after the mid-1950s, the Bank followed a strikingly different path from that taken by U.S. bilateral and other development institutions. Between one-third and one-half of U.S. economic aid to Southern Asia over the years 1951 to 1957 was for agriculture, health, and education.[91] In the case of Thailand, 30 percent of U.S. bilateral aid between 1950 and 1954 was for agriculture, while public health also received a large share.[92] Over the years 1949 to 1950, the Export-Import Bank lent more for agriculture than did the World Bank.[93] The agricultural and human resource thrust of U.S. aid was a direct response to the political emergency centered in rural Asia; peasants were the prime target and milieu for communist mobilization. In country after country, the policy was to prevent "another China," an objective that was reinforced by the Korean War. Poverty, perceived as the seedbed of communism, was visibly and overwhelmingly concentrated in agriculture. At the same time, agricultural science and medicine were advancing rapidly, and the expected payoffs from extension services to farmers, and from primary health measures such as malaria eradication and vaccination, were high.

If the sector mix of U.S. aid was in large measure dictated by the location and urgency of the political emergency centered in Asian peasant economies, it was, at the same time, consonant with popular beliefs in postwar America. Programs to spread education, health, and farm technology struck a chord with American faith in the individual, in human capacities, and in the power of technology and scientific progress. Truman could propose to stem communism over much of the globe armed, initially, with no more than a $45 million Point Four program of technical assistance. As Dean Acheson said, quoting Truman, "For the first time in history, humanity possesses the knowledge and skill to relieve the suffering of these people." Acheson continued, "[American] material resources available for foreign aid [are] limited [but American] technical knowledge [is] inexhaustible."[94] "Point

91. Charles Wolf, Jr., *Foreign Aid: Theory and Practice in Southern Asia* (Princeton University Press, 1960). The exact proportion ranges from 34 to 48 percent, depending on the allocation of a large "general and miscellaneous" category. Military aid is excluded.

92. Robert J. Muscat, *Thailand and the United States: Development, Security, and Foreign Aid* (Columbia University Press, 1990), chap. 4.

93. Cited by Mason and Asher, *World Bank since Bretton Woods*, pp. 499–500.

94. Truman, cited by Acheson, *Present at the Creation*, p. 265. Truman's 1949 budget proposal to the Congress requested $7 billion of foreign aid for Europe and the "rim." He

Four means people and American knowhow," wrote the *New York Times*.[95] The Rockefeller Foundation, subsequently joined by the Ford Foundation, was in the van of a scientific crusade to modernize agriculture in poor countries, starting in the 1940s with the precursor of CIMMYT, a hybrid-corn and wheat research center in Mexico, and IRRI in the Philippines in 1960. The U.S. Agency for International Development assisted the launching of agricultural universities in India in the early 1960s, with extraordinary dividends in the offing in the form of the Green Revolution. Faith in the wand of technology and education was not uniquely American. The Food and Agriculture Organization (FAO), United Nations Educational, Scientific, and Cultural Organization (UNESCO), International Labor Organization (ILO), World Health Organization (WHO), and UNICEF set out to teach modern farming, educate the population, train workers, and improve public health.[96] The 1951 United Nations report argued: "The first major obstacle to the general advance in technology in under-developed countries is . . . the lack of an educational and administrative structure."[97] And in 1955 Arthur Lewis argued even more forcefully: "As for priority, expenditure on bringing new knowledge to peasant farmers is probably the most productive investment which can be made in any of the poorer agricultural economies."[98]

The approach to rural development leaned heavily on education and technology, but institutional change was at the core of the effort. During the late 1940s and early 1950s, the United States pushed through land reforms in Korea and Japan. (When the landowners were American rather than Asian in Guatemala, it just as forcefully prevented land reform.) More important, many governments of underdeveloped countries closely identified modernization with radical social change in the countryside. President Ramon Magsaysay of the Philippines stressed rural development, local government, and health, while Taiwan and Korea were investing heavily in education and rural development. In Peru, a powerful new political party, Acción Popular, took its name from self-help rural development efforts. In India, the effort took the form of a community development program, started with the support of the United States and the Ford Foundation in 1952, that rapidly became nationwide. The hope was to bring about a peaceful, "voluntary" revolution by precipitating and assisting self-help at the village level. By 1959, twenty-five countries had followed India's lead in establishing community development

---

later sent a follow-up request for $45 million to fund the Point Four program. Robert A. Pastor, *Congress and the Politics of U.S. Foreign Economic Policy, 1929–1976* (University of California Press, 1980), p. 269.

95. Felix Belair, Jr., "Point Four Bringing Hope to Many Distressed Areas," *New York Times*, April 20, 1952, International Supplement, p. 5.

96. WHO was perhaps the most effective of these small agencies at this time.

97. United Nations, *Measures for the Economic Development of Under-Developed Countries*, p. 29.

98. W. Arthur Lewis, *The Theory of Economic Growth* (London: George Allen and Unwin, 1955), p. 187.

programs.[99] And, hidden from the rest of the world, China launched health, educational, and agricultural reforms. Community development lost momentum, but in China, two decades of mass executions, mass "resettlement," and disruptions that produced a man-made famine[100] would be followed by a dramatic rise in food production and in life expectancy.[101] Measured by the hundreds of millions of persons drawn out of early death and chronic hunger, China, through brutal social engineering, and to the permanent confounding of any possible single index of "human welfare," recorded the largest contribution to poverty reduction in the century.[102]

The canvas of the developing world was thus a scene of frontal, energetic, life-and-death engagement with rural poverty and human development. Against that backdrop, and with a great deal of conviction, the Bank set out on an independent course, not to the rural and human welfare front lines of the war on want, but instead to the tasks of ordnance and logistics—to build roads, railways, ports,

99. Lane E. Holdcroft, in Carl K. Eicher and John M. Staatz, eds., *Agricultural Development in the Third World* (Johns Hopkins University Press, 1984), pp. 46–58.

100. Mass executions of "counterrevolutionaries" were carried out during 1950–51. The Chinese government reported that 800,000 persons had been tried, and, in a 1957 speech, Chou En-lai stated that 16.8 percent, or about 150,000 persons, had been executed. See Richard Madsen, "The Countryside under Communism," in Roderick MacFarquhar and John K. Fairbank, eds., *The Cambridge History of China*, vol. 15 (Cambridge University Press, 1991), p. 625: "Up to perhaps 800,000 landlords were eventually executed as 'counterrevolutionaries.'" Stuart Schram, in *Mao Tse-tung* (Penguin Books, 1966), p. 267, considers that a more accurate estimate is between one and three million executions; Schram cites Jacques Guillermaz, *La Chine Populaire*, 3d ed. (Paris: Presses Universitaires de France, 1964), p. 47. The famine followed Mao's 1959 Great Leap Forward. Madsen states that the ensuing social chaos combined with bad weather to produce "one of the greatest human tragedies of the twentieth century. According to recent demographic analyses, around 20 million people died directly from starvation between 1959 [and] 1962" (p. 642). The forced migration of millions of persons, or resettlement, resulted from the creation of communes and collectivization, and expulsions from urban areas.

101. In China, the gross value of agricultural output grew 4.2 percent annually from 1953 to 1986. But growth was modest between 1958 and 1978 (2.9 percent), and rapid over 1978–86 (6.3 percent). Life expectancy rose from thirty-four years in 1952 to seventy in 1990. See Dwight Perkins, "China's Economic Policy and Performance," in Roderick MacFarquhar and John K. Fairbank, eds., *The Cambridge History of China*, vol. 15 (Cambridge University Press, 1991), p. 517. In India, value added originating in agriculture rose at 2.3 percent annually over 1960/61–1986/87. For the longer period 1949/50–1988/89, the value of crop production rose at 2.5 percent, with a deceleration from 3.1 percent in 1949/50–1964/65 (the years before the Green Revolution) to 2.5 percent in 1967/68–1988/89 (after the revolution). See World Bank, *India, 1991 Country Economic Memorandum*, vol. 2: *Agriculture—Challenges and Opportunities*, Report 9412-IN (Washington, D.C., August 23, 1991).

102. Carl Riskin, "Food, Poverty, and Development Strategy in the People's Republic of China," in Lucile F. Newman, ed., *Hunger in History: Food Shortage, Poverty, and Deprivation* (Basil Blackwell, 1990), pp. 331–52.

and power stations, and to teach governments to balance budgets, pay debts, plan expenditures, and repair roads.

That choice of lending policy made sense from the calmer perspective of 1818 H Street, several removes from the urgencies of political and economic survival. It was the common sense of American board and seminar rooms that economic growth was the indispensable and principal tool for reducing poverty in developing countries, and that efforts to shortcut this process by raising expenditure on welfare would be counterproductive. Such measures would be temporary palliatives, at the expense of savings and productive investment; direct and immediate attacks on mass poverty would only squander limited national resources. Conversely, growing production would mean a gradual but inevitable rise in living standards. These beliefs, that growth would spread or "trickle down," and that there existed a trade-off between growth and distribution, served to rationalize patience in the face of poverty.

A third concept, that growth meant, above all, industrialization and urbanization, reinforced the argument for patience. Economic laws seemed to dictate that relief for the poor must arrive not only gradually but also in a pecking order, with factory and urban workers ahead and peasants at the end of the queue. More than patience, for the current generation of rural poor, economics seemed to imply resignation.

That hard-headed wisdom was aptly reflected in the title of James Morris's 1963 book on the Bank, *The Road to Huddersfield.* Morris's metaphor for development is a reference to one of the Yorkshire mill towns where "our modern world was born"[103] through

> the building of factories . . . [and] migration of thousands of people from gentle countryside to raw new town. . . .
>
> It was no lily road to well-being. . . . Factory conditions were appalling. Housing was often repulsive. The treatment of child workers was one of the disgraces of European history.
>
> The Huddersfields were the pace-makers, but today there is scarcely a nation of the earth that does not wish to follow them down the highway to the mills.[104]

Ten years earlier, a United Nations report had stated that "economic development has to be thought of largely in terms of industrialization. . . . [Though] due importance should be attached to agriculture in national development, it is nevertheless true that industrialization forms the decisive element of economic development."[105] Hollis Chenery, who as the Bank's chief economist through the 1970s

103. Morris, *The Road to Huddersfield,* p. 4. The book was commissioned by Eugene Black during the last months of his term as president and was published shortly after the arrival of Woods.

104. Ibid., pp. 7–9.

105. United Nations, "Report of the Sub-Commission on Economic Development of the United Nations Economic and Employment Commission" (ECM147), December 18, 1947, p. 6, in IBRD, Secretary's memorandum 328, January 14, 1948.

would help McNamara push agricultural lending, opened a 1955 article on development with the sentence: "Industrialization is the main hope of most poor countries trying to increase their levels of income."[106]

For the most part, the proposition was an extrapolation of historical experience in the richer nations. The empirical association between economic growth and the shift from primary to secondary production was given prominence by the work of Allan Fisher and Colin Clark before the war.[107] The notion was strengthened by theories that converted the empirical correlation into a causal relationship. For the Anglo-Saxon mainstream, the most heralded explanation of development came to be that proposed in 1954 by Arthur Lewis. Lewis posited that growth was the direct, arithmetic consequence of the transfer of low-productivity workers from a backward, largely agricultural sector to a modern, high-productivity, largely industrial and urban sector.[108] The simple, transparent mechanics of that model outweighed the sensible qualifications that Lewis never tired of making, when for instance he noted the strong complementarity between agricultural and industrial modernization.[109] The unrigorous consequence was to reinforce the use of "industrialization" as a synonym for "growth," and the unwitting reduction of agriculture to the status of a declining and passive sector, a role that discouraged agricultural and rural approaches to reduce poverty. The Lewis model came late in the day, from the point of view of the ideas that influenced Bank lending allocation during the 1950s, but it confirmed and strengthened the less rigorous, commonsense notions of the bankers, lawyers, administrators, and even economists whose day-to-day decisions were shaping the Bank's lending policy in that decade, a policy that continued with little change through most of the 1960s.

A much-cited 1961 article on the role of agriculture in development illustrates the extent to which the industrialization thesis came to dominate thinking over the 1950s.[110] Written by Bruce Johnston and James Mellor, leading advocates for agriculture during the 1970s and 1980s, the article argues that farmers should be taxed and squeezed through price policies to finance investment in manufacturing, mining, transportation, and public utilities. They see the investment needs of

---

106. Hollis B. Chenery, "The Role of Industrialization in Development Programs," *American Economic Review*, vol. 45 (May 1955), p. 40.

107. Allan G. B. Fisher, *The Clash of Progress and Security* (London: Macmillan, 1935); Colin Clark, *The Conditions of Economic Progress* (London: Macmillan, 1951).

108. W. Arthur Lewis, "Economic Development with Unlimited Supplies of Labour," *Manchester School of Economic and Social Studies*, vol. 22 (May 1954); Lewis, *Theory of Economic Growth*.

109. See, for example, W. Arthur Lewis, "The Industrialisation of the British West Indies," *Caribbean Economic Review*, vol. 2, no. 1 (May 1950); reprint entitled *Industrial Development in the Caribbean* (Port of Spain, Trinidad: Kent House, 1951).

110. B. F. Johnston and J. W. Mellor, "The Role of Agriculture in Economic Development," *American Economic Review*, vol. 51, no. 4 (September 1961), pp. 566–93.

agriculture as "moderate" and those of the modern, nonagricultural sectors as "formidable," and they note that "if communist countries have an advantage in securing rapid economic growth, it would seem to lie chiefly in their ability to ride roughshod over political opposition [to the taxation of farmers]."[111] Johnston and Mellor were echoing Hans Singer, who had argued in 1952 that, because, "in nearly all underdeveloped countries opportunities exist for raising agricultural output by comparatively cheap methods, such as improved seeds, local irrigation, better rotation, better tools, etc.," the bulk of investment should be allocated to non-agricultural activities, despite the much smaller fraction of the population employed outside agriculture.[112]

Sociologists and economists suggested that urbanization was in itself a positive factor. In 1952 British historian G. D. H. Cole wrote that "urbanisation, then, is the outstanding mark of modernity."[113] In 1955 Henry Bruton developed that view, arguing that the conditions for development

> are more likely to thrive in an urban environment than elsewhere. . . . Workers come into contact with new and different ideas and new ways of doing things, [which] contribute to increased flexibility and fluidity of the social system. . . . Such changes facilitate and indeed encourage the adaptation . . . of improved economic processes. . . . Industrialization results . . . in the emergence of an environment which, rather than impeding technical and social innovations, makes change a part of the routine of the economic process.[114]

An additional argument for patience was provided by Simon Kuznets. Studying a cross section of industrialized countries, Kuznets discovered a long-run cycle in income inequality, increasing in the early stages of growth, and decreasing in later stages.[115] By suggesting that inequality was at once an inevitable companion to growth, and self-correcting, Kuznets's findings reinforced the case for getting on with growth rather than worrying over distribution.

111. Ibid., p. 579. At the time, Johnston and Mellor were assistant professors at Stanford and Cornell universities, respectively; Mellor later became the director of the International Food Policy Research Institute, an organization supported by the World Bank through the Consultative Group on International Agricultural Research (CGIAR).

112. Hans Singer, "The Mechanics of Economic Development," in A. N. Agarwala and S. P. Singh, The Economics of Underdevelopment (Oxford University Press, 1963), p. 390.

113. G. D. H. Cole, Introduction to Economic History, 1750–1950 (London: Macmillan, 1952), p. 3.

114. Henry Bruton, "Growth Models and Underdeveloped Economies," in Agarwala and Singh, The Economics of Underdevelopment, p. 265. Arguments for a causal link from urbanization to development were set out in several articles published in Economic Development and Cultural Change, in October 1954 and January 1955; by Bert Hoselitz in the Journal of Political Economy in 1953; and in the American Economic Review in 1955.

115. Simon Kuznets, "Economic Growth and Income Inequality," American Economic Review, vol. 45 (March 1955), pp. 1–28. This behavior of income distribution is often referred to as the "U-curve" hypothesis.

Radical alternatives to neoclassical theories were equally unsupportive of policies that might have favored the rural or urban poor. Raúl Prebisch, at the head of
the United Nations Economic Commission for Latin America (ECLA), without
directly addressing the question of sectoral priorities, nonetheless added to the bias
against agriculture by pressing the urgency of import substitution based on protection, while arguing that technical progress in agriculture inevitably created a
surplus of labor.[116] Marxist theory, in turn, though not explicit with regard to
sectors, accepted low wages and growing inequality as the inevitable concomitant
of capitalist growth. Leftists were faced with an inconsistency between the logic of
Das Kapital, which implied that attempts to intervene in favor of wage levels and
public welfare would delay the eventual, revolutionary solution, and the usefulness
of redistributionist demands as a means to power. Once established, however,
leftist regimes in Eastern Europe repressed rural incomes and urban wages to
finance industrialization. Similarly, Africa's socialist, one-party states in the 1960s
would find themselves at odds with the trade union movements that had carried the
brunt of the fight against colonialism.[117]

It was thus with all the authority of both common sense and economic theory
that the Bank could chide India, in 1958, for flirting with redistribution.

> Not least amongst the dangers to be guarded against in the present stage of India's
> development is the pursuit of welfare at the expense of efficiency.
>
> The government's policy of progressively reducing inequalities, if carried beyond a
> certain point, may be difficult to reconcile with the aim of rapid economic development.
> This policy, which operates mainly through high marginal rates of direct taxation and
> through limitations on the salaries of public employees, is liable to encourage widespread
> evasion amongst the very rich, whilst penalising the honest and efficient businessman or
> civil servant, discouraging private foreign investment and inhibiting the growth of a
> progressive middle class.[118]

The warning was repeated two years later in a report on India's five-year plan:
"Investment in social services will . . . be on a very modest scale in relation to the
needs. The mission does not in general advocate any increase in the financial

116. United Nations, Economic Commission for Latin America, Economic Survey of
Latin America 1949 (New York, 1949), pp. 49, 83.

117. W. Arthur Lewis, "A Review of Economic Development," American Economic
Review, vol. 55, no. 2 (May 1965). Lewis wrote, "Recognition of the connection between
wages and employment has opened up a gulf between trade-union leaders and political
leaders in new states, especially where government is the chief employer of labor, or is
concerned about the adverse effects of high wages on exports, import-substitution and
employment, or even prefers high profits to high wages because it can tax profits more easily
than wages. Governments have therefore begun to think in terms of an incomes policy"
(p. 15).

118. IBRD, Current Economic Position and Prospects of India, Report AS-68a, July 28,
1958, pp. 39–40.

provision for welfare programs and it believes that the only satisfactory answer to the problem in rural areas lies in greater local efforts."[119]

The Bank's firm putting aside of welfare matters would have been approved by Rene Dumont, Raúl Prebisch, and Arthur Lewis, who provided some of the most powerful statements on development policy during these years. Dumont, in *False Start in Africa*, criticized FIDES (Fonds d'Investissements pour le Développement Economique et Social), France's aid program in Africa:

> The basic error of FIDES was the primacy it gave to the "social" sector. . . . In Guinea, Mali and Morocco there is a deep-rooted desire for education and public health. . . . Any policy which prides itself on its "social" orientation in a backward country is sacrificing the hope of increasing production in order to gain immediate satisfactions. In the long-run, it is anti-social. . . . Improvements in social welfare could be financed by the beneficiaries themselves. . . . In this way, schools and hospitals, and other "social" benefits will be the result of development, and be considered in a sense as a reward.[120]

Prebisch's views have been reported by Benjamin Higgins, who assisted UNESCO during the early 1960s in its campaign for increased government spending on education. After seeing the UNESCO document prepared for a conference to be held in Santiago in 1962, Prebisch "threatened to withdraw the CEPAL [United Nations Economic Commission for Latin America] delegation and boycott the conference. . . . In his view, Latin America still needed a great deal of physical capital accumulation before it could start thinking seriously about major expansion or improvement of educational systems, and he did not want to have resources dissipated by large-scale investment in human capital."[121] Similarly, some years before, Arthur Lewis had opened his *Theory of Economic Growth* saying, "Our subject matter is growth, and not distribution."[122]

In avoiding agriculture, social services, and redistribution and concentrating instead on economic infrastructure, the Bank was swimming with the intellectual current during the 1950s. But the initial, and paramount, consideration that shaped lending policy was financial. When Robert Cavanaugh, the Bank's chief fund-raiser from 1947 to 1959, was asked whether the New York stock market would have reacted adversely to Bank financing of education, public health, and housing, he said, "If we got into the social field . . . then the bond market would definitely feel that we were not acting prudently from a financial standpoint. . . . If you start financing schools and hospitals and water works, and so forth, these things don't

119. IBRD, Bank Mission to India, "India's Third Five-Year Plan," Report AS-80a, August 10, 1960, p. 47.

120. Rene Dumont, *False Start in Africa* (Praeger, 1969), pp. 47–48. The book was originally published in French in 1962.

121. Benjamin Higgins, *The Road Less Travelled: A Development Economist's Quest* (Canberra: National Centre for Development Studies, 1989), pp. 98–99.

122. Lewis, *Theory of Economic Growth*, p. 9. Lewis admitted that "it is possible that output may be growing, and yet that the mass of the people may be becoming poorer."

normally and directly increase the ability of a country to repay a borrowing."
Cavanaugh felt that lending to social sectors could hurt the Bank despite the
United States government guarantee of Bank obligations: "With the guarantees
that we have, [buyers of Bank bonds] would not worry about getting their money
back but they'll make us pay more for it."[123] Garner's rejection of Colombian health
and education projects, saying "We're a bank," reflected the same perception.
More generally, Garner saw the Bank constrained in all its operations by expected
financial market reaction: "We've always had to say to ourselves, 'If we do certain
things in a certain way, will that tend to build confidence in the Bank, or will it tend
to undermine confidence in the Bank?'"[124] The developmental need for social
investment was not rejected, but, at the time, the Bank could distinguish between
governmental priorities and its own lending priorities. As Alexander Stevenson
recalled, "We might have thought that education or health was important, but the
Bank wasn't lending in those sectors."[125]

The Specific Project

The allocation of lending by type of activity was less a conscious decision than a
fallout from the Bank's dependence on Wall Street and from a loan policy, centered
on the specific investment project, that developed in response to that dependence.
Both social sector and agricultural lending were put at a disadvantage by that
policy, mostly in consequence of their high proportional content of local currency
and recurrent costs, and comparatively lesser need for the large-scale items of
imported and visibly productive capital goods that best favored the Bank's image in
Wall Street.

The influence of Wall Street on the Bank's lending policies began at Bretton
Woods. Before offering the first bond issues, the Bank's lending rules were being
shaped by several provisions in the Charter written with an eye to its future
relationship with financial markets. Above all, it was to be a financial marriage
broker and, only in extremis, a bride. Thus, using guarantees and participations, it
was to "facilitate," "promote," and "encourage" private investment. And, if marry it
must, it would do so under strict rules; only "when private capital is not available on
reasonable terms" was it to "supplement" private investment by lending directly.

Cautious and protective rules were set out for such cases of direct lending. The
Bretton Woods delegates shared a conviction that much of the prewar collapse in
international markets could be traced to loose lending, and the Charter would be a

123. Robert W. Cavanaugh, interview, World Bank Oral History Program, July 25, 1961,
pp. 63–64.
124. Garner, Oral History, July 19, 1961, p. 45.
125. Alexander Stevenson, interview, World Bank Oral History Program, November 18,
1985, p. 7.

shield against foreseeable temptations and pressures.[126] The most important of those provisions was the stipulation that, except in special circumstances, loans made or guaranteed by the Bank be for *specific projects*.[127] Other provisions encouraged the Bank to lend for capital rather than intermediate goods, and for foreign exchange rather than local currency costs, and enjoined the Bank to lend for productive purposes, not consumption, and to ensure that loans were used only for the purposes for which they were granted.[128] To verify compliance, the Charter mandated end-use control: the Bank "shall make arrangements to ensure that the proceeds of any loan are used only for the purposes for which the loan was granted."[129] These various requirements became ingredients of the Bank's dominant lending mode, "the specific project approach." Admittedly, when faced by the reconstruction emergency in 1947, and later, when approached by highly credit-worthy borrowers such as Australia, Belgium, and Italy, the Bank felt at liberty to make nonspecific program loans, arguing "special circumstances." And, three decades later, "special circumstances" would justify large-scale structural and sectoral adjustment lending. But Garner and Black were uneasy about such experiments and gradually moved away from them toward greater orthodoxy. Their sense of the market undoubtedly coincided with that of the Bretton Woods delegates, understanding that in banking it was as important to look sound as to be sound.[130]

The specific project approach was particularly suited to create an image of soundness.[131] Garner described end-use control as simply "sound business practice," a practice that, as he saw it, had been neglected by banks when lending

126. Aron Broches recalled: "There were a number of people in Bretton Woods under the impact . . . of the happenings of the '20s and '30s. There was a lot of talk about the unsoundness of . . . borrowing abroad to finance local expenditures. And the examples were generally the borrowing by Germany in the '20s for such public amenities and facilities as swimming pools and sports parks, borrowings by municipalities, and so forth . . . there was a general wave of revulsion against that sort of thing which, we think, is reflected in the charter." Aron Broches, interview, World Bank Oral History Program, July 11, 1961, p. 39.

127. "Loans made or guaranteed by the Bank shall, except in special circumstances, be for the purpose of specific projects of reconstruction or development." IBRD, *Articles of Agreement*, art. III, sec. 4 (vii). Chapter 10 of this volume discusses the Bank's interpretation of "special circumstances." The issue of interpretation first arose in connection with reconstruction loans, and with proposals for development loans of a program nature to Australia, Italy, and the Belgian Congo during the 1950s, and it acquired renewed salience in relation to the Bank's structural adjustment lending in the 1980s.

128. Ibid., art. III, sec. 5(b).

129. Ibid.

130. William Bennett, who helped market Bank bonds and obtain a rating from Moodys, recalls that "impact" or program lending "would have been frowned on in the early days of the Bank. They swore by the gods that they would only lend for sound projects, soundly run, soundly financed, and so forth." Bennett, Oral History, January 20, 1988, p. 9.

131. One effect of the Bank's thorough end-use supervision would be a remarkably scandal-free record in the disbursement of its funds.

overseas in the past.[132] More accurately, Garner should have said "sound banking practice." Investors were comforted when they could "see" the use to which their funds had been put. S. R. Cope explained, "The market likes the idea of specific projects. There's a feeling that, if you know exactly where the money goes, it must be a sound thing."[133] In the matter of supervision, as in the formulation of other operational norms, the Bank edged forward always looking over its shoulder to gauge the impact on confidence.[134] Belief was encouraged when funds were assigned to the purchase of large, discrete items of capital equipment from abroad, and it was reinforced when a project appeared to be self-liquidating, that is, when it would directly produce the revenues required to pay back a loan. By contrast, the "use" or final destination of monies lent to farmers for working capital, or to a ministry of education to purchase locally produced school supplies, was easier to question. The repayment rationale for project lending was stressed by Andrew Kamarck in a 1961 interview. Then economic adviser on Europe and Africa and later head of the Bank's Economic Research Department, Kamarck summarized the reasons for project lending. One was that projects were a door to influence on borrower management and policies. Another, he wrote, was that "project lending . . . does help to insure that the loan will be serviced; that there will be no default. When a loan is tied to a particular project, the people in the country, the general public, associate the Bank with that particular project. . . . [I]f there is a change in the government . . . their willingness to continue to service an existing debt is greater than if the loan were made for some purpose which vanished as far as the economy as a whole is concerned and you couldn't identify it."[135]

Visibility, verifiability, and apparent productivity were the touchstones for projecting an image of supervised, controlled, safe "quality" lending, and these criteria were best satisfied by the large-scale, import-intensive, long-lived investment project. Dams, power stations, and roads could be described, photographed, and trusted in a way that funds spent on intermediate goods or short-lived assets or salaries could not. But if specialization in economic infrastructure at first "seemed prudent to the management," in Mason and Asher's account, it came to be reinforced by the expertise that the Bank acquired in such projects.[136] More than in

132. Garner, Oral History, July 19, 1961, pp. 9–10.

133. Cope, Oral History, August 9, 1961, p. 37.

134. Benjamin King suggests that Wall Street's reaction had become a myth. "I was manager of the second loan to Norway in 1955 in conjunction with a Wall St. bond issue. The first loan had been, disingenuously, characterized as a loan for shipping. I proposed coming clean on the second one and saying it was for imports in general. I was told it would not sit well on Wall St., but the fellow at Harriman Ripley [Wall St. brokers] said he didn't give a damn." Letter, Benjamin King to Richard Webb, undated, November 1993. See also King, Oral History, July 24, 1986, p. 14.

135. Kamarck, Oral History, August 10, 1961, pp. 17–18.

136. Mason and Asher, World Bank since Bretton Woods, pp. 151–52, 189–90.

later periods, the Bank's lending choices were constrained by a sense of its own "comparative advantage."

The fifth annual report explained that the Specific Project Provision of the Charter was a "safeguard," designed "simply to assure that Bank loans will be used for productive purposes."

> If the Bank were to make loans for unspecified purposes or for vague development programs which have not been worked out in terms of the specific projects by which the objectives of the program are to be achieved, there would be a danger that the Bank's resources would be used either for projects which are economically or technically unsound or are of a low priority nature, or for economically unjustified consumer goods imports.[137]

Behind the specific project mode was not only a disinterested, if tutelary, concern that borrowers benefit by making the best use of Bank funds, but also a concern for the Bank's creditworthiness. In 1950, Black described the Bank's lending policy as "a new step forward in the history of international investment" that would satisfy "the need for re-establishing the integrity of international loan contracts . . . [and] the ability and willingness of the borrowers to repay them. The standards we have established have, I think, done much towards reviving and proving the idea that international investment can be carried on with adequate rewards both to the borrower and the lender."[138]

Black also announced that the Bank had finally established its credit, and, a year later, informed the United Nations Economic and Social Council (ECOSOC) that "the Bank does not now face any difficulty in raising sufficient funds."[139] But the rationale that had shaped the Bank's loan policy was by then settling into an orthodoxy that Black and Garner preferred to leave undisturbed through the decade.

One reason was that the Bank soon learned that it could dress balance of payments and general development assistance as specific project loans. When B. K. Nehru objected to the imposition of the project mode for the Bank's first loan to India—the funds were assigned to India's railways—Davidson Sommers replied:

> Why do you fight these theological battles with us? We have now found you a project which satisfies our concept of a project, namely the development of the Indian railways, which can absorb twice as much as the entire Bank lending program for a definite period of time, and it performs all the purposes of a specific project loan and a foreign exchange loan, and yet from your purposes is just as flexible as a balance of payments loan.[140]

137. IBRD, *Fifth Annual Report, 1949–1950*, p. 8.

138. IBRD, *Summary Proceedings: Fifth Annual Meeting of the Board of Governors, Paris, France, September 6–14, 1950* (November 30, 1950), pp. 10–11.

139. Eugene R. Black, address before the Economic and Social Council of the Economic Social Council of the United Nations (ECOSOC) at Santiago, Chile, March 6, 1951, IBRD Press Release 237, p. 2.

140. Sommers, Oral History, August 2, 1961, pp. 34–35. According to Sommers, Nehru retorted that, for India to get an adequate volume of financing "we're going to have to pick so many projects . . . [that] it will just take too damn long to get the total that we need."

By September 1958 the Bank could respond rapidly to a balance of payments emergency in India with $160 million in three "project" loans for railways and power, of which $151 million was disbursed in little over a year. And when the Bank worked out the details of its two-part loan for the Belgian Congo, it was at pains to reconcile the balance of payments and general development intent of the loan with a project appearance. As S. R. Cope remembered in 1961,

> We felt that since even then the importance of projects in our thinking had been increasing, that we ought to have something like a project in this deal. We, therefore, selected OTRACO, which is a transport monopoly in the Belgian Congo, as the project, and that we would limit our disbursement to expenditure on OTRACO which we had investigated as being a sound project to carry out. And so, we could claim to the outside world that this was no exception to our general rule that proceeds of Bank loans had to be allocated in some way or other to specific projects.[141]

When Cope's interviewer, Robert Oliver, put the point more bluntly, "Doesn't it really in fact turn out that the Bank . . . puts a great emphasis on specific projects partly for public relations reasons and partly . . . to satisfy the market . . . [that] the Bank's bonds are tied to something physical which can be seen and pointed to thereafter[?]" Cope replied, "Yes I would agree."[142] Summarizing the Bank's first two decades, J. H. Williams wrote, "At no time . . . has a President of the Bank felt free to ignore investor reaction to the way the Bank is making loans."[143]

The specific project took root for another reason, suggested by Garner during an interview. Emphasizing the importance to the Bank of market confidence, he noted, "It's been a useful thing . . . a very useful argument, to tell people why the Bank must pay attention to financial opinion and judgments."[144] As the demand for Bank loans grew, the local expenditure limitation, for instance, became an increasingly useful filter, as had been intended at Bretton Woods. According to Cope, the Bank felt that if it

> lent freely for local expenditure, it would be opening the floodgates to application from countries that we're not anxious to lend substantial amounts to for projects which we felt were of a low priority [such as] municipal improvements in Latin America or elsewhere. . . . [W]e felt that we should emphasize whatever barriers there were in the Articles of Agreement to [avoid] being flooded with requests for financing of that sort. . . . [T]he arguments against local expenditure financing have been practical and empirical rather than theoretical.[145]

---

141. Cope, Oral History, August 9, 1961, pp. 25–26.

142. Ibid., pp. 40–41.

143. J. H. Williams, "International Bank for Reconstruction and Development," paper presented to the Fourth Maxwell Institute on the United Nations, Bretton Woods, N.H., August 27–September 1, 1967, p. 3.

144. Garner, Oral History, July 19, 1961, p. 45.

145. Cope, Oral History, August 9, 1961, p. 13.

Cope's reference to the use of "whatever barriers there were" hints at rationing and administrative discretion. To some extent, in blaming Wall Street and the Charter, Black and Garner were undoubtedly making room for their own commonsense views about development, a degree of managerial discretion that increased over the decade, rising with the Bank's credit ratings and prestige, and with the growing demand for loans. The personal prejudices of Black and Garner were undoubtedly hard to distinguish from their reading of the Wall Street mind, and one is left wondering if, for instance, had Garner been born in a town with piped water in each home, he might have agreed to lend for municipal water services.

The insistence on specific investment projects was born as a piece of banking psychology. It was thought that, though loans were guaranteed by borrower governments, clients were more likely to repay a debt incurred for a visibly productive project; and further, that specific projects would inspire confidence in the Bank's investors. Good project choices as well as good clients would thus ensure the Bank's own creditworthiness. Within a few years of the Bank's opening, however, much of the original, acute concern for repayment had abated and what remained became attached instead to the overall state of a borrower's economy, and especially, its balance of payments, rather than to the outcome of specific projects. The Bank correspondingly increased its attention to the secondary and general effects of projects on the borrower's economy. Indeed, when critics argued that the Bank examined the merits of particular projects in isolation, the Bank replied that, "in fact, [it] does precisely the opposite," by investigating the priority of each project in the context of national development programs.[146]

But if critics were misled, the blame attached principally to the Bank, which in its choice of projects, loan descriptions, and other public statements continually drew attention to the financial and technical merits of individual projects rather than to judgmental assessments of country development programs. Indeed, it was the very image of a loan portfolio made up of stand-alone, self-justifying, individually "sound" projects that helped the Bank overcome market suspicion of foreign lending. But, though it continued to seek out investments with enclave virtues, from an early date the Bank was also beginning to look beyond the specific project: it looked for coherence with other investments.[147] It actively discouraged uneconomic projects; and, more generally, it sought to influence a borrower's development policies and practices.

A certain schizophrenia thus began to develop. Much of the Bank's mind continued to be occupied with the need to meet exacting standards for each of its projects. Beyond the natural concern for financial image, this effort was further justified on tutorial grounds: Bank projects were meant to become showcases to spread better project management in the developing countries. At the same time,

146. IBRD, *Annual Report, 1949–1950*, p. 9.
147. As it argued in ibid.

it began to broaden its evaluations and advice to encompass more and more of the borrower's economy. Increasingly, it identified its mandate with "extra-project" contributions to the overall quality of a borrower's development management. To some extent, these two distinct concerns came to be embodied in the organizational separation of tasks between project specialists and area staff, the first responsible for the accounting, legal, and technical requirements of good specific projects, the second for the economic and diplomatic requirements of successful intervention beyond the project.

This broadening role was initially seen as a reinforcement of good project lending: most underdeveloped countries needed assistance in the selection, preparation, and management of viable investment projects. But the drive to assist and advise soon went beyond the strictly ancillary requirements of Bank projects. The Bank was in fact beginning to pursue a more ambitious role as tutor and influencer, using its advantageous position as a low-cost, long-term lender and its comfortable administrative budget. Eventually, ends and means would seem to trade places: individual projects would come to be seen mostly as instruments for influencing the larger development effort.

Yet there was a further reason for setting objectives that went beyond the specific project: even as it drew attention to the concrete merits and close supervision of its projects, the Bank was aware that the end use of its funds was not easily determined. To the extent that funds are fungible or substitutable within a government budget, or through the reallocation of foreign exchange, the actual "use" of a loan may differ and extend far from its official, specified purpose. Like water poured into a pond, the additional funds could have effects distant from the point of entry. In a fungible world, project evaluation and the study of spending priorities would be valuable as means to improve the use of resources and to reassure investors, but they would be misleading as a basis for judging the impact of Bank financing. In such a world, the effects of the Bank's "pitcher of water" would be distributed in nearly invisible ways through a multiplicity of governmental budget items and uses of foreign exchange. "Specificity" would be spurious, and the Bank, and the buyers of its bonds, would be less confident about the use being made of their money.

It is hardly surprising, therefore, that the financial sector, utterly dependent on confidence, goes about its business on the assumption that money, once lent, remains concrete and identifiable in the way in which it is used. Investment bankers must proceed as if "end use" can be determined, and the productive contribution of loans can be identified by their direct impact. As a "mere bank" during the 1950s, it was second nature for the Bank, and convenient from the perspective of its marketing task, to adopt the same working assumption, subjecting projects—its pitchers of water—to rigorous tests and assessing its own contribution to development on the assumption that the specific investment project was the measure of its loans.

The assimilation of this functional credo by the Bank was not entirely smooth, for the reason that the institution already carried the seeds of being more than a bank. The Bank seemed bound to ask itself whether success in establishing its own creditworthiness was truly accompanied by economic development. The professional instincts of its economists had been trained to "see" the generally invisible and indirect effects of economic activity. Economists were a minority in the early Bank, especially among the senior staff, and, as noted above, the director of the Economic Department, Leonard Rist, was a career banker. Nonetheless, their presence helped to stir debate about lending policy.

The question of fungibility was posed, frontally, in the annual report for 1949–50, as part of a discussion of the Bank's lending policies.[148] After noting that resources are scarce, and that, in consequence, Bank investment must be devoted to those undertakings that contribute most to strengthening the economy of borrowers, the report goes on to state that "the Bank recognizes, of course, that, by financing one particular investment project, it may be releasing resources already available to the borrower for some other investment activity."[149] This admission undercut the principal justification for the specific investment project; whatever their nominal purpose, it said, Bank loans were perhaps financing "some other" activity. Indeed, though the report limits the admission to the possibility of "some other investment," the acknowledgement fell short; funds that are released may be consumed rather than invested. The report quickly discouraged the idea that fungibility might imply any loosening in the rigor of project evaluation. The Bank's practice of careful evaluation, it says, improves the use of resources and acts, in effect, as an educational device, providing an object lesson that frequently improves the quality of a borrower's investment projects in general: "It may reasonably be hoped that, as the underdeveloped countries become more generally familiar with the Bank's method . . . they may tend gradually to apply the same standards to the investment projects which they finance from their own resources. This may well prove in the long run to be a most valuable by-product of the Bank's lending technique."[150]

This argument, that Bank projects served as classrooms or how-to-do-it demonstrations through which its staff could transmit skills applicable to non-Bank investments and to the development efforts generally of borrowing countries, became a powerful internal justification for the specific project approach. By pointing to the educational externalities of Bank projects, it sidestepped the question of their true or net impact on resource allocation. In effect, if "specificity" was admitted to be uncertain, because of fungibility, the project could nonetheless be justified as a vehicle for the Bank's educational and tutelary messages.[151]

148. Drafted by Richard Demuth and Benjamin King.
149. World Bank, *Annual Report, 1949,* p. 9.
150. Ibid., pp. 9–10.
151. Although it could stress the educational role of project investments, the Bank, as a bank, could not admit to ignorance of their "end use." The candid discussion of this question

The undoubted value of educational externalities, however, failed to persuade Paul Rosenstein-Rodan, Rist's deputy in the Economic Department and, in effect, the Bank's senior professional economist from 1947 to 1952. Rosenstein-Rodan had been arguing persistently in favor of large-scale program lending, partly on the grounds that lending was fungible. He dismissed the preference for specific projects as a banker's device to ensure that "the project is certain and concrete," so that the risk "appears very much less." He was at a loss to explain "the psychoanalytical problem why a bunch of intelligent people" should be taken in by this "optical illusion."[152] The Bank may think that it had financed an electric power station, he said, "but in fact financed a brothel."[153]

Others agreed. John de Wilde described the Bank's project choices: "We make a fetish here in the Bank of saying, 'We only finance high-priority projects.' Of course, by financing high-priority projects, if indeed we do this, most of us recognize that implicitly we finance projects at the margin, since presumably resources are exchangeable."[154] At times, it even became convenient to draw attention to fungibility. S. R. Cope, for instance, justified a loan to the Netherlands by telling the Board: "The form which the loans take is not particularly important. . . . [I]t makes very little difference whether we have a loan for a general reconstruction program or whether we have it tied down to a specific project or enterprise. In both cases the loans increase the foreign exchange resources of the country and enable it to expand its investment."[155] On another occasion, turning the argument around, Harold Larsen cited fungibility to defend the Bank against the criticism that it would not lend for social sectors; "to which I reply that it has always been that our funds are substitutable."

> In one of my missions to a Latin American country, the Minister of Finance requested specific finance for housing and hospitals. I asked him what his own government's investments and expenditures were, and he said they were putting it into power and roads, and they were satisfactorily taken care of, but he was now short of money for other purposes. We pointed out to him that we would finance the roads or power, which would release his money for financing the social sector.[156]

---

in the *Fifth Annual Report* was not repeated. Even more, as Richard Neustadt noted, "The tendency of bureaucratic language to create in private the same images presented to the public should never be underrated." Having "sold" doctrines through their public statements, officials may be "stuck" with their consequences. In Richard E. Neustadt, *Presidential Power: The Politics of Leadership* (John Wiley and Sons, 1960), p. 139. Over the decades, the Bank has invested much of its analytical effort debating sectoral "priorities" for its investments, a debate that presupposes some degree of nonfungibility.

152. Rosenstein-Rodan, Oral History, 1973, p. 7.

153. Ibid.

154. Gerald Alter, Harold Larsen, and John de Wilde, interview, World Bank Oral History Program, July 1961, p. 12.

155. Meeting of Executive Directors, January 16, 1951.

156. Alter and others, Oral History, July 1961, p. 19. A Mexican delegation confronted the Bank with the same criticism during a visit to Washington in 1956. Western Hemisphere economist Jonas Haralz replied with the same argument. Interview with the author.

For social investments, it seems, it was Catch-22. They were unattractive as specific projects; but if specificity was considered "an optical illusion," the Bank could retort, "in that case, finance them yourself, since our funds are substitutable anyway."

Despite the awareness, above all by economists, that the Bank could not fully ascertain where its money was going, and despite even the official recognition that these views received in the 1950 annual report, the Bank remained wedded to the specific investment project approach. It made several program loans for development purposes during the 1950s, but they had an exceptional character, and only two, to the Belgian Congo and Iran, were to underdeveloped areas, a behavior consistent with the use of specific projects to ration lending when it came to less creditworthy borrowers. Garner took a more rigid line than Black, disagreeing, for instance, with Black's approval of the Italian program loan.

Albert Hirschman also came to be associated with the Bank in its early years. Hirschman left a position in the U.S. Federal Reserve to work as an adviser in Colombia between 1952 and 1954. That experience was enormously fruitful for his own thinking, and for the young science of development economics. Yet, like Rosenstein-Rodan, he remembered his relationship with the Bank as sterile and frustrating.[157]

From today's perspective it would seem felicitous that Rosenstein-Rodan and Hirschman, two pioneers of development economics, came to be associated with the Bank in its first years, but the relationship turned out a disappointment for both of them, and for the Bank.[158] Following their scientific noses, the two economists set off on intellectual quests that produced powerful, though competing visions of the development process. What those visions had in common was a fascination with externalities; both questioned the common sense of appearances and explored the less visible consequences of economic behavior. Little wonder that their banker colleagues, striving to persuade investors that the world is more predictable, visible, and attractive than it really is, were not at ease with these scientific explorers. In a business required to build Potemkin villages, the wiser course was to keep economists well leashed, not roaming behind the facades.[159]

157. Albert O. Hirschman, "A Dissenter's Confession: 'The Strategy of Economic Development' Revisited," in Gerald M. Meier and Dudley Seers, eds., *Pioneers in Development* (Oxford University Press, 1984), pp. 90–91.

158. See ibid., pp. 90–91. In a section titled, "Revolting against a Colombian Assignment," Hirschman notes that, though employed by the Colombian National Planning Council, he had a "special relationship" with the World Bank, which had advised in the creation of the Council and had recommended him for the post. Asked by the Bank to prepare a detailed development program, he "felt that one of the things Colombia needed least was a synthetic development plan compiled on the basis of 'heroic estimates.'" Furthermore, "The task was supposedly crucial for Colombia's development, yet no Colombian was to be found who had any inkling of how to go about it."

159. Barend de Vries, an economist who joined the Bank during the 1950s remembered that "the work of economists in the mid-1950s . . . was subordinated to that of the operations staff. People at the time would hide the fact that they had economic training, and division chiefs or operations officers would often chide economists for the work they were doing. My

With customary thoroughness, Garner followed through in 1952, using an administrative reorganization to cut the size and authority of the Economic Department. Economic research was downgraded and most economists were placed at the service of regional loan offices.[160] Garner was relieved when Rosenstein-Rodan resigned in 1954, commenting, "I frankly never thought that the Bank was his dish of tea. . . . [T]he Bank was not the place for the development of broad economic policies or studies."[161] According to Bank economist Albert Waterston, Rosenstein-Rodan "did not make any real impact on the policy of the Bank because someone like Bob Garner wouldn't even talk to him. . . . [E]ven on me he had much less influence than you would expect, for a very good reason. The World Bank was essentially a pragmatic organization. We did not start with a theory . . . and deduce actions. . . . That was a way which did not sit well with bankers."[162]

Cracks in the Marble

It was the Bank's conception of its proper role, during the 1950s, that it should put a stern face on poverty, and the preceding sections have attempted to explain that position. "Poverty" was not part of the Bank's Charter or working language, the subject was never the centerpiece of a statement by the institution during this time, and its projects seemed distant from the poor. Yet, if for the most part the Bank appeared to be unmoved by the extent and urgency of world poverty—and it should perhaps be emphasized at this point that this was a matter of functional image, not of personal sympathies or motivations—it did often register awareness of human needs in speeches and reports. More important, its stance did not prevent an organizational drift in the direction of poverty lending. In some respects

---

own division chief, Albert Waterston, who later had a career in the Economic Development Institute, made fun of the work of 'his' economist." Interview with Charles Ziegler, January 21, 1986.

160. Rist saw this change "as a deliberate intention to humiliate people." Leonard Rist, Oral History, July 1961, p. 60. However, many economists reassigned to lending departments went on to become senior officials. Gerald Alter, for instance, became director of the Western Hemisphere Department. (Conversation about George Woods with Robert Oliver, July 13, 1985, p. 7.) By downgrading research and putting economists to work in operations, Garner in effect increased the role of economic analysis.

161. Garner, Oral History, July 19, 1961, p. 98. According to William Bennett, Rosenstein-Rodan "was invited to leave." Bennett, Oral History, January 20, 1988, p. 9.

162. Albert Waterston, interview, World Bank Oral History Program, May 14, 1985, pp. 2–3. The Bank had quietly dispensed with its Advisory Council, a panel of economists and businessmen, though Article V of its Charter mandated at least one annual meeting of the Council. After two sessions, in 1948 and 1949, the Bank simply failed to call a new meeting. When the matter was brought up at the May 24, 1951, Board meeting, the Board decided to do nothing.

—above all the creation of IDA at the end of the decade—it was the very success of the Bank's marble front that thrust poverty lending onto its lap.

Shortly after leaving the Bank, John McCloy wrote: "It must never be forgotten that low productivity and living standards are as much the product of poor government, unsound finance, bad health and lack of education as of inadequate resources or the absence of productive facilities. The attack on backwardness . . . must be made on many fronts."[163] Robert Garner, giving a farewell address in 1961, seemed to be equally mindful of the "many fronts": "I would emphasize the importance of . . . a sensible plan of balance among agriculture, industry, transport, power, communications, with such provision for housing, education and medical services as resources permit."[164] President Black referred to poverty, inequality, and the health and education needs of underdeveloped countries in many of his earlier addresses. In 1950 he noted the "dangerous fallacy . . . that the standard of living of the masses can be raised without some alteration of those economic structures which permit a relatively few people to enjoy most of a nation's income," while reminding his audience of the need for health and education.[165] He used a commencement address in 1951 for an eye-opening illustration of the privileged lives of American youths, comparing their survival and schooling chances with a peer group in India.[166] That same year he spoke of the need for land tenure reform to a meeting of ECOSOC.[167] In 1953 he told a Wall Street group that he had "seen at first hand some of the underprivileged millions . . . faced with the specter of hunger," and spoke of their needs.[168] These comments, however, became less frequent during the second half of Black's term as president.

The Bank's survey missions, often drafted by respected external consultants and addressed to developing-country governments, were given a freer voice and were often outspoken about inequality and social needs.[169] Most also pointed to agriculture as the priority sector. A notable example was the 1951 report on Guatemala,

163. John McCloy, "The Lesson of the World Bank," *Foreign Affairs,* vol. 27, no. 4 (July 1949), p. 555.

164. Robert Garner, address to Board of Governors of the International Finance Corporation, in IFC, *Summary Proceedings: 1961 Annual Meeting of the Board of Governors, Vienna, Austria* (September 21, 1961), p. 7.

165. Eugene Black, speech to the Board of Governors, in IBRD, "Verbatim Report of the Fourth Session of the Bank, Held at the Bank of Paris," September 8, 1950, Bank sess. no. 4, p. 7.

166. Eugene Black, commencement address to the University of Chattanooga, June 11, 1951, p. 2.

167. Black, address before ECOSOC, Santiago, Chile, March 6, 1951, p. 6.

168. Black, "Some Considerations Affecting Foreign Aid," p. 4.

169. Though signed by external consultants, the writing often fell to Bank staff, suggesting that the "freer voice" of the Survey Missions, as compared with economic reports written for Bank decisionmaking, was more a case of wearing different hats than having different views.

drafted by Saskatchewan economist George Britnell, which criticized "absentee landlords . . . interested only in immediate cash income however ruinous the productive methods used. . . . In the lower Pacific coastal region, potentially one of the richest and with fairly adequate railway transport, some of the best land has been held in complete idleness."[170] The Guatemalan upper classes were criticized for holding prices unnecessarily high, seeking exorbitant profits, and investing them abroad. The report said that agriculture was the key development sector, noting that without rural poverty alleviation there would be no market for industrial development, and that, owing to the extreme inequality of income, additional taxation of the rich would not reduce growth. The reports on Colombia and Nicaragua called for balanced investment to meet both economic and social needs. The Guatemalan and Colombian reports were closely read and drawn upon in the formulation of development plans, although in Guatemala's case political factors intervened to prevent Bank lending. Land tenure was highlighted by a 1956 follow-up mission on agriculture in Colombia: "The present pattern of land use in Colombia," it stated, "is one of the most serious obstacles to increasing agricultural production."[171] Though the language referred to use, rather than ownership, the study was clearly pointing a finger at inequality. A report on Thailand urged priority attention for the poor Northeast region.[172] The report on Malaya endorsed the government's major commitment to education and health services, commending Malaya's British administrators for their achievement in this area: "Not long ago, Malaya was one of the unhealthiest places in the tropics. Today it is among the healthiest."[173] The report on Turkey expected that the "first and most important result [of the proposed investment program] should be to stir Turkish agriculture out of the lethargy in which it has remained for centuries. . . . Any improvement which benefits the greater part of the population will by that very fact contribute greatly to economic progress . . . an awakened, more efficient and progressive agriculture will provide the basis for further industrial development."[174]

What the Bank was hearing about poverty, distribution, social needs, and the key role of agriculture from its own studies was reinforced by the rising chorus of aid demands from poor countries and a burgeoning "aid community" in rich countries. But its response stopped short at occasional acknowledgments by senior officials, statements that were at once moral reminders, and a way to explain and justify the

170. IBRD, *The Economic Development of Guatemala* (Washington, D.C., 1951), p. 26.

171. IBRD, *Report on Colombian Agriculture*, June 27, 1956, p. 3. The joint FAO-IBRD mission, led by Sir Herbert R. Stewart, included Montague Yudelman, later director for rural development in the Bank, between 1973 and June 1978.

172. IBRD, *A Public Development Program for Thailand* (Johns Hopkins University Press, 1959), pp. 7, 18–19.

173. IBRD, *The Economic Development of Malaya* (Johns Hopkins University Press, 1955), p. 546.

174. IBRD, *The Economy of Turkey: An Analysis and Recommendations for a Development Program* (Johns Hopkins University Press, 1951), p. xxiv.

institution. It did not go on to examine the possible implications for policy and operations. What should and could the Bank do to reduce poverty, over and above promoting general economic growth in poor countries?

Lecturing in Brazil in 1950, Jacob Viner posed the "should" question (without mentioning the Bank). Instead of measuring development in terms of per capita income, he said,

> Suppose that someone should argue that the one great economic evil is the prevalence of a great mass of crushing poverty, and that it is a paradox to claim that a country is achieving economic progress as long as the absolute extent [of poverty] . . . has not lessened or has even increased? . . .[T]he numbers of those living at the margin of subsistence or below, illiterate, diseased, undernourished, may have grown steadily con- sistently with a rise in the average income of the population as a whole. . . .
>
> Were I to insist, however, that the reduction of mass poverty be made a crucial test of the realization of economic development, I would be separating myself from the whole body of literature in this field.[175]

Viner went no further with this daring thought, but his question lights up ethical (and statistical) territory that the Bank was not exploring.

In fact, the Bank was reticent to examine what might be done for the poor even inside the technically aseptic bounds of aggregate output maximization. It did not go out of its way to look for projects that combined high rates of return with a faster spread of the incremental income beyond the project boundaries, or, for that matter, that worked through "trickle-up," nor did it discuss or advocate policies that could improve the distribution of benefits to the poor.

Perhaps the closest approach to such an effort consisted of a few encounters with regional allocation as an instrument for making growth work more directly for the poor. By and large, Bank projects were located in or served major cities and the more productive regions, or opened new areas for settlement, such as the Mag- dalena and Cauca valleys in Colombia. In Thailand, however, the Bank repeatedly emphasized the needs of the poor Northeast region, though it made few concrete proposals. It was not until 1962–63 that these urgings were translated into a mission whose main objective was to contribute to the solution of the Northeast problem, an initiative, however, that ended with a tragic helicopter accident that killed several members of the mission.[176] In Brazil, the regional distribution of poverty was cited by staff in 1952 to justify a $15 million energy loan designed to serve the principal cities and their hinterland in Brazil's Northeast: "this is a backward area of Brazil . . . [where] raising the standard of living . . . [is an] urgent national necessity."[177] By contrast, most of the funds provided to Pakistan up to 1960 were

---

175. Jacob Viner, *International Trade and Economic Development* (Oxford University Press, 1953), pp. 99–100.

176. Mason and Asher, *World Bank since Bretton Woods*, p. 691.

177. Meeting of Executive Directors, May 26, 1950.

invested in the less poor western half of the country. Returning from a visit in 1958, Knapp noted: "I assume that we continue to regard West Pakistan power development as top priority, although I note it would be better if we could do more in East Pakistan."[178] One economist recalls:

> There were times when we felt painfully alone in our attention to income distribution. I well remember a trip to Ho and Bolgatanga in Northern Ghana (then the Gold Coast) in November 1952. The North was in sub-Saharan dry savannah belt and very poor, in contrast to the south, rich in cocoa, timber, gold, manganese and diamonds. And that is why we went. The northerners were ethnically different from the southern sophisticates, who, we discovered, had never been there and could care less.[179]

But early in the decade the Bank ventured into an explicit and dramatic effort to address poverty through regional allocation, in southern Italy. A modest, first loan of $10 million in 1951 to the Cassa per il Mezzogiorno was followed by six additional loans between 1953 and 1959. In all, $299.6 million was provided to support the regional development efforts of the Cassa. Receiving the proposal for the first of these loans, the Board was told that regional trickle-down was ineffective in Italy: Industrialization in the north would benefit only the north, with very little positive effect for the south.[180] This spark of heresy fell on damp ground; the Mezzogiorno loans remained an isolated initiative. Arguably, attention to regional poverty in an already industrialized country was not a precedent for countries in which the great majority lived in crushing poverty. Also, the loan was spurred by political urgency, created by postwar fears of a communist electoral victory in Italy. However, it may have been the personalities involved that most effectively shut the door on precedent. President Luigi Einaudi of Italy, a respected professor of economics and personal friend of Rosenstein-Rodan, had written Black to say how glad he was that so knowledgeable a person as Rosenstein-Rodan was available to handle the loan, a hint that Black preferred not to ignore.[181] Rosenstein-Rodan's involvement produced an innovative loan design, the "impact loan," especially in its program character and regional poverty focus, but the design had to be imposed on Garner and, in any case, was probably too idiosyncratic for the 1950s institution.

Other instruments that might have improved the distribution of project benefits at no (or little) cost to growth, such as the sectoral allocation of investment, or more poor-friendly standards and technologies, seemed to be even further from the

---

178. Mason and Asher, *World Bank since Bretton Woods,* p. 669.

179. Letter, King to Webb, November 1993.

180. Meeting of Executive Directors, August 21, 1950. Paul Rosenstein-Rodan argued, however, that the failure of income to spread was not symmetrical; though income would not spread from north to south, it would flow in the opposite direction, from south to north, as investment in the south created purchasing power and demand for goods from the north.

181. Rosenstein-Rodan, Oral History, 1973, p. 12.

Bank's ken. Lending to social sectors was off limits, while agriculture was less bankable than energy, transport, and industry, leaving the Bank little leeway on the sectoral side. Taking stock of its unimpressive record on agriculture, the Bank pointed out, rightly, that roads, ports, and railways provided support to farmers and helped make agriculture more efficient.[182] On the other hand, the Bank's "project" concept, which favored large-scale investments and high engineering standards, made it difficult to support feeder roads.[183] Whether or not the Bank was missing an opportunity to alleviate poverty more rapidly by not steering its own funds to regions and sectors in which output gains might accrue more directly to the poor, depends, of course, on the extent to which those funds were fungible in borrower budgets and balances of payments. Because the Bank's financial image was built on the idea of the specific project, it would have been contradictory to defend its lending policy on grounds of fungibility, even if, in private conversation, Bank officials might reject a borrower's request for housing and hospital finance saying, "our funds are substitutable," as Larsen had replied to a South American government.[184]

The Bank could have sidestepped fungibility by encouraging governments to allocate their overall national budgets in directions more favorable to the poor, and by assisting borrowers in the search for such opportunities. In fact, an even more frontal attack on poverty, through redistribution, had been hinted at in the 1950 annual report and in statements by Black and Garner. In practice, however, the Bank was inhibited from any such course by its dependence on the conservative financial community, and by its own professional conviction that, for the poor, patience was the best rule; redistribution would reduce savings, while "a rising tide lifts all boats." Also, in the polarized ideological climate of the 1950s, even mild reformist proposals were politically suspect, so that, for instance, the Bank found it difficult to work with governments that had conspicuous redistributive programs, such as Guatemala under Arbenz and Ceylon under the Sri Lankan Freedom Party. Beyond the allocation of its own funds (which, in any case, may have been fungible), the Bank of the 1950s lacked the prestige and financial weight to press governments further in the direction of poverty alleviation than they were already set to go, as the Bank must have known in some uninhibited corner of its mind.

Nonetheless, the Bank was carried in the direction of poverty lending during the decade. This happened, for the most part, because the institution evolved into a suitable instrument for that purpose, and because a need for development instru-

182. IBRD, Memorandum from the Secretary, R-759, document submitted to the U.S. Senate Banking and Currency Committee, December 30, 1953, p. 73.

183. As argued by OED's 1970 study on Colombia. According to the report, "The Bank never considered this type of impact in its appraisals in a formal way." IBRD, Operations Evaluation Division, *Bank Operations in Colombia: An Evaluation,* Report Z-18, May 25, 1972, p. 62.

184. Alter and others, Oral History, July 1961.

ments arose out of the changing nature of the cold war. And indirectly, by its perceived success, the Bank probably contributed to the expansion of aid flows to poor countries through other institutions.

By the mid-1950s both the Soviet Union and the United States had come to believe that their survival depended in large measure on "winning" the third world. One implication, according to John Foster Dulles, was the need "to make political loans and 'soft' loans on a long term basis."[185] Against conservative objections to soft lending, Dulles argued, "It might be good banking to put South America through the wringer, but it will come out red."[186]

Black had been one of the conservative objectors to soft loans from the moment the idea was first mooted at the beginning of the decade. He argued that "loans of this kind are . . . part loan and part grant. They . . . are not always apt to be regarded as serious debt obligations. Like all other 'fuzzy' transactions, they therefore tend to impair the integrity of all international credit operations."[187] At the end of the decade he objected to the growing linkage between development aid and cold war objectives:

"Diplomats and military strategists [who] offer economic aid in exchange for a military alliance or a diplomatic concession . . . are certainly not serving the interest of orderly economic development; in fact they may well be abetting and perpetuating conditions which in a short time will render their military alliances and diplomatic concessions quite hollow victories."[188] Such arguments had little force against the rising sense of emergency. Early in 1956, Dulles stated that "East and West are in a contest in the field of development of underdeveloped countries. . . . Defeat . . . could be as disastrous as defeat in the arms race."[189] Black and his colleagues were caught up in a political tide that lifted the volume and urgency of development aid during the last years of the Eisenhower administration. Poverty in underdeveloped countries came into sharper focus; the arguments for "patience" and reliance on economic growth were softened by an acceptance of the need for some social concessions, by which policymakers understood welfare-related investments, in housing, water supplies, health services, and education; and, because it was to be run by the Bank, Black changed his mind on "fuzzy loans," agreeing in 1959 to the creation of IDA, though, to put some distance between IDA and the IBRD, he at the same time insisted that IDA loans be called "credits."

When the Eisenhower administration finally moved to escalate economic aid to underdeveloped countries, between 1957 and 1958, the Bank stood out as a

185. Cited in Walter LaFeber, *America, Russia, and the Cold War, 1945–1992* (McGraw-Hill, 1993), p. 177.

186. Ibid., p. 177.

187. Black, "Some Considerations Affecting Foreign Aid," p. 7.

188. Eugene R. Black, Cyril Foster Lecture, Oxford University, March 3, 1960, pp. 12–13.

189. Clifton Daniel, ed., *Chronicle of the 20th Century* (Clifton, Mo.: J L International, 1992), p. 776.

plausible vehicle. As a multilateral institution, it softened both the reality and the appearance of political dependence for borrowers. And because voting was based on capital subscriptions, the United States could exercise a degree of control over the use of its contributions. Furthermore, the IBRD's businesslike model of international economic assistance, crafted above all by Garner, based on market rates, high project standards, supervision, project assistance, and borrower creditworthiness was widely perceived as genuinely productive by comparison with bilateral and United Nations aid, and in addition as relatively disinterested. The Bank of the 1950s provided an argument against American suspicion of governmental "assistance," magnified when it came to foreign governments. In fact, the Bank's perceived success as a quality lender helped to legitimize economic aid in general and thus to lighten the political burden of selling foreign aid to the American public. The U.S. government, moreover, was aware that its capital contribution was highly leveraged, first because other members provided about two-thirds of paid-in capital, and then through IBRD borrowing, which multiplied the volume of lending made possible by paid-in capital contributions (table 15-1). Hence, the Bank provided a relatively inexpensive mechanism, from the standpoint of the taxpayers, for foreign aid.

The most important—and ironic—consequence for the Bank was the creation of IDA. As a reward for being a tough and effective lender, it was offered soft funds. IDA greatly extended the Bank's capacity to assist the poorest countries, and to lend for social needs that, at the time, were considered less productive than economic infrastructure, and, often, not creditworthy by the standards of the IBRD. Though IDA free money was to play the lead role in carrying the Bank toward poverty alleviation, the Bank's success as a market borrower during the 1950s was to be an important factor.[190] That achievement, built as much on its image as a serious banker as on the U.S. government guarantee, and crowned in 1959 by a triple-A rating, allowed the Bank to borrow increasing amounts during the next two decades, multiplying its capacity to lend to poorer countries and poorer groups and vindicating Black's judgment that, if "the emphasis were put on . . . quality, the quantity would be forthcoming."[191] The United States quickly approved a capital increase in 1959 that gave the institution room for increased borrowing.

The Bank of the 1950s also provided a blueprint and an encouragement for the creation of regional and subregional multilateral development banks over the following decades, which, taken together, have probably meant a net increase in the overall supply of capital to poor countries. The first to be established, in 1959, was the Inter-American Development Bank, closely modeled on the IBRD, though

190. Free, that is, to the Bank. IDA terms were exceptionally soft for borrowers, but were nonetheless "credits."

191. Meeting of Executive Directors, July 11, 1950.

proposed, in part, as a reaction to the IBRD's lending policy, responding in particular to Latin American complaints that the IBRD was unwilling to finance agriculture and social overhead.[192]

Furthermore, in the course of its operations over this period, the Bank developed procedural tools that gave it the capacity, and to some extent, the inclination, over the following decades, to engage in poverty alleviation, as external circumstances and its own evolving priorities carried it in that direction. In the first place, with the growth in membership to thirty underdeveloped countries by 1960, the Bank acquired an exceptional degree of access and fund of experience regarding the poor countries (table 3-2), preparing it for a role as adviser and facilitator to the large number of new, poor nations that gained independence during the 1960s. Also, one of the Bank's more important instruments for leveraging and influencing assistance to poor countries, the consultative group, had been pioneered with the India Aid Consortium in 1958.

Of particular importance as future "steering" devices, when the institution later sought to channel growth toward the poor, were two operational features of the 1950s' Bank. One was the specific investment project; another, the evaluation of a borrowers' overall development program. The two worked as complementary instruments, the Bank's yin and yang of intervention. Whether through project specifics or through the grand design of economic policy, the Bank involved itself in the borrower's whole economy, and, increasingly, identified its own objectives with the borrower's overall performance rather than with the results of specific projects. In either case, the Bank was honing tools that would be needed for the inherently interventionist business of poverty alleviation within countries. When the Bank launched a war on poverty in the 1970s, it would do so principally through exercises on the project keyboard—their allocation across sectors, regions, and types of borrowers—and by redesigning other project specifics. When it reemphasized poverty alleviation in the late 1980s, it would place greater stress on the policies, institutions, and overall structure of public expenditures that made up a borrower's development program.

192. And indeed, over its first decade (1960–69), the Inter-American Development Bank allocated 51 percent of its lending to agriculture and the social sectors. By contrast, the IBRD assigned 3 percent over the 1950s and 17 percent over the 1960s to those sectors.

FOUR

Approaching the Poor, 1959–1968

FROM THE approval of the first credit granted by the International Development Association in May 1961 to the end of the decade, before Robert McNamara's agenda began to make its imprint, Bank operations moved a long way toward the poor. If the primary thrust of lending continued to be economic growth, and, in that way, poverty reduction, Bank operations also became more poor friendly. For the most part, this came about simply because the Bank phased out lending to developed countries. But it was also the result of a broadening of the Bank's portfolio. The Bank began to lend increasingly for activities where its money and advice were more likely to provide direct benefits to poorer groups within borrowing countries. More generally, the Bank reshaped itself during this period in ways that shortened the distance to future, more radical attempts at poverty alleviation.

The new poverty orientation was principally a matter of its choice of customers. Although the International Bank for Reconstruction and Development continued to do business with high-income countries such as New Zealand, total Bank Group lending in Europe, Australia, New Zealand, and Japan dropped from 43 percent of commitments in the 1950s to 21 percent over 1961–69, and to only 7 percent during 1968 and 1969.[1] By contrast, and with the help of IDA, one-third of total

1. See tables 3-1 and 4-1, which show development lending before and after the start of IDA, up to the McNamara presidency. Table 3-1 covers the period through April 1961, before the first IDA credit in May 1961. Table 4-1 covers the period from May 1961 to June 1969 (fiscal year 1969) and is based on the assumption that loan commitments made during McNamara's first year (fourteen months) largely reflect lending decisions and preparation carried out under Woods.

Table 4-1. *IBRD and IDA Lending, 1961–69*[a]

Millions of U.S. dollars

Borrower[b]	Number of borrowers	IDA	IBRD	Total
Total	93	2,217	7,219	9,436
High income	16	15	1,644	1,659
Middle and low income[c]	77	2,201	5,575	7,776
Middle income	43	354	4,113	4,467
Low income	34	1,847	1,462	3,309
India	1	1,044	405	1,449
Pakistan	1	413	375	788
Power and transportation	68	852	3,593	4,445
Agriculture, education, and water	49	604	941	1,545

Source: World Bank data.

a. Commitments from May 1, 1961, the date of the first IDA credit, through June 30, 1969.

b. The following list of borrowers, by income group, shows total borrowing by country (in millions of U.S. dollars). High-income countries: Australia 100, Austria 5, Denmark 25, Finland 142, Greece 13, Iceland 20, Ireland 15, Israel 82, Italy 100, Japan 495, New Zealand 103, Norway 25, Singapore 99, South Africa 45, Spain 188, and Taiwan 203. Middle-income countries: Afghanistan 9, Algeria 21, Argentina 321, Bolivia 24, Botswana 4, Brazil 366, Cameroon 31, Chile 128, Colombia 444, Congo 31, Costa Rica 39, Côte d'Ivoire 23, Cyprus 35, Ecuador 31, El Salvador 31, Gabon 20, Guatemala 28, Iran 211, Iraq 23, Jamaica 53, Jordan 12, Korea 113, Malaysia 194, Malta 8, Mauritius 7, Mexico 607, Morocco 86, Panama 4, Papua New Guinea 9, Paraguay 33, Peru 137, Philippines 142, Portugal 58, Senegal 23, Swaziland 10, Syria 9, Thailand 206, Trinidad and Tobago 49, Tunisia 99, Turkey 176, Uruguay 31, Venezuela 298, and Yugoslavia 287. Low-income countries: Benin 5, Burkina Faso 1, Burundi 3, Central African Republic 4, Chad 6, Ethiopia 103, Ghana 63, Guinea 66, Guyana 12, Haiti 0.4, Honduras 43, India 1,449, Indonesia 51, Kenya 63, Kenya/Tanzania/Uganda 22, Lesotho 4, Liberia 8, Madagascar 26, Malawi 28, Mali 9, Mauritania 10, Nicaragua 30, Niger 8, Nigeria 214, Pakistan 787, Sierra Leone 8, Somalia 9, Sri Lanka 16, Sudan 101, Tanzania 62, Togo 4, Uganda 29, Zaire 6, Zambia 53, and Zambia/Zimbabwe 8.

c. As defined in *World Debt Tables, 1992–93,* p. 154.

lending over the 1960s was allocated to India and Pakistan, two of the world's poorest and most populous nations, while the number of smaller low-income borrowers jumped with decolonization, especially in Africa (table 4-1). The original sense of the Bank's name changed; by 1969 the "World Bank" had become a bank for poor countries. Likewise, "development" no longer meant any expansion in the world's physical productive capacity, regardless of location. When the Bank used the occasion of its twentieth anniversary to reflect on its purpose, stating that its principal continuing mission was to assist the development of "the economically less developed countries," it was clearly referring to poor countries, not the un-developed resources of an Australia or Norway.[2] "Development" had acquired a morally discriminatory sense, becoming a near synonym for poverty alleviation across countries, that is, for raising poor countries toward the income levels of the rich.

The Bank also moved closer to poverty by diversifying the sectoral allocation of its credits. It increased the share of agriculture and opened its doors to education, urban water supplies, and sanitation. Loans to agriculture—the overwhelming source of livelihood of the poor—rose from 2 percent of pre-IDA development

2. World Bank, *Annual Report, 1965–1966,* p. 5.

Table 4-2. *Sectoral Allocation of IBRD and IDA Lending, 1961–69*[a]
Millions of U.S. dollars

Sectors	IDA	IBRD	Total
Agriculture	395	764	1,159
Education	152	92	244
Finance	40	768	808
Industry	7	327	333
Mining	0	85	85
Nonsector[b]	29	0	29
Power	141	2,555	2,696
Program lending[c]	555	0	555
Telecommunications	119	158	277
Transportation	714	2,372	3,086
Water supply and sanitation	66	99	165
Total	2,218	7,220	9,437

Source: World Bank data.
a. May 1, 1961, through June 30, 1969.
b. Technical assistance and commercial vehicle import credits.
c. Industrial import credits to India and Pakistan.

lending to 11 percent during the 1960s, and reached 20 percent in the last two years of the decade (table 4-2).[3] Education and water received only 4 percent between 1961 and 1969, but a much larger allocation was in the pipeline of projects in the stages of identification, appraisal, or negotiation. Support for development finance companies grew rapidly as well, creating a lending mode that would later become an instrument for targeting benefits to the poor, especially small farmers.

Whether Bank credits actually resulted in higher domestic spending on agriculture, education, or clean water is perhaps impossible to determine, since Bank funds may have substituted for other sources of financing in the fiscal and foreign exchange accounts of borrowers. Moreover, the growth of these more poverty-related sectors was far from being a guarantee of faster or more direct poverty reduction. In fact, the first beneficiaries of most of these lending initiatives were better-endowed farmers, a handful of secondary school students, and relatively well-off urban residents. Nonetheless, in agriculture the Bank was becoming engaged in an activity in which a large, if not overriding, share of output was produced and owned by relatively poor households. And in education it was creating productive assets with an egalitarian potential.

Finally, the Bank's finances, procedures, and concepts changed in ways that made poverty lending easier and that prepared the organization for even further movement in the direction of poverty in subsequent decades. The reshaping was largely pushed on the Bank from the outside, most directly by the creation of IDA, but also by the less visible force of ideas and social pressures that accompanied the

3. See chapter 8 on lending for agriculture and rural development.

political and conceptual emergence of "underdevelopment," understood as international inequality. Internally, the Bank found room to adapt to those external forces, as financial constraints were relaxed early in the decade, as George Woods succeeded Eugene Black in the presidency, and as the institution matured, bringing greater confidence and flexibility and an increasingly diversified staff.[4] Though Black, Woods, and later Mc-Namara each affirmed in turn that the Bank was a development agency, not a bank, this formulistic characterization rang truer in the 1960s than the 1950s. By the end of the 1960s, the institution was far readier to countenance the proposition that would be advanced by McNamara and outside critics that it should and could do more for the poor than promote economic growth—and counsel patience.

Even as it approached the poor in these ways, however, the Bank strained to remain and to appear to remain the same hard-nosed 1950s institution: one that focused on creating the conditions for national economic growth, lending only for highly vetted projects that promised a direct payoff in increased production, in countries where macroeconomic policies gave confidence of repayment, while shutting out considerations of distribution and relative poverty within borrowing countries. In particular, it insisted that IDA was intended for productive, not "social" or "soft" projects. Over the 1960s the Bank was largely successful on both fronts; it preserved the operational standards and procedures that it had developed during the 1950s and protected its image as a quality lender.

Indeed, the Bank appeared to turn a deaf ear to the steady demands from borrowers and a burgeoning aid community for a softer attitude to social needs. It seemed to ignore even the parting, somewhat revisionist reflections of Robert Garner, the man most responsible for the institution's strict character. His 1961 farewell address, mentioned above, contained some second thoughts: "Feudal society, with wealth and power in the hands of a few . . . must disappear if there is to be economic progress. . . . So I put high on the list of public policy positive efforts to see that the benefits of growth be spread widely."[5] Garner, moreover, was echoing doubts that had begun to arise in the U.S. foreign policy establishment. Undersecretary of State Douglas Dillon, for instance, speaking to the Senate Foreign Relations Committee in the aftermath of Fidel Castro, had pointed to the distributive failure of previous development efforts: "While there has been a steady rise in national incomes throughout [Latin America], millions of underprivileged have not benefitted."[6] Yet, despite its professions of business as usual and unbend-

4. See chapter 18.

5. Robert Garner, address to Board of Governors of the International Finance Corporation, *Summary Proceedings, 1961 Annual Meeting of the Board of Governors*, September
21, 1961, Vienna, Austria, pp. 7–8.

6. Cited in Milton S. Eisenhower, *The Wine Is Bitter: The United States and Latin
America* (Doubleday, 1965), p. 249. From 1961 to 1965 Dillon served as Kennedy's secretary
of the Treasury. Through his strong support for expanded foreign economic aid and for the
creation of IDA, Dillon also had a major impact on the Bank's future.

ing manner, the institution was in fact being transformed. Pulled by political and intellectual currents, its operations drifted toward the poor over the 1960s.

Enter "Underdevelopment"

From the beginning of the cold war through the late 1950s, a moving spotlight played over the countries that bordered China and the Soviet Union. A central tenet of Western foreign policy was that communism should be contained within its borders and, after 1950, that the burden of that policy should shift from Europe to the poorer rim nations, running from Turkey and Iran through Pakistan and India to Indochina, Taiwan, Korea, and the Philippines. Containment was pursued through a mix of military alliances and intervention, large-scale military and economic aid, and special diplomatic effort. Little of this attention, least of all economic aid, spilled over to other parts of the developing world; as late as 1960, the United States was allocating only about 2 percent of that economic aid to Latin America, and less to Africa.[7] The Bank, conversely, seeking both financial safety and policy leverage, by and large avoided the rim, with the major exceptions of India and Pakistan. But as the 1950s ended, floodlights began to illuminate the larger stage of the third world. One after another, hitherto obscure nations claimed international notice. Even more, "the developing world" became an entity in itself, a concept that began to influence foreign policy and institutional responses in richer countries. Economic development emerged as a shared global enterprise, linking poor countries that had little in common but poverty, and tying rich and poor through the mutual need for security and a growing sense of moral obligation.

For the most part attention followed the widening course of the cold war. The idea of a clearly defined "Free World," with its implied notions of a "rim" and "containment," was thrown out of focus in 1955 with the creation of a nonaligned movement at the Bandung Conference. Between 1956 and 1958 attention turned to the Middle East, drawn by nationalist coups and leftward turns in Egypt, Iraq, and Syria between 1956 and 1958, and dramatized by the dispatch of marines to Beirut and by alarm over oil supplies. In 1958 the focus shifted to Latin America, where Vice President Richard Nixon was met by stone-throwing mobs, jolting U.S. complaisance about the southern neighbors. Months later, the region was demoted by the National Security Council: "Latin America is and must be dealt with primarily as an underdeveloped area."[8] This was a minor prelude to the alarm that followed Fidel Castro's victory and slide into communism during 1959. The rim had suddenly skipped to America's backyard. Shortly after, the United States

---

7. Stephen G. Rabe, *Eisenhower and Latin America: The Foreign Policy of Anti-communism* (University of North Carolina Press, 1988), p. 135.

8. A National Security Council statement (NSC5902/1) setting out the rationale for foreign assistance, approved by Eisenhower on February 12, 1959. Quoted in ibid., p. 12.

intervened in an attempt to depose Castro in Cuba, and Rafael Trujillo in the Dominican Republic, while the United Kingdom rigged elections in British Guyana to block a Marxist candidate, Cheddi Jagan.[9] Most of Africa became a contested area of the cold war, as nationalism and socialism converged in the independence movement. The breakdown of Belgian control over the Congo and French control over Algeria raised fears that colonial administrations would be replaced by nationalist and leftist regimes, as in fact had occurred with Sékou Touré in Guinea.

The broadening geography of the contest brought a shift in foreign policy, from localized containment of communism to generalized competition for political allegiance, accompanied by efforts to forestall communism through economic and social development. A university textbook on development economics began: "The Cold War is not going very well for the western world. Soviet or Chinese influence is infiltrating into many of the undeveloped countries, in Asia, Africa, and Latin America."[10] There was a greater readiness to engage in military combat, but also an expansion and diversification of economic assistance. Moreover, engagement across a wider front placed a premium on the political and diplomatic character of aid giving, favoring regional, consortium, and multilateral arrangements. But it was not only security that drew attention to the poorer countries and that helped to produce a surge of collective awareness and commitment in the cause of development. Much was a response to evolving ideas and perceptions.

From small beginnings after World War II, information on the developing countries had grown into a flood, fed by a surge in the number of scholars and organizations devoted to development, assisted by air travel, given scientific weight by the multiplication of statistics (especially censuses), and distributed to the general public through a mushrooming network of print, radio, and television. Writings on development became voluminous. Viner's 1953 remark that "literature on 'economic development' has in recent years reached massive proportions," became a refrain over at least a decade, as each annual crop of development authors was newly impressed by the explosion in his or her field.[11] Development

9. Robert A. Packenham, *Liberal America and the Third World: Political Development Ideas in Foreign Aid and Social Science* (Princeton University Press, 1973), pp. 75–81.

10. Stephen Enke, *Economics for Development* (London: Dennis Dobson, 1963), p. vii. In 1962 Barbara Ward, arguing for more development assistance, similarly pointed out, "We should realize soberly that the world-wide struggle is not necessarily 'going our way.'" Ward, *The Rich Nations and the Poor Nations* (W. W. Norton, 1962), p. 134.

11. Introduction to a lecture, "The Economics of Development," delivered by Viner in 1950 at the National University of Brazil. Jacob Viner, *International Trade and Economic Development: Lectures Delivered at the National University of Brazil* (Oxford: Clarendon Press, 1953), p. 94. A. N. Agarwala and S. P. Singh introduce *The Economics of Underdevelopment* (Oxford University Press, 1963), with a reference to the "enormous proportions" of the "fresh literature" (p. 3). According to Bank economist J. H. Adler, "In the first years of the decade of the 1960s an unprecedented outburst of intellectual interest in the

studies continued to blossom in the 1960s, sustained by the excitement of discovery as well as political and humanitarian urgency. Surveying the scene in 1962, a historian noted, with unabashed ethnocentricity, "It is only today that it has become possible . . . even to imagine a whole world consisting of peoples who have in the fullest sense entered into history," a revealing if unintended testimony to the revolution in Western perceptions.[12] Black had used almost identical words a year earlier: "Even today the bulk of Africa's more than 200 millions are only beginning to enter world society."[13]

Discovery arrived with optimism: an increased belief in the possibility of widespread and rapid development and in the efficacy of outside intervention to bring about that development. The first students of the underdeveloped areas, looking from a Western perspective, had been struck by cultural differences and had been quick to see in those differences "obstacles" to development. The field became highly interdisciplinary, drawing anthropologists, sociologists, and political scientists, along with economists. Its principal journal, established at the University of Chicago in 1953, was named *Economic Development and Cultural Change*. Economists dabbled in sociology to explain economic stagnation. Hindu reverence for cows became a popular symbol, a shorthand, to explain the historical failure of "primitive" or "backward" peoples to achieve material progress. Max Weber was rediscovered, and his indictment of Catholicism seemed doubly applicable to the otherworldliness of Eastern religions.[14] Religion, institutions, and other cultural differences were boiled down to a societal "lack of will," the missing prerequisite for progress.[15] The 1950 *UN Report on Development* noted that, "economic

---

process of economic development occurred. It produced an avalanche of studies, new concepts and new methods of analysis." Adler, "The World Bank's Concept of Development—An In-House *Dogmengeschichte*," in Jagdish Bhagwati and Richard S. Eckaus, eds., *Development and Planning: Essays in Honor of Paul Rosenstein-Rodan* (MIT Press, 1973), p. 41.

12. E. H. Carr, *What Is History?* George Macaulay Trevelyan Lectures, delivered at Cambridge University, January–March 1961 (Alfred A. Knopf, 1962), p. 199.

13. Eugene Black, "Tale of Two Continents," Ferdinand Phinizy Lectures, delivered at the University of Georgia, April 12 and 13, 1961, reprinted in *The Diplomacy of Economic Development and Other Papers* (Atheneum, 1963), p. 87. Nathaniel McKitterick, speechwriter to Black and Woods, downplayed the input of both presidents. Instead, McKitterick made "copious use of individuals within the Bank," and he saw the speeches less as personal statements than as "the public record of the head of the Bank." Nathaniel M. McKitterick, interview, World Bank Oral History Program, July 24, 1985, pp. 1, 2.

14. This argument is now turned on its head by Mahn-Je Kim, a leading economic adviser in South Korea during the 1960s and 1970s, who attributes Korea's economic success to Confucianism. See chapter 2 in volume 2 of this history.

15. IBRD, *Annual Report, 1950–1951*, p. 15. Similarly, the United Nations report, *Measures for the Economic Development of Under-Developed Countries* (New York: UN, May 1951), considered that "some governments have not any *adequate will* to develop. . . . The part of the world most afflicted with this is probably the Continent of Africa, some of

progress will not be desired in a community where the people do not realize that progress is possible."[16] The Bank was echoing this (Anglo-American) common wisdom when it thought necessary to affirm, in 1951, "The people of a country must have a purposeful desire to develop their human and natural resources."[17] Its first Survey Missions had sought at least partial explanations for economic back-wardness in social and cultural features. In Guatemala, it was the "cultural isolation and the defensive attitude of the Indians"; in Cuba, "unconstructive attitudes"; in Ceylon, a lingering caste system and "conservative pressure [of] religious forces"; and in Jamaica, a "lack of energy and cooperation."[18]

By the 1960s, however, development economists seemed to have brushed aside these sociological cobwebs. Optimism was buoyed by the postwar economic boom, including strong growth rates in many Latin American and African nations (table 4-3). Per capita growth in the developing world was less striking, owing to population growth, but even those figures were high by historical standards. The Marshall Plan and the Tennessee Valley Authority had caught the popular imagina-tion as demonstrations that economic development could be engineered. John Kennedy heightened the activist mood, using his inaugural speech to "pledge our best efforts" on behalf of "those people in huts and villages of half the globe," and proposing that economic aid be increased, separated from military aid, and com-mitted for several years.[19] Faith in the deus ex machina powers of technology and science was high, reinforced by the space race, and by news of medical and agricultural breakthroughs.[20] Though population growth had accelerated with

---

whose governments are too proud to borrow for colonial development" (p. 83, emphasis added). W. Arthur Lewis devoted the first substantive chapter of his *Theory of Economic Growth* (London: George Allen and Unwin, 1955) to "The Will to Economize." But anthropomorphic metaphors pretend to more than is really understood about collective behavior. A society whose members are all brimming with a "will to develop" may nonethe-less stagnate if the interaction between individuals causes those energies to cancel out.

16. United Nations, *Measures for the Economic Development of Under-Developed Countries*, p. 13.

17. IBRD, *Annual Report, 1950–1951*, p. 15.

18. IBRD, *The Economic Development of Guatemala*, Report of a Mission (1951), p. 7; IBRD, *The Economic Development of Jamaica*, Report by a Mission (Johns Hopkins University Press, 1952), p. 7. Another explanation of poverty was hot climate. Barbara Ward argued in 1962: "Nor is the climate of tropical regions precisely designed for work. When the temperature rises to ninety degrees and the humidity to ninety per cent, you do not feel like rushing out and solving one of the first problems in Euclid. Even less do you want to cut a tree—favorite occupation of Victorian gentlemen." Ward, *Rich Nations and the Poor Nations*, pp. 39–40.

19. The Kennedy administration made the development process "sound a little too easy," according to Arthur Schlesinger, *A Thousand Days: John F. Kennedy in the White House* (Houghton Mifflin, 1965), p. 588.

20. Improved corn and wheat varieties, developed by an international agricultural re-search center (Centro Internacional de Mejoramiento de Maiz y Trigo, CIMMYT) located in Mexico and initially financed by the Rockefeller Foundation, helped Mexico become self-

Table 4-3. *The Postwar Boom: GDP Growth Per Annum 1950–68*[a]

Countries	1950–59	1959–68
OECD	5.5	4.5
Less developed	4.7	5.0
Africa	4.2	3.2
Egypt	4.6	5.7
Kenya	3.5	4.6
Nigeria	3.7	4.9
America	4.8	4.8
Brazil	5.5	4.7
Colombia	4.6	4.8
Mexico	6.1	6.8
Peru	4.4	6.0
Asia	4.3	5.2
India	3.3	3.3
Pakistan	2.5	5.5
Philippines	5.6	5.4
Thailand	4.4	7.6
Europe	6.2	7.1
Turkey	5.2	5.5
Yugoslavia	7.5	6.9

Sources: OECD countries: OECD, *National Accounts of OECD Countries,* 1970; less developed countries: Development Centre, OECD, *National Accounts of Less Developed Countries,* 1968 and 1970; these figures cover 114 countries and territories for 1950–59 and 121 countries and territories for 1959–68.

a. Annual compound growth rates weighted by GDP.

medical breakthroughs, the cyclical outbreak of Malthusian fears was interrupted over much of the 1950s and early 1960s in the face of rising world food production and even a growing concern for food surpluses.[21] Drawing lessons for the development cause, Andrew Shonfield affirmed in 1960 that "peoples do not differ so drastically as to make the deliberate application of science to the massive production of wealth . . . possible for one [people] and impossible for the other."[22] In 1966 John Adler, director of the World Bank's Economic Development Institute, used the tenth anniversary of that teaching center to ask, "What Have We Learned about Development?" "The most important lesson," he wrote, is that "the poverty of

sufficient in grains by 1958. J. George Harrar, *Strategy toward the Conquest of Hunger: Selected Papers of J. George Harrar* (New York: Rockefeller Foundation, 1967).

21. Fred Sanderson, "The Great Food Fumble," *Science,* vol. 188, no. 4188 (May 9, 1975), p. 503; and Thomas Poleman, "World Food: A Perspective," *Science,* vol. 188, no. 4188 (May 9, 1975), pp. 510–13. For the postwar years, Sanderson and Poleman find major outbreaks of pessimism in the late 1940s, mid-1960s (1965–66 India droughts), and 1973–75 (USSR crop failure; rising world food prices).

22. Andrew Shonfield, *The Attack on World Poverty* (Random House, 1960), pp. xi–xii. Shonfield was a widely read financial journalist for the *London Observer.*

nations is not preordained and immutable. . . . As a result economists concerned with development have become 'activists.'"[23]

For the most part, activism meant more money. Economists were coming to see development more and more as a direct function of physical investment. Seduced by the mathematical conceit of the Harrod-Domar family of growth models, and using fresh concepts that bristled with a sense of financial urgency—big push, vicious circle, balanced growth, take-off, and two-gap models—economic doctrine was increasingly in harmony with the foreign policy need for rapid and large-scale responses to the spreading security emergency.[24] Doctrine converged as well with the unflagging message of the domestic and borrower aid lobby, that the developing countries needed and were capable of absorbing more aid. Official reports on aid written in the late 1950s reflected this convergence, expressing increased confidence in the absorptive capacity of developing countries, and in the efficacy of economic aid and once-over reforms.[25]

In rich countries, the moral faculties were stimulated by the new visibility and "nearness" of the poor, and by their own passage into affluence.[26] Charity or obligation alone would have produced little in the way of development assistance; even the historical, cultural, and wartime closeness of Britain had failed to move Congress to approve an emergency postwar loan to that nation until it was persuaded by Soviet threats in Europe and Iran. And when Paul Hoffman, former head of the Marshall Plan, congratulated Dwight D. Eisenhower for his aid advocacy, he drew

23. John H. Adler, "What Have We Learned about Development?" *Finance and Development*, vol. 3, no. 3 (September 1966), pp. 159–60. According to Davidson Sommers, "Our vision of what was possible grew as our vision of what the reality was became clearer. . . . Americans didn't have either the advantages or disadvantages of being colonial administrators. They had a political and social sympathy with developing countries. [Black and Woods's] disadvantage of local Wall Streetism was joined by the advantage of the American idea that change is possible and desirable. . . . [A]ll of us after World War II, up until at least 20 years later, were fairly idealistic." Davidson Sommers, interview, World Bank Oral History Program, July 18, 1985, p. 15.

24. The concurrence extended to ideology and funding links. According to David Wise and Thomas B. Ross, *Invisible Government* (Bantam Books, 1964), the MIT Center for International Studies, which pioneered much of the new doctrine, received financing from the Central Intelligence Agency (CIA). With U.S. support, Harvard social scientists were deeply involved in Pakistan. Kennedy later drew on both universities to create a foreign policy staff.

25. The most notable were Max F. Millikan and W. W. Rostow, *A Proposal: Key to an Effective Foreign Policy* (Harper and Brothers, 1957); William H. Draper, chairman, *Composite Report of the President's Committee to Study the United States Military Assistance Program* (Washington, D.C.: August 17, 1959).

26. See John Kenneth Galbraith, *The Affluent Society* (Houghton Mifflin, 1958). Galbraith, however, argued that affluence was *reducing* concern for inequality in the United States. But concern for poverty increased. An influential study was Michael Harrington, *The Other America: Poverty in the United States* (Macmillan, 1962).

attention to Eisenhower's choice of words in justifying aid. Eisenhower had called aid an "investment for peace." "Semantics are important," said Hoffman, and he "could think of no two words that handicap a program more than *foreign* and *aid.*"[27]

Yet domestic affluence and foreign visibility were on the increase, suggesting that newly prompted sentiment did in fact increase the quotient of sincerity in the term "foreign aid" and thereby reinforcing the case for development assistance as a means to national security, access to resources and markets, and, in the case of former colonial powers, the rescue of some degree of imperial glory. Moreover, the moral argument probably helped to sustain large annual foreign aid appropriations as the national self-interest case became stretched by the increasing number and dispersion of recipients. This reinforcement was needed over the second half of the 1960s and early 1970s, when escalation in Vietnam and enlarged domestic social expenditures combined to strain the U.S. budget.[28]

The role of sentiment was boosted by the redefinition of poverty as hunger, and then, in the mid-1960s, as a "food crisis." The case for the existence or imminence of large-scale hunger was argued repeatedly through the two postwar decades, mainly on the basis of independent calculations, by the Food and Agriculture Organization and the U.S. Department of Agriculture, of food "balances" and nutritional availabilities in relation to requirements. Those figures, showing large food deficits and nutritional inadequacies in the underdeveloped countries, were used to support notions of overpopulation, imminent food shortages, and social collapse. For most of the period, such arguments made little impression on the prevailing optimism, and later estimates produced more moderate "deficits." But, the "food crisis" acquired powerful credence in 1965 with the onset of a two-year drought in India (see chapter 8).[29] Its plausibility, moreover, was increased by the

27. Blanche Wiesen Cook, *The Declassified Eisenhower: A Divided Legacy* (Doubleday, 1981), p. 314.

28. In the early 1960s foreign aid continued to be preponderantly American. For a study of American foreign aid, see Robert A. Packenham, *Liberal America and the Third World* (Princeton University Press, 1973). After noting the difficulty of separating real determinants of aid from "sheer rhetoric," Packenham concludes, "At no time was all economic and technical assistance principally used for developmental ends; during . . . most of the fifties and the latter half of [the] sixties . . . security ends were dominant" (p. xix).

29. The case for a "crisis" was strengthened even before 1965 by a slowdown in Indian agricultural growth from 1958 to 1964, and by a resurgence of political concern for rural poverty in India during the preparation of the Third Plan. Revised—and higher—estimates of Indian population growth added to the concern. A more skeptical explanation for the crisis atmosphere is suggested in the briefing for Woods before the September 1964 Annual General Meeting: "Nehru's death [and the] indisposition of his successor Lal Bahadur Shastri, have created an atmosphere of political uncertainty and confusion which very likely has something to do with the current food 'crisis.'" World Bank, "India Briefing Paper," August 12, 1964, p. 9. According to Poleman, "World Food," pp. 510–11, both FAO and U.S. Department of Agriculture figures overestimated food and nutritional deficits, especially in the 1950s. He suggests that both agencies had political objectives:

emergence in those same years of the conservationist movement in the rich countries, which, though it spoke principally to a domestic audience, drew attention to population growth, soil erosion, depletion of fisheries, desertification, and other environmental changes that were part of the concern for food adequacy.[30]

Aid rhetoric came into its own when Kennedy moved from Eisenhower's defensive, containment stance in the cold war to a more aggressive call for American leadership: "I ask you to join with me in a journey into the 1960s, whereby we will mold our strength and become first again."[31] Shifting the rhetorical weight a degree, from interests to values, Kennedy appealed to America's sense of mission, melding obligation with self-interest in a "development cause." Where Eisenhower had strained to persuade others, including his conservative Secretary of the Treasury George Humphrey, of the security benefits of economic as against military aid,[32] Kennedy raised the debate to one of more transcendent issues— America's leadership and "way of life"—a shift that permitted a more comfortable foreign policy embrace of the development cause. Kennedy's tinge of missionary imperialism, with its implied burden, strengthened aid advocacy. At the same time, American development aid motivations became more similar to those of the colonial powers, especially France and Britain.

National and international programs and organizations to provide development assistance were set up to respond to underdevelopment. There were two bursts of institution building. The first, from 1945 to 1950, saw the ratification of the Bretton Woods Agreement, the creation of most of the United Nations system, and the establishment of bilateral aid agencies in the United States, Britain, and France.[33]

one of the USDA's was to strengthen the case for U.S. farm price supports, and the FAO's was to lobby for foreign aid.

30. Environmental awareness and protective legislation—aided by Rachel Carson's *Silent Spring* (Houghton Mifflin, 1962)—grew rapidly over the decade. The year 1970 saw the creation of the Environmental Protection Agency (EPA) in the United States, and the celebration of the first Earth Day.

31. Campaign speech cited in David Farber, *The Age of Great Dreams* (Hill and Wang, 1994), p. 28. Kennedy was alluding to the post-Sputnik perceptions of a U.S. lag in the space race and in missile strength: the "missile gap."

32. Clarence Randall, Eisenhower's special consultant on foreign economic policy, speaking to the National Association of Manufacturers, also noted that "our own domestic economy requires the world for its market," but though "the entire world must buy American products . . . the others have nothing with which to balance their trade budget." Eisenhower thus mobilized business and media support—especially through C. D. Jackson and Henry Luce of Time-Life for a "Foreign Economic Policy Battle Plan." Cook, *Declassified Eisenhower*, pp. 312–13.

33. American bilateral aid, easily the largest program for over two decades, was dispersed over several agencies and was subject to almost continuing change in organization and terms of reference. Its core, the Economic Cooperation Administration, created in 1948 to administer the European Recovery Program, evolved into the Mutual Security Agency (1951), the Foreign Operations Administration (1953), the International Cooperation Administra-

The Food and Agriculture Organization was created in 1945. The International Monetary Fund and the Bank opened in 1946, along with the United Nations Children's Fund and the United Nations Educational, Scientific, and Cultural Organization.[34] The United Nations family expanded over 1947 and 1948 to include two regional organizations, the Economic and Social Council for Asia and the Pacific (ESCAP), and the Economic Commission for Latin America (ECLA), and another specialized agency, the World Health Organization. Though the regional and specialized agencies of the United Nations were designed to play a nondiscriminatory, global (or regional) role, in practice most evolved into development institutions, directing their principal efforts to poorer countries. This happened rapidly in the case of those agencies governed by one-country, one-vote rule, and more gradually in the case of the Bank and the IMF. The first program designed with a truly third world objective was Truman's Point Four program, which appeared in 1949, but its funding was less than 1 percent of aid flows at the time. The year 1949 also saw the establishment of the United Nations Expanded Program of Technical Assistance (EPTA), and the Overseas Committee of the Organization for European Economic Cooperation (OEEC). Finally, the Colombo Plan was launched in 1950.

In 1956 the International Finance Corporation was created to augment the World Bank's lending powers in the private sector, but with that exception, institution building was interrupted for much of the decade. The already established United Nations agencies, however, put increasing emphasis on promoting development in poor countries and took on an advocacy role in North–South redistributive politics.

The "second day" in the creation of development institutions occurred between 1958 and 1962.[35] The Development Loan Fund was added to U.S. bilateral assis-

---

tion (1955), and the Agency for International Development (1961). An important separate arm was the Export-Import Bank, which, though established in 1934, took on new life in 1945 with sizable increases in its capital and borrowing authority. Its direction moved from European relief and reconstruction to the support of rim countries, and then to the economic development of poorer nations. Aid was largely economic in 1946–51, military in 1952–56, and increasingly economic again in 1957–68. Except for the Marshall Plan (1949–52), two-thirds of aid over 1946–68 consisted of soft loans and one-third grants. France set up FIDES in 1945. Britain approved the second Colonial Development and Welfare Act the same year; it was first approved in 1940.

34. The International Labor Organization was a prewar creation of the League of Nations.

35. George Humphrey, who as secretary of the Treasury had resisted efforts to increase economic aid, resigned in April 1958. And, referring to economic aid, "once Humphrey resigned, Eisenhower told Dulles to run with it." Cook, *Declassified Eisenhower,* p. 320. The administration as a whole was by then convinced of the security argument for broader assistance to developing areas. Urgency was added in 1958 by the world recession and its sequel of balance of payments crises in much of the developing world, and also by cold war events in the Middle East.

tance in 1958. The European Investment Bank (EIB), including its developing country window, the European Development Fund, the United Nations Economic Commission for Africa (ECA), and the first informal aid coordinating effort, the India Aid Consortium, also made their appearance in 1958. The next year saw the creation of the Inter-American Development Bank and the Special United Nations Fund for Economic Development (SUNFED). Institution building continued in 1960 with the establishment of IDA; the Canadian International Development Association (CIDA), Canada's bilateral aid agency; the metamorphosis of the OEEC into the Organization for Economic Cooperation and Development, which included a development secretariat; the related creation of the aid-coordinating Development Assistance Group (DAG), which in 1961 became OECD's standing Development Assistance Committee (DAC); and a second country aid consortium, for Pakistan. Momentum continued in 1961 with bilateral arrangements, the Kuwait Fund, a Ministry of Cooperation in both France and Germany, a Swiss cooperation service, and Japan's Overseas Economic Cooperation Fund (OECF), and also with multilateral arrangements, and, within the IDB, a soft-window Social Progress Trust Fund. Another initiative in international aid coordination was the Interamerican Committee for the Alliance for Progress.[36] The development institution edifice was largely completed by 1962, with the establishment that year of bilateral organizations in Belgium, Denmark, and Norway, OECD's Development Centre, and the first consultative group in Nigeria. Institution building continued at a slower pace after the 1958–62 burst of activity, with the notable additions of the African Development Bank in 1964 and the Asian Development Bank in 1966.

Although early postwar agencies—the bilaterals, Bretton Woods, and other United Nations agencies—had no clear mandate to help develop poor countries, but drifted in that direction through the 1950s and 1960s, the second group, created over 1958–62, were almost entirely dedicated to that function from birth. In the space of little more than a decade, between the mid-1940s and late 1950s, a previously unheedful world became intensely conscious of international inequality. The global map was redrawn around two new axes, the East–West political divide, and the fault line between rich and poor nations.

"Underdevelopment" was brought into the scene by the cold war, intellectual discovery, and moral feelings. But its lasting power owes much to institutionalization; the concept became embedded in the official development institutions, which consisted of a large number of bilateral and multilateral organizations that, by

36. The establishment of this Committee followed Kennedy's highly publicized offer of $20 billion in public and private funds to support Latin American economic development and social reform. A committee of "Nine Wise Men" to review and endorse national development programs and aid requests was replaced in November 1963 by a unit operating under the Organization of American States, the CIAP (Interamerican Committee for the Alliance for Progress).

original design or later adaptation, set out to remedy an unacceptable, uneconomic, and dangerous fact of international life. Civil society also responded through a plethora of organizational and private acts of assistance, motivated at times by religious and political agendas, and often by spontaneous charity. Above all, it was at the intellectual and official levels that underdevelopment installed itself as a way to categorize the world and define international relations. The word was made flesh. The new organizations became standing reminders of international inequality. More actively, because they thrived in proportion to public awareness of and concern for the development problem, bureaucratic self-perpetuation became a mechanism that reinforced and propagated the North–South division.

At one level, "underdevelopment" signified no more than the bare statistical fact of inequality. At another, the concept was charged with implications. It connoted security risk and a redistributive obligation, and both notions acted to legitimize intervention by "the aid community" in the affairs of the underdeveloped. Furthermore, the strong early association of underdevelopment with the spheres of national security and international politics lent an air of urgency to subsequent policy response and suggested that governmental institutions should be involved and that large financial transfers were needed. For several decades the "development effort" had empowered governments, as compared with civil society; had encouraged governments to rely on money as a solution rather than on qualitative inputs such as institutions, policies, attitudes, and organizational capacities; and had repeatedly tripped over its own impatience. At the same time, the recognition that relative poverty *between* countries was a compelling criterion for public action, though prompted more by fear than obligation, gave force to moral attitudes (if not necessarily to morality) as an element in international relations. The issues of poverty, inequality, and human rights *within* countries arrived a decade later, on the coattails of poverty *between* nations, but, as a weak echo, lacking a strong identification with national self-interest.

Through the 1950s, the Bank was by and large insulated from this evolving context by its financial and managerial autonomy, and its relative smallness.[37] Some adaptations were made during 1958 and 1959, in the form of rudimentary aid coordination, several emergency balance of payments loans, and increased lending. But it was the establishment of IDA in 1960 that breached the institutional walls, bringing the Bank face to face with a redefined, revitalized development mission, now charged with political urgency, a larger cast of characters, and a strong association with poverty.

37. Gross disbursements by IBRD in 1956 reached $166 million, barely 5 percent of the $3,316 million in loans and grants disbursed to underdeveloped countries by other public and multilateral sources that year. And in 1961, on the eve of IDA, the figures were $434 million, 7.5 percent, and $5,768 million, respectively. See World Bank, *World Debt Tables*.

IDA Yeast

When the U.S. proposal for an International Development Association arrived at the Bank in July 1959, Secretary of the Treasury Robert B. Anderson had already cleared the idea with prospective donor governments. Bank officials, notably Davidson Sommers and Richard Demuth, had worked informally with Treasury personnel. In its broad outline, IDA was a fait accompli. But the proposal was silent on allocation. It fell to the Bank to decide for whom and for what the money would be used. This question stirred the institution for several years.

The IDA Charter

A first round of debate took place as staff and executive directors drafted a charter for submission to the Board of Governors in January 1960. But the Charter was not the last word. Debate continued in part because, in drafting the Articles, the institution chose ambiguity as a way to protect its managerial prerogative and lending practices. "Questions could be ducked by having the charter in broad general terms," suggested Sommers in a staff discussion. And "he hoped that the charter would be left quite unprecise. . . . The good things in the [IBRD's] charter were the vaguenesses."[38] However, there was another reason why debate was not closed with the Charter: the drafting decision to leave the door open coincided with a change of season.

From the beginning, senior Bank staff and executive directors agreed on the guiding principle for absorbing IDA: repayment terms would be soft, but project and policy requirements would not. Eligibility for IDA financing would be determined not by the particular character of a project, but by a borrower's balance of payments, specifically, by a lack of "IBRD creditworthiness," that is, a lack of foreign exchange to meet repayments on IBRD market-based lending terms. IDA would lend to borrowers who showed the necessary capacity to make profitable use of the funds but were constrained by large external debts or weak export prospects. India and Pakistan were very much on the collective mind. In October President Black said to delegates at the closing session of the Bank-IMF annual meetings: "This pledge I give you. . . . IDA will not be a 'soft lender.'"[39]

To make good on his pledge, however, Black would have to face several challenges. One was that IDA had been conceived as a substitute for SUNFED and it carried the genes of its third world and United Nations parentage. The debates

---

38. Davidson Sommers, cited in IBRD, "Rough Notes of Staff Loan Committee Meeting," SLC/M/760, August 11, 1959, pp. 2, 7. Sommers made a similar recommendation on the question of IDA's ability to make equity investments: "It would be easier if the matter was left vague and each country told its own story to its legislature" (p. 4).

39. IBRD, IMF, IFC, "Verbatim Report of the Closing Joint Session. . . ," 1959 annual meetings, Board of Governors, Washington, D.C., sess. no. 2, October 2, 1959, "Remarks of Eugene R. Black. . . ."

regarding the SUNFED proposal were a ten-year history of developing-country and aid-lobby demands for expanded, softer, less conditioned development assistance, frequently of the "social," "program," and local currency kind. Failing to make SUNFED disappear, the United States had decided to try cooptation. Richard Demuth, reporting to Bank colleagues on his informal conversations with U.S. officials, explained that IDA "was not a U.S. affirmative program," but "a desire to assuage Congress" and "to keep off SUNFED."[40] Concessions to the original goals of SUNFED might therefore be required to achieve those political goals, particularly since third world representatives in the Bank's Executive Board and Board of Governors would have a say, if not a meaningful vote, in the outcome. Further ahead, IDA raised two pitfalls. First, the continual need for replenishments would increase political pressures on allocation, as Sommers noted at the first Staff Loan Committee discussion of the U.S. proposal.[41] More insidious was the danger within: where IBRD lending had been disciplined by dependence on the market, rigor in IDA lending would depend on self-discipline. Many staff members, restricted to unadventurous power and transportation projects and champing at the developmental bit, would be aware that IDA had loosened their Wall Street reins.

Much of the allocation debate centered on "social" lending. In discussions with Demuth and Sommers before the official proposal was submitted in July, the U.S. administration had not insisted on an explicit commitment on this issue. The Bank knew, however, that political expectations transferred from SUNFED to IDA included social lending and that the United States felt pressed to satisfy those expectations to some degree. The proposed Inter-American Bank Charter, for instance, on its way to approval in December 1959, enjoined that institution to lend for social overhead.[42] Indeed, by Eisenhower's later account, the emphasis on IDB's social mandate was less a sop to populist Latin American regimes, as Sommers seemed to suggest, than a deliberate reformist intervention by the United States. The decision to proceed with the IDB, wrote Eisenhower,

> was highly significant. Traditional unilateral aid was sustaining a prevailing social order which was unjust to the masses of the people, but we could do nothing directly about this without violating the policy of non-intervention in the internal affairs of other nations. The creation of the new bank changed this, for now the Americas had a multinational instrument, secure against control by any one country, for bettering the life of people throughout the Americas; if this instrument insisted upon social reform as a condition of extending development credit, it could scarcely be charged with "intervention."[43]

40. IBRD, "Rough Notes of Staff Loan Committee Meeting," SLC/M/760, p. 3.

41. Sommers said: "IDA exposed us to more Congressional scrutiny." Ibid., p. 7. He further noted that its creation "posed some dangers to the Bank. We would be supplicants to the Governments for money." IBRD, "Rough Notes of Staff Loan Committee Meeting," SLC/M/7624, September 3, 1959, p. 3.

42. IDB, *Articles of Agreeement,* art. I, sec. 2(v).

43. Dwight D. Eisenhower, *Waging Peace: 1956–1961* (Doubleday, 1965), p. 516.

Demuth communicated this heightened political urgency, telling the Staff Loan Committee in August that "there would be a lot of pressure for IDA to go into social projects." But Sommers foresaw "a good deal of eyebrow-lifting about the Bank getting into soft lending."[44] When the Committee returned to IDA in September, there was little hint of willingness to adapt:

> *Mr. Sommers.* Bank projects should be the normal field of IDA projects but others should not be excluded. Municipal waterworks and sewerage systems might be somewhat unusual. Health and educational projects would not be excluded by name but would not be likely to be financed.
>
> *Mr.* [William] *Iliff.* What was SUNFED to have done?
>
> *Mr. Sommers.* Social overhead projects. No one agreed on what these were. . . . He felt that a good deal of talk about financing social overhead was just atmosphere and would not be pressed hard except perhaps in the case of waterworks.
>
> *Mr.* [Dragoslav] *Avramovic.* What about education?
>
> *Mr. Sommers.* [I]t would be most difficult for an international organization to get embroiled in this. . . .
>
> *Mr.* [Raymond] *Cope.* It was more a question of words. We should give a strong hint that IDA would not lend in the social field, without excluding it.[45]

Two weeks later management summarized its position to the Board: "IDA's financing would be largely concerned with directly productive projects of the type normally financed by the Bank, but . . . social projects would not be excluded. We would prefer to avoid any reference to health and education projects."[46]

IDA's country allocation was less controversial. The chief question concerned the eligibility of "Dependent Overseas Territories." Though Britain and France were pressing for the inclusion of colonies, several staff members objected. Peter Cargill noted that "if the U.K wanted to step up development in the U.K. colonies it could afford to do so." Eugene Black felt that IDA loans to colonies would be tantamount to "siphoning major portions of [IDA] subscriptions back to the metropolitan countries."[47] This objection was extended by Cope to "the wards of the U.S., e.g. Korea." The point was developed by Burke Knapp: "Were there not cases in which countries were sufficiently established as wards of the U.S., to be treated paramountly as colonies[?]" Sommers qualified this, noting that Black thought that, "while IDA would only be able to invest in Korea and Viet-Nam on a

44. IBRD, "Rough Notes of Staff Loan Committee Meeting," SLC/M/760, p. 7.

45. IBRD, "Rough Notes of Staff Loan Committee Meeting," SLC/M/7624.

46. Staff Loan Committee memorandum, "Management Position on IDA," SLC/0/1018, August 26, 1959, draft, p. 3.

47. Comments by Cargill, in IBRD, "Rough Notes of Staff Loan Committee Meeting," SLC/M/7624, p. 2. Sommers's position was again in favor of vagueness, but "there would have to be very special justification for IDA loans to [colonies]." IBRD, "Rough Notes of Staff Loan Committee Meeting," SLC/M/760, p. 1.

token basis . . . it would be helpful to the Bank and to these countries occasionally to have relations with the Bank instead of having them all with the U.S."[48]

As yet, relative poverty (per capita income) had not been mentioned as a basis for allocation among developing countries. Sufficient unto the day, perhaps, was IDA's abrupt cleavage of Bank membership into rich and poor, and the restriction of IDA eligibility to the latter. Reasoning from the principle that IDA existed only for debt-capacity reasons, Bank staff referred to relatively rich countries such as Argentina and Venezuela as possible borrowers when IDA eligibility was first discussed. But circumstances were already shepherding the Bank toward poverty-based allocation, using per capita income as an allocative criterion: from its origin as a basis for the North–South division, per capita income was later extrapolated to decide allocation within the South.

One circumstance was the pro-India inclination of IDA's management. Indeed, the Bank wished to embrace IDA in part because it saw that India was reaching debt-repayment limits for IBRD borrowing. In addition, India's planning and administrative reputation ensured a supply of bankable projects. "India could take up any amount" of IDA, said Knapp. Though a per capita criterion justified a substantial allocation to India, Board and borrower pressures were pulling in the direction of a broader geographic distribution. In this context, the relative income criterion came to the assistance of management, providing a rationale for the lion's share assigned to India and a defense against the demands of other developing countries, particularly those in Latin America whose advocacy had been instrumental in the founding of IDA, and who now objected as they saw the fund being stolen from under their noses.[49]

More generally, IDA created a need for rationing. Thus, Cope noted, "We had got to contrive artificial alternatives to the creditworthiness limits we used now." At this stage, however, as staff members met in late 1959 to ponder the implications of IDA, they went no further toward a relative income criterion than Knapp's statement that there was "a gap" within the less developed areas, and that IDA's "emphasis would be on the more undeveloped countries."[50]

After this initial positioning by Bank management, the debate shifted to country representatives. At the Annual Meeting, from September 29 to October 1, third-world governors chose to assume that IDA would lend for "projects not normally covered by Bank lending," for "nonrevenue-producing schemes," and for local currency costs.[51] The governor for Ecuador proposed that IDA "should have in

48. IBRD, "Rough Notes of Staff Loan Committee Meeting," SLC/M/7624, p. 4.
49. The creation of the Inter-American Development Bank, however, reinforced the per capita and extreme poverty arguments for favoring India.
50. IBRD, "Rough Notes of Staff Loan Committee Meeting," SLC/M/7624, pp. 2, 3.
51. IBRD/IDA/IFC Press Release 48 and 71. Remarks at Third Session of the 1959 Annual General Meetings by Abdel Magid Ahmed, governor for Sudan, and K. A. Gbedemah, governor for Ghana, October 1, 1959.

mind the social conditions of the people," and lend for "housing, school buildings, education of the masses, public health and sanitation [which] have a major and fundamental effect on . . . economic development."[52] In his closing remarks Black sought to quell these expectations, but his effort was undermined by the U.S. delegate, Douglas Dillon, who, alluding to IDA, welcomed the "opportunity to broaden further the lending facilities available to the Bank so that it may play its part more effectively in the historic struggle of man against poverty and disease." More pointedly, Dillon suggested that "high technical standards" in IDA projects would not rule out "financing pilot projects in some fields of social overhead."[53] Following the meetings, the debate was transferred to the Board's Financial Policy Committee, which was composed of all the executive directors but which provided a less formal arena for discussion without voting.

In the Financial Policy Committee, a forceful advocate for social lending by IDA was Jorge Mejia-Palacios, executive director for Colombia, who was supported by the directors for Canada and Australia. The Canadian, Louis Rasminsky, held that "IDA should be free to venture into fields that the Bank could not properly venture into, such as social projects."[54] Mejia's most telling argument was that "there are some operations the Bank does not undertake, not for lack of legal authority, but because of considerations related to its need to borrow in the market."[55] Mejia also offered the prescient observation that, to the extent that "IDA was motivated by political rather than economic considerations . . . social projects were more important than economic ones [because] it would be easier to sell the idea to the parliaments."[56]

On the other side, the directors for Germany and the Netherlands, Otto Donner and Pieter Lieftinck, respectively, were adamant in supporting the management position, namely, that IDA and IBRD lending should not differ other than in their terms of repayment. Donner, presumably with newly independent nations in mind, even rejected the idea that IDA could be used to assist particularly weak countries: "There might be countries which are not viable at all economically, so that even if they follow sound practices, they cannot be brought to a situation in which they can stand on their own feet. Such countries . . . would present a political rather than an economic problem, and . . . should [not] be a matter for IDA."[57] But T. Graydon Upton, the U.S. director, reminded his purist colleagues: "Mr. Dillon had said at the Annual Meeting

52. IBRD/IDA/IFC Press Release 67. Remarks at Third Session of the Annual General Meetings by Isidro Ycaza Plaza, governor for Ecuador, October 1, 1959.

53. Statement by the Honorable C. Douglas Dillon, undersecretary of state and alternate governor of the Bank for the United States, at the discussion of the Bank's annual report, September 30, 1959.

54. IBRD, "Memorandum of Meeting of Financial Policy Committee," IDA/5911, October 26, 1959, p. 4. The citation refers to the paraphrased version in the memorandum.

55. IBRD, "Memorandum of Meeting of Financial Policy Committee," IDA/599, p. 9.

56. IBRD, "Memorandum of Meeting of Financial Policy Committee," IDA/5911, p. 4.

57. IBRD, "Memorandum of Meeting of Financial Policy Committee," IDA/599, p. 6.

that pilot projects in the field of social overhead might be appropriate for IDA," and though "the United States would emphasize productive projects of an economic character [it] recognizes the strong interest on the part of several countries in the financing of the so-called 'social projects.'"[58] The final proposal sent to member countries in January and ratified in September stated, with suitable vagueness, that IDA financing would be available for purposes "of high developmental priority."

Commenting on the Articles, Black said, "We can do what we want. The charter of IDA gives the management and staff the right to do almost anything."[59] Black was exaggerating. In fact, the Board had compromised between the competing tugs of financial and political criteria, using the device of an "Accompanying Report of the Executive Directors" to the proposed Charter to interpret the Articles of Agreement and narrow the room for managerial discretion. On allocation, the attachment explained first that colonies would be eligible along with "less-developed member countries." Second, it allowed that a project could be of "high developmental priority" even though it was not "revenue-producing or directly productive." Thus, "projects such as water supply, sanitation, pilot housing and the like are eligible . . . although it is expected that a major part of the Association's financing is likely to be for projects of the type financed by the Bank."[60] Third, clearly broadening the intent of the Bretton Woods stricture that Bank lending should be only for specific projects, except "in special circumstances," the Accompanying Report stated that, in addition to the window provided by special circumstances, IDA was to interpret the words "specific projects" "to include such proposals as a railway program, an agricultural credit program, or a group of related projects forming part of a developmental program."[61] The Accompanying Report device helped protect the Bank's financial image by keeping the Charter clean of any reference to social projects. At the same time, management was licensed to use IDA in ways that would indeed depart from established practice. These could include allocative experiments; lending that, though "productive," did not have the "directly productive" or "revenue-raising" character that best enhanced the IBRD's financial rating; and financing for packages of projects that blurred the distinction between project and program lending.

The staff and Board debates on allocation had an additional, if less direct "loosening" effect on Bank lending policy. One director questioned the implicit association between "social" and "unproductive" and suggested that it was the short- or long-run nature rather than level of productivity that was at issue.[62] The

58. Ibid., pp. 11–12.

59. Cited by James H. Weaver, *The International Development Association: A New Approach to Foreign Aid* (Praeger, 1965), p. 100.

60. IDA, *Articles of Agreement and Accompanying Report of the Executive Directors of the International Bank for Reconstruction and Development*, p. 3.

61. Ibid., art. V, sec. 1 (b), and paras. 13–15, p. 3.

62. Comment by Carlos Brignone, executive director for Argentina, in IBRD, "Memorandum of Meeting of Financial Policy Committee," IDA/5911, afternoon session, p. 5.

director for Malaya, Ismail bin Mohamed, developed this point by noting that in many countries technical and professional skills were a bottleneck to development. Other code words of the 1950s Bank were questioned—such as "high priority," "sound project," "program and project lending," "inability to borrow," and "directly productive"—and thus began a dialectic that would help open the door to a more flexible lending policy.[63]

Early IDA Lending

As they awaited formal ratification by the governors, the staff began to draft operational rules for IDA. Despite the Accompanying Report, the Bank's official position remained that IDA lending would not differ from that of the IBRD, and that IDA's reason for being was related to debt-servicing capacity, not to the nature of the investments to be financed. Speaking to a meeting of the Economic and Social Council of the United Nations in April, Black objected to the picture of IDA, painted by some journalists, as a "lady of easy virtue," though admitting that IDA's easier terms gave it "feminine virtues of sympathetic understanding and helpfulness."[64] Seeking to dampen expectations, he pointed to Africa's lack of absorptive capacity: "Until the human resources of the new African nations are more fully developed . . . the opportunities for the wise and effective utilization [of credits] will necessarily remain limited."[65]

But the genie had been let out of the bottle; institutional debates and decision-making were broadening out and rapidly diverging from the Bank's starchy self-image. A meeting of the Loan Committee in June 1960 saw a lively, freewheeling discussion of lending options for IDA.

> *Mr. Knapp.* . . . Training schemes, land settlement, and agriculture were better than water supply, sanitation, and housing. . . . He would prefer to do things in rural areas.
>
> *Mr. Demuth.* It seemed appropriate for IDA to help clean up health menaces.
>
> *Mr. Knapp.* Improvements in the water supply just removed one of the limits to crowding in the cities. . . . With water supply projects one would get into local politics. . . . What would IDA do in India? The Bank had not got far into food supply, agricultural development and village projects there. Why shouldn't IDA assist in these in India?

63. Mejia-Palacios noted that "inability to borrow" from the IBRD, proposed as a criterion for IDA access, "was often not inability at all but reluctance of the lending institutions to lend." See IBRD, "Memorandum of Meeting of Financial Policy Committee," IDA/599, p. 7.

64. Eugene R. Black, address to 29th Session of the Economic and Social Council of the United Nations, New York, April 7, 1960, p. 9.

65. Ibid., p. 11. Black's argument was double edged: it provided a rationale for lending for education. Phillip W. Jones, *World Bank Financing of Education: Lending, Learning and Development* (London: Routledge, 1992), p. 34, cites this speech as a recognition by the Bank of the developmental need for education, at least in Africa. However, at this time, Black did not suggest Bank financing for education.

Mr. Rosen. . . . These would be just as messy for IDA.

Mr. Knapp. IDA had that missionary function.

Mr. Rosen. It would not be fair or possible for IDA to finance where the Bank had not been prepared to go for doctrinal reasons.

Mr. Demuth. How could we expect the same people to be crusading and adventurous in the case of IDA and not so in the case of the Bank?

Mr. Knapp. . . . IDA would press the Bank plus IDA into undertaking more things.

Mr. Rosen. . . . The Bank had made a mistake in not undertaking water supply projects in the past. They were just as important as those for the supply of electrical power. . . .

Mr. Demuth. If IDA did nothing but Bank projects there would be a revival of support for the establishment of SUNFED.

With regard to country allocation:

Mr. Knapp. . . . [P]rincipal priority should be given to the poorer of the Part II countries. . . . Korea was a ward of the U.S. . . . We should save our fire for cases that were more meaningful.

Mr. Demuth. . . . Korea and China [Taiwan] should be eligible if a good project came along, but . . . keep the amount low.

Mr. Knapp. Lending by IDA to colonial territories was a very dubious proposition. If IDA financed African wards of France and the U.K., it might just as well finance wards of the U.S. . . . The Committee expected . . . not to have IDA pick up the white man's historical burden.[66]

The shaping of IDA lending policy continued during 1960 and 1961, at times through the discussion of general issues, such as lending for water supply and guidelines on local currency and cost sharing, but also through the accumulation of ad hoc responses to specific situations that were presented to the Bank. Many of the credit proposals that arrived at the Loan Committee's desk appeared to be stamped "Urgent."

A sense of emergency surrounded the first proposal for an IDA credit discussed by the Loan Committee, for a project in Jordan. The Loan Committee had found Jordan uncreditworthy in February 1958: "The country's solvency depends on aid. . . . But where next year's grants will come from is by no means clear. . . . We are not even prepared to hold out [hope] even in some remote future." The Committee refused to lend despite its own admission that "Jordan is clutching at the Bank as at a last straw."[67] Five months later, however, the Middle East was in a new crisis; a pro-Nasser army coup had overthrown the neighboring Iraq monarchy and crippled the Baghdad Pact. American and British marines were dispatched to support pro-Western regimes in Beirut and Amman, respectively. Twenty-one-year-old King Hussein of Jordan, beset by internal opposition and a large influx of Pales-

66. IBRD, "Rough Notes of Staff Loan Committee Meeting," SLC/M/6015, June 13, 1960, pp. 9–10.

67. Ibid., pp. 1–2.

tinian refugees, looked unlikely to survive. IDA provided the Bank with a way to assist, and in October 1960, weeks before IDA had opened for business, the Loan Committee considered a credit for water supply in Amman. The project was Amman's own top priority. There seemed to be no question regarding approval, despite the innovative character of the project; it was only a month later that the Loan Committee met to discuss lending for water supply as a general issue. The Jordan debate focused instead on whether precedents would be established, especially regarding cost sharing and the self-liquidating nature of the project. Admitting, in effect, that rules were being bent, Joseph Rucinski, director of South Asia and Middle East Operations, affirmed: "We were not setting general policies for the future of IDA but for the Jordan project only," while Knapp said, "In the case of IDA, we wanted to have general principles but we might strain them a little in a particular case."[68]

The process of accommodation was recorded in Committee minutes. One principle that gave way, for instance, required borrowers to contribute a substantial share—commonly half or more—of project costs.

> *Mr. Knapp.* The Bank's policy would be not to finance the whole. It would be unhealthy to give the projects to the municipalities as completely free gifts. . . .
>
> *Mr. Demuth.* This case was worrisome because it was the first IDA one and if we financed up to 90% of the total cost, we would have established a difficult precedent.
>
> *Mr. Knapp.* . . . IDA might be prepared to finance 70%. . . .
>
> *Mr. Rucinski.* If the municipalities were supported by the Federal Government [which] in turn, supported them from external aid, this would amount to window-dressing. . . . If the municipalities could raise 20%, would we still have 10% of window-dressing?
>
> *Mr. Knapp.* Yes. We should get anything in substance we could. . . .
>
> *Mr. Rosen.* It would then be a question of how much you scrutinized the Jordanian budget. There would be other cases similar to this in Korea, Viet-Nam, Laos, Cambodia, etc.[69]

Another principle was that "sound" projects should be self-liquidating; that is, they should generate enough revenues to cover project debt service. Here, too, the Committee considered a compromise.

> *Mr. [Walter] Armstrong.* We had been going on the basis that the Jordanian projects would have to be self-liquidating.
>
> *Mr. Demuth.* He questioned whether these projects had to be self-liquidating. It was not a necessary criterion that waterworks should be on what we would consider normally to be a sound financial basis.
>
> *Mr. Knapp.* He would hate to start . . . on the basis that they were not going to be sound. . . . IDA should be regarded as having a self-liquidating policy for its financing.[70]

68. Memorandum, Edward Symonds to files, "No Hope for Jordan—Staff Loan Committee Meeting," February 3, 1958.

69. IBRD, "Rough Notes of Staff Loan Committee Meeting," SLC/M/6030, October 21, 1960, pp. 1, 3.

70. Ibid., pp. 4–6.

It was eventually agreed that IDA would finance 70 percent of total costs, and "while part of the costs . . . might be met by an agency of a friendly Government . . . it was important that no more than 70% of the cost . . . be financed *explicitly* by foreign aid."[71] Later accounts, however, showed that local contributions, even when defined retroactively to include pre-project investments, financed only 6% of total cost.

Several of IDA's early loans were for projects in Latin America, another region in crisis during 1960. Honduras, Chile, Nicaragua, Colombia, Costa Rica, and Paraguay were all borrowers during IDA's initial two years of operation. These credits coincided with a more general turn of events; between 1959 and 1960, Latin America received the full benefit of Fidel Castro's revolution. The first effects had already appeared with the decisions to establish an Inter-American Development Bank and to surrender—after long resistance—to Latin American demands for commodity price stabilization; a coffee agreement was signed in September 1959. The aid momentum increased in early 1960, following Cuba's sweeping expropriations, its trade pact with the USSR, and Eisenhower's trip to South America. "Upon my return," he wrote, "I determined to begin . . . historic measures designed to bring about social reforms for the benefit of all the people of Latin America."

> Constantly before us was the question of what could be done about the revolutionary ferment in the world. . . . We needed new policies that would reach the seat of the trouble, the seething unrest of the people. . . . One suggestion was . . . to raise the pay of the teachers and start hundreds of vocational schools. . . . [We] had to disabuse ourselves of some old ideas . . . to keep the Free World from going up in flames.[72]

In April, Secretary of State Christian A. Herter informed the Pan American Union of a sharp change in American foreign policy toward Latin America, including a decision to support land reform. Dillon presented a new aid program to Congress in August, which called for $600 million in funding for soft loans by the Inter-American Development Bank and stressed social expenditures to contend with income inequality and outdated institutions, two serious impediments to progress. The bill was promptly enacted.

The perception of crisis in the region continued into 1961, and Kennedy escalated the response: "Next to Berlin it's the most critical area. . . . The whole place could blow up on us. . . . I don't know if Congress will give it to me. But now's the time, while they're all worried that Castro might take over the hemisphere."[73] In March 1961 Kennedy demanded action to avert chaos in Bolivia. His staff decided to "ignore proposals by both the International Monetary Fund and State Department that Bolivia needed a good dose of an anti-inflationary austerity, and instead

71. Ibid., p. 5. Emphasis added.

72. Eisenhower, *Waging Peace,* pp. 530, 537.

73. John F. Kennedy, cited in Richard Goodwin, *Remembering America* (Little, Brown, 1988), p. 147.

should offer immediate economic assistance. . . . Things were grim enough without calling for further sacrifice from those who had nothing to give."[74] A week later Kennedy announced the Alliance for Progress with Latin America, a ten-year program for cooperation and development, stressing social reform, with large-scale aid to countries that "did their part."

Midway through these policy developments, while Eisenhower was still president, southern Chile had suffered a severe earthquake. In his presentation to Congress, Dillon proposed that $100 million be earmarked for Chilean earthquake reconstruction.[75] The Bank first discouraged any idea that it could provide relief, citing macroeconomic problems, but a mission sent to Chile returned with a favorable report on Chile's creditworthiness and on the high quality of Chile's development projects for agriculture and feeder roads.[76] A month after the earthquake, in fact, Knapp had spoken of using IDA for a possible "show of sympathy."[77] Despite Chile's relatively high per capita income in relation to other developing countries, a "blend" (combined) IBRD-IDA loan, principally for road reconstruction in the earthquake-affected area, was approved in June 1961.

IDA's first credit, for a highway in Honduras, had been approved a month before. At this time, the Caribbean littoral was in turmoil, with U.S. officials alarmed over Castroite guerrillas in Colombia and Venezuela, and leftist movements in the Dominican Republic and Panama. Like Jordan, Honduras was the poorest country in its particular region, suffered from weak government, and appeared particularly open to subversion. When Eisenhower returned from South America in March, his new policies included "civic-action" programs that would involve the Latin American military in building dams and roads and in implementing other developmental projects. By the end of 1961, U.S.-financed engineering battalions were operating in Bolivia and Honduras and were preparing to go to Guatemala.[78] Outbreaks of violence in Costa Rica and Honduras occurred during a November 1960 Bank mission to Central America. Over the next five months the Bank rapidly selected and approved a project for the construction of a highway through the poorest and least promising region of Honduras, a highland area that bordered on similarly impoverished and densely populated highlands in Guatemala and El Salvador. Feeder roads into the poor countryside were to be added. The proposed road, a southern extension of the Western Highway that already served

74. Ibid., p. 153. In his speech Kennedy drew an analogy with the Marshall Plan.

75. Eisenhower, *Waging Peace,* pp. 537–38.

76. The road and agricultural projects had in fact been appraised and approved in 1956, but, for creditworthiness reasons, lending between 1958 and 1960 was limited to power. Despite the reappraisal, fiscal deficits and inflation remained high during the early 1960s. Memoranda: S. R. Cope to Burke Knapp, June 1, 1960; Knapp to files, June 13, 1960; Roger A. Chaufournier to Orvis A. Schmidt, August 19, 1960, with attached Report of Mission.

77. IBRD, "Rough Notes of Staff Loan Committee Meeting," SLC/M/6015, p. 2.

78. Rabe, *Eisenhower and Latin America,* p. 138.

richer commercial areas in northwest Honduras, had recently been appraised and turned down.[79] The Bank was clearly taking development to "the seat of the trouble," as Eisenhower had proposed, and was just as clearly breaking with the commercial and growth-oriented criteria that had steered the location of its transportation projects over the 1950s.[80]

The discussion of a proposed credit to Nicaragua revealed new stages in the evolution of IDA policy.[81] Staff now referred to relative income as an established allocative principle, comparing per capita income estimates for Nicaragua with those for recent borrowers Honduras and Sudan. Another innovation arose when a staff member objected that Nicaragua was creditworthy for IBRD borrowing. Management replied that the lack of creditworthiness, as a fundamental criterion for IDA eligibility, had been reinterpreted: IDA eligibility could be claimed as a preventive measure, if continued IBRD borrowing threatened to "use up" a country's borrowing capacity.[82] Finally, the proposed IDA credit raised a public relations issue related not to questions of financial creditworthiness, but to normative considerations. This arose when the Committee chairman announced that the Board would have to be informed that President Anastasio Somoza owned large holdings in the proposed irrigation project area.

> *Mr.* [Aron] *Broches.* I am told that the Somoza family is in everything and it would be difficult to find anything in Nicaragua which did not raise this problem.
>
> *Mr.* [Robert] *Cavanaugh.* I am concerned that we would appear to be fostering an arrangement under which people will be urged to sell land that the President wants. . . .
>
> *Mr.* [Simon] *Cargill.* If the project itself is satisfactory I don't believe that the interest of the President is such a problem that the whole thing should be held up. . . .
>
> *Mr. Rucinski.* I agree that it is too late to turn it down.
>
> *Mr. Aldewereld.* The problem of the land holding and Somoza ownership is an unfortunate one but it is one we have been aware of from the very start and I think it is too late to raise the question now.

79. Ibid., p. 147.

80. IBRD, "Appraisal of the Honduras Western Highway Extension and Supplementary Projects," Report TO(IDA) 2, May 3, 1961. A May 1958 Bank loan had financed the more commercially viable stretch of the Western Highway, from the port at San Pedro de Sula to Santa Rosa de Copan. Funds had been included to study the "Extension." However, "plans for the Extension were completed in 1959, but because of unexpectedly high cost estimates, the Government instructed the Consultants . . . to restudy the economic justification" (para. 8). But the IDA mission sent a year later asserted: "The project is technically sound, economically justified and necessary" (p. 11). The viability of the Extension was predicated on major complementary investments by the government, which, however, were not carried out.

81. In 1960, USAID completed an East-West Highway traversing the mountainous and poor northeast region of Thailand, a choice of route in which security reasons superseded economic grounds. Robert J. Muscat, *Thailand and the United States: Development, Security, and Foreign Aid* (Columbia University Press, 1990), pp. 97–98.

82. IBRD, "Rough Notes of Staff Loan Committee Meeting," SLC/M/6118, May 2, 1961.

Mr. Reid. . . . The large holdings amount to about a sixth of the irrigable property. This isn't anything like the situation in Dez [in Iran] where a few people owned the whole works.[83]

As they listed practical reasons for going ahead with the credit, the staff were ambiguous, stating the problem in terms of external image, yet seeming to argue against their own sense of propriety regarding the use of IDA funds.[84]

An IDA loan to Ecuador for farm credit caused the Loan Committee to take an unusually long, hard look at social and political issues in June 1961:

Mr. Knapp. Ecuador would appear to be the next country on the list to go "Fidelistic." . . . What is the political risk of the submerged Indians, representing half or two-thirds of the population, who are still completely out of the political and economic picture? . . .

Mr. [John] de Wilde. Ecuador has a good record. . . . [I]sn't [this] a strategic time for the agencies . . . such as the Bank to step into the picture . . . and . . . prevent a deterioration in the political situation?

Mr. Knapp. . . . That is the sort of salvage job that the U.S. must perform.

Mr. Broches. Where does Ecuador stand on the index of social injustices Mr. Kennedy has been referring to?

Mr. [Orvis] Schmidt. While there is great disparity in the distribution of wealth in Ecuador, this is less so than in other countries in Latin America. . . . The Indians up on the mountains are still quiet although the Government has not really been doing very much on their behalf.

Mr. Demuth. In looking at the Latin American feudal countries . . . to be realistic we must assume that revolutions are going to occur and only hope that the [new governments] will honor the obligations of former Governments. . . .

Mr. Aldewereld. Colonialism is certainly bad in Ecuador . . . even . . . worse than in the Far East. Something violent is going to happen. . . . I think that our projects do serve to relieve internal pressures. . . . I agree that we might consider more IDA money because of these political risks.

Mr. Knapp. . . . But political situations do lead to defaults.[85]

IDA also stirred the Bank with questions of sectoral allocation. IDA was to consider lending for water supply, raising the issue of consistency with IBRD's effective ban on such projects.[86] The rapid acceptance of Jordan's request for a water supply loan had already set a precedent. In October 1960 the staff began to discuss future policy toward loans for water supply, and by November 7 the

83. Memorandum, M. H. R. Jordan to Staff Economic Committee, "A Project in Nicaragua—Bank or IDA," April 12, 1961.

84. IBRD, "Rough Notes of Staff Loan Committee Meeting," SLC/M/6118, pp. 6–7. Dez was a multipurpose irrigation and power project in Iran, approved early in 1960.

85. This loan was prepared over the early months of 1961, coinciding with preparations in Nicaragua for the Bay of Pigs invasion on April 17. By May, as Rucinski said, the loan was "too late to turn down."

86. IBRD, "Rough Notes of Staff Loan Committee Meeting," SLC/M/6124, June 14, 1961, pp. 1–4.

Technical Operations Department (TOD) had submitted a draft policy statement to the Staff Loan Committee (SLC). The draft saw large potential benefits: "Few projects. . . incorporate as great a potential for directly benefitting the vast majority of the people . . . as does water supply improvement." Moreover, as Robert Sadove of TOD noted, water was an important industrial input and thus "not essentially different from electric power."[87] Nonetheless, the draft tried to discourage lending for water supply, citing large administrative difficulties in such loans and drawing a distinction between projects whose economic effects "extend considerably beyond . . . themselves" and the "lesser priority" of those that "merely alleviate hardships."[88] This position was disputed by Gerald Alter of the Western Hemisphere Department, who saw considerable justification in water projects.[89] In the SLC debate, Bank staff seemed to agree on two points. One, as stated by Knapp, was that though "there was no logical reason to make a distinction between the Bank and IDA in accepting water supply projects . . . there is a background of pressure for IDA investments in social projects."[90] The other was that the economic contribution of such projects would be difficult to establish, beyond Demuth's general supposition that "good water leads to better, more efficient labor," a view loosely supported by Leonard Rist's anecdote about an IMF colleague: "When Mr. Prasad went on home leave to Poona, he and all his family were sick. . . . Most everybody in [India] is sick at least one month out of every year from bad water." But, said Stevenson, the question was "whether water supply projects have a productive or a consumptive purpose." Martin Rosen noted that, in principle, measurement of the economic contribution of water supply was no different from that of feeder roads. Knapp, who chaired the Committee, remained reluctant: "Water is the first thing the people want but we have to distinguish between . . . amenities which raise the standard of living, and . . . projects which will benefit the economy. . . . Our emphasis should be on the latter." Senior staff seemed resigned to but unenthusiastic about water supply lending.

In the course of the November 1960 water supply discussion, Demuth mentioned: "Some countries think that education should be included in projects to be financed by IDA." Knapp dismissed the topic for the moment: "That raises another question entirely. That of the market for the Bank's obligations."[91] The Wall Street

87. In the Executive Board's "Accompanying Report" to IDA's Charter, as noted in this chapter, in the section "The IDA Charter."

88. Memorandum, Robert Sadove to S. Aldewereld and P. J. Squire, "The Bank's Policy Towards Municipal Water Supply Projects," October 5, 1960, pp. 4–5. Sadove became the architect of TOD's position on water supply.

89. Ibid., p. 2.

90. Memorandum, Gerald Alter to William Diamond, November 8, 1960. Alter's region (Latin America) began to receive substantial lending for water supply from the Inter-American Development Bank in 1960.

91. IBRD, "Rough Notes of Staff Loan Committee Meeting," SLC/M/6035, November 23, 1960, p. 9.

Bank was very much alive; and whereas "amenities" such as waterworks could at least claim to be revenue generating, in addition to having a capital-intensive similarity to the Bank's traditional work in infrastructure, both virtues seemed to be absent in the case of education. Nonetheless, as with water, the arrival of IDA was considered to imply the possibility, even probability, of lending for education. That same month, Knapp acknowledged that education was an investment but in effect ruled out Bank lending on the grounds that education was a subject for grants, not loans. That November, economic staff director Rist began to study the economics of education lending, particularly the criteria that could be used to measure the economic contribution of educational investments. In March 1961 he reported that technical schools provided suitable investment opportunities for both IDA and the IBRD, but he also made a case for the value of general basic education.[92] Staff members interviewed in July 1961 spoke about education lending with the same mix of resignation and reluctance that they had expressed about water supply loans. John de Wilde cautiously admitted, "We have now declared in principle that at least through IDA we might be prepared to look at some investments in these fields" but also stressed the Bank's comparative advantage, the inherent subjectivities of a soft sector, and the "politically very hot issues" that would be raised. Still, "[We] have our fingers crossed." Harold Larsen said, "We're going to try and find out quite quickly in the educational field. This is for the International Development Association, not the Bank."[93]

The biggest change wrought by IDA may have been the quietest: IDA smoothed the way for a transition from true "specific project" loans to program lending in its various guises. A large step in that direction had been taken during 1958–59 when the Bank responded to India's balance of payments crisis by rapidly disbursing project loans and by taking a leading role in the creation of the India Aid Consortium.[94] The crisis had persisted, however, and the Bank's continuing role in India was threatened by that country's high foreign debt and the Bank's own large exposure there. India's delegation to the Annual General Meeting in September 1959 was told to expect less from the Bank.[95] The appearance of IDA soft money at that point rescued the lending relationship and, in doing so, kept alive an experiment with program and consortium lending that was planted on good soil, being strongly legitimized by India's political priority, administrative respectability, and

---

92. Ibid., pp. 6–9.

93. Jones, *World Bank Financing of Education,* p. 38.

94. Gerald Alter, Harold Larsen, and John de Wilde, interview, World Bank Oral History Program, July 1961, p. 21.

95. See chapters 3, 9, and 10. The first meeting of the India Aid Consortium was called a "meeting on India's foreign exchange situation" and was seen as a rescue mission. Lending to richer countries was already markedly "program" in nature, especially the original reconstruction loans; the series of loans to Italy, Australia, and Japan; and the colonial loans to Belgium and the Congo. A program loan was also approved for Iran in 1956. With the Iran exception, however, loan decisions and disbursements for developing countries were tied to projects rather than to aggregate foreign exchange or fiscal needs.

extreme poverty. Furthermore, the Board had expressly relaxed the rule against program lending for IDA in its Accompanying Report to IDA's Charter.[96]

When the Staff Loan Committee met in September 1961 to review a proposed $60 million loan for an Indian coal project, it engaged in an uninhibited discussion of innovations in lending policy. With regard to the real nature of the loan, Knapp said: "I suggest that the words 'balance of payments loans' be deleted in the report, not because it's not true that this is a balance of payments loan, but because the word has come to have a derogatory sense." In addition, IDA was beginning to affect its sister institution, loosening IBRD discipline. Thus Rucinski argued that since the intended beneficiary of the loan was the government rather than the coal industry, the period of repayment to the IBRD should be lengthened, since "India's need for foreign exchange is so important that in considering our lending it outweighs other considerations." Aldewereld countered that a repayment term of twenty to twenty-five years would "seem to be giving an IDA character to Bank operations." To protect the IBRD, William Diamond suggested: "Since we are providing funds for the Government I would prefer to see an IDA credit rather than a Bank loan." Knapp agreed that softer terms were appropriate because "we are talking about a loan to assist the Indian economy and using the coal industry program as a vehicle for this assistance." Cargill, however, objected: "All of the arguments that have been given for deviating from Bank policy are . . . arguments for IDA," adding, "I thought that the commitment of $200 million [from] the Bank and $200 million from IDA over the next two years was made particularly so the Bank would not have to deviate from its usual practices. . . . I don't understand why abandonment of those practices is now being urged."[97]

Two Banks

The unrestrained spirit of IDA was unsettling to the Bank. A staff economist visiting a Middle East city in November 1960 wrote of the difficulties his mission faced: "There continue to be the expected misapprehensions about IDA. . . . [When we] visit a town or village, the mayor and council produce a list of projects. . . ."[98] After striving for fifteen years to achieve Wall Street respectability, the Bank

96. Memorandum, Raymond J. Goodman to files, "Notes of a Meeting with the Indian Delegation to the Annual Meeting, 1959," October 7, 1959. Effective disbursed loans to India amounted to 14.6 percent of total effective lending by the Bank in June 1961.

97. According to John Adler, IDA led to "a radical departure" from project lending "by using a large part of IDA funds for programme loans (to India and Pakistan)." Moreover, "in part the decision to engage in programme loans was motivated by the desire to provide as quickly as possible foreign exchange 'relief.'" Adler, "The World Bank's Concept of Development," p. 44 and note 34.

98. IBRD, "Rough Notes of Staff Loan Committee Meeting," SLC/M/6125, June 16, 1961, p. 6.

watched as IDA suddenly materialized and conjured up the 1940s' augury that the Bank would grow up to be a soup kitchen. Already IDA was being drawn on to provide balance of payments and disaster relief, to support politically beleaguered areas, and to serve as the vehicle for entry into what the Bank called "soft" sectors.[99] And in India, though masked by the sophistication of its civil service, cold war priority was joining forces with a compelling argument about a balance of payments gap and with the practice of Consortium pledging to put IDA allocations on the road to become an obligatory financial contribution, or dole.[100] In addition, country relative income, or "need," was establishing itself as a basis for IDA allocation, in conflict with strict output maximization, or, as would be described in a 1963 paper on IDA lending policy, with the rule that "IDA is out to 'buy as much development as possible.'"[101] Where the IBRD could approve or deny financing on the grounds of creditworthiness, IDA had no equivalent defense. Its allocation was necessarily "a value judgment, pure and simple; and it's not only a value judgment [since] most of the members of the board have political reasons for their distributions. The French would like to give it all to Chad."[102]

Black at times appeared to be carried along. When he addressed ECOSOC in April 1961, he dutifully noted that "IDA will apply the same high standards . . . as does the Bank," but stressed IDA's broadening range of activity:

> The range of these projects is wide, both in geography and type. . . . They include water supply, irrigation works, road development, port facilities, rural electrification, telecommunications and industrial estates. Under its charter, IDA is to support projects which can contribute most to the development of the country concerned, whether or not they are directly productive. IDA will finance all the kinds of projects which the Bank finances and a broader range as well.[103]

The following month, Black strongly objected to staff that IDA lending was excessively concentrated in Latin America and in traditional sectors. "We cannot be seen to use IDA to do what the private sector should be doing." Instead, he suggested, "What . . . is wrong with things such as agriculture in India?"[104] A Bank mission

99. Letter, Ray Goodman to Geoffrey Wilson, November 9, 1960.

100. IDA was used for the Bank's first loan to Taiwan, in August 1961, supplementing large-scale United States assistance. Chinese shelling of Quemoy was heaviest during 1958 but renewed in June 1960 to coincide with Eisenhower's visit to Taiwan. Knapp complained about the loss of leverage, saying that U.S. aid to places such as Taiwan and Korea, "put IDA in a position of being a last resort lender." IBRD, "Rough Notes of Staff Loan Committee Meeting," SLC/M/6015, p. 1.

101. Soon to be escalated by the Chinese invasion.

102. IBRD/IDA, economic staff, "IDA Lending Policy," Report EC-119b, November 26, 1963, esp. p. 15.

103. Benjamin King, interview with Richard Webb and Devesh Kapur, October 21, 1991, pp. 19–20.

104. Eugene R. Black, address to the Economic and Social Council of the United Nations, New York City, April 24, 1961, pp. 6–7.

leaving for India was instructed to come back with a dozen agricultural projects, leading to a burst of lending to that sector. The loans were highlighted in IDA's next (and Black's last) annual report (1961–62) by the unusual device of listing all lending to India that year under the subtitle, "Credits for Agricultural Development."[105]

It is understandable, then, that even as the Bank allowed itself to move in those directions—taking up IDA's "missionary function" in Knapp's words, and becoming "crusading and adventurous" in Demuth's words—it sought to raise walls that would defend it from secretaries of state, village mayors, and its own adventurous inclinations. Its defense consisted chiefly in the Bank's original formulation, that IDA's reason for being was exclusively to soften debt servicing and enable countries to borrow more; in all other respects, IDA and the IBRD were one and the same.

Indeed, though events drew him into acceptance of IDA innovations, Black was at most a reluctant convert. When he lauded IDA's "widening" role at the ECOSOC in April 1961, he was playing to a developing-country audience, seeking to dampen further demands. A few days earlier that same month, speaking in his home state, Georgia, he had sent a conservative message to American policymakers, a counterpoint to the newly installed Kennedy administration's foreign aid rhetoric. Admitting the "glaring inequalities in income in South America," he said, "the corrective most usually suggested is more social services." But "inequalities in income are a necessary by-product of economic growth [which] makes it possible for people to escape a life of poverty. . . . As for social services, they too are made *possible* by economic growth."[106] Five months later, at the Annual General Meeting, he continued on a conservative note: "Several Governors have urged that IDA be administered in accordance with the dictates of our hearts." Such a course, he said, would defeat "our ultimate development objective" and "betray the responsibility that is ours."[107]

Black's reaffirmation of the Bank's "heartlessness" served a banker's purpose, protecting the institutional image and making it easier to say "no," but the statement was inaccurate. The current that was driving IDA and the Bank into new activities and countries was produced less by sentimentality than by political fear, intellectual innovation, and the Bank's own organizational urge to expand; and IDA was providing room for those motivations. Underdeveloped country elites seeking to finance education, health, and housing were less tuned in to the "dictates of the heart" than to the noise of mobs, poll results showing strong communist support, and intelligence reports on guerilla activity. When Eisenhower and then Kennedy set out to support and step up those "social" efforts, the predominant American and recipient government objective was to stave off revolution. Eisenhower's visit to a low-income housing project in Santiago had made an impression, and self-help

105. Black cited by Willi Wapenhans, interview with John Lewis and Devesh Kapur, September 6, 1991, pp. 10, 12.

106. IDA *Annual Report, 1961–62*.

107. Black, *Diplomacy of Economic Development*, pp. 110–11.

housing efforts were quickly high on the development assistance list.[108] It was no coincidence that Pedro Beltran, Peru's arch-conservative prime minister in 1960, had determined on a similar priority.[109] With the help of a Maryknoll priest, Beltran launched a system of mutual savings and loan associations to finance middle-income housing. Indeed, political scientists of the time were arguing the modernizing, stabilizing, and therefore developmental virtues of the middle classes and of property ownership.[110]

Knapp perhaps best expressed the Bank's somewhat disapproving, somewhat bewildered attitude to the philanthropic nature of IDA in the course of an interview just two months after the Association's first credit. Whereas the IBRD had never had to ration money, he said, IDA imposed a "very perplexing and difficult and burdensome problem . . . [which] inevitably takes us into the realm of political . . . and arbitrary judgments on allocation." With IDA, he said,

> we have somewhat more freedom of action. . . . We can lean a little in the direction of . . . social projects rather than directly productive economic projects . . . less investment in future productivity and more satisfaction of current welfare requirements, like housing, water supply. . . . Our sort of doctrine . . . has been that those things were the fruits of economic development and that we would rather invest in the means of economic development and let countries develop the taxable capacity and the productivity that would enable these amenities to be provided.[111]

That is, IDA, more exactly the United States, was imposing "social lending" against the Bank's own better judgment. But, standing on the threshold of IDA operations, Knapp underestimated the pressures for change. Over the decade the institution did more than "lean a little" toward what it continued to call "soft" lending. To do so it found arguments to overcome its own doctrinal reluctance and ways to enfold IDA's inherent gift-giving nature inside its banker's suit.[112]

In part, the difference was about bearing and language. There was a Republican, anti–New Deal cast to the characterization of social lending as "soft" and to its injunctions against "welfare objectives" and "dictates of the heart." Conversely, many saw the new development advocacy and soft money as asking the

108. IBRD, Press Release 71, remarks by Eugene Black, Closing Joint Session of the Boards of Governors, Vienna, September 22, 1961, pp. 2–3.

109. Eisenhower, *Waging Peace,* p. 530. A fuller account is provided in Eisenhower, *The Wine is Bitter,* pp. 248–50.

110. Beltran was also an influential, behind-the-scenes advocate of the $500 million Social Progress Trust Fund created to provide the Inter-American Development Bank with its own IDA, and, in particular, to finance social infrastructure. Yet, over several decades, Beltran used his newspaper *La Prensa* to wage unrelenting war on Peru's "Communists," a group that included centrist politicians such as Fernando Belaunde.

111. Brazil's equally conservative Roberto Campos, who served as minister of finance under the military junta between 1964 and 1966, had chided the United Nations ECLA in 1956 for neglecting education.

112. J. Burke Knapp, interview, World Bank Oral History Program, July 1961, pp. 32–33.

Bank to wear its heart on its sleeve. However, more was at stake than the face put on poverty. Real poverty-related choices quickly surfaced in the course of efforts to define an IDA lending policy. This happened first and most clearly with regard to the country allocation of IDA, where, with relatively little hesitation, the Bank began to use per capita income as a criterion for eligibility and allocation. Poverty as an explicit lending criterion also began to peep around from behind the "economic" considerations raised in the early discussions of lending for agriculture, education, and water.

At the start of the 1960s the Bank thus found itself in a new world with a new assignment. These circumstantial developments—the appearance of "underdevelopment" and of IDA—began to push the institution toward the poor. At that time, however, its main character, image, and business remained those of the market-based, hard lender molded by Black and Garner. Old and new terms of reference—the financially cautious 1950s institution and the new "missionary function," as Knapp described it—differed in their implications for poverty, both in terms of overt concern and of the unintended or secondary effects of allocation criteria. From about 1960, this dual personality settled in as a permanent feature of the institution.

When George Woods delivered his first Annual General Meeting speech in September 1963, he tried to satisfy both conceptions of the Bank. He set out an adventurous agenda, describing new lending approaches required, he said, to meet the evolving problems of the developing countries, but, summing up, he took care to reassure underwriters that his guidepost for change would be "to maintain unimpaired and unquestioned the Bank's financial integrity and its reputation as a sound financing institution."[113] In seeking a balance between these different and in some ways contradictory requirements, Woods was picking up where Black had left off. Woods went on to "lean" further in the direction of the new terms of reference than Black, just as later McNamara moved even closer to the poverty agenda. Though their positions changed, reflecting presidential personalities as well as changing public opinion about development, all three presidents wrestled with and sought to resolve the contrast between the Bank's Wall Street and poverty-alleviating personas.

Those institutional efforts, as expressed in decisions on policy, administration, and lending over the 1960s and 1970s, are the subject matter of the next sections of this chapter and of chapter 5. As a preface to that account, attention should be

---

113. The Bank's original inclination had been, rather, to minimize the comparability of IDA and the IBRD by making IDA a provider of grants not loans. This proved politically unacceptable. According to Knapp, the Bank then resorted to setting IDA terms "just as close to grants as you could get away with politically," and decided that "repayment should be extended as long as one could, with a straight face, say 'this is still a loan.'" J. Burke Knapp, interview, World Bank Oral History Program, October 6 and 29, 1981, p. 48. See chapter 17 in this volume.

drawn to the general outcome and its probable reasons. As it turned out, the two roles—respectable bank and friend of the poor—coexisted with surprising ease, perhaps even advantage. Measured by lending volume, image, and influence, the Bank flourished through the next decades. The personality contradiction, or "blend," was perhaps more asset than liability.

One plausible explanation of that outcome is that the Bank showed administrative and public relations skill in managing the IDA-IBRD graft (though "skill" tends to be defined after the event). Another helpful factor was the institution's rapid expansion through the 1960s and 1970s, since overall growth provided room to accommodate both agendas. In addition, the political pressure for rapid and overt responses to poverty abated over the decade, as the United States in particular backed off from efforts to induce preventive and democratic reforms, choosing to rely instead on the repressive and developmental abilities of authoritarian regimes.[114] The appearance of new development institutions and growth of bilateral aid served also to lessen political pressures on the Bank. France, the United Kingdom, and other European nations increased their assistance to Africa. In Latin America, the Inter-American Development Bank provided $987 million for social infrastructure in the region between 1961 and 1970, more than twice the Bank's lending for similar projects in *all* regions during that period (table 4-2). The Bank was given time to adjust.

Yet the blending of market-based financial intermediation with poverty-alleviation was more than a gradual habituation to an awkward marriage. What proved more important in the longer run was an institutional innovation: a major enhancement of the Bank's perceived role as coordinator, adviser, teacher, and authority on development. The change was a matter of degree because technical assistance had been a growing component of the Bank's development lending since the beginning. But the trend accelerated during the 1960s, and the emphasis in Bank operations now moved a long way beyond its role as a source of finance, to dispensing opinion and advice, principally to borrowers but also to the larger aid community. If the Bank had built its reputation on being a hard lender, it could now sustain that image by dispensing hard advice and being a demanding judge. This

114. George D. Woods, "Closing Comments," in World Bank, *Summary Proceedings, 1963 Annual Meetings of the Board of Governors,* pp. 8–15. According to the account of George Wishart (Woods's personal assistant), Woods succeeded in reassuring his audience. William Iliff, a former senior vice president, reportedly told Wishart: "That speech went very well . . . it's gone down fine with the underwriters. . . they felt they could trust George Woods absolutely. . . . [H]e wasn't going to sponsor a 'give-away' program business." Wishart, interview, World Bank Oral History Program, 1983, pp. 44–45. But Harold Graves (director of information under Black and Woods) had a different recollection: the speech, he said, "caused ripples of alarm through the investment houses," requiring "a special exercise . . . to calm people down and say 'Look this is not going to threaten the integrity of the Bank's financial operations.'" Graves, interview, World Bank Oral History Program, July 24, 1985, p. 29. Both accounts underline the continuing hold of financial markets over the Bank.

growing tutelary and judgmental role was closely linked to its lending—loans to newly independent African nations, for instance, demanded substantial technical assistance—but it also blurred the distinction between Wall Street and IDA and provided a new basis for justifying and judging the Bank's activity.

Creativity came to play in another, more gradual way to resolve the role conflict. This happened through the eventual, serendipitous "discovery" that particular types of poverty-related lending, such as small-farmer and primary schooling projects, were indeed as highly productive and so as fully justified on output grounds as traditional lending for power and highways. Whatever the degree of rationalization involved, the end result was that the Bank found arguments and evidence to support operational poverty initiatives and took a growing lead itself in this intellectual work.

The Woods Agenda

Black's retirement and replacement by George Woods on January 1, 1963, accelerated the Bank's accommodation to new circumstances. Growth and change became pronounced during Woods's term of five years and three months. Though both were Wall Streeters, Woods found it easier than Black to adapt, and he added his own inclinations and goals to the outside pressures that were carrying the Bank in a more "adventurous" direction.

Woods was an unlikely radical. Recommended to President Kennedy by Black, he came to the Bank at the age of sixty-one from a lifetime in investment banking, leaving his position as chairman of First Boston Corporation. His talent and career had focused narrowly but brilliantly on financial planning, on advising on the most advantageous and marketable combinations of debt and equity instruments for particular investments. The choice of Woods was undoubtedly influenced by his solid reputation in the international financial market. In 1962 U.S. balance of payments problems were signaling that the Bank would need to expand its access to foreign bond markets; it was a moment to reaffirm, not risk, the Bank's image of financial soundness.[115] Moreover, when he arrived at the Bank, Woods had had more personal and working contact with the institution than any other president at the time of their appointment, with the possible exception of Black, who had briefly but fully served as U.S. execu-

---

115. There was little choice. During the 1960s and early 1970s authoritarian governments governed in most of the developing world. According to Packenham, *Liberal America,* p. 13, only ten of eighty-five developing nations were democratic in 1967. The popular term "Free World" had lost all literal meaning early in the 1950s. Eisenhower's late-1950s revival of democracy as a foreign policy priority, intensified by Kennedy in 1961–62, was rapidly reconsidered and set aside after six military coups in Latin America during 1962 and 1963, spreading insurgency in Asia, and the birth of one-party states in Africa.

tive director.[116] Woods's career became threaded in with those of Black and the World Bank in 1951 when First Boston and Morgan Stanley were chosen to organize and lead the syndicate for retailing World Bank bonds.[117] Woods advised Black on bond marketing but soon extended the relationship into foreign advisory missions. "Mr. Woods seemed to be very interested in going on missions abroad," recalled Marie Linahan, who worked as secretary to John McCloy, Black, and Woods.[118] Woods's missions spanned the decade between 1952 and 1962 and were concerned with the financing of a steel project in India; development finance companies in India, Pakistan, and the Philippines; an aluminum smelter in Ghana; and the negotiation of Suez Canal stockholder claims after its expropriation. Also, with four other members of the banking community, he served on an advisory panel to review IFC investments. Nonetheless, after his appointment Woods rapidly and almost casually challenged several tenets of the 1950s Bank. He was aptly described by Raúl Prebisch as the Bank's Pope John XXIII.[119]

Woods brought little in the way of a blueprint or innovative program for the Bank. In his first decisions he appeared to share Black's conception of the institution as a cautious, image-conscious, prestige lender. Yet he soon defined a "developmental" agenda. His openness in that direction was less a consequence of doctrine than of its absence; he was less fettered by taboos of the 1950s Bank, the commonsense rules that, as in any successful enterprise, had been elevated to dogma. It may also be relevant that the Wall Street careers of Black and Woods had been spent on opposite sides of the balance sheet: Black had sold bonds; Woods specialized in investing. At the same time, he brought a new enthusiasm and an energetic, even impatient pragmatism to the assignment. Within six months of his arrival, Woods had defined the agenda that guided most of his subsequent initiatives in financial, operational, and lending policies. It was in character that this broad agenda emerged as a response to a strictly financial issue and that it first took the form of a memorandum to the Board's Financial Policy Committee.[120] The memorandum was a brief but perceptive sketch of developing-country needs, but

116. With regard to Woods's appointment, Sommers said: "George Woods was . . . a leading figure, if not the leading figure, in the Wall Street investment banking community [and] . . . was interested in something outside of his close knit Wall Street sphere of activity." Sommers, Oral History, July 18, 1985, p. 5. According to William Bennett, former financial journalist and the Bank's principal contact with Wall Street rating services from 1949, "Kennedy wanted to have a man who was known widely as a very able American investment banker and financier and a very successful one." Woods "seemed . . . the ideal man to bring in." Bennett, interview, World Bank Oral History Program, January 20, 1988, p. 20.

117. Black served as U.S. executive director from March 1947 to July 1949 before becoming president.

118. The arrangement survived until 1968.

119. Marie Linahan, interview, World Bank Oral History Program, July 19, 1986.

120. Cited by Roger Chaufournier, interview, World Bank Oral History Program, July 22, 1985, p. 22. The comparison was made by Raúl Prebisch, after Woods's April 1964 speech to UNCTAD. Arthur Karasz, the Bank's European Office representative, writes that Prebisch

its genius was to match that diagnosis with an innovative view of the Bank's financial and operational possibilities.

The issue that triggered Woods's July 1963 paper was a financial paradox; the Bank faced a combination of high earnings and diminishing investment opportunities. Traditional clients were reaching borrowing limits and, as it then seemed, the more urgent infrastructure requirements of borrowing countries were well on the way to being met. The "excess reserves" question predated Woods. It had been the subject of a 1957 paper and, more recently, of a 1962 weekend seminar that Woods attended.[121] Excess earnings were a "problem" for political and image reasons. The Charter seemed to suggest, and management agreed, that the payment of dividends was the proper though politically unpalatable course.[122] High profits in a development institution were an inducement for borrowers to press for lower loan charges, and, in the words of Germany's Otto Donner, for "adverse comments" by the press and by parliaments of industrialized nations facing balance of payments problems who were at the same time being asked for additional payments on their capital subscriptions and for new IDA contributions. For Donner, "the problem of dealing with surplus earnings . . . was urgent,"[123] and it remained a contentious issue in the Board during the first months of Woods's appointment.[124] Woods first favored the payment of dividends but soon changed his mind in the face of Board opposition. In February 1963 he started to look for a rationale that would justify keeping net income within the Bank while at the same time avoiding the politically unsatisfactory image of a development bank that was earning unseemly high profits.

The solution that began to emerge took the form of new and "riskier" lending. Such lending would at once expand the Bank's investment opportunities and, by being more venturesome, justify its increasing reserves.[125] Working with Richard

---

was "full of praise for Mr. Woods" after the speech. Memorandum, Karasz to Richard Demuth, April 3, 1964. Pope John XXIII, almost seventy-seven at his election in 1958, proved an unexpected revolutionary, stressing human rights and appealing to richer nations to help the poor.

121. Memorandum to Financial Policy Committee, FPC/638, "Bank Financial Policy," July 18, 1963. The memorandum evolved, undergoing several revisions, from a first draft dated January 15.

122. Harold Graves, interview, World Bank Oral History Program, July 25, 1985, p. 31.

123. This opinion was expressed in "Bank Financial Policy," a paper drafted by Demuth and sent to Woods on April 17, 1963, through Geoffrey Wilson.

124. Donner, in IBRD, "Memorandum of Meeting of Financial Policy Committee," FPC/6311, August 2, 1963, p. 6. Donner referred in particular to possible decisions to withdraw or withhold approval of the use of the 18 percent portion of their subscriptions in Bank capital.

125. Edward S. Mason and Robert E. Asher, *The World Bank since Bretton Woods* (Brookings, 1973), wrote that Bank net annual income was increasing "at an almost indecent rate," p. 407.

Demuth, Woods first resorted to his own stock-in-trade, industrial investment. A memorandum prepared by Demuth in April suggested project loans for specific "pioneer industries" and program loans to meet the foreign exchange requirements of growth across broad industrial sectors. It also proposed that the Bank seek a modification of its Charter to allow private sector lending without government guarantees.[126] This creative exercise proved heady. Demuth's next draft, dated June 17, contained additional adventurous proposals: longer repayment terms for the IBRD, loans for school buildings and for "long-term agricultural improvement schemes," and an ambitious expansion in technical assistance.

The addition of agriculture between the April and June drafts may have been influenced by Pierre Moussa's objection that the stress on industry would discriminate against smaller and poorer borrowers and "make the Bank look too much of a 'reactionary' institution."[127] What is certain is that Woods was impressed by a meeting that took place in London in early May with Lord Howick, chairman of Britain's Colonial Development Corporation and former governor of Kenya. Howick persuaded Woods of the possibilities for a broader approach to agricultural lending, moving beyond large-scale irrigation works to meet the credit, storage, roads, and other needs of individual farmers. Returning from the trip, Woods wrote Demuth:

> I have been wondering more and more about working into the memorandum the idea of assisting private agriculture. Apparently in various parts of the world entities for this objective are coming into being. Lord Howick . . . told me in London last week of such a development in the Cameroons. The Deputy Prime Minister . . . of Malaya . . . told me what he is doing and planning along these lines in Malaya.
>
> These conversations, among other things, have made me wonder whether we are stressing private industry too much. . . . Acceleration of exports is more likely to come from enlarging extractive and agricultural activities.[128]

The June draft argued that additional technical assistance was needed for the proposed broadening of lending and the special assistance that would be required by new members. With the recently independent African nations in mind, it stated: "To lend money wisely in such countries involves a much greater investment of human skills." Similarly, new lending activities "will require considerable preinvestment work [and] . . . technical and managerial assistance during the course of execution."[129] As director of the Development Services Department, which over-

126. Richard Demuth, interview with the authors, January 17, 1995.

127. Demuth, "Bank Financial Policy," with attached memorandum, "Use of Bank Earnings to Finance Private Sector Industry."

128. Memorandum, Pierre Moussa to Richard Demuth, "Draft Memo on Bank Financial Policy," April 24, 1963, p. 1. Moussa was director of operations for Africa.

129. Memorandum, George Woods to Richard Demuth, May 13, 1963. According to his personal assistant, Woods was initially reluctant to lend for agriculture, "for almost exactly the same reason as not paying for the school teachers' salaries or the doctors' salaries." Wishart, Oral History, 1983, p. 41. It is noteworthy that Woods appears to have been

saw technical assistance, Demuth was a knowledgeable advocate for the expansion of those services. Also, as noted earlier, Demuth had been responsible for the Bank's exploratory discussions with UNESCO and other sources of expertise on education since 1961.

The final version of the Demuth-Woods memorandum, completed in July and presented that month to the Board, contained minor but indicative changes: in the list of new lending options, agriculture had been moved to the top, with land redistribution added as an item worthy of Bank support.[130] Woods's final proposal to the Board's Financial Policy Committee, submitted on July 30, had become a far-reaching agenda. Rather than passively accept the curtailment of lending opportunities and deal with the Bank's embarrassment of riches by cutting interest charges, paying dividends, or building up liquid reserves, Woods recommended an aggressive and costly plan to create investment opportunities through new types of lending and new clients. Woods's agenda implied riskier lending, a larger staff, more hands-on development assistance, and in general, a relative increase in the Bank's nonfinancial role. The idea of direct poverty alleviation, as distinct from or additional to the general increase in incomes made possible by economic growth, played no part in the shaping of this program. Indeed, the first educational and nonirrigation agricultural projects seemed to target the least poor within those sectors.

Woods was delighted with the emerging program.[131] It provided the plausible argument for keeping earnings in the Bank that he had requested. In addition, it seems probable that Woods began to see the outline of an answer to a more personal need, the creation of a "Woods Bank." Though Woods and Black were

---

especially influenced by persons outside the Bank. Woods, somewhat self-conscious about his proletarian, Brooklyn upbringing, was perhaps particularly open to persuasion by Lord Howick, formerly Sir Evelyn Baring. In addition to Howick's colonial experience, he was a member of one of the most prestigious investment banking families in Europe. It is interesting to record that Howick could both advocate loans for smallholders and explain Mau Mau brutality to Woods with the cultural cliché: Africans are intelligent "but 200 or 300 years behind the thinking of countries such as our own." More advanced nations had recently accomplished a world war, the Holocaust, and Hiroshima. Cited in Wishart, Oral History, 1983, p. 55.

130. Memorandum from the president, "Bank Financial Policy," June 17, 1963, pp. 4, 13.

131. "In some cases improvement of agriculture . . . may call for assistance in meeting the financial requirements following upon a program of land distribution." IBRD, "Bank Financial Policy," FPC/638, pp. 8–9. The proposal, however, did not extend to the financing of landowner compensation payments. Only three months before, Woods had brushed aside a suggestion that the Bank support land reform in Latin America, saying that the "the poor peon" had no management ability, and was often "just plain lazy." Letter from George Woods to (Reverend?) Willsie Wood, April 12, 1963. The characterization has Woods's bluntness but was probably common currency among contemporaries. A compendium of self-justifying clichés regarding the poor—lazy, inept at management, freeloaders—it was seemingly untouched by Woods's travel and work in India and other developing countries.

associates and friends over a long period, Woods found it difficult to work in Black's shadow, presiding over an institution popularly known as "Black's Bank," and surrounded by staff, executive directors, journalists, and foreign leaders who, over Black's fifteen years as either executive director or president, had been helped in their careers, influenced in their thinking, or simply charmed by Black's courteous, winning personality. Woods's surge of enthusiasm for the budding "developmental" and innovative character of his program suggests that more than intellectual conversion was at work.[132]

Board members from poorer countries applauded, describing the proposal as "the best thing that had happened to the Bank since . . . IFC and IDA," "a substantial incentive to economic development," "consistent . . . with present-day requirements," "far-reaching and very, very bold." Woods was commended for his "vision, courage and initiative."[133] Directors from developed countries worried. The German representative doubted the wisdom of loans for purposes "so far afield from economic infrastructure." Referring to difficulties that had arisen in the first loan for education, he said, "The Bank's experiences in the Tunisian case should serve as a warning."[134] Most rich-country representatives opposed Bank lending for education. Support for expanding technical assistance was grudging: several directors stressed the need to stick to established areas of expertise and avoid duplication with other agencies. The Nordic representative said that her countries would prefer "that no IDA-like operations be introduced in the Bank [and that] what might be called the more improvident credits should continue to be left to IDA."[135] An even sharper opinion was given by the Dutch director: the Bank, he said, should be extremely cautious in changing its policies. Otherwise, "instead of remaining a true bank . . . it would gradually change into a development assistance fund." The Bank, he said, "could not meet every urgent need in the field of development . . . [and] should not embark on IDA-type or IFC-type financial activities."[136] Moreover, "the financing of spare parts and raw materials was not the business of the Bank."[137]

132. As reported by Richard Demuth, interview with the authors, January 17, 1995.

133. William Bennett said of Woods: "Everyone I know likes to psychoanalyze him, including me. . . . [H]e wanted to be admired. . . . He wanted people to feel about him the way they felt about Gene Black." Bennett, Oral History, January 20, 1988, p. 18. As it happened, Woods's testy, combative, distrustful personality, combined perhaps with worsening health, resulted in an exceptionally conflictual presidency. His contemporaries often recall Woods's sense of rivalry with Black and general competitiveness.

134. Statements by several members in "Memorandum of Meeting of Bank Financial Policy Committee," FPC/6311, July 30 (dated August 2), 1963, pp. 9, 20; and "Memorandum of Resumed Meeting of Bank Financial Policy Committee," FPC/6312, August 6, 1963, pp. 3–4.

135. IBRD, "Memorandum of Meeting of Bank Financial Policy Committee," FPC/6311, p. 8.

136. IBRD, "Memorandum of Meeting of Bank Financial Policy Committee," FPC/6315, September 23, 1963, p. 3.

137. IBRD, "Memorandum of Meeting of Bank Financial Policy Committee," FPC/6311, p. 15.

Opposing visions of the Bank showed up in a semantic disagreement. The term "IDA-type" activities had come into regular use by Board (and staff) members, but Woods and Knapp refused to acknowledge the term. At one point Woods expostulated that he really did not know what the expression "IDA-type" meant, and, as for "so-called IDA-like loan business, he disclaimed it."[138] The real debate was not over definitions but how the institution should house and finance the new activities that Woods was proposing. Conservative Board members wanted to restrict IBRD money to "conventional loans," confining the new activities to IDA and the IFC. This segregation, they thought, would best protect the purity of the Bank.[139] Woods, though sensitive to the image problem, was nonetheless resolved to make the innovations a part of both the IBRD and IDA—indeed, to "disclaim" any difference in the activities of each—and therefore, to change the institution as a whole. These broader and contradictory visions bore on the immediate question of profit allocation. Woods wanted to plough them back into the IBRD, whereas the Board wanted to transfer some part at least to IDA. Since Woods strongly objected to the transfer, Dutch and German directors suggested a compromise, the creation of a special fund within the IBRD, a General Development Assistance Grant and Loan Account, funded out of profits and earmarked for Woods's proposed "soft uses." But this, too, was refused by Woods who, despite his disclaimer, was determined to make the entire Bank more "IDA-like."

Against much staff and Board skepticism, Woods announced his new lending and technical assistance plans at the September 1963 Annual Meeting. Though he stayed within the bounds of proposals discussed by the Board, he presented them in a third-world idiom that, according to Harold Graves, raised underwriter eyebrows.[140] He suggested that developing-country problems were not entirely the result of their own deficiencies, citing weak commodity prices, high debt burdens, and import barriers to rich-country markets. As for the Bank, "We must . . . leave this proven ground and venture onto less familiar terrain."[141]

138. IBRD, "Memorandum of Resumed Meeting of Bank Financial Policy Committee," FPC/6312, p. 22.

139. IBRD, "Memorandum of Meeting of Bank Financial Policy Committee," FPC/6315, p. 8.

140. John Williams attributed the juridical separation of IDA from the Bank to "substantial concern at the time about the possible adverse effect on the Bank's market image"; hence, "IDA was created as a separate institution only to preserve the chastity of the Bank." John H. Williams, presentation to Fourth Maxwell Institute on the United Nations, Bretton Woods, August 27–September 1, 1967, p. 10.

141. Graves said that the speech was "energized" by Bank economist Dragoslav Avramovic. When Woods heard Avramovic present his ideas at a staff meeting, his face "lit up" and he said: "This is what I want to talk about. You are now the chairman of my drafting committee." Avramovic transformed the speech into a pro-developing-country address, challenging rich countries to deal with commodity prices and the needs for debt relief and industrialization. Even so, according to Graves, Woods's speech "bore a marked resemblance to Black's last speech." Robert Oliver, A Conversation with Harold Graves I, Conversations about George Woods and the World Bank, Washington, D.C., July 17, 1985.

A week after the Annual Meeting, Woods met with staff at Williamsburg to begin to fill in the details of his agenda and obtain Board approval for specific changes. Policy papers for education, agriculture, industry, and IDA lending had been drafted and were debated and approved. Complementary financial measures—lower loan charges, longer lending terms, and the decision to transfer IBRD profits to IDA—were also prepared and approved over that period.[142] Most of the policy innovations had been approved by early 1964.

For the remainder of his term, Woods turned his attention from lending policy to the funding of IDA. With Black, he had been persuaded that IDA's soft money could be used to strengthen the creditworthiness of IBRD borrowers and therefore of the IBRD itself.[143] The Bank's long-standing catechism that easy money was detrimental to borrowers—because it undermined conditionality, incentives for good use of capital, and the development of private investment flows—was put aside when it became necessary to deal with the institution's own balance sheet problems.[144] But Woods's growing absorption with IDA suggests that the original financial justification was overtaken by an enthusiasm for the developmental role that IDA was opening up for the Bank.[145]

---

142. Annual address by George D. Woods, *Summary Proceedings: 1963 Annual Meeting of the Board of Governors,* September 30–October 4, 1963, p. 11.

143. A report, "Proposed Bank/IDA Policies in the Field of Education," was approved by the Financial Policy Committee on November 26, 1963. The agriculture policy paper, approved by the Committee on February 6, 1964, is discussed in chapter 8. "IDA Lending Policy," report no. EC-119b, was approved by the Committee on November 26, 1963. Harold Graves recalled: "One of the first things Woods did . . . was to set in motion a whole series of studies [about agriculture and industry]. . . . [W]e had paper, paper, paper on all these subjects. This had never happened in the Bank before. . . . We wrote all this stuff down in a big policy manual, and the Bank has been writing everything down ever since: *ad nauseam.*" Graves, interview, World Bank Oral History Program, July 17, 1985, p. 16.

144. After Black had agreed to IDA, Davidson Sommers was sent to persuade Wall Streeters that it was a good idea. Sommers said to Woods: "George, if you were a banker who had two branches, one . . . making regular loans on the basis of creditworthiness and the other [with] grant money that you could make available to borrowers that were in trouble, don't you think that would improve the quality of your regular loans?" Woods replied: "I certainly do, and I am now an IDA supporter." Sommers, Oral History, July 18, 1985, p. 7.

145. A January 15, 1963, draft Board paper on Bank loan charges, for example, had argued against any reduction in the Bank's loan charges: "The management's view," it stated, was that it was "important not to weaken the incentive of the less developed countries to accept the disciplines and . . . policies" that would allow them to become self-sufficient market borrowers. IBRD, "The Bank's Policy Concerning Reserves, Loan Charges and Dividends," draft, January 15, 1963, pp. 2–3.

By the mid-1960s Woods was fully occupied by IDA.[146] In 1965 he told senior staff that IDA's replenishment "was the biggest problem for the future."[147] He was disappointed by the size of IDA's first replenishment in 1964 and then became despondent and almost obsessed by the delays and frustrations that accompanied the second replenishment, which was not obtained until after his departure in 1968. His former chief economist, Irving Friedman, recalls Woods saying: "What I want, to succeed in doing as president . . . is to see that IDA becomes more important than the [IBRD]. There is no future in the World Bank Group unless IDA becomes more important than conventional lending."[148] This statement would have been anathema to the 1950s Bank. By implication, it depreciated the developmental virtues of lending on near-commercial terms, oft-repeated by Black, and the very basis for the Bank's earlier perceived success as both borrower and lender, a recipe not only replicated in the new regional development banks but invariably recommended as sound policy for the development finance companies of borrower countries.[149]

In addition to lobbying for replenishments, Woods was responsible for three major initiatives in support of IDA. First, when he realized that IDA's second replenishment was falling well short of expectations, he reconsidered the Board's proposal that part of Bank profits be used to supplement IDA capital. In 1963 he had opposed the idea on the grounds of image: "a direct transfer of a portion of the Bank's net earning to IDA at this time would adversely affect the Bank's standing in the financial communities of the world."[150] Moreover, Latin American countries, largely excluded from IDA, objected to the transfer. Its legality was also in doubt,

146. Julian Grenfell said: "I think there was a transformation of Woods in the second half of his term of office: he came to an understanding that the [World Bank] could do a lot more than he had imagined. . . . He moved out of being an autocratic head of the World Bank to being an international statesman." Grenfell, interview, World Bank Oral History Program, July 15, 1986, p. 6.

147. Robert W. Oliver, *George Woods and the World Bank* (Lynne Rienner, 1995). According to Oliver, in 1965–66 "Woods was devoting 90 percent of his energies to IDA" (p. 111).

148. Ibid., p. 204.

149. Irving Friedman, interview, World Bank Oral History Program, March 1974, p. 62. At the time of the IDA negotiations, said Friedman, "Woods was getting more and more nervous. . . . There was nothing that preoccupied his mind in the same way as the IDA Replenishment. [It absorbed] 90 percent of his energies. . . . He is not doing administration. . . . He is hyped on the idea" (pp. 61–62). According to Graves, "The big thing on Woods' mind [in 1967] . . . [was] IDA replenishment." Graves, Oral History, July 17, 1985, pt. 1, p. 19.

150. Yet Robert Asher and Edward Mason, during an October 1973 interview, also agreed that IDA was "the key" to the Bank's future. "Story of Bank Went 'Surprisingly Smoothly' Say Bank Historians," *Bank Notes,* October 1973, n.p.

since, to protect the IBRD, the IDA Charter had prohibited IDA from borrowing from the Bank. In July 1964, however, the Bank's general counsel reversed himself, deciding that his previous objection, based on the Charter, did not apply to outright grants from the IBRD to IDA,[151] and thus cleared the way for approval of the first transfer from Bank earnings to IDA.

Second, Woods used his last major speech, in Stockholm in 1967, to make a dramatic plea for expanded development assistance, leaving no doubt that he was referring to concessional, rather than IBRD funding. Drafted by Barbara Ward, the speech asserted that "our worldwide crisis today [is] . . . vaster and deeper and even more complex" than at the time of the Marshall Plan. He spoke of "the risk of stark crisis—in food, in work, in hope—for over half the human race."[152] And he called for a new, expert review of the situation, a "grand assize," a proposal that later took the form of the Pearson Commission.

His third initiative was a low-profile attempt to influence McNamara with regard to future IDA lending policy. In February 1968 Woods asked Ben King, a staff economist, to prepare a report on IDA policies, instructing him to recruit a young team and not to consult the vice presidents, saying he was looking for fresh ideas. He wanted, according to King, a radical report.[153] Further, the indirect target, as King saw it, was IBRD lending policy. King's report began: "Undoubtedly the central question for IDA is whether its main purpose is to alleviate poverty."[154] It proposed that "IDA should devote its main effort to the development of its most impoverished member countries," and that "value judgments" must be made, in practice, between the use of aid as "a moral commitment and as an engine of growth." This formulation challenged the official insistence that IDA's only rationale was balance of payments need and was directly rebutted by Irving Friedman: "I believe that the balance of payments criterion embodied in the IDA Articles of Agreement is essentially sound and the omission of the poverty criterion from the Articles is sound." Thus "some poor countries may not qualify [for IDA funds] and some richer countries may."[155] In the end, Woods's attempt at an end run around the vice presidents appears to have been frustrated; after Woods's departure, King's report was thoroughly revised for presentation to the Board. Yet it was seen by, and

151. Woods may have wanted to respect Black's promise to the markets that there would be no financial linkage between IDA and the IBRD. IBRD, "Bank Financial Policy," FPC/638. According to Broches, however, Black told Woods that "you won't find me snapping at you" if Woods went ahead with the transfer. Aron Broches, interview, World Bank Oral History Program, November 7, 1985, p. 2.

152. Memorandum from Aron Broches, general counsel, July 27, 1964, distributed by the secretary as SecM64-183 on July 28, 1964. Broches's previous opinion was written in his memorandum of February 12, 1963 (FPC/636).

153. George D. Woods, "Development—The Need for New Directions," address to the Swedish Bankers Association, Stockholm, October 27, 1967, p. 4.

154. Benjamin King, conversations with the authors.

155. IBRD, "Report of the Working Group on IDA Policies," draft, May 24, 1968, p. 4.

may have influenced, McNamara, since IDA lending policy evolved in the direction of many of the operational proposals contained in the report.

The financial embarrassment of riches that had provoked Woods's innovations was short lived, and indeed, Woods's last two years as president were lean times for the institution, a turn that checked the growth of both lending and administrative spending. Similarly, the political tide that had pushed IDA onto the Bank and that changed the developmental landscape in other ways had begun to ebb even before mid-decade. By then, however, Woods's agenda was firmly embedded in Bank organization, procedures, and lending policy. It was equally important that the more diversified and tutelary institution of the later 1960s seemed more in tune with the evolving public expectations of the time. The rather accidental circumstances of 1963—the Bank's financial situation and Woods's arrival—thus precipitated changes that strongly enhanced the Bank's development role.

Operational Trends

Previous sections of this chapter have reviewed three developments—the emergence of "underdevelopment," the creation of IDA, and the arrival of Woods—that strongly influenced the institution in the early 1960s. This section is about the impact of those events on the course of operations over the decade. The review is selective and is guided by the question of the Bank's actual or potential engagement in poverty alleviation. To what extent did operations respond to a concern for need and poverty, at the cost of or to complement the dominant economic growth objective? And did operations evolve in ways that made future responses to need and poverty easier to carry out?

Of course, more pressures came to bear on Bank operations during the 1960s than those precipitated by the dramatic events of the first years of the decade. The Bank's original character, anchored in a continuing market dependence and a belief that direct poverty alleviation measures would reduce growth, was not easily moved. In addition, there were major new developments: the Bank went from financial ease to stringency, cold war priorities evolved, India's long-running crisis gripped the institution's president, and Woods's leadership weakened. Those developments are discussed in the context of four themes: the expansion in the level and variety of Bank operations, the growing interaction with other lenders and donors, the emergence of relative poverty between borrowers as a criterion for allocation, and the extent to which relative poverty within countries began to appear as an element in decisionmaking.

The Bank's Size

The combination of IDA funding, strong earnings, new membership, and Woods's more aggressive lending and technical assistance program produced a remarkable

Table 4-4. *The Size of the Bank: Growth by Periods*[a]

	Fiscal years: two-year averages					Annual growth			
	1948–49	1959–60	1968–69	1980–81	1993–94	Pre-IDA[b] 1948–49 to 1959–60	1960s[c] 1959–60 to 1968–69	McNamara[d] 1968–69 to 1980–81	Post-McNamara 1980–81 to 1993–94
Administrative expenses[e] (FY1993 US$ millions)	35	81	261	825	1,455	8	14	10	4
Staff									
Total	414	657	1,859	5,470	7,106	4	12	9	2
Higher level	...	270	829	2,513	4,075	...	13	10	4
Membership									
Number of countries[f]	47	68	109	137	177	3	5	2	2
Borrowers									
Number (annual)	4	21	51	80	90	16	11	4	1
Number of loans[g]	7	44	103	302	445	19	10	9	3
Lending commitments[h] (FY1993 US$ millions)	1,093	4,100	7,194	20,208	26,043	13	6	9	2

Sources: World Bank annual reports; IFC annual reports; Review of World Bank financial and operating programs; fiscal year administrative budgets.

a. Fiscal years ending June 30.

b. Postreconstruction lending under Black before IDA.

c. Black and Woods lending after creation of IDA. McNamara became president April 1, 1968, but most loan commitments during 1968 and early 1969 can be attributed to Woods.

d. McNamara resigned June 1981. The debt crisis began in August 1982.

e. Actual expenses, real FY1993 US$ millions based on price index used by World Bank budget office.

f. IBRD membership for all years.

g. Includes IBRD loans since FY1947, IFC investments since FY1957, and IDA credits since FY1961.

h. Real FY1993 US$ millions using IBRD and IFC commitment deflators. IFC totals include loan and equity commitments.

expansion of the Bank during the 1960s, particularly after the appearance of IDA in 1961. Table 4-4 provides a perspective on that growth, comparing the evolution of key dimensions of the Bank during four main periods: Black's 1950s, the Black–Woods 1960s, McNamara's 1970s, and the post-McNamara years.[156] Though lending rose in absolute terms, the expansion of the institution was perhaps most noteworthy in other dimensions, especially in the geographical and sectoral diversification of its loans and in the extent of economic, policy, and aid coordination work.

Between 1961 and 1969 loan commitments rose at the rate of 10.4 percent a year, while the number of annual loan operations jumped from thirty-one to eighty-two (table 4-4). Lending began for water supply and sanitation, education, and tourism and greatly expanded for agriculture, especially nonirrigation projects and for development finance institutions. In general, the Bank's portfolio broadened as credit for activities other than traditional power and transport infrastructure projects increased from 29 to 46 percent of the total. Though data on projects at the stage of identification or preparation are incomplete, they suggest a swelling pipeline; the number of projects at those preliminary stages rose from 50 in 1962 to 121 in 1966.[157] In 1961 the Bank had 68 members, 21 of which borrowed that year; in 1969 there were 110 members and 51 borrowers. During the period covering fiscal years 1961 through 1969 the Bank made its first loan to 50 new borrowers, 27 of which were in Sub-Saharan Africa, 10 in Northern Africa and the Middle East, 7 in Latin America, and 6 in Asia.

As the July 1963 memorandum had foreseen, new borrowers, new sectors, and expanded technical assistance all meant "a much greater investment of human skills."[158] In effect, the number of employees, level of administrative spending, and, most notably, the size of the professional staff all grew explosively. The number of professionals rose from 283 in 1960 to 917 in 1969, a rate of 14 percent a year, the most rapid of any decade. The Economic Department grew fourfold. The Bank's administrative budget more than tripled, rising most rapidly (20 percent annually)

156. Memorandum, Irving S. Friedman to S. R. Cope, "IDA Paper," June 14, 1968.

157. Growth figures are in real terms, measured in constant 1993 U.S. dollars and between two-year end-point averages. Table 4-4 excludes the start-up growth rates of the 1940s. To better relate operations to presidential policies, it should be kept in mind that a preexisting loan pipeline largely determines lending volumes for at least a year or two. Prior administrative decisions and arrangements also carry over to affect the initial trends in membership and administrative spending by a new president. For this reason the Black-Woods 1960s are defined to include fiscal year 1969 (through June 1969). The fiscal 1969 lending spurt was in part a consequence of Woods's efforts to secure IDA's second replenishment, but also a consequence of McNamara's immediate and successful campaign to increase borrowing. The reason for using 1959–60 as a starting point for the 1960s is to capture the impact of IDA from 1961.

158. Agricultural lending (chapter 8), nonagricultural project lending (chapter 8), IBRD finances (chapters 15–17), IDA (chapter 17).

over the period between 1960 and 1966. As may be seen in table 4-4, rapid growth was experienced in other periods in the Bank's history, and the volume of lending in particular grew even more rapidly over the start-up 1950s and during the 1970s under McNamara. However, if a broader measure of activity is applied—giving weight also to the number of borrowers, individual loans, and the level of economic and advisory work—growth over the 1960s must be considered to have been as substantial as, if not greater than, that of other decades.

It bears mentioning that institutional growth during the 1960s spanned three presidencies: operating expenses, for instance, grew 33 percent in real terms during Black's last two years in office, 140 percent over Woods' tenure, and another 11 percent during McNamara's first year.[159] As already mentioned, another feature of the expansion is that it was interrupted by a brief period of financial tightness during 1967–68. The Bank's coffers and borrowing capacity were brimming as the decade began, following the General Capital Increase in 1959, successful borrowings in new markets outside the United States, the accumulation of a large liquid reserve, and subscriptions and contributions to IDA.[160] Though U.S. balance of payments difficulties had first appeared in 1960, IBRD lending remained unconstrained. When denied access to U.S. financial markets in 1966, the IBRD resorted to borrowing in Europe and drawing down reserves.[161] In 1967, however, the IBRD found itself in the unusual situation of a cash squeeze, aggravated by a delay in the replenishment of IDA capital; these circumstances made it necessary to cut back on administrative spending and disbursements by the IBRD and IDA. But project preparation and economic work continued, and both IBRD and IDA lending recovered rapidly when funding became available again in 1968.

Aid Coordination

As the Bank became, in Demuth's words, crusading and adventurous, it found itself playing more and more as a member of a larger development orchestra. In pursuit of both market image and policy leverage, the 1950s Bank had sought to distance and differentiate itself from the soft, more visibly political aid provided by bilateral and UN agencies. It dealt with the Export-Import Bank and with the specialized UN agencies as rivals. Because it avoided lending in the rim countries (except India and Pakistan, and less continuously, Turkey), it appeared to distance

159. IBRD, "Bank Financial Policy," FPC/638, July 1963, p. 4. Actually, by mid-1963 both employment and administrative spending were already growing rapidly—at 12.8 percent and 19.6 percent per year, respectively, between 1960 and 1963.

160. In constant 1995 dollars and by fiscal year, administrative expenses rose from $74.7 million in 1960 to $99.5 million in 1962, $238.8 million in 1968, and $266.6 million in 1969.

161. The General Capital Increase in 1959 raised IBRD's authorized capital from $10 billion to $21 billion, without any increase in paid-in capital. By 1968 bond placements outside the United States accounted for 60 percent of the IBRD's outstanding debt. The contribution disbursed to IDA in 1960 was $650 million.

itself from the cold war. This role as a solo player began to erode with Black's ventures into international diplomacy and with the Bank's decision to chair a concerted response to India's balance of payments emergency in 1958, a collective action that was formalized as the first Aid Consortium.

Aid concertation between the Bank and other members of the development assistance community increased with IDA. In part, it was imposed on the Bank by bilateral donors, each of which saw its IDA contribution as one arrow in its aid quiver, an imposition whose weight increased as former colonies became borrowers. Another reason lay in the "adventurous" nature of lending opened up by IDA; as the Bank entered the unfamiliar territory of nonirrigation agricultural projects, water supply, education, and other new activities, it sought expertise in the specialized agencies of the United Nations, particularly FAO, UNESCO, and WHO, a policy encouraged by Woods and announced in his speech to the first meeting of the United Nations Conference on Trade and Development (UNCTAD) in 1964. Mason and Asher noted that, although Woods's policy of cooperation later appeared normal and self-evident, at the time "most people in the Bank felt that the 'normal' way for it to expand its lending in a new field would be to hire the necessary experts."[162] Davidson Sommers remembered a Bank that was standoffish and "supercilious" in its attitude to other international organizations. He suggested to Woods that the Bank was in such a strong position that it could benefit by cooperating with these other international organizations, particularly the ones that had strong technical staffs.[163] According to Julian Grenfell,

> When Woods decided that it was not enough for the Bank simply to focus on infrastructure . . . he said, "Look, we will have to have a major expansion in [education, agriculture, industry, program loans]. . . . Why are we not using the expertise of the individual agencies to identify and prepare projects that could be the subject for investment by the World Bank instead of us relying on our relatively small staff to do the same work?"[164]

If Woods indeed pushed cooperation, it is also the case that, much earlier, in October 1960, discussing the Bank's first water supply project at a Staff Committee meeting, Knapp had asked whether WHO had been consulted. "The whole question of IDA and the UN agencies was becoming a hot subject. We might set up an informal relationship . . . and get off on the right foot about this."[165] Similarly, when

162. The formal denial of permission to float bonds in the United States capital market in 1966 (see chapter 15) was preceded by several years of informal discouragement. Ralph Hirschtritt, deputy secretary of the Treasury responsible for the multilateral institutions and former U.S. executive director, said: "Usually we didn't have to formally deny it. This was discussed and we would tell the Bank to look elsewhere, actively; after . . . maybe they could come here." Hirschtritt, interview, World Bank Oral History Program, November 22, 1985, p. 9.

163. Mason and Asher, *World Bank since Bretton Woods*, p. 571.

164. Sommers, Oral History, July 18, 1985, p. 11.

165. Grenfell, Oral History, July 15, 1986. Willi Wapenhans reported that as early as 1963 George Woods had looked at a number of agriculture projects and told staff that "if you can't

Rist began to study the economics of education lending in 1961, he sought advice from academic experts and from organizations such as the OECD and UNESCO.

From 1961 onward there was considerable correspondence between UNESCO and the Bank, especially with Demuth on the Bank side.[166] There was "acute sensitivity on both sides about each other's territory," but "UNESCO was indisputably the lead UN agency in education, with a solid reputation, global influence and a strong network of experts."[167] On the other hand, UNESCO was poor, so the relationship prospered, driven by mutual interest and helped by Demuth's skillful diplomacy. The Bank entrusted much of its sectoral investigation and project identification work to UNESCO, compensating the organization for the salary cost of a group of experts (approved by the IBRD) recruited to carry out preinvestment work on projects designed for Bank or IDA financing. Initially, it kept its own education staff deliberately small. More, it borrowed a UNESCO official, Ricardo Diez Hochleitner, to serve as the Bank's first education chief, from 1962 to 1964, a relationship that continued when the official returned to UNESCO to head the UNESCO–World Bank Cooperative Agreement through 1968.[168]

A similar cooperative agreement signed with the FAO helped pave the way for the Bank's expansion of lending to agriculture, while a less formal working relationship (finally formalized in 1971) developed with WHO as the Bank more gradually expanded its lending for municipal water and sanitation. Reviewing the WHO relationship in December 1964, the Bank concluded that "a continuation of the very satisfactory cooperation which had been obtained in the past would be very desirable for future joint or supplementary activities."[169] Gradually, however, the Bank increased its in-house capacity in each of these lending fields, so much that, writing in the early 1970s, Mason and Asher were moved to "confess to some surprise . . . at the course of the Bank's own administrative expenditures for agriculture and education since the 1963–64 decisions to rely heavily on FAO and Unesco. . . . Obviously, the Bank has been increasing its own stable of specialists in these sectors more rapidly than have the units in FAO and Unesco that are financed by the joint programs."[170] In either case, as it drew on the expertise of

---

do better than that we'll get the FAO to participate in planning the preinvestment of the projects." Cited in ibid., p. 28. Grenfell also recalled that Woods's friendly UNCTAD speech in 1964 had caused "a great deal of dismay" among staff (p. 29).

166. IBRD, "Rough Notes of Staff Loan Committee Meeting," October 21, 1960, p. 1.

167. Jones, *World Bank Financing of Education*, p. 46.

168. Ibid., p. 47. Demuth disputes this view, saying that "UNESCO did not have a single educational expert on its staff until its agreement with the Bank." Demuth, personal communication to authors, 1995.

169. This precedent was followed in 1969 when McNamara created the Population Projects Department, appointing Dr. Kandiah Kanagaratnam, a Singaporean and senior United Nations official as its first director.

170. Minutes of the Working Group on Procedures for Cooperation between WHO and IBRD, December 10–11, 1964, p. 1.

others, and as it expanded its own technical "stable," the Bank was increasing its operational capacity and potential influence.

Cooperation also became a door that let in the broader, more systemic, and usually more socially oriented perspectives and concerns of the United Nations agencies. "Unesco sector reports on education . . . [had] a powerful educative effect on Bank staff," according to Phillip Jones.[171] The Bank restricted lending through the 1960s to what it saw as strictly "developmental" investments in education, which it defined as technical secondary and vocational schools, yet, through the reports and personal interventions of its director general, René Maheu, and of Diez Hochleitner, UNESCO was an untiring advocate for more attention to literacy, informal education, primary schooling, and educational policy. In the same way, WHO drew the Bank's attention to health, and FAO to land tenure and smallholder agriculture. In 1965 the Bank's Agriculture Department compared its policies with those of FAO and reported there were no basic disagreements, but that

> if there are differences, they appear to lie more in the degree of emphasis to be given to improvement of income distribution as compared to economic growth. [In particular] the tendency of FAO to give priority to small farmers and the Bank [to] economic and financial viability . . . [and] FAO's concern with regional inequalities in income and the Bank's preference for projects producing high returns. . . . [Also], FAO recommends that labor costs be priced at half the market price.[172]

These outside perspectives and nagging had little effect on projects during the decade, but probably helped prepare the Bank for its poverty orientation in the 1970s.

Poverty between Nations

During the 1960s the Bank was transformed from a source of capital for rich and poor nations alike to a lender that, in practice, lent only to poor countries.[173] Both IDA and the IBRD were part of that change. In the case of both institutions the proximate cause was financial scarcity and its consequence: the need (and the opportunity) for rationing. Relative income differences between countries, a concept rarely mentioned before 1960, quickly became an accepted criterion in the subsequent allocation, or rationing, of IDA and IBRD funds.

This happened first, most suddenly, and most visibly with IDA. The concept of relative income was formally introduced into the Bank through IDA's Charter which, in contrast to the universality that characterized Bretton Woods, defined the Association's purpose as economic progress for *the less developed areas* of the world, and which split the Bank's membership into rich and poor countries,

171. Mason and Asher, *World Bank since Bretton Woods*, pp. 572–73.
172. Jones, *World Bank Financing of Education*, p. 52.
173. Memorandum, S. Takahashi to files, August 3, 1965.

diplomatically termed "Part I" and "Part II."[174] The idea of relative poverty soon gained added acceptance and currency as it became necessary to decide the allocation of IDA's limited budget. The Bank's engrossment with India and Pakistan—strongly justified by the relative poverty criterion—may have quickened that acceptance.[175]

An effort to codify IDA lending policy in November 1963 listed "need or poverty" along with "performance" and "creditworthiness" as criteria for IDA allocation.[176] The paper proposed a "means test" for IDA eligibility, suggesting a per capita income cutoff of $250. Going further, it suggested the application of distributive weights as a tool for allocation: "Allowance should presumably be made for the value judgment that it is more desirable to increase income in poorer countries than in countries that are not so poor. Thus income streams in different countries should be 'utility weighted.' . . . The poorer a country is, the more valuable a given increase in income will be."[177]

Distributive and utility weights, and the underlying pretension that the poverty criterion could be applied in a scientific manner, were not mentioned again for another decade, but the elementary version of that concept, the income per capita cutoff, became standard IDA practice.[178] The practice was sanctioned by a Board

174. The full transformation extended from the 1950s, with the graduation of four European borrowers (France, Luxembourg, Netherlands, and Belgium) into the 1970s. Last loans to other "rich" borrowers were: Japan (1966), New Zealand (1972), Iceland (1974), Finland (1975), Iran (1975), Israel (1975), Singapore (1975), Ireland (1976), Spain (1977), and Greece (1979). But, as noted earlier, most of the change occurred during the 1960s: Bank Group lending to rich borrowers (and their colonies) had fallen from 43 percent during the 1950s to 7 percent over 1968–69.

175. IDA, *Articles of Agreement,* art. I. Part I and Part II countries were defined in a list (Schedule A) attached at the end of the Charter. Of the seventeen Part I members, fourteen were sometime borrowers from IBRD. Demuth comments: "It was startling (but very satisfactory) that the Executive Directors accepted the staff's division of members into Part I and Part II countries without any acrimonious or lengthy debates." Richard H. Demuth, personal communication, 1995.

176. A history of early aid coordination states: "Aid to India is the one operation to which the aid-givers as a corporate entity, as distinct from individual aid-givers with special interests, appear irrevocably committed." John White, *Pledged to Development: A Study of International Consortia and the Strategy of Aid* (London: Overseas Development Institute, 1967), p. 29. Andrew Shonfield introduced an overview of development in *The Attack on World Poverty,* p. xii: "The reader will notice that Indian experiences and problems are constantly cited by way of example . . . because I regard India as a special kind of test case for the West. If we can manage this one, we should be able to deal with the rest." Knapp's briefing note to Woods before the 1963 Annual General Meeting negotiation with Indian officials says: "It is assumed that the Bank continues to lend in both India and Pakistan after the presently agreed margins are exhausted. . . . If the Bank [falls short] the burden would be shifted to IDA."

177. IBRD, "IDA Lending Policy," Report EC-119b, November 26, 1963, prepared by the Economic Staff.

178. Ibid., pp. 8 and 14.

Table 4-5. *IDA Commitments to Countries Classified by Per Capita GNP*[a]
Annual averages

		FY1961–68		FY1969–73	
Classification of recipients	Number of countries	Millions of U.S. dollars	Percent	Millions of U.S. dollars	Percent
Poorest (up to $120)	32	181	79	564	76
Indian subcontinent	2	157	69	356	48
Indonesia	1	—	—	90	12
Other[b]	29	24	10	118	16
Intermediate ($121–250)	29	21	9	109	15
Above $250	4	27	12	59	8

Source: "IDA Lending Policies," IDA/R73-7, February 7, 1973, p. 4; and Benjamin King, "Report of the Working Group on IDA Policies," Draft, May 24, 1968, annex IIB.

a. Per capita GNP figures are from *1972 World Bank Atlas*.

b. Other countries include Afghanistan, Burma, Burundi, Cameroon, Central African Republic, Chad, Congo (B), Congo (K), Dahomey, Ethiopia, Gambia, Haiti, Kenya, Laos, Malagasy Republic, Malawi, Mali, Nepal, Niger, Nigeria, Rwanda, Somalia, Sudan, Tanzania, Thailand, Togo, Uganda, Upper Volta, and Vietnam.

debate in August 1964, though the cutoff was approved as a "guideline," not an absolute limit. This policy, and the $250 figure, remained unchanged until a new Board decision in July 1968 proposed a slight increase in the figure, to "perhaps $300." A later Board decision, in March 1973, raised the amount to $375 and began the practice of annual inflation adjustments to maintain that figure in real terms.[179]

The allocation of IDA over the decade by countries classified by income level is shown in table 4-5. The picture is dominated by the large allotment—69 percent— to India and Pakistan, where GDP per capita was under $100. A group of twenty-five countries defined as the "least developed" by a 1971 United Nations resolution, and which excludes India and Pakistan, received 8 percent.[180] Countries above the $250 cutoff, such as Chile, Costa Rica, and Colombia, received 12 percent, but most of that amount was committed during the first years of IDA, before the relative income criterion took firm hold. The combined effect of the per capita income criterion, Indonesia's absence from the scene, and the enormous difficulties that attended lending—at traditional Bank standards—to new African members, was an exceptionally high concentration of IDA operations in the Indian

179. Members of the Staff Economic Committee were in "general agreement that the solution based on an income cut-off was theoretically inferior but might be necessary from an operational point of view." Memorandum of August 21, 1963, from Doreen Crompton to Staff Economic Committee summarizing Committee meeting on August 9, p. 3.

180. Memorandum from the secretary, "Meeting of Financial Policy Committee, July 23, 1968: Chairman's Statement on Discussion of IDA Policies," IDA/SECM6875, July 31, 1968; paper on IDA lending policies, IDA R737, February 7, 1973. For a detailed account of IDA distribution policy, see chapter 17.

subcontinent.[181] For the only time in IDA's history, IDA commitments to India and Pakistan during the 1960s surpassed those of other IDA-eligible countries in per capita terms: $2.30 for India and Pakistan and $1.42 for other IDA members.

By the middle of the decade IDA's poverty orientation was visibly reflected in its country allocation. What was more important though less evident was that in practice relative poverty had begun to displace the Bank's official criterion for IDA soft lending, namely, the existence of a balance of payments constraint on foreign borrowing at commercial terms. Today's poverty, measured by average national income, became a shorthand, a credible proxy for tomorrow's debt repayment problems. The exceptions—very poor nations with strong foreign exchange positions such as Nigeria and the Philippines, and less poor countries constrained by high debt burdens such as Turkey—were few and did not challenge the seeming strong association between poverty and long-run foreign capital need.[182] This conceptual melding was reflected in Woods's explanation that IDA was established to make soft loans "to countries too poor to borrow at conventional rates."[183] Similarly, John Adler explained, the Bank "recognized that by and large the poorer countries among the developing countries had less freedom of action in the setting of their economic policies and obviously a longer way to go on the arduous path of development than the better-to-do countries in the group, *and therefore were more deserving of grant-type assistance.*"[184]

The transformation of IBRD into a poor-country lender came about through graduation, as better-off clients stopped, or were discouraged from, borrowing, mostly during the 1960s and 1970s. France and Luxembourg did not borrow after their reconstruction loans, approved in 1947 and 1948, respectively, nor did the Netherlands and Belgium after 1957 and 1958.[185] The concept of graduation was implied in the Charter, which requires that "in the prevailing market conditions the borrower would be unable otherwise to obtain the loan under conditions which in the opinion of the Bank are reasonable for the borrower."[186] Given the likely

181. This concept was pushed by France, which wished to favor the small, Francophone countries, mostly in Africa.

182. There were no loans to Indonesia under President Sukarno.

183. "The Philippines presented the apparently paradoxical picture of a low-income country [which] did not make any immediate claim for IDA assistance, since the remaining margin of creditworthiness [for commercial term borrowing] was unlikely to be exhausted in the near future." IBRD, "Notes of Meeting of Staff Economic Committee on October 24, 1963," p. 1. Turkey, which exceeded the $250 cutoff but was highly indebted, received $92.5 million in nine IDA credits during the 1960s.

184. George Woods, "The Development Decade in the Balance," *Foreign Affairs,* vol. 44, no. 2 (January 1966), p. 208.

185. John Adler, "The World Bank's Concept of Development—An In-House *Dogmengeschicte,*" in Bhagwati and Eckaus, *Development and Planning,* p. 44. Emphasis added. In the sentence quoted, Adler is referring to actual practice during the 1960s.

186. Four members never borrowed: the United States, Canada, the United Kingdom, and Germany.

correlation between market access at "reasonable" terms and a borrower's economic strength, graduations would have been the expected consequence of a process of development by individual nations accompanied by an opening of world capital markets. Yet the 1957 and 1958 loans to the Netherlands and Belgium were not seen, at the time, as "last" loans. It was in late 1963 that the Bank began to consider the systematic exclusion of better-off members from access to borrowing.

That consideration followed the appearance of an imminent scarcity of IBRD resources, a direct consequence of the U.S. balance of payments deficit that surfaced in 1960 and grew worse over the decade. In 1964 the U.S. Treasury requested that the Bank restrict borrowings in the domestic market. Two years later, the request became a formal denial of permission to borrow. Over late 1963 and early 1964 staff began to discuss whether Bank loans should continue to be available to the more advanced countries that could easily borrow at market rates of interest.[187] In March 1964 Austria, which had borrowed in 1962, approached the Bank for a new loan and was told by Knapp that its prospects of borrowing in New York were good and if so, "we would expect [it] to do so . . . [and] not come to the Bank merely to seek the advantage of a lower interest rate."[188] In mid-1965 the Staff Loan Committee complained that Spain was failing to borrow in private capital markets and noted that "the Bank might find it necessary in the next year or so to introduce some rationing of its lendable funds and that in such circumstances the Bank might have to reduce the amount of lending it presently contemplated for Spain."[189] Other less poor borrowers were similarly being discouraged.[190]

By October the staff had fixed on the idea of charging better-off countries a higher interest rate—a reverse discrimination—as a disincentive to borrowing, despite the paradoxical implication that creditworthiness would be penalized. Woods justified the proposal saying that he was particularly concerned with raising money during the coming six months.[191] Probable victims objected; for the Australian director, the scheme "would turn the Bank into more of an aid institution" and "aid and welfare were matters for IDA." But his sharp reminder that the Bank "had hitherto . . . followed accepted market principles" was countered by another director who noted that "charging what traffic would bear" was accepted business practice.[192] Woods instead openly stressed the distributive rationale, noting that all IBRD loans enjoyed a subsidy, and further that the Bank's technical assistance was not distributed on a pro rata basis to all borrowers. Hence it was "reasonable that

187. IBRD, *Articles of Agreement,* art. III, sec. 4.

188. Oliver, *George Woods and the World Bank,* p. 168.

189. Memorandum, J. Burke Knapp to George D. Woods, "Austria," March 4, 1964.

190. IBRD/IDA, "Minutes of Meeting of Loan Committee Held on July 12, 1965," LC/M/6514, August 2, 1965, p. 2.

191. Memorandum, J. Burke Knapp to George D. Woods, "Austria," March 4, 1964.

192. IBRD, "Memorandum of Meeting of Financial Policy Committee," Bank/FPC/6419, December 17, 1964.

those who had already achieved some credit standing should be subsidized less. The completely unsophisticated new country . . . should enjoy the maximum benefit." The higher rates were approved, mostly because, as Donner put it, where "the Bank had before had more freedom and was not constrained by a lack of financial resources . . . the situation was now completely different."[193] This policy lasted only a few years, but, as a signal and as a financial disincentive, the measure helped the Bank wean most of its better-off borrowers. Australia, Austria, Belgium, Denmark, the Netherlands, Malta, Norway, Italy, and Japan all received their last loans between 1957 and 1967.[194] Moreover, the temporary measure served notice that the IBRD, too, and not only IDA, had a heart.

Adler remarked on the "discovery" during the 1960s of relative income differences among developing countries:

> The suggestion that the "discovery" that there was a difference between countries with a *per capita* income of $100 and, say, $600, constituted a change in the Bank's outlook may seem almost ridiculous. It must be remembered, however, that until the early 1960s, the theoretical writing on development and the practice of agencies providing development finance did not make that distinction.[195]

Yet it bears noting that, though relative poverty became a visible basis for the country allocation of both IDA and IBRD funds, in its public explanations the Bank played down that fact, stressing instead the country creditworthiness and project quality considerations that went into the loan decisions of both institutions.

Poverty within Nations

Encounters with internal inequality became more frequent as lending was diversified, economic work took on a broader, countrywide development focus, and aid coordination increased the Bank's interaction with socially minded United Nations agencies. But the logic of need had come alive and was sustained by IDA and stimulated by new operations. The 1963 IDA policy paper followed that logic when it went on from a discussion of the per capita income cutoff for country

193. Ibid., pp. 3, 4.

194. Ibid. "In February 1965 the Bank introduced a 'market eligible' rate for those countries that were able to 'cover their external capital needs mainly in private markets.' This rate was to be no more than 1 percent above the standard Bank lending rate and was intended to approximate the market rate at which such countries could borrow. . . . [It] remained in effect until late 1967." When a proposal to reintroduce higher rates for higher-income borrowers was discussed by the Board on January 21, 1975, the president's memorandum discussing the measure described it as "based essentially on equity grounds." Memorandum to Executive Directors, "Review of IBRD/IDA Program and Financial Policies," R74256, December 12, 1974, p. 24.

195. A later round of graduations, during the 1970s, covered middle-income, oil-rich, and rapid-growth countries such as Spain, Greece, Portugal, Finland, Israel, Iraq, Iran, Taiwan, and Singapore.

allocation to propose that relative income also be considered in the allocation of IDA funds within countries:

> It might therefore be judged proper . . . to take into account the extent to which an IDA credit will help to raise incomes in the more backward areas of a country. . . . The phenomenon of a "dual economy" is well exemplified today in many of the under-developed countries. . . . Many countries . . . are saddled with regressive systems of public finance. In such cases it could be argued that the adoption of appropriate measures of income redistribution should be made a condition of IDA lending.[196]

The suggestion was dropped; the Bank was not ready to extend its recognition of an allocative claim from poor countries to poor groups within countries. Nonetheless, such questions were becoming common in operations, even if they were kept largely in the background.

One such issue was land reform. Surprisingly, this exceptionally sensitive measure was among the first to be raised and openly discussed. Woods's 1964 policy paper on agriculture stated that tenure reform was likely to be "an essential condition" to agricultural development in some areas.[197] The early appearance of this radical proposal, however, was in context with the turn taken by cold war politics, which had produced a spate of concern over the communist potential of inequitable social arrangements. Under the umbrella of the Alliance for Progress, the United States offered large-scale aid to Latin America conditioned on major social changes, including land reform. Even conservative economists spoke out: Arnold Harberger affirmed that "a society simply cannot thrive with 50 percent of its people alienated from the mainstream of activity," and that "come what may, agrarian reform is in the cards in many parts of Latin America."[198] Land reform was in any case already high on third-world political agendas: the early 1960s saw agitation, land takeovers, and reform legislation in Indonesia, Iran, the Philippines, and in no less than fourteen Latin American nations.[199] Meanwhile, India was struggling to implement reforms initiated at the state level. Simultaneously, the FAO embarked on an aggressive campaign advocating tenure reform.

A 1962 Bank mission to Colombia concluded that "the slowness with which the benefits of economic growth had accrued to the people in general, and to the

---

196. Adler, "The World Bank's Concept of Development," p. 44.

197. IBRD, "IDA Lending Policy," Report EC-119b, p. 11.

198. IBRD/IDA, "Report of the President to the Executive Directors on Proposed Bank/IDA Policies in the Field of Agriculture," Report FPC/641, January 17, 1964, p. 5. The report doubted, however, that the Bank could finance the purchase of land, a position that would be repeated in future statements on land reform.

199. Arnold Harberger, "Economic Policy Problems in Latin America," *Journal of Political Economy*, vol. 78, no. 4 (supplement to July/August 1970), p. 1010. The comment was originally made as part of the concluding remarks at a 1966 conference, "Key Problems of Economic Policy in Latin America," organized by the University of Chicago in 1966.

low-income farmers in particular" was a major development problem.[200] But, it argued, "safeguarding and nurturing the currently productive segments of the agricultural economy" was more important than rapid redistribution, and the Bank settled in to support Colombia's policy of mild and largely ineffectual reform.[201]

A mission to Mexico in 1966 produced a more radical critique of land tenure and of the "general bias of Government policy in favor of the larger and more efficient producers," but the report was shelved after objections by senior staff and Mexican officials.[202] For the most part Bank operations avoided the political and administrative complications of land reform, despite occasional questions raised by economic reports and the political impetus behind the issue early in the decade. An internal retrospective review of the Bank's work in agriculture during the 1960s makes no reference to land reform.[203]

If one element of Woods's developmental agenda came to be associated with the poverty objective, it was the increase and diversification of agricultural lending. The interest in more agricultural lending had first arisen as a solution to the problem of how to lend to very poor, largely agrarian, new African members. But even then, the policy was also associated with a concern for the poorest *within* countries, a view reinforced by perceptions of a "food crisis." Raúl Prebisch, for instance, who was advocating radical land reform during the first (1964) UNCTAD conference, praised the "enlightened" lending policy announced by Woods at the meeting.[204] In later decades, the perceived linkage between agriculture and poverty alleviation became even stronger.

One result of that closeness was that agriculture became the operational terrain where staff were most explicit in drawing the line between output and poverty considerations. A major instance was a 1964 Bank report on Indian agricultural policy, which argued that the

200. Major legislative agrarian reforms were passed in Venezuela (1960), Colombia (1961), Costa Rica (1961), El Salvador (1961), Chile (1962), Dominican Republic (1962), Guatemala (1962), Honduras (1962), Panama (1962), Nicaragua (1963), Paraguay (1963), Brazil (1964), Peru (1964), and Ecuador (1965). Actual implementation was weak, at best, in almost all cases.

201. As reported in IBRD, "Operations Evaluation Report: Colombia," vol. 6, "The Agricultural Sector," October 31, 1971, p. 14.

202. Memorandum, Wolf Ladejinsky to J. Evans, "Mexico—Economic Mission Back . . . Office Report," April 14, 1966; and conversation with Enrique Lerdau who headed the economic mission. Lerdau recalls that the report nonetheless became—in his term—a piece of *zamizat* (Russian underground literature) in the Bank. The chief objector was J. Evans, head of Agricultural Projects.

203. World Bank, "Agriculture," Sector Program Paper R72100, May 2, 1972. An account of agriculture in South Asia by Bank economist Inderjit Singh, *The Great Ascent: The Rural Poor in South Asia* (John Hopkins University Press, 1990), discusses land reform under the telling subtitle: "The Missed Opportunity."

204. It was at this meeting that Prebisch compared Woods to Pope John XXIII.

basic reason for the slow rise in the productivity of Indian agriculture seems to be that Indian farm policy has been directed largely toward social welfare objectives. . . . [P]olicy has been oriented to the two-thirds of the farm families tilling less than five acres. . . . [T]his group would be ill-equipped to undertake the type of management necessary for rapid increase in output on a mass basis. Yet Indian farm policy continues to be directed toward the alleviation of poverty rather than the expansion of output.[205]

Therefore, "policy should be reoriented to the needs of medium and large sized farmers." Gradual land reform, it said, was creating uncertainty and was "pointless . . . if production expansion is a serious public objective." And, though recognizing that "the low-income farm problem is real and must be treated," it argued that the only ultimate solution lay in the growth of nonfarm employment. "Whatever is done [within agriculture] it cannot be with the intent of more than a holding action."[206] The subsequent Bell Mission Report on India stressed the priority of agriculture but made no reference to poverty alleviation or to relative need, and its discussion and proposals were framed entirely in terms of aggregate output. The implicit priority given to production was later reflected in preferential support for better-off farmers in the Punjab. Reviewing India's problems in 1967, Friedman attributed them to the governmental excess of objectives, which included not only growth of exports and other production but also improving the distribution of income and promoting full employment. "My personal view," he said, "is that they will not be on a firm foundation for growth until they have clearly decided that increased growth and improved efficiency is the number 1 priority."[207]

Lending for education and water supplies reflected a similar tension between their perceived "social" or not strictly productive nature and the continuing conviction that all Bank investments and advice should seek the maximum contribution to economic growth. As with agriculture, the Bank's response to this conflict was to be particularly emphatic about the productive justification for individual water and education projects.

In the case of water supplies, "production" was associated with revenue generation, that is the possibility of collecting water rates, and with industrial consumption.[208] Through the decade staff members struggled with a sense that water supplies were a "social" contraband. One official noted that lending for water projects "has been accepted in principle. But in practice, there seems to be more reluctance to lend for [water supply projects] than for, say, roads or power plants."[209]

205. IBRD, "Some Observations on Indian Agricultural Policy," draft, September 1, 1964, p. 1. This statement of the Bank's position differed from that of many in the aid community and in the government of India. See chapter 8.

206. Ibid., pp. 3, 23.

207. Memorandum, Irving Friedman to George Woods, "India," April 24, 1967, p. 5.

208. In a memorandum to the files, May 13, 1966, H. G. van der Tak argued the need for a paper on water supply projects that would "refute the suggestion that water supply projects need to be of low priority because they are so-called 'non-productive'" (p. 1).

209. Memorandum, C. A. Ryshpan to Walter Armstrong, "Economic Appraisal of Water Supply Projects," July 11, 1966.

In 1966 there developed a concern to cool the enthusiasm for water supply lending. Knapp cautioned against an excessively fast growth in such lending, while Michael Hoffman worried about the problem "posed by the energy with which the World Health Organization is producing urban water supply projects which, if carried out, would require huge amounts of capital."[210] Kamarck suggested that as "an immediate deterrent" to WHO's enthusiasm, "more attention should be given to possible unfavorable side effects of improved water supply," such as higher population growth and overcrowding.[211]

Somewhat defensively, the Water Supply Projects Department insisted on strict financial and productive justification of their projects. One official wrote: "Water must be paid for at whatever its cost. . . . This does not exclude the city paying for water used at public taps and which the poor people must have. It does insure, however, that the water utility is not being asked to run the welfare agency."[212] Since much of the poverty-alleviation effect of water supply projects arises in the form of hard-to-measure indirect benefits, or public health externalities, such effects were in practice discounted—in comparison with the weight given to more measurable revenue generation—at the moment of project appraisal. One result was to downplay sewerage in relation to water supply.[213] Another poverty-related consequence was rural-urban allocation. On this, an official listed reasons to justify an urban bias, such as ease of project implementation, faster population growth, more local financial support, and even cultural attitudes:

> Urban communities are generally regarded as pacesetters in cultural innovation, and it may be difficult or impossible to convince rural inhabitants of the need for better standards of water service . . . if their urban brethren have not accepted them first. It is because of these many factors that the World Bank has found few instances where rural water projects could meet its criteria for investment.[214]

Knapp had earlier sought to soften this bias, recommending that Bank projects should avoid the largest cities: "I am not saying we should go for the villages and the hamlets but I wonder if we couldn't make a more effective contribution by con-

210. Memorandum, A. M. Kamarck to Michael Hoffman, "United Nations Development Program—Urban Water supply," March 21, 1966. In a memorandum from J. Burke Knapp to Siem Aldewereld, December 27, 1966, Knapp wrote: "I would like to talk to you upon your return about whether we are not 'plunging overboard' on water projects."

211. At the same time, Hoffman wrote the UNDP—which assisted the Bank by financing project identification—to express the Bank's strong interest in water supply lending. Memorandum, Kamarck to Hoffman, March 21, 1966.

212. Letter, Harold Shipman, deputy to the assistant director, Water Supply Projects Department, to Richard Pelz, chairman, Interdepartmental Task Force, Water for Peace, U.S. Department of the Interior, July 14, 1966.

213. Memorandum, Harold Shipman to David Knox, October 21, 1968. Shipman asked, "Is the Bank's present policy of water first, sewerage second, one which should be continued?"

214. Letter, Shipman to Pelz, July 14, 1966, attachment.

centrating on the secondary cities and towns. . . . [I]t seems to be preferable on social . . . grounds to cultivate some degree of decentralization."[215] Two years before, however, Demuth had turned down a proposal from the Pan American Health Organization for a joint program to develop rural water supplies throughout Latin America.[216] In the end, it was the Inter-American Development Bank that invested heavily in such projects.

Contrary to the Bank's original expectations, most of the financing for water supply projects during the decade was provided by the IBRD rather than IDA. The high points given to revenue generation and to financial rates of return made water supply projects suitable for IBRD financing. At the same time, the need for assistance in this sector, as well as the administrative capacity to administer water supply systems, seemed relatively greater in the more urbanized middle-income, non-IDA countries. Yet, though water supply lending thus avoided the poorest in several ways—through the choice of countries, urban over rural, and project designs targeted for revenue rather than public health—the record on project implementation was nevertheless troublesome. A 1971 review of water supply lending stated: "The most important lesson is that lending in this sector is more difficult than had been expected. . . . [M]ost borrowers have been poorly managed. . . . We now recognize that local officials and water managers are generally less able, less accustomed to thinking in hard financial and economic terms, and more exposed to direct political pressure than in other public utility sectors."[217] This conclusion tended to support the fear, shared by most senior staff members during the 1960s, that welfare-oriented lending would be costly in terms of efficiency and production, but, as it happened, the cautionary lesson was probably untimely and unwelcome, emerging just as the Bank was gearing up for a much larger charge into the poverty-alleviation arena.

The priority of output was kept well in sight in education lending also, perhaps with less effort than in the case of water supplies: education had no forceful welfare or poverty aspect that thrust itself forward on the Bank's attention as did the issue of public health. Woods's first policy statement noted that "educational expenditures serve social and cultural, as well as economic objectives," but, for Bank lending, "I believe that only economic factors should be taken into consideration."[218] That primacy was ensured, first by choosing investments in the most visibly and immediately "productive" forms of education, especially vocational and techni-

216. Memorandum, J. Burke Knapp to Hugh Ripman, "Selection of Water Supply and Sewer Projects," July 6, 1965.
216. Memorandum, Richard Demuth to files, "Pan American Health Organization Proposal for a Rural Water Supply Program," October 15, 1963.
217. IBRD, "Water Supply and Sewerage," Sector Program Paper R7184, April 22, 1971, pp. 8–9.
218. IBRD, "Education." Report to the Financial Policy Committee regarding proposed Bank/IDA policies in the field of education, October 31, 1963, p. 2.

cal training at the secondary and higher levels. Second, the Bank sought to justify and tie in its educational projects with the manpower gaps revealed by other Bank projects in the borrowing country.[219] Third, the Bank's characteristic insistence on high engineering and other technical standards and on isolated specific projects—an insistence probably sharpened by the inability to calculate convincing rates of return for educational investments—meant the rejection of cheaper, more replicable, and more poverty-oriented forms of educational investment. Marble cladding on the walls of the inaugural project's technical secondary schools in Tunisia became a symbol of that implicit choice.[220]

Yet education did not escape the image that, in Ballantine's words, "it wasn't an economic thing . . . especially [for] the more conservative who grew up in the banking business or Wall Street. . . . It was social, or it was consumption. Not investment."[221] Unlike water supplies, which could be self-financing through revenues, education was not "suitable" for the IBRD. IDA made 78 percent of education loans up to 1968, fulfilling the original expectation that such lending would be tied to that organization. Yet education gave the Bank an instrument for providing support to relatively poor countries, and it became a means to reinforce lending for agriculture and other more "developmental" investments that needed training and strong technical assistance components.

Like water supplies, however, education loans provided an apprenticeship in the implementation difficulties that would be faced by later poverty lending, in particular, a greater involvement with weak local administrations and need for local subcontracting.[222] Ballantine recalled: "These were not turn-key operations. You were working with very primitive executive capacity, especially when we got into the rural area. The projects weren't big enough to draw in a contractor from outside. . . . So you were dependent on local people. . . . We had to cope with a lot of local stuff."[223]

Reprise: The Logic of Need

There was always a seed of income redistribution—from affluent to needier nations—in the Bank's purpose, despite the early avoidance of normative language and a plausible reading of the Bank's Articles that its "prime task" was to foster capital flows between countries on an income-blind basis.[224] The seed was fathered

219. Duncan S. Ballantine, interview, World Bank Oral History Program, November 21, 1986, pp. 2–3.

220. Jones, *World Bank Financing of Education*, pp. 57–58.

221. Ballantine, Oral History, November 21, 1986, p. 23.

222. OED, Review of "Bank Operations in the Education Sector," report no. 2321, 1978.

223. Ballantine, Oral History, November 21, 1986, p. 22.

224. Alec Cairncross, *The International Bank for Reconstruction and Development*, Essays in International Finance 33 (Princeton University, March 1959), pp. 5–6.

by the de facto association between financial need and relative poverty, and, one could say, mothered by the Bank's paid-in capital and member government guarantees, which provided the necessary subsidy. If conception was mostly an accident, that was another matter. The redistributive purpose began to come into view when the Bank was displaced from its primary European reconstruction task and rededicated to "development," a move that greatly increased the apparent association between claims to Bank resources and relative poverty between nations. From the first, the Bank took to its development role with a sense of mission and tutelary responsibility that, it argued, was needed to ensure "sound" lending. But the extraordinary success of the 1950s Bank in leveraging its subsidy in the financial markets tended to bury, in both fact and appearance, the redistributive possibility and its publicly funded means (see chapter 3). Much of that success was a reward for strict adherence to the role of a market-based, production-focused institution, a policy that was aided by the Bank's smallness, the inclinations of its principal officers, and a prevailing development model that equated any response to immediate need with *less* poverty alleviation in the long run. The Bank was *not* another New Deal institution, was the repeated message. Substantial lending to developed countries in Europe and to Japan and Australia reinforced the "soundness" of the Bank's portfolio, though, for a time, it distanced the Bank from its redistributive potential. Market dependence, in turn, protected the Bank from the growing demands for a more charitable lending policy, a role that the Bank saw as merely palliative. Strangely, it was Bretton Woods's most ethical progeny that was the illicit child, and that was loudly denied.

But new political and conceptual tides, peaking between 1958 and 1961, pressed the Bank into more immediate service on behalf of poverty and need. Going further than moral and political suasion, they irrupted into the very precincts of the Bank with the creation of IDA, an institutional arrangement as incongruous then as would have been a merger between Salomon Brothers and the Ford Foundation. In 1963 the instincts of a new president—George Woods—caught the political mood with an agenda for change, adding the rhetoric of "new horizons" and a "developmental" role to the operational changes already begun by Eugene Black. Reluctant Board members and senior officers were no match for the external pressures, and many were in fact caught up by the adventure of charting a more developmental role for the IBRD and debating the essential poverty purpose of IDA. "IDA funds were for the needy," said the French director in 1964, countering his German colleague's insistence that IDA should emphasize economic results and not "rush wherever the red lamp of poverty lit up."[225] From the early 1960s, poverty and need had become open contenders with output in allocation decisions.

225. IBRD, "Memorandum of Resumed Meeting of IDA Financial Policy Committee," IDA FPC/6410, August 12, 1964, p. 6. Statement by Donner, memorandum of meeting of IDA Financial Policy Committee on "IDA Lending Policy," FPC/649, August 10, 1964, p. 4.

As already noted, Bank operations moved a long way toward the poor over the 1960s. At the same time, the scale of operations multiplied in several dimensions—staffing, membership, economic work, lending and aid coordination—greatly increasing the Bank's potential financial as well as advisory contribution to poverty reduction. Yet the assessment of this decade has been ambiguous.

The most negative view emerged almost immediately, in 1968, when Robert McNamara, succeeding Woods, used his first Annual General Meeting to describe the development effort as a "sharply disappointing picture" that had produced "cosmetic" results and a "deep sense of frustration and failure" in the poorer nations, where "growth is concentrated in the industrial areas, while the peasant remains stuck in his immemorial poverty, living on the bare margin of subsistence."[226] That view, followed by McNamara's own more radical efforts to alleviate poverty, amounted to an implicit deflation, if not criticism of the 1960s Bank. Mason and Asher, writing in 1970–71, also mute the scale of change in the 1960s and, in particular, the growing weight of "social" objectives, but they do so from an opposite perspective, of undisguised skepticism with regard to the appropriateness of social criteria in the Bank's work.[227] Contemporary staff members give the 1960s more credit. Knapp reflected that "there was certainly no sense at that time of a direct attack on poverty, but it certainly did begin to develop . . . long before [McNamara] came in 1968. George Woods used to speak quite eloquently about poverty problems and it was he who began our orientation of agricultural lending towards small farmers."[228] John Adler saw "a significant modification of the Bank's view on the development process."[229]

Much of the ambiguity is deliberate. The Bank was more concerned to avoid the appearance of succumbing to a political and relief role than to advertise its humanitarian impulses. It protected its reputation as an institution committed to raising production and to playing by market rules, minimizing the appearance of bending before social demands, denying any difference between IDA and the Bank when it

---

Donner had said: "The poverty criterion. . . could not be considered a principle of prime importance in determining allocation of IDA resources among the Part II countries. It would lead to the false conclusion that a project located in a poor country should be financed by IDA even though its economic results were poor and worse than those of another possible project elsewhere. If the United States had adopted this principle after World War II, the Marshall Plan would not have been born, Europe would not have recovered so quickly, and other broad shoulders would not now be available to share with the U.S. the obligation to help the countries that were still poor." But Donner's insistence on the logic of maximum output was a rearguard action, which few directors or staff members supported in full.

226. Robert McNamara, address, "To the Board of Governors, Washington, D.C., September 30, 1968," in McNamara, *The McNamara Years at the World Bank* (Johns Hopkins University Press, 1981), pp. 3–5.

227. Mason and Asher, *World Bank since Bretton Woods*, pp. 475–76, 733.

228. J. Burke Knapp, interview with the authors, October 22, 1990.

229. Adler, "The World Bank's Concept of Development," pp. 42–43.

came to project standards, and downplaying the role of need in IDA allocation. At first, Black and Woods even refused to muddy the waters by transferring profits from the IBRD to IDA. Woods's rhetorical innovations—"new horizons" and "developmental purpose"—were cautious and followed up by reassurances to Wall Street that little had changed. Over the decade, they came to appear even more cautious in contrast with Kennedy's "War on Poverty," Johnson's "Great Society," and, more important, with the beginnings of a generalized questioning of the 1950s development model that arose in poor countries, United Nations organizations, and universities.

Unusually, then, action exceeded rhetoric with respect to social goals, but how far did "need" and "poverty" actually go during this period as they encroached on the traditional objective of economic growth in Bank decisions and in its thinking? This chapter has so far chronicled the forces that pushed a social agenda: the political and intellectual empowerment of "underdevelopment," the creation of IDA, and Woods's more liberal agenda. What held back even greater change?

Several barriers—some carried forward from the 1950s, others peculiar to the 1960s—restrained further innovation during the 1960s: continuing dependence on financial markets, the lack of an alternative model, the boom-bust financial and political cycle of the decade, and presidential style.

Dependence on Financial Markets

By the end of the 1950s, the Bank had reason to lower its guard with respect to financial image. With the help of the Bank's AAA rating and the opening of world capital markets, borrowing grew rapidly over the decade. It doubled, for instance, between 1957 and 1959. Entering the 1960s, financial image was enhanced when no less than the chairman of one of the Bank's underwriters (First Boston) was appointed to succeed Black. Woods arrived to find that large reserves and high earnings were at the top of the Bank's list of "problems" to be addressed. In this context of easing financial constraints, it seems easy to understand the confidence with which he launched an adventurous proposal for a riskier lending policy. The tyranny of presumed market reaction to loan policy seemed to endure more as convenient management myth than as reality.[230]

Yet this relaxation was a matter of degree, and Woods's venture reflected his underwriter's capacity to calculate the market finely, not a disappearance of the constraint. Independently of their personal convictions regarding the place of economic and social objectives, management and Board continued to believe that the Bank could not put its borrowing capacity at risk by appearing to wander from production—preferably visible and of short gestation—as the overriding criterion for investment. At most, the straightjacket had become a cage.

230. As illustrated by Ben King's account of a loan to Norway. See chapter 3.

Lack of an Alternative Model

Restraint was more than a matter of financial dependence. It was also in the mind. Though more and more voices were raised through the decade questioning the orthodox development model, no "sound" alternative was thought to be available.

It was not for lack of authoritative academic arguments. The concept of human capital had been pioneered in the 1950s, developing out of studies suggesting that physical capital played a small role in explaining long-run per capita growth in the United States and pointing to a "residual factor," identified with education, invention, and entrepreneurship, as the key determinant of growth.[231] In 1961 Hans Singer spoke of "a shift in our whole thinking about . . . development"—from physical to human capital, but it was T. W. Schultz's translation of that idea into an economist's terminology, as "human capital," that energized and broadened its acceptance.[232] Though the emphasis was placed on education, the concept of human capital was already being extended to health.[233] As a potential alternative development model, "investment in people" had the virtue of being uncontaminated by distributive considerations—its University of Chicago promoters saw a source of growth, not equity—though, in fact, it was plausibly an avenue to both growth and a broader distribution of benefits.

A further development soon followed: T. W. Schultz, again, took the lead in extending the concept to remodel the image of the peasant farmer, whose backwardness was then commonly attributed to "irrationality" or noneconomic behavior. In a 1964 book Schultz argued that the low productivity of peasants reflected a lack, not of economic calculation nor of entrepreneurial inclinations, but of more productive technology and factors of production. The corollary, that resources provided to small farmers could yield high returns, suggested the possibility of a more equitable development pattern. Research findings—many draw-

231. Moses Abramovitz, *Resource and Output Trends in the United States since 1870*, Occasional Paper 52 (New York: National Bureau of Economic Research [NBER], 1956), pp. 6–12. See also NBER studies by John W. Kendrick, *Productivity Trends: Capital and Labor*, Occasional Paper 53, 1956; and Solomon Fabricant, *Basic Facts on Productivity Change*, Occasional Paper 63, 1959. Similar findings by Robert Solow and Edward Denison were also compelling and widely discussed. But early findings on the "residual" were obtained from already industrialized countries.

232. Hans Singer, "Education and Economic Development," in Singer, *International Development: Growth and Change* (McGraw-Hill, 1964), p. 66. Theodore W. Shultz, "Investment in Human Capital," *American Economic Review*, vol. 51 (March 1961), p. 11. In his presidential address to the Annual Meeting of the American Economic Association, December 28, 1960, Schultz had named the World Bank among those responsible for a "one-sided effort" to transfer physical capital alone to the developing countries "in spite of the fact that . . . knowledge and skills [are] the most valuable resource that we could make available to them," and, more broadly, had implicated the Bank in "our export of growth doctrines," which had contributed to the neglect of human capital (p. 16).

233. See, for instance, Enke, *Economics for Development*, pp. 398–418.

ing on the 1960 round of national censuses—that small farms had higher yields and labor productivity than large farms began to abound, providing "respectable," that is, output-based, support for land redistribution.[234]

Moreover, the concept of investment in people—extended to support for small farmers—rapidly moved beyond academia into the hands of development practitioners who were potential rivals of the Bank. Benjamin Higgins, who was then working with UNESCO, recalls:

> When the "residual factor" burst on the scene . . . UNESCO was quick to say, "the residual factor, of course, is education." ILO was equally quick to add, "true, but a major component of education for development is manpower training." FAO stressed the importance of training farmers. WHO was a bit slow in pointing out that the "residual factor" might include improvements in nutrition and health as well. In any case the economics of education became the vogue. OECD set up a special program.[235]

In 1963 Jan Tinbergen persuaded the Dutch government to finance the creation of the United Nations Research Institute for Social Development (UNRISD) and in 1966 Hans Singer published an article with the then surprising title, "Social Development: Key Growth Sector."[236]

These ideas and bureaucratic initiatives did indeed influence the Bank, providing arguments, a competitive spur, and technical support for a small and growing involvement with agriculture, education and water, and rapidly expanding technical assistance. As a general concept, however, human capital was new, competing for attention in a crowded and effervescent intellectual field. In any case, academic credentials would have been only a first step toward displacement of the received wisdom applied by development practitioners, in particular, the intuition that any concession to welfare would delay long-run development.

Those intuitions were put in evidence when Walt Rostow, Kennedy's national security adviser and an influential economist, gave a lunch talk to Bank senior economists in late 1963. He said that the central problem of development was not the poor–rich gap between nations but the poor–rich gap within the developing countries. He called for more stress on agriculture and on cheap, mass-market

234. A seminal article by Sol Tax argued that risk aversion by peasants in Guatemala was rational considering the available options. Tax, "Changing Consumption in Indian Guatemala," *Economic Development and Cultural Change*, vol. 5, no. 2 (January 1957), pp. 147–58. The commonly cited evidence on "higher yields" of small farms referred to land and labor productivity, not to other forms of capital. The debates and policy on land reform are discussed in more detail in chapter 8.

235. Benjamin Higgins, *The Road Less Travelled: A Development Economist's Quest* (Canberra, Australia: National Centre for Development Studies, 1989), p. 97. Higgins, a Canadian, worked on Indonesia, taught at MIT, and wrote a widely used textbook in development economics.

236. H. W. Arndt, *Economic Development, The History of an Idea* (University of Chicago, 1987), p. 89.

manufactured goods. Dragoslav Avramovic, the acting head of the Economic
Department during 1963 and 1964, was a critic of the orthodox development
model. Reporting to Woods on Rostow's talk he said: "It is the bitter truth that
many, perhaps most rural areas . . . after 15 years of development efforts, have
remained as miserable as they have always been." Moreover, "small farmers can, up
to a point, be just as efficient . . . as the very large ones." His critique of trickle-
down and optimism regarding smallholder farming would later be the core tenets
of McNamara's war on poverty, but (as Avramovic pointed out) in 1964 his views
were in the minority: "The majority of [senior economists] were fairly critical of Dr.
Rostow's idea. . . . There were only a few of us who came in defense."[237]

Senior staff reluctance to address questions of internal equity remained strong
by the time of Woods's departure, as is suggested by the fate of the proposal for a
new IDA lending policy prepared by Benjamin King at Woods's request.[238] The
proposal indeed made a strong case for a more poverty-based allocation of lending
between countries. But when it came to helping poorer groups within a country,
the possibility of using IDA was ruled out. IDA was said to lack the resources and
necessary expertise for "direct relief of the poor *per se.*" Furthermore, King's report
doubted whether "IDA has a mandate to intrude into the essentially political
domain concerned with inequalities in income distribution within a country."
However, the report did countenance the use of IDA to address internal inequities
if "the dual nature of the economy [constituted] a very real obstacle to development." Poverty alleviation was admissible, not for its own sake but as an instrument
for overall economic growth. Even these mild concessions were deemed too radical
for the final version of the IDA lending-policy report.

It is a rare occasion when a body of busy, practical men suddenly revise long-
standing professional views. When they do, the explanation is more likely to be found
in external circumstances than in intellectual reconsideration. In this case, however, the
notable turnabout in financial and political circumstances over the 1960s acted to
reinforce rather than to undermine a development paradigm that placed priority on
growth and was skeptical regarding attempts to shortcut the reduction of poverty.

Financial and Political Cycles

The decade opened with a crest of awareness and political concern regarding
underdevelopment. One reason was decolonization, but for the main source of

237. Memorandum, Dragoslav Avramovic to George D. Woods, February 13, 1964,
pp. 2–4. Rostow was discussing ideas given in an October 1, 1963, speech at New Orleans.
Avramovic was acting head of the Economic Department during 1963–65 and then was
appointed director of a new department called Special Economic Studies. He was succeeded by Andrew Kamarck in the Economic Department.

238. IBRD, "Report of the Working Group on IDA Policies," draft, May 24, 1968, p. 23.
Drafted at Woods's request under the supervision of Ben King.

development funds, the United States, the more important cause was a sudden metastasis of the cold war. As part of a wide-ranging institutional and financial response by the West, the Bank was given IDA funds—with a nudge into social lending—and a capital increase that reinforced its already strengthened borrowing capacity in the markets. There was in addition a mood of confidence in the West regarding technical and governmental capacities, boosted by European and Japanese recovery, American growth, and visible progress in many underdeveloped nations. Thus encouraged and reinforced, the Bank launched into a major program of expansion, sectoral broadening, and outreach to the newly independent nations. But, even as it geared up to respond, the political mood began to change and financial access to be restricted. By 1967–68 the Bank found itself overextended, in poor relations with the U.S. administration, and facing a new mood of pessimism with regard to aid and development.

One element in that political reversal was a retreat from democracy as a major foreign policy objective. When John F. Kennedy called for expanded aid, he went further than Eisenhower in linking democracy to economic and social reform. Democratic rebirths in several Latin American nations at the turn of the decade led one writer to characterize the period as "the twilight of the tyrants."[239] The push for social emergency spending—through IDA, the Inter-American Development Bank, and bilateral aid—was seen as a way to buy political support for fragile new democracies that in turn were thought to be the best bet against subversion.[240] A measure of that conviction was the U.S. decision to subvert a non-communist dictator in the Dominican Republic.[241]

The elevation of democracy in the hierarchy of aid and security objectives was short lived, however. Authoritarian governments became the rule in the developing world during the 1960s, following a series of military coups in Latin America and the birth of one-party states in Africa. Increasingly absorbed in Vietnam and less immediately concerned with subversion in its backyard, the United States muted its rhetoric on democracy and fell back on a policy of reliance on, and accommodation to, nondemocratic regimes. Authoritarian governments, less preoccupied by

239. "Since 1955 six dictatorships have vanished from the scene," wrote Tad Szulc in *Twilight of the Tyrants* (Holt, 1959), p. 3, referring to Argentina, Colombia, Venezuela, Peru, Brazil, and the Dominican Republic. Also, Turkey's military government held elections in 1961.

240. The U.S. economic aid response to earlier cold war emergencies in Asia was also heavily weighted to poverty alleviation—especially food, peasant agriculture, health, and rural infrastructure—as distinct from development projects. Likewise, after 1964, aid to Thailand came to be heavily concentrated in the poor Northeast region.

241. Castro's revolution was seen as a direct consequence of Fulgencio Batista's dictatorship. Hoping to prevent a repetition in the neighboring Dominican Republic, the U.S. supported a coup that ousted Rafael Trujillo in 1961. Richard N. Goodwin, *Remembering America: A Voice from the Sixties* (Little, Brown, 1988), p. 210. Similarly, in 1963 the United States decided to remove the corrupt strongman of Vietnam, Ngo Dinh Diem.

political survival and possessed of longer planning horizons and more freedom to impose technocratic agendas, were often at home with the Bank's traditional policy and lending preferences: stabilization and production-oriented investments.[242] The initial rush of pressure on the Bank to support social reforms and direct poverty alleviation thus gradually ebbed over the 1960s.[243] Pressure on the Bank for social lending was also relieved by the appearance of the Inter-American Development Bank, which assigned half of its lending over the decade to the social and agricultural sectors.

There was a corresponding, though even sharper cycle in the Bank's financial situation, affecting both IDA and IBRD funding. Support for IDA in the United States was hurt by rising public and congressional doubts about the purpose and efficacy of foreign aid, and by U.S. fiscal problems.[244] U.S. economic aid rose rapidly between 1958 and 1961 but then stagnated, eroded by inflation and spread more thinly over a larger number of beneficiary nations.[245] Other donors also failed to respond. Though the United Kingdom created a Ministry of Overseas Development in 1964, the size of its aid program declined over the decade. Total Overseas Development Assistance (ODA) from donor to less developed countries peaked in 1964, at $49.4 billion (in 1990 dollars), and then declined to $27.5 billion in 1969. In 1964 Woods was already telling a Council on Foreign Relations audience that "Disappointment with the results of foreign aid is widespread."[246]

All this occurred despite the sense of urgency created by reports of food shortages in developing areas, especially in India during the mid-1960s.[247] Two-thirds of IDA disbursements over 1961–69 was allocated to the Subcontinent, a region that seemed to be in a permanent state of crisis. The scope for IDA credits

242. In addition to the spread of military regimes in Latin America, several authoritarian regimes, such as those in Spain, Portugal, Taiwan, and Korea became major new borrowers during the decade.

243. In Thailand, however, the Vietnam War produced a doubling of U.S bilateral aid over 1965–74, and a focus on its poorer Northeast region that bordered Vietnam.

244. "The novelty and glamour of aiding exotic lands have worn off," wrote Robert E. Asher in 1969, who quotes a frustrated U.S. aid administrator as saying, "The loudest signal they get from Capitol Hill . . . is one of indifference. Attribute this indifference to anything you like: Vietnam, the problems of our cities, higher taxes, lack of understanding of what development means, neo-isolationism. You name it." Asher, *Development Assistance in the 1970s: Alternatives for the United States* (Brookings, 1970), pp. 99–100. See also Milton J. Esman and Daniel S. Cheever, *The Common Aid Effort* (Ohio State University Press, 1967), p. ix: "A noticeable relaxation of interest in development assistance" occurred in 1965.

245. Joan M. Nelson, *Aid, Influence, and Foreign Policy* (Cambridge, Mass.: Center for International Affairs, Harvard University, 1968), p. 5. Asher, *Development Assistance in the 1970s*, pp. 1–2, noted: "The Foreign Assistance Act of 1968 provides the smallest appropriation since the program began in the 1940s" (pp. 1–2).

246. George Woods, speech to Council on Foreign Relations, New York City, May 27, 1964.

247. The decade included wars with Pakistan and China.

to other areas, especially the newly independent African nations, was reduced during these critical first years of self-government, though, at the same time, the credits were more difficult to put together and disburse. More significantly, and in contrast to the easy course of IDA's first replenishment in 1964 (covering disbursements over 1965–67), the second replenishment (for 1968–70) was a troubled, touch-and-go, almost four-year affair that greatly frustrated and distracted Woods. In consequence, IDA disbursements were more than halved, from $342 million in 1967, to $255 million in 1969, and $143 million in 1970, even as the number of potential IDA recipients was rising. Since the share of IDA allocated to projects in agriculture, education, and water supplies was twice as high as that assigned by IBRD lending during the decade, the IDA cutback had a disproportionately larger effect on those projects.

The IBRD's funding problem, which resulted from the U.S. balance of payments deficit, had the effect of gradually limiting the growth in lending. The impact was cushioned and delayed by the Bank's high cash reserves, which Woods began to draw down, and by increased borrowings in other markets. Over 1966–68, however, IBRD commitments were held back to $854 million a year, below the levels achieved in 1965 ($1,023 million) and 1962 ($882 million). Reversing its long-standing claim that lending was not constrained by funding but only by a scarcity of good projects, the Bank began to argue that borrower absorptive capacity was not being met and that additional funding was required. The cash squeeze extended to hiring and administrative expenses, checking the enthusiastic growth of missions, technical assistance, and economic and sector studies with which the Bank had been pushing the frontiers of its work in new sectors and in the smaller, generally poorer new borrowing nations.

Presidential Style

Despite the rapid change of the 1960s, Woods was in fact frustrated as an administrator, unable to follow through on much of the energetic and innovative course that he set out at the start of his presidency. He was helped at first by the Bank's tradition of presidential respect, his own considerable executive capabilities, and by U.S. and public support for a more politically responsive lending policy. And he was an activist, by contrast with Black's slower end-of-term pace, when external pressures demanded Bank responses. But as the political context grew less supportive, Woods found himself thwarted as a leader; his personality and management style proved handicaps for the assignment.

The immediate obstacles to change were the settled views of senior staff and conservative Board members. Woods was forceful, argumentative, and given to long Board and staff debates, but he was neither winning nor persuasive. Charisma and diplomacy might have been more effective in working conversion and enrollment in the developmental direction that he was hatching. Though he won the loyalty of many subordinates, he alienated others with an abrasive, brusque, distrustful manner; his habit of delegating much less than Black; and the nature of some of his appointments.

He also failed to develop an effective cadre, a core group of like-minded staff dedicated to clarifying his developmental intuitions, putting them into operational form, and pressing them on foot-dragging colleagues. At the same time, he did perceive the need, and, he thought, a solution: more economists.

> If the Bank were still a Bank, I wouldn't need any economists at all because I know how to give bank loans. But . . . with IDA I don't know how to deal with it and I therefore need economists to give me advice on what to do with this. . . . If we can't have a big IDA, I don't want an economics staff, because . . . as long as the Bank is bigger than IDA, we'll [never] transform the Group into a development agency.[248]

The idea of economists as revolutionaries was implied in Woods's 1964 remark to the professional staff: "Gene Black is afraid of economists. I am not."[249]

Woods went on to expand the size and status of the Bank's economic staff. Between 1965 and 1969 the Economic Department grew from 20 to 120 members. The Economic Committee was to coordinate the Bank's economics work and to express an opinion on each project. Economic missions increased in size and scope.[250] Country evaluations and efforts to influence national policies broadened from the earlier focus on ingredients of borrower creditworthiness (balance of payments, monetary stability, and foreign debt) to a wider consideration of the components of national development. Growing aid coordination reinforced the need for a countrywide view, and hence for economists. On the poverty front, the Bank published a major study that addressed the problem of lending to the many new, poor African members, John de Wilde's *Experiences with Agricultural Development in Tropical Africa*.[251] Roger Chaufournier remembered the 1960s as the "economists' golden age."[252]

The economists, however, proved tepid revolutionaries, and even weaker as bureaucratic shock troops. A key appointment, that of Irving Friedman as chief

248. Friedman, Oral History, March 1974, pt. 1, p. 48. Interviewed in 1961, Aldewereld also linked the need for economists to IDA: "Now that we are going into the finance of water, mostly out of IDA funds, we asked the economics staff to give some thought to the general economic justification of water supply projects."

249. Cited by Andrew Kamarck, "The Economics Complex and Economic Research in the Bank," May 10, 1993 (processed), p. 2.

250. Many earlier missions, especially those sent to carry out "survey" reports published as books, had been large, while others became "permanent"; that is, they involved several-year residencies, but the norm increased under Woods.

251. John C. de Wilde, *Experiences with Agricultural Development in Tropical Africa* (Johns Hopkins University Press, 1967).

252. Roger Chaufournier, "The Coming of Age," *Finance and Development* (IMF/World Bank), vol. 21, no. 2 (June 1984), pp. 32–35.

economist, was unfortunate on both scores. A former IMF official, Friedman had little inclination or background for the institutional and noneconomic issues that arise prominently in social projects and in lending to very underdeveloped countries. Andrew Kamarck, who headed the Economic Department, also showed little sympathy for the social agenda. In any case, economists—unless acting as line administrators—mostly remained on the edge of operations, often rebuffed by the operational staff, while the Economic Committee carried little weight in loan decisions.[253]

With time, the economists would turn out to be more potent as agents for change. Thus they helped to legitimize social sector lending by developing arguments and methodologies to establish economic rates of return.[254] The director of education projects, struggling for acceptance by his colleagues, hired economists "to make us respectable in the Bank and to actually treat this as an economic activity."[255] Friedman noted the economists' proclivity to go beyond strict project considerations:

> The moment you get economists involved . . . they want to know what kind of secondary benefits . . . you may get . . . outside the simple financial cost-benefit analysis. I found this was just growing like Topsy . . . all these additional social and economic costs and benefits. . . . You got to the point where you started to ask yourself such questions as, Well, what if it causes eye disease, like the Volta River did? What if it creates an environment in which too many people will flock to the cities?[256]

But through the 1960s there was scant questioning of the premise that output and poverty alleviation were at odds. The 1963 proposal by the economic staff that the Bank tackle regional poverty in dual economies and condition IDA credits to more egalitarian policies had been premature and was rapidly forgotten. Lending policy for education and agriculture, the cutting edge of Woods's social agenda, was developed largely by the projects staff and Knapp's Loan Committee.[257] And

253. One member, Peter Wright, complained: "The SEC [Staff Economic Committee] meetings to consider country economic reports are rapidly becoming a farce." Memorandum, Wright to Dragoslav Avramovic, March 10, 1964. In 1965, Woods wrote senior staff to defend Friedman from accusations of overstepping his authority. "The operations of the Bank with respect to economic matters have been at a low ebb for a long period. . . . I am anxious to lean over backward to change this situation. I want to give the Economic Committee maximum dignity." He added that newly appointed Economic Department directors were a beginning to rehabilitation. Memorandum, Woods to A. Broches, "Economic Committee," March 10, 1965 (copies to Knapp, Wilson, Aldewereld, and Demuth).

254. A notable instance was Mark Blaug's report, *A Cost-Benefit Approach to Educational Planning in Developing Countries*, EC-157 (December 20, 1967). His methodology was then applied in a case study of Kenya by Hans Thias and Martin Carnoy in July 1969.

255. Ballantine, Oral History, November 21, 1986, p. 11.

256. Friedman, Oral History, March 1974, pp. 45–46.

257. Richard Demuth recalled that when Jim Evans, head of agricultural projects, was told in 1963 of Woods's new policy for agriculture, "his normally dour face burst out into a

though economists looked beyond projects, most had been schooled in the doctrine that there was a "conflict between performance and need."[258] From the perspective of his initial enthusiasm for a "developmental" redirection of the Bank, in which agriculture and social needs would play a large role, Woods had chosen poorly when he sought lieutenants. In any case, he proved more effective at expanding the number of economists than their influence.

According to Friedman, Woods lamented the lack of support for his concept of the evolution of the Bank "from a bank to a development agency":

> As [Woods] put it, "The people here don't see the image that I have." . . . The only guy who had this vision was Dick Demuth . . . everyone else to a man . . . didn't understand what [Woods] was talking about. . . . [Demuth] must have done a lot of hard thinking in terms of the IDA and the recognition of the poverty problem as against the developmental problem. . . . With the others . . . the Bank was the Loan Committee. . . . They were just being good, hard-headed bankers.[259]

In addition to his difficulties with the staff, Woods was embroiled in drawn-out disagreements with the Board, bad relations with the U.S. secretary of the Treasury, Henry Fowler, and a major policy confrontation with India. As Stanley Please remembered, whereas in the 1950s "all the Western world thought India did everything right . . . suddenly in the 1960s everybody felt that it was all going sour."[260] The Indian setback was a hard blow; India was his principal borrower, and the country with which he most closely identified his own potential success. These personal conflicts and disappointments, aggravated by health problems, seemed to feed on each other, increasing his frustration, reducing his effectiveness as an administrator and potential world leader, and checking the momentum created by his 1963 developmental agenda.

---

smile a mile wide. He said that's what the members of the Agriculture Department had been wanting to do for ten years, and had been held back from doing." Demuth, interview, World Bank Oral History Program, March 19, 1984, p. 4. Duncan Ballantine, head of education projects, was known for his strong personality.

258. IBRD, "IDA Lending Policy," EC-119b, p. 11.

259. Friedman, Oral History, March 1974, pp. 27–286. In the end, it was the lawyer, Richard Demuth, and one economist, Dragoslav Avramovic, who came closest to fulfill the function expected by Woods. Though they were respected individuals, the two were heavily outgunned.

260. Stanley Please, interview, World Bank Oral History Program, August 26, 1986, p. 8.

FIVE

Poverty Moves Up

IN ALL that George Woods did to push the Bank toward development and poverty, the most far-reaching move may have been his choice for a successor.[1] Robert McNamara, during his long term as president from April 1968 to June 1981, applied himself with energy, talent, and single-mindedness to expand the Bank, to redefine it as a "development agency," and—most controversially—to move poverty up front, from the rear of the bus. Over some two decades, poverty reduction had been the unspoken but expected indirect consequence of economic growth. McNamara would insist that it be explicit and "direct."

1. Woods wanted a successor who shared his own convictions regarding the Bank's development mission. He occasionally lunched with McNamara at the Pentagon and knew that the secretary had publicly argued for more attention to economic development: "[There was] an irrefutable relationship between violence and economic backwardness [and] security means development." Robert S. McNamara, address to the American Society of Newspaper Editors, Montreal, May 18, 1986. When Woods broached the subject of the presidency in April 1967, McNamara informed Lyndon Johnson and put the idea on ice. The proposal proved serendipitous, giving Johnson a way to ease McNamara's departure from the Cabinet in November. McNamara later wrote: "I do not know to this day whether I quit or was fired." Robert S. McNamara, *In Retrospect: The Tragedy and Lessons of Vietnam* (Times Books, 1995), p. 311. McNamara, in turn, called Woods "a good bridge" between the Black and McNamara Banks, saying that Woods had moved the Bank closer to becoming a development institution, and that "his [McNamara's] work would have been ten times harder . . . if there hadn't been this period when Woods came in." Julian Grenfell, interview, World Bank Oral History Program, July 15, 1986, pp. 13–14. See also Robert W. Oliver, *George Woods and the World Bank* (Lynne Rienner, 1995), pp. 224–25; Deborah Shapley, *Promise and Power: The Life and Times of Robert McNamara* (Little, Brown, 1993), p. 416.

He brought to the challenge a sense of moral mission and persuasive ability. And though, at fifty-one, he was the youngest appointee, he had earned a reputation for taking on bureaucratic Goliaths, at the Ford Motor Company and then as secretary of defense, and for being the first civilian to successfully dominate the Pentagon generals.[2]

The poverty mission was signaled within months of his arrival and then reiterated, with increasing specificity, through the first half of his term. But rhetoric outran implementation. Having stated the goal, he found it harder to devise the means or to move the institution. Five years elapsed before he was able to announce a major new "poverty-oriented" form of lending: integrated rural development projects for small farmers.

Indeed, if McNamara's intent were to be judged by how he spent his day or deduced from his first and most dramatic achievements, his main objective seemed rather to be the sheer expansion of lending. He shocked the Board at their first meeting by stating that lending would be doubled. His private agenda was dominated by fund-raising. From 1969 to 1973 loan commitments jumped 131 percent.[3] In any case, McNamara was notably uninformed about the developing world and so appeared to lack credentials as a judge of ongoing development efforts, much less as the originator of a better approach. When he did launch into criticism, in 1968, he was doing so before it became the fashion.[4] Going further, McNamara's tragic experience as secretary of defense, and his driving, missionary personality lent themselves to the dismissive view that there was an element of immediate, personal need and precipitation in the way in which he took up the cause of poverty alleviation. Certainly, at the time, staff members were inclined to put down the rhetoric as a way to excite rich countries into a revival of interest in development, if not also as the peculiarity of an unusual new president—the first nonbanker and the first with political experience. That interpretation, comforting to Bank officials, was given credence by McNamara's professional and methodical approach to management. Moreover, his financial audacity seemed to be governed by an awareness of Wall Street and political sensibilities.[5] Above all, he endorsed the Bank's insistence on the overriding need for economic growth.

2. Reported to the authors by John Steinbruner, who wrote a study of the Department of Defense under McNamara.

3. In constant dollars. Most of the jump occurred over fiscal 1968–70.

4. William Clark, a former director of Britain's Overseas Development Institute, wrote that McNamara was "quite naive about development and the Third World." He also remarked that Walt Rostow had been patronizing on McNamara's appointment, saying, "He doesn't know about development." "Notes on Part IV: The McNamara Years," unpublished notes, n.d., pp. 3, 26. Paradoxically, as McNamara was pointing to the failure of trickle-down in 1968, Hans Singer, an apostle for the social agenda during the 1950s and 1960s, now wrote that social objectives should not be carried too far.

5. Arguing caution on program lending, McNamara "underlined the reaction in Wall Street if the Bank Group went into program lending in a major way." Memorandum,

Nonetheless, the Bank was set on a new course, though the fact was hidden at the time by the institution's reluctance to acknowledge the change, by the haziness of the new direction, and by a characteristic ambiguity in McNamara's position: he refused to admit that new poverty alleviation might come at the expense of old growth promotion. One of his earliest acts became a potent agent for change. This was the simple distinction between economic growth and poverty reduction; the one would no longer be a synonym for the other. In his first public speech, at the September 1968 Annual General Meeting, he noted that, since 1960, in the developing world "the average annual growth thus far has been 4.8%. . . . And yet . . . you know and I know that these cheerful statistics are cosmetics which conceal a far less cheerful picture. . . . [M]uch of the growth is concentrated in the industrial areas, while the peasant remains stuck in his immemorial poverty, living on the bare margin of subsistence."[6] Whether or not the affirmation was empirically true, it challenged a key article of the Bank's creed, the belief that rising national income in a less developed country would benefit its poorer citizens.

To understand that challenge it is necessary to examine the importance of doctrine for the Bank. From its earliest days as a development lender, the institution had understood its mission as one that extended beyond "mere" financing to the provision of technical assistance and development advice. In the beginning this tutelary and educational role was justified as ancillary to sound lending in backward societies, but it soon grew into a major purpose in itself, one that was identified with, and in fact came to represent, the Bank's emerging "developmental," rather than strictly financial character.[7] In time, it became a matter of debate whether financing or advice was the Bank's most valuable contribution to borrowers. For many officials, lending came to be seen chiefly as a means to influence, a way "to buy a seat at the table." And by the late 1960s the Bank was feeling its tutelary muscle: large economic missions were becoming routine; country economic analysis and subsequent policy discussions with borrowers had broadened to cover a wide range of national and sectoral issues; and senior government officials of developing countries were being trained through the Economic Development Institute and

---

Mahbub ul Haq to John H. Adler, "Meeting of the Review Group on Brazil" [notes on meeting on Brazil CPP held on November 16, 1970], December 4, 1970, para. 4. On India's debt problems he wrote in a private note to the files: "It is important to avoid involvement in rescheduling. . . . Many accepted last rescheduling in connection with food crisis years; but what will *Barron's* and *Financial Times* say next time? We must avoid rescheduling because we are subject to market; this is not true for other creditors." Memorandum, Robert S. McNamara to files, "India," February 9, 1970.

6. He described the state of world development as "a sharply disappointing picture," and spoke of "a mood of frustration and failure." Robert S. McNamara, "To the Board of Governors, Washington, D.C., September 30, 1968," in McNamara, *The McNamara Years at the World Bank* (Johns Hopkins University Press, 1981), pp. 3–5.

7. A proposition politely but clearly stated in the *Annual Report, 1949*. See chapter 3.

influenced through an expanding research and publications program.[8] This blossoming missionary role made doctrine increasingly important.

A fundamental tenet of the institution was that hard-won economic growth would eventually spread to most of the population in a developing country. This belief justified persistent efforts to persuade borrowers of the advantages of discipline, sacrifice, and trust in the market, and therefore of the need to hold the line against political temptation. The point was not academic or obvious. Seductive, contrary arguments were everywhere put before governments by false prophets—populists, sentimentalists, and leftists—who pressed for redistribution and more immediate welfare for the poor. Questioning the spread or "trickle-down" of growing national output to the poor, McNamara was in effect admitting that development was not succeeding and thereby undercutting the case for patience and reliance on the market.[9]

But the admission prepared the way for a more interventionist strategy, one that would attack inequality by modifying and improving on the market mechanisms that acted to distribute the benefits of economic growth. Just as the United States had recently turned to "affirmative action" to speed racial integration, McNamara would resort to administrative means—controls and quotas—to reduce poverty in the developing world more directly. The Bank had previously seen fit to intervene in the allocation of resources; it would now similarly intervene with regard to the distribution of benefits.[10] It would be at the heart of the new approach to be explicit

8. Courses at the Economic Development Institute had 14 participants in 1956 (its first year), 22 in 1960, 145 in 1965, and 306 in 1970. By 1980 the number had leaped to 1,269. These figures understate the importance achieved by EDI in its first decade, when seminars were much longer, lasting six or more months versus the later practice of one-month courses, and students were higher-level government officials. For 1956–60, see World Bank, "Economic Development Institute," R65-86, June 8, 1965, p. 3. For 1965–80, see World Bank, "The Future of the Economic Development Institute," R83-114, April 25, 1983, p. 41.

9. The metaphor "trickle-down" has excited much semantic objection. It pictures capitalistic growth as a distributionally uneven process with benefits spreading only gradually and perhaps incompletely from a few to the majority. It is sometimes used pejoratively, to stress unfairness, and sometimes with a happier intent, to emphasize the ultimate sharing. The fundamental questions, rarely addressed, would seem to be how long does trickle-down take, and how much reaches the bottom? For Louis Emmerij the issue is that "economic growth is effective in achieving social objectives . . . but it might take three to five generations. In other words, the transition period would be humanly and politically irresponsible." "The Employment Problem and the International Economy," *International Labour Review*, vol. 133, no. 4 (1994), p. 457.

10. Though it was evident that resource allocation helped shape income distribution, economists argued that all citizens would be better off if output was first maximized and then redistributed. But, because wealth meant power, redistribution could be blocked. In addition, redistribution, especially when well targeted, could be difficult and costly. The thrust of the Bank's new policy was to make market outcomes more equitable in the first place and so reduce the need for redistribution.

about poverty, no longer just when speaking of allocation between countries, but when addressing the taboo issues of domestic inequities and relative needs.

McNamara's distinction between growth and poverty reduction did much more than excite the generosity of rich countries. The distinction became a wedge. Prying open the idea of development to bare its growth and equity components McNamara laid an operational cornerstone for the 1970s. The measure of progress became two-dimensional. As he sought to point the way and measure advance, McNamara would question each policy and project from the distinct and separate perspectives of output and poverty reduction. Reluctant staff were not allowed to apply a double standard—using "precise" figures when they referred to expected output effects and vague estimates when claiming "poverty reduction." Despite much grumbling, statements about poverty impact were required to be backed up by statistics, and staff had to scurry to find or create data on income distribution and on the number and living standards of project beneficiaries. More than anything, the unabashed insistence on being open about relative needs and the refusal to disguise moral claim under the ambiguous robes of the term "development" provided McNamara with a powerful instrument for raising the priority of poverty alleviation in Bank operations. Certainly, that conceptual step outlasted McNamara's concrete operational experiments for the poor.

The sudden upgrading of poverty alleviation under McNamara was an exceptionally personal decision. Need and poverty had surfaced in many ways as a criterion for Bank operations during the 1960s. McNamara's stance on poverty, however, was far more explicit and aggressive than anything yet countenanced by the institution. If he eventually created a core group of advisers and managers who appeared to share his vision, the intensity of his commitment set him apart. Within the Bank's upper echelon he remained an almost solitary beacon for the poor in his conviction—or sheer insistence—that more rapid poverty reduction could indeed be engineered. But outside the Bank, his position was less lonely. McNamara's initial 1968 statement was ahead of most officialdom and academia, but it was soon followed and even overtaken by a wave of questioning and reformulation of development doctrine.[11]

McNamara's motivations were certainly complex, with visible strains of generous and missionary impulses, but also of national security thinking, as well as the confidence of a preeminent social engineer. The security reason had been advanced in a 1966 speech at Montreal in which he had argued that national security and world poverty were closely related: "Security is not military hardware . . . without development there can be no security."[12] He had strong authority for that

11. McNamara's critique was still novel in February 1970 for many of the academics and officials who attended the Columbia University conference. Recollection of Joan Nelson (personal conversation) and one author of this history.

12. McNamara, speech to the American Society of Newspaper Editors, May 18, 1966. Earlier, in testimony as defense secretary to a hearing of the Senate Foreign Relations Committee on June 14, 1961, McNamara had described economic and military aid as complementary. *Congressional Quarterly Almanac*, 1961, p. 299.

view: six years as secretary of defense during a major war and the lesson provided by the failure of a predominantly military solution in Vietnam. But the thesis had deeper roots—in the beginnings of the cold war and Marshall Plan response, and the later security motivations for the geographical and institutional multiplication of development aid. Where the development specialists of the 1970s were awakened to poverty by doctrinal and empirical reexamination, McNamara was, in a sense, serving as a time capsule—carrying into the 1970s the rationale and poverty orientation of U.S. economic aid during the security-driven 1950s and 1960s. U.S. aid in that period had been shaped by a sense of urgency about rural poverty and characterized by easy terms and emphasis on small-scale agriculture, village self-help, and rural health, education, and roads. The principal (and small) exception to that pattern of development assistance had been the World Bank, an exception only marginally corrected by its latter-day, post-IDA "developmental" turn.[13]

On his arrival, McNamara did not appear to pause to consider the reasons and possible advantages that lay behind the Bank's different style of development assistance. His clean-slate approach to the Bank was in character: his personality, business school training, and belief in "scientific management" epitomized the American can-do spirit.[14] It was an outlook that gained energy because it was unconcerned with history, institutions, or the limits of social control. Proposing to "eradicate" world poverty, he seemed to defy the Vietnam setback and reaffirm his managerial confidence.[15]

It is likely that McNamara had also been influenced and informed by contacts that were part of his close association during the 1960s with the Kennedy family

---

13. This was despite the 1963 effort (see chapter 4) by Walt Rostow, then McNamara's colleague at the National Security Council, to encourage the Bank to move more rapidly into poverty lending.

14. The young McNamara was drawn to and was good at numbers. He has recounted how professors at Berkeley taught him to see math as "a process of thought," saying: "It was a revelation. To this day, I see quantification as a language to add precision to reasoning about the world." McNamara, *In Retrospect*, p. 6. He quickly excelled at the Harvard Business School, where thinking was then captured by theories of management control, statistical control, and control accounting. During the war he helped create an apparatus for statistical control, applying it to air force operations. After the war, much of the military "Stat Control" team—the "Whiz Kids"—was recruited to rescue Ford Motor Company through scientific management, where McNamara rose to president. Both character and training seemed to predispose him to believe in the scope for social control. In public office McNamara put his trust in technocracy, managerial systems, and benign authority, repeatedly underestimating the complexity, perversity, resilience, and mystery of the social systems, whether markets or political structures, that he set out to change.

15. In his first address to the Board of Governors, at the 1968 Annual General Meeting, he said, "There is every reason for hope. In the past few generations the world has created a productive machine which could abolish poverty from the face of the earth." McNamara, *The McNamara Years*, pp. 14–15.

and other liberal thinkers and activists of the decade who were stimulating public concern on environment, population, and development. These included Barbara Ward, who became a friend and adviser after he began his term at the Bank. His awareness of social policy may have been heightened while serving in the Kennedy and Johnson administrations, when domestic poverty surfaced as a political issue in the United States, stirred up by widely discussed studies, such as Harrington's *The Other America,* Frank Riessman's *The Culturally Deprived Child,* and the Moynihan Report, and prompting Kennedy's War on Poverty and Johnson's Great Society programs.[16] One week after McNamara took office at the Bank, his meeting with senior staff was cut short by riots and a curfew following the killing of Martin Luther King. He often likened the neglect of poor countries to that of American blacks.[17]

McNamara's contention that trickle-down was not working had been novel for mainstream academics and international agencies in 1968. By 1973, however, the new official wisdom was that trickle-down had come to an end.[18] The criticism quickly became a chorus that converged with, strengthened, and influenced McNamara's own thinking on poverty. This historical coincidence between McNamara's

16. Michael Harrington, *The Other America* (Macmillan, 1969); Frank Riessman, *The Culturally Deprived Child* (Harper and Row, 1962). Daniel Patrick Moynihan was assistant secretary of labor in the Department of Labor and the principal author of an initially confidential report submitted to Lyndon Johnson in March 1965: U.S. Department of Labor Office of Policy Planning and Research, *The Negro Family: The Case for National Action* (GPO, March 1965). It "became one of the most controversial documents in the history of American social science," according to Michael R. Katz, *The Undeserving Poor: From the War on Poverty to the War on Welfare* (New York: Pantheon Books, 1989), p. 24. The U.S. domestic war on poverty was in fact ending in the late 1960s, so that its possible influence on McNamara and others in the development community amounted to a reincarnation.

17. William Clark, "Robert McNamara at the World Bank," *Foreign Affairs,* vol. 60, no. 1 (Fall 1981), pp. 167–73.

18. Reviewing a batch of reports on development assistance, Robert Asher wrote in early 1971 that "a broad measure of consensus exists [that] more attention should be paid to the social and civic dimensions of the development process—to employment creation . . . income distribution . . . participation . . . corruption . . . social justice." "Development Assistance in DD II: The Recommendations of Perkins, Pearson, Peterson, Prebisch, and Others," *International Organization,* vol. 25, no. 1 (Winter 1971), p. 102. James P. Grant, in "Development: The End of Trickle Down," *Foreign Policy,* vol. 12 (Fall 1973), pp. 43–65, spoke of "a major rethinking." And Arun Shourie, in "Growth, Poverty and Inequalities," *Foreign Affairs,* vol. 51, no. 2 (January 1973), p. 340, claimed: "Trickle-downism is thus on the wane." An influential conference was instigated by Barbara Ward and held in two stages, at Williamsburg and Columbia University in February 1970, to discuss the Pearson Report. It was attended by a solid representation of "official" academic and government economists. But Ward deliberately broadened the group to include younger economists and representatives from developing countries. The view that trickle-down was not working for the poor produced what some described as a "double take." "One could almost see the shifting of ideas taking place at the conference." Conversation with Joan Nelson, June 30, 1993.

private impulses and conceptions and a changing development paradigm may have been decisive for the energetic course of poverty-alleviation efforts in the Bank during the 1970s. Despite the clarity and force of his rhetoric, and the sharp moralistic advice that he dispensed privately on visits to poor countries, McNamara was in fact slow to translate those intentions into operational specifics. For that he needed practical knowledge to design concrete, workable antipoverty measures and projects; and that in turn depended on a willing, enthusiastic staff. Both requirements became easier to meet when other development agencies, academics, and public opinion joined the search for a new development model. McNamara's poverty crusade might have amounted to very little had it been launched a decade earlier or later.

Even with outside support, imposing the poverty agenda on the Bank was a struggle. In that respect the contrast with IDA is interesting. Like IDA, the poverty crusade had its roots in the cold war, and both were grafted onto the Bank; neither was a product of institutional evolution. But IDA arrived as a definitive, once-over constitutional change. McNamara's program, instead, was imposed gradually and against much resistance, requiring the full force of his own commitment, personality, and intellect, as well as legitimation and intellectual input from outside the Bank. McNamara was building on the changes begun under Black and Woods, yet the effort to further upgrade social needs as opposed to growth proved to be a major struggle against the Bank's market-based upbringing.

Nonetheless, despite the obstacles that first delayed and later reversed its advance, the concern for poverty became the Bank's trademark for the 1970s, which suggested that it suited the doctrines, politics, and institutional needs of the time. And though poverty lending was delayed, constrained, and later disowned by many in the Bank, the cause may have been given a lasting boost because taboos were broken, concepts changed, and a new generation of staff members—more open to the poverty goal—was inserted into the Bank's staffing pipeline.

The poverty mission engaged McNamara on several fronts. One was the Bank itself, which he set out to redesign to better serve his particular blend of growth—as a "development agency"—and poverty reduction objectives. A second was the "donor" community, rich lenders and givers from whom he sought a much increased financial base. The third consisted of leaders of poor countries, whose commitment to equity would be a precondition for the effectiveness of Bank assistance. A fourth was the intellectual front: a vastly expanded level of spending on research became a means to exert influence on the development community.

On the home front, the development of poverty-oriented lending meant a variety of conceptual, administrative, and operational changes. William Clark wrote that McNamara had been "shocked to find we don't help the poorest because Bankable projects [are] not suitable for them."[19] Some lending initiatives were

---

19. William Clark notebooks, written as an outline for a memoir. The quotation is from "Notes on Part IV: The McNamara Years."

announced in the 1968 speech: in addition to a doubling of the total financial effort, he proposed a greater share for the poorest countries, more attention to Africa and Latin America, and support for population policy, education, and agriculture. With less drama, he carried out a series of administrative changes that culminated in a major reorganization in 1972. That combination of motivational, lending, and procedural measures became the most energetic attempt in the Bank's history to wrench it onto a new course.

It was the donor front that McNamara tackled with most urgency and that seemed to be his main preoccupation at first. Certainly he saw additional funding as indispensable to his ambitions for the Bank as a development agency. But there was another reason for that distribution of effort: when it came to fund-raising, both the goal and the necessary steps—intense lobbying and well-planned public relations—were comparatively clear to him; furthermore, they were tasks that he could carry out to a large extent by himself. The design of a poverty-lending strategy was, by contrast, a riddle, a vague aspiration that would need time, trial and error, and the involvement of many persons.

The third effort, an attempt to draw the attention of developing-country leaders to inequities and welfare needs in their countries, was, like fund-raising, a task that McNamara could carry out to a considerable extent on his own, combining it with the ambitious program of travel that he set for himself to become acquainted with developing countries and their leaders. This advocacy was broadened through new administrative procedures that gave him the opportunity to review systematically the overall development strategy for each borrowing country and guide his staff with regard to the principal policy messages that he wished to transmit to borrowers, notably a greater emphasis on poverty and equity.

The campaign evolved after McNamara's 1973 announcement at Nairobi that the Bank was planning to carry out a large rural development effort focused on small farmers, as a vehicle for direct poverty alleviation. That announcement is often identified with the launching of McNamara's war on poverty and was indeed a turning point, but one between two stages in the poverty effort.[20]

The initial stage, covering McNamara's first five years in the Bank, can be characterized as a time of intellectual and operational gestation during which the Bank, through studies, consultation, and experimentation, sought to define a poverty-alleviation policy and, above all, suitable lending operations. Administrative changes were carried out as McNamara endeavored to increase his control over the Bank. Much of what was accomplished to upgrade poverty as an objective was done during this period, through influence and advocacy. Using speeches, announcements, research publications, country strategy discussions, new administrative procedures, and conversations with government leaders, McNamara campaigned to

20. For a thorough and thoughtful account of McNamara's war on poverty, see Robert L. Ayres, *Banking on the Poor: The World Bank and World Poverty* (MIT Press, 1983); it focuses largely on the period 1973–80 (see p. 22).

raise the priority of poverty and also to achieve a substantial increase in the Bank's funding.

After the Nairobi announcement, attention shifted from design to execution. Putting the strategy into practice engaged the Bank at two levels, that of national politics and policymaking and the more prosaic level of project implementation. Borrowers needed to be desirous or persuaded of a more direct approach to poverty alleviation. But also, the projects had to work on the ground: they needed to be well implemented at the investment stage and well managed once they were running. In practice, good policies and good projects were interdependent: implementation failed more often when borrower interest was low; conversely, projects that were inappropriately designed or implemented were less likely to create enthusiasm and win the support of the borrowers.[21] Poverty-oriented operations, especially lending and research, increased steadily, peaking during the later 1970s. Work on policy design was more continuous: the approach to poverty was debated through the decade.

The next three sections look more closely at the McNamara years. They cover the revolution in thought that accompanied and supported McNamara's poverty agenda, the mix of rhetoric and administrative reorganization that made direct poverty alleviation a major objective for the Bank, and the specific lending and advisory approaches devised to achieve this objective. Much of the conceptual and rhetorical effort was carried out over the period 1968–73, but the search for practical lending approaches continued, with major debates and new initiatives, through McNamara's entire presidency. How these plans were put into action—by influencing borrower policies and through new-style "poverty projects"—is the story of chapter 6.

Critique of Trickle-Down

The loss of confidence in national economic growth as a sufficient means to reduce poverty—what David Morse in 1970 called the "dethronement of GNP"— was sudden and widespread.[22] Data showing rapid population growth, widening income distributions, and limited growth in industrial employment were brought

---

21. This lesson, that borrower participation and "ownership" were important not only to ensure more poor-friendly policies but also to make poverty projects work, became clearer with time, as is discussed in chapter 7.

22. David Morse was secretary-general of the ILO from 1958 to May 1970. Morse, "The Employment Problem in Developing Countries," speech at Seventh Cambridge Conference on Development, September 1970, in Ronald Robinson and Peter Johnson, eds., *Prospects for Employment Opportunities in the Nineteen Seventies* (London: Cambridge University Overseas Study Committee, 1971), pp. 5–13. The 1970 Nobel Peace Prize was awarded to the ILO and received by Morse on behalf of the organization.

forward to support this revisionist hypothesis. But the suddenness of the intellectual change, and the casual, incomplete, and tardy nature of the evidence suggest that data were used to confirm rather than to arrive at the new consensus.[23] Several factors came together to precipitate the shift in perceptions, but an explanation must begin with some words on the extent and implications of the phenomenon.

The new paradigm was old wisdom for much of the world. Outside the small but powerful development establishment centered in Washington and in prestigious Anglo-Saxon universities, intellectuals and officials were more inclined to skepticism than belief in the proposition that market-based economic growth would spread equitably to the masses. The contrary affirmation—that the poor were not sharing and were unlikely to share in growth—was widely held, and the belief was sustained by a substantial body of conceptual and empirical study.[24] Indeed, it was a founding principle of Marxism.

23. For example, "The poorest sections of the population have gained little, if anything, from the growth of some 5 per cent per year (in real terms) of the economy since the mid-1950s." Cite in ILO, *Towards Full Employment: A Programme for Colombia* (Geneva: International Labor Office, 1970), p. 14. Many seemed satisfied that continuing wide income extremes were sufficient evidence that the poor were no better off. Ian M. D. Little, *Economic Development: Theory, Policy, and International Relations* (Basic Books, 1982), p. 209, observed that once people had decided that trickle-down was not working, "work began to try to prove this case." Later studies questioned the dismissal of trickle-down. Interestingly, one of the first careful reviews of the evidence was by Marxist economist Bill Warren, who disputed the claim that income and welfare had not been reaching the poor. Warren, "The Postwar Economic Experience of the Third World," in Rothko Chapel, ed., *Toward a New Strategy for Development* (Pergamon Press, 1979), pp. 144–68. Observers generally underestimated income gains by the poor from productivity growth and changes in the structure of employment.

24. The Economic Commission for Latin America of the United Nations has published numerous statistical studies of income distribution in Latin America and insightful discussions of its technological, political, and sociological determinants. See, for example, United Nations, *The Economic Development of Latin America*, Report E/CN.12/659 Rev. 1 (New York, 1964), pp. 62–73. For a more analytic survey, see "Income Distribution in Latin America," *Economic Bulletin for Latin America*, vol. 12, no. 2 (October 1967), pp. 38–60. Studies by the FAO, the University of Wisconsin Land Tenure Center, and others during the 1950s and 1960s argued that land reform was a prerequisite for rural poverty reduction. From the early 1960s, Harry T. Oshima argued that a strong pro-rural policy was indispensable for employment and equity. See his "A Strategy for Asian Economic Development," *Economic Development and Cultural Change*, vol. 10, no. 3 (April 1962), pp. 294–316. Both ECLA and the ILO were signaling the emerging "employment problem" through the 1960s. According to Werner Baer and Michel Herve, "Employment and Industrialization in Developing Countries," *Quarterly Journal of Economics*, vol. 80, no. 1 (February 1966), pp. 88–107, the lack of industrial labor absorption had both technological and policy determinants. For a respected, pessimistic opinion on the issue, see Gunnar Myrdal, *The Asian Drama: An Inquiry into the Poverty of Nations* (New York: Twentieth Century Fund, 1968).

The disagreement, then, went well beyond academic difference. Each view was an ideological axiom, a scientific belief that sustained, or rationalized, a particular stance with respect to the roles of state and market. Indeed, optimism or pessimism regarding the trickle-down effect was close to an ideological litmus test. The political function of the competing axioms seemed to preclude academic review and debate. Its strong political associations probably explain why, when the paradigm was challenged, its reformulation was carried out within the framework of orthodox concepts and institutions, mostly ignoring the evidence, arguments, and personalities associated with more radical perspectives. But both critiques led to a similar, reformist conclusion: that market and social mechanisms were failing the poor, and that policy changes and interventions were needed to improve distribution.

One of the first major research efforts to dent trickle-down confidence was a historical review of industrial and trade policies in developing countries undertaken by the Development Centre of the Organization for Economic Cooperation and Development. The work was directed by Ian Little, Tibor Scitovsky, and Maurice Scott and published in 1970. Though its focus was growth and the cost of excessive protection, the study also implicated import protection as a cause of limited job creation.[25] Free-trade proponents were among the first to draw attention to what was being called the employment problem, and even to suggest that some growth should perhaps be sacrificed for the sake of employment, that is, for poverty reduction.[26]

Unemployment in the development context—expressed as "the employment problem"—could be understood intuitively as a corollary of the already familiar Lewis model, the dominant development paradigm.[27] In the Lewis model, growth and poverty reduction both hinged on the redistribution of labor, from unproductive farms—where, as some argued, work was a form of "disguised unemployment"—to industry and other modern, mostly urban activity. The possibility of raising productivity on small farms or in urban informal activities was downplayed

25. Ian Little, Tibor Scitovsky, and Maurice Scott, *Industry and Trade in Some Developing Countries* (London: Oxford University Press, 1970). The negative employment effects of import protection and capital subsidies had been noted before. See, for example, Baer and Herve, "Employment and Industrialization in Developing Countries." For a review of the study by Little and others, along with two reports on the employment problem by the ILO and OECD, see Derek T. Healey, "Development Policy: New Thinking about an Interpretation," *Journal of Economic Literature*, vol. 10, no. 3 (September 1972), pp. 757–97. Healey remarked on the simultaneity of their "very similar results" and saw the "new thinking" as the outcome of an overwhelming accumulation of evidence.

26. See Little and others, *Industry and Trade in Some Developing Countries*, p. 92: "In present circumstances, when the employment problem is already crucial, it may thus be necessary, to some extent, to be ready to sacrifice growth of output for more early employment."

27. By contrast, when Keynes had sought to direct attention to persistent unemployment in industrial countries, he had elaborated a full-fledged "General Theory."

in the model. The future lot of the rural poor was therefore tied to job creation by modern factories. Any failure by industry (and other modern activities) to create jobs would mean continuing "unemployment," and therefore poverty, for the rural population.[28]

Recasting poverty as "unemployment" opened the door to more explicit and energetic debate on the common issue. The persistence of mass poverty despite impressive economic growth could be admitted and explained in terms that were at once ideologically aseptic and, to the neoclassical economist, familiar. Instead of revolution, or even redistribution, poverty could be tackled by eliminating price distortions. And once poverty reduction was identified with "job creation," win-win solutions became possible: more jobs would raise production and help the poorest simultaneously. Sensitive and wooly issues of political power, institutions, race and caste, resource endowments, and culture could be put aside. The proxy notion of an "employment problem" thus became a bridge from orthodoxy to interventionism in development policy, much as cyclical unemployment had legitimized Keynesian fiscal policy.[29]

The leadership in the development and diffusion of the employment problem was by and large a collaborative effort of the International Labor Organization and the newly created Institute for Development Studies (IDS) of Sussex University. In 1969 the ILO launched a World Employment Program that carried out seven country studies over the period 1970–75.[30] Also in 1969, Dudley Seers, the director

28. A model of rural-to-urban migration rounded out the picture by explaining urban unemployment—a concept extended to embrace the urban informal sector—in terms of "rational" market behavior and market distortions. Michael P. Todaro, "A Model of Labor Migration and Urban Unemployment in Less Developed Countries," *American Economic Review*, vol. 59 (March 1969), pp. 138–48.

29. A more structural explanation of unemployment was that modern technologies, imported by developing countries, had been developed by and for rich countries and were thus biased against employment. A rhetorical side benefit of "poverty as unemployment" was to provide a statistical shortcut to prove that the poor were not sharing in growth: stagnant incomes could be deduced from the yawning gap between a growing labor force and the small number of industrial jobs created each year. Little effort was made to obtain direct evidence on the trend in incomes of the poor.

30. The World Employment Program (WEP) was a sudden decision by David Morse, who had been looking for a fiftieth-anniversary theme for the ILO. The WEP consisted mostly of a substantial research program, large policy-oriented country studies, and regional offices, notably in Latin America. Colombia was chosen for the first country report, following a visit to the ILO in 1969 by President Carlos Lleras Restrepo. Directed by Dudley Seers, the report stood "trickle-down" on its head. Arguing from GDP and employment projections, it stated that growth would not solve poverty at an acceptable rate and that policy should put employment first, letting growth emerge as a by-product. Subsequent reports, however, moved away from the "unemployment" theme, developing their own, individual slants on the issues of growth and poverty. The reports covered Colombia (1970), Sri Lanka (1971), Kenya (1972), (Iran) 1973, Philippines (1974), and Sudan and the Dominican

of IDS, excited many people with an address in which he debated "the meaning of development," calling for less attention to GDP and more to poverty, employment, and social objectives in general.[31] The employment problem was the theme of the Annual Development Conference in Cambridge University in 1970, where David Morse, the retiring head of the ILO, remarked that GNP had been dethroned.[32] The entire issue was reviewed by David Turnham in 1971 in an influential monograph published by the OECD.[33]

The need to reexamine development policy was also pressed from a less intellectual but politically influential quarter that spoke directly to politicians and development officials. The most effective messages were delivered by two widely read books, *Development Reconsidered* by Edgar Owens and Robert Shaw (1972), and *Small Is Beautiful* by E. F. Schumacher (1973).[34]

Republic (1975). Louis Emmerij succeeded the first director, Maurice Blanchard, and ran the program from 1970 to 1976. Both Emmerij and Richard Jolly attribute the principal inspiration for the WEP message to Hans Singer. According to Jolly, Singer, with David Owen, had prepared a study on unemployment for the Archbishop of Canterbury in 1936 and studied under John Maynard Keynes. He directed WEP's Kenya study and suggested its "redistribution from growth." Seers and Walter Galenson became the first WEP advisers. International Labor Organization, *World Employment Program: Research in Retrospect and Prospect* (Geneva: ILO, 1976), p. 7; David Turnham, *Employment and Development: A New Review of Evidence* (OECD, Development Centre Studies, 1993), pp. 175–88; Louis Emmerij, interview, November 1995; Richard Jolly, interview, November 18, 1995.

31. Dudley Seers's address to the Society for International Development (SID) in New Delhi in November 1969 was published as "The Meaning of Development," *International Development Review,* December 1969. Gerald Meier's annotated collection of articles on development, *Leading Issues in Economic Development* (Oxford University Press, 1964), contained no reference to poverty or distribution. The second edition (January 1970) included an introductory section, "The Meaning of Development," but did not reproduce any of the trickle-down critique literature. The third edition (August 1975), however, devotes its opening section to several articles on the redefinition of development objectives, the employment problem, and redistribution with growth.

32. These studies and debates make clear the extent to which the relabeling of poverty as an "employment problem" proved a powerful and politically versatile attention getter. All manner of villains were cited—including market distortions, power exercised by business groups and unions, large landowners, and multinational corporations—to explain the failure of a modern sector to create jobs—and hence relieve poverty. In that way the concept served a constructive purpose: it diverted attention from a stalemated ideological debate to a search for common solutions through "job creation," which would improve both equity and growth. When it came to concrete actions to address poverty, however, the broad concept provided little (or too much) operational guidance.

33. David Turnham, assisted by Ingelies Jaeger, *The Employment Problem in Less Developed Countries: A Review of Evidence,* Development Centre Studies, Employment Series 1 (OECD, 1971).

34. Edgar Owens and Robert Shaw, *Development Reconsidered: Bridging the Gap between Government and the People* (Lexington, Mass.: Lexington Books, 1972); Ernst

Owens and Shaw spoke as aid officials with field experience. Their criticism of "capital-intensive endeavors in the big cities and on large farms" coincided with one of the main strains of the employment problem critique, but they went on to argue that the key to development was participation by the poor in the development process, harkening back to the philosophy of the community development movement of the 1950s.[35] Their populist tone struck a chord with some members of the U.S. Congress and helped reorient the U.S. aid program in 1973 toward a concentration on basic human needs, a shift that was referred to as the "New Directions" legislation.[36] A similar view was being put forward by James Grant, president of the Overseas Development Council (ODC), a Washington organization created to support foreign aid. Indeed, Grant had engineered the Owens and Shaw collaboration.[37] Schumacher's book, subtitled *Economics As If People Mattered,* had a far wider reach. Its intuitively appealing argument and lively style helped to make it a best-seller during the 1970s. It was both a commonsense brief for intermediate technology, which meshed with the employment problem argument, and a cultural cri de coeur, in the spirit of Gandhi, that echoed with the cultural rebellions of the 1960s in the United States and Europe and with the budding environmental movement of the early 1970s.

If most of the trickle-down critique was kept on respectable ground by proposing strategies that offered to improve both growth and distribution, it was joined by an element of straightforward moral objection. This occurred in several instances

---

Friedrich Schumacher, *Small Is Beautiful: Economics As If People Mattered* (Harper and Row, 1973). In April 1971 S. R. Sen, the Indian executive director, sent McNamara a copy of an article by Schumacher that stated: "Industrialisation—splendid! But will the poor people be involved? . . . . As we look back upon 'development' during the 1960s . . . development has gone ahead in many places, but The People, the poor, the great majority have been by-passed." McNamara sent it on to Chenery with a note saying "Murray Gell-Mann [Nobel Prize–winning chemist] made the same suggestion to me a few weeks ago." Memorandum, S. R. Sen to Robert S. McNamara, "Choice of Technology for Developing Countries with Substantial Labour Surplus," April 9, 1971, with attachments.

35. Owens and Shaw, *Development Reconsidered*, p. iv.

36. Aid allocation would be guided by a country's stress on self-reliance, participation by the poor, and small-farmer productivity. Two admirers were Representative Bradley Morse (Republican of Massachusetts), a proponent of the New Directions legislation approved in 1973, and Representative Donald Fraser (Democrat of Minnesota), who introduced Title IX, on participation, into the 1966 aid bill. Fraser saw Owens as one of the true "practitioners" of political development. Rolf H. Sartorius and Vernon W. Ruttan, "The Sources of the Basic Needs Mandate," *Journal of Developing Areas*, vol. 23 (April 1989), pp. 331–62.

37. James P. Grant, *Growth from Below: A People-Oriented Development Strategy,* Development Paper 16 (Washington, D.C.: Overseas Development Council, 1973). The ODC published other essays on this theme, including Barbara Ward's *A "People" Strategy of Development,* Communique on Development Issues 23 (ODC, 1974). Grant gave an account of his role in the Owens and Shaw book in an interview with Sartorius and Ruttan, October 16, 1987.

where the moral claim was difficult to ignore. One that struck home with the Bank
in particular was the partition of Pakistan, a disaster immediately linked to the
history of development and policy bias in favor of West Pakistan. Though bias could
be blamed on the political dominance of West Pakistan, aid officials and Pakistan's
own development planners accused themselves of reinforcing and legitimizing the
bias toward West Pakistan by favoring output over need considerations. That
leaning had worked in favor of the West and in that way had contributed to the
eventual tragedy. Such was the admission of Edward Mason and Robert Asher,
writing on the Bank's role.[38] And such was the dramatic confession of Mahbub ul
Haq, former chief economist of the Pakistan Planning Commission.[39]

Moral sentiments may also have been prodded by hope rather than catastrophe
when several developing countries took egalitarian turns. In Peru, a left-leaning
military government carried out a radical and widely applauded land redistribution
in 1970 and embarked on other redistributive measures. The "Peruvian experiment" was viewed with sympathy outside the country.[40] Yugoslavia's model of
worker management seemed to offer a highly promising, alternative route to
equitable growth. At about the same time, poverty surfaced as an explicit political
issue in India, with the publication of a study by V. M. Dandekar and N. Rath in
1970 and Mrs. Gandhi's adoption of *garibi hatao* ("eliminate poverty") as a campaign slogan.[41] Tanzania provided another egalitarian experiment that aroused

38. Mason and Asher, *World Bank since Bretton Woods*, pp. 670–75. Mason and Asher
write that the outcome may have been inevitable, but that "gnawing doubts persist. Even if
the tide could not have been turned, could the Bank and the members of the Bank-sponsored consortium have acquitted themselves more impressively?" They go on to note that
the Bank "was not vigorous" in the pursuit of rural development and regional balance, and
"did not actively support the Comilla [community-based] approach to rural development.
. . . Nor . . . did it support or encourage the drive for social justice envisaged by the [Third
Five-Year Plan, 1965–70]." This comment on the Bank is especially poignant because, as was
well known, it amounted to a self-questioning by Edward Mason, who had overseen much of
the foreign development advice given to Pakistan from the late 1950s through the 1960s.

39. See Mahbub ul Haq, *The Poverty Curtain: Choices for the Third World* (Columbia
University Press, 1976), esp. pp. 3–11. An orthodox, growth-centered economist and planner
in the early 1960s, ul Haq began to express doubts in the late 1960s, notably in an early 1968
lecture at McGill University. In April 1968 in Karachi, he "created major shock waves" by
criticizing the concentration of wealth "in the hands of only twenty-two family groups," and
the maldistribution of public services (pp. 5–6). Ul Haq's self-criticism influenced Bank
thinking.

40. For a collection of articles on the military government's policies, see Abraham F.
Lowenthal, ed., *The Peruvian Experiment: Continuity and Change under Military Rule*
(Princeton University Press, 1975). Peru's access to foreign capital was complicated by the
expropriation of foreign-owned properties.

41. Mrs. Gandhi's poverty initiatives were stymied for the most part by a succession of
external shocks, especially the 1973 oil shock, the conflict with Pakistan, and opposition from
within the Congress Party. Yet her initial stance brought "poverty" into political discourse

opinion and hope within the development establishment, even more after Julius Nyerere's January 1967 Arusha Declaration.

The moral issue arose more directly when the Green Revolution was challenged on distributive grounds during the first years of the decade. A barrage of accusations were made that Green Revolution technology was, in practice at least, favoring better-off farmers and better-off regions and was also working to reduce the demand for labor by encouraging mechanization.[42] The OECD's review of the employment problem expressed further doubt: "The potential of the 'green revolution' for employment and income distribution, especially in the longer term, are much less clear than the potential for increasing output."[43]

However, the rethinking of development policy should perhaps be understood in a more general perspective. Going beyond the country cases just mentioned— Pakistan, Peru, India, and Tanzania—Albert O. Hirschman has suggested that development economists were becoming aware that rapid economic growth could have deleterious side effects: "The series of political disasters that struck a number of third world countries from the 1960s on . . . were clearly *somehow* connected with the stresses and strains accompanying development and 'modernization.' These development disasters, ranging from civil wars to the establishment of murderous authoritarian regimes, could not but give pause to a group of social scientists."[44] Questions about development were being asked not only in Indochina, but also throughout Africa, where extravagant expectations attached to independence were not being met; in Indonesia, where rural reconstruction and welfare had become an overwhelming priority after the 1965–66 civil war; in Malaysia, shaken by race riots and underlying ethnic inequalities in 1969; in Chile, where policies of gradual redistribution and social welfare had not prevented the election

---

and probably reinforced a warm relationship with McNamara. A former Indian rural district officer remembers that "poverty became a big deal" only with Mrs. Gandhi's campaign "one-liner," and he was thereupon instructed to prepare the first "poverty plan" for his district. Vijay Jagannathan, interview, August 11, 1993. Widespread debate on the distribution of the gains from development was stimulated by V. M. Dandekar and Nilakantha Rath, "Poverty in India—Dimensions and Trends," *Economic and Political Weekly* (India), vol. 6, no. 1 (1970), pp. 25–48.

42. This criticism was debated almost continuously over the 1970s and 1980s in India, notably in the pages of *The Economic and Political Weekly*. Earlier literature includes Francine R. Frankel, *India's Green Revolution: Economic Gains and Political Costs* (Princeton University Press, 1971); Harry M. Cleaver, "The Contradictions of the Green Revolution," *American Economic Review Papers and Proceedings*, vol. 72 (May 1972), pp. 177–86; and Keith B. Griffin, *The Political Economy of Agrarian Change: An Essay on the Green Revolution* (Harvard University Press, 1974).

43. Turnham, *The Employment Problem*, p. 103.

44. Albert O. Hirschman, "The Rise and Decline of Development Economics," in Hirschman, *Essays in Trespassing: Economics to Politics and Beyond* (Cambridge University Press, 1981), p. 20.

of Allende's socialist regime; and in Mexico, where student riots in 1968 had shaken the smooth-running political and economic machine of the Institutional Revolutionary Party (PRI). As noted, even the Green Revolution was suspected of a dark side. At a staff meeting in 1969, McNamara commented: "There was no doubt that the 'green revolution' would predominantly increase the income of the rich peasants and thereby create additional social stress."[45] At the Williamsburg Conference in 1970, just before he was recruited by the Bank, Hollis Chenery had indeed "paused" (in Hirschman's phrase) to reflect when he proposed that, instead of seeking a *maximum* rate of growth, societies should target a lower *optimum* rate. The latter would sacrifice some growth in favor of social objectives.[46] Put in a more positive light, the reconsideration may have been induced by the very success of the development effort during the 1950s and 1960s with respect to its first priority: the achievement of rapid economic growth. That comparative success gave some breathing room to neglected social objectives, and even to intellectual ebullience.

The Bank could hardly have avoided being influenced. It had already proved responsive to external opinion and politics during the 1960s. Moreover, sensitivity to outside opinion was heightened as the Bank continued to move toward an increased developmental role, a role strongly associated with IDA and so subjected to the politics and evolving views that lay behind approval of congressional appropriations. After his retirement, William Clark wrote that "during twelve years [there was] never a time when funds were not pending in Congress," and "we learnt that [on IDA] we only had [a] margin of about five votes and if they were lost we were dead."[47] It was not only opinion in donor countries that came to matter more: a "developmental" as distinct from pure banking role meant, above all, a capacity to influence borrowers. Influence, in turn, rode on reputation: professional, intellectual, and moral. Coming as it did in the van of the development rethinking of the 1970s, McNamara's initiative was well timed to strengthen the Bank's moral and developmental leadership. The widespread critique of growth-oriented development by intellectuals and development institutions had become one more justification for

45. World Bank, Minutes of President's Council Meeting, March 24, 1969. Mason and Asher refer to internal debates during 1969 and 1970 on the wisdom of tractor imports to India and Pakistan. The incident is recounted to illustrate not an open concern for distribution per se, but the possibility of undesirable political consequences from investment decisions. Thus one argument cited is that "the 'green' revolution might well turn red." Mason and Asher, *World Bank since Bretton Woods*, pp. 249–50 and fn. 28.

46. Hollis Chenery, "Targets for Development," in Barbara Ward, J. D. Runnalls, and Leonore D'Anjou, *The Widening Gap: Development in the 1970s* (Columbia University, 1971), p. 27. After becoming the Bank's chief economist in May 1970, he no longer spoke of a trade-off between poverty alleviation and growth. However, he did not share the Bank's inhibition against a straightforward moral justification for poverty alleviation.

47. Like Woods, McNamara saw IDA as paramount to the Bank. When the Pearson Commission delivered its draft report, recommending that IDA be removed from the Bank and put under separate administration, McNamara said "I'd rather put the Bank under IDA." The recommendation "got removed by our pressure," says Clark in "Notes on Part IV," p. 13.

waning development assistance budgets: McNamara had noted in 1968 that the will to provide aid "was never lower."[48] By contrast with his nonconformist role within the Bank on the poverty objective, outside the Bank McNamara appeared as the standard-bearer for a new majority, enhancing the institution's capacity to call forth additional support for the International Development Association and the International Bank for Reconstruction and Development. With time, that external image worked to legitimize and even to spur the changes that McNamara was seeking in the Bank. This stance was double edged when it came to borrowers, however: if the Bank's standing and influence in the developing world was generally enhanced, in many countries the new insistence on the poor also became an irritant and obstacle to lending relationships.

Gestation

For five years, from 1968 into 1973, there was a notable contrast between McNamara's forceful calls for more equitable development and the organization's slow, relatively unheralded reshaping of lending and advisory work.[49] But critical change was taking place. What came to be called poverty lending—loans for agriculture in general, for small farmers in particular, and for water supply and education—gathered momentum through the early 1970s.[50] These first years also saw a great deal of advocacy, administrative change, and policy exploration to increase the weight of poverty alleviation in Bank operations (tables 5-1a and 5-1b).

To that extent, the 1973 announcement that lending for small-scale agriculture would be vigorously expanded was more an official confirmation than a launchpad. Similarly, the publication of *Redistribution with Growth* in early 1974, a research report on policies to improve income distribution and employment, provided an intellectual rationale for the approach that the Bank was already taking to poverty—through "bankable" or production-oriented poverty lending.[51] These two widely cited official statements seemed finally to precipitate the realization, inside and

48. McNamara, "To the Board of Governors, . . . September 30, 1968." That year, the McNamara Bank was the beneficiary of the largest percentage replenishment in IDA's history—negotiated during Woods's term. But aid budgets as a whole began to decline. In 1967 U.K. overseas aid fell in real terms for the first time, despite Prime Minister Harold Wilson's earlier, enthusiastic commitment to development assistance.

49. This led Mason and Asher, who closed their draft in late 1971, to remark that in the field of income distribution and employment creation, "to date, there continues to be a sizable gap between the public pronouncements of some of the Bank's spokesmen and its day-to-day practice." Mason and Asher, *World Bank since Bretton Woods*, p. 732.

50. World Bank, Operations Evaluation Department, *Rural Development: World Bank Experience, 1965–86* (1988), table 1, p. 11.

51. Hollis Chenery, Montek S. Ahluwalia, C. L. G. Bell, John H. Duloy, and Richard Jolly, *Redistribution with Growth* (Oxford University Press, 1974), p. v. Though remembered for this argument, the book in fact contains a variety of viewpoints, including an article by Clive Bell on the importance of political factors.

Table 5-1a. *IBRD and IDA Lending during the McNamara Period, Fiscal 1969–82*[a]

Millions of U.S. dollars

Borrowers[b]	FY 1969–73	FY 1974–82	Total
Total	11,215	79,207	90,421
High income	811	770	1,581
Middle and low income[c]	10,404	78,437	88,840
Middle income	6,499	48,248	54,747
Low income	3,905	30,188	34,093
Middle and low income by sector	10,404	78,437	88,840
Transport, power, telecommunications	4,922	27,153	32,075
Agriculture, social[d]	3,267	31,694	34,961
Agriculture	2,101	22,623	24,724
Education	531	3,380	3,911
Population, health, and nutrition	71	489	559
Urban development[e]	25	1,374	1,399
Water supply and sewerage	540	3,828	4,367

Source: World Bank, "Financial Database Information."

a. The McNamara period includes commitments from July 1, 1969, through June 30, 1982, based on the assumption that loan commitments made during FY 1982 largely reflect lending decisions and preparation carried out under McNamara.

b. High-income borrowers (11): Bahamas, Cyprus, Finland, Greece, Iceland, Ireland, Israel, New Zealand, Singapore, Spain, and Taiwan. Middle-income borrowers (55): Algeria, Argentina, Barbados, Bolivia, Bosnia-Herzegovina, Botswana, Brazil, Cameroon, Chile, Colombia, Congo, Costa Rica, Croatia, Djibouti, Dominica, Dominican Republic, Ecuador, El Salvador, Fiji, Gabon, Guatemala, Indonesia, Iran, Iraq, Jamaica, Jordan, Korea, Lebanon, Macedonia, Malaysia, Maldives, Mauritius, Mexico, Morocco, Oman, Panama, Papua New Guinea, Paraguay, Peru, Philippines, Portugal, Romania, Senegal, Slovenia, Solomon Islands, Swaziland, Syria, Thailand, Trinidad and Tobago, Tunisia, Turkey, Uruguay, Venezuela, Western Samoa, and Yugoslavia. Low-income borrowers (48): Afghanistan, Bangladesh, Benin, Burkina Faso, Burundi, Central African Republic, Chad, China, Comoros, Côte d'Ivoire, Egypt, Equatorial Guinea, Ethiopia, Gambia, Ghana, Guinea, Guinea-Bissau, Guyana, Haiti, Honduras, India, Kenya, Lao, Lesotho, Liberia, Madagascar, Malawi, Mali, Mauritania, Myanmar, Nepal, Nicaragua, Niger, Nigeria, Pakistan, Rwanda, Sierra Leone, Somalia, Sri Lanka, Sudan, Tanzania, Togo, Uganda, Vietnam, Yemen, Zaire, Zambia, and Zimbabwe.

c. As defined in *World Debt Tables, 1994–95*, vol. 2, p. xxiv.

d. Social sectors include education; population, health, and nutrition; urban development; and water supply and sewerage.

e. Figures represent 70 percent of total urban development lending; see World Bank, "Retrospective Review of Operations," Report 3919, April 22, 1982, p. 50.

outside the institution, that its poverty crusade was to be a wholehearted commitment. The statements were thus a culmination of five years of advocacy and administrative change, during which McNamara pressed the moral claim of poverty and the organizational search for growth-with-equity solutions.

Advocacy

More than any other president, McNamara used speeches as a form of carefully planned communication, with the Bank itself as much as with the outside world. The speeches often brought announcements of major initiatives, news at times even to the Board. Always, they were powerful inspirational messages. For the

Table 5-1b. *IBRD and IDA Lending during the McNamara Period, Fiscal 1969–82*[a]

Percent

Borrowers[b]	FY 1969–73	FY 1974–82	Total
Total	100	100	100
High income	7	1	2
Middle and low income[c]	93	99	98
Middle income	58	61	61
Low income	35	38	38
Middle and low income by sector	100	100	100
Transport, power, telecommunications	47	35	36
Agriculture, social[d]	31	40	39
Agriculture	20	29	28
Education	5	4	4
Population, health, and nutrition	1	1	1
Urban development[e]	°	2	2
Water supply and sewerage	5	5	5

Source: World Bank, "Financial Database Information."

a. The McNamara period includes commitments from July 1, 1969, through June 30, 1982, based on the assumption that loan commitments made during FY 1982 largely reflect lending decisions and preparation carried out under McNamara.

b. See table 5-1a.

c. As defined in *World Debt Tables, 1994–95*, vol. 2, p. xxiv.

d. Social sectors include: education; population, health, and nutrition; urban development; and water supply and sewerage.

e. Represents 70 percent of total urban development lending; see World Bank, "Retrospective Review of Operations," Report 3919, April 22, 1982, p. 50.

° Less than 0.5 percent.

most part they were efforts to present "state-of-the-art" reports, or navigational fixes, on what became a meandering, decade-long quest for ways to do more than lament the fact of mass poverty. The September 1968 speech had been sharp in its criticism and ambition, even raising the hope of an "eradication" of world poverty. It spoke of solutions in general terms only—doubling the Bank's lending, stressing agriculture, education and the most poor countries—but it was soon followed by more specific statements on social needs and policy.

When it came to a concrete formulation of the problem, the first idea was population control, and this became the dominant note in his 1969 speeches, at Notre Dame, in Buenos Aires, and at the Annual General Meeting. Population control was a likely first approach to poverty alleviation for McNamara. Like the Green Revolution, it appeared to offer a simple, technical solution that could be provided from the outside, with vast potential benefits. The obstacles to population control, identified with official attitudes and anachronistic religious beliefs, seemed amenable to audacious, persuasive advocacy. The idea was strongly legitimized for McNamara by his early tutors, Barbara Ward and her circle and the Ford Foundation, and by the endorsement of U.S. aid officials. At the same time, though population growth was an undoubted handicap to the poor, McNamara was avoiding, or postponing, a solution to other, fundamental causes of poverty: low productivity and lack of political power.

On May 1, 1969, McNamara dramatized and widely publicized his position on population restraint by taking his case, as it were, into the heart of enemy country, the Catholic University of Notre Dame, and by speaking graphically of the "degrading conditions . . . sprawling camps of packing crates and scrap metal. Children on the street. . . . Broken men . . . despondent mothers" that characterized slums in "any major city in the developing world."[52] Then, knowing that his statements were likely to cause some skittishness on Wall Street, he carried out a preemptive strike. Speaking to the New York Bond Club, he said that though he indeed intended to emphasize agriculture, education, and population, these were "the best investments," and that the Bank was "not a philanthropic organization and not a social welfare agency."[53] In September 1969, at his second Annual General Meeting, he reaffirmed and developed his view on the need for an enhanced and direct approach to poverty, referring now to the problems of unemployment and urbanization. Addressing the Columbia University conference on the Pearson Report, in February 1970, he spelled out in even more detail the way in which the poor had been left behind during the First Development Decade, making, for the first time, a direct reference to skewed income distributions.

He envisaged Bank involvement and established a Population Projects Department that year, but it was evident that, above all, he was taking on a missionary role and playing that role with audacity and a touch of drama, seeking an understanding with the Pope, and generally, bearing witness:[54] "This is a thorny subject which it would be very much more convenient to leave alone. But I cannot."[55] In addition to making speeches, McNamara aggressively pressed the cause of population control in conversations with national leaders, especially between 1968 and 1970, upsetting Argentinean officials yet drawing approving responses from others, such as newly elected President Luis Echeverría in Mexico and General Soeharto in Indonesia. As a leading solution, however, population control had a short life. Enthusiasm was dampened by difficulties—including borrower reluctance and the rivalry of other development agencies—in translating the objective into lending programs. At the same time, other approaches to poverty alleviation were surfacing. Population control remained on the Bank's list of poverty-related concerns, but the emphasis placed on this goal fell off rapidly after 1970.

52. Robert S. McNamara, "To the University of Notre Dame, Notre Dame, Indiana, May 1, 1969," in McNamara, *The McNamara Years at the World Bank*, p. 45.

53. Robert S. McNamara, "To the Bond Club of New York, New York, May 14, 1969," in McNamara, *The McNamara Years at the World Bank*, p. 55.

54. He also upset Roman Catholic officials in Buenos Aires with a speech on population control. This choice of venue was odd: population growth in Argentina—1.4 percent a year over the 1960s—was one of the lowest in the developing world.

55. McNamara, "To the Board of Governors, . . . September 30, 1968," p. 12.

A new formulation of the poverty problem—unemployment—was already making its appearance in 1969. Unemployment in turn came to be closely linked to the idea of excess urbanization. Its appearance in McNamara's rhetoric coincided with the attention that began to be generated that year by the ILO's World Employment Program, and also by work being carried on at the OECD Development Centre, including a major review of the issue that McNamara had read.[56] As with population, the Bank found it difficult to translate employment into suitable lending programs. The concept was not discarded, and efforts to apply it in operations continued, but its moment in the rhetorical spotlight was brief.

In the gradual buildup of poverty rhetoric, the Pearson Commission Report struck a somewhat discordant note. Conceived as Woods's "grand assize," the report had been intended principally as a tonic for the flagging aid effort, not as a reconsideration of development doctrine. Nonetheless, the Commission's conservative message—none of its ten conclusions spoke of poverty, basic needs, or inequality—became public in late 1969 just as the trickle-down critique was emerging.[57] The coincidence was a provocation and led to the Columbia University conference, which—under Barbara Ward's management—became an important forum for radical views. The meeting, in fact, seemed to go beyond an academic exchange of views: a majority of participants signed a manifesto calling for more poverty-oriented development policies.

One of the most influential and questioning voices at the meeting was that of McNamara. In addition to making standard references to malnutrition, illiteracy, and unemployment, he now, for the first time, spoke of the environment, land reform, public health, and "severely skewed" income distributions. He announced some operational initiatives, but, reflecting the Bank's continuing uncertainty about lending approaches for poverty alleviation, the proposals amounted to merely more research and more coordination with other UN agencies. His Annual Meeting speech in Copenhagen that year was by and large a repetition of the points made at Columbia.

During this period McNamara was backing up public advocacy with private sermons. Lecturing Mexico's delegation to the Annual Meeting, he indicated "concern for Mexico's growing social problems, with special reference to the approxi-

56. Attending a conference in 1969, McNamara borrowed the draft report, prepared by David Turnham, from Monty Yudelman, then director of the OECD Development Centre. Yudelman said: "And much to my surprise . . . he read the whole damned thing. He gave it to me the next morning and said he enjoyed reading it and that he had learned something from it but that there were some mistakes on page 72—one of the footnotes or something like that." Montague Yudelman, interview with John Lewis and Devesh Kapur, September 12, 1991, p. 1.

57. The middle-of-the-road report seemed to please few. It was ridiculed by conservative economist Harry G. Johnson in "The 'Crisis of Aid' and the Pearson Report," a lecture delivered at the University of Edinburgh, Scotland, March 6, 1970.

mately 15 million peasants who had been virtually bypassed by the country's progress."[58] President Echeverría seemed responsive to a poverty focus, proposing that the Bank lend for a large program of feeder roads. The Bank hesitated, arguing that many other facets of Mexican policy, such as big irrigation schemes and cheap credits to large farmers, were regressive.[59] In 1970 McNamara pressed the Moroccan government with regard to the distribution of benefits from the proposed Rharb-Sebou irrigation project:

> When I emphasized to Tazi [Morocco's executive director] again that we could not tolerate private individuals manipulating the project to advance their personal gain, he admitted that the Minister of the Interior had been distributing the land to his friends. . . . When I asked point-blank whether these actions were known to the King, he said nothing was done in Morocco without the King's knowledge and support.[60]

In Pakistan that year, the government protested McNamara's public reference to the growing inequalities between East and West Pakistan.[61] McNamara also raised the social issue in discussions with government officials in the Philippines.[62] Finally, Brazil became an archetype of unequal development and McNamara continually returned to the theme in his dealings with that country.

A large part of the next Annual Meeting speech, in 1971, was given over to social objectives. Both the analysis and operational suggestions were innovative. Nutrition was now seen as a productive investment and as susceptible to targeting. Also, the discussion of unemployment was more comprehensive and was directly related to two operational proposals: support for small farmers and policy changes that would favor labor-intensive industrialization. To bring the latter proposal down to earth, the published version of the speech actually included a practical guide, a list of potential labor-intensive manufacturing activities suitable for developing countries.

Further developments made their appearance in several speeches given in 1972. At UNCTAD III in Santiago, McNamara stressed the theme of income inequality and so the need for equity-oriented policies, such as more progressive taxes, land

58. Memorandum, Enrique Lerdau for the record, September 23, 1970, p. 1.

59. Memorandum, R. Nelson to files, October 1, 1971; E. Peter Wright to Robert S. McNamara, June 1, 1972; Edgar Gutierrez for the record, December 18, 1972.

60. Memorandum, Robert S. McNamara, conversation with Mr. Tazi, September 9, 1970. Benjenk later reported: "The subject [of land distribution] has also been raised repeatedly . . . with the King himself last September," and that protests by tenants in the proposed project area had led to a riot in which police had killed six people. Memorandum, M. P. Benjenk to Robert S. McNamara, "Briefing for visit of Moroccan Finance Minister," December 30, 1970, p. 1. A year later a new government was more accommodating, at least in its rhetoric, proclaiming "a new direction, paying more attention to social goals." Memorandum, R. H. Springuel for the record, "Morocco—Visit of the Prime Minister, H. E. Karim Lamrani," October 5, 1971, p. 2.

61. Memorandum, P. P. M. Cargill to files, September 24, 1970.

62. Memorandum, Gordon H. Street to files, September 25, 1970.

redistribution, and tenancy security. Although he highlighted inequality, a message tailored to Latin America's scandalous income and wealth disparities, the speech began what would become a continuing shift in emphasis, away from equity and toward "the absolute poor."[63] Thus he proposed that a poverty program be defined in terms of "the bottom 40 percent" of the income distribution, and that such a program should include measures to raise small farmer productivity, and educational reforms. This reformulation was given a strong push six months later at the 1972 Annual Meeting, where he focused on a critical analysis of the trickle-down assumption and went on to propose what amounted to a basic needs program, saying that governments should establish "growth targets in terms of essential human needs: in terms of nutrition, housing, health, literacy, and employment."[64] "Such a reorientation of social and economic policy is primarily a political task," he admitted, but he carried the thought forward to questions about the political systems of many if not most of his borrowers. Population control was not mentioned.

The 1973 Annual Meeting speech at Nairobi was a rich diet of both inspirational and operational messages. What is remembered is the announcement that lending for smallholder agriculture would be sharply increased and would become the chief instrument for poverty alleviation. Perhaps because the statement essentially confirmed an ongoing expansion of smallholder lending, it was credible as an operational announcement. There was no similar operational experience to back up and give credibility to other proposals for social improvement made over those years, as in the fields of nutrition, employment, and population control. The speech contained a second operational proposal: that the economic measuring rod be modified. A "new index" of economic progress would be developed, one that would give greater weight than existing measures to income gains by the poor.[65] This

63. By 1972 the terms "absolute poor" and "bottom 40 percent" had become familiar. They had been part of the language of the 1970 Columbia University conference, where Richard Jolly, from the University of Sussex, was especially emphatic on the subject. In a later recollection, McNamara associated his use of "absolute poor" with the debate with Delfim Netto over Brazilian income distribution. Robert S. McNamara, interview with the authors, October 3, 1991, p. 33. The speech followed shortly on Fishlow's presentation on Brazil, which had centered on inequality rather than poverty.

64. John L. Maddux, who drafted most of McNamara's speeches, saw this passage as "an intellectual precursor of what later became known . . . as the 'basic human needs' approach" in *The Development Philosophy of Robert S. McNamara* (World Bank, 1981), p. 18. But the endorsement did not extend to Bank financing of health. An excellent writer, Maddux added much to McNamara's public impact. His first collaboration was the Montreal speech. Angela Maddux tells this story: working in the Bank's Paris office during 1966, she was moved by an account of the then defense secretary's Montreal speech in the *International Herald Tribune* to say: "That's the man who should be president of the Bank." What is more, she later met—and married—the man behind the speech. John L. Maddux, interview with authors, June 30, 1993.

65. Cost-benefit based on total output is distribution blind. Even valuing the *proportionate* increase in each person's income *equally* would weight most evaluations considerably toward the poor.

daring—explicitly normative—idea was more fully explained in *Redistribution with Growth*, but, in contrast to the impact of the small farmer announcement, it was quietly and soon forgotten.

The 1973 speech also marked a further escalation in rhetoric. Reinforcing the shift from equity to poverty, he stressed "absolute poverty," which, he said, was "a condition of life so degraded by disease, illiteracy, malnutrition and squalor as to deny its victims basic human necessities." He made a blunt moral appeal, saying that to tolerate such conditions was to fail to fulfill the "fundamental obligations accepted by civilized men." Finally, though he had spoken of eradicating poverty before, he now set a target: "We should strive to eradicate absolute poverty by the end of this century."[66]

First Steps

Staff members were at first skeptical, reluctant, and "surprisingly resistant to progress," in Clark's recollection. Clark, who became McNamara's antenna to both the outside world and internal opinion, told him: "The staff did not really believe in the poverty thesis," which they saw as "McNamara's and Mahbub's favorite toy." Even Chenery "at first resisted the swing towards poverty lending," seeing the notion of target groups as "a boy scout's approach."[67] Staff members were embarrassed by McNamara's emotional lectures on poverty.[68] Commenting on a draft for one McNamara speech, Knapp wrote: "I would avoid as much as possible the concept of 'need,'" and on another, that it should be "less strident." "Don't overdo" the poverty message, he advised. A year later, Knapp told McNamara that his references to income inequality in the Columbia University speech had disturbed Latin American members, suggesting interventionism.[69] John Holsen remembers, "We economists did not take McNamara's poverty message seriously," and when McNamara invited Albert Fishlow in early 1972 to present his findings on inequality in Brazil, there was a negative reaction to bringing in "an outsider." But, said Holsen: "It was the only way McNamara could shake us up. We were very stubborn."[70]

66. Robert S. McNamara, "To the Board of Governors, September 1973," in McNamara, *The McNamara Years at the World Bank*, pp. 238–9, 259.

67. Mahbub ul Haq, interview, World Bank Oral History Program, December 3, 1982, pp. 11–12.

68. Shapley, *Power and Purpose*, p. 499.

69. Memorandum, J. Burke Knapp to Robert S. McNamara, January 24, 1969; World Bank, Minutes of President's Council Meeting, April 13, 1970, p. 2.

70. John Holsen, interview with the authors, March 12, 1992. Albert Fishlow, "Brazilian Size Distribution of Income," *Papers and Proceedings of the American Economic Association*, vol. 62 (May 1972), pp. 391–402. McNamara invited Fishlow to present his research findings at the Bank during the spring of 1972. Fishlow's statistical analysis and academic credentials impressed McNamara, tipping the scales in a long-running internal debate over the seriousness of Brazil's distributive deficiencies and encouraging McNamara to take a tougher line, including holding up a loan.

One executive director's reaction to a proposed nutrition loan was: "This is soup kitchens," once again conjuring up Wall Street's postwar dismissals of New Deal programs.[71] According to Ravi Gulhati, the social objective was "seen as an illegitimate activity . . . not part . . . of the Bank's mandate," and as being the wrong way to go.[72] Mason and Asher, who had been observing the Bank and interviewing officials while writing their history between 1968 and 1971, were undoubtedly reflecting the contemporary views of senior management when they editorialized: "A serious question arises concerning the relevance of these [social] considerations to the Bank's objectives . . . the question whether, if [social objectives] run counter to economic growth, the Bank is in a position to substitute its judgment concerning appropriate public policy for that of a borrowing member country."[73]

But several appointments came to assist McNamara with his plans for the Bank. William Clark, who joined the Bank on the same day as McNamara, as vice president for external relations, had assisted Anthony Eden and then directed the British Overseas Development Institute, an organization created to promote the foreign-aid cause.[74] He had the European and third-world experience and contacts that McNamara lacked, and he shared McNamara's gusto for a role on the world stage. Eugene Rotberg, recruited in early 1969 as treasurer, played a strong supporting role in helping McNamara multiply IBRD funding (see chapter 16). The next key appointee was Mahbub ul Haq, who had attended the Williamsburg Conference, and whose recantation of growth-oriented development intrigued McNamara. From April 1970 ul Haq became McNamara's unofficial poverty activist in the Bank, becoming director for policy planning in 1972.[75] He served

71. Purviz Damry, interview with the authors, June 27, 1991, pp. 3–4. According to Damry, former secretary and vice president, some officials saw projects for small farmers as "throwing good money after bad" and felt that McNamara "was off on a new adventure." In Damry's view, the staff did not always appreciate that "trickle down didn't work," and that "it was better to go straight to the poverty recipients. . . . But it took some time to get people to understand what all this meant."

72. Ravi Gulhati, interview with the authors, July 9, 1991, p. 4.

73. Mason and Asher, *World Bank since Bretton Woods*, pp. 476, 478. Yet the historians also shared the prevailing staff view that the Bank's future lay in IDA. Interviewed in 1973, Asher stated that the one change he would like to see was: "to make IDA bigger. The Bank will have a rough future if IDA doesn't get larger." Mason said: "We both agree, everyone agrees, that the future of the Bank depends on how much money will be available to IDA." The idea that hard lending had a disciplinary and educative value important to development, a conceptual mainstay of the 1950s Bank, had been left behind.

74. Clark met and collaborated with Woods in 1967 on the "grand assize." In December, Woods offered Clark a position as director of information and public affairs, but, because McNamara's appointment had just been made public, Clark was invited to a joint interview with Woods and McNamara.

75. Ul Haq was first appointed as an economist in 1969 and well before becoming a director had been an influential adviser in the search for ideas on direct poverty lending. Ul Haq recalls his first encounters with McNamara as conflictive: McNamara "suggested . . .

McNamara as a sounding board and articulate promoter in the search for and selling of poverty-related policies and lending.

Hollis Chenery became the Bank's chief economist in June 1970.[76] His economic staff, in addition to research and statistical documentation, was charged with much of the burgeoning agenda of policy work, as the Bank explored possible lending initiatives and procedures.[77] Chenery was a responsive assistant and trusted adviser in poverty-related tasks, despite the fact that he was a late—and never unconditional—convert to the McNamarian "no trade-off" proposition, that is, that poverty alleviation was possible at no sacrifice to growth. Instead, in a somewhat discordant vein, but one that bespoke integrity, he insisted on the purely moral justification for poverty-alleviating measures.[78] Ernest Stern left a senior position in the Agency for International Development to join the Bank in 1970 as a deputy to Chenery. He quickly became one of the most influential voices close to McNamara, serving as "translator" between the economists and the senior operational staff. McNamara's "poverty team" had an additional member in Barbara Ward with whom he met often during his first years in office and who was probably the greatest single influence on him during that formative period. Another outside adviser was Maurice Strong.[79] Also, in the same month that McNamara joined the Bank he became a trustee of the Ford Foundation, then directed by his former government colleague McGeorge Bundy, and he found in that organization many of the ideas that oriented his initial thinking about development.[80] This influence was perhaps most evident in his strong, initial commitment to population control. Up to mid-

---

that [ul Haq's] kind of belligerent questioning of growth . . . was totally uncalled for," and ul Haq came close to leaving the Bank in 1971. Ul Haq, Oral History, December 3, 1982, p. 2.

76. Chenery was a professor at Harvard University and had been deputy administrator for AID. McNamara was slow in arriving at this appointment. He had inherited Irving Friedman as economic adviser, who remained in the position close to eighteen months, and also hired Guy Orcutt, an Australian econometrician, to head economic research for a brief tenure before appointing Chenery in May 1970.

77. Demuth thought that McNamara "relied on economists . . . too much for policy planning." The decision to delegate policy planning to the economists under Chenery was discussed at a President's Council meeting at which, according to Demuth, everyone except Chenery disagreed with the proposal. Bill Gaud (vice president of the IFC) said that his one regret while director of AID was having put the policy responsibility under the economists. Richard H. Demuth, interview, World Bank Oral History Program, March 19, 1984, pp. 24–25.

78. In this he followed Andrew Kamarck, former Economic Department director, who favored using distributive weights in social-benefit evaluations, a method that would openly tilt investment decisions toward the poor.

79. Ul Haq, Oral History, December 3, 1982, p. 9.

80. "When I became World Bank president, I borrowed or 'stole' many of their ideas concerning population planning, poverty reduction, agricultural research, and environmental preservation—ideas enormously helpful, to the World Bank and me, in dealing with problems in developing nations." McNamara, *In Retrospect,* fn., p. 235.

1970 at least, there was much to justify the comment by staff members that the Bank's new lending policy was being developed by outsiders.[81]

With time, many staff members came to be persuaded of the real possibility of combining growth with equity, or, in any case, of its historical necessity for the Bank. Thus Knapp, reflecting a decade later on the Bank's evolution during the 1970s, said: "We didn't find much conflict between building up economic productivity [and] achieving a more equitable distribution of income." Helping the poor, he said, meant building up productive capacity, mobilizing the energies and talents of additional people, and ensuring political and social stability. "I always felt that one of the strongest arguments for . . . more attention to basic needs was simply that, if [neglected,] the creditworthiness of the country was threatened and the basic interests of the Bank as a creditor institution were endangered."[82] Others remained unconvinced. Demuth, for instance, also looking back from the 1980s, said: "During McNamara's presidency . . . the emphasis was on removing poverty rather than on increasing productivity. My own view . . . is that the role of the Bank is to increase the productivity of countries so that they can deal with their own poverty. I don't believe it's feasible for the Bank to run a global poverty alleviation program."[83] Demuth retired from the Bank in 1972, but many who privately shared his opinion held key positions through the decade.

It is difficult to say to what extent McNamara was aware of disagreement in the ranks. He made some key appointments and nudged a small number into retirement, but the changes were remarkably few and gradual; for the most part he worked with the management team in place. On the other hand, "little effort was made to bring [people] on board," according to Gulhati, referring to the senior staff inherited by McNamara. Rather, it was the gradual promotion of more malleable younger officials, and large-scale recruitment, through which much of the staff was eventually "brought on board."[84]

Returning from the Williamsburg Conference, William Clark briefed

about two hundred members of the staff in the Boardroom on the results of the Pearson Commission and of this conference. [I said] "You're going to hear a lot more about the bottom 40% and about development from the bottom up." I got a very cool response from the older members of the Bank and a puzzled but very friendly response from what was then called the 530 Club . . . it met in Room 530 . . . and involved the younger people in the Bank. . . . The Club was to be a sort of ginger group and was somewhat frowned on by the senior staff.[85]

81. Hearing McNamara present his new lending proposals at the February 1970 Williamsburg Conference, a surprised Irving Friedman, who still held the position of economic adviser, turned to a colleague: "Don't look at me." Graham Donaldson, interview with the authors, October 13, 1995.

82. J. Burke Knapp, interview with the authors, October 2 and 29, 1981, pp. 7–8.

83. Demuth, Oral History, March 19, 1984.

84. Ravi Gulhati, interview with the authors, July 9, 1991, p. 11.

85. William Clark, interview, World Bank Oral History Program, October 4, 1983, p. 14.

To managers, McNamara appeared remote, aloof, and deaf to objections, especially arguments that a problem was not susceptible to a precise, definitive solution.[86] He seemed as much unwilling as unable to perceive difficulties and disagreement, relying on his own strong convictions and confidence in the power of intelligence, managerial rules, and systems.

Much of McNamara's attention was taken up by the redesign of administrative procedures and by what seemed to become the dominant objective in itself, the expansion of funding and lending. The latter proved a greater challenge than anticipated after an unsuccessful first issue of Swiss bonds and a worsening U.S. balance of payments problem. Political distractions and setbacks intervened. Still pursued by his role in Vietnam, McNamara jeopardized support for IDA by openly backing Bobby Kennedy's candidacy. He then suffered deeply at Kennedy's assassination; and, with Nixon's election, found himself facing a less sympathetic executive branch.

A major managerial innovation was the Country Program Paper (CPP), introduced in 1968, which became a convenient medium for raising social and distributive issues. The CPP, prepared by the respective regional department, usually on an annual basis, opened with a discussion of country politics and then reviewed the economy, external financing, and the evolution of the Bank's own loans, and on that basis proposed a five-year lending program for each potential borrower. Its confidentiality—it was not accessible to borrowers or Board members—invited frank exchanges on sensitive matters, and its broad canvas accommodated the variety of economic structures, institutions, and policies that come to bear on equity and poverty. Since McNamara generally participated in the discussions, the CPP became an administrative pivot and therefore a powerful lever for his leanings and suggestions.[87]

Brazil became the test case for the CPP and a target for the Bank's new distributive focus. Thus, setting out guidelines for the first set of CPPs in June 1968, he asked that the development of the Northeast of Brazil be regarded as "a key problem" and added that a special meeting would be devoted to that issue. He drew attention to population growth, requesting that it be regarded as "a key development problem" in Colombia, and that Mexico and one African country each be considered as a "laboratory for population analysis." He further instructed that lending to Africa upgrade agriculture and also consider the payoff to primary versus other levels of schooling; that the program for Ethiopia contain a statement on the "feudal land tenure system, and our desire to test the willingness of the government to make changes"; that the paper on Thailand discuss plans for the

---

86. Many staff members have attested to McNamara's seeming inability, even refusal, to accept disagreement—except from a small number of close aides. Faced with a contrary opinion, he would neither debate nor openly express anger, but rather "switch off."

87. Until 1974, after which he delegated smaller countries to Knapp.

(poor) northeast region; that the "dichotomy between rich and poor (10 acres and less) farmers" in India be highlighted, as well as that country's "unwillingness to take advice on agriculture"; and that the paper on Korea give "recognition to the inadequate attention given by Korea to agriculture and the desirability for the Bank to press for policy changes."[88]

Other organizational changes sought two seemingly contradictory objectives: to establish greater (centralized) control over Bank operations, and to increase the (decentralized) authority of regional and country units. To achieve the first objective McNamara created a Programming and Budgeting Department (P&B) in 1968, modeled on similar organizational innovations at Ford Motor Company and the Pentagon and based on the "scientific management" techniques that he had learned and taught at the Harvard Business School.[89] P&B became the instrument for greatly expanding the use of numbers in the conduct of Bank business. By reducing multiple, complex, individual decisions and transactions to summary statistics, McNamara sought to make the institution more transparent and subject to control. The wisdom of relying heavily on quantification for the conduct of an organization whose activities, both as banker and adviser, are essentially judgmental and qualitative, has been much debated. As a dirigiste mechanism, however, P&B served McNamara's purpose in bringing about a rapid reorientation and expansion of the Bank.

The creation of P&B was complemented and reinforced by other administrative changes, such as the establishment of the Economic Programming Department, and later, the Policy and Planning Department, which together verified that loan proposals followed policy guidelines as well as the established country lending programs. In 1970 he established the Operations Evaluation Unit (the OEU: it later became the Operations Evaluation Department) to prepare project performance audit reports on loans once they had been fully implemented. Formal control by top management was reinforced by the creation of two key project departments within the vice presidency of central projects, the Rural Development Department (in 1972), and a parallel Urban Projects Department (in 1973), both designed to act as innovating, poverty-oriented project design, experimentation, and even lending units. These various administrative changes gave McNamara a greater capacity for deciding, issuing, and policing instructions with regard to the desired poverty impact of lending.

The subversive potential of such changes was revealed by one of the first assignments taken on by the OEU, a review of all Bank operations in Colombia. As mandated, the OEU was allowed independence, a freedom that was taken to heart by a team of young, middle-level officials directed by Christopher Willoughby.

88. World Bank, Minutes of President's Council Meeting, June 1, 1968.
89. Shapley, *Promise and Power*, p. 251; Roger Hilsman, "McNamara's War—Against the Truth: A Review Essay," *Political Science Quarterly*, vol. 111, no. 1 (Spring 1996), p. 159.

Their report was remarkably critical of the Bank's past neglect of poverty and social considerations in its lending relationship with Colombia. Indeed, it seemed to go further than McNamara had expected and became the focus of considerable criticism from both staff and the Colombian executive director.[90] It concluded that "if development is measured by reduction of poverty, Colombia has developed marginally if at all," and that Bank support had aggravated the urban-rural income differential and had contributed to the frustration of land reform.[91]

The second objective, greater regional authority, was achieved through a major administrative reorganization of the Bank in late 1972. The changes were nominally based on the recommendations of an external consulting firm, which, however, was well briefed on McNamara's own administrative vision. The most notable change consisted in the creation of five regional vice presidencies responsible for loan and project operations. In essence, project staff, previously centralized in a strong, influential project department that set common standards and evaluated and approved all projects within their respective fields, were now dispersed across the regional units and placed under the authority of the region- and country-oriented directors and vice presidents. The effect was to increase the weight of countrywide lending criteria as against the specialized technical criteria of project staff. This change complemented the already established CPP system, and together they opened doors to the introduction of new lending considerations, especially the social and distributive criteria that McNamara pursued.

Yet, despite major administrative innovations, McNamara felt frustrated. Lending was rising rapidly, but most of the loans were more of the same: power, transportation, and industrial projects absorbed close to two-thirds of new commitments between 1968 and 1973, while agriculture and education projects did not target the poor. Control over operations and a breakthrough on ways to lend to the poor remained elusive. Before the 1972 reorganization, according to Baum, McNamara complained that "even after a year or two in the Bank he had not gotten a handle on the institution . . . not yet found a way in which he could operate the levers of command. These levers were very much in the hands of Burke Knapp and the Loan Committee."[92] Certainly, it was in character for McNamara to see the problem in terms of managerial arrangements rather than of staff conviction or, perhaps, of an overambitious goal.

Defining a Strategy

How to make development work more directly for the poor vexed the Bank over the whole of McNamara's presidency. There were actually two sides to the ques-

90. Virgilio Barco, president of Colombia from 1986 to 1990.
91. World Bank, Operations Evaluation Unit, "Report on Colombia" (1971), pp. 40–41.
92. Warren Baum, interview, World Bank Oral History Program, 1986, p. 6.

tion. The most pressing concerned what the Bank itself should do: what new types of lending would accelerate poverty reduction without lowering traditional standards, and what nonlending operations—grants, research, and technical assistance —would reinforce poverty alleviation? The second concerned the borrowers' agenda: what distributive policies and programs should be recommended by the Bank to its clients?

This search for an operational strategy was carried out in parallel with the administrative or housekeeping reforms and sermonizing described earlier, but it was most intense between 1971 and 1976. For close to three years, from 1968 into 1971, the Bank appeared to be casting about for that "better way" to make development work for the poor. It turned to outsiders for ideas and followed a variety of uncertain leads, searching for loans that would be simultaneously "bankable" by World Bank standards and "poor-friendly." From 1971, however, McNamara's initial, almost solitary advocacies and proposals developed into a more substantial, group effort, with the Bank considering a variety of approaches until it finally focused on small farmer projects, at Nairobi in 1973. But the search for a better poverty strategy continued over the rest of the decade.

Before Nairobi, 1968–73

The initial approach to social objectives was uncertain and groping. Repeatedly, time was lost backing the wrong horse. This occurred first with population control, which, as noted, drew much of McNamara's attention but failed to develop into a significant lending program. It was also the case with other ideas for helping the poor, such as nutrition, employment generation, housing, land reform, and the use of distributional weights, all of which proved operational nonstarters. Each was relevant to poverty, but none met the Bank's need for "bankable" projects—large-scale, foreign exchange, mostly hard-terms loans that would be acceptable to borrowers and attractive to the Bank's principal shareholders.

More generally, the search for bankable solutions was initially hindered by the long-ingrained habit of defining the problem in terms of equity and income distribution rather than of poverty (or absolute poor). The two definitions—equity and poverty—coexisted, and in a way competed, since they had different policy implications. But it was equity and income distribution that were the legitimate, sophisticated, compelling concepts, with rich histories in economic theory and political debate. By contrast, the poor were ignored by economic science and considered vaguely disreputable in discussions of public policy, being traditionally associated with welfare programs, benevolent societies, and soup kitchens. Chenery's large research program focused on income distribution, not poverty, an emphasis appropriately reflected in the title of its first important product, *Redistribution with Growth: Policies to Improve Income Distribution in Developing Countries in the Context of Economic Growth.*

This way of posing the objective, as a redistributive and therefore conflictive exercise, best exemplified by land reform, had a motivational advantage for the poverty cause: poverty, of its own, might elicit charity—a tepid emotion—but inequality was a scandal and a challenge. On the other hand, defining the problem as one of inequality, and thus of redistribution, became a barrier to action: the definition magnified the perceived political constraint and increased the probable complexity of any lending operation. It was only when the Bank escaped the conceptual grip of "equity" that it broke through into large-scale poverty lending.[93] Putting equity aside, the Bank could focus on the more politically acceptable and—as it first appeared—administratively limited goal of providing resources to the poor. That solution was given an intellectual blessing by *Redistribution with Growth,* despite the original, distributive terms of reference of the study. Equity did not disappear from the Bank's language: it lived on as a useful rhetorical theme for speeches, sophisticated research, and policy dialogues with borrowers, but it was by and large put aside in the formulation of "poverty lending" approaches.

The greatest obstacle to a fast start on poverty operations, however, was that McNamara refused to consider purely welfare solutions. When it came to possible poverty initiatives, he made clear his intention that poverty alleviation should not be a rationale for accepting lower productivity standards in Bank projects.[94] Despite the radical image created by his speeches and advocacy, he repeatedly insisted that economic productivity was a necessary criterion for Bank loans. Poverty alleviation was simply added as a second necessary criterion. Flaunting the conventional wisdom that a "trade-off" between welfare and production was inevitable, McNamara was being a stubborn fool—or a new Columbus—and in either case at odds with the establishment. But when it came to the need for economic growth he was a mainstream believer. "There is no sense in simply redistributing the same size pie," he told the Board in October 1968.[95] And, responding to the United Nations Educational, Scientific, and Cultural Organization in 1973, he wrote: "In the long run no direct efforts against poverty and unemployment can succeed without sustained economic growth. Hence, while the Bank Group is increasingly directing attention and assistance to employment and the distribution of income, the transfer of real resources for development assistance [that is, growth] continues to increase."[96] Growth was necessary to poverty reduction and an essential purpose of every Bank loan and policy recommendation.

93. This position was signaled in McNamara's speeches to UNCTAD III and the Annual General Meeting in 1972.

94. Memorandum, Robert S. McNamara for the record, "Meeting on Mr. McNamara's UNCTAD Statement," January 7 and 12, 1972.

95. Meeting on October 9, 1968.

96. Memorandum, Robert S. McNamara to Philippe de Seynes, undersecretary-general, UNESCO, March 23, 1973.

McNamara's identification with the earlier Bank went further than an endorsement of the growth objective; he was also cautious when it came to straying from the traditional insistence on project lending. In late 1970 McNamara addressed a meeting of senior colleagues:

> [Many] advocated that the Bank Group must quickly get into program lending and local currency financing. He . . . was prepared to take a very liberal stand on this issue but at the same time he would like to caution everyone that program lending should not be tantamount to irresponsible performance on the part of the developing countries. . . . [T]he African Finance Ministers had called on him to complain that too many restrictions were being placed [on] project loans and that they would prefer to have non-project lending. He felt that most developing countries which asked for program assistance were not willing to accept performance conditions which had to go with such lending.[97]

If he was slow then to develop operational formulas for poverty alleviation, it was to a large extent because he was demanding in terms of *both* orthodox and radical criteria: the traditional goals and restraints of the institution and the new objective of direct poverty reduction. Trying to satisfy output and need at the same time, he was sailing an uncharted sea.[98]

It is not surprising therefore that during the first years of that search he found himself looking for a solution that, in the minds of most colleagues, did not exist. Each initiative to study some social aspect of development or to push for social objectives in country lending programs, for instance, seemed to emerge out of his personal concern, conversations, and observations during travel and thinking rather than as a proposal brought forward by staff. Such was the case when the Bank turned to consider unemployment, nutrition, regional poverty, and land tenure. Also, there was little support from outside the Bank, where the rethinking of development policy was only beginning. The mix of ideas and competitive impact that came from the ILO's World Employment Program, from the United Nations 1971 interagency project on food and nutrition (PIA/PNAN), and from other external sources began to be felt only in the early 1970s. Further reinforcement of McNamara's agenda in those years came from a growing number of studies on income distribution.

Equity and poverty—as matters to be tackled directly—barely appeared in McNamara's first agenda, the action list that he drew up for himself in May 1968,

---

97. Memorandum, ul Haq to Adler, "Meeting of the Review Group on Brazil," p. 1; notes on Meeting on the CPP for Brazil held November 16, 1970. McNamara held to this line through the decade, frequently rejecting proposals by his vice presidents for program loans in specific cases.

98. The accommodation of output and need came to be expressed in the concept of "redistribution with growth," as proposed by Keith Marsden, "Towards a Synthesis of Economic Growth and Social Justice," *International Labour Review*, vol. 100, no. 5 (November 1969), pp. 389–418; and by Hans Singer, *Employment, Incomes and Equality, A Strategy for Increasing Productive Employment in Kenya* (Geneva: ILO, 1972).

shortly after arriving at the Bank. Of ninety-eight items only one concerned poverty, when McNamara reminded himself to "consider . . . the financing of housing, health, and urbanization." The list was dominated by administrative and financial measures to increase presidential control over the institution and to raise the volume of lending.[99] Subsequent lists drawn up periodically through 1972 all show the same concentration on management and funding, with almost no reference to lending policy and the poor. Minutes of weekly meetings of the President's Council[100] also show scant attention to poverty alleviation through early 1971, despite the fact that McNamara used the second meeting, on April 8, 1968, to commend Edward Mason's report on education and express his disappointment that education projects were not receiving the same attention from staff members as other types of projects.[101]

The few references to social issues at President's Council meetings from 1968 to early 1971 were mostly to population control, though ecology, including the appointment of an ecology adviser, was also brought up several times. Following his visit to Iran in late 1969, McNamara requested a review of experience with land reforms. That year also, when he commented on the "social stress" created by the Green Revolution, he went on to say that he "preferred to postpone discussion of this controversial matter to a much later date."[102] Strikingly, when a senior Bank official proposed support for preventive health services in Jamaica, McNamara replied that "he was reluctant to consider financing of health care unless it was very strictly related to population control, because usually health facilities contributed to the decline of the death rate, and thereby to the population explosion."[103] Letting rationality get the better of common sense, McNamara was in effect saying that disease should not be controlled pending a reduction in birth rates. Between November 1970 and January 1971 McNamara was impressed by two non-Bank reports on the employment problem, an "excellent paper" by Hans Singer affirming that unemployment levels in less developed countries were 20 to 30 percent and were "bound to increase further," and a draft OECD (Turnham) report on employment, both of which he sent on to Chenery asking for recommendations on how the Bank could best address the problem.[104]

99. McNamara chron. files. Untitled document, May 25, 1968. The files contain similar though shorter lists prepared in August 1969, January 1971, October 1971, and January 1972.

100. Created by Woods and continued by McNamara, it included the vice presidents, general counsel, and chief economist and served as the president's principal advisory group for day-to-day control over the affairs of the Bank. It was more a discussion and information forum than decisionmaking group.

101. Mason's report, a wide-ranging policy review of the education sector, had been requested by Siem Aldewereld after consultation with McNamara in late 1967.

102. World Bank, Minutes of President's Council Meeting, March 24, 1969.

103. World Bank, Minutes of President's Council Meeting, March 3, 1969.

104. Memorandum, Robert S. McNamara to Hollis B. Chenery, November 14, 1970, attached to H. W. Singer, "International Policies and Their Effect on Employment," n.d.,

By 1971 the search for a poverty strategy was no longer a quixotic, one-man enterprise and was broadening across a wide front of institutional activities and potential operational areas. Poverty alleviation was becoming an increasingly open and accepted objective in country and project discussions. Issues and proposals regarding poverty impact were beginning to be raised by operational staff, and policy studies on potential new lending areas and poverty-related issues were multiplying. Working with a rapidly expanding economic staff, Chenery initiated research on income distribution. This momentum was largely the effect of Mc-Namara's steady advocacy and recruiting, and organizational changes, but it was also helped along by a growing outside stimulus and support.

The most visible outside influence was the ILO's World Employment program. Writing in 1972 on Bank-ILO relations, Michael Hoffman said: "I think we are going to be under considerable pressure to introduce a specific employment dimension into all our project appraisals and President's Reports."[105] In Colombia, Ceylon, Kenya, and the Philippines, the Bank followed on the heels of the ILO with its own large-scale studies.[106] When McNamara endorsed public-works programs in 1972, FAO's World Food Program (WFP) proposed a cooperative effort. The WFP was then engaged in food-for-work and nutritional projects in eighty-eight nations.[107] Academic criticism and public doubts on development efforts were growing: U.S. aid legislation was moving toward its basic needs, "New Directions" reformulation; Fishlow's findings on Brazilian inequality and Teresa Hayter's radical critique of aid were both published in early 1971.[108] Political events between

---

processed. A report titled "The Employment Problem and Bank Operations" (Report R72-94), was completed on April 21 and presented to the Board on May 2, 1972. It was later issued as *The Employment Problem and World Bank Activities,* Bank Staff Working Paper 148 (March 1973), prepared by David J. Turnham (who had done the original OECD study) and E. K. Hawkins.

105. Memorandum, Michael L. Hoffman to Richard H. Demuth, "Employment and Bank/ILO Relations," April 7, 1971. Hoffman recommended that the Bank use ILO staff for employment analysis in Bank projects and in return offer the ILO a way to move forward: "So far about all they have done is to organize these big advisory missions and make pronouncements about the importance of employment. We could help ILO to tie its efforts to visible results [and to take] credit for increasing the employment impact of Bank Group projects."

106. World Bank, 1972, 1974, 1976.

107. In his address to the 1972 Annual General Meeting, McNamara had said: "Unemployment . . . must be attacked head-on [through activities such as] the building of market roads; construction of low-cost simple housing; reforestation programmes; expansion of irrigation and drainage facilities; highway maintenance and similar low-skill, labor-intensive . . . projects," an agenda that overlapped with not only the WFP efforts but those of many voluntary agencies, such as CARE, Church World Service, and Catholic Relief Services, as well as bilateral aid sources. Robert S. McNamara, "To the Board of Governors, Washington, D.C., September 25, 1972," in McNamara, *The McNamara Years at the World Bank,* p. 224.

108. Teresa Hayter, *Aid as Imperialism* (Penguin Books, 1971). The New Directions aid legislation was finally passed in 1973. McNamara requested that replies to Hayter and to *Washington Post* editorials by Barnet be prepared. Hayter was especially influential in Europe.

1969 and 1971, especially Allende's election in Chile, Algerian and Peruvian socialism and oil nationalizations, civil war in Pakistan, and Indira Gandhi's election
on a poverty-oriented platform may also have given an edge to the search for a new
strategy. A more personal influence came to bear with McNamara's visits to six
African countries between January and May 1971.

Several areas with a potential "social" contribution were studied. Much of this
study had the long-run and rigorous character of academic "research"; but much
was "policy work," consisting of broad reviews of existing knowledge on particular
issues, as a basis for guiding Bank lending and advice. The research was almost
entirely the responsibility of the Economic Department, which after the 1972
reorganization became a vice presidency, named the Development Policy Staff
(DPS) under Hollis Chenery. Policy work was assigned instead to ad hoc teams that
generally pooled specialists with staff from DPS and its organizational twin, also
created in 1972, the Central Projects Staff (CPS).

The agenda for "social" topics reflected McNamara's urge to reconnoitre. Studies
were initiated at his direct request, often at meetings of the President's Council.
His annual speeches had something of the character of marching orders: each
speech led into "follow-up" plans. Less than a month after his 1971 Address to the
Governors, the economics staff reported on changes carried out in the research
program. Five of the seven topics covered by the research program now dealt with
social issues. Research on agriculture was to stress small farmers and landless
laborers. And a major study on the policy implications of income distribution was
being initiated, though "some of the more controversial and politically sensitive
aspects . . . such as the distribution of landholdings, regional priorities, and policies
for redistributing wealth" were not receiving much attention. Other initiatives dealt
with employment, population, and nutrition.[109] This drive to explore and widen the
scope of Bank activities extended beyond the poverty agenda: forestry, fishing,
tourism, and the environment were also added to what was becoming—as critics
would later say—a "full-service bank."

Even so, reflecting the continuing weight of traditional lending, by June 1972,
four years into McNamara's term, the research program continued to have "a heavy
emphasis on transportation and public utilities, while . . . new areas of interest such
as employment, urbanization, income distribution and rural development are only
reflected modestly in new proposals for fiscal year 1973."[110] On the other hand,
traditional operations were themselves being nudged toward social objectives. A
1969 policy statement for the International Finance Corporation, for instance,

109. Memorandum, J. P. Hayes and P. D. Henderson to Hollis B. Chenery, "Follow-up to
McNamara's Address," October 27, 1971, p. 2. The study of income distribution was
directed by Irma Adelman.

110. Memorandum, Ernest Stern to Research Committee, "Bank Research Priorities,"
June 5, 1972.

rephrased that institution's purpose: whereas before it had said, "IFC's activities are similar in many respects to those of a private investment banker," the new statement added, "Its investments must do more than meet the test of the market."[111] Moreover, two of the poverty-oriented research themes taken up during this period, income distribution and distributional weights in cost-benefit analysis as a way to steer projects toward the poor, were indeed effective in calling attention to the problem, but neither proved helpful for the formulation of lending operations.[112]

When McNamara began to look beyond population control—his first enthusiasm—he turned to nutrition and employment.

NUTRITION AND HEALTH. Beginning in April 1971, McNamara took a closer interest in nutrition. As a Brookings Institution trustee, he was aware of Alan Berg's work, published in a 1973 book, *The Nutrition Factor.* He referred to that work at a President's Council meeting, decided on Bank representation at a United Nations panel on the topic, asked Chenery to follow up with a series of seminars and possible material for his Annual General Meeting speech, and said that he "foresaw eventually the need for a separate section somewhere in the Bank's staff to deal with the problems of malnutrition."[113] The month of May saw the culmination of discussions begun in 1969 to create an international financing consortium to support agricultural research, the future Consultative Group on International Agricultural Research, meetings supported by McNamara and chaired by the Bank. In November 1970, Dr. James Lee, a biochemist, was appointed science adviser, with nutrition included in his responsibilities. A January 1972 report, *Possible Bank Actions on Malnutrition Problems,* led to the creation of a nutrition unit. That year also McNamara was moved to an extraordinary health-related initiative: the sponsorship of an international donor consortium to eradicate river blindness in West Africa. The effort, modeled on the recently created CGIAR, was highly successful.[114] By 1972 the Bank had started including health components in agriculture, population, and education projects.

111. The new statement also said that, while profitability remained an essential investment criterion, economic benefit to the country was now to be "equally essential." IFC's new, more developmental role under McNamara also took the form of increased lending to smaller and poorer countries and, in effect, consisted of the cross-subsidization of the greater risk and cost of such investments by IFC's safer and more profitable clients. See chapter 13.

112. The notion that the value of a dollar depends on the income of its recipient: in particular, that a dollar creates more welfare when received by a poor person than by a rich person.

113. Considerable impetus to food and nutrition planning was given by the 1971 International Conference on Nutrition, National Development, and Planning held at MIT, followed by the creation in 1972 of the International Nutrition Planning Program at that university, funded by the Rockefeller Foundation and USAID. World Bank, Minutes of President's Council Meeting, April 12, 1971, p. 2. See also Minutes of President's Council Meetings of April 19 and May 10, 1971.

114. However, the CGIAR and river blindness initiatives became the exceptions to the rule that, until the early 1990s, the Bank chose not to engage in grant funding of international or cross-national public good projects.

A nutrition policy paper was drafted during 1973 in parallel with the preparation of the Nairobi speech. The paper admitted that "the case for an investment in better nutrition on more direct *economic* grounds . . . has only recently been advanced and is as yet less clear" and then went on to what was essentially a moral argument. Better nutrition, it said, would "imply a more equitable distribution of income . . . encourage more effective population planning . . .[and] improve the level of well-being."[115] The actual operational proposal was modest: that the Bank "assume a more active and direct role in nutrition," and finance two projects, in Brazil and Iran, as a start. When the paper was discussed by the Board in November 1973, after Nairobi, McNamara further clarified that "the Bank was not thinking of participating in mass food distribution programs" and "would limit itself to development-oriented work." The Board was nevertheless worried and discouraged. "Most speakers had difficulty in conceiving what was envisaged in nutrition projects," and several saw nutrition as tackling the effects but not the causes of malnutrition. Unusually, the Board extracted from McNamara the conditions that not only would the two projects be considered "experimental" but that they would not be negotiated before each was discussed with the Board.[116]

If the Board was reluctant to engage in nutrition lending, in the case of health it was McNamara who hesitated. He reacted negatively to separate staff recommendations that the Bank support health programs in Jamaica and Colombia; and Bank lending for this sector remained limited to minor components in other projects.[117] It was not until June 1973 that he requested a health policy paper.[118] Yet his objection was certainly a question of suitability for the Bank, not of policy for the borrowers, since he advocated health along with nutrition spending in speeches at Columbia in 1970 and at the Annual General Meeting in 1972.

EMPLOYMENT. In January 1971 McNamara asked Chenery "how the Bank best could address itself to the critical unemployment problems facing LDCs."[119] A

115. World Bank, "Nutrition Policy," Sector Program Paper R73-247, October 31, 1973, pp. 3, i–ii.

116. IBRD/IDA, "Summaries of Discussions at Meeting of the Executive Directors of the Bank and IDA, on November 27, 1973," SD73-52, December 21, 1973, paras. 30, 45.

117. An early 1969 request by Colombia for a public health project foundered when Colombia refused to make family planning an explicit objective. "Bank Operations in Colombia: An Evaluation," Operations Evaluation Unit Report Z-18, May 25, 1972, pp. 155–57, later made the case for Bank support for public health in Colombia. Christopher Willoughby, who drafted the report's—unsuccessful—recommendation on health, tells that, seven years later, as he was leaving the Board meeting that had (finally) approved the creation of a Health Department in the Bank, he found himself walking next to McNamara and reminded him of the 1972 refusal. McNamara said, "Too early is as wrong as too late." Willoughby, interview with the authors, April 26, 1995.

118. Memorandum, Anders Ljungh, Office of the President, to Hollis Chenery, "Policy Paper on Health," June 1, 1973.

119. World Bank, Minutes of President's Council Meeting, January 4, 1971.

unit was created within the Economic Department called the Population and Human Resources Division, with responsibility for employment questions. The Bank examined the possibility of collaborative work with the ILO, and an agreement between the two institutions led to the use of ILO economists in some Bank missions during 1970 and 1971, and, in turn, to the involvement of Bank economists in the large-scale ILO country studies in several countries.[120] Although in the opinion of Bank officials the ILO in reality had few economists to lend and little expertise relevant to Bank economic work, the Bank persisted in this tentative relationship, perhaps because it sensed the force of the ILO's political initiative. As Edward Hawkins, the Bank's liaison officer with the ILO, noted:

> At first sight it is puzzling that countries with whom the Bank has a close relationship, large spending programs and frequent economic reports should approach the ILO for employment missions. The answer may well lie in the feeling that employment is in some way a separate issue from the development questions discussed by the Bank; there may also be a political motivation involved, in the expectation that the subsequent report can be used publicly to support particular policies. The request for the first [ILO] mission to Colombia, for example, was linked to the wish of the then President to be able to make a public impact with the report in the closing days of his administration. The recent request from the Philippines appears also to be timed in relation to the next presidential elections in 1973.[121]

Hawkins went on to note that the Bank had, in fact, focused on employment and social objectives in its own recent economic report on the Philippines, but that the report had not yet been available to the Philippines, and also that "presumably Bank reports cannot be easily used for political purposes." The larger conclusion of Hawkins's analysis was the image of "two international agencies . . . engaged in scarcely distinguishable similar activities for the same countries . . . hardly an encouraging prospect." But Hawkins also saw the matter in a way that was traditional in the Bank: the ILO, he said, "is a *labor* organization and not an *employment* organization—concerned essentially with social rather than economic questions."[122]

A paper titled *The Employment Problem and Bank Operations* was finally presented to the Board in May 1972.[123] Its preface noted that it had little to offer: though it dealt with "one of the principal issues facing the poorer member countries . . . very little as yet is known that can be used as a basis for action." Hence, "the interim nature of this report." At the same time, and in slight contradiction, it assured readers, the Bank had already begun to respond to the problem, a claim based on several recent economic reports that had incorporated employment considera-

120. Memorandum, E. K. Hawkins to Hollis Chenery, "Cooperation on Employment with the ILO," April 24, 1972.

121. Ibid., p. 5.

122. Ibid., p. 5, n. 1, and p. 6.

123. World Bank, "The Employment Problem and Bank Operations."

tions.[124] The report was skeptical on the value of project-based analysis ("There is little virtue in trying to spell out the amount of employment created in any particular project") and stressed the macroeconomic and policy-based nature of the problem.[125] Nonetheless, staff argued that employment was central to equity, "because, for the mass of people in the developing world, better access to productive activity . . . was the only practical way to improve income distribution."[126] Several Board members worried about a possible conflict between output and income distribution. One "hoped the bank was not heading towards sacrificing growth as a primary objective." But a more fitting comment was that of a director who compared the employment and population problems, pointing out that "the latter was slow to yield projects and results," forcing the chairman to admit that "the analogy was extremely close."[127] The Bank continued to be frustrated in its search for a clear poverty strategy.

During this period the Bank worked on two other employment-related studies: one, begun in February 1971, on the technical feasibility of substituting labor for equipment in civil construction, and the other, begun in 1972, on rural and urban public works. One component consisted of a study of the employment effects of tractor mechanization in West Pakistan and Gujarat State of India. Studies of the possibility of technical substitution continued through the decade and generated reports on each phase of the research, including country experiments.[128] The second initiative, proposed to the Board on January 3, 1973, led to separate reports on rural and urban public works produced in 1976.[129]

URBANIZATION. Urbanization became a subject of study from 1968, when McNamara created an Economics of Urbanization Division under Richard Westebbe in the Economic Department. A "White Paper" on the subject was prepared over 1968–70 and became a special section in the Bank's *Annual Report 1970.*[130] A policy paper was requested in 1971 and the Urbanization Sector Working Paper

124. Ibid., pp. i, 24.

125. Ibid., pp. 27, 32.

126. IBRD/IDA/IFC, "Summary of Discussion at Meeting of the Executive Directors of the Bank and IDA, May 15, 1972," SD72-75, June 14, 1972, p. 1.

127. Ibid., pp. 2–3.

128. The first phase produced a report, IBRD/IDA, *Study of the Substitution of Labor and Equipment in Civil Construction: Phase II Final Report,* Staff Working Paper 172, vol. 1 (1974). Subsequent reports, including a "Guide," were published in 1975, 1976, 1978, 1985, and 1986.

129. Memorandum to the Board, "Study of Rural and Urban Public Works Programs," Sec M73-7, January 3, 1973; World Bank, "Rural Public Works and the Bank: Background Analysis," March 24, 1976, reviewed by staff on January 12, 1976; IBRD/IDA, "Issues in Bank Financing of Rural Public Works," PRC/C/76-1, March 24, 1976; World Bank, *Public Works Programs in Developing Countries: A Comparative Analysis,* Bank Staff Working Paper 224 (February 1976).

130. World Bank, *Annual Report, 1970,* pp. 57–63.

completed the following year.[131] The principal message of these papers was conceptual, indicating the need for an integral or systems view of urbanization as a framework for choosing and evaluating projects and for providing policy advice. For Westebbe, "a main purpose was to get Bank operations to recognize the urban economy as an economic unit." This broader view would become helpful for the discussion of investment choices that bore on poverty and employment, such as those having to do with technical standards and with the coverage of urban services, and also for the analysis of the relationship between the rural and urban economies.[132] Westebbe became involved in an operational debate regarding a proposed beltway for the city of Sao Paulo in Brazil. The debate became an early test of the poverty criterion: McNamara chose not to finance the beltway on the grounds that Bank funds should be assigned instead to the poor Northeast of Brazil. More important, the report contributed to an emerging poverty strategy by advocating sites and services projects, mass transit, and simpler and cheaper provision of power, water, and sewerage.[133] When the report appeared, the Bank's first sites and services project, in Senegal, was already on the way to Board approval.[134] In discussing this report, many Board members continued to be skeptical of the Bank's social involvement, arguing against sites and services projects, for instance, on the grounds that the housing problem was so large that "the Bank could not hope 'to make a dent in it.'"[135]

WATER SUPPLY AND SEWERAGE. While economists and project staff debated the rarefied concept of "urban development," urban lending in practice consisted almost entirely of water and sewerage projects. A Sector Program Paper on Water Supply and Sewerage was presented to the Board in April 1971. The paper, which reviewed Bank experience in the sector since the first loan in 1961, contained an early warning of some of the implementation difficulties that would face future "poverty lending." It noted that lending in this sector "is more difficult than had been expected," requiring planning assistance, intensive supervision, and much needed institutional improvement. Moreover, "We now recognize that local officials and water managers are generally less able, less accustomed to thinking in hard financial and economic terms, and more exposed to direct political pressure." And, "institutional improvement is much more difficult to achieve than engineering improvement."[136] The sector project staff responsible for the paper lamented:

131. World Bank, Minutes of President's Council Meeting, June 14, 1971; June 21, 1971; April 3, 1972. The sector paper was completed April 28, 1972.

132. Richard Westebbe, interview, World Bank Oral History Prgram, January 25, 1988, p. 17.

133. IBRD/IDA, Urbanization Sector Working Paper, April 28, 1972, pp. 28–43.

134. It was approved in fiscal 1972.

135. IBRD/IDA/IFC, "Summaries of Discussions at Meeting of the Executive Directors," SD 72-23, May 23, 1972, p. 8.

136. World Bank, "Water Supply and Sewerage," Sector Program Paper R71-84, April 22, 1971, pp. 8–10.

The water/sewage sector shares one basic characteristic of other public utilities . . . it sells services to the public. But in the minds of many people it has a stronger "social service" character. It is frequently classified, even in some Bank reports, as "social" rather than "economic infrastructure," perhaps because no other public utility more closely affects the daily lives of people.[137]

On the issue of urban bias, the paper admitted and defended the concentration of lending in urban areas, and though it agreed that rural water projects were also justified, it made the telling point that "to date, none has been presented [and] not many such projects are likely to appear unsolicited. . . . The reasons which cause governments to neglect urban water and sewerage needs apply with even greater force to rural areas."[138] Nonetheless, Roger Chaufournier, then vice president for West Africa, urged "increased attention to rural water supply as one facet of rural development which includes measures for health, credit, tertiary roads, markets, etc."[139] The executive director for India, S. R. Sen, saw an antipoor bias in the Bank's excessive standards: "It appears that the Bank approach has been too much 'perfectionist' and has tended to introduce too much 'technology' and standards which are too much out of line with the level of technology and standards in other sectors in the same area. The result has sometimes been a T-model Ford car fitted with the latest Cadillac engine trying to move in a convoy of bullock carts."[140]

Yet, despite the sector's "social" taint, water supply projects were sufficiently "productive" and comparable in other ways to traditional economic infrastructure to establish a foothold over the 1960s and expand rapidly in the early 1970s, without explicit resort to nonproductive justifications. The ability to charge for services, and thus pay their way—in principle if not often in practice—allowed water supply lending to jump from an average $27 million a year over 1968–70 to $180 million over 1971–73—and to do so quietly, with little "new policy" fanfare. On the other hand, the constant struggle by sectoral spokesmen to minimize and downplay the "social" character of water supply may have been too successful, hiding its potential as an instrument for poverty alleviation at a crucial moment of change in the Bank's lending criteria.

EDUCATION. There was a notable expansion and diversification of lending for education during the early 1970s, including support for primary schooling, and for nonformal, adult, and literacy training. Commitments for education projects tripled from an average of $62 million during 1968–70 to $194 million during 1971–73. The phase would later be described as "the McNamara revolution" in Bank policy toward education.[141] Yet, though education would come to be seen—in the 1990s—

---

137. Ibid., p. 4.

138. Ibid., p. 10.

139. Memorandum, Roger Chaufournier to S. R. Cope, March 9, 1971.

140. Statement by Dr. S. R. Sen on the Sector Program paper, "Water Supply and Sewerage," May 19, 1971, EDS71-22, p. 1

141. A detailed account is provided by Phillip Jones in *World Bank Financing of Education: Lending, Learning and Development* (London: Routledge, 1992), chap. 4. Jones also argues that "the poverty focus promoted by Robert McNamara after 1973 had far less impact on the education sector than is frequently supposed" (p. 93).

as a powerful device for poverty alleviation and distributive fairness, neither poverty nor equity entered into the arguments that were put forward to justify this policy
change during the early 1970s. As in the case of water supply, the new policy was
defended solely on the grounds of productivity.

The "revolution" began in an unlikely way, with a sober, cautiously worded
report by Edward Mason in 1968.[142] Mason's principal recommendation was for a
gradual broadening, from concentration on secondary-level vocational or technical
schooling toward primary and university. The report contained no reference to
equity, poverty, or noneconomic educational objectives. Support for literacy programs was justified on strict productivity grounds, because when "attached to
particular areas of economic activity [they] can have a more immediate effect on
productivity than any type of formal education."[143] Mason thought the emphasis
placed on secondary, technical, vocational, and teacher training was "still appropriate," but that "the time has come for a substantially greater latitude for
exceptions."

The call for a broadening of the scope of education lending was warmly received
by the director for education projects, Duncan Ballantine, who went on to propose
pilot projects in new educational areas, including nonformal education, and in
particular, support of educational broadcasting for the rural and poor population.
At the time, there was much enthusiasm for nonformal schooling. One of its
principal promoters, Philip Coombs, influenced Ballantine and authored a Bank
publication on nonformal education.[144] Though approached by Coombs and others
in the United States as a productive tool, especially in the form of farmer education, the idea had political and social overtones. It was, in fact, acquiring the nature
of a "movement" in some developing areas, joined by a mix of religious and private
aid organizations and activist political groups, that saw mass education as the key to
both development and democracy. Radio stations became the principal medium of
teaching.[145]

Ballantine drafted a policy paper on education lending for Board review in July
1970. The paper reconfirmed that productivity was the basic criterion for Bank
lending but recommended some broadening and experiment in new educational
fields.[146] When McNamara had posed the question of the relationship between

142. As mentioned earlier, the report, delivered to the Bank in February 1968, drew
McNamara's attention and favorable comment in a meeting of the President's Council in
April 1968.

143. Edward Mason, Report on Education, February 15, 1968, cited in Jones, *World
Bank Financing of Education*, p. 95.

144. Philip Coombs and Manzoor Ahmed, *Attacking Rural Poverty: How Nonformal
Education Can Help* (Johns Hopkins University Press, 1974).

145. The movement was especially strong in Latin America, from the early 1960s. Paulo
Freire and Ivan Illich became leading ideologues, and the Catholic Church was deeply
involved. See David Lehmann, *Democracy and Development in Latin America: Economics,
Politics and Religion in the Post-War Period* (Temple University Press, 1990), pp. 96–104.

146. "Lending in Education," R70-147, July 23, 1970, for Board meeting on August 4, 1970.

education and development in March 1969, he had "guessed . . . that functional illiteracy was a major obstacle."[147] It is notable that, despite his intuition and the opening provided by Mason, the policy paper contained no reference to literacy. Also, the proposed engagement with primary education was to be limited to experimental and demonstration projects. There was no reference to equity or poverty.

SMALL FARMERS AND NAIROBI. As mentioned earlier, agriculture was already the core of a low-profile but incipient "poverty strategy" during the 1960s. Though it spoke of "social" needs rather than "poverty," the pre-McNamara Bank had nonetheless developed a sense that, whether on moral or political grounds, some exceptions were necessary to the rule that resource allocation should be guided only by productivity; some concession was required to the claim of relative need.

That "social" response had come to be associated principally with support for agriculture, and especially, with an increasing share of smallholder projects. The linkage was in part a historical accident: "relative need" presented itself during the 1960s most clearly in the guise of the newly independent, very poor, and extremely underdeveloped African nations. Obligated to respond to the needs of these new members, the Bank had few lending options outside smallholder agriculture. Pushed by Woods and then McNamara, agricultural lending jumped almost threefold in real terms from mid-1966 to mid-1973, rising from 13 percent to 27 percent as a share of total—pre-Nairobi—Bank commitments (chapter 9). The proportion of lending that favored small farmers went up from 24 percent over 1965–67 to 37 percent over 1971–73.[148]

McNamara's endorsement for this trend was announced in his first Annual General Meeting speech, in which he promised that "the sector of greatest expansion in our five-year program is agriculture," a commitment that he frequently repeated over his first years.[149] Why, then, did five years go by before agricultural lending was recognized and announced, at Nairobi, as the obvious centerpiece of a poverty-alleviation strategy?

One reason is that not all agricultural loans were considered "poverty lending." This distinction had been understood by Woods who, with new, African borrowers in mind, had discussed the need and potential for smallholder support at the time of his decision to push agriculture. But the distinction was downplayed during the 1960s, when most agricultural lending consisted of irrigation and livestock projects that directly benefited a social cross section of farmers and laborers in a given rural

147. Memorandum, Robert S. McNamara for the record, March 6, 1969.

148. World Bank, Operations Evaluation Department, "Rural Development: World Bank Experience, 1965–86," table 1, p. 11.

149. Robert S. McNamara, "Address to the Board of Governors at the Annual General Meeting, September 30, 1968," in McNamara, *The McNamara Years at the World Bank,* p. 11.

area, or of loans to well-off and even rich ranchers and farmers. The "poverty" component of agricultural lending would be smaller if measured in the stricter sense defined by McNamara, counting only those projects in which a majority of the benefits accrued directly to "absolutely poor" persons.

The distinction did not appear in McNamara's 1968 statement. Beginning that year, however, it began to be brought out of the shadows by his own poverty rhetoric, which increasingly spoke of the "absolute poor" rather than of rural population in general. The relationship of agricultural development to poverty alleviation was further confused by the criticism that the Green Revolution's new technologies had tended to favor better-off farmers, increasing rural inequity, and even reducing employment and wages for the landless. A 1970 paper prepared by the Bank's Economic Department for the Board repeated this accusation:

> It is already apparent that these [new technologies] have widened income disparities firstly because the geographical and other physical requirements for change are unevenly distributed and secondly because the institutional framework of credit supply, etc., frequently favors particular groups. The employment implications of investment in agriculture are coming to be recognized as crucial to the determination of the distribution of benefits.[150]

These concerns, which McNamara echoed during 1970 and 1971, did not reduce confidence in the primary output-raising and food-producing potential of the Green Revolution, but they questioned the simple correlation between agricultural growth and poverty reduction.

The hesitation on agriculture was also supported by doubts concerning the practical feasibility of large-scale, productive smallholder lending. McNamara's visit to East Africa in 1970, where experiments with integrated smallholder development schemes had some success, and where he was impressed by the personality and leadership of Julius Nyerere, became a stimulus.[151] On returning, McNamara wrote: "It was clearly essential to assist small-holder schemes in the region," and "some form of package approach to rural development might be possible." He noted, however, that "Ojaama [sic] villages in Tanzania were so far without much substance."[152] The widely documented growth of output on small

150. World Bank, "The Disposition of the Increment to Agricultural Income," SecM70-38, January 30, 1970, p. 2.

151. Clark waxed enthusiastic after hearing Nyerere's exposition on how he planned to make the smallholder more productive, calling it the "breakthrough of the century." Clark, "Notes on Part IV," p. 27. But Brakel's report on Tanzania stated that "raising agricultural production and income of smallholders through the Ujamma concept is still lacking appropriate quantification and a practical operational approach." Memorandum, W. Brakel to files, "Salient Points Raised during Mr. McNamara's Visit to East Africa—January 7–10, 1970," January 28, 1970, pp. 3–4.

152. Memorandum, Robert S. McNamara for the record, March 5, 1972. The usual spelling is "Ujaama."

farms in Asia using new technologies was an obvious and probably much greater source of encouragement.

But doubts lingered. McNamara was dissatisfied by staff efforts to develop a concrete lending strategy for small farmers. After reading a draft of the 1972 Sector Paper on Agriculture, he asked that it "deal more fully and explicitly with the problems of the small farmer [whose] needs are so large and problems so complex that neither the Bank nor anyone else at present knows of economic solutions."[153]

Other factors intervened. As already mentioned, several possible solutions to poverty—population control, employment, nutrition, health, urbanization, and water supply—created temporary enthusiasm and were the subject of considerable attention and study over the period 1968–73. Decisionmaking was interrupted and delayed by the 1972 administrative reorganization of the Bank. In the end, the decision to home in on small farmers was to some extent a process of elimination in the search for a bankable solution.

The confidence that finally led McNamara to commit himself to substantial lending to small farmers thus developed slowly and had only become firm by the middle of 1973. The move to a commitment was accelerated by administrative and staffing changes made in mid-1972, in particular the creation of a "rural development" unit separate from the Agriculture Department, despite strong objections from the agricultural projects staff and the resistance of vice presidents.[154] At a fall 1972 meeting to discuss a report advocating Bank support for rural development and poverty alleviation, the vice presidents "weren't terribly keen on it. They didn't see any reason why there should be special emphasis. They felt it was too difficult. They felt this wasn't in their purview."[155] A key staffing change placed Montague Yudelman in charge of the central Agriculture Department. He was brought in "because they said the president wanted to do something about rural development."

After Yudelman's appointment, a year went by before the decision to concentrate on smallholder lending became a firm commitment. It was characteristic of McNamara's use of public announcements that the final stage of a major policy decision came to be closely related to the drafting of the 1973 Annual General Meeting address. McNamara felt pressed to make a concrete proposal regarding poverty, but an early (February 1973) draft of the speech did not yet focus on rural poverty. The reappearance of food shortages in Asia, discussed at President's Council meetings in November 1972, probably helped to tip the balance. It was reported that rice shortages were "global," affecting Indonesia, Bangladesh, Vietnam, India, and China.[156]

153. Memorandum, Robert S. McNamara for the record, "Agriculture Sector Program Paper Meeting, April 5, 1972," April 10, 1972.

154. Memorandum, Robert S. McNamara for the record, October 20, 1972, and March 9, 1973.

155. Montague Yudelman, interview with the authors, September 12, 1991.

156. World Bank, Minutes of President's Council Meetings, November 6, 1972 and December 11, 1972. Jean Dreze and Amartya Sen, *Hunger and Public Action* (Oxford: Clarendon Press, 1989), pp. 126–33. A drought in western India lasted from 1970 through 1973.

McNamara's decision was firm by June 1973, when he called a meeting to discuss the draft. Staff continued to express doubts. Baum was concerned about the novelty of "the whole approach to the rural poor," Chenery saw the need for a more balanced approach that included health and education, and Yudelman and Pedro Pablo Kuczynski worried about the feasibility of the ambitious output goals that were being set for small farmers. Ul Haq explained the underlying concept as one of "redistribution of growth" rather than of existing income or wealth, a definition borrowed from Hans Singer's recent ILO report on Kenya and one that would become the signature concept for the Bank's approach to poverty alleviation. Stern, however, highlighted the rhetorical function of the announcement and strongly endorsed the speech, saying that "the rededication of the Bank is important and he felt a need . . . to show that a drastic change can be made in people's lifetime."[157]

After Nairobi, 1974–81

Though Nairobi defined what would be the principal instrument, the Bank continued to look for ways to broaden and improve the poverty strategy: it sought an urban analogue to the small farmer, it debated a more radical "basic needs" approach, and it continuously tinkered with its previously defined policies.

URBAN POVERTY. Directly after Nairobi, the Bank set out to identify ways to reach the urban poor. It searched for an urban equivalent to the small farmer, that is, a targetable population that could be the recipient or direct beneficiary of productive investments, not simply of welfare transfers. By this time there were few voices in authority willing to question the wisdom of opening yet a new front in the poverty war. One protest was registered by Peter Cargill, vice president for finance: "I am surprised . . . that [urban poverty] should be regarded as an important topic for Mr. McNamara's speech this year. None of the social problems, including this one, with which we have been busy these past few years, can really be resolved except in the context of economies which have a reasonable rate of growth."[158] The process involved the preparation of policy and research papers and was carried forward under the shared and often conflictive direction of the economics staff, with Chenery and ul Haq at the helm, and the Urban Projects Department headed by Kim Jaycox. An Urban Poverty policy paper was completed in 1975, and sector papers were prepared on sites and services (April 1974), housing (May 1975), urban transport (May 1975), and urban poverty (1976). Urban poverty became the main thrust of McNamara's 1975 address to the Annual Meeting.

A task force was then created to ensure implementation of the urban poverty objective, but the group found itself frustrated in the search for an operational approach. The first problem was that of defining a target group. A March 1976

157. Memorandum, Robert S. McNamara for the record, "Meeting to Discuss 1973 Governors' Speech, June 22, 1973," June 25, 1973.

158. Memorandum, P. P. M. Cargill to Hollis Chenery, "Note on Urban Poverty," May 14, 1975 (copies to Burke Knapp and Robert McNamara).

report by the task force stated, "It is clear that on the urban side we will have no equivalent of the small farmer. . . . We need something similar to farm size. . . . It is therefore proposed that . . . the urban poor be defined in terms of an easily observable proxy. Lack of access to a safe water supply is an obvious choice."[159] But the report went on to suggest a heterogeneous variety of lending activities that were not easily related to that operational definition of the poverty target, and that was made up of two distinct elements: employment creation, and the provision of urban services. Knapp commended the report's caution and moderation, saying that it "properly emphasizes the uncertainties and difficulties that we face in this area."[160]

Attention began to shift away from direct targeting of Bank investments on the poor to the enhancement of indirect benefits through increased urban employment. In effect, the strategy was falling back on the trickle-down approach. Employment was to be created through "improved industrial sector work," "design improvement for direct capital-intensive industrial lending," "increased activity in labor-absorptive branches of industry," and more convincingly, "increased support to small enterprises" and "innovative support of informal sector enterprise."

The second leg of the urban poverty strategy proposed by the task force dealt with urban services, an area in which, in principle, the concept of targeting the poor was more applicable, but in which the Bank's productivity standards were more distant. The proposal stressed sites and services and slum-upgrading projects, and water supply and sewerage, but also more general assistance to improve "overall urban efficiency" through institution building, better urban finance, and effective land management.

In July 1977 Jaycox admitted that "progress on implementing the program is somewhat disappointing,"[161] and in October McNamara allowed that, with respect to poverty, "as far as rural areas . . . the Bank . . . knew how to do it. . . . For urban areas, however, this indeed remained an unresolved issue."[162] Such conundrums bedeviled the urban poverty program through the decade, though they were partly offset by an unusual degree of enthusiasm and group commitment within the urban projects staff. One effect of this mix of high energy and an inherently difficult task, however, was that the urban "crash program" was in a constant state of experimentation and reformulation.

159. World Bank, "Urban Poverty Action Program: Interim Report of Urban Poverty Task Force," SecM76-208, March 24, 1976, p. 6.

160. Memorandum, J. Burke Knapp to Robert S. McNamara, "Draft Board Paper on Urban Poverty Program," March 22, 1976.

161. Memorandum, Edward V. K. Jaycox to Robert S. McNamara, "Urban Poverty Program," July 21, 1977.

162. Memorandum, Robert S. McNamara for the record, "Meeting of the Research Advisory Panel on Income Distribution and Employment (RAPIDE)," October 10, 1977.

REFINING THE SECTORAL APPROACHES. Along with the urban effort, the Bank continued to experiment with and modify other sectoral lending policies and methods of implementation in ways that might improve their contribution to poverty reduction. Thus immediately after Nairobi, Bank staff focused attention on the operational definitions that would be used to enforce the poverty intent of agricultural lending, and also on the development of the concept of area and integrated smallholder projects. They stressed the implementation of what would be a "rural development" as distinct from an "agricultural" investment policy. Lending policies in other sectors were similarly continuously reviewed and changed, as was the case with population, nutrition, education, water supply, and roads. This process of constant review led to a late but critical reconsideration: the establishment of a Health Department in 1979 and the decision to fund stand-alone health projects in addition to health components in other projects.

BASIC NEEDS. A more fundamental rethinking on policy began in 1976 with the emergence of the proposal concerning "basic needs." The concept was put forward as a significant escalation, even radical redefinition, of the poverty strategy and it excited debate over several years. In essence, it proposed giving greater weight to need, as distinct from output, as a criterion for deciding resource allocation: fundamental human needs, certainly nutrition and basic health, but potentially extending to less "basic" needs such as clothing and shelter, and even to nonmaterial "needs" such as human rights and cultural values, were included by proponents.[163] If "redistribution with growth" consisted in giving each person a fishing rod—a more productive plot to a small farmer, or a business credit to an urban workshop—"basic needs" would be "an approach that enables the poor to earn *or obtain* their 'basic needs.'"[164] That is, with or without a fishing rod, food would be guaranteed.

When basic needs showed up on the Bank's agenda, the proximate cause seemed to be, again, an ILO initiative.[165] Seeking to revive and push forward the

163. "BN [basic needs] encompasses 'non-material' needs. . . . They include the need for self-determination, self-reliance, political freedom and security, participation in making the decisions that affect workers and citizens, national and cultural identity, and a sense of purpose in life and work." Paul Streeten, "The Distinctive Features of a Basic Needs Approach to Development," Basic Needs Paper 2, World Bank Policy Planning and Program Review Department, August 10, 1977, p. 2. Streeten worked with Mahbub Ul Haq in the PPR Department and was principal author of Paul Streeten and others, *First Things First: Meeting Basic Human Needs in Developing Countries* (Oxford University Press, 1981). The book, in effect the Bank's "final word" on the debate, made no reference to nonmaterial "needs." Launching the basic needs movement, the ILO also spoke of "a healthy, humane and satisfying environment, and popular participation in the making of decisions that affect the lives and livelihoods of the people and individual freedoms." ILO, *Employment, Growth and Basic Needs: A One-World Problem* (Geneva: ILO, 1976), p. 7.

164. Streeten and others, *First Things First,* p. vii (emphasis added).

165. The Bank was similarly prodded into following up on "the employment problem" by the ILO.

distributive concerns of the early 1970s, the ILO in June 1976 organized a new conference, "Employment, Growth and Basic Needs," with the central proposition that the war on poverty be recast as a "basic-needs strategy."[166] The concept was echoed in McNamara's address to the Annual General Meeting of the Board of Governors a few months later. He spoke of "a serious reexamination of earlier growth strategies . . . causing governments to focus more directly on . . . the hundreds of millions of individuals whose basic human needs go unmet."[167] At that point, the statement was ahead of events, but almost immediately McNamara met with Chenery, Clark, and Stern to follow up. He told them that "we should think of a dramatic change in the intellectual leadership role of the Bank over the next five years" and suggested that "meeting basic human needs or eliminating absolute poverty by the end of the century" could be proposed as an approach to the Third Development Decade.[168] Stern cautioned, "We had not done much work related to this and we did not even know whether it was possible or even desirable."[169]

Over the next four to five years the Bank sought answers to those questions: was basic needs "desirable or even possible"? Country and sectoral studies were carried out; the global cost of meeting basic needs was estimated; and, gradually, proponents and opponents moved toward a compromise. Debate was favored by the ambiguity of the proposal and by its ideological overtones. Greater government intervention in both production and distribution seemed to be a necessary corollary of the approach; some proponents spoke of "supply management" and "selective

166. ILO, *Employment, Growth and Basic Needs*. McNamara was also stimulated by the 1976 Tinbergen Report to the Club of Rome, "Reshaping the International Order." Chenery disapproved of the report, saying it "could only be carried through in a strongly socialist economy." McNamara "said that it was dangerous that documents like the Tinbergen report were floating around the world . . . based on very shallow analysis." Minutes of President's Council Meeting, November 22, 1976, p. 2. The ethical proposition that societies should guarantee their members minimum physical rations of the necessaries of life had been advanced by international organizations, including the ILO, before World War II. It was encouraged and legitimized by scientific discoveries in the fields of physiology and nutrition and scientific optimism regarding food production. Eugene Staley wrote that work on defining "norms for healthful and humane living . . . has progressed farthest in the field of nutrition. . . . Efforts are now being made to extend similar methods into such fields as housing, medical care, clothing, and opportunities for education." Staley, *World Economy in Transition* (New York: Council on Foreign Relations, 1939), pp. 61–62. Reported in Douglas Rimmer, "'Basic Needs' and the Origins of the Development Ethos," *Journal of Developing Areas*, vol. 15 (January 1981), p. 228.

167. Robert S. McNamara, "To the Board of Governors, 1976, Manila, Philippines, October 4, 1976," in McNamara, *The McNamara Years at the World Bank*, p. 337.

168. Memorandum, Robert S. McNamara for the record, "Meeting to Discuss Future Work on Development," attended by McNamara, Chenery, Clark, and Stern, October 22, 1976, p. 1.

169. Ibid.

interventions in the production and distribution processes."[170] Ambiguity was inherent in the subjective nature of the term "needs." Despite casual references to nutritional standards, "needs," even for food, were open to a wide range of definitions, and therefore costs. McNamara added to the ambiguity: when staff debated the issue of growth versus needs, he continually insisted that he wanted both, cutting off any discussion of acceptable trade-offs.[171]

He thus encouraged all sides, but this apparently open position would stymie the basic needs proposal over the decade. As conceived and implied in its name, "basic needs" was an ethical proposition. By the late 1970s, moral obligation had become the established assumption behind the Bank's poverty-alleviation objective. In Bank practice, it was understood that productivity calculations for rural development, water supply, feeder road, and urban shelter projects could contain a degree of tolerance and optimism that, in effect, masked an ethical intent. But naked moral claim was not an admissible criterion for specific lending decisions. Proponents of basic needs were therefore required to justify their proposals in terms of cost and economic return and to assume the burden of proving that economic growth would not be impaired. This proved difficult during a time when majority opinion was at best agnostic on the productivity of spending on education and health and even more skeptical of an economic rationale for large-scale nutrition and shelter programs. Meanwhile, opponents—a majority among the staff— were allowed to describe the proposal as "a mistake," "haircurling," a "superfluous new idea," a "slogan," and "dirigisme."[172] Objectors, including Chenery and Stern, repeatedly insisted that there *was* a trade-off with growth. McNamara responded by asking for further research on the subject, postponing his endorsement of a large-scale basic needs lending program. By 1981 that option had been closed out by mounting economic instability, political conservatism, and McNamara's departure.

170. T. N. Srinivasan, "Development, Poverty, and Basic Human Needs: Some Issues," *Food Research Institute Studies,* vol. 16, no. 2 (1977), pp. 18–19. At a meeting of the President's Council to debate Srinivasan's paper, Chadenet referred to the "strong emotions behind the basic needs approach," which, some believed, "implied [a] change of political systems." McNamara stated: "It was true that some people considered basic needs a code word for a package of economic and political changes," but "this was way beyond the role of the Bank and would not be very fruitful to discuss." Minutes of President's Council Meeting, June 13, 1977, p. 1. Also Streeten, in "Distinctive Features of a Basic Needs Approach to Development," argued that income inequality led to the "import or domestic production of over-sophisticated products" which "frustrated the pursuit of a Basic Needs approach." Instead, it was necessary to ensure a supply of "appropriate products" (p. 3).

171. Memorandum for the record, "Meeting on March 16, 1977, to Discuss Issues Paper by Streeten."

172. Memorandum, Adalbert Krieger to Robert S. McNamara, "The Basic Needs Approach," September 16, 1977. Krieger was an Argentinean and vice president for Latin America. His most damning epithet was that basic needs was "populist." The substance of his objection was the alleged trade-off between "consumption" gains and investment.

Though the effort was frustrated at the time, basic needs research and advocacy of the 1970s prepared the ground for later policy change. In particular, two of the items in the basic needs agenda—basic education and primary health—would become the new and principal vehicles for direct poverty alleviation during the 1990s. The process that brought this about is discussed in chapter 7. Under McNamara the Bank had gone a long way in raising the weight attached to need at the expense of output as an allocative criterion for lending. But the limit, the high-water mark for that advance, fell short of the basic needs proposal.

SIX

Waging War on Poverty

WHEN THE Bank set out during the 1970s to make economic growth work more favorably for the poor, it used two, almost inseparable instruments: projects and influence. As this "war on poverty" progressed, however, project statistics—their volume, type, and beneficiaries—became the public measure of poverty alleviation. By contrast, success or failure in efforts to influence borrower policies were rarely reported. In a sense, there were two parallel campaigns, one consisting of highly publicized, visible lending for "new-style" poverty projects, the other of discreet reform mongering in which the Bank used the weight of its financial, intellectual, and moral influence to nudge borrowers toward more egalitarian and benevolent policies. There is little doubt that in the Bank's understanding it was the policy war that promised the most significant gains toward distributive objectives. McNamara shared that judgment, despite the impression given by his quantitative, project rhetoric. Why then was the spotlight invariably positioned on lending?

The most evident explanation is that investment is the Bank's chartered business, an official purpose that the institution took care to respect. Admittedly, at an early date it entered into and pursued a deepening affair with "development," adding increasing layers of nonfinancial activity—project assistance, development advice, and research—and, more and more, defining itself as a development agency. But if it stretched the founders' intent, it remained faithful to form; most of that "developmental" activity was packaged into and around loans. What the Bank called "operations" existed only when lending was involved.

Loans, in any case, were the principal medium for developmental influence, whether through the lessons and institutional innovations that came with projects or the financial muscle they gave to right-minded factions in the borrowing country, or the creation of direct negotiating leverage on policy decisions. The contribution of projects to influence went beyond project-level tutoring and the purchase of a hearing in decisionmaking councils; lasting policy change needs to be embedded in widespread convictions, practices, and institutions. Projects are a means to that embodiment.[1]

Moreover, visibility is often at odds with influence: McNamara used speeches and a formidable (and expensive) economic research effort as public routes to build authority; but—until structural adjustment lending—it was the institutional wisdom that the effectiveness of more direct efforts at persuasion was enhanced by being kept in the shadows. For these various reasons, the importance of lending was increased and not diminished by a preoccupation with influence.

At the same time, lending does not always advance the cause of policy. Loans are motivated by a miscellany of considerations. The hope for influence is usually present but often is not the determining justification for a loan. Not infrequently, the Bank has put policy influence and other long-run development objectives aside to see a country through balance of payments or fiscal difficulties, or even to support a regime. Also, much lending takes on the character of a habitual transaction, with few immediate expectations beyond a capital transfer and desire to sustain a long relationship. When influence is not the primary objective, the effect of financial support may be to undermine rather than promote the policies recommended by the Bank. Lending was thus both a tool and an obstacle to McNamara's efforts to influence borrower policies with regard to poverty alleviation.

Though lending and policy influence were thus closely interconnected, each took on a distinct operational character. Most notably, whereas poverty lending engaged a large part of the staff, the policy dialogue was carried out at a senior level, sometimes by McNamara himself. That dialogue is the main concern of this chapter. Because encounters over policy were highly country specific, and because so little was reported at the time on the events of that "quiet war," the discussion centers on several country cases and then briefly considers what could be called the war on the ground: poverty lending, or the more visible effort to redesign and redirect investment to favor the poor with a larger share and faster delivery of its benefits. Poverty lending, which relied principally on rural development projects, is also discussed in chapters 7 and 8.

---

1. Explaining the Bank's reluctance to engage in poverty policy-based lending, Alexander Shakow said: "Poverty reduction [was] not so much a matter of a simple policy change. . . . [It] requires an investment in the training of lots of people, in building institutions. . . . [The] fear was that . . . policy loans [be used] to enact change in something that is not susceptible to simply *a* decision or *a* rule of government but instead requires many years of investment in decisionmaking." Alexander Shakow, interview with authors, July 2, 1992, pp. 9–10.

Influencing Policies

McNamara's early broadside on opinion—through speeches, private sermons, research, and publications—was consistent with, and in large part a consequence of, his view that the Bank's larger objective was to influence borrower policies and institutions, a conviction that also, undoubtedly, played to his missionary bent. Though the message was novel and the advocacy more forceful, McNamara's focus on policy influence was in harmony with two decades of Bank thinking and practice.

Over the 1970s, as the Bank repeatedly engaged in private discussions and "negotiations" with individual borrowers, the wider impact of national policies on the less well-off shared the agenda with specific "poverty projects." According to Mahbub ul Haq:

> [McNamara] always felt that the Bank's money was going to be a small part of the total development of these countries. He felt that the signals that we set on this issue and the policy framework that we brought in were far more important than trying to do all of it ourselves. After all, the Bank's total lending to developing countries financed roughly less than 1 percent of the development expenditures of these countries. He was very uncomfortable with this figure, but I kept mentioning it to him all the time. I tried several times, unsuccessfully, to put it in one of his speeches and to show that the Bank was not the world, but he felt very uncomfortable and would take it out each time.
>
> However, he understood that 1 percent cannot change the profile of poverty in these countries, except by setting the right signals. That's why he put so much emphasis on economic sector work, on his policy speeches, on country dialogue, and on signals.[2]

William Clark, in a private note, made the same observation: "Bob feels that advice Bank gives is more important than money. Hence DPS [Development Policy Staff] and DDR."[3] McNamara put this message into his own words during an October 1968 visit to Canada, where he told senior government officials: "Many developing countries badly needed changes in social and economic policies. Canada . . . was in a unique position to advise and persuade them. . . . Canada's willingness to provide advice in these fields was probably more important than its financial contribution. . . . If Canada . . . would endorse the Bank's advice . . . this might often tip the scales. . . . [A]ll [McNamara] had in mind was to use economic aid as a lever for economic policy changes."[4]

The quantitative triviality of Bank lending was pointed out in a paper, on the employment problem, presented to the Board in May 1972:

> Bank lending . . . covers, on average, less than 2 percent of the total capital expenditures of the member countries. . . . Its significance lies rather in the possible impact of the Bank as a source of ideas and technical assistance. . . .

2. Mahbub ul Haq, interview, World Bank Oral History Program, December 3, 1982, p. 14.

3. William Clark, unpublished notes, undated, "Notes on Part IV: The McNamara Years," p. 21 (obverse).

4. Memorandum, Robert S. McNamara for the record, September 9, 1968.

The possible demonstration effect of projects implies the need for rather careful formulation of a system for incorporating employment and poverty redressal aspects within a coherent framework of analysis relating the various objectives of project lending. . . . [T]here is little virtue in trying to spell out the amount of employment created in any particular project. . . . [T]he evolving project methodology of the Bank seeks to contribute to employment policy by influencing governments, through work on actual projects, to move towards general policies favorable to employment and income creation.[5]

The same month McNamara said, with regard to the Bank's role on employment: "The basic contribution of the Bank would be in its advice to governments, its review of employment policies and its work with specific institutions rather than through its projects."[6]

Four years later, discussing the Bank's economic work program with senior staff,

Mr. McNamara disagreed with the view that the Bank obtained its major impact through its project and technical assistance work. Although this work, of course, was essential, it did not influence the population at large in our borrowing countries, nor did it influence donor policies. The development community was influenced by soundly based ideas and it was an essential part of the work of [the Development Policy Staff] to find such ideas and turn them into strategies for development.[7]

McNamara returned to this point in his last Annual Meeting speech, in 1980: "In the longer run . . . it is the non-financial assistance of the Bank that is of even greater value than its financial support."[8]

The centrality of policy was certainly deeply believed by the Bank's two chief operational managers through the decade: Burke Knapp, who as chairman of the key Loan Committee from 1956 to 1978 had made the search for policy influence a central and constant criterion for loan decisions, and Ernest Stern, his successor as vice president for operations from 1978, who fully shared, and, in the circumstances of the 1980s, was able to take Knapp's preoccupation with policy influence several degrees further. There was a growing presence of economists in the Bank, from Hollis Chenery through his research staff to the regional economists who had been bureaucratically elevated by the 1972 reorganization, and whether from professional bias or because they were less caught up in the captivating bustle of lending, they weighed in on the policy side of the scales. But if there

5. World Bank, "The Employment Problem and Bank Operations," R72-94, May 2, 1972, pp. 26–27.

6. Memorandum, Ernest Stern to files, May 2, 1972. Record of McNamara meeting with Mr. Jenks, director-general of ILO.

7. Memorandum, Robert S. McNamara for the record, "Second Meeting to Discuss Future Work on Development," December 1, 1976. The attendees were McNamara, Chenery, Stern, and Clark.

8. Robert S. McNamara, "To the Board of Governors, Washington, D.C., September 30, 1980," in McNamara, The McNamara Years at the World Bank (Johns Hopkins University Press, 1981), p. 653.

was a meeting of minds on the priority of policy, there were different expectations regarding the scope for influence.

Years of exhortation and arm-twisting with borrowers had made Bank managers sensitive to the constraints on policy influence in general, and on social policy in particular. Attending to what Knapp called "the social dimension" had been, and continued to be, bounded by the need to accommodate borrower priorities and politics in the context of the Bank's long-run lending relationships. Some countries, for instance, were unwilling to incur hard currency debt for social expenditures; others balked at large-scale investments in the "uneconomic" backward areas that were home to poor small farmers. And, during the troubled decade of the 1970s, many countries were caught up in balance of payments and political emergencies that pushed aside not only the poverty goal but also the Bank's more traditional developmental concerns.[9]

Quarreling with the Operations Evaluation Unit over its contention that the Bank had not done enough for the poor in Colombia, Enrique Lerdau responded with a fine description of the inherent limits of the lending relationship:

> [The Bank] must behave in a way that reconciles its perceptions of equity and efficiency with those of the governments of LDC's; even though the latter may reflect group interests which in many ways are not identical to national interests as defined by us. It must find a continuous accommodation between its sense of mission on one side and national sovereignty on the other, however spurious we may consider the invocation of the latter in particular instances. The key words are reconciliation, accommodation, adjustment. The fact that the Bank has been able to function at all was, I think, only made possible by giving these words pretty heavy weight.[10]

Nonetheless, McNamara pressed ahead to influence distributive policies, using the opportunity provided by periodic, often annual reviews of Country Program Papers, and drawing for this purpose considerably on the analyses and opinions of Chenery and his rapidly growing staff, particularly the unit headed by ul Haq. By 1978 the growing attention to domestic policy concerns of borrower countries prompted a President's Council statement of consensus that, owing to "the Bank's increasing involvement in issues of economic management in countries infringing on the political and social field, a far broader dialogue between the Bank and LDC policy makers was required."[11]

9. For example, the 1973 and 1979 oil shocks, Vietnam War, coup in Chile, Idi Amin in Uganda, revolution in Iran, Watergate, East Pakistan secession war, Yom Kippur War, Khmer Rouge in Cambodia, civil war in Lebanon, coup in Argentina, and wars and coups in Pakistan, Nicaragua, Angola, Zaire, Ethiopia, and in many other countries in Africa.

10. Enrique Lerdau to Christopher Willoughby, January 31, 1971, commenting on the Report on Colombia by the Operations Evaluation Unit. Lerdau's commentary evokes the title of Eugene Black's lectures on development and the role of the Bank: Eugene R. Black, *The Diplomacy of Economic Development* (Harvard University Press, 1960).

11. Memorandum, William Clark and Attila Karaosmanoglu to Robert S. McNamara, "Third World Program—Anarttina," March 29, 1978.

What did these expressions of concern for borrower policies lead to? Did the Bank open the eyes, soften the hearts, or twist the arms of borrowers with regard to their own poor? The following, arbitrarily chosen case studies, of Brazil, Guatemala, Malaysia, Kenya, India, Bangladesh, Chile, the Philippines, and Tanzania provide a sense of the complex, varied, and in the end, largely frustrating experience represented by the effort to intervene in borrower distributive policies.

Brazil

The most visible and sustained attempt to influence a borrower's policies as they bore on poverty and inequality was made in Brazil, where inequality was extreme, blatant, dramatized by recurrent droughts in the poor northeast, and aired by a developed and only partly repressed intellectual community and press and an outspoken, socially active Catholic Church.[12] The sense of scandal was heightened by Brazil's economic success and middle-income status; inequality was easier to tolerate in the poverty-ridden countries of Asia and Africa.[13] For those who had concluded that orthodox economic growth was not working, Brazil provided the readiest "evidence."[14]

The Bank and government at first seemed to be of one mind on the priority of social needs, particularly in the poorer Northeast. Visiting McNamara in May 1968, the Brazilian minister of the interior stressed that "the Northeast is a critical area for development," that more emphasis would in future be placed on food crops, and that it was "important to establish a better balance between agriculture and industry by accelerating agriculture."[15] It was not an implausible attitude for a right-leaning military government that had intervened to stifle a rising popular movement. Elsewhere, authoritarian governments were responding with a similar focus on rural poverty.

A year after the distributive issue in Brazil was brought to the fore, the Country Program Paper seemed to commend the regime and to downplay distributive worries. It spoke of Brazil's "spirit of national affirmation," "national pride shared by all parts of the political spectrum," "outstanding progress," and of the

12. Repression was greatest during the first decade of military rule, between 1964 and 1974, and began to ease under the "abertura" policy of President Figuereido.

13. Attending a lecture by Stephen Marglin—recently returned from India—in the late 1960s, Arthur Lewis brushed off Marglin's energetic call for massive redistribution in India "from the top 10 percent to the rest." "In India," said Lewis, "the top 10 percent is everybody." Shane Hunt, personal communication, September 1, 1995.

14. A later Bank study concluded that income and welfare rose rapidly for the poorest in Brazil during the high-growth 1960s and 1970s. Guy Pfefferman and Richard Webb, "Poverty and Income Distribution in Brazil," *Review of Income and Wealth*, vol. 29, no. 2 (June 1983), pp. 101–24.

15. Memorandum, Gerald Alter to files, "Meeting of Mr. McNamara with Minister of Interior of Brazil, General Alfonso de Albuquerque Lima," May 23, 1968.

government's "vigorous effort to develop the less developed parts of the country." And whereas "social unrest was initially handled by repression, . . . positive programs are now having an increasing effect." "Brazil's social and political problems," the paper continued, "can only be resolved gradually and in a climate of sustained economic growth." A final consolation was that the U.S. Agency for International Development and the International Development Bank were taking up the burden of social lending.[16] There was substance to the arguments: 10 percent of the Northeast region's GDP was received as a transfer from the central government.[17]

The Bank's supportive stance continued during 1970 and 1971, but patience with slow social progress appeared to fray, perhaps because McNamara, now accompanied by Chenery and ul Haq and stimulated by the International Labor Organization and others, was becoming bolder in his poverty-alleviation ambitions. The 1970 CPP praised Brazil's "large-scale attack upon these basic socio-economic problems" and defended the smallness of its allocation for poverty loans, saying: "We are trying to avoid spreading the Bank thin."[18] McNamara agreed. He "expressed his satisfaction with the more recent pace of development in the Northeast of Brazil and congratulated the Brazilians on their approach to the problem." But he "then raised [questions] concerning certain weak points in the picture, particularly with respect to the extent of illiteracy, nutritional problems and distribution of income."[19] And he was "disturbed by the fact that Brazil was not doing very much for better income distribution or for employment." For the moment, however, these questions were left hanging.

The subsequent annual review of lending to Brazil was again accommodating: the 1971 CPP spoke of the government's "strong effort to alleviate regional income disparities" and of its "appropriate responses, worthy of our support." Indeed, the report saw a "significant improvement in equity" dating from a 1967–68 measure in favor of industrial workers.[20] A more convincing argument for not interfering was that Brazil's best bet was to "take the advantage of the present momentum . . . by pressing for the highest feasible growth"—GDP had risen 9.5 percent in 1970—which "would substantially alleviate unemployment."[21]

16. "We do not propose any Bank lending for . . . education and water supply. . . . There has emerged a clear division of labor between the AID and the Bank . . . in Brazil. . . . The IDB is also interested in . . . education, water supply and sewerage and agriculture." IBRD/IDA Economic Committee, "Brazil: Country Program Paper," draft, EC/O/69-125/1, November 25, 1969, pp. 1–3, 26.

17. Estimated as 2 percent of Brazil's GDP. Ibid., p. 6. The funds were mostly for industrialization-promoting subsidies and infrastructure.

18. World Bank, "Country Program Paper—Brazil," November 27, 1970, pp. 3, 20.

19. Memorandum, Gerald Alter for the record, "Meeting of Mr. McNamara with the Minister of Interior of Brazil, Jose Costa Cavalcanti," February 17, 1970.

20. World Bank, "Country Program Paper—Brazil, November 23, 1971, pp. 4, 18.

21. IBRD/IDA Economic Committee, "Brazil: Note of Meeting on October 7, 1971," EC/M/71-44, October 19, 1971, pp. 1, 2.

But the Bank also felt that it lacked the capacity to press Brazil into more aggressive poverty alleviation. In 1970 McNamara had argued that "the government was not prepared to do anything about income distribution in the short run, and as such, it was unrealistic to make it a condition for lending. . . . Brazil had rejected our proposal to constitute a Consultative Group just in order to avoid pressure in their policy performance."[22]

Several officials suggested that lending to Brazil should be cut. Knapp pointed to the Bank's large exposure and political risk in Brazil: "We should be quick and ruthless to cut back if the situation deteriorates. . . . Events in Argentina showed how quickly a promising outlook could change for the worse."[23] Bernard Chadenet, deputy director of the Projects Department, said that the Bank's image would suffer from its support for a repressive government. McNamara agreed that there was "a tremendous amount of repression," and that "one could not close one's eyes," but he argued that repression

> was not necessarily a great deal different from what it had been under previous Brazilian Governments, and it did not seem to be a lot worse than in some other member countries of the Bank. Was Brazil worse than Thailand? Probably not, but events in Brazil are much more publicized! We should go ahead with the program. . . . He did not agree with the proposition that we should turn off the program if the situation deteriorates. . . . Once we had made the decision to go in on a large scale, we could not salvage our investments by discontinuing our lending. "[The Brazilians] are so big. They are going to tell us to go to hell."[24]

The last was prompted by Brazil's rejection of Bank overtures to create a consultative group and to establish a resident mission in Rio, proposals that Brazil rightly perceived as steps to achieve influence. McNamara argued for staying the course: "No viable alternative to Government by the generals seemed open. The Bank had to face the facts of political repression in many of its member countries. The response was not to lend less, but rather to support efforts within the country toward economic growth and social equity."[25]

The following year McNamara was provoked into a more aggressive position. In January 1972 he was impressed by Albert Fishlow's statistical findings showing severe and increasing inequality in Brazil. That month he was drafting a speech for the United Nations Conference on Trade and Development and ordered that "specific examples should be mentioned, such as Brazil, where neither the urban nor the agricultural poor have benefitted from the economic growth over the last

22. Memorandum, Mahbub ul Haq to John H. Adler, "Meeting of the Review Group on Brazil," December 4, 1970, p. 2.

23. World Bank, "Notes on Brazil Country Program Review, December 2, 1971," December 9, 1971. Argentinean President Onganía had been ousted by a coup in June.

24. Ibid.

25. World Bank, "Country Program Paper—Brazil," December 13, 1971, p. 41.

decade, as was evident from Professor Fishlow's findings."[26] The study became a subject of debate between the Bank and Brazil's minister of finance, Delfim Netto. Delfim Netto had commissioned his own study of Brazil's income distribution, and rebutted that "people in the lowest decile of income earners had had a real growth in income of 24 percent between 1960 and 1970."[27] Delfim Netto was argumentative rather than diplomatic in the face of what he saw as an obsession. Reacting to a draft Bank report he "opined with some asperity that 85 percent of the economic report was devoted to income distribution."[28]

The second event occurred in December, when a proposed livestock project for Brazil was criticized in the Board on the grounds that its primary beneficiaries would be a small number (seven hundred) of large and well-to-do ranchers. The tables were turned on McNamara: he was being held to task for presenting a project "inconsistent" with his own statements regarding "the need to ensure that the benefits of development were diffused among the poorer sections of the population," having "specifically mentioned Brazil in this connection." The loan, Board members said, "would help to build up the unfortunate 'image' of the Bank as an institution that helped the rich."[29] McNamara found himself defending the loan, arguing that "a severe maldistribution of income . . . was characteristic of many developing countries," that "neither the Bank nor the governments of these countries . . . had a ready answer," that "steps towards more equitable distribution usually met with strong political resistance," and that, "in view of the difficulties, it was not surprising that, at the present stage, the Bank's principles were running ahead of its practice." Thus, "given . . . the intractability of the problem of redistribution, and its prevalence in developing countries, to condition further lending on substantial progress in dealing with this problem would amount to a suspension of lending."[30] Several months later Knapp insisted on a defense of the livestock loan:

26. Memorandum for the record, "Meeting on Mr. McNamara's UNCTAD Statement, January 7, 1972," January 10, 1972. Chenery was present. He noted that Raúl Prebisch had written on the subject and suggested that material could be quoted.

27. Memorandum, Robert Skillings to files, "Brazil—Meeting with Minister of Finance," July 27, 1972. In September Netto argued with a Bank mission that Fishlow's hypothesis was that distributional equality would improve welfare whereas a second study, by Carlos Langoni, did not. His own policies assumed that absolute income growth was a "much stronger" determinant of welfare than (re)distribution. "Were he to accept the Fishlow hypothesis, he said, Brazil would have to abandon the price mechanism and resort to a socialistic form of economic organization." Memorandum, Roger P. Hipskind and Francesco Abbatte to Gerald Alter, "Brazil: Economic Mission—Back-to-Office Report," September 22, 1972.

28. Roger P. Hipskind to files, "Brazil—December 12, 1972, Meeting with Minister Delfim Netto," January 8, 1973, p. 3.

29. World Bank, "Summaries of Discussions at Meeting of the Executive Directors of the Bank and IDA, December 19, 1972," SD 72-55, January 4, 1973, pp. 7–8.

30. Ibid., pp. 8, 10.

I must say that I think that we have sometimes tended to be too apologetic about our support for commercial livestock projects. I think that these stand on their own feet. . . . They are no substitute for measures to redistribute income and specifically for projects in support of poor farmers: but no one should suppose that every project financed by the Bank . . . can make a direct contribution to these objectives.[31]

After the Board embarrassment, however, McNamara became more determined to press the issue.

By this time the usually imperturbable Chenery had become an activist on Brazilian inequality. "The main issues facing us in Brazil," he argued, "are the likely effect of our operations in bringing about a fairer distribution of the benefits of growth [and the] brunt of our influence in Brazil at the present time should be directed at social justice"; in view of the Bank's large lending program, he added, it was not unrealistic to expect some influence.[32]

The effect of these proddings showed up during the discussion of Brazil's 1973 CPP. The rapporteur, after prefacing his notes with the remark, "This one-hour meeting was fascinating," continued:

No time was spent on the usual macro-economic issues. The question of income redistribution and equity dominated the session. . . . Mr. McNamara . . . requested Mr. Alter to resubmit an operations program . . . to define more precisely the projects designed to increase equity. . . . Mr. Alter objected that he could not firm up the social portion of the program that fast. . . . Mr. Alter was overruled by Mr. McNamara, who insisted he wanted to put some flesh on these social sector projects. No alternative projects in other sectors were acceptable to him. . . . Despite further protestations . . . Mr. McNamara repeated he would refuse "hard" projects in the traditional sectors as substitutes for "soft" projects in the social sectors.[33]

Alter protested that insistence on difficult social projects—understood principally as small-farmer projects—might mean not meeting the Bank's overall lending target. McNamara "quickly objected" to the argument, saying that "loans are only a means to our objective which is development."[34]

When regional officials proceeded to negotiate this new policy with Delfim Netto, the minister "expressed skepticism that there could be economic lending to small ranchers."[35] The Bank's position, however, was reinforced when, at Nairobi that year, the Bank publicly committed itself to a small-farmer lending strategy. Brazil was chosen as a country for "special effort" to implement that strategy. By

31. Memorandum, J. Burke Knapp to Gerald Alter and Warren Baum, "Livestock Development in Latin America," October 26, 1973.

32. Memorandum, Hollis B. Chenery to Robert S. McNamara, "Brazil—Outstanding Policy Issues," February 16, 1973.

33. Memorandum, Alexis E. Lachman to John H. Adler, attaching "Notes on Review of CPP on Brazil," February 28, 1973.

34. Ibid.

35. Memorandum, Gunter K. Wiese to Robert S. McNamara, "Brazil—Briefing Memo . . . ," March 23, 1973, paras. 4, 2.

March 1974 the region could state that the Brazilian government "on the whole welcomed our initiative" and report on a great deal of joint work on smallholder projects in the Northeast, a substantial research program, a nutrition component, and agricultural research and extension projects. The change of government in 1974, though it delayed the negotiations, seemed to promise an easier course for the poverty agenda with the replacement of the combative, growth-oriented Minister of Finance Delfim Netto by Mario Simonsen, the head of Brazil's dynamic adult literacy program. But if the battle for political acceptance appeared to be won, the poverty program now became hostage to the limitations of public administration.[36] Land redistribution, a prerequisite for some area development projects, and project preparation in general "moved very slowly." Moreover, specific policy disagreements continued, notably on the issue of Brazil's highly subsidized interest rates to farmers. The effort to develop projects for lower-income groups was proving "an uphill task."[37] The CPP review recognized that "an effective program did not yet exist." McNamara nonetheless insisted that the poverty-oriented program "was imperative" and stated that he was willing to concede on interest rate subsidies: "He would not want a disagreement over interest rates to stand in the way of implementing such a program."[38]

Taking stock a year later, in early 1975, McNamara was faced with a dilemma. Baum had reported delays in the poverty program and pointed out that "the Brazilian Government's commitment to large-scale programs for improving small farm productivity [is] lacking." McNamara seemed to lose patience. He wrote Knapp: "I have long suspected that this was the case. If the Brazilian Government has no program for increasing the productivity and the level of income of large numbers of its poor, are we justified in continuing lending to it? I think not."[39]

Yet political and financial factors now made a cutoff or drastic reduction in lending less thinkable. General Ernesto Geisel had assumed the presidency announcing a democratic opening ("abertura"), acknowledging the need for a more

36. The new government backed its more liberal rhetoric with social measures: an expansion of social welfare, including its extension to rural workers, new health and nutrition programs, and fiscal proposals to redistribute resources from richer to poorer states and to substitute sales and income for payroll taxes. But Alter saw no fundamental change: "Like the old Government, the new is relying on a high rate of growth to increase the incomes of the poor." Memorandum, Gerald Alter to Robert S. McNamara, "Brazil—Impressions Gained from Recent Visit to Brazil," June 10, 1974, p. 2.

37. World Bank, Country Program Paper—Brazil, March 27, 1974; attachment 6, "Program of Action for Promoting Increased Productivity of Small-Scale Farmers in Northeast Brazil," March 25, 1974; memorandum, John H. Adler and Mahbub ul Haq to Robert S. McNamara, "Brazil Country Program Paper—Outstanding Policy and Program Issues," April 5, 1974.

38. World Bank, "Country Program Paper—Brazil," March 27, 1974, p. 14.

39. Memorandum, Robert S. McNamara to J. Burke Knapp, March 18, 1975.

energetic social effort and creating a new program—POLONOROESTE—for rural development in the Northeast. Also, the continuing growth "miracle" (11.4 percent a year over 1970–73) strengthened the argument for attacking poverty through employment creation. Finally, Brazil's balance of payments and growth momentum suddenly looked vulnerable after the year-end 1973 jump in the price of oil.

What seemed to carry the most weight, however, were the Bank's own financial priorities. Within weeks of McNamara's "are we justified in continuing lending" outburst, the Bank was jolted by the U.S. refusal to support the Bank's fund-raising Third Window proposal. At the review of the CPP on Brazil, McNamara explained to surprised colleagues that though previously "we could borrow as much money as we needed . . . *as of this morning* things are different."[40] For that reason above all, he said, he was trimming Brazil's proposed lending program. He said that "if the Government of Brazil had not started its own income distribution policy in the North East [POLONOROESTE], he would have proposed a much bigger cut."[41] A second financial restriction came into play: the Bank's large exposure to, and so dependence on, Brazil. Brazil's interest payments on IBRD debt were projected to exceed 100 percent of the Bank's net income. "This is hell," McNamara exclaimed, since "in a liquidity crisis one was not sure what Brazil would do with respect to interest and charges."[42] The exposure risk reduced the Bank's leverage, all the more in that poverty loans were slow to arrange and to disburse, whereas financial concerns put a premium on immediate cash flows.[43]

McNamara's "are we justified" exclamation came to mark the peak rather than an escalation of the effort to influence Brazil on poverty. Brazil's poverty-related policies, which had dominated the 1973 and 1974 discussions, were scarcely touched on in 1975. From that year attention shifted away from the original and larger question of what Brazil was doing for (or to) its poor to how much of the Bank's own lending program (which financed about 2 percent of Brazilian investment) was allocated to poverty lending. Matters of research and statistical documentation on poverty were also continually brought up.

At subsequent CPP reviews McNamara pressed to increase the weight of "social," particularly small-farmer projects, in total lending. In 1975 such projects represented about 35 percent of the program; by 1979 the share was 57 percent. Further increase ran into the rising need for adjustment-related support of Brazil's "precariously vulnerable" balance of payments, aggravated in 1979 by the second

40. Memorandum, George Zaidan to John H. Adler, "Meeting of the Review Group: Brazil," May 30, 1975, containing notes on meeting of the CPP review group on Brazil held on May 21, 1975, pp. 1, 4. The rapporteur, once again, prefaced the account with an editorial "this meeting . . . was, by a wide margin the most interesting this year."
41. Ibid., p. 3.
42. Ibid., p. 4.
43. See chapter 15 on Brazil.

oil shock and "the Brazilian government's strong wish that we remain in the traditional sectors of electric power and transportation."[44] By 1981 the concern over creditworthiness had become acute: "Brazil's total foreign debt, approaching $60 billion, exceeds that of any developing country and any major default could have serious implications for the international financial system." Hence, "a large part of [the lending program] has resource transfer as its primary objective and little policy impact."[45] The Bank's leverage was further curtailed by the manyfold expansion in easily tapped and unconditioned commercial bank credit made possible by recycled petrodollars.[46] From 1975 government policies, which had changed more in rhetoric than in substance, were rarely criticized and instead often commended for their concern for social objectives.[47]

This position was not unopposed within the Bank. In the rather intellectual and catholic environment of the 1970s institution, disagreement was readily tolerated. There were many insistent critics of Brazilian social policies—notably land tenure, education, and health—especially in the Bank's economics and policy units, which, after all, were only carrying on with the poverty mission and country policy priorities that McNamara had professed since his arrival. Some of these objections were made in the 1978 CPP discussion: Herman G. van der Tak stated, "It was indeed urgent for Brazil to develop a strategy to alleviate poverty"; Stern said the CPP "should have [addressed] what could be expected from the Government; how would it deal with poverty." But McNamara limited his comments on Brazilian policies to issues of creditworthiness and exports and commended a study carried out by the regional staff—who were less enthusiastic about intervention in poverty matters—that concluded trickle-down had worked better than critics (including

44. World Bank, "Brazil—Interim Program Memorandum," draft, November 2, 1979, pp. 7, 18. See also World Bank, "Country Program Paper—Brazil," draft, March 1975, p. 23.

45. Memorandum, Mahbub ul Haq to Robert S. McNamara, "Brazil CPP: Major Policy Issues," May 29, 1981, pp. 1, 2.

46. Over 1976–78 Brazil could borrow more cheaply from commercial banks than from the World Bank. Between 1976 and 1978 the cost of funds borrowed from the IBRD was 8.7 percent, and from all commercial sources 6.9 percent. See table 15-5.

47. The 1978 CPP stated that "Brazil has clearly departed from the earlier 'laissez-faire' approach to public involvement with poverty, in favor of what it calls 'redistribution with growth,'" World Bank, "Country Program Paper: Brazil," draft, September 6, 1978, p. 20. Returning from Brazil, McNamara told the President's Council on November 19, 1979, that he was impressed by the commitment of the Brazilian government to poverty alleviation and improving income distribution. World Bank, "Minutes of President's Council Meeting," November 19, 1979. Policy change proved to be cosmetic. The 1980 CPP stated: "The present government has done more than any of its military predecessors to move toward a more democratic system and, *at least in public statements,* stress the importance of a more equitable society. . . . The Government continues to affirm its commitment to *poverty alleviation and improved income distribution* as primary objectives." World Bank, "Country Program Paper: Brazil," December 5, 1980, pp. 2, 11. Emphasis added.

himself) had been alleging.[48] By 1981 ul Haq's discussion of "major policy issues" in Brazil was focusing on debt and creditworthiness, with only a passing reference to Brazil's "flagging attack on poverty."[49]

The effort to influence distributive policy in Brazil for the most part took place between 1972 and 1974. Shortly after, in late 1975, Knapp compared the Brazilian experience with that of Iran, where the Bank was also struggling to influence distributive policy: "The Bank would probably have to cave in to the [Iranian] Government's policy as we had done in Northeast Brazil and Nigeria."[50] If the assessment seems hard, it reflected the ambition that had accompanied the effort. A longer view would credit the Bank with some influence on Brazilian attitudes and sense of the possible through poverty projects, research, and advocacy.

If the Bank was stymied in its frontal attack, was it because Brazil was a particularly tough nut, or because the Bank itself moved from an overreach on distributive goals to a more balanced pursuit of its several objectives? Most clearly, persistence with regard to income distribution was hampered after 1975 by rising balance of payments and exposure concerns, and by the government's shift to a more redistributive rhetoric.

Guatemala

The distributive issue was sharply etched in Guatemala. Casual observation revealed highly unequal land ownership and ethnic privilege. Colonial inequality had been aggravated by unequal appropriation of the new wealth created by the eradication of malaria, which opened rich Piedmont and coastal lands suitable for cash crops. The perception of injustice was magnified by its ethnic correlation, by uncaring governments, and by the seeming consequence of that state of affairs: persisting and extreme social violence. Guatemala's inequality was thus part real and part image. A review of evidence in 1973 found little basis for firm statistical statements, particularly when it came to a comparison with other "bad" cases, yet

48. Memorandum, Guenter H. Reif to K. Georg Gabriel, "Meetings of the Review Group: Mexico and Brazil," September 27, 1978, with attached note, "Brazil Country Program Review Meeting, September 20, 1978." Chenery's comment on this study was more guarded: "Even the critics in DPS were impressed by the amount of work done in this area." A 1978 study of nutrition and basic needs in Brazil directed by Peter Knight provided a highly documented and strong condemnation of governmental neglect in the areas of nutrition, and basic health and education. The study of poverty and distribution was published as Guy P. Pfefferman and Richard Webb, *The Distribution of Income in Brazil*, World Bank Staff Working Paper 356, September 1979.

49. Memorandum, ul Haq to McNamara, May 29, 1981.

50. Memorandum, J. Burke Knapp for the record, October 3, 1975. Knapp spoke too soon with regard to Iran: soon after this statement the Bank ceased to lend. See chapter 9.

Guatemala's "inordinate" inequality was the starting point for almost every Bank report and discussion on that country during the period.[51]

Bank opinion was uniformly critical and often scathing from the beginning of the decade. In 1970 an Issues Paper on Guatemala stated: "The distribution of income is extremely skewed, even by Latin American standards. . . . Past Governments have rarely lived up to their words, and little suggests that present rulers will be of different caliber."[52] At the CPP discussion in January 1971, McNamara "found inequalities . . . quite shocking" and thought "the country might blow up unless there was a significant change in its policies." When it came to specifics, the Bank's most repeated charge was that Guatemala's tax ratio was too low, an accusation that steered clear of the deeper land tenure question, and that pointed to increased government spending on rural infrastructure and social services as the definition of a more acceptable distributive policy. In 1972 a suggestion that the International Development Association could be used to channel funds "to the Guatemalan Indians" prompted the indignant reply: "Should we subsidize the callousness of the rich?"[53]

That assessment did not change over the decade. In 1979 McNamara, generalizing about Central America in a remark that was pertinent above all to Guatemala and El Salvador, said that "he had stayed out of these countries for 11 years because their governments were immovable, oppressive and corrupt." Stern added: "Politically it would be important to bring Marxists into the hemispheric system in order to moderate them."[54]

The Bank's response was to cut lending. Guatemala seems to have been the only country where lending was reduced over the entire period on unequivocal grounds of distributive policy.[55] The cut was severe, though some lending continued: ten loans were made over the period, mostly for infrastructure, but lending per person was notably low. Upon introducing the 1971 CPP, regional economist Peter Wright had stressed that "we could not influence the Government by total withdrawal," and both McNamara and Knapp had agreed, though through the period the Bank hovered between threats of full or at least "drastic" cuts and the argument that some lending was needed for leverage. Thus Stern decided in 1979 that it would be best to continue approving one project per year. Wright had recommended in 1971

51. The review of evidence was a background report for the 1973 CPP.

52. Memorandum, J. Chaffey to Economic Committee members, "Issues Paper—Economic Committee Meeting on Guatemala," December 16, 1970.

53. Memorandum, Alexis E. Lachman to John H. Adler, April 4, 1972, with attached "Notes on Guatemala Country Program Review Meeting."

54. Memorandum, Robert S. McNamara for the record, "Meeting on the Future of Central America," July 31, 1979. The "staying out" reference was most applicable to Guatemala, where lending between 1968 and 1981 totaled only $2 per person. In El Salvador it was $3 and in Nicaragua $4. Another small country, Malaysia, received $63. Though large countries generally fared worse in allocation per person, Brazil received $4 and Colombia $9.

55. Lending to Zaire was also curtailed during part of the decade for similar reasons.

that the Bank should lend in sectors "where there was some possibility of exercising leverage," which, given the government's preferences, meant infrastructure rather than social projects, and Stern now reaffirmed that policy.[56]

The stridency in Bank commentary on Guatemala was probably as much a reaction to that country's deaf ear as to its extreme inequality and regressive policies. The complaint that the government did not listen became a refrain. In 1979 Stern said that the "Government was short-sighted and the Bank had no influence at all," and an exasperated McNamara stated that there was "nothing the Bank could do."[57] The problem predated McNamara: from 1956 to 1967 Guatemala had refused to settle debt arrears, in effect precluding Bank loans. In 1971 Guatemala was considered "not a very popular country with the management."[58] Ironically, once the debt was settled Guatemala's strong creditworthiness opened commercial bank doors and so had the effect of reducing Bank influence. Guatemala enjoyed low debt, monetary stability, and a strong balance of payments and maintained parity with the dollar into the 1980s; it did need emergency aid after an earthquake in 1976, and the Bank assisted, but the relationship quickly returned to its earlier form. Leverage was also undercut by U.S. political support and an ample supply of funds on concessionary terms, especially from USAID and the IDB. "The other lending agencies so far have not been willing to make their assistance conditional on improved Government policies," wrote Sidney Chernick in 1979.[59] This competition was especially damaging for poverty lending, since, "apart from the Government's lack of commitment to social reform, it shows no inclination to borrow on Bank [IBRD] terms for social projects."[60]

The Bank was thus thwarted in Guatemala with regard to poverty and distribution. Its uncompromising stance did not force open government doors, and it was unable even to exercise indirect influence through poverty lending.

Malaysia

Malaysia presented the Bank with a puzzle: here was a nation that placed redistribution at the center of its economic policy but that defined redistribution in terms of ethnic and political needs, rather than strictly income. What is more, the central notion of Malaysian policy, as conceived and set out in the Second Malaysian

56. Memorandum, John H. Adler to Mahbub ul Haq, January 18, 1971, with attached notes of "Meeting on the CPP for Guatemala. . . ."

57. Memorandum, McNamara for the record, July 31, 1979. Stern was citing and endorsing the CPP evaluation.

58. Memorandum, Adler to ul Haq, January 18, 1971.

59. Memorandum, Sidney E. Chernick to Ernest Stern, "Guatemala CPP—Major Policy Issues," July 20, 1979, p. 2.

60. Memorandum, K. Georg Gabriel to Ernest Stern, "Guatemala CPP—Outstanding Policy and Program Issues," July 23, 1979.

Plan—though using different and fuzzier language—was to "redistribute with growth."[61] Malaysia had adopted—two years before the concept was formulated and baptized by the ILO and subsequently by the Bank—what would become the central concept of the Bank's own poverty strategy, namely, that redistribution would be carried out at the margin by steering the allocation of new resources, rather than by transferring ownership of preexisting wealth.

Racial divisions—above all between Malays and Chinese, though Indians added a further ethnic complication—had bedeviled Malaysia since its independence in 1960. Against the background of a recent large-scale communist insurgency and continuing terrorism, it is scarcely surprising that racial riots in May 1969 proved traumatic, and that the avoidance of such sparks should become a national priority. The Bank's first reactions to what came to be called the New Economic Policy (NEP), still in preparation at the end of 1970, seemed shallow in their perception of this context. A back-to-office report spoke of "disappointing" preparatory work and "prolonged debates" on broad objectives that had "delayed and disrupted" work on specifics.[62] Aware of the drift toward pro-Malay affirmative action measures, the Bank counseled in early 1971 that Malaysia "be wary of diversions of development resources and effort to programs of benefit to Malays as a group (as distinguished from production, employment and the disadvantaged generally)."[63] It worried that such a policy "would tend to have some disincentive effects," that "limited planning capacity" would be "used excessively on the establishment of the social objectives," and that administrative difficulties were "worsening rather than improving because of the government's preoccupation with upgrading the role of the Malays."[64]

The following year the Bank continued to shake its head, saying: "To some extent, the goals of economic development and racial justice were conflicting," and

---

61. The "Second Malaysian Plan, 1971–75" set forth what came to be known as the New Economic Policy (NEP). According to Just Faaland, J. R. Parkinson, and Rais Saniman, *Growth and Ethnic Inequality: Malaysia's New Economic Policy* (London: C. Hurst, 1990), the Plan "had no direct precedent in Malaysia or in other developing countries. Indeed, it was a forerunner of what was later known as the 'Strategy of Growth with Equity' or 'Redistribution with Growth' or the strategy of 'Basic Needs'" (p. 75). They also write that the design of the New Economic Policy was not assisted by external agencies, who were "at best passive and mute" (p. 203). The NEP was a response to race riots in May 1969 and to the underlying ethnic divisions between Indians, Chinese, and—the largest and poorest group—Malays. Jacob Meerman, *Public Expenditure in Malaysia: Who Benefits and Why* (Oxford University Press, 1979), described the NEP as "quite modern, with its overwhelming emphasis on distributing *increases* in product. . . . Redistribution of existing assets is anathema. Neither expropriation, . . . nor land reform is considered in the NEP" (p. 28).

62. Memorandum, Shinji Asanuma and Jean-Marie Jengten to Raymond J. Goodman, "Malaysia: Economic Mission, Back-to-Office Report," November 24, 1970.

63. World Bank, "Country Program Paper: Malaysia," EC/0/71-30/1, February 12, 1971, p. 2.

64. Ibid., pp. 8–9.

"the pursuit of the objective of social restructuring led the government to play down the importance of free enterprise development." The Bank worried that measures that sought ethnic balance amounted to inefficient "diversions" of resources from more productive uses and would create administrative bottlenecks and private sector uncertainties. Even more it feared that growth would be held back deliberately because "growth is associated with widening racial income disparity."[65] In McNamara's view: "The neglect of more urgent matters seems to be a terrible price to pay for the stress on racial balance."[66]

Visiting Malaysia in early 1972, McNamara heard Minister of Finance Tun Tan Siew Sin explain Malaysian policy and its political roots. McNamara did not comment on the ethnic policy directly but vigorously lectured the minister on the need to insist on rapid growth. He said that Plan targets should be exceeded and "more ambitious future objectives" be set, adding that "if such steps were not taken the Bank would be quite concerned about the employment situation and the possibility of achieving a more even distribution of income."[67]

In May 1973 the Bank began to hedge its bets, admitting that the ethnic policy approach "has been cautious and there is not any indication, as yet, of diversion of resources from other programs. Nonetheless, there is at present some apprehension among non-Malay investors."[68] A year later the Bank could no longer lecture Malaysia on growth: the country's gross national product (GNP) had risen 13 percent in 1973 and investment was rising through 1974. Already in 1973 Knapp had opened the CPP review meeting saying that "the objectives of the Malaysian Government coincide with those of the Bank and that we should have no hesitation about assisting the country."[69] The CPP, however, now signaled what would become the Bank's new line of pressure: "because of political necessity," ethnic redistribution was working to favor urban middle- and upper-income Malays, whereas the government should also attend "the equally serious problems of rural poverty and rapid employment creation."[70] The NEP would now be criticized not as inimical to growth but to the poor.

Happily, the Malaysian government was open to this argument and had, in fact, already "requested the Bank to look into this difficult area."[71] Whether the initiative lay with the Bank or the Malaysian government, the rapprochement was successful and developed into a strong poverty-oriented Bank-lending program. The Bank

65. IBRD/IDA, Economic Committee, "Note of Meeting on Malaysia," EC/M/72-18, March 21, 1972, pp. 1, 2.

66. World Bank, "Notes on Malaysia Country Program Review Meeting, April 3, 1972," April 5, 1972.

67. Memorandum, Robert S. McNamara for the record, "Malaysia—Meeting with Minister of Finance . . . ," February 2, 1971, p. 2.

68. World Bank, "Country Program Paper: Malaysia," May 22, 1973, p. 7.

69. World Bank, "Notes on Malaysia Country Program Review Meeting, June 8, 1973."

70. World Bank, "Country Program Paper: Malaysia," May 22, 1973, p. 4.

71. Ibid., p. 5.

defined the ethnic policy as a political requirement that "we had to accept"; Malaysia in turn concurred with the Bank's reminders on the rural poor. To an unusual extent, the Bank's lending program through the decade was concentrated in agriculture. At the same time, Malaysia became a "country of concentration" for the Bank's poverty research. Knapp referred to Malaysia as "one of our best clients."[72] The smooth relationship was grounded on much more than the poverty orientation of lending: Malaysia also boasted rapid growth, monetary stability, excellent creditworthiness, and good project implementation.

Even as this relationship was being celebrated, the Bank continued to press for policy improvements. In 1976 McNamara complained—and threatened to reduce lending—because Malaysia was not proceeding with a family planning project: "He repeated more than once that if the Malaysians do not want to go ahead with the population project then he would not be willing to go ahead with the proposed [lending] program."[73] The pressure escalated the next year after the appointment of a disciplinarian, Shahid Husain, as regional vice president.[74] The 1977 CPP again criticized ethnic policies, particularly those implemented through the Industrial Coordination Act, which, it said, were having "adverse consequences on the overall level of private investment. . . . This . . . approach to redress racial inequities has the potential of inflicting serious damage to the engine of Malaysia's growth—the private investor."[75] The CPP also renewed the charge that racial redistribution conflicted with poverty redressal. Though recognizing that "Malaysia's commitment to assist its low income groups has been strengthened significantly in the past few years," an improvement for which "the Bank can justifiably take some measure of credit," it insisted that racial goals "may seriously undercut efforts to reduce poverty."[76] But the CPP's emphasis on reducing the pace of Malayanization was itself criticized within the Bank. Husain did not dispute the CPP arguments, but said that "he had discussed with the Prime Minister and other Cabinet members the advisability of moderating some of the NEP measures. However, the policy of racial restructuring was the paramount political issue in Malaysia; the redistribution of economic and political power was the government's main concern . . . the Government was adamant."[77]

Both sides were working to sustain the relationship. McNamara and Husain accepted the political constraint; Malaysia showed genuine interest in receiving Bank assistance on poverty alleviation, as was evident in the strongly rural, poverty-

72. World Bank, "Malaysia Country Program Review Meeting, June 4, 1976."
73. Ibid.
74. Husain's disciplinary approach also surfaced in Colombia and Indonesia. See chapters 9 and 10.
75. World Bank, "Country Program Paper: Malaysia," December 16, 1977, p. 6.
76. Ibid., pp. 13, 15.
77. Memorandum, Guenter H. Reif to files, "Malaysia CPP-RVP Review Meeting," January 27, 1978, paras. 6, 9.

oriented composition of the Bank's lending program. Visiting Malaysia in June 1978, McNamara was told by Tengku Razaleigh, the minister of finance, that "the Government intends to follow more and more the Bank's policy of raising the incomes of the rural poor through integrated rural development schemes." According to an account of the trip, it was considered "a great success." McNamara received excellent media coverage and a citation stating that "Malaysians see Mr. McNamara as a giant in the field of international economic development."[78]

Staff responsible for Malaysia nonetheless made a new effort in 1980 to overcome the inhibitions of senior management with regard to Malaysia's distributive policies. The staff proposal was influenced by the basic needs approach, for which Malaysia had been chosen as a major case study.[79] The 1980 CPP set out an ambitious proposal that, in effect, would have conditioned Bank financial support on "the implementation of national policies that are essential to a successful eradication of poverty." "Essential" policies would include more small-farmer projects but also "a large redistribution program" of government transfers that would "directly supplement the incomes of the poor." The justification for what amounted to a welfare program was that "there will be a large number of residual poverty families with few obvious ways out of poverty through production increases," such as the very large number of padi and rubber farmers with tiny holdings.[80]

What the report brought out was that poverty reduction had been more limited than many believed, and that income distribution was worsening: for the poorest 40 percent of the population income had risen only 10–15 percent between 1970 and 1978, whereas for the rest it had increased by more than 60 percent. It was becoming clear that the concentration on rural projects, with substantial Bank support, had created an exaggerated image of the extent of poverty alleviation. The persistence of poverty, said the CPP, was in part due to "the concentration of public expenditures on a few major programs with substantial benefit to a limited number of poor households. The prime example of this is the land development program which has accounted for almost 60 percent of expenditures in agriculture but has affected only about 10 to 15 percent of the agricultural households in poverty."[81] In other words, Malaysia, with Bank support, had substituted project showcases—or hopefully, demonstration projects—for broader poverty-alleviation policies. This charge was to be repeated later, in the 1985 CPP, and with fuller documentation. But in 1980 the staff proposal was put aside. The management review meeting of the CPP, chaired by Stern, concluded:

78. Memorandum, Robert S. McNamara for the record, "Malaysia—Mr. and Mrs. McNamara's Visit to Malaysia, June 9–13, 1978," June 23, 1978, paras. 5, 17.
79. Jacob Meerman, *Public Expenditure in Malaysia: Who Benefits and Why* (Oxford University Press, 1979).
80. World Bank, "Country Program Paper: Malaysia," draft, October 8, 1980, paras. 4, 37, 39, 54.
81. Ibid., para. 23.

"Because the issue of poverty in Malaysia was inextricably linked with the politically sensitive question of restructuring along racial lines, it was agreed that the Bank's approach would not be prescriptive, but would be confined to highlighting the choices available to the Government."[82] What was missing in this statement, as it had been in all statements by Bank officials since the NEP was introduced, was a full recognition of racial coexistence as an intrinsic societal value, and also as solid political ground for development.

Kenya

In late 1969 Kenya stood out as one of the most promising countries in Sub-Saharan Africa. As noted in the 1969 CPP, Kenya had set out on independence in 1963 under "the astute leadership" of President Jomo Kenyatta, had "held latent tribalism in check," had formulated a development plan that emphasized equitable distribution, had chosen gradual Kenyanization, and, in contrast to a majority of new African nations, notably its neighbor Tanzania, had elected capitalism. Since 1963 GDP had grown at 6 percent a year, investment had trended upward, and macroeconomic management had been sound. In addition, agriculture had shown "remarkable progress."[83]

The CPP also observed greater "inequality between the haves and have-nots" and the emergence of a "new elite among the Africans." But the government was aware of these problems, and in its election manifesto the ruling party laid "particular attention on the need for a more equitable distribution of incomes."[84] The government seemed especially interested in rural development schemes, but, the Bank noted, "much too little is known about the political, social and economic background of rural peoples in Kenya" and the government had "wisely decided to adopt an experimental or pilot project approach." Fourteen such pilots were in existence. Discussing rural development, a Bank report laid heavy stress on "local initiative," echoing the 1966 Kericho Conference, whose conclusions had "already had a notable influence on government policy." With regard to self-help, Kenya was in an "enviable condition." "Staggering efforts" had been carried out, leaving "no doubt about the genuine level of motivation which exists at the local level." Potential donors were warned that the "Government has rightly decided that the [rural development] schemes should be implemented through the existing machinery of government. . . . This means that there is no scope for a separate project in the normal sense used by most donors."[85]

82. World Bank, "Country Program Paper: Malaysia," postscript, October 31, 1980, based on management review meeting held October 29, 1980.
83. World Bank, "Country Program Paper: Kenya," December 10, 1969, paras. 11, 18.
84. Ibid., paras. 15, 16.
85. World Bank, "Economic Development Prospects in Kenya," pt. 2, October 22, 1969, Report AE-06A, pp. 22–24. Also annex B, "Rural Development," pp. 1–6.

From 1969 through 1972 the Bank focused on financial support rather than policy interventions, including distributive policy. Distribution was not raised again as a CPP issue until 1972, when it was noted that "unlike the Tanzanians [Kenyans] had not yet made a decision on the proper trade-off between growth and distribution," but that the forthcoming ILO employment mission might be of help in that regard.[86]

The government, staffed by well-trained and respected technocrats, was cooperative but urged the mission to moderate the radical message of an earlier (Colombia) ILO employment mission. The mission leader, Hans Singer, accommodated Kenya's market-oriented leanings and made that evident in the apt title given to the report, "Redistribution from Growth."[87] The term, expressly coined *for* Kenya, was later borrowed and slightly modified—to redistribution with growth— to state the essence of Bank policy on income distribution. The ILO mission seemed to coincide with and possibly reinforce "a significant shift in [the] Government's attitude to the disparities of income. . . . It has been accepted . . . that a fast rate of growth will not, by itself, ensure an equitable distribution of income." For the CPP authors, the new budget had "a distinctly egalitarian flavor," though this seemed to consist mostly of excise taxes on luxury goods.[88]

But questions of distribution were almost immediately set aside by the oil shock. From mid-1973 through the end of 1976 the Bank was above all concerned with Kenya's "increased resource needs." Moreover, because Kenya adopted a homegrown, well-managed adjustment program, which by contrast with Tanzania relied more on policy change than borrowing, the Bank could say that "Kenya warrants a large increase in the scale of financial assistance."[89] Increased lending, however, gave McNamara the opportunity to press rural development lending and to address the sector-level administrative and institutional deficiencies that were holding back investment and production in smallholder agriculture. This emphasis did not prevent occasional, worried observations on the broader social and political scene. In 1975 McNamara said that the CPP was "unduly generous in its assessment of

86. IBRD/IDA, Economic Committee, "Note of Meeting on Kenya and East African Community," EC/M/19, March 23, 1972. Area department representatives noted that Kenya's income distribution had been unequal and that "the Kenyans were aware of their lack of success in narrowing the gap between the rich and the poor and were trying to find a solution to the problem."

87. Richard Jolly, interview with the authors, November 18, 1995. Philip Ndegwa played a key role as liaison between the ILO and government. A key policy statement of May 1965, approved by Kenya's assembly in Sessional Paper 10, referred to as "Kenya's economic 'bible,'" had affirmed a market-oriented course complemented by a redistribution with growth strategy. It called for growing incomes, equitably distributed. Colin Leys, *Underdevelopment in Kenya: The Political Economy of Neo-Colonialism, 1964–1971* (University of California Press, 1975), pp. 221–22.

88. World Bank, "Country Program Paper: Kenya," draft, January 1973, p. 7.

89. World Bank, "Country Program Paper: Kenya: Postscript," August 7, 1974.

Kenya's political system and its stability," a concern that, for staff and in McNamara's mind, was closely associated with that for equity.[90]

Equity reemerged as an issue at the end of 1976 prompted by political clouds: an opposition leader was assassinated, people were growing dissatisfied with "widespread corruption," restlessness was increasing "at the universities and in the trade unions which also hampered the Government's anti-inflationary austerity program," and there were "tensions with Uganda and Somalia." Most worrying, as Kenyatta entered his late eighties, was the "succession question."[91] Meeting to discuss Kenya, Knapp thought that previous Bank lending to the country now looked "excessive," and he expressed concern for the Bank's political risk. McNamara, in turn, found that the area staff as well as the Kenyan government had paid too little attention to "the problem of raising the low productivity elements of society." He thought that the lack of data on income distribution "might be an indication of the fact the Government was not sensitive to this matter; this was the clear impression he had when he talked to the Government." When Stanley Please defended Kenya's trickle-down record, McNamara disagreed, and, suggesting that the Bank had been insufficiently critical, said that "no country was getting as good a deal." But the meeting produced no agreement on concrete lending or policy steps, beyond a decision to carry out more research on poverty trends.[92]

A year later, in early 1978, the regional staff found "growing land and income concentration" and "no significant change in the per capita income of the lowest 40% of rural households." Additional bad news came from Kenya's foreign relations: "instability in the Horn of Africa, the unpredictability of neighboring Uganda, the deterioration of relations with Tanzania and the final collapse of the EAC [East African Community]."[93] Nevertheless, the CPP was restrained in suggesting a policy stance: "While we must continue to press for needed policy changes, we should be realistic as to what we can expect to achieve," adding "the Bank's exposure is already high."[94] The vice president for East Africa, Willi Wapenhans, agreed that Kenya's poverty problem was "serious enough to warrant front attack" but then asked what, concretely, could be proposed:

> The Bank early emphasized the importance of improving the plight of the small farmer. Kenya followed our advice and raised producer prices of staples. However, the higher prices had not affected much the smallholder . . . as most of them were in the subsistence

90. "Kenya Country Program Review Meeting, October 1, 1975."

91. Memorandum, John H. Adler to Robert S. McNamara, "EAC, Kenya and Tanzania CPPs . . . ," December 14, 1976, p. 3. A principal Kenyatta challenger, though former supporter, Josiah Kariuki, had been murdered in early 1975. Other opposition figures were persecuted.

92. Memorandum, G. Zaidan to John H. Adler, December 21, 1976, with attached "EAC, Kenya, and Tanzania Country Program Review Meeting, December 16, 1976."

93. World Bank, "Country Program Paper: Kenya," February 13, 1978, paras. 6, 17.

94. Ibid., para. 59.

sector. . . . [C]redit, most public services, education, etc. had also not reached them. We had created an impression that we would be able to reach the smallholder, but if we take our agricultural projects apart, how much of the subsistençe sector . . . could we reach. . . . We had not yet developed efficient instruments to deal with the rural poverty problem. . . . For Kenya . . . in the next few years there would be no choice but emphasizing direct productive sectors and exports.[95]

McNamara had agitated for greater emphasis on income distribution by Kenya but in his summing up he steered around the issue. Instead, he insisted that more attention should be given to population growth, limited his other comments to operational matters, and offered what seemed to be an explanation of his noncommittal stance: "The real trouble was between now and the decision on President Kenyatta's succession."[96]

The year 1978 proved a high point for Bank discussion of equity and poverty in Kenya during the McNamara period; these subjects soon receded from view in the face of a new oil shock. In addition to Kenya's foreign exchange needs, the Bank was worried about its exposure, which became the main topic of discussion at the 1979 Kenya review meeting. Also, at this time of transition from Kenyatta to Daniel Arap Moi, the Bank was especially intent on supporting key "reformist" ministers, most notably Finance Minister Mwai Kibaki. The collapse of the East African Community acted as a further inhibitor, as the Bank stepped in to assist and mediate a settlement of the former community's tangled finances.[97] The CPP for 1979 contained only a token reminder that the Bank should seek projects to benefit the poorest 20 percent.[98] The 1980 CPP similarly referred briefly to possibly the "biggest socio-political problem" now, the "pervasiveness of the corruption," but it again abstained from any policy discussion beyond the macroeconomic concerns.[99] In the 1981 CPP there was not even a passing reference to these matters.

An awareness of poverty and equity hovered over Kenyan policy discussions through the decade and occasionally broke through into the policy proposals and dialogues with the Kenyan government. Most of the time however, other pressing concerns seemed to justify postponing the issue. Also, instead of confronting the government on central distributive issues, particularly land tenure, the Bank chose to support what it saw as progressive stances on some social fronts. This was especially the case with Kenya's large rural development project effort, its strong

95. Memorandum, Shu-Chin Yang to files, "Kenya CPP: RVP Review Meeting, February 13, 1978."

96. Memorandum, Guenter H. Reif to K. Georg Gabriel, March 22, 1978, with attached "Kenya—Country Program Review Meeting, March 1, 1978."

97. Victor H. Umbricht of Switzerland, who became the principal mediator, described the process in *Multilateral Mediation: Practical Experiences and Lessons* (Boston: Martinus Nijhoff, 1989).

98. World Bank, "Country Program Paper: Kenya," June 18, 1979, with attached postscript, August 1, 1979.

99. World Bank, "Country Program Paper: Kenya," draft, December 18, 1980, para. 23.

population control effort, and the beginning of an environmental policy in the form of wildlife park conservation.

More generally, the Bank adopted a protective, tolerant, and supportive attitude to what it saw as a potential model performer in a region scourged by socialist experiments, political instability, and abysmal public administration. Kenya was credited with market policies, a comparatively enlightened leadership, seemingly tolerable levels of corruption, a strong group of technocrats, and considerable stability. The Kenyan government deflected incipient pressure with credible professions of distributive concern, particularly in 1973 and 1978–79. When the area department expressed strong concern about land concentration and lagging rural areas, external events in 1978—a second oil shock, the political succession, and the EAC breakup—intervened most pressingly to downgrade their urgency. A later interpretation would see much deterioration in the distributive situation during the 1970s, as corruption became ingrained, wealth became concentrated, and the limited focus of rural development projects left many of the rural poor unattended and were often ineffective even where they did exist. Nonetheless, Kenya did succeed in maintaining relatively good economic performance and in expanding its social services during that period.

India

Through the 1970s poverty and income distribution received little attention in the Bank's policy dialogues with Indian officials. The topics were sensitive, the relationship especially deferential, and the agenda crowded by political and financial crises and delays and shortcomings in project execution. In any case, the Bank's attitude had long been that India needed nudging *away* from distribution and *toward* production. And when McNamara pushed the Bank leftward, Mrs. Gandhi, elected in 1971 on an antipoverty platform, took India even further—measured by intentions—in the same direction.

On the whole, the Bank had little quarrel with what it saw as the progressive leaning of Indian policies. After a 1976 visit McNamara recorded that India's priorities were "sound, . . . mentioning agriculture, family planning, and energy self-sufficiency." In 1977 Stern, then vice president for South Asia, said: "There were now no major policy differences between the Bank and India." And after another visit in 1978, McNamara wrote: "In the ten years since I have been visiting India as President of the Bank there has been a dramatic change in the attitude of the political leaders, at all levels, towards the problem of poverty. . . . On . . . this latest visit, all were talking about the need to move or reduce it."[100]

100. On McNamara's view of India's priorities, see Stern's memorandum to files, December 9, 1976, which pertains to McNamara's visit to Mrs. Gandhi. Stern's 1977 statement is from N. Ramachandran, memorandum to files, "Proceedings of the RVP Review Meeting of October 26, 1977, on the India CPP," October 27, 1977. McNamara's remarks are from

Nonetheless, questions were continually raised within the Bank, if not with Indian officials. Telling colleagues that income distribution, unemployment, urbanization, and social problems "should command the urgent attention of the Area Department," in 1970 McNamara went on to request a paper on why land reform had not been implemented. And referring to a statistic in the CPP that more than 100 million persons earned less than thirty-two dollars a year, he asked several times how they were really surviving or what their future was. According to the minutes: "Nobody really seemed to know, so the subject was closed."[101] Eighteen months after Mrs. Gandhi's election, the CPP noted that "economic progress achieved during the last twenty years has not filtered down. . . . Disappointed expectations have, with the passage of time, added increasing urgency to the demand for greater social justice. . . . Under the slogan 'garibi hatao'—'abolish poverty'—Mrs. Gandhi committed her Government to respond to this demand."[102]

However, it continued, "this has not been done in any comprehensive fashion."[103] A year later the Bank noted that India's plans to raise consumption by the poorest 30 percent through subsidies were likely to face "formidable" practical and political difficulties and, "at best . . . to remain a futile theoretical exercise." There was a trace of ideology in that position: the Bank was especially objecting to the proposal for consumption-oriented subsidies, going on to say, on "redistribution-with-growth" lines, that "without expanded production . . . only poverty can be equitably distributed."[104] In a thoughtful note to McNamara, William Gilmartin set out to explain "the inhibitions which seem to beset Mrs. Gandhi and her Government." His starting point was the "gloomy panorama," a litany of "poor harvests . . . industrial shortages . . . [and] slow, uneven and poorly distributed agricultural development" and other woes. Furthermore, there was a "virtual paralysis of policy when it comes to . . . social justice . . . agrarian reform and agricultural taxation. . . . These are measures which run head-on into the interests of those who constitute the real power foundations of the Congress Party; the larger and better-off farmers and land owners of rural India." The Congress Party, he said, was a "government of kulaks."[105]

Hopes for more forceful implementation of the poverty agenda, including an ambitious Minimum Needs Program, were raised when Mrs. Gandhi declared a

---

Robert S. McNamara, "Notes on Visit to India, October 1–12, 1978," p. 4, in McNamara Contact Files.

101. Aide memoire, "Meeting on the CPP for India . . . ," August 12, 1970, p. 3.

102. IBRD/IFC, Economic Committee, "India: Country Program Paper, EC/O/72-95, August 17, 1972, p. 2.

103. Ibid., p. 2.

104. World Bank, "Country Program Paper—India," November 16, 1973, paras. 7, 8.

105. Memorandum, William M. Gilmartin to Robert McNamara, "Mrs. Gandhi's Economic Options and Political Inhibitions," November 1, 1973, pp. 1, 9. Arun Shourie made the same argument in "Growth, Poverty and Inequalities," *Foreign Affairs,* January 1973, pp. 340–52.

state of emergency giving herself extensive executive powers.[106] On the political implications of this act the CPP took a tolerant view, pointing out that though the emergency was "traumatic for the intelligentsia and for the opposition parties," it had a different meaning for the poor, for whom "the periodic right to vote" is hardly significant, given their "economic insecurity, subjection, and desperate want." Instead, under the emergency, "Mrs. Gandhi may use the opportunity to attempt to fulfill her pledge to 'abolish poverty.'" The CPP went on to note that important redistributive measures had already been promised: implementation of land ceilings and of minimum wage laws, abolition of bonded labor and cancellation of rural debt owed to moneylenders.[107] McNamara was further encouraged by Mrs. Gandhi's family planning program: "At long last India is moving to effectively address its population problem," he wrote, adding matter-of-factly that, initially, "sterilization will be the major contraceptive method," and that "the authorities believe that some form of pressure (sterilization laws, loss of government jobs, increase in the marriage age, compulsory abortion) will be required."[108]

This burst of reformist optimism was short lived. The emergency lasted less than two years. Mrs. Gandhi was voted out in March 1977, and the one "social" measure that her government pursued aggressively, the sterilization campaign, "was widely regarded as a key factor in the Congress [Party] defeat." The 1977 CPP predicted that under the new Janata government emphasis would shift to productivity and growth.[109] When McNamara visited India again in 1978 he saw a greater awareness of poverty but came away with many sad observations:

> The revolutionary changes needed to affect agricultural productivity, management of the environment and health and nutrition of the mass of the people have scarcely begun . . . the much-awaited rural transformation has not occurred . . . cooperatives have failed to flower. . . . The most anguishing plight is that of rural labor. . . . Agricultural laborers and marginal farmers (less than one acre) and their families may total 275 million people. No one in India sees clearly any satisfactory and early resolution of the circumstances of their profound misery. . . . Communalism . . . remains a troublesome element. . . . The ruling Janata Party is a weak coalition. . . . There is no sign that the Government of India recognizes the ineffectiveness of the present [population] strategy. . . . The corruption of political and economic power is said to be evident everywhere. . . . One is beginning to see a few modest steps . . . for example Maharashtra's guaranteed employment plan, Rajasthan's Antydaya [sic] Plan . . . and Mafatal's rural development scheme [but all] of these plans . . . will face the shocking rigidities of the social, political and economic structure, particularly that of caste. . . . To this day they prevent tens of millions of untouchables from using the same well which serves their fellow villagers.[110]

106. World Bank, "India: Country Program Paper," November 12, 1975, p. 2.
107. Ibid., pp. 2, 7.
108. Robert S. McNamara, "Notes on Visit to India, November 6–12, 1976," p. 3.
109. World Bank, "Country Program Paper: India," November 7, 1977, pp. 2, 11.
110. McNamara, "Notes on Visit to India, October 1–12, 1978," pp. 1–4.

Behind the disappointment on distributive policies lay a more general frustration. Discussing the 1972 CPP, Peter Cargill had said "we have no leverage on the Indians." Siem Aldewereld had agreed, saying that "the chances of success with the Indians were minimal and he was altogether very pessimistic."[111] A year later, and responding to a statement in the CPP that "our leverage to press for fundamental policy changes is limited, especially in view of the extreme sensitivities in India to any outside interference,"[112] McNamara opened the CPP review announcing that "he wanted to focus on policy. . . . Specifically, how do we exert policy influence on India, and in what area?" Cargill commented: "I fully share the desperation of the CPP. I would hate to be a loan officer for India because nothing ever happens." Knapp reasoned that "IDA lending levels are sacrosanct targets. Hence we may have locked ourselves in a position that impedes leverage," suggesting that "sector by sector, project by project, we should step up our leverage." But McNamara "expressed some doubt," saying "for example, Mrs. Gandhi cannot do anything about land reform, which is a political problem."[113] A 1978 retrospective on the Bank's economic and sector work by Peter Wright and Attila Karaosmanoglu gave a mixed review: despite the "extreme sensitivity" of Indian officials, "something of a policy dialogue does take place," and the Bank's economic and sector work makes "a silent contribution." Nevertheless, they said:

> India is a country very much set in its ways and there is little disposition on the part of the [government of India] to contemplate radical new departures in economic policy . . . senior officials see themselves as being increasingly hemmed in by political constraints . . . our impression [is] that they exercise less authority than . . . ten or fifteen years ago.[114]

On the substance of the Bank's work in India, the report contains a detailed discussion of many economic and sectoral topics but makes no mention of equity or poverty.

As Knapp suggested in 1973, influence was constrained by the Bank's own strong commitment to Indian aid. Chenery noted: "The generally held assumption that we are anxious to commit the annual tranche of IDA availabilities by the end of each fiscal year may limit our influence on Indian policy."[115] Underpinning that "anxiety" was the perennial assumption that India would stand or fall to the extent that its foreign exchange "gap" was or was not "filled." Chenery's own theorizing on

111. Memorandum, Alexis E. Lachman to John H. Adler, September 28, 1972, with attachment, "Notes on India CPP Meeting, September 18, 1972," p. 2.

112. World Bank, "Country Program Paper—India," October 29, 1973, p. 33.

113. Memorandum, Alexis E. Lachman to John H. Adler, December 5, 1973, with attached "India Country Program Review Meeting, November 30, 1973."

114. Memorandum, Peter Wright and Attila Karaosmanoglu to Hollis B. Chenery and David Hopper, December 20, 1978, with attached paper, "Evaluation of Economic and Sector Work in India," December 20, 1978, p. 23.

115. Memorandum, Hollis B. Chenery to Robert S. McNamara, "India Country Program Paper: Major Policy Issues," November 29, 1973, p. 2.

development, stressing inflexible foreign exchange and savings "constraints," reinforced that view.[116] In 1970 he had written that "India is the outstanding example of aid shortages contributing to reduced growth," and in 1972 he said that India's slow growth was "the result of a history of too little aid."[117] Few in the Bank would have put so much weight on aid availability: the more common view was that policies and institutions were the critical determinants of growth.[118] Yet when it came to balancing lending against policy insistence, the Bank acted *as if* foreign exchange assistance was critical, and therefore untouchable.

Going further, it was the concept of aid itself that seemed to become "sacrosanct" in India. When Mrs. Gandhi's government proposed to reduce net foreign aid to zero, aiming at "self-reliance," McNamara told M. G. Kaul, India's secretary of finance, that such a policy was "dangerous and counterproductive" and that "it was unrealistic to expect that India could be able to continue her development efforts at a reasonable pace without a positive transfer of foreign aid."[119] Yet aid barely amounted to 1 percent of Indian GNP during the decade and, by the Bank's own account, there was much room for improvement in Indian export and savings performance and for the substitution of domestic effort for foreign aid. Even Stern, a firm believer in the room for balance of payments adjustment and for the more efficient use of resources—as a general proposition—became an adjustment pessimist when confronted with the prospect of a reduction in India's IDA share to accommodate China's entry as an IDA borrower. Seeking to minimize the cut, he argued in 1980 that "India faces a large balance of payments gap," and that its "debt servicing capacity will deteriorate substantially in this decade."[120]

McNamara's forceful statement, scotching the idea of financial self-reliance, suggests that more was at stake than India's interest. Because of its size, democracy, cold war location, extreme poverty, and comparatively good administration, India had become the aid-advocate's best argument. Any criticism that downgraded India's image as a highly deserving borrower would have weakened the general

116. Chenery was a major contributor to what came to be known as "two-gap" models of development. These models, which downplayed the role of price mechanisms and of supply elasticities, helped to rationalize foreign aid, particularly during the 1960s.

117. Hollis B. Chenery, "Targets for Development," in Barbara Ward, J. D. Runnalls, and Lenore D'Anjou, eds., *The Widening Gap: Development in the 1970's* (Columbia University Press, 1971), p. 45. See also memorandum, Lachman to Adler, September 28, 1972.

118. Though it was consistent with his writings in the early 1960s on "two-gap" models of development, Chenery's statement on India was an exception to the more balanced position he was taking in the 1970s.

119. Memorandum, Jochen Kraske to files, "India—Mr. McNamara's Meeting with Mr. M. G. Kaul," August 16, 1973, p. 2.

120. Memorandum, Ernest Stern to Robert S. McNamara, December 12, 1980. He saw only two choices: "a further reduction in the rate of growth"; or "substantial borrowing from supplier credits and private banks." Balance of payments adjustment, as an alternative, was not mentioned.

case for development assistance. A "self-reliant" India would have been even more damaging, turning into a striking, reverse argument against the need for aid (or, for that matter, for a "development establishment"). As it turned out, the oil crisis almost immediately made the proposal—and McNamara's reaction—academic. From the beginning of his presidency McNamara had taken on the role of spokesman for the aid and development effort as a whole and it is in that capacity, as keeper of the larger development assistance enterprise, that his repeated concessions to India's "sensitivities" as well as his vehement insistence on its "need" for aid can more easily be understood. India's assigned role as an aid showcase thus added to the constraints that hemmed in the capacity to press for policy change.

Bangladesh

Independence in 1971 was followed by years of economic and political disruption. A reluctant Bank was forced into what Knapp in 1974 called a "relief" role.[121] The situation in Bangladesh was "heart-rending," he said. Performance on Bank loans "is unquestionably poor and donors feel they are caught in the web of circumstances." McNamara said he "was disheartened," and that "Providing emergency relief was not our business." Cargill defended Bangladesh, pointing out that little more could be expected in the way of project performance after the personnel losses caused by the civil war. "What aid we give," he added, "will need to be on humanitarian grounds."[122] A year later Knapp worried that IDA's "humanitarian" lending to Bangladesh could damage IDA's image at a time when the Bank had begun to negotiate a "replenishment," or new commitment of funds to IDA by donors. In 1976, to deal with the problem of continued and undisciplined large-scale program lending to Bangladesh, McNamara proposed an innovation that anticipated future adjustment loans: he "insisted on such lending being conditioned (in writing in a Fund type agreement) on basic macro economic policy variables that are measurable." Stern quashed the idea. "He felt we could deal with macro policies outside the context of program lending."[123] His preference was to

121. The Bank had played an unusually supportive role in East Pakistan's first steps to independence. In 1968 it began to point out to Pakistani authorities that resource allocation discriminated against East Pakistan. Memorandum, Robert S. McNamara for the record, May 9, 1968. After rebellion broke out in the East, the Bank bravely spoke out on subsequent acts of destruction and cruelty by West Pakistan forces, and led a donor suspension of aid to West Pakistan.

122. Memorandum, N. Ramachandran to John H. Adler, "Meeting of Review Group—Bangladesh," November 7, 1974, with attachment, "Bangladesh Country Program Review Meeting, November 6, 1974."

123. Memorandum, G. Zaidan to John H. Adler, "Meeting of the Review Group: Bangladesh," November 29, 1976, with attachment, "Bangladesh Country Program Review Meeting, November 24, 1976." Stern added that, though "the Bengalis could prepare a macro plan if we asked them to; he remained skeptical that tying this to a program loan would make

continue to struggle for policy influence and project discipline within the context of traditional program and project loans.

Poverty and equity appeared only briefly and late in the decade in Bangladesh policy reviews within the Bank, and there is no record of such discussions with the government. The 1977 CPP noted the challenge posed by large-scale landlessness (37 percent of the rural population), population growth, and acute malnutrition, a condition that begged for more direct solutions than those of "redistribution with growth."[124] Ul Haq unsuccessfully pressed McNamara on the subject, citing a USAID study that "agrarian reform had not been implemented effectively . . . [and] that Bangladesh is not the nation of smallholders that had generally been assumed, but is characterized more by insecure tenancy and large scale landlessness."[125] The topic was raised again in 1980, in an unusually penetrating discussion of local political structures:

> Villages seem to be divided into several factions. . . . The factions each appear to be headed by a better-off village member and include dependents loyal to the faction leader based upon his providing protection, access to Government benefits, loans and other financial support. In this atmosphere of factional competition, efforts to form village wide institutions (such as cooperatives) are likely to fail; those in control of a pump may be unwilling to share the water with farmers belonging to another faction.[126]

An independent study found that benefits from Bank-financed tubewells were almost entirely appropriated by local elites, but, the authors state, their findings failed to move Bank officials.[127] From the heights of Washington, the distinction between "village poor" and "village elites" has often seemed a quibble. Yet the obstacle in this case was probably less unawareness of politics and institutions than jadedness and frustration produced by past efforts; it was to some extent a backlash to the apparent failure of attempts to intervene in rural institutions, most notably the Comilla approach. The 1974 CPP stated: "Efforts to ensure the development of rural institutions have faced severe difficulties. The three interconnected programs which constituted the core of the rural development approach pioneered at Comilla . . . had all ground to a halt before independence and have been in disarray ever since."[128] The importance of local organizations and political structures—and the will to tackle them—would be discovered anew by the Bank a decade or more later.

---

a difference." Three years later Stern helped to design the first macroconditioned structural adjustment loans.

124. World Bank, "Country Program Paper: Bangladesh," n.d., 1977, pp. 7–8.

125. Memorandum, Mahbub ul Haq to Robert S. McNamara, "Bangladesh CPP: Major Policy Issues," January 12, 1978. The USAID report referred to was "Report on the Hierarchy of Interest of Land in Bangladesh," September 1977.

126. World Bank, "Country Program Papers: Bangladesh," draft, March 5, 1980, p. 20.

127. Betsy Hartmann and James K. Boyce, *A Quiet Violence: View from a Bangladesh Village* (London: Zed Press, 1983), p. 265. The authors met with the acting head for South Asia operations at the Bank in January 1979.

128. World Bank, "Country Program Paper—Bangladesh," October 16, 1974, annex, p. 2.

In the 1970s, however, conversations with Bangladeshi officials were over-whelmingly concerned with raising total production and with improving the im-plementation of investment projects. Those two objectives seemed to become one: the financial rescue of Bangladesh and the protection of IDA's reputation. Both directed attention to the project pipeline—to achieve compelling IDA disburse-ment targets, and to ensure that, in design and execution, IDA projects would be seen to be "productive" rather than "relief" operations. With an entire country—and IDA—in the balance, whether project benefits went to those at the bottom of the ladder or to those a few rungs up became a perfectionist detail.

Chile

Chile was the scene of dramatic experiments in social policy during the decade: Allende's massive redistribution (1970–73) was followed by severe wage repression and cuts in social spending (1974–79); the latter stage was in turn overlapped and gradually succeeded by a new, highly targeted welfare policy. It seems extraordi-nary, then, that distributive policy was almost entirely absent in the Bank's policy dialogue with that country.

The Bank was certainly unprepared for such a dialogue. Reviewing Chilean prospects in July 1970, three months before Allende's election, McNamara predicted that Chile would be a paradigm for the scenario that he was incubat-ing and that would later be called "redistribution-with-growth": a future of smooth, consensual sharing in growth. "He considered the degree of social consensus being achieved in Chile to augur well for the long-run stability of the country, especially by comparison with other countries where the longer-run sig-nificance of current economic gains was uncertain because of the lack of progress toward building a national consensus on social and political issues."[129] Instead, distributive policymaking took Chile into political extremes, bloodshed, and economic extravaganza.

A year after Allende's unexpected election, and after a major land reform, wage increases, health care expansion and other energetic though disorderly redistribu-tive measures, a Bank mission reported on macroeconomic prospects but offered no commentary or advice on Allende's social objectives, nor on how they could be pursued without destabilizing the economy.[130] Except for two small loans nego-tiated but not approved until after the coup, the Bank did not finance Allende's government (see chapter 15). In a private memorandum to McNamara, Mahbub ul Haq criticized that posture:

129. World Bank, "Country Program Paper: Chile: Postscript," July 13, 1970. McNamara left no room for the accident of electoral arithmetic, which allowed the election of a revolutionary with only 36 percent of the vote.

130. "Chile Mission Back to Office Report," December 17, 1971. The mission visited Chile during September and October 1971.

We failed to support the basic objectives of the Allende regime, either in our reports or publicly. If we had done that, we could have been freer to make the legitimate point that "economic" costs of these objectives were unnecessarily high and could be reduced by proper economic management. We could have gone further and shown what set of economic policies would have been consistent with these objectives. Instead we mumbled about exchange rates, fiscal balance and price distortions, without ever trying to establish a link between our theology and Allende's concerns.[131]

Lending recommenced after the September 1973 coup but from 1974 to 1979 amounted to only $127 million. Relations with Chile continued to threaten IDA, this time because the Carter administration joined European governments to object to the country's record on human rights. In July 1976 McNamara stated that "high level U.S. sources had informed him that there was some opposition to Chilean lending within the American Administration and that a favorable U.S. vote on Chile was not assured. Even assuming American support . . . the vote on Chile would produce a divisive split at the Board and be harmful to the Bank's capital increase and IDA replenishment initiatives."[132]

Internal opposition was expressed by ul Haq, who proposed that lending be postponed until the Bank was "reasonably satisfied that the Pinochet Government's development strategy is not merely restoring the unstable elitist economic society that had led to the upheaval in Chile in the first place." But colleagues showed little sympathy for ul Haq's concerns about the "prohibitive" cost of the stabilization program "for the poorer classes" or his allegation that it had "worsened the country's distribution of income."[133] The charges brought a heated defense of lending, and by implication, of the junta's policies, from Adalbert Krieger, the regional vice president. Policy remained as described in a 1974 memorandum: "The need to transfer resources is the overriding element in the proposed strategy."[134] Nonetheless, lending remained small, and by not being more supportive at that time of need, the Bank lost the opportunity to exercise leverage.[135]

In 1978 internal reviews began to criticize Chilean social policies and to propose intervention in that field. The 1978 CPP stated hopefully: "A resumption of lending

131. Mahbub ul Haq, "The Bank's Mistakes in Chile," April 26, 1976, p. 2. A copy sent by McNamara to Chenery contained a handwritten note asking, "How do you propose to use?" suggesting a seminar. The following day, however, McNamara changed his mind; Chenery received a note from McNamara's assistant saying, with respect to Haq's memorandum, "McNamara said to ignore."

132. Memorandum, F. J. Aguirrre-Sacasa to files, "Chile—CPP Management Review," July 20, 1976, p. 2.

133. Memorandum, Mahbub ul Haq to Robert S. McNamara, "Chile Country Program Paper—Majority Policy Issues," July 12, 1976.

134. Memorandum, Robert Armstrong to John H. Adler, "Chile CPP—RVP Draft," November 13, 1974, p. 2.

135. Memorandum, ul Haq to McNamara, July 12, 1976. Ul Haq's statement was in direct contradiction with McNamara's favorable diagnosis of pre-Allende Chile, cited earlier.

would lay the basis for a constructive dialogue with the members of the economic team aimed at causing them to adopt policies which would better blend their primary concern with growth and efficiency with the Bank's own views on equity." But Bank leverage was now diminished by past hesitation, by Chile's strong economic recovery, and by the willingness of commercial banks "to oblige."[136] In fact, Chile's finance minister, Sergio de Castro, refused to borrow from the Bank over 1978–79.

In the event, Chile, on its own, fashioned two model social policy innovations, both contributing to what became a powerful safety net through some fifteen years of severe recession. First, an extensive "minimum employment program" (Programa de Empleo Minimo) that at its peak provided a minimum wage to 13.5 percent of the labor force.[137] The second took the form of welfare targeting—taken to an extreme degree. The health policy in particular almost exclusively emphasized primary care for mothers and small children. During this time of economic crisis infant mortality in Chile fell from 82 per thousand live births in 1970 to 24 in 1982. The minimum employment program traded safety-net effectiveness for productivity—the unemployed were receiving income long before their labor could be put to truly productive uses—though it gradually moved toward a more effective use of work gangs and even to combining employment with training programs. In the same way, the severe targeting of health and education tended to transform these services from human capital investments into purely welfare programs.[138] Both innovations raised eyebrows at the Bank, where acceptable social policies, even in the late 1970s, continued to exclude transfers or pure redistribution, though a decade later it would embrace the safety-net concept. If the Bank was unable to influence Chilean social programs, it seemed both unwilling and unable to object to the broader policy changes that had major long-run distributive consequences. Chile's new economic growth model, in effect, traded an increase in poverty and inequality for faster growth.[139]

Philippines

President Ferdinand Marcos of the Philippines was an especially successful negotiator. American bases, communist insurgency, and well-cultivated political

136. Proposed modifications to Chile CPP, distributed in memorandum from Francisco Aguirre-Sacasa, "Chile—Regional Vice President's Review of the CPP," December 5, 1978, paras. 60g, 78, 81. The Bank's "own views," however, evolved, and a decade later were giving high marks to Chilean distributive targeting.

137. Dagmar Raczynski and Pilar Romaguera, "Chile: Poverty, Adjustment, and Social Policies in the 1980s," in Nora Lustig, ed., Coping with Austerity: Poverty and Inequality in Latin America (Brookings Institution, 1995), table 8-5, p. 285.

138. Ibid., pp. 306, 310–15.

139. Poverty increased *before* government transfers but was substantially reduced *after* transfers. Household spending by the poorest quintile fell 40 percent between 1969 and 1988 and rose 24 percent in the richest quintile. Different sources agree that poverty increased between 1970 and 1990. Ibid., pp. 286–90.

support in the United States gave him a strong hand, and he was a persuasive influencer. For well over a decade he obtained continually renewed support while parrying the Bank's persistent and emphatic insistence on the need for "social reforms."

Opening the decade, a 1970 review of the Philippines stated: "the Bank, in further negotiations with the Government, will place great emphasis on more adequate public revenues and on the whole complex of corruption, inefficiency and social inequities."[140] McNamara continued to press the issue in 1971. He proposed a cut in IDA lending because "he was not all persuaded that the Philippines had performed. . . . He cited specifically endemic corruption and income distribution."[141]

The following year Bank policy toward the Philippines was prepared against an uncertain political background: Marcos had suspended the writ of habeas corpus, seen the opposition win a surprise victory in off-year Senate elections, and survived an assassination attempt. Above all, Marcos "now seems preoccupied with retaining effective control after the Presidential elections of 1973," not being allowed to succeed himself. The annual policy review went to some length in identifying and analyzing the roots of inequality in the Philippines. Yet it saw room for hope: "Nearly all sections of society—including the ruling oligarchy—are beginning to recognize that something must be done to break down the economic gulf between rich and poor." Indeed, the principal critic seemed to be Marcos himself:

> I come to speak of a society so sick it must either be cured and cured now or be buried in a deluge of reforms [a] political system corrupted by a social and economic order that is best described as oligarchic. . . . The freest government cannot long endure when the tendency of the law is to create rapid accumulation of wealth and property for a few and to render the masses poor and dependent.[142]

What especially seemed to persuade the Bank was his team of "able and dedicated" technocrats: "to President Marcos' credit . . . he has retained his team of tech-nocrats despite his political pre-occupations."[143]

When the CPP was finally reviewed by McNamara and senior management in July 1972, the entire "reform" issue was dropped. The minutes state:

> A rather surprising meeting! No more of the criticism of earlier years (politics, corruption, income inequality), but a rather general feeling that we should increase our lending program. And a flabbergasted Area Department trying to defend the cautious position taken in the CPP! The order of the day is to work within the system. (Politics not necessarily worse than in Thailand but more publicized.) . . . [W]e should aim to lend on average $120 million a year in FY74–78, 50% more than proposed.[144]

140. World Bank, "Notes on Philippines Country Program Review Meeting, August 12, 1970."
141. World Bank, "Notes on the Philippines CPP Meeting, August 12, 1971."
142. World Bank, "Country Program Paper: Philippines," July 1972, pp. 2–3.
143. Ibid., p. 3.
144. World Bank, "Notes on the Philippines Country Program Review, July 28, 1972," prepared by H. Schulmann on August 15, 1972.

Two months later Marcos declared martial law. Military and police spending began to multiply, tripling in real terms between 1971 and 1977. H. W. Brands, citing U.S. Ambassador David Newsom, wrote: "Until the onset of martial law Marcos' greed had not seemed exceptional. . . . But beginning in the mid-1970s it grew to breath-taking proportions." A Filipino legacy of this period was the term "crony capitalism." Newsom wrote of the dilemma of working with "essentially Machiavellian, authoritarian Filipino leaders."[145]

At the moment, however, what was visible and impressive to the Bank was that long-postponed tax measures, land reform and other "important and potentially far-reaching" reforms were approved, respected technocrats were empowered, the investment climate improved, and the economy boomed. Extrapolating from these achievements, the regional staff speculated hopefully that people seemed "prepared to give President Marcos an opportunity," and that "however much one regrets the demise of representative government . . . there can be no doubt that the Philippines now has a stronger government that is giving a firmer sense of purpose and direction to economic development. . . . [T]he Philippines is now in a better position to tackle its deep-seated economic and social problems."[146] McNamara endorsed this hopeful attitude. Summarizing the senior management review, the rapporteur editorialized: "A miracle has occurred in the Philippines. Philosophically, it is distressing, however, that the miracle occurred under the auspices of a military dictatorship. Mr. Cargill said he didn't believe the miracle would continue, 'but while it does,' interjected Mr. McNamara, 'and only as long as it does, let us continue to support it.'"[147] A year later McNamara continued to insist that he "wanted to press ahead while the going was good."[148]

Doubts and worries began to arise after the mid-1970s, but the Bank's commitment was not easily reversed. The 1976 Annual General Meeting was held in Manila and, to coincide with the meeting, the Bank prepared a supportive economic report on the Philippines. That year the regional vice president, Bernard Bell, brushed aside worries concerning political stability and risk to the Bank arising from continuing poverty and inequality: "Mr. Bell said that the risk in lending to the Philippines was lower than for Malaysia or Korea."[149] By 1978,

145. H. W. Brands, *Bound to Empire: The United States and the Philippines* (Oxford University Press, 1992). Brands cites a U.S. Embassy April 1983 study that documented the acquisition of control over private firms by government-controlled agencies by means such as tax-financed "rescue" operations. Boards of acquired firms were then filled with Marcos's cabinet members and their relatives (p. 313).

146. World Bank, "Country Program Paper: Philippines," December 4, 1973, pp. 2–3.

147. Memorandum, Alexis E. Lachman to John H. Adler, December 27, 1973, with attachment, "Philippines Country Program Review, December 19, 1973."

148. World Bank, "Philippines Special Program Review Meeting, July 22, 1974," dated July 31, 1974.

149. Memorandum, G. Zaidan to John H. Adler, June 15, 1976, with attachment, "Philippines Country Program Review Meeting, June 4, 1976."

however, a more forceful objection surfaced from the Bank's Policy Review Department: "Wealth and income inequalities remain large. . . . The Marcos Government, though ostensibly committed to poverty redressal, appears to be making haste slowly."[150] Management agreed "to urge the Government to tackle basic poverty issues more vigorously."[151] As McNamara's term ended, however, Heinz Vergin wrote him to say that in the Philippines, by comparison with the Bank's influence on industrial policies, its "impact on policies relating to poverty alleviation is less obvious."[152] Ul Haq put it more clearly: "The real question mark is the seriousness and commitment with which the Philippines authorities intend to implement poverty alleviation."[153] Some continued to argue that Marcos had sought to modernize and improve equity but had been defeated by an oligarchical economic and political establishment.[154] By this time, though, the Philippines had been overtaken by stabilization problems and the Bank had begun to emphasize "the urgent need for structural adjustment."[155]

Tanzania

In Tanzania, honest and selfless leadership proved as entrapping as the Machiavellian variety. The regime's moral tone provided a justification for McNamara to once again bet on the powers of authority to remake society. The Bank became strongly committed to Nyerere's communal socialism and welfare schemes.

In 1973 the Bank's loyalty was enthusiastic: "Tanzania is making genuine rural progress . . . [and] deserves every encouragement and support. We are inclined to give Tanzania an excellent performance rating. "[156] But soon loyalty was expressing itself as a plea for patience: a subsequent review saw administrative problems but insisted that President Nyerere "is a pragmatist at heart," and that "in judging Tanzania's economic performance it is important to bear in mind that the country is 'traversing' to new forms of social and economic organization which it is hoped will stimulate the growth of GNP and improve its distribution in the long term."[157] Questions regarding the centerpiece of Nyerere's rural program—"ujamma," or

150. Memorandum, P. Landell-Mills and J. McGibbon to Russell Cheetham, "Philippines CPP: RVP Review Meeting," May 8, 1978

151. World Bank, "Country Program Paper: Philippines: Postscript," June 30, 1978.

152. Memorandum, Heinz Vergin to Robert S. McNamara, "Philippines CPP—Outstanding Policy and Program Issues," April 1, 1981.

153. Memorandum, Mahbub ul Haq to Robert S. McNamara, "Philippines CPP: Major Policy Issues," April 6, 1981.

154. Russel Cheetham interview with the authors, February 5, 1992. Jeanne Fitzpatrick, in Brands, Bound to Empire.

155. Memorandum, Heinz Vergin to Robert S. McNamara, "Philippines CPP—Outstanding Policy and Program Issues," April 2, 1981.

156. World Bank, "Country Program Note: Tanzania," draft, February 12, 1973, pp. 6, 15.

157. World Bank, "Country Program Paper: Tanzania," draft, March 14, 1974, pp. 2–3.

forced, large-scale resettlement of rural inhabitants into villages—were put aside by the 1975 country review: "It is too early to say whether the villagization . . . will contribute to agricultural productivity, but the potential is there."[158]

By 1978 the weaknesses of the Tanzanian model were fully evident, as Nyerere openly recognized.[159] This only served to strengthen the argument for continuing support: Tanzania's "impressive" qualities, such as its "moral and determined leadership" and "emphasis on growth with equity," were now boosted by "increasing pragmatism," "willingness . . . to make difficult political decisions," and to admit the "country's mistakes and failures." This combination of moral virtue and pragmatism, said Bank officials, "promised the economic success of Tanzania's 'African Socialist' framework."[160]

A retrospective review by the Operations Evaluation Department criticized that commitment: the Bank had failed "to communicate its concerns over policies" and had "abandoned the position of an 'honest broker' and of an impartial expert. By becoming a quasi-partner of the Government, the Bank had to temper its opposition."[161] Ironically, the term "partnership" was often the Bank's way of describing its role in a positive sense.[162] Partnership implies commitment and certainly "tempering of opposition" rather than an intrusive and disciplinarian use of aid. The developer's dilemma between patient fostering of borrower capacities and "ownership," on the one hand, and prompt correction of "errors," on the other, was magnified by the scale of Nyerere's plans for social and economic change. The initial decision to support so ambitious an experiment carried a longer-term commitment and a higher degree of risk than with less ambitious government programs. Looking back it seems clear that a withdrawal of support at the first signs of trouble would have reduced the costs of the experiment. But rapid withdrawal would also have been inconsistent with the Bank's initial approval of Tanzania's plan to create a model of African socialism.

Sri Lanka

The Bank's objection to nonproductive transfers was at the center of its difficult interaction with Sri Lanka. When the relationship was reviewed in 1990 by the OED, the report stated that "Sri Lanka may be unique among mixed economies in achieving a massive transfer of resources from the elite to the poor."[163] From its

158. World Bank, "Country Note on Tanzania CPP," May 19, 1975.

159. Julius K. Nyerere, *The Arusha Declaration Ten Years After* (Dar es Salaam: Government Printer, 1977).

160. World Bank, "Country Program Paper: Tanzania," draft, January 5, 1978, p. 22.

161. OED, "Tanzania: World Bank–Tanzania Relations 1961–1987," Report 8329, January 16, 1990, vol. 1, pp. 41, 55.

162. The Bank-inspired Pearson Commission Report was titled "Partners in Development."

163. OED, "The World Bank and Sri Lanka. A Review of a Relationship," Report 6074, February 24, 1986, p. 5. The study was directed by Professor Gustav Papanek.

independence in 1948, Ceylon (Sri Lanka from 1972) set out to ratify and strengthen the social welfare policies already in place under British rule, reducing death rates, illiteracy, and malnutrition to an extent that rivaled that of much richer countries. By the 1970s, according to the OED, "Sri Lanka began to be cited as the outstanding example of a country that came close to meeting its people's basic needs." Yet Bank lending and influence in Sri Lanka was small until the late 1970s. Obstacles included the nationalization of foreign assets, nationalistic sensitivity, lack of fiscal discipline, and, famously, Sri Lanka's expensive policy of subsidizing the consumer price of rice.

The rice subsidy was already drawing attention in 1953 when John Exter, an American expatriate governor of the Central Bank of Ceylon wrote Eugene Black: "By all odds the most important factor has been the food subsidies. . . . For more than two years now food subsidies have eaten up at least about 18% of current revenue and at most about 35% . . . this policy has been suicidal. . . . Your mission recommended gradual elimination. This information is still highly secret in Ceylon, but the decision has now been taken to eliminate the subsidies completely on July 1."[164] In the event, the subsidy was only temporarily reduced; it lived on as a continuing bone of contention with the Bank.[165] During the early 1970s the Bank's attitude to Sri Lanka was at a nadir, following the 1970 election of Mrs. Sirimavo Bandaranaike after a campaign in which Bank conditionality had been a major issue. In 1972 Cargill said that he had "no expectation the Ceylonese government will take any of the steps it ought to be taking"; Knapp referred to "Ceylon's dismal performance"; and said that "the country is on the dole and a caretaker program is needed"; Aldewereld "was very negative on any assistance"; and McNamara said that "Ceylon is politically sick . . . [its] economy is shot through with wrong incentives . . . [but] if we walk away, bankruptcy and default might ensue."[166] Token lending continued. As William Diamond put it in 1974, "For several years, we have held to a 'wait and see' position towards Sri Lanka and have restricted lending to one small project a year, whose principal purpose was to maintain our dialogue."[167] He explained the Bank's rationale:

164. Letter, John Exter to Eugene R. Black, May 15, 1953. Exter began his personally typed letter explaining that his delay in replying was "because I have not felt free to dictate some of these things to a Ceylonese stenographer." Much care was taken to avoid the appearance of Bank imposition. Exter pointed to the "opposition by poorly informed people who fear onerous and unacceptable conditions, or who regard the Bank as the opening wedge of American imperialism."

165. From independence, power seesawed between the free-enterprise "Conservative" UNP and the Fabian Socialist or Freedom Party (SLFP). Bank lending was strongly associated with UNP terms in office. Yet the rice subsidy was created by the UNP, during its first government (1947–56).

166. Memorandum, Alexis E. Lachman to John H. Adler, "Meeting of the Review Group on Ceylon," May 24, 1972, with attachment, "Notes on Ceylon Country Program Review Meeting, May 18, 1972."

167. Memorandum, William Diamond to Robert S. McNamara, "Sri Lanka . . . ," May 29, 1974.

[Sri Lankan] policies, while they may have promoted income equality, also had the effect of inhibiting growth and thus, in due course, undermining the beneficial effects of improved income equality. In particular, the budget was weighed down by heavy consumer subsidies (including a free food ration). . . . We have repeatedly discussed these matters with the Government in the course of a continuing dialogue going back almost ten years . . . aid to Sri Lanka could be recommended only on humanitarian and political, not on economic grounds.[168]

A year later, Sri Lanka's general performance still "disappointed Mr. McNamara very much," and "Mr. Knapp asked whether Sri Lanka's access to Arab and Iranian money was undermining our leverage." Consortium contributions to Sri Lanka, said Knapp, were "'give-away money' which the Bank should not do."[169]

In 1976 a Bank official reflected on the unsatisfactory relationship: the Bank's attitude had "fluctuated," and despite "a consensus" on the need for drastic change in financial policies, the government "resisted any policy change, and in any case, lacked the political capacity" for economic reform.[170] The Bank, in turn, had failed to find a formula that combined stable growth with equity:

Sri Lanka continues to be a challenge for the Bank. . . . If as an institution, the Bank has acquired expertise in dealing with foreign exchange, fiscal and monetary and investment policies in growth oriented economy, little has yet been gained in combining the macro-economic analysis and employment generation with social justice. We should make a special attempt . . . to help the Government to put together a development strategy within the framework of its social objectives.[171]

Chenery defended lending, noting that Sri Lanka's performance was considerably better than Tanzania's, which he considered the relevant comparison, and yet support given Tanzania was much higher.[172] The inconsistency spotted by Chenery stands out more clearly in a later perspective. Sri Lanka's annual economic growth per capita between 1960 and 1978 was far from "dismal": at 2.0 percent, it exceeded the average for all low-income countries (1.6 percent). And despite its "suicidal" fiscal policies, inflation remained relatively low, at 9.5 percent a year over 1965–80.[173] Moreover, growth accelerated in the late 1970s and 1980s, in part as a result of policy improvements but presumably also helped by the substantial

168. Memorandum, William Diamond to Robert S. McNamara (through Mervyn L. Weiner), "Sri Lanka—Aid Group Meeting and Bank Posture," May 1, 1974.

169. Memorandum, George Zaidan to John H. Adler, "Meeting of the Review Group: Sri Lanka," May 28, 1975, with attachment, "Sri Lanka Country Program Review Meeting, May 21, 1975."

170. Memorandum, M. Devaux to Mahbub ul Haq, "Sri Lanka CPP-RVP Review Meeting," June 10, 1976, p. 1.

171. Ibid., p. 2.

172. Memorandum, G. Zaidan to John H. Adler, "Meeting of the Review Group: Sri Lanka," July 21, 1976.

173. World Bank, *World Development Report 1980*.

population control efforts and human capital investments of the 1960s and 1970s. For the longer period 1965–86, Sri Lanka's per capita growth was 2.9 percent, exceeding that of most countries that received strong Bank support.[174] With more opposition than support from the Bank, Sri Lanka sustained a commendable and balanced equity, welfare, and growth performance over two decades.

Poverty Lending

When the Bank set out to "eradicate" poverty, its greatest hopes were placed on bringing about more enlightened, caring, and equitable behavior by its borrowers; but the day-to-day effort in this campaign was dedicated for the most part to its own "poverty projects." These were understood as investments in which the distribution of benefits would especially favor the poor. Though the search for investments that would reach the poor directly led the Bank to explore a wide spectrum of activities, most poverty lending in practice came to be concentrated in two areas: agriculture and urban water supplies.

The term "poverty lending" came to be identified principally with rural develop-ment projects for poor farmers, housing and infrastructure services for the urban poor, credits to small enterprises, health components in other projects, and with a few other small projects whose benefits could be targeted to bring about a direct increase in the productivity and income of the very poor. Most of these projects were thought of as innovations and sometimes described as "new-style" projects; "poverty projects" were indeed designed and redesigned almost continuously through the decade as the Bank sought to overcome implementation problems and to improve their targeting. Progress in the poverty war came to be equated with the volume and innovative character of this specialized subset of the Bank's overall lending activity.

Note, however, that the unusual attention given to those projects and the very term "poverty lending" have been a source of confusion regarding the Bank's contribution to poverty reduction. That contribution, per dollar invested, was surely enhanced by the more direct flow of benefits to the poor in the case of such projects—that is, when they were successful as investments—but the larger volume of Bank lending that continued to be made up of economic infrastructure and support for development finance companies did not cease to make a contribu-tion to economic growth, and so indirectly, to poverty alleviation. What the first achieved through better targeting the second to some extent made up through larger volume, and perhaps, better project performance. In addition, and though

174. For instance, per capita growth rates over 1965–86 were Colombia, 2.8; Mexico, 2.6; Turkey, 2.7; Pakistan, 2.4; India, 1.8; Kenya, 1.9; Tanzania, -0.3; and Chile, -0.2. Sri Lanka's life expectancy in 1986 was seventy years, almost equal to that of Chile (seventy-one). See World Bank, *World Development Report 1988*, table 1, pp. 222–23.

this also tended to be ignored in the attention given to the "new-style" projects, the poverty contribution of traditional lending was on balance increased during this period, usually through simple locational and design changes that left them short of the "poverty project" category but nonetheless provided a further boost to the overall effort. "Poverty lending"—in the stricter sense that became the Bank's usage—should be understood as a reflection of the importance that such lending took on for the institution itself. *Visible* poverty alleviation was becoming increasingly important to the funding of IDA through the decade, and, one suspects, to institutional self-justification and motivation. Beyond the Bank, the visibility of poverty projects took on a symbolic role for the development cause in general. This is not to deny, however, the considerable role played by the Bank's other lending and developmental activities.

The widely shared perception that equated poverty alleviation with "poverty projects" was reflected in a thorough account of that project effort published by Robert Ayres in 1983.[175] The Bank's own retrospective report, *Focus on Poverty*, also concentrated on "poverty projects" in the strict sense, but reminded readers that indirect poverty reduction not be disregarded:

> There has been a tendency in the Bank in recent years to describe projects in these growing sectors and subsectors as "poverty" lending, and the rest as "non-poverty" lending. This has been useful shorthand for suggesting degrees of emphasis on activities especially likely to benefit poor people. It should be used carefully, however, as it would be misleading to imply that only selected sectors or programs have a significant impact on poverty. It also tends to downplay the often important direct and indirect effects of other sectors and programs.[176]

According to that report, poverty lending made up about one-quarter of the Bank's lending between 1968 and 1981. The proportion rose through the decade, from 5 percent in 1968–70 to 29.5 percent in 1979–81. Small-farmer projects accounted for about 55 percent, water supply and sewerage for 25 percent, other urban poverty loans for 10 percent. What would later come to be called human resource investments—primary schooling, health, nutrition, and population—accounted for 7 percent.[177]

These statistics, however, are approximations because "poverty project" was never an exact or official category, except, for a time, in the case of agriculture.[178]

175. Robert L. Ayres, *Banking on the Poor: The World Bank and World Poverty* (MIT Press, 1983).

176. World Bank, *Focus on Poverty: A Report by a Task Force of the World Bank* (World Bank, 1982), pp. 3–4. The task force was created in September 1981 and headed by Alexander Shakow.

177. Three-year averages of the share of Bank and IDA lending to "Directly Poverty Oriented Sectors" provided in ibid., table 2, p. 24, are 1968–70, 5.0 percent; 1971–73, 15.3 percent; 1976–78, 27.4 percent; 1978–81, 29.5 percent.

178. An agricultural project in which 50 percent or more of the direct benefits were expected to accrue to the rural poor was called a "rural development project," a term which,

Which schools, water and sewage facilities, roads, family planning services, or urban transport improvements were classified as poverty projects was left to judgment and a measure of bureaucratic expedience. This definitional imprecision—who was "poor" and who got project benefits—was an early signal of the difficulties that the Bank was taking on when it established poverty reduction as an independent criterion for evaluating projects.

The criterion for poverty lending became stricter under McNamara. When the Bank had first moved away from its most bankable infrastructure or industrial loans, the term "social" was used to describe and justify agricultural lending in general, all education and water supply projects, and even, at times, infrastructure that was not self-financing, such as roads.[179] But as the Bank refined its statistical measures of income distribution and ventured closer to very poor beneficiaries in some projects, the clearer it became that much of what the Bank had considered "social" lending had benefited middle- and upper-income groups rather than the poor. On the other hand, statistics on poverty lending published during the 1970s undoubtedly contain an upward bias caused by McNamara's rigid lending program targets and by bureaucratic incentives to show that targets were being met.

The enterprise was characterized by both enthusiasm and contentiousness. Its supporters, concentrated in new organizational enclaves—Development Policy Staff and the Rural Development and Urban Projects departments—were dismissive of the Bank's traditional work, confident of their revolutionary program, and zealous in its execution. According to Mervyn Weiner, "There was an insulation of ideas and influence between the side of the Bank in which [Chenery and ul Haq] operated and the side of the Bank where the Bank's day-to-day business was being done."[180] The larger and older Bank, which notwithstanding the 1972 reorganization continued to hold the spending levers in its hands, tended to disguise rather than overcome its skepticism. Not surprisingly, in their project-finding missions they were quick to see difficulties in proposed poverty loans and to endorse the objections of local officials. Moreover, many of their fears were soon realized; poverty lending proved itself complex, slow, and costly in terms of departmental administrative budgets. Pressed to avoid project slippages and meet departmental lending targets, officials who in any case felt an intuitive reluctance against poverty projects now had personal reasons to object to—and sometimes evade—projects that consumed an exaggerated share of their time and resources.

As with all its lending, what the Bank sought through poverty loans was much more than a direct capital transfer to some impressive but inevitably small fraction

---

confusingly, the Bank used to denote an agricultural poverty-oriented project. In practice, of course, which benefits would be "direct" and who would receive them were judgments necessarily left to the not disinterested lending officials. For a brief discussion, see OED, *Rural Development: World Bank Experience, 1965–86,* 1988, p. 4.

179. Peter Wright, interview with the authors, October 9, 1992.

180. Mervyn Weiner, interview with authors, April 30, 1993, p. 9.

of the world's poor. By themselves, Bank investments would not go far toward the direct and expeditious eradication of poverty proposed at Nairobi. The Bank's eye was set, rather, on hoped-for multiplier effects: the greater objectives were demonstration, education, conversion, and thus replication, a developer's version of the miracle of the loaves and the fishes.

There was an element of missionary enthusiasm and conviction in the way in which this project effort was carried out. Rural development projects, for instance, became the equivalent of pulpits from which the Bank preached a new faith to disbelieving local officials (and unconverted Bank colleagues), namely, that "ignorant," peasants, cultivating "uneconomically" small lots on marginal soils and in poor climates, at great distances from roads and markets, would nonetheless turn in economic rates of return comparable to those on power projects and on modern agricultural and industrial investments. Urban projects, such as sites and services and slum upgrading, had a similar educational and motivational purpose. In the case of infrastructure projects such as water supply and rural roads, the missionary effort consisted principally in overcoming the bias toward high technical standards of both Bank project specialists and their counterparts in borrowing countries. Conversion would follow to some extent from the many opportunities for "sermons" that arose in the course of project implementation, but mostly, from demonstrated success.

In that sense, poverty projects had an inherent showcase character; and it was important that their visible success be ensured. It was also helpful to persuasion that the projects be presented as innovations.

Beyond project replication, poverty lending also strengthened the Bank's efforts to influence distributive policies more broadly: committing its own money, the Bank legitimized its advocacy. Both moral and technical force were increased when it came to sector policies that bore some relationship to particular projects. Small-farmer projects, for instance, opened the door to discussions on policies concerning irrigation management, agricultural research and extension, and farm prices or to pressure for better sector institutions.

Finally, well-publicized poverty lending served the institutional image at a time when the U.S. Congress and European parliaments were putting more and more weight on the Bank's social and poverty-related purposes before approving IDA budget appropriations. Poverty lending came to the Bank's defense at a particularly difficult juncture during the Carter administration, when the United States pressed to make human rights a lending criterion. The Bank defended itself by differentiating between "economic" and "civil" rights, and pointing to its social loans as a pursuit of human "economic" rights. Stern proposed that "the Bank should hammer away at the point that it was less effective in addressing basic economic rights if it had to face the civil rights issue." Knapp added: "Basic human needs should not be narrowly defined," and he "urged the new paper to hit hard on the conflict between economic and civil rights, in order to widen the economic rights loophole."[181] The two most important project vehicles used to reach the poor more directly were rural development projects and urban housing, both of which encountered implementation difficulties.

Rural Development

Beginning in the mid-1960s, loans that sought to raise the production and welfare of poor farmers grew steadily to a peak level of US$2.8 billion per year (1990 dollars) between 1980 and 1982, almost 11 percent of total lending in those years. The most rapid growth in commitments occurred during McNamara's first years in the Bank as Woods's pipeline came into effect, and then during the two to three years following Nairobi. First developed with an eye to Sub-Saharan Africa during the 1960s, small-farmer loans spread to every region. As the organizational form of the projects and the mix of components evolved, the central objective remained constant, namely, to supply key agricultural inputs and infrastructure—water, credit, fertilizer, seeds, technology, roads—to small farmers.

The assumption was that very poor smallholders would respond to the availability of those additional inputs by raising production. And—despite their powerlessness before local and national elites—they would hold on to a sufficient portion of the increment to meet the rate of return, or "productivity" standards, that the Bank set on all its lending. A prior assumption was that the suppliers of those inputs—government agricultural experts and service providers and their corresponding Bank counterparts—would divine the right technological "packages" for an existing agriculture and society that, for the most part, was unfamiliar to them, and would retail those packages to a large, dispersed, frequently not organized and sometimes internally conflictive population.

There was also organizational change within the Bank. These projects were first the work of the Agricultural Projects Department, which was responsible for all agricultural lending before the term "poverty-oriented" came to be used. In 1973, following the Bank's major reorganization, agricultural staff and project initiation were dispersed to the area departments along with most other project work, but a renamed Agriculture and Rural Development Department (ARDD) under a new director, Montague Yudelman, was charged with the initiative for poverty-oriented, or "rural development" projects. Yudelman's staff became the pioneers and shock troops in the effort to design, sell, and implement rural development projects. Their work was then gradually transferred to the originally reluctant area departments so that, by the end of the decade, most agricultural poverty lending was originating outside ARDD.

The two principal elements in rural development projects were credit and the area concept. Credit became a central tool for all agricultural lending, including

181. Memoranda, Robert S. McNamara for the record, meetings on February 13 and 16, and March 2, 1978.

that directed at the rural poor. It was provided most often through "credit projects," but also as a component in a "livestock" or "tree-farm" or "tube-well irrigation" or any "small-farmer" project. Credit was in itself an important input, but it had a further advantage as an instrument for targeting, in that funds, and thus purchasing power over other inputs, were provided directly to selected individuals. It is notable that, though the Bank had pioneered development finance institutions, which lent mostly for industry, and had built up a strong technical and managerial capacity in that field, what eventually became a large financial portfolio of agricultural credit came to be managed separately, by technical staff responsible for agricultural projects and their regional, usually nonspecialized division and departmental supervisors.

The concept that rural development projects should be carried out in geographically bounded areas came to characterize most of the Bank's rural development projects, including not only "area" and integrated rural development projects, but also irrigation, tree-crop, livestock, and other agricultural projects that had a functional or subsectoral focus but that frequently limited their geographical scope. The area concept suited the poverty targeting objective but was also a way to satisfy the Bank's traditional mandate for "specific" projects. Sector and countrywide loans for agriculture would have taken on a program nature and would have demanded much larger loans.

Although rural development lending grew steadily through the period, the lending statistics masked an extraordinary psychological and perceptual cycle in the Bank. The launching of small-farmer lending in the 1960s had been accompanied by considerable enthusiasm. That energy and conviction rose even further in the years following Nairobi. Many pilot projects were promoted into full projects before being tested. A group of enthusiasts now shared McNamara's sense of missionary urgency, direction, and assuredness. This was the sense of McNamara's comments to the Board immediately after Nairobi:

> [There is some fear] that our objective is to redistribute poverty. Nothing could be further from the truth. It may be that we will find some circumstances in which an increase in the welfare of . . . the lowest 40 percent cannot be achieved while increasing the productivity of the land and the labor in that area. I have not seen any such situation as yet.[182]

And to Board members who pointed to the ambitious nature of his targets he said:

> I couldn't agree . . . more. The question is how fast are we going to move forward. . . . As fast as possible . . . faster than other institutions that I am familiar with, much faster. We are going to try to move forward faster than many governments are going to be willing to accept. But it is still going to be very slow. And the reason is, quite frankly, we don't know how to do some of these things.[183]

182. Board meeting October 9, 1973.
183. Ibid., p. 11.

As project proposals came up for approval, they confidently painted large income and output gains for poor beneficiaries.[184] Bank officials arrived in country after country to explain the virtues of rural poverty lending. Between March and June 1973, for instance, Bank missions set out to persuade Brazilian officials to support loans for small farmers, land reform, and agricultural settlement. The Brazilian minister of finance was not easily convinced: "He cited . . . the need to ensure economic viability of land reform programs; the uneconomic scale of small farms; and the inability to profitably conduct ranching operations on other than a large scale basis."[185] At a subsequent meeting the Bank turned to a more narrowly focused approach. The mission leader, Warren Baum, argued that sectorwide programs for agriculture were insufficiently targeted, that industrial development would take too long, and that colonization would be expensive and "suggested that one type of project which could and should be mounted to help close the gaps left by existing programs would be an *integrated rural development project.*" Baum went on to emphasize that "the Bank, based on its experiences . . . was convinced that economically viable programs could be designed for low income farmers," assuring the minister "that the Bank would not encourage uneconomic projects."[186] When Prime Minister Olaf Palme of Sweden asked in 1975 whether the Bank "efficiently reached the poor and raised their productivity," McNamara replied that "the Bank did exactly that and to underline his point he sent a letter to Palme with ten case studies of rural development projects."[187]

Staff members raised a number of objections, about the "low capability . . . of local organizations," the "scarcity of people . . . who know how to help," macroeconomic dangers (including the external terms of trade and the possible impact of increased production on farm prices), and the inefficient and corrupt public administration in many borrowing countries.[188] Other "obstacles" to rural development lending were internal: Bank policies and procedures were not adapted to many features of these new multisectoral rural development projects. Such

184. The fifty-six "new-style" projects approved in fiscal 1974 projected an average annual increase in income for beneficiaries of 7.3 percent over about eight years. World Bank, "Rural Development and Bank Policies: A Progress Report," OED Report 588, December 2, 1974, p. 42. One project in northeastern Brazil expected net family income of participating farmers to double in six years; another in Mexico saw the incomes of 45,000 farmers doubling in eight years; in Tanzania a project would double project village per capita incomes in five years; in Korea, it was to rise at 7.5 percent a year over seven years; in the Philippines, the increase would be between 100 and 400 percent in different project areas. Ayres, *Banking on the Poor,* p. 99.

185. Memorandum, Gunter K. Weise to Robert S. McNamara, "Brazil—Briefing Memo," March 23, 1973.

186. Memorandum, Eldon H. Senner to files, "Brazil—Meeting with Finance Minister," June 8, 1973. On Bank discussions between Bank mission headed by Warren Baum and Brazilian Minister of Finance on May 14, 1973.

187. Minutes of President's Council Meeting, November 17, 1975.

188. A small sample of staff concerns following the Nairobi speech: B. Harvey to Mahbub ul Haq, December 5, 1973; Mustafa Yulug to Adi Davar, November 6, 1973.

obstacles included the tendency of new projects to include social sector components that were not part of the Bank's usual work and skills, the inapplicability of international competitive bidding in the case of projects that required much small-scale and local construction and purchasing, their high local cost and recurrent cost components, complex Bank disbursement procedures not geared to large numbers of small purchases, the difficulty of quantification, and the clash between high preparation and supervision requirements and limited departmental budgets. Management responded with a paper that downplayed each of these worries.[189]

These administrative obstacles proved less binding than staff had feared. Though many of the worries concerning policies and procedures were justified at the time, the Bank was in fact adjusting rapidly, loosening restrictions on local and recurrent cost financing for instance, and developing new disbursement and bidding procedures. In addition, the force of sectoral, country, and poverty lending targets turned the staff into willing collaborators in that loosening and, at times, circumvention of rules, allowing the enterprise to move forward and to achieve the extraordinary lending levels noted before.

By 1981 much of the ardor behind rural development had evaporated. Indeed, the Bank's original enthusiasm seemed to be matched by the sharpness of its self-criticism. The objective basis for the critique was persuasive: in comparison with more traditional lending, rural development projects had run up an exceptionally problematic record; a large number were being classified as "failures" by the OED. Substantive critiques, focusing on Sub-Saharan Africa, began to appear, bearing out Uma Lele's earlier (1975) report. The Berg Report (1981) and an OED review of rural development lending were principally discussions of obstacles and problems, foreseen and "unforeseen." In 1979 Shahid Husain addressed a conference on rural development, mixing official optimism with a daunting list of what remained to be done. He noted that, though six years had gone by since Nairobi, there was still "a major gap in knowledge . . . on rainfed tropical agriculture," where the bulk of the rural poor in Africa lived; that "people's attitudes and institutions are more difficult to change than technology"; that there was a need for "special action to prevent discrimination against the smaller and poorer rural families," for "management reform and institutional change, including the patterns of land-holding tenure and tenancy," and for "sound policies and programs."[190]

Housing for the Poor

The Urban Development Department was created in 1972 (one year before the Agriculture and Rural Development Department) and by the end of fiscal year

189. Memorandum, J. Burke Knapp to all operational staff, "Bank Policies, Procedures and Practices: Do They Raise Obstacles to Effective Rural Development Programs," March 14, 1974.

190. S. Shahid Husain, "Address to the World Conference on Agrarian Reform and Rural Development," Rome, July 12, 1979.

1974 had approved nine projects totaling $160 million in as many countries. In terms of poverty alleviation, however, the urban effort was not only delayed; it was also far smaller. Total urban development lending over 1972 to 1982, much of which was not targeted to the urban poor, amounted to only 4 percent of Bank lending.[191]

What did the Bank do in terms of projects, and how did those projects affect the urban poor? The composition and emphasis of the program evolved continuously. Over the period as a whole, however, the principal area of lending was housing. The stress on housing, and more broadly on service delivery to the poor, was for the most part a second-best result. It came about as the Bank failed in a decade-long attempt, involving policy exercises and pilot small-enterprise projects, to identify a lending approach that would satisfy the twin criteria of being poverty targeted and productive. The objective was to identify urban analogues of the small farmer and of the corresponding rural development project. The frustration of that search left housing for the poor, by default, as the principal vehicle for an urban poverty effort.

The housing program first took the form of sites and services projects (projects providing new home sites and public services to an area), but the emphasis soon shifted to upgrading schemes to improve both housing and infrastructure in existing slums. An in-house review of urban development projects from 1972 to 1981 noted that 58 percent of all projects were for housing, and these represented 46 percent of total urban development lending. The first housing loan, in 1972, preceded the definition of an urban poverty policy by several years. This loan provided $8 million in IDA credit for a sites and services project in Senegal. The credit was expected to reach 160,000 families in the principal cities of Dakar and Thies—though by the following annual report, the number of beneficiaries had been cut to 140,000.

One of the most promising ways of combating the increasing problem of urban poverty, the 1972 annual report argued, was to provide "home sites and public services for families in the lower income brackets who can provide a substantial amount of self-help in building their own homes and can afford minimal payments to amortize the cost."[192] The project was doubly novel for the Bank, which as yet had minimal experience with income targeting in urban lending, or with the technical, political, and administrative aspects of sites and services projects.

The objective was to develop a new approach to the provision of affordable housing for the urban poor, an approach that moreover would prove financially replicable by achieving significant cost recovery and therefore a limited level of public subsidy. The Bank's larger objective was to demonstrate a model that could

191. Lloyd Rodwin, "Some Lessons and Implications of the World Bank's Experience in Urban Development," in Benjamin Higgins and Donald J. Savoie, eds., *Regional Economic Development: Essays in Honor of François Perroux* (Boston: Unwin Hyman, 1988).

192. World Bank, *Annual Report, 1972*, p. 23.

be used to persuade developing countries to move away from a tradition of costly public housing schemes that tended to favor a small number of middle-income families. The basic concept was to limit public provision to land and basic infrastructure, leaving the new homeowner to construct the home. That is, sites and services projects would provide serviced land, including roads, water supply, sanitation, drainage, electricity, construction loans for housing, and social services, including educational and health facilities. Later projects would include employment-generating schemes.

In Nigeria in 1978, at the time of appraisal of a Bank sites and services project, the cheapest house financed by the public sector cost $40,000. The shelter unit in the project was estimated to cost only $1,600. But disappointment at the limited reach and slow implementation of sites and services projects led the Bank to turn to slum upgrading as a way of reaching much larger numbers of beneficiaries and to accelerate implementation. These projects worked with existing settlements, with minimal demolition and relocation, and they provided infrastructure networks. Both kinds of projects would ensure title for homeowners in exchange for service fees and substantial self-help efforts in building and maintaining the housing units.

These housing projects faced two main difficulties; they were often unable to reach the intended poor beneficiaries; and they incurred considerable project implementation problems. Sites and services projects tended to be out of reach for the poorer segments of the targeted beneficiaries. OED's report on urban development concluded that sites and services failed because the schemes were too costly. Despite the explicit and critical determination that standards would be lowered to affordable levels, the period of implementation saw a process of "standards creep," in design and other standards, both for the home sites and for the levels of provision of public services; substantial subsidies became necessary to complete the projects, making replication too costly. The OED report states that "the poor could only afford sites and services programs, however, when they were heavily subsidized— not a replicable approach given tight budgetary constraints in most cities."[193] According to the departmental review from 1972–82, the total number of households served by all Bank shelter projects was approximately 1.9 million.[194] In 1977 the department also estimated that 20 percent of all urban lending was poverty oriented. But it appears that few belonged to the lowest income deciles of the population; instead, most of the benefits went to the middle poor, and even the middle classes.

The Bank eventually started phasing sites and services projects out and moved toward slum upgrading. The OED report states: "Portfolio experience points to

193. World Bank, "Twenty Years of Lending for Urban Development 1972–92: An OED Review," OED Report 13117, June 14, 1994, p. 32.

194. World Bank, *Learning by Doing: World Bank Lending for Urban Development, 1972–82* (World Bank, 1983), p. 46.

upgrading programs reaching poorer beneficiaries than sites and services components did; for example, Indonesia's KIP supported by five successive Bank-financed projects benefiting 3.7 million urban inhabitants, 70 percent of whom were reported to be poor. . . . Sites and services components of shelter projects generally benefitted higher-income groups than squatter upgrading did."[195] The Bank instituted cross-subsidies as a way to provide access to lower-income families without giving up on the overall financial recovery targets for the projects. The OED urban development report was surprised to find that "the objectives of only half the shelter and integrated urban projects mentioned poverty alleviation," and the report notes that "few completed urban projects in South Asia were concerned with alleviation; project designers did not make specific references to poverty targeting in large cities where the urban poor are a large and visible majority."[196]

The Bank began to find it difficult to reconcile poverty impact with cost recovery and rate of return targets. In Tanzania, the Bank refused to proceed with another housing project because the government likewise refused to recover costs by charging users. Despite such pressures for relaxation, the Bank insisted that, through appropriate design and good implementation, it would be possible to develop model projects that would be both poor targeted and economically viable.

Independently of the difficulty of building at sufficiently low costs to reach the extremely poor, the projects found their benefits being appropriated by higher-income persons. "In some projects," the OED report notes, "higher-income households appropriated benefits intended for the poor, albeit on a small scale," but it does not give any figures for appropriation.[197] This was often a consequence of upgrading: improved communities attracted higher-income inhabitants while poorer segments were unable to keep up with payments for housing or services. Even in model projects, such as the Jakarta *kampungs*, varying income groups coexist together, and it is inevitable that some higher-income groups will benefit from improvements. It proved difficult to identify the poor in an urban setting where both employment and residence change more often than in rural areas. In El Salvador many families were unable or reluctant to participate in the sites and services projects because they did not have the time or the money to construct their homes; women were excluded because of the casual nature of income and employment.

Urban development projects required much energy and expense in ironing out project problems, for example, with land tenure and titling. Ownership on project sites was frequently a matter of dispute and therefore caused implementation delays and increased project costs. The OED report states: "Slow acquisition of land slated for development considerably delayed implementation of many urban projects worldwide. As owners held out for better compensation from govern-

195. World Bank, "Twenty Years of Lending," p. 32.
196. Ibid., p. 17.
197. Ibid., p. 33.

ments, cumbersome procedures delayed the first project in the Philippines."[198] This problem also held up sites and services projects in La Paz, El Salvador, and Brazil. In Côte d'Ivoire, difficulties arose over the purchase of title to land in Bank project sites by non-Ivorian citizens. In the end, the Bank had to make land acquisition a condition of project approval, sometimes relying on expropriation.

Another complication that delayed implementation was the dislocation of previous residents at project sites and consequent need for resettlement. According to Bank estimates, 7 percent of original settlers were dislocated or had to be resettled because of housing projects. The highest percentage of resident relocated (30 percent) was found in Rabat.[199]

The effort to reach the poor by lowering design standards ran up against existing housing codes and regulations in borrower countries. In Côte d'Ivoire, the government balked at the "affordable" housing and service standards proposed by the Bank, which government officials saw as providing substandard housing conditions.

The Bank took pains to increase institutional capacity, and the most widely cited case of a successful effort is the Calcutta Metropolitan Development Authority (CMDA). In Jordan the Bank pushed for the creation of an Urban Development Department to replace the existing National Housing Corporation. The high public visibility of housing projects may have contributed to a greater degree of political interference. This occurred in Morocco, where the king pressed for the redesign of an upgrading project, requesting that the project site be razed. He was finally persuaded to accept the original design, but the interference led to implementation delays. Similar problems arose in Kingston, Jamaica, because of a riot, and in the Philippines, where Imelda Marcos took a direct interest.[200]

Despite these many implementation difficulties the Bank frequently cites its *kampung* projects in Indonesia and the Tondo project in the Philippines as examples of successful urban-poor housing efforts. Yet the focus on housing and service delivery repeatedly proved difficult to replicate, even as urban populations rapidly increased. The Cameroon-Douala and Yaoundé Water Supply project, for instance, seemed to lose the race with population growth. According to the project completion report: "The project did not improve the water service to the urban poor. In fact, due to a rapid increase in the urban population, but virtually no increase in the number of standpipes, the percentage of population served fell from an estimated 69 percent in 1968 to 54 percent in 1973."[201] By itself, the Bank's

198. Ibid., p. 42.

199. Figure cited by Ayres, *Banking on the Poor,* p. 191.

200. Ibid., pp. 181–85.

201. World Bank, "Project Performance Audit Report, Cameroon-Douala and Yaoundé Water Supply Project," OED Report 1350, SecM76-761, November 12, 1976, p. A7.

project was insufficient to meet the needs of the poor population as a whole; successful and rapid replication of the Bank's approach was indispensable to the success of the effort, but the Bank was unable to spark such a response.

Overview

The Bank made some effort to follow through on its conviction that borrower policies were at the heart of poverty alleviation and equity. Commentaries and statistics on income distribution became routine in country economic reports and CPPs.[202] Intermittently, the subject was brought up in senior management discussions of country lending and policy priorities. But the important step from strategy sessions to action, which in this case meant communications of various sorts designed to persuade or pressure borrowers toward more progressive policies, was rare. Moreover, the efforts that were made seem to have achieved little. The reasons lay in part in external circumstances, and in part in the Bank.

Crusades are not launched on waves of common sense, so it is no surprise that potential influence was overestimated. But the crusade was also unlucky. It could not be seen that a coming flood of petrodollars over the decade would weaken the Bank's leverage. In addition, social goals proved weak competitors when it came to the allocation of the Bank's scarce persuasive capital. Social goals were imprecise, still polemical, and geared to the long run. By comparison, balance of payments "gaps," food supply "needs," scheduled debt repayments, and outbursts of inflation presented themselves as uncontroversial, well-defined, and seemingly precise claims on immediate attention. Even the guardians of the poverty agenda—mostly Chenery and his staff—seldom objected when financial and political emergencies crowded out social objectives, as happened repeatedly.[203]

Events were unfriendly to the poverty mission during the 1970s. The security fears that had spawned IDA and pushed the earlier expansion of social lending became less compelling. But as the cold war faded, world economic instability increased, threatening more and more borrowers with shipwreck. Social objectives were set aside as the Bank turned to balance of payments loans and to policy dialogues on macroeconomic policies. Paradoxically, both bonanza and impoverishment contributed to the loss of leverage.

The check on influence was greatest in the oil-producing countries, such as Iran, Mexico, Nigeria, Venezuela, and Indonesia, which were empowered by the cash, by the increased political deference of rich countries, and by McNamara's plan to

202. It is remarkable, however, that throughout the decade the attention to poverty and equity was almost always a response to questions, requests, and proddings by McNamara.

203. Ul Haq's memo on Bank policy toward Chile was an articulate but ineffectual exception.

capture oil funds for the Bank. In Iran, for instance, the Bank had already been suffering from inattention before the oil price hike, but it swallowed its misgivings on the Shah's hasty plans for instant modernization and maintained a supportive stance.[204] Over 1973 and 1974 various Bank officials stated, for instance, that the Bank wanted to be "more closely identified with HIM's [His Imperial Majesty's] social reforms";[205] that Iran "is prepared to move towards the social goals supported by the Bank"; and, in a summary of senior management opinion on the 1974 CPP, that "there was no disagreement with [Iran's] program."[206] Meeting with the Shah in July 1973, McNamara said:

> We had but one objective and that was to assist him in the dramatic revolution which he had under way in Iran; that our technical assistance was . . . much more valuable than our financial assistance, but by its very nature . . . might well lead to controversy and if the controversy ever reached the point where it was unproductive, I wanted him to inform me directly.[207]

Supportive statements, and even McNamara's offer of a hot line to his office, failed to appease the Shah. HIM became impatient with advice contrary to his plans—"controversies"—and lending ended in 1975.

Oil had a similar, distancing effect in Indonesia, though both sides took care to maintain the appearance of a continuing close partnership.[208] A first indication of change was a 1974 warning by Bernard Bell that henceforth "the Bank's ability to influence policy will depend to a larger extent than before on the size of its lending program." During the following years various officials complained of information

204. Shourie wrote: "On the question of receptivity to our sage advice, the Iranians have been quite intransigent . . . the South Asia Department had noted that 'Iran had not hitherto been disposed to take much notice of Bank advice.'. . . Leverage . . . is invoked most often for countries that are fairly well off on their own—the Portugals, Malaysias and Irans. I have never understood how we always manage to persuade ourselves that these relatively well off countries are indeed the ones that will be most willing to do as we see fit." Memorandum, Arun Shourie to Hollis B. Chenery, "Iran CPP: Points for Discussion at the Economic Committee Meeting," March 17, 1972.

205. Memorandum, Gregory B. Votaw to Robert S. McNamara, "Iran—Audience with HIM," July 26, 1973. Votaw also warned: "In the past the Shah has reacted very negatively to evidences of Bank leverage to force policy changes in Iran; he is proud of Iran's independence. Today we think we are working to support reforms he has decided to carry out, but he may still fear that Bank enthusiasts occasionally infringe on Iranian sovereignty" (p. 2).

206. Memorandum, Alexis E. Lachman to John H. Adler, June 17, 1974, with attachment, "Iran Country Program Review Meeting, June 14, 1974."

207. Memorandum, Robert S. McNamara to files, "Conversation with the Shah of Iran at Blair House—July 27, 1973."

208. See chapter 8. From 1968 through 1972–73 money and well-meshed personalities—Suharto's adviser Widjojo Nitisastro and the Bank's representative Bernard Bell—empowered the Bank. The weakening of influence began when McNamara replaced Bernard Bell as the resident representative, and it was reinforced by the oil boom.

"blackouts," lack of "a frank and open manner," "cool" and "indifferent" attitudes, and even "outright antipathy" and "little leverage."[209] In 1978 Husain and Bell agreed that "for some time now . . . there has been little discussion of developmental policies and issues."[210] Stern wrote of a "massive misunderstanding" in the relationship,[211] and Husain informed McNamara:

> I have a very uneasy feeling about the nature of this relationship. It has been too personal. . . .
> I have been appalled to see how little and how restricted the discussion of our economic
> reports on Indonesia has been. . . . [T]he discussion that has taken place has been in the nature
> of negotiations on wordings and phrases and much less on objectives and policies.[212]

In addition, leverage was curtailed in countries that were not oil producers but were financially favored for other reasons. Thus Arab nations such as Syria and Jordan became recipients of large-scale aid from Arab producers; oil money spilled into Anwar Sadat's Egypt in the form of workers' remittances as well as Arab bilateral aid; and when Arab aid to Egypt was cut off after Camp David in 1978, U.S. bilateral aid mushroomed. For much of the period, Thailand, Pakistan, and Turkey received substantial cold war aid.

When the 1977 Pakistan CPP drew attention to that country's "poor performance in the social sectors and family planning" Stern commented: "Indeed, it has been the same story for 25 years. Pakistan is the one country in South Asia where there has been little concern for the poor." But Stern, then regional vice president, defended his nonsocial priorities for Pakistan: "Our attention has been focussed, properly in my view, on getting the [government of Pakistan] to get its economic house in order."[213] Yet leverage seemed no more effective in the economic realm: the 1979 CPP on Pakistan complained that "the Bank's dialogue on macroeconomic policies has little impact."[214]

209. Memorandum, Bernard R. Bell to Robert S. McNamara, September 25, 1974; memorandum, Thompson to Bell, August 14, 1975; Resident Staff in Indonesia (RSI), "Note on Development in Indonesia," June 20, 1977; memorandum, Fateh Chaudri to Kirmani, December 8, 1977; memorandum, Pierre Landell-Mills to Pieter Bottelier, January 9, 1979; memorandum, J. Goldberg to A. Golan, January 10, 1979.

210. Letter, S. Shahid Husain to Jean Baneth, January 10, 1978. Also, World Bank, Resident Staff in Indonesia, "Note on Development in Indonesia," June 20, 1977; memorandum, S. Shahid Husain to Robert S. McNamara, briefing for meeting with Indonesian delegation, September 26, 1977.

211. Letter, Ernest Stern to Terence Hull, December 15, 1978. The characterization was actually Hull's, and Stern was implicitly accepting Professor Hull's conclusion based on a study of Indonesian attitudes.

212. Memorandum, S. Shahid Husain to Robert S. McNamara, "Indonesia—Organization of the Bank's Work," February 16, 1979.

213. Memorandum, Ernest Stern to Robert S. McNamara, "Pakistan," November 28, 1977.

214. Memorandum, Sidney Chernick to Ernest Stern, "Pakistan CPP: Major Policy Issues," May 14, 1979.

But losers far outnumbered oil shock beneficiaries. Fuel importers were impoverished; others were simply destabilized by a mix of volatile world circumstances and misguided domestic policies. In all these cases the Bank's ability to influence distributive policies was reduced. This came about in two ways.

First, as already noted, where economic and political stability were threatened, the Bank felt compelled to maintain its financial support and to concentrate its dialogue on balance of payments and stabilization policies. This happened in India, Bangladesh, Kenya, Tanzania, Brazil, Côte d'Ivoire, and many smaller Sub-Saharan nations.[215] In some cases the "compulsion" to lend could be traced directly to the safety of the Bank's own portfolio; but the more general reason was the protection of a long-run relationship, and so, of future possibilities for influence. To some extent, also, the Bank was pressed to lend by the increased presence of other lenders: bilateral donors, often working with the Bank in Consultative Groups, tended to fall into "relief" lending with fewer qualms than the Bank; and commercial banks, with large volumes of petrodollars to place, became alternative and unconditioned sources of credit.

Second, during hard times poverty lending lost favor. At such moments the Bank sought projects that would raise output quickly, particularly exports, be easy to implement, and permit the large, rapid disbursements needed for balance of payments support. These requirements were more easily met by traditional infrastructure and productive projects, including commercial rather than subsistence agriculture, and by program loans, rather than by complex, usually smaller and still problematic poverty projects. Poverty loans thus turned out to be luxury goods, affordable only in good times. And since Bank projects were the standard platform, or point of entry, for policy dialogues, the shift in lending toward nonpoverty lending weakened the Bank's position when it came to persuasion and policy pressure in the spheres of poverty and equity.

If the 1970s as a whole were unfriendly to the poverty agenda, the timing of events within the decade was also unfortunate. Enthusiasm for distributive objectives peaked twice, first over 1972–73 with the culmination of the search for a poverty strategy and its announcement at Nairobi, and again during 1977–78, when many country strategy discussions returned to the subject with renewed emphasis. The 1977–78 revival gained strength from the basic needs movement, but it was also expedient: it served as an evasive tactic against President Jimmy Carter's efforts to impose human rights guidelines on Bank lending. On each occasion, however, the upswelling of concern for poverty occurred on the eve of an oil shock. Poverty and equity initiatives were quickly set aside as the Bank and its borrowers turned to deal with macroeconomic problems.

The argument for short-run financial support often shaded into a political rationale: the continuity of a regime or group of technocrats would be considered a country's best chance for long-run development. Such judgments were necessarily

215. See chapter 12.

intuitive. They were strongly influenced by personalities, all the more because McNamara was given to definite, instinctive responses to individuals, the most notable instances among borrowers being his trust and support for Indira Gandhi in India and Julius Nyerere in Tanzania. Nor was long-term commitment necessarily an early, once-over decision. It could be instead the result of a series of short-term tests of wills and wits with the borrowing country.

External events were unfavorable, but the scant success in influencing distributive policies also had causes inside the Bank. One was that poverty did not really achieve the degree of priority suggested by the Bank's official position. When circumstances presented a choice, it was poverty and equity, invariably, that were set aside. This reflected the continuing leanings of the staff, and for that matter, of their counterpart officials in developing countries. McNamara was unable to break the hold of old beliefs, that GNP was the overriding priority and that poverty alleviation implied a trade-off with growth. Attitudes did change; there was an increasing recognition of and willingness to address poverty more directly, as McNamara noted on returning from a trip to India in 1978. But the core beliefs remained. In fact, when critical financial issues were in the balance, McNamara himself seemed to agree to their priority, in case after case, notwithstanding his own rhetoric. In 1980 he told senior colleagues that "the fundamental issue facing the Bank was the one of financing current account deficits in LDCs, and that its work on poverty alleviation would have to be done in conjunction with this."[216]

A second internal cause was that the Bank fell behind in its effort to develop a policy road map for poverty and equity, a list of concrete measures to be proposed to borrower governments. Statistics on income distribution remained sketchy and debatable, and the standards by which to judge them were even more so.[217] In contrast to the weight of professional authority and experience that the Bank brought to bear on matters of production and economic stability, its recommendations with regard to poverty and inequality were patently subjective and poorly informed.

The statistical weakness showed up in the debate with Brazilian authorities. After his initial outburst on Brazilian inequality, McNamara found himself facing

216. Minutes of President's Council meeting, February 11, 1980.

217. Statements about distributive "badness" were typically based on unstated ethical judgments concerning the importance to be attached, for instance, to extreme poverty, urban-rural income differences, regional inequality, excess riches, and whether those riches were invested productively (landed wealth was "bad"; industrial wealth was not criticized). Different countries were judged by different standards, as a result of data availability, popular opinion, and personal biases. In CPPs, Korea's distribution over the decade was judged almost entirely by one statistic: the ratio of rural to urban incomes. In Brazil, regional poverty was singled out. In Mexico, Malaysia, and Kenya, it was rich versus poor farmers. "Badness" was also judged with reference to rudimentary country and historical comparisons, such as those embodied in the "Kuznets curve." In practice, evaluations were impressionistic and changeable.

heated refutations, which were partly borne out by evidence collected later by the Bank. Over most of his term, McNamara found himself struggling between the impulse to take a stand and his nearly obsessive respect for statistical grounding. His requests for further research worked in favor of area managers who were happy to postpone the distributive issue, especially since in the meantime new priorities had often arisen to command the immediate agenda. In 1978 Stern doubted that the forthcoming first issue of the *World Development Report* should include a table on income distribution: there were not enough data, he said, partly because the Bank had not "stimulated much interest in the subject in the research community."[218] The more significant shortfall was not in measurement but prescription: despite an unprecedented research effort, which drew heavily on development thinking outside the Bank, policymakers in the 1970s seeking to alleviate poverty were provided with a list of options that was skimpy and often ambiguous.

Aggressive redistribution was avoided, partly as an act of political accommodation, but also out of fear that productive costs would exceed distributive benefits. Measures such as land reform, nationalization of large firms, steep wealth and income taxes, and steps to fight corruption were occasionally discussed within the Bank—especially land reform—but were dismissed as too "politically sensitive" to press on unwilling borrowers. And when such measures emerged from a revolutionary regime, they generally arrived pell-mell on a wave of inexperienced and fervid policymaking that disrupted production, created financial disorder, and alienated donors with anti-Western rhetoric. Most damaging to Bank lending— and thus to potential policy influence—was the fact that revolutionary redistribution was frequently extended to foreign-owned assets (rich nationals were permissible targets.)[219] During the early 1970s one or more of these transgressions became obstacles to Bank involvement in the equity-oriented programs of Algeria, Peru, Guinea, and Chile, and at the end of the decade, of Nicaragua. Tanzania, however, was a major exception.

Pure welfare spending, or income transfer with no convincingly "productive" outcome—a category that through the 1970s included primary education and health—was also frowned on. The full embrace of health and education as productive investments was germinating under cover of the basic needs proposal of the late 1970s, but its official recognition came at the close of the McNamara period,

218. Memorandum, Ernest Stern to Robert S. McNamara, "WDR—Income Distribution Data," May 11, 1978.

219. By the 1970s, Bank officials were giving more weight to financial disorder and pricing distortions than to expropriations, but expropriations were legally easier to use by donor countries who wished to punish expropriators by vetoing loans. When assets of non-Western countries were involved, as in Uganda, the Bank made no objection. The U.S. ban on lending to Peru pending compensation of expropriated U.S. Standard Oil properties was debated by the Bank over several years, over McNamara's objections. In the case of Algeria, the opposition came from France.

most publicly in the 1980 *World Development Report*. Likewise, the politically attractive idea of employment-generating public works programs was viewed with skepticism and cautiously accepted in only a few cases, such as Mexico's PIDER program, where they seemed to serve a productive and not mere unemployment relief purpose. A 1976 report stated: "Past public works programs have been tilted heavily in favor of economic and social infrastructure compared to directly productive projects. . . . The importance of creating productive assets through public works cannot be stressed too strongly."[220]

There were exceptions to the ban on nonproductive transfers. One was the cautious acceptance of cross-subsidies within power, water, and other bounded systems for the sale of public goods and services. It came to be accepted that poor customers could be charged lower rates if shortfalls were made up from richer customers. Cross-subsidies had been accepted in water supply and power projects in the 1960s. The principle became standard in the 1970s and was extended to sectorwide policies. Another exception applied in poverty-oriented credit projects or project components. In 1974 McNamara overruled staff objections to interest rate subsidies for small farmers in Brazil.[221] By 1979 Stern could write that the subsidization of loans to small enterprises "is in fact pretty common practice" and was "entirely consistent with Bank policy."[222] Another acceptable transfer was, in effect, a geographical cross-subsidy; the Bank took the lead in encouraging some governments—notably those of Brazil and Thailand—to favor backward regions in their countries through budgetary allocations.

Unresolved contradictions between macroeconomic prescriptions and social justice showed up in several policy areas. The rule that what was good for stable growth was necessarily good for poverty and equity was questioned at times, with regard, for instance, to low-wage policies, "excess" devaluation, and price distortions. In fact, farm price supports, backed up by subsidies, were seen as pivotal poverty-reducing and growth-promoting interventions in many cases, as in Korea's and Indonesia's rice-pricing policies. Conversely, "taxes" on agriculture in the form of overvalued exchange rates, import protection, pricing, and other policies were not criticized by the Bank in the 1970s, though in the 1980s they would come to be regarded as major culprits of bad distributional outcomes.

Other policy areas that would be deemed critical to poverty alleviation in later years were also absent from the 1970s agenda. The importance of empowerment

---

220. World Bank, "Rural Public Works and the Bank: Background Analysis," Development Economics Department, March 24, 1976, p. 21. Knapp considered the paper "very useful and stimulating" and suggested that it be widely distributed within the Bank. Memorandum, J. Burke Knapp to Robert S. McNamara, April 5, 1976.

221. Memorandum, Ernest Stern to C. Koch-Weser, "Pending Assignment—Urban Poverty Lending," July 30, 1979.

222. Letter, Ernest Stern to Francine Frankel, July 20, 1976. Memorandum, Robert S. McNamara for the record, on Brazil, January 28, 1974.

and participation by the poor in policy and project formulation and execution had been common wisdom during the 1950s and 1960s, and it had been applied through community development initiatives and other forms of participation and self-help, especially by the rural poor, yet it played little role during the 1970s, a victim of the spread of authoritarian governments, but also of a doctrinal swing within the Bank.[223] Deeper social causes and forms of poverty, such as sex and racial or caste discrimination, were also absent from the agenda. Finally, though McNamara showed early concern for the environment, this aspect of development—as a cause of poverty and of loss of welfare in particular—was largely set aside in Bank lending and in its policy prescriptions at the time. The sidelining of health reinforced that neglect, given the close interrelation between preventive health and environmental care.

Shortly after McNamara's departure, a task force reexamined poverty alleviation. It noted: "Poverty issues have seldom featured significantly in dialogues . . . [and the Bank] has often failed to raise at the highest levels, politically sensitive issues of the poverty impact of efficiency adjustments." Nonetheless, coming full circle, it reaffirmed the greater significance of policy influence over that of projects noting that the "Bank's lending amounts to less than 2% of total investment in developing countries," whereas "policy changes . . . can have much greater impact on the well-being of large numbers of poor people." But the report did not ask why the Bank, after expressing almost exactly the same opinion ten years earlier, had not achieved more in the way of influence, nor therefore what was needed to make future efforts more fruitful.

If the Bank made little headway in nudging borrowers into policies more favorable to the poorer citizens of their countries, how much did the Bank achieve through its own, direct poverty lending? The starting point for an answer is, of course, the statistic just cited from the task force conclusions, namely, that the "Bank's lending amounts to less than 2% of total investment in developing countries." And poverty lending, at its peak amounted to about one-third of that 2 percent. This same realization was the point of departure for the policy-influencing efforts carried out over the decade and reviewed in the preceding country case studies of this chapter.

But more is involved in a judgment on "poverty lending." On the plus side there is the possibility, indeed likelihood, that Bank poverty projects induced some replication. The extent of replication was undoubtedly reduced by the difficulties—and even frequent image of "failure"—of many Bank rural development and urban poverty projects. In addition, Bank projects enjoyed hidden subsidies, such as preferential bureaucratic treatment, that would have made replication difficult even in cases of Bank "successes." On the other hand, these projects helped to break down the mental barrier that saw an inevitable conflict between serving the

223. World Bank, *Focus on Poverty*, pp. 18–19.

poor and serving the general good. Even to chip away at that powerful and self-serving notion, which is simply the other side of the coin of the idea that "what is good for General Motors is good for the country," was to improve the odds for other, perhaps more successful, poverty-alleviating approaches in the future.

The short-run arithmetic of poverty lending, however, was surely disappointing. In addition to the very small proportionate figure involved, there is the very large question of fungibility that must be answered. And even favorable assumptions regarding the degree of fungibility must allow that some important part of the funds invested by the Bank in poverty projects served, at the margin, to allow borrowing governments to carry out other expenditures that did not necessarily benefit the poor. There can be no answer to the question of the extent of fungibility, but common sense and a minimal knowledge of government decisionmaking suggest that the net contribution made to the poor through those projects was significantly less than official lending figures would imply.

One returns therefore to the intangibles. Whatever was achieved by the Bank's poverty projects must be found, to a large extent, in their contribution to breaking down mental barriers, raising motivation, teaching, indirect influence on policies, and a general nudging of borrowers toward greater openness and a capacity to develop their economies in ways more directly favorable to their poor.

Confidence in social engineering drove the crusade. Seeking to intervene not only in production but also in income and wealth distribution, the Bank was entering relatively untrodden territory. But it did so with much assurance that the enterprise was feasible. Like putting a man on the moon or developing hybrid rice strains, a well-financed, scientific crash effort, manned by "the best and the brightest," could be counted on to come up with the requisite formulas. A further though rarely discussed assumption was that, once such formulas had been demonstrated through Bank projects, they would be widely replicated.

In practice, intervention in distributive policies proved difficult. National agendas were crowded with long-run development goals and with immediate, circumstantial needs. Other variables also affected the outcomes, such as the political interests of the Bank's rich shareholders and the institutional concerns of the Bank itself. Poverty projects proved equally frustrating. In the end, project eggs were placed in a surprisingly small number of baskets: rural development projects, urban housing for the poor, and water supply projects. Though these categories conceal important differences, and many other kinds of lending also made a contribution to direct poverty alleviation, a retrospective view must necessarily wonder that a social, and global, revolution—seeking to eradicate poverty in developing countries— could have been expected from so limited a tool kit. This reflection influenced the Bank's approach when it returned to poverty alleviation in the next decade.

SEVEN

Demotion and Rededication: 1981 to the mid-1990s

WHEN Tom Clausen succeeded Robert McNamara as the president in June 1981, the poverty theme, which had been faltering, was abruptly muted in Bank decisionmaking and public statements. Then, almost as suddenly, it reappeared in 1987 and again permeated policy debates and documents, even taking center stage in *World Development Report 1990*. By 1991, it was being pronounced the Bank's "overarching objective."[1]

This changing course pertained only to poverty alleviation in the stricter sense of investments and policies that worked *directly* for the poor. Its outward signs were a slowing down in the search for what McNamara called "poverty projects" and an easing up of the weight placed on poverty in internal directives and public statements.

But it should be emphasized that views diverged on the significance of this shift in focus. The Bank that McNamara joined a decade earlier had for the most part not believed in rapid solutions to poverty. And, although many had been caught up in the optimism of the 1970s, doubt in the Bank was renewed by the poor performance of that era's poverty-oriented lending innovations. Those who believed that the main chance for the poor lay in economic growth saw little to lament or to remark on in the slackening of direct poverty alleviation during the 1980s. Instead, they saw a steady continuity of purpose and relevance in what had always been the Bank's main business—growth-oriented projects and policy advice. Even at the peak of McNamara's poverty crusade, some two-thirds of lending had been allocated to power, transport, industry, urban development, and other investments not specifically targeted to the poor.

1. World Bank, Operational Directive 4.15: Poverty Reduction, *The World Bank Operational Manual* (December 1992), p. 2.

The policy swing away from strict poverty lending was also moderated by administrative inertia. Though poverty was on the back burner between 1982 and 1987, many loan approvals reflected the goals and bureaucratic decisions of an earlier period: a pipeline of projects, already identified and partly negotiated, was making its gradual way to the Board. Disbursements on pre-1981 project commitments were even less sensitive to current priorities. Although the phrase "poverty lending" now resounded less often and less rigor was enforced in targeting, poverty projects in McNamara's strict sense—small farmers, water supply, primary education, health, population and rural roads—still accounted for one-fifth of Bank lending between 1982 and 1987, not far below the one-third recorded by McNamara. Also, if poverty lending was slightly reduced during the 1980s, intellectual and administrative foundations were laid for new approaches to direct poverty alleviation that would emerge in the 1990s.

Another point to note about the evolution of the Bank's poverty policy is that it was partly influenced by dramatic external developments. During the 1970s and early 1980s, the countries of Asia—both the "tigers" and populous low-income countries such as India, China, Pakistan, and Indonesia—recorded high rates of income growth and poverty reduction. The idea that growth could be an engine of poverty reduction reemerged. Another important development to recast the entire poverty-versus-growth issue was the debt crisis. Since it threatened rich and poor alike, matters of distribution or redistribution seemed less urgent. The Bank had just spent a decade looking for ways to reengineer economic growth to favor the poor more rapidly while also debating whether to complement trickle-down with "basic needs" commitments, all questions of long-run allocation and sustained policy commitment. Now attention turned to more short-run objectives, and the distributive question became how to carry out rapid stabilization, policy reform, and institutional change in a manner friendly to the poor.

The swing back to direct poverty alleviation, like the shift away, was associated with presidential change. Barber Conable replaced Clausen in June 1986 and quickly began to signal the new direction. This time the policy reversal was less sudden. Conable knew little about the Bank, development, or the history of poverty-alleviation efforts. He also lacked experience in the management of large organizations, a deficiency that contributed to what became a costly interruption of Bank operations during a slow and wearing reorganization over much of 1987. Nonetheless, the policy change gathered steam in each year of Conable's term. Lewis Preston, Conable's successor in June 1991, endorsed that reorientation.

Yet a closer look at events suggests that presidential inclinations played only a supporting role. The policy evolution was driven in the main by other circumstances. Most visibly, Bank priorities moved with shifting G-7 politics and with the unfolding debt crisis. Equally important, perhaps, was an institutional cycle of fatigue and renewal. When "poverty lending" returned to fashion, the emphasis was on short-run welfare and on human resources, to complement stabilization efforts. Also, by accepting loans for social emergency programs—for flood, famine, earthquake, and war relief—and for "basic needs" such as feeding and nutrition programs, Bank operations became more "welfare" in character. This extraordinary evolution in the Bank's policy and operational stance from 1981 into the early 1990s—more a matter of rhetoric and fashion than of lending volume—is the subject of this chapter.

Demotion: 1981–86

On July 1, 1981, Clausen's first day as president, Mahbub ul Haq circulated a list of policy research topics, including a request to staff member Michael Lipton to prepare an "analysis . . . to see if current concern with adjustment problems is having an adverse impact on Bank's poverty focus."[2] In subsequent discussions Lipton referred to this request as "the erosion hypothesis."[3] Though ul Haq was anticipating Clausen's leanings, the sense of erosion in the commitment to poverty had been developing for some time. It had been reflected, for instance, in briefings prepared for Clausen, one of which stated: "Many countries will be concerned primarily with establishing external balance over the coming years. . . . The danger . . . is that longer-term goals, including that of alleviating poverty, may get lost."[4]

It was already happening. Financial instability had been growing through the 1970s, crowding out the poverty cause. In 1977 Ernest Stern explained why the Bank had closed its eyes to Pakistan's retrograde record on social policy: "Our attention has been focused, properly in my view, on getting the [government of Pakistan] to get its economic house in order."[5] From 1979 debt and balance of payments problems, along with a few cases of rescheduling, dominated the policy agenda of many countries. And in the Bank, the main concern in many country lending programs was exposure levels and repayment prospects.[6] Ul Haq, whose running commentary on country lending programs through the 1970s had prodded officials to remember social objectives, acquiesced as Country Program Papers turned their attention to financial problems. McNamara endorsed the urgently needed macroeconomic policies and fast-disbursing, typically nonpoverty types of lending.[7] Those internal, managerial signals were reinforced in 1979 by the public announcement of structural adjustment lending at the Belgrade Annual General

2. M. Lipton to PPR staff, July 17, 1981.

3. For example, M. Lipton to Pierre Landell-Mills, *Policy Brief on Alleged Recent Erosion of "Poverty Focus" in Lending,* July 21, 1981.

4. Briefing File for President Clausen, June 1981, Development Policy Staff briefing, appendix II, p. 6.

5. E. Stern to McNamara, November 28, 1977. Stern wrote: "Pakistan is the one country in South Asia where there has been little concern for the poor."

6. See chapter 12.

7. See the remarks in chapter 5 concerning the way in which stabilization problems superseded efforts to influence distributive policies in Brazil, Kenya, the Philippines, and Tanzania.

Meeting and by the second oil shock. Thus, in May 1982—before the debt crisis erupted—Stern was asked to explain the absence of population projects in the Bank's portfolio. One reason, he said, was: "In times of economic crisis, *as now*, the automatic response of national planners is to reduce allocations to human resource development (including population) in favor of shorter term [productive] investments."[8]

That month a discussion of what was being done in response to Sudan's debt arrears to IDA concluded that new IDA loans to Sudan had "turned to directly productive investments . . . [and] refrained from poverty-oriented projects (with high recurrent costs) at a time when the government also is redirecting resources from health, education and rural development."[9] Another important factor was the poverty mission's growing fatigue. Successive experiments with rural, urban, and social projects designed to favor the neediest had proved troublesome, costly, and unsatisfactory, despite continuing reformulations. At first, these difficulties only fueled further innovation, but reports of "project failure," as the Bank defined it, tended to bear out the predictions of skeptics and to disillusion those who had been willing to believe in the possibility of improving on trickle-down. Skepticism turned to cynicism when officials, pressed by the pressure to lend and the intrinsic difficulties of poverty projects, found themselves resorting to administrative and semantic expedients to exaggerate the direct poverty impact of their projects.[10]

Much criticism of poverty projects had surfaced in the relatively open atmosphere of the Bank in the 1970s. One that had considerable impact was a 1975 study of rural development in Africa by Uma Lele that questioned the Bank's policy of area-based, integrated rural development.[11] The urban poverty approach was a

8. Memorandum, Ernest Stern to M. Syeduz-Zaman, May 17, 1982, emphasis added. Stern admitted: "On the basis of the lending proposals presented to the Board in Fiscal Years 81 and 82 only, one may question the strength of our population program." The perception of crisis was strong before the Mexican announcement in late 1982. GDP growth in the OECD countries had fallen from 3.3 p.a. over 1970–80 to 1.2 percent in 1981. World trade growth dropped from 26 percent in 1979 and 21 percent in 1980 to –1 percent in 1981. GDP in the developing countries rose 5.0 percent in 1980 and only 2.2 percent in 1981. The Bank's *Annual Report 1982* stated "dangers of further recession and decline seem serious" (p. 19). The recession did indeed deepen in 1982: OECD growth fell to –0.2 percent and LDC growth to 1.9 percent.

9. Draft background paper by Percy Mistry for IDA retrospective study, *Who Misled Whom. IDA's Involvement in Sudan*, May 28, 1982, p. 2.

10. Wilfred Beckerman, "The Measurement of Poverty in the Context of the World Bank's Activities," undated draft, probably written 1980–81. According to Shakow, Beckerman's finding that poverty "body count" data were spurious contributed to the decision by management to abandon the effort to distinguish "rural development" (that is, projects for the rural poor) from other "agricultural" projects. Interview, June 25, 1996. Costas Michalopoulos commented: "When I came to the Bank in 1982 I was absolutely astonished to find that this part [poverty alleviation] of the World Bank's thinking—which was quite visible to the outside world—had not permeated at all the Bank's operations." Personal communication to authors, February 1990.

11. See discussion in chapter 9.

topic of continual debate across departmental units, especially in the face of a growing body of negative evidence, some coming directly out of Bank staff field experience. Discussing Kenya's lending program in 1978, Willi Wapenhans admitted in frustration that the Bank had created an impression that it would be able to reach the smallholder but did not yet have the capability to deal with the rural poverty problem.[12] More systematic reviews began to appear toward the end of the decade. In a 1978 assessment of a set of early rural development projects in Sub-Saharan Africa, the Operations Evaluation Department recorded many weaknesses.[13] This regional effort was criticized even more sharply in the Berg Report of 1981.[14]

Those charged with promoting and monitoring the institution's poverty-oriented endeavors had also begun to complain, particularly about management's lack of attention. A special unit—URBOR—had been created within the Urban Projects Department to encourage and help regional departments to intensify the poverty bias of their urban lending and to replicate the "new-style" urban poverty projects developed by Urban Projects staff. In 1979 the unit's chief, Friedrich Kahnert, remarked on the lack of support from senior management: "Strong public statements continue to be made about the importance the Bank attaches to its poverty programs. This is not always followed up in practice."[15] URBOR's budget was cut in fiscal 1979, and its reports on the Bank's employment promotion work were ignored by management. A subsequent study of the Bank's urban work sought to explain why poverty was no longer being given high priority :

> As the McNamara era drew to a close, the relaxation of constraints that had created a relatively free space for urban activities also drew to a close. There was a reassertion in the urban area of the traditional limits, which took the form of attention to staffing coefficients and a much keener competition for space in country lending programs . . . and a relative downgrading of urban priorities. "Urban" now had to accommodate to constraints from which it had been temporarily spared.[16]

In March 1981 the director of Urban Projects, Anthony Churchill, sought to reduce the weight of poverty in his department's work: "Throughout the development of the Bank's urban lending program, there has been no confusion on our part

12. See chapter 6.

13. OED, *Rural Development Projects: A Retrospective View of Bank Experience in Sub-Saharan Africa*, October 13, 1978, report no. 2242. The review, which covered eighteen projects appraised and approved before 1973, estimated an average rate of return of 15 percent, which was equal to that of other projects in the region but well below original predictions.

14. World Bank, *Accelerated Development in Sub-Saharan Africa: An Agenda for Action* (Washington, D.C., 1981). The principal author was Elliot Berg.

15. F. Kahnert to Baum, July 12, 1979.

16. Cheryl Mattingly, Lisa Peattie, Don Schon, *Urban Practices in the Bank: Notes Toward a Learning Agenda* (MIT Press, April 1984).

over the fact that poverty alleviation is only one among many multiple objectives."
Moreover, "urban poverty alleviation depends heavily on the workings of the urban
economy and . . . it is difficult to trace all of the impacts of individual projects."[17] In
brief, there was little scope for direct—that is, targeted and identifiable—urban
poverty alleviation. Poverty reduction would thus have to depend on growth and
trickle-down.

Churchill's view was widely shared within the Bank. W. L. Pease, an agricultural
economist working in the African region, protested:

> I think we are chasing butterflies . . . and imposing foreign concepts of morality. . . . In an
> agricultural context . . . we should be investing strictly from the point of view of a
> development banker. I am unconvinced that the trickle-down theory is inapplicable in
> agricultural development because . . . history shows that it does work. . . . If our assistance
> benefits better off farmers, so be it. We are probably creating a far stronger and more
> lasting base for the country that way than by acting the philanthropist.[18]

McNamara's inaugural vision had been that technology, scientific management,
and beneficent leadership could rapidly and substantially reduce poverty in the
developing world. It was a vision that for a time had excited much of the Bank. But
by 1981 that vision had faded within the institution and even in McNamara's own
mind.

In 1980 Munir Benjenk, the former head of operations in Europe and the
Middle East, became vice president for External Relations. After Clausen was
appointed president, Benjenk approached him with decided views on the appropriate image for the Bank. Defining himself as one of the "closet conservatives"
of the McNamara era, he thought that in the new political environment it would be
to the Bank's disadvantage to be identified with McNamara. The Bank, he advised
Clausen, should signal a break, a "bend" in the road, and "make peace with more
conservative public opinion."[19] This message sat easily with Clausen, who had told
ul Haq at an early meeting that poverty alleviation did not figure in his thinking at
all and who considered the poverty focus no more than a "thin veneer."[20]

Clausen's first address to the Board of Governors in September 1981 touched on
but did not stress poverty, and the overall message was more in line with Benjenk's
recommendation. During most of his tenure Clausen made pro forma references
that did little to conceal an overriding concern for macroeconomic policy, free
markets, and international cooperation. In contrast, McNamara expressed an almost missionary zeal in his day-to-day harping on the poverty theme with col-

17. A. Churchill to Bevan Waide, March 30, 1981.

18. W. L. Pease to Mr. Ali, acting chief, WAPA4, *Measurements of Poverty*, August 7, 1981.

19. Interview with authors, January 20, 1995.

20. Mahbub ul Haq, interview by Robert Asher, December 3, 1982, World Bank Oral
History Program, p. 16. Ul Haq's statement is disputed by other senior officials. Yet Clausen
rarely touched on the subject in staff discussions.

leagues and borrower officials. Clausen—perhaps misleadingly—did little to suggest an energetic, urgent concern for and belief in the possibility of rapid poverty alleviation. Instead, his speeches and the institution's *World Development Reports* stressed stabilization, balance of payments adjustment, and the market economy, all of which seemed consistent with a former private banker's priorities.[21] Even the Bank's traditional preoccupation with investment projects seemed to give way to a concern with short-term balance of payments and fiscal assistance.

In September 1981 an effort was made to rescue the sinking poverty mission. At ul Haq's prompting, and following on his request to Lipton, a task force was established to examine the Bank's approach in this area, one of its major objectives being "to counter staff uneasiness" regarding new Bank priorities. The report, *Focus on Poverty*—also known as "the Shakow Report," after the study director, Alexander Shakow—criticized many aspects of the effort to reduce poverty yet saw progress. It proposed that greater emphasis be placed on influencing borrower policies and on making "nonpoverty" projects—such as roads, power, and industry—work better for the poor, implicitly criticizing an excessive reliance on "poverty projects." It recognized the importance of economic growth, though it downplayed the idea that poverty alleviation necessarily implied less growth: "There are broad and important areas of complementarity between the twin objectives of efficient economic growth and alleviation of poverty."[22] Admitting past shortfalls, the report nonetheless reaffirmed the priority and feasibility of a more poor-friendly path to development.

When senior management met to review the report, they were told that "Bank interest in the poverty issue had eroded. . . . What they read in the press, their understanding of some donor attitudes, and the absence of significant Bank statements . . . led them to express doubts and concerns on whether the Bank will remain as strongly committed as before." The Managing Committee "agreed that clear signals ought to be sent both within and outside the Bank to counter this perception."[23] But some members had reservations. Stern was uncomfortable with the report. He saw no need for the proposed changes in procedures and policy and refused to comment on the draft, calling its purpose "obscure" and recommending that it not be sent to the Board.[24] In the end, the report went to a Board seminar, where it received "strong and supportive comments from all speakers." Several

21. At a Brookings Institution conference in 1982 he spoke of his confidence in and admiration for the "competitive, creative, energetic marketplace . . . [his] home for thirty-one years," saying, "I know it works . . . I loved it. And I still do." A. W. Clausen, remarks before the Brookings Institution seminar on "The Future Role of the World Bank," January 7, 1982, Series 3962 (President's papers—A.W. Clausen—Speeches).

22. World Bank, *Focus on Poverty*, 1982.

23. Managing Committee meeting on March 1, 1982.

24. Stern to Shakow, March 25, 1982. Chenery was the responsible vice president, but in Shakow's opinion the initiative for the study was almost certainly ul Haq's. Interview, June 25, 1996.

directors agreed that Bank project reports "did not now have the emphasis on poverty alleviation that the Task Force stated was desirable." One executive director commented: "The Bank was more comfortable with its traditional efficiency emphasis, and the equity side had not yet been given adequate strength."[25] The report was published in September and widely circulated but did little to stop the demotion of poverty.

The timing was unlucky: publication coincided with the announcement of Mexico's debt default and major escalation of the debt crisis. Moreover, it was delivered into a new political atmosphere, less sympathetic to development assistance and to poverty objectives. There was a decidedly rightward shift when Margaret Thatcher took office in mid-1979, Ronald Reagan in late 1980, and Helmut Kohl in 1982. The Managing Committee had alluded to this shift in its discussion of "some donor attitudes" that were signaling less commitment to poverty.[26] But the U.S. Treasury was blunt: Undersecretary Beryl Sprinkel argued that governments and international institutions should take on no function that could be performed by the private sector. Early in his term Sprinkel commissioned a study to determine whether the World Bank had "socialistic" tendencies[27] and held back on replenishments for the International Development Association and capital increases for the International Bank for Reconstruction and Development requested by the Bank. This pitch of aggressiveness soon moderated, but the U.S. Treasury remained an unsympathetic, if not hostile, patron, an attitude that almost certainly reinforced Clausen's inclination to tone down the poverty rhetoric.

The institution was turning against McNamara's poverty agenda. Although many in the Bank, especially members of the Bank's policy and research departments, were certainly "uneasy" about the signs of backsliding in the Bank's poverty commitment, what carried more weight was the operational staff's growing concern about complications and delays associated with poverty operations. Poverty was seen as an obstacle to lending performance, defined for the most part as lending volume. When Shakow followed up his report with a proposal suggesting that special poverty briefs be included in each CPP, the regional staff objected strongly to what they saw as

> additional work without any obvious justification. They felt that the concern for poverty in Bank work was superficial. This was borne out by the fact that whenever any project or program was to be cut due to budgetary reasons, it was the poverty-related projects that were deleted. The rhetoric on poverty is confined to top management and has no practical bearing on what is expected by management from the working level.[28]

25. Cited in memorandum, Waide to Baum, April 22, 1982.

26. Minutes of Managing Committee meeting, March 1, 1982, p. 3.

27. Hobart Rowen, *Self-Inflicted Wounds, From LBJ's Guns and Butter to Reagan's Voodoo Economics* (Times Books, 1994), p. 300. For a fuller discussion of the U.S.-Bank relationship, see chapter 6 by Catherine Gwin in volume 2 of this work.

28. A. M. S. Ahmed and J. W. van Holst Pellekaan to M. Yudelman, *Poverty Report*, January 11, 1983.

By 1981 the poverty crusade was beset from outside and from within. Arriving at this juncture, Clausen found it relatively easy to bring about a change of stance. The poverty mission was now rapidly abbreviated and downgraded.[29]

Clausen's choice of Anne Krueger, a polemical conservative economist, to replace Hollis Chenery as chief economist contributed both in substance and in appearance to a decreased role for poverty studies.[30] Krueger made no bones about her ideological agenda, which coincided with the Reagan administration's market orientation, and set about it with energy. Issues of equity and poverty were not prominent in her research agenda. Frank Vogl, Clausen's public relations adviser and a strong supporter of Clausen's record, wrote in 1985:

> What we hear far less today from ERS [Economic Research Staff] is talk of the ability of nations to secure economic growth and income redistribution at the same time and of the ability to find ways by which the poorest in poor countries can contribute to the overall economic strengthening of their nations. These subjects were at the heart of the Bank's economic research in the 1970's.
>
> The shift in the research focus, combined with other factors, has clearly left many observers of the bank with the view that the Bank has moved to the political right.[31]

The appointment gained added political significance because it followed an attack in a *Wall Street Journal* editorial on Albert Fishlow, another candidate for the position. The *Journal* berated Fishlow for being an "ideological clone" of McNamara and for focusing his research "on things like income distribution in Brazil."[32]

References to poverty became scarce in operational documents such as Country Program Papers, Country Strategy Papers, Managing Committee discussions, and briefings for Clausen, suggesting the principal messages that he should convey to country delegations at the annual meetings. The topic is rarely mentioned in Clausen's and Stern's correspondence over that period. CPPs and CSPs for countries in which poverty had previously been high on the policy agenda, such as the Philippines, Brazil, Thailand, and Mexico, now only occasionally mentioned the problem. The relaxation of targeting was most evident where the effort had been

---

29. Ul Haq goes further, saying that poverty was disowned by his colleagues. He recollects that at an early senior staff meeting with Clausen, in the face of Clausen's evident disinterest, only ul Haq had admitted to being sympathetic to the Bank's poverty role. Interview with authors.

30. Vogl suggests that it was deliberate. Letter to authors.

31. Briefing memorandum from Frank Vogl, acting vice president for External Relations, to Jose Botafogo, who was to become vice president for External Relations, January 1985, p. 17. Sent to authors by Vogl on February 13, 1990. Although Vogl's point is true, Krueger did support one major poverty-related research project—the Living Standards Measurement Study program (LSMS), which had been initiated by Chenery—that would underpin much of the Bank's 1990s poverty work.

32. *Wall Street Journal,* November 21, 1980, p. 28. Fishlow had publicly opposed the appointment of Chicago economist Arnold Harberger as head of the Harvard Institute of International Economics on the grounds that Harberger had supported the Pinochet regime in Chile.

greatest—in agricultural lending. Administrative targets and controls had succeeded in steering a much larger share of agricultural lending to the poorest farmers: the ratio rose from less than one-fifth to more than half during the 1970s. This ratio began to decline in the early 1980s. One evaluation concluded that only 28 percent of agricultural lending over 1985–89 was targeted to the poor, though all targeting estimates are statistically suspect.[33] Nonetheless, many sector and project evaluations by OED prepared during the late 1980s and 1990s point to a lessening in the targeting effort and a corresponding increase in attention to productivity considerations.[34] The fading of poverty as an explicit objective from operational work was reflected in the titles and summaries of published Bank reports. In 1985 only 1 percent of those reports mentioned "poverty" in their titles or abstracts; the figure had been 6 percent in 1980 and rose to 12 percent in 1995.[35]

Yet Clausen did take up the cause of Sub-Saharan Africa.[36] Even before joining the Bank, he had indicated that lending to Africa would rise significantly under his leadership, and during his term in office the Bank did indeed launch several such initiatives.[37] Perhaps he found it easier to respond to a geographically and financial-

33. Review and Analysis Division, Policy Review Department, World Bank, *Targeted Poverty Projects Supported by the World Bank: An Overview of Operations Approved During 1985–89*, November 1991, pp. 2–3. As noted above, officials had strong incentives to exaggerate the poverty reach of their projects during the 1970s; also, comparisons between the 1980s and 1970s are weakened by changing administrative practice. This estimation problem is also cited by Jonathan Sanford, "The World Bank and Poverty: A Review of the Evidence on Whether the Agency Has Diminished Emphasis on Aid to the Poor," *The American Journal of Economics and Sociology*, vol. 48, no. 2 (April 1989), pp. 151–164. An April 1988 OED study, *Rural Development. World Bank Experience, 1965–86*, reports a decline from 61 percent to 39 percent between 1980–82 and 1983–85. The report also cites several indicators of lessened concern for poverty in agricultural lending, pp. 11–15. Figures for the period 1969–87 are: 1969–71, 17 percent; 1972–74, 38 percent; 1975–77, 52 percent; 1978–80, 51 percent; 1981–83, 55 percent; 1984–85, 40 percent; 1986-87, 53 percent, according to *Status Report on the World Bank's Support for Poverty Alleviation*, prepared by the Strategic Planning and Review Department, February 26, 1988 and presented to the executive directors. A late 1980s trend was measured by the Policy, Planning and Research Department, in their *Annual Review of Development Effectiveness. FY88* (ARDE, December 14, 1988), p.8, which appeared to use different criteria, but found a decline in poor-targeted agricultural loans from 61 percent in 1987 to 51 percent in 1988. This was the second ARDE, a series of annual reports intended "to serve the President and members of the President's Council by monitoring . . . the progress made in achieving the Bank's development objectives," *ARDE FY87*, p. 1.

34. For example, OED, *Interim Assessment of Brazilian Rural Development Projects, 1986*.

35. Statistics compiled by Robert Wade. See chapter 13, volume 2.

36. See chapter 12.

37. Interview with *The Times*, June 1981. Reported by Frank Vogl, February 13, 1990. Vogl served as Clausen's spokesman and director for information from 1982 to 1990.

ly bounded version of poverty. Whatever the case, his personal inclination was strongly reinforced by circumstances that pushed the Bank into a deeper involvement with the region during the decade. Beginning in 1983 drought began to cause severe food shortages in much of Africa. By 1984 and 1985, world attention was gripped by large-scale famine in Ethiopia, Sudan, and the Sahel.[38] In April 1984 the Bank made a $2 million donation to the World Food Program, a decision which the Managing Committee "strongly supported . . . as a good and astute gesture," though it worried over the precedent being set.[39]

The developing crisis in Africa came together with an earlier United States decision to sharply reduce its contribution to IDA for the period 1985–87.[40] When the rigidity of this position was realized, the Bank began to consider the possibility of "a special fund" to supplement IDA.[41] The Bank approached other Part I countries and slowly won commitments. As late as November, however, Qureshi could report only that "he rated the chances for special funding at about 50-50 with the major stumbling block remaining the British and the Germans." But he "noted that the current public awareness of the drought in Ethiopia provided an opportunity for the Bank to harness public support for a Sub-Saharan Africa program."[42] The Bank's proposal was approved soon after: a Special Facility for Sub-Saharan Africa was established in May 1985 with a total contribution from non-U.S. donors of $1.84 billion. The Bank added a further "contribution" of $150 million out of its own operating surplus, arguing that projected net income was exceeding expectations.[43]

In the context of Africa's crisis, the Bank's earmarking initiative proved a successful fund-raising device, serving to moderate the overall reduction in conces-

38. One of the most dramatic accounts was a BBC report by Michael Buerk and Mohammed Amin from Ethiopia in late 1984, when the crisis was reaching its peak. Anthony O'Connor, *Poverty in Africa. A Geographical Approach* (London: Belhaven Press, 1991), pp. 90–97. Millions suffered hunger and forced migration, but O'Connor believes that publicity and resulting international aid averted a much larger disaster (p. 92).

39. Minutes of Managing Committee meeting of April 9, 1984.

40. Despite a major campaign by the Bank, the U.S. reduced its contribution from $3,240 million for IDA 6 (1981–83) to $2,250 million for IDA 7 (1985–87).

41. Minutes of meeting of Managing Committee held on December 12, 1983. This meeting appears to have been the first occasion when a special fund was mentioned.

42. Minutes of meeting of Managing Committee held on November 12, 1984.

43. This transfer was first proposed to the Managing Committee on January 7, 1985. Minutes of meeting. The allocation of net income for concessional lending is, in practice, paid for out of interest received from IBRD borrowers, principally the middle-income countries and thus amounts to a cross-subsidy—an unwilling cross-subsidy, since such transfers have generally been imposed by the Bank's main shareholders against the wish of middle-income borrowers, who preferred a reduction in interest charges on their own loans.

sional assistance that resulted from the Reagan administration's decrease in development assistance.[44] The fund-raising "opportunity" referred to by Qureshi was not only a matter of Africa's needs. The Bank and donors knew that the Special Facility would, to an extent, serve a refinancing function at a time when many African nations would have been unable to meet debt servicing without new concessional financing.

In a different way, the Clausen Bank took a long, though little-noticed, step toward the acceptance of social criteria for its lending, as distinct from productive criteria. This happened through the growth in what the Bank called "Emergency Recovery Loans" (ERLs). Two of these loans were prompted by the drought in Africa: in 1985 ERLs were approved for Ethiopia ($30 million) and Sudan ($20 million). But other emergencies—cyclones, floods, and earthquakes—soon also became the justification for emergency lending, especially during FY1985 and FY1986 at the end of Clausen's term.

The Bank has also had a continuous if low-profile tradition for "emergency" lending. Indeed, the concept was akin to the reconstruction lending that Keynes called "the primary" purpose of the Bank.[45] The earliest emergency loan made after the Bank had closed its reconstruction operation appears to have been an IDA credit to Chile—Chile's first and last access to IDA—granted for road reconstruction following an earthquake in 1960.[46] Despite the importance attached to the reconstruction purpose in the Charter, however, the Bank shied away from the concept. Few "emergency" loans were made during the 1960s, and though their number increased during the 1970s—over thirty were approved by McNamara— they remained a sporadic and minor category of lending.[47] Moreover, when the Bank did respond to emergencies, it sought to present the loans as standard, developmental project loans. This long reluctance was closely tied to the Bank's strong preference for project lending and the strict interpretation that it gave to the project concept for most of its first three decades. Certainly the rapid, flexible, and relatively unconditioned responses required for emergencies conflicted with the cautious, slow, and restrictive rules and procedures that characterized normal project lending. But in addition, emergency loans had a "relief" character that the Bank sought to avoid even through the 1970s. In searching for ways to reach the poor, for instance, McNamara had worked hard to develop loan instruments that

---

44. The Special Facility was accompanied by several other initiatives directed at Sub-Saharan Africa, listed in chapter 12. The proposal set a target of $1.6 billion but modifications, including exchange rate movements, raised the actual approval to $2.0 billion.

45. See chapter 2.

46. See chapter 4.

47. "Emergency Recovery Loans" according to Bank's database in November 1996. A study by the Food Security Unit of the Africa Technical Department, *Food Security and Disasters in Africa: A Framework for Action*, June 25, 1991, lists several drought relief loans approved in 1974 that are not included in the Bank database.

could be justified as essentially "productive" in character, minimizing program lending in the process. And when the Bank began to multiply emergency lending during the 1980s, it developed guidelines that insisted on the "recovery . . . not relief" character of that lending.[48]

Thus when the Bank began to expand emergency lending, it had already traveled a long distance away from a rigid adherence to productive criteria and closer to a greater openness toward social needs. That distance can be measured by its long resistance to emergency lending and its constant effort to minimize the appearance of accepting a relief role. The timing of the expansion—the first jump occurring in 1979–80, and the second in 1984–85—suggests that, once the Bank had loosened its inhibition against program lending, ERLs became an instrument for providing rapid balance of payments and fiscal relief to debt-burdened bor-rowers. Three aspects of the Bank's move toward a more socially responsive position should be noted: though social need was a factor, the principal motivation appears to have been balance of payments assistance; both the McNamara and the Clausen Bank played down social motivation in justifying its loans; and, perhaps for the very reason that "poverty" rhetoric was played down, the two administrations made essentially the same response.

In addition to his plans to assist Africa, Clausen also stated early in his presidency that he intended to raise the priority of agriculture.[49] But in prac-tice the share of lending for agriculture fell steadily, from 28.6 percent of total commitments made during 1981–83—largely from McNamara's pipeline—to 20.9 percent in 1987–89, when Clausen's final lending decisions were reaching the Board. The decline would continue into the 1990s, falling to 16.7 percent by 1993–95.[50]

The Bank remained more attentive to social conditions than it seemed. Indeed, one reason for that attention—creditworthiness—demanded confidentiality. As a lender to governments, the Bank had always kept a close eye on the politics of its borrowers. This was partly due to the Bank's practice of judging the opportunities for policy reform and good project performance. But another part consisted of what bankers would later come to call "political risk" analysis. A central proposition of that analysis is that poverty and inequality are sources of political instability, and, hence, of lending risk. In contrast to the more formal, technical, and largely public nature of its macroeconomic assessments of creditworthiness, the Bank's political analysis has been intuitive and discreet. Paradoxically, such analysis also has been more independent of the doctrinal leanings of the time than its economic evalua-

48. World Bank, Operational Directive 8.50, *Lending by the Bank for Emergencies,* approved October 1988.

49. Agriculture was one of three priorities (along with energy and Sub-Saharan Africa) announced at Clausen's first address to the Board of Governors, on September 29, 1981.

50. World Bank, *Poverty Reduction and the World Bank: Progress and Challenges in the 1990s* (1996), table C-1, p. 68. See chapter 8 for further discussion of agricultural lending.

tions. The Clausen administration was no exception to this practice. In fact, with the eruption of the debt crisis, the administration had particularly strong reasons to be alert to political and social circumstances.

Social and political conditions in borrower countries were tracked in periodic reviews of lending programs, especially in CPPs, as a basis for in-house judgments on creditworthiness, and not, as in the 1970s, for the purpose of prompting specific policy or lending recommendations. The 1984 review of Mexico referred to unemployment as a danger to the political sustainability of reforms. Worries over "continued social stability" also arose in Indonesia between 1983 and 1985, triggering staff discussion on equity, ethnic discrimination, corruption, and unemployment. The Indonesia CPP for 1983 affirmed that "support for the regime has rested largely on its ability to achieve economic growth and a reasonable sharing of the benefits of growth."[51] The 1984 paper saw "rising unemployment and potentially increasing social unrest" as "the single biggest problem confronting Indonesia in the coming years."[52] And in 1985, it warned: "The poverty and employment outlook is of acute concern . . . in the current political environment."[53] At a management discussion on Chile in 1986, the regional vice president, David Knox, saw "a difficult period involving considerable risk to the Bank. . . . This made it imperative to monitor the social impact of the program, particularly given the great volatility of the political environment."[54]

Human Resources

Social conditions were on the Bank's agenda for another, less self-centered reason, though again with a low profile: the Clausen Bank supported and helped to develop what became a new paradigm for poverty alleviation. Whereas in the 1970s the Bank had sought to provide the poor with productive physical assets, the new approach stressed welfare needs and "human resources." Stymied by the perceived failure of its 1970s' efforts, the Bank throughout most of the 1980s found itself without practical alternatives to replace, in volume and targeting efficacy, the rural development and urban service projects that had been its main antipoverty lending instruments. Yet the alternative was in fact in the works; over the decade the Bank was gearing up an operational commitment to "social" lending—especially education, health, nutrition, and family planning—while simultaneously sharpening the poverty focus of those services. Moreover, by lending for social emergency programs, for relief in cases of flood, earthquake, famine, and war, and for "basic

51. Indonesia CPP 1983, p. 2.
52. Luis de Azcarate to Operations Policy Sub-Committee, Indonesia CPP: OPSC review, November 8, 1984, "Topics for Discussion," p. 1.
53. CPP 1985, p. 7.
54. Minutes of Managing Committee, May 12, 1986.

needs" such as feeding and nutrition programs, Bank operations became more daringly "welfare" in practice, if not in rhetoric. The reformulation was gradual. It had roots in the 1970s, was encouraged under Clausen, and blossomed in the late 1980s. This section returns to the 1970s, briefly interrupting the 1980s story, to stress the continuity in the development of human resources as a new approach to poverty alleviation.

These social services had been part of the basic needs agenda of the 1970s. The weight of advocacy, however, would shift from the 1970s welfare argument to a 1980s productivity rationale. The public face of these services was thus adjusted to suit the political times: upheld as "needs" in the 1970s, they became "human resources" in the 1980s.[55] By avoiding an untimely appeal to welfare or to the language of equity and distribution, the Bank in the 1980s opened the lending door for these services by emphasizing their productive virtues. Growing from a small base, the volume of "human resource" lending remained a small share of the Bank's operations through Clausen's term. And they were unable to offset the decline in rural development and other 1970s-style poverty projects. Nonetheless, the increasing number of these operations helped to build up administrative and technical capacity and to create a pipeline of potential projects. But, as has been noted, the expansion of human resource lending in the 1980s was set in motion by administrative steps and doctrinal changes that took place during the previous decade.

The most far-reaching organizational measure was the creation of the Population, Health, and Nutrition Department (PHN) in October 1979. From that date, PHN Department staff and budgets provided a supply-side push to sector lending. Expansion was also encouraged that year by the decision to allow stand-alone health loans; previously, health operations had been limited to small components of population, rural development, and other projects.[56] The decision not only opened the door to large health-sector loans but also freed population efforts from the no-health-lending restriction that had held them back.[57] Over the 1970s the Bank's population advocacy had done much to legitimize the developmental significance of family planning.[58] But missionary impact may have been purchased at the cost of

55. See chapter 6.

56. Health components began to be added to other projects from 1970. George Simmons and Rushikesh Maru, Working Paper WPS 94, PHN, World Bank, *The World Bank's Population Lending and Sector Review*, September 1988, pp. 1–2.

57. OED, "Twelfth Annual Review of Project Performance Results. A World Bank Operations Evaluation Study," 1987, p. 123.

58. K. Kanagaratnam, who was the first director of the Population Projects Department from 1969 and then population adviser when the department was melded into PHN in 1979, wrote a candid admission of its operational limitations but argued that it had "moved population activities away from the shadow of the traditional position in which it had been perceived as a social and welfare program." K. Kanagaratnam to Norman Hicks, "IDA Retrospective Review—Population Sector" (draft for background paper for the "IDA Retrospective Review," April 30, 1982.

a less effective operational approach. Riding on a sense of urgency, McNamara's efforts leaned toward frontal, targeted, supply-side intervention, exemplified by Indira Gandhi's strong-arm sterilization program.[59] Later wisdom would be that a more roundabout, demand-based approach, in which family planning was integrated with and partly disguised by health and nutrition projects, would be more effective and lasting.[60] From 1979, PHN and direct health operations helped to bring about that transition.[61] The change was reinforced by the beginning of direct lending for nutrition in 1976, with a loan to Brazil. The India Tamil Nadu nutrition project, later a model for the Bank's nutrition work, was approved in 1980.[62]

Education lending grew strongly during the 1970s, from $163 million annually in 1970–74 to $336 million in 1975–77. And the thrust carried into the early 1980s: $590 million annually in 1980–84.[63]

Promising as this early growth in volume was, however, it was actually the changing orientation of education loans that facilitated subsequent expansion. The shift was prompted by a combination of events: Ballantine's departure as department director and the publication of three major sector reviews, an OED evaluation of education projects (1978), an external panel report (1978), and a sector policy paper (1980).[64] One change was Bank-wide: in the late 1970s attention shifted from concrete and delimited projects to sectorwide institutions and national policies. In the education sector the turn was encouraged by the publication of *Review of Bank Operations in the Education Sector*, a harshly critical OED evaluation of project experience in education. The report brought to light many project deficiencies later seen to be common in Bank operations. Because education had

59. See section on India, chapter 6.

60. According to Kanagaratnam, McNamara was: "very uneasy . . . about the effectiveness of the Bank's approach to reducing [fertility] . . . because we do not seem to know about the linkages [between causes]. This means we do not know where to put the emphasis." K. Kanagaratnam to files, meeting of External Advisory Panel on Population with Mr. Mc-Namara, December 17, 1975. Population policy became a North-South political issue at the 1974 Bucharest World Population Conference, where LDCs imposed their view that fertility should be treated as a result, not a cause, of development. McNamara, instead, saw population control as a condition for development. He opposed "waiting for development" and so "letting fertility take care of itself."

61. The suspicion that an indirect, health-based approach to family planning represented a failure of commitment persisted for some time. In 1982 Stern wrote an executive director: "Where there remain barriers to explicit population programs it may be possible to include provision for family planning when supporting improvements in health systems. *This is in no sense the submerging of population by health.*" Stern to M. Syeduz-Zaman, May 17, 1982. Emphasis added.

62. OED, "Twelfth Annual Review," pp. 123, 131–32.

63. Phillip W. Jones, *World Bank Financing of Education* (London: Routledge, 1992), p. 184.

64. OED, *Review of Bank Operations in the Education Sector*, December 1978; *External Advisory Panel on Education Report*, October 31, 1978; *Education Sector Policy Paper*, 1980.

been chosen for the first such sectorwide review, however, it created the immediate impression that education was an inherently difficult sector for Bank project involvement.[65] The OED report recommended that the Bank "systematically address the broader needs of the education systems rather than those of the project, and that this concern be moved to the center of the Bank's strategy for educational financing."[66]

A second, more gradual change consisted of a growing acceptance of the importance of basic and primary schooling, which rose from 4 percent of all education loans in 1970–74 to 14 percent in 1975–79. The 1978 and 1980 reports encouraged this trend: the external panel in particular stressed the joint equity and productivity benefits of rural and female education.[67] And when the education sector policy paper was presented to the Board—by coincidence only a few days after the award of the 1979 Nobel Prize in economics to Theodore Schultz and Arthur Lewis— strong support was expressed by the U.S., U.K., and most other Board members for a basic education emphasis.[68] Both of the new directions—toward institutional development and policy reform and toward primary schooling—lent themselves to larger, sectorwide education loans in later years.

The way forward for social sector lending was made easier by doctrinal change. Though basic needs proponents were frustrated in the main, their arguments and empirical studies worked to erode the preconception that social lending was essentially "redistribution" and "consumption." Research and policy papers contested the belief that social programs involved a choice between welfare and growth. Researchers found evidence that primary education and health were directly productive.[69] The 1980 World Development Report incorporated and supported much of that argument. The WDR defined the concept more broadly as "human development, an important complement to the [Bank's previous] approaches to poverty alleviation," and argued that productivity as an objective should be balanced with welfare. At the same time it avoided the ambition, interventionist tinge, and welfare rationale of the basic needs approach.[70] In its introduction to a

---

65. The OED report highlighted insufficient emphasis on borrower participation and insufficient concern to build up institutional capacity. It also noted that the effort to influence management and general educational policies through project covenants had had little success. OED, *Review*, 1978, p. iv.

66. OED, *Review*, 1978, p. ix.

67. *External Panel*, 1978, p. 6.

68. Jones, *World Bank Financing of Education*, p. 160.

69. Including Norman Hicks, "Growth vs. Basic Needs: Is There a Trade-Off?" *World Development*, 7 (1979), pp. 985–94; Schlomo Reutlinger and Marcelo Selowsky, *Malnutrition and Poverty*, World Bank Staff Occasional Papers number 23 (Johns Hopkins University Press, 1976); Marcelo Selowsky, "Income Distribution, Basic Needs and Trade-Offs with Growth: The Case of Semi-Industrialized Latin American Countries," *World Development*, 9 (1981), pp. 73–92.

70. *World Development Report 1980*, p. iii. Stress was placed on the productive potential of a better-schooled and healthier population, but the Report was clear in accepting that education, health, and nutrition were in themselves "ends of development" (p. 2).

discussion of human development issues the Report said: "Ten years ago this chapter would have been written very differently. In certain areas thinking has changed substantially."[71]

There was considerable continuity then in the Clausen-Stern push toward human resources. Both shared McNamara's special interest in family planning, but their commitment was especially remarkable in that it ran against attitudes in the U.S. administration. These attitudes had undergone a surprising reversal, from strong support in the 1970s to ideological antagonism. Clausen ignored a warning by Senator Charles Percy, chairman of the Foreign Relations Committee, that on this matter the Bank was out of whack with the U.S. administration."[72]

As senior vice president for operations and chairman of the Managing Review Committee, Stern was in an exceptionally strong position to press for particular objectives, and one that he consistently pushed was family planning. Population policy, and so health, were repeatedly highlighted in CPPs and other policy and programming discussions on India and Bangladesh, for instance.[73] When the committee met to review the Bangladesh CPP in 1983, Stern called attention to population, urging the staff to avoid delays: he "emphasized that improvements in the . . . program should be implemented as soon as they were identified."[74]

Stern's campaign for attention to population concerns was carried out, for the most part, at the level of country program decisions. In 1982, for example, he ordered that "CPPs should not be circulated unless they contain a discussion of the population issue."[75] His insistence and authority were largely responsible also for the choice of population as the theme for *World Development Report 1984*, the only socially oriented topic addressed by the reports between 1983 and 1989.

Set in motion by McNamara and endorsed by Clausen and Stern, human resource lending found a third stimulus in the macroeconomic crisis of the 1980s. Because social programs and consumer subsidies tend to be large in government budgets, pruning that spending—and raising fee income from services—had long been a priority in Bank macroeconomic policy dialogues. In the context of the debt crisis, this objective took on added prominence. By engaging in social sector projects, the Bank found that, instead of simply pressing for blanket spending cuts, it was in a position to discuss with and persuade sector officials of the importance of finding alternative ways to finance, allocate, and deliver those services. Social projects thus became a friendlier and more constructive way to lead borrowers by the hand toward austerity, even as such services were being made more equitable and poverty oriented. Killing two birds with one stone, social service projects were

71. *World Development Report 1980*, p. 46.

72. A. W. Clausen, interview with the authors, June 8, 1992.

73. See, for example, India 1983 CPP, pp. 7, 45.

74. Basil Kavalsky, through E. Stern, to members of the Managing Committee, *Bangladesh CPP*, July 21, 1983.

75. Ernest Stern to Heinz Vergin and Basil Kavalsky, September 17, 1982.

discovered to be a powerful tool for the occasion: they served the adjustment, and thus productivity and growth, objective; and they served the equity and poverty objectives.

Debate

The perception that poverty had been demoted grew stronger each year after 1980. The Bank's concern over inequalities and political instability and attempts to encourage a still small level of social sector lending did nothing to counter that image. But management differed on the appropriate response. In 1983 a staff member in the public relations office warned that "the Bank's activities have, in fact, become markedly less focused on reducing poverty. This is a potential public relations problem," and, "Many staff feel that the pressure is off" with respect to poverty.[76] In March 1983 the Managing Committee discussed an annual report on urban operations and "questioned whether poverty issues were being given less weight than previously. In the case of housing," the authors admitted, "targeting projects to the poor is possible but they are extremely difficult to replicate. Thus, there had been some shift towards middle-income housing."[77] The perception of heartlessness was reinforced by the messages of key policy papers prepared for health and for education.[78] In discussing how to finance their sectors, the solution for each lay in user fees, in various guises.[79] The Bank's annual reports between 1983 and 1986 carried few references to poverty: the 1983 report had no section on the topic for the first time in many years, an omission repeated in 1984 and 1986; and the 1985 report had a brief sentence.[80] Clausen's Annual General Meeting speeches contained references to poverty alleviation, but the central messages concerned other topics. In January 1984, when the Managing Committee turned to the question of how to persuade major shareholders to go along with a General Capital Increase, Frank Vogl warned that "the strongest supporters of the Bank remained those who viewed aid from a humanitarian perspective," and therefore, that "the Bank should emphasize the aspects of its work that appealed to this perspective."[81]

76. David Beckmann, Information and Public Affairs Department, through Julian Grenfell to Frank Vogl, December 20, 1983. The second quote is from p. 35 of a report attached to the memorandum documenting the demotion of poverty in Bank operations.

77. Minutes of Managing Committee meeting, March 28, 1983.

78. World Bank, *Financing Education in Developing Countries. An Exploration of Policy Options*, 1986. *Financing Health Services in Developing Countries. An Agenda for Reform*, 1987.

79. The four reforms proposed in the health paper—"charge users," "provide insurance," "encourage the nongovernment sector," and "decentralize"—all sought in effect to transfer the health-financing burden from central government to users, local government, and charities. Ibid., pp. 3–6.

80. World Bank, *Annual Reports* for 1983–86.

81. Minutes of Managing Committee meeting to discuss paper prepared by Frank Vogl of the External Relations Department, *Politics and the Future Role of the Bank,*

Looking back at this period, a 1988 OED report asked: "The Bank's Poverty Focus: Waxing, Waning or Wavering?" It noted that "speeches by senior Bank officials have been devoted to global macroeconomic problems, domestic policies and international cooperation, except for a January 1985 speech by the president which focused on poverty issues."[82] The question was also raised by the Board. In 1984 the Canadian executive director remarked on the Bank's move to "more emphasis on *efficiency* objectives at the expense of *equity* objectives."[83]

For most staff members, the shift in emphasis was apparent in their work instructions. Poverty lending had been an onerous requirement, unhelpful to careers. Designing projects to reach the very poor meant greater administrative effort and risk. Compiling poverty statistics was felt to be artificial, and motivation was dampened by the knowledge that much "poverty lending" was spurious. McNamara's armylike apparatus of work rules, including time sheets and poverty body counts, had become a demeaning substitute for the commitment and judgment of the professional.[84] The relaxation in pressure for targeting was therefore noticed and welcome.

In 1985 these personal impressions were given official confirmation by an evaluation of loan operations in fiscal 1984 by the Operations Policy Staff.[85] This report had been carried out following a management decision of September 1983, Operational Policy Note 2.07, that had attempted at once to simplify and to extend the practice of poverty monitoring at country and project levels.[86] The Operational

---

EXR/MC84-14, on May 10, 1984. Though the Committee concurred, there was no noticeable change in the Bank's external message until 1986.

82. World Bank, *Rural Development, World Bank Experience, 1965–86,* 1988, box 2.2, p. 15.

83. Morris Miller, executive director for Canada, to R. Munzberg, "JAC—Bank's Poverty Focus," February 9, 1984. Miller attached a paper containing proposals for more effective monitoring of poverty work.

84. Poverty reporting requirements increased over the 1970s—always ahead of compliance. An internal review of rural development projects noted that: "Mr. Stern directed that the percentage of benefits accruing to various income groups should be indicated in Staff Appraisal Reports. Very few Appraisal Reports attempt to comply with this direction." A. Musa to M. Yudelman, *Poverty Reporting—Comments,* November 17, 1982. A typical staff member's reaction to these requirements was: "You can see the plight of the poor if you just walk around." J. R. Peberdy to van Gigh, November 7, 1979. Cited by Wilfred Beckerman, "The Measurement of Poverty in the Context of the World Bank's Activities," May 1981.

85. Country Policy Department, *Focus on Poverty,* June 1985.

86. At the May 1985 meeting of vice presidents, Mr. de Azcarate recalled that OPN 2.07 had sought "to reduce the emphasis on the quantification of the poverty focus in individual projects." The OPN had been influenced by the report on the Bank's poverty measurements prepared by Wilfred Beckerman of Oxford University in May 1981, which agreed with the view prevalent among staff that most of the effort devoted to measurement was unjustified. Despite this effort to simplify, poverty monitoring remained a constant requirement—and source of aggravation—through the 1980s. Thus, on April 24, 1985, "it was decided to extend poverty monitoring of Bank lending to, among others, the industry sector. . . . A recent check

Policy Note also instructed the Country Policy Department to "prepare annually a brief Bankwide overview of poverty work." The resulting report found "a decline in the amount of lending for the sectors considered to offer the most direct benefits to the poor, i.e., rural development, primary education, population, health and nutrition, small-scale enterprises, urban development and water supply and sewerage, from an average of 28% of total lending in FY79–83 to 22% in FY84."[87]

Several staff members noted that "the current preoccupation with reviving stagnant economies has necessarily taken precedence over the distribution of benefits within economies." But many objected to the suggestion that the poverty effort had declined. Stern acknowledged that there existed "serious problems of public relations, monitoring and management on poverty," but argued that, despite adjustment lending, there was considerable scope for improving the poverty effect of other operations. One speaker attributed the statistical decline in poverty lending to implementation difficulties. Others noted that projects alone were an inadequate means of measuring poverty efforts.[88] A summary of the meeting prepared for circulation in the Bank stressed the setback to poverty lending and the need for additional effort: "adjustment programs should try to mitigate their effects on the poor," and lending operations in general should "focus more deliberately on poverty alleviation through appropriate project design."[89]

The influence of donor opinion on Bank priorities at this time is suggested by the contents of a report prepared during 1984–85 in an effort to support its case for a general capital increase before G-7 finance ministers. Explaining the report's agenda to the Board, D. J. Wood said:

> You may be surprised that some issues have not been included at all. Why for example, are we not looking at the Bank's role in poverty alleviation? The answer is that we are building on the consensus of the 1970's with regard to the development objectives of the institution. We are deliberately taking some things for granted. Although this planning exercise is a means of reassessing our sense of direction, we do not see it as involving questions about our fundamental purpose and objectives.[90]

In the context of accumulating evidence that poverty projects had been unsuccessful, criticism that the issue was being neglected, and the well-known lack of interest by G-7 finance ministers, Wood's remark was a transparent rationalization for

---

of Appraisal Reports on industry projects approved in FY86, revealed that this situation was in fact not being adhered to." Memo by A. R. Khan, January 17, 1986.

87. Office of the senior vice president, Operations, to files, minutes of operational vice presidents' meeting of April 24, 1985.

88. Minutes, May 6, 1985.

89. Shahid Husain to department directors and division chiefs, regional offices, OPS, EIS, "Focus on Poverty: A Review of Bank Operations in FY84," July 2, 1985.

90. Statement by Mr. D. J. Wood at informal Board seminar on "Future of the Bank," June 8, 1984.

silence. The voluminous papers and minutes of meetings produced over seven months by this exercise contained only fleeting references to poverty.[91]

The image of downgrading continued to gather strength after Clausen's term ended. In May 1987 a Nordic symposium was held in Helsinki to discuss the question "Has the World Bank Abandoned Its Focus on Poverty Alleviation?"[92] Indeed, external criticism surged after 1985, much of it centered on the austerity at the heart of the adjustment effort. The most resounding objection came from the United Nations Children's Fund, which published a collection of papers in 1987 under the title, *Adjustment with a Human Face*. These papers were case studies of the "social costs of adjustment," that is, of worsening health, education, employment, and incomes in countries undergoing economic adjustment.[93] The argument was muddied by a failure—or refusal—to distinguish between the "social costs" of corrective measures and the costs of the preceding macroeconomic disequilibria.[94] Nonetheless, the book was well timed politically and achieved rhetorical success. "Human face" became part of the adjustment language, discomfiting the Bank.

But by 1987–88 it was the Bank itself that had decided most firmly that it had strayed from its poverty mission. This message was amplified and transmitted in several major reports, beginning with a status report requested by Barber Conable five months after his appointment was announced. The report, prepared under the direction of Shahid Husain, was delivered on April 7, 1987.[95] A separate task force on food security in Africa called for additional or enhanced efforts to address poverty in that region more directly, *over and above macroeconomic adjustment*.[96]

Delivering his conclusions, Husain wrote Conable that, in the task force's view, social lending remained strong, but that "the perception externally and even among many staff" was that the Bank had drawn back from its concern for poverty. "It would be very easy," he continued, "to add up the substantial program of activities which is ongoing or planned in this area and to argue both to ourselves and the

91. Yet, at the initial Board seminar, executive directors insisted on the inclusion of poverty in the agenda and minutes of the meeting record that, in fact, members were assured that "the poverty focus will be reviewed" for the purposes of the report. Serena Han Clarke to executive directors and alternates, June 15, 1984.

92. "Economic Development and Adjustment in the Third World, A Symposium on the World Bank's Role," Helsinki, May 11–12, 1987.

93. G. A. Cornia, R. Jolly, and F. Stewart, *Adjustment with a Human Face* (Oxford University Press, 1987). Though other research questioned the validity of UNICEF's studies, the book carried the day with public opinion.

94. Subsequent rebuttals of the UNICEF case likewise overlooked the distinction between the results of unplanned, market-imposed adjustment and those of planned adjustment measures.

95. In December 1986 Conable appointed a task force to consider "once again" the Bank's approach to the alleviation of poverty and to recommend new initiatives.

96. World Bank, *The Challenge of Hunger in Africa: A Call to Action* (1988).

outside world that the Bank's poverty focus is unchanged. *Neither I, nor my colleagues on the Task Force, believe that is the current reality.*"[97]

Many in the Bank thought that all this questioning and criticism missed the mark, and this was more than plainly expressed by Ernest Stern to a delegation of German parliamentarians in 1986. "Adjustment programs," he said, "are very beneficial to the lower-income groups."[98] He was referring to a direct benefit, not to the eventual trickle-down that would follow adjustment and renewed growth.

Stern's principal argument was that overvalued exchange rates along with other practices such as export taxes on agricultural commodities and import tariffs "all burdened agriculture." Moreover, the fiscal and protectionist policies that were responsible for the crisis "very clearly benefit the rich."[99] For instance, import protection, food subsidies, and health and education expenditures, as currently designed, favored urban, often middle-class inhabitants, not the rural poor. Similarly, high wage policies merely helped workers "in the modern sector of the economy which employs only a small proportion of the total population . . . with the result that inflation was fueled."[100] In this view, the cry against the "social costs of adjustment" was a misperception because those who would be hurt by adjustment were typically urban dwellers, not the rural poor. "Every study that has ever been made," Stern emphasized, "shows, very clearly, that even the people who live in the slums have a larger income, a larger real income, than those on the farms." If people thought differently, it was because "we see the slums, and they're terrible. We don't see the tremendous poverty in the rural areas, and that poverty is worse in every country than it is in the slums."[101] Stern took the standard complaint—"too much adjustment"—and stood it on its head.[102]

Stern was going beyond the uncontroversial argument that for the longer run the poor needed a growing economy. This long-run argument did not rule out

---

97. Shahid Husain to Barber Conable, April 7, 1987; emphasis added.

98. Remarks by Ernest Stern to a visiting delegation of members of the German Parliament, October 29, 1986. But after the UNICEF outcry, the Bank retreated, no longer insisting that "adjustment is good for the poor" in public statements. Yet the conviction persisted. Kim Jaycox, vice president for Sub-Saharan Africa, arguing for structural adjustment in 1993, wrote: "Expenditures in health, education and so forth have increased as a result of structural adjustment in every country. . . . The elites are the ones that really suffer. The rural poor, even the informal sector have a big advantage out of structural adjustment because they get access to foreign exchange at least at some price . . . [and] their farm market prices are up. Their access to inputs is up. . . . The elites . . . [p]eople who have their kids in Switzerland in school . . . always say the poor are the ones being hurt." "Regional Briefing for Executive Directors and Alternates on the Africa Region," February 3, 1993.

99. Remarks by Stern, October 29, 1986.

100. Ibid.

101. Ibid.

102. On this occasion he did not resort to another much-cited argument—that because inflation hurt the poor more than the rich, adjustment, by ending inflation, improved equity.

short-run "social costs" and was therefore compatible with a "human face" middle road, or a "balanced approach." But if adjustment was pro-poor even in the short run, compromise would have been illogical.

Anne Krueger shared Stern's position, and one of the more important research projects carried out under her vice presidency was "Comparative Study of the Political Economy of Agricultural Pricing Policies," which was directed by Maurice Schiff and Alberto Valdes. The study strengthened the empirical basis for the "adjustment is pro-poor" case by measuring the overvaluation or exchange-rate "tax" on agriculture.[103]

Critics, already provoked by the no-compromise implications of the "adjustment is pro-poor" argument, were additionally excited by the seemingly unfeeling insistence on quick adjustment—what came to be called a "shock" or "big bang" approach. The reasons for this preference were both political and economic: "getting it over with" before political opposition was mobilized, and reaping the economic benefits of a return of confidence. For its proponents there was no "unfeeling" aspect to this prescription, and, in 1984, Stern found an elegant way to make that point by circulating extracts from a pamphlet written in 1965 by Escott Reid.[104] Reid spoke of the diplomatic skills, sympathy, and compassion that were necessary to good policy dialogues in poor countries. He said:

> The international diplomat of development, once he appreciates something of the problems of the political leaders of poor countries, will put his advice . . . on a delicate and difficult choice between alternative policies, not as "This alternative is clearly better than that" but rather "If you choose this alternative, you will slow down your rate of economic growth.". . . For it is the extent of the slowdown which is the real economic cost of . . . choosing a softer course of action, which is politically easier, instead of a harder course which will give a higher rate of economic growth.[105]

Gentle and sympathetic encouragement of the "harder course" was Stern's version of "adjustment with a human face." Not given to polemics, this indirect message to colleagues seems to have been the closest that Stern came to debating with an increasing number of critics. Stern's adjustment optimism was shared with bankers

103. See chapter 9. The pro-devaluation argument briefly revived a very old debate on the social effects of farm exports. The United States Public Broadcasting System aired a program on "The Politics of Food" in December 1986 and January 1987 which argued that export crops were enriching a few farmers and hurting the poorest. The argument was endorsed by Bruce Babbit, then a Democratic presidential candidate. Reported in article by Lucy Komisar, *Journal of Commerce,* February 25, 1988. In fact, it is difficult to generalize about the distributional effects of pro-trade adjustment policies. This was the conclusion, for instance of a study, undertaken at the request of IMF Managing Director Johannes Witteveen, by Omotunde Johnson and Joanne Salop, "Distributional Aspects of Stabilization Programs in Developing Countries," *Staff Papers,* International Monetary Fund, vol. 27, no. 1 (March 1980), pp. 1–23.

104. Director of the South Asia and the Middle East Department, 1962–64, and author of *Strengthening the World Bank* (Adlai Stevenson Institute, 1973).

105. Ernest Stern to operational vice presidents, June 18, 1984. Quoted from Escott Reid, *The Future of the World Bank: An Essay* (Washington, D.C., 1965).

and financial authorities who, by happy coincidence, would also benefit from—indeed, would be the most immediate beneficiaries of—rapid adjustment by borrowers. In a note to David Mulford, assistant secretary for international affairs at Treasury, Stern wrote in 1986: "with appropriate policies . . . the turn-around in the creditworthiness of the highly-indebted countries can come fairly quickly.[106]

"Appropriate policies," above all austerity, would necessarily hurt the Bank's image as an advocate of the poor. But, for the adjustment advocate, the Bank's loss was the borrower's gain because to achieve forceful adjustment and a quick turn-around it was as important to seem as to be hard faced. This was a consequence of the rarely discussed role of psychology in adjustment. Public discussions of adjustment dealt with policies, but two key objectives—getting borrowers to act and restoring financial confidence—were matters of motivation and belief. To dwell on the possible impoverishing effects of debt repayment and adjustment would give grounds to political opposition and to those who proposed temporizing half-measures. Likewise it would tend to confirm fears that adjustment would not be carried through, delaying the return of confidence. A "human-face" posture, because it would delay or water down an immediate, sharp response to the financial emergency, would in the end be crueler.

It is understandable that a heightened awareness of public statements, especially the Bank's doctrinal message and the spin given to country assessments, became part of its adjustment agenda. The tightening of message control was most evident in the Economics vice presidency, where the climate went from academic openness to ideological rigor. Debt forgiveness and the social costs of debt repayment and adjustment became taboo subjects.[107] Message control was also felt in operational departments. The vice presidency for Latin America and the Caribbean was admonished for publishing a monograph entitled *Poverty in Latin America: The Impact of Depression.* The study concluded that "the effects of the crisis on the poor are extremely serious." Its most provocative thought was "the very real possibility that rapid growth will fail to resume in the next five years," and therefore, "that it would be unwise to wait for resumed growth before reforming government agencies dealing with education, health, nutrition, and other social services."[108] Though the monograph followed and was in fact prompted by the

106. Ernest Stern to David Mulford, February 7, 1986.

107. When Benjamin King, former director of the Development Economics Department, was called back from retirement to succeed Krueger, he described the atmosphere on his return using terms such as "taboo," "censorship," and "suppression of free speech."

108. Guy Pfeffermann, *Poverty in Latin America: The Impact of Depression* (World Bank, 1986), p. 6. Pfeffermann forecast: "It is reasonable to expect that per capita consumption and employment will grow very modestly if at all in most of the region's countries, unless external circumstances change substantially. Except in Brazil and Colombia, Latin America's development effort has been set back a decade." David Knox, vice president for Latin America, had proposed the study as a follow-up to Baker's September 1985 second thoughts on adjustment at Seoul, where the "Baker Plan" was announced.

realization that adjustment would not be quick, its message was ahead of the Bank's position. That position would soon change radically.

The Bank felt little need to persuade the public that adjustment was the best course for the poor. The financial emergency was expected to end soon. A public campaign was thus an unnecessary risk. More importantly, at this time a conservative U.S. Treasury, relatively unconcerned with social issues, was calling the tune for the Bank while at the same time shielding it from public outcries—and threats to funding—that originated in liberal constituencies of the U.S. Congress and abroad.[109] The Bank was able to ignore not only criticisms of its alleged neglect of poverty and "social costs of adjustment" but of newer issues such as the environment and women's rights. In any case the effort to persuade the world that through adjustment lending the Bank was acting in the best short-run interests of the poor was foredoomed. And the principal reason was the Bank's own past rhetoric.

For years the Bank had drawn attention to the specific and visible characteristics of its *projects*. In the 1950s and 1960s it was to stress their "productive" nature, so that annual reports were made impressive by photographs of towering, concrete dam walls and stretches of freshly laid tarmac. During the 1970s the Bank highlighted instead the physical features of smallholder and urban slum projects showing peasants in rice fields and barrio residents laying sewers to create graphic images of a Bank involved shoulder to shoulder with the poor. In addition, an emphasis on statistics—and therefore on the measurable—added to the impression that what mattered was concrete and countable. Efforts to improve bureaucracies and policies were certainly mentioned, but not in headlines. All this was fundraising wisdom: investors were comforted and donors satisfied by "seeing" where their funds had ended up. But, having played to and therefore endorsed the commonsense illusion that what mattered was what could be seen, the Bank was at a disadvantage to explain the undoubtedly real but hard-to-see benefits for the poor of adjustment loans.

Even for much of the Bank's own staff it was the tangible evidence—fewer "poverty projects," less targeting, and cuts in social spending by borrowers—that persuaded them that direct poverty alleviation had been demoted, a conclusion that was reflected in the Husain study mentioned above.[110] The Bank had internal-

109. June 1985 statements by two Treasury officials regarding Treasury priorities for the multilateral development banks contain no reference to poverty or other social issues; they deal only with privatization, macroeconomic policies, and financial and management issues. Memorandum from M. Qureshi to A. W. Clausen, *U.S. Position on MDBs,* July 8, 1985, attaching copy of speech by James W. Conrow, deputy assistant secretary, U.S. Treasury, at the Asian Development Fund donor's meeting in Rome, June 17, 1985; and copy of letter from Bruce E. Thompson, Jr., assistant secretary (Legislative Affairs), U.S. Treasury, regarding Treasury views on MDB policies and upcoming replenishments. During the 1970s the Bank had grown increasingly dependent on and attentive to the U.S. Congress.

110. The conviction with which staff members identified a poverty focus in projects bears out, once again, Richard Neustadt, cited in chapter 3: "The tendency of bureaucratic

ized its own rhetoric. Outsiders were even more inclined to equate project practice with priorities. There was no disagreement on the fundamental need for adjustment to return to a process of long-run, *indirect* poverty reduction, but the *direct* poverty effects of adjustment remained controversial into the 1990s.[111]

At the time, however, changing circumstances—the drawing out of the debt crisis, growing political objections to adjustment policies, and turnover at the top of the Bank—made the "social cost of adjustment" debate academic.

Rededication: After 1987

In September 1987, Barber Conable, who had succeeded Clausen in June 1986, formally "rededicated" the Bank "to the fight against poverty." The occasion was, again, an Annual Meeting speech. The announcement was not sharply distinguished from Conable's earlier declarations on the same theme nor from other items in a litany of priorities.[112] Nonetheless, the statement can be taken to mark what became a change of direction for the Bank. To begin with, it set a new rhetorical tone. From this time the Bank would repeatedly refer to itself in "born again" terms. Soon it would have declared itself "renewed," "reorganized," and "rededicated." And poverty, it promised, would be "reaffirmed," "reintegrated," and "revitalized." Four years later, Lewis Preston, Conable's successor and a former Wall Street banker, opened his presidency by taking that rhetoric to a new height. Poverty, he said, was the Bank's "overarching objective." Reporting on the speech and seemingly unaware of Conable's recent rebaptism of the Bank, the *Financial Times* wrote: "World Bank refocuses its gaze on plight of the world's poor. . . . If Mr. Preston is serious, the bank could be entering a new phase."[113]

---

language to create in private the same images presented to the public should never be underrated." *Presidential Power,* p. 139. The point is developed by Robert Packenham, who added: "public statements force the policymaker to work with the goals and expectations established by those statements because congressmen and various aid constituencies do not forget the rhetoric even if the official may want to." *Liberal America and the Third World.*

111. During this period the IMF remained firmly convinced that "there is no support for the view that adjustment programs generally hurt the poor as a group. The rural poor often benefit directly from adjustment programs." IMF, *The Implications of Adjustment for Poverty: Recent Experiences with Fund-Supported Programs and Lessons,* paper presented to the Development Committee meeting, September 26, 1988, p. 1.

112. Indeed, in a personal interview with the authors in which he recounted the highspots of his term, he did not mention his statement on poverty at the 1987 Annual Meeting. April 13, 1986.

113. In his September 30, 1987, address to the annual meeting of the Board of Governors, Conable said that he had "renewed," "reorganized," and "rededicated" the Bank to poverty. The 1987 Husain report on poverty alleviation spoke of "reintegrating" poverty concerns. Poverty was said to have been "revitalized" at a meeting of the PRE Committee, November 21, 1990. A progress report on "Implementing the World Bank's Assistance

Defining itself by contrast to its past and trumpeting its commitment to poverty and to other newly assumed social commitments, especially the environment and gender equality, the turn-of-decade Bank found energy, enthusiasm, and external approval. In so doing it was implicitly devaluing the old Bank.

But the move from rhetoric to operations was gradual. Though it took fewer years than the gearing up of McNamara's poverty campaign, which at the time was a more radical redirection of the institution, this second attempt to bring the Bank closer to the poor was delayed by similar obstacles—internal resistance, false starts, doubts regarding the proper weight of productivity and need as criteria for allocation, and a need to develop large-scale lending instruments. Most of those start-up difficulties were faced by Conable between 1987 and 1991. By the time Preston arrived in June 1991, the Bank had changed substantially in terms of staff commitment to social objectives, size and composition of its "social lending" portfolio, and conceptual underpinnings for that new role. Even so, change was far from over. Indeed (viewed a decade later), the process of reexamination and change that started or at least accelerated after 1987 seems to have become a permanent characteristic of the Bank. And much of that effervescence—or instability—continues to revolve around the competing claims of social and economic objectives.

There seems to be nothing in Conable's background to suggest that he would become an advocate for the poor. A small-town lawyer from New York state, he had a long and respected career as a Republican member of the U.S. House of Representatives. His specialization in finance—he became the ranking minority member of the House Ways and Means Committee—had brought him into close contact with senior Republican officials, particularly George Bush and Secretary of the Treasury James Baker. And it was Baker who, by Conable's account, inveigled him into the Bank presidency. By contrast, before joining the Bank, McNamara as secretary of defense had considered and developed strong opinions regarding the security implications of underdevelopment—even overstepping Cabinet protocol to speak publicly on the issue—and he had been a fellow traveler, as it were, of the liberal thinkers and program administrators of the Kennedy-Johnson War on Poverty.

Nor was Conable's initiation one likely to induce strong social commitment. His briefing dealt mainly with the Bank's macroeconomic adjustment and growth-promotion business, and though he was a newcomer to the third world, the briefing contained little to open his eyes to the scope and nature of underdevelopment and deprivation or to the Bank's own history of hopes, commitments, and frustrations in attempting to find faster solutions to those needs.

Yet the briefing did contain a short, pointed exception to that broader omission. Reviewing its lending for agriculture and rural development it said:

Strategies to Reduce Poverty," presented to the Development Committee meeting on April 28, 1992, began by stating that "poverty reduction has been 'reaffirmed'" (p. 1). The 1986 AGM speech also spoke of "rededication," and that year Conable appointed the Husain Task Force on Poverty. *Financial Times*, October 23, 1991, p. 4.

abject poverty and chronic malnutrition remain unresolved. . . . Alleviation of *chronic poverty* remains a major goal of the Bank's operations in this sector. How to more effectively assist poor people in acquiring skills and productive assets so as to escape from poverty remains a major challenge for the Bank, however. In addition to promoting long-term economic growth, carefully designed programs are needed to alleviate hunger in the short term.[114]

The suggestion that the Bank might become involved in alleviating "short-term" hunger would have been a radical proposal for an institution traditionally careful to avoid a "relief" role, or even its appearance, and all the more so in the conservative political context of the 1980s. But Conable's arrival came on the heels of a burst of drought relief and other short-term emergency loans: in 1985–86 the Bank approved eight such loans totaling $649 million. Conable was thus presented with a Bank principally concerned with macroeconomic and growth objectives, with a small but growing involvement in human resource lending, and a recently expanded role— which bordered on relief—in the alleviation of immediate human deprivations.

It is understandable that a career politician, with no background in development, financial markets, or corporate management, would proceed gradually when it came to proposals for new priorities and even more slowly in putting them into effect. Conable's capacity to act, moreover, was greatly hampered by two unexpected developments: he was abandoned by the U.S. administration that had appointed him; and he fell into a traumatic and protracted administrative reorganization of the institution.[115]

Yet at the same time Conable's outsider role, in relation to both the U.S. administration and the self-contained, professional bubble of the Bank, may have made change easier to bring about. Piqued by the unfriendly attitude of U.S. officials, he also felt

114. The briefings were largely the work of Ernest Stern whose mandate as senior vice president for operations covered, in his own words, "the core of the Bank." Ernest Stern to Barber Conable, *Briefing Materials—Operations,* April 30, 1986. Quotations are from letter of transmittal and p. 5 of section on Operations Policy Staff. Discussing education the briefing notes the need for more primary schooling and literacy but points out the cost of expanding coverage and the probable setback effect of adjustment programs: "Despite the high returns to education and the magnitude of needs . . . macroeconomic considerations will dictate sharp fiscal austerity for the sector in most countries . . . the adjustment process will inevitably impact strongly on education" (p. 8).

115. Major shareholders, led by the United States, voted against the Bank's proposed administrative budget for 1986–87. Though this occurred two days before Conable took office, the decision was tantamount to a vote of no confidence in the incoming president. Conable would need a supportive U.S. Treasury during his term for the approval of administrative budgets, capital increases, and IDA replenishments. Instead, he quickly learned that his friendship with James Baker and other U.S. administration officials would count less than the continuing hostile attitude towards the Bank of U.S. Treasury officials, and especially of David Mulford, the undersecretary for International Affairs. The reorganization was an effort to reduce administrative costs, in response to the position taken by the major shareholders. Interviews with the authors, May 8 and August 19, 1996.

freer and more motivated to develop his own views. Later he would refer to his stance on social issues with some pride and contrast it with what he saw as a fixation with adjustment by U.S. officials as well as by the previous Bank administration: "Growth isn't bad . . . but the Bank's purpose is the reduction of poverty and not just better macroeconomic figures."[116] In this outsider role he was both reinforced and nudged toward social issues by his wife, Charlotte, an activist for women's education and other social concerns before and during his tenure at the Bank, with whom he enjoyed a productive professional partnership. She invariably traveled with him, collecting impressions and information on living conditions and social programs, and participated in Bank meetings and debates on social issues. Conable dedicated much of his first two years in office to visiting developing countries, and, by his own account, these visits strengthened the views that he was developing on social topics.

In September 1987 Conable turned his back on this frustrating start. He announced the end of the administrative reorganization and began taking a more determined stance on social issues. In 1986 he had stressed that growth was necessary for social improvement, saying that growth would be the "healing antidote" to the "poison of poverty." Now, he said, "growth, by itself, is not enough." It was a return to the McNamara starting point. Conable went on to outline direct poverty-alleviating measures in the style of McNamara.[117] Over the rest of his term the institution engaged in a repetition of McNamara's early search for an operational poverty strategy: this was the institution's second attempt to find ways to improve on trickle-down.

Social Agenda

The administrative reorganization of the Bank became a major facilitator for the redirection of policy. Two senior appointments that were to some extent accidentally associated with the reorganization were especially important. Conable's decision to switch Stern and Qureshi into the positions of senior vice president for Finance and Operations, respectively, brought a more willing collaborator to the operational side of the poverty initiatives that were being set in motion. Stern continued to participate in senior management discussions, but was weakened in his ability to impose his doubts and disagreement regarding those initiatives.

A second influential staffing change followed Anne Krueger's resignation as vice president for Economics and Research and her replacement by Stanley Fischer in the fall of 1987. At first skeptical, Fischer was quickly won over to the poverty proposals that emerged over the next three years. He upgraded poverty in the research agenda and during 1989 agreed to the choice of poverty as the 1990 World Development Report theme, helping in the working out of its message.

---

116. Interview with authors, April 13, 1996.
117. World Bank, *The Conable Years at the World Bank: Major Policy Addresses of Barber Conable, 1986–91*, pp. 3–11, 31–41.

Two other organizational changes strengthened the role of poverty alleviation. One emerged directly from the reorganization: the Population, Health and Nutrition and the Education and Training departments were joined and then decentralized. Originally part of the Operations Policy Staff, these departments had functioned as central pools of expertise in their fields, carrying out research, formulating policy, and providing specialized manpower to the regional offices on demand. The decentralization of these human resource specialists —into offices called "Population and Human Resources Divisions"—gave each region an operational capacity and a bureaucratic incentive for human resource lending.

A second administrative step consisted in the creation in 1988 of a class of high-priority activities, called areas of "special operational emphasis." These operational categories, which included poverty alleviation, human resource development, women in development, and the private sector, were budgeted and monitored separately. That effort had been interrupted by the reorganization, and then, by Husain's appointment as vice president for Latin America. Thanking Husain for proposals that would "reintegrate" poverty concerns "back into the center of [the Bank's] operations," Conable affirmed that he was "committed to assuring active Bank leadership in this area."[118] In July 1987 he appointed a new group under Attila Karaosmanoglu and gave it more explicit presidential recognition. The new effort represented a broadening of the Bank's involvement: where the Husain report had been developed under the aegis of the former central Operations Policy Staff, the new team was representative of the Bank as a whole, for it included members from the regional offices and the Finance and Economic departments.

The same day, W. David Hopper, who would oversee the new task force, drew attention to its political importance to the Bank. He wrote Conable that the Annual Meeting speech had

> generated high expectations within and outside the Bank that the Bank will be giving higher priority to poverty issues. . . . Parliamentarians from the U.S. and Europe have recently begun sending strong letters of encouragement for a strengthened Bank focus on poverty . . . there is a strong political need to provide evidence of the Bank's serious attention to poverty questions. . . . The report should be produced as soon as possible so as to be of maximum use internally to support GCI [General Capital Increase] discussions.[119]

Karaosmanoglu's report, presented in May 1988, took Conable's "rededication" to be a mandate for an exceptionally broad review, including a large number of sectoral and country studies, and for adventurous proposals. But Conable remained uncertain as to the administrative status and weight that he intended to attach to

118. Barber Conable to Shahid Husain, *Preliminary Report of the Poverty Task Force,* July 28, 1987. Conable was referring to the report delivered by Husain on April 7. He apologized that the "hectic reorganization" had "resulted in your preliminary report receiving far less prompt attention than both the report and the subject deserves."

119. David Hopper to Barber Conable, follow-up to the Poverty Task Force, July 28, 1987.

the effort. He presented an early version to the Policy Committee asking whether it should be discussed by the Board. Hopper now downplayed the report, stressing that it was not a statement of policy, and other senior staff remained unconvinced regarding a return to poverty alleviation.[120] When a draft was reviewed by the Operations Committee in February, discussants warned that "poverty alleviation programs generally require significant Bank resources for ESW [economic and sector work], project preparation and project supervision." In addition, several members noted that the paper "did not adequately highlight the limits to our knowledge of the poor . . . [and] might inadvertently raise expectations about what can be done in the near term."[121] The report was criticized by the Board, some of whom argued that it proposed a "welfare" approach to poverty amelioration and did not stress enough the importance of growth. Some also objected that the "core" program would force the Board to preapprove operational details that were not yet known.[122] In the view of staff members, the Board's reaction was tantamount to disapproval. Moeen Qureshi, senior vice president for operations, responded by writing to the regional vice presidents:

> I have been very concerned to learn that following the Board discussion, there has been a perception among the staff that poverty amelioration is no longer at the forefront of our operational strategy. I stress that this is incorrect. . . . [I]t is essential that poverty profiles be prepared for all countries. . . . It is also essential to develop core poverty programs for selected countries.[123]

In the event, neither of the report's two principal recommendations were adopted at the time. What Conable called the "key" recommendation called for the identification and implementation in each country of a "core poverty program," consisting of a set of "strategies and operations whose primary and immediate objective is the alleviation of poverty, particularly extreme poverty."[124] A second proposal consisted of poverty-oriented program loans, extending the Bank's experience with structural adjustment loans (SALs) and sector adjustment loans (SECALs) into the poverty area. Numerous and detailed modifications in lending procedures were suggested to facilitate the proposed loans. These innovative suggestions were accompanied by a straightforward recommendation that additional concessional funding be sought to carry out the effort, referred to as a Special Poverty Fund.

Conable approved of the proposals, seeing the Core Poverty Program as a way to "stimulate stronger efforts to reach the utterly poor and the destitute."[125] In May he wrote: "I support in principle the proposed CPP [Core Poverty Program]

120. Minutes of the Policy Committee, February 24, 1988.

121. Minutes of the Operations Committee, February 8, 1988.

122. Minutes of Board meeting, July 26, 1988.

123. Qureshi to regional vice presidents, poverty and Bank operations, December 12, 1988.

124. Barber Conable to members, Policy Committee, *Task Force on Poverty Alleviation,* May 13, 1988.

125. Minutes of the Operations Committee to consider report of the Poverty Task Force, April 27, 1988, p. 3.

approach [and] the notion of policy based, fast disbursing Poverty Program Loans," but he postponed a decision on the Special Poverty Fund.[126] The proposals ran into criticism within the Bank. Stern "considered that the CPP [Core Poverty Program] concept was not a very good idea . . . [and that] there was a proliferation of special approaches (for example on the environment or on the private sector) which fragment management control and reduce the response flexibility." However, Stern did acknowledge the "potential political attractiveness of this approach." The "special approaches" amounted, in essence, to earmarking—funds could be raised by the Bank but for specified purposes—and, after venting his objectives, Stern's reference to "political attractiveness" was in effect an admission that the Bank should perhaps resign itself to a curtailment of managerial autonomy as the price for obtaining the additional funds.

The "poverty program loan" was vetoed by the Bank's Legal Department, which argued that there was no authorization for such lending in the Articles.[127] The Core Poverty Program, in turn, was held back because of its procedural vagueness, which became an obstacle—or an excuse—for the unwillingness of operational departments to accept the implied radical change in lending procedures or the return to poverty targeting. Conable's "rededication" appeared to have gotten off to a false start, though it was credited with creating a greater awareness of poverty and of the operational difficulties that would arise as the Bank continued to move toward poverty lending. As it happened, when large-scale poverty lending was renewed in the Bank's agenda, it was less as a result of the task force exercises than of new circumstances and initiatives.

In parallel with the Karaosmanoglu effort, Conable established the Task Force on Food Security in Africa in 1987, as mentioned above, headed by Kim Jaycox. The initiative had strong political roots: food self-sufficiency was a powerful political banner in the region.[128] At the same time, the physical images of famine in Africa during the 1980s had been a major stimulant of concern and aid for the region. By the late 1980s, moreover, Bank frustration at its own inability to respond to African poverty and to do so in a direct and visible way was running high: rural development projects remained in disrepute; urban poverty projects were at one remove from rural hunger; and, however mistakenly, adjustment measures were perceived as being irrelevant, if not actually an aggravation, to short-run deprivation. The report was completed in May 1988.

126. Barber Conable to Moeen Qureshi and Attila Karaosmanoglu, May 23, 1988.

127. Ibrahim Shihata, legal memorandum to executive directors, May 10, 1988 (SecM88-517). Going beyond the strict legal difficulties in the proposal, Shihata added: "A serious question arises in my mind on whether a government which must be paid in order to adopt policies beneficial to its poor population, should receive funds from the Bank to be used for items not known in advance to the Bank and not necessarily related to poverty alleviation."

128. Alberto de Capitani to Willi Wapenhans, June 7, 1988, commenting on the task force report. De Capitani went on: "Whether it is also a good conceptual framework remains to be seen . . . there are reasons to be skeptical."

Management reviews were not enthusiastic. They cited above all, the conceptual and operational confusion and overlaps implied by any effort to address "food security" along with all other Bank work on African development and the additional administrative burden implied.[129] Nonetheless, a compromise solution created a small Food Security Unit within the Africa region and published a brief report, *The Challenge of Hunger in Africa: A Call to Action*.[130] This solution went some way toward meeting the political—and funding—need for a show of special action, with relatively little cross-interference with the Bank's normal work program.

In 1987 Conable launched a second poverty-directed initiative focused on Africa, the Social Dimensions of Adjustment program (SDA). Its objective was strongly conceptual—to create data and methodologies for developing highly targeted poverty programs in the region, to teach African governments, and to execute pilot projects. It emphasized the integration of social welfare and income objectives. The SDA was largely a French government initiative, though it was jointly funded and carried out with UNDP regional offices—by 1990, in twenty-nine African countries. The French influence extended to the staffing of the Bank's SDA unit, which had a large proportion of French nationals. In practice, the SDA mostly limited its work to statistical procedures and data collection, doing little to spark new lending approaches as had been intended.[131]

International financial developments set the stage, in particular. When the Baker Plan was announced in September 1985, with its implied reconsideration of adjustment prospects, hopes for a rapid solution to poverty faded. Austerity would not be enough; debtors would have to grow their way out of the debt.

An immediate corollary of that reconsideration was concern for the political sustainability of adjustment. Suddenly, "the social costs of adjustment" leaped into high priority. Whether they were real or merely apparent became academic; what mattered was the public perception. Rather than insist that adjustment was good for the poor, the Bank was now ready to admit some social costs. Thus there was no objection this time when Guy Pfeffermann wrote, in 1989: "When countries adjust, the visible costs (such as unemployment among former government workers and cuts in health and education spending) inevitably precede the resumption of growth and employment creation. I call the interval the 'crossing of the desert.'"[132]

129. Minutes of the Operations Committee, May 6, 1988. Minutes of the President's Council meeting, June 10, 1988.

130. Published in 1988.

131. RAF/86/037, United Nations Development Program, *Assessment of the Social Dimensions of Adjustment in Sub-Saharan Africa (SDA)*, prepared under the direction of Enrique Lerdau, August 1990. The Bank considered the evaluation "lacking in objectivity" and "damaging to our SDA effort," and prepared a 50-page rebuttal.

132. Guy Pfeffermann, "Poverty Alleviation," in Gerald Meier, ed., *Politics and Policy Making in Developing Countries* (San Francisco: International Center for Economic Growth, 1991), p. 186.

This concern took hold in the Bank and found an immediate outlet in support for Social Emergency Funds or Social Action Programs, known more generally as "safety nets."

The rapid crystallization of this response owed much to a timely Bolivian initiative, the Social Emergency Fund created in December 1986. A staff member, Katherine Marshall, recalled that the Bank was at first skeptical about what it saw as "a vast, under-designed public works scheme that had unhealthy shades of relief activities in which the Bank's charter prohibited involvement." But two novel factors helped to persuade the Bank. Instead of the usual welfare and employment-guarantee goals of such programs, Bolivia's plans and staffing for the proposed Fund took on a decided private sector and "productive" orientation. Political considerations weighed in as well. According to Marshall, "Vital in the effort to gather support was the increasing attention being paid at the Bank and other institutions to the issue of 'social costs of adjustment,' dramatized by a major UNICEF report urging 'adjustment with a human face.'"[133] Sensitivity to the politics of the situation was increased by "the chance presence in Bolivia of a Bank consultant . . . who was a politician (a British Member of Parliament). . . . He helped [to] convince the Bank staff that the need for highly visible action to address social issues was crucial . . . [and] that all the adjustment measures and outstanding economic management would be useless if political forces swamped and overturned the government."[134]

The timeliness and businesslike design of Bolivia's program helped make it a model for the Bank. Other Social Emergency Funds were soon created, especially in Latin America and Sub-Saharan Africa. According to Qureshi,

> In the context of adjustment operations government expenditure is frequently curtailed in an attempt to achieve macroeconomic balance. Consistent with Bank policy, it is imperative that we seek to protect vulnerable groups against cuts in public expenditure . . . protecting the poor during adjustment is a primary concern of the Bank . . . expenditures should, to the extent possible, be maintained in real terms for primary education, primary health care and other programs benefiting the poor.[135]

133. On how the Bank came to support Bolivia's program see Katherine Marshall, "Genesis and Early Decades," in Steen Jorgensen, Margaret Grosh, and Mark Schacter, *World Bank, Bolivia's Answer to Poverty, Economic Crisis, and Adjustment* (World Bank, 1992), pp. 25–32. Marshall writes that the program was led by "a well respected and dynamic Bolivian business man, Fernando Romero [who] took some pride in asserting that he had never served in government" (p. 26). By 1995 programs existed in twelve Latin American countries, and eleven Sub-Saharan Africa countries. Philip Glaessner, Kye Woo Lee, Anna Maria Sant'Anna, Jean-Jacques de St. Antoine, *Poverty Alleviation and Social Investment Funds. The Latin American Experience*, World Bank Discussion Paper 261, 1994, p. iv; Alexander Marc, Carol Graham, Mark Schacter, Mary Schmidt, *Social Action Programs and Social Funds. A Review of Design and Implementation in Sub-Saharan Africa*, World Bank Discussion Paper 274, 1995, pp. vii–viii. The spreading variety of these programs make definition difficult. The common feature is rapid provision of welfare to large groups of very poor people through temporary jobs or distribution of welfare-related goods and services.

134. Ibid., p. 26.

135. Moeen Qureshi to regional vice presidents, April 14, 1989.

A second circumstance was the burgeoning movement to rely more on non-governmental organizations, and more broadly, the growing public awareness of Bank activities and intrusiveness of the media and public opinion in this regard. Although that opinion was concerned primarily with environmental issues, a sizable constituency also worked on behalf of poverty, in part through some donor governments that were especially responsive to poverty, notably those of the Nordic countries and Canada, and in part through the direct intervention of northern-based NGOs and public opinion. During 1988 the Canadian director, Frank Potter, wrote Conable:

> Poverty alleviation as you know has been a subject of ongoing debate between Canada and the Bank. . . . Canada would like to see a clearer operational backstop . . . which would require that when cuts in key poverty programmes are required a statement should be made in the documents and in the presentation to the Board . . . [thus] flagging cases of cutbacks in social expenditures.[136]

The involvement of NGOs was illustrated in January 1991, when a policy paper, *Assistance Strategies to Reduce Poverty,* was about to be submitted to the Board. As in the case of other major position papers, the U.S. executive director had received a copy before it was distributed to other members of the Board. On reading it, he organized a meeting of its authors, Part I executive directors, and representatives from donor-country NGOs.

> The NGOs in attendance were very well informed, apparently having seen a leaked copy of an earlier draft of the Board paper. Mr. Boehmer, an executive director, complained about the difficulties such leaks have made for Board members, who themselves not having seen the paper were not in a position to respond to NGO questions, concerns and observations. There were questions about reviewing the poverty OD [Operational Directive] with the Board *and NGOs* before it is issued.[137]

Mounting external pressure found its source of leverage in the Bank's funding dependency on donor governments. From 1986 to early 1988 the Bank was involved in two funding struggles, the replenishment for IDA 8 (which would finance IDA disbursements over 1988–90) and the approval of a General Capital Increase. The Bank's sensitivity to external opinion and pressures had been increased by its failure in the preceding IDA 7 negotiations, held in 1984–85, to prevent the United States from forcing through a 25 percent cut, the first reduction in IDA's history. Even after the establishment of a supplementary special facility for Sub-Saharan Africa, total concessional funds available to the Bank were reduced by 18 percent. Though it had appeared that Clausen's poor relations with the U.S. administration had been partly to blame, Conable had been almost immediately cold shouldered

---

136. Frank Potter to Barber Conable, *Poverty Alleviation,* August 26, 1988.

137. Enzo Grilli and Hans Wyss to Moeen Qureshi, January 23, 1991, p. 2, emphasis added. During the session, the U.S. executive director apologized for having failed to invite representatives of the poorer borrowing countries.

by the U.S. Treasury over the level of the Bank's administrative budget. But the challenge for the Bank was now far more than its relationship with the U.S. Treasury. Environmental and other special interest groups were exerting influence through Congress, other donor parliaments, and the media. And because the Bank's hand with Treasury had been strengthened by the Baker Plan announcement of a major financing role for the Bank, the focus of the financing effort was turning from Treasury to Congress.

The former congressman was well prepared to understand and to deal with those new pressures. He was helped by the existence of a committee established in 1982 for cooperation between nongovernmental organizations (NGOs) and the Bank. A few months after arriving at the Bank, in November 1986, Conable took advantage of the committee's Annual Meeting to begin to develop a funding campaign. A Bank report noted that between July 1985 and November 1986 the extent of Bank-NGO contact and collaborative activity had "surged." The committee themes included, as Conable noted in his presentation, "poverty alleviation, women in development, environment, debt management and, more broadly the social impact of austerity measures and restructuring."[138] The Bank's internal report on this meeting noted: "Certain NGOs have expressed doubts about the commitment and effectiveness of multilateral development banks in reducing poverty. For example, poverty was a major theme of the book and conference about the World Bank which the Overseas Development Council organized in June 1986. Another U.S. NGO, Results, helped organize expressions of concern from some members of the U.S. Congress."[139]

At about this time Frank Vogl, of the External Affairs Department, proposed a public relations effort to head off what he saw as potentially troublesome pressure on the women-in-development theme:

> I most strongly believe that the issue of women in development is a major one that could enter the political arena in a major way at any time, with interest groups urging the Board to do far more in this sector. Such interest groups are, in my opinion, likely if aroused to be at least as influential as groups working on environmental issues. We dare not be caught by surprise.[140]

Pressure on the Bank continued to grow. In September 1987, for instance, NGOs organized a press conference at which a letter was presented that called for "greater [poverty] program effort" from the Bank and that carried the signatures of

138. Address of Mr. Barber Conable to the Sixth Annual Meeting of the Bank-NGO Committee (Nov 5, 1986). Bank report on *Cooperation Between Nongovernmental Organizations and the World Bank. Fourth Progress Report*. International Relations Department, October 20, 1986.

139. *Cooperation*, p. 2.

140. Frank Vogl, IPADR, to Jose Botafogo, VPE, *Women in Development*, October 31, 1986.

153 members of the U.S. Congress and 40 senators.[141] When the committee met again in November 1988, Conable's briefing reported: "When the Bank-NGO Committee last met in Washington two years ago, you generated great enthusiasm by indicating your intention for the Bank to work together with NGOs more than in the past. . . . Good progress has been made."[142]

The campaign for the General Capital Increase peaked later, in early 1988, and, though it concerned the IBRD and not IDA directly—and by this time IDA had become virtually the Bank's "window for the poor" in the eyes of both Bank officials and the outside—the campaign nonetheless included poverty as a major theme. A campaign "Master Plan" prepared in March 1988 listed "Poverty/Church Groups" among the constituencies to be addressed:

> The Bretton Woods Committee has agreed to try to develop a coalition of poverty groups who might be willing either to mute their criticisms of the Bank's structural adjustment programs, or perhaps support the GCI legislation.
>
> We will talk to UNICEF about the possibility of doing a joint briefing on the "Human Face of Adjustment." Such a briefing was suggested to us by UNICEF several months ago.
>
> Treasury must prepare regular reports for Congress on the Bank's involvement with NGOs, poverty programs, women's programs, micro-enterprises, etc. We are cooperating with them on this.[143]

The plan also proposed that a speech to be given by Conable in Germany in May focus on the human dimensions of the adjustment. The draft GCI resolution proposed to the Board on January 29, 1988, in listing the Bank's "Lending Objectives" in its justification for the capital increase, cited as the first of those objectives: "The Bank will reassert and expand its role in the attack on poverty through a targeted program focused on eradicating the worst forms of poverty."[144] The proposal went on to highlight several targets: the low-income countries of Asia, protection of the poorest groups in countries that are undertaking adjustment programs, education and health, and women in development.[145]

The Ninth Replenishment, to cover IDA credits over the period July 1990 to June 1993, was also negotiated by Conable. It placed even higher priority on poverty alleviation and "requested that IDA's executive directors review on an annual basis how well those priorities were being pursued."[146] This requirement led

141. Harry K. Nicholas to Julian Grenfell, *Congressional Letter on Poverty*, September 23, 1987.

142. Alexander Shakow to Barber Conable, *Bank-NGO Committee Annual Meeting— November 2, 1988*, October 14, 1988.

143. Francisco Aguirre-Sacasa, director, EXT, to Barber Conable, *GCI Master Plan*, March 11, 1988.

144. Memorandum from the president to the executive directors, *General Capital Increase*, January 29, 1988, R88-25.

145. Ibid., p. 4.

146. World Bank, *Annual Report 1994*, p. 170.

to a strengthening of the Bank's program of poverty assessments; at the same time, it became an inducement to more energetic poverty lending. "In the context of soliciting support for the IDA 9 replenishment," said Qureshi, "the President has assured potential donors that poverty alleviation will continue to provide a special focus to IDA assisted programs."[147]

To a much greater extent than in the 1970s, the Bank's dedication to poverty alleviation in the late 1980s was a response to outside pressures. Driven by funding "needs," it felt compelled to adapt its rhetoric and operations to meet the demands made by liberal political constituencies that controlled swing votes in donor-country parliaments. More broadly, the Bank found itself subjected to an increasingly intrusive public scrutiny. The institution began to be judged by the standards of a general, unprofessional, and largely uninformed public that placed much weight on graphic or easily perceived evidence of social impact. Visible, direct poverty alleviation took on a special weight in those judgments. But public opinion was not constrained by a professional understanding of the Bank's essentially economic and production-oriented purpose and capacities; there soon appeared to be no boundaries to what could be expected and demanded from the Bank.

Thus the call for greater attention to poverty—a demand that the Bank could easily and even willingly respond to—was only one of several social goals that an uninformed public could associate with and demand of the Bank. Indeed, other social values, especially the environment and women in development, had greater powers of con-vocation, mobilization, and funding impact on the Bank than third world poverty. In fact, the pressure from environmental groups was felt more keenly by the Bank during this period than the call for poverty alleviation. The Bank's response with respect to poverty was thus part of a movement toward a broader and potentially unlimited agenda of social objectives.

The Conable Bank was pliant in the face of these pressures. Indeed, Conable became an enthusiastic activist for causes such as poverty alleviation, primary and especially women's education, family planning, NGO involvement, and the environment. But if the Bank gave in so readily, it was to a large extent because much of what was being demanded could be accommodated by rhetoric—including administrative relabeling—and by rule changes of uncertain future compliance.

Reining In

By the end of the decade it was becoming apparent that the Bank was less ready to shoulder the new social responsibilities than it had been to take them on. Several factors made implementation difficult.

First, there was a need for an intellectual framework that would reconcile the Bank's continuing and indeed reaffirmed pursuit of adjustment, growth, and free

147. Moeen Qureshi to regional vice presidents, April 14, 1989.

markets with its rebirth as a poverty-oriented lender. The need for such a framework had been made evident by the debates and confusion that had characterized the 1987–88 task force debates. Opinion among senior staff remained conservative; they found it difficult to imagine the possibility of a drastic reorientation back to poverty objectives; and they were certain that any such change would mean administrative complications and added costs. Conable himself was unfamiliar with operational issues and could do little to steer the search. And second, new lending vehicles were required; old (McNamarian) "poverty projects" had been discredited.

The intellectual framework was crystallized in the 1990 World Development Report. As usual, the WDR distilled and gave coherence to recent Bank thinking and practice. The report was an especially well-timed and well-tailored intellectual construction for the direction that the Bank was in any case largely constrained to follow. Its "dual" strategy for poverty alleviation was, in effect, a compromise, combining poverty-targeted and even welfare lending with a reemphasis on growth and trickle-down. It conceded that adjustment could indeed have "social costs," justifying compensatory interventions and subsidies, but reaffirmed the central role of economic growth.

The operational need for new "poverty projects" found a solution in two areas: adjustment safety nets and human resource lending. In lending for safety nets the Bank was taking a long step toward what had been its childhood nightmare—that it would become a soup kitchen. Yet the proposal found ready acceptance, a measure of the extent to which the Bank had drifted away from its earlier rule that all loans be justified on strict productivity grounds. A decade earlier, McNamara had shied away from the welfare connotations of employment schemes and health projects, endorsing the traditional productivity rule.

The second main vehicle proposed for reaching the poor directly—human resource lending—was also, to some extent, made possible by the weakening of the productivity criterion. A new, more developed empirical case had been built up over the 1980s for the human capital concept originally argued in the 1950s and 1960s. It argued that education was an investment with large, even extraordinary, rates of return. This concept had been extended, more loosely, to investments in health, nutrition, and family planning. Yet despite the vigorous argumentation and statistical regressions, the argument that education, health, and other social spending had impressive rates of return was in the end a highly intuitive and speculative proposition, as it always had been, and its sudden acceptance now had much to do with operational timing. Most important, there was a need for newly minted, "innovative" approaches to direct poverty lending, unsullied by the wear and tear of practical experience, as had become the case with rural development and urban poverty projects. And, equally important, human resources lent themselves to the large and often fast-disbursing, programlike loans that were needed at a time of continuing balance-of-payments and debt-repayment pressures. Thus, the prospect of human resource lending did not raise the hackles of Bank managers in the way that a return to rural development and urban poverty projects would have done, perhaps because the activity was relatively new and had not yet entered a stage of implementation problems and negative OED ratings, perhaps also because such projects were inherently more difficult to subject to rate-of-return tests. "Softness," or nonmeasurability, which in earlier times had damned certain types of lending, now became a plus.

The enthusiastic reception by management and Board of the 1990 World Development Report led to an immediate follow-up in the form of a policy paper, "Assistance Strategies to Reduce Poverty."[148] And in 1991 also the Bank approved Operational Directive 4.15, which interpreted the general policy lines in the form of concrete instructions to regional operational staff. By 1991 the Bank had gone a long way toward reestablishing the intellectual and administrative apparatus for a renewed effort at poverty alleviation.

But other factors worked to restrain the Bank's burgeoning social agenda. One was the change in leadership that occurred in June, when Lewis Preston, a lifetime banker and former chairman of Morgan Guaranty, succeeded former congressman Barber Conable. Known as a successful manager, Preston conceived his role narrowly as bringing his administrative skills to an undermanaged institution.[149] Also, with Preston, Ernest Stern returned to the helm of Bank operations. Preston created a new hierarchical structure, appointing three managing directors to run the Bank under his supervision. Stern became a managing director, but also chairman of the key Operations Committee.

Preston subscribed to the heightened poverty rhetoric launched by Conable. He took up and repeated Conable's new definition of poverty as the Bank's "overarching purpose."[150] But neither Preston nor Stern shared Conable's enthusiasm for a broad social agenda. Preston said: "This institution never turns down an assignment; it must learn to say no."[151]

Stern was a skeptic both on trickle-down ("I don't believe this happens") and on targeting ("I am not a great fan").[152] When asked to comment on a proposal that would become the "Program of Targeted Interventions," he wrote: "I am not a

148. World Bank, 1991. The WDR team leader, Lyn Squire, was also the principal author of the policy paper.

149. Interview with the authors, February 10, 1993.

150. Perhaps unconsciously, this term served a double agenda: it appeared to raise the degree of priority of poverty; but it also worked as a device to rein in an uncontrolled social agenda and, in addition, to reimpose economic criteria. The environment, women in development, and other objectives were let in the door—through the arch of poverty—as instruments of raising income rather than as ends in themselves.

151. Interview with the authors, February 10, 1993.

152. Letter from Ernest Stern to Stanley Fischer commenting on draft Review of Adjustment Lending, February 27, 1990. He added, "[Trickle-down] is even less likely in a situation of rapidly changing relative prices." In a separate comment he said: "As we should know by now, reduction of poverty is not synonymous with income growth in low-income countries." Memorandum to Munir Benjenk on draft speech for DAVOS, January 16, 1984.

great fan of these highly directed, quantified objectives. . . . The way this is laid out leaves, in my view, the management inadequate flexibility and there is an inadequate balance between the multiple objectives which I believe the Bank must serve. . . . I also thought that calling something 'A Program of Targeted Interventions' sounded like something out of Star Wars."[153]

Speaking publicly as a Bank official he sounded more optimistic. In the mode of a pep talk, he congratulated the development community for its renewed attention to income distribution. This attention, he said, reflected a "deepening" of knowledge of the development process: "How the benefits of growth are distributed is, in fact, a central issue in development. Central not only because it affects the long-term prospects for political stability and national cohesion, but also central because it is a major reason why the development community is concerned about development."[154] A few years later, though, writing privately to Stanley Fischer, he threw cold water on the idea that rich countries were really concerned about distribution: "In most bilateral aid programs . . . poverty alleviation was but a minor objective most of the time. It still is."[155] On Bank policy, he publicly celebrated the institution's learning process regarding equity:

> In the early 1970s, the Bank began to focus increasingly on the question of equity, how development strategies and investment programs could be designed to more rapidly improve the lives of the millions of desperately poor in our member countries by increasing their ability to produce more. It involved a major shift in our lending in agriculture to emphasize smallholder farmers. . . . Ten years later we can say with confidence that this increased concern for equity, for the growth of income of the lower-income groups, has not come at the expense of growth. . . . The evolution of the Bank has yielded an institution which today has competence in the productive, social and infrastructure sectors of the economy; which can draw on over thirty years of experience with development issues, ranging from export competitiveness to income distribution.[156]

A decade later, however, in a private setting—a farewell ceremony on his retirement in January 1995—he sounded skeptical about efforts to improve on trickle-down: "I never was, and am still uncomfortable with the distinction people try to make between development and alleviating poverty. . . . I also believe that growth . . . is the only solution to the reduction of poverty and inequalities."[157]

153. Ernest Stern to Paul Isenman, draft poverty policy paper, November 26, 1990, p. 2.

154. Address on "The Role of the World Bank at the Meeting to Celebrate the 40th Anniversary of the United Nations Monetary and Financial Conference," Bretton Woods, July 13, 1984, p. 4.

155. Memorandum, Ernest Stern to Stanley Fischer, May 17, 1990. Stern wrote to agree with views expressed by a visiting Australian delegation. The Australian note stated that: "The WDR [1990] places excessive weight on anti-poverty objectives. Most aid programs have, quite explicitly, political, *multiple* objectives: humanitarian, strategic, commercial. Even 'humanitarian' objectives cover a wider range of objectives than only anti-poverty goals." And therefore, the WDR's evaluation of donor aid programs from the point of view of antipoverty objectives alone was "inappropriate."

156. "Role of the World Bank," July 13, 1984, pp. 405.

157. Farewell speech by Ernest Stern, January 26, 1995.

Both Preston and Stern leaned toward a conservative interpretation of the Bank's priorities and procedures and sought to reestablish the priority of output considerations. In his farewell speech, Stern drew implications for Bank policy that echoed Eugene Black's vision of the Bank: "I do not think we should ever confuse development assistance with charity because charity cannot be a concept among nations . . . that is why I believe that a Bank, requiring repayment, anchored in financial discipline, supported by sound project analysis, by the monitoring and evaluation of results and by a sense of accountability, is the best channel for assisting development effectively."[158]

Room to pursue a poverty agenda was in any case suddenly curtailed by the collapse of the USSR. After 1992 a large bloc of new east European and Central Asian (ECA) member countries began to absorb much of the Bank's administrative budget and managerial attention. The impact went beyond a competition for resources: it affected the very nature of the Bank. The ECA became a new category within the Bank's membership—"transition economies" that needed restructuring rather than development, exhibited less of the extremes of wealth and poverty of the developing world, and objected to being grouped within the underdeveloped world. Indeed, though physical destruction was not involved, it was evident that the Bank's role in eastern Europe would be more comparable with that of its reconstruction origins than with its later development and poverty-alleviating functions. When a vision statement, "Learning from the Past, Embracing the Future," was written for the fiftieth anniversary of Bretton Woods in 1994, the Bank accommodated eastern European demands by redefining itself: instead of a Bank whose "overarching" purpose was the alleviation of poverty, it now called itself an institution for "helping borrowers reduce poverty and raise living standards."[159]

The new definition blurred the sharp focus on poverty that had been achieved in Preston's earlier characterization. The Bank backtracked toward its self-image of the 1950s and 1960s; the special claim of relative need was weakened. Subsequent statements of purpose were consistent with a watering down of the poverty objective. The Bank's 1995 annual report stated: "The World Bank . . . has one central purpose: to promote economic and social progress in developing nations by helping raise productivity." The 1996 annual report stated: "Poverty reduction and sustainable development remain the central objectives." In 1995 the following text was added to the Bank logo: "The World Bank. A partner in strengthening economies and expanding markets to improve the quality of life for people everywhere, especially the poorest."[160] This definitional adjustment seemed appropriate after the incorporation of the ECA bloc. The Bank's membership had already included a sizable group of "middle-income" countries in Latin America (GDP per person

158. Stern, farewell speech.

159. Our emphasis. Interview with Sarwar Lateef, October 31, 1994. Lateef was the principal author of "The World Bank Group, Learning from the Past, Embracing the Future," July 12, 1994.

160. World Bank, *Annual Report 1995*, p.4; *Annual Report 1996*, p. 14. The logo appears on back cover page of both reports.

$2,690) and the Middle East ($1,950) whose needs were significantly different from those of poorer members. The arrival of the ECA (GNP per person $2,080) pushed the Bank further toward a middle-income clientele: the region absorbed 19.8 percent of Bank lending in 1996, while Sub-Saharan Africa received 12.8 percent.[161] It was part of this accommodation to its middle-income and transition clientele that when health was chosen as the theme for the 1993 World Development Report, the paper dealt as much with the management and financing of largely curative health systems in relatively developed countries as it did with the more urgent primary care needs of the world's poorest.

In 1995, the new director for external affairs, Mark Malloch Brown, carried out a "customer survey" which became the basis for staff briefings. External perceptions and expectations of the Bank, it found, were not favorable to the poverty mission. The Bank's image suffered when it was identified as an "aid" agency, and when it was seen as moving toward "humanitarian," "refugee," and "relief" actions. Outsiders did not share the Bank's poverty lexicon, which was viewed as sentimental and not real. Bank critics tended to blame McNamara's "missionary" approach to poverty and development. In short, staff were encouraged to play down the poverty theme. And, defining the Bank at a news conference, Brown said: "We're a bank. We're not an aid agency."[162]

Implementation of a social agenda in any case required expertise and manpower that the Bank lacked. The need was most evident in specialized areas such as the environment and health. In the case of poverty the awareness of a skill deficit developed gradually because it was tied to evolving ideas regarding the way to approach poverty. Increasingly, poverty alleviation was seen as an integrated or package problem requiring the solution of each item in a menu of social needs— education, female education, and other aspects of the women-in-development agenda, environment, health, water supply, protection against forced resettlement, protection of indigenous peoples, food security, and other items. Moreover, for each of these needs the solution required participation and sense of ownership by the intended beneficiaries. In addition, honest and efficient judiciaries, systems of property titling, broad-based economic growth, and macroeconomic stability were all considered necessary requirements, and even these macroeconomic and broad institutional objectives were now seen to depend on ensuring adequate participation and sense of ownership in decisionmaking. Finally, in each case it was seen that

161. Lending data in World Bank, *Annual Report 1996,* appendix 13, p. 248. GNP per person refers to 1992. Data from World Bank, *World Development Report 1994,* table 1, pp. 162–63.

162. Presentation by Peter Stephens, adviser to the director of external relations, to Bank staff members, April 1995. Brown cited by the Associated Press, May 16, 1995. Brown arrived with a Madison Avenue background; his press statement was billed by Reuters as the "unleashing [of] an advertising campaign." AP said that the Bank was "for the first time . . . waging an ad campaign."

the need was not only for better rules or policies, but for better institutions, a conclusion that implied a further manpower requirement difficult to meet—expertise in institutions.

Through the early 1990s the Bank rapidly expanded the number of sociologists, anthropologists, experts in participation and in institutions, and other social specialists. Yet as late as 1996, the Bank decided that it was falling far short of meeting the staffing requirements created by the new social and poverty agendas. A report, "Social Development and Results on the Ground," called for further, large-scale recruitment of what came to be called "Nessies," or noneconomist social scientists, and for upgrading in their operational involvement and responsibility.[163] By the mid-1990s, the Bank was finding that its capacity to carry out a social agenda was constrained and that, in any case, its clients were less enthusiastic regarding that agenda.

Overview

In the crusade against poverty in the 1970s, the problem had been defined, simply, as inadequate income. However loud the objection to engaging the Bank in matters of distribution, the issue was nonetheless presented in language familiar to the economist: production and income were two sides of one accounting identity. Indeed, the central proposition in McNamara's strategy was that, with small farmers and many urban poor, production and income could be raised simultaneously. A mid-decade proposal to redefine the poverty goal in terms of "needs" had been quashed; another proposal, to use subjectively determined distributive weights in project evaluation, was ignored. Through the decade the Bank was determined not to stray from what it saw as objective, measurable goals of production and low incomes.

When Conable launched a second crusade, the objective became diffuse. New goals sprang up, spilling out of economics into other fields. Inadequate income, or "poverty," remained a central objective, and to some degree—using the concept of an "overarching" goal, and by discovering the poverty relevance of the environment and of gender equality—it was called on to legitimize each of the other social goals. But the number and variety of social claims and concerns were clearly, to some degree, social claims on their own. This was true, for instance, of gender equality, the universal right to education, protection or security against hunger, minimum nutrition and health standards, the individual capacity to control family size, the environment, the right not to be forcibly resettled, the suffering caused by natural disasters and wars, the "special" claim of Sub-Saharan Africa, and even the victims of macroeconomic adjustment programs. This expansion cannot be attributed to

163. World Bank, "Task Group Report: Social Development and Results on the Ground," SecM96-1063, October 18, 1996.

Conable's personal inclinations, though as a politician he was quick to sense and accommodate the external demands and opportunities that prompted each new responsibility.

To find the original cause, one might look back to McNamara's introduction of need as an explicit allocative criterion. Yet need had surfaced as a criterion even earlier, in Woods's and even Black's country and sectoral allocation of lending. Indeed, the Bank's drift away from its market-disciplined, "productive investment" origins toward an increasingly social, need-based definition of its goals probably started with the switch from reconstruction to development banking.

From the beginning the Bank has been prodded to take on greater responsibilities. The United Nations was an active and articulate source of proposals for social and increased lending that badgered the Bank through the 1950s. In the 1960s, decolonization, the cold war, and a growing intellectual and political recognition of underdevelopment came together to press the Bank to play a broader development role. Social objectives and their constituencies blossomed in the 1970s: new platforms included the environment, women, and human rights; and new constituencies arose among church groups, Social Democrat governments, and Western NGOs.[164] The influence of most of these groups increased during the 1980s and 1990s.

The Bank's capacity to resist those urgings has been proiportional to its financial independence. For that reason, its vulnerability greatly increased when IDA grant money was added to IBRD market borrowing. The institution quickly became preoccupied with concessional lending.[165] IDA also allowed capriciousness to color external pressures in that donor-government policies were frequently inconstant and individual parliamentarians and single-interest groups gained disproportionate leverage through parliamentary mechanics.[166] Despite the room for intervention

164. One expression of those views was the 1980 Brandt Report, which was initiated by McNamara but which found an independent voice and drew up an aid agenda and even proposals for reform of the Bank that McNamara found inconvenient and irritating. Though its main thrust was North-South resource transfer, the Report proposed a variety of new social emphases and programs, for example, food security, agrarian reform, malnutrition, and impoverished areas.

165. Woods's biographer, Robert Oliver, noted that by 1965–66 "Woods was devoting ninety percent of his energies to IDA." Chapter 4, p. 72, fn. 139. In 1973, Robert Asher and Edward Mason were interviewed on their just-published history of the Bank. Asked to recommend one change in Bank policy, Asher said: "I would make IDA bigger. The Bank will have a rough future if IDA doesn't get larger in comparison with Bank lending." Mason's reply was: "We both agree, everyone agrees, that the future of the Bank depends on how much money will be available to IDA." *Bank Notes*, October 1973.

166. The Charter had intended the full-time Executive Board to be a buffer against uninformed and changeable governance by the Bank's owners. When John McCloy weakened the Board in 1947 to gain managerial freedom of action, he also deprived the Bank of that safeguard. The budget appropriation processes that approved IDA funding contained even less in the way of checks against the imposition of unwise demands and conditionalities on those funds.

created by IDA in 1960, little effort was made to intervene in the first two decades, though it increased between the 1960s and 1970s.[167] The effects of dependence on donors became more evident during the 1980s. In the late 1980s, however, outside influence began to change in character, becoming more intensive and more varied in its objectives. For the first time, the U.S. government, as dominant owner, was no longer able to keep other constituencies from having a major influence. The loss of the U.S. executive shield opened the Bank to an exploding set of pressure groups, focused on a wide range of social objectives. This external development coincided with Conable's arrival.

Conable then appeared to open a Pandora's Box of social responsibilities. Certainly, he shook out new and renewed tasks for the Bank with enthusiasm, in apparent contrast to his conservative predecessor. But this new approach also coincided with a changed external context, which would have imposed much of the new agenda on any Bank president. In fact, the Bank already had an eye on many of the items on Conable's list: McNamara had drawn attention to the environment, hiring a special adviser in the early 1970s; the post of adviser on women in development had been created in 1977;[168] natural disaster relief lending, in cases of earthquakes, droughts, and monsoon floods had a long tradition at the Bank;[169] and support for nutrition, health, and primary education had been growing during the 1980s. Throughout its history the Bank has shown a readiness to take on new social responsibilities. Though the rate of change appeared to accelerate with his arrival, Conable was following established precedent in adapting to the facts of financial dependence and evolving public opinion.

If IDA 9 used indirect methods to move the Bank toward more targeted poverty lending, the Tenth Replenishment, negotiated during 1992–93, took a large step toward dirigisme. IDA 10 mandated a detailed list of poverty-related actions and targets that impinged substantially on managerial discretion. Conable seemed to welcome rather than to fight those demands, opening the door for what, by the mid-1990s, has come to be a partial takeover of Bank administration by donors, NGOs, and the media.

As a proportion of total population, world poverty has been declining throughout the Bank's life. Yet approximately one billion persons, one-fifth of the

167. The Bank was shielded at first by its own low profile, by U.S. dominance as a donor, and by U.S. executive control over the aid budget. Pressure groups needed time to build up lobbying knowledge and skills. During the 1970s McNamara parried outside pressures with political skills and broadened the Bank's funding sources. See chapter 18 of this work. See also Gwin, *U.S. Relations with the World Bank, 1945–1992*. Chapter 13 contains a detailed account of the way in which environmental NGOs learned how to press the Bank.

168. Gloria Scott, *World Bank Projects and Women* (World Bank, May 18, 1979).

169. For example, earthquake reconstruction in Chile (1960); the earthquake in Peru (1970); earthquake in Guatemala (1977); monsoon in Bangladesh (1970); famines in Iran, Nicaragua, and India; and drought in Sub-Saharan Africa.

world's population, continue to live in extreme poverty: the "eradication" proposed by the Bank a quarter century ago remains a distant goal.[170] Most of that poverty remains rural, and the Bank has criticized itself for "a significant decline of commitment to rural development."[171] It has pointed to its own failure to create income growth in Sub-Saharan Africa.[172] And, in its repeated announcements of new antipoverty approaches, it effectively confesses to a frustration of past efforts. Vice President Ismail Serageldin, for instance, recently heralded microcredit as a poverty solution, saying: "It is within our grasp to *start* making a dent in eliminating poverty."[173]

In practice, the Bank continues to direct most of its lending and advice to promote economic growth and to provide balance-of-payments and fiscal assistance. And, to these authors, it seems likely that whatever contribution has been made by the Bank to poverty reduction has been principally the result of that general support for economic stability and development rather than of its efforts to bring about more direct poverty alleviation. As is evident from the preceding chapters, the Bank's own view of those efforts to improve on trickle-down has been largely critical. And, though the issue is rarely brought up, much of what is called "direct poverty lending" remains haunted by the question of fungibility. In 1996, Michael Bruno, vice president and chief economist, reminded his colleagues that "Money is fungible and, in particular, money from foreign assistance. Much of the money that we channel to the government does not go to the objective that is written on the piece of paper."[174]

170. World Bank, From Vision to Action in the Rural Sector, August 5, 1996, p. 1.

171. Ibid., p.4.

172. See chapter 12.

173. Speech at the Microcredit Summit, cited by the Associated Press, January 31, 1997 (emphasis added).

174. Address to the Bank's Sociological Group, May 3, 1996. The address was given months before his death.

EIGHT

Agriculture and Rural Development

FOR AN institution that in the 1970s would become agriculture's most active and generous official international promoter, the World Bank got off to a slow start. The UN's Food and Agriculture Organization was launched a year before the Bank. It quickly entered into a variety of development initiatives in the late 1940s. During the 1950s agriculture and rural development (ARD) were high on the agendas of some of the new bilateral aid programs as well as those of such nonofficial interveners as the Rockefeller and Ford foundations.

Although the Bank did not entirely bypass agricultural issues and lending, it had different preoccupations in the early years. Under the presidencies of George Woods (1963–68) and, even more, of Robert McNamara (1968–81), however, attention to and investment in agriculture surged, thanks to forces outside the institution as well as changes within. Since 1981, the Bank's ARD activities have been mixed, but ebbing.

Slow Start

During its first fifteen years the Bank put only a modest effort into agriculture; arguably, it was lopsided. In 1961 a total of twelve professionals covered the institution's agricultural program worldwide, and most of them were engaged in irrigation and drainage work.[1] In part, this reflected the institution's comparative

---

1. Willi Wapenhans, interview with John Lewis and Devesh Kapur, September 6, 1991.

advantage: surface irrigation projects were typically large and capital intensive. They were of a piece with the rest of the Bank's infrastructure emphasis; indeed, in certain dual-purpose cases, irrigation and power projects were one and the same. However, much of the irrigation priority was owed to the Bank's Indus Basin initiative, and the motivation in that project seems to have been as much diplomatic as developmental.

The partition of India and Pakistan in 1947 split the vast, complex, Indus Basin irrigation system into two dysfunctional pieces, adding to the explosiveness of the relations between the two countries. Eugene Black, who had become president of the Bank in mid-1949, was anxious to help reduce the tensions between these potential major clients of the institution, both to defuse the problem and to demonstrate the effectiveness of the Bank to the investment community. An opening was provided by a *Collier's* magazine article in August 1951 in which David E. Lilienthal, formerly of the Tennessee Valley Authority (TVA), pressed for a joint, binational solution to the Indus puzzle and proposed that the Bank become involved as a technical expert and honest broker.

With this introduction and the blessings of the British and American governments, before the end of September 1951 Black was able to get the parties to accept—Pakistan, willingly, India, more hesitantly—the Bank's offer of its good offices. Thereupon began a nine-year stop-and-go negotiation that several times nearly failed but that finally yielded the Indus Water Treaty in 1960, in good part because of the skill and perseverance of Black and his aide, William Iliff. The story is well told elsewhere, and there is no need to detail it again.[2] Before the Bank was done, however, it had scored a great success in Indian as well as Pakistani eyes, and, indeed those of the world at large. At least for the time being, it had helped rebuild hydrological coherence in a binational Indus system. It contributed to and organized support for three dams: the Beas in India, the large Mangla dam, and (later) the giant Tarbela in Pakistan.

The Indus initiative set the pattern for a water-management focus that would persist. But the aggregate agricultural program remained modest. This was not surprising. The lawyers, investment bankers, and policy economists who populated the young Bank had no particular appetite or aptitude for agriculture. Indeed, there was a cultural gap between Bank people and the plant breeders, agronomists, extensionists, agricultural economists, and other farming specialists who tended to staff foundation and bilateral-agency agricultural operations. Such staffers delivered technical assistance that was largely "disembodied" from capital transfers. They spent much of their time posted in developing countrysides. The Bank, by contrast, was headquarters-centered; its main concern was to transfer capital, and

2. Harold N. Graves, "The Bank as International Mediator: Three Episodes," in Edward S. Mason and Robert E. Asher, eds., *The World Bank since Bretton Woods* (Brookings, 1973), pp. 595–646.

when that task needed to be packaged with technical assistance, Washington was likely to contract out the technical assignment.

In these early years the Bank was preoccupied, above all, with establishing the institution's creditworthiness in the New York financial market. The kinds of projects that best served this purpose were those promising directly to generate returns that would service the Bank's loans. Many agricultural projects were not self-liquidating in this sense. Also most required funding of local costs (rather than imports). Not only was the Bank inhibited against such financing by its Articles; it was reluctant to sacrifice the greater accountability that concentration on foreign exchange funding afforded.

At the outset the Bank saw itself more as a capital transfers specialist, less as a comprehensive development promoter obligated to pursue all major aspects of development, whatever the institution's comparative advantage. In any event, many of the chief development pundits of the period—Arthur Lewis, Raúl Prebisch, Ragnar Nurske, P. C. Mahalanobis, Albert Hirschman, Walt Rostow—seemed to be reassuring as to the Bank's lack of agricultural emphasis: they focused on industry as the engine of development.[3] Traditional agriculture was the sector from which resources of some kind needed to be extracted in behalf of industrialization.

There was yet another factor that slowed Bank venturing into agriculture in the early years: uncertainties over the extent to which the uplift of food and other farm output in the developing regions would depend on or be retarded by reforms in the ownership of and tenurial rights to agricultural lands, and uncertainty over the extent to which such reforms were politically feasible in host countries and appropriate causes for such outside interveners as the Bank. At the end of the 1950s, views of all these issues were blurred and disputed; accumulating evidence of the presence or absence of scalar economies in agriculture was patchy and mixed; in developing regions, the outlook for serious land and tenurial reforms by nonviolent means appeared to be poor; with recipient countries resistant, few in donor governments were pushing either their own bilaterals or such multilaterals as the Bank to agitate for land reform; and yet some respected analysts saw little prospect for either output or equity breakthroughs in agriculture until land policies were structurally transformed.[4] The field looked like a good one for a prudent agency to leave to others.

3. Albert O. Hirschman, *The Strategy of Economic Development* (Yale University Press, 1958); W. Arthur Lewis, "Economic Development with Unlimited Supplies of Labor," *Manchester School of Economic and Social Studies*, vol. 22, nos. 139–91 (May 1954); Raúl Prebisch, *The Economic Development of Latin America and Its Principal Problems* (Lake Sucess, N.Y.: UN Department of Economic Affairs, 1950); Ragnar Nurske, *Problems of Capital Formation in Underdeveloped Countries* (Oxford University Press, 1953); P. C. Mahalanobis, "Some Observations on the Process of Growth of National Income," *Sankhya*, September, 1953; W. W. Rostow, *The Stages of Economic Growth: A Non-communist Manifesto* (Cambridge University Press, 1960).

4. Gunnar Myrdal *Asian Drama: An Inquiry into the Poverty of Nations* (New York: Twentieth Century Fund, 1968), chap. 26, pp. 1255–59, 1301–86; Thomas R. Carroll, "The

In January 1964, at the beginning of his second year as president of the World Bank, George Woods addressed a major paper to his Board in which he noted that agriculture, which employed two-thirds of the working population of the less developed world, had received only 8 percent of the dollars loaned from the opening of the International Bank for Reconstruction and Development through June 30, 1963. The new agency, the International Development Association, had channeled 24 percent of its credits to agriculture, but the sector's portfolio was still small. This was still the case eight years later: "Bank Group lending in the field of agriculture was very slow to develop. In the period before 1963 less than 9 percent of total lending was directed to this area."[5] Woods did not denigrate the past effort, but projected an expansion: "The Bank and IDA have in the past devoted considerable attention, effort and resources to promoting improvements in agriculture, but the importance of this sector in the development process requires, in my opinion, that we give it still higher priority in the future."[6]

Promoting Agricultural Expansion in the 1960s

When Woods assumed the presidency of the Bank at the start of 1963, some of the shift toward agriculture had already begun. This was the result of the launching of IDA in 1960. Eugene Black, when the Bank was borrowing its resources in the market, was in favor of creditworthy projects in creditworthy countries. He was not a great fan of agriculture's claims. But when he switched his stance and welcomed IDA into the Bank Group, he recognized that the new soft credits should flow mainly to the needier countries heavily dependent on agriculture (see chapters 4 and 17). More agriculture lending—for example, to agricultural credit projects and for a couple of modest ($16 million) "comprehensive agricultural projects" in Africa—began to be encouraged. But this was a mere prelude to what Woods began demanding when he took over in 1963.

The Woods Shift to Agriculture

For an investment banker, George Woods reached the World Bank with a surprising head of pro-agriculture steam. He shared Black's perception of the rising importance of IDA within the Bank's portfolio and of the major role of agriculture

Land Reform Issue in Latin America," in Albert O. Hirschman, ed., *Latin American Issues: Essays and Comments* (New York: Twentieth Century Fund, 1961), pp. 161–20; Doreen Warriner, *Land Reform and Economic Development,* National Bank of Egypt 50th Anniversary Commemoration Lectures, Cairo, reprinted in Carl K. Eicher and Lawrence W. Witt, eds., *Agriculture in Economic Development* (McGraw-Hill, 1964), pp. 272–98.

    5. Mason and Asher, *World Bank since Bretton Woods,* p. 203.

    6.IBRD/IDA, "Report of the President to the Executive Directors on Proposed Bank/IDA Policies in the Field of Agriculture," FPC/64-1, January 17, 1964, p. 1.

in IDA countries. But in his travels—for example, in India, at times as a Bank consultant—he had developed his own appreciation of the salience of rural issues.[7]

As soon as he had taken stock of the scene, Woods mandated a quick doubling of the institution's agricultural program. He said if the feasible recruitment of agricultural specialists could not keep pace with such an expansion, he was prepared to enlist FAO in the preparation of Bank projects.[8] The Agriculture Projects Division, shocked at the rate at which its business was to grow, agreed to share the work: the Bank itself would continue to identify projects, but FAO would undertake the technical preparation of some of them. This suited Woods, who favored collaborations with the specialized UN agencies and proceeded to enter into a formal partnership with FAO, which was succeeded later by one with the United Nations Educational, Scientific, and Cultural Organization.[9]

In his January 1964 paper George Woods painted developing-country agriculture as an atomistic industry in which most production units were very small, fragile, and weakly supported by physical as well as social infrastructure. They faced inadequate incentives in fragmented markets. Large "foreign plantations" and "big estates" might have a competitive edge, but most rural populations depended on small farms and herds, and the crucial development issue was to help these become "viable in a modernizing economy." Woods was at ease with the idea of land reform programs, which, although the Bank lacked the authority to fund them directly, it "might well assist . . . by financing roads and other necessary installations and the provision of necessary technical, financial and organizational services to the new holders."[10] Moreover, Woods emphasized the need for "'agrarian reform' in the broadest sense—including improvement not only in land use and, where appropriate, in tenure arrangements, but also in government agricultural services, in price and other economic policies, in marketing and in the supply of credit and farm requisites."[11]

---

7. Robert W. Oliver, *George Woods and the World Bank* (Boulder, Colo.: Lynne Rienner, 1995).

8. A contemporary Bank official remarks that this was the only perceived alternative to in-house staffing because consultancy capacity in the private and unofficial sectors was so small. By the 1990s such capacity had increased so radically that the IBRD-FAO arrangement referred to in note 10 was being called redundant.

9. IBRD, "Agreement with the Food and Agriculture Organization of the United Nations (FAO)," Board of Governors Resolution 201, adopting proposal R64-26/IDA R64-6 of March 19, 1964. The agreement aimed at promoting financing as well as technical assistance to intensify support of agricultural development. Under the agreement, the FAO was to find prospective projects and bring them to the Bank, which would then determine if they were eligible for financing. Bank staff were divided in their attitude toward the IBRD-FAO agreement: some wanted access to FAO at large, whereas others, echoing a general distrust of UN agencies, preferred the creation of a special collaborating unit within FAO. The latter position prevailed. Willi Wapenhans, interview with the authors, September 6, 1991.

10. IBRD/IDA, "Report of the President to the Executive Directors on Proposed Bank/IDA Policies in the Field of Agriculture," FPC/64-1, January 17, 1964, p. 15.

11. Ibid.

The Bank, its president recognized, was better suited for some things than others. It had been heavily involved in irrigation, drainage, and flood control projects and should remain so; these tended to be large and capital-intensive endeavors. He called for a large increase in agricultural technical assistance, but, as indicated, was prepared to see much of this farmed out. He wanted to see the Bank active in helping build "agricultural institutions" in recipient countries. What he had in mind, however, were operating institutions engaged in marketing, inputs supply, and smaller-scale irrigation (the sorts of organizations that came to be called "parastatals" in Africa), rather than in education or research. In retrospect, it is noteworthy that Woods said almost nothing about research. He did urge the Bank to play a major role in agricultural credit, however, if "complemented by other elements of 'agrarian reform'" and kept to a rather carefully detailed set of guidelines.[12] In what became the style of the 1960s, Woods's 1964 prospectus recommended that agricultural promotion efforts be concentrated on specific high-return project areas and that governments be encouraged by Bank/IDA loans to engage coherently in all the various elements of rounded agrarian-reform packages.

Finally, in ways not confined to agriculture, the paper challenged several of the Bank's orthodoxies. First, because of agricultural investment's heavy dependence on local cost financing, Woods undertook to look into a relaxation of the standing inhibition against such funding. Second, recognizing that many of agriculture's import requirements were, like fertilizer, recurrent costs normally not deemed to be eligible for Bank investment financing, the president suggested an exception: the "purchase of fertilizers or other supplies, as an essential part of the intensive development of a project area, should also be acceptable for a limited period, provided we are satisfied that adequate local resources will thereafter be able to finance continued use of those prerequisites."[13] And third, although the paper favored a trend toward cost-covering user charges for newly provided agricultural facilities, "we should continue to make no hard and fast rule that projects must be financially self-liquidating."[14]

The Bank's move toward agriculture in the mid-1960s was, without doubt, internally—more particularly, presidentially—motivated. When Woods arrived at the Bank, Pakistan's Mangla project was in train, but views differed over the whole drainage strategy for West Pakistan, and the question of the huge Tarbela dam proposed for the Indus Basin itself was unsettled. The economic rationale for Tarbela was in dispute and its external funding incomplete. During his first year Woods stopped in Pakistan, hit it off with President Ayub Khan and promised that the Bank would undertake a study that would once and for all settle the country's water management issues.

12. Ibid., p. 8.
13. Ibid., p. 18.
14. Ibid., p. 20.

Woods's choice for this task was the first sitting member of the Board of Executive Directors in Bank history to be drafted for a technical assignment. The draftee was Pieter Lieftinck, economist, former finance minister in the Netherlands, and previous Bank consultant. He was given a team of his choice, autonomy from all Bank executives save the president, and as much time as necessary to complete what was to be an exhaustive study. It was indeed a massive work—some 30 manuscript volumes—to have been finished by its designated authors by 1967. Some questions surround the authorship of the report, however, in that some Bank veterans suggest it was for the most part the unattributed work of a London consulting firm. In any event, the report was a highly professional piece of work, which, with some straining, reached an economic justification for the Tarbela dam; and it also steered Pakistani water management doctrine somewhat away from the ideas in a report filed by an American expert (Roger Revelle) three years earlier.[15] In retrospect, the Lieftinck study conspicuously failed to solve Pakistan's drainage problems for the long run.[16] But it did reestablish the Bank's reputation for water policy expertise and, within the institution, set a new standard for the placement of project analyses into sectorwide and economy-wide frameworks.

External Changes

The Bank's shift toward agriculture during Woods's presidency was also driven by factors outside the institution, which, in turn, played back into the Bank, in part via its so-called Bell Mission to India in 1964–65. By the mid-1960s the development promotion community was seized with the importance of agricultural production, especially in the aftermath of some devastating crop failures in company with a growing inadequacy in long-run supply. Geographically, both factors were centered in South Asia. By the late 1950s agriculture looked less like an engine than a brake on growth in that part of the world. Third-world populations were increasing faster than expected. The rate of expansion in South Asian food production, on the other hand, had slowed down. As a result, India began drawing on PL 480 food imports from the United States and would continue to do so through most of the 1960s. Already by 1959 a team of eminent American and Indian specialists recruited by the Ford Foundation was warning, in a "Food Crisis" report, that Indian development was about to be bottlenecked by food shortages and that this situation could be avoided only by a sharp reallocation of resources together with major changes in program design.[17]

15. Pieter Lieftinck, A. Robert Sadove, and Thomas C. Creyke, *Water and Power Resources of West Pakistan: A Study in Sector Planning* (Johns Hopkins University Press, 1968–69), three volumes.

16. World Bank, "World Bank in Pakistan: Review of a Relationship, 1960–1984," vol. 2, OED Report 6048, SecM86-0119, January 27, 1986, pp. 50–67.

17. Government of India: Ministry of Food and Agriculture and Ministry of Community Development and Cooperation, *Report on India's Food Crisis and Steps to Meet It* (New Delhi, April 1959).

According to the new thinking, however, the increased needs were coupled with improved prospects for response. For one thing, peasant farmers could be expected to respond to better economic incentives. Until now such farmers had been given little chance to prove themselves. In many countries, including those of South Asia, they had been trapped in repressed markets with controlled prices. Moreover, foreign advisers of an anthropological bent had spread the view that it would be crudely ethnocentric to expect local villagers to respond to Western-style economic incentives. One had to sort out the patterns of indigenous motivation before trying to design reforms.

As the 1960s dawned, support began emerging for the contrary hypothesis, that peasant farmers are actually incentive prone. This concept arose from a small base of solid village studies, two of which would provide the springboard for T. W. Schultz's seminal 1964 treatise, *Transforming Traditional Agriculture*.[18] But many policymakers did not need a great accumulation of scholarly evidence to persuade them of the importance of incentives in the rural regions of developing countries. Indeed, this was the official view of successive Indian ministers of food and agriculture (although not equally of the Planning Commission) from the early 1950s onward. A recommendation in behalf of incentive prices for farmers featured a report of a Foodgrains Enquiry Commission in 1957. This was repeated more forcefully by another official committee in 1964, which also (and with greater promise of adoption) repeated recommendations for two implementing mechanisms—a standing Agricultural Prices Commission to keep calculating and setting incentive product prices and a Food Corporation that would develop a buffer stock and, by purchases and sales operations, keep food prices within a reasonable range.[19]

Three other new elements of the agricultural development environment were taking shape by the beginning of the 1960s. First, new technologies and new institutions to generate and propagate them were being developed. Dramatic breakthroughs were being achieved in plant breeding. Institutionally, the Rockefeller Foundation was the chief instigator. New high-yielding wheats were being generated by research in Mexico that, in 1966, would be organized within the framework of the country's wheat and maize institute (CIMMYT).[20] Earlier, in 1960, the International Rice Research Institute (IRRI) in the Philippines became the first of the formally established international agricultural research centers. The movement would spread to other crops, regions, and ecological settings.

18. The two studies were Sol Tax, *Penny Capitalism: A Guatemalan Indian Economy* (Smithsonian Institution, Institute of Social Anthropology, 1953); and W. David Hopper, "The Economic Organization of a Village in North-Central India," Ph.D. dissertation, Cornell University, 1957. Schultz's book was published by Yale University Press.

19. John P. Lewis, *India's Political Economy: Governance and Reform* (Oxford University Press, 1995), chap. 3.

20. Centro Internacional de Mejoramiento de Maiz y Trigo.

The improved yields achieved with the new technology were not uniform across crops and regions, but where they were good, as in the case of the high-yielding wheats and rices, they were explosively good. Their success depended on—and, by the same token, motivated—a second sea change beginning in the early 1960s: an inputs revolution. Chemical fertilizer—both its supply, whether via imports or domestic production, and its distribution—became vastly more important, as did pesticides. The new seeds had to be multiplied and distributed reliably. The most successful new varieties required assured and predictable water supplies. Agricultural credit became more urgent, as did trustworthy markets.

A third new, or intensified, aspect of the agricultural development environment was institutional. In many countries the agricultural public sector—ministries, departments, parastatals—were filled out in ways that would be challenged in the 1980s. Cooperatives were well established in many countries, but by the 1960s a number were being strengthened or newly established. Support prices and buffer-stock operations, as in India, began to appear. National (not just international) agricultural research institutions were on the rise, along with agricultural universities and other training facilities. And extension systems were being more tightly focused on farm production.

In the midst of all this ferment, agricultural development doctrine achieved a new thematic statement, in the brief but pivotal book by Theodore Schultz already mentioned. *Transforming Traditional Agriculture* did not initiate the technological and policy changes of the 1960s. But, appearing in parallel, it gave them a lucid rationale. Schultz's two central and related propositions became the new conventional wisdom. First (just as Sol Tax and W. David Hopper had found in their village studies), traditional farmers were disposed to optimize economically. Hence, traditional agriculture tended to be fairly efficient already, within its existing technological frame; mere exhortation and extension could not expect to squeeze out a great deal of improved performance. Second, therefore substantial, sustainable output growth had to be dynamic; it required new and improved technologies that could raise the whole production function. Thus Schultz provided a scenario for the Green Revolution before the phenomenon even had a name. Although he started the book in 1959 and finished it in May 1963, it may not have been available in the Bank before Woods addressed his paper to the Board eight months later.

Whereas the preceding agriculture-accenting factors were enduring changes that were not easily reversed, two back-to-back droughts in the populous countries of South Asia in 1965–66 and 1966–67 created a sudden jolt worldwide. In these two crop years South Asian grain output was more than 15 percent below the levels of 1964–65.[21] This turn of events, which saw food aid shipments to India alone approach annual rates of 10 million tons, caused some observers to panic.[22]

21. Donato Antiporta and Randolph Barker, "Food Production and Demand," in Asian Development Bank, *Rural Asia: Challenge and Opportunity,* Supplementary Papers, vol. 1 (Manila: Asian Development Bank, 1978).

22. See the discussion of William Paddock and Paul Paddock, *Famine 1975!* (London: Weidenfeld and Nicolson, 1967), later in the chapter.

To make matters worse, the poor production was not confined to South Asia. Peru, too, reported a decline in its agricultural annual growth rate, from an average 5 percent during 1950–55 to 3.6 percent in 1955–60 and 2.1 percent in 1960–65. Events in Africa were even more alarming: its population growth of 2½ to 4½ percent was outpacing modest farm output growth in the range of 1½–2 percent.

The Bell-Crawford Intervention

By 1963 the World Bank team following events in India became convinced that various lags in the country's development performance warranted a more searching review.[23] The new president of the Bank, himself familiar with and concerned about the Indian economy, accepted the proposal and augmented it. The review would be wide ranging, the mission would be large, its members would spend several months within the country, and unlike routine Bank missions, it would be led and in part staffed by people from outside the institution. The American economist, Bernard Bell, was recruited to head the mission. In August 1964, President Woods persuaded an old acquaintance, India's finance minister, T. T. Krishnamachari, to agree to the exercise, and the first members of the Bell Mission arrived in October of that year.

The Bell Mission is memorable particularly for its part in the attempt by the Bank, along with the United States as a bilateral donor, to encourage the government of India to consider certain reforms of trade and industrial policy. This episode (from 1964 through 1968) can be viewed as a precursor of the Bank's "policy-based lending" era that began in 1980 (see chapter 9).

For the purposes of this chapter, it is important to consider the agricultural part of the Bell Mission's work, not so much because of its impact on India but because of its effect on the Bank. The Mission reached outside the Bank for its whole agricultural contingent—in part, at least, because the Agricultural Projects Division was so heavily engaged in trying to implement the program expansion on which the president was insisting. At the suggestion of people in the Food and Agriculture Organization, Bell recruited Sir John Crawford, a distinguished Australian civil servant, as the head of his agricultural group, and Crawford gathered an interesting and able set of colleagues, including the same village-studying Canadian who had contributed to the Schultz thesis, W. David Hopper.[24]

23. It included Alexander Stevenson and Peter Wright in Washington and Benjamin King and Romano Pantanali in New Delhi.

24. Hopper at this time was with the Ford Foundation in New Delhi and would soon move to the Rockefeller Foundation offices there (he would wind up as a senior vice president of the World Bank). Others on the team included, from FAO, the Chicago-trained French economist Louis Goreux (who would wind up at the IMF), and Wolf Ladejinsky, Soviet émigré and U.S. Department of Agriculture statistician who in the postwar period had become a fabled propagator of land reform in East Asia and a student of Asian rural institutions.

The Crawford group compiled a long and lucid analysis of the condition and needs of Indian agriculture. It was emphatic about the need for stepped-up research, and it made a strong case for incentive producer prices and (via the Food Corporation of India) a market-stabilizing buffer stock system (although evidently comments from Bank staff had strengthened this aspect of the report).[25] Crawford and his colleagues pressed hard in behalf of commercial fertilizer use and therefore urged a dramatic scaling up of domestic fertilizer production, arguing that there was room for all players in that expansion—whether in the public, private, cooperative, or foreign-private sectors. The group focused on improving the distribution of cooperative and private inputs, and, like the Ford Foundation's "food crisis" team and the Indians' own current agriculture programs, argued that efforts to raise agricultural output needed to concentrate initially on the country's more responsive farming areas.

In the Indian context, these were useful ideas, but not new ones. Many of them had been pressed by factions within the government of India itself since the middle 1950s. The rest had been advocated, first, in fragmented form, then more coherently, by the American agencies represented in Delhi: the Ford and Rockefeller foundations and the U.S. Agency for International Development. USAID began to use program loans to encourage agricultural reform in the fall of 1964 and found a responsive partner in the new minister of food and agriculture, C. Subramaniam, who had taken over when Lal Bahadur Shastri had succeeded to the prime ministership upon Jawaharlal Nehru's death at the end of May.

Minister Subramaniam was even bolder than his American mentors in his readiness to import the new high-yielding varieties of wheat and rice and to build the indigenous research capacity needed to sustain innovation in producing new varieties. He pressed ahead with price reforms and their implementing institutions. He sought a rapid expansion of efficient indigenous fertilizer production of whatever sectoral stripe and was prepared to attract foreign private investors to the industry. He embodied all of this in a New Agricultural Strategy (the opposition was softened by the severity of the drought that worsened as the year progressed) that he sold to the cabinet and Parliament in December 1965.

In their comprehensive summary, Crawford and his colleagues articulated and reinforced the New Agricultural Strategy. But the strategy had been instigated by the Americans and even more by some of the Indians themselves.[26]

---

25. Wapenhans, interview, September 6, 1991.

26. The agricultural side of the Bell Mission and its relationship to both Indian and American initiatives in the 1950s as well as the 1960s are dealt with at greater length in Lewis, *India's Political Economy*, chaps. 3 and 4.

In later years, the Bank sometimes laid too much claim to the Green Revolution. And in this respect, the formidable 1982 study, *IDA in Retrospect* (written to put IDA's best foot forward at the time of an IDA replenishment), was rather flagrant. Readers might understand the study to say the Bank helped steer India's new-technology, price-support, food-corporation and other pivotal decisions during 1964–66. Moreover, there is a quotation from Subramaniam that might be read to endorse this account.[27] Subramaniam, whose main reform transactions had been with the Americans, understandably became deeply angry over the humiliation President Lyndon Johnson inflicted on the Indians by his "short-tethering" of food aid during 1966–68 (they had, as it were, to sit up and beg for driblets every couple of months). Subramaniam was happy, by comparison, to praise others.[28] But he would not dispute the claim that the Bank's excellent group of agricultural consultants were codifiers, not originators.

What the Bell exercise did, however, was introduce a reinforced set of agricultural perspectives into the Bank. John Crawford himself went back to Australia, but he remained a continuing trusted adviser to Woods and others in the Bank.[29] Subsequently, he became the first chairman of the Technical Advisory Committee (TAC) to the Consultative Group on International Agricultural Research (CGIAR) network of international agriculture research centers that the Bank joined in setting up.[30] After a brief interval, Bernard Bell continued to play major roles in the Bank. David Hopper, after a decade as first president of Canada's International Development Research Centre, joined the Bank as vice president for South Asia in 1978. But the intellectual and programmatic impact these people had on the institution depended not only on their personal presence. Even though the agriculture volumes of the Bell report theoretically were restricted, they were widely circulated inside and outside the Bank. And in a general way, it can be said that from 1966 onward the institution leaned toward a Crawford-style span of agricultural attention and set of policy preferences.

27. Subramaniam is quoted in IDA, "IDA in Retrospect: The First Twenty Years of the International Development Association," IDA/SecM82-244, July 6, 1982, Box 4.3 (subsequently published as IDA, *IDA in Retrospect: The First Two Decades of the International Development Association* [Oxford University Press, 1982]): "These were major innovations; to be fully implemented, they needed a tremendous amount of assured resource flows. It was at that time that the World Bank's President promised India this flow of concessional resources for a number of years. It was the marriage of scientific development, institutional support, and IDA funding that contributed to the remarkable success of Indian agriculture." There are two ironies in the foregoing. First, the enhanced program aid flow that George Woods "promised" the Indians in the spring of 1966 was in support of trade and industrial liberalization cum devaluation, and was not primarily in support of agriculture. Second, and sadly, the promised enhanced flow withered after the first year. It failed to provide reliable underpinning for anything. See chapter 9 of this volume; and Lewis, *India's Political Economy*, chap. 5.

28. IDA, "IDA in Retrospect," pp. 4, 25–26, and Box 4.3.

29. Wapenhans, interview, September 6, 1991.

30. Consultative Group on International Agricultural Research.

The Late 1960s and Regional Priorities

As to expansion of the Bank's agricultural program, George Woods had his way. Figure 8-1 shows the growth of agricultural lending in the Bank's portfolio. Figure 8-2 shows annual Bank and IDA commitments for agriculture. Project resources take time to move through the pipeline. Robert McNamara became president in April 1968. Thus all commitments through fiscal year 1970 were the work of the Woods era—spanning, in effect, 1965 to 1970. During these years, agriculture's shares of both IBRD and IDA lending increased rapidly, as did the number of agricultural projects. With the institution's lending totals also rising, Woods's goal of doubling the real transfers to agriculture was more than realized.

Tables 8-1 and 8-2 show regional and subsectoral aggregate breakdowns of agricultural lending. Because of the low starting level, the *rate* of growth of allocations to agriculture was higher during the Woods presidency than in any subsequent period. Both in Asia and in Europe, Middle East, and North Africa (EMENA), lending was concentrated on irrigation and drainage to a striking extent during the first two decades. In Latin America, this pattern varied somewhat more, owing to the importance of livestock projects. In the African case, where Bank/IDA lending only started in the 1960s, total allocations were far smaller, indeed, only about one-quarter of the amount in each of the other regions.

If the Woods regime had seemed a little light on the subject of agricultural research at the beginning of 1964, it made up for that failing before the end of its tenure. In 1966 the Bank, aware both of the pivotal role that the new biological-chemical technologies were assuming and the limits that private foundation support for them was approaching, employed Campbell P. MacMeekan, a New Zealand professor of animal husbandry, to conduct a comprehensive survey of the present state and problems of development-oriented agricultural research worldwide. MacMeekan's report, at the end of six months of traveling, foreshadowed the launching of the CGIAR during the McNamara presidency.[31]

Some comments of the Pearson Commission aptly sum up World Bank agriculture under George Woods. Headed by Lester Pearson, the former prime minister of Canada, the Commission was first proposed by Woods. Several of its staff had worked or would work, at the Bank, and its 1969 report (like the institution's commitment/disbursement numbers for that year) can be associated with the Woods era.[32] The Pearson Commission's assessment of agricultural development stated in part:

> Until quite recently, it seemed that the hopes for rapid economic progress in many of the poorest countries were doomed by very slow growth of the huge agricultural sector. . . .

31. Wapenhans, interview, September 6, 1991.
32. The new president, Robert McNamara, having recruited Pearson, displayed a very active interest in the work of the Commission.

Figure 8-1. *World Bank Lending for Agriculture, Fiscal 1948–95*[a]

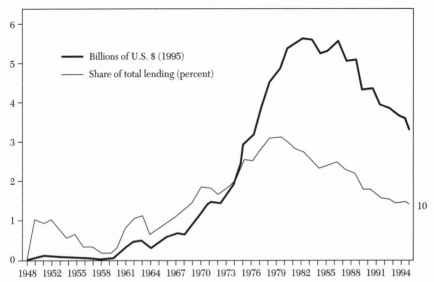

Source: World Bank data.
a. Three-year moving averages.

Figure 8-2. *Agriculture Lending: Share of IBRD and IDA, 1948–95*[a]
Annual averages, billions of U.S. $ (1995)

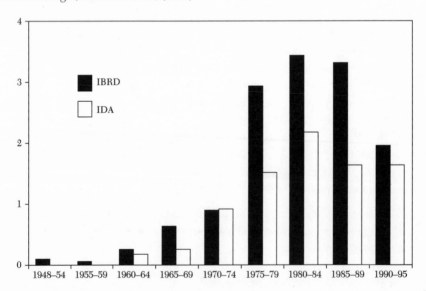

Source: World Bank data.
a. The IDA lending began in 1961.

Table 8-1. *Agriculture Lending by Region, 1959–95*
Percent share

Region	Through FY 1959	1960–69	1970–79	1980–89	1990–95
Africa	0	13.7	14.5	15.2	14.9
Asia	42.2	42.9	40.6	43.7	48.1
Europe and Central Asia	0	3.3	11.3	9.5	8.9
Latin America and Carribbean	41.5	28.1	17.9	24.2	19.5
Middle East and North Africa	0.0	7.7	7.5	7.4	8.5
Other	16.3	4.4	8.2	0	0

Source: World Bank, Loan and Credit Database.

Table 8-2. *Agriculture Lending by Subsector, 1959–91*
Percent share

Subsector	Through FY 1959	1960–69	1970–79	1980–89	1990–91
Agriculture credit	10.9	11.6	15.5	15.4	10.5
Area development	2.6	7.7	21.8	18.5	17.0
Fisheries	0	2.1	1.1	0.6	0.9
Irrigation drainage	49.7	54.6	32.2	27.0	22.9
Livestock	0.0	17.5	9.4	2.6	0.5
Agro-Industry	4.1	1.5	6.0	7.4	3.2
Perennial crops	0	3.3	7.5	5.3	5.3
Research/extension	0	0	3.7	4.6	6.4
Forestry	2.2	0.3	1.9	3.5	7.7
Agriculture adjustment	0	0	0	9.9	18.1
Other[a]	30.5	1.3	0.7	5.1	7.7
Total	100	100	100	100	100

Source: World Bank data.
a. Includes agriculture.

These dire forecasts could not take into account the progress that has now been made in seed research, in irrigation practices, in extension work, and in agricultural education. They also ignored the impact price incentives could have. . . . As controls over production were relaxed and prices for farm products were made remunerative, farmers proved willing to adopt a new technology with amazing rapidity. . . . The Green Revolution has been a matter of both new technology and new policy. Although it is too early to say how deep and how rapid the impact will be and whether similar breakthroughs will be repeated in other parts of the world, the prospects for growth obviously look very much brighter.[33]

33. Lester B. Pearson, *Partners in Development: Report of the Commission on International Development* (Praeger, 1969), pp. 32–35.

The focus here is plainly on growth. The authors were less preoccupied with low-end poverty and the landless.

The ARD-Intensive 1970s

The story of the Bank's ARD work in the McNamara years is one of robust expansion. But it is also a complex one, made up of a fair assortment of interwoven strands.

The Factors in Play

At least five factors contributed to the changing emphasis on agriculture and rural development during the 1970s.

TWO GOALS, WHETHER OR NOT CONFLICTED. For the World Bank, as for other pro-development interveners, raising agricultural, more particularly, food, output in the developing countries remained a matter of urgent concern. In 1967, in their *Famine, 1975!* William and Paul Paddock had announced that the population explosion already had so outdistanced the planet's capacity for food production that disaster in the developing world was inescapable. Not even American food aid could prevent it; such should be used, they argued, to save (and, incidentally, guide) those developing countries that were salvageable. Those that were not, such as India, Egypt, and Haiti, according to the Paddocks' "triage" program, would simply have to waste away.[34]

That this fraternal collaboration between a third-world traveling agronomist and a retired U.S. foreign service officer was given a serious hearing in the United States and some other countries of the Organization for Economic Cooperation and Development in 1967 is strange enough. But then, as already mentioned, the 1965–67 droughts in South Asia had induced a measure of hysteria in northern countries. What is noteworthy is that nine years later a reputable publisher decided to reissue the same Paddocks' book, only with a change of title.[35] This was because food-supply concerns persisted. Indeed, prompted by fresh droughts, particularly in the Soviet Union, that soaked up the bulk of buffer stocks in the United States (where surplus-generating policies were in process of being tamed) in 1974 anxiety prompted a World Food Conference. And this Rome conference, in turn, launched a set of new or renewed food promotion multilaterals: a reinforced World Food Program, the World Food Council, and the International Fund for Agricultural Development.

34. Paddock and Paddock, *Famine 1975!* p. 22.
35. William Paddock and Paul Paddock, *Time of Famines: America and the World Food Crisis* (Little, Brown, 1976).

Thus agricultural expansion remained a key goal of development policy in the 1970s, and the Bank, retaining the momentum of the Woods years, would remain a major pro-production player. But there was also a new cause—or, rather, an established cause—that took on new fervor. As chapters 2–7 of this volume make clear, the whole development effort can be viewed as a (partly self-conscious) attack on poverty. But in the 1960s in many places and programs, relief of intracountry poverty (whether relative or "absolute") had been pushed aside, at least rhetorically, by the focus on output growth. At the end of the decade, however, the international development community experienced a kind of global double take. Looking at the record of the 1960s, it found that "trickle-down" was not good enough; it was taking too long. Attention shifted to questions of equity.

There were demands for direct attacks on low-end poverty to supplement whatever benefits to the poor the promotion of growth might bring. These revisionist voices were more pragmatic than ideological. They wanted, not to displace growth, but to combine redistribution with it, and to do so without generating unacceptable social and political turmoil. But the revisionists' priorities shifted toward equity and, de facto, posed the question—in the World Bank and elsewhere—of how sharp the trade-off between equity and growth appeared to be.

The relevance of agriculture to poverty alleviation was inescapable: most of the poor in the third world were rural people dependent on indigenous food supplies. But there was also an income connection. The largest class of the rural poor in most areas, even larger than landless laborers, were small farm proprietors, tenants, and sharecroppers operating small holdings. This, given its land assets, was the class most accessible to developmental interventions. And there was growing evidence (contrary to what George Woods had feared in 1964) that small holdings were not inherently inefficient. In many places and crops, their outputs per hectare compared favorably with those of much larger farms. Smallholder agriculture became a vast target for antipoverty efforts trying to raise the productivity of the poor.

TWO POLICY DESIGNS: SINGLE-TRACK, MULTITRACK. At least since the community-development efforts of the 1950s some programs had focused on the multiplicity and interrelatedness of the needs of poor village-based societies: agricultural uplift with its various ramifications, but also education, health, infrastructure, off-farm employment, reduced inequalities, and greater self-management. And reciprocally, impatient with the diffusion and complexity of such "development-in-the-round" efforts, there have been reactions favoring first-things-first, single-track, trimmed-down, sharper targeting of agriculture per se.

This choice would be played out in the Bank in the 1970s. Both of its sides would have partisans, and it would not be, in fact, a binary choice: programs could have different degrees of multiplicity; conceptually, the agricultural production function could be extended to include inputs supply, credit, marketing, and other ancillary activities; and even education, health, nutrition, and population programs could be viewed as indirect modes of crop-production uplift. Conversely, as already indicated, preferred methods of promoting crop production could be supported as critical types of poverty alleviation.

Thus, while the single-track and multitrack designs overlapped the substantive pro-growth and pro-equity choices, they by no means coincided with them. But the tension between single and multiple modalities—the extent to which multiple subjects would be "integrated" into agricultural projects—would be evident in much of the institution's ARD work in the 1970s. Furthermore, the organizing principle for selecting and interrelating the multiple subjects of multitrack, integrated rural development projects (IRDP) would be geography. For the Bank, as for other donors in the 1970s, the prototypical IRDP would become an *area* development project.

TWO PACES: SLOW AND FAST. The Bank in the 1970s would drive itself to do a greatly increased volume of lending, especially in its ARD work. It would try to increase the pro-poor fraction of the expanding ARD total but this, by itself, did not make it easier or harder to move money along priority-to-equity than priority-to-production channels. Nor, a priori, were multiple-target area projects better money movers than single-track projects. For example, investments in agricultural credit, in contrast to agricultural research, could be designed quickly and (not irresponsibly) disbursed in a hurry.

There was, however, a consideration of pacing that cut across the generality of the institution's ARD business. In any given project or other specific operation, should the priority be to get it right, or to get on with it? What should be the trade-off between quantity/timeliness and quality/performance? The issue is inherent in any large calendar-paced operation, but for Bank ARD it was all the more critical when ARD became a central theme of the McNamara years.

At the same time, getting on with it could mean weak enforcement of loan conditions, especially ancillary policy conditions. A good number of 1970s agricultural project loans would carry policy covenants anticipating those in sector adjustment loans in the 1980s, a cotton investment project, for instance, including conditions with respect to cotton prices or deregulation of output markets. But then, under pressure to get on with the lending, enforcement of these undertakings could become perfunctory.

WITHIN THE BANK: DISTINGUISHABLE CASTS OF PLAYERS. By the early 1970s certain cadres of staff had identified themselves with some of the contrasting themes just noted.

—There were the technical agriculturalists. These included applied scientists, agricultural engineers, agronomists, and micro (for example, farming-systems type) agricultural economists. As noted, there were few technical agricultural staffers at the beginning of the 1960s, but their numbers grew steadily during that decade. The agriculturalists were allied with and managed by the Central Projects Staff. Together these were the get-it-right project people. They were likely to be concerned more about production than equity, and before the reorganization of 1972 they tended to control lending decisions.

—There were generalist operators, now beginning to be augmented by young professional (YP) types, who later would come to dominate the set. Their priorities between the production and equity goals were more difficult to predict. They were not, as a group, particularly ideological; they took their signals from management. But they were can-do, get-on-with-it specialists, who were conspicuous, after 1972, for the supervision they exercised over older technical specialists.

—Finally, there were redistributional reformists who pressed pro-equity values into the rural scene. Perhaps the most prominently engaged was Montague Yudelman who, as he was about to leave the OECD Development Centre in Paris, impressed McNamara with his encouraging good sense about the potentialities of smallholder agriculture. Hired as a rural development adviser, Yudelman arrived when the 1972 reorganization was dispersing most personnel of the old central agriculture department to Washington's regional operational offices. Yudelman was selected to head a diminished but still central ARD unit. Others who could have been given the reformist label, although not working full-time on rural matters, were chief economist Hollis Chenery and a number of his colleagues in the Bank's research wing: Chenery's recruit, Mahbub ul Haq, who became head of the policy-analysis staff situated midway in the research-operations spectrum and ul Haq's recruit, S. Javed Burki, who would long outstay him.

The absence of one component from this typology of personnel is deliberate. By the time the Bank entered the 1980s it would be hard to address agricultural issues without a significant input from macroeconomic economists concerning trade, exchange rates, relative internal and international prices, and fiscal, monetary, and related matters. But these were not subjects of lively ARD concern in the Bank as the 1960s turned to the 1970s.

LEADERSHIP. The development policy community would no doubt have increased its attention to agriculture and rural development in the 1970s with or without the World Bank, and the Bank would have joined that trend with or without Robert McNamara. But there is no question the new president took a strong personal hand in the Bank's and the decade's ARD story.

McNamara was an indefatigable but shrewd expansionist. He enthusiastically embraced both farming growth and rural equity, and he was allergic to trade-offs. It would become institutional doctrine that there was no need to sacrifice output expansion to the strengthening of the poor or to accept a quality discount in large-volume lending. His files showed and his immediate staff knew that the president was not blindly committed to this position, but the institution was made strongly aware of it.

On the other hand, McNamara was not similarly wedded to single- or multiple-track programming for rural projects, one or the other. He felt that the Bank had room for both in its portfolio. Though certainly a person of strong opinions, McNamara also recognized what he and his institution did *not* know; hence his appetite for research. Furthermore, he was comfortable accommodating a diversity of views within the Bank, and in open-ended ARD matters he would be more inclined than many of his staff to defer to client preferences, particularly in the case of borrowing countries whose leaders he admired. Julius Nyerere would be one such case. Above all, the new president imparted a thrust and enthusiasm to the Bank's ARD work that, despite its complexity, raised both the energy and expectations of the institution. How this work changed in the 1970s can best be understood by examining the Bank's pro-production and pro-equity agendas and its regional operations.

The Mounting Commitment to Agricultural Production

The first forays of the McNamara Bank into agriculture were direct extensions of the Woods approach, albeit with a continued rapid expansion of lending. As chapter 4 of this book makes clear, the new president arrived in 1968 with a pro-poor agenda. But this related to the overall welfare of poorer countries, of poorer regions within those countries, and of the poorer fraction (in his September 1972 annual speech to the Board of Governors it became "the poorest 40 percent") of developing-country populations. Of course, agriculture was recognized as the sector on which vast numbers of the poor depended. But initially McNamara focused mainly on the *outputs* of food and exports the sector produced. It was "the indispensable foundation of a healthy economy,"[36] a sector currently experiencing heartening (Green Revolution) productivity gains. In his very first speech to the governors, the president singled out agriculture—"which has for so long been the stepchild of development"—for greatest expansion in the Bank's new five-year program.[37]

The most striking aspect of the World Bank's investments in agriculture and rural development (and in the expansion of food production within that total) was, indeed, the vast increase in their scale. The sheer size of this expansion, which continued throughout the decade after the initial McNamara surge, eclipsed the effort of all other external lenders in the field. In real terms, Bank lending for ARD during the 1970s grew at an annual rate of 13.5 percent, rising in 1990 dollars from less than $1.5 billion in 1970 to almost $5.3 billion in 1980.[38] At the sight of this

36. Robert S. McNamara, "To the Board of Governors, Washington, D.C., September 29, 1969," in McNamara, *The McNamara Years at the World Bank: Major Policy Addresses of Robert S. McNamara 1968–1981* (Johns Hopkins University Press, 1981), p. 78.

37. Robert S. McNamara, "To the Board of Governors, Washington, D.C., September 30, 1968," in McNamara, *The McNamara Years at the World Bank*, p. 11.

38. Early in his tenure McNamara told Warren Baum and James Evans (Yudelman's predecessor as head of the Agriculture Division of the Projects Department) that he was prepared to give them all the staff they needed to reach the rising agricultural lending targets. They concluded that 25 percent a year was the fastest the division could recruit and absorb staff. This defined the division's personnel budget for several years before 1972. Baum correspondence, June 1994.

increase, other promoters of agricultural development often asked whether the Bank's ARD operations were as innovative and creative as they were large and solidly financed. Whatever the mixed answers to that question, the institution clearly displayed initiative as well as scale in the areas of agricultural research and extension.

Research, Extension, and the CGIAR

The Bank's growing interest in agricultural research, evident under George Woods, burgeoned under McNamara. The new president arrived with a broad commitment to the importance of research Bank-wide.[39] As a new trustee of the Ford Foundation, he was hearing about the financial needs (already noted within the Bank by the MacMeekan Report) for carrying forward the research into high-yielding varieties of foodgrains (HYVs) begun by the Rockefeller and Ford foundations. When the foundations proposed a series of conferences of bilateral and multilateral aid agencies (the first in April 1969) to consider the establishment of a new network of international agricultural research centers (IARCs) to be funded mainly in the public sector, McNamara was quick to join. He became the ringleader at these "Bellagio" conferences, which culminated, in May 1971, in the formal launching of the consultative group (CG) system, in the operation of which the Bank would play a leading role.[40]

THE CG FORMULA. Four of the international centers, established under the auspices of the Rockefeller and Ford foundations, were already in operation before the CGIAR framework was formally constructed: these were IRRI in the Philippines, CIMMYT in Mexico, the Institute of Tropical Agriculture in Ibadan (IITA), and the Latin American Center for Tropical Agriculture in Colombia (CIAT). Because of their shared origins, these centers had certain characteristics in common:

—The Rockefeller and Ford Foundations gave the new centers access to the best American technical resources without the overburden of U.S. foreign policy.

—The IARCs had an almost single-track mission, which was to raise the food productivity of developing countries. Later, in 1985, the system's goal would be revised to state that production should be promoted "in such a way that the nutritional level and general economic well-being of low-income people are improved."[41] In the mid-1990s the CG began to give more attention to natural

39. One of the present writers was in a conversation in the early 1970s with McNamara, Hollis Chenery, his chief economist and research vice president, and David Bell, executive vice president of the Ford Foundation. McNamara expressed readiness to scale up the Bank's research outlays to a level that startled even Chenery.

40. Warren Baum, who chaired the Consultative Group for International Agricultural Research (CGIAR) for ten years beginning in 1974, described its origins in *Partners against Hunger: The Consultative Group on International Agricultural Research* (World Bank, 1986), chap. 2.

41. FAO, "TAC Review of CGIAR Priorities and Future Strategies," TAC Secretariat, August 1985, p. vi.

resource management. Initially, however, equity was a secondary consideration for the CGIAR.[42]

—From the beginning, the CG had an entrenched commitment to professional excellence. This preoccupation sometimes placed considerable distance between the IARCs and their host-country environments, but, on balance, it enhanced their effectiveness.

—Although the scientists and other professionals attracted to the IARCs had outstanding credentials, they were primarily interested in applied, utilitarian, and field-oriented questions and were dedicated more to the system and its productivity than to individual scholarly achievement.

The CGIAR's organizational formula was distinctive. As the centers multiplied, they would become an issue. The group was highly decentralized; individual IARCs were their own masters and had their own governing bodies. Donors could distribute their support across the set as they wished.[43] Quality control and coherence were maintained by intensive semiannual groupwide meetings and by an elaborate (and costly) regime of internal and external reviews.

In the new system the World Bank was a counterpoise to the FAO. Initially the latter had been skeptical about the idea of an independent group of IARCs but eventually joined the United Nations Development Program (UNDP) and the Bank as a cosponsor of the new scheme. The FAO even agreed to provide quarters for one of the group's two secretariats—that of the dominant Technical Advisory Committee (TAC). The CG's secretariat for administrative and fiscal matters was quartered at the World Bank, and it was agreed that the CGIAR, consisting of representatives of the system's donors, would be chaired by a senior officer of the Bank. This design imparted a healthy balance and internal tension to the system, while also enabling each secretariat to remain fairly independent of its institutional host.

42. In a 1975 conference on agricultural research Sir John Crawford, first head of the CG's technical secretariat, put the matter this way: "Food was given absolute priority. Within food, crop priority was given to food grains. It is fair to say that our concern was production, and we did not in our early work debate extensively the question of maximizing production versus optimizing farm income distribution, whatever that may mean. We did, however, keep before us the need to strive for technologies which were applicable to small-scale farming for the simple reason that many of the world's underfed people are poor, so-called subsistence farmers." J. G. Crawford, "The Future of the International System: A View from the Inside," in Thomas M. Arndt, Dana G. Dalrymple, and Vernon W. Ruttan, eds., *Resource Allocation and Productivity in National and International Agricultural Research* (University of Minnesota Press, 1977), p. 592.

43. Warren Baum points out, however, that the Bank, as donor of last resort, together with USAID and several other donors who followed the Bank's lead, helped ensure that all the centers were financed roughly in accordance with the annual program/budget recommendations of TAC and the CG Secretariat.

SUPPORT AND PERFORMANCE. The CG system has been one of the greatest successes in the annals of development promotion. There was a rush to support it. During the system's first ten years (1972 through 1981) the number of donors (governments, multilateral bodies, and foundations) increased from sixteen to thirty-three, and nominal contributions grew at an annual rate of 22 percent—about twice the growth rate in nominal Official Development Assistance worldwide.[44] Two donors led the list: USAID, with about one-quarter of the total, and the World Bank, with 10 percent (mainly out of its earnings).

Moreover, the enthusiasm for the CG formula was quickly reinforced, indeed, inspired, by evidence that it paid off. Studies of the output effects of the new HYV wheat and rice technologies—which were actually "first-generation" HYVs produced by CIMMYT and IRRI before the formation of the CGIAR—began to appear in the early 1970s. The news was remarkably good. All but one of twenty or more studies reviewed in one 1975 survey "reported extraordinarily high rates of return to investment in research," on average amounting to about 50 percent a year.[45]

Specialists from developing and developed countries alike celebrated these results at a meeting in Virginia in January 1975. What they found particularly encouraging was that these achievements promised not to be one of a kind. Although it is true that the expanding CG system probably would never again equal CIMMYT's and IRRI's degree of early success, the average returns to subsequent agricultural research, while uneven and more modest, have been substantial. Robert Evenson, a leading expert in the field, has pointed out that the new research systems "have been productive, and they have contributed to the welfare of many groups—especially consumers. The IARC system has been particularly effective."[46] As they evolved over the 1970s, however, some doubts began clouding the agriculture research story.

IARCS, NATIONAL SYSTEMS, AND THE BANK. In a development context, research is an instrumental activity; it is as good as, and no better than, the productive applications it achieves or inspires. And *international* research centers are no better than the improvements to which they contribute in developing country farming, in good part through the intermediation of *national* research systems. The growing concern in the 1970s was that relations between the new IARCs and national agricultural research systems (NARS) would prove to be more competitive or substitutional than complementary.[47] Perhaps IARCs would bid aid

44. CGIAR Secretariat, "CGIAR Funding: 1972–1993," January 1994.

45. Robert E. Evenson, "Agricultural Research and Extension in Asia: A Survey," in Asian Development Bank, *Rural Asia: Challenge and Opportunity*, Supplementary Papers, vol. 2 (Manila: Asian Development Bank, 1978), p. 27. The reference is to James K. Boyce and Robert E. Evenson, *National and International Agricultural Research and Extension Programs* (New York: Agricultural Development Council, 1975).

46. Robert E. Evenson and Carl E. Pray, *Research and Productivity in Asian Agriculture* (Cornell University Press, 1991), p. 29.

47. For example, Evenson raised such questions in "Agricultural Research and Extension in Asia."

resources away from NARS, or perhaps developing-country governments would slack off on their own research efforts, thinking that they could obtain the research results they needed from one of the new IARCs.

Yet most IARC products did require local adaptation, and if the new basic innovations became more widely available, they might actually stimulate local research.[48] Once it became evident that this was indeed happening, a donor such as the World Bank had to decide how it should divide its research support between the generators of primary innovative information (the IARCs) and NARS (the practitioners of adaptive research). Although in most cases the Bank hoped to do more for both, national research projects proved difficult to design and carry out.[49]

EXTENSION AND ITS INTERFACE WITH RESEARCH. In most countries, developed and developing, there tends to be a cultural gap between agricultural research and extension; that is to say, research employs more highly trained personnel. Conceptually, of course, the two activities are closely linked: research produces information for extension. However, this connection was slow to emerge in the developing regions. In the 1950s and 1960s extension activity ran well ahead of indigenous agricultural research activity in the developing areas of Asia and Africa, as governments sought to propagate research borrowed from elsewhere and found extension, in terms of trained and trainable personnel, more feasible to do as well as far cheaper in terms of cost per worker. In both regions, research spending picked up sharply during the 1970s, in part because of the effects of investments in the IARCs. In Latin America, where the push in extension outlays did not start until the 1960s, extension and regional research spending increased sharply in the 1970s.

Not only was the Bank strongly behind the research bandwagon—both its IARC and NARS components—but it also developed a special role in agricultural extension. In the early 1970s it acquired the services of a dynamic Israeli agricultural worker, Daniel Benor, who had developed a highly ordered and replicable system of agricultural extension. Measured by host-government acceptance and later by evaluations, Benor's Training and Visit (T&V) system, propagated largely under Bank auspices, was a big hit—to an extent in Turkey, then resoundingly, in a number of Indian states, then elsewhere.[50]

48. Evenson and Pray, *Research and Productivity in Asian Agriculture,* chap. 1.

49. Letter, Warren C. Baum to John P. Lewis, June 5, 1994. At the same time Baum does not recall debate over whether, when it came to supporting NARS, it was better to do so directly or instead to leverage the NARS by giving extra support to IARCs.

50. The system's first published explication appeared in 1977, in a pamphlet: Daniel Benor and James Q. Harrison, "Agricultural Extension: The Training and Visit System" (World Bank, 1977). An enlarged, revised edition with Michael Baxter as an added author appeared in 1984. See also the detailed work, Daniel Benor and Michael Baxter, *Training and Visit Extension* (World Bank, 1984); and the evaluation by Michael M. Cernea, John K. Coulter, and John F. A. Russell, eds., *Agricultural Extension by Training and Visit: The Asian Experience* (World Bank, 1983).

By 1984, forty countries had had some experience with T&V, and eight of these, along with eight Indian states, had introduced the system to all of their farming areas. The system consisted of a carefully structured hierarchy of extension managers and deliverers, supplemented at each level by technical specialists. Also structurally important were the village extension workers (VEWs), who were required to feed back their learning from the field. VEWs attended regular weekly or fortnightly training sessions explaining timely seasonal farming practices, and then they imparted these practices, in reliably regular fortnightly visits, to their assigned clients, partly through the mediation of selected "contact farmers."

In contrast to the integrated rural development strategies the Bank was also pursuing in the 1970s, the T&V system was entirely directed toward agricultural production. Its themes were trustworthy regularity and hands-on delivery of small specific bites of information by personnel who were not sophisticated in a general sense but were highly motivated and well schooled in the lessons for the fortnight and had good access to specialists on various aspects of agriculture.

Although some extension specialists have found fault with the Benor system in recent years (see the discussion later in the chapter),[51] it clearly helped diffuse technological know-how to large numbers of low-skilled personnel in a short time. What somewhat surprised agricultural development promoters of the period, however, was the vigor with which the Bank trumpeted its own brand of extension. Bilateral donors were inclined to attribute this to the dearth of other institutional innovations in agriculture that the Bank could claim as its own.[52]

CGIAR GROWING PAINS. Arguably, the CG system worked as well as it did because it had a limited number of operating units. By design, the group had a weak center. The system floated in multilateral space. Its large mixed bag of donors was self-appointed, and its constitution was unwritten. The group made decisions by consensus; differences were delegated to committees and subcommittees, and if the latter could not report a consensus the chairman could hear, the issue was shelved. The structure was particularly awkward when major reallocations had to be made among the constituent IARCs.

The system worked well enough while two conditions prevailed. First, an escalating budget throughout the 1970s kept allocation problems at bay. Second, the small number of IARCs facilitated collegial relations among the centers, which

51. See B. E. Swanson, B. J. Farmer, and R. Bahal, "The Current Status of Agricultural Extension Worldwide," in FAO, Agricultural Education and Extension Service, Human Resources, Institutional and Agricultural Reform Division, *Report of the Global Consultation on Agricultural Extension* (Rome: FAO, 1990), pp. 43–75.

52. Another aspect of the T&V system ties back to the new departures in agricultural development in the 1960s, more specifically to Theodore Schultz's thesis that because shrewd peasants already were exploiting existing technology aggressively, new growth required new technology. Because of its routinized, standardized, small-bites character, the T&V system was better at moving average farmers into closer approximation to existing best practice than it was in propagating the (often complex) new practices, processes, and products emerging on the leading edge of the technological frontier. The success of T&V suggests that, although Schultz was more right than not, he exaggerated. In the developing-country farming industry (in the language of Harvey Leibenstein), there still was a lot of "x-inefficiency" to be rooted out.

helped them maintain the kind of (quality-oriented) homogeneity on which the effectiveness of the system depended. There were forces pressing for proliferation from the start, however, not the least of which was the very success of the formula itself and the support this had generated. Conceptually, the credentials for membership in the system were not tightly drawn. Of the original four centers, IRRI and CIMMYT were specialists in one or two crops, presumably with applications throughout the third world. But CIAT and IITA were regionally oriented: they were centers for tropical agriculture in their respective regions (Latin America and Africa), and they dealt with a broad array of crops, and, in the case of CIAT, even livestock.

Thus the door to differently defined research enterprises was open. Two livestock-oriented centers were added in Africa. Potatoes got their own center in Peru. Ecological issues were the focus of attention at the International Crops Research Institute for the Semi-Arid Tropics (ICRISAT) in Hyderabad, India. And crop research was not even an explicit mission in the International Food Policy Research Institute (IFPRI) in Washington, and the International Service for National Agricultural Research (ISNAR) in the Hague, the first such centers to be established in industrial countries. ISNAR was dedicated to the promotion and the improved management of national research systems in developing countries.

By the end of the CGIAR's first decade, the number of IARCs had risen to thirteen. In supplying the system with a steadily increasing financial contribution, as well as providing its presiding officer and one of its secretariats, the World Bank supported each step of this expansion. But when funding flattened out in the 1980s, and all the while new IARCs were still being proposed, some people in the Bank, as well as in other donor agencies, began to wonder whether what had been a very good thing was not becoming unwieldy.

Infrastructure and Direct Physical Inputs

Space is too limited here to review all of the World Bank's operations in the 1970s that bore on farm production, but, plainly, the institution did not abandon its traditional bent toward infrastructure lending or forget that farming had to be market oriented in order to be networked into the market economy. Thus the Bank funded rural electrification—for example, in the Philippines—but pushed the idea of recovering costs through electricity charges. In its transportation lending, it encouraged countries to allocate a larger share of their national transportation budgets to feeder roads and to delegate greater funding capacities and responsibilities to local governments. And it tried to demonstrate that satisfactory rural roads could be built cheaply, as in the case of the roads included in three Nigerian rural development projects between 1975 and 1980.[53] But there were also some constraints on the Bank's public works ventures, as explained later in the chapter.

53. World Bank, *World Development Report 1982: Agriculture and Economic Development*, p. 72.

IRRIGATION, DRAINAGE, AND WATER MANAGEMENT. Lending for irrigation and water management, the Bank's primary subsector of agricultural investment in the 1950s and 1960s, continued in this position into the 1970s, mainly in Asia, the Middle East, and Latin America. The Bank matched its allocation priorities to those of the developing countries themselves. Thus investment in irrigation increased sharply in the developing world, reaching close to $15 billion by 1980. The irrigated area had grown by 2.2 percent a year since 1960 and now constituted one-fifth of the harvested area in developing countries. Furthermore, this irrigated sector was producing two-fifths of the crops and using three-fifths of the fertilizer employed in agriculture. During the same period more than half of the developing world's increase in farm output came from new or rehabilitated irrigated areas.[54]

Water management projects certainly had a long history in the Bank, in part because they suited it. Such projects tended to run to large numbers and were well served by a seasoned technical staff traveling from Washington, especially when that staff could coordinate their activities with a competent technical organization in the host government. The Bank's water-management business in the 1970s can be illustrated by its dealings with two contiguous clients, Pakistan and India. Forty-one percent of the institution's ARD lending in Asia in the 1970s went to irrigation and drainage projects, and Asian projects accounted for 55 percent of the Bank's investments in the subsector worldwide.

In the field of surface irrigation, the Bank continued to contribute to major dam building, but it also became more heavily involved downstream, in intermediary and localized distribution. The Bank contributed to country allocations of investment to groundwater as well as surface irrigation and in the groundwater field assisted in the development of tubewells, both the large, deep, and mostly public variety and the small, shallow, mostly private kind. In the case of small tubewells, its usual strategy was to influence recipient-government policies and help with the provision of credit. To complete its span of involvement, the Bank continued to participate in drainage investments, albeit while failing to persuade host governments to keep pace with the need.

As any fair assessment of the World Bank's role in irrigation in South Asia is likely to point out, the activity was broadly successful and productive during the 1970s. It was essential to the pace of expansion that was achieved in agricultural production, especially that of food, most notably, foodgrains. The effectiveness of the high-yielding varieties on which the growth of foodgrains mainly depended relied in turn on assured water supplies, and thus on expanding irrigation. Good responses to increased fertilizer inputs required congenial hydrology. Expanded irrigation was a pivotal component of the Green Revolution, and the World Bank was a key player in the expansion.

54. Ibid., p. 62.

In South Asia, however, water management had many ups and downs, and some of the problems continued well past the 1970s. Irrigation's impact on the environment, for one, was a growing concern, as was the plight of persons displaced by water projects. How to allocate investment between surface and groundwater irrigation was another vexing issue, and it was only made worse by politics. In Pakistan, for example, key officials persuaded President Ayub Khan to make Tarbela dam a national priority. The report issued by the Lieftinck group struggled to produce an economic justification for the dam. It noted that the cost of increasing the surface water supply from Tarbela would be three times as much per acre-foot as the cost of augmenting the supply of irrigation water from groundwater sources.[55] But by slowing the flow of the river, the dam would help maintain the supply of fresh groundwater. Tubewells encountered equally difficult complications, often of a quasi-political nature. One annoying problem was that the system of large public tubewells begun with American aid in the late 1950s (with Bank funding later joining in)—which was to provide "vertical" drainage to combat waterlogging and salinity—was being pushed toward freshwater sites by those more concerned about getting additional water on the land than about drainage. Another problem was the growing competition between large public tubewells and smaller private tubewells.

The Lieftinck group skirted these problems with a consummate sense of not rocking the boat:

> The main emphasis in irrigation development in the years up to 1975 is to get more water onto the land. The drainage effect of public tubewells will be important; in some areas, the groundwater table needs to be lowered before additional surface supplies from Tarbela can prudently be absorbed. But the past preoccupation of public tubewell development with reclamation of saline and waterlogged lands should be reduced in favor of efforts to exploit groundwater resources for irrigation purposes. At the same time, public tubewell development should not be undertaken in large areas where private tubewells are spreading rapidly. The public tubewell program tries to steer a middle course, including projects in areas which are predominantly underlain by fresh groundwater and where the reclamation problems are not the most severe, but excluding areas where conditions are the most favorable to continued rapid growth of private tubewells. Extensive surface drainage schemes, included in the program, will help to lower the water table and thus provide valuable support to tubewells, whether private or public, and enable additional surface supplies from Tarbela to be absorbed subsequently. The public tubewell projects generally cover substantially smaller areas than those of the past. Nearly 50 percent of the public sector expenditures on irrigation and drainage works in the recommended program are allocated to public tubewells.[56]

In most countries irrigation also presented a set of equity problems. In surface systems, large landholders often obtained preferred access to the water. Whether by dominating cooperatives or otherwise, local elites tended to benefit dispropor-

55. Lieftinck, Sadove, and Creyke, *Water and Power Resources of West Pakistan*, vol. 1, p. 226.

56. Ibid., p. 230.

tionately from public tubewells. But they also could dominate in the private well side. They were more likely to own or control enough land to accommodate the command area of an efficient private tubewell; and they were apt to have readier access to mechanized land-leveling services.[57]

Especially in India, but also elsewhere, many water-related issues had to do with macro- and micromanagement. Reportedly, one reason the Bank shied away from funding main surface irrigation systems in favor of smaller downstream projects was its unwillingness to exempt the government of India from a requirement calling for international competitive bidding in major construction projects.[58] The question of how best to irrigate small areas was another source of conflict, both in India and in the Bank. Should cultivators be required to adapt their cropping to a (presumably) fixed and proportionate pattern of water distribution, or should the waterings be varied to suit the needs of different crops in different plots in the same command areas? The first formula was found to work well in the Punjab of India, but it was resisted in South India, where the "water-to-crops" pattern proved to be highly conducive to corruption. In the Punjab of Pakistan, however, the crops-to-water approach appeared to lack the resistance to distortions and cheating demonstrated across the border.[59]

Irrigation and drainage projects also had a time-horizon problem, which was more serious here than in some other sectors. Such projects, in the Bank and elsewhere, were deeply committed to the cost-benefit mode of project appraisal. Yet the use of a reasonable shadow-price of capital—say, a discount rate of 10 percent—for purposes of rationing scarce capital across a set of competing investments implied that benefits accruing beyond, say, fifteen years hence had little bearing on current investment choices. Decision makers in the Bank long had known that such a rule was simplistic and that some way had to be found to give weight to the interests of future generations. At the same time, benefit-cost calculations, in the abstract, promised systematically to give slight value to investments in drainage—whose benefits lagged far behind the benefits of the expanded flows of irrigation water. Yet in the absence of adequate drainage, after a time more irrigation could lead to waterlogging, salination, and reduced soil fertility.

57. See Inderjit Singh, *The Great Ascent: The Rural Poor in South Asia* (Johns Hopkins University Press, 1990), pp. 128–35.

58. Robert Wade, "The World Bank and India's Irrigation Reform," *Journal of Development Studies,* vol. 18 (January 1982), pp. 171–72.

59. On the overall issue, see W. I. Jones, "A Review of World Bank Irrigation Experience," in *Water Policy and Water Markets,* Selected Papers and Proceedings from the World Bank's Ninth Annual Irrigation and Drainage Seminar, Annapolis, Maryland, December 8–10, 1992, edited by Guy LeMoigne and others, World Bank Technical Paper 249, 1994, pp. 40–41. On corruption, see Robert Wade, "The System of Administrative and Political Corruption: Canal Irrigation in South India," *Journal of Development Studies,* vol. 18, no. 3 (April, 1982), pp. 302–04.

In fact, the Bank has not been inattentive to drainage in its water policy inter-ventions.[60] Its Pakistan projects focused on salinity, waterlogging, and drainage from the outset. But the Bank did not succeed in persuading its borrowers to remain drainage minded. Meanwhile, the Pakistanis, as noted, gave precedence to the spread of freshwater. The surge of private tubewells increased both aquifer salinity and the need for surface drainage. The drainage lag into the 1980s could be attributed, as much as anything, to the formidable scale of the need by then. It dictated larger expenditures than could be fitted easily into annual budgets.

In the case of India, Bank documents from the late 1970s reflect little concern about drainage. The institution's annual economic reports on India for those years—all very attentive to agriculture and, more particularly, to irrigation—make almost no mention of drainage. The topic finally turns up in the 1979 India economic report, at the end of a long section on irrigation, but is raised in a sober, noncommittal way:

> The emphasis in the plans for irrigation is always on the water supply side, while the drainage system . . . is treated as a secondary item. Drainage problems usually develop as a consequence of irrigation. . . .
>
> It is difficult to assess the magnitude of existing drainage problems in irrigated areas in India. [Yet] it is clear that drainage problems do constitute a real threat to the value of [irrigation] investments.[61]

Note, too, that South Asian water management in the 1970s was crosscut by geopolitics. The position in Pakistan already has been noted. In India many data on surface flows remained classified because of disputes with East Pakistan, then Bangla-desh, over sharing the water of the Ganges. More generally, there were various visionary, but technically plausible, proposals for sharing all the "Eastern waters" of the Brahmaputra and the torrents coming down from Nepal, as well as the Ganges. Such schemes promised rich returns to all three of the countries putatively involved, and they fascinated such outsiders as Robert McNamara. But they hypothesized more tampering with Indian autonomy than any Indian government of the period was willing to consider. Clearly, South Asia's water management issues were highly complex in the 1970s. The question is, what role did the World Bank play in tackling them? For one thing, it was an informed lender; for another, it was active, somewhat pliant, and prudent.

Throughout the decade the Bank had a good deal of in-house water manage-ment expertise and was connected with more outside. Yet in dealing with South Asian borrowers for water-related projects, the Bank was not particularly doctrinaire. It recognized that each borrowing country had its idiosyncracies and that most, especially India and Pakistan, had their own cadres of irrigation en-gineers and other specialists; also that many of the particular issues under debate were not sharply opposed. They were different routes to similar objectives.

60. Jones, "A Review of World Bank Irrigation Experience," p. 36.
61. World Bank, *Economic Situation and Prospects of India*, Report 2431-IN, April 9, 1979, pp. 46–47.

As to project designs, therefore, the Bank tended to defer to the borrowers, particularly when it came to details. This worked well, first, because the relevant design alternatives were not that far apart. Second, thanks to the magic of the new agricultural technologies, the output responses to any sensible options for augmenting irrigation were likely to be high. And, third (in sharp contrast to parallel African cases), the borrowers had at the ready enough administrative and technical capacity to put the resources being wholesaled to them by the Bank and other donors to fairly effective use.[62]

There were counts on which the Bank could be faulted.[63] Those in the Operations Evaluation Department who reviewed the Pakistan record felt the Bank had been remiss in not fostering more and better indigenous water research in that country.[64] Throughout the 1970s, the institution's water management work could have been more aggressive on the equity front. It could have been bolder and less pliant in pressing for earlier attention to drainage. And, retrospectively, one could wish for earlier and more effective attention to environmental defense.

FERTILIZER, PESTICIDES, AND SEEDS. Although the Bank's work on fertilizer has been conducted by "industry" rather than ARD units, agriculture promoters inside and outside the Bank consistently have recognized that fertilizer plays a role in agriculture. During the 1970s, the Bank's inputs story played up the fertilizer theme even more than water management. There was no doubt at the time about the importance of the linkage between chemicals and crops, although environmentalists would later have something to say about this. Nor was there

62. While we think this paragraph in the main is correct, it may exaggerate the Bank's passivity. Gabriel Tibor, who worked as a lead Bank engineer on Indian irrigation for ten years in the 1970s and early 1980s, has called to our attention the Bank's very active technical assistance role—promoting improved engineering education and participant training, propagating new technical doctrines, pondering stratagems to reduce the effects of corruption, and winning (Tibor reports convincingly) "unqualified praise" by Bank technicians' Indian counterparts.

63. Not all, however, were apparent at the time. A 1983 staff memo remarked: "The Bank's TA efforts in [the irrigation] area have had the greatest impact on the planning and design of the Narmada Basin Development. . . . [T]hrough an extensive four-year involvement, the Bank and its consultants have established a highly competent planning organization which works with a large group of local consultants. Foreign consultants, in joint ventures with Indian firms, have actively participated in the planning of the project and an internationally recruited dam review panel has been guiding the design of the Sardar Sarovar dam. . . . As a result major technological innovations are introduced in the project." Staff memo to W. Thaluitz, Director, ASP, "Technical Assistance in Project Lending (Irrigation Sector) . . . ," April 8, 1983, p. 4. In the light of the Narmada uproar a decade later, the preceding is reminiscent of a pattern of repetitive overcorrection that is not limited to ARD or even to the Bank. An institution will get some things right but forget others. Then later it overcorrects, forgetting what it had right the first time. Policy tends to zigzag around a reasonable track.

64. World Bank, "World Bank in Pakistan," p. 11.

much doubt in the Bank and elsewhere that the larger fertilizer-using countries should move as rapidly as their markets together with their managerial and technical capacities would allow toward producing their own finished fertilizers. This view was modified as the decade proceeded, but only in the context of a role in which the Bank excelled—namely, that of, not just funder, but global industry analyst.

In the 1960s the World Bank had been slow to get started in financing fertilizer plants, in comparison with, say, USAID. In the 1970s it built its new plants portfolio with a vengeance: of the thirty-two fertilizer operations the Bank undertook world-wide during the decade, twenty-six involved the financing of new plants.[65] But exuberant support for new construction was soon scaled back. As urea became the nitrogenous fertilizer of choice, the Bank would finance urea production from the ground up only if the country had natural gas as a feedstock. Otherwise it was cost effective for indigenous urea producers to import their ammonia base from suppliers who had an abundant supply of cheap gas. During the 1970s and 1980s together, the Bank provided the foreign exchange for some 15 percent of fertilizer production capacity in developing countries, but its funding of new plants was giving way to investments in the renewal and upgrading of existing facilities and in fertilizer distribution systems. In the 1980s only about one-quarter of the institution's fertilizer loans would be for new plants, and the Bank would move heavily into financing fertilizer imports in support of agricultural and related reforms.[66] Meanwhile, "a major part of the Bank's fertilizer work involve[d] persuading borrowers to forego unwise or excessively risky investment projects."[67] In many cases such persuasion succeeded; at the same time, OED has found that those plants the Bank did help build tended to perform well.

This record does not sound like that of an institution bent, simply, on shoveling out money. Neither, however, had the Bank suddenly become overwhelmed with prudence. It was a case, rather, of the McNamara Bank's expansionist proclivities being superseded by its adoption of the role of global indicative planner.

To many observers in the early 1970s it was clear that, worldwide, chemical fertilizers had become a highly turbulent industry. Demand shocks were emanating from the Green Revolution in Asia. The new technologies coming on line, particularly in the case of nitrogenous fertilizers, were characterized by large economies of scale and plunged earlier processes into obsolescence, almost without regard to input and factor price differentials. These new technologies put new twists on plant location decisions as particular feedstocks—natural gas and naphtha—became dominant; and then, in 1973–74, the first oil shock widened the advantage of gas over naphtha.

---

65. *Improving the Supply of Fertilizers to Developing Countries: A Summary of the World Bank's Experience,* World Bank Technical Report 97, Industry and Energy Series, Washington, D.C., 1989, p. 50.

66. Ibid.

67. Ibid, pp. 50–51.

Moreover, this was an industry characterized by high degrees of concentration. Multinationals, some of them oil companies, together with a few megacooperatives made most of the fertilizer in the North; and they along with state enterprises were building the industry in developing countries. At the time, only a few international engineering firms were in a position to design and construct the new giant ammonia and urea plants.

Yet concentration did not mean coherence. On the contrary, three factors caused this lumpy, centerless system to lurch into violent investment cycles. First, the new technologies were highly capital intensive. Second, and related, plant gestation periods were relatively long. Third, information was poorly networked among the global industry's decision makers. All of these problems were fairly plain, but it took the World Food Conference and the contemporaneous "fertilizer crisis" of 1974 to bring the international community into full voice on the subject. The conference "recommended that the international agencies, as a matter of urgency, establish and regularly maintain an authoritative analysis of the medium- and long-term fertilizer supply and demand situation, and provide, on a global basis, information that would assist investment agencies in avoiding cyclical imbalances between supply and demand."[68]

Fully sharing these perceptions, the World Bank in 1974 decided to expand its Industry Projects Department to include a unit charged with maintaining a database on world fertilizer supply, demand, and balances. From the beginning of 1975, the Bank joined with the FAO and the UN Industrial Development Organization (UNIDO) in conducting a continuing industry-monitoring process. The World Bank/FAO/UNIDO Fertilizer Working Group institutionalized not only a useful routine and a division of labor among the three lead agencies, but pursued a policy of open membership for all manner of interested parties that maximized the networking effect. Participants in the group have included other multilaterals; international, regional, and national trade associations; fertilizer trading countries; and various bilateral representatives, including at times, for example, ones from China and the Soviet Union.

During the 1970s the Working Group established the pattern of meeting twice a year. Before the first meeting, the FAO published fertilizer production, demand, and trade figures for the previous year, and the Bank canvassed the major producing and consuming countries for views of the fertilizer situation in their areas. In the meetings, estimates of demand and of supply were made country by country. Members spent a good part of the first meeting airing their differences. In the second they reached a nonbinding consensus that the Bank was authorized to broadcast: "The Bank acts as the custodian of the data, and with the help of other members of the Group it prepares the regional and world supply, demand and balance figures."[69]

68. Ibid, p. 65.
69. Ibid, p. 67.

These widely noted annual estimates prompted producers to stabilize the world's fertilizer production around its still vigorously rising trend. The Bank was well cast for its central role in the process. It knew agriculture's needs for fertilizer and had a great deal of working contact with the fertilizer industry. Bank staff had, and maintained, the necessary technical and analytical expertise—both sectoral and macro—that the exercise requires. Moreover, the institution's fertilizer analysis in the 1970s and thereafter was sensibly pragmatic: it viewed the quasi-private, quasi-public, oligopolistic characteristics of the global industry as properties that, instead of being wished away, should be worked with. The Bank's fertilizer people, who made a proud record in the 1970s, thought the world's fertilizer oligopolists should be helped to guide themselves into collectively more constructive behavior.

Food Production: Other Inputs

The World Bank in the 1970s was very mindful of the other inputs needed to expand food production, but in most of its borrowing regions and countries these inputs were not high on the list of its lending priorities. Thus in the human resources field, aside from the investments in research and extension already discussed, the Bank seemed to think well of the agricultural university initiatives that had been undertaken by other donors, especially USAID. But it did not seek to replicate them itself. It articulated the importance of serviceable marketing institutions to agriculture, for both supplying inputs and moving outputs, and it built pro-marketing components into some of its rural development projects in such countries as Mexico, Cameroon, and the Philippines. The Bank intensified the support of agricultural credit that it had begun back in the 1960s—spelling out the rationale for such lending in its Agricultural Credit Policy Paper in 1975. However, the story of agricultural credit is better told in the framework of the 1980s.

Historically, one paradox arises: during the 1970s, especially in Africa, the Bank put a good deal of thought as well as lending muscle into the development and support of a variety of agricultural marketing and processing parastatals. Yet in the 1980s it encouraged the dismantling of the same parastatals. Such reversals were even more common in parastatals concerned with tree and other export crops than those dealing with domestic food.

Pro-Poor Rural Development

Poverty-oriented rural development was the second of the Bank's main ARD goals for the 1970s. It is an interesting fact that Robert McNamara's Nairobi speech, which stands as the greatest articulation of his pro-poor teaching and was most of all about smallholder agriculture, did not come until 1973, well into the president's sixth year in office. Poverty had been a theme from his first annual speech onward. But it took some time for him to actually spell out the agricultural side of the antipoverty diagnosis cum program.

There were two fairly distinct elements to what became the McNamara Bank's anti–rural poverty agenda (in shorthand, the RD side of ARD). The first, given its doctrinal statement in the Nairobi speech itself, was the smallholders thrust. The second, which became prominent only in a Rural Development Sector Policy Paper of February 1975, was billed as an elaboration of the Nairobi-speech strategy. But, unlike the speech, it dwelled on the integrated, multitarget (soon-to-become) area project format.[70]

Once it was articulated, the smallholder rationale was straightforward. A major exposition appeared in *Redistribution with Growth,* the treatise reconciling growth and equity efforts on which, at McNamara's behest, Hollis Chenery and colleagues collaborated with a group from the Institute for Development Studies, Sussex, in 1974.[71] The premise was that small holdings, especially in densely populated countrysides, were not—certainly did not need to be—inefficient. There was also a pragmatic premise that fell short of some of the Bank's rhetoric of the 1970s: namely, that radical land reform was probably unavailable under nonrevolutionary political conditions. Thus the category of the rural poor who could best be reached directly with productivity-raising interventions were small-farm proprietors. Via them, their laborers, tenants, and other dependents could also benefit.

What made the smallholder strategy a major antipoverty initiative was that most of the small proprietors were poor and that, together with their dependents, there were a lot of them. The interventions could be single-track, pro-agriculture measures, and their collective uplift would (additively) be large.

However, the Operations Evaluation Department's main evaluation of the Bank's 1970s experience with rural development has little use for a single-track, head-counting concept of its subject. The February 1975 sector paper, it notes, "described the operational goals of RD as 'improved productivity, increased employment and thus higher incomes for target groups, as well as minimum acceptable levels of food, shelter, education and health.' It followed that the program 'must embrace a wide range and mix of activities.'"[72] For the evaluators, the essence of "rural development," according to "common usage of the words in

---

70. As a drafter of the 1975 paper, Graham Donaldson says there was no intent to quarrel with the Nairobi speech. However, in operational implementation, the latter devolved into a numbers-of-the-poor concept of "rural development" that, as the text indicates, Donaldson's OED agricultural unit faulted.

71. Hollis Chenery and others, *Redistribution with Growth: Policies to Improve Income Distribution in Developing Countries in the Context of Economic Growth* (Oxford University Press, 1974).

72. World Bank, "World Bank Experience with Rural Development, 1965–1986," OED Report 6883, October 16, 1987. This report was later published as World Bank, OED, *Rural Development: World Bank Experience, 1965–86* (World Bank, 1988), p. v.

their broad sense," was the pursuit of an interrelated set of sectoral and subsectoral targets. And *area development projects,* addressing a collection of such targets in a defined local geographic jurisdiction, represented "the heart of the rural development experience as originally proposed."[73]

Instead, for scorekeeping purposes to which the evaluators later objected, Bank operators adopted a different, poverty-based, definition of "rural development." RD projects were any projects in developing-country rural areas—and only those—in which a majority of the beneficiaries were appraised to fall below the poverty line. Thus an exquisitely designed project, synchronously raising the quality of life in many facets of a bounded rural landscape, would fail to qualify as "rural development" if half its beneficiaries were not certifiably "poor," whereas a single-track project to fertilize tobacco farming would be RD if it had a majority of poor participants. It is not clear who had the better of this dispute over the defining characteristic of RD. If RD was part of a poverty-alleviation strategy, then the nose-counting definition had some merit. What was clear (at least in the minds of the OED evaluators) was that operations were driven to use the number-of-poor criterion because it was simpler and quicker. There was pressure to move money, to increase the number of ARD loan signings, and to increase the RD share of the ARD total. In other words, "Get on with it" took precedence over "Get it right."[74]

In any event, expansion pressures affected both varieties of RD projects, whether or not they changed the allocations between them. There always was incentive to add numbers to the single-track, pro-poor family of projects; and some kinds of single-track schemes, say, agricultural credit projects or components, were easier to enlarge than others. Similarly, in area projects there was pressure to make the areas larger, to add subsectoral components, and to raise the number of first-round and early-round pilot ventures.

To reiterate a point made earlier, because of its history and configuration, the World Bank was an inevitable wholesaler. Expansion pressures tilted it further toward wholesaling, making it more dependent than ever on recipient countries' institutional and managerial capacities to "retail" resources, knowledge, and technology. Where the client lacked that capacity, the path of least resistance (masquerading as enlightened implementation) led directly into one of the pathologies of aid administration: special, segregated, donor-dominated project authorities that drew talent and focus away from the borrowing country's regular public administration. The Bank's RD project work in the 1970s, especially in Africa, was speckled with such creations, most of which would net out as being counterproductive within a few years.

---

73. Ibid., pp. xiv–xv.
74. Warren Baum indicates that the new numbers-of-poor form of rural antipoverty assessment was adopted because it was the least laborious mode for the regional staffs and, hence, the only mode to which they would agree. Letter, Baum to Lewis, June 5, 1994.

The pace of the area-projects expansion was explosive. The number of projects rose from five in the period 1968–70 to seventy-two in 1977–79; the number of area projects in the RD category climbed from three to sixty-two during the same period, and lending for the latter (in constant 1984 dollars) rose from $14.5 million a year to $556.4 million annually, which translates to an annual growth rate of 50 percent![75]

The RD area projects were complicated. Their average size in constant dollars nearly doubled during the 1970s. They were designed to an ambitious prescription—they were to benefit large numbers of the rural poor, have a low cost per beneficiary, have a rate of return at least equal to the Bank's assumed opportunity cost of capital of 10 percent, have a mix of productive and welfare components, and achieve local participation in decisionmaking.[76]

In the event, local participation in the design and implementation of the area projects was scant, and, judged by the Bank's standard economic-rate-of-return yardstick, performance was disappointing. According to the OED retrospective review of the experience, 51 percent of the RD area projects failed to achieve an economic rate of return (ERR) of 10 percent, thereby performing somewhat more poorly than RD projects as a whole. Regionally, the poor performance was concentrated in Africa. Whereas in other developing regions a comfortable majority of OED-audited area development projects achieved an "acceptable" ERR, in West Africa nine of twenty-one and in East and Southern Africa twelve of fifteen did not.

Area development projects during the 1970s were not uniquely concentrated in Africa; more such lending, for example, was done in Asia. But the *relative* concentration in Africa was striking; area projects altogether dominated the Bank's ARD portfolio for that continent. Further, the problems in the area projects category were typical of the difficulties that, during the McNamara years, beset the Bank's ARD work throughout most of Africa.

Thin Spots in the RD Strategy

The McNamara Bank set such an ambitious agenda on the quantitative side that it was bound to shortchange some of its declared, but operationally more difficult, goals. Two such goals in the rural-development realm were, first, land and tenurial reforms and, second, expanded nonfarm rural employment.

Rhetorically, both of these were very much a part of the McNamara multitarget RD effort. Both, for example, figured explicitly in the Nairobi speech as the first component of a

strategy for increasing the productivity of small-holder agriculture:

75. World Bank, OED, *Rural Development*, chap. 3.
76. Ibid.

Acceleration in the rate of land and tenancy reform.

[In addition to reorganizing the support structure for smallholder agriculture,] the structural changes [are] necessary. . . . And the most urgent . . . is land and tenancy reform. Legislation dealing with such reform has been passed. . . . But the rhetoric of these laws has far outdistanced their results. . . .

This is extremely regrettable. No one can pretend that general land and tenancy reform is easy. It is hardly surprising that members of the political power structure, who can own large holdings, should resist reform. But the real issue is not whether land reform is politically easy. The real issue is whether indefinite procrastination is politically prudent.

We are ready to assist land and tenancy reform programs by providing the follow-up logistical support required by the small farmer, and to help in the technical and financial aspects of land purchase and consolidation.

We are prepared to finance rural public works programs as well as multi-purpose rural development projects.[77]

During the 1970s there was no noteworthy resistance to Bank participation in land reforms on the part of Part I member countries. But there also was no decisive advocacy from that side. As McNamara remarked in 1973, borrowing-country elites were allergic to such reforms. And few operators in the Bank, striving for a performance record of solid project-lending expansion, were prepared to tangle their programs in contentious land policy issues. It will be noticed that the readiness to support the land reform McNamara had promised in the foregoing quotation was circumspectly phrased. Even so, it seldom materialized.

The story in rural public works was similar. In the Nairobi speech, the statement committing the Bank to the support of such nonfarm employment was explicit but brief. The two preceding annual speeches in 1971 and 1972, however, had dilated on the subject. It is arguable, of course, that the Bank went some distance toward implementing this intention in some of the infrastructure lending already noted and in many of its area development projects that included construction components, especially roads.

Nevertheless, the institution avoided or hesitated over rural works projects of a scale calculated to make a serious dent on the unemployment problem spelled out in McNamara's 1971 annual speech. In this very period the Bank shied away from major efforts of this kind initiated by some of its major borrowing countries. In 1974 the Bank earmarked $6.5 million for assisting the government of Indonesia in training staff for INPRES, an ambitious rural works program. But it did not become a financial contributor to the larger program.[78] In India the Bank was well aware of the massive, domestically run, Guaranteed Employment Scheme begun

77. Robert S. McNamara, "To the Board of Governors, Nairobi, Kenya, September 24, 1973," in McNamara, *The McNamara Years at the World Bank*, pp. 249, 251, and 258.
78. World Bank, "1974 Briefing Paper: Indonesia," September 25, 1974, annex 3.

in Maharashtra State in the early 1970s. But it made no move to support it. And in Mexico it stalled visibly and repeatedly before buying into the Echeverría administration's large, works-centered rural development program (PIDER); when it did join, the Bank was at pains to tilt its inputs toward "productive" rather than "employment" components.[79]

Among the reasons for the Bank's reticence about large-scale rural works programs, two were conspicuous. First, all the labor and most of the other direct inputs to such construction were to be procured locally; there was some continuing reluctance in the Bank to do local-cost funding. Second, rural public works tended to be administratively and programmatically messy. Many of the roads, bunds, and other structures constructed did not stay built; thanks in part to inadequate engineering, they washed out. Part-time unskilled workers were hard to manage. Works projects were prone to corruption. And critics of rural works saw them as second-best instruments for fighting poverty: while their immediate employment and income benefits might accrue to the poor, many of the assets created tended to complement and make more valuable the lands disproportionately held by the rural elites.

Yet, if the Bank had been sufficiently keen on launching a major attack on the rural employment problem, these difficulties need not have been overwhelming. The institution could have opted for more local cost financing. It could have met the problems of administrability, flawed engineering, and failed local accountability head-on. In the 1970s, answers to these issues were emerging in different country settings. If they had a common theme, it was that the Bank needed to decentralize: to devolve more of the choice of works projects, and more of the responsibility for contributing to and implementing them, to local jurisdictions.

Regional Notes

This account of the Bank's agricultural activities would not be complete without some mention of its regional activities: in Asia, the Middle East and North Africa, Latin America, and other parts of Africa.

ASIA. As an ARD lender, the Bank was most active in Asia during the 1970s. Although its worldwide ARD lending soared during the decade, Asia's share of that global total rose from less than 30 percent to nearly 45 percent (see table 9-2). Part of this surge simply reflected the demographic size of Asian farming: the Asian countries in which the Bank worked had three times as many farmers as there were in all of Sub-Saharan Africa.

But as mentioned in the section on irrigation and water-management activity, there was another reason for Asia's lead during the decade of greatest ARD expansion: regional conditions suited the Bank's comparative advantage for whole-

---

79. World Bank, "Study of Bank/Mexico Relations, 1948–1992," OED Report 12923, April 1, 1994.

saling large sums to borrowers with relatively well-developed administrative and technical capacities for implementing projects. This was notably the case with water-management projects, which, although their 1960s share of the ARD total was squeezed by other subsectors, still accounted for a heavy plurality (about 41 percent) of the institution's total ARD lending in Asia over the 1970s. Agricultural credit lending, rising to about 15 percent of total regional ARD, was equally absorbable. Moreover, regional operations, using the official "nose-counting" definition of RD, were able to contribute to the Bank's expanded RD goal by labeling more lending in Asia "area (rural) development" than would be logged in Sub-Saharan Africa's more spotlighted area development efforts.[80]

Asia's comparative readiness for Bank ARD lending was evident in a different subsector: extension. That Daniel Benor's T&V system of expansion caught on so well in a number of Indian states was not accidental. They had already established extension bureaucracies that by this time could be shaped into reliable mechanisms for delivering limited messages and providing feedback on their impact.

THE MIDDLE EAST AND NORTH AFRICA. The World Bank's ARD lending in the EMENA (Europe, Middle East, and North Africa) region during the 1970s was like its Asia operations, only more so. There was an overwhelming concentration on the water-management and agricultural-credit subsectors. Both of them were regarded as relative strengths of the Bank at the time, and, considering the comparative populations of the Asia and EMENA regions, the levels of activity on a per capita basis were quite intense. EMENA received about half the water-management lending that went to Asia and more than two-thirds the agricultural-credit loans.

LATIN AMERICA. Bank ARD lending to Latin America and the Caribbean scarcely hit stride in the McNamara years. In terms of current dollars, the level in the 1980s would be nearly three times that in the 1970s. Subsectorally, the alignment was quite distinctive. Water management was important, but not dominant, as it was in Asia and the Middle East. Lending for area development was the largest single subsectoral total, reflecting the region's major multitrack rural development initiatives, for example, in Brazil and Mexico.[81] And livestock lending was larger in absolute and relative terms than in any other region.

AFRICA. Without question, the most stressful regional story in the Bank's 1970s ARD experience was that in Africa. This is not immediately apparent from the lending numbers: lending in Africa—although it grew faster than that in any other region—still accounted for only 16 percent of the ARD total over the 1970s. But Africa was a problem area. Here political independence was at its newest. Political diversity was the greatest: the region had some forty states, half of them with fewer than 5 million inhabitants, and a set of governments that varied greatly

80. Amnon Golan, interview with John P. Lewis and Devesh Kapur, March 9, 1994.
81. See "Profiles," nos. 1 and 2 in World Bank, OED, *Rural Development*, pp. 63–71.

in their economic and other agendas, degrees of sophistication, and level of commitment to agricultural uplift. The institutional capacity for development was uneven and limited. Dependence on foreign aid was unparalleled, and the Bank was further ahead of counterpart donors than was the case in any other region.

Yet as the largest and leading donor in Sub-Saharan Africa, the Bank had to relate to an extraordinary proliferation of other bilateral and multilateral interveners—a good twenty-five in some countries, with a dozen or more unofficial donors and assisters to boot. This well-intentioned multitude had little in the way of common doctrine. Thus undermanned host governments not only had to deal with more external development agents than their calendars could accommodate, but they often had to try to digest sharply conflicting advice concerning the same macro, sectoral, and subsectoral issues.

Bank management recognized that the institution needed to try to bring some coherence into the region's rural development scene. But this was going to be difficult to do because the Bank did not speak with one voice. In different countries, different Bank specialists and operators handed out different appraisals and prescriptions. The cleavages were the kinds of methodological and cadre differences noted earlier. One in-house assessor of the Bank's African agricultural performance, economist Uma Lele, saw the record as essentially bifurcated.[82] There were pronounced differences between the general policy analyses the Bank included in its country economic reports and its widely separated agricultural analyses, whether in the same reports or elsewhere.[83] Whereas some of the Bank's agricultural policy analyses made good sense, actual ARD operations took a different tack. They were extrapolated directly from McNamara's 1973 Nairobi speech and the 1975 Rural Development Sector policy paper, and they were driven, partly by the decade's money targeting, into a proliferation of large projects, especially large-area development projects. In terms of their staffing and cross-sectoral articulation, these grew faster than the Bank and, more particularly, African governments were ready for.

Hence the Lele critique came down to juxtaposing, against the area-development, integrated agricultural development project (IADP) model, which places maximum demands on the readiness of the host government's institutional and administrative capacities, a *sequential* scenario focused precisely on capacity building. The Bank, Lele argued, should promote, first, the building of human and

---

82. Writing from within the institution, Uma Lele produced *The Design of Rural Development: Lessons from Africa*, rev. ed. (Johns Hopkins University Press, 1979). After a variety of in-house studies, in the late 1980s and early 1990s, she presided over the preparation of a multivolume World Bank study, *Managing Agricultural Development in Africa* (MADIA).

83. Both types of discrepancies are emphasized (with respect to Kenya, Tanzania, and Malawi) in Uma Lele and L. Richard Meyers, *Growth and Structural Change in East Africa: Domestic Policies, Agricultural Performance, and World Bank Assistance, 1963–86*, pts. 1 and 2, MADIA Discussion Paper 3 (World Bank, 1989).

institutional infrastructure: planning and policy analysis capacities; the building of cadres of indigenous expertise (instead of the importation of so much technical assistance); and the nurturing of agricultural research, education, and extension. These in her view, were things to which the Bank gave too little attention in the 1970s in Africa; it was too busy trying to do too much else.

Lele became involved in the denouement of the McNamara Bank's most telling ARD country case: Tanzania. Tanzania was not representative; it was more extreme than the average. But the country was prominent, and the Bank's ARD transactions with it, like those of such well-intentioned donors as the Nordics and Netherlands, displayed the pitfalls of donor indulgence—in particular the problems that can ensue when one charismatic leader (McNamara) becomes captivated by another (Julius Nyerere).

Nyerere was the Nehru of Africa: cerebral, materially selfless, of robust morality, loved as well as revered. McNamara, less inclined than his predecessors to impose ideological stereotypes on clients, was an early, unstinting admirer. Under his leadership, Bank operations, although they seldom failed to raise pointed questions, were inclined to give Tanzanian rural policies and programs the benefit of the doubt from the early *Ujamma* days onward.[84] It may not have been before a new agricultural technical chief was posted for the subregion and made his inaugural trip to Tanzania in 1978 that President McNamara heard a strongly negative report on Tanzanian agriculture and on the state of the Bank's rural projects in that country.[85] Tensions in the ARD field between the Bank and the government increased until, in 1982, the same agriculture technical chief presided over the issuance of a major report on Tanzanian agriculture of which Uma Lele was the principal author.[86] By this time, according to Lele's recollection, President Nyerere ruefully admitted the soundness of much of the Bank's critical diagnosis.[87]

The report, differing from the norm in that it relied on a number of background papers from experts in the Bank and from Tanzanian officials and did not arise from a single formal sector mission to Tanzania, stated: "Agriculture has suffered from over a decade of insufficient resources, weak institutions, and inappropriate policies, and its decline threatens to continue unless there are major changes in these areas."[88] An urban bias in domestic policies (which gave priority to the industrial

---

84. *Ujamma* literally translates as "familyhood" but has come to mean "socialism"; it was Nyerere's rural development plan stemming from his 1967 Arusha Declaration, which sought to implement a socialist society in Tanzania. The *Ujamma* concept called for communal work and ownership of land, and equitable distribution of basic necessities, but later included forced peasant relocation into villages.

85. Stephen Eccles, interview with John P. Lewis and Devesh Kapur, March 23, 1994.

86. Ibid. World Bank, "Tanzania: Agricultural Sector Report," OED Report 4052-TA, August 19, 1983. A green cover draft was issued in October 1982.

87. Uma Lele, personal conversation with John P. Lewis, mid-1980s.

88. World Bank, "Tanzania," p. 162.

and social service sectors, and public sector monopolies) was identified as the main culprit, responsible for draining financial and manpower resources out of the countryside. The comprehensive report also called for a reduction in the role of parastatals and the public sector, legalization of the private sector in agricultural input and output marketing, production, agro-processing and transport, and for positive producer incentives. This was much in line with the direction in which the Bank was heading in the early 1980s. The report called donors to task for their uncoordinated aid efforts in Tanzania and recommended program aid (in the form of structural adjustment loans) as well as guaranteed food aid to protect the most vulnerable groups.

ARD in the 1970s: An Assessment

The Bank had a complex ARD agenda in the 1970s that throughout the period was focused on the double goals of production and equity. The institution's performance, and image, bore the stamp of the incumbent president, but McNamara himself was more complex than his ARD reputation.

The president was known as an expansionist determined to drive ARD lending up a steep incline while favoring smallholders and the absolute poor, yet not detracting from growth. The design was overambitious in terms of the growth-equity trade-off; not all warranted pro-equity tilts were costless. As to development-in-the-round philosophies, the rural antipoverty program was weak when it came to land policy and nonagricultural employment. And in its effort to move money and be multisectoral, the effort pulled too far, too fast in the case of area development programs, most particularly in Africa, where there was a yawning lack of institutional and trained manpower.

As mentioned earlier, the ARD side of McNamara's antipoverty agenda delivered resources to a large number of needy people, and many small cultivators achieved lasting gains in productivity. In Africa, however, a harsher conclusion probably is in order. The Bank's interventions may have delayed the development of effective, self-reliant cadres and institutions. But this is far from the entire ARD story for the 1970s. Both the Bank and McNamara played key roles in institutionalizing good and relevant agricultural research. If it was the Bank's fate to take on the proprietorship of the Benor extension system and promote it rather loudly, the recipients benefited. More important, the institution not only performed well in the "wholesaling" fields where its comparative advantage lay, but it did so in ways that befitted its leader.

Thus in the water-management area, the Bank moved large quantities of money, especially in Asia, constructively. But it also did so in a way that was characteristic of McNamara, although not of his reputation. The Bank was fairly permissive as far as recipient technical preferences were concerned. Although he was a man of strong opinions, McNamara, unlike some Bank veterans, was not one to insist that recipients follow detailed project prescriptions if they had good reasons for preferring alternative methods.

Similarly, in the fertilizer field, a substantial volume of transfers was coupled with a systems-analyst role for the Bank that not only suited the Bank's comparative advantage; it *sounded* like vintage McNamara. That this happened actually was a tribute to initiatives that could be taken at the middle level, in the spaciousness of the Bank's intellectual and bureaucratic structures. The boss evidently had little to do with it. But it was entirely of a piece with his ongoing preoccupation with the advantages of systematic planning, both during his tenure at the Bank and before. In short, on balance both the institution and its leader had good reason to be satisfied with their ARD work in the 1970s. But if the story already was complex, it would become more so in the years following.

Agriculture and Rural Development since 1980

The early 1980s were a time of change both inside and outside the World Bank. One of the Bank's two longest-sitting presidents left in mid-1981. After rapid real growth over the twenty years ending in 1981–84, IDA replenishments were flattening. And the character of the institution was altered by the era of structural adjustment lending launched in 1980.

Among the major changes of this period was the contraction in the Bank's program in agriculture and rural development. For various reasons—some sector-wide, some sector specific, and some region specific—ARD's share of Bank/IDA lending began to lose ground. Interpretations were not sorted out until well into the 1990s.

The Shift in Sectoral Strategy

A number of complex factors accounted for the shift in sectoral strategy.

WHY THE SLOWDOWN IN AGRICULTURAL LENDING?   One thing, certainly, that affected the Bank's ARD activity from July 1981 onward was the departure of McNamara. Succeeding presidents did not replicate McNamara's ardor for smallholder agriculture or his concern for the rural poor. Once his pull on the sector was removed, perhaps it was simply natural for the Bank to reduce the resources and attention committed to agriculture. After all, the sector almost invariably generates a declining share of GDP as countries develop. Perhaps it was time for Bank inputs to agriculture also to begin tapering.

Taper they did. From a level of $5.4 billion (1992 dollars) in the early 1980s, annual Bank/IDA lending for agriculture declined to an average of $3.9 billion in the four fiscal years 1990–93. Agriculture's share of the institution's total lending dropped from 30 percent to 20 percent.[89] Neither inside nor outside the Bank, however, were observers ready—without further scrutiny—to attribute the decline in agricultural loans simply to the natural progression of nonagricultural activity. In the late 1980s, the Bank appointed a working group chaired by R. L. P. Harris to examine the trends in agricultural lending.[90] At the same time, the Group of 24 (of IMF/IBRD developing member countries) retained a pair of outside analysts, Michael Lipton and Robert Paarlberg, to prepare a report on the same subject.[91] The two documents agreed on the dimensions of the decline and the continuing importance of agriculture. The working group's study concentrated on the relative growth of the nonagricultural economy in several large countries and emphasized the shortfalls in the recent ARD project implementation record, as well as the adverse effects of recipient country policies. In contrast, Lipton and Paarlberg underscored the effects of discretionary changes in *Bank* policies: the displacement of investment lending by SALs and a retreat in the volume of lending for irrigation and agricultural credit.

Moeen Qureshi, the senior vice president for operations, and Michel Petit, the French agricultural economist who had joined in 1988 as the Bank's new head of agriculture and rural development, shared the sense that the institution's ARD strategy was in some disarray. When Qureshi asked Petit to work up a proper sector strategy paper, however, Petit ran into bureaucratic turbulence: the regional agricultural chiefs told him not to think of writing such a piece without their input—but then had no time to participate.

At this point, the Board's newly emerging activism came into play. It was agreed that the staff was to prepare a new set of sector policy papers to be discussed with the Board. When Petit managed to book a projected agricultural paper at the head of the queue, his regional counterparts agreed to join the exercise. The prolonged, iterative negotiation of the document yielded, by mid-1993, a strategy statement measurably different from, although a linear descendent of, one that might have been written in the late 1970s.[92]

ALTERED DOCTRINE: LESS INTERVENTION. The 1980s were years in which the World Bank, along with most of the policy world, was preaching the positive, growth-promoting merits of governments withdrawing from much of the economic management they had been attempting. In agriculture specifically, a leading public policy prescription became: Do less. This doctrine of disengagement had been anticipated by the end of the 1970s: the net effect of (direct)

89. World Bank, Agriculture and Natural Resources Department, *Agricultural Sector Review*, July 1993.

90. World Bank, "Lending for the Agricultural Sector," Report of the Working Group on Lending for the Agricultural Center, August 31, 1989, processed.

91. Michael Lipton and Robert L. Paarlberg, *The Role of the World Bank in Agricultural Development in the 1990s* (Washington, D.C.: International Food Policy Research Institute, 1990).

92. World Bank, *Agricultural Sector Review*.

agricultural intervention policies in developing countries . . . is to create disincentives to agricultural production; prices of food products and raw materials have been held down, partly in the belief that this would assist industrial development, but also in response to political pressures from urban groups. [Policies holding down agricultural prices have] impeded the direct contribution of agriculture to economic growth and to the balance of payments, and encouraged rural and urban migration. [They] have tended to lead to inefficient resource allocation, both between agriculture and industry and within agriculture, reducing agricultural output and employment below what [they] would otherwise have been. . . . Without higher incentives, the effectiveness of other efforts toward expanding food production will be constrained. . . . While it is difficult to specify what the correct prices are from the point of view of economic efficiency, there are good arguments to suggest that . . . agricultural prices should be raised toward those levels prevailing in international trade.[93]

Like others, the quoted study recognized that some direct government interventions—for example, supporting producer prices, subsidizing inputs—had benefited farmers. But it found that, typically, the positive interventions had been swamped by the negative ones. This was one of the main messages of the *World Development Report 1986*, which focused on trade and pricing policies in world agriculture:

While governments have played an important role in agriculture through expenditures on activities which the private sector does not have the incentive to provide, their role in providing a sound environment for private markets should not be underestimated. Although significant progress has been made in a few countries, other governments could do more by eliminating parastatal monopolies and by improving the legal and institutional framework required for the functioning of competitive private markets.[94]

Furthermore, as the 1980s wore on, the proposition that governments could increase the net gain from farming by withdrawing from most or all direct interventions into agricultural markets (while trying to see to it that markets operated reliably and fairly) was outclassed by growing perceptions about the effects of *indirect* interventions. These latter were policies that, although addressed to the economy generally, spilled unequal effects on agriculture. The most important, motivated in many developing countries by import-substitution strategies, were import (tariff and nontariff) barriers and overvalued currencies. These policies raised agriculture's costs, squeezed its earnings, and worsened the sector's terms of trade with the rest of the economy. Such indirect interventions are the equivalent of hidden taxes on agriculture.

All of this was laid out in principle from the beginning of the decade and earlier—for example, in the World Bank's major 1981 study, *Accelerated Develop-*

93. World Bank, "Agricultural Prices, Subsidies and Taxes: A Summary of Issues," paper prepared jointly by the Agricultural and Rural Development Department and the Policy Planning and Program Review Department and circulated to the Executive Directors, SecM79-342, May 11, 1979.

94. World Bank, *World Development Report 1986*, p. 104.

ment in Sub-Saharan Africa, drafted by a team headed by the University of Michigan economist, Elliot Berg.[95] The theme was reiterated in various 1980s documents including the *World Development Report 1986.* But what brought the point into vivid relief was the appearance in 1992 of one of the summary volumes of a Bank-funded study of the political economy of agricultural pricing policy. This volume, written by Maurice Schiff and Alberto Valdés, digested the results of the eighteen country studies of which the research had consisted.[96] For the eighteen sample countries, the studies reviewed the de facto taxation—direct and indirect—they had levied on agriculture during twenty-five years, 1960 through 1984. The findings were striking. For the whole sample, average direct taxation of agriculture was 8 percent of agricultural GDP. *Indirect* taxation was nearly three times as much—22½ percent—making average total taxation of the sector about 30 percent. For the "representative" group of ten countries, the figures were: direct, 12 percent; indirect, 24; total, 36 percent.[97]

Moreover, this was not just a matter of twisted unit values; the aggregate resources that policies had been withdrawing from agriculture were formidable:

> The transfers out of agriculture have been enormous. The net effect of total (direct plus indirect) interventions averaged 46 percent of agricultural GDP from 1960 to 1984. These transfers ranged from 2 percent for the protectors (Korea and Portugal) to 140 percent of actual agricultural GDP in Sub-Sahara African countries. Such enormous transfers must have severely depressed private investment and growth in agriculture.[98]

The Schiff-Valdés thesis was not new. But the 1992 statement was fuller blown than earlier findings. What it said was that all of the development community's old fears about "urban bias" deserved to be renewed.[99] There had been a widespread sense that, because many farmers (at least the medium-small ones, if not the

---

95. The Berg Report's indirect-taxation-of-agriculture argument is a theme of Peter Gibbon, Kjell Havnevik, and Kenneth Hermele, *A Blighted Harvest: The World Bank and African Agriculture in the 1980s* (London: James Currey, 1993).

96. The eighteen, divided into groups by their comparative degrees of discrimination against agriculture, were (1) the extreme "taxers": Côte d'Ivoire, Ghana, Zambia; (2) the representative taxers: Argentina, Colombia, the Dominican Republic, Egypt, Morocco, Pakistan, the Philippines, Sri Lanka, Thailand, and Turkey; (3) the mild taxers: Brazil, Chile, and Malaysia; and (4) the only two of the eighteen that, when account is also taken of direct interventions, actually protected (that is, applied the equivalent of a negative tax) agriculture: Korea and Portugal. It should be noted that the sample did not include the two giants, China and India.

97. Maurice Schiff and Alberto Valdés, *The Political Economy of Agricultural Pricing Policy,* vol. 4, *A Synthesis of the Economics in Developing Countries* (Johns Hopkins University Press, 1992), p. 201.

98. Ibid., p. 200.

99. The term—and the focus—belong to Michael Lipton, *Why Poor People Stay Poor: A Study of Urban Bias in World Development* (Canberra: Australian National University Press, 1977).

smallest and the landless) had developed some political voice and muscle, the worst pro-urban, antiagricultural policy tilt was over in many countries. The Schiff-Valdés findings argued the contrary—particularly because, over the twenty-five years of their study, discrimination against agriculture had *increased* in most of their sample.[100]

Earlier alarms about antiagricultural discrimination did not escape challenge within the Bank. It was argued that the distortions, the de facto "taxes" being estimated, were based on official prices, whereas these were largely irrelevant for subsistence farmers and those trading on parallel markets. The market-distortions analysis was said to overlook the inadequacies of input supplies and of research and extension systems. It ignored the fact that the price distortions reflected the short-term preoccupations of leaders and their lack of commitment to implementing reforms in workable sequences.[101]

All the same, much of this questioning had been sorted through by the time the 1992 study appeared and had no effect on its findings. Policy mix, it concluded, was extremely important, and the best thing many developing country governments could do for their agricultural sectors was to reduce government-caused distortions in their national after-tax (and after-subsidy) price structures. Furthermore, if the World Bank wanted to promote agriculture, it should be talking at least as much to finance ministries as to ministries of food and agriculture.

ALTERED IMPLEMENTATION: ADJUSTMENT LENDING. The Bank's introduction and development of SALs from 1980 onward (see chapter 9) had spillover effects on agriculture. Structural adjustment reforms curtailed subsidies and other budgetary transfers to farming and increased the costs of imported inputs. Moreover, as chapter 9 indicates, from the early 1980s onward the United Nations Children's Fund and others claimed that structural adjustment was having a costly impact on the rural poor. On these matters, however, the Bank maintained a comparatively united front. It certainly wanted to cushion the impact of adjustment reforms on the poor, but, for all the institution's internal pluralism, Bank executives and analysts were nearly unanimous in their sense that macroeconomic structural adjustment was good—indeed, necessary—for the long-term health of agriculture in borrowing countries. This was a theme of the 1993 sector strategy paper. It said bad macropolicies were partly responsible for the observed ineffectiveness of the Bank's agricultural projects compared with its other investment lending.[102] Furthermore, "in many countries macroeconomic and industrial protec-

100. In fairness, it should be noted that the norm against which analyses of the Schiff-Valdés type measure indirect taxation of agriculture—namely, global prices—is itself distorted by subsidies of the industrial countries. See chapter 10.

101. Such was the gist, for example, of Kevin Cleaver's "The Impact of Price and Exchange Rate Policies on Agriculture in Sub-Saharan Africa," World Bank Staff Working Paper 728 (1985). This paper caused considerable internal discord.

102. OED "rated only about one-half of completed agricultural projects as satisfactory in 1989–91, down from two-thirds in 1974–88. Moreover, agricultural projects consistently

tion policies strongly discriminated against, even plundered, agriculture; [but] this situation is changing as many countries pursue structural adjustment."[103]

The same logic applied to sectoral adjustment in the agricultural sector itself. The sentence immediately following the one just quoted read, "Farming in many countries has also suffered from poor agricultural policy, both through direct taxation and indirect taxation occasioned by cost-ineffective parastatal marketing agencies; this situation, too, is changing as many countries pursue sectoral adjustment."[104]

Agricultural sector loans were nothing new; they had been used for decades— especially in the 1970s—to finance inputs, whether imported or domestic, to farming activities pursued beyond the boundaries of particular projects. And not infrequently such lending had been associated with discussions of policies and policy reform with recipient authorities. What was different about sectoral *adjustment* lending, however, was that—just as in the case of structural adjustment loans—the policy reforms at issue became more sharply defined and promissory. Bank loans or IDA credits were made on specified conditions, whose performance, presumably, would determine the availability of subsequent lending.

The use of sector adjustment lending programs for agriculture burgeoned in the 1980s: they rose from three loans in 1983 totaling $125 million to eleven loans in 1986 totaling more than $1.3 billion.[105] Chapter 9 indicates part of the reason: SAL circuits were getting overloaded; there was a perceived need to disaggregate comprehensive adjustment loans that were becoming burdened with too many policy targets and conditions to be easily enforced. Increasingly, it seemed preferable to the Bank—and, not infrequently, preferable to the borrowing government as well—to pursue policy reforms via stand-alone SECALs, sector by sector.

In agriculture such policy lending seemed here to stay. Yet it was paradoxical: a program that invited governments to promote agriculture by intruding less on the workings of the market invited the same governments (and those, such as the Bank, aiding them) to intrude more with respect to market-framing policies. For the Bank, this anomaly had another dimension: the terrain of intervention—namely, national policies dealing with agriculture prices, taxes, de facto taxes, subsidies— was far more sensitive, more controversial, closer to the inner core of the recipient's sovereign autonomy, than the particulars of almost any agricultural investment project.

That was not the only paradox of sectoral adjustment lending. One of the motivations for shifting Bank resources from agricultural investment lending, first

---

performed less well than projects in other sectors. . . . [T]he share of satisfactory agricultural projects continues to be 10 to 20 percentage points below the satisfactory ratings obtained in other sectors." World Bank, *Agricultural Sector Review*, p. i.

103. Ibid.

104. Ibid.

105. Data from World Bank Group Financial Database.

to SALs and then, in a more focused way, to SECALs, was that many Bank/IDA agricultural projects had been doing poorly—indeed worse than a decade earlier—according to OED evaluations. This was notably the case for many area development and agricultural credit projects. But by the early 1990s, when enough experience with agricultural SECALs had accrued for them to begin to receive their OED ratings, the scores were no better than the typical agricultural project ratings.[106]

Again, however, the Bank's evaluators and agricultural specialists converged in their reactions.[107] The patchy performance of SECALs did not necessarily mean they had been ill designed or poorly administered. Their bad news was different from the project bad news. Bank agriculturists thought that the SECALs' motivating assessment—that policy reforms were needed—had been quite right. But they had launched a higher-stakes game, entering a field of greater sensitivity than project loans. This game promised, if anything, a higher failure rate, but also a higher payoff. The shift toward SECALs made it doubly important to achieve the high measure of borrower "ownership" of reforms on which, as chapter 9 describes, the Bank placed rising value in the 1980s.

AGRICULTURE'S IN-HOUSE SHRINKAGE. Agriculture's relative decline after 1980 as an object of Bank/IDA lending was partly reflected in, partly driven by, the field's smaller, less sector-specific, voice within the institution.[108] One can cite at least three respects in which agriculture lost some of the center staging it had enjoyed under McNamara.

Policy Analysis. The economics invoked by the new agricultural strategy tended to be more macro in its preoccupations, with less emphasis on microeconomics of the farm-management type that had been featured in the 1970s. Much of the early analytical work that informed interfaces with clients about agricultural SECALs came from the Bank's clusters of general economists rather than agricultural economists, and the interfacing tended, as noted earlier, to be more with finance ministries than ministries of food and agriculture. It is symbolic that Maurice Schiff of the Valdés-Schiff study was from the Bank's general economics, not its agricul-

---

106. See, for example, World Bank, "World Bank Structural Adjustment Operations: The Second OED Overview," Report 10870, June 30, 1992. This report reviewed the evaluations of twelve agricultural SECAL-type loans approved during 1980–86. Half could be judged satisfactory, half not. By its "Annual Review of Evaluation Results 1992" in October 1993 (Report 12403), OED could report that thirteen out of a set of twenty-one agricultural SECALs (62 percent) were satisfactory. This compared with 64 percent of all agricultural loans. In Africa the agricultural SECAL satisfactory rate was 44 percent, compared with 46 percent for area development projects.

107. OED and AGR staff members, interviews with the authors, May 10 and May 31, 1994.

108. Both the Harris report and the comments on the Lipton-Paarlberg report (see nn. 90 and 91) assembled by Michel Petit from AGR staff attributed part of the decline in agricultural lending to personnel capacity problems, that is, to the thinning out of staff with relevant technical experience and expertise, as explained later in the chapter.

tural economics, shop, and that a ringleader of the whole study, who wrote its final volume, was none other than the Bank's former chief economist, Anne Krueger.

Staffing and Expertise. By the early 1990s there was a near consensus within the World Bank's agricultural complex that it had suffered a severe erosion of technical expertise during the preceding decade or so—across nearly the whole array of the program's established subsectors. As noted, many division-level respondents emphasized this point in the internal correspondence triggered by the Lipton-Paarlberg paper. The erosion was the natural product of aging not sufficiently offset by timely and effective recruitment (to which, arguably, management was insufficiently attentive).

But there were at least two extenuating circumstances. First, the institution's administrative budget tightened markedly during the 1980s; recruitment, even of replacements, was more constrained. Second, with the shift in sector strategy—not only in its policy reactions but toward such new priorities as environment, biotechnology, and women in development—the assortment of specialties to be accommodated within constrained personnel budgets was considerably diversified.

Coping with Hunger. One other change of doctrine shifted the focus from agriculture-specific to general economic and social phenomena. A revisionist view of the subject of hunger and food security, dating from the late 1970s and early 1980s, was not peculiar to the World Bank. But it was nicely articulated in a 1986 Bank report, *Poverty and Hunger: Issues and Options for Food Security in Developing Countries.*[109] The key discovery (unsurprising in retrospect) was that hunger, even in the form of famines, was not mainly a function of insufficient food production. It could be the result of failed transport and logistics, even of insufficient information in the system. But usually it was a poverty problem. Most of the hungry, most of the time, were poor people who lacked the income (or the employment that could generate the income) to procure available food supplies. The policy focus shifted from agricultural supplies to income entitlements.

Subsectoral Changes

After 1980 Bank lending to some ARD subsectors proceeded on quite different vectors and at a different pace from those of the 1970s. Four subsectoral aspects were particularly important at this time: environment and natural resource management, agrarian reform and local empowerment, agricultural credit, and research and extension.

ENVIRONMENT AND NATURAL RESOURCE MANAGEMENT. More than nearly any other industry, a country's agriculture has a pervasive encounter with its physical environment. It was inevitable, therefore, that the World Bank's increasing attention to environmental issues during the 1970s (described in volume 2, chap-

---

109. World Bank, *Poverty and Hunger: Issues and Options for Food Security in Developing Countries* (World Bank, 1986). Principal author: Shlomo Reutlinger.

ter 13) would have an impact on its agricultural program in the 1980s. The 1993 *Agricultural Sector Review* provides a compact statement of the agriculture-environment connection:

> Since a nation's farmers are the custodians of many of its natural resources, agricultural development has a direct bearing on how these resources are managed. In low income countries, the nexus of rural poverty, rapid population growth, and low-productivity farming is leading to the degradation of land, water, and forest resources, many of which are critical for sustaining the livelihoods of the poor. Agricultural intensification that increases the productivity of scarce resources is crucial to relieving these pressures. In middle and high income countries, increased productivity is also required to help resolve the increasing conflict between rural and urban demands for natural resources. When yields are raised by increasing the use of chemicals or diverting more water for irrigation, however, there are increased possibilities for misusing these inputs and causing pollution, pesticide poisoning, and waterlogging and salinization of irrigated lands. If agricultural intensification is to be desirable and sustainable, it must be based on environmentally friendly technologies and management practices.[110]

Later in the same document, while emphasizing the importance of pro-environment macropolicies, the Bank listed a half-dozen sectoral reforms that borrowing countries can pursue in behalf of sustainable agriculture, and it set out a three-pronged strategy for itself: strengthened environmental impact assessments, a broader brand of economic and sector work on environmental issues extending beyond the boundaries of particular projects, and lending directly aimed at countering environmental degradation. To prove that the last was more than a statement of intent, the paper supplied summary descriptions of antidegradation project loans already made to eleven developing countries.[111] (For elaboration, see volume 2, chapter 13.)

AGRARIAN REFORM AND LOCAL EMPOWERMENT. By the end of the 1970s the World Bank had been typecast as a comparatively conservative institution in matters involving rural social and political power structures. The issues emphasized here are land reform and, in the case of rural public works, not only their scale but the voice given local participants—poor participants—in the selection and conduct of works projects. In the 1970s, the World Bank sometimes had talked a bold rhetoric, but it actually soft-pedaled land reform. And although it engaged public works in a small way in a number of area development and other projects, it avoided forays into supplemental employment programs, especially ones organized along participatory, "bottom-up" lines.

On these counts, however, the Bank was due to surprise observers somewhat in the 1980s and 1990s, particularly in view of its slight overall shift to the right after 1980. In matters of rural reform, ideas that were considered radical by the stand-

110. World Bank, *Agricultural Sector Review*, p. 5.
111. Ibid., pp. 23–24.

ards of the 1970s have found a strong voice in the pluralistic Bank of recent decades. In the case of land reform, the boldest single initiative failed; but in the case of bottom-up rural employment promotion, new patterns seemed to be taking root. In both cases the Bank's conduct was more progressive than its reputation.

During the 1980s the institution had mixed success with projects in which it sought to assist the mapping, regularization, and registration of agricultural land titles, an issue that in the 1990s became important in the former Soviet Union.[112] But these efforts only tinkered, albeit nontrivially, around the edges of the rural economy's land variable. By contrast, in the Philippines in 1987 there was an opportunity to reorganize the whole structure of land-society and land-output relations.

During the Marcos years Philippine land reform had been attenuated and ineffective, with the country's elites and the regime both resisting it for different self-serving reasons. The question was whether the takeover of President Aquino in 1986 was sufficiently revolutionary to constitute the kind of pro-reform shock that had worked in such places as Japan, Korea, and Taiwan after World War II. President Corazon Aquino came from the landed elite herself, but she had a mission, and she had the right to rule by presidential decree until a new Congress resumed normal legislative functions in late July 1987. Some members of the government thought the World Bank could help persuade Mrs. Aquino to lock in thoroughgoing land reform during her window of opportunity. Others expected the Bank, were it invited to join the debate, to take a more cautious, incremental line that would help avoid radical outcomes.

Things came to a head in January 1987, following a bloody riot earlier in the month by farmers demanding land. At the meeting of the consultive group in late January, the government asked the donors to provide financial support for land reform and asked the Bank to review a draft Accelerated Land Reform Program (ALRP) drawn up by the government's Inter-Agency Task Force on Agrarian Reform. The Bank's East Asian vice president decided to seize the moment and, if closer inspection of the circumstances warranted, to go for all-out reform. Accordingly, Martin Karcher of the regional staff agreed, if he could pick the other members, to head the Bank's review team. The team, deemed rather radical by the U.S. State Department personnel on whom Karcher had been encouraged to call before departing for the Philippines, spent an intensive second half of March 1987 in Manila and then, back in Washington, worked urgently to produce, by mid-May, a report that outreformed the draft ALRP in three critical respects. Instead of an incremental introduction, it would have extended the ALRP's land ceiling of 7 hectares at once, across the board, even to the sugar holdings of such planters as Mrs. Aquino's family. It would have interpreted the country's constitutional re-

112. World Bank, "Russian Federation, Land Reform Implementation Support (LARIS) Project," Staff Appraisal Report 12711-RU, May 26, 1994.

quirement that those dispossessed of land be paid "just compensation" as being satisfied by compensation equaling the sworn valuations owners had been required to place on their land during the Marcos years (thereby, at this point, hoisting them by their own petards). Finally, instead of subjecting the recipients of reallocated land to thirty years of amortization payments (a practice on which most beneficiaries had defaulted under Marcos's land reform), the Bank reviewers would simply have charged each of them a one-shot payment of 600 pesos, that is, about $30.

These recommendations sparked a tug-of-war within the Aquino government. The case in their favor was weakened when it was reported in the press that the "World Bank itself would not be able to finance compensation payments (to landowners) for the transfer of land." On the theory that such expenditures were not production enhancing, Japan and the United States—among other donors— took the same position. Yet in fact this was not a major obstacle to Bank participation. A substantial reform exercise would have entailed other expenditures nearly as large that the Bank *could* fund; but the press report was interpreted as an antireform vote by the World Bank.

What probably counted for more in influencing the vote of the harried President Aquino, however, was her uncertainty regarding the extent to which the Bank would stand behind the Karcher recommendations. Here the performance was mixed. Attila Karaosmanoglu, the vice president for East Asia and the Pacific, who would become one of the institution's first trio of managing directors during the Preston presidency, signed on to the Karcher proposals, but he was the highest officer to take a clear stand. Two factions formed within the institution: one consisting of regional economists inclined toward more caution, the other composed of supporters seeking to reinforce Karaosmanoglu's commitment and, through him, win the endorsement of top management.

There was no clear resolution to the standoff because, like other issues that spring, this one was overwhelmed by the vast confusion generated by denouement of the Bank's 1986–87 reorganization (see chapter 18). By the time the dust of the reorganization had begun to settle, Mrs. Aquino had come down on the side of caution. Shortly before the new congress met, she signed an executive order that left most of the critical land policy decisions to the legislature, with the result that in 1990, the Philippine government acquired a grand total, nationwide, of 22 hectares of private land for redistribution![113] In the process of shooting a blank, however, the Bank had revealed a disposition toward a new degree of progressiveness in the land policy field.

In the case of the Bank's new perspectives on rural employment in the late 1980s and early 1990s, the innovations rested on a base of self-criticism, and their theme

113. Sheila S. Carond, "The Lost Revolution," *Foreign Policy*, vol. 84 (Fall 1991), p. 169.

became decentralization. The object of this criticism was the area of integrated rural development projects that had been so widely embraced in the 1970s. These, as the 1987 OED rural development review said, had been variously flawed.[114] They were much too complicated and multifaceted to be well managed. They overburdened the administrative systems of recipient governments, a problem they tried to meet by creating cordoned-off project authorities, typically in nonenduring ways that had pathological consequences for established public administrative systems.

In the first place, then, the new thinking in the Bank—which now accepted the institution's role as a wholesaler of assistance to rural development, including rural employment— placed greater emphasis on the qualities of recipient governments as intermediaries. But, in the second place, recognizing the top-down limitations of central national governments in their attempts to arouse rural development, the new thinkers in the Bank were interested in seeing decisions, resources, administration, and accountability all transferred to lower levels.

This decentralization thinking was not simply an expression of increased support for nongovernmental organizations.[115] The idea was to expand the capacities and responsibilities of local *governments*. The advocates of this strategy were not unmindful of the limitations and risks of official decentralization.[116] Categories of decisions might be delegated so far down a hierarchy that they spilled externalities well beyond the decisionmaking jurisdiction; and localities still in the hands of unreconstructed elites might be harsher than national governments in their treatment of the disadvantaged. To avoid the first problem, governments would have to calibrate decentralizations to the subjects. To avoid the second, humane national regimes would need to monitor their downward delegations of authority in behalf of fairness; it would be even more important to engage in an economic and political strengthening of the poor, to enable them increasingly to fend for themselves.

The new thinking centered around fiscal issues. In most countries most of the time, the comparative advantage of higher levels of government to raise revenue did not match that of lower levels to spend it effectively and responsively. This called for net transfers downward. But also, and separately, there was a role for *matching* grants that would motivate local jurisdictions to augment their total resources; accept (as World Bank vernacular has it) greater "ownership" of the jointly funded programs, projects, and activities; and insist on greater transparency

114. World Bank, OED, *Rural Development*.

115. It was concentrated in part in the Agriculture and Natural Resources Department and the central economics staffs. Their thinking, as well as identities, were displayed in a March 1994 request for funding of research on "Decentralization, Fiscal Systems and Rural Development." World Bank, "Decentralization, Fiscal Systems and Rural Development," revised proposal, June 24, 1994.

116. These were detailed, for example, in ibid., annex 1, "Literature Review: Decentralization, Fiscal Systems and Rural Development."

and accountability in the conduct of public business. This benign matching-grant leverage was, in principle, as available to external earmarked funds that the likes of the World Bank passed through national governments as it was to the grants of their own funds that the same governments made to lower jurisdictions.

Intellectually, it was something of an achievement for the World Bank to have spelled out such thinking (and the plans for augmenting research) to the extent that it did before the mid-1990s. But, more important, operations to implement the approach had begun. The distinguishing characteristic was a new degree of permissiveness, both on the part of the Bank and of its national-government intermediaries, as to the uses localities would make of the matching grants. Fiscal decentralization meant self-restraint was to be practiced by both of the senior parties; it meant, within broad limits, letting the locals choose their own expenditure priorities.

It is this last point that connects the decentralization initiative loosely but reliably with the rural employment issue. The matching grants may be earmarked for labor-intensive construction but leave it to local groups to decide which construction to do—roads, or, say, local irrigation works. Even when the grants are more widely discretionary, local assemblies and authorities are inclined to opt for structures or services that are labor intensive.

As of mid-1994, the two instances in which the Bank had moved to implement its decentralization thinking were both in Latin America. The Fondo de Desarrollo Rural Integrato (Integrated Rural Development Fund) in Colombia was a modest fund to which the Bank and the IDB both contributed. But the design (which consisted of a wide range of discretionary uses, distribution tilted toward poorer people and poorer regions, capacity building, enforcement of technical and environmental standards) was insightful and replicable. In Mexico, the Municipal Solidarity Funds (FMS) introduced in 1990 were designed "to demonstrate how a locally managed fund may be a successful alternative for managing rural investment in technically simple infrastructure."[117] In 1994 the program was functioning in most of the thirty-one states of Mexico and had financed about 75,000 projects over a four-year period. In 1992 the Bank, calling it the Decentralization and Regional Development Project, contributed $32.5 million to the program for 653 rural municipalities. These were, to be sure, limited interventions by the Bank. But their promoters hoped they augured a further move into more participatory rural development for both the Bank and many of its borrowing countries.

AGRICULTURAL CREDIT. This is a subsector in which the World Bank experienced a major round of revisionism in the 1980s, in a way that was distinct from, albeit related to, the general doctrinal changes under way in the institution. Then, in the 1990s, there were some second thoughts. Until the 1980s the Bank had long been one of a number of external agencies assisting the provision of special institutional credit to developing-country agriculture, especially for small

117. Ibid., annex 1, p. 68.

and medium-sized farms. Bank/IDA agricultural credit lending accounted for about 12 percent of all the agricultural lending the institution had done up to the end of the 1960s. So far, most of the loans for agricultural lending had gone to the Latin American and EMENA regions, but the product was spreading. Indeed, by the middle 1970s it could be presumed that most well-rounded agriculture promotion packages would include provisions for short-term production lending to farmers (for example, for fertilizer, perhaps administered by cooperatives); and they might also support investment lending for productive assets (for example, for terracing or tubewells) by some type of agricultural development bank.

In 1975 the Central Projects Staff compiled an Agricultural Credit Sector Policy Paper that codified the Bank's rationale for such lending. The purpose, according to a 1993 OED review, was not to fragment the financial market further; it was to fill a gap in the market attributable to "banker discrimination against agriculture and especially against small farmers."[118] The idea was to deliver to farmers financing for production and modernization that would otherwise be unavailable to them at reasonable prices. It was not to collect their savings, which were presumed to be scant, and, in any event, were not very responsive to interest rates. Accordingly, specialized rural outlets targeted resources (domestically and externally provided) at relatively concessional rates on those small and medium farmers who qualified for the loans. Often the apex funders offered subsidies to induce commercial banks to establish rural branches to serve as distributors of such credit.

Once it gathered momentum, lending along these lines built rapidly, reaching peaks in the early and middle 1980s. As table 8-2 shows, it then fell into a sharp decline from 1990 onward. For the entire period 1948–92, agricultural credit lending accounted for 26 percent of total agricultural lending. After the 1980s, it became a small fraction of an agricultural program that was itself diminished.[119]

It took two things to topple agricultural credit projects as a favorite mode of World Bank lending. One was the institution's own operating experience, as perceived by many of its operators and, in particular, its evaluators. In the late 1980s a large percentage of agricultural credit projects and of the credit components of other agricultural projects were being given unsatisfactory performance ratings by the OED. Credit given as a "component" of diversified agricultural projects got worse ratings than those for the predominantly credit projects. Although the situation varied greatly from region to region, the whole set of "unsatisfactory" ratings was high for the twenty years of projects reviewed: 23 percent for all regions, and 46 percent of projects in Sub-Saharan Africa, which had the worst showing. These trends, if anything, were worsening.[120]

118. World Bank, "A Review of Bank Lending for Agricultural Credit and Rural Finance (1948–92)," OED Report 12143, June 29, 1993, para. 8.
119. Ibid.
120. Ibid.

Such ratings and the case-by-case disappointments they reflected were suffi-cient to get the attention of regional and sector management. But they were scarcely enough to account for the scale of the fall from grace suffered by "tradi-tional" agricultural credit lending. The other toppling factor was an onslaught of revisionist thinking about agricultural credit that, starting very quietly in the early 1970s and growing in concert with other more general revisionist doctrine, had taken over Bank agricultural credit policy by the end of the 1980s.

What became the new school of Rural Financial Market reform (RFM) started smaller than a man's hand with a single article, "Agricultural Credit in Latin America: A Critical Review," by an associate professor of agricultural economics at Ohio State University, Dale W Adams, in 1971.[121] Drawing on his field experience and an examination of Latin American data, Adams questioned the assumptions of the traditional credit model—that agricultural finance could be treated as if it were segregated from general finance; that credit could be targeted on farmers at subsidized interest rates without repressing saving and distorting the financial system. He began to gather a set of like-minded adherents. The insurrection incubated in USAID's expanding program for small-farm supervised credit. In the Bank it migrated first to an EDI course in 1976. "By the early 1980s, the classes were increasingly associated with expression of the 'emerging' view. . . . The center of critical opinion had passed from USAID to the Bank."[122] Following Adams's lead, "the emerging view" advocated raising farm interest rates to (formal) market levels, eliminating subsidies, using rural financial institutions to mobilize deposits as well as lend resources, and reducing the insulation of such institutions from the rest of the financial system.

Interestingly, the ginger group of new agricultural credit thinkers seems initially to have been quite distinct from two other intellectual movements heading in a similar direction. One followed the lead of such general financial theorists as Edward Shaw and Ronald McKinnon of Stanford University, who were shaping doctrines of financial deepening and financial liberalization.[123] The other was the resurgence of mainstream neoclassical market economics that gained a new grip on the Bank's thinking in the 1980s. There can be little doubt that these larger waves of doctrinal change helped speed RFM toward acceptance.

121. Dale W Adams, "Agricultural Credit in Latin America: A Critical Review of External Funding Policy," *American Journal of Agricultural Economics,* vol. 53, no. 2 (May 1971), pp. 163–72.

122. World Bank, "A Review of Bank Lending for Agricultural Credit and Rural Fi-nance," p. iv. Among the conceptional insurgents within the Bank were J. D. Von Pischke, Avishay Braverman, and Hans Binswanger.

123. See Ronald F. McKinnon, *Financial Liberalization and Economic Development: A Reassessment of Interest-Rate Policies in Asia and Latin America* (San Francisco: Inter-national Center for Economic Growth, 1988); Edward S. Shaw, *Financial Deepening in Economic Development* (Oxford University Press, 1973).

Indeed, the role of the first of these parallel waves—in behalf of general financial reform—was explicit and pivotal. At the request of Senior Vice President for Operations Moeen Qureshi, a Task Force on Financial Sector Operations (under the chairmanship of Fred Levy) prepared a report presented to the Board in August 1989. After several iterations, this led to an Operational Directive on Financial Sector Operations at the end of February 1992. But the Task Force's impact on agricultural credit, which the Task Force treated as, essentially, a subsector of the financial sector, appeared to register—and register sharply—as soon as 1990:

> The thrust of the Task Force recommendations was to move the Bank toward a liberalized regime of financial intermediation and market-based interest rates. In response to the argument that targeted subsidies were essential to serve the credit requirements of many of the Bank's "target" groups, the Task Force replied that these programs were prone to abuse and failed to secure their objectives anyway. On all these points the objections of the Task Force and the RFM group converged. . . .
>
> The response by the staff working on agricultural projects was immediate. Operations that were in the pipeline were evaluated against the new guidelines and the majority were reformulated, suspended or dropped.[124]

While the Levy Task Force certainly meant what it said, it had not, according to OED, "anticipated the strength of the reaction" to its recommendations.[125] Nevertheless, two forces tempered the turn away from lending for agricultural credit. One had to do with expedience. During the 1980s, as is emphasized in chapter 10, the Bank was under heavy pressure to find vehicles that could quickly disburse loans. The institution was reluctant to let adjustment lending carry the whole burden of quick resource transfers for fear of impairing its capacity to lever policy reforms. At the same time, nonconditioned (or only lightly conditioned) nonproject loans had fallen out of favor.

All of this increased the usefulness of project loans that could disburse quickly without impairing effectiveness. Loans to general development finance institutions (DFIs) were one such type. But in other countries—Mexico and Brazil are cited as examples—agricultural credit loans seem to have served the same function.

The other element that might temper the decline in agricultural credit lending was the concern about how sweeping a change the RFM critique should be allowed to trigger. Some outside the Bank have argued that the new conventional wisdom has overshot the mark.[126] And from inside, the 1993 OED review has pointed out that "traditional" agricultural credit lending, while flawed, has on balance been constructive. According to this review, the RFM critique did cut away deadwood

124. World Bank, "A Review of Bank Lending for Agricultural Credit and Rural Finance," p. v.

125. Ibid.

126. See John W. Mellor and Bhuphat M. Desai, *Institutional Finance for Agricultural Development: An Analytical Survey of Critical Issues* (Washington, D.C.: International Food Policy Research Institute, 1993).

usefully, but it did not salvage enough good parts of the old-style lending. The pace of reform should be slowed, it suggested; while the integration of agricultural finance into general finance should proceed, agricultural finance should be remade, in parallel, into an integral part of agricultural strategy.

The Bank's final position on this matter was blurred, however, by the fact that the OED and the sectoral-policies wing (which adhered more closely to the RFM reform doctrine) negotiated an overview for the sector review that was markedly less critical of the new doctrine than was the body of the report.[127] As a result, regional agricultural division chiefs, relying on the body of the report, found renewed authorization for a volume of agricultural credit projects that the Levy report had seemed to deny them, while the overview confirmed the need for the financial reforms that executive directors favored.

It is also important to note that the body of the 1993 OED review contained a nuanced preview of the prospects for Bank agricultural credit lending in Latin America that may prove to be not far off the mark for the subsector more generally:

> Whatever occurs, the traditional form of subsidies will disappear. Some "preferential" rates for farmers (positive but somewhat below market) will survive, because governments will insist on them. And the region may start experimenting with special concessional rates for private investments with ecological externalities, and with subsidies aimed at bank branches to support their transaction costs for farmer lending. But the emphasis is going to pass from direct support to subsidized small farmer credit to institutional and infrastructural assistance aimed at "leveling the playing field" to permit small farmer access to existing credit systems.[128]

RESEARCH AND EXTENSION. After 1980, when the Bank's total lending for agriculture was in decline, its support of agricultural research remained steady; it has been broad (half of all agricultural loans have had a research element) and animated in its encouragement of reforms in recipients' research operations. The institution published an agricultural research sector policy paper in 1981. In the next eleven years it loaned amounts averaging more than $4 million to thirty-five free-standing research projects and spread some $200 million annually across the research components of more than three hundred other projects.

Even though many of these latter elements (in the view of the Bank's leading agricultural research specialist) were too small to have much impact on recipients' research policies and practice, the institution kept pressing borrowers to strengthen their national agricultural research systems (NARS) by improving their planning and management and maintaining adequate recurrent cost budgets. Indeed, the Bank stretched its norms by contemplating some recurrent cost funding itself.[129]

127. View of members of the AGR Department.

128. World Bank, "A Review of Bank Lending for Agricultural Credit and Rural Finance (1948–1992)," OED Report 12143, June 29, 1993, p. 148.

129. A. J. Pritchard, senior adviser, Agriculture and Natural Resources Department, "World Bank Investment in Agricultural Research Policy and Strategy: Past and Future," n.d., ca. 1993–94.

The institution's other main connection to agricultural research remained its linkage to the CGIAR. The Bank continued to fill the chair and provide administrative staffing for the CG, and also to act as its funder of last resort. It raised its contribution (as before, in grant form, drawn mainly from IBRD profits) from $14.6 million in 1981 to $37.1 million in 1991. The CG system became even more heavily dependent on the Bank's financial support with the sharp decline in the contributions of other donors, particularly USAID.

The financial squeeze on the CG came at a particularly awkward time as the number of IARCs admitted to the group continued to climb. Membership had risen to eighteen centers by 1993. Plainly, the Bank was being moved into an even more central role for keeping the CG system whole and healthy. For their part, Bank staff demanded more voice in determining the uses to which Bank allocations to the IARCs would be put.[130] This augured poorly for the autonomy of the centers. On the other hand, it appeared that appreciation of contributions of CG expertise to Bank programs might encourage self-restraint on the part of the larger institution.

Along with research, agricultural extension remained a lively issue in the period after 1980. The subsector continued to vie for resources, and to keep the debate spirited. A central issue here was the merits and limitations of the Bank's brand of extension, that is, the training and visit system. By the time the debate gathered steam, much of the relevant decisionmaking lay well in the past. Thus of the projects surveyed in an April 1994 OED review of agricultural extension, two-thirds of the free-standing extension loans and three-quarters of the loans with extension *components* had been approved by the end of 1981. There was also a geographic slant to the set. Although only 4 of the 33 free-standing extension loans supported methodologies other than T&V, only 2 of the 33 were in Latin America (one of these was not T&V), whereas all 17 of the South Asian freestanders were T&V. On the other hand, the sample of loans with extension components leaned heavily to non-T&V methodologies (47 versus 27) and all of the 19 Latin American loans with extension components supported non-T&V methods.[131]

The weightiest criticism of the T&V system came in the 1990s, particularly in the 1994 OED review.[132] In essence the complaint was that the T&V system supplied too standardized, inflexible, and regimented a form of extension. The OED and other critics sought a brand that was better tailored to the particularities of its clients and their locale, that was more participatory and less lockstepped, and

130. Ibid.

131. World Bank, "Agricultural Extension: Lesson from Completed Projects," OED Report 13000, April 29, 1994, annex I, tables 1 and 2.

132. Among the challenges from outside the Bank was that of the University of Manchester's David Hulme. See his "Enhancing Organizational Effectiveness in Developing Countries: The Training and Visit System Revisited," *Public Administration and Development*, vol. 12, no. 5 (December 1992), pp. 433–45. This prompted a reply in the December 1993 issue of the same journal from V. Venkatesan of the World Bank, which elicited a quick rejoinder from Hulme in the February 1994 issue. Inside the Bank there was an accumulating literature partly critical of T&V. It included the following works: Dina L. Umali and Lisa

that elicited more creativity from its professionals. Such seemed to be the predominant view among extension specialists—including those seeking to introduce more flexibility, diversity, and adaptability into the still so-called T&V system itself.

Interestingly, the OED assessment was questioned by the Bank's Africa Region, which, although allegedly not opposed to the evaluation department's philosophy, found much to say for the systemwide, single-track discipline T&V sought to provide.[133]

Perhaps the debate lacked a clear enough time frame (or stages-of-development frame) to produce a consensus. When T&V first burst into use in South Asia in the 1970s, existing agricultural technology, predating the Green Revolution, was being underexploited; the new technologies were technically fairly simple; they were capable of being broken down into small seasonal and teachable sound bites that suited wide geographic areas; existing extension systems had been bogged down in multiple purposes; in the idiom of community development, village workers had been charged with pursuing a variety of performance targets simultaneously; and the available village workers, the implementing personnel, had weak training and limited capacities.

The problem was to make a teaching and research-feedback system with weak teachers and weak return-transmitters of field experience work better, more quickly, and more broadly areawide. The propagators of the system had to point out these weaknesses delicately, for one was trying to build the self-confidence and morale of these very same workers. But embedded in the Benor system's documentation are numerous references to the personnel constraints under which the typical T&V venture begins.[134] These constraints were well recognized by other commentators.[135] To address this problem, Benor designed a clear, no-nonsense, command system, with a single purpose, a clear command structure, well-packaged inputs of information and expertise, clear messages to the clients, and answers to

Schwartz, *Public and Private Agricultural Extension: Beyond Traditional Frontiers,* World Bank Discussion Paper 236 (World Bank, 1994); and Charles Ameur, *Agricultural Extension: A Step beyond the Next Step,* World Bank Technical Paper 247 (World Bank, 1994).

133. World Bank, "Agricultural Extension: Lessons from Completed Projects," box 5: "Differences between OED and AFR on Interpretation of Findings," pp. 50–52.

134. Daniel Benor, James Q. Harrison, and Michael Baxter, *Agricultural Extension, the Training and Visit System* (World Bank, 1984), pp. 18–19, 58; Benor and Baxter, *Training and Visit Extension,* pp. 14ff., pp. 45ff.

135. "It is important in designing new technology to note the educational level and technical competence of the average field-level extension worker is not high. The T&V system aims to offset this by providing simple programmed messages to field workers at regular intervals. It is questionable whether this approach is adequate for training farmers in the adoption of more complex techniques such as integrated pest management, organic farming, or alley cropping." International Food Policy Research Institute/International Service for National Agricultural Research, *Towards a New Agricultural Revolution: Research, Technology Transfer, and Application for Food Security in Africa* (The Hague: ISNAR, 1981), p. 35.

predictable queries. The village workers responded with enthusiasm; they were glad to be put to straightforward work, and the results gave them a sense of achievement. Moreover, their clients were pleased; for the most part, the system delivered.

But what seems obvious in retrospect is that, from the beginning, T&V should have been treated as a transitional expedient. In country after country, as personnel, information, and research capacities developed, extension programs should have evolved into more differentiated, participatory, and (in some cases) privatized operations. This change is now taking place in developing countries, and there has clearly been a matching evolution in the Bank, whether or not under the T&V label.

It is a pity that what should be seen as a spectrum of available modes of extension (as dissent in the Africa region makes clear, certain circumstances still invite the standardized and routinized approach) has been viewed as a competitive face-off between T&V and "other" systems. This, it would appear, has two related explanations. The Bank maintained a proprietary, rather jealous, attachment to the T&V logo longer than was appropriate; and in Daniel Benor the training and visit system had a charismatic propagator whose presence, whether or not he intended it, tended to freeze his invention in time.

Outstanding Regional Developments

After 1980 the Bank's ARD experience continued to be differentiated by regions, as explained earlier in the chapter. Two of these regions merit further comment: Sub-Saharan Africa and China.

AFRICA BELOW THE SAHARA. For the Bank in the 1980s, Sub-Saharan Africa was partly, but only partly, a revisionist case. The centrality assigned to agriculture in the Bank's diagnosis of African development problems was notably upgraded. By 1989, in its most ambitious special report on this region, the institution declared: "In contrast to the past, the future strategy [proposed by the Bank for Sub-Saharan Africa] sees agriculture as the primary foundation for growth."[136] "Transforming agriculture and expanding its productive capacity is the prerequisite for improving living standards in Sub-Saharan Africa."[137]

There also was one important substantive change in the Bank's ARD agenda for Africa, one abundantly foreshadowed in the debates and disappointments of the 1970s: the emphasis on integrated, multifaceted, area rural-development projects disappeared. Although such lending continued to account for sizable fractions of the institution's regional commitments well into the decade, the Bank recognized that it had made excessive claims on indigenous implementation capacities. Furthermore, a major OED review of rural development lending in 1987 concluded

136. World Bank, *Sub-Saharan Africa: From Crisis to Sustainable Growth* (1989), p. 8.
137. Ibid., p. 89.

that it "was often a mistake" to pursue "a project-based rural development strategy in the absence of benign macro policies."[138]

Otherwise, however, little was unfamiliar in the "new" ARD strategy for Africa. In its elaborate details, it sounded remarkably like what was being recommended for the rest of the developing world or had already been proposed for Africa. Some of the strongest advice was in the new idiom of governmental disengagement:

> The private sector, including cooperative and grassroots organizations, should be given a bigger role. Agricultural products should be freely marketed. Prices should reflect supply and demand to stimulate and regulate production. Private investment in production, agricultural processing, and farm input supply should be promoted, not constrained by excessive regulations and administrative controls or legislation. Rural financial intermediation by commercial and cooperative banks and credit unions should be encouraged, rather than hampered by government regulations.[139]

As for other recommendations, all of the things governments did for African agriculture needed to be done better. But the list of things was familiar: better and better-managed national research systems, more effective extension, better agricultural training, more attention to rural infrastructure, legal and administrative arrangements to ensure greater security of land tenure, programs to assist women as farmers and traders. To be sure, the 1980s saw greater emphasis in the Bank on the roles of human-resource and institutional development as critical inputs to African agriculture. And by the end of the decade attention to the links (some positive, some negative) between agricultural expansion and environmental protection was greatly increased.

Yet, against the record of the past, the prospectus was not heartening. Indeed, on reflection, there was a kind of desperate wishfulness about the treatment of agriculture in the 1989 Africa report. If the GDP of nations in Sub-Saharan Africa was ever going to reach average annual growth rates of 5 percent (arguably, the minimum acceptable with even dampened population growth), average agricultural growth had to be cranked up to 4 percent annually, according to the models on the subject, and the yields of productive land would have to rise to 3 percent a year. This pace of average agricultural growth had never been managed in Sub-Saharan Africa, nor anywhere else in recent times. Yet, declared the report, it *had* to be achieved, and to support this and the rest of Africa's goals, foreign aid to Sub-Saharan Africa had to be increased—at least through 2020. Although in that year Africa's reliance on external resources to finance development and on food imports was expected to be "much smaller than today," net transfers to Sub-Saharan Africa, which were about $12 billion, or 8 percent of GDP, in 1990, were projected to rise to $19 billion, or 9 percent of GDP, in 2000. Even at 5 percent of

138. World Bank, "World Bank Experience with Rural Development, 1965–1986," OED Report 6883, October 16, 1987, p. x.
139. World Bank, *Sub-Saharan Africa*, pp. 106–07.

GDP, they were still expected to approach $28 billion in 2020. "With a proper policy framework," said the 1989 report, such inflows would not need to promote aid dependency. Korea was cited as a reassuring example.[140]

Battered aid veterans of the period had difficulty taking these estimates seriously. The Bank, for all its efforts, could not see the light at the end of the tunnel. The problem of African agriculture was not generically different from the problems elsewhere. It was just deeper. Its institutional deficits were greater. And it was broken up into more pieces of both agroclimatic and political geography. The need for effective "retailing" of transfers was unparalleled. And, although the Bank's Africa region greatly augmented its field representation during the 1980s and 1990s, it still was not satisfied with its ability to encourage good retailing.

CHINA. The period of China's membership in the World Bank (from 1980) and the Bank's subsequent conduct of a very active China program has coincided with a stretch of rousing performance by Chinese agriculture. It is easy, and not altogether mistaken, to imagine a causal connection. The surge in China's agricultural output and productivity can be attributed in large part to a set of reforms introduced in 1978, well before interactions with the Bank took hold. Econometric evidence unmistakably indicates that one of the most influential reforms was the shift in productive organization from collective farming to the "household responsibility system" begun experimentally, even furtively, in some Chinese provinces in 1978. The swift propagation of this institutional change was coupled with price reforms and others substituting markets for planning, all under way before the arrival of the Bank.[141] Table 8-3, borrowed from the source just cited, outlines the pattern of agriculture growth in China during 1978–84 and in the periods preceding and following.

Members of the Bank staff working on China in the 1980s and 1990s are spirited, however, in claiming to have contributed to the Chinese success. From the beginning of the relationship, Bank officials were engaged in supportive dialogue with the Chinese reformers; in 1987 they formalized their influence in a rural-sector adjustment loan that supported the liberalization of producer and consumer grain prices and established a major rural financial institution. In 1991, after Tiananmen Square, the Bank offered a $500 million investment loan for grain production that encouraged the decision in favor of desubsidizing urban grain prices. Also in the grain field, the Bank helped improve the country's bulk handling and transport facilities. It provided support for commercialized bank lending for agriculture, the introduction of new animal breeds and plant varieties, an array of incrementally improved technologies, and decisive improvements in Chinese forestry.

---

140. Ibid., p. 175.

141. Justin Yifu Lin, "Chinese Agriculture: Institutional Challenges and Performance," in T. N. Srinivasan, ed., *Agriculture and Trade in China and India: Policies and Performance since 1950* (San Francisco: ICS Press, 1994), chap. 2.

Table 8-3. *Average Annual Growth Rates of Agricultural Output in China,*
1952–87[a]

Percentage

Period	Agricultural output value	Crop output value	Grain output	Cotton output	Oil crops output	Population
1952–78	2.9	2.5	2.4	2.0	0.8	2.0
1978–84	7.4	5.9	4.8	17.7	13.8	1.3
1984–87	4.1	1.4	–0.2	–12.9	8.3	1.3

Source: Ministry of Agriculture, Planning Bureau, *Zhongguo nongye tongji ziliao, 1987* (China agricultural statistical material, 1987) (Beijing: Agriculture Press, 1989), pp. 28, 34; Ministry of Agriculture, Planning Bureau, *Zhongguo nongcun jingi tongji ziliao doguan, 1949-1986* (A comprehensive book of China rural economic statistics, 1949-1986) (Beijing: Agriculture Press, 1989), pp. 112–15, 146–49, 189–92; State Statistical Bureau, *Zhongguo tongji nianjian, 1988* (China statistical yearbook, 1988) (Beijing: China Statistics Press, 1988), p. 97.

a. Reproduced with permission from Justin Yifu Lin, "Chinese Agriculture: Institutional Challenges and Performance," in T. N. Srinivasan, ed., *Agriculture and Trade in China and India: Policies and Performance since 1950* (San Francisco: ICS Press, 1994), table 2.10, p. 39.

Finally, it was the Bank's sense that, because of the tightness of China's domestic budgets, the Bank's lending choices had had a strong impact on internal priorities. For example, six years of Bank preparation was largely responsible for the launching of the Yellow River's first flood control dam. But at least as influential, in the view of Joseph Goldberg, agriculture chief in the Bank's China Department, was the Bank's *rejection* of projects:

> Projects and programs we have rejected have tended to die, from [several hundred a year] misconceived micro-level investments . . . to large dangerous programs, such as reconversion of areas to communal farming, programs of investments in huge Russian-style slaughterhouses, expansions of irrigation pumping to uneconomic elevations, construction of plants without toxic effluent control systems, unsustainable exploitation of natural resources . . . construction of uneconomic dams, etc.[142]

All in all, according to Goldberg, the Bank's input to Chinese agriculture was one of which it was proud.

Conclusion

Agriculture and rural development have cut a wider swath through the history of the World Bank than agriculture's share in developing-country GDPs would suggest. It was a while before the Bank's programming caught up with the fact that most of the people in its client countries farmed for a living. Soon, however, it became apparent that poverty was primarily a rural issue, and that trade and industrial outcomes depended on agriculture as much as it rested on them. In the

142. Memorandum, Joseph Goldberg to Devesh Kapur, "World Bank History Project—Bank Contribution to Chinese Agriculture," March 1, 1994, para. 9.

1960s and 1970s the Bank went into agriculture and rural development in a big way.

The Bank's agriculture-related activities and operations can claim a measure of leadership within the institution. There was no productive or service sector—industry, utilities, finance, education, health—in which, by the late 1970s, the Bank had developed greater authority and expertise, in comparison with other institutions and assemblies of talent. The Bank's ARD work was balanced in its attention to micro and macro issues. It was informed by a large volume of high-quality analysis and research. And, during its agricultural heyday, the Bank was a very big spender; it invested heavily in strengthening existing programs and in starting new ones.

Although that prodigious flow has now subsided, it did demonstrate that the ability and willingness to risk large sums on highly uncertain outcomes sometimes can achieve breakthroughs attainable in no other way. In the Bank's case under McNamara, when the institution had achieved the momentum and quasi autonomy to do so, it was unfortunate that one of its most proliferated, highest-risk bets—on area development programs—to a large extent failed. In a sense, the situation seemed all the worse because of the candor and thoroughness of the institution's self-evaluations, not only by OED but also by the other critical faculties the Bank constantly turns on itself. These evaluations confirmed what had been fairly apparent: that, in agriculture and rural development, the Bank is almost inherently a wholesaler; and that its success depends on its effectiveness in promoting the good retailing of ideas and resources among its developing-country recipients.

The area development experience, most particularly in Africa, was disappointing mainly because agriculture had by then fallen to a lower level on the Bank's agenda. Agricultural claims on the institution's lending and administrative budgets are still in retreat. In terms of personnel and expertise, the Bank's comparative advantage in ARD is slowly eroding; the glory days of Bank ARD seem to be over. The situation invites several conclusions.

First, the decline of agriculture at the Bank, if it is real, is to be regretted, because no other agency in the international development community seems poised to take over the leadership the Bank has exercised in this field for twenty years; and despite declining agricultural fractions of GDP, developing-country agricultures will still need external assistance for the next several decades, as is painfully evident in Sub-Saharan Africa (even if, as most parties to the problem hope, external efforts can inspire increasing self-reliance).

Also, in the kind of analysis represented by the Schiff-Valdés findings, one sees a more general case for continued and pointed World Bank involvement in—and *about*—developing-country agriculture. Urban bias remains alive and well. The forms of direct and indirect taxation that manifest such bias appear to deserve continuing attack by friends of development.

There is a further argument for renewed agricultural activism at the Bank, as has been stated most explicitly by C. Peter Timmer.[143] Agricultural strategy, like general development strategy, need not consist of a one-dimensional approach, whether fully market oriented or fully interventionist. As "the East Asian model" (or miracle) has demonstrated, countries can use and value the market, and yet be prudently interventionist. In the agricultural case, revisionism has strongly relied on the market. But a more ambitious strategy would be to steer the agricultural market more actively, for the purpose, for example, of stabilizing food prices, ensuring social benefits valued outside the market, or providing indirect reinforcements to growth.

There is yet another good reason for renewing agricultural budgets and staff in the Bank. Lately, the sector has been experiencing a surge in complexity—as exemplified by the rapidly expanding field of biotechnology. Comprehensive coverage of ARD calls for new sets of experts who add to, but do not substitute for, those who retire and (since their specialties remain relevant) who need replacing. As noted in chapter 18, however, one answer may be to develop a small but very knowledgeable and adept core group of agricultural technical specialists who succeed in making good and flexible use of a larger band of able consultants and other sources of external expertise.

A further conclusion is that—if the institution's ARD work were to receive a new ration of budgetary and staffing support—what the Bank would do on the side of the agriculture production function seemed fairly straightforward in the middle 1990s. It would press for the suppression of disincentives to agriculture, hidden and otherwise. It would encourage its clients to adopt (and then reliably implement) a coherent set of agriculture-related policies, macro and micro, sectoral and subsectoral. The policies would be either cautiously noninterventionist or shrewdly interventionist, depending on the preferences and capacities of the borrowing regime. A financially replenished Bank also would press ahead with some sizable infrastructure and water management programs (appropriately vetted for environmental and social impacts) that fitted recipient priorities and capacities and suited the Bank's wholesaling modalities. In agricultural credit, the probable disposition would be to proceed pragmatically, supporting specialized farm finance when the need is plain but tying such elements to the general financial system, not isolating them from it.

As to matters of equity, the Bank has reached the mid-1990s with a set of perceptions and practices that may address most macro aspects of rural poverty and disadvantage as seriously as was the case in the 1970s and, save for sparse funding, perhaps more effectively. There are two dimensions of the rural equity scene, however, in which the Bank has been found wanting in the past. It has seldom

---

143. C. Peter Timmer, "Agriculture and Economic Development Revisited," *Agricultural Systems* (England: Elsevier Science, 1992).

mustered operational initiative or seriousness about land reforms; and it has been diffident in its attempts to address the problem of nonfarm, nonmarket employment. Some fresh breezes have been stirring in this direction lately. It is too early to tell how seriously to take them, but they are promising. In particular, its recent employment program initiatives in Latin America find the Bank experimenting with what may be the answer to its endemic problem of how to be a better wholesaler. The answer may be by learning to rely more on the retailer, while pressing said (national-government) retailer itself to test how much it can responsibly delegate decisions and accountability downward within the domestic system.

NINE

Policy-Linked Lending: I

THE WORLD Bank is widely known for its efforts to influence the behavior of borrowing governments through the transfer of persuasive ideas and information. This characteristic is evident in almost everything the Bank does. Of particular interest in this chapter and the next are its efforts to affect the public policies of borrowing countries. The work of a multilateral public sector lender, by its very nature, invites such activity. Yet in the case of the Bank, another of its characteristics has often taken center stage: its mandated focus on projects.

This discussion concentrates on "macropolicies" that affect general economic performance and deals only lightly with such sectoral matters as agriculture, social programs, and environment. Although promoters of development have various instruments at their disposal—for example, technical assistance, publication, and research—the Bank tends to rely greatly on loan-linked policy persuasion, since it transfers substantial financial resources to developing countries. The response to this strategy differs from country to country. Big countries such as Brazil, India, and China have tended to resist external policy influence, in part because their receipts of official transfers usually have been *relatively* small. There are exceptions, of course. Bangladesh is a large country and its aid receipts in the 1970s were large, but it was so impoverished and beleaguered that donors hesitated to enforce strong policy conditions.

Making a loan is not the only way to lever policy. Withholding a loan also may induce reform. The effectiveness of nonlending as a leverage tool depends on how easy it is for would-be borrowers rebuffed by the Bank to find alternative funding, as well as how firmly the institution has defined and pursued its policy preferences.

The Early Bank's Macropolicy Views

To understand the *process* of policy influence at work in World Bank lending, it is useful to know what kinds of macropolicies the institution would like its borrowers to pursue. Such information makes it easier to see how actions in a particular country in a particular period matched up with Bank norms, and also how and when the norms changed. The problem with such an exercise, however, is that the Bank operates on a loan-by-loan, case-by-case, country-by-country basis, and it has seldom, if ever, set forth comprehensive catechisms of its macropolicy views. Even the annual *World Development Reports* from 1978 onward do not provide systematic policy summaries.

Nevertheless, the current central tendencies in the Bank's views on macropolicy are not too difficult to identify. A summary of those views can therefore provide a serviceable framework for examining departures and changes of emphasis in the Bank's first half century.

Macropolicy Preferences

The Bank's preferred client policies can be classified in relation to their stance on the role of government in the economy; markets, and private versus public sector activities; trade and industry; exchange rates; fiscal and monetary affairs; and foreign transfers, borrowing and investments, and foreign debt.

THE ROLE OF GOVERNMENT. From the 1940s through the 1960s the Bank tended to be somewhat to the right of non-Marxist conventional wisdom in regard to the role of government in the economy. That wisdom—shaped by the Great Depression, the Keynesian policy revolution, wartime economic experience in the countries of the North and West, and the independence movements and anticolonialism in newly emerging countries—favored mixed economies that were neither wholly capitalist nor wholly socialist. Public policy was expected to play a leading economic role. The World Bank in its early decades, staffed in part out of New York's financial district and needing above all to demonstrate its soundness to the financial market, was more conservative than most of its member governments with respect to the appropriate scale of their market interventions and the private-public division of labor.

But the conservative bent was limited. As it faced up to its enforced shift of attention from war-ravaged to developing economies, the Bank not only accepted, it advocated—frequently it even required—national economic planning. Although adapted to particular national circumstances and traditions, the kind of planning that was encouraged typically was comprehensive. Its multiyear projections of outputs and incomes sought to be internally consistent. With specified monetary, fiscal, and regulatory interventions, markets were expected to implement the projections. And the planning was more than academic; it endeavored to steer budgeting and other policies with some authority.

MARKETS AND PRIVATE VERSUS PUBLIC SECTOR CHOICES. With most of its clients starting from a highly regulated context, the Bank in its early decades usually was in favor of thinning out administrative controls, the goal, however, being to reduce controls, not eliminate them. Competition was a benign orderer of activity, but it often needed administrative supplementing or strengthening.

As to the question of private or public ownership, such leaders as Eugene Black, Robert Garner, and George Woods had a strong preference for private industrial enterprises, although many Bank people recognized there was a spectrum rather than a dichotomy of ownership modes. Infrastructure, including "public" utilities, was a different matter. The Bank adopted the continental European practice of typically endorsing the assignment of such activity to the public sector.

TRADE AND INDUSTRIAL POLICIES. The early Bank favored international trade; it inclined toward openness. But "development" was preoccupied with industrializing, which tended to mean import substitution; and because of the infant-industry problem, import-substitution industrialization (ISI) entailed protection. Thus the Bank's trade and industrialization recipe in the 1950s and 1960s was to seek both import-substitution and export-promotion industrialization via a liberalized price rationing of inputs, protected by tariffs and partly ordered by national economic planning.

The Bank's tendency to accept second-best (but realistic) solutions in the 1940s to 1960s can be seen in the way it agreed to export subsidies—in part because of the inaccessibility of the next item.

EXCHANGE RATES. At the outset, the Bank faced multiple rates in many borrowing countries. It favored a convergence toward a single-market rate. Under the Bretton Woods system, rates were supposed to stay put while domestic fiscal and monetary management flexed to them. Thus events forced exchange rates to change only occasionally, and such changes were primarily a concern of the International Monetary Fund.

FISCAL AND MONETARY POLICIES. In the 1950s and 1960s the Bank recognized that most borrowing countries were trying to serve two goals:

—*Stabilization,* which tempered price and employment turbulence. Usually this meant inflation fighting. However, there were regional differences of degree, for example, between South Asia and much of Latin America. The whole substantive territory in the early decades tended to be IMF turf.

—*The promotion of growth and efficiency.* This was done by planning, building indigenous saving and investment, decluttering the market of unnecessary controls, building human capital (for example, by strengthening education), and expanding exports. As between the Bretton Woods institutions, The foregoing were usually viewed as Bank concerns, although the IMF did not remain silent on such issues.

In its first two decades, however, the Bank gave comparatively little attention to what would become a third macro welfare goal for its borrowers, namely, internal equity. Growth promotion was expected to reduce disparities in income and wealth between countries, but later there would be more concern for reducing them also *within* developing countries.

FOREIGN TRANSFERS, BORROWING AND INVESTMENTS, AND FOREIGN DEBT. The International Bank for Reconstruction and Development would not have existed if its owning governments did not see an advantage in well-vetted flows of external resources going to developing countries under public multilateral auspices. As explained in other chapters, the IBRD flows consisted of private resources publicly managed. When funds from the International Development Association were added, these came mainly from the taxpayers of owner governments. In the 1950s and 1960s, the typical inclination of Bank management and the development promotion community was to bargain with political authorities for expanded resource transfers. Some commentators, however, were beginning to raise the specter of aid dependency.

Foreign private investment, patently an important issue for many developing countries, was nevertheless treated with great ambivalence from the beginning of the concerted development effort after World War II. In such developing regions as Sub-Saharan Africa and parts of South Asia, the scale of private foreign investment available was small relative to the need for external capital. Potential suppliers, like their governments, often pressed for more access than they were prepared to take up. Conversely, some host governments and indigenous competitors were neurotic in their hostility to foreign private investment. The Bank, however, in both its IBRD and International Finance Corporation guises, maintained consistent, yet not unrealistic, support for direct foreign investment in borrowing countries.

Foreign debt was an elusive subject. The Bank and its borrowers groped for guidelines. Once in the 1960s, Mexican authorities declared to the Bank that they would not permit Mexico's debt-service ratio to exceed 10 percent—a ceiling that would look remarkably conservative in a dozen years.[1] Twenty years later, Mexico would come a cropper over the matter. The issue was due to be somewhat better (although less than precisely) sorted out in the Bank's later decades—just as would the question of what limits on lending and country exposure would be prudent from the viewpoint of the institution's own creditworthiness.

Coping with Emergencies

Any development player was responsible to itself for making short-run responses to emergencies. And any public player was responsible to its political masters for such responses, in particular to such events as debt crises and sea changes in

---

1. Mervyn L. Weiner, personal communication. According to Weiner, a Bank staffer working on Mexico at the time, this declaration was contained in a letter from Mexican Minister of Finance Antonio Ortiz Mena to the director of the Bank's Western Hemisphere Department, Orvis Schmidt. The ratio referred to was that of debt-service charges to export earnings.

borrowing countries' terms of trade. In the case of the Bank, as the decades unfolded, responsibility for such fire fighting rose as the institution's centrality and weight in the international economy increased.

Policy Promotion through the 1960s

By the 1960s the Bank would witness the emergence of a major tension between country policies, on the one hand, and project lending, on the other. Yet there was an appearance of benign coexistence between these two aspects of the new Bank's activities. The Bank was mandated to be mainly a "project" lender, whatever that was (implicitly, the institution also was invited to give content to the project concept). At the same time, the Bank's highest priority at the outset was to establish its own creditworthiness in the New York financial market, and this called for both policy and project implementation. For one thing, in justification of its portfolio, the institution needed to show that the governments borrowing from it were creditworthy because they had or were adopting sound economic policies. Once the policy worries of the Bank's creditors were somewhat allayed, the creditors were reassured by a portfolio consisting mainly of discrete projects whose productivity could be appraised in ways that abstracted from the political environments surrounding the projects.

The Early Policy Focus

On the reconstruction side of its mission, the new institution was thrown abruptly into general-purpose nonproject lending to war-damaged member countries, first to France, then to the Netherlands, Denmark, and Luxembourg. Although there was considerable discussion of macropolicies with the French, the rest of these program loans had little influence on policy. But they showed that the "special circumstances" that under the Articles were to be identified so as to permit the use of the nonproject loan format could in fact be readily established, and therefore that if the nonproject vehicle was needed for direct, unambiguous policy leverage, it seemed to be available.

The first developing country to request a loan was Chile. In 1946 Chile asked for a single loan of $40 million to cover a whole list of hydroelectric, forestry, urban, and suburban transport and railway schemes. The Bank responded, first, that the omnibus request should be disaggregated into separate project components; and, second, that the whole bundle could not be moved until it had been cleared on national policy grounds. Substantively, Chile had to show that it had adopted an orderly process for disposing of the arrears on its prewar international debts.[2] This

2. World Bank, "Memorandum with Regard to the Outstanding External Debt of Chile," Secretary's Memorandum 30, November 21, 1946.

pattern became a norm. Other countries presented requests for lists of projects, and the Bank regularly invoked policy questions as they considered the overall creditworthiness of the would-be sovereign borrower.

It became evident that the young Bank's viewing of a project request depended on the policy environment the project would occupy, indeed, on the project's place in the country's overall development program. Economic planning came into vogue in and for developing countries; it was encouraged by external bilateral and multi-lateral development promoters, including the Bank. Countries turned to the Bank for technical assistance to their early planning efforts. Thus at the end of the 1940s the World Bank, joining a variety of United Nations and bilateral agencies, began to dispatch an array of country missions broadly instructed to determine and report countries' development needs. A first such mission, partly staffed and funded by the Bank, was an elaborate one to Colombia led by the American economist, Lauchlin Currie, who later settled in Colombia. Follow-ups to the Currie report led to fiscal and monetary reforms, easing of foreign exchange controls, a liberalization of capital imports and exports, and transportation reforms. By 1955 the Colombia report had been succeeded by more than a dozen other major country missions and studies. Two of these, to Syria and Jordan, were led by the redoubtable Dutch former professor and finance minister, Pieter Lieftinck, who was the Bank's first resident representative in Turkey and in the later 1950s became an executive director of the IBRD. Meanwhile the institution had sent country missions to Turkey, Nicaragua, Guatemala, and Cuba in 1950, to Iraq and Ceylon in 1951, to Jamaica in 1952; a joint working party with Mexicans reported on their country in 1951; and further reports were made on British Guiana and Nigeria in 1953, on Malaya in 1954, and on Jordan in 1955. In every instance the resulting high-profile country report recommended substantial policy reforms, especially in the macro area.

The Bank's project business was growing quite steadily through these years. But as its country reports accrued, the institution was strongly inclined to inject country policy, more particularly, country macropolicy, considerations into its loan transac-tions. Eugene Black articulated the position in a 1951 letter to William McChesney Martin, chairman of the U.S. Federal Reserve System:

> As the International Bank acquired more experience in development, it has come to realize that the project-by-project approach, even when projects are judged in the light of the general economic situation of the borrowing country, leaves a good deal to be desired. Although projects proposed for external financing may, in relation to the general economic situation, appear to warrant a top priority, their real significance can be understood only in the light of the country's other proposed investments and the resources available to it. For example, if the projects would be carried out even in the absence of a foreign loan and if the investment program includes other projects of doubtful economic merit, the real effect of the foreign loan may be to release funds for uneconomic ventures.[3]

3. Letter, Eugene Black to William McChesney Martin, n.d., 1951.

Brazil became a notable instance of Bank policy focus. In 1951, when coffee prices were high and the development outlook in Brazil was bright, Burke Knapp, who was due to become the most enduring senior executive in Bank history, was coopted from the Bank for a year to lead the U.S. side of a joint Brazil–United States Economic Development Commission. At the time both the Bank's president and vice president, Eugene Black and Robert Garner, respectively, were moved to speculate that over the five-year planning period under discussion the Bank might invest $250 million to $300 million in Brazil, remarks the Brazilian government viewed as a "moral commitment." The Commission produced a respected report replete with projects for presentation to the Bank.

Meanwhile, however, the country's foreign exchange prospects turned sour, inflation accelerated, and the government blocked foreign remittances of earnings and the repatriation of capital. The Bank decided to make no new loans until this last policy had been reversed and, more broadly, until effective stabilization measures had been put in place. The government felt the Bank had reneged on its offered support for the development plan. The Bank felt that its pro-reform pressures on the government were aborted (in 1953) by the U.S. government's decision to bail out Brazil with a U.S. Export-Import Bank loan of $300 million for three years.

Reflecting on the matter some years later, Burke Knapp, who by 1953 was back in the Bank and, as head of its Western Hemisphere Department, was conveying the institution's stabilization message to his Brazilian friends, said Brazil was considered to be "one of the two or three classic cases of how inflation leads to balance of payments disequilibrium and hence to destroying [the borrowing country's] creditworthiness."[4] He said that what the Bank had been recommending, more specifically, was a balanced budget, restricted credit to the private sector, currency devaluation, and some import austerity. As Roberto Campos recalled many years later, this was a case of attempted policy leverage by the withholding of transfers. Eugene Black was adamant. His policy-based proscription of further lending to Brazil persisted almost without interruption until George Woods resumed lending in 1965.[5] Looking back on the episode "from the vantage point of 1971," analysts Edward Mason and Robert Asher doubted that the prolonged straining of relations with the institution's largest Latin American member had been warranted:

> The Bank seriously over-estimated its capacity to influence macroeconomic policies. Furthermore, its judgment of creditworthiness seems to have been rather static and limited. Brazil's gross national product grew at a rate of 6.8 percent a year in real terms in the 1950s. And although the rate of inflation continued at 15 to 20 percent until 1959 and foreign exchange policies left much to be desired, Brazil would hardly have been judged not creditworthy by present standards.[6]

4. J. Burke Knapp, interview, World Bank Oral History Program, July 1961, p. 9.

5. Roberto Campos, "Half a Century Later," *O Estado de S. Paulo* (Brazil), July 31, 1994, contained in World Bank, *Development News Weekly Supplement*, August 26, 1994.

6. Edward S. Mason and Robert E. Asher, *The World Bank since Bretton Woods* (Brookings, 1973), p. 662.

Brazil was by no means the only country in which Bank project loans were denied or delayed on policy grounds in the 1950s and 1960s. Such was also the case in Ceylon in both the 1950s and 1960s, in Colombia in 1957, in Korea in 1963, and in Turkey in 1954. In the last case, the Turkish government ejected the Bank's resident, Pieter Lieftinck, for what it perceived as undue interference in sovereign affairs. As in the Brazilian case, this last began a long policy-motivated interruption in the Bank's Turkish operations. Thus it would have been hard for a casual observer to detect any muting of the World Bank's policy voice during this period. Yet it can be argued that such a weakening was under way.

The 1950s and 1960s: The Projects–Policy Relationship

While borrowers' macropolicies constituted alluring targets for an institution such as the Bank, they also were somewhat forbidding. They were politically risky. It was not unwise to stand above the high-policy, low-politics fray and do solid project work.

To implement its mandated project focus, the Bank had to define what a project was and become a project specialist. The essence of a project was that it was bounded. It usually had a limited, specifiable geographic scope. Economists commonly defined it as an *investment* undertaking. But a project could, under plausible circumstances, finance current account expenses. What most clearly differentiated it from a policy or program was its finiteness. Psychologically, trying to influence the design and implementation of a project that a lender was helping finance was less intrusive than trying to influence those recipient policies that, among their various ramifying effects, would help establish the context in which the project would operate.

In 1946–47 the World Bank, staffed mainly with bankers, lawyers, and macro-economists, had little experience with or expertise in dealing with discrete projects. In 1946 the first annual report noted: "For the time being, it is contemplated that the engineering and technical staff of the Loan Department will be kept to a minimum and that, to the maximum extent practicable, the technical services required by the Bank will be secured on a consulting basis."[7] Thus it was that M. J. Madigan, whom Mason and Asher have memorialized for his brevity, became the Bank's sole overt engineering adviser. Madigan was a consultant, and his technical report on two Mexican power projects read—in its entirety!—as follows:

> I visited Mexico several times during the last year, and made inspections of the properties of the Mexican Light and Power Company and the Federal Electricity Commission. I checked over the proposed programs of expansion and am satisfied that they are reasonable and in line with good engineering practice. The staffs of both the Mexican Light and Power Company and the Commission are competent and I feel sure can carry out the program proposed.[8]

7. IBRD, *First Annual Report by the Executive Directors,* Washington, D.C., September 27, 1946, p. 8.

8. Mason and Asher, *World Bank since Bretton Woods,* p. 159.

Table 9-1. *World Bank Staffing, 1949–63*

| Date (July) | Total engineers | Total agri-culturalists | Loan/technical departments[a] | | Area departments[b] | | Total bank staff |
			Total staff	Percentage of total bank staff	Total staff	Percentage of total bank staff	
1949	4	1	55	13	...	...	412
1950	8	2	68	16	...	...	428
1951	9	2	76	17	...	...	455
1953[c]	14	2	67	15	107	23	461
1954	16	4	76	15	114	23	502
1956	21	3	90	16	105	19	548
1957[d]	22	2	91	16	128	22	575
1958	23	2	107	17	130	21	624
1959	25	1	111	17	133	20	652
1960	31	2	126	18	137	19	714
1961	36	5	154	19	154	19	826
1962[e]	37	7	158	18	182	20	889
1963	39	8	180	19	217	23	963

Source: World Bank personnel rosters for all years. Rosters for 1955 are missing.

a. Before the 1952 reorganization this column represents the Loan Department, which included technical staff. From 1953 onward the column represents the Technical Projects Department. Hence the drop in numbers between 1952 (84) and 1953 (67); the rest of the old Loan Department went elsewhere.

b. Area departments were established in the 1952 reorganization.

c. Three area departments established: Asia and Middle East; Europe, Africa and Australia; and the Western Hemisphere.

d. Asia and Middle East area department split into Far East, and South Asia and Middle East.

e. Area departments consisted of Africa, Europe, Far East, South Asia, and Western Hemisphere.

Actually, the preceding exaggerates the institution's early technical innocence slightly: from 1947 the Bank had three in-house engineers on its staff, but, until General R. A. Wheeler, formerly of the U.S. Army Corps of Engineers, was brought aboard in March 1949, the personnel lists had these three disguised as economists. Nevertheless, even allowing for four engineers instead of one in 1947–48, a virtual revolution in Bank staffing had occurred by 1960, most of it after the 1952 reorganization. From 1953 to 1960 (see table 9-1) Bank staff grew at an annual rate of only 6.5 percent. The growth of the technical staff averaged 16 percent a year. It is true that, except in 1961, the absolute number of project people never got as big as the combined area departments, but there were three of those; relatively speaking, the technical staff outgrew them all.

This was a surprisingly quiet change. Indeed, the documentation suggests that it was almost ignored. In all of the Bank's annual reports for fiscal years 1946 to 1961, the only comment appears in the tenth, for fiscal 1955 (a ten-year retrospective): "As the number and variety of proposals presented to it has increased, the Bank has steadily had to add to its staff specialists particularly concerned with the assessment and execution of projects."[9]

9. IBRD, *Tenth Annual Report, 1954–1955*, p. 33.

A number of factors were at work here. One was clearly the prudence factor: it was circumspect to stay out of the kind of political fire into which the Bank had gotten in Brazil. There was some opportunism: supplies of available personnel were conducive to technical expansion. As Asian and some African countries became independent, growing numbers of European colonial civil servants, many with development-relevant skills and experience, became available. The personnel profile of the Bank altered in a pro-projects direction. There was also a division-of-labor factor. By the late 1950s work sharing between the two Bretton Woods institutions had further been sorted out. The IMF was to keep a cautionary watch on developing-country finances; arguably, it could run macroeconomic inter-ference for the Bank while that institution attended to its projects. Moreover, by the end of the decade, one reason for the Bank's focus on country policies had lost some of its urgency: the Bank no longer needed to work so hard to prove that, from a policy perspective, its portfolio of borrowers warranted the Bank's achieving a high credit rating itself. In 1959 World Bank bonds won the AAA rating for which the institution had been striving. The rating still had to be defended, but doing so was less onerous than getting there in the first place.

All of these elements in the institutional environment contributed to the rise of the Bank's project work, but some internal factors played an important role as well. The institution's own creditworthiness was fortified by its funders' sense that the Bank was doing solid and sophisticated project work, and management took pride in supporting high standards of project quality. Thus there is no question that the World Bank had become a far stronger project shop by the end of the 1950s and that senior management was content with that development. The question was whether, in the process, the countries-areas-policies side of the institution had lost ground. Had the projects side of operations taken charge? Some forty years later, veterans of the Bank remained deeply divided over this question.

One of the strongest voices acclaiming the dominance of projects was Warren Baum, who joined the Bank as an economist at the end of the 1950s, quickly was engaged in project activity, and, as vice president and chief of the Central Projects Staff, wound up as a principal custodian of the institution's project conscience. Baum emphasized that by insisting on project quality and therefore granting the technical experts whatever time they needed to get the quality right, management had accorded the Projects Department (founded in the reorganization of 1952) control of the timing of Bank operations. In retirement in 1986, Baum still savored the power the projects people had enjoyed.

> The Projects Department had enormous power because the Area departments could not appraise projects or supervise them except by getting a decision from the Projects Department to allocate staff for that purpose. So as Assistant Director-Transportation, I had the power to decide which of the transportation projects of the Area departments would proceed, and on what schedule. . . . [A] lot of tension grew out of this control. Of

course the basic source of the tension is the one which is inherent in Bank operations between the country focus and the project focus.[10]

In 1985, Baum's predecessor as head of Bank projects, Siem Aldewereld, had remarked in an oral history interview, "The reorganization of '52 . . . put the Projects Department into a prominent position, the center position in the World Bank."[11] Aldewereld had earlier observed that, following the reorganization in 1952 "the total responsibility for all aspects of project appraisal and supervision was put in my department, the department of technical operations, and I think it has worked out well."[12]

The theory of how project work came to dominate Bank operations was spelled out by Stanley Please, who joined the institution in the 1960s.

> The process of identifying, preparing, and appraising a project takes time, and calls into being teams of people both in the country and in the Bank—appropriate technical staff (agronomists, engineers, educators), financial analysts, economists, and so forth. Members of these teams wrestle with complex technical, financial, and economic problems, and frequently have links with other teams working on related projects in the same sector or subsector. This work takes on a life and schedule of its own, and continues into the implementation stage. Many delays are, of course, likely to occur at all stages as a consequence of project-related technical problems or nonavailability of domestic financing or cofinancing. However, the inner dynamics of the technical, financial, and administrative arrangements associated with the project cycle generate a momentum of project development and implementation within a project agency and within the Bank. It is extremely difficult and often costly—but not, of course, impossible—to interfere with this process in order to address broader problems than those directly relating to the project.[13]

In the 1970s Please shared his views about how the Bank's project emphasis had weakened its policy-reform potential with Ernest Stern, who at the end of that decade would become the most authoritative member of the school advocating that opinion. Stern and Please agreed on the overlapping question about loan vehicles: nonproject loans, they thought, were better than project loans at conveying macropolicy influence. But this last was not yet the main issue in the 1950s, which was, simply, whether the institution's project work had gotten the upper hand over its country policy efforts. Baum, Aldewereld, and others said that it had. William Iliff, who had spearheaded the 1952 reorganization, gave a nuanced, on-balance yes: The area departments established in the reorganization were key in developing country-specific expertise and promoting constructive relations with borrowers.

10. Warren Baum, interview, World Bank Oral History Program, July 23, 1986, p. 4.

11. Siem Aldewereld, interview, World Bank Oral History Program, November 2, 1985, p. 16.

12. Siem Aldewereld, interview, World Bank Oral History Program, July 13, 1961, p. 29.

13. Stanley Please, *The Hobbled Giant: Essays on the World Bank* (Boulder, Colo.: Westview Press, 1984), p. 27.

They had to signal the creditworthiness of a country for a Bank loan to be made. But then, said Iliff, the new Technical Operations Department became central:

> The technical aspects of these operations had become so important that we decided to cut away altogether from the loan department the technical examination of projects which had hitherto been carried out within the loan department, and this led to our recommendation that a technical operations department should be established whose job it was, in short, to review the technical, the economic, the financial and the managerial aspects of every project that came to the Bank for financing.[14]

On the other side of the debate, however, there is a chorus of the Bank's old hands—among them, Benjamin King, Peter Wright, Richard Demuth, and Mervyn Weiner—denying that the development of the institution's project work ever needed to impair its effectiveness as an intervener for policy reform. Leading this chorus is Burke Knapp who, as the chairman of the institution's Loan Committee, was at the pinnacle of its operational decision structure for more than twenty years.[15] Knapp dismisses the Baum-Please claims as exaggerations. In the 1950s and 1960s, he says, every loan proposal came to the Loan Committee from a task force chaired by an area department. To be sure, the committee almost always accepted the views of the Projects Department and heeded its requests for more time; and the committee was always mindful of the president's injunction to optimize project quality in the interests of borrower and lender creditworthiness. But the ruling committee was chaired by a veteran of an area department who was determined to maintain a constructive projects-policy balance.

This standoff can be resolved as follows. Together the project and the policy advocates reflect the fact that virtually any external pro-development agency tends to be crosshatched by two organizational principles. One is geographic. Work dealing with the agency's country clients—concerning, for example, country policies— is likely to be organized by country desks and regional bureaus. At the same time, the Bank and other such agencies also have required *technical* expertise; and their technical experts, their disciplinary specialists, tend to be grouped largely in sectoral and subsectoral units. In the Bank the technical work was mostly project work—grouped in the 1950s and 1960s into the Projects Department.

This basic matrix structure in the operational aspects of the World Bank was altogether normal. What was different, compared with other international operations, was the *absence* of country-area-policy dominance. In virtually every bilateral aid agency that took shape in the 1950s and 1960s the pattern was the same as in foreign ministries; the "line" organizations were made up of country desks organized into regional sections or bureaus. The agencies' technical units were deployed as staffs supporting the line units. But (this also, incidentally, was the typical military pattern) the line controlled.

---

14. William Iliff, interview, World Bank Oral History Program, August 12, 1961, pp. 3–4.

15. The Committee, by the way, never took a vote during that period, which attests to the influence of the chairman.

In the World Bank from 1952 to 1972, however, there *was* no clear line-staff distinction in institutional operations. The Projects Department and the area departments shared power. Each was to behave as quasi line, quasi staff, with the Loan Committee and its chief marrying the two in a balanced way. For many of the players, the arrangement worked well enough. But it was disquieting to many of the pro-policy and area players. As they looked at the surge in voice and clout that projects work had achieved within the institution during the 1950s, as well as at the dominant role of the regional line units in other aid agencies, not to speak of external affairs and defense ministries, they felt the culture of the institution had tilted against them.

Windows on Policy

In the early 1960s area- and country-organized units in the Bank were looking for ways to make the influencing of borrowers' policies a more central aspect of Bank operations. Three such tactics were tested in Latin America during the 1960s, India in the middle and later 1960s, and Indonesia from the later 1960s to 1972.

Latin American Programs of Projects

In the Latin American region, area executives decided not to compete with the institution's project emphasis, but to adapt it to their policy-influencing purposes. Veteran Bank economist Barend de Vries has commented on the atmosphere in the Latin American regional division: "It was the fastest stepping, most exciting group, under the leadership of Burke Knapp. We had a very good, active group of economists and operators working."[16] Even after Knapp moved on to other positions, the Western Hemisphere Department, later the Latin American and Caribbean (LAC) region, of the Bank retained its distinctiveness. Its leadership was assumed by Orvis Schmidt, then during the Woods presidency, by Gerald Alter. Both were known as strong, effective area-program executives.

Under Alter, the Latin American region was greatly concerned about the macroeconomic policies of borrowing countries. As he recalls it,

> We put a much greater emphasis than most of the other regions did on the general economic policy aspects of the Bank's work. At a very early stage when I became chief of the Western Hemisphere department, I recognized that the Bank's project lending needed to be put into a much broader context than some of the other departments seemed to be doing.[17]

The Bank's main policy concern in this region was aggregate demand management. In good part, said Alter, the focus on macroeconomics was

> produced by the simple fact [that] the inflationary forces in Latin America were generally stronger, and you just could not avoid facing up to the macro aspect of the problem. . . .

16. Barend de Vries, interview, World Bank Oral History Program, June 28, 1990, p. 2.
17. Gerald Alter, interview with John Lewis and Devesh Kapur, November 13, 1990, p. 1.

Even in the simple fields, as, for example, electric power, transport—the traditional infrastructure sectors—we were always running into the problem of the rate covenant in the Bank's loans, which required, in an inflationary environment, adjustment processes. And that ran into the whole question of stabilization policy.[18]

The Latin American region's answer to this policy problem was to reaffirm the practice initiated in the late 1940s: it organized sets of projects into country programs, and it made the availability and pacing of these programs contingent on the country's adoption of policy reforms that had been discussed with the Bank:

As the thing developed, and particularly in the latter part of the regime of Mr. Woods, I became increasingly convinced of the necessity of the Bank to prepare, particularly in the Western Hemisphere department at that time, lending programs which consisted of a program of project lending, extending over two or three years in the future, with some determination of what kind of policy changes we felt the country should make in order for us to respond in the appropriate manner to their willingness to undertake these policy changes. We had to, of course, take into account the readiness of the projects.[19]

This pattern of lending was resumed in Brazil after the takeover of the new military government in 1964. The Bank dispatched to Brazil its largest economic mission up to that time.[20] Its recommendations became the basis of a large lending program in transportation, steel, and electric power. The mission's work ended in a letter of agreement on economic policies between the Bank and Brazil, and George Woods conducted a day-long meeting with the Board on the Brazilian economy, using the mission's report as a text. The same approach was being applied in Mexico, Colombia, and elsewhere.[21]

In the 1960s Alter's Latin American operation was conducted with crisp effectiveness. It collaborated closely with the IMF's Latin American program under Alter's counterpart, Walter Robichek, as well as with bilateral donors, notably the U.S. Alliance for Progress. But proponents of the complementarity of the Bank's

18. Ibid., p. 1.

19. Ibid., p. 2.

20. The mission consisted of twenty economists including Shahid Husain (who was later to head the Brazil Division and subsequently serve as vice president, LAC), Richard Goode (who subsequently became the head of the Fiscal Affairs Department of the IMF), Hans Adler (who led a special transportation team), and Shigeharu Takashi (who did the work on agriculture). It was received by the Brazilian finance minister, Octavio Gouvea de Bulhoes, and the Brazilian planning minister, Roberto Campos, and concluded with a two-hour meeting with the president.

21. See the discussion of Mexico later in the chapter. As noted, Colombia had been the site of the Bank's first country mission and had sustained a special relationship with the Bank. In 1968 Burke Knapp's briefing of the newly arrived President McNamara identified Colombia as "a country which is of special interest because of our sponsorship of a consultative group . . . and because of our specially intimate relationships with the IMF and AID in attempting to influence Colombian economic and financial policies." Memorandum, J. Burke Knapp to Robert S. McNamara, "Briefing Paper on Colombia," May 6, 1968.

projects and policies sides would argue that the LAC program was no exception to mainstream Bank practice; it was just mainstream practice done right, so that the objectives of good project work and constructive policy influence both could be served—and without conscripting the unorthodoxy of nonproject lending to the pro-policy cause. Both before and after McNamara's arrival, there had been debate over whether and when "the Bank should make program loans—nonproject loans." But it was Alter's recollection that during his period in the LAC region, although "nonproject lending . . . of course lent itself very easily to this kind of general policy discussion with the government on some of the chief elements in both their macro policies and their micro policies . . . we did not really get into this field very much."[22]

If the "program-of-projects" mode of lending was indeed the mainstream way of melding the Bank's policies and projects agendas, why did it not prevail in other regional programs and beyond the 1960s? There are two answers. In the view of one school of practitioners, who would become dominant by the end of the 1970s, the easy compatibility of project detail and macropolicy influence in the same project-lending transactions was a myth. In the view of Please and Stern, for example, the lender's persuasive energies tended to be spent on project details, and the rhythms of country policy and projects work were not easily synchronized. The other answer was that the program-of-projects vehicle for policy influence tended to get devalued by the circumstances of the 1970s. The Bank itself came to assign a higher priority to program expansion than to policy conditionality; it changed its program priorities to favor poverty alleviation; and alternative, much more lightly conditioned, sources of credit became available after the first oil shock. Meanwhile, at least for those not deeply skeptical about project-macropolicy compatibility, the Latin American operation had been demonstrating one technique for escaping the grip of excessively narrow project-mindedness.

Leverage in India

In the early 1960s the Bank was just beginning to establish a view of India's—and also of neighboring Pakistan's—policy requirements. The problem for India was not to stabilize demand, as was the case in Latin America, but to reform agriculture (see chapter 8) and to liberalize trade and industry. In the eyes of the Bank and the U.S. Agency for International Development, the other donor with which the Bank was closely associated in delivering this aid, industrial and trade liberalization had both internal and external dimensions. Internally, it meant thinning out the self-perpetuating clutter of economic regulations and controls that had accumulated over the lives of successive governments and was stultifying India's markets and sapping efficiency. Externally, because its currency had become over-

22. Alter, interview, November 13, 1990, p. 2.

valued, the Indian government had raised its import barriers—not only tariffs but quantitative controls and bans—in an effort to implement import-substitution strategies and shrink balance of payments deficits. Trade liberalization would mean reducing the barriers, diminishing the accumulated drag on exports, simplifying or eliminating foreign exchange licensing, rationalizing exchange rates, and getting the effective exchange rates for imports and exports into closer balance.

In seeking these various policy objectives, the Bank showed a disposition to use a new kind of lending instrument. With IDA already launched and India its largest client, the Bank began some nonproject lending for "maintenance" industrial imports in 1964. Except for an agreement by the government to simplify import controls, the first of these loans was not policy conditioned. But the instrument, as it were, was at the ready. At this time the Bank also took on a round of heavy policy analysis.

The new Bank president, George Woods, had done some previous work with India, and when in 1964 regional staff recommended a more intensive look at India's economic situation (the Third Five-Year Plan for 1961–66 was falling well short of its goals), Woods opted for more intensity than the staff had intended. The leader of the review team was to be the respected American economist, Bernard Bell, from outside the Bank. Woods authorized Bell to recruit colleagues from both inside and outside the institution, agreed to broad terms of reference for the mission, and persuaded his old acquaintance, T. T. Krishnamachari, the Indian finance minister, to agree to the exercise.

The Bell mission worked hard and long, first in New Delhi, then in Washington, and informally in tandem with U.S., in particular, AID, people in both places. It was decided that the United States would continue to lead in pressing agricultural reforms, while the Bank, interacting as appropriate with the IMF, would be the front-runner for liberalization, including the embedded and touchy issue of devaluation.

Both the multilateral and the bilateral reform promoters worked with members of the Indian cabinet, especially Minister of Agriculture C. Subramaniam and Minister of Planning Asoka Mehta. But their heaviest dealings were with a group of senior officials and government economists including L. K. Jha, secretary to the prime minister, S. Bhootalingam; senior secretary in Finance, I. G. Patel, economic adviser in the same ministry; and Pitamber Pant of the Planning Commission. This inner group of economic bureaucrats played key roles in maintaining policy momentum across the transition from Prime Minister Lal Bahadur Shastri to Prime Minister Indira Gandhi when the former died in January 1966. Moreover, when the political level of the government fell into de facto stalemate after the February 1967 election, these were among the core group of officials who pressed ahead to implement the reforms that by then had been broadly decided at the political level.

Along with some of their close colleagues, the members of this subset of advisers and administrators were sophisticated pragmatists. They had come to favor a shift toward deregulation and freer markets on its merits. But, given the abundance of contradictory rhetoric as well as political and bureaucratic inertia, the reason they opted for liberalization when they did was straightforward. As L.K. Jha put it, "That was what George Woods told us we had to do to get aid."[23] New American aid commitments had been interrupted, partly because of the brief war between India and Pakistan in September 1965. IDA's first replenishment was lagging. The interveners saw little chance of reviving aid, especially program aid, on the scale Indian planning required—nor did those wielding the leverage *want* this to happen—until reforms were in place.

The Bell mission produced a massive and comprehensive report consisting of thirteen volumes. The first of them detailed sixteen actions "required on the part of India," ranging from restraint in defense spending to increased foreign private investment. Except for the breadth of the policy intrusion, the core official group had little difficulty with the gist of the recommendations—except for the very first: in plain English Bell demanded a major devaluation, whether formal or de facto. While seeing the case for such a move themselves, the insiders knew the subject was politically explosive. To most politicians, most of the vocal Indian press, and the informed public, lowering the rupee during an era of fixed exchange rates would look like lowering the flag under external pressure.

The issue between India and the Bank, acting in behalf of the India Aid Consortium, was negotiated by George Woods and Asoka Mehta in Washington in the spring of 1966. The operative question was that of liberalization; the agricultural reforms, as indicated in chapter 8, were already in train. Devaluation was needed to raise the rupee prices of imports enough to let prices instead of direct controls do much of the job of rationing scarce imports. The Bank pressed for it, the Gandhi government secretly decided to make the move, Mehta indicated an array of other promising measures, and the parties agreed on a quid pro quo: what the Indians understood to be a best-effort promise from Woods to raise $900 million of nonproject money from the aid consortium annually for the next three years.

To the dismay of some of its own cabinet members, the Indian government sharply devalued the rupee in early June 1966. The political firestorm that followed exceeded most expectations. The polity, it turned out, already rubbed raw by President Lyndon Johnson's "short-tethering" of food aid, was thoroughly out of patience with external "pressurizing" (see chapter 8). The country that summer suffered a meteorologically improbable second drought in a row, and between the devaluation and the drought, Mrs. Gandhi's wing of the Congress Party fared badly in the February 1967 parliamentary election.

23. John P. Lewis, *India's Political Economy: Governance and Reform* (Oxford University Press, 1995), p. 136. This subsection draws freely from this source.

Thus the Bank's Indian venture into policy-conditioned lending was commonly perceived to be a political disaster, and for some time neither the bilateral donor community nor the Bank itself was disposed to go the same route. At the same time, looked at from the perspective of the insider group of economic officials who would run the economic side of Indian public affairs for the next couple of years, the policy-levering experiment was a considerable success, except for one thing. The insiders already had swallowed the bitter pill of devaluation. The latter was in place, and the effects were not allowed to erode quickly: postdevaluation inflationary pressures were contained.[24] The officials implemented a number of partial but significant decontrolling and liberalizing steps that, as it turned out, could not be greatly or easily reversed.

Thus, on balance, the pro-reform venture might have been judged a limited success, *except* that the money side of the transaction fell apart. It took many months longer to get together the first $900 million installment of program money than had been expected, and during the second and third years the consortium, with the United States marginally in the rear, did not even come close. The insiders felt swindled. Their disgust with external pressurizing now matched that of their political masters, and the government determined never again to become so aid dependent. It built its foreign exchange reserves. Instead of retreating into greater protectionism, by 1969 it throttled back on public investment, on future aid requirements, and therefore on projected growth, more than either of its principal donors, USAID and IDA, thought appropriate.

The Indian experiment in the use of conditioned nonproject lending in support of designated policy reforms taught mixed lessons. But it had to be a learning experience for the World Bank if for no other reason than the number of future players who were involved.[25] Edward Mason and Robert Asher single out the episode as the sharpest use of pro-policy leverage up to 1973, and, at least superficially, the way the Indians were induced to commit 1966 to a set of liberalization reforms against the promise of increased flexible assistance looks like a direct antecedent of the structural adjustment lending that would be invented fourteen years later. However, there were some important procedural differences. The loan instruments involved were not particular loans linked to particular reforms but rather a whole program, indeed, a multidonor program, of program loans, linked to a reform agenda. Most of the Indian undertakings were less precise, less contractual, than what would become the SAL pattern. And a number of them grew not

24. During the seven years preceding 1966, the official wholesale price index rose at an annual rate of 6.5 percent. In the seven years following 1966 the average annual increase was 7.4 percent.

25. These included, along with Bernard Bell himself, David Hopper, Jean Baneth, and Stanley Please of the Bell Mission, as well as, among those involved on the USAID side, Hollis Chenery, Ernest Stern, and Paul Isenmen. John Lewis, one of the authors of the present study, was director of the USAID mission at the time.

out of promises of future change, but out of donor-recipient interchange (what would come to be called "dialogue") and were already adopted. Nevertheless, in retrospect the genealogy from 1966 to 1979 would look fairly obvious.

Togetherness in Indonesia

In Latin America the Bank used programs of project lending to advance its policy views concerning the inflationary tendencies of some countries in the region. In India it used nonproject lending, by itself and in concert with some of its consortium allies, to press for agricultural and liberalization reforms. In Indonesia from the late 1960s onward, the macroeconomic reform preferences it wished to promote were largely shared by a key group of Indonesia policymakers, but the modalities of the relationship were close and congenial enough to generate a considerable measure of policy influence.

In the Sukarno years, ending in the mid-1960s, Indonesia had little more than a nominal connection with the World Bank, which it quit in August 1965, as it did the IMF. Robert McNamara's recollection, that the rebirth of the Bank's relationship with Indonesia dated from his visit to Jakarta in June 1968, is elliptic. But he is certainly right that the relationship, once regenerated, was nearly unique.[26] The recollection is that, soon after his arrival at the Bank (April 1, 1968) the new president spotted Indonesia as the most populous poor country, save China, with which the Bank was doing no business and resolved to make it one of his first country visits.

The visit was indeed decisive, but the way had been prepared by various developments, some of which reached back before the final turbulent and bloody years of the Sukarno era. In particular, in the late 1950s the Ford Foundation had provided fellowships to a few bright young Indonesians for Ph.D. training in economics, mainly at the University of California, Berkeley, where they became immersed in Western economic theory and policy analysis. The first of them, Widjojo Nitisastro, received his degree in 1961. Widjojo and four others came home to university posts. But when General Suharto assumed executive power in March 1966 he made this whole group of newly minted economists advisers to his government. By 1967 Widjojo was the formal head of BAPPENAS, the official

26. McNamara's vivid memory of the way he came to focus on Indonesia was expressed in an interview with the authors on April 1, 1991. Neither the latter nor Bank documentation attributed geopolitical considerations to the renewal of Bank interest. However, it is clear that the bilateral aid donors, who, with the United States in the lead, had instituted a consultative aid group under the chairmanship of the Netherlands (the Inter-Governmental Group for Indonesia) in late 1966, were highly mindful of the country's Southeast Asian location and of the recent violent communist insurgency, the resumption of which it was a major purpose of both the Suharto regime and the Western donors to forestall. See the memoir by the then-resident American ambassador, Marshall Green, *Indonesia: Crisis and Transformation, 1965–1968* (Washington, D.C.: Compass Press, 1990).

planning agency, and soon all five "technocrats," as they were called, were holding ministerial portfolios.[27]

The same set of economists would continue to rotate through the country's top macroeconomic posts for a quarter century. What the new World Bank president would find in June 1968 was that this group had already accomplished a great deal in the three years since Suharto had taken command, amidst horrendous inflation and staggering foreign debt. Average prices were rising at an annual rate of 600 percent. Exports had dropped 24 percent since 1959. Debt-service obligations exceeded export earnings, and foreign exchange reserves had fallen to $17 million, which translated to about nine days of imports.

The government announced it would rejoin the IMF and the World Bank and called for a meeting of creditors to reschedule the country's debts. Only when this had happened in September 1966 was the stabilization program on which the technocrats had been working set out in a series of presidential decrees. Among other things, the latter raised formal interest rates, stopped central bank credits to state enterprises, ended consumer goods subsidies, abolished all quantitative import restrictions, and devalued the rupiah. In October 1966, the country's bilateral concessional donors constituted the Inter-Governmental Group for Indonesia. The IGGI, which had its first formal meeting in February 1967, pledged new aid to cushion the stabilization program.

The apparent results of the program were striking. Austere budget and credit policies helped bring inflation down from 635 percent in 1965 to 6 percent in 1970. An export surge helped relieve the country's balance of payments and fiscal imbalances. A World Bank–financed study viewed the record with some awe:

> The most remarkable aspect of the 1966 stabilization program was that the drop of inflation was accompanied by economic expansion rather than contraction. Real GDP in 1967 . . . was actually 2 percent higher than in 1966. This unusual phenomenon . . . was the result of increased productivity achieved through better allocation of resources, an increase in exports induced by devaluation, and foreign aid, which reduced inflation by making imported consumer goods available and by increasing the output of domestically produced goods manufactured with imported capital goods.[28]

Meanwhile, from 1966 on, the Washington multilaterals had been reestablishing contact with Indonesia. The Fund, integrally involved in the debt-relief exercise, posted a resident, Kemal Siber, in Jakarta, and the Bank began a cautious orderly process of reengagement from the time the Indonesian finance minister and

27. In the early Suharto years the ministerial lead on the government's economic side was shared by the Sultan of Jogjakarta and by Sumitro, who had studied economics in Rotterdam, in part under Pieter Lieftinck. Sumitro had been minister of finance in the mid-1950s and had returned from exile in 1967. But the continuity of the ("Berkeley") technocrats from 1966 onward captures the essential story for the purposes of this chapter.

28. Wing Thye Woo, Bruce Glassburner, and Anwar Nasution, *Macroeconomic Policies, Crises, and Long-Term Growth in Indonesia, 1965–90* (World Bank, 1994), p. 30.

central bank governor called on Burke Knapp during the 1966 annual meetings. Bank economists traveled to Indonesia in the summer of 1967 to prepare for an economic study and then visited at length in the fall to conduct the study. By January 1968 Jakarta was heavy with Bank travelers. Vice President Mohamed Shoaib visited. So did Asia Director Peter Cargill. The chief author of the Bank's new Economic Memorandum on Indonesia came back to present his report to the government. The possibility of having a resident Bank team in Jakarta had already been discussed, and certain administrative issues were joined well before McNamara's intervention: Bernard Bell, who had dealt with Indonesia in his pre-Bank career, agreed with those who thought the mooted resident mission should report to the Projects rather than the area department, and he seemed to favor less autonomy than did Peter Cargill of the area department for what would come to be called the Resident Staff, Indonesia (RSI).

Indeed, Robert McNamara was well prepared for his arrival in Jakarta in mid-June (he had sent Shoaib and Bell ahead to see if his visit would be timely). Furthermore, on the Indonesian side, he was received by a remarkably seasoned set of young policy managers who already had been operating with a great deal of success. It still is correct to say that the McNamara visit may have been the most consequential that a Bank president has paid to a borrowing country. It galvanized the president into making Indonesia, from the Bank's side, an instant special case.

McNamara hit it off with his fellow Berkeley alumnus Widjojo and Widjojo's colleagues.[29] He and President Suharto admired each other, and the Bank president on the spot adopted unique modalities for a country program. On June 15 he told a press conference: "This is the first time that the World Bank has established this sort of a Resident Mission in a developing area. . . . [Y]our problem in Indonesia demands a unique solution and a greater concentration of effort than we have applied anywhere else in the world."[30] Bernard Bell was confirmed as the president's lieutenant for Indonesian operations. The program was to be run from Jakarta; the resident mission would become larger, more senior, and, in its technical capacities, more diverse than any of its contemporaries. And from Jakarta, Bell would have a direct line to the president of the Bank; no one else in the institution could countermand his recommendations.

From the outset, the policy-influencing strategies for Indonesia were striking for their procedural character. On substance, there was little disagreement over policy that was reserved to the technocrats and their Bank advisers. This was the zone of macroeconomic policy centering in the finance ministry and the planning establishment. President Suharto (he had assumed the office in 1967) was a general, and

29. For accuracy, note that one of the technocrats, Mohammed Sadli, got his M.S. in engineering economics at MIT, rather than at Berkeley. He received his Ph.D. in economics from the University of Indonesia.

30. Robert S. McNamara, "Statement at a Press Conference by Robert S. McNamara," Djakarta, Indonesia, June 15, 1968.

his government, in good part, was a government of generals, many of whom were corrupt. One of them, a former army medical officer, General H. Ibru Sutowo, played (much to his chief's liking) a swashbuckling role as the leader of the country's growing and aggrandizing oil industry. These other zones of public affairs would pose problems for the Bank in future years.

But President Suharto—motivated, it would appear, by the country's dire macroeconomic problems his regime had inherited—had carved out the finance-planning zone as one in which his professional economists would hold sway. And they, as the Fund already had learned, had no basic argument with the kind of macroeconomic policies the Bank was disposed to recommend. They were committed to balance in the formal fiscal budget (the parallel "oil budget" would become something else) as well as to monetary conservatism, prudent foreign borrowing, and heavy reliance on market processes. Also, like President Suharto himself, the technocrats, despite a penchant for austere demand management, wished to avoid any uprising by the rural poor and to maintain urban rice supplies.[31]

But all of this substantive togetherness did not render the Bank's policy advice redundant. On the contrary, the technocrats craved all they could get, as long as it was not broadcast. They wanted analytical help and close-in discussion. Procedurally, this was the classic case of intimate, ongoing, everlasting dialogue, with few if any spurs or prods in evidence. While they were engaged in daily policy discussions, the Bank and the government of Indonesia acted like a couple of old cronies.

The closeness was rare in Bank annals. It differed markedly from the arm's-length formalism of the Bank's programs-of-projects lending in Latin America and its quasi-adversarial relations with India. The affability of the Indonesian relationship was partly a matter of personalities. Bernard Bell, strengthened by his mandate from McNamara and perhaps by lessons learned in India, and already known to his Indonesian advisers, was a highly effective interlocutor. His nondoctrinaire pragmatism suited the Indonesian temper. The story is told how, in his first year, he transformed a fault-finding critique of Indonesian performance that had been made in his absence by a Bank traveler from Washington into a review of performance gains and joint donor-recipient opportunities for improvement that made the ensuing IGGI meeting a positive experience for all concerned.[32]

The personal skills of the technocrats were at least as important. They were not only gifted and affable but were self-confident enough to receive much close-in advice without being captured or intimidated. They relied on an assortment of advisers. Even before the Bank arrived, there were some sent by Professor Jan Tinbergen as well as a platoon of specialists from Harvard's Development Advisory

31. Woo and others, *Macroeconomic Policies, Crises, and Long-Term Growth in Indonesia,* p. 37, emphasize the concern to forestall any revival of leftist insurgency in the countryside.

32. David Cole, Harvard Institute of International Development, Jakarta, interview with John Lewis, Richard Webb, and Devesh Kapur, November 26, 1991.

Service; later, counselors came from three American and European investment banking houses and a few others were bilaterally supplied. The technocrats were attentive to all these pundits and then called their own shots, in ways the Bank (the adviser bringing the most money) typically approved.

The intimacy of the Bank's early relationship with Indonesia can also be traced to political structuring. Whereas in India there was a sharp contrast between a group of "insiders" and a larger polity, Indonesia had no larger polity to speak of in 1970. The country had a weak overt political opposition with a small voice, some business interests, anxieties about rural groundswells, and the generals. Dominating the entire scene, however, was the president, who made the technocrats and the Bank mutually dependent. The Bank needed the access to presidential decisions that the technocrats afforded. At the same time the latter greatly valued the way the Bank, while it was favorably influencing other donors and investors, was also helping them maintain their presidential mandate.

As was inevitable, the honeymoon ended in 1972. Bell's direct access to the boss, especially when not replicated elsewhere in the Bank's institutional structure, put too much strain on the normal administrative process to endure. Tensions between Washington and Jakarta escalated. In September 1971, in a delayed monthly letter to McNamara, Bell reported an improvisation. General Sutowo of the oil combine, Pertamina, had come to him ("Pertamina being, fortunately, a go-go organization [that] has had fewer hesitations than most others about the rate at which fertilizer consumption will grow")[33] on the verge of accepting a high-cost French and U.S. Export-Import Bank deal for a new fertilizer plant. Bell persuaded him to hold off on the deal by tentatively committing substitute IDA funding. The problem was, it was a *public* sector factory and this was a time when the Bank was not yet comfortable with the financing of public sector manufacturing.

At this point, the Bank's top managers may well have felt that Jakarta-centered decisionmaking had gone too far, as was certainly suggested by the rounds of anguish the government of Indonesia emitted the following summer when it learned Bell was being withdrawn. McNamara stood fast against this onslaught, but his explanation—that now that the 1972 reorganization was opening up some new vice presidential slots, he wanted Bell to have one of them, in Africa—sounded rather weak.

The Bell honeymoon did not end in an annulment, however. Although the relationship became less idyllic, it remained organizationally and procedurally distinctive, substantively complex, and (with Bernard Bell now based in Washington and once again involved) it had to grapple with some of the issues sidestepped in the initial years. In fact, Indonesia is a policy case that is interesting to follow through the 1970s, and discussion of it is resumed in a later section of the chapter.

33. Letter, Bernard R. Bell to Robert S. McNamara, Letter no. 809, September 2, 1971, p. 3.

The McNamara Transition

The three cases just sketched do not adequately represent the varieties of policy activism into which area units of the Bank entered during the 1960s. For example, the absence of Sub-Saharan Africa, even though it was barely emerging from colonialism, is conspicuous in the light of the heavy claims the region would impose on World Bank attention from the 1970s onward. But even more troublesome to well-paced narration is the way these cases bridge into the McNamara presidency without, as it were, proper punctuation.

Robert McNamara burst on the Bank in a way no other president has. As he recollects it, one of his initial themes was policy reform along the lines some of the area units of the Bank had been pushing.[34] He certainly had congruent interests: he was an efficiency addict, had a distinguished background in business, and (as he would demonstrate in his opposition to U.S. budgetary deficits in the 1980s) favored responsible macrofinance. Ideologically, McNamara was to the left of his predecessors. While greatly valuing the efficiency of a market mechanism bounded by sensible public policies, he was less hostile to public enterprises than earlier presidents, and he saw a major role for the state in developing countries. But none of this put him on sharply different macropolicy tracks from the ones the institution had been promoting.

What was different was the intervention of other new priorities. The new president was determined to increase the scale and broaden the impact of the Bank/IDA operations. In support of this, he was deeply committed to a new regime of country programming. He was equally determined to tackle poverty far more aggressively than the Bank had heretofore done. He would become determined to find ways to do more for smallholder agriculture, and, to the extent possible, for other classes of the rural poor.

A number of other subjects found a place on McNamara's agenda at or soon after the time of his arrival. Population was one of these. Environment, urban development, and education were others. Macropolicy reform was one of these second-order goals. The latter were not unvalued. They were simply crowded aside, in part only because time and energies were finite. In addition, the priority accorded program expansion diminished the opportunity for pro-reform leverage. And this effect was aggravated by external developments before the 1970s were half over. The net result was that, the 1970s (until their final year) were a period in which most of the Bank's policy-influencing efforts were upstaged and ineffective. Yet the decade witnessed doctrinal changes that were to become more influential later.

---

34. Robert McNamara, interview with John Lewis, Richard Webb, and Devesh Kapur, Washington, October 3, 1991.

Policy and Its Promotion in the 1970s

Those interested in seeing the World Bank play a more active role in influencing borrowing members' policies, especially macroeconomic policies, encountered unexpected impediments in the 1970s. Among these inhibiting factors were the "money targeting" that McNamara initiated and that gathered momentum after the reorganization of 1972, the "oil shock" of 1973–74 and its consequences, and a set of political complexities that helped shape operations. The question is, precisely how did these factors affect the substantive content of the Bank's policy messages? Were changes of consequence under way, whether or not the messages could be effectively delivered at the moment? Was there an as-yet-unassembled but stronger policy-influencing regime gathering steam in the 1970s? Did the availability of other sources of foreign exchange weaken Bank leverage on behalf of macropolicy reform? In which countries? These are issues that arose before the Bank encountered "the bend in the road" in 1979–80.

Inhibiting Factors

One of the earliest factors to inhibit the Bank's influence on policy reform was of McNamara's own making.

MONEY TARGETING AND REORGANIZATION.   Policy promotion within a frame of country programming was one of the themes with which McNamara came on board. His intention was to "focus on policies and on the preparation of leading programs stretching several years into the future as a backdrop for the individual operation."[35] Insofar as there was a contest between policy and project, in 1972 the president presided over a reorganization that appeared to strengthen the area/ policy hand. Most of the personnel of the great central projects departments were dispersed to the regional units and put under the command of regional vice presidents, who tended to be either country economists or operations-managing generalists in what would become the Young Professional mold. In 1990 Warren Baum still expressed strong regrets over the way this reorganization reduced the power of the projects side of the house.[36]

What this move did, however, was not so much diminish the constraints on the linkages between loan programs and macropolicy reforms as switch them elsewhere. The newly empowered area chiefs were now overwhelmed with sharply increased lending targets. Area managers were told to expand their investment lending radically; hence their personal incentives to meet the new goals became

35. Alter, interview, November 13, 1990, p. 2.
36. Warren Baum, interview with John Lewis, Richard Webb, and Devesh Kapur, November 13, 1990.

very strong. The president's intention was decidedly to expand without sacrificing project quality. How well this second purpose was served is still in dispute. In any event, the expansion effort left the heads of regional and country operations little room for adding policy burdens to their project transactions. The net effect of the Bank's internal changes in the early 1970s on policy-based lending might have been a standoff. But before one could tell, the whole issue was bumped aside by the most important economic happening of the decade: an exogenous force that jolted the entire economic world from the path it had been following.

THE OIL SHOCK. This jolt was the first oil shock of 1973–74. As far as development and North-South matters were concerned, the 1970s were filled with headliner themes. Issues ranging from antipoverty, pro-employment, rural development, redistribution, and basic needs suddenly figured heavily in the institution's agenda, following McNamara's arrival (see chapter 5). Equally ground-shaking was the great North-South dialogue that became overt in the (spring 1974) Sixth Special Session of the UN General Assembly. Therein the South articulated its demand for a New International Economic Order (NIEO), which remained a headline until late 1981.

Without question, however, the defining event of the decade, which, among other things, triggered and empowered the NIEO cause, was the abrupt fourfold rise in petroleum prices imposed by Organization of Petroleum Exporting Countries, at the turn of 1973–74. Much of world's economic history of at least the succeeding half dozen years—and, quite plausibly, of the next decade and a half—can be traced back to this event. This is not to say that all the bad—or the good—that ensued was "caused" by OPEC's action. But because the jolt was so sharp and its impacts had such wide ramifications, the subsequent experiences of many countries and groups of countries were far different from what they would have been without the shock.

In the Bank, the oil shock had a profound effect on the Bank's evolving possibilities for influencing borrowers' policies. In the first place, the Bank itself immediately was seized by and preoccupied with the impact on its oil-importing developing-country members.[37] Like the Fund, the Bank was concerned to get some quick-disbursing loans to the "most seriously affected countries" to offset part of the increased petroleum claims on their foreign exchange. And this was simply a question of immediate damage repair; there was little thought of stipulating policy reforms that would help borrowers adjust to enduring changes in their terms of trade.

37. Robert S. McNamara, *The McNamara Years at the World Bank* (Johns Hopkins University Press, 1981), pp. 278–81. See also Hollis Chenery, "Restructuring the World Economy," *Foreign Affairs,* vol. 53, no. 2 (January 1975), pp. 242–63; and Hollis B. Chenery, "Restructuring the World Economy: Round II," *Foreign Affairs,* vol. 59, no. 5 (Summer 1981), pp. 1102–20.

As for policy-influencing loans, the bigger shift was in the way the oil shock weakened borrowers' receptivity to such influence. Of the resulting changes, the largest was the way commercial bank lending became an alternative for official loans to the oil-importing middle-income countries, notably in Latin America and East Asia. The oil price hike handed Saudi Arabia and the other oil-laden, lightly populated oil exporters enormous windfalls, much larger than they could invest immediately. For safekeeping, they deposited these surpluses in American and European commercial banks, where the depositors, sated with their windfalls, were content to accept very low interest rates. The banks thereupon recycled the OPEC savings to borrowers in newly industrializing countries (NICs) and middle-income countries (MICs) eager to invest to sustain their rapid growth rates of the 1960s. With the commercial banks competing for their business, the borrowing countries got their loans at bargain rates, indeed—in view of the general inflation to which the oil price hike had contributed—often at negative real rates. Few of the borrowers hesitated when the banks persuaded them to accept variable rather than fixed interest rates for the first time. After all, the current rates were low, and this cheap money came without policy strings or even lectures. The World Bank, meanwhile, prodded by its own targets, continued to do a large volume of mostly project lending. But its ability to attach policy, as opposed to project, conditions was undercut by the ready availability to the NICs and MICs of commercial-loan alternatives.

Bank clients became averse to Bank-type policy advice for a second strong reason: a whole new set of donors had been created. For the balance of the 1970s the major oil exporters, with Kuwait and Saudi Arabia in the lead, became (in terms of percentage of GNP) more generous donors of Official Development Assistance than any member of the Organization for Economic Cooperation and Development had ever been. Their aid was provided by regional and OPEC-wide as well as national agencies; and they inspired and contributed disproportionately to a new universal multilateral organization, the International Fund for Agricultural Development (IFAD). Most of this new aid flowed to other Arab, Islamic, and North African countries. It made the recipients less dependent on the World Bank for a time; and, in the South-South idiom, the new donors hesitated to intrude on their recipients' policy prerogatives.

Third, the oil shock overlapped with the conversion of several populous previous aid recipients into major oil exporters. In Nigeria and Mexico, oil production boomed soon after prices surged, and both countries lost most of their eligibility for official concessional loans. Hence they used their oil assets to plunge heavily into unconditioned commercial debt. Indonesia—the most populous of the oil exporters (other than the then Soviet Union)—kept its aid flow and Bank-centered policy dialogue ongoing in the cordoned-off sector of government operations described earlier. But its separated oil economy burgeoned and, like Mexico, plunged it into debt.

Except for Indonesia, this last set of countries, like the Arab oil exporters and their aid dependents, and like the NICs and MICs of East Asia and Latin America, lost their appetite for intensive policy-laden loans from official lenders. It would take a second (1979) oil shock plus the interest rate shock the latter prompted to make many of these borrowers once again receptive to pro-reform leverage, in part by increasing the need for fast-disbursing transfers, in part by diminishing (after some lags) the presence of alternative lenders.

POLITICAL COMPLEXITIES. At this writing many third-world countries are moving not only toward market-favoring and liberalizing economies but also toward more democratic governance. Although one cannot know how long the democratic trend will persist, it is useful to be reminded how different things were in the 1970s.

During Robert McNamara's time at the World Bank, the borrowing regimes varied widely not only in terms of their arbitrariness, repressiveness, legitimacy of access to power, and presence or lack of popular participation, but also in their socioeconomic systems, which extended from formal communism to laissez-faire capitalism. The great variation in this regard was one of the things that prompted the institution's founders to prescribe a nonpolitical operating mode. This suited the president who took over in 1968. McNamara came to the Bank from a comparatively short, high-profile, and controversial political career. He joined an institution with a preference, congruent with his own, for official political neutrality.

Thus the new president was not politically uncomfortable with President Suharto's autocratic Indonesian regime. In the fall of 1968 he described himself to an Ethiopian delegation as "an admirer of the Emperor," and two years later, when he met Haile Selassie, he found no reason to doubt Ethiopia's need for heavy defense spending.[38] Yet in the fall of 1974, scarcely tripping over the intervening coup, the president's in-house correspondence about Ethiopia remained quite positive, encouraged by the improved outlook for land reform.[39] The situation was similar in Chile, where some accused the Bank of flip-flopping from Allende to Pinochet, but the effort could be interpreted as doing appropriate business with the reigning government of whatever political hue. The Bank's overt concern with both Chilean regimes was their capacity and readiness to conduct efficient project operations, while the institution tried to ward off excessive U.S. influence.[40] Later in the 1970s, McNamara, despite his own history, was prepared to resume lending to Vietnam.

38. Memoranda, M. A. Burney for the record, "Meeting of Minister of Finance of Ethiopia with Mr. McNamara—Relations with Ethiopia," October 5, 1968; and Michael L. Lejeune for the record, "Interview with the Emperor of Ethiopia," November 25, 1970.

39. Memorandum, S. Shahid Husain to Robert S. McNamara, November 1, 1974.

40. Memoranda, Robert S. McNamara, "Conversation with Salvador Allende Gossens, President of Chile, Santiago, April 14, 1972," n.d.; and J. Burke Knapp to files, December 18, 1973.

Under the exigencies of IDA renewal, however, he was forced to accept U.S. congressional restraint (see chapter 17).

The Bank's approach to borrower's politics had two abiding characteristics during the McNamara years: first, management sought a measure of autonomy from owner pressures, especially from attempted steering by the United States; and, second, management had an intrinsic preference for *political* (as opposed to economic-policy) neutrality. Both tendencies came into play with respect to the U.S. push for the injection of human rights considerations into Bank decisions during the Carter administration. McNamara seemed to resist this initiative with particular zeal, as if to demonstrate that his autonomous persuasions were non-partisan; he was as ready to resist Democratic U.S. directives as he was Republican. But second, as a matter of substantive conviction, he drew a deep contrast (as he still did in interviews many years later) between what he called economic and political human rights. For the first, in its antipoverty and related initiatives, his Bank was an embattled activist. The second were better left to others. The same economic-political cleavage is evident in the distinction McNamara accommodated between the promotion of (properly bounded) markets as organizing mechanisms and private ownership of various means of production. The former were inescapably important as a matter of efficient and productive economic policy; the latter was driven more by local idiosyncrasies and tended to be a subject for home rule.

It is arguable that, with respect to McNamara's political neutrality, there was one exception: Pakistan in the matter of East Pakistan's transformation into Bangladesh in 1971–72. But it is easy to exaggerate the case. McNamara seldom forgot his official role-playing. Thus it was the president's seasoned director and vice-president-to-be, Peter Cargill who starkly assessed the circumstances, notably the fear that pervaded East Pakistan in the first half of 1971. Cargill articulated the Bank's estimate of the way politics had led to economic failures, and presumably it was from somewhere in the McNamara-Cargill complex that his report leaked to the press. But McNamara's own official encounters with Pakistani officials and leaders in Washington and Pakistan remained couched in economic policy terms. Documents suggest that McNamara may have viewed Pakistan's follow-on Z. A. Bhutto regime with some dyspepsia. But the Bank's approach remained rational, if stern, and mindful of Pakistan's development needs.

Very shortly, moreover, South Asia afforded another, perhaps, defining, example of Bank political neutrality. In June 1975, with her so-called Emergency measures, Indira Gandhi abruptly interrupted Indian constitutionalism. Rights were abridged, opposition leaders jailed, and normal political processes superseded. For all Indians and India watchers, even those who saw justifications in Mrs. Gandhi's actions, this was a traumatic business. The third world's nearly sole (and overwhelmingly largest) remaining case of constitutional democracy was aborted in a day. Scarcely anyone interested in development, democracy, or South Asia remained silent. And yet if one peruses the Bank's presidential papers, they are remarkably free of all traces of India's "Emergency," not just in the Bank's public utterances but in intramanagement memoranda and in meetings with senior Indians. Thus the record of President McNamara's meeting in September 1975 with C. Subramaniam (now Mrs. Gandhi's finance minister) expresses the president's great concern about external perceptions of India's economy, without so much as a glancing reference to her politics. McNamara finished a November 1976 trip expressing more satisfaction than he had in previous visits to India. He left sensing, he said, "a disciplined, realistic approach to development programs and a willingness to find practical solutions to economic problems rather than an attitude of falling back on 'socialist ideologies' and didactic debate."[41] Bank people did ask whether there were negative reactions to the new vigor of the government's population-control efforts but officially seemed to be reassured by the negative answers.[42] Quite clearly, the McNamara Bank of the 1970s favored the activist white-smock image of boldness as to clients' economic policies, including those of the equity-enhancing sort, but of prudence in the political sphere.

Yet another element of political complexity that inhibited the Bank's policy-reform efforts in the 1970s was the frequent weakness of its capacity for influencing policy. Repeatedly and perhaps increasingly, at least in Africa, the Bank found it could have very little pro-reform influence on countries whose politics were disorganized, inattentive, or otherwise preoccupied. Of the many available, Ghana is a prime example. A medium-sized African country (nearly twelve million people by the end of the 1970s) Ghana was the first to win independence (1957), appeared to be among the more progressive, and had a sizable sophisticated elite. In his first years President McNamara and his colleagues in the Bank's West African Department had a number of meetings with senior Ghanaian officials, for example, the finance minister, Joseph Mensah, a former UN Secretariat economist. But try as the Bank people would to get the government to do a properly intensive and ambitious piece of national planning, little happened. And then in early 1972 there was a coup, followed in the rest of the decade by a series of coups. As a result, things never stabilized sufficiently to arrest the erosion of economic activity and capacities. The Bank, like other interveners, did not have sufficient force or voice to get the government's attention well enough or long enough to stop the decline and start a sustained recovery.

This situation was not peculiar to Ghana. For an institution bent on policy reform, the experience should have been humbling. Indeed, many in the Bank

41. Memorandum, Robert S. McNamara, "Notes on Visit to India: November 6–12, 1976," n.d., p. 3.

42. Travelers to Delhi at the time found it hard to avoid a firestorm of unofficial reports of "forced sterilizations," and within four months the Congress Party had the unprecedented experience of failing to return a single candidate to the Lok Sabha from across the whole of northern India, by common consent because of the reaction to the regime's sterilization program.

were quite realistic about the limitations on their ability to influence borrowers' policies. But the institution as a whole did not fall into deep self-doubt. The Ghanaian experience is discussed further in chapters 10 and 12.

The Substantive Policy Messages

If Robert McNamara was cautious about the Bank intervening in borrowing-country politics, he was bold in advancing institutional views and initiatives in the realm of economic policies. During the latter part of the 1970s, as had been the case with the Pearson Commission ten years earlier, the Bank was instrumental in the creation of the Independent Commission on International Development Issues under the chairmanship of Willy Brandt.[43] McNamara's office records show he had explicitly remarked on the operational importance of broad policy ideas in a small meeting with his colleagues Hollis Chenery, William Clark, and Ernest Stern on December 1, 1976.

> Mr. McNamara (the meeting's recorder wrote) disagreed with the view that the Bank obtained its major impact through its project and technical assistance work. Although this work, of course, was essential, it did not influence the population at large in our borrowing countries, nor did it influence donor policies. The development community was influenced by soundly based ideas and it was an essential part of the work of DPS [the Development Policy Staff] to find such ideas and turn them into strategies for development.[44]

As discussed in chapters 5 and 6, the most celebrated policy of the McNamara Bank was its attack on the poverty of the poor in poor countries. Plainly, this was the decade's most important amendment to the summary sketched near the beginning of the present chapter, of the macropolicies the Bank preferred in its early years.

As the 1970s unfolded, the institution listened to and sometimes, as an interested observer, addressed the interbloc (North-South) negotiations about a "New International Order" that broke loose in 1974, triggered by the oil shock. Although items on that agenda—trade, transfers, commodities, and the like—were ones on which the Bank had positions, the latter were not notably different from those it had held right along.

Three other aspects of macro thinking at the Bank in the 1970s bore on the policy line it would follow in the 1980s, when the influencing process became less inhibited. But these precursive elements played differently. The first was important but little changed. The second was innovative and then rejected. The third fed positively into the 1980s, laying the groundwork for a sharpened policy line.

43. The Brandt Commission report was titled *North-South: A Programme for Survival: Report of the Independent Commission on International Development Issues* (London: Pan Books, 1980).

44. "DPS" was the Development Policy Staff under Chenery. Memorandum for the record, "Second Meeting to Discuss Future Work on Development, December 7, 1986," 792/2/216, December 2, 1976.

MACROPOLICY: FISCAL AND MONETARY. At the risk of doing injustice to particular analysts or country reports, one might say that the Bank's macroanalysis during the 1970s, while workmanlike and extensive, was fairly routine.[45] The focus on demand-management issues, in particular, varied among countries and regions. The issue was more urgent in Latin America than in South Asia. Yet the standard topics under this heading—monetary and credit management, government expenditure budgeting, the raising of taxes and other domestic resources, the exchange rate, net flows of external resources—were the stock-in-trade of all country reporting. During the 1970s, as throughout the Bank's history, nearly all of its country economists maintained a competent grasp of such issues. Yet the institution was largely insulated from the considerable heat of academic macroeconomic debates during the decade, some of which sparked bitter attacks on Keynesianism, a new blossoming of monetarism, and the rise of rational expectations theory. None of this cutting-edge theorizing penetrated World Bank operations very much. The institution's country and regional economists knew their countries' data and the latter's limitations. They used pragmatic blends of Keynesian and monetarist analytics in reports that often were long on common sense and on understanding which policy alternatives were politically feasible.[46]

The brand of macroeconomic policy analysis the Bank pursued remained largely unchanged through the 1970s. Just as a general-practitioner physician practices a great deal of internal medicine, Bank country economists and country and regional executives practiced a lot of country macroeconomic policy analysis in the 1970s. When they reached the next decade, they had a large repertoire at the ready. But they had innovated very little.

This was also the case with countries' external indebtedness—and, for that matter, with *internal* borrowing and credit expansion. Debt—internal and external borrowing—had been an aspect of developmental expansion from before the beginning of modern concerted national development efforts after World War II. It remained so in the 1970s. The oil shock administered a jolt to national balance sheets that made many countries more heavily dependent on borrowing. For some it was a foretaste of the 1980s. But the phenomena of borrowing, overborrowing,

---

45. It is true the Bank had its own formal macroeconomic model, the so-called RMSM (two-gap) model for framing its general economic analysis. This formula—Keynesian and national income in its vocabulary—contrasted with the IMF's (monetarist) Polak model. The two were definitively identified, compared, and reconciled in pieces that Mohsin S. Khan and Nadeem U. Haque wrote when Bank vice president Anne Krueger borrowed them from the Fund in the early 1980s to reinforce the Bank's central economic staff. But as the Khan-Haque treatment makes clear, these models were not really competitive and certainly were not trailbreaking. They were useful logos; they represented their agencies' respective subject matters and policy preoccupations. But analytically they were simplistic. The actual economics being practiced in the country and regional offices of both agencies was considerably more sophisticated than these models. But it also broke few trails and did not need to.

46. See also volume 2, chapter 12.

and subsequent coping mechanisms were not new. Intellectually, they presented very familiar terrain for influencing policy, if and when the Bank's influencing capacities grew.

The decade did see one firming of the Bank's debt-adjustment doctrine. As a sometime encourager of governments and private firms that had lent to developing countries to lengthen, soften, even forgive their loans after the fact, the institution became emphatic in its stance that the Bank itself could do no such thing: the structure of transfers and interventions, and their ramifications, depended on the spotlessness of its own creditworthiness (see chapters 11 and 14–16).

THE IMPORTANCE OF PRIVATE OWNERSHIP. A major component of the preferred policies on which the Bank broke new ground at the start of the 1970s, but from which it was already retreating by the start of the 1980s, was private ownership (see chapter 13). The question of concern to the Bank was the significance for developing countries of the linkage between markets and private ownership of such means of production as industrial factories. Throughout its life the World Bank has expressed an appreciation of the organizing and efficiency-enhancing capacity of self-adjusting, or only lightly regulated, markets. At least as a seriously considered view, this was not a vote for anarchistic, state-of-nature markets; when it was speaking carefully, the Bank always recognized that flexible, self-regulating markets need to be legally bounded and serviced. Moreover, the Bank also saw a need for government interventions in cases of market failure, for example, as a consequence of natural monopolies. But otherwise—in the 1940s, 1950s, and 1960s as well as the 1970s—the institution always was pro-market. This was a matter of technocratic (rather than ideological) good sense.

In the 1950s the World Bank of Eugene Black and Robert Garner went further: as to suppliers of goods and services, it believed a satisfactory market had to be occupied mainly by *private* firms; along with market structuring and flexibility, private ownership was critical. The Bank was comfortable funding public sector (goods and services-selling) industries only in the case of natural monopolies, as found, for example, in infrastructure. This stance, which remained dominant Bank policy through most of the 1960s, was distasteful to the governments of many of the Bank's borrowing members. In the early postwar decades—whether because of unhappy experience with foreign investors, rebellions against colonial regimes, the inadequacies or perceived untrustworthiness of indigenous entrepreneurs, socialist sentiments, or impatience to get on with development faster than the private sector seemed to promise—many developing-country governments had strong preferences for the public sector. Although the gap was partly bridged by some bilateral donors and (in some countries, not others) by foreign private investors, this made for a considerable mismatch between what the Bank offered and what its clients wanted.

President McNamara took a different position. The shift may have been influenced by the fact that broadening the permissible targets for Bank lending was consistent with the new president's determination to increase the volume of lending. There is little doubt, however, that at this point the Bank rejected the equation of the market and private ownership on its merits: ownership was less important than who *controlled* industrial enterprises, and in the case of many large industrial corporations, both private and public, in developing as well as developed countries, control lay with hired professional managers (that is, private or public bureaucrats) who were not major owners. So the simplest market models did not apply; private and public corporations blurred together conceptually; there was a whole spectrum of mixed types of ownership and control.[47]

In the McNamara Bank, all of this was taken to mean that country mixes of ownership reflected local histories, ideologies, and politics, and, given the liberation of markets, interveners such as the Bank should be slow to second-guess local ownership choices. The shift in doctrine was welcomed by a variety of mixed-economy borrowers, and it was reflected in Bank loans for a number of public sector manufacturing enterprises that would not have been made under the older Black-Garner dispensation.

During the 1970s, however, the Bank's markets-ownership distinction was not easily or cheerfully accepted by many Bank staff, and certainly not by some of the institution's (especially Part I) owners. It did not become an intellectually and doctrinally entrenched decision before it was upended. As the track record of state-owned industrial enterprises accumulated during the 1970s, it was disappointingly bad in many of the Bank's borrowing countries. However, for the purposes of this discussion, attention will focus on the principal abandonment of the McNamara distinction, as set forth in the Berg Report of 1981.

By the late 1970s the Bank was painfully aware of the complexity and difficulty of Sub-Saharan Africa's development predicament. The Bank agreed with its Africa governors that the situation demanded special attention. In mid-1980 the Bank recruited Elliot Berg, a market-oriented development economist long specialized in Africa, to lead a quartet of Bank analysts in the preparation of a report, *Accelerated Development of Sub-Saharan Africa,* published in the fall of 1981. This was the Bank's first major input to a contrapuntal dialogue that, launched by the Organization of African Unity's *Lagos Plan of Action* in 1980, was to take place between the World Bank and Africa's regional multilateral institutions.[48] The report had multiple effects. It rejected the markets-ownership distinction that the Bank

47. In the case of the United States, the separation of corporate ownership and control was highlighted in A. Berle and G. Means, *The Modern Corporation and Private Property* (New York: Commerce Clearing House, 1932). In 1994 the whole literature on the relationship of markets and ownership (that is, private versus public sector choices) was authoritatively reviewed and augmented in Joseph Stiglitz, *Whither Socialism?* (MIT Press, 1994).

48. Organization of African Unity, Assembly of Heads of State and Government, *Lagos Plan of Action for the Implementation of the Monrovia Strategy for the Economic Development of Africa* (Addis Ababa: Organization of African Unity, 1980).

had been making for most of a decade, and under which it had been aiding and investing in a number of African parastatal agencies and enterprises (see volume 2, chapter 5). The argument was pragmatic rather than ideological. The report found that Sub-Saharan parastatals, including ones the Bank had been assisting, were so emphatically inefficient that the institutional norm became to seize all possibilities for converting state-owned enterprises to private ownership. This was especially the case for Africa, but the Berg Report marked a crumbling of the distinction between market and private sector for the institution in general.

TIGHTENING THE FOCUS ON EXPORT EXPANSION. As the World Bank worked its way through the 1970s toward the more policy-aggressive 1980s, some of its policy doctrines became sharper and simpler. Such was the case with the markets and ownership issue, just noted. During the 1970s the institution tended to separate the two aspects and differentiate its approach to particular country cases. As the private sector bandwagon began rolling at the end of the decade, the markets and ownership issues were reamalgamated; the Bank's policy preference for liberalized private enterprise became less equivocal and more nearly universal. The same thing was going on with respect to recommended trade policy during the 1970s.

Typical development strategy in the 1950s and 1960s had had a protectionist tilt. Countries trying to accelerate growth needed to raise imports faster than their exports (either traditional or "nontraditional") tended to grow "naturally," that is, unassisted. Especially under conditions of "export pessimism," therefore, many developing countries opted for import-substitution industrialization; they protected indigenous substitutes with tariffs or quantitative restrictions (QRs).

Causing exports to rise faster than would have occurred in the absence of policy effort was, of course, an alternative or complement to ISI (or IS, for short). The two were co-strategies for reducing a country's trade deficit to a sustainable level by shifting some of its productive energies from "nontradables" to "tradables" and thereby either adding to the export side or reducing the import side of the trade balance. In the late 1960s and early 1970s, the Bank, as a development promoter, had good things to say about both of these substrategies. Thus, for example, in 1970, in one of his earlier papers as a Bank consultant, Bela Balassa (who was a protagonist of the Bank's conceptual transformation in the trade-policy area during the 1970s) was carefully evenhanded in his recommendation that borrowing members of the Bank should pursue comparative-advantage industrialization by *either* IS or export promotion (EP).[49] Balassa noted that the choices between the two would vary among countries, with larger countries, for example, relying less on exports and more on their internal markets.[50] During much of the Bank's country-

49. Bela Balassa, "Industrial Protection in Developing Countries," Economic Department, World Bank, June 1, 1970, *passim*, but esp. pp. 42–43.
50. Ibid., p. 14.

by-country work in the 1970s, it was fairly common to find the institution supporting IS. For instance, in its 1972 CPP for the Philippines, the Bank not only
accepted, it actively favored, an IS strategy. The 1976 CPP again emphasized import
displacement, albeit with tariffs, not QRs, the preferred means of protection.

A reappraisal of the institution's trade-policy choices appeared in a pivotal
advisory paper in 1979: "It is noteworthy that, until the early seventies, the Bank's
economic and sector missions to developing countries used to adopt benevolent
attitudes towards (protectionist) import-substitution policies, while they now advocate vigorously for fairly neutral incentive systems combined with reasonably
liberalized trade regimes and realistic exchange rates."[51]

This phrasing—"fairly neutral incentive systems"—indicates the kind of export
promotion that Bank analysts such as Balassa had in mind. For some time, in some
regions and countries, there had been strong advocacy of highly interventionist
export subsidies to promote nontraditional exports. This, for example, was the line
Raúl Prebisch's Economic Commission for Latin America had taken with its Latin
American members in the early 1960s.[52] Instead, during the 1970s the World Bank
became increasingly committed intellectually to a trade-liberalizing (both tariff-
reducing and subsidies-reducing) form of "export promotion." Writing in the
1980s, advocate Jagdish Bhagwati explained the nomenclature: "By EP strategy,
the literature now simply means a policy such that, on balance, the effective
exchange rate for exports (EER_X) is not significantly different from that for imports
(EER_M). . . . In short the effective exchange rate does not show a 'bias against
exports.'"[53] The reason for this apparently lopsided terminology was that, for political economy reasons, it took a great deal of policy effort for governments to make
exporters' incentives as attractive as those of firms producing substitutes for imports.

By the late 1970s export promotion in the foregoing sense was on its way to
becoming the World Bank's party line for trade policy. This tightening of focus
(from IS on the one hand and EP on the other, to a no-nonsense concentration on
EP) was a significant change for the Bank. It invited more rigorous policy leverage
than the more variable and accommodating stances on trade policies earlier in the
McNamara presidency. And given the institution's penchant for and protocols of
objective analysis, it helped for a shift of this kind to be situated on a base of solid
research. If it was to underpin policy levering in the 1980s, it helped for that
research to be systematically readied in the 1970s.

51. Jurgen Donges, "Incentive Policies and Economic Integration," in World Bank,
"Report of the Research Advisory Panel on Industrial Development and Trade," May 1, 1979
(transmitted to the Executive Board, June 22, 1979), appx. 1, p. 9.

52. Raúl Prebisch, *Towards a Dynamic Development Policy for Latin America* (New
York: United Nations, 1963).

53. "Rethinking Trade Strategy," in J. P. Lewis and Valeriana Kallab, eds., *Development
Strategies Reconsidered* (New Brunswick, N.J.: Transaction Books for the Overseas Development Council, 1985), p. 92.

A 1979 paper (the appendix to the Research Advisory Panel on Industrial Development and Trade) spells out the way these research needs were met. One of the advisory panel's members produced a paper evaluating nine Bank research projects, some of them country specific, dealing with trade and industrialization policy. The leading one, "Development Strategies in Semi-Industrial Countries," was by Balassa. Theoretically innovative but heavily empirical in its effort to assemble and analyze comparable data from six developing countries with different industrialization and trade strategies, this study, started in 1971, yielded a report of 1,200 pages, issued in 1978. Along the way its methodology had influenced the other studies.

Having assessed them all, the author concluded that the work (with participants both inside and outside the Bank) had been of high professional quality, the authors had made methodological advances, their work had for the most part complemented related work in other official and academic institutions, the work had been particularly successful in serving the needs of the Bank's operating departments, and the studies had succeeded in enlisting interest and participation in developing countries.[54]

These studies all emphasized export promotion cum trade liberalization as a trade-balancing strategy for developing countries, of whatever size and in whatever region. Belassa built his empirical and theoretical case insistently, even doggedly. Few other economists rivaled his devotion to the theme. One of them was Anne Krueger, at the end of the 1970s, still at the University of Minnesota.

Components of a Policy-Influencing Regime

Inhibited from pressing a policy-influencing campaign in the 1970s, the World Bank nevertheless further readied three components that would contribute to such a campaign in the 1980s: economic and sector work (ESW), country program papers (CPPs), and program lending. With the 1972 reorganization's emphasis on country programming and the augmentation of region- and country-specific economic staffs, ESW was stepped up markedly. In retrospect, the Bank gave the activity high marks:

54. The author of the evaluation was Jurgen Donges of Kiel. The other members of the committee were Assar Lindbeck of Stockholm, chair, Edmar Bacha of Brazil, Gerardo Bueno of Mexico, Jae Ik Kim of Korea, Richard Nelson of the United States, and Kirit Parikh of India. The committee's report was dated May 1, 1979 (see note 51 in this chapter). In terms of intellectual ancestry, Bela A. Balassa's study, *Development Strategies in Semi-Industrial Countries* (IBRD, 1969), had been anticipated not only by some of his own work but by that of Ian M. D. Little, Tibor Scitovsky, and Maurice Scott, *Industry and Trade in Some Developing Countries: A Comparative Study* (Oxford University Press, 1970). Donges's evaluation remarked: "In fact the operational staff is to a large extent convinced of the relevance of this research, and has expressed this by applying the findings of the research in country economic reports and policy analyses." Donges, "Incentive Policies and Economic Integration," appx. 1, p. 8. Donges also details developing-country response here.

Some of IDA's most important contributions to development have been made through the discussions it has with governments on a broad range of policy issues. Considerable time is spent on general economic and sector work before any actual project lending takes place. Economic reports survey macroeconomic conditions and the main sectors—agriculture, industry, and energy. They tend to study the key issues of investment and savings; public finances; the balance of payments, particularly the performance of exports; and overall prospects for growth. They act as the starting point for discussions with governments on the nature and severity of their development constraints, and on the policies and resources needed to overcome them. Sector reports go into more detail on sectoral developments—specific bottlenecks, investment programs, and government policies—and set the stage for project identification. These reports are valued not only by the borrowing country but also by other donors and institutions, since they are usually the most comprehensive and up-to-date assessment of the country's economic prospects and development strategy. The fact that detailed reports are produced periodically for each country underlines IDA's belief that each economy is unique and changing. While IDA recognizes that every government has its own economic philosophy and is free to choose its own development goals, it does point out distortions and inefficiencies that hinder resource mobilization.

Macroeconomic and sectoral policies are naturally interrelated, and they often have a direct bearing on the success or failure of individual projects. It is difficult to sustain a good project in an unfavorable environment. Furthermore, fruitful policy dialogue can do more to influence a country's development than even a series of good projects.[55]

Like the other precursors of policy-based lending that appeared in the 1970s, however, ESW was not by itself very influential. It was well done and well received in many countries. But commonly it failed to induce the policy reforms to which it pointed. Standing alone, ESW lacked financial leverage. Particularly under circumstances in which the Bank had expansionist reasons to push its project loans, there was a gap between the institution's policy analysis and its lending.

The CPP exercise that became a key element of Bank operations was another pivotal but incomplete component of a policy-influencing regime. The CPPs summed up the best operational thinking of the Bank's country and regional units crisply, systematically, and comprehensively to assist top management in deciding what general shape the Bank's operation should take in the country in question during the next few years. The CPPs reached over the heads of projects to focus on policy, even to probe sharply into the qualities of a regime and its governance. One could imagine them as the themes of some candid policy dialogues between the Bank and particular clients. The only trouble was that the CPP was highly confidential; it and the debate it engendered were conducted out of earshot of the other party. That party's Bank counterparts would leak to the borrower some of the gist of the CPP exercise, but the CPP remained more of a black box than a good policy-influence instrument.

---

55. World Bank, *IDA in Retrospect: The First Two Decades of the International Development Association* (Oxford University Press, 1982), pp. 56–58. Because of the subject of the report, the references are exclusively to IDA, but they could extend as well to IBRD.

The third component of the decade's unassembled policy-influence mechanism was the minor tradition of nonproject or *program lending* that had been carried into the decade. The propriety of this strain of activity regularly was challenged, but once again, various ad hoc reasons for sustaining it were discovered. During the 1970s the Executive Board accepted the guideline (not a ceiling or target) that 6–10 percent of Bank/IDA lending could be in nonproject form; actual commitments averaged 6 percent. About one-tenth of IDA's lending during its first two decades (1961–81) had been in nonproject form. Most such loans had had the same two functions that had been assigned to the new "structural adjustment" round of nonproject lending (SAL) that had just begun in 1980: "These 'program credits,'" it was said, "can be disbursed rapidly and are intended to ease severe foreign exchange constraints." But also they "have generally been accompanied by policy advice aimed at improving a country's overall performance."[56]

Through the 1970s, however, program lending, in terms of the folklore if not the constitutional law of the Bank, retained only borderline legitimacy, and it was used mostly in South Asia, entirely in cases with special circumstances. India was the largest such instance; about half the program lending had gone to India, starting in the 1960s. Then, when the United States retired from the role of the principal provider of program aid to India after the Bangladesh War, IDA stepped into that gap. Once it was constituted, Bangladesh itself became the second largest recipient of IDA program aid.

As the 1982 *IDA Retrospective* claimed, most of the pre-SAL program lending had at least a loose connection to recipient policy reform. This was least true of nonproject lending to Bangladesh; the impoverished new country could barely keep its nose above water and remained an unadorned claimant for balance of payments rescue. Even so, Bank management became increasingly impatient with Bangladesh's plea for special treatment as the decade proceeded. In 1979 the senior vice president for operations wrote the vice president for South Asia, rejecting the latter's proposal of more program lending for Bangladesh in "the absence of a program to support": "Having taken the first step last year in reducing general purpose lending for balance of payments support, since the basic situation has not changed, I see little to be gained by reversing ourselves."[57]

In India, where the nonproject lending was said to be for "industrial import programs," each annual program was indeed accompanied by policy discussions that, in the Bank's view, helped lead, especially in the middle 1970s, to "some broader policy shifts, including import-licensing reform, improved export promotion policies, and general anti-inflationary macroeconomic policies."[58] And elsewhere the policy linkage had a real bite. Program lending was stopped in both Sri

56. Ibid., p. 54.
57. Memorandum, Ernest Stern to W. David Hopper, vice-president, South Asia, "Bangladesh–IDA Allocations," August 24, 1979, p. 1.
58. World Bank, *IDA in Retrospect*, p. 56.

Lanka and Pakistan because of Bank dissatisfaction with recipients' macroeconomic policies. Such lending to India also ceased after 1976, but not on policy
grounds. Rather, it was because improvements in the Indian balance of payments
had diminished India's special-circumstances claim for program assistance. Thus
although its pro-reform uses had looked rather promising, the nonproject loan
vehicle had not yet been accepted for mainline service.

Cases of Diminishing Leverage

It stood to reason that the strength of the World Bank's policy voice in a country
was linked to the relative indispensability of the Bank's loans. It is useful to examine
that proposition in a few country cases. Two good candidates are Indonesia and
Mexico, both populous countries that commanded heavy World Bank attention by
the early 1970s. Indonesia, as explained earlier, had been singled out for special
Bank treatment by the new President McNamara in 1968. Mexico was spotlighted,
for one thing, because it was the only developing country to border the United
States. The Bank had strong macropolicy views it was inclined to share with both
countries. But each of them developed major and growing oil exports as the decade
proceeded, and—although matters unfolded differently in the two cases—the
availability of external resources threatened to weaken the Bank's policy influence.

Iraq and Iran provide two other interesting examples. Although both were less
important demographically and were the focus of less attention at the Bank, they
illustrate nondependency on Bank transfers. Both were flush with oil money; one
was strongly identified with the Soviet camp, the other with the United States. In
terms of policy, the Bank had little success in moving either.

The Indonesian Relationship Matures

From 1972 onward the Bank experienced substantive and procedural changes
in its relations with Indonesia. The country's economic indicators are arrayed in
table 9-2. Although less hospitable after Bernard Bell's departure, Indonesia continued to accept a strong and influential resident mission.

On its side, the Bank greatly increased its policy targets. Initially (as Robert
McNamara's summary at the end of his June 1968 visit of Indonesia's near-term
needs had suggested) the Bank, like the government of Indonesia itself, was mainly
concerned with achieving the real as well as the financial dimensions of stabilization.[59] Increasingly, especially after financial stabilization was given a further (debt-
relief) leg up by the Paris Club on April 24, 1970, the Bank urged Indonesia to pay

59. The near-term needs, McNamara suggested, were to maintain the stability of the
price of rice, in part via U.S. food aid; import fertilizer as well as food; cope with the present
scarcity of external loan capital, especially soft-loan, capital; and secure an orderly reduction

Table 9-2. *Indicators: Indonesia, 1964–82*
Period averages

Indicator	1964–67[a]	1968–73[b]	1974–79[c]	1980–82[d]
GDP (billions of $US)	...	12.1	42.8	88.4
GDP (billions of 1987 $US)	...	29.6	42.1	56.2
GDP per capita (1987 $US)	...	242.9	306.1	371.3
Oil share of total exports (%)	35.4	45.5	44.8	63.3
Exchange rate (rupiah per $US)	149.6	367.8	454.2	640.1
Budget deficit/GDP (%)	...	(2.6)	(0.7)	(0.5)
Long-term debt (billions of $US)	...	4.7	13.1	19.7
Total debt service/exports (%)	...	16.6	18.2	15.3
IBRD/IDA net flows (millions of $US)	...	30.3	188.3	392.5
IBRD/IDA net transfers (millions of $US)	...	32.6	128.6	248.4
Percentage of population below poverty line	...	...	36.7	27.8
Average annual growth rates (%)				
Real GDP	1.6	8.1	7.2	5.0
GDP deflator	517.0	15.0	15.6	9.4
Real GDP per capita	(1.0)	5.4	5.7	2.6

Sources: IMF, *International Financial Statistics;* World Bank, *World Debt Tables;* World Bank, *World Tables;* William Easterly and others, eds., *Public Sector Deficits and Macroeconomic Performance* (Oxford University Press, 1994), p. 530; Wing Thye Woo, Bruce Glassburner, and Anwar Nasution, *Macroeconomic Policies, Crises, and Long-Term Growth in Indonesia, 1965–90* (World Bank, 1994), pp. 168 and 171; *Indonesia: Strategy for a Sustained Reduction in Poverty* (World Bank, 1990), p. 152; *Monthly Statistical Bulletin,* Republic of Indonesia, 1970, Table IV.1.

a. 964–67: Figure for exchange rate is from 1967 and the GDP deflator growth is for 1966–67.

b. 1968–73: GDP and debt indicators are period averages for 1970–73. Real GDP and real GDP per capita growth for all periods are derived from figures in 1990 rupiah from IFS.

c. Percentage of population below poverty line for 1974–79 is the average of 1976 and 1978.

d. The average of 1980 and 1981 is shown from 1980–82.

attention to longer-term policy. In terms of the language of the time, the Bank has in fact been somewhat more "plan" minded than the government, which tended, more than many of its developing-country contemporaries, to be oriented toward market solutions, less toward quantitative plan modeling. The Bank, however, in its dialogue with the government of Indonesia, was more committed to certain themes than to planning per se. Predictably and straightforwardly, the themes included the production of indigenous foodgrains and export promotion. During the middle and later 1970s the Bank, as well, supported and assisted the government's controversial program of official and subsidized transmigration of families from Java to the outer islands.[60] But the Bank also became more concerned, than it had appeared to be during the "honeymoon" Bell years, with the conduct of Indonesia's oil business, in particular, and the matter of corruption, in general.

---

of Indonesia's debt-servicing burden. Note, "IBRD President McNamara's Principal Conclusions of Indonesian Problems as Prepared by the Indonesians," n.d., President's File.

60. See the extensive explanatory statement of the relevant area director to the Executive Board: S. Shahid Husain, "Board Statement by S. Shahid Husain—January 4, 1979."

In 1972 Bell himself sent a long cable from Jakarta describing the draft CPP put forward for that year as too euphoric. The positive achievements, he said, depended too much on a few gifted and dedicated individuals. Political power was held by the military, which had a tradition of corruption that was "unacceptable to small but potentially vigorous elements of the public."[61] What was alarming was not so much that an old habit of malfeasance was being perpetuated; it was the *scale* of the resource diversion and mismanagement that was now being made possible by the country's ongoing oil boom. The account of the 1966–70 stabilization and growth triumph given earlier in this chapter skips over the degree to which oil expansion contributed to growth and exports. From 1967 to 1973 the volumes of the country's oil production and oil exports both rose about two and a half times. Oil prices more than doubled. Oil's shares went from 2.7 percent to 12.3 percent of GDP and from 36 to 50 percent of the country's export earnings.

All of this was *before* the first oil shock. Revenue from the oil sector, which had been less than 350 billion rupiahs in 1973, jumped to more than 800 billion in 1974, and in 1975 to nearly 1,200 billion.[62] What made this expansion doubly significant was that, by President Suharto's design, it empowered a second Indonesian development program that was competing with the one presided over by the technocrat group. Recent commentators speak of the contest waged between the technocrats and Sutowo's "technicians" (that is, the military and engineers).[63] Instead of being given to conservative demand management, aid funding, and the market, the "technicians" pursued a program of large-scale, public sector, import-substitution industrialization that used its oil assets and earnings to fund its capital-goods and other imports by means of heavy foreign commercial borrowing.

The president wanted the government's oil combine, Pertamina, to "dynamize" the system. He was willing to have Sutowo withhold much of the industry's earning from central government budgeting and accounting, to have contracts steered to firms supplying the largest kickbacks, and to deploy the earnings at presidential discretion. Pertamina turned with zest to becoming a conglomerate. It "improved harbors, managed a hotel chain, ran a tanker operation, developed residential and commercial estates, built roads and hospitals, and established insurance subsidiaries in Hong Kong, Los Angeles, Singapore, and Tokyo. . . . [B]y February 1975 [Pertamina] was the largest corporation in Asia outside Japan."[64]

61. Cable, Bernard R. Bell to Robert S. McNamara, February 11, 1972.
62. At the official exchange rate, this was an increase from less than $1 billion to nearly $2 billion and then to nearly $3 billion. The data in this and the preceding paragraph are from Woo and others, *Macroeconomic Policies, Crises, and Long-Term Growth in Indonesia*, p. 55, table 7.1. If it is assumed that the relevant Indonesian prices were rising about 20 percent a year (an estimate derived from the World Bank's annual World Development Indicators), the country's oil revenue in 1974 and 1975, respectively, was about 680 billion and 880 billion in 1973 rupiahs.
63. Ibid., pp. 40–41. Alternatively, some commentators call the "technicians" "technologists."
64. Ibid., p. 58.

The technocrats were on the defensive and so was the Bank. Robert McNamara had expected to discuss Pertamina and corruption when he visited Jakarta in February 1974, but instead he focused on Indonesia's need prudently to manage the enormous windfall that, with the oil shock, was just coming to hand. At this point it looked probable that the Sutowo economic program would prevail. Indeed, the following September, Bernard Bell (now involved again, as the regional vice president for East Asia) commented on "the somewhat faltering and hesitant response of the economic team to the new circumstances."[65]

Meanwhile the Bank was maintaining polite relations with General Sutowo. The conversation was restrained when he visited McNamara in July 1973 and again at the end of January 1975, at the very time the Pertamina "crisis" was igniting. The groundwork reached back three years when, in conjunction with a standby agreement obtained from the IMF, the government of Indonesia decided it needed to curb foreign debt accumulation throughout the sector; it imposed a requirement that all foreign borrowing by government entities of any kind had to be approved by the Ministry of Finance. When Pertamina ignored this directive (and the United States, the country's largest bilateral donor accordingly suspended its aid), the government set up a more lenient rule for Pertamina in order to bring the corporation on board: it could borrow short term (that is, less than one year, for operating capital) and long term (more than fifteen and a half years) without Ministry of Finance permission, but it required the latter for durations in between. Pertamina thereupon went heavily into short-term borrowing. When short-term rates shot up after the oil shock, the banks from which Pertamina had borrowed balked at rolling over the short-term loans without a review of the whole Pertamina operation, and in February 1975 the company wound up in technical default.

The government hastened to cover the Pertamina shortfall, to forestall cross-default reverberations, and the company's own credit was quickly retrieved, but not without profound managerial and policy changes. The conglomerate was disassembled, arrangements channeling company earnings into the central budget were reaffirmed and made effective, and the company's accounting and regulatory practices were brought under control.

In October 1975, at the behest of Bell, who had been talking to the technocrats, McNamara addressed reflections on the matter to President Suharto. He sought to lock in the disposition of the "Pertamina Affair," saying, in part, "I appreciate the difficult nature of many of the decisions involved, and I applaud the comprehensive and systematic way in which you have moved to reestablish appropriate priorities to reorder plans and arrangements for the investment program and to meet financial problems. I am reassured by the action you have taken to ensure that there will not be a recurrence in the future of the recent unfortunate events."[66] McNamara went on to say that he would be expressing this confidence to the international financial

65. Memorandum, Bernard R. Bell to Robert S. McNamara, "Indonesia—Increase in the Lending Program for FY75 and FY76," p. 2.
66. Letter, Robert S. McNamara to President Suharto of Indonesia, October 9, 1975, p. 2.

and business community and was basing on it plans for a progressive increase in IBRD lending to Indonesia during the coming four fiscal years. (Indonesia was no longer eligible for IDA credits.)

As for Indonesian corruption in general, the Bank clearly had this issue in view from the beginning of its (1968) renewed relationship with the country. But the relevant documents convey little sense that the phenomenon had to or could be fully eradicated. Indeed, McNamara himself did not warm to the issue until late in his tenure, at which time he became quite vociferous. In his final presidential visit he gave almost the same message verbatim to assembled ministers, then to Vice President Malik, and finally to President Suharto, face to face. McNamara explained that "it was also necessary to maintain the emphasis on reducing corruption. Outside Indonesia, this was much talked about and the world had the impression, rightly or wrongly, that it was greater in Indonesia than in any but perhaps one other country. . . . It was like a cancer eating away at the society."[67]

The reasons why McNamara spoke up strongly now and not earlier may have been several. As Jean Baneth, director of the Resident Staff, Indonesia, reported, the Indonesians themselves had now become much more open in their discussion of the corruption problem. Related and perhaps most important, the demise of Pertamina had flushed out the whole subject of official probity and made it easier for an intervener, particularly a long-standing and still close and friendly intervener like the Bank, to weigh in. Still it is interesting that President Suharto, almost fulsome in the warmth and abundance of his appreciation of McNamara in this last meeting, is recorded as making no trace of a response to the démarche on corruption.

In terms of policy, there was quite clearly a prophylactic reaction to the Pertamina affair. From 1975 onward, Indonesia was, for a populous oil exporter, a near model of prudent financial management. The most striking instance of such behavior was the surprise devaluation the government announced in October 1978— a sizable one of 51 percent:

> There was clearly no balance of payments problem, nor was this devaluation associated with significant trade liberalization. The government was primarily concerned with the consequences of the Dutch Disease—the adverse effects of real appreciation since 1972 on non-oil export industries. The real appreciation had resulted from the combination of a fixed nominal exchange rate and domestic inflation well above world levels, averaging nearly 20 percent from 1972 to 1978. It can be regarded as part of the domestic economy's adjustment to the boom in petroleum and gas income.[68]

---

67. Memorandum, Jean Baneth to files, "Meeting with President Suharto—May 15, 1979," May 22, 1979. (The other country may have been Zaire.)

68. I. M. D. Little, Richard N. Cooper, W. Max Corden, and Sarath Rajapatirana, *Boom, Crisis, and Adjustment: The Macroeconomic Experience of Developing Countries* (Oxford University Press, 1993), p. 225. Corden is the principal author of chapter 8, from which this is drawn.

The government of Indonesia used the devaluation to protect the country's "non-booming" tradables. Foreseeing an eventual decline in oil exports, the Indonesians anticipated a future balance of payments problem for which they wanted to preserve non-oil export industries.[69] The effect was to narrow the adjustment problems the country would encounter in the 1980s.

But what of the World Bank? Its documents suggest that the devaluation almost took the Bank by surprise and subsequently was appraised with some skepticism. By early January Vice President Husain was saying kind things about it,[70] as President McNamara did in May.[71] Jean Baneth, the Bank's resident director in Jakarta, reports that he was aware of the discussions preceding devaluation, had opportunities to give his views, and informed the regional vice president (orally, to minimize the risks of leaks); yet the subject "was definitely not at the center of our concerns." The Fund was more involved, and more in favor of devaluation, as were a couple of Harvard advisers.[72]

This account is consistent with the sense that there was a slow drawing apart between the technocrats and the Resident Staff after the Bell residency. And, in the curbing of Pertamina the technocrats and the Bank had jointly dodged a bullet. Previously, the former had been in charge only of a quadrant (finance and planning) of Indonesian policy. But by overreaching, Sutowo had brought the oil economy also into the realm of orthodox macropolicy. Likewise, the Bank's influence, if less intimate, broadened.

With respect to oil per se, McNamara and Bell pressed Sutowo to strike a better (for Indonesia) bargain with the internationals marketing Indonesian oil. More broadly, from the beginning of the 1970s the Bank urged the building of non-oil exports. Equally hardy was its emphasis on agriculture and rural development. In comparison with Nigeria, another populous oil exporter, Indonesia "devoted a much higher proportion of public development and capital expenditure to agriculture and rural development. This move would have helped offset the depressing effect on agriculture of the real exchange rate appreciation."[73] Similarly it is likely that the Bank's recurrent emphasis on social and educational budgeting strengthened Indonesian inclinations along those lines. There is an appearance that dialogue—even routinized dialogue—had accumulated some weight.

The procedural aspect of the 1970s relationship basically concerned the sustainability of the unusual organizational regime President McNamara had established for the Indonesian program. Indonesia was the presidentially designated jewel in the Bank's operational crown. Did it continue to deserve such special treatment? By the late 1970s there was a sense that much of the uniqueness had

69. Ibid.

70. Husain, "Board Statement by S. Shahid Husain, January 4, 1979."

71. Letter, Robert S. McNamara to President Suharto, June 19, 1979.

72. Jean Baneth, personal communication, August 12, 1994.

73. Little and others, *Boom, Crisis, and Adjustment*, p. 39.

leached out of the Bank's collaboration with Indonesia. Moreover, the Jakarta-centered aspect of field-headquarters relations was encountering mounting Washington resistance. Transactions between the Bank and its client became, to a large extent, preoccupied with the problem of slow project loan disbursements. These delays, presumably because of the Bank's continuing drive for lending expansion, caused the institution endless heartburn. Repeated Indonesian testimony blamed them on the brittleness and inflexibility of Bank procedures. The Bank, on the other hand, resisted demands for reduced supervision.

In the late 1970s two Bank personalities proposed major changes in relations with Indonesia. In the spring of 1977 Shahid Husain, always a vigorous executive, took over the East Asian vice presidency. He thought the Indonesia program had gone a bit to seed. He soon proposed "a broad institutional relationship with the government of Indonesia as distinct from a narrow personal relationship which has been the hallmark of the past."[74] From the documentation it is hard to be sure of the chemistry between Husain and the Indonesians. In August 1978 Minister Widjojo, still the dominant voice in the finance-planning quadrant of Indonesian affairs, appeared to go out of his way to praise Husain's contribution to the government's formulation of its third five-year plan.[75] Yet Husain projected a more active and encompassing array of joint studies and other engagements with counterparts in the Indonesian government than the country's authorities, at this stage in their history, seemed to desire. He also wrestled with a reallocation of tasks and responsibilities between Washington and Jakarta that, while it retained special prerogatives for the director of RSI, left no doubt that the latter reported on big issues to the regional vice president.

As he approached the end of his own Jakarta tour, Jean Baneth, the RSI director, proposed a sharply contrasting operational style. The reason the Bank was having so much trouble with project disbursements, said Baneth, was that it was trying to do more detailed lending than it was cut out for. To paraphrase Baneth's words, the Bank should turn to wholesaling; it should switch to large sector loans and deliberately overprogram, leaving it to the recipient government, now more matured in its economic operations, to determine the disbursement pace. Compared with projects, the access to resources that such broad sector loans would provide would afford the Bank more policy leverage, which, however, should be used "with extreme care," and only after the Bank had mastered the intricacies of the sector.

In these démarches, Husain and Baneth framed the procedural possibilities for the Indonesian program. Neither of their recipes was implemented. The net outcome, as of the end of the 1970s, was that the relationship between the Bank

74. Memorandum, S. Shahid Husain to colleagues, "Management of the Indonesian Program," October 25, 1979, p. 1.

75. Memorandum, Office of the President, "Meeting with Mr. Widjojo, Indonesian Minister of State for Economy, Finance, and Industry, and Ambassador Ashari, August 7, 1973," August 10, 1978.

and Indonesia was much less nearly unique than it had been projected to be a dozen years earlier. Yet the atypically large Resident Staff probably did contribute to a slow but significant seepage of policy influence. Collectively, the staff also came to understand Indonesian perspectives and institutions in some depth. A process of ongoing two-way learning had become regularized. And yet (China not yet having quite come over the horizon) there was little move to replicate the field-centered format elsewhere.

A Second Case: Mexico

If all developing countries are exceptional, Mexico, whose economic indicators are shown in table 9-3, is one of the most exceptional. It is large in both population and area and is the only developing country contiguous with the United States. Mexico has a long history of independence. In the 1920s it began a long run of political stability, and in 1940 it started a thirty-year stretch of high average economic growth, on its own, well before international interveners began their efforts to promote development. Mexico had another distinction: throughout the decades of its interaction with such interveners as the World Bank, its government had a good measure of economic and administrative sophistication.

Mexico provides another good example of the Bank's efforts at, and difficulties in, influencing borrowers' policies. This is a country whose government has long been strongly allergic to external arm twisting. In November 1969 the briefing paper the Western Hemisphere Department gave Robert McNamara for his first presidential visit to Mexico warned: "Mexico is the last country in the world in which the overt exercise of leverage can be expected to pay off."[76]

At the same time, Mexico was then an outstanding example of the "programs-of-projects" mode of policy influence widely employed in the Latin American region under Gerald Alter. In the Mexican case, the slogan was "graduated response": the totality of the Bank's project lending to the country responded tacitly but perceptibly to what the lender perceived to be the quality of the borrower's macro-economic policies. The Bank's evaluations gave high marks to Mexican policies and performance in the 1960s. The Bank had not yet developed a doctrinal aversion to the kind of protectionist, import-substitution strategy Mexico was pursuing, especially in instances such as this: the country was achieving real annual GDP growth approaching 7 percent while the peso/dollar exchange rate remained stable, and inflation averaged less than 4 percent annually. The World Bank's response bespoke its satisfaction: its loans to Mexico in the 1960s (for power, roads, irrigation, and agricultural credit) ran at an annual rate three and a half times that of the 1950s.

76. November 26, 1969. Quoted in World Bank, *OED Study of Bank/Mexico Relations, 1948–1992*, Operations Evaluation Department Report 12923 (April 1, 1994), p. 49.

Table 9-3. *Indicators: Mexico, 1965–82*
Period averages

Indicator	1965–70[a]	1971–76	1977–82
GDP (billions of $US)	38.3	69.6	159.7
GDP (billions of 1987 $US)	68.4	85.4	123.2
GDP per capita (1987 $US)	1359.3	1513.1	1854.1
Budget deficit/GDP (%)	(3.5)	(3.0)	(8.7)
Exports (billions of $US)	2.9	5.3	18.9
Oil share of total merchandise exports (%)	3.0	7.0	52.8
Real exchange rate (pesos per $US)[b]	12.9	14.2	17.5
Long-term debt (billions of $US)	6.0	11.7	40.7
Total debt service/exports (%)	44.3	40.4	57.2
IBRD net flows (millions of $US)	75.9	106.8	244.9
IBRD net transfers (millions of $US)	44.7	46.0	93.8
Percentage of population below poverty line[c]	72.6	58.0	48.5
Average annual growth rates (%)			
Real GDP	6.8	6.6	7.3
GDP deflator	3.5	15.8	27.7
Real GDP per capita	3.3	3.3	4.7
Real exports	2.4	4.7	20.6

Sources: IMF, *International Financial Statistics;* World Bank, *World Debt Tables;* World Bank, *World Tables;* Easterly and others, eds., *Public Sector Deficits and Macroeconomic Performance,* p. 530; Angus Maddison and Associates, *The Political Economy of Poverty, Equity, and Growth: Brazil and Mexico* (Oxford University Press, 1992), p. 228; Carlos M. Urzua, "Five Decades of Relations between the World Bank and Mexico," 1995, table I; Jesús-Augustín Velasco-S., *Impacts of Mexican Oil Policy on Economic and Political Development* (Lexington, Mass.: Lexington Books, 1983), p. 187. World Bank, *Special Study of the Mexican Economy: Major Policy Issues and Prospects,* Report 2307-ME, vol. 2, statistical appendix, 5/30/1979, p. 38.

a. 1965–70: Figures are from 1970; GDP deflator and real exchange rate are 1965–70 averages.

b. Real exchange rate is computed using GDP deflator and world export unit index (1970 = 100). See Maddison and Associates, *The Political Economy of Poverty, Equity, and Growth,* p. 228.

c. Figures for percentage of population below poverty line are from 1964–70, 1970–76, and 1976–82 from Urzua.

Starting its six-year term in 1970, the Luis Echeverría administration moved to a far more populist, interventionist, deficit-spending, pro–public enterprise program than that of its predecessor. While Bank economists deferred in some measure to this political shift, most were critical. However, there were some restraining factors. For one thing, there was an ideological convergence at the top: not only did the two presidents—Echeverría and McNamara—share many of the same social priorities.[77] There was great personal empathy between them when they met in late 1971. In point of fact, their shared sentiments (except, perhaps, for a series of integrated rural development loans) appeared to have little effect on the composition of the Bank's Mexican portfolio. But Bank staff were inhibited from advocating more conservative financial management. There was a related doctrinal shift. The Bank's attitudes toward public sector manufacturing were changing. The institution made two loans to state-owned steel mills in 1974 and 1977.

77. Ibid., pp. 5, 49.

In the main, however, the Bank was constrained from wielding a heftier conservative influence on macroeconomic policy by two broader factors, mentioned earlier in the chapter: first, the Bank was driving itself to expand (development-warranted) project lending in Mexico as elsewhere; and, second, new oil wealth, as well as the commercial borrowing it enabled, reduced Mexican willingness to hear—at least to follow—Bank advice.

In the third and fourth years of the Echeverría administration expressions of Bank concern about Mexico's financial management were on the rise. In Mexico City in August 1973 Gerald Alter told the Ministry of Finance that the Bank "wanted to be sure the external debt would not be allowed to get out of hand."[78] The following year staff remarked that draft documentation of the Mexican economy "paints too rosy a picture. The 'manageable' fiscal deficit is growing bigger. . . . I believe we risk some unpleasant surprises later on if we do not have our eyes wide open now."[79] The Bank urged the government to raise taxes.[80] The following March Burke Knapp complained that a Bank report did not set a tight enough benchmark when it indicated that Mexico's debt-service ratio could safely rise to 25 percent during the coming decade.[81] In September 1975, meeting with the Mexican delegation to the annual meetings, President McNamara noted that "Mexico . . . faced [a] very difficult 6–12 months ahead and could encounter serious debt management problems. He urged . . . that the Government watch for this most carefully."[82]

Yet while sounding such alarms, the Bank kept raising its lending to Mexico. The annual rate for the first half of the 1970s was about three times that of the 1960s. Clearly, this no longer was a case of "graduated response." It expressed the generally expansionist mode the Bank had adopted. But also two other considerations had come into play. Staff in the summer of 1975 argued that

> the Bank profile in Mexico should not be lowered precipitately. Probably the most important [reason is] . . . the impact on Mexico's creditworthiness of a sharp withdrawal by the Bank; Mexico had stretched its credit in the world's capital markets to a point where any explicit loss of confidence on the part of an agency like the World Bank would have disastrous consequences on the country's creditworthiness.[83]

78. Memorandum, Ian Scott, economist, LACI, to files, "Mexico: Meeting with the Ministry of Finance, August 2, 1973—11 A.M.," August 14, 1973, p. 6.

79. Memorandum, John A. Holsen, senior economist, LACI, to Adalbert Krieger, director, LACI, "Mexico: Comments on the Special Program Paper ('RVP Draft')," May 14, 1974, p. 2.

80. World Bank, "1974 Briefing Paper—Mexico," September 23, 1974.

81. Memoranda, Adalbert Krieger to Enrique Lerdau, director, LACI, "Mexico: Economic Performance," March 10, 1975; and Shiv S. Kapur, division chief, LACI, to Adalbert Krieger, "Mexico: Economic Performance," March 14, 1975.

82. Memorandum, Shiv S. Kapur, division chief, LACI, for the record, "Meeting of McNamara with the Mexican Delegation on September 2, 1975," September 3, 1975, p. 3.

83. World Bank, "1975 Annual Meeting Briefing—Mexico," August 18, 1975, p. 3.

Second, on the reassuring side, worries were dampened by Mexico's oil assets: "It can be argued that petroleum exports can be 'tuned' so as to maintain the debt service ratio within reasonable bounds. . . . [I]t is particularly timely to examine just how significant the scope for adjustment through petroleum exports is going to be in the 2 or 3 years ahead."[84]

Tension between the government of Mexico and the Bank increased during the final year of the Echeverría presidency. Trying to cope with a mounting foreign exchange crisis, the government devalued the peso twice, lowered export taxes, and still had to suspend foreign exchange transactions and seek IMF assistance.

But in the (December 1976) first weeks of the new José López Portillo administration, just when the Bank's advocates of sterner policy conditionality thought they might prevail, the government was able to announce that new discoveries of oil during the preceding three years had radically increased the country's proven reserves. The Bank immediately counseled that the new resources be husbanded prudently, with output expanding just enough to meet domestic demand and oil exports being held to "only 1.25 million barrels per day in order to pay for imports to promote growth and create jobs, without causing inflation or excessive dependence on oil sales."[85] But the expansionists in the administration had the bit in their teeth. Quickly they raised the daily export ceiling to 1.5 million barrels a day. They began to borrow heavily both domestically and internationally.

When the GDP growth rate in both 1977 and 1978 was disappointing and, at the same time, borrowing ballooned, the government, instead of pulling back on its development budget, once again was saved by its geologists. At the beginning of 1979 it was able to announce that proven petroleum reserves had doubled from 20 to 40 billion barrels, making the country's holdings the world's sixth largest. The government also signed a large natural gas sale to the United States; it charged ahead with its investment and foreign borrowing program.

> The Portillo administration undertook high-cost initiatives that increased the economic participation of the state in the national economy as well as the share of the national debt to overseas. The public sector deficit went from 7% of GDP in the seventies to 14% in 1981 and 18% in 1982; the national debt rose to about $90 billion in 1982, about three-quarters of which was owed by the public sector.[86]

During the López Portillo period the Bank not only loaned with less than normal purpose and wielded little influence, but it monitored the Mexican economy less successfully than usual. The informational slippage may have occurred in part because the Bank had put itself at arm's length from the fortunes of the Mexican oil industry; in 1977 it incurred much government displeasure by sticking to established institutional policy and refusing to invest in Mexican oil

84. Memorandum, Guy Pfeffermann, senior economist, LACI, to Thomas Hutcheson, LCIDA, "Recent Developments in Mexico," May 27, 1975.

85. World Bank, *OED Study of Bank/Mexico Relations,* p. 15.

86. Ibid., p. 16.

development on the grounds that alternative financial sources were readily available. Also contributing to the relevant informational lapse was the inordinate delay in Mexico's debt reporting; and the Bank did not succeed in getting the government to expedite it to any extent.[87]

Bank documents of the late 1970s reflect a curious ambivalence about Mexican prospects:

> [February 3, 1978:] The Mexican government almost certainly will experience a large increase in the resources at its disposal by the early 1980s. Our most recent projections show that . . . the balance of payments will show a surplus on current account by 1982. . . . At present, large foreign indebtedness and a sizable public finance deficit are the direct outcomes of recent (1974–76) public sector inability to mobilize . . . resources. However, large increases in export revenues, mainly from petroleum and products, should make both the foreign debt problem and the management of public finance much easier to manage by the 1980s. . . . The debt service ratio of 32.6 percent in 1976 will increase progressively to 53.1 percent in 1978, and thereafter will decline to 49.4 percent in 1980 and to about 30 percent in 1982.[88]

> [November 19, 1979:] Both the increase in Mexico's external public debt and especially the increase in the debt service ratio, which in 1979 may become as high as two-thirds of its exports of goods and non-factor services, suggest a very critical situation. In fact the truth is exactly the opposite.[89]

> [September 11, 1981:] In particular, we share with the Bank the concern with issues like inflation and its impact on resource allocation, and the question of balance of payments disequilibrium that has persisted in spite of the oil exports.[90]

The monitoring was mixed enough to let the Bank, for all the attention it was giving Mexico, be caught somewhat off guard by the country's August 1982 debt crisis. All told, the 1970s' part of the story of policy influencing in Mexico is not one from which the Bank emerges with much distinction. But a base had been laid from which substantial improvements would be possible.

Iraq and Iran: Weak Leverage and Nonlending

World Bank lending to Iran and Iraq in the 1970s illustrates the comparative lack of Bank leverage with countries having access to alternate sources of funds. Both countries had abundant oil money; one was identified with the Soviet camp,

---

87. Memorandum, Catherine Slappey to John Holsen, "Debt Reporting by Mexico," January 26, 1978; letter, Jesús Silva-Herzog, Mexican finance minister, to Devbrat Dutt, division chief, World Bank, December 21, 1978.

88. Memorandum, Adalbert Krieger to Robert S. McNamara, "Mexico: Your Meeting with Rafael Izquierdo," February 3, 1978, p. 3, annex 1, pp. 3, 6.

89. Memorandum, Jorge García Mujica to files, "Mexico's Public External Debt and Related Coefficients," November 19, 1979, p. 1.

90. Letter, Mexican Minister of Finance David Ibarra to President A. W. Clausen, September 11, 1981.

the other with the United States. By the mid-1970s the Bank's relations with Iraq and Iran had deteriorated and its lending had ceased, as had any policy-influencing effects of the nonlending. In both cases, the Bank's cessation of lending had little effect on the client.

Before 1972, the Bank's relationship with Iraq had been perfunctory; it involved only two loans (one in 1950 and the second in 1967). The resumption of operations in 1972 was also short lived. There were two loans each in 1972 and 1973 (for a total of $120 million), after which the Bank stopped lending. The resumption had been formally opposed by the United States (because of disputes related to compensation following the nationalization of the Iraqi Petroleum Company), as well as by Iran (whose relations with Iraq were at a low ebb). The Bank (McNamara) did not see merit in these objections and decided to go ahead with the loans, but the transactions soon faced rough sailing. A telecommunications loan stalled because the Iraqi government would not agree to any "contractual understanding on tariffs, be it in the form of a rate-of-return covenant or any other formula." The Iraqi minister agreed with the Bank on the principles that supported such a covenant: the relation to costs, the fact that the service was not an obvious vehicle for redistributional subsidies, and the need to generate surpluses for investment. But the minister would not accept any binding obligation that would restrict his government's freedom to set prices as it saw fit. In four cases (involving telecommunications, irrigation, and grain storage) the Iraqis repeatedly raised the sovereignty issue. That the Bank soon ceased its operations in Iraq made little difference to the country. During the rest of the 1970s and the 1980s Iraq continued to enjoy access to a wide variety of commercial and governmental sources of money.

The Bank's lending to Iran began in 1957. During 1957–74, Bank lending amounted to $1.2 billion in thirty-three loans, of which some $188 million's worth was canceled. In comparison with fiscal 1966–70, when lending averaged $40 million a year, the Bank's 1969 CPP proposed to boost commitments to $125 million a year, to "improve the terms of Iran's borrowings and more importantly to assist the Government in improving the quality of its investment program."[91] By conventional criteria, the early 1970s were impressive years for Iran, with output growth at 10–12 percent. Yet defense expenditures skyrocketed and the rural sector lagged. The fifth five-year plan formulated in 1972 gave priority to the agriculture sector. To assist in project identification and preparation, the Bank in 1973 set up a Tehran resident Agriculture Task Force (ATF), which it regarded as one of its most ambitious ventures in agriculture.[92] The Bank sharply increased the volume and range of its lending, adding education, population, and urban transport, as well as agriculture to its earlier infrastructure focus. Lending to Iran in 1973 was projected

91. Actual lending in 1971–75 averaged $150 million per year.
92. Memorandum, Gregory Votaw to Robert S. McNamara, "Iran—Audience with HIM, July 27, 1973," July 26, 1973, p. 2.

at $240 million a year, representing 15 percent of Iran's gross foreign borrowings during its fifth five-year plan.

Even as the Bank was committing itself to greater involvement in agriculture and social sectors, it decided to support state-owned agroindustrial complexes. But the Shah's vision of rural modernization was too different to be thus assuaged. He was already impatient with "effete Western intellectuals" criticizing agro-business and raising questions about land reform. He claimed that there was an "'intellectual conspiracy" abroad to undermine his achievements and aspirations in the rural areas. It was widely observed that the government's large-scale schemes entailed collectivization and were pushing out peasants. The Shah accused Bank staff of joining such redistributive criticism. Actually, the Bank staff's stronger objection was that the agribusiness corporations were unlikely to attract investors. Eventually, Sir John Crawford was called in to smooth the Bank's agricultural agenda.

Problems also beset the institution's thrust in Iran's education sector. The Bank wanted to finance "rural, vocational, technical and secondary education" projects, but the government asked that it support one or more of three university-type projects. The Shah was particularly keen on one of them (Arya Mehr Technical University). As oil revenues climbed rapidly, Iran began to find the Bank's institution-building procedures too time consuming. Like the Iraqis, the Shah "reacted very negatively to evidences of Bank leverage to force policy changes in Iran." McNamara sought to reassure the Shah: "In conclusion, I emphasized we had but one objective, and that was to assist him in the dramatic revolution which he has under way in Iran."[93]

While Bank lending to Iran climbed to $265 million in fiscal 1974, it dropped to $53 million in fiscal 1975, before ceasing completely. Relations had already soured when the Bank overrode Iran's objections on lending to Iraq for the lower Khalis (irrigation) project. The Bank had concluded that the objections were of dubious merit: Iran was the upper riparian state and the Bank interpreted its objections as essentially political, not technical.

Clearly the sharp acceleration of oil revenues after 1973 greatly affected Iranian attitudes. Following meetings between the Shah and McNamara in February 1974, an agreement was reached that the Bank would lend only for "nontraditional" sectors, and, at the same time, through offsetting resource transfer agreements Iran would cease to be a net borrower from the Bank. The Bank's role would change from project financing to technical assistance. The agreement soon foundered over ambiguities as to whether the offset arrangements were on a commitment or disbursement basis. Iran's loans to the Bank disbursed almost immediately whereas the Bank's loans to Iran took many years to be drawn down.

93. Robert McNamara, "Conversations with the Shah of Iran at Blair House," July 27, 1973.

From mid-1974 the Bank began to encounter difficulties in all its operations in Iran. Project execution suffered and many projects became "problem cases." The Bank was unsuccessful in obtaining Iranian contributions to the Third Window (intended to attract extra OPEC funds to Bank programs) or to IDA 5. Relations became quite sour. In July 1976 the Bank closed its technical assistance mission in Tehran. Iran's policymakers "complained bitterly of an unsympathetic and sometimes arrogant attitude on the part of the Bank."[94] Iran even refused to provide data on its economic position and its external balances.

Matters began to improve following a meeting between McNamara and Hushang Ansary (then minister of finance) at the Manila annual meetings in 1976. There appeared to be a softening of attitude on the Iranian side. Several reasons seemed to account for the change, despite the country's access to financial resources and the private expert consultancy services it could theoretically have purchased. While the Iranians appeared to be keen to obtain the Bank's technical expertise, the stronger reason may have been political. By this time the Shah's regime was coming under increasing criticism in the foreign press for human rights abuses, lavish defense expenditures, and corruption. The country's claim to leadership in OPEC was being challenged by Saudi Arabia. And in international fora on North-South debates, Kuwait and the United Arab Emirates were projecting themselves more positively, in part through their voice in the multilateral institutions. The Shah's aversion to external criticism thus seems to have motivated the effort to bring back the Bank to Iran. In addition, there were internal reasons. Associating with the Bank could help legitimize internal development programs (see chapter 2 in volume 2). Bank reinvolvement also could help mitigate the excessive corruption that was by now apparent in the large Iranian projects that were under way.

The Iranian overtures won over senior Bank staff. The then department director recommended that the institution consider Iranian requests for assistance favorably in view of its "highly commendable economic performance over the last 15 years, and the recent progressive policy initiatives of the Government" and its "eminent creditworthiness and high absorptive capacity."[95] However "progressive" the measures, they were too late. Internal events in Iran proved overwhelming, and from 1978 to 1989 there was no official contact between the Bank and Iran, except for some informal encounters during annual meetings.

The cases of Indonesia, Mexico, Iraq, and Iran in the 1970s broadly confirm that financial independence of the World Bank is associated with reduced susceptibility to Bank influence, although Indonesia is somewhat different in this regard. Presi-

94. World Bank, "Briefing Note, Islamic Republic of Iran," November 9, 1989, p. 3.
95. Memorandum, Martijn J. W. M. Paijmans, director, EMENACPI, to Robert S. McNamara, "Iran—Discussions Held in Tehran from January 29 to February 5, 1977," February 28, 1977.

dent Suharto's cordoning off of the macro (finance-planning) zone of policy from manipulation by his military colleagues, the special chemistry between technocrats and Bank early on, and the near accident of Sutowo being brought up short—all these factors combined to yield responsible policy when the Bank no longer had much leverage.

Mexico, similarly situated in many ways, was a more conventional case of limited influence slipping further as competing resources mounted. In Iraq and Iran, there was never much influence, or perception of influence, to start with.

The Great Bend in Events

The years 1979 to 1981 proved to be a time of turning in global affairs, at least in those of the "North," the "West," and the developing countries. The world, of course, affected the World Bank, but change, especially in the realm of policy promotion, also was internal to the institution.

Landmark Years Globally: 1978 to 1981

Nineteen hundred seventy-nine was an exceptional year. It started with the Iranian revolution. This led directly, albeit with a lag of a few months, to a lurching rise in petroleum prices. Within six months the international price of crude oil rose 125 percent; within twelve months, 160 percent. The second oil shock had none of the buoyancy that had characterized aspects of the first. The oil exporters, whose real prices meanwhile had sagged, did not have the same sense of windfall or surge of generosity toward their developing-country brethren. The jump in oil prices was very widely expected to initiate a grinding secular rise that did not materialize. At the same time, there was little of the offset from other commodity prices, whose rise had softened the first oil shock's blow to many oil importers. This time changes in non-oil primary terms of trade were negative.

The biggest economic impact of the oil shock, however, was on interest rates. By the start of 1979 the United States and other OECD governments were catching their breath; they thought stagflation had nearly been put to rest. The onslaught of a new oil price surge prompted a last-straw resort to rigorous monetary restraints. In the United States in July, Paul Volcker was made chairman of the Federal Reserve, and by October the Fed's shift to monetary targets was administering a "Volcker Shock" to interest rates. For the many developing countries that by now had taken variable-rate loans from foreign commercial banks, interest bills began to encroach more heavily than oil bills on their balances of payments. Moreover, as part of the same exercise, the effective value of the U.S. dollar rose radically, augmenting both the cost of oil and of servicing dollar-denominated debt.

Meanwhile, in June 1979, Margaret Thatcher's election as British prime minister was the harbinger of a political sea change that acquired the appearance of inevitability incrementally, as subsequent events accrued. In November, the Iranian seizure of American hostages strengthened the likelihood that Ronald Reagan would join Mrs. Thatcher in the leadership of the North-West a year later. In December, a Soviet invasion of Afghanistan may have increased that probability; in any event, by raising U.S. defense spending, it levered a further hike in the American military budget when the new administration acceded.

Rhetorically, ground was shifting under the feet of the developing countries. As already noted, heady NIEO demands had been registering in United Nations fora from 1974 onward. The Brandt Commission, encouraged by the World Bank, achieved a comprehensive and ambitious statement by its combined Southern and Northern membership in early 1980. But then, partly because of the way the second oil shock was causing OECD perspectives to sour, any prospect for consensus began to fall apart. In late August in New York, a special session of the UN General Assembly convened that was to have negotiated an International Development Strategy for "the Third Development Decade" (DD III). But the strategy was upstaged by an added starter: the negotiation (proposed by the organization of the nonaligned nations) of a "new round of global negotiations." Preparations for the new round were high level and heated, but they never got beyond a procedural stalemate: if the proposed negotiations were to be held under the oversight of a (New York-based) ad hoc common body, would the latter be able to consider recommendations concerning the Bretton Woods intermediaries (for example, concerning the governance of the IMF) resisted by the intermediaries themselves? In the end, the United States, the United Kingdom, and Germany blocked a positive answer, and the preparatory exercise got no further.

By 1981 the NIEO campaign had lost most of its energy. In an attempt at revival, President López Portillo of Mexico and Chancellor Bruno Kreisky of Austria picked up a suggestion of the Brandt Commission: they invited a carefully chosen selection of twenty-two heads of government to join in a summit at Cancun, Mexico, in October, meant to focus and reinvigorate the global reform effort.[96] The meeting was well tempered but thoroughly hollow. Mrs. Gandhi was polite to Ronald Reagan and vice versa. But there was no meeting of minds about an altered North-South balance.

Moreover, the third world's losses rhetorically were being matched in the realm of real events. In the early 1980s unequal outcomes for South and North were rife in the areas of budgetary and foreign exchange deficits and adjustment

96. By the time of the conference, Chancellor Kreisky was succeeded as cochairman by Prime Minister Pierre Trudeau of Canada. The participants were Algeria, Austria, Bangladesh, Brazil, Canada, China, Côte d'Ivoire, Federal Republic of Germany, France, Guyana, India, Japan, Mexico, Nigeria, Philippines, Saudi Arabia, Sweden, Tanzania, United Kingdom, United States, Venezuela, and Yugoslavia.

discipline. As the World Bank's chief economist wrote the secretary-general of OECD in 1990,

> Twenty-five years ago the industrialized countries' current account surpluses largely matched the deficits of the developing countries. This pattern was altered in the periods of high petroleum prices, when the surplus of the high income oil countries financed increased deficits in the developing world and small deficits in the OECD—the recycling of "petrodollars." However, as oil prices declined, the data suggest that OECD current account deficits increased. This appears to reflect growing deficits in the U.S. and in the rest of the OECD, except for Japan and Germany.[97]

Fiscally, the most flagrant non–role model for the developing countries was the United States, which—by cutting its taxes; increasing governmental, especially military, spending; and raising the consumed share of its income—lived off the rest of the world to an unprecedented degree.

The North-South operational differential was evident, as well, in the trade area, where the developed countries exhorted the developing countries to open their markets at the same time the OECD countries were nudging up their trade (especially nontariff) barriers, circumventing the General Agreement on Tariffs and Trade (GATT) with unilateral trade sanctions, and allowing the Uruguay round to stall over intra-OECD arguments. The double standard was also operative financially. "The debt crisis" was certainly a problem for the borrowing developing countries. But in the (North-led) international community, at the onset of the crisis, such concerns were upstaged by anxieties about the survival of international commercial banks and the global financial system to which they belonged. Foreign aid compounded the financial constraint on development; the growth of aid slowed markedly.

Finally, the double-standard phenomenon had various sectoral manifestations, for example, in agriculture and in armaments. Organized agricultural groups in developed countries repeatedly inspired Part I member directors at the World Bank to argue against loans to competitive farming in developing countries. At the same time, substantial tariffs and subsidies in the OECD countries continued to protect domestic farming. And the same Part I governments that encouraged the Bank to discourage Part II military spending often had militaries and industries of their own energetically selling armaments to third-world customers.

The Turn of Events inside the Bank

The global changes of 1979 to 1981 washed over the World Bank, of course. But internal shifts were under way that were not in the first instance ideological.

SALS: DESIGN OF A NEW PRODUCT. As Robert McNamara approached his (self-imposed) termination date, he was dissatisfied with the way the Bank's normal

---

97. Letter, Stanley Fischer to Jean Claude Paye, secretary-general, OECD, May 22, 1990, p. 1.

project lending was imparting macropolicy influence to borrowing governments. Ernest Stern, the new operations chief McNamara had appointed in the second half of 1978, was even more displeased. He was impressed by the number of cases he already had encountered—Egypt, Pakistan, Turkey, Bolivia, Ghana, Zaire, El Salvador—where country lending programs needed to be reduced or delayed for the lack of good or sufficient macroeconomic policies.[98]

Stern in particular, but with McNamara not dissenting, was a partisan of the greater use of program loans for policy purposes.[99] The first public articulation of proposed nonproject lending for "structural adjustment" came from the president in his speech to the UN Conference on Trade and Development at Manila on May 10, 1979. The story of how that reference came about indicates that, at this point, "structural adjustment" already was a shared concept within the Bank but for McNamara remained a fairly matter-of-fact one. The president, inclined to project the Bank as a wide-ranging participant in policy debates, had enlisted Mahbub ul Haq and others in drafting a speech on the obligation of the industrialized countries to open their markets to the exports, especially the nontraditional, manufactured exports, of the developing countries. Twice, at sessions to review drafts of the speech, Attila Karaosmanoglu, then director of one of the country programs departments for the Europe, Middle East, and North Africa regional office, urged that McNamara comment on what the Bank could be doing to support trade policy reform, so that he would not be perceived as a nonplayer bearing unsolicited advice. Karaosmanoglu's recommendation was rejected, but at a third such session, when he renewed his proposal and Hollis Chenery and Ernest Stern (who had now joined this series of meetings) supported it, the proposal was accepted.[100] The following was added to the Manila speech:

> In order to benefit fully from an improved trade environment the developing counties will need to carry out structural adjustments favoring their export sectors. This will require both appropriate domestic policies and adequate external help.
>
> I would urge that the international community consider sympathetically the possibility of additional assistance to developing counties that undertake the needed structural adjustments for export promotion in line with their long-term comparative advantage. I am prepared to recommend to the Executive Directors that the World Bank

98. Memorandum, Ernest Stern to Robert S. McNamara, "Review of the FY 1979 Lending Program," February 26, 1979.

99. A decade earlier, when Stern was USAID's assistant administrator for programs, he had written a memorandum stating that "while the Bank Group has been very effective in exerting leverage on borrower policies at the project and sector level, its leverage at the macro-economic level could be greatly enhanced by willingness to resume program lending." Cited in memorandum, John H. Adler to Robert S. McNamara, "AID's Attitude to the Third IDA Replenishment," December 18, 1969.

100. Attila Karaosmanoglu, interview with John Lewis, Richard Webb, and Devesh Kapur, November 17, 1994.

consider such requests for assistance, and that it make available program lending in appropriate cases.[101]

Pursuers of the policy-influence theme can note, in this statement, the focus on exports as the particular object of restructuring, the uninhibited invocation of program lending, and the absence of conditionality. Even though the last was a big gap in what would become the norm, the statement qualifies as the beginning of formal SAL documentation. A far more extensive, albeit in-house, version would be logged within the week.

On May 16, 1979, Stern wrote McNamara a long memorandum that began: "Some time ago we discussed briefly whether the Bank could better condition its country lending programs by linking them, more explicitly, to the macro-economic policies of our member governments. As you know, I consider this a principal issue for the evolution of the Bank in the years ahead."[102]

The operations vice president proposed a launching of conditioned program loans in support of macroeconomic policies to selected, mostly middle-income, countries that were ready and able to reform. His advocacy was cautious. Indeed, the May 16 memo's list of "considerations which would argue against proceeding on this course" was one longer than the favorable list (seven points versus six). SAL, said Stern, would give the Bank an uncomfortably high political profile; it would "lead to much more intensive, and political, Board participation" and an "explicit shift to such a policy will be strongly resisted by the developing countries." The memo was quite explicit about the scale of the innovation the operation chief envisaged: "Such negotiations are necessarily complex and we could do them only for a few countries annually after a considerable effort at preparation [even though] we may be seen . . . as neglecting important policy issues [that we do not take up]."[103]

McNamara's reaction to Stern's thoughts on the subject was favorable, and their scheme soon was accelerated by events. By midsummer 1979 the new oil shock had sharply increased the need for oil-importing countries to obtain quick-disbursing transfers. By contributing to the interest shock that helped generate the debt crisis that hit three years later, the oil shock indirectly created a need for quick-disbursing transfers that outclassed the direct need in 1979. But even that direct need posed by oil price inflation was not trivial. It strengthened the case for what would become structural adjustment lending, and from the beginning it determined a deep characteristic of the mode: SALs would inherently come to have a double purpose. They would move money, and they would try to move policy. Some proponents (for example, McNamara) arguably were more interested in the first

101. Robert S. McNamara, "To the UN Conference on Trade and Development, May 10, 1979," in McNamara, *The McNamara Years at the World Bank*, p. 549.
102. Memorandum, Ernest Stern to Robert S. McNamara, "Macro-Economic Conditioning," May 16, 1979, p. 1.
103. Ibid., pp. 3–4.

purpose, some (for example, Stern) more in the second; and under certain circumstances (such as the debt crisis) the relative importance of one of the two purposes would be raised. But under all circumstances all serious proponents sought both purposes.

McNamara and Stern both say they talked through the outlines of what became SAL en route to Belgrade in late September 1979 for the Bank-Fund annual meetings that year. The president followed up his brief favorable May-in-Manila reference to adjustment lending with another in his Belgrade speech. He and Stern continued to fill out the design during the rest of the year.

In terms of SAL's macropolicy content, as discussed in chapter 10, the need of so many countries to close balance of payments gaps would dominate the reform agendas of early structural adjustment lending. The SAL designers were very mindful of the need to take account of the Bank's relations with the IMF. Adjustment lending would use a (program) form of lending identified with the Fund. It would be addressing borrowers' macropolicies that, at minimum, partly overlapped those featured in Fund lending. The innovation also had to be sold to a Board reflecting many Part I member countries disposed, as between the Bretton Woods institutions, to accord seniority to the Fund. All of this tended to put a constraint on the Bank's procedural choices. The latter could have varied between an ex-ante, contractual, preconditioned mode wherein the borrower would make fairly precise undertakings as to future policy reforms, whose performance the lender would evaluate as a basis or not for further lending—call it the IMF model; and an interactive ex-post mode wherein, when the borrower had undertaken reforms growing out of the dialogue between the borrower and the Bank, the Bank would reward the borrower with a loan, if, on balance, it approved the borrower's policy action.

In adjustment lending, the substantive relations between the two institutions also required careful tending. It was Bank policy to defer to the IMF with respect to such "core" macropolicy areas as general budget balances and (most particularly) exchange rates. But the Bank had to have an informed view of the client's entire macro scene, and, conversely, the Fund developed expertise and opinions about many functional and sectoral subjects (for example, government wages, privatization) that seemed more naturally to invite Bank attention. The only solution would be a great deal of interchange between and cross-referencing of the two institutions' operations.

There was, in the thinking of 1979–81, however, one key principle for dividing labor between the two institutions.[104] This was a time allocation. Indeed, it determined the nomenclature assigned to Fund "stabilization" (for which also read,

104. From 1960 to the middle 1970s, there had been another dividing principle. The Bank had (IDA) soft money; the Fund did not. However, this boundary was broken by the Fund's so-called trust fund distributions in the 1970s, and it would be again in the mid-1980s.

short-term adjustment) programs, on the one hand, and to the Bank's "structural adjustment," on the other. Stabilization was concerned with steadying aggregate demand in the short run. "Structural" problems, conversely, concerned stubborn imbalances with enduring causes—for example, a persisting shift in the terms of trade—that called for an adjustment in the *structure* of borrowers' production (more tradables, fewer nontradables)—not just for stabilizing demand.[105]

There were other time elements in the design. First, recipients of SALs would receive transfers quickly for adjustments that would be time consuming. The problem of conditions enforcement posed by this gap between funding and the policy impact would be met either by tranching loans or giving a series of them (wherein receipt of later loans would be premised on performance under earlier ones). Second, in principle, structural adjustment, while time consuming, would be a one-shot affair: once the payments imbalance under attack was corrected (with, for example, the structure of production being reordered toward more tradables), both the Bank and its borrowers could revert to former development priorities.

The new design had yet another component: if program loans were to be pressed into a more salient and stressed structural adjustment use, the other marginal, less conditioned, kinds of program lending that had been used in the earlier years would need to be abandoned. Otherwise there would be a "Gresham's law" problem; borrowers would choose the easier, less demanding form of program borrowing.

1980: SAL LAUNCHED. On February 5, 1980, in a paper that was compact for one expounding a major (even if temporary) change of direction, Bank management sought Board approval of its decision to launch a new line of SALs. The paper noted that recent changes in the international economy were "posing increasingly acute problems for many of the developing countries." The changes included "the increase in the price of oil, continued high levels of inflation and prolonged periods of slow growth in the OECD economies." The affected countries, which faced "deteriorating terms of trade and growing current account deficits" had to "consider how they can adjust their development patterns and economic structures" to the changed international environment.[106]

105. Two other usages of "structural" or "structural adjustment" were not being invoked when the Bank adopted the term in 1979. First, "structural" change was a familiar concept among development theorists. Development, instead of involving simply extrapolated (albeit) accelerated growth, tended to require systematic shifts in the structure of output from primary to secondary and tertiary sectors of production. This was a familiar view of such empiricists as Colin Clark and, indeed, Hollis Chenery, as well as of Marxist and neo-Marxist writers. Second and quite different, "structural adjustment" had been viewed as needed therapy for industrialized economies adopting liberalized trade policies, thereby reducing the protection of industries in which they lacked comparative advantage.

106. World Bank/IDA, "Lending for Structural Adjustment," R80-22, IDA/R80-17, February 5, 1980, p. 1.

According to the paper, the new lending program with which the Bank would help countries meet the new challenges would have the following features:

—The loans indeed would be policy based. Their distinguishing function would be to promote dialogue with the borrowing country about various aspects of development policy and policy reform.

—They would provide finance over a period of several years in direct support of specific policy reforms.

—The loans would be of the nonproject variety, providing the wherewithal for imports not linked to specific investment programs.[107]

The February 1980 paper did not attempt to predict which reforms any single country-specific structural adjustment program would feature, but it suggested possibilities: revision of investment programs, squaring them with available resources and seeking quicker yields; reforms improving incentives, infrastructure, and marketing on behalf of export diversification; reductions in protection to make domestic industries more competitive; and policies concerning domestic resource mobilization, price incentives, and efficient resource use.

The common structural adjustment themes across countries and programs, according to the paper, would be "increased efficiency of resource use and improved responsiveness of the economy to changes in economic conditions."[108] Although particular SALs would disburse quickly, lending for structural adjustment "must be conceived as an association with a borrower in a program of structural change over three to five years which will require financial support and technical collaboration throughout this period."[109] Finally, the paper noted that, while SALs would complement IMF operations, they would differ in the range of reforms addressed and the time frame over which the reforms would be expected to take effect.

Struck by the succinctness of the proposal, the Board pressed certain questions before it acquiesced, later in the spring, in the new departure. The directors were particularly curious about relations with the IMF. Was the Bank moving in on the Fund's turf? Was it going to dilute or second-guess Fund prescriptions? If not, on the other hand, were not two IMFs more than most borrowing countries could stand? Management's response had to tread a fine line: in its SA operations the Bank would be dealing with policy issues lying outside the Fund's core fiscal, monetary, and exchange rate agenda. It would not and could not avoid the latter subjects, but it normally would take pains to coordinate its macroeconomic views with those of the Fund: to the point that, in practice, successful SAL recipients usually already would have a Fund (standby or ESF) program in place. At the same time, the SAL innovation would not be allowed to lead the two institutions into the legal (and political) trap of "cross-conditionality."[110] (How, exactly, the two institu-

107. Ibid.
108. Ibid., p. 3.
109. Ibid., p. 4.
110. World Bank, "Structural Adjustment Lending," R80-122, IDA/R80-83, May 9, 1980.

tions could coordinate their activities without at least implicit cross-conditionality was discreetly sidestepped.)

The directors asked as well about the intended scale of structural adjustment lending and about the relation of the latter to the Bank's other, including other nonproject, lending operations. Although somewhat cryptic, management's responses emphasized opportunities for SALs and sector and project loans all to focus synergetically on common policy objectives; management appeared to estimate that something on the order of $600 million to $800 million would be allocated to structural adjustment lending in fiscal 1981.[111] Their doubts somewhat assuaged, the directors authorized the new category of lending twelve weeks before the start of what turned out to be the last year of the McNamara presidency.

CHANGING THE GUARD. In retrospect it is clear that a major change of ideology was in process at the turn of the 1970s into the 1980s. Inside the Bank, this was not the way it felt to Robert McNamara (he was not a part of it) or to Ernest Stern (he was a pragmatist). But A. W. (Tom) Clausen, coming from the headship of the Bank of America to succeed McNamara in 1981, was a representative of renewed capitalist doctrine concerning the limits of governments and the virtues of flexible, self-adjusting markets. Under Clausen, the Bank would become a major propagator of revisionist policy messages.

Other personnel changes punctuated the transition. Mahbub ul Haq, perhaps the institution's most eloquent antipoverty advocate, left soon after McNamara, and so did Hollis Chenery, the vice president for research and chief economist. The recruitment of Chenery's replacement first signaled, then helped shape, the institution's new doctrinal priorities.

The fief of the next vice president for research and chief economist would not be all it had been; the sectoral and policy analysis portions were transferred to Ernest Stern's operations complex. But the headship of what remained—general country and international economics and research management—still was the leading professional economics job in the institution, and McNamara and Chenery sought to settle the question of replacement before either left. They favored Albert Fishlow, then of Yale University; and for a time, until a slashing attack on Fishlow's alleged interventionist propensities appeared in a *Wall Street Journal* editorial, it looked as if President-elect Clausen would go along. After Clausen's arrival the matter was referred to a panel of distinguished outside economists chaired by Sir Arthur Lewis, and from the short list that the panel recommended, Clausen chose Anne Krueger of the University of Minnesota.

Krueger, a distinguished representative of the neoclassical school of development and trade policy, would place a heavy pro-markets, anti-interventionist imprint on the Bank's research and policy-analysis programs. She reshuffled the

111. That is, something on the order of 5.0 percent to 6.5 percent of the combined IBRD-IDA commitments that were projected for that year.

central economics staffs into closer conformity with her own views and quickly became an articulate and unyielding spokesperson for the new policy priorities.

One World Bank document, mentioned earlier in the chapter, highlighted the institution's intellectual transition as the 1970s gave way to the 1980s: the Berg Report of 1981.[112] The way, in its treatment of African parastatals, the report abandoned the distinction between the market and the private sector provides one example of its focus. The Organization of African Unity's *Lagos Plan of Action,* in explaining the beleaguered state of Sub-Saharan African development, had placed much of the blame on the international environment and on the policies of non-African governments and institutions contributing to it.[113] Other analysts, for example, Uma Lele, had emphasized that African governments and agencies, with outside assistance, needed to build human and institutional development capacities, along with physical infrastructure.[114]

Berg, by contrast, came down heavily on the responsibility of specific African policy errors for Africa's predicament. The report did not deny the presence of other problems. But its strongest recommendations, along with an endorsement of increased aid, were those for reforms by African governments. Thus the report strongly reinforced the new structural adjustment rationale: recipient policies *really* mattered, and it was the Bank's duty to lever needed reforms. The World Bank now headed into the operational phase of its heavy engagement with policy-based lending.

112. World Bank, *Accelerated Development in Sub-Saharan Africa: An Agenda for Action,* Report 3558, Office of the Senior Vice President, Operations, R81-211, 1981.

113. Organization of African Unity, *Lagos Plan of Action,* 1980.

114. Uma J. Lele, *The Design of Rural Development: Lessons from Africa* (Johns Hopkins University Press, 1979; 3d printing with a new postscript). Also OECD, *Development Cooperation 1980* (Paris: OECD, 1980), chap. 2.

TEN

Policy-Linked Lending: II

BY THE end of 1981 the World Bank had a new president drawn from the private banking sector. It was on the verge of getting a new chief economist who would put a strong neoclassical imprint on its staff. The Bank had a new structural adjustment line of business that was becoming more ideologically affiliated than its originators had intended. Structural adjustment loans would take on a still higher profile within the year when the debt crisis hit the "highly indebted" countries. Some of the Bank's government owners had become sharply more conservative and events were wrapped in a global shift of politico-economic philosophy that would look in retrospect more decisive than it felt at the time. Influenced by these changes, the macropolicy doctrines the Bank imparted to its borrowers underwent revisions.

Revisionism: Macro Views in the 1980s

A number of changes in macro views were in store for the 1980s. One of the more important—sometimes called the hallmark issue of the decade—had to do with the roles of government and markets in the economy.

The Roles of Governments and Markets

Although it was still admitted that "market failures" had to be coped with, government failures now began attracting more attention. While never an absolutist, the Bank joined the antigovernment, pro-market trend. In general it favored policies that freed markets, stripped away controls, cut back subsidies, and reduced other distortions that governments, by their interventions, were seen to impose on market outcomes.

Export Expansion Fueled by Import Liberalization

Export growth tended to be urged on nearly all borrowing governments, small and large, very poor and less poor—and exports, making their way by comparative advantage, were to be facilitated, not by subsidies, but by reducing import barriers that reined in export competitiveness. This part of Bank doctrine became narrower and more emphatic.

Public versus Private (Product-Marketing) Enterprises

The Bank became once again a less inhibited, more doctrinaire advocate of private product-marketing enterprises, as the 1981 Berg Report had recommended. The changes in doctrine were incremental, however. Previously, in choosing norms for good industrial performance, the Bank had concentrated on the quality and independence of management, whatever the variety of ownership. Now ownership issues once again became paramount. Nationalizations—"wrong-way" changes in ownership, from private to public—were discouraged. Where there was a choice, it was hoped that new starts would go private. Where ownership was mixed, shifts to increase private shares, in part through sales to public or foreign investors, were favorably regarded. But, especially in the earlier 1980s, the Bank remained highly interested in improving the quality of *public enterprise management* (on the implicit assumption that the firms in question were likely to stay public). It was only by mid-decade—first, with Secretary James Baker's speech in Seoul in 1985, then with the institution's involvements in Eastern Europe and the former Soviet Union—that *privatization* became a major item on the Bank's policy-promotion agenda.

Exchange Rates

In the 1980s and early 1990s the Bank became less deferential to the International Monetary Fund in the matter of exchange rates. Because the Fund was characteristically preoccupied with inflation, it shied away from devaluations that tended to raise members' indigenous prices. The Fund also, arguably, had a Gallic inclination to avoid interfering with the tie to the French franc in the Francophone countries of Africa that formed the Communauté financière africaine (CFA). The Bank, on the other hand, with its heightened commitment to export promotion, was more active in encouraging borrowers to devalue.

Fiscal and Monetary Policy

The main macropolicy tools the World Bank used in promoting reform in the 1980s were the familiar ones, but the agenda fanned out. The Bank continued to recognize the two differentiated goals it had distinguished from the beginning (stabilization and growth). It kept attending, albeit less aggressively, to a third purpose that had been greatly scaled up in the 1970s (internal equity), and much emphasis and priority were attached to a fourth purpose (adjustment), which became the focus of the 1980s.

In the 1980s the Bank became less diffident (in relation to the IMF) about mixing into the issue of short-run, aggregate-demand smoothing stabilization. In too many countries too much of the time in the 1980s inflationary instability was too preemptive and flagrant for the Bank to hang back. Intervening, its stance characteristically was—indeed, like the Fund's—austere, with the caveat that demand restraint not be allowed to abort export promotion.

The Bank's conception of the principal means of promoting *growth and efficiency* had not changed from the 1970s and before, except that now there was an even greater tendency to emphasize the importance of such inputs as technology, education, producers' health, and the effects of governance on the economic environment.

As an aside, it might be noted that, conceptually, the majority view in the World Bank during the 1980s was hostile to propositions that would have added "incomes-policy" and directed-investment amendments to the monetary and fiscal instrumentation for pursuing the stabilization and growth objectives. But in the 1980s and 1990s the Bank found itself having to cope with "heterodox" stabilization policies in several Latin American countries and with the so-called East Asian model of activist industrial policy.

The third of the four fiscal and monetary policy purposes that the Bank recognized in the 1980s and 1990s has been elaborated in the "poverty chapters" of this book. Defenders of Bank continuity deny that this focus disappeared with Robert McNamara, but at least it submerged. As elaborated briefly in this chapter and more extensively in chapter 7, the priority reached a new phase of heavy attention beginning with the *World Development Report 1990* and its emphasis on poverty.

The fourth purpose of fiscal/monetary policy did not move to center stage until the 1980s. Adjusting the economy's external and internal balances to a resumed or new state of sustainability was not a new idea conceptually, but in the 1980s it achieved an altogether new order of importance. The changes required were often, even typically, structural; and they were preemptive. In terms of resource uses, they might temporarily encroach on either or both growth and equity, but they needed to be accommodated if countries were to regain an opportunity to concentrate on those goals.

Budgetary and Financial Institutional Development

Budgetary and financial institutional development in the 1980s and 1990s was sufficiently different from and additive to broad fiscal and monetary policy reform to deserve a separate listing. As the Bank traversed the 1980s, the distinction between "Type I" and "Type II" or "first- and second-generation" reforms became familiar. In the first round of macro (including monetary/fiscal) reforms, changes tended to be fundamental and sweeping. Like the reduction of a tariff rate, they were almost self-implementing, "stroke-of-the-pen" shifts. But then came the second generation, often requiring heavy, painstaking implementation. Increasingly, as a reforming government and the external influencers pursued a reform agenda, they found themselves engaging in such things as government expenditure surveys, detailed rationalizations of tax laws and tax administration, and the overhaul of financial institutions.

Transfers, Foreign Investment, Debt, and Creditworthiness

The biggest happening in developing countries' external finance in the 1980s was the debt crisis, discussed in chapter 11. That chapter also dwells on the issue of creditworthiness, that of both the Bank and its borrowers. Thus it and the present two policy chapters, and, indeed, the finance chapters need to be read as a package.

The official-transfers component of the Bank's macropolicies doctrine for the 1980s and 1990s was an extrapolation from earlier decades. The Bank still favored such transfers, thinking that they served a useful purpose. Nevertheless the real growth of concessional transfers, including those of the International Development Association, seemed to be ending. Net official nonconcessional transfers, of the International Bank for Reconstruction and Development and others, had turned or were turning negative, in part because of reflows and in part because some borrowers had less appetite for official transfers. In the case of very poor countries, especially in Africa, there was growing concern about the scale and habits of aid dependency. At the same time, the outlook for foreign commercial bank lending to developing countries was mixed and uncertain.

In the wake of these developments, the World Bank experienced something of an identity crisis in the 1990s. Was it, some asked, no longer primarily a resource transfer agent? Had it become mainly a purveyor of other products, such as macropolicy advice? To what extent would the one continue to depend on the other, and what did the prospective combination say about the future relevance of the institution? At least one thing was clear: the Bank of the 1980s was a less equivocal, more forthright, promoter of foreign private investment in its borrowing countries.

The SALs-SECALs Era

In 1982 the Bank introduced a variant of structural adjustment lending in the form of sector adjustment loans. These loans were for occasions on which the Bank preferred or perceived a readiness for a more concentrated adjustment exercise, the borrower preferred the sectoral approach to opening up its whole macro-economic spectrum to an adjustment review, or a sectoral reform was following up and complementing macro reform. SECALs were not widely used until mid-decade but then for a time became more frequent than SALs. Conceptually and procedurally, however, the two formats were close cousins.

Adjustment loans in the 1980s claimed not much more than a quarter of the dollar volume of the World Bank's new commitments, but they were the most prominent and contentious part of the Bank's product. Borrowers sensed an emotional if not a logical inconsistency: SALs intruded most heavily on clients (policy-making was the latter's most distinctively sovereign activity) at a time when the institution was counseling governments to intervene less into their own economies. SALs claimed a disproportionate share of the time and nervous energy of both Bank management and the Executive Board. Quickly they became the institution's pivotal activity.

Almost at once tension built up between the inclination to do policy lending selectively, and very well, and the way demands for expansion of the programs piled up faster than the instigators had expected. Between March 1980 and September 1981 the operations vice president turned back ten SAL proposals, citing the proposed borrowers' lack of readiness or their access to other resources, these negatives being compounded in some cases by inadequate preparation on the Bank's side.[1] He counseled the regional vice presidents: "I cannot emphasize too strongly that structural adjustment lending must be in support of a program of specific and monitorable policy, institutional and other changes, which we are convinced has a high probability of being implemented by the borrower."[2]

The SAL mill ground slowly. In fiscal 1980, the program's first operational year, loans of the new style to Turkey and Kenya (both were modified to fit the new design) were the only two approved. Five more made it onto the books in fiscal 1981 and only six in each of the two following years. Nor was the new mode yet claiming a large fraction of total Bank/IDA lending. In fiscal 1981 the fraction was less than 6.5 percent.[3]

Meanwhile an expansionist dynamic had been turned loose. The foreign exchange requirements generated by the second oil shock focused attention on the new SALs. Within the Bank a new fashion took hold. Making tough-minded, conditioned, policy-based program loans became the done thing. The operations chief tried to check the bandwagoning. As he told a regional vice president at the end of 1980:

1. In chronological order, the applicants were Pakistan, Argentina, Turkey II, Brazil, Sudan, Egypt, Peru, Thailand, Kenya II, and Zaire. This information is from the Stern files. (Some of these proposals prevailed later.)

2. Memorandum, Ernest Stern to regional VPs, "Structural Adjustment Lending—Internal Bank Processing," May 22, 1980, p. 1.

3. Of commitments. World Bank data.

As you know I am in full agreement with the Region's strategy to move increasingly to sector lending. This is desirable from the Bank's view in terms of relevant policy discussion and workload and many of the countries of the Region have the necessary institutional capacity for such an approach. But this shift must be done gradually and sensibly. The strong impression I receive is that the Regional staff accept this as the current fashion without having the intellectual/policy/and institutional underpinnings in place. This leads to confusion and loan proposals . . . which are inadequately defined.[4]

But the expansionist momentum already was strong by early 1982, and it became insistent for what would be called "the highly indebted countries" (HICs)—most of them in Latin America—after Mexico triggered the debt crisis in August of the same year.

The SAL designers who had suppressed weaker, less conditioned forms of program lending for Gresham's law reasons now suffered the consequences. Strictly speaking, SALs and SECALs were not the only vehicles for conveying quick-disbursing balance of payments money. To some extent such things as agricultural credit loans were bent to the same purpose. But adjustment loans were now the Bank's program loans of choice, and pleas for quick-disbursing money concentrated on them.

Which Clients?

The designers' original expectation—that SALs would be for select middle-income countries—was not what transpired. In part this was because the agreement of the second party to each SAL decision—that is, the recipient government—was by no means automatic. The new loans always had a genuine double purpose; even when the need for quick-flowing funds was most urgent, the policy-reform side of the transaction was never simply cosmetic. Governments had to be fairly serious about the reform and be willing to accept intrusions into their policy decisions. Thus India avoided any form of Bank adjustment lending until 1992. During the 1980s Pakistan accepted only one SAL (in 1982) and then shifted to more sectorally circumscribed SECALs. Choosing various sector loans, Mexico (beginning in 1983) and China (with a rural sector loan in 1988) avoided the nomenclature and some of the standard procedures of SALs.

Indeed, the average population size of countries opting for SECALs, once they came available, was much larger (even when China is left aside) than that of SAL acceptors. But little can be made of this distinction. Through 1989, Kenya, Korea, Morocco, the Philippines, Thailand, and Turkey were, like Pakistan, all SAL recipients with populations in excess of twenty million. What is striking, compared with initial expectations, is the extent to which Sub-Saharan African countries (most of them low-income countries) became objects of Bank adjustment lending.

4. Memorandum, Ernest Stern to E. V. K. Jaycox, acting regional vice president, East Asia and Pacific, December 8, 1980.

Like Turkey, Kenya was one of the first (1980) two SAL countries because the governments and the Bank already were working on conditioned program loans when the new program started. Thereafter, SALs in Africa went to Mauritius, Côte d'Ivoire, Ghana, and Togo during 1981–83, and SECALs to Uganda and Zimbabwe. But then, with the Sub-Saharan countries caught in interest rate and terms-of-trade squeezes, with debt burdens rising, short-term IMF loans running out, and the countries in severe economic decline, SALs and SECALs to Sub-Saharan Africa came in a rush during the balance of the 1980s. From 1984 through 1989, twenty-one countries—Nigeria, Sierra Leone, Zambia, Guinea-Bissau, Mauritania, Burkina Faso, Madagascar, Burundi, Guinea, Zaire, the Central African Republic, Congo, the Gambia, Niger, São Tomé, Gabon, Mali, Mozambique, Benin, Cameroon, and Somalia—received adjustment loans.

What better fitted the earlier expectations was the way Latin America provided the other concentrated group of recipients. Bank analyses retrospectively treated conditioned program loans to Jamaica, Bolivia, and Guyana (1979–81) as SALs.[5] From then on recipients in Latin America (Mexico, Panama, Uruguay, Brazil, Costa Rica, Colombia, Chile, Argentina, Ecuador, Honduras, and Venezuela) constituted the bulk of the decade's highly indebted countries.

Bank adjustment lending in the 1980s had a clientele throughout the developing world. It was numerous and diverse, and it fitted no single paradigm.

How Much Adjustment Lending?

In the abstract, the question of quantity was a puzzler. A project loan had to fund a reasonable fraction of an assessable project, but how much did a decision for reform cost? Enough to get a hearing? To ease the pain of adjustment? Ease it how much? Was it not true that, whereas too little adjustment support from outside could fail to get attention or to provide the cushioning for reform, too much could delay reform and become a substitute for it? Would not too much cushioning entrench aid dependency? Where was the optimizing mean?

Debates along these lines remained conceptually lively, but for the World Bank and its owners in the 1980s, the issue was foreshortened: adjustment lending was supply constrained. Plainly, to be of any consequence at all the new mode had to be nontrivial in its scale. But all resources available to Bank/IDA for adjustment lending were supply constrained. This was self-evidently the case with taxpayer-funded IDA (see chapter 17). But it was also true for IBRD lending. Even though it was still in principle comparatively easy to go to the private market for fresh resources, some members (notably the United States) now resisted such expansion as a way of dampening the whole Bank program. But there was a more specific rein on the volume of Bank *adjustment* (that is, SAL and SECAL) lending. Adjustment

---

5. World Bank, "Report on Adjustment Lending II; Policies for the Recovery of Growth," March 1990, annex table 5.5.

Table 10-1. *World Bank Adjustment Lending, 1980–93, by Country Categories*
Annual averages, millions of 1990 U.S. dollars

Loan and borrower	1980–82	1983–86	1987–90	1991–93
Adjustment lending	1,412	3,553	5,597	4,744
Adjustment lending/total loans (percent)	7	18	26	23
SAL/total AL (percent)	87	40	45	51
SECAL/total AL (percent)	13	60	55	49
Borrowers				
Africa	320	916	1,305	1,049
Percentage of total AL	23	26	23	22
Number of loans	3	10	18	14
East Asia	301	389	687	147
Percentage of total AL	21	11	12	3
Number of loans	1	1	3	1
Europe and Central Asia	440	572	498	924
Percentage of total AL	31	16	9	19
Number of loans	1	2	2	4
Latin America and Caribbean	95	1,257	2,284	1,527
Percentage of total AL	7	35	41	32
Number of loans	2	5	9	10
MENA	0	229	437	474
Percentage of total AL	0	6	8	10
Number of loans	0	1	2	2
South Asia	256	189	386	621
Percentage of total AL	18	5	7	13
Number of loans	2	1	3	4
HICs[a]	165	2,020	3,015	1,743
Percentage of total AL	12	57	54	37
Number of loans	1	7	11	13

Source: World Bank Financial Database.

a. Highly indebted countries are Argentina, Bolivia, Brazil, Chile, Colombia, Costa Rica, Côte d'Ivoire, Ecuador, Jamaica, Mexico, Morocco, Nigeria, Peru, Philippines, Uruguay, Venezuela, and Yugoslavia (until April 1993). Does not include 1993 loan to Slovenia for $80 million.

lending was program lending, and program lending had been acceptable only under "special" circumstances. Thus one had to get specific Executive Board approval to do it, and the Board promulgated relative ceilings on the activity—as did the IDA deputies with respect to IDA SALs and SECALs.

At the start of the SAL era, the program-loan ceiling was 10 percent of new commitments. By the late 1980s, this was nudged up to as high as 25 percent, and if, at one time or another, such giant clients as India and China were counted as not competing for program-loan dollars, the quota left for other recipients was larger. It was larger still (considering the fact that program loans typically were drawn down much faster than project loans) as a share of disbursements.

All the same, non–project loan resources remained scarce relative to the claims on them. This helped skew early thinking about the most appropriate SAL clients;

Table 10-2. *World Bank Adjustment Lending, 1980–91: Frequency of Policy Conditions*
Annual averages

Policy condition	1980–82		1983–86		1987–90		1991	
	No.	Percent	No.	Percent	No.	Percent	No.	Percent
Supply-side, growth-oriented policies								
Trade policies	47	17	118	18	192	11	162	11
Industry sector	23	8	56	9	76	4	23	2
Energy sector	24	9	27	4	74	4	23	2
Agricultural sector	54	19	143	22	224	13	112	8
Social sector	3	1	2	0	34	2	101	7
Financial sector[a]	12	4	54	8	211	12	240	16
Public institutions and regulations	21	7	49	7	202	12	219	15
Public enterprise reforms	26	9	79	12	288	17	161	11
Other	2	1	8	1	42	2	68	5
Absorption-reduction policies								
Fiscal policy[b]	57	20	98	15	287	17	298	20
Monetary policy (money supply)[a]	2	1	5	1	13	1	25	2
Switching policies								
Exchange rate[b]	8	3	16	2	36	2	20	1
Wage policy[b]	2	1	5	1	47	3	31	2
Total	282	100	657	100	1725	100	1483	100
Total number of adjustment operations	8		19		31		31	
Average number of conditions per operation	34		35		56		48	

Source: Adjustment Loan Database, ALCID, as of September 20, 1991; report generated on April 16, 1993.
a. Money supply was included in financial sector in the source, but it has been separated for this table.
b. Exchange rate and wage policy were included in fiscal policy in the source, but they have been separated for this table.

the latter were not the generality of project-funded low-income countries but rather a select group of middle-income countries with reforms at the ready. (As already indicated, this was to be overtaken by the urgency of African needs.) Resource scarcity skewed choices of loan vehicles. A single program loan might be a plausible vehicle for trying to reach several sectoral policy targets; it was tempting to get as many different kinds of good policy mileage out of a given loan as possible.

There was also the question of additionality. Was adjustment lending to come on top of and not displace the Bank's established lending programs? In the aggregate, the answer was clear: institutional totals could not increase appreciably (although disbursement rates could confound this somewhat); but adjustment lending could be at least partially additive for reform-minded countries, at the diffused expense of others.

Tables 10-1 and 10-2 provide an overview of the quantitative and conditioning dimensions of adjustment lending. Total adjustment lending during the 1980s and early 1990s peaked at about 30 percent of total Bank/IDA disbursements during 1987–90. It declined to a level of 20 percent in 1991–93. SECALs leaped to

60 percent of the structural adjustment total in 1983–86. Thereafter SALs and SECALs each claimed half the total.

How Many Policy Targets?

The key issue of adjustment lending was what reforms were to be promoted. But also there was a sheer numbers question: How many conditions or other policy targets was an individual adjustment loan supposed to serve? Despite the general cautiousness of early SAL administration, adjustment loans immediately began to sprout a multiplicity of targets. The first SAL to Senegal in December 1980 (its second tranche was later canceled) was not atypical. The loan had grown out of a shared dialogue with the newly reform-minded Senegalese government, but when it came to writing the loan text, the Bank specified no less than thirty-two measures that the government of Senegal was obliged to undertake, most of them specifically monitored by the Bank. The timely performance of all of them was to be a condition for release of the loan's second tranche, and thirteen of them were to be started or completed, monitored or discussed, within the first three months of the life of the loan.[6]

This was something like the norm. As the 1980s progressed, virtually every serious review of adjustment lending recommended, as the Economic Department's "Review of Adjustment Lending I" (RAL I) put it, that there be "fewer, better-monitored" conditions. Yet by the time of RAL II (1990) the average count of conditions or other specific undertakings per loan already was fifty-six, and it kept growing.[7]

There were, of course, explanations for the profusion of targets. Some of the reforms reinforced others. Bureaucratically, some recommended reforms had technical and sectoral advocates within the Bank, and it was easiest for SAL managers to acquiesce in their inclusion. As indicated, multiplying the number of conditions per loan appeared to increase the reform mileage—or imagery—that could be gotten from limited policy-loan money. However, the combination of target multiplicity with an ex-ante, contracting adjustment-lending procedure invited high averages of visible nonperformance.

For Which Reforms?

Substantively, the Bank's policy-based lending in the 1980s evolved at several levels. Its primary focus was on macroeconomic policies, broadly defined; this set

---

6. John P. Lewis, "Aid, Structural Adjustment, and Senegalese Agriculture," in Mark Gersovitz and John Waterbury, eds., *The Political Economy of Risk and Choice in Senegal* (London: Frank Cass, 1987), pp. 283–325.

7. The RALs (reviews of adjustment lending) and other official evaluations of the activity are identified later in the chapter.

of core policies widened as the decade proceeded. Second, a group of what can be called *"enhanced* adjustment" targets developed (to stretch "the adjustment umbrella"). Related was another set of reform targets that, as things sorted out, were promotable by separate, stand-alone loans. Finally, there was the question of how the reform effort interfaced with other Bank goals. Adjustment lending, as noted, had twin purposes; it sought to promote reform *and* provide flexible foreign exchange. But what more should be said about goals other than reform during the period of high-profile project-based lending operations?

On the issue of which policy targets policy-based lending tried to promote, the story after 1980 was relatively straightforward. The targets started out being quite tightly focused. But throughout the decade, the tendency was to enlarge the target set, which eventually threatened to fall or fragment of its own weight. Adjustment therapy was what policy did to correct an unsustainable, potentially calamitous, financial imbalance in the economy, and the imbalance of focus was in the borrowing country's external accounts. Uncorrected and uncompensated for, it could cripple a national economy. Ernest Stern never retreated from the view that balance of payments repair was the only appropriate goal of structural adjustment lending. In 1989, when he no longer was operations chief, he told a Bank conference:

> It is my personal conclusion—one which is certainly not universally shared—that structural adjustment lending ought to be anchored in balance of payments problems. . . .
>
> We provide quick disbursing loans because the actions being undertaken by the government have some balance of payments impact . . . we can help defray. To me, that justification has been and continues to be the basic anchor of structural adjustment lending.[8]

By then, this was an unacceptably restricted view of structural adjustment lending's macro agenda.[9] At the same time, it was fairly encompassing. Strict constructionists like Stern saw adjustment extending to two policy sets. In the first place, it included measures that served *directly* to raise exports relative to imports: exchange rate adjustments (albeit, Fund-led) and commercial policy changes that promoted exports in part by liberalizing imports. Such measures shifted the structure of production from such "nontradables" as domestic services not traded internationally to "tradables," that is, exports and substitutes for imports.

In the second place, SAL was interested in budgetary and monetary determinants of domestic imbalances, notably government deficits. But, for strictly construed structural adjustment, these were important not in their own right, but

---

8. Ernest Stern, "Evolution and Lessons of Adjustment Lending," in Vinod Thomas, Ajay Chhibber, Mansoor Dailami, and Jaime de Melo, eds., *Restructuring Economies in Distress: Policy Reform and the World Bank* (Oxford University Press, 1991), p. 4.

9. In 1988, when the draft review of adjustment lending (RAL I) went to the President's Council for clearance, it contained a recommendation to do adjustment lending only when there was a balance of payments need. After reflection the president decided the recommendation should be dropped from the version that went to the Board. Communication from Stanley Fischer, January 1996.

because of their linkage to balance of payments variables; they were *indirect* determinants of payments outcomes.

By the middle 1980s this strict constructionist view of adjustment lending rankled with many Bank people. Not all macro reforms in which the Bank was interested had much of a balance of payments spillover. Trying always to tackle an economy's macro maladies via external balances could be foolishly roundabout at times. Often the dominant imbalances were internal; often inflation was primarily an internal problem; sometimes runaway domestic debt was more of a challenge than foreign debt. Moreover, these internal problems could be structural: domestic savings incentives could need strengthening; investment allocations could need changing for reasons other than improving future balance of payments; government capital and current budgets could invite reordering; public sector efficiency and the public versus private sector division of labor could demand reform.

The idea that macro adjustments always had to have a balance of payments hook was particularly regrettable in the eyes of the Bank's Latin American and Caribbean wing. Latin America, on average, had been more inflation prone than the other regions, and the inflationary propensity was internally rooted. Latin American governments in the 1970s and early 1980s encouraged borrowing from foreign commercial banks, but often less to solve external payments imbalances than to ease internal budgetary constraints.[10] Thus Bank functionaries who wished to assist economic restructuring in Latin America found it awkward to have to justify proposed loans on the basis of payments needs. In 1990 the Bank's chief economist, Stanley Fischer, accused Latin American and Caribbean countries of doing some "creative accounting." Venezuela and Colombia faced no immediate external financing gaps. But the countries were reluctant to undertake critical trade reforms for fear of negative fallout on their balance of payments. The regional staff solved the problem by projecting a sufficient payments gap to warrant the loans required to cushion confidence and get the reforms rolling.[11]

Whether or not they needed to be linked to their balance of payments effects, macropolicies that came within the orbit of structural adjustment lending can be classified under three headings: lending that affected aggregate demand and, when the latter was curbed, reduced "absorption"; on the supply side, lending that affected productive growth and efficiency; and as a subset of the second category, lending that had the "switching" effect of transferring inputs from producing outputs of goods and services not internationally traded to the production of tradables. Table 10-2, indicating the distribution of conditions in the Bank's 1980–91 adjustment loans, is organized around these categories.

10. See Karin Lissakers, *Banks, Borrowers, and the Establishment: A Revisionist Account of the International Debt Crisis* (Basic Books, 1991), chap. 3.

11. Memoranda, Stanley Fischer to Shahid Husain, LAC vice president, "Venezuela—Financial Sector Adjustment Loan," May 8, 1990; Stanley Fischer to Senior Vice President Moeen Qureshi, June 14, 1990.

Time was an evolving dimension of the new lending regime. According to SAL's original theory, the Bank-type adjustment was concerned with medium- and longer-term reforms, including changes in an economy's productive structure. This much stayed put. But otherwise matters of timing changed as experience accrued. Effective adjustment, it turned out, took much longer than the original SAL design had imagined. There were two effects. The chronological mismatch was aggravated between the delivery of a quick-disbursing loan and the time when its reform purposes were programmed to be accomplished. But more important, the idea of putting growth promotion on hold while an adjustment detour was negotiated became unrealistic. The revised agenda became adjustment *with* growth—both in the minds of Bank staff and as articulated by U.S. Treasury Secretary James Baker when he presented the "Baker Plan" at the Bank-Fund annual meetings in October 1985 (see chapter 11).

Internal Tensions: Heyday, yet Constraints

The adjustment program's spread tendencies came into their own in 1987. The idea of getting more benefits out of given loan transactions appealed—good politician that he was—to Barber Conable, the new president who had come on board in mid-1986. But in addition, the incidence of SALs was enhanced when Conable's 1987 reorganization switched the Bank's two senior vice presidents. Both were exceptionally able and, although there was some tension between them, they respected each other and collaborated well enough. But there was a difference in style. Ernest Stern, the long-standing chief of operations, had been trying to hold adjustment lending down to size. Moeen Qureshi, who had been the senior vice president for finance, was more permissive as Stern's successor, more inclined to give his regional and other staff their heads. As is explained in chapter 18, the reorganization had accentuated interregional differences within the Bank. With more domestically focused as well as debt-motivated loans for the Latin American and Caribbean region, a surge of African adjustment loans, and the president and senior vice president for operations keeping a looser rein on structural adjustment proposals in general, the latter 1980s were a heyday for the Bank's adjustment lending, before problems that would accrue had fully emerged.

What did begin to take form was a realization of the Type I, Type II distinction noted earlier (it is emphasized in the country case on Ghana later in the chapter). The line between the two sets is not precise, but in contrast to "stroke-of-the-pen" changes, Type II reforms needed to be administered in an iterative fashion. They required institutions to be built and operational capacities to be generated. Such agencies as the Bank had a lower rate of success with second-generation interventions, which were harder for both borrower and lender. But they became more common as the adjustment program matured. As Table 10-2 indicates, loans after 1986 had a greater incidence of public enterprise reforms and many more conditions concerning public institutions and regulations. Contracts with governments to privatize revenue-producing enterprises began to appear, and the promotion of financial sector reform picked up sharply.

If the Conable presidency was the heyday of adjustment lending, the initiative still ran into certain boundaries. One constraint was self-imposed, ideological, and deeply rooted in Bank thinking. It had two manifestations. As explained in chapter 9, the Bank's macroeconomic analysis in the 1970s, while competent, was comparatively routine. It could have been said that the absence of a missing element in the analysis also was routine in the period's applications of market-oriented development economics. The missing element was the "incomes-policies" hypothesis that broad-gauged wage- and price-setting decisions are in some degree independent variables that policy can seek to influence constructively. This was still a respectable view in the policy debates among some members of the Organization for Economic Cooperation and Development, although less common than it had been in the 1950s and 1960s. But, as the earlier sketch of the Bank's 1980 macropolicy doctrine has indicated, the thought scarcely appears in Bank documentation, the grounds, it seems, being that such attempts to steer product and factor prices constructively are bound to create the kinds of rents and allocative distortions that market liberalization seeks to reduce. The issue, however, emerged in the later 1980s. Mexico in 1987 was one of a series of Latin American countries adopting "heterodox" anti-inflationary programs with incomes-policies components. The Bank could not turn a blind eye to such programs, but it was ill at ease with them. The same was true in Turkey.

The Bank's same inhibition against managed price and wage making had a second manifestation: the institution had little appetite in the 1980s for interventionist industrial policy. It had so little regard for governmental initiatives to "pick winners" and alter comparative advantage in the manner that had been practiced with alleged success by South Korea and Taiwan that Japanese representatives began to lobby insistently for more attention to the more interventionist "Japanese" mode of industrial development.[12] The result—the study, *The East Asian Miracle,* which appeared in 1993—gave only grudging support to interventionist doctrine and did not signal any substantive shift in adjustment lending—at least none that was evident by the mid-1990s.[13]

The International Monetary Fund provided a third substantive constraint on the World Bank's choice of macro reform targets. The nature of the intra–Bretton Woods tension warrants some emphasis.

12. See Alice H. Amsden, *Asia's Next Giant: South Korea and Late Industrialization* (Oxford University Press, 1989); Robert Wade, *Governing the Market: Economic Theory and the Role of Government in East Asian Industrialization* (Princeton University Press, 1990); also volume 2, chapter 6.

13. World Bank, *The East Asian Miracle: Economic Growth and Public Policy* (Oxford University Press, 1993).

The Bank and the Fund: The Argentina Case

The Fund's seniority on the subject made the Bank reluctant to enter one of the two principal fields of direct balance of payments influence. The Bank pushed trade policy but at the start of the 1980s hesitated to press exchange rate reform. The latter was Fund turf. As is discussed in chapter 12 here and in chapter 5 of volume 2, the constraint skewed Bank/IDA interventions in Francophone Africa.

Another Fund-related inhibition became evident from the mid-1980s onward when the Bank began to bore into public finance issues: compared with the Bank, the Fund had developed a near monopoly in the area of taxation analysis. This seems to have no particular rationale, but as became apparent in a revealing and thoughtful two-day conference held by the two institutions and outside experts in June 1987, the imbalance was well embedded in the comparative staffing patterns.[14] It was only by a heavy use of consultants and fresh hiring that the Bank achieved status as a tax-reform adviser by the end of the decade.

In 1982 Ernest Stern contributed a paper on Bank structural adjustment financing to a conference on IMF conditionality.[15] Commenting on the paper, Michael Bruno, who in 1993 would become the World Bank's vice president/chief economist, raised several questions, which, as he said, "a visitor from outer space might now ask":

> Is there any clear, inherent separation of functions (between Fund and Bank) left other than accidental institutional history? What is the difference between a Bank's structural adjustment loan (SAL) or a Fund's EFF [Extended Fund Facility] if correctly interpreted? Would the Fund agree to adopt Bank conditionality on a SAL? Is it really the case, as seems to be claimed in Ernie Stern's paper, that the difference only lies in the "orientation and expertise of Bank staff"? That surely cannot be a viable and lasting reason for institutional separation. I would certainly not want to be misunderstood on this point. Having long been critical of past lack of cooperation between these two great neighboring institutions, I have found the recent evolution of relationships (joint meetings of senior staff, increasing number of joint field missions, and so on) most welcome.[16]

Bruno's puzzlement may well have deepened as the 1980s proceeded, for Michel Camdessus, who became managing director of the Fund in 1987, was active and persuasive in securing augmented soft-money funding for the Fund and engaging it in the promotion of structural adjustment reform (and even structural adjustment terminology) that increased the substantive overlap with the World Bank.

14. Heywood W. Fleisig, ed., "Improving Tax Policy Advice: Lessons and Unresolved Issues from Asian Experience," Internal Discussion Paper, Asian Regional Series, reporting a seminar of June 25 and 26, 1987, World Bank Report IDP-35, June 1989.

15. Ernest Stern, "World Bank Financing of Structural Adjustment" in John Williamson, ed., *IMF Conditionality* (Washington, D.C.: Institute for International Economics, 1983), pp. 87–108.

16. Michael Bruno, "Comments," chapters 4–6 in Williamson, ed., *IMF Conditionality*, pp. 127–28.

One way to illuminate Fund-Bank relations in the 1980s is to review the dramatic tensions that developed between the two institutions in regard to Argentina and other Latin American countries in the years 1987–89. In the Argentina case, the World Bank departed from its normal practice of making a government's acquisition of an IMF agreement (standby or EFF) a de facto precondition for a Bank SAL. In October 1988 the Bank presented to its Executive Board a go-it-alone set of adjustment loans for Argentina. Although the loans were accepted, the European and Australian directors excoriated the president and Bank management for imprudence. As early as December, moreover, Bank staff found themselves unable to recommend a tranch release for lack of borrower performance, as they reported to the Board in March 1989. In volume 2 of this work Jacques Polak characterizes the Bank's Argentina foray as a "disaster" and "debacle." The experience caused President Conable in mid-1989 to enter into a new "concordat" with Managing Director Camdessus of the Fund that provided a more explicit division of labor and plan of cooperation between the two institutions. Polak's chapter on the World Bank and the IMF, including its account of the 1987–89 Argentine case, is written from the perspective of a Fund veteran. Certain Bank readers have by and large approved its rendering of the Argentina episode.[17] There is another version, however, that deserves airing.

17. Notably, Ernest Stern in a letter of November 1992 and Stanley Fischer in one of October 1992, well after his departure from the Bank and before his joining the Fund as its first deputy managing director in 1994. Fischer wrote Polak, "Your account of the 1989 dispute and of Argentina is very good. I have reason to believe Conable would not have made the Argentine loans without strong American pressure, but that is not something that anyone can do more than speculate about." Letter, Stanley Fischer to Jacques Polak, October 17, 1992, p. 4. Stern noted, "[The Argentine case] occurred after the Bank's famous reorganization. The Senior Vice President for Operations, the LAC management and the new Chief Economist . . . had a very strong perception that the Bank was too subservient to the Fund on macroeconomic assessments and that it should be more independent. A relatively new President was persuaded to drop the long standing rule that there should be no Bank adjustment program without a Fund agreement. . . . After that experience, the rule was restored."

In a January 1996 communication, Stanley Fischer made this further comment: "In 1987 when I signed up at the Bank, I perceived the Fund as strongly pursuing a mistaken no-debt relief strategy, that drove its macroeconomic advice in Latin America. Under those circumstances I wanted the Bank to challenge the Fund's views when they needed challenging. However, in the Argentine case I saw the Bank making exactly the same mistake as the Fund, and opposed the Argentine loans (see my memo to Conable and Qureshi that is quoted by Polak). In general, and no doubt reflecting my academic heritage, I believe it is good for the Fund to have its macro (and other) assessments challenged by informed people. Thus I think the Bank should have the capacity to do independent macro assessments, and that disagreements between the staffs should be brought to the attention of management, as the 1989 memorandum of understanding requires. It is a mistake for the two staffs to give conflicting advice; those conflicts need to be sorted out in Washington. The division of responsibilities that emerged in the 1989 agreement is workable and broadly sensible." Letter, Stanley Fischer to John Lewis, January 14, 1996, p. 2.

Tensions between the two institutions had been accumulating since the 1971 breakdown of the Bretton Woods fixed exchange rate system robbed the Fund of its principal, originally assigned functions. There had been encroachments and counterencroachments on each other's turf—Fund access to concessional funds, Bank engagement in macropolicy reform—and considerable rivalry. In the early years of the debt crisis of the 1980s, the Fund had the limelight and money, and the Bank objected to the way allegedly pat IMF prescriptions appeared to contribute to borrowers' economic hemorrhages. It is a wonder relations between the two remained as peaceful as they did, but there were the makings of an explosion.

It was triggered when the Bank's 1987 reorganization changed both the senior vice president operations and the vice president for Latin America. Almost immediately a scuffle ensued over a proposed adjustment loan for the power sector in Brazil. The Brazilian government's new finance minister thought he had the approval of such a loan from Managing Director Camdessus of the Fund (with which Brazil did not have a current agreement). But there was confusion over the sequencing of commercial bank loans vis-à-vis the fresh IMF standby Minister Bresser Pereira proposed to get; and meanwhile (in August 1987) Richard Erb, the Fund's deputy managing director, attacked the Bank for acquiescing (implicitly as a novice) in Brazil's insufficiently austere fiscal targets. The Bank's new senior vice president for operations wrote an indignant response, and an acerbic exchange ensued, each party addressing copies of its paper to the U.S. Treasury as de facto referee.

Relations were further riled in May 1988 when Camdessus gave a pro-Fund description of the division of labor between the two institutions to which Stanley Fischer, newly arrived as the Bank chief economist, strongly objected.[18] Fischer (who would succeed Erb) continued to spearhead the Bank's resistance to the Fund's early draft of a new concordat between the institutions.

One other point should be made about the context in which "the Argentina case" arose. The Board of the Bank was extremely restless during the 1987–89 period with the assertive adjustment interventions being proposed by the Bank's LAC wing in rivalry with or substitution for the IMF. The number of Part I abstentions from, even opposition votes to, such actions was highly unusual.[19]

The Fund, by the end of 1987, had compiled a difficult history with Argentina's civilian government. IMF's European and Australian Board members were very hawkish as to conditionalities to be imposed on Argentina. They rebuked Managing Director Camdessus for a visit to the Alfonsín government in Buenos Aires in

18. Memorandum, Stanley Fischer to David Hopper, "Mr. Camdessus' Summing-up on PFP's," May 26, 1988.

19. World Bank, Summaries of Discussions of Meetings of the Executive Directors of the World Bank, IDA, and IFC, December 22, 1987 (SD87-73), January 12, 1988 (SD88-4), September 15, 1988 (SD88-54), and October 27, 1988 (SD88-58), involving loans to Brazil, Mexico, Argentina, Honduras, and Argentina again.

December and pressed the Fund in its next standby to Argentina to impose strict conditionalities, which Bank personnel found so rigorous that they alerted the Fund that the government was sure to fall short. The government quickly did just that—by May 1988—and the Fund, in the eyes of Bank staff, had boxed itself out of a constructive role in Argentina for some time to come.

Meanwhile the Bank people, who had been spending more time in Argentina than their Fund counterparts, found the latter's macroanalysis stereotypical, excessively short ranged, and thin. To revive noninflationary growth, they thought, Argentina would require some basic institutional and management reforms that Fund models were not capturing. In particular, according to the Bank, these models were missing off-budget transfers from the central bank to the Argentine states that were contributing a large hidden component to the country's structural deficit.

Neither the Bank analysts nor their superiors took kindly to what they regarded as dismissive treatment by Fund staff. At the same time, in the summer of 1988 the Bank was invited by Argentina's finance minister to take on, in effect, a combined Fund-Bank role and negotiate a joint stabilization and adjustment program, involving a Fund-type macro loan and a set of sectoral adjustment loans. Close colleagues understood that President Conable had been encouraged by Managing Director Camdessus to proceed. In any event, Conable decided to do so. The loans were negotiated and, as noted, presented to the Bank Board in October.

Given Argentina's past spotty record on conditionality, the decision, as Conable emphasized in a special trip to President Alfonsín before the 1988 annual meetings, was a risky one. In view of the risk, the loan package design would provide the bulk of the money in later tranches while the conditions were front loaded. The decision to proceed was motivated partly, a number of parties agree, by U.S. government pressure, although this abated in the late summer when James Baker left the Treasury to run the George Bush election campaign. The United States, in turn, may in part have been motivated by the same concern Shahid Husain attributes to Bank management in a commentary on the Polak chapter: the viability of Argentina's first constitutional democracy in a generation was precarious. A second multilateral rebuff, especially in advance of an upcoming Argentine election, might have been fatal.

However bold its risk taking, the Bank monitored the borrower's performance assiduously. The failure, Bank apologists insist, was on the side of the Argentine regime. Its reform undertakings had not been unrealistic; it simply lost the energy and will to perform them. This the Bank's country staff detected in a scant two months, and the loan was turned off with little loss of institutional funds. Meanwhile, said the apologists, the risk taking, by gaining some time and avoiding some turbulence, helped move the system toward orderly elections.[20]

20. The foregoing account is based on exchanges with the department director and regional vice president most directly involved as well as with President Conable.

The Bank's regional vice president for Latin America and the Caribbean has argued that the Argentina case's contribution to Bank-Fund relations was considerably more positive than one might have expected.

> The post-1989 division of labor in Argentina allowed the Bank, in consultation with the Fund, to take the lead in the institutional underpinnings of macroeconomic policy: tax administration, a new public finance law to control expenditures, privatization of public enterprises, civil service reform to downsize public employment, [and] a new Charter for the monetary authority establishing limited powers of money creation and lending to the Government. The Fund, in consultation with the Bank, took the lead in discussions on short-term targets and the general architecture of the macropolicy framework. Other areas were shared and depended on internal resources, tax policy, and provincial finances. As a result, structural changes led to improvements in macroeconomic performance and growth. Collaboration was genuine—including joint missions, advance readings of drafted policy positions and mission briefs, and frequent staff consultations on short- and medium-term projections. Though there is still room for improvement, this story is mirrored in country after country.[21]

Lending for Enhanced Adjustment and Beyond

It is not surprising that, during the thrust toward policy-based lending in the 1980s, while the adjustment umbrella was being stretched to cover growth promotion (whether or not pointedly related to balance of payments), it also was made to encompass aspects of equity, namely, poverty reduction and its analogue, social sector reform.

This reflected a changed institutional view. In the earlier, strict constructionist years of the decade, the official line would have agreed with OED's flat assertion in its 1986 review of adjustment lending:

> SALs were never intended to and are not an appropriate instrument to address directly the longer-term actions needed for poverty alleviation. To the extent that policy measures under the SALs affect income distribution and employment, complementary financial and non-financial assistance should be devised . . . so that the most effective and appropriate instruments can be used to address the adverse social effects of adjustment.[22]

But the preceding was something of a last gasp. Strong attacks on SALs and SECALs for not alleviating poverty were coming from outside the Bank, notably from the United Nations Children's Fund, in a program that became known by the name given its major publication, "Adjustment with a Human Face."[23]

---

21. Letter, S. Shahid Husain to Richard Webb, October 2, 1992, p. 7.

22. World Bank, "Structural Adjustment Lending: A First Review of Experience," Operations Evaluation Department (OED) Report 6409, September 24, 1986, p. 80.

23. UNICEF's campaign, in terms of written product, culminated in Giovanni Andrea Cornia, Richard Jolly, and Frances Stewart, eds., *Adjustment with a Human Face* (Oxford University Press, vol. 1, 1987; vol. 2, 1988). UNICEF's first salvo, however, was an un-

Through the middle 1980s, sections of the Bank aided various country and area-focused attempts to build defense-of-the-poor elements into their adjustment programs. A notable effort was launched in Bolivia, where Bank staff in 1986 helped the government organize a poor-cushioning follow-up to radical fiscal and monetary reform.[24] Similarly, in Ghana the Bank chaired a multidonor Program of Action to Mitigate the Social Costs of Adjustment (PAMSCAD; see the Ghana case study later in the chapter). At the African regional level, the Bank undertook to join the United Nations Development Program in the Social Dimensions of Adjustment (SDA) project. By the early 1990s, as the Bank was becoming heavily involved in Eastern Europe and the former Soviet Union, social safety nets were fairly common elements in Bank adjustment programs.

Once the Conable presidency was well launched, the Bank's principal response to the pro-poor critique of SALs came from the top down. As is detailed in the earlier part of this work, it was institutionalized in a series of studies and commitments that included the pivotal World Development Report 1990 and, carrying on into the Preston presidency, an operational directive that highlighted poverty alleviation as the principal objective of all the Bank's (both investment and non-project) lending activity (see chapter 7).

Beyond poverty alleviation, the further question was what other policy changes Bank policy-based lending might encourage. As the 1980s came to a close, each of the following subjects had adherents inside and outside the institution: private enterprise development, reduced military spending, enhancement of the role of women, environmental protection, good governance, observance of human rights and the rule of law, and democratic government.[25]

In the case of the Bank, promotion of democratic governmental processes per se, let alone the application of loan leverage in their behalf, continued to be seen as proscribed by the institution's apolitical mandate. This is not the case with such bilateral donors as the United States, Germany, and the United Kingdom, and with the European Bank for Reconstruction and Development (specifically mandated to be pro-democratic). Although prodded strongly by the United States in the aftermath of the Tiananmen Square repression, the World Bank also resisted the

---

published paper by G. K. Helleiner, G. A. Cornia, and R. Jolly, "IMF Adjustment Policies and Approaches and the Needs of Children," later published in World Development, vol. 19, no. 12 (December 1991), pp. 1823–34. This was succeeded by various representations to the World Bank and the rest of the international donor community.

24. Through the Emergency Social Fund (ESF), the wages of the average ESF worker were 12.8 percent higher, the work week 9.5 hours longer, and weekly earnings 32 percent higher than what would have been without the ESF. John Newman, Steen Jorgensen, and Menno Prathan, "How Did Workers Benefit from Bolivia's Emergency Social Fund?" World Bank Economic Review, vol. 5 (May 1991), pp. 367–93.

25. This list is taken from Joan M. Nelson, Global Goals, Contentious Means: Issues of Multiple Aid Conditionality, Policy Essay 10 (Washington, D.C.: Overseas Development Council, 1993).

direct advocacy and loan conditioning of "political" human rights, arguing, like McNamara, that the institution's proper role is to advance the economic human rights of the poor—and, indeed, of all developing-country citizens.[26]

On the other hand, since the mid-1980s, the Bank's apolitical boundaries have been enlarged to encompass governance in the sense of efficient, orderly, and accountable general public administration. The quality of government, of course, has always been critical to matters in which the Bank has been engaged. But until recently it was not considered in the direct purview of Bank influence. This is one of the things the crisis in Africa changed. The quality of government had become so patently integral to economic reform and progress in Sub-Saharan Africa that by the early 1990s improvements in government (for example, reductions in the numbers of public employees and increases in their per capita compensation) had become common and critical parts of many adjustment loans. The rationale was elaborately articulated in the Bank's large special 1989 study, *Sub-Saharan Africa: From Crisis to Sustainable Growth*.[27]

Arms reduction is a mixed case. The subject plainly is sensitive as well as political and was typically avoided by the Bank until—in the aftermath of the cold war—the presidents of the Bank, first Conable, then Preston, joined Managing Director Camdessus of the Fund, in making borrowers' allocations to defense a matter of greater Bank-Fund concern.[28] The initial strategy was to deal with the issue indirectly, with the Fund specifying ceilings on total public expenditures and the Bank promoting floors on social expenditures, thereby encouraging borrowing governments to squeeze defense spending. The Bank, as part of its observation of borrowers' fiscal policies in the context of adjustment lending, became engaged in closer reviews of public expenditure programs from the mid-1980s onward.[29] This entailed attention to the transparency of expenditure accounting, including that for defense, as well as comparisons with such other spending categories as education and health, and attention also to comparable spending in other countries.[30]

---

26. However, the votes on loans of individual members, the United States being one, sometimes have reflected their political human rights concerns.

27. World Bank, *Sub-Saharan Africa: From Crisis to Sustainable Growth* (1989), pp. 55–59.

28. See annual address by Barber B. Conable, president of the World Bank, *1989 Annual Meetings of the Boards of Governors: Summary Proceedings* (World Bank, September 26, 1989), p. 16; World Bank, "Bank Work on Military Expenditure," SecM91-1563, December 9, 1991; and World Bank, "The General Counsel's Statement on Whether Public Expenditure and Military Expenditure in Particular Fall within the Bank's Mandate," SecM91-1563/1, December 13, 1991.

29. As distinct from its earlier focus on public *investment* reviews.

30. See World Bank, "Review of Public Expenditure Work," Office of the vice president of Development Economics, January 1995; and Martha de Melo, "Public Investment/Expenditure Reviews: The Bank's Experience," World Bank, Country Economics Department, 1988, processed.

Two others on the list of possible collateral SAL goals require little separate comment. The issue of enhancing the role of women has won increasing salience in Bank doctrine and programs; yet in a quick canvass of the institution's newer policy goals, issues concerning women can be treated as a major subset within the poverty and social sectors category. Private enterprise development can be viewed as an instrumental means of facilitating efficient growth. However, it is given separate attention in chapter 13, as are environmental matters in volume 2, chapter 13. Environmental protection has joined poverty alleviation and social-sector improvement as a major amendment to the macroeconomic goals of policy-based lending. In taking up environment as a policy priority, the Bank was arguably more reactive and less self-propelled than in its antipoverty initiatives. But by the mid-1990s the priority was routinely asserted.

There could be some dispute, if these subjects were to be adopted as policy priorities by the Bank, over which of them (such as poverty alleviation) would be accepted as enhanced adjustment targets and which of them (perhaps environment protection) would become stand-alone, other-than-adjustment, policy targets. There are some reforms—for example military de-escalation—whose proponents may strongly advocate encapsulation under "adjustment" because of the awkwardness of determining what separate dollar value should be placed on the (downsizing) reform. But by and large, the adjustment-or-nonadjustment issue may be reminiscent of angels and pins; it can be consigned to the subject of target overload and deconstruction.

The Interface with Other Bank Goals

Although the inherent ambivalence of policy-based program loans seems clear enough, there are times and places where now and then a policy loan's money-moving purpose becomes more insistent. Such was the case with loans to many African countries, especially from 1983 onward. Many of these loans were designed in part to help the borrowers meet obligations coming due to the IMF. It will be remembered that the Bank's original SAL design did not foresee extensive lending to African low-income countries. But the combination of the second oil shock and declining commodity prices left many poor African countries desperate for foreign exchange. They turned to the Fund and borrowed extensively. But Fund loans (which are not called loans) are short-duration instruments, and the borrowers were having to repay the IMF long before their basic international accounts had rallied. Thus Africa's amortization charges rose from $2.3 billion in 1980–82 to $8 billion estimated for 1985–87.[31]

The situation posed an urgent challenge to the international payments system. The African countries needed to recoup much of the net inflow of capital they were

31. World Bank, *Toward Sustained Development in Sub-Saharan Africa: A Joint Program of Action* (1984).

losing, but, perhaps even more, they needed to avoid defaults to the Fund. The Fund, as disciplinarian of the system, could not ignore the receipts due. Yet commercial lenders were not about to provide the Africans with resources to repay the Fund, and many bilateral donors also were reluctant. The World Bank helped to keep the system whole. It made available large numbers of the one kind of quick-disbursing loan it now was stocking (SALs and SECALs), *not* without policy strings, but quickly and with less meticulous conditioning than otherwise would have been imposed. Most observers saw this as responsible behavior. Not to have sought a pragmatic balance between the two goals at issue would have been reckless.

At the same time, tilted ambivalence can become a slippery slope. The kind of corner cutting many respected as an alternative to an Africa-IMF debacle became demoralizing as it became more widespread. In adjustment lending's heyday, the Bank, in the words of a senior staff economist who later became an executive director of the IMF, increasingly found itself on a treadmill. Funding, both concessional and nonconcessional, was scarce relative to the need for adjustment lending. The macroeconomic arithmetic that was used in the quantification of broad, non–project loan cases was inherently discretionary; it left more room for judgment than the typical project analysis. There was an insistent bias toward optimism in the documentation of adjustment-lending proposals: with scarce funds, estimates of country performance had to be optimistic for the Bank to project closure of the resource gaps perceived. And the projections almost always turned out to be high, leaving de facto gaps the next time around that fresh (loosely conditioned) "adjustment" lending had to be used to close.[32]

In this kind of action the Bank was protecting its own hide as well as that of the borrower, and the fashion among Bretton Woods critics has been to treat such behavior as at least slightly reprehensible. It is regrettable if self-protection led to a fudging of the figures. But self-protection per se needs no apologies. If it was appropriate for the World Bank to help the Monetary Fund avoid defaults, it owed itself the same service for the same system-maintenance reasons.

Program lending, by accelerating disbursements, rapidly increased the Bank's exposure in selected countries, and thereby its financial risks (table 10-3). As discussed in chapters 14–16, the Bank took offsetting steps to manage the risks— instituting financial reserves and provisions—which it had not used before. From 1980 onward the risk side of adjustment lending never got out of hand. Yet as early as 1984 the two senior vice presidents were considering ways to reduce the likelihood of borrower defaults. Mentioned were the easing of conditionality requirements, relaxing creditworthiness assessments, and using IDA to maintain disbursements to IBRD borrowers. None of these alternatives found favor with

---

32. Enzo Grilli, interview with John Lewis, Richard Webb, and Devesh Kapur, July 5, 1993.

Table 10-3. *Adjustment Lending as a Ratio of Total Commitments and*
Disbursements for the World Bank Group, 1984–92
Millions of U.S. dollars

Fiscal year	Commitment ratio	Disbursement ratio
1984	0.17	0.11
1985	0.11	0.15
1986	0.22	0.16
1987	0.26	0.27
1988	0.26	0.24
1989	0.29	0.25
1990	0.27	0.38
1991	0.26	0.28
1992	0.26	0.31

Source: World Bank, *World Debt Tables*, 1984–92.

Stern and Qureshi. Yet the senior managers also wanted urgently to avoid defaults.[33] As it turned out, they got their wish in large part. The World Bank escaped a wave of defaults without extensively resorting to contrived means of avoidance.

Procedural Choices

In engaging in policy-based lending during the 1980s the Bank made several procedural choices. The first had to do with *loan vehicles*. Which kinds of lending instruments were the better conveyors of policy influence? Ostensibly, this had been decided at the outset of the decade: the chosen vehicle was the non–project policy loan, and in reciprocity, for Gresham's law reasons, a cloud was thrown over the use of nonproject loans for anything outside of policy-influencing lending. As noted, in 1982 the decision was taken to divide adjustment lending into the comprehensive, systemwide variety (SALs) and sector-specific adjustment loans (SECALs).[34] Yet as the decade proceeded, the pro-nonproject procedural choice became less decisive and unblurred than the folklore of both the Bank and its critics admitted. One of the abiding reasons for making policy-based loans non–project loans was, of course, to move money rapidly. This always meant that, especially in the case of "structural" loans, disbursement would come earlier than the intended impacts of the policy reforms being promoted. Hence it was decided to use sequential disbursements (tranches or series of loans) to strengthen lender control and the accountability of both the borrower and the lending agency. But as program lending proceeded in the 1980s, one line of thinking (although in the end

33. Memorandum, Ernest Stern to Moeen A. Qureshi, March 21, 1984.
34. Retrospectively, 1980 and 1981 sector loans to Sudan and Tanzania were assimilated as SECALs. World Bank, "Report on Adjustment Lending II," annex table 5.5.

it came to little) argued for a variety of slower-disbursing nonproject loans (called development policy loans) to match up with slower-registering reforms.[35]

So-called hybrid loans constituted another blurred vehicular choice. Secular non–project adjustment loans were tied together with substantively related "investment" loans under this labeling and in the mid-1980s had some vogue, which then abated as it was recognized that the coupling could actually occur without benefit of specific nomenclature.

As the case mounted for disaggregating adjustment policy targets, the rationale also grew for stand-alone, single-purpose policy loans that were arguably components of an "adjustment" program. In principle, there might also be an occasion for policy-based loans that lay outside the adjustment realm altogether; however, the same function probably could be served well enough by one or another of the Bank's array of established loan types.

The second set of procedural choices concerning policy-based lending in the 1980s had to do with the *modalities* of policy lending: ex-ante versus ex-post conditioning, lender-driven versus interactive specifications of reforms, didactic influence versus dialogue, borrower "ownership" or not. Here, too, the Bank seemed to have made its choice at the start of the decade, opting for a no-nonsense, ex-ante, contractual, IMF-style mode. But in fact, there was considerable variance as the years unfolded. At least three major country cases involved deviations from the SAL procedural norm, and there were others.

Mexico was the most striking early on. Traditionally the government had been hyperallergic to policy leverage, and the sentiment did not disappear when, in late 1982, it became more urgent to get the nonproject inflows to which Bank-advocated policy reforms were tied. Bank staff found a procedural substitute for a reform agenda for Mexico that was less distasteful to the client than a standard-issue SAL would have been. A "special action program" was joined with an "export development loan" (retrospectively Bank-classified as an adjustment loan) in 1983. The alternative was pragmatically embraced by Senior Vice President Stern, who explicitly ruled against trying to press the Mexicans into accepting the normal SAL format. From here on Bank dialogue with the Mexicans on macro and sectoral policy matters was augmented and routinized.[36] Later in the decade, when the government had become acclimated to the adjustment loan nomenclature, it asked for one, but after the fact: it felt the "Bank should recognize and reward the country for what had been already done."[37] The Bank granted three $500 million SECALs with little forward conditioning.[38]

35. Proposed in the 1984 "Future Role of the World Bank" exercise.

36. Memorandum, Nicolas Ardito Barletta to Warren Baum, "Mexico—SAP for Agricultural Projects," July 11, 1983.

37. Memorandum, Rainer B. Steckhan to Moeen A. Qureshi, "Mexico," November 18, 1988, para. 9.

38. They were partly rolled into the Bank's participation in Brady Plan operations for Mexico.

By early 1988 the Bank finally took, and the government of Mexico accepted, a step that characterized its other two prominent instances of "dialogue"-style modalities. The Bank established a resident mission. But the relationship had been significantly close and cordial for some time.[39] In Indonesia, the first great resident mission country, the institution also found occasion in the late 1980s to depart from the standard SAL scenario. The Bank's top managers agreed (and defended the move in the face of Executive Board skepticism) that Indonesia should get a large SECAL without the usual second-tranch arrangement for assuring performance. The reason: the government, being engaged in ongoing dialogue with the Bank, already had taken the reform steps stipulated in the new loan.[40]

Once the World Bank had negotiated the opening to China in 1980, it worked diligently and well to establish rapport with the giant country. The Bank engaged in full company with the People's Republic in a heavy run of economic and sector work to improve internal as well as external understanding of the Chinese economy, and, in the process, to highlight development policy issues. But as early as October 1984, the Chinese finance minister was at pains to lay down ground rules about policy influence: "The minister explained China's view that assistance to the developing countries should be unconditional. . . . [T]his did not mean that the Bank could not offer advice and ideas. The World Bank could put these forward and they would be considered if they were useful. But the Bank should not impose its views."[41]

The Bank essentially conducted itself accordingly. It maintained a close and cerebral Beijing-centered relation with the government under strong and differentiated leadership in Washington. After the Tiananmen Square violence, bank leadership was preoccupied with shielding the Bank's economic program from political fallout. But the institution's manners as to policy remained educative, interactive, and flexible. These special procedural adaptations in China, Indonesia, and Mexico were markedly different from the Bank's policy-influence modalities in Sub-Saharan Africa. The African case was so central and difficult in the institution's 1980s experience that it is given separate attention in chapter 12.

A final procedural change of some salience concerned donor consortia and consultative groups. CGs, of course, were not new to the 1980s or to countries receiving program loans. But under adjustment lending conditions there was a sense among lenders as well as borrowers that the CGs became livelier fora of policy advice and donor coordination. The Bank had become more active and vocal

39. Detailed analysis of the Bank–Mexico relationship can be found in World Bank, "OED Study of Bank/Mexico Relations, 1948–1992," OED Report 12923, April 1, 1994; and volume 2 of this work, chapter 2.

40. Cheetham to files, November 21, 1988.

41. Memorandum, J. Richard Baumgarner to files, "China—Regional Meeting with Chinese Delegation to Annual Meeting," October 2, 1984, para. 15 on meeting with Minister of Finance Wang Bingqian.

in its promotion of macropolicy reform, and other bilateral and multilateral donors, typically taking their lead from the World Bank, became more engaged themselves in such policy promotion. Previously in some country and project-lending cases, CGs had been mainly mechanisms for eliciting donor pledges. Now, their meetings became venues for more explicit, focused, and coherent policy dialogues.

Overload and the Reach for Disaggregation

By the end of the 1980s the scale—the spread—that adjustment lending had attained began to be, if not self-limiting, self-challenging. The overt challenger within the Bank was Stanley Fischer, new chief economist, who had come aboard in 1988 for what would be a three-year term. There were two principal complaints about the state at which policy-based lending had arrived. One was that multitargeting had an adverse impact on the functioning of both the Bank and recipient governments, neither of which had the time or the capacities to vet and implement dozens of policy conditions simultaneously. Under the orthodox SAL format, this meant one of two things: many (often, most) of the conditions were not enforced. Or, if on the other hand the Bank did play by the book and held up a whole (second-tranch or second-loan) operation over one minor delinquency, it appeared unreasonable.

Plainly, what gave the SAL process an appearance of frailty, indeed, of toothlessness, was the basic choice of modalities that had been made in 1979–80. The system looked ineffectual because the borrower was under ex-ante contract to do a number of things the borrower and lender jointly did not succeed in getting done. Realizing this, in the early 1990s, some in the Bank felt it was time to get tougher and slow down tranch release or the writing of follow-on loans or even to cancel more policy loans where performance was slack. But in fact there was little stomach for this. As for the toughest sanction—that is, loan cancellation—there were in the 1980s only a handful of such actions.[42] Instead, a positive rationale was growing for softening the modalities as a way of promoting borrower "ownership" of reforms emerging from lender-borrower dialogue.

42. A note to Executive Director Murray A. Sherwin from Heinz Vergin ("Structural Adjustment Lending—Tranche Conditions," January 27, 1989) mentions eight such cases, but in two of these (Jamaica 2d Export Development Fund and Sudan agriculture rehabilitation) only small remaining fractions of the loan (less than 10 percent) were canceled, and in one (Korea 2d Industry and Finance Sectors Loan) 17 percent was canceled because the private sector found the on-lending terms too onerous. Thus the five "genuine" cancellations were Senegal, $16.3 million of $60 million (unsatisfactory agricultural marketing privatization); Panama, $50.2 million of $100 million (pensions reform unmet and inability to secure external funds); Jamaica, entire $30.1 million canceled (because of unagreed changes in foreign exchange auction system); Yugoslavia, a $90 million fertilizer sector loan was withdrawn (for various reasons); and Burkina Faso, $4.47 million of a $13.7 million fertilizer credit (a study was not completed on time).

The other complaint about the type of policy-based lending the Bank was practicing in the late 1980s was the one Stanley Fischer was more inclined to emphasize: it was breeding aid dependency, especially in Africa. Fischer was not diffident about taking on the in-house system. In November 1989, he told a group of the Bank's operations staff:

> The Bank is *de facto* making adjustment lending a permanent, or at least a very long-term, part of its collaboration with individual countries. Would this be a good thing? I believe not, in large part because I also believe we greatly underestimate the dangers of aid or external dependence. These extend not only to the Dutch disease phenomenon, that in providing external resources we appreciate the exchange rate and slow the development of exports, but also to the slowing down of the creation of independent policy capacity in developing countries. It has often been said that adjustment lending is addictive. That it is, not only for the Bank, but especially for member countries.... [I]t is very hard to get off the habit, because of the pain that will be suffered while the habit is being kicked. There are elements of addiction also for the Bank in the impact of adjustment lending on the profile of net disbursements.[43]

Ernest Stern, now senior vice president for finance, took umbrage at the possible cloud Fischer's remarks could cast on the institution's creditworthiness. Fischer conceded that he should have engaged the creditworthiness question positively and directly, but added that "there are more, and more important reasons than the risks you refer to for making that change [toward investment lending]—not least a concern that long-term dependence on [adjustment] lending may blunt members' adjustment efforts."[44]

In one sense the Bank had had in mind for a long time the goal toward which Fischer was reaching, namely, a more parsimonious use of adjustment lending. That was much of the rationale for adopting sector-specific SECALs as a branch of the SAL innovation in 1982. But the evolution Fischer advocated would go farther. Beyond those collateral-reform purposes (for example, governance) that might need the protective cover of an omnibus adjustment loan, the decision would be to give other collateral-reform objectives their own free-standing loan vehicles.

The substitute vehicles might (following Fischer) be simply refurbished investment loans; or perhaps new-style "investment loans" where both parties inverted the priorities and made the loan's policy message, not its project content, its primary purpose; or maybe resuscitated hybrid loans or the elusive freestanding, conditioned *non*-adjustment policy loan. If one, or some combination, of these alternatives should be the wave of the future, the SAL/SECAL wave would be flattened, disaggregated, spread out. But, as a matter of Bank priorities, the salience of policy-based lending would continue.

43. Stanley Fischer, "Long-term Operational Strategy for the Bank," draft presentation prepared for Operations Retreat, November 17, 1989.
44. Memorandum, Stanley Fischer to Ernest Stern, March 16, 1990.

Evaluations of Adjustment Lending

Not surprisingly, almost from the start of new-style, policy-based lending in 1980, there was great interest in assessing the effectiveness of the effort. It is difficult to regard a category of lending never exceeding a third of the World Bank's loan operations as the institution's bellwether activity. Yet policy-based lending became just that in the 1980s. For the Bank's borrowing clientele, it often was controversial and abrasive. It promised to unleash unwelcome changes on many of their privileged groups. It seemed to threaten the poor and disadvantaged. And it rubbed national sovereignties the wrong way.

Within the Bank, SAL, the institution's house brand of policy-based lending in the 1980s, revised the Bank's analytical work agenda. It changed staffing and consultant requirements and radically altered the allocation of management time. Thanks to quick disbursement, SAL required the Bank to cope with greater financial risks including increased country exposures. It made the institution more interventionist at a time when it was urging reduced interventionism on its borrowers.

It is natural that, inside and outside, there was great curiosity about whether and how well the SAL brand of policy-based lending worked.[45] Within the institution there was a stream of on going assessments by the Bank's regional and central-staff offices. The Operations Evaluation Department made two major reviews, in 1986 and 1992.[46] In 1988, U.S. Treasury official David Mulford summoned the Bank's new vice president and chief economist, Stanley Fischer, to his office and demanded that the Bank's economics complex undertake a comprehensive assessment of adjustment. What the gesture lacked in grace it made up in product: a series of three Bank reviews of adjustment lending (RAL I, II, and III, in 1988, 1990, and 1992).[47] There have been other notable in-house studies of adjustment lending experience, for example, in Sub-Saharan Africa.[48]

---

45. Among the many external studies of the issue was Paul Mosley, Jane Harrigan, and John Toye, *Aid and Power: The World Bank and Policy-Based Lending* (New York: Routledge, 1991); and Nicholas Stern's chapter in volume 2 of the present work. Professor Stern (no relation of Ernest Stern) identifies the rationale of structural adjustment lending as the Bank's most important conceptual innovation. The Bank's openness to such enquiries deserves emphasis. It facilitated both the Mosley and the Stern studies.

46. World Bank, "Structural Adjustment Lending: A First Review of Experience," OED Report 6409, September 24, 1986; World Bank, "World Bank Structural and Sectoral Adjustment Operations: The Second OED Overview," OED Report 10870 (SecM92-951), July 13, 1992.

47. World Bank, *Adjustment Lending: An Evaluation of Ten Years of Experience*, Country Economics Department, Policy and Research Series, 1 (1988); World Bank, *Adjustment Lending Policies for Sustainable Growth*, Country Economics Department, Policy and Research Series, 14 (1990); and World Bank, *Adjustment Lending and Mobilization of Private and Public Resources for Growth*, Country Economics Department, Policy and Research Series, 22 (1992).

48. Ajay Chhibber and Stanley Fischer, eds., *Economic Reform in Sub-Saharan Africa* (World Bank, 1991); Tony Killick, "The Developmental Effectiveness of Aid to Africa,"

The methodology of policy-based lending evaluation is complicated. Which should be assessed: input (that is, the adequacy or not of recommendations, decisions, and actions by the two parties) or output (that is, the recipient economy's performance)? Legalistically—contractually—inputs have the better of the argument: If the issue, for example, is what action should trigger the second tranch of a SAL, it is, for fairness reasons, better to hinge release on the taking of a previously specified policy measure (say, a tariff reduction) than the achievement of a specified economic result, say a certain GDP growth rate. The first is more nearly subject to the borrower's control; all manner of other, beyond-control variables can intervene to affect the outcome.

Yet operationally—practically—it was the outcomes that interested both participants in and observers of the SAL process. Both inside and outside the institution the serious evaluators (leaving aside those driven by a priori negatives) examined this series of issues:

—In the case of a particular SAL operation, what was the nature, size, and quality of the Bank's reform effort? Was it serious, or in good part cosmetic?

—With respect to the loan recipient as reformer, how did the recipient receive, adapt to, and interact with the lender's initiative? What if any, were the non-Bank inputs to the reform, homegrown or by non-Bank interveners? What was the strength, quality, and sustainability of the reform, whatever its provenance? How well was it implemented? Did the borrower take ownership of it?

—What was the linkage between the reform actions (whatever their source) and the relevant outcomes, which implied the question, what was the role (at least collectively) of other independent variables?

Each of the above is a debatable question, and, of course, the uncertainties multiply as one argues one's way through the series. Yet, empirically, the assessments tended to converge. There were differences. For example, Paul Mosley, in commenting on an estimate of SAL country performance and effectiveness by Vittorio Corbo and Patricio Rojas that had been used in RAL II and then was spelled out in a paper for a 1990 conference already cited, faulted the authors on their failure to take account of the strength of a borrowing government's reform commitment. The Bank defined its category of "early-intensive adjustment lending" countries simply by the earliness and/or number of a borrower's SALs. But Turkey (Mosley rightly said), as a deeply committed adjuster in the earlier years of

World Bank, International Economics Department, Policy, Research, and External Affairs Working Papers, WPS 646, April 1991; Ibrahim A. Elbadawi, Dhaneshwar Ghura, and Gilbert Uwujaren, "World Bank Adjustment Lending and Economic Performance in Sub-Saharan Africa in the 1980s: A Comparison with Other Low-income Countries," World Bank Policy Research Working Papers, WPS 1000, October 1992; World Bank, "Adjustment in Sub-Saharan Africa: Selected Findings from OED Evaluations," SecM93-824, July 29, 1993; World Bank, Adjustment in Africa: Reforms, Results, and the Road Ahead (Oxford University Press, 1994).

the program, certainly belonged in a different class from Kenya, whose government paid little more than lip service to its early SAL.

The Bank's assessments of performance related to adjustment lending have not been euphoric. Stanley Fischer thought RAL I (1988) offered statistical evidence that was "moderately but certainly not conclusively favorable to adjustment lending."[49] RAL II (1990) conveyed what came to be the norm: serious adoption of adjustment tended to be associated with somewhat faster growth; it was not systematically or strongly related to reduced equity; but it was typically associated with *reduced* investment, private as well as public.

Given the contrary output and investment trends, the adjusters appeared to be using capital more efficiently. Mosley added to the Bank's explanations of the relative slowing of investment. Like others, he noted that less public investment, instead of making room for more private capital formation, often reduced the supply of preconditions for the latter. He also suggested that governments found it easier to channel program loans than project loans into consumption uses. But other commentators disagreed with this last. A 1994 IMF working paper on Sub-Saharan Africa, for example, found that the increased imports of spares, components, and raw materials that program loans made possible relaxed supply bottlenecks that had been impeding the use of productive capacity.[50] Thus SAL not only raised productivity by economizing on capital; in some cases it gave a quick and direct lift to output.

RAL III (1992), echoed in part by the second (June 1992) OED review of adjustment lending, found a positive relationship between the seriousness and scope of adjustment reforms and the growth of real income.[51] Within the time frame thus far available, the investment effects remained mixed. Initially adjusting countries experienced an investment sag. Of it the OED reviewers said:

> With respect to *investment and resumption of growth,* most of the countries experienced an investment pause during the adjustment period. This is the expected result of cutbacks in public investment and the increase in uncertainty that comes with the actual or potential crisis that generates the need for adjustment. In about half of the countries with an investment pause, a recovery of investment had already begun in the postadjustment period. For the others, it is too early to see the results. It is clear, however, that the positive relationship between investment and growth is reestablished after the adjustment period, and that real devaluation contributes to postadjustment growth.[52]

The 1992 OED review ventured two other interesting points. First, it suggested that thirteen of the thirty-four countries in its sample with sufficient data to support

49. Interview, Boston, February 1993.
50. Michael T. Hadjimichael and others, *Effects of Macroeconomic Stability on Growth, Savings, and Investment in Sub-Saharan Africa: An Empirical Investigation* (Washington, D.C.: International Monetary Fund, 1994).
51. World Bank, "World Bank Structural and Sectoral Adjustment Operations: The Second OED Overview."
52. Ibid., p. 57.

such analysis faced unsustainable debt burdens. (To oversimplify, the real interest rate on their debt exceeded their real GDP growth rates; thus, in the absence of debt relief or a strong change of circumstances, they promised, by borrowing to service their debt, to spin their way to default.) The OED found that further manageable fiscal adjustment could stabilize the debt-GDP ratio in seven of the thirteen countries. But Congo, Côte d'Ivoire, Nicaragua, Sudan, Zambia, and Zimbabwe were in serious trouble. According to the assessment, they were cases in which adjustment, rather than being overdone, had not gone far enough.

The other innovative contribution of OED's 1992 SAL review was an attempt to measure the increasingly remarked-on issue of borrower "ownership" of structural adjustment reforms.[53] Efforts to quantify the phenomenon are inherently controversial. But by aggregating individual subjective estimates the reviewers at least engaged the problem. They concluded:

> The countries that exhibited ownership that was both consistent and of the highest degree with respect to the programs that constitute our sample [of forty-two countries] are Chile, Indonesia, Korea, and Mauritius. The countries that exhibited the lowest degree of ownership . . . are Bolivia, Brazil, Côte d'Ivoire, Guyana, Nigeria, Senegal, Sudan, Tanzania, Togo, Uruguay, and Zaire.[54]

In leaving the matter of SAL assessment and evaluation, it can be noted that the concern, inside the Bank as well as outside, that has been lavished on the issue is admirable. More and better evaluation means better learning from experience. But strident critiques of adjustment lending often forget the relevant question: Compared with what? In most developing countries at the start of the "adjustment revolution" the status before the fact no longer was available. Adjustment's core macro problem consisted of imbalances, especially abroad, that could not be sustained. They tended to come to a self-prolonging head during 1978–85. In the absence of sufficiently generous grants and other soft transfers, there was no way pain could be completely avoided. Many in the Bank were concerned to find by what policies, with what combination of transfers and self-help, the burdens of adjustment could be curbed. The Bank and its clients proposed imperfect answers, which with learning arguably improved. But wand waving was not an option.

Both the Bank and its critics were guilty of overkill in their assessments of adjustment lending. External reviews of SAL linked it to all manner of economic, environmental, and social ills. In many cases the critics let ideological predilections turn correlation into causality. For its part the Bank (although not in many of its formal evaluations) often claimed too much. Both sides tended not to dwell on the deep roots of problems, the longer time horizons needed, the entrenched character of political and social structures, and the unforgiving global environment.

53. The issue itself had been prominent in RAL I.
54. World Bank, "World Bank Structural and Sectoral Adjustment Operations: The Second OED Overview," p. 176.

A Cluster of Other Country Cases

A few countries obviously cannot represent the universe of World Bank clients; yet more detailed accounts of transactions with particular borrowers are needed to leaven generalized discussions. The four cases of Turkey, the Philippines, Colombia, and Ghana provide some insight into the workings of policy-influence lending in the Bank. In the 1980s the institution had a heavy policy involvement with all four countries. Politics was writ heavy on all four. Three of them (Colombia was already there) made turbulent transitions to pluralistic modes of government. In the Philippines the Bank had to deal, back-to-back, with two very different regimes. In terms of economic policy, all four countries suffered different degrees of debt crisis. All four pursued outwardly oriented reforms. And all four governments in company with the Bank mouthed the stabilization verities, but with different degrees of success.

If any of these four countries was closest to the center of Bank attention in the 1980s it may have been Turkey. Here the account runs back into the 1960s and extends through the early 1990s. In the 1980s the government and the Bank jointly pursued a predominantly single-track (exports-centered) agenda. The theme one takes from the case is the need for balance between external and internal policy.

In the Philippines the theme is political. Not only did the Bank have to deal with two contrasting governments; in each instance there was a sharp cleavage between the governing regime and the bureaucracy, the latter of which (as in Turkey) sustained considerable continuity from one regime to the next.

In Colombia the story line is the tension, in a more republican and politically ordered context, between (short-term) stabilization and (longer-term) supply-side adjustment issues—involving the government's relations with the IMF and the Bank as the respective expositors of the two concerns, as well as the institutions' relations with each other.

Ghana's 1980s story may be the most satisfying scenario of World Bank contribution to macroeconomic reform. There was policy balance on the government's side and sensitivity and appropriateness on the part of the Bank, until the emergency was succeeded by less authoritarian politics. The case illustrates (a matter discussed further at the end of the chapter) the episodic character of macropolicy repair.

The Bank and Turkish Macropolicy

The Bank's relationship with Turkey in the 1980s was greatly influenced by events of earlier decades.

BEFORE 1980. From 1923 Turkey was governed by a secular, authoritarian, modernizing regime that adopted democratic procedures in 1950. As a recipient of Marshall Plan aid, the country was a founding member of OECD when the latter was converted from OEEC in 1960. The last explains why OECD, rather than the

World Bank or another multilateral or bilateral agency, chaired the aid consortium for Turkey when, from 1960 onward, the country was perceived to warrant development assistance.

In 1950 the Turkish polity had a few principal governing elements. There were two party groups in the political center headed by Kemal Ataturk's Republican People's Party (RPP) on the one hand, and, on the other, by Adnan Menderes's Democratic Party, succeeded later by the Justice Party of Suleyman Demirel. But these two leading parties had other fragmentary factions surrounding them and usually (especially in the 1970s) had to govern—if and when they did—as the leaders of coalitions.

The country's highly structured and indoctrinated bureaucracy, whose roots reached back into the Ottoman Empire, held power in its own right.[55] During the interval between the world wars and after the second of them, the Turkish bureaucrats, governing from the top down, were accustomed to implementing Kemalist policies.[56] Yet their code called for them to serve any effective national authority. They were typically aligned with and subordinate to their fellow elitists in the military officers corps. Commentators often cast Turkish military leaders in the role of Platonic guardians: reluctant to intervene in civilian affairs, they did so in pursuit of the military's notion of the common interest when the civilians were perceived as having become too stalemated, corrupt, or inept. During the World Bank's encounter with Turkey, the military was moved to take over in 1960–61 and again in 1980–83; and it placed the government under strict tutelage in 1971–73.

An adequate political sketch, especially for the later decades, also must include interest groups. Robert McNamara met with two dozen industrialists, bankers, and trade association people during his first presidential trip to the country (July 1968). The labor unions had a Kemalist tradition, and organized agriculture had considerable voice, especially with the pro-rural Democrats. In the Ataturk and post-Ataturk periods, however, Turkey was a country in which political decision tended to be monopolized by the central structures of the state itself. Indeed, "etatism," constitutionally committed to centrally planned, highly regulated economic management, was the norm of all the centrist parties in the 1960s and 1970s.

Economically, like Mexico, Turkey was a country in which average production and incomes had grown quite vigorously in the decades before the World Bank started up. Real GDP, having risen by about 7 percent a year from the mid-1920s until the late 1930s, had an annual growth rate of about 5 percent in the 1950s and 6.5 percent from 1961–63 to 1977–79.[57] In the late 1960s and early 1970s, Turkey

55. Serif Mardin, "Turkey: The Transformation of the Economic Code," in Ergun Ozbudun and Aydin Ulusan, eds., *The Political Economy of Income Distribution in Turkey* (New York: Holmes and Meier, 1980), pp. 23–53.

56. The terminology invokes Ataturk's original name, Mustafa Kemal.

57. Bent Hansen, *Egypt and Turkey: The Political Economy of Poverty, Equity, and Growth* (Oxford University Press, 1991), table 6.3, pp. 268–69.

experienced a surge in worker migration to Western Europe. This generated remittances that dampened external deficits while the exodus provided a safety valve against rural and urban unemployment. Early in its modern period the country exhibited a propensity for slipping into inflation. Under Ataturk, the RPP had an opposite (fiscally and monetarily austere) tradition, but, especially during periods of Democratic-Justice populist government, Turkey was given to rapid monetary expansions and soft-budget constraints. Inflation got increasingly out of hand in the 1970s.

The Bank had had a rough start in Turkey. After Pieter Lieftinck and his resident office were ousted in the early 1950s, Eugene Black resisted impulses within the Bank toward early renewal. According to some Turks, the hostility lingered in George Woods's time. In 1972, Menduh Ayter, recently returned to the State Planning Organization, recalled for McNamara the tensions that had existed between the organization and the Bank a decade earlier. McNamara gave a studied technocratic reply: no longer, he said, would Bank officers be permitted to express the kind of political and ideological partisanship that Ayter alleged had been shown in the 1960s. More to the point, the president bespoke a lending stance toward Turkey he had adopted in 1968, when he pronounced the annual rate of Bank/IDA lending to the country ($12 million) ridiculously small. He favored vigorous expansion. By 1972, the rate of gross transfers had moved into the $100 million to $200 million range and still was rising briskly.

The Bank in the 1970s was at pains in Turkey not to overreach. The Bank was not the chairman of the consortium. Until recently, its financial input had been small. It expressed great concern for the quality of project design and implementation.[58] And it was conspicuously neutral politically. Thus, while it would have undisguised enthusiasm for the market-oriented reform measures Demirel and his technocratic colleague, Turgut Ozal, would adopt at the beginning of the 1980s, the Bank was very attentive to Bulant Ecevit, the RPP (social democrat) prime minister in the 1970s. Indeed, for Ecevit, in 1978 alone, McNamara, at some pain to normalize operating procedures, gave the government—in order to help its anti-inflationary record—a temporary waiver on the electrical utility's need to raise power tariffs, adopted a procedurally less offensive means for concerting policy understandings than Bank staff had proposed, and nursed another program loan for Turkey past considerable Board opposition. Moreover, the Bank seemed to take special pains to attribute benign motives to the Turkish military and avoid exhibiting displeasure at its interventions. The institution's formal comments to the effect that the military takeover in 1980 would not displace the Bank's lending intentions were extremely polite.[59]

58. Memorandum, Adi J. Davar for the record, "Turkey: Discussions during Mr. McNamara's Visit," May 14, 1975, concerning McNamara's meeting with Prime Minister Demirel, April 24, 1975.

59. Memoranda, Roger Chaufournier to Robert S. McNamara, "Turkey: Latest Political Developments," September 16, 1980; Adi J. Davar for the record, "Turkey: Visit of Turkish Ambassador with Mr. McNamara," September 23, 1980.

Substantively, in addition to its close-in project work, the Bank had been making its case on broader subjects. These, addressed by means of ESW and policy discussions, had included agriculture, population, and other social-sector issues. But in terms both of its centrality to near- and medium-term Turkish affairs and of apparent Bank influence, one topic stood out from the rest: industrial and trade policy.

Turkey had been adamantly—in fact, in its 1961 constitution, almost constitutionally—committed to an import-substitution strategy of industrialization, supported by protection against imports and coupled, especially in the 1960s, with a heavy allocation of investment to the public sector. By 1977 the policy was running into a major financial breakdown. Imports were high; in the face of European stagflation, exports and workers' remittances sagged, and the country encountered a major foreign debt crisis four or five years before the problem became common. OECD, with heavy help from Germany and with the rest of the consortium joining in, in 1978 ran a rescue operation whose effects were partially aborted by the second (1979) oil shock.

THE 1980 SWITCH, WITH SUPPORTIVE FUNDING. A widely perceived prospect for change was signaled by Demirel's succession as prime minister in late 1979, but few expected the radical turn of policy into which Demirel's deputy, Turgut Ozal, talked his official colleagues in a multiday "retreat" in January 1980. The program that emerged was celebrated in an enthusiastic reunion (beside his earlier interactions with the Bank as a Turkish planner, he had worked two years in the Bank's Industry Division in the 1970s) Ozal had with McNamara and some of his senior staff in the president's office a few weeks later. The government's program priority was given to "increasing export incentives; improving external debt management; studying the system of protection; eliminating the budget deficit; encouraging private saving, and rationalizing and reducing the level of public investment."[60] But the heaviest accent was on the first item on that list.

The Turkish reform agenda was greatly influenced by the structural adjustment thinking that, at the time, was taking shape in the Bank. Reciprocally, the Turkish program became a prototype for the institution's structural adjustment loan series. (Interestingly, the convergence caused a procedural hiccup at the very start of SAL operations. The latter put great stock, especially at the outset, in ex-ante conditionality: after receiving a SAL the recipient was to adopt reforms specified and encouraged by the loan. But in the Turkish case an exception had to be made straightaway: the borrower on its own already had taken the reforms to which it agreed.)

The shift of the Bank–Turkey relationship from its prickly earlier state to cordiality by the start of the 1980s owed much to effective "bridging" by high-level

---

60. The language is from World Bank, "Evaluation of Structural Adjustment Lending in Turkey: Program Performance Audit Report of the Fourth and Fifth Structural Adjustment Loans (Loans 2321-TU and 2441-TU) and Overview of SALs I-V," OED Report 7205, SecM88-443, April 13, 1988, p. 3.

Turks in the Bank. Aside from Ozal, two were especially important. Attila Karaos-manoglu had hired Ozal (and, indeed, Demirel) into the Turkish planning organization in the early 1960s and supervised him for a while when Karaosmanoglu was back from the Bank as a deputy prime minister and economics chief in the early 1970s. Karaosmanoglu encountered Ozal again in Washington when the former returned to the Bank. As the player with the highest combined rank in the two organizations, the Bank and the government of Turkey (at the Bank he became one of its first three managing directors), Karaosmanoglu personified a constructive Bank–Turkey interface. Munir Benjenk was Karaosmanoglu's Bank-side boss for many years. Benjenk, a native of Istanbul, who had a deep grasp of Turkish politics and culture, was vice president for Europe, Middle East, and North Africa throughout the 1970s. The presidential files show him helping to forestall incipient clashes between the government and the IMF and, in general, supplying Mc-Namara with a flow of insightful advice.

The Turkish leadership with which the Bank had to interact in 1980–83 was once again the military. The generals and their counterparts in the other services liked the Ozal program. They took charge once more in September 1980, keeping on Ozal as their civilian deputy. They returned government to a democratic mode in May 1983, when Ozal's Motherland Party was popular enough to elect him prime minister over the military's sponsored candidate. Ozal, it turned out, would be Turkey's central leader for another decade.

The country was a favored adjustment client. It got not one but five Bank SALs by 1985. One reason Turkey appeared to adjust well was that official donors staked it to what, by subsequent standards, was an unusually generous transfer of adjustment-cushioning resources. In the first three years of the 1980s, despite a heavy outflow of interest payments, net external public resource transfers to Turkey remained positive, helping the country couple growth with adjustment. "Other heavily indebted countries did not enjoy this luxury . . . ; they were forced to generate a [net resource transfer] of 4–5 percent of GNP almost as soon as their debt crisis hit in 1982."[61]

There were reasons for the comparative generosity to Turkey. For one thing, the country simply got a head start; it hit its financial crisis four years ahead of the big debt crisis, and it was comparatively easy for donor governments and multilaterals to find transferable resources. Also there were geopolitical reasons for supporting Turkey, to which the Bank theoretically turned a blind eye.[62] The Iranian revolution, Turkey's mooting of a closer move to the Soviet Union, and the latter's invasion

61. Dani Rodrik, "Premature Liberalization, Incomplete Stabilization: The Ozal Decade in Turkey," in Michael Bruno, Stanley Fischer, Elhanan Helpman, and Nissan Liviatan, eds., *Lessons of Economic Stabilization and Its Aftermath* (MIT Press, 1991), p. 331 and tables 9.3 and 9.4.

62. Personally, as a global statesman, McNamara was not blind to Turkey's geopolitical salience, as a revealing 1979 exchange between Helmut Schmidt, then the chancellor of the Federal Republic of Germany, makes clear.

of Afghanistan, all intensified Turkish claims on Western concern. International politics would continue to overlay the country's macroeconomic story. Thus in 1991 Gulf War reparations would overtake the economic policy calculus, and thereafter reform policies would be upstaged by the country's move toward a customs union with the European Union together with a cluster of other external political concerns.[63]

But there was as well—for the Bank, in particular—a special ideological reason for the focus on Turkey. Turkey made itself the example par excellence of export-led growth. The attractiveness of export promotion in any country facing an unsustainable balance of payments gap was self-evident, but for the Bank the "fit" was more than pragmatic. Turkey seemed to vindicate the whole Balassa-Krueger line of policy analysis that had taken center stage at the turn of the decades. The strongest theme of the economic reform program that Turgut Ozal and his associates initiated in January 1980 was export promotion, and decision makers at the Bank embraced the program like a parent.

As the decade wore on, some of the enthusiasm went out of the Bank's Turkish venture. In the 1990s IMF would emerge as, for this country in its then predicament, the more consequential Bretton Woods partner. And some of the anomalies of Bank-supported reforms would become plainer. But euphoria did not wane quickly. As late as the end of August 1988 in a briefing note to EMENA Vice President Willi Wapenhans as the 1988 Country Strategy Paper for Turkey was about to be considered in the Bank President's Council, staffer Albert de Capitani declared, "Among the Bank's clients, Turkey represents one of the most spectacular success stories."[64]

THE FIVE SALS PHASE: PRIORITY TO EXPORTS. The five SALs the World Bank wrote for Turkey from 1980 to 1985 were the most it made to any client during the institution's first half-dozen years of adjustment lending. Indeed, among the reasons for switching to SECALs thereafter was the feeling of Bank clients and owners that, if, as projected, structural adjustment was a time-bound exercise, time for this adjustment should have run out with the signing of the fifth loan in a row; that, in any event, Turkey was getting more than its fair share of quick-disbursing flexible money.

For both Turkey and the Bank, the policy emphasis of the whole series was on export promotion, first, by various adjustments in commercial policy (export subsidies, import liberalization, increases in export prices, including those of state enterprises) that added to the profitability of exporting; and second, by currency devaluation.

Ongoing devaluation was the conspicuous core of the program. At the start of reforms in early 1980 the nominal exchange rate got knocked down about 70 per-

63. For an analysis of Turkey's troubled role as "pivot of Europe and Asia," see "Turkey: East, West, Which Is Best?" *Economist*, vol. 33, no. 7890 (November 19, 1994), pp. 23–25.

64. De Capitani to Wapenhans, August 30, 1988.

cent, bringing a decline of 30 percent in the real effective exchange rate. Then after periodic adjustment until May 1981, a regime was adopted of a daily downward crawl that implemented the rule of "purchasing power parity plus." Through 1988 there were annual *real* devaluations in the range of 2–10 percent. These together with sporadic devaluations thereafter, in particular, the plunge of the lira that occurred in 1994, meant that by the latter year the size of one U.S. dollar's worth of Turkish liras, compared with the end of 1979, had risen some 900-fold.[65]

The purpose of devaluation was to sharpen the competitiveness of Turkish exports, and because of the linkage to export expansion, the Bank did not let deference to the IMF temper its enthusiasm for the measure. At this point in Turkey, the Bank was less outspoken about a second pro-competitiveness factor: in manufacturing, real wages had peaked in 1977. They began a formidable decline that continued through most of the 1980s. Obviously, one of the determinants of real wages was domestic price inflation. But the wage trend was also the product of deliberate "labor market repression" involving restraints on unions and industrial wage bargaining.[66]

During the period of the five SALs, neither the government of Turkey nor the Bank in its specification of loan conditionalities was literally single track in its focus on exports. The whole array of familiar macro objectives was addressed. But part of the record consists of the ways in which, and the reasons why, the export priority outweighed the others.

STABILIZATION AND OTHER SECONDARY PRIORITIES. The five Turkish SALs tended to repeat one another: they covered the full panoply of macropolicy objectives and conditions—for example, to reduce inflation, increase domestic resource raising, eliminate the budget deficit, rationalize public investment, tighten monetary policy, deregulate interest rates, reform state enterprises, and liberalize imports while maintaining a realistic, flexible exchange rate.[67] It would have been presumptuous in 1980, a year when Turkish inflation exceeded 100 percent, to suggest that inflation fighting was not in the forefront of the minds of both the Turkish government and the World Bank; and during the two succeeding years, the growth rates of the price indexes were in fact brought down to about 30 percent. OED concluded that the reform program was partly responsible.[68]

But other factors contributed to the subsidence of inflation. For one thing, fresh inflows of external resources helped Turkey (just as oil earnings had done in

65. Ziya Onis and James Riedel, *Economic Crises and Long-Term Growth in Turkey* (World Bank, 1993), pp. 39–40.

66. Hansen, *Egypt and Turkey*, p. 415.

67. The examples are taken from all five SALs as summarized in World Bank, "Evaluation of Structural Adjustment Lending in Turkey, Program Performance Audit Report (PPAR) of the Fourth and Fifth Structural Adjustment Loans and Overview of SALs I-V," OED Report 7205, April 13, 1988.

68. Ibid, p. xii.

Indonesia fourteen years earlier) combine radical inflation reduction with growth. But the way the 1980 inflation rate spiked was rather freakish: "Most of the 109% inflation in 1980 happened in the first two months, when there was a very large devaluation and a very large increase in public-sector prices. If one averages out these [administered] price increases, in 1980–83 inflation was 46%, in 1984–1988 it was 44%, and in the years of the late 1970s it was also around 40–50%. *It is arguable that Turkey is not an example of incomplete stabilization but a case of no stabilization at all.*"[69] This last is the telling point. It was much too early to be celebrating even a partial defeat of inflation.

Through the period of the five SALs—and beyond—the government of Turkey and the Bank never stopped talking, analyzing, and conditioning in behalf of stabilization. The dialogue was intense. But implementation was weak. The 30 percent price rise in 1982 turned out to be the lowest of the decade. There was a bump to 50 percent in 1984. The price indexes climbed more than 60 percent in each of the years 1988 and 1989, and this was simply a warm-up for heavier inflation to follow.

As the 1980s proceeded, there was a major political dimension to this performance, to which we will come shortly. Cynics might suggest that the Turkish authorities felt not unkindly toward inflation because it sharpened the competitiveness of industrial real wages. But there is no need to impute conspiracy. The issue was simply one of priorities. The priority that ongoing devaluation was accorded neutralized the exports-dampening effect of domestic inflation, thereby taking much of the starch out of inflation resistance.

If this was how objectives were ranked by the Ozal government, it is noteworthy that the ranking seems to have been shared by the World Bank. Every 1980s Bank report on Turkey, early and late, gave space and emphasis to the need for further and more effective monetary, fiscal, and other moves in behalf of domestic stabilization, but there was an ambivalence. The draft of the retrospective OED report on the five SALs issued in April 1988 was an example. It voiced an alarming analysis of the country's emerging budgetary and internal debt exposure centering around the fact that real Turkish interest rates since 1980 had assumed a level 10–20 percent or more above average world real interest rates, driven in good part by expectations of ongoing real depreciation of the lira.[70] Interest rates related ominously to the public budget:

> The primary deficit [net of interest expense] has been close to zero since 1981, so interest payments account for nearly the entire deficit. This means that the Government is borrowing to finance its interest payments. . . . [F]inancing a fiscal deficit at a real rate of interest that exceeds the growth rate of tax revenues given the prevailing tax structure

69. "Comments by Sweder van Wijnbergen" in Bruno and others, *Lessons of Economic Stabilization and Its Aftermath*, p. 355; emphasis added.
70. World Bank, "Evaluation of Structural Adjustment Lending in Turkey . . . ," pp. 33–45.

draws the country's finances into an inherently unstable position. . . . [T]he ratio of debt to GNP will [tend to] grow continuously.[71]

Yet up front the same sober report was strongly upbeat: "Turkey's commitment to the program of structural adjustment was solidly expressed throughout the life of the SALs. At the policy level a variety of measures were introduced to improve the efficiency of resource allocation and to strengthen export competitiveness."[72] Four months later, in the CSP exercise, Bank management decided to favor a $1 billion annual lending level for Turkey that would carry the institution's exposure in the country farther above the preferred ceiling, and, in his related briefing note for the regional vice president, de Capitani made the "spectacular success story" assessment already quoted. As noted, Turkey and the Bank were engaging all the right macro subjects; they had few blind spots. And some of the country's stabilization difficulties could be attributed to the kind of Phase I, Phase II distinction that is evident in other country cases. Reforms were becoming more difficult as increasingly they entailed major institutional modification or rebuilding. The central example of state economic enterprise (SEE) reform is discussed later in the chapter under the heading "Reform Politics."

An overlapping point can be put differently: during the first half-dozen years of the 1980s Turkey's priority need was indeed export-led growth, and the government's programmatic priority was well chosen. But increasingly, from the mid-1980s onward, the adjustment need shifted to reforms of the fiscal roots of the balance of payments, for which devaluation was not the answer. Further, the IMF was at work, side by side, and stabilization, for all of the Bank's verbal attention, was the Fund's greater responsibility. The Bank, with export expansion working so well, felt it could remain concentrated on growth promotion.

Yet one scarcely has to look beyond the price index records—which never stabilized and ran uphill toward the end of the 1980s—to conclude that, for all its dither, the domestic stabilization effort was remarkably soft. This was the net effect of the Ozal government, and the softness was not effectively resisted by the Bank ("effectiveness" being signaled, for example, by the kind of pointed cutback in adjustment lending that was intermittently considered but never decisively adopted). For both parties, there was a disconnect between a disappointing domestic stabilization effort and external success. Within the Bank the distinction was still being made in a draft CSP as late as mid-1991: "Notwithstanding . . . domestic financial instability, Turkey's economic growth remained high and the external accounts displayed a strong improvement throughout the decade, which, combined with a continued accumulation of official reserves, led to a marked improvement in international creditworthiness."[73]

71. Ibid., 4.17, p. 49.
72. Ibid., p. vii.
73. World Bank, Country Operations Division, Country Department, EMENA, "Turkey: Country Strategy Paper," draft, May 28, 1991.

Table 10-4. *Economic Indicators, Turkey, 1970–93*[a]
Period averages

Indicator	1970	1977–79	1980–83	1984–92	1993
GDP (billions of $U.S.)	12.7	56.6	54.7	78.6	174.2
GDP (billions of 1987 $U.S.)	28.0	46.5	49.4	69.7	112.0
Agriculture share of GDP growth (percent)	0.6	0.3	0.4	0.5	(0.3)
Total investment/GDP (percent)	22.5	23.5	19.9	22.2	22.7
Budget deficit/GDP (percent)	(3.5)	(9.4)	(7.7)	(5.0)	...
Current account balance/GDP (percent)	(0.3)	(3.4)	(3.8)	(0.8)	(0.9)
Exports (billions of $U.S.)	1.0	3.9	8.4	19.4	30.4
Exchange rate (Turkish liras per $U.S.)	11.5	24.5	143.8	2179.7	20296.7
Unemployment (percent of labor force)	12.0	9.6	11.4	9.0	7.2
Average annual growth rates (percent)					
Real GDP	8.9	1.1	4.4	5.1	...
GDP deflator	17.9	56.3	32.5	52.7	...
Real exports	17.7	4.5	19.5	6.6	...
Average daily real wage	(6.7)	(6.6)	(2.5)	11.0	...

Sources: IMF, *International Financial Statistics;* World Bank, *World Tables;* William Easterly and others, *Public Sector Deficits and Macroeconomic Performance* (Oxford University Press, 1994), p. 530; OECD, *Labor Force Statistics,* OECD, 1970–90 and 1971–91, pp. 434–35; *Main Economic Indicators* (Ankara: Turkish Prime Ministry, March 1994); *Statistical Yearbook of Turkey* (Ankara: Prime Ministry State Institute of Statistics, 1977–94); Guy P. Pfefferman and Andrea Madarassy, *Trends in Private Investment in Thirty Developing Countries* (World Bank/IFC, 1989), p. 12; Jack D. Glen and Mariusz A. Sumlinski, *Trends in Private Investment in Developing Countries, 1995* (World Bank/IFC, 1995), p. 14.

a. Export figures are deflated with the manufactures unit value index (1992 = 100) to compute real exports growth. Unemployment for 1993 is the first quarter estimate from *Main Economic Indicators;* other unemployment figures are from *Labor Force Statistics.* Average daily real wages are computed with figures from the *Statistical Yearbook of Turkey* and deflated by the CPI (1987 = 100). Average daily wage figures for 1985–87 are not available; the period averages are 1980–84 and 1988–92.

THE POLITICS OF REFORM. What so cheered the World Bank was Ozal's sharp turn toward the market and away from detailed government interventions into market decisionmaking. The turn toward global as well as internal openness, fueled by robust export expansion, was the kind of economic program the Turkish military reinforced when it took charge once again in September 1980, retaining Ozal as prime minister. In a mixture of expediency and class tilt, the military–Ozal regime was distributionally conservative. As noted, it presided with few regrets over a prolonged slide in industrial real wages—one that, its supporters argued, started from a wage-bargaining field that had been rigged to favor organized labor from the 1961 constitution onward and had produced a rash of union growth, strikes, and turmoil in the 1970s. The results, in the 1980–83 holiday from party politics, were sinking real wages, constrained, strike-forbidden unions, and (with export and GNP growth) soaring corporate profits.[74] But, as table 10-4 indicates,

74. Hansen, *Egypt and Turkey.*

with opportunities for migration to West European countries narrowed, economic expansion also did little to reduce Turkey's distressingly high rate of involuntary unemployment. Furthermore, in its earlier phases the Ozal era (he graduated to president in 1989 and succumbed in 1993) was sparing in its expenditures on human resources and social services. Budget restraint was not as tight as anti-inflation demand management required, but the budget pulled back on the social sectors.

The World Bank rather reminds one of the Bank in Chile in the 1970s. It was slow to second-guess Turkey's politics. But it got progressively nervous about the drift of the country's distributional policies. In 1991 the Bank remarked to itself:

> Internal economic policies . . . have continued to be influenced by the country's political cycle. . . . Central to Turkey's current internal political situation is the view that the burden of adjustment and the benefits of growth have not been shared equitably among the population, that poverty continues to be a serious problem, particularly in the Eastern parts of the country, and that social indicators are lagging behind those of other middle-income countries. Popular discontent on socio-economic inequities has become increasingly vocal.[75]

The Turkish polity appeared to have undergone an important transformation between the 1970s and 1980s. Economic policy opted for a shift toward liberalization. But there seemed also to be a political shift, from reliance on a military balance wheel to dependence on the contentions of civilian politics.

From Ataturk onward the system was state dominated with the military intervening intermittently (the rhythm was about every ten years) to correct or reverse the excesses of civilian rulers. With the relaunching of democracy in 1983 the military may have decided (neither they nor others could be sure) to return to the barracks permanently, leaving future emergencies to be coped with by a substitute civilian cycle of budgetary overshoot followed by anti-inflationary redress. In a familiar diagnosis, analysts see in the Turkish polity a set of coalitions of political parties, party fragments, and interest groups that may, depending partly on their recent interplay, be comparatively civil or boisterous in their collective action. But their common characteristic is that they seek a larger composite reward than the system has to distribute. The preoccupying task of government is to mediate interfactional peace.[76]

In the peacekeeping milieux of the 1980s, the government of Turkey, when political circumstances pressed, tended to mediate by undertaking inflationary

75. World Bank, "Turkey: Country Strategy Paper," pp. 5–6.

76. In a way, of course, the view of claimants wanting more than the whole pie is a universal explanation of inflationary demand, but certain writers—for example, Mancur Olson for the United States (*The Logic of Collective Action: Public Goods and the Theory of Groups* [Harvard University Press, 1965]); Pranab Bardan for India (*The Political Economy of Development in India* [Oxford, England: Basil Blackwell, 1984]); and Ziya Onis for Turkey (in Onis and Riedel, *Economic Crises and Long-Term Growth in Turkey*)—have given the point great emphasis.

rates of public spending. A government so driven is drawn to conducive structures and instruments. The 240 or so SEEs the government owned by the early 1980s provided such a potential. The typical SEE was demand expanding: it failed to generate as much public revenue as expected, was inefficiently costly, and claimed public subsidies. A regime seeking to mediate among hungry interests was reluctant to "privatize" such institutions. Although the World Bank continued its advocacy, Turkey's privatization program was slow to get moving and accelerate, and it remained so well into the 1990s.

Moreover, a device for relaxing public budgetary discipline was developed and routinized as the 1980s proceeded. "Extra budgetary funds" increasingly became vehicles for enlarging and disguising the flow of funds through SEEs. Thus equipped, composite public budgets became quite opaque, nearly impervious to strict fiscal control.

The swathe that the World Bank had been cutting in Turkey narrowed in the first half of the 1990s. The Bank's quantitative input—particularly adjustment lending—dropped.[77] The decline of Bank loan disbursements was especially sharp compared with those of other external donors, lenders, and investors.[78]

In the aftermath of the 1987 election, the government was preoccupied with the way inflation was accelerating. But, even more, not only was the government failing to cope with, but it was helping perpetrate, a breathtaking rebound in real wages in manufacturing. In a postelection populist phase the country ricocheted from "wage repression to wage explosion."[79] By the early 1990s the whole economic scene was remarkably turbulent. Consumer prices in the fourth quarters of 1992 and 1993 were, respectively, 338 percent and 572 percent of their 1990 average. The growth of exports in 1993 stalled; it was only 6 percent. But the domestic economy boomed; real GNP grew 8 percent, and financial activity surged. Investment, both foreign and domestic, boomed, and the young stock market became one of the world's most bullish: average values recorded a sevenfold rise during the course of 1993.

At the beginning of 1993, Michael Wiehen, the Bank's director for Turkey, spelled out his frustration to management. He emphasized the ineffectiveness of

77. Average Bank commitments of all loan types to Turkey between 1986 and 1990 were US$845.2 million annually; commitments between 1991 and 1995 averaged only US$428.5 million a year. Commitments for *adjustment* lending between 1981 and 1988 averaged US$345.5 million a year. However, the commitment for adjustment lending in 1989 was US$29.9 million.

78. IMF, *International Capital Markets: Developments and Prospects,* various issues, and World Bank annual reports, various issues.

79. Ismail Arslan and Merih Celasun, "Sustainability of Industrial Exporting in a Liberalizing Economy: The Turkish Experience," in G. K. Helleiner, ed., *Manufacturing for Export in the Developing World: Problems and Possibilities* (London: Routledge, 1995), p. 141. They quote the State Planning Organization's report that from 1988 to 1991 the index for the real wages in the 500 largest industrial firms rose from 100 to 229 for private firms and from 100 to 288 for public enterprises.

the country's popular new finance minister.[80] In her company he had recently met with Prime Minister Demirel:

> I laid out the Bank's assessment of the economic situation in Turkey; I told him that we estimated the [public sector borrowing requirement] for 1992 to be around 15–16%, and inflation above 65%; worst of all, that neither the budget deficit nor the inflation rate could be expected to come down in 1993 significantly without major action on resource mobilization . . . expenditures . . . and SEE privatization/restructuring. . . . I also said to him I considered it disastrous that the Central Bank could not prepare a monetary program for 1993 because of the totally unrealistic macro program. The PM said he "agreed fully" with the Bank's analysis, but that for political reasons he could not move on most of the fronts. I argued with him, for example on the SEE issue . . . to no avail.[81]

Wiehan added that the "Bank's message has been delivered loudly and clearly," by others as well as himself. Three months later, in the midst of 1993's runaway inflation and an unsustainable domestic boom, President Ozal died of a heart attack.

Turkey's story is thus a turbulent one: it had devolved from its phase of impressive, export-led, but instability-accumulating, growth during the first two-thirds of the 1980s to violent fluctuations and mounting instability thereafter. Of the two Bretton Woods institutions, the Fund became the more relevant. Whether the decline was cyclical or secular, current Bank influence had diminished.

The Philippines, 1972–92

As an object of World Bank attention to borrowers' macropolicies, the Philippines had similarities to Indonesia. It was Southeast Asian and populous—less than Indonesia, but the size of Thailand and South Korea. It had a colonial past, although the United States continued to exert greater influence (for example, in the matter of military bases) than did the Netherlands on Indonesia. Since independence the Philippines had had a much longer and deeper flirtation with democracy than had Indonesia. But with President Ferdinand Marcos's declaration of martial law in 1972, both countries were ruled by authoritarian governments. As of that time, Indonesia had the lower GNP per capita, but, after a hectic 1960s, it was on the way to growing faster (4.1 percent annual average over 1970–74) than the Philippines (2.6 percent).

The dominant theme of the present twenty-year Filipino case concerns the problems and limitations an apolitical external technocracy encountered in trying to lever macro reform. The case is distinctive for the dualism of the government involved: simultaneous dualism between a senior bureaucracy and its political masters, and sequential dualism between the two back-to-back regimes (Marcos

80. Tansu Ciller, later to become prime minster.
81. Memorandum, Michael H. Wiehen to Ernest Stern, "Re: Turkey," January 19, 1993, pp. 1–2.

and Aquino) with which the World Bank had to deal. Substantively, as in a number of other countries, there was a persistent tension between the policy problems of (short-term) stabilization and (longer-term) growth.

THE BANK AND THE GOP JOIN FORCES. World Bank lending to the Philippines went back to 1958, and some measure of Bank monitoring further than that. But relations with the Philippines were very thin. This was one of the many countries, once he arrived, of which Robert McNamara remarked that Bank lending was low. In fiscal 1971, when only two projects totaling $22.3 million were approved, it was still low, but deliberately so: McNamara and his staff were annoyed at the way the Philippine legislature was stalemating policy reforms.

Thus the Philippines was an instance in which martial law triggered the takeoff of Bank lending. Marcos dismissed the legislature and started ruling by presidential decree in August 1972. McNamara and the Bank staff welcomed the move. A month later the Bank president told the finance minister, Cesar Virata, who had moved to the position from the University of the Philippines in 1970:

> In the past we had been disappointed that measures designed to achieve economic and institutional reforms had not achieved legislative approval. He [McNamara] added that, provided the political environment was stable and the Administration was making an effective attack on the fundamental economic problems, the Bank was fully prepared to more than double its current rate of lending if an adequate number of projects could be prepared in time.[82]

McNamara emphasized his disappointment that the forthcoming fiscal 1973 Philippine program was no more than $30 million. But he urged a new departure.[83]

Henceforward the Bank and the Philippine government were committed to a joint expansion venture. Day to day, the effort was in the hands of two competent bureaucracies. On the Filipino side Marcos recruited an array of senior technocrats, heavily from the universities. Virata was one, and pivotal; he would become prime minister as well as finance minister in the early 1980s and stay with Marcos until the end. Gerardo (Jerry) Sicat was another; he served as minister of planning and director-general of the National Economic and Development Authority. Later he became chairman of the Philippine National Bank—government owned, the country's largest commercial bank. In the mid-1980s, Sicat would join the World Bank in Washington. There were a number of other senior, enterprising, and well-trained economic officials.

Bank staff enjoyed working with these counterparts and were themselves spirited and engaged. Their prototype was Russell Cheetham, in effect the Philip-

82. Memorandum for the record, "Philippines—Meeting of the Philippine Delegation to the 1972 Annual Meeting with Mr. McNamara on September 29, 1972," October 2, 1972, p. 1.

83. McNamara visited the Philippines three times during his presidency: in October 1971, again in October 1976 (for the annual meetings held in Manila), and finally in May 1979.

Table 10-5. *Economic Indicators, the Philippines, 1972–92*[a]
Period averages

Indicator	1972–82	1983–86	1987–92
GDP (billions of $U.S.)	21.7	31.3	42.6
GDP (billions of 1987 $U.S.)	28.0	32.9	36.9
Current account deficit/GDP (percent)	(5.1)	(2.5)	(3.5)
Budget deficit/GDP (percent)	0.5	(3.7)	(3.4)
Exports (billions of $U.S.)	5.0	8.3	13.3
Total debt service/exports (percent)	26.8	33.8	27.5
Long-term debt (billions of $U.S.)	10.3	25.9	30.4
Average annual growth rates (percent)			
Real GDP	5.5	(4.2)	2.7
GDP deflator	12.6	22.3	11.7
Real exports	7.6	3.0	9.1

Sources: IMF, *International Financial Statistics;* World Bank, *World Debt Tables;* World Bank, *World Tables;* William Easterly and others, *Public Sector Deficits and Macroeconomic Performance* (Oxford University Press, 1994), p. 530.

a. Budget deficit/GDP figures from Easterly and others are for 1981–90. Export growth rates are computed by deflating export figures using the manufactures unit value index (1992 = 100).

pine desk officer during much of the 1970s. Cheetham, in and out of Manila, became highly conversant with Filipino culture, politics, and economics. He was venturesome—for example, pressing possibilities for World Bank promotion (albeit not direct funding) of serious Philippine land reform. In the end the initiative did not succeed in either Manila or Washington, but it helped establish the bona fides of Bank staff.[84] Cheetham was a vigorous programmer of Bank lending, and in 1976 he was one of the authors of a widely noted Bank book on the Philippines.[85]

The Philippine economy had a trend growth rate in real GNP of 6 percent during the 1970s (table 10-5). Fixed investment rose from 16 to 25 percent of GNP. Government promotion helped push up nontraditional manufactured exports, and agriculture, thanks in good part to the "Green Revolution" in rice (in which the World Bank had some hand) did particularly well. Later some observers would call the expansion "debt driven;"[86] foreign commercial banks' brisk recycling of OPEC oil earnings countered the dampening effects of costlier oil imports. But, although it was risk laden, this was not inherently unhealthy as long as the export growth rate did, and would continue to, exceed the real interest rate on foreign borrowing.

84. Russell Cheetham, interview with John Lewis, Richard Webb, and Devesh Kapur, Washington, D.C., February 5, 1992.

85. Russell J. Cheetham and Edward K. Hawkins, *The Philippines: Priorities and Prospects for Development: Report of a Mission Sent to the Philippines by the World Bank* (World Bank, 1976).

86. James K. Boyce, *The Philippines: The Political Economy of Growth and Impoverishment in the Marcos Era* (London: Macmillan, 1993).

The Bank was abetting the Philippine expansion: business-cycle-minded people would say, "pro-cyclically." The Bank's loan commitments to the country, which had been $30 million in fiscal 1973, jumped to $165 million in fiscal 1974 and continued to climb. They totaled $400 million for sixteen projects in fiscal 1980. But operational problems began to mount. Projects became slower disbursing, and, as they came on stream, their estimated rates of return diminished. In 1979 an alarming 63 percent of the Bank's Philippine projects were deemed to be "problem projects" by OED. Moreover, the effectiveness of the policy messages attached to projects had become worrisome as early as 1975. "The question is whether Marcos will follow through to implement reforms he has promised. He has not really pursued land reform with constant vigor. Industry is protected and not much interested in exports."[87]

That was the question—the temper of the leader. How close a match was Marcos for President Suharto? In Indonesia, with his inoculation into macroeconomic sobriety renewed by the Pertamina affair, Suharto continued to endorse the economic planning and fiscal decisions of his seasoned technocrats. In the martial-law Philippines, President Marcos started that way; he let Virata, Sicat, and their colleagues call the macroeconomic tune. But contrasts began to appear. Marcos was not just a warrior against the old landed gentry; he was a creature of a new subset of rural oligarchs; two of them, Roberto Benedicto and Eduardo Cojunco, ran, respectively, the government's sugar-marketing and coconut-marketing monopolies. Corruption spread more and more indiscriminately from the top of the system, without the out-of-bounds areas that had been maintained in Indonesia. And the first lady was a phenomenon. Increasingly, in part in her role as minister of human settlements and in charge of metropolitan Manila, she became a kind of second chief executive, deploying resources and nervous energies toward a competing national agenda.

In a 1992 interview, Russell Cheetham estimated that the Virata-Sicat group largely lost its grip on events during 1979–81.[88] That the Bank, half aware of it, was trapped by the situation was registered in a briefing paper the institution's regional office provided the new president, A. W. Clausen, in 1981. The country's natural and cultural endowments "combined with good economic management by highly competent technocrats in the cabinet, allowed many impressive gains to be made during the 1970s."[89] However, things could have gone better, the paper said, and there were problems—maldistribution, a balance of payments constraint, and strains on public administration. But number two on the list of four problems was politics:

87. Memorandum, Gregory B. Votaw to Robert S. McNamara, "Phlippines: Your Meeting with Mr. Marcos," November 18, 1975.
88. Russel Cheetham, interview with John Lewis, Richard Webb, and Devesh Kapur, February 5, 1992.
89. World Bank, "Country Brief: Philippines," briefing paper prepared for A. W. Clausen, 1981, para. 1.

Second, past development has taken place in an autocratic political environment, and the increasingly sophisticated technocratic structure does not appear to be supported by a strong political base. The "New Society" program initiated by President Marcos in the 1970s was intended to bring greater economic equality by stripping away the political and economic power of the old oligarchy, but many now believe that the old oligarchy has only been replaced by a new one. Opponents of the current regime have voiced their resentment over the lack of civil liberties, increasing corruption, continuing ineffectiveness of the bureaucracy, and abuses of power by the military. Traditional political activity has been suppressed since 1972 under martial law (now abolished) and by the self-imposed exile of major opposition leaders. Although the president is setting the stage for a gradual transition to more democratic rule, considerable uncertainty remains with respect to the Philippines' political future.[90]

Yet the same paper wound up positively: "The dialogue between the government and the Bank is an excellent one." There had been various good joint studies, consultative group meetings, and joint project implementation reviews. Sectorally, the upcoming lending agenda was comprehensive. "The allocation to industry will increase, reflecting the capital role of this sector in resolving the balance of payments and employment problems in the 1980s and our progress in reaching agreement on needed policy reforms."[91] Meanwhile the Bank was charging ahead with new-style conditioned program lending to the Philippines. In October 1979 McNamara and Shahid Husain, then vice president for East Asia, had told Cesar Virata the Bank was willing to support program lending for industrial tariff reduction and export promotion. Already (in May) telling the Bank what it wanted to hear, President Marcos had volunteered the rationale for industrial imports liberalization as an instrument of indigenous output and exports expansion:

> There was a need for gradually eliminating the protection provided for the industrial sector in order to encourage efficiency and ensure competitiveness of the Philippine manufacturing products in world markets. He [Marcos] stated that this process, in fact, had already begun, and that as a first step the Government was planning to limit the maximum level of tariffs to 50%. This limit would be further reduced and gradually eliminated over the next few years on an industry-by-industry basis.[92]

By September 1980 (the new structural adjustment lending mode meanwhile having been inaugurated), the ground was well prepared for the contemplated loan to be launched as SAL I. It focused on export promotion, import liberalization, and

90. Ibid., para. 4.

91. Ibid., paras. 9, 10.

92. That 50 percent was a good downward adjustment target in 1979 highlights the degree of trade liberalization that was achieved by many developing countries in the period thereafter. Memorandum, Hedayat Amin-Arsala, senior loan officer, to files, "Philippines— Mr. McNamara's Meeting with His Excellency Ferdinand E. Marcos President of the Philippines," May 31, 1979, p. 1.

reorganization of the industrial sector.[93] SAL I was followed in May 1981 by a $150 million Industrial Finance Project Loan, and then by SAL II for $300 million in April 1983.[94] The latter, however, whose negotiation was preoccupied with Bank-IMF relations,[95] was superseded before it could become effective by the financial crisis the country had entered in 1981.

DEEPENING TROUBLES, 1981–86. At the start of 1981 a prominent business-man heavily into Filipino commercial credit fled the country, leaving behind an estimated 500 million to 800 million pesos ($63 million to $101 million worth) of debt. At first the crisis that had been triggered was confined to nonbank money markets and institutions, but it started a crumbling of confidence in the country's financial system. Two of the largest investment houses and the holding companies behind them failed; doubts and runs spread to rural and thrift banking institutions; and in 1982 the government's spending attempts to shore up the scene widened both the budget and balance of payments deficits. In 1983 failures spread to the comparatively stronger and safer commercial banks. By the end of the crisis in 1986, bank credit to the private sector would decline by 53 percent in real terms. The two largest banks, the Philippine National Bank and the Development Bank of the Philippines, would become de facto insolvent and the 80 percent of their assets that were nonperforming would be transferred to a new government holding pen, the Asset Privatization Trust.[96] Meanwhile foreign commercial banks, reluctant to increase developing-country exposure in the aftermath of the 1982 Mexican debt crisis, suspended new credits to the Philippines.

But other factors commingled with the financial. Most notably, in August 1983 the prominent opposition politician, Senator Benigno Aquino, self-exiled to the

93. The project completion report for SAL I and II prepared by the region in 1984 indicates substantial implementation of policy objectives. See, "Philippines—Structural Adjustment Loans I and II (IBRD Loans 1903-PH and 22656-PM): Program Completion Report," dated July 30, 1984, attached to World Bank, "Project Performance Audit Report: Philippines First and Second Structural Adjustment Loans," OED Report 5813, SecM85-975, August 21, 1985.

94. The 1981 loan was subsequently reclassified as an adjustment loan.

95. After being withdrawn from the Philippines for most of 1982, the Fund finally agreed in February 1983 to a standby that promised monetary and fiscal tightening, continued use of a flexible exchange rate policy, and prudent debt management. The Bank delayed SAL II until after the new standby was in place: "Our second SAL is closely linked to a new IMF standby. However, we have indicated to Prime Minister Virata that we cannot proceed with our support for a medium-term program of structural adjustment unless we are assured that the measures which the country is taking to deal with its short-term problems are adequate, i.e., we will continue processing of SAL II up to the negotiations stage but the loan will not be presented to the Board until an agreement with the IMF has been reached." Memoran-dum, S. Shahid Husain to A. W. Clausen, "Philippines—Your Meeting with Mrs. Marcos," September 15, 1982.

96. This account is based on Jean-Claude Nascimento, "Crisis in the Financial Sector and the Authorities' Reaction: The Philippines," in V. Sundararajan and Tomás J. T. Baliño, eds., Banking Crises: Cases and Issues (IMF, 1991), pp. 175–233.

United States, was assassinated upon his return at Manila airport. The assassination, Gerardo Sicat said, did "an enormous damage of setting back a large part of the timetable of development in the nation. This event alone scored neatly in undermining the credibility before the world of the present government, whether deserved or not. It took away the confidence that was already shaky at that point and made it a large event of consequential dimensions, thus aggravating a crisis that was already rearing its head."[97]

In terms of the real economy, gross domestic saving and investment tumbled in 1983–84 and real GNP plunged in 1984. Prices soared. The political economy was a first-class mess. For the World Bank, an important macropolicy message was driven home. On October 17, 1983, the balance of payments squeeze forced the government to announce the first of five 90-day moratoria on repayments of foreign debt principal. The IMF standby fell apart; negotiations that began at once to replace it would take fourteen months; and the Bank's structural reforms were shunted aside. SAL I reforms reducing tariffs and quantitative barriers were abandoned, and the measures were replaced for a year by quantitative controls. Furthermore, in consultation with the IMF, an import surcharge of 10 percent was put in place.[98] In emergencies, quite plainly, the Fund short run took precedence over Bank longer run.

What the Bank could do in the short run was limited. In calendar 1983 it stepped up disbursements to the Philippines (as opposed to commitments) to $600 million from the previous year's $251 million. And it articulated loyalty to an old friend: in September 1984 when management recommended a $150 adjustment loan for agricultural imports and the U.S. executive director protested that there was insufficient evidence of the government's willingness to address developmental problems, management recommended that the Philippines' excellent relations with the institution be rewarded. The loan was approved with the United States opposing and one other abstention.

But then, as a matter of fact, commitments of new Bank loans to the Philippines *were* cut back, quite drastically. The two-year average of $478 million in fiscal 1982–83 fell to $219 million in fiscal 1984–85. In their reform and other development efforts, the Bank and the government both were on the defensive.[99]

97. Gerardo P. Sicat, "A Historical and Current Perspective of Philippine Economic Problems," Philippine Institute for Development Studies, Monograph Series no. 11, June 1986, p. 4. This work is a reprint of Sicat's article by the same name in *Philippine Economic Journal*, vol. 24 (1985), pp. 24–63.

98. Mosley, Harrigan, and Toye, *Aid and Power*, p. 52.

99. An April 1985 CPP, so concerned to forestall leaks that its copies bore individual serial numbers, expressed a management policy, after the Benigno Aquino assassination, to shift the fiscal 1984–85 lending program toward quick-disbursing, non–project loans and make a concerted effort to increase disbursements during the 1984–86 period. However, the overall program proposed for 1984–88 was sharply reduced from what had been projected in the previous (1993) CPP.

Before proceeding to what next transpired, with the impetus coming from well outside the orbit of World Bank lending, it is time to pause briefly for diagnosis. What had happened to bring such deep trouble to the Filipino economy in 1981–86? Several answers are possible. In an interpretation suggesting that a multilateral should avoid even thinking, let alone acting, politically, Jean-Claude Nascimento, a Philippine IMF staffer, offers a remarkably narrow view of the troubles. There is no mention of the change of government to come, or of Senator Aquino. Instead there is a meticulous examination of lapses in the liberalization of foreign capital, of interest rates, of monetary controls, of weaknesses in the banking structure, in supervisory authority and rules, and in lending practices. The conclusion "is that factors within the financial system caused and exacerbated the crisis": "Although the political and economic climate of the late 1970s and early 1980s increased the fragility of the financial sector, weaknesses of the regulatory framework and loose banking practices triggered and exacerbated the crisis."[100]

When, out of office, Gerardo Sicat was invited to give his assessment of the situation and its roots to the annual meeting of the Philippine Economic Association in 1984, he provided a rich and rounded contrast to Nascimento's subsequent circumspection. What the Philippines was suffering, he said, was full-scale economic malaise, indeed a "witches' brew" of problems, and it did not originate from 1981 only. Way back there had been failures to exploit advantages offered by U.S. time-bound trade preferences, failures to devalue, and a mistaken ISI strategy. There had been a profusion of controls, subsidies, and rents reflecting misguided good intentions. Aggregate demand policy had been soft and indulgent; responsible officers had become preoccupied with firefighting.

Sicat reserved his vehemence, however, for the breakdown of order and control. The result was a grievous distortion of priorities.

> The nation is "gifted" with an international convention center out of proportion to its need, a large film palace that is a vain imitation of the Parthenon in Athens, many specialized hospitals clustered together but designed to cure separate organs of the human anatomy. There is a government university that is nothing but a public embarrassment both before our people and before the world.[101]

Sicat continued at length in this vein. His blast came well over a year before the end of the Marcos regime. But it signaled the end. Like others, the World Bank wondered what would come next.

PRESIDENT CORAZON AQUINO. The Marcoses did not fall to a revolution in February 1986; they were fired. A popular uprising aided by the country's chief soldier, Fidel Ramos, dismissed them and installed as president Corrie Aquino, the slain senator's widow, who was widely believed to have won the election whose results the Marcoses were trying to suppress.

100. Nascimento, "Crisis in the Financial Sector and the Authorities' Reaction," p. 177.
101. Sicat, "A Historical and Current Perspective," pp. 34–35. Sicat's reference is not to the University of the Philippines but the new health university Mrs. Marcos was sponsoring.

The World Bank approached the transformed scene warily. President Aquino was barely in place when Attila Karaosmanoglu, vice president for East Asia and the Pacific, reported to Senior Vice President for Operations Stern:

> We expect that the decision making process will be more difficult than in the past, because of a more collegial nature of the new team, the enhanced role of the legislative branch, and the populist tendencies of the new Government. Assuming the new Government has the willingness and ability to come to clear decisions on economic policy issues, we should be able to resume our country assistance related activities within a reasonable period of time.[102]

The Aquino assassination continued to haunt the scene. Mrs. Aquino was not prepared to take advantage of the mandate (the ability to rule by decree for seventeen months) with which she had been equipped. She was insecure in her power, looked for support to the old landed elite she knew in the Congress, relied too much on flawed personal advisers, and dismissed a number of able bureaucrats.[103]

Nevertheless it soon became apparent that the new administration would continue to rely on external assistance. It sought improvements in relations between the Bank and the government, and it was well disposed toward market-liberalizing reforms. The Bank was ready to respond. Before the end of 1986 the country's long balance of payments crisis seemed to be over: the stabilization program that the IMF had encouraged had helped turn the Philippines' current account to a surplus of nearly $1 billion in 1986, and a new standby was negotiated with the new administration in October of that year. But the Bank anticipated a need for further quick-disbursing loans:

> The present relative calm on the balance of payments front is not due, unfortunately, to a good performance of exports, but to the stagnation of import demand. Financing problems will begin to emerge more clearly in 1987 and 1988, when the current account is expected to return to a deficit as the economic recovery will increase import demand. . . . Our proposed Economic Recovery Loan (up to $300 million), . . . should be seen in this context. We do not exclude possibility of a delay in processing this loan, as the Government will have to take some fairly hard political decisions regarding the reorganization of government banks and on trade liberalization, and it may take time.[104]

The $300 million economic recovery loan that was signed in March 1987 initiated a balanced push on the two sides of adjustment lending. The institution was forthcoming with quick-disbursing money. At the same time, it pursued a pro-reform dialogue that stipulated reforms in four areas: tax increases, further trade liberalization, a closer vetting of public investments, and reorganization of

102. Memorandum, Attila Karaosmanoglu to Ernest Stern, "Philippines—Current Political Situation and Operational Implication," February 26, 1986, p. 2.

103. Assessment of an experienced Philippine observer.

104. Memorandum, S. M. L. van der Meer to Barber B. Conable, "Philippines: External Debt and Financing Needs," August 15, 1986, pp. 1–2.

specified government financial institutions. As the OED reported, the government was in agreement; "much of the required action was taken prior to release of the first tranche."[105]

A second SAL for $200 million was approved in June 1988. It was designed to facilitate the privatization of state enterprises, and the administrative complexity of implementing sell-off arrangements delayed the loan's third tranch by six months. But by the extended deadline in February 1992 the privatization targets had been surpassed.[106]

The country's current account began to slip again in 1989 and, with geopolitical complications, it worsened in 1990:

> In the last twelve months the country has endured a prolonged drought, a powerful earthquake, major floods and prolonged breakdowns in power facilities. But the real damage has been man-made. Continued coup attempts and the disintegration of the Aquino coalition have eroded the ability of President Aquino to take corrective action. The Middle East crisis has aggravated the problem. The country is now on the brink of a major economic crisis that threatens to undo the progress made since 1986.[107]

Far from abandoning the country, the Bank entered into its most active policy-based lending period in the Philippines. From May 1989 to December 1992, the Bank approved five adjustment loans committing a total of $924 million, and an additional $390 million for energy sector adjustment in 1990. This was a time when the function of SALs as a resource vehicle dominated. On three occasions the U.S. executive director took the comparatively unusual step of abstaining from the approval of a sector adjustment loan—motivated, many thought, by Philippine-American differences over the islands' U.S. military bases, although the U.S. executive director's overt objection was to what he called weak governmental conditioning. Nevertheless, the Bank moved the money.[108]

An important dimension of the World Bank's program lending operations with the Aquino administration was the institution's demonstration to other creditors of support for and contribution to the country's restructuring of the $4.4 billion of foreign debt falling due between 1987 and 1992.[109] This was an effect of the 1987 economic recovery loan, and later, under the so-called Brady initiative (see chap-

---

105. World Bank, "Program Performance Audit Report—Philippines: Economic Recovery Program (Loan 2787-PH) and Economic Recovery Technical Assistance Project (Loan 2788-PM)," OED Report 10866, SecM92-1027, June 30, 1992, p. xi.

106. World Bank, "Project Completion Report: The Philippines—Reform Program for Government Corporations," Report 11768, SecM93-0368, April 2, 1983, para. 4.3.

107. Memorandum, Gautam Kaji to Barber B. Conable, "Philippines: Update," September 24, 1990, p. 1.

108. U.S. executive directors abstained on the following loans: Financial Sector Adjustment, May 1989; Energy Sector Project, February 1990; and Environmental and Natural Resources Sector Adjustment, June 1991.

109. World Bank, *World Debt Tables*, various issues.

ter 11), the Bank provided debt and debt-service-reduction loans to the Philippines in January 1990 and again in December 1993. The scheme was to reduce debt through cash buyback and debt-service reduction. With the two loans the Bank, in company with such other lenders as the Fund, commercial bankers, the U.S. Treasury, and the Japanese EXIM Bank, restructured a very large face value of Philippine debt.

Another aspect of relations between the Bank and the government that had little net result—namely, a possible collaboration in behalf of major land reform—was the most interesting of the Aquino period. But it was not, strictly speaking, macro-economic policy; it has been treated in chapter 8. At the end of June 1992, President Aquino handed over the reins of government to her democratically oriented military champion, General Fidel Ramos—who, as president, would be strongly (and effectively) stabilization and reform minded.

COMMENTS. The Bank is mandated to be apolitical, and in the Philippines in the 1970s and 1980s it largely was. Its relations with the national economic bureaucracy were seamless and managed to be cordial with two very different leaderships. The habits and loyalties built in the Bank's business with the Marcos government yielded a measure of entrapment as the moral quality of the regime declined. But, as elsewhere, the Bank tended to avoid such issues, minding the probity of its own operations rather than challenging the growing decadence of Philippine budgeting. On the other hand, when the government's leadership changed, the Bank was quick to reengage its policy-cum-transfers mission.

As in other countries, the substantive message of the Bank's Philippine macro-policy experience was the complementarity of stabilization and structural (including trade and industrial policy) reform. The same lesson was encountered in Turkey. In the Philippines a conventional answer—the stereotypical division of labor between the World Bank and the IMF—was more readily at hand; and, after lapses in the early 1980s, was successfully practiced.

Throughout this case one is reminded of the tension between, but also the interdependence of, resources and reforms. There was no ducking the need for Philippine policy changes to regain financial balance and promote efficiency. Yet the transfers the Bank provided and those of other lenders it catalyzed were often as important, sometimes more so, than the accompanying reforms—and often they were integral to the reforms themselves. (Note, however, that excessive transfers can postpone and overburden reform. A successful marriage of transfers and policy promotion must tread a narrow path.)

Finally, the country is another case of the way the mechanics and responsibility of long-term lending tend to hobble a bellwether development agency. There were times in the 1970s, in the early 1980s, and in the Aquino years when the logic of policy influence argued for giving less—even altogether less—policy-based lending until the implementation of certain reforms was at least under way. But concerns for the client, for the relationship, and for the responsibilities of a "residual donor" to keep the whole transfer scenario whole intervened. Such concerns were not necessarily soft headed. But they weakened the policy influence of policy lending.

Colombia: Bank Lending, Bargaining, and the Speed of Reform

Colombia's relationship with the World Bank had been special almost from its inception. The country was very open to analysis and constructive criticism. It was the first to have a mission sent and be reported on (the "Currie report" after Lauchlin Currie). It received the "programs-of-projects" lending featured in the LAC region in the 1960s. Sectorally, the Bank played a pivotal (if not altogether successful) role in the development of Colombia's electric power.[110]

In the 1980s the Bank's adjustment lending led to major tensions between the government and the Bank, and also the IMF. In the mid-1980s the institution went to extraordinary lengths to facilitate the flow of resources—both its own and, more important, those of commercial bank funds—to help a trusted client steer its way through difficulties. For a time the Bank tried hard to accommodate Colombia's aversion to the Fund. Later it reversed itself (but not its purpose) insisting on an IMF standby for the country, together with drastic liberalization in financial markets and trade.

DEBT, STABILIZATION, AND FUND-BANK RELATIONS. In the period leading up to the debt crisis, Colombia was different from its Latin American neighbors. It almost avoided the crisis altogether. Had it not been for Mexico's financial breakdown in 1982, and the Venezuelan and Ecuadorian crises of 1983, Colombia probably would not have had a serious debt problem. In 1980 the country had enjoyed four decades of economic growth and comparative stability. During the course of the tumultuous 1980s it would achieve the LAC region's highest GDP per capita growth rate (see table 10-6).[111] The country was consistently run by prudent economic managers. Such observers as Albert Hirschman had emphasized Colombia's bent toward consensus making and gradual change.[112] This characteristic had not forestalled extreme violence, but it had brought moderate average economic success; it allowed Colombia to escape severe debt and pay its creditors. In 1982–83, however, external shocks combined with President Belisario Betancur's moderately populist expansionist program to deplete the considerable foreign exchange reserves the administration had inherited and bring balance of payments difficulty.

Decreasing coffee prices in the late 1970s, together with the tightening of commercial bank credit in 1982, led Minister of Finance Edgar Gutiérrez Castro to implement

---

110. See World Bank (1990) "Colombia: The Power Sector and the World Bank, 1970-1987," OED Report 8893, 3 vols., June 28, 1990. The Bank's long involvement in the power sector would eventually lead to a power SECAL in December 1987.

111. John Williamson, "The Progress of Policy Reform in Latin America," in Williamson, ed., *Latin American Adjustment: How Much Has Happened?* (Washington, D.C.: Institute for International Economics, 1990), p. 408.

112. See Albert O. Hirschman, *Development Projects Observed* (Brookings, 1967).

Table 10-6. *Economic Indicators, Colombia, 1980–92*[a]
Annual averages

Indicator	1980–82	1983–87	1988–92
GDP (billions of $U.S.)	36.3	36.6	41.9
GDP (billions of 1987 $U.S.)	29.5	33.1	40.5
Current account balance/GDP (percent)	(4.8)	(3.0)	2.9
Budget deficit/GDP (percent)	(7.2)	(4.1)	(2.0)
Exports (billions of $U.S.)	5.4	5.8	9.6
Total debt service/exports (percent)	22.1	35.1	37.4
Long-term debt (billions of $U.S.)	5.9	11.5	15.3
Average annual growth rates (percent)			
Real GDP	1.6	4.6	3.3
GDP deflator	23.8	25.1	25.9
Real exports	(2.6)	6.4	6.5

Sources: IMF, *International Financial Statistics;* World Bank, *World Debt Tables;* World Bank, *World Tables;* William Easterly and others, *Public Sector Deficits and Macroeconomic Performance* (Oxford University Press, 1994), p. 530.

a. Budget deficit/GDP figures from Easterly and others are for 1980–90. Export growth rates are computed using export figures in pesos deflated by export price index in pesos (1990 = 100) from *IFS.*

a "heterodox" stabilization program with strong import controls and nationalization of failed banks.[113] The country fared well enough through 1982, but Venezuela's devaluation of its currency in February 1983 had a harsh impact on Colombia—the trade between the two was extensive.[114] International commercial banks reduced lending and hardened their terms for Colombia after the start of the Mexican crisis in August 1982. The country needed to reschedule even its relatively small amount of debt,[115] and in 1983 the balance of payments became an urgent problem.

In a way reminiscent of heterodox policies in Argentina, Brazil, and Peru, Colombia put on its import brakes. In fact, it had a history of doing so—as Rudolf Hommes would remark many years later, at about the time he became the reformist minister of finance in 1990.[116] In 1983 World Bank staff monitoring Colombia reported:

113. For a discussion of the Colombian economy in this period, see Jose Antonio Ocampo and Eduardo Lora, *Colombia: Country Study No. 6* (Helsinki: WIDER, 1987).

114. In 1982, Colombia exported 75 percent of its goods within the region to Venezuela. Memorandum, José B. Sokol and Vinod Thomas to Miguel Schloss, "Colombia—Recent Problems in the External Sector," March 19, 1984, table 3. Bank staff reported that "had the massive Venezuelan devaluation not taken place, [Colombia] might have been better placed to handle the current situation: declines in exports to Venezuela alone have accounted for over 25% of the fall in the current account receipts over the last 12 months." Memorandum, José B. Sokol and Vinod Thomas to Miguel Schloss, "Colombia External Sector Problems and Responses," April 23, 1984, p. 2.

115. Medium- and longer-term foreign debt was about 18.9 percent of GNP in 1982.

116. "Colombia has a long tradition of reverting to import licensing when current account deficits become large." Rudolf Hommes, "Colombia," in Williamson, *Latin American Adjustment,* p. 217.

Colombia will have to approach the international capital markets during 1984–88. The recent debt problems of other Latin American countries make it all the more important for the Government to assign this task a very high priority. Moreover, it will also require increasing support and assistance from multilateral lending agencies. The adverse developments on the external debt of many countries have discouraged additional commercial bank financing to the Latin American region and, in effect, have also limited Colombia's ability to significantly tap those markets in the near term despite the country's creditworthiness and recent policy actions to maintain it by increasing public sector resource mobilization, depreciating the exchange rate faster, and strengthening the financial sector.[117]

By October, at the Bank-Fund annual meetings, Minister of Finance Gutiérrez told Bank representatives

that reserves have been falling over the entire year, that export performance was disappointing, and that Colombia has thus become a net capital exporter. In answer to a question on external resource mobilization efforts, he indicated that the Government, after deliberately staying out of the international capital markets during the first half of this year, was now in a process of "breaking the ice," and that they were on the verge of concluding an external loan of about $220 million (involving a wide range of US, German, Japanese, Canadian and British banks).[118]

The World Bank increased 1983 disbursements on current loans by 27 percent.[119] At the same annual meetings Minister Gutiérrez asked the Bank for structural adjustment lending. The Bank was slow to respond—the first adjustment lending, the Trade Policy and Export Diversification loan, was not approved until May 1985—but given the country's starting posture and the events of 1984, the Bank's hesitation was understandable.

When Bank representatives met with President Betancur in February 1984, they painted a bleak picture of the country's reserve prospects: "The president seemed to understand clearly that in order for reserves not to continue to fall dramatically, Colombia would have to obtain the required external resources, and for this to happen, economic policy as well as the economic team would have to appear creditable to the international banking community."[120] The president indicated that there would be a significant shift in economic policy, but it was slow to appear.[121] The next month, negotiations with the government concerning a stabili-

117. Memorandum, José B. Sokol and Vinod Thomas to Miguel Schloss, "Colombia—Scope for Additional External Financing," July 14, 1983, p. 1.

118. Memorandum, Miguel Schloss to files, "Colombia: Annual Meeting Discussions," October 4, 1983, p. 1.

119. Ibid., p. 2.

120. Memorandum, Miguel Schloss to files, "Meeting with President Belisario Betancur and Former President Carlos Lleras Restrepo," February 14, 1984, p. 2.

121. Internally, Bank staff were impatient: "I continue to be struck by the difficulties the Colombians have had in, first, recognizing how the changes in the international environment

zation program had progressed to a point where the Bank felt it appropriate to mention the Fund, even though it knew this had been a contentious subject for Colombia ever since a devaluation had failed in 1966. Internally, Bank staff reported: "The relationship with the IMF has not been particularly close, and a renewal of political sensitivities at this point in time could undercut the Government's economic program. Nevertheless, a routine IMF consultation mission has been scheduled for April."[122] In mid-May, President Betancur, modifying his resistance to reform, authorized his veteran minister of finance, Edgar Gutiérrez, to negotiate policy adjustments, and the minister approached the Bank for a $300 million export promotion loan. But Colombian policy flipped again in June after the Dominican Republic had suffered poststabilization riots and Colombia itself encountered a series of security threats, including the assassination of the minister of justice and increased kidnapping. Also an anticipated surge in coffee prices promised to help mitigate the perceived external payments crisis. Yet, Colombian officials, aware of their eroding basic reserves, had been edging away from heterodox, toward orthodox, reform. At this point, change still was coming at Colombia's familiar pace, but acceleration was on tap.

SPIRITED BARGAINING. According to Bank records, it was expected in May 1984 that the minister of finance would be replaced, but with no significant change in government policy. When Roberto Junguito took over in July 1984, the move was not heralded as significant. Yet Junguito would, in a short time, usher in the country's first adjustment lending.

Working with the Bank and the IMF, which sent an Article IV mission to the country in July 1984, Junguito devised a standard orthodox stabilization recipe.[123] When he tried to sell it to President Betancur, the minister met with stiff opposition specifically on the Fund's role in the program.[124] Colombian officials told the Bank in October 1984 that "based on the historical relationship between the Fund and Colombia and the nature of the Colombian democracy with its vibrant press and independent Congress, a Fund program is likely to be counterproductive in obtaining the political support for the necessary adjustments."[125] A few days earlier, Junguito had told top officials at the Bank that he "did not feel that the Colombian debt profile and economic problems warranted a formal Fund operation and that

---

constrained their own action, and, thereafter, to bring about the necessary adjustments with sufficient determination to arrest the deteriorating trend. The Bank, both at headquarters and Resident Mission, by virtue of not having to deal with day to day matters, is in an ideal position to distinguish the central from the peripheral, and help the Colombians to focus on those matters with greater impact." Telex, Miguel Schloss to Melvin Goldman, July 24, 1984, pp. 2–3.

122. Memorandum, Sokol and Thomas to Schloss, March 19, 1984, p. 3.

123. Roberto Junguito, interview with the authors, March 1993.

124. See Ocampo and Lora, *Colombia*, p. 27.

125. Memorandum, Melvin Goldman to files, "Colombia—Meeting of Delegation with Mr. Knox," October 5, 1984, pp. 1–2.

the country intended to make the necessary adjustment by itself."[126] The Bank undertook to help him devise a suitable stabilization program without the Fund.

Vice President David Knox summarized the plan in a letter to the Colombians which was promptly leaked to the press on October 29, 1985. The leak served to call attention to the crisis at hand and to mobilize domestic support for the program. It was clear that the Colombians were going to carry out the stabilization program on their own terms. When Knox visited the country in December,

> the President expressed worry about the potential political fall-out of an IMF relationship even to the point of questioning seriously the advisability of the presence of an IMF mission in the country while the Congress deliberates on the fiscal package during its January extraordinary session. [The President] mentioned specifically that he understood that many of the measures taken and to be taken would not be popular and that he was prepared to suffer the consequences. At the same time, it was made clear that matters of timing and style, i.e. the politics of presenting the adjustment program were to be his domain and that he would at times appear to waiver on certain actions, but that this would only be for tactical reasons to achieve the targets of the adjustment program.[127]

Clearly it would take some time for adjustment lending to be negotiated and approval to be gained from the Bank's Board. The country needed to seek an additional line of international credit. The government asked the Bank to start querying international private banks on the possibility of extending Colombia commercial credit. The banks, accustomed to IMF approval and a bit leery of the Bank's technical capacity to oversee stabilization programs, insisted on IMF involvement. But the country remained adamant, resisting Bank pressures to include the Fund. In January, "Mr. Stern was emphatic in explaining that the Bank does not intend and does not have the capability to replace the Fund and that therefore, any thought that the Bank would undertake substantial short term monitoring should be discarded."[128] But Junguito was tenacious. He appealed to Paul Volcker to pressure the commercial banks, the World Bank, and the IMF.[129] The U.S. Treasury was also involved in urging the Colombian case, while Clausen and Stern joined in lobbying the Fund.[130] Bank staff helped prepare the January 1985 "road show" the Colombians took in selling their stabilization program to commercial banks. They sought a loan or loans totaling $1 billion.[131]

Pressure from the United States was crucial in the final compromise. Agreement was reached in April 1985 for a sui generis monitoring arrangement, under

126. Memorandum, Melvin Goldman for the record, "Colombia—Meeting with Mr. Clausen, September 21, 1984," October 1, 1984, p. 2.

127. Memorandum, Miguel Schloss to files, "Mr. Knox's visit to Colombia," December 14, 1984, pp. 1–2.

128. Telex, Goldman to Schloss, January 21, 1985, para. 7.

129. Ministerio de Hacienda y Crédito Público (Colombia), *Memoria del Ministerio de Hacienda* (Bogotá, Colombia: Banco de la República, 1986), p. 73.

130. Roberto Junguito, interview with the authors, March 1993.

131. Miguel Schloss, interview with the authors, February 1993.

which the Fund would follow developments of the stabilization program as closely as it would have under a standby agreement. The Fund agreed to stand by without a formal standby agreement.[132] The price, which Colombia was more than willing to pay, would be no flow of Fund resources. The Bank, then, would step in with its own financing as a sign to the commercial banks of burden sharing, and commitment to Colombia. The Bank had an interest of its own in keeping the country in good standing: its exposure in Colombia was high, where its loans accounted for 20.4 percent of public and publicly guaranteed long-term debt outstanding and disbursed.[133]

The Bank rapidly negotiated its first structural lending to Colombia; the Trade Policy and Export Diversification loan for $300 million was signed in May 1985. The details of the loan had been mostly worked out after the Bank's mission to Colombia the previous August.[134] Loan conditions laid emphasis on more liberal trade. They called for reduction of the public sector deficit, a slowdown in monetary expansion, currency devaluation, limited trade liberalization, and a scaling down of external borrowing. Subsequently the Bank judged the loan to be a major success.[135] Almost complete implementation was achieved and, more important, the loan was instrumental in persuading commercial banks to continue their lending to Colombia. The result was the $1 billion commercial bank "Jumbo" loan signed in December 1985.

More adjustment lending came in May 1986 when the Trade and Agricultural Policy (TAP) loan for $250 million was signed. This loan supported the macro-economic adjustment program and financed imported inputs for export, but with the added goal of changing agricultural policy. Several of the undertakings integral to the loan were articulated outside the loan document:

> Agreements, embodied in letters from the Coffee Federation to the President of the World Bank, indicated that coffee price increases would be contained, diversification

---

132. The Fund made it clear that this was an exception, both for Colombia and other countries. Reporting on an IMF Board meeting in December 1985, Bank staff indicated that "The Fund envisages a return to Article IV Consultations in accordance with the standard cycle." Memorandum, Jayati Datta-Mitra to Turid Sato, "Colombia: IMF Board Meeting," December 8, 1986, p. 2. In addition, the IMF Board was concerned that this case not set a precedent for other borrowers. "It was emphasized that the approval was strictly an exception, a strictly isolated experiment, and did not constitute a precedent for other cases. Even with such proviso, a number of EDs were concerned that this action could lead to moral/political obligations in other cases, and that uniformity of treatment among members had to be safeguarded." Memorandum, Miguel Schloss to Vinod Dubey, "Colombia—IMF Board Meeting," July 29, 1985, p. 3.

133. World Bank, *World Debt Tables, 1990–91*, vol. 2, p. 70. By 1987 the Bank's debt share in Colombia reached its apogee at 29.7 percent.

134. See memorandum, José B. Sokol and others to Miguel Schloss, "Colombia—Back-to-Office Report," August 2, 1984.

135. World Bank, "Project Performance Audit Report, Colombia: Trade Policy and Export Diversification; Trade and Agricultural Policy Loans," OED Report 9258, SecM91-615, April 26, 1991.

encouraged and fertilizer subsidies eliminated. A second agreement concerned increases in the real interest rates to positive levels and the freeing of three key rates—contained in a letter from the Finance Minister to the Bank President. Third, there were unwritten agreements to depreciate the real exchange rate. All these actions were taken and were fundamental to the implementation of the TAP.[136]

Several of the agricultural reform measures that had been agreed to were not implemented on time, however. Without the long process of consensus building characteristic of Colombian policymaking, agricultural policymakers resisted having the ministry of finance change sectoral policies in the processing of a World Bank loan.[137]

Moreover, changes in Colombia's economic situation had altered the bargaining context. In the case of the first loan, some of the intended reforms already were in place, and the Bank did not have to press the Colombians heavily to make the needed financial reforms, in particular devaluation. While the World Bank encouraged orthodox stabilization, Colombia's political leaders were similarly minded. By 1986, when the TAP was implemented, world coffee prices had risen (in 1985) and the stabilization program was producing rapid results. Many of the quarterly targets agreed upon with the Fund were exceeded in 1985–86. The overall public deficit fell from 6.7 percent of GDP in 1984 to 4.2 percent in 1985; for 1986, no deficit was expected. Helped by higher prices of coffee and higher exports of coal and petroleum, the balance of payments deficit on current account shrank fast and was in surplus by 1986.

By early 1986 it was becoming clear the government had few further plans for major import liberalization or export promotion. According to a Bank official, "the 1984–86 trade liberalization did not fundamentally alter the inward orientation of productive incentives."[138] But a new phase of Bank-Colombia relations was in the offing.

THE BANK AGAINST GRADUALISM. Colombia, with the help of the Bank, IMF, and commercial lenders, had weathered the pre-1986 balance of payments threat quite well. But now new requirements loomed in the form of power loan adjustments. In July 1986 the Bank was estimating the country's needs for commercial-bank loan rescheduling and by December Washington was preparing a power SECAL for Colombia.[139] The loan was instrumental in securing $1 billion in parallel cofinancing from Japan for the power sector.[140] But negotiations, extending

136. Ibid., p. ix.
137. Ibid.
138. Kristen Hallberg and Wendy Takacs, "Trade Reform in Colombia: 1990–94," in Alvin Cohen and Frank R. Gunter, eds., The Colombian Economy: Issues of Trade and Development (Boulder, Colo.: Westview Press, 1992), p. 261.
139. Memorandum, Jayati Datta-Mitra to Miguel Schloss, "Colombia—Country Strategy for Resource Mobilization," July 16, 1986, p. 2.
140. See World Bank, "Project Completion Report, Colombia: Power Sector Adjustment Loan (Loan 2889-co)," SecM94-942, August 17, 1994. This financing, known as the "Concorde" loan, was signed in January 1988.

over a year, were difficult; they required several redesigns "to achieve a balance between quick disbursements and inducements to sector adjustments."[141] In the end, the loan incorporated three tranches, all of which had to be renegotiated; the third tranche eventually was canceled in 1990.

Once again, the Bank had come to the support of Colombia with needed financing. This time, however, the price was structural change and trade liberalization—the more rapid the better. Until now, Colombia had succeeded in stabilizing its economy and skirting long-term structural reforms. The gradualistic, consensus-driven nature of Colombian policymaking had been at work. Liberalization was incremental.[142] Moreover, the sense that the country had weathered the crisis of the mid-1980s adroitly was tending to dampen further liberalization. Many Colombians felt the crisis had been brought on by external factors, not by poor domestic policies.[143] In addition, Colombia was almost unique in obtaining commercial credit in the face of reduced credit flows to the region.

The Bank in mid-decade was forthcoming in its lending to the country, and its appraisals favorable. Bank staff advised President Clausen in 1985, "You may wish to congratulate Mr. Betancur for the formulation, by the authorities themselves, of a truly 'Colombian' adjustment program which combines stabilization with growth."[144] The Bank reorganization under President Barber Conable in 1987, however, brought a jolting change to relations. In the high turnover of staff, some tacit understandings that had existed between Colombia and the Bank were lost. Shahid Husain was named vice president for the LAC region, and a hostile relationship would develop between him and the Colombian finance minister, Luis Fernando Alarcón. Along with Husain, Katherine Marshall became chief of country operations for Colombia. Within the Bank both were known as no-nonsense managers.

The change in perspective concerned the timing of policy reform: the Bank came down on the side of swiftness. By 1988, regional Bank staff were convinced that Colombia had to reform faster if it was going to have sustainable economic growth. The institution began intensive pressure on the country, signaled by the June 1988 Country Strategy Paper. The CSP was notable for its conviction on the benefits of reform:

> Colombia could do much better if it followed bolder policies, given its strong resource base and macroeconomic management framework. Faster growth would benefit most

141. Ibid. (attached Memorandum to the Executive Directors and President).

142. In 1986 the percentage of items on the free-import list nearly tripled but average tariffs increased from 21.1 percent in 1985 to 27 percent in 1987 as tariffs were substituted for quantitative restrictions. Miguel Urrutia, "Colombia," in John Williamson, ed., *The Political Economy of Policy Reform* (Washington, D.C.: Institute for International Economics, 1994), p. 291.

143. Ocampo and Lora, in *Colombia,* are strong advocates of this position.

144. Memorandum, Andre R. Gue to A. W. Clausen, "Colombia—Meeting with President Betancur," March 29, 1985, p. 1.

Colombians but above all should make possible faster progress in alleviating poverty and increasing employment; this should help to lessen social tensions. . . . We conclude, therefore, that bolder policies will be essential in virtually any likely scenario; the question is when that will become unmistakably apparent. *The groundwork for a far-reaching reform effort, aimed essentially at increasing growth in industry and agriculture, and entailing important steps towards opening the economy, should be established as a matter of priority.* . . .

The timing and direction of future trade reform are not clearly defined. It is disquieting that almost no action in the direction of reform has been taken since June 1987. . . . Trade policy must remain high on Colombia's reform agenda. This will call first, for additional analysis, principally to establish the extent of coverage of domestic production by import restrictions . . . and second a carefully orchestrated dialogue on trade issues involving both high level discussions and bottom-up, subsector specific analysis to demonstrate options for reform and their consequences. This effort must aim to demonstrate that, in Colombia, the costs of liberalization . . . would be outweighed by increased efficiency of investment, output, and exports.[145]

Bank management agreed with the recommendations. In a meeting on June 20, 1988, President Conable "appreciated the direct and honest style of this CSP," while Stanley Fischer was concerned about "how the Bank could further encourage the adoption of bolder policy reforms."[146] Regional staff took this as a green light to charge ahead. In September, the Bank sent a programming mission on trade to Colombia which perceived increased willingness on the part of Colombia to reform. Husain reported something of a breakthrough to President Conable in February 1989, stating that despite the "somewhat difficult" policy dialogue over the past two years, "reflecting [the Colombians'] own internal political and administrative problems which have delayed action on many fronts, and our own disappointment at their unwillingness to address important issues, notably on trade and financial sector policies," progress had been made in several areas, "notably on poverty issues."[147]

Nevertheless, Husain noted that Colombia had failed to achieve broadly based trade policy reform in connection with the two previous adjustment loans. A less productive programming mission took place in March 1989, with negotiations reported to be protracted and tense albeit polite. The Bank was taking a hard line on Colombia, which sought more adjustment lending: "Quick-disbursing loans for gradual reform programs," said the staff, "are problematic in a fundamental sense; they do not meet our guidelines for adjustment lending."[148] In addition, in a break

145. World Bank, "Colombia: Country Strategy Paper," June 10, 1988, pp. 3, 12–13.

146. World Bank, "Minutes of President's Council—June 20, 1988," July 18, 1988, pp. 3–4.

147. Memorandum, S. Shahid Husain to Barber B. Conable, "Colombia—Briefing on Visit by Members of the Economic Team," February 3, 1989, p. 2.

148. Memorandum, Katherine Marshall to Ping-Cheung Loh, "Colombia: Programming Mission—March 5–10, 1989," March 14, 1989, p. 3.

with the past, LAC regional management, having been burned by its Argentina experience, insisted on IMF involvement: "As to the macroeconomic context, we have suggested to them that not only would we want to review, and reach an agreement on, a medium-term macroeconomic framework, but also would insist on an IMF program."[149] These conditions were unacceptable to the Colombians. When regional staff responded by urging Colombia to follow the example of Argentina, Bolivia, Mexico, and Venezuela (the other rapidly reforming economies in the region), the message rubbed the government the wrong way. Relations deteriorated to the point that Minister of Finance Alarcón, who had stepped in for former Minister Gaviria when the latter left to campaign for the presidency, sent a letter directly to President Conable in June 1990 expressing concern about "the negative opinions expressed on various occasions by high officials within the Regional Vice Presidency for Latin America and the Caribbean, with respect to the improvements achieved by the country in its macroeconomic stabilization process and structural adjustment." He went on to complain about "abrupt changes in the rules of the game of negotiations of credit operations"[150] and anxiously pressed for quick-disbursing loans, which the country needed to cover amortization payments coming due. But the response of the regional vice presidency was firm:

> The Colombia Country Strategy Paper to be reviewed by the Operations Committee on June 13, 1990 stresses the deep-seated nature of Colombia's slow and consensus driven policy-making processes, which leads us to see a very high probability for gradual reform. Given recent experience, this is likely to constrain possibilities for adjustment lending, and to result in negative net disbursements in the short term. . . . You may wish to indicate to Minister Alarcón that the effort to add specifics to the Bank's macroeconomic conditionality is universal and not specifically directed at Colombia. The need for specific criteria is applied to all countries, independently of whether they have or have not a program with the Fund. A review of the Bank's experience with quick disbursing lending has led our research department to conclude that major weaknesses in the past were due to the lack of specification in defining a macro-economic program. Colombia is in some degree a "test case" for the development of criteria in this area. This is an issue which has great impact for other countries, such as Brazil and Argentina, for the future. . . . The main problem derives from Colombia's perception of itself, that it is a unique case, different from other countries. Therefore, normal current Bank procedures would not apply to Colombia. It is important that we see the implication of any possible special treatment of Colombia for our dealing with other countries.[151]

The Bank stuck to its guns. In fact, it insisted on not lending to Colombia until after the 1990 elections and the inauguration of the new president—even though

149. Memorandum, S. Shahid to Barber B. Conable, "Colombia—Bank Strategy and Operations," October 13, 1989, p. 2.

150. Letter, Luis Fernando Alarcón Mantilla, Colombian minister of Finance and Public Credit, to Barber B. Conable, May 31, 1990, pp. 3–4.

151. Memorandum, Pieter P. Bottelier to Barber B. Conable, "Colombia—Visit of Finance Minister," June 4, 1990, pp. 1, 3–4.

the Colombians, and Minister Alarcón in particular, expressed willingness to enact trade reforms in January 1990.[152] An observer close to events in late 1989 has noted that while President Barcos's chief of staff was opposed to trade liberalization, exporters "were beginning to see that protectionism was incompatible with exports in a world more and more unwilling to allow Colombia to maintain trade policies no longer accepted anywhere else."[153]

The last adjustment loan in the series here under review, the Public Sector Reform (PSR) loan for $304 million, was signed in December 1990 by the newly installed Gaviria administration. Relations quickly improved and trade reforms, to which the new administration was deeply committed, were rapid. How radical a break this was from Colombia's history of gradual reform often goes unnoticed. The country reached the PSR loan conditions on trade in less than eighteen months, rather than the five years originally expected, and in less than nine months industrial quantitative restrictions, covering 82 percent of domestic manufacturing production, were eliminated.[154] "Colombia," concluded one observer, "has apparently implemented and consolidated fundamental reforms without the rest of the world noticing that it was doing anything other than having trouble with the drug barons."[155]

What brought on this abrupt change? What role did the Bank play in the process, and how much effect did its withholding of funding have? The radical shift from gradualism to rapid reform undertaken by the Gaviria administration stems from a decade of policy experiments, some in accordance with the Bank and Fund doctrine, others by Colombia idiosyncratically. The lessons learned over the decade eventually led to a break with tradition. Even so, President Cesar Gaviria, who proved to be an ardent free trader, and his minister of finance, Rudolf Hommes, directly benefited from the mild reforms initiated by the seemingly reluctant Minister of Finance Alarcón in early 1990. Gaviria did not have to take the political fallout of instituting an unpopular structural adjustment program, but he did accelerate the program drastically. At the same time, Gaviria entered office under propitious economic times. In addition to the discovery of massive oil reserves in Cusiana, a revival of coffee prices brought unexpected strength in the balance of payments.[156] It was this turn of good fortune combined with a joint desire to see through the adjustment loan on which they had been working that inspired the government and the Bank's regional office to put forward the hypothetical balance of payments gap of which the Bank's chief economist was sharply critical.

152. Memorandum, Hari Prasad to files, "Colombia—Discussions of the Minister of Finance with Mr. Husain," January 23, 1990, p. 1.

153. Urrutia, "Colombia," p. 302.

154. World Bank, "1991 Annual Meetings Brief," LAC Region Brief, September 24, 1991, p. 2; World Bank, "Colombia: Macroeconomic Consistency and Structural Reforms," Report 9764-CO, May 20, 1992, p. 33.

155. John Williamson and Stephan Haggard, "The Political Conditions for Economic Reform," in Williamson, ed., *The Political Economy of Policy Reform,* p. 541.

156. See World Bank, "Colombia: Macroeconomic Consistency and Structural Reforms."

Clearly, the institution had had a hand in identifying the need for reform. Husain's strategy to put pressure on Colombia seems also to have been effective at the outset of the 1990 reform process. But the Gaviria administration took owner-ship of the process and rapidly implemented reforms well beyond the Bank's expectations. Even so, although gradualism was thrown out the window, the habit of consensus making remained. Many of reform's previous opponents had changed their minds. A Bank staff member explained that "the private sector in Colombia had become convinced that integration of the economy with world markets is necessary for long-run growth. . . . By the late eighties, it had become clear that the import substitution model of development in Colombia was limiting increases in efficiency, higher economic growth, and improvements in the standard of living."[157]

Ghana: African Test Case

In the 1980s Ghana became a favored site of World Bank attempts to wield macropolicy influence in Sub-Saharan Africa. It was a substantial country with a dramatic and, in terms of indigenous capacities, self-reliant history, and in their intervention, in the eyes of many, the Bank's agents served both the borrower and the lender well.

Chapter 9 noted the Ghanaian economy's downhill slide almost from inde-pendence (in 1957) onward, but especially during the 1970s. Things went from very bad to worse in the early 1980s. There was an extended drought. The country's terms of trade sagged further. And in 1982 more than 1 million Ghanaian workers were forced home from Nigeria, adding more to consumption needs than they did quickly to output. One is tempted to say that, as of 1982, the country had nowhere to go but up, but the cases of Zaire, Somalia, and Liberia argue otherwise. The turn in Ghana was a purposeful achievement for which credit belongs to the combina-tion of local leadership and external assistance.

Flight Lieutenant Jerry Rawlings, who executed his second Ghanaian coup the last day of 1981, was no twice-born apostle of market economics. He was a pragmatist who, like other Ghanaian leaders before him, was, if anything, a statist. But most of all he was a scourge of privilege and corruption. He attacked the rent seekers, the old bureaucratic elite, and came to perceive the rents-reducing virtues of a freer market. Rawlings recognized the country's need to alter its export-import balance, therefore the advantage of devaluation; also the need for internal fiscal balance and monetary restraint. Without particular passion he arrived at a set of macropolicy views broadly consistent with those of the IMF and the World Bank. He was helped in his reasoning by the local Fund and Bank residents; he was helped more by such Ghanaian contemporaries as Jonathan Frimpong-Ansah, then in commercial banking in the United Kingdom, and the close advisers Joseph Abbey and Kwesi

---

157. Hallberg and Takacs, "Trade Reform in Colombia," pp. 295–96.

Botchwey. Both were trained economists. Abbey was a leading domestic official and represented the country abroad. He was as highly respected by the Washington multilaterals as he was fiercely independent. Rawlings recruited Botchwey, a credentialed intellectual Marxist, in 1982 to be chief of the financial secretariat of the Permanent National Defence Council, that is, Ghana's ruling government, from the time of Rawlings's takeover. Botchwey was a practical intellectual. Years later, when he had become minister of finance and economic planning, he would admit no conflict between his ideological origins and the government's market-friendly reforms: "I see things as they really are on the ground and I see them in the way that they originate and develop, I don't come to any socio-economic reality with any preconceived ideals. I believe these things must be investigated empirically."[158]

BASIC RECOVERY AND MACRO ADJUSTMENT. The Economic Recovery Program (ERP) emerging from the dialogue in which Rawlings had been engaging with such new advisers as Botchwey, was announced in April 1983.[159] It centered on a persisting program of devaluation. From 2.75 to $1 the cedi was lowered to 25:1, 30:1, 90:1, and then in 1986 to 330:1; and in that year a system of ongoing foreign exchange auctioning (involving the likelihood of continuing devaluation) was adopted. In the early rounds of basic reforms, imports were liberalized. Prices were partly decontrolled. Farmers were buoyed by a major increase in the prices the government paid for their cocoa. Taxes were increased, government budgets were squeezed, and by 1986 the public deficit had been virtually eliminated. The monetary regime was tightened. By the second half of the 1980s inflation was radically reduced.

What needs to be emphasized, especially in contrast to the earlier Turkey case, is that Ghana, with the Bank in close support, quickly reached for and kept seeking a balance between outward orientation and domestic stabilization. The key export-promotion tool—aggressive devaluation—was the same. Ghana had nothing like Turkey's success with its nontraditional exports; markets and industrial structures and experience were not equally conducive. But tree crops recovered from their pre-1983 repression, and other export capacity began to be marshaled. Meanwhile there were some strong, if interrupted, moves toward internal stability. The government implemented its whole agenda of orthodox macro reform energetically, and by 1987 the familiar judgment within the Bank was that macro financial reform had been nearly concluded: successfully.[160] This economic story is reflected in the economic indicators shown in table 10-7.

158. "Economy: Memories Are Very Short," West Africa, no. 3980 (January 10–16, 1994), pp. 27.
159. The present account draws on various selections in Donald Rothchild, ed., Ghana: The Political Economy of Recovery (Boulder, Colo.: Lynne Rienner, 1991), especially Naomi Chazan, "The Political Transformation of Ghana under the PNDC [Permanent National Defence Council]," pp. 21–48; also World Bank, "Ghana: Country Assistance Review," OED draft, February 7, 1995.
160. Retrospective comments of engaged Bank officials.

Table 10-7. *Economic Indicators, Ghana, 1971–93*[a]

Annual averages

Indicator	1971–80	1981–83	1984–87	1988–91	1992–93
GDP (billions of $U.S.)	3.1	4.1	4.9	5.9	6.5
GDP (billions of 1987 $U.S.)	4.6	4.3	4.7	5.7	6.5
Contribution to GDP growth					
Agriculture (percent)	0.6	(2.9)	1.9	1.3	0.5
Industry (percent)	(0.3)	(2.5)	1.6	0.8	0.8
Service (percent)	0.3	0.7	2.4	2.5	2.9
GDP per capita (1987 $U.S.)	466.5	375.0	368.1	389.9	401.1
Current account balance/ GDP (percent)	(0.4)	(5.7)	(1.6)	(2.6)	(7.3)
Budget deficit/GDP (percent)	(6.2)	(4.6)	0.8	2.2	(2.5)
Long-term debt/GDP (percent)	25.1	29.2	33.2	43.4	50.4
Exports (billions of $U.S.)	0.8	0.7	0.8	1.0	1.2
Total debt service/exports (percent)	7.6	18.8	31.5	42.0	24.7
Public sector real monthly earnings (1987 = 100)	96.0	48.6	79.0	135.7	221.3
Average annual growth rates (percent)					
Real GDP	(0.3)	(5.5)	5.0	4.3	4.8
GDP deflator	38.4	68.6	34.4	30.1	25.2
Real exports	1.1	(22.7)	3.9	2.7	6.8

Sources: IMF, *International Financial Statistics;* World Bank, *World Debt Tables;* World Bank, *World Tables;* Ishrat Husain and Rashid Furuqee, *Adjustment in Africa: Lessons from Country Case Studies* (World Bank, 1994), p. 165; Michael Holman, "Ashanti Is a Remarkable African Success Story," *Financial Times* (London), August 4, 1995, p. 8; Susan Horton and others, *Labor Markets in an Era of Adjustment,* vol. 2 (World Bank, 1994), p. 394; William Easterly and others, *Public Sector Deficits and Macroeconomic Performance* (Oxford University Press, 1994), p. 530.

a. GDP per capita figures are calculated using GDP and population figures from World Bank, *World Tables.* Budget deficit/GDP figures from Easterly and others are for 1971–88. The budget deficit/GDP figure for the last period is from 1993 from the *Financial Times.* Export figures are deflated with the manufactures unit value index (1992 = 100) to compute real exports growth. Public sector real monthly earnings are based on linked indexes from Husain and Furuqee, *Adjustment in Africa;* and Horton and others, *Labor Markets in an Era of Adjustment.*

LENDING, MODALITIES, AND OWNERSHIP. The fact of substantive congruence is not all that needs to be said about macropolicy relations between the government of Ghana and the World Bank in the 1980s. For one thing, the Bank invested in reform; it made major loans in support of the policy preferences it shared with the government. Early on the Monetary Fund lent more in short-run credits: 359 million SDRs in August 1983 with another 120 million pending. But after the Bank's long hiatus, from June 1983 onward that institution began routing a series of long-term IDA adjustment loans to Ghana—one sectoral adjustment loan a year during 1983–86 with sizes ranging from $28.5 to 76 million. This was bold behavior, given the government's repetitively disappointing record as a developer and borrower before 1983. As OED's draft Country Assistance Review in 1995 remarked:

It was a main contribution of the Bank (and the IMF) that they supported in a timely fashion the Government's emergent reform program, a risky thing to do in 1983. This was not only because the new Ghanaian team lacked any track record in managing reform, but also because some of its members had a record of anti-market actions and anti–Bank/Fund rhetoric. Against this background, staff in charge of the Ghana program made a strong case for accepting these risks—at the risk of their own credibility—and the Bank made a substantial upfront commitment of resources.[161]

In its 1991 Program Performance Audit Report of three Ghana SECALs, OED had judged that in some cases the Bank's risk taking had gotten ahead of staff preparedness.[162] But, as the 1995 draft Country Assistance Review emphasized, once lending to Ghana resumed, the institution became heavily engaged in building the numbers and quality of staff working on that country. Simultaneously a strong team of economists and policy analysts formed on the government's side. The combined effect contributed to the distinctive procedural character of macro-policy relations between Ghana and the Bank in the 1980s and 1990s.

A great deal has been said in this and preceding chapters about country "owner-ship" of reform programs. Ghana in the 1980s was a comparative hotbed of home-owned reform. As noted, the Bank—and the Fund—were brave to back the government's recovery and adjustment efforts as much and as quickly as they did. But there was no reason to doubt the origin or proprietorship of the efforts: ERP and the related reforms were the government's creations. Sarwar Lateef, Bank economist sent to conduct a seminar on adjustment policy with P. V. Obeng soon after the latter's appointment as chairman of the Committee of Secretaries (de facto prime minister) in July 1985, tells a fascinating story of the proceedings:

> We set up a week-long set of meetings which start from ten in the morning and go until seven in the evening where he [Obeng] brought everybody, the whole cabinet, the defence council, the committee for the defence of the revolution, the trade unions, the national employers association in the private sector, and he invited the press. The ground rules were that they couldn't report on what was happening, but he said, "Look, I want to make clear that there are no secrets between us and the Bank or anybody else. We are not trying to negotiate . . . in private. . . ."
>
> . . . Each day was devoted to a key issue, and the idea was to first get agreement on the objectives and then discuss what are the ways of arriving at them. And he was very clever. He . . . chose chairmen who were not necessarily sympathetic to the proposal. . . . He never chaired anything himself. He sat in the audience. And so those guys then ended getting some ownership of the areas. . . .
>
> [W]e [the Bank people] introduced the subjects, and we issued the paper which was circulated the night before . . . and then they would comment on it [in particular] where

161. World Bank, Operations Evaluation Department, "Ghana: Country Assistance Review" (1995), pp. 36–37.

162. World Bank, Operations Evaluation Department, "Program Performance Audit Report: Ghana: Reconstruction Import Credits I & II (Credits 1393 and 1573) and Export Rehabilitation and Export Rehabilitation Technical Assistance Projects (Credits 1435, SF-9 and 1436)," February 13, 1991, draft.

they felt . . . we had not done our homework properly. One sector, cocoa, where we had not done our homework, they . . . really completely obliterated the positions we were taking. They were a very bright lot. . . .

But at the end of this week we . . . were all friends. . . . They saw that they had been managing; most of the discussion was between them. We were sitting in. . . . And the minutes recorded the areas of consensus and agreement.[163]

The 1985 exercise helped trigger a level of concessional aid to Ghana that peaked at 18.4 percent of GNP in 1987–98. This was not Africa's highest country aid level during the 1980s, but it amounted to a heavy donor input and would cause second thoughts about aid dependence. Dependence, the 1995 Country Assistance Review (CAR) retrospectively noted, exposed the country to a level of donor-driven management that would be dangerous if it became permanent.

PHASE 2: HARDER. In 1992, when the Ghanaian government requested that the Bank send an eminent economist, the World Bank responded by breaking with its normal procedure and sending Ravi Kanbur as its representative in Ghana. Kanbur had recently come to the Bank from an academic career. In 1993 he gave the first annual social science lecture of the Ghana Academy of Arts and Sciences, in the course of which he highlighted what was becoming a much-remarked contrast in the reforms interveners were urging on countries of Sub-Saharan Africa. "Type I" reforms, he said, included "restoration of macro economic balance; establishing realistic exchange rates; removal of quantitative controls, particularly in trade;[164] reduction of taxes on agriculture; and rehabilitation of basic infrastructure." They could be contrasted with Type II, which included "private sector development; export promotion;[165] divestiture of state-owned enterprises; public sector restructuring and downsizing in some areas; financial sector rehabilitation and liberalization; and the reallocation of public investment and expenditure towards basic health, education, and infra-structure."[166]

In Ghana (as in other SSA countries) the distinction between the two types became also a contrast of the first phase versus the second, since the first set of changes, as a group, had come earlier, chronologically. Type I reforms certainly were not all easy, but they were administratively simpler than Type II, and some of them were politically easier. To borrow a phrase from Kanbur and others, Type I reforms can be called "stroke of the pen" changes. From the late 1980s onward the burden of need shifted toward more complex and iterative (Type II) institutional, capacity-enhancing changes. Politically, reform was facing a more

163. Sarwar Lateef, interview with the authors, December 16, 1992, pp. 9–10.
164. "QRs" (quantitative restrictions) were the more egregious kind of trade restrictions.
165. The reference was to institutionally implemented export promotion.
166. Ravi Kanbur, "Welfare Economics, Political Economy and Policy Reform in Ghana," World Bank Policy Research Working Paper 1381 (November 1994), pp. 18–19.

conflicted agenda in the 1990s. But what needed to be done also had become intrinsically more difficult.[167]

AID COORDINATION AND PAMSCAD. In Ghana, as it had in most of, at least non-Francophone, Sub-Saharan Africa, the World Bank had become the ring-leader among aid donors. Its own credits were a minority fraction of total conces-sional transfers to the region, but they were the largest fraction, and the Bank was the influential pattern setter. It both exhorted and sought to coordinate the other donors. This was very much the case in Ghana. Consultative group (CG) meetings, with the Bank in the chair, were resumed in 1983. They became "the main formal instrument of aid mobilization."[168] They helped accelerate certain government policies, let the government make its case for aid and the program, facilitated information and stocktaking by government and donors alike, and strengthened the hand of reform elements within the government. More detailed aid coordination was left to sector meetings organized by the Bank in Accra—indeed, the CAR faulted the government for being an insufficiently active aid coordinator itself, particularly as to the prioritizing of competing claims on Ghanaian technical and analytical capacities. But from ERP onward, among the outsiders, the Bank was the leading player and was perceived by the other donors and the government of Ghana to be a constructive one.

It may be unexpected to have the subject of aid coordination lead directly into that of the Program to Mitigate the Social Costs of Adjustment. The latter was instigated by those donors to Ghana, especially UNICEF, who feared that adjust-ment reforms would not maintain a sufficiently "human face" to the social and antipoverty needs of the country. The PAMSCAD program was endorsed en-thusiastically by the 1987 meeting of the Ghana CG, and thirteen donors pledged more than $80 million to it in a February 1988 pledging conference. But in the execution process the program became a cautionary tale of hypercomplexity. It was to contain twenty-three individual projects, to be implemented by portions of seven ministries coordinated by two special units. The program was to generate employ-ment, compensate retrenched workers, minister to basic needs, provide child feeding, and promote education and community initiative.

The contributions to PAMSCAD were slow to come in, and slower to be disbursed. There were severe administrative tangles. Arguably, the choice of the geographic sites of projects was pulled more by internal politics than by compara-

---

167. See the thoughtful article by Ghanaian political scientist, Eboe Hutchful, "Why Regimes Adjust: The World Bank Ponders Its 'Star Pupil,'" *Canadian Journal of African Studies*, vol. 29, no. 2 (1995), pp. 303–17. Hutchful makes a further point: for all of its vaunted neoliberalism, the Rawlings regime from 1982 onward tended to be, in terms of the present analysis, McNamaran in one aspect of its states-and-markets views. It was an advocate of liberalized markets but was not equally wedded to the privatization of public sector marketing enterprises.

168. World Bank, "Ghana," OED Country Assistance Review, p. 65.

tive needs. The scheme for monitoring PAMSCAD performance under a related multicountry Social Dimension of Development program addressing medium- and longer-term social sector issues was never established. As voiced by Joseph Abbey, the perception of PAMSCAD by key Ghanaian officials was sharply negative. Likewise, a multidonor evaluation of PAMSCAD in 1990 gave the program poor marks. In particular, it had been more successful at providing benefits to "some 45,000 retrenched government employees who in general found the severance pay . . . adequate" than in helping "small farmers in the northern regions."[169]

What OED's disappointed commentary did not emphasize was that most of PAMSCAD's disjointed complexity was directly attributable to the multiplicity and self-assertedness of the donors involved. The Bank was presiding over sophisticated CG meetings and giving its donor colleagues good macro briefings. But it had not succeeded in persuading the government to be sufficiently assertive in laying down sector policy lines and taking charge of coordination problems. According to Kanbur, however, progress was in sight. By the middle 1990s the most important opportunities for substantive donor coordination were being provided by carefully planned and conducted public expenditure reviews, and the donors, accepting the Bank's cues, were adopting the role of interested bystanders. The donors were leaving the whole design and implementation of the expenditure reviews to the government—with predominantly satisfying results.[170]

REFORM POLITICS. The obvious political question the Ghana case raises is the extent to which reform—and the Bank's effectiveness in the promotion of reform—have rested on the authoritarian capacities and disposition of a reform-minded government. Arguably it took authoritarianism to launch the 1983 program in Ghana. Implementation of reforms through the balance of the 1980s was driven in part by authoritarian official measures (and by fear of same). Following its own pattern in other countries, the Bank was prepared to play the role of what we have called the "white-smocked" economic technician: the Bank was not easily distracted from its chosen economic mission by the politically authoritarian nature of a regime serious about improved economic policies.

The political space in which the Rawlings government operated during the earlier years of reform was almost bound to diminish. Affairs had been in such an extremis state by 1983 that all interest groups were temporarily enervated, and the regime encountered little effective resistance to the pro-agriculture measures it enacted, benefiting small farmers who were slow to develop political muscle. The

169. Ibid, p. 99.

170. Interview with Ravi Kanbur, May 11, 1995. There were notes of regret from some Bank staff, however, that the 1994 government-run public expenditure review did not consider the overall macro framework or forward-looking plans for improving the current (election-aggravated) fiscal situation. Such issues, it was argued, were better dealt with in the earlier (1985, 1989, and 1992) Bank-run PE reviews. World Bank, office of the vice president of Development Economics, "Review of Public Expenditure Work," app. D, p. 34.

change came at the comparative expense of urban constituencies—especially the entrenched bureaucrats and the remarkably large array of some three hundred nonfinancial public enterprises the government inherited from the country's decades of Nkrumah-style socialism. But the urban interests were only laid low, not destroyed, and as the economy revived, they revived. They made increasingly insistent demands for democratization. The government conceded in stages. First, it permitted a 1988–89 set of district assembly elections in which 59 percent of the country's registered voters participated in electing members of Ghana's 110 local assemblies. Then in late 1992 a national election was held in which Flight Lieutenant Rawlings stood for president, but at severe temporary economic cost.

Shortly before the election civil servants, long the subject of relative wage restraint, were given a sudden 80 percent raise. The increase raised the country's fiscal deficit from some 1 percent to 6 percent of GDP; it brought a 50 percent increase in the money supply. The inflation rate, which had been lowered to 10 percent in 1992, ballooned; the exchange rate depreciated sharply; and private, including foreign private, investment collapsed. The new president, Rawlings, won a 58 percent majority in the multiparty election, and the government set about rebuilding its macropolicy rigor with considerable success. But by 1995 another presidential election (in 1996) loomed, Rawlings again was a contender, and macro concessions once more were made. Government spending surged, inflation rose again, to the 30 percent neighborhood, the cedi dropped, and interest rates topped 35 percent while nearly one-third of the Ghanaian work force was counted as unemployed. Joseph Abbey was quoted as saying, "The government is no longer solely focused on the economy. . . . I think the requirements of politics are a distraction."[171]

By mid-1995, ruing the intervening costs, Botchwey reported the Ghanaian economy back again on a growth track. He wished the World Bank, in administering loan conditions and calendars could be "a little more sensitive to [recipient] politics." But he said this "with some equivocation. . . . [T]he Bank or other donors [should not] indulge people who misuse their money."[172] Was Ghana, then, still a model for Africa? "Yes," he said, "in that the fundamentals are sound, and it shows that if preparations are made the country can get moving. But the lesson is that if your full potential is not liberated, you will limp along with 5 percent growth. That's not bad. But it is not nearly as good as it could have been."[173]

SUMMING UP. There is a good deal in the case to be celebrated. Ghana, with its tradition of intellectual and policy-analytical sophistication, by the mid-1990s had as good a prospect as any Sub-Saharan African country north of South Africa of evolving a formula for successful economic development by democratic means.

171. Stephen Buckley, "Ghana Finds Politics at Odds with Economics," *Washington Post,* April 16, 1995, p. A20.
172. Michael Halman, "Survey of Ghana," *Financial Times* (London), interview with Dr. Kwesi Botchwey, August 4, 1995, p. 9.
173. Ibid.

The formula would involve a working balance between popular representatives and a professional bureaucracy, interdependence between market flexibility and government oversight, and an incidence of public and private enterprises tilting (albeit not precipitously) toward the latter, with a substantial presence of foreign private enterprise and investment.

In principle, with its expertise and its recent pro-development and pro-reform determination, Ghana was well positioned to succeed in difficult "Phase II" institutional reforms. But the government would need to take charge of coordinating the various inputs of its valued but dissonant aid donors. A common view among those observing the Bank in Africa has been that the achievement of better-integrated multidonor and recipient efforts would be assisted by the transfer of more of the Bank's Ghana-focused staff from Washington to residence in Accra. Interestingly, however, one veteran of the institution's Ghanaian experience has volunteered that, until more Bank staff have altered the style of their participation, it would be a mistake to bring them closer to the field for longer periods.

What the last remark invokes is a paradox that runs throughout the Ghana case, namely, that it is an outstanding example of recipient ownership of macro reforms. But the procedural nub of the Bank's policy-influencing process in the adjustment era was conditionality. And there was a lurking incompatibility between ownership and conditionality, whether or not they were joined at the surface. The argument of the chapter has been that policy-influencing procedures are evolving away from precise, ex-ante, conditionality.

Sub-Saharan Africa, broadly considered, has, since the early 1970s, been the most frustrating region for the World Bank's "policy mongering." Ghana, as of the early 1990s, was, arguably, the most encouraging country instance of such Bank efforts. But the experience in Ghana did not contain enough of a breakthrough—it did not provide a sufficiently replicable model—to obviate our need for a region-wide discussion of the institution's Africa dilemma (see chapter 12).

Policy Influence: Conclusions

The saga of the World Bank's efforts to wield macropolicy influence on its borrowers leaves a variety of impressions. Some are broader points that emerge from but transcend the more detailed, heavily procedural, matters on which we have concentrated. Some are process conclusions themselves. And some are net impressions with which one leaves the policy influence issue.

Broader Points

To intrude on a borrowing government's policy choices (these chapters have focused on macropolicies) was at once irresistible and hazardous for a concerned and financially empowered multilateral such as the Bank. Making policies—

effectively—was the most pivotal activity in which borrowers engaged, and, as the Bank's capacity to wield influence grew, the institution's disposition to be constructive together with the demands of its funders and investors for accountability in the use of their monies made policy interventions inevitable. But from the viewpoint of sovereign borrowers, such intentions were also most sensitive. They loaded the risks and hurtful consequences (to be sure, also, the good consequences) of external advice mainly onto the borrowers. On the borrowers' side, the sense of unevenness was compounded by the dominance OECD members possessed in the governance of the Bank.

The turn toward the heavier practice of macropolicy influence had major effects on the World Bank institution. It shaped the thrust of the Bank's work and program and surely gave many staff and managers a sense of power exercised. But the costs were heavy. With a higher profile, the institution was more exposed to attack. The Bank already was elitist. But the SAL-SECAL era gave it more opportunity to consort with and importune the top leaders of governments. With ministers of finance as principal counterparts, it was harder to sustain the quality of relations in depth with the technical ministries and agencies with which Bank projects were lodged. The critiques of declining Bank project work and diminishing technical capacity in the 1980s were written by and large by Bank staff. But the hypothesis that the performance was in some measure reciprocal to the rise of policy lending cannot be ruled out. Certainly what became the familiar Wapenhans Report complaint of excessive attention to loan making, not enough to implementation and "supervision," was consistent with the Bank's preoccupation with policy-based lending during the 1980s.[174]

The effects that macropolicy-linked lending had on borrowers were the pivotal question. Within it, the issue was whether the Bank's substantive policy stances were borrower friendly, that is, borrower constructive. Although they had a high measure of continuity, the stances varied through time. Furthermore, the institution struggled to maintain a high measure of prescriptive equity, albeit not literal equal treatment, across its diverse universe of borrowers. This last task was inherently half thankless, but the Bank's coping warranted no loud reproaches— except in Sub-Saharan Africa, where the Bank's failures were widely shared.

The institution's substantive macropolicy positions in the 1980s and 1990s were broadly mainstream, and its endorsement helped keep them that way: mostly neoclassical in their economic doctrine, but not unexceptionally or rigidly so. The strongest theme was openness, both between economies and within them. In particular there was enthusiasm for liberalization-led export expansion. The Bank saw a lot for governments to do to maintain viable and even-dealing markets as well as to support social services and help and defend the poor. The institution was

174. World Bank, "Effective Implementation: Key to Development Impact," Portfolio Management Task Force Report (Wapenhans Report), R92-195, dated September 1, 1992, unpublished, submitted to the Board in December 1992.

centrally focused on economic growth along with adjustment. Increasingly it recognized the dependence of these goals on painstaking institutional development. Its advocacy of inflation resistance was certainly not unblemished, but in general it pressed the virtues of external and internal balance, of financial self-restraint and, over the longer run, of national self-reliance.

To most of the governments receiving them, these messages were not bolts from the blue, but they did get attention. They provided information and argumentation to contestants in government and to other parties of influence who shared the Bank's views. The Bank helped to cross-reference policy discussion across countries. And the loans that carried the messages sometimes tipped decision balances or facilitated implementation of reform.

A sketch of the more pervasive effects of policy lending must also note those on the Bank's Part I members. Substantively the industrialized country members largely approved of the macropolicy messages the Bank sent its borrowers, although some, especially the Nordic countries, the Netherlands, and sometimes the Canadians, felt the institution was not sufficiently attentive to the "human face" needs of the poor.[175] As the bilateral donors in the later 1970s and early 1980s became increasingly persuaded of the importance of linking aid to macropolicy persuasion, they shifted from simply leaving it to the Bank and the IMF to perform that function to following (in their consultative groups and otherwise) the Bank's lead in the design and prosecution of their own policy-linked lending.

The Bank as leader and consortium chairman of multidonor policy-linked lending undoubtedly facilitated some convergence of doctrines and practice among donors. Pro- and anti-Bank interests would continue to argue over whether the semiconverged result was more constructive for recipients than would have been the case had the Bank been abstracted from macropolicy lending altogether.

A final broad comment: one reason the Bank was interesting as a policy promoter was that it was directed to be, and in considerable measure became, a financially powerful political eunuch. Obviously the institution was not blind to political issues, nor unresponsive to its nation-state masters. But its full-timers sought a measure of autonomy, and their apolitical mien served that purpose. Yet it offered no guarantee of institutional independence. The zone of independence around the Bank was diminished, when, first, under IDA, the institution began to draw substantial public revenues from its members, and second, began intruding more aggressively into their policymaking.

Process Points

In the Bank's first fifty years, the policy dimension of its work had a particular evolution reflecting the institution's project-lending mandate. Geographically oriented policy work was there from the beginning, but in the 1950s and 1960s, in

175. The allusion is to UNICEF's "Adjustment with a Human Face."

the eyes of some Bank units and people, it was upstaged by the vigor with which the institution implemented its mandate to become primarily a *project* lender. Different players in the Bank perceived different mixes of complementarity and conflict between the area-policy and sector-project sides of the institution, and the balance shifted through time: for example, moving a notch in 1972 and again (and more dramatically) in 1979–80. But by the late 1980s (although this was not necessarily a positive symptom of institutional health), most of the passion had gone out of the policy-projects conflict. Synergies of project and policy work not only were preached; they were more commonly practiced.

If loans have been the vehicles of the policy influence here under discussion, the evolution of the Bank's vehicular choices has been one of the story's more active issues. The task of picking loan vehicles along the project-to-nonproject axis was related to, but differed from, the policy-versus-project question. Constitutionally, nonproject lending started out under a cloud for the Bank; its availability was limited to special circumstances. This interfered with the inclination in some Bank quarters to use program loans, unencumbered with the particularities of a project, to convey broader kinds of policy influence. In practice, however, the legal inhibition to nonproject lending turned out seldom to be formidable.

Meanwhile, especially in the 1960s, especially in Latin America, the Bank made considerable strides in making do with country "programs" of project loans as instruments of macropolicy influence. There were, however, parallel or competing experiments in strengthening the institution's policy voice. In one of these particularly, in India, the use of non–project loans was unabashed, albeit sharply criticized both by some staff and some of the institution's Part I and Part II members.

Vehicular issues were not prominent during the 1970s; influence wielding was beleaguered by more basic problems. But in 1979–80 vehicular questions jumped life-size into the center of the Bank arena with the launching of structural adjustment (non–project) loans. The 1980s revealed the variety of alternatives along the vehicular spectrum: SECALs as well as SALs; hybrid loans; slower-disbursing adjustment loans; stand-alone, other-than-adjustment policy loans; and broader and narrower investment loans (as project loans now were called). But the flagship vehicle was the SAL, and, according to the present account, the SAL was burdened and overburdened with more and more reform targets until it threatened to sink of its own weight. The trend of recent years, then, has been to "disaggregate" policy-based vehicles and specialize them to fewer tasks. But policy-specializing lending does not appear to have been reverting to its pre-1979 state.

Conditionality and modalities create another tension in the story. Alternative means for promoting lender-borrower agreements on macro reform agendas are arrayed along a modalities axis. At the extreme toward which the Bank strongly inclined in the earlier structural adjustment years, the model was before-the-fact conditioning of (preferably) measurable, precise, and monitored reforms, with performance disciplined by the withholding of second-tranch or next-of-a-series loans. The alternative of a more interactive Bank-borrower dialogue involving greater borrower initiative was less precise in yielding the reforms the Bank preferred. But as the 1980s unfolded, it became evident that the success of policy-influencing efforts depended overwhelmingly on how deeply a country committed itself to a set of reforms. Interactive dialogue was the much likelier mode to encourage such "ownership."

Thus one encounters a major paradox in the policy-influencing venture. Fundamentally, there was a tension between conditioning and ownership. In practice the Bank has softened, accommodated, and semantically sanitized its conditioning no little amount—especially in the case of big countries. More generally in the late 1980s and early 1990s there was a growing awareness that excessive conditioning leads to revealed toothlessness. But the opposite hazard was that shapeless dialogue might move very little. If they were to be productive, interventions into the policymaking of a sovereign client could not avoid at least a lurking prickliness.

"Policy loans" are given for some kind of policy-performance consideration. Their denial or delay could also influence policy-borrowers' policy decisions. There were instances of withheld loans, some policy influential, as far back as the 1950s. In the 1980s some exasperated reformers felt the Bank should tighten up its release of policy-designated money substantially. But defenders of the lending said this could put a blight on emerging cases of reform ownership, let alone block SAL's *other* inherent purpose, that is, to move quick-disbursing funds in response to resource needs.

The Bank's policy influence has tended to outweigh that of such other non-governmental interveners as foundations and nongovernmental organizations because the Bank has brought influential quantities of resources to the policy table. It is important to remember the distinction if one extrapolates a future in which the World Bank's transfer function is greatly diminished.

Given their contiguity historically, geographically, and functionally, it is not surprising that relations between Bank and Fund figure prominently in the policy-influence story. The two agencies have engaged in much mutual encroachment since the early 1970s. Once the Fund undertook to do concessional lending, adopted development promotion as a main purpose, and weighed into micro institutional analysis while the Bank, under the banner of policy-based lending, engaged the whole panorama of macropolicy, the division of labor between the two became shadowy. But the cultural differences are embedded and have changed little. Each institution has some value as a check on the other; and the political chances of an amalgamation in the near future are small.

The lesson of this review is that each agency, including its respective management, needs to work harder at living constructively with the other. The division of labor can be somewhat rehabilitated and clarified. Working procedures can be more reliably connected, and exchanges of personnel, including at senior levels, can be beneficial. Thus, just as it was useful for Moeen Qureshi to move from the Fund to IFC/Bank some years ago, the move of Stanley Fischer to the number two spot at the Fund in 1994 augured improved Fund-Bank compatibility.

The Time Line: Some Net Impressions

At the bottom of the policy-influence story one emerges with three impressions, all with a time dimension.

In the first place, the Bank's macropolicy experience teaches that consequential reforms—changes in government regimes and their programs—often take more time than their designers, promoters, and funders anticipate. This is true for both the borrowing countries and the interveners. Thus the time span of structural adjustment—what was expected in 1980 to be a major but finite, one-shot adjustment—was underestimated. A bevy of delaying and distracting factors intervened. Time horizons had to be stretched.

The second lesson may not be proven by the foregoing analysis, but it is strongly suggested, and it is the most sobering: policy fixes seldom last. Innovations take hold, sometimes with enthusiasm and great effect. Frequently, as this chapter has emphasized, they require a follow-on phase of institutional development, and sometimes these are long lasting. But in the macropolicy reform case, the new departure goes on to overreach and deteriorate. Hegelian cases are possible: a thrust and counterthrust may yield a synthesized new thrust. But the safer lesson is simply that given policies, no matter how soberly adopted, are likely to be episodic. However, that is not to denigrate them or what they accomplish. History, among other things, is a series of such episodes. In the eyes of many, a number of the policy efforts of recipient countries in which the World Bank participated in the 1980s were quite effective; for a time they justified themselves; but then they frequently were superseded—and the policymakers went on to other policies. The final time-line lesson is not depressing; it is just humbling for an external intervener like the World Bank. In a world still dominated by nation-states, the role of an official external intervener into a borrower's broad economic policies tends and needs to be doubly episodic. OED's 1995 Country Assistance Review of the Bank in Ghana chose as its principal theme sustainability. This was a good choice if the subject was the country's own policy program. (As just pointed out, it probably was going to take longer than expected, but it should not have been expected to last forever.) But sustainability of policy intervention would not have been an appropriate theme for the outsider.

The record suggests that the multilateral lender should be on call; it should sustain an accessible presence and maintain its knowledge of the local situation. But its operational interventions should be temporary, occurring only as local decisionmakers' efforts generate needs for exceptional nonsustainable assistance. The self-image of the outsider should be more that of a resourceful plumber or other skilled service contractor than of a side-by-side partner.

This is not to say that the effectiveness of a multilateral as a pro-development intervener is likely to be less than that of bilateral donors; the reverse probably is true. Nor is it being suggested that the presence of the Bank—physical or conceptual—on a developing-country scene should be a stop-and-go affair. Typically the institution will have ongoing project and technical-assistance business. But the record indicates that intervention into national macro policymaking is a high-risk activity; it is more likely to be constructive when practiced sparingly and intermittently.

ELEVEN

The Latin American Debt Crisis

As, pent in an aquarium, the troutlet
Swims round and round his tank to find an outlet
Pressing his nose against the glass that holds him,
Nor ever sees the prison that enfolds him;
So the poor debtor, seeing naught around him,
Yet feels the limits pitiless that bound him;
Grieves at his debt and studies to evade it,
And finds at last he might have as well have paid it.
        —Bartlow S. Vode in Ambrose Bierce, *The Cynic's Word Book,* 1906

THE 1980s were a wrenching period for numerous low- and middle-income countries. Particularly hard hit were the fragile low-income economies in Sub-Saharan Africa, as was already painfully apparent by the end of the 1970s. But times were also trying for the middle-income countries, especially in Latin America, which were swept into an economic maelstrom just as they appeared poised to continue the economic advances of the previous decades. Bewildered by events that defied simple explanations, most Latin American countries would find the 1980s an abrupt departure from the past.

The simultaneous economic travails of a large number of countries unfolded on two, virtually separate, paths—one traversed by low-income countries and the other by middle-income countries. The key distinguishing variable, as seen in table 11-1, was the magnitude and share of commercial bank debt and debt service in 1981, just before the eruption of the crisis.

In the case of countries that were later categorized as severely indebted low-income countries (SILICs), almost all of which were situated in Sub-Saharan Africa,

Table 11-1. *Debt of Severely Indebted Developing Countries, 1981*[a]
Billions of U.S. dollars

Creditor	Low-income countries	Middle-income countries
Total debt	74.7	278.3
Official creditors	39.9	43.8
Commercial banks	10.3	130.6
Debt service	6.8	52.1
Official creditors	1.8	5.2
Commercial banks	2.2	30.8

Source: World Bank, *World Debt Tables*.

a. Defined as countries in 1989 in which three of four ratios were above critical levels: debt to GNP (50 percent); debt to exports of goods and all services (275 percent); accrued debt service to exports (30 percent); accrued interest to exports (20 percent).

the debt was largely owed to official creditors. Although even at the beginning of the decade, commercial bank debt service was a heavy burden on the enfeebled economies of this region, it was relatively small in absolute terms. Consequently, their impairment did not pose a serious threat to the financial health of the banks. More important, external debt was but one facet of the much deeper economic crisis afflicting this region.[1]

In contrast, commercial bank debt and, even more, commercial bank debt service of the severely indebted middle-income countries (SIMICs), were significant in both relative and absolute terms. The geographic concentration of the debtor countries in Latin America and of the creditor banks in the United States was to prove crucial both to the definition of the crisis and the manner in which it was managed. What came to be known as the "debt crisis" was the potential systemic risk posed to the United States and the global financial system; the economic distress of the debtor countries was, at least in the early years, secondary to the individuals and international institutions that mattered. But their close intertwinement would fundamentally affect the trajectory of events.

In the many analyses of the debt crisis, the World Bank was conspicuous for its absence through the first half of the decade, in contrast to the International Monetary Fund, the Federal Reserve, the U.S. Treasury, and sundry other actors, all of which played a role.[2] It gradually emerged from the shadows following the

1. The Bank's role in the debt crisis in low-income countries is addressed in chapter 12.

2. For an institutional view of the Bank's role in the debt crisis see Sebastian Edwards, *The Latin American Debt Crisis* (World Bank, 1994). A more forthright analysis is Percy Mistry (a former Bank official and senior advisor to Moeen Qureshi), "The World Bank's Role in the Debt Crisis Affecting the Highly-Indebted Countries," report to the Group of Twenty-Four, January 1991. The Bank's analytical role is examined in Beatriz Armendariz de Aghion and Francisco Ferreira, "The World Bank and the Analysis of the International Debt Crisis," London School of Economics, November 1993. The issue is also examined in chapter 12 of volume 2.

Baker proposals, becoming more conspicuous after the Brady initiative. Is this interpretation valid? If it is, the Bank's low profile over much of the period poses several questions. The hound that did not bark is a most curious event, especially as it was vigorously barking at so many other issues. Why did the institution keep such a low profile? Was its lack of visibility more a question of style than of substance? How valid are criticisms that not only *could* the Bank have played a more conspicuous role, but that if it had, it *somehow would have mattered*? Examining the Bank's role in the debt crisis is important for another reason: it may help to better explain the constraints and difficulties facing multilateral institutions when their members' interests fundamentally differ.

This chapter focuses on the Bank's role in the middle-income countries, most of which were in Latin America, but which also included countries in Africa (Côte d'Ivoire, Morocco, and Nigeria), Europe (Turkey and Yugoslavia), and Asia (Philippines). The complexity of the crisis was reflected in the nature of the Bank's response, especially to the financial aspects of the debacle. The fact that these were middle-income countries and therefore borrowed from the International Bank for Reconstruction and Development (rather than the International Development Association) had significant financial implications for the institution, issues that are also discussed in chapter 16. At the same time, for the Bank the debt crisis became inextricably linked to its efforts to restructure economic policies in these countries, issues that are examined in chapter 10.

Prelude

Most accounts of the debt crisis trace its roots to the first oil shock and the subsequent role of commercial banks in recycling the gushing balance of payments surpluses of the oil producers accompanied by profligate borrowing countries.[3] The financial intermediation had several distinctive characteristics: the intermediation was primarily market based, a concomitant to the failure to redistribute international liquidity through official channels; commercial banks played a leading role in that intermediation; lending by the commercial banks was organized through syndicates; and the dominant financial instrument was the variable interest rate loan. Although there was no dearth either of greed and naïveté on the part of lenders or of economic mismanagement and financial profligacy on the part of borrowers, the decisionmaking was quite "rational" given the negative real interest rates that prevailed during much of the latter half of the 1970s.[4] In hindsight, these

3. See for example, Robert Devlin, *Debt and Crisis in Latin America: The Supply Side of the Story* (Princeton University Press, 1989); Karin Lissakers, *Banks, Borrowers and the Establishment: A Revisionist Account of the International Debt Crisis* (Basic Books, 1991).

4. An extreme example of perverse borrower-lender behavior was Zaire. By the time Zaire was forced to reschedule its debts in 1978, its external debt had grown at about 35

structural features of financial intermediation in the 1970s make the fragility of the system seem all the more manifest. When, following the second oil shock, Federal Reserve Board Chairman Paul Volcker announced in October 1979 that his institution would target monetary aggregates in order to wring out inflation in the United States, he inadvertently lit the fuse: it was a matter of time before the volatile mixture exploded.

For its part, the Bank had been concerned about the debt burden of developing countries throughout the 1970s. This concern was strongly reflected in the institution's annual reports and Robert McNamara's speeches. References to the "debt problem" of developing countries were so frequent that they had an almost ritualistic air to them, usually ending with exhortations to the international community for additional capital flows at more concessional rates, which it was thought would alleviate the problem. By the end of the decade, the gloomy assessments of the 1978 portfolio analysis review had led the Bank's finance vice president, Peter Cargill, to urge McNamara to impress upon the institution the need for substantially greater attention to country creditworthiness.[5] As in any rapidly expanding banking institution, concerns with growth in the 1970s had edged out the more prosaic concerns of creditworthiness. The result, as the new operations chief noted to his regional vice presidents, was that country-level projections had a built-in optimistic bias on balance of payments outlook, more than was warranted by the world economic outlook.[6]

The number of countries experiencing arrears or seeking multilateral debt renegotiations had increased from three to eighteen between 1974 to 1978. LIBOR had surged from 7.5 percent in December 1977 to about 16 percent in late 1979. Although inflation had surged as well, real interest rates were rapidly climbing to their highest levels in the decade (figure 11-1).

Citing the rapid growth in private capital flows to developing countries, the development of new financing techniques, and the reemergence of the recycling problems following the second oil shock, McNamara expressed his concerns to his senior managers "about the state of [the Bank's] work on international capital flows and financial markets," deeming it "essential . . . that we intensify our efforts in this area."[7] As a consequence, the debt issue acquired a renewed analytical prominence within the Bank. Staff analyses noted that a common characteristic in these coun-

---

percent a year since 1970, with most of the borrowing having come from commercial sources at hard terms. In contrast, the IBRD made one loan to Zaire in the 1970s ($100 million) and another in the 1980s.

5. Memorandum, I. P. M. Cargill to Robert S. McNamara, "Riskiness in IBRD's Loan Portfolio," October 25, 1978.

6. Office memorandum, Ernest Stern to regional vice presidents, "Identification of Country Creditworthiness Issues in CPPs," December 15, 1978.

7. Memorandum for Mr. Qureshi, "Subject: Work on Capital Market Flows," September 1979, p. 1, processed. McNamara assigned primary responsibility for the work to the Bank's Finance complex, given its expertise in this area.

Figure 11-1. *Nominal and Real LIBOR, 1973–92*
Percent

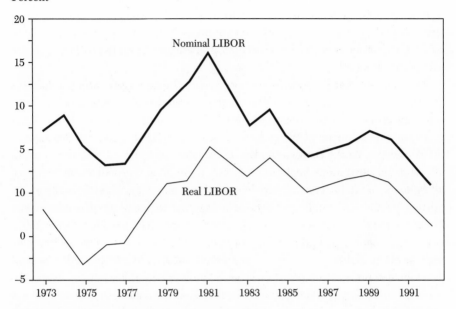

Source: *International Financial Statistics; World Economic Outlook.*

tries was an inability to raise new funds from private capital markets once liquidity shortages emerged. There were apprehensions that if "perceived creditworthiness changes and private banks are unable to extend new loans over and above the usual rollovers, we may see a large number of countries in extremely difficult situations."[8] Further analysis of the debt problems of developing countries now resulted from the background work done for the new flagship publication of the Bank, the *World Development Report,* which had an up-front analysis of global trends. Thus staff files indicate serious thinking on "liquidity" versus "solvency" issues, estimates of the increasing recourse to, and credit risks rising from, short-term debt, as well as increased efforts to keep track of the countries facing debt-servicing difficulties.[9] However, there was insufficient understanding of the risks implied by the shifts

8. Memorandum, Surinder Malik and C. Doultsinos to Jean Baneth, "Bank Borrowers Experiencing Debt Servicing Problems," October 29, 1979, p. 2.

9. For instance, in a memorandum to Attila Karaosmanoglu, D. Joseph Wood directed his attention to the "now commonplace . . . distinction between the kind of debt problem facing the low-income countries and the kind facing the middle-income countries. The latter group is often said to have a liquidity problem, whereas the former group is said to suffer from an inadequate transfer of real resources." Memorandum, Wood to Karaosmanoglu, "Debt Problem of the Middle-Income Countries as a 'Liquidity Problem,'" February 21, 1979. Knud Ross, "The Nature of Short-Term Debt," May 14, 1979.

from fixed interest rates to floating rates.[10] And the focus on real interest rates, while undoubtedly valid, underplayed the cash flow problems that could result from high nominal rates. Moreover, with one notable exception—the advent of structural adjustment lending—the operational changes were for the most part modest. It was one thing to flag a *potential* problem; it was quite another to decide what to do about it.[11]

The Bank was hardly alone in its concern with the debt issue. Morgan Stanley's "World Financial Markets" issued a warning on the looming debt problems that was well covered in the financial press.[12] The Brandt Commission, no doubt reflecting the influence of the codirector of its secretariat, Dragoslav Avramovic, previously the World Bank authority on external debt, urged that the "various international institutions begin immediately to study and articulate the range of likely debts and debt servicing problems as they emerge . . . and the likelihood of existing private and public institutions being able to meet these needs."[13] The Development Committee set up a task force on nonconcessional flows in September 1979. A draft report prepared a year later, while noting the problems raised by high levels of debt, the increases in interest rates, and the limited access of developing countries to international bond markets, was still sanguine about "the generally encouraging trend of the flow of non-concessional resources to NODCs [non-oil developing countries] in 1980 and the early part of 1981. This situation is particularly noteworthy as it marks a departure from the earlier pessimism about the short-term prospects for external borrowings by NODCs; such pessimism was wide-spread at the time the Task Force was set up."[14]

However, the final report, submitted six months later, would be more cautious, reflecting the deteriorating situation in the interim.[15] The IMF also got into the act

10. In the case of the major borrowing countries, floating interest loans as a percentage of public debt rose from 18.4 percent in 1974 to 32.5 percent in 1978 to 45 percent in 1981. World Bank, *World Development Report, 1985,* table 2.4, p. 21.

11. A review meeting in 1979 called to discuss a draft of "A Review of Creditworthiness Analysis in the Bank and Tentative Guidelines" (prepared by the Policy Planning and Program Review Department and finalized in July 1980) was inconclusive with "many disagreements about the various recommendations made by the paper." Memorandum, Ramanbhai Bhakta to files, "Creditworthiness Analysis and Tentative Guidelines," December 17, 1979, p. 1.

12. Morgan Stanley, "World Financial Markets," October 1980, as reported in Peter Montagnon, *Financial Times* (London), "Foreign Debt Risk Warning by Bank," October 9, 1980.

13. *North-South, a Programme for Survival: Report of the Independent Commission on International Development Issues* (Cambridge, Mass.: MIT Press, 1980), p. 239. Willy Brandt was chairman of the commission. Another assessment on similar lines was "The World Economic Crisis," a report prepared by the Commonwealth Group of Experts, particularly chapter 3, on the balance of payments problems facing developing nations.

14. Report of the Task Force on Non-Concessional Flows, draft, September 1981, processed. The task force was chaired by Alfredo Phillips, deputy director Bank of Mexico. Its members included Michel Camdessus and Fred Bergsten.

15. Task Force on Non-Concessional Flows, "Non-Concessional Flows to Developing Countries," report to the Development Committee, May 1982.

in 1980, putting together a paper on the debt of developing countries.[16] Like the Bank, the Fund continued to be sanguine that "the prospects for continued large-scale access to banking credits, by non-oil developing countries, appear to be reasonably positive at the present time."[17] An internal staff note commenting on the Fund study noted, "Clearly, there is considerable overlap between this paper, the work program for WDRIV and the ongoing work of the Finance Department and EPD,"[18] prompting a senior manager to note, "What a crowded field!" In connection with the work for *World Development Report 1980,* staff analysis judged that the binding constraint on non-concessional flows would be the ability of developing countries to service their debts rather than the ability of the banking system to recycle funds.[19] Yet the 1980 report would project large positive net transfers to developing countries through 1990, while finessing the implications for gross lending implied by these numbers.[20]

Despite their profusion, these studies suffered from three major lacunae: by focusing almost exclusively on the external sector, they underplayed the linkages between the emergence of debt problems and fiscal and monetary developments within developing countries; they failed to examine the transmission of far-reaching changes in U.S. fiscal and monetary policy; and no one envisaged the possibility— or consequences—of panic sweeping over the commercial banks.

By 1980, although significant commercial bank reschedulings had already occurred in Peru, Turkey, Nicaragua, Sudan, and Zaire, the fears of a more generalized problem appeared to abate. The commercial banks continued to be confident. When India— one of the few large developing countries that had eschewed commercial bank borrowings in the 1970s—went to the IMF in 1980–81, commercial banks strongly lobbied the new team at the U.S. Treasury to curb India's access to the Fund's facilities. The banks argued that if India was granted such access, despite the IMF's conditionalities, they would be deprived of business. This "crowding-out-the-market" argument struck a sympathetic chord in the new U.S. Treasury team. Indian officials lobbied European capitals and received a more sympathetic hearing from Volcker and the Federal Reserve Board. The loan was finally approved with the United States abstaining.[21]

16. Bahram Nouzad and Richard C. Williams, *External Indebtedness of Developing Countries,* IMF Occasional Paper 3 (May 1981).

17. Richard C. Williams and others, *International Capital Markets: Recent Development and Short-Term Prospects,* IMF Occasional Paper 7 (August 1981), p. 4.

18. Memorandum, Nicholas Hope to files, "IMF's Work on Debt," August 7, 1980. EPD was the Economic Analysis and Projections Department.

19. Memorandum, Jean Baneth to K. Georg Gabriel, "Preliminary Notes on Capital Flows," February 4, 1980.

20. The projections for *World Development Report 1980* assumed a real interest rate of 1 percent. A sensitivity analysis of the projections, assuming a real interest rate of 3 percent, indicated that the debt servicing ratios would become unsustainable. According to Baneth, McNamara asked that the latter simulation be dropped. Jean Baneth, interview with the authors, October 1993.

21. I. G. Patel, interview with the authors, September 26, 1990; Catherine Gwin, interview with the authors, February 20, 1992. At the time the loan was the largest ever granted

Table 11-2. *Euphoric Lending: The Growth of Commercial Banks' Assets,*
1978–81

		Percentage growth from December 1978		
Location of bank assets	*December 1978 (billions)*	*To December 1979*	*To December 1980*	*To December 1981*
Mexico	23.3	32	76	138
OPEC (non-Mideast)[a]	31.1	28	44	51
Latin America[b]	55.9	28	58	84
Selected Pacific Asia NICs[c]	14.8	31	66	97

Source: Philip A. Wellons, *Passing the Buck: Banks, Governments and Third World Debt* (Boston: Harvard Business School Press, 1987), p. 23, table 6-3.

a. Algeria, Brunei, Ecuador, Gabon, Indonesia, Nigeria, Trinidad and Tobago, Venezuela.

b. Excludes Mexico.

c. Malaysia, Republic of Korea, Taiwan, and Thailand.

In Mexico, as the two front-runners vying for anointment as the presidential candidate of the ruling PRI—David Ibarra of Treasury and Miguel de la Madrid of Planning and Budget—jockeyed for position, disputes broke out over the rival camps' diverging assessments of future lending prospects by the commercial banks. The Ibarra camp was bearish on continued access to commercial bank loans, in contrast to the confident bullishness expressed by the de la Madrid camp. To resolve the issue, President José López Portillo decided to poll the foreign banks on their lending intentions. The banks, "fearing that the government was about to put a lid on borrowing, and would use the polling results as a basis on which to ration mandates, greatly inflated their lending projections."[22] Mexico would borrow record amounts in the next eighteen months (table 11-2).

The Bank's economic report on Mexico, prepared in mid-1981, raised several concerns about the financial and macroeconomic situation but met with a hostile reception during discussions with a visiting Mexican economic team. The report's suggestion that the growing current account deficit on the balance of payments was the result of "the excessive resort to foreign borrowing" was brushed aside. "The increase in foreign borrowing," countered the team, was "dictated by the increased profitability of investment in Mexico."[23] The Mexican team included Carlos Salinas, then director-general in the Ministry of Programming and Budgeting. Salinas had

---

by the IMF. Ironically, the Indian economic team was severely criticized in India for "selling out" the country's interests to the IMF and by implication the United States.

22. Lissakers, *Banks, Borrowers and the Establishment*, p. 83.

23. Memorandum, Gabriel Sciolli to Nicholas Ardito Barletta, vice president, Latin America, "Mexico—Your Meeting with Mexican Delegation on July 14, 1981," July 10, 1981, p. 2.

hitched his wagon to the fortunes of de la Madrid and was unhappy at the Bank's less-than-enthusiastic endorsement of Mexico's continued access to international capital markets. A Bank staff economist who wrote a dissenting annex to this report was subsequently ostracized following furious representations by Salinas.[24]

The World Bank lent $1.1 billion to Mexico in 1981, by far its largest commitments to date. At the end of 1981, the Bank's draft Country Program Paper for Mexico was projecting annual GDP growth for Mexico of 8.1 percent between 1983 and 1985 and 8.5 percent for the remainder of the decade. The economic report, discussed with the Mexican authorities in early 1982, projected smoth sailing for the economy and downplayed the policy risk of overindebtedness. The new Bank president, A. W. (Tom) Clausen, who had recently presided over some heavy lending to Mexico by the Bank of America, reiterated the Bank's confidence in Mexico's prospects following his visit in March 1982. In a letter to President López Portillo he noted,

> Our meetings in Mexico City with your top aides reinforced my confidence in the economic leaders of your country. You, Mr. President, can be rightfully proud of the achievements of the last five years. Few countries can claim to have achieved such high growth rates, or have created so many jobs. . . . I wish to congratulate you on the many successes already achieved.
>
> As I stated during our meeting, the recent setback for the Mexican economy is bound to be transient, and we will be happy to be of assistance during the consolidation process.[25]

Meanwhile a significant manifestation of a commercial bank debt problem was occurring in Eastern Europe, in Hungary and Poland. Poland's $4.6 billion rescheduling in the summer of 1981 had been the largest to date. However, at the time neither country was a member of the Bank (or Fund), although Hungary would soon apply for membership. The problem was contained despite strident opposition from the Reagan administration.[26] As Walter Wriston apparently explained to Lloyds Bank Chairman Jeremy Morse in March 1982, "Americans shouldn't 'make trouble because we're about to have a problem in Latin

24. Memorandum to files, "Mexico: Present Economic Situation—Problems and Policies," August 14, 1981. The economist (at this writing still with the Bank) had taken a much more alarmed view of Mexico's macro prospects in 1981 and wrote up his dissenting economic analysis in the form of a memo to the files. His subsequent career at the Bank was jeopardized; after an embattled few years, he was reinstated after a legal battle. Pieter Bottelier, interview with the authors, January 19, 1993.

25. Letter, A. W. Clausen to His Excellency José López Portillo, president, United Mexican States, March 19, 1982, p. 1.

26. In fact, the U.S. government's actions for a time appeared to be expressly designed to push Poland into default for a variety of reasons: it would punish the country for imposing martial law; it would put increased financial burden on the Soviet Union; and also reinstill financial discipline in the Western banking system. See "A Case for Default?" The Banker, April 1982, p. 7.

America.'"[27] Wriston's allusion to problems closer to home was undoubtedly influenced by the repercussions of the Falklands War in March–May 1982, which triggered a U.K. freeze of $1 billion in Argentine assets held in U.K. banks and an Argentine counterfreeze on debt payments due to U.K. banks, which caused considerable anxiety about a broader Argentina debt moratorium. While the crisis was becoming evident, fear of self-fulfilling expectations led to discretion by all parties concerned.

In Peru, the central bank, uneasy about the government's expansionist fiscal policies, refused to lend to the government. In a cautionary tale to later overexpectations on the virtues of central bank independence, the government simply solved its daily cash crisis by having the minister of finance (a former senior official of a prominent U.S. commercial bank) each day place "a telephone call to some [foreign] bank. Public enterprises alone borrowed about $500 million, or 2.5 percent of GDP, in short-term credits [in 1982]."[28]

In May 1982 the Bank's senior vice president for operations, Ernest Stern, attended a meeting of the International Financial Group. At the meeting, commercial bank representatives considered themselves heavily exposed and concurred that strong competition had led to unfortunate results, with excessively low spreads and some imprudent lending, but they did not expect much change. Stern reported back to Clausen, "unrealistic as it may sound, there was extended discussion of 'pulling out' from lending to LDCs before they finally concluded that this was not realistic."[29] The Bank's management was more concerned about the dramatic increase in the Fund's activities in 1982, which it feared "could create future problems if the IMF was not prepared to refinance the repayments when they fell due."[30]

Yet the news of the crisis that Jesús Silva-Herzog, the Mexican finance minister, brought to Washington on Friday, August 13, 1982—that Mexico would be unable to service its external debt obligations—caught almost everyone in the Bank, as it did nearly everyone else, by surprise. The institution had several able staffs—in its finance and research departments, in the central operations complex, and in the Latin American regional department—engaged in monitoring and analyzing the debt issue. As the principal international agency collecting data on external debt of developing countries, the fact that the Bank was caught so off guard needs some explanation.

27. Steven Solomon, *The Confidence Game: How Unelected Central Bankers are Governing the Changed Global Economy* (Simon and Schuster, 1995), p. 199. At the time, in addition to his responsibilities at Citibank, Wriston was also chairman of President Ronald Reagan's Economic Advisory Council.

28. Richard Webb, *Peru*, Country Study 8 (WIDER, 1987), p. 2. At the time the author was the governor of the Banco Central de Reserva del Peru.

29. Memorandum, Ernest Stern to A. W. Clausen, "Ditchley Conference," May 14, 1982.

30. World Bank, "Minutes of August 16, 1982 Meeting," Managing Committee, p. 2.

There were several reasons for this failure of perception. The most obvious was the nature and magnitude of concurrent exogenous shocks: the second oil shock on the oil-importing developing countries (and in Mexico's case the decline in oil prices in 1981); the adverse effects of the recession in the countries of the OECD between 1980 and 1982 on developing-country exports; and the "scissors" effect of unprecedented high interest rates and declining terms of trade facing these countries.

A second reason was technical weakness in both the capacity of developing countries to manage capital flows and in the Bank's debt-reporting system. Managing capital flows is a technically complex undertaking and many developing countries had failed to develop the requisite institutional capacity. Although the Bank had been in the forefront of providing technical assistance to help countries set up debt-reporting systems, these systems had not kept pace with the changing nature of debt, particularly short-term and private nonguaranteed debt.[31] Furthermore, countries were not likely to be up-to-date on their debt reporting if a prospective crisis loomed. By mid-1982 Mexico was between twelve and eighteen months behind in supplying the Bank with debt information.[32] And even if the debt-reporting systems had been better, they were unlikely to have picked up either the magnitude of the capital flight that was occurring or the rapid growth of borrowings that occurred between 1979 and 1981, an increasing share of which was short-term debt.[33] Although the Bank adopted a much firmer stance after the debt crisis erupted, even going so far as to link continued lending to timely compliance with the external debt-reporting requirements, there were limits to what could be achieved, as the 1994 Mexican crisis would demonstrate.

Third, as the figures in table 11-2 indicate, the commercial banks' lending euphoria was so strong that the availability of information is unlikely to have reversed the invariable triumph of fads over logic.

31. There was a technological aggravation as well. Enrique Lerdau, then a director in the LAC region, noted in a memo to Hollis Chenery, "While the Bank is designated as the central recipient agency for external debt data, we as yet have no resources or model programs which our clients can use as they computerize their external debt systems. Indeed, I understand that our own system is so complex and so specific to our needs that it cannot be used even as the beginnings of a model by our clients." Memorandum, Enrique Lerdau to Hollis Chenery, "Technical Assistance in External Debt Compilation," January 30, 1980.

32. A memo to files reported on a conversation with Mr. José Luis Flores of Hacienda concerning external debt information on Mexico. "I pointed out to him that we have not received updated Form 2 since December 30, 1980, and Form 1 since June 1981. Mr. Flores explained that computer difficulties in registering foreign public debt has been the reason for the delay and he assured me that all efforts would be made to furnish the required information before . . . mid-August." Memorandum, V. Nercissiantz to files, "Mexico—External Debt," July 15, 1982.

33. Although a crude estimate of capital flight can usually be gleaned from the "errors and omissions" item in the current account, figures for which are typically available with a lag

A fourth reason the onset of Mexico's debt crisis in August 1982 took the World Bank by surprise was that the Bank had been focusing on the plight of the poorer oil-importing countries, somewhat less on middle-income oil-importing countries and least on a middle-income, self-confident, oil-exporting country like Mexico. While in Mexico's case Bank staff, as indeed many others, were bedazzled by the possibilities that seemed to gush from its oil wealth, in fact prospects for the other large middle-income countries of Latin America—Argentina, Brazil, and Mexico— had been widely regarded as rosy, so much so that since 1979 the U.S. Treasury had begun to press the Bank to "graduate" these countries from its lending. The complacency bred of success not only adversely affected the institution's analytical work (especially in the Latin America region) but also led these borrowers to be indifferent to even the muted warnings in the Bank's economic reports.

Yet another source of myopia was the intrinsic dilemma that bureaucracies saddled with sensitive decisionmaking always have had to struggle with. Imprimatur organizations face particularly vexing difficulties in organizing their public predictions in ways that guard against the tendency of prophecies to become self-fulfilling. For the Bretton Woods institutions, creditworthiness and exchange rate concerns are perhaps the most difficult and delicate matters in this regard. As the 1994 Mexican crisis would demonstrate more than a decade later, perceptions of creditworthiness are cruelly fickle, and history is a poor guide. Consequently, as has been noted for some time,

> Given the Bank's prominent role and its need to maintain its own financial health, it is highly unlikely that it would ever become a purveyor of "gloom and doom" through its financial projections. Any dire predictions by the Bank are likely to be self-fulfilling. There is always the danger, however, that the Bank's buoyancy in describing financial prospects could contain an element of self-deception.[34]

Under the new Donald Regan Treasury, as the Bank faced an unprecedented hostile attitude on the part of its largest shareholder, it was even less likely to call attention to issues where information and analysis were decidedly uncertain. This "keep-the-head-down" attitude was reinforced by the transition in the Bank's presidency. The new president, a commercial banker himself, whose grip on the institution was as yet tentative, was an unlikely candidate for leadership on an issue as complex and as plagued with uncertainty as this.

But last, and perhaps most important, it is unclear what the Bank could have done, even if it had come to the conclusion that a major problem was at hand. By

---

of a few quarters. The World Bank later estimated that between 1979 and 1982, capital flight from Argentina, Mexico, and Venezuela was on the order of $68 billion, nearly two-thirds of gross capital inflows in the same period. World Bank, *World Development Report, 1985*, p. 64.

34. Charles R. Frank, Jr., "Comment: Debt Adjustment: The Tyranny of Bankers, Brokers, and Bondholders," in John P. Lewis and Ishan Kapur, eds., *The World Bank Group, Multilateral Aid and the 1970s* (Lexington, Mass.: Lexington Books, 1973), p. 129.

the beginning of the decade the inertial forces were simply too strong to be checked by such a relatively minor actor on the global financial stage as the Bank. And knowledge and beliefs notwithstanding, the role of Cassandra is an unenviable one, and rarely a popular one. Soothsayers are rarely rewarded for their prescience.

Phase I, 1982–85: Belt Tightening

The crisis had been precipitated by a complex set of cumulative factors: external shocks; inept borrowing-country policies made worse by vested interests of governing elites; commercial bank cupidity and naïveté; and inadequate regulatory mechanisms. Although the relative weight of these factors would be debated endlessly, the fateful event at this juncture was the almost complete reversal in private capital flows after mid-1982. In the ensuing panic, as the commercial banks began to pull out, the gap between private and collective rationality widened and the crisis deepened.

Initially, leadership, characterized by a sense of both urgency and tough-mindedness, was provided by public sector leaders of the international financial community, most particularly by Jacques de Larosiere, the managing director of the IMF, and Paul Volcker, chairman of the U.S. Federal Reserve System, aided by Gordon Richardson of the Bank of England and Fritz Leutwiler, chairman of the Bank for International Settlements (BIS). Their goal, for reasons evident in table 11-3, was dominated by an overwhelming anxiety to defend, not just or primarily, individual commercial banks, but those of the United States and the global financial system. The anxiety was fed by the scale of the risks the banks had incurred and the pace at which incapacities to service their stocks of debt spread from Mexico to other countries.

The way private commercial banking dominated the lending side of the debt had two effects in the initial stage of the crisis. First, it meant that once "the whistle blew," fresh lending ground to a halt. Jacques de Larosiere, in the first round of Mexico's 1982 "rescue," had indeed brow-beaten the lenders into some forced or

Table 11-3. *Concentration of Commercial Debt, 1982*

Borrowers		Lenders	
Country	Percentage of developing-country debt	U.S. banks	Loans to developing countries as percentage of total capital
Mexico	17.3	Nine largest	229
Brazil	16.6	Next fifteen	160
Three largest	41.3	All others	69
Six largest	58.4	All U.S. banks	152
Ten largest	68.8		

"concerted" lending, but this the banks did most reluctantly and, as the crisis proceeded, as little as possible. Presumably, if Mexico's loans had come from public agencies less focused on a profitable bottom line in the short term, the lenders would have sought to provide the borrowers with more cushion. Second, the syndicate structure, with the multiple bank lenders consisting of an inner circle of center city banks and a periphery of provincial banks aggravated the free-rider problem, and the consequent difficulties of organizing "concerted lending."

With an overriding concern for preserving the stability of the financial system, the crux of the initial strategy was to restore confidence in the financial system. To this end, IMF programs and debtor country announcements were instituted to provide plausible expectations of debt servicing by debtor governments. By the end of 1982, with the Mexican restructuring in place, the strategy's basic tenets had jelled:

—The crisis was to be treated primarily as a short-term liquidity problem to be resolved by the IMF and the central banks, and the focus was to be on the "big-four": Argentina, Brazil, Mexico, and Yugoslavia.

—Debts of the private sector were to be converted into sovereign debt.

—A partly collective approach would be taken to any important decision on steps pertaining to the debt; the collective approach applied to the creditors, while the debtors were to be treated on a case-by-case basis.

—Debtors were to maintain interest payments in full so as to avoid any provisioning for reserves by the banks; relatedly, although rescheduling would be part of the agenda, there would no hint of debt forgiveness or concessional interest rates.

—New loans by commercial banks were to be conditioned on the debtor country promising to pursue austerity measures, the promises to be ensured through a standby agreement with the IMF.

It was crucial that the appearance of near normalcy be maintained to preserve confidence. Given the immense uncertainties, an important aid in this respect was the concept that the problem was one of liquidity rather than of solvency. This diagnosis became the generally accepted view in Washington, supplanting an earlier New York consensus, symbolized by Citibank Chairman Walter Wriston's brave assertion that since sovereign states "don't go out of business," they were unlikely to go broke either.[35] Intellectual support for this thesis was provided by William Cline, based at the influential Institute for International Economics, in Washington D.C., who predicted that a 3 percent OECD growth rate would

35. Henry Wallich (a governor of the Federal Reserve Board) was later credited with having "memorably described the notion of sovereign immunity from default as being as elusive as the smile on the vanishing face of the Cheshire cat." Peter Montagnon, "Two Principles of 1970s Lending that Now Seem Dubious," *Financial Times* (London), July 30, 1992.

resolve the problem.[36] The reliability of long-term macroeconomic forecasting, even in developed country settings, is seldom significantly better than that of soothsayers. Here, despite the much greater uncertainty, both with regard to data and structural interrelationships, the alacrity with which the Cline study was seized upon was a testament more to its attractiveness than its reliability. A moderate upturn in the global economy in 1983 and the Republic of Korea's success further bolstered its message.

The solvency-liquidity distinction might appear to have been largely a hair-splitting exercise, of greater academic than operational significance. If a liquidity problem persists for more than a few months, then liquidity and solvency distinctions are, for all practical purposes, indistinguishable.[37] The need to draw a sharp distinction was, however, important to help sell the particular strategy of crisis management being followed. It was logical for an illiquid creditor to pursue a debt-raising strategy to service its external obligations and thereby defend its creditworthiness. On the other hand, insolvent debtors required a debt-reducing strategy.[38] As the central banks and the IMF wrestled the commercial banks into "concerted lending," thereby requiring the banks to increase their exposure, this distinction provided a strong rationale for the approach. Furthermore, the very focus on the distinction ensured that the debate could be passed off as a matter involving economic rather than political judgments.

At the same time, the institutions that were thrust into the breach—the IMF and the central banks—were by their mandates required to preserve monetary and financial stability and thus had innately short-term concerns. Within that framework, their achievements would be creditable in the immediate aftermath of the crisis. The problem would not prove to be a short-term predicament, however, and the great disparity between its magnitude and the institutional resources

36. William R. Cline, *International Debt and the Stability of the World Economy* (Washington D.C.: Institute for International Economics, 1983). Cline's affirmation, of course, carried the usual caveats about "acts of God." A decade later, Cline would claim that he had been essentially right all along. William Cline, *International Debt Reexamined* (Washington, D.C.: Institute for International Economics, 1995).

37. Strictly speaking, it can be argued that a country with sufficient resources to service its debt, but temporarily unable to convert these resources into the foreign exchange required to service its debt, faces a liquidity problem. It is insolvent only if its assets are less than its external obligations. Such a criterion would imply that few countries would ever be insolvent; after all, they could always sell the country's assets to pay off the debts. In reality, what matters is the extent to which a country can realistically be expected to mobilize domestic resources to pay off external obligations. And what constitutes "realistic" invariably entails strong political judgments.

38. Barry Eichengreen and Peter B. Kenen, "Managing the World Economy under the Bretton Woods System: An Overview," in Peter Kenen, ed., *Managing the World Economy—Fifty Years after Bretton Woods* (Washington D.C.: Institute for International Economics, 1994), p. 47.

brought to bear upon it would be more than apparent with the benefit of hindsight. A crucial variable was the unwillingness, or perhaps inability, of the G-5 countries, and in particular the United States, to shoulder a greater responsibility. In part, this was because, as Lewis Preston, then chairman of J. P. Morgan (and later president of the World Bank), would later state, "I'm not sure anyone in the Reagan administration understood. . . . They were ideologues, free marketeers. They were trapped in their own ideology."[39] Ideological predilections notwithstanding, the trajectory of the debt crisis would be steered largely by U.S. interests, and later those of other G-7 members.

Despite their public unhappiness at being strong-armed into concerted lending, commercial banks, especially the large money-center banks, were quite willing to acquiesce in viewing the crisis as a short-term phenomenon. Financially, the immediate consequences were quite profitable because of higher spreads and front-end fees on new and restructured loans.[40] Another reason was that the management of these institutions was now in the hands of the very people who had made these loans in the first place—international lending had been the fast track to senior management positions in the 1970s—rendering it more difficult for these institutions to take a broader view of the problem.[41]

When a nation encounters more external obligations than it has the resources to meet, it has only three possible courses of action, aside from unilateral default: run up arrears, borrow further, or adjust the imports-exports balance (or some combination of these). From very early on, however, it became quite evident where the relative balance would lie. With additional borrowings available only in ever smaller quantities and with limited room for rapid export expansion, the countries faced a Hobson's choice as long as they continued to faithfully service their external obligations: severe demand compression that drove down imports and per capita national income.

An almost exclusive emphasis on stabilization became the standard IMF medicine administered to countries requiring financial assistance. But the large devaluations that were made part of this package, in the attempt to bring the external accounts into surplus, queered the stabilization pitch. As the debt-servicing burden of the private sector surged, governments succumbed to pressures to socialize the large private sector debt. Since governments had to finance domestically the resources to purchase the foreign exchange required to service

39. Cited in Solomon, *The Confidence Game*, p. 225.

40. Citibank's earnings in 1983–84 from Brazil alone were 20 percent of its total worldwide earnings. Dividends declared by the large U.S. money-center banks in 1984, two years into the crisis, were double those in 1980. Lissakers, *Banks, Borrowers and the Establishment*, p. 194.

41. Most commentaries on the crisis suggest that the leadership of continental banks (German and Swiss in particular) was prepared to take a long-term view from quite early on. However, since their exposure to Latin America was relatively modest they had less to lose, and little influence on the negotiating stance of the country advisory committees.

their external debt, the budgetary implications of devaluations were severe.[42] With no recourse to external resources, the overwhelming part of the government deficit was financed through local borrowings, with the result that domestic debt increased, undermining stabilization efforts. Budgetary pressures arising from debt servicing were compounded by the severe stress on government revenues caused by sharp declines in production. The precipitous decline in production, and especially the duration of the recession, was one of the most underestimated consequences of the crisis associated with orthodox stabilization programs, although it was not entirely unforeseen.[43] The effects were damaging: fiscal deficits stubbornly persisted, despite major cutbacks in government expenditure. It was almost inevitable that these deficits would get monetized with sharp inflationary consequences.

Compounding the difficulties in analyzing the scope of the problem were the large uncertainties in most forecasts. The Cline study and the IMF's analysis were two among many that occupied a vast penumbra of plausible possibilities. The conclusions of such studies were couched in language suggesting that if, over the next few years, the country reduced aggregate demand, and if certain assumptions on world growth, interest rates, and commodity prices held within certain plausible ranges, debt service would be manageable, without "undue" compression of domestic demand, the latter clearly raising issues of political feasibility. The projections used were midpoints of ranges (usually with large variances). Since the funding packages were already so tight—both financially and in getting the hundreds of creditors on board—there was little interest in giving serious consideration to contingency plans if the assumptions underlying the projections did not work out. On the contrary, the compulsions to underestimate the problem were overpowering, given the strong political need to maintain confidence in the financial system and sell the program domestically in the debtor countries. At some indiscernible point, assumptions would jell into convictions and gradually harden into dogma. In attempting to walk the tightrope between what was economically desirable and what was financially and politically feasible, projections became politically contaminated,[44] with estimates of capital flight particularly malleable to pressures to ensure that financial packages were "fully funded."[45]

42. An early exposition of the problem can be found in Helmut Reisen and Alex van Trotsenburg, *Developing Country Debt: The Budgetary and Transfer Problem*, OECD Development Centre Studies (Paris: OECD, 1988).

43. For an early critique on these lines see the report of the G-24, published in Gerald K. Helleiner, "Balance of Payments Experience and Growth Prospects of Developing Countries: A Synthesis," *World Development*, vol. 14 (August 1986), pp. 877–908.

44. As Volcker put it candidly in referring to the IMF's numbers, "The Fund was the Fund—I don't need to say any more. . . . We don't have to discuss what kinds of programs they put in. Those are negotiated numbers. But they're the only ones in town." Solomon, *The Confidence Game*, p. 217.

45. For instance, Fischer noted in a memo to his IMF counterpart, "Bank staff are concerned with the Fund's projections of substantial return capital flight in the financial gap

This is what happened in Peru, which in January 1983 was faced with an unprecedented natural calamity: rainfall and oceanic conditions changed drastically owing to an irregularly occurring flow of warm surface water off the coast, a phenomenon known as El Niño. In March 1983, the IMF projected Peru's 1983 GDP to grow at 0.9 percent, exports at 8.8 percent, and inflation at 55 percent. The actual rates were –12.3, –8.0, and 111 percent respectively.[46] The macroeconomic models of the Bank and Fund were simply ill-equipped to deal with the implications of such large declines in GDP with its implied effects on the structural interrelationships between financial variables and the real economy.

One factor that received limited attention was that in some cases limitations in debt repayment capacity were not necessarily the result of foreign exchange problems but of the inability to mobilize domestic resources. Governments often lacked the political wherewithal to tax enough or to obtain enough resources to actually buy the foreign exchange, even if it was available. And no one—not the governments or the commercial banks—was willing to confront the issue of capital flight. The benefits of the borrowings had been privatized and the costs socialized in the sense that capital flight had removed the money, and governments could not capture private foreign assets to offset public liabilities.[47]

The Bank's Initial Response

The Bank's role in the initial years of the crisis was peripheral.[48] The signals from the G-5 were quite clear: the Fund, together with key central banks, would manage the process with the purpose of stabilizing the financial system. Given the analytical framework of the IMF—grounded in a balance of payments approach—its central role helped strengthen the short-term liquidity view of the crisis. Almost immediately after the crisis broke, commercial banks approached the Bank to seek its

---

analysis for some countries. We are unaware of the economic analysis on which such projections are based, and believe that it would generally be a self-denying prophesy to argue that a financing gap will be closed by return capital flight, which depends above all on confidence in overall macroeconomic and financial stability." Memorandum, Stanley Fischer to Jacob A. Frenkel, "Coordination of Forecasts," June 27, 1989. In his reply Frenkel concurred that "the issue you raise concerning projections of return capital flight in financial gap analysis is one which, as you are aware, *embraces considerations other than purely analytical ones.*" Memorandum, Jacob A. Frenkel to Stanley Fischer, "Coordination of Forecasts," July 14, 1989, pp. 1–2. Emphasis added.

46. This discussion draws on Webb, *Peru.*

47. Between 1978 and 1983, U.S. commercial bank claims on foreigners in the Latin American region increased by $131 billion. At the same time their liabilities to foreigners in the region increased by $82 billion for a net increase of $49 billion. For the role of the commercial banks, see Lissakers, *Banks, Borrowers and the Establishment*, chap. 6, "Capital Flight: Their Savings and Ours."

48. For instance, Joseph Kraft's extensive and oft-cited account does not mention a single World Bank person. Kraft, *The Mexican Rescue* (New York: Group of Thirty, 1984).

assistance in increasing cash flows to Mexico to help restore confidence in the face of Mexico's perceived liquidity problem. As chance would have it, at that time the Bank's projected disbursements to Mexico were just about breaking even with repayments. In fact, the crisis measures being taken by the Mexican authorities were slowing down Bank disbursements as the authorities struggled to find counterpart funds. Therefore "there was not much more we could do to help in Mexico's cash flow problems."[49]

The Bank moved cautiously in the initial years of the crisis. Notwithstanding later criticism, the Bank had limited flexibility on the financial front. The major shareholders had mandated overall lending ceilings on the IBRD in agreeing to the 1979 General Capital Increase (GCI; see chapter 17). After 1980, two new and large IBRD borrowers, China and India, further reduced the Bank's lending room.[50] At the same time, the Bank's lending procedures and instruments, in contrast to those of the Fund, were not designed for large-scale, quick-disbursing loans. Its new lending instrument, structural adjustment loans, did indeed provide it with greater flexibility, but there was little consensus both among management and among the Board members on the extent to which the new instrument ought to be deployed. The G-5's insistence that the IMF take the lead, coupled with large uncertainties inherent in the early years of the crisis, led the Bank to align its financial role with its assigned second-tier status, fearing it might endanger its financial health otherwise. Several members of the Bank's Board, led by Germany and Japan (who did not share the relaxed views of the United States and United Kingdom) felt strongly that the Bank should not stray too far from its project-lending role. These constraints caused the ceilings on IBRD adjustment lending to rise only gradually.

In early 1983 management proposed a two-year "Special Action Program" to accelerate disbursements under existing and proposed loan commitments and to shift the structure of lending to quicker-disbursing "high-priority operations."[51] Steps were taken to streamline disbursement procedures, as a result of which net disbursements increased by nearly $1 billion between 1980 and 1984 and another $1.8 billion between 1985 and 1989.[52] Privately, however, the Bank's management

49. IBRD, "Minutes of August 23, 1982 Meeting" Managing Committee, p. 1. The minutes in this case were noting Clausen's comments.

50. Although India was not a new IBRD borrower, it had been largely an IDA borrower in the 1970s. The paucity of IDA resources would result in its becoming one of the largest IBRD borrowers in the course of the decade.

51. IBRD, "World Bank Program of Special Assistance to Member Countries, 1983–84," R83-22, IDA/83-10, January 28, 1983.

52. The changes were of a procedural nature and involved an expansion in the use of statements of expenditure and revolving funds. The amounts advanced in each period through so-called special account advances were recovered in subsequent periods. Advances in the two periods totaled $1 billion and $5 billion, respectively. The Latin American region was the biggest beneficiary, accounting for nearly 40 percent of the special account advances. E-mail, Constance Ely to Devesh Kapur, with attachment, "Special Account Advances and Recoveries by Region in 1980s," September 24, 1993.

harbored few illusions about the impact of these increases, in view of the magnitude of the problem.[53] Before the crisis had flared, the Bank had planned a 1982–86 IBRD lending program of $60 billion.[54] Actual lending levels over the period would be slightly less than the planned figures, in part because of shortfalls in IBRD lending in fiscal 1985–86, despite the obvious financial distress afflicting many Bank borrowers.

The World Bank's early diagnosis of the problem concluded that "even though some developing countries face serious debt problems, a generalized debt problem seems highly unlikely."[55] Clausen, in one of his first major public speeches, addressed himself to the debt crisis, maintaining that it was "a problem of liquidity rather than solvency,"[56] and consequently a short-term problem, a view widely shared in official circles. A more systematic analysis was carried out in mid-1983.[57] Since up-to-date debt statistics were not available from the Bank's debt division, a task force enrolled twelve country economists to do the work. The study focused on the balance of payments and consumption per capita. Issues relating to the fiscal transfer aspect of debt servicing (that is, the need to transfer real resources from the private to the public sector in order for the latter to service debt) were not considered. The conclusion of the country simulations was that for nine of the twelve countries, even with optimistic savings and export assumptions, debt service would translate into a prolonged decline of per capita consumption.[58] Barely six months after Clausen's strong affirmation of a liquidity—and therefore short-term—view of the crisis, the Bank's Managing Committee, in examining the study's

53. The minutes of the January 24, 1983 meeting of Managing Committee note that the discussion then turned to "how the Special Action Program could best be publicized in a way that did not draw attention to the relatively low levels of net resource transfers involved." IBRD, "Minutes of January 24, 1983, Meeting," Managing Committee, p. 2.

54. As per figures in the 1981 (and 1982) budget memoranda. See chapter 16.

55. Helen Hughes, "External Debt Problems of Developing Countries," draft of internal World Bank document, February 1983, p. 42.

56. Letter, A. W. Clausen to Donald T. Regan, March 7, 1983. The speech in question was the annual Jodidi lecture at Harvard University. One of the authors recalls McNamara strongly sharing this view at the time.

57. The study came about at the behest of Shahid Husain, then vice president of the Operations Policy Staff, who had worked on debt issues with Drag Avramovic in the 1960s. Since most of the critical countries were in the LAC region, Guy Pfefferman, that region's chief economist, was asked to lead the study reporting to Bevan Waide, then director of the Country Policy Department.

58. The countries consisted of Argentina, Brazil, Chile, India, Indonesia, Ivory Coast, Korea, Mexico, Morocco, Philippines, Turkey, and Yugoslavia. While the results of such simulations can be quite sensitive to the structural characteristics of the models, most were predicated on plausible scenarios of growing per capita incomes and declining debt-service burden. However, since these scenarios all envisaged increasing domestic savings and rising exports, the burden of debt payment was borne by per capita consumption which continued to fall over the medium term.

conclusions, noted "that the major debtors even under the most optimistic circumstances would continue to face a difficult situation over the next ten years."[59]

By the end of 1983, the commercial banks had reached agreements with eighteen debtor countries, rescheduling $35 billion of debt and granting $14 billion of additional credit. Drawings on the IMF's facilities had increased by about $9 billion in three years (1981–83).[60] However, a few of the key players were beginning to recognize the longer-term nature of the crisis.[61] Privately the Bank's management was pessimistic about any quick turnaround on the debt crisis.[62] Returning from a conference held at the New York Fed, Stern reported, "We are clearly the most pessimistic about the adjustment process and the resumption of growth. The IMF scenario and the views of the commercial banks are much more upbeat."[63] Differing objectives—short-term balance of payments versus long-run consumption growth—meant different criteria for success, and thus the fact that perceptions of success differed was quite understandable. Yet, despite a growing unease, both within the Bank and outside it, about the strategy's effects on the debtor countries, there were tremendous inhibitions on going public with these doubts.[64]

Meanwhile, the internal task force's analysis on the implications of the crisis for the Bank's borrowers were turned over to a different department, which prepared a report released in mid-1984.[65] It was poorly received by key members of the Bank's management, in particular by Anne Krueger and Ernest Stern, whose unhappiness stemmed from two major concerns. The first related to the use of financial figures based on the "net transfer" concept:

59. IBRD, "Minutes of September 19, 1983, Meeting," Managing Committee, p. 2.

60. Eichengreen and Kenen, "Managing the World Economy under the Bretton Woods System," p. 43, table 6.

61. For instance, in October 1983 Volcker had concluded that the debt strategy of less developed countries would take "years, not months. And we had better recognize the stakes are too high to fail." Solomon, The Confidence Game, p. 245.

62. Letter, A. W. Clausen to Jacques Delors, April 24, 1984. "As you know the debt problem will be with us for a long time."

63. Memorandum, Ernest Stern to members of the Managing Committee, "Conference at the Federal Reserve Bank of New York," OPS/MC84-22, May 11, 1984, p. 1.

64. One of the authors of this study, in his capacity as governor of the central bank of Peru, made a public statement in June 1984 that Peru faced a difficult choice between continuing to service its external debt and meeting import levels needed for growth. His government had recently failed to meet its fiscal targets under a Fund standby agreement. The implied suggestion that Peru should at least consider a partial unilateral moratorium provoked an outcry by Peru's steering committee that, in turn, caused a panic in the government. He was accused by the then prime minister of "stabbing the country in the back." Impeachment proceedings were initiated against him on the grounds that his statement had ruined Peru's foreign credit. See Webb, Peru.

65. IBRD, Operations Policy Staff, "Debt and Adjustment in Selected Developing Countries," SecM84-698, July 23, 1984. The report was prepared by Sidney Chernick and Basil Kavalsky under Bevan Waide's direction in the Country Programs Department.

Am not prepared circulate paper which analytically based on net transfer concept. Much of what is said, despite a few disclaimers, is based on proposition that net transfers undesirable, and fails recognize analytical distinction between current payments and capital account. Despite extensive treatment of debt cycle at outset . . . and statement that borrowing is trade across time idea that interest is payment for use of capital is forgotten thereafter. Interest payments unfailingly described as burden.[66]

Stern's position was shared by many of his colleagues and predecessors. Loan repayments fell into the capital account, while interest payments were rewards for the use of foreign capital and belonged, like other factor services, in the current account. In this view, continuously positive net transfers implied continuously rising levels of debt and, therefore, as Burke Knapp put it, was tantamount to a gigantic Ponzi scheme.[67] Still, the stringent opposition to the use of the net transfer concept appears to have been as much for tactical reasons as for anything else.

At the same New York Federal Reserve meeting, Stern reported that "the issue of net transfers was raised and was greeted with a veritable fire storm of negative comments, from several governors and other participants. The World Bank was also attacked by several speakers for having endorsed this concept."[68] But there was a more pragmatic reason for the Bank to shy away from a public use of the net transfer concept:

If we hold the commercial bank [sic] responsible for maintaining net transfers . . . then we are saying that . . . the World Bank itself at some future point can be held responsible for not maintaining positive net transfers. We are arguing in other fora that one thing that distinguishes the World Bank from other banks, and justifies our separate treatment in rescheduling, is that we maintain net disbursements—not net transfers. If we accept the net transfer argument in a public speech by the President, our basis for rejecting attempts to draw us into rescheduling when our net transfer payments are no longer positive will be much weaker.[69]

However, such a stance did not distinguish between the long term and the short term. Although positive net transfers should not be considered necessary in the long term, they may well be desirable in the short term on occasion. As observers would later note, for the debtor countries the "transfer" problem entailed the need to generate outflows of real purchasing power and was therefore a significant indicator of the constraints on GDP growth. It was also an important determinant of the sustainability of their debt

66. Fax message, Ernest Stern to Luis de Azcarate, director, CPDDR, May 15, 1984.

67. Burke Knapp, interview with the authors, March 1995. The argument that net transfers to a banking institution would eventually have to turn negative because of the simple arithmetic of compound growth rates is incorrect. For net transfers to be zero, all that is needed is that the nominal level of debt increases at the actual interest rate, which means that the real level of debt grows at the real rate of interest, the so-called Domar rule.

68. Memorandum, Ernest Stern to members of the Managing Committee, "Conference at the Federal Reserve Bank of New York," May 11, 1984, p. 1.

69. Memorandum, Ernest Stern to Munir Benjenk, "Draft Speech for Davos," January 16, 1984, p. 2.

accumulation process.[70] Moreover, "repayments and interest payments were both made in money, and the theoretical distinction was irrelevant to policymakers who had to cope with fluctuations in the cash flow from the financial side imposing a restructuring of their economies which was sometimes radical, sometimes impossible."[71] In reality, although Bank staff were conscious that any reference to net transfers in external discourse could invoke management wrath, Bank Country Strategy Papers were replete, as indeed they had long been in the past, with such references as concerns about the Bank's portfolio risks grew over the decade.[72]

Stern also criticized the mid-1984 report for hiding the "most important issue; namely countries did not have the capacity (sometimes technical, sometimes institutional, sometimes political, sometimes all of the above) to react flexibly to changing circumstances." Furthermore, it put the onus on external causes "instead of emphasizing the failure of, and need for, flexibility in economic management in a world economy which is not likely to get much less volatile."[73] Stern's comments embodied a shift in the institution's center of gravity, in the relative weighing of factors internal to a country (economic policies and institutions) and the external circumstances (terms of trade, interest rates, sudden withdrawal of lending) affecting their worsening fortunes.

This shift was most dramatically reflected in the analysis emanating from the research complex of the Bank following a change of leadership in that part of the Bank. On the one hand, World Development Report 1982 had claimed that "the developing countries, despite the rise in their current account deficits from $40 billion in 1979 to $115 billion in 1981, have been much more successful than the industrialized countries in adjusting to the new situation."[74] On the other hand, World Development Report 1986 asserted that "at the root of the poor performance and debt problems of developing countries lies their failure to adjust to the external developments that have taken place since the early 1970s, coupled with the magnitude of the external shocks."[75]

70. Edmar L. Bacha, "External Debt, Net Transfers, and Growth in Developing Countries," World Development, vol. 20, no. 8 (August 1992), pp. 1183–92.

71. Göran Ohlin, "The Negative Net Transfers of the World Bank," in UNCTAD, International Monetary and Financial Issues for the 1990s, vol. 5 (UNCTAD, 1995).

72. Thus, after Mexico's Brady agreement in 1989, the statement by the Bank's president, Barber B. Conable, addressed to the "International Banking Community" noted: "A fully funded package would help reduce uncertainty, as net transfers abroad are reduced in a manner consistent with Mexico's need to maintain a moderate current account deficit." September 15, 1989. Emphasis added.

73. Fax message, Ernest Stern to Luis de Azcarate, director, CPDDR, May 15, 1984.

74. World Bank, World Development Report 1982, p. 7.

75. World Bank, World Development Report 1986, p. 33. A later Bank research paper noted that concerted G-3 monetary contraction following the second oil shock imposed heavy costs on the region. In its absence, Latin America GDP would have been 5 percent higher in the 1980s. Chris Allen and others, "How OECD Policies Affected Latin America in the 1980s," World Bank Working Paper WPS 954, 1992.

Although the shift in tone was partly ideological, it was also partly functional, driven by the systemic imperatives of the debt crisis. Analyst Carlos Diaz-Alejandro, investigating the way the crisis was playing out in its second year, felt the many transgressions in debtor nations' domestic policies paled in comparison with the magnitude of the external shocks between 1979 and 1982.[76] This suggestion drew a sharp response from Stern:

> I really think it is time to stop whining about how immature LDC managers are and how they need special protection at every turn. The countries which borrowed $10–15 billion a year are playing in the big leagues. They thought they had the capacity—they often said so. They did so with their eyes open. They were very proud of what they were doing at the time—and much of what they did was sound. But they miscalculated. That can happen, and the cost of miscalculation can be high. But, if they want to be partners in an open and interlinked international economic system, it is time that they equip themselves to do so properly, and you should not put the burdens of failure on the shoulders of everyone but themselves—it is not. I believe it is a view they, in fact, share.[77]

Stern's frustration was shared by many in the Bank who felt that arguments such as Diaz-Alejandro's implied that these countries wanted to have their cake and eat it too. In the years leading to the crisis, several of the countries then in deep waters had treated even the Bank's mild warnings with indifference, making it clear that they knew what they were doing and did not need anyone to tell them otherwise. And now they were shouting for rescue.

Moreover, few in the Bank disagreed that since 1973, the developing countries in particular had had to face unprecedented shocks. However, the Bank interpreted this fact as underscoring the case for more flexibility in the economic structures of these countries to absorb external shocks, and therefore the need for structural reform. On the other side were those who argued for global mechanisms to act as shock absorbers, thereby mitigating the consequences of such shocks. Many in the Bank, however, felt that their advice to the borrowers should be based on the world as it was, rather than as it ought to be. As Stanley Fischer would later put it: "I very much fear giving them [the less developed countries] any encouragement to believe the international community will do much to help them, and thus tend to emphasize that they have to handle their own problems."[78] It was felt that little was served by creating expectations that were not going to be met and thereby postponing the adjustment that would have to occur in any case.

---

76. Carlos F. Diaz-Alejandro, "Latin American Debt: I Don't Think We Are in Kansas Anymore," *Brookings Papers on Economic Activity*, no. 2 (1984), pp. 335–404. In placing the state of play of the debt crisis in the Land of Oz, Diaz-Alejandro was drawing an analogy between the Wizard of Oz and the role of a "hapless" IMF: "a mythologized contraption through which weak human beings speak," (p. 383).

77. Letter, Ernest Stern to Carlos F. Diaz-Alejandro, September 10, 1984, pp. 3–4.

78. Memorandum, Stanley Fischer to Ibrahim Shihata, May 26, 1990.

In 1984 David Knox took over as the new vice president for Latin America, his predecessor, Ardito Barletta, having departed to become a presidential candidate in Panama. Knox recalls that one of his first questions was "'What is the Bank doing about the debt crisis?' And the answer I got was, by and large, 'very little.' And I said, 'Why? Surely this is critical, vital to these countries, and should we not be trying to do something?' And again the answer was, 'But surely that's what the Fund has been trying to do. . . . We shouldn't be meddling around with them too much.'"[79]

Knox's feeling that the Bank had become too subservient to the Fund was shared by Bank staff who were becoming increasingly frustrated by the short-term nature of the Fund's programs when the countries involved needed longer-term support. At the time the Bank was engaged in an extensive internal exercise termed "The Future Role of the World Bank," the principal purpose of which was to lay the groundwork for a capital increase.[80] At a May 1984 retreat for senior operational managers in connection with this exercise, a proposal was mooted that the risks of adverse external contingencies

> can and should be addressed through a different type of debt restructuring agreement than we have had in the past. The new style agreements should cover amortization falling due over, say, a three year period. . . . [T]he Bank's contribution to such multi-year restructurings should not be seen mainly in terms of the net new money we provide, although I do not believe we can be effective unless we are in a positive net transfer position throughout the multi-year period.[81]

Shortly thereafter, the Bank informally met with some bankers in London to gauge their interest in supporting such a multiyear restructuring program as a complement to a World Bank structural adjustment program in cases where a Fund standby arrangement might not be feasible.[82] The bankers made it very clear that as far as they were concerned the Bank had no credibility in these programs. Only the IMF was acceptable to the banks for these sorts of restructuring operations.[83] Although discussions with the Fund were initially fruitless, since it continued to insist that the current strategy was fine and consequently saw little need for anything different, it soon changed its mind on the virtues of multiyear restructuring.

In June 1984 eleven Latin debtors met in Cartagena, Colombia, to discuss their own strategy. This was six months after a planned secret meeting of the finance

79. David Knox, interview with Richard Webb and Devesh Kapur, May 21, 1992.
80. The exercise involved a dozen working groups, which consisted of some hundred individuals drawn from different parts of the Bank.
81. Presentation by D. Joseph Wood on "Role of the Bank" at Senior Operational Managers' Retreat, Bedford Springs, Pa., May 3–5, 1984, pp. 10–11.
82. Nicholas Hope, interview with the authors, September 1992.
83. Ibid.

ministers of Argentina, Brazil, Colombia, Mexico, and Peru had fallen through.[84] The June meeting was a more public affair, although little came of it. With talk of a Latin debtors' cartel now in the air, an impasse in the newly democratically installed government of Argentina's negotiations with the IMF, and a financial "hump" facing the debtors as the effects of the first round of reschedulings came due, the commercial banks made a moderate concession by moving away from annual rescheduling to multiyear rescheduling arrangements (MYRAs) at reduced interest rates. Whether by design or happenstance, the move forestalled a prospective revolt against the prevailing debt strategy. The choice of the cooperative debtor, Mexico, as the first country to be granted a MYRA, both demonstrated the rewards of cooperative behavior and ensured that Mexico would not defect.

MYRAs provided a safety valve by mitigating the immediate financial pressures that had been building up. Equally, they served to rekindle confidence in the management of the debt crisis. A strong impression was generated that finally Mexico was going to get out of the woods. This arrangement could then be extended to the other big debtors and thence to the smaller ones. But MYRA proved to be another Band-Aid for Mexico. And even as MYRAs were extended to several other countries, global economic performance began to stumble again. The political pressures against further squeezing expenditures in the face of mounting negative net transfers and collapsing economies were simply insupportable. Unsurprisingly, most of the countries could not stick to their programs.

Meanwhile, the Bank's Latin American region initiated another study to try to identify those countries that had liquidity problems and those that had solvency problems (and, in the case of the latter, needed debt reduction rather than more "concerted" lending); analyze the many proposals that were being made for dealing with the debt crisis (well over a hundred proposals had been made, but they all came down to a few basic ideas) and present a typology; and recommend the one that seemed most suitable.[85] The study recommended purchasing debt at a discount from the commercial banks and rescheduling them over longer terms, with write-offs in extreme cases, combined with SAL-type assistance from the Bank.

David Knox, then regional vice president for Latin America, informally sounded IMF staff on the study's conclusions, but their strong reaction persuaded him that sending the paper formally would simply create a storm.[86] In the Fund's view, a Bank study arguing that many of the countries were not solvent (and that merely

---

84. Silva-Herzog, interview with the authors, July 20, 1995. The meeting was to be hosted in Cuzco, Peru, by the Peruvian finance minister, Carlos Rodriguez Pastor, who, however, suddenly resigned. According to Silva-Herzog, the resignation was so sudden that at least one of the ministers actually showed up, not knowing that the meeting had been canceled.

85. Frederick Z. Jasperson, "Proposals for Dealing with the Developing Country Debt Problem: Their Impact on Economic Growth and Creditworthiness of the Heavily Indebted Latin American Countries," November 1984.

86. Knox, interview, May 21, 1992.

more lending would not help) would torpedo its efforts to orchestrate "involuntary lending." This would lead commercial banks to jump ship (something they were already trying to do).

The principal obstacle to the debt-purchasing proposal, as in the case of so many others, was the problem of financing it.[87] In this respect the scheme was similar to several proposals that suggested putting part of the developing-country debt into a shell, backed by the international community, which would go out and borrow money to buy these assets. Any proposal that argued that a small amount of capital could be leveraged into a large pool of assets was understandably attractive. The Bank's Finance complex had in fact already spent more than a year intensively examining one option—christened "The Bank's Bank"—an arm's-length financial subsidiary of the IBRD whose financial structuring would have allowed it to be much more highly leveraged than the IBRD. For a number of reasons (discussed in chapter 16) this proposal did not garner support.

But the reactions to the study's recommendations within the Bank also revealed the dilemmas facing both the Bank and the development community. While recognizing that some sort of debt relief was required to get these economies back on track, many among Bank staff and shareholders were ambivalent about a greater Bank involvement in debt workouts (such as allowing its resources to be used to finance a debt forgiveness scheme), out of concern that such a move would divert the institution from its main task: providing development finance to the poorer countries.[88]

The Intellectual Hiatus

As noted earlier, during this period the Bank's analytical work on the subject was largely confined to its operations complex, notably its Latin America region and the central policy staff. Many observers would later attribute the institution's circumspection—especially the absence of any public pronouncements or analysis that would appear to countenance some form of debt relief—to its dependence on financial markets for its own funding. Yet, perhaps unexpectedly, the boldest stance on the debt crisis was emanating from its Finance complex. Although its efforts to leverage the Bank's financial flows by creating an institutional affiliate ("The Bank's Bank") failed, it was nonetheless a serious attempt at institutional innovation. The Bank's treasurer, Eugene Rotberg, who enjoyed a formidable reputation in financial markets, bluntly noted in late 1984 that the commercial banks should stop operating under the assumption that the principal of their developing-country loans would eventually be repaid.[89]

87. An early suggestion to this effect had emanated from Peter Kenen in 1983. See Peter B. Kenen, "A Bailout Plan for the Banks," New York Times, March 6, 1983, p. F3.

88. A strongly articulated view to this effect was Willem H. Buiter and T. N. Srinivasan, "Rewarding the Profligate and Punishing the Prudent and Poor: Some Recent Proposals for Debt Relief," World Development, vol. 15 (March 1987), pp. 411–17.

89. "World Bank Treasurer Warns of 'Pretense' on Repayments," International Herald Tribune, November 14, 1984.

But overall, there was little doubt that for much of the decade the institution maintained a low dialectical profile. This was particularly true of the one part of the Bank that a priori would have been expected to take the lead in stimulating research and discussion on this issue: its research complex, which was also responsible for the annual *World Debt Tables*. This abnegation poses a puzzle given that its staff and budgetary resources devoted to the study of development issues vastly overshadowed those of any other institution. During this period, the institution's eloquence on policy failures by developing countries, and on the consequences of these policies for their economic predicament, was remarkable. However, the simultaneous prudence demonstrated by the institution, with regard to the international causes of the debt problem appears in retrospect to be equally remarkable. After all, the issue's salience at the time could hardly be overemphasized.

In contrast to the Fund, which is often caricatured as the multilateral equivalent of the Catholic Church, the Bank has been likened to a contentious collection of Protestant sects. Substantially greater room for differing views and more vigorous debate (albeit within certain parameters) had been an important characteristic of the Bank's research work in the 1970s. But during the period 1983 to 1986, the Research Department underwent a profound change. The "let a hundred flowers bloom" philosophy, which undoubtedly had also yielded weeds, was displaced by an outlook that was the research management equivalent to planting only genetically engineered products. An episode related to the analysis of the debt issue provides a somber illustration of the problem.[90]

In June 1985, Jeffrey Sachs, a professor at Harvard University, presented a paper at a retreat for staff from the research complex entitled, "Conditionality and the Debt Crisis: Some Thoughts for the World Bank." He was subsequently invited to extend this paper for submission to the *World Bank Economic Review* (a new research journal launched by the Bank) by its managing editor, Mark Leiserson. The subject was topical and Sachs's eclectic views would establish the independence of the new research publication, inoculating it against the suspicion that it was simply another Bank mouthpiece. The article received favorable reviews at a meeting of the journal's editorial board (in March 1986), and it was slated for publication in the journal's inaugural issue.[91] Questions were raised regarding the political sensitivity of the article, but the editorial board decided not to stand in the way of publication.

Sachs's paper, reflecting on the Bank's shift into loans conditioned on macroeconomic policy reforms, argued that the role for conditionality-based lending was

90. The next few paragraphs have drawn heavily on a host of internal Bank memoranda.

91. The article received favorable comments from three external referees and two editorial board members assigned to read it. There were, however, some reservations about the paper's technical analysis and its relation to the paper's central arguments. A special technical review was sought from three outside referees who concluded that while some qualifications were in order, the technical analysis was not crucial to the central arguments in the paper.

"more restricted than generally believed, because enforcement of conditionality is rather weak and our knowledge of what constitutes 'good behavior' is limited." It further argued that "the incentives for a country to abide by conditionality terms are also likely to be reduced by a large overhang of external indebtedness. . . . The IMF and World Bank should encourage debt forgiveness by private sector creditors in cases of extreme indebtedness, rather than trying to plug a large financial gap."[92]

Sometime during the following month, Vice President Krueger, to whom the Economic Research Staff (ERS) reported, read the paper and evidently disapproved of it. Her stance was transmitted through the research administrator (Deepak Lal, who was also the editor's administrative superior), who asked that the article be withdrawn from consideration. The editor questioned the propriety of the action, given the Bank's officially stated purpose in establishing the journal as an independent journal, over which censorship would not be exercised except in extremis. The editor's protests, that he could not recognize the authority of a single member of the editorial board to issue instructions that were the province of the whole editorial board, were overruled by the vice president. At this point the editor resigned from his job.[93] A few months later, the editor of the other new research journal launched by the Bank—the World Bank Research Observer—also resigned, citing serious differences with the working style of the research administrator.

These events can be understood in the context of the evolution of the organizational framework of the Bank's research after the arrival of Anne Krueger as vice president in 1982 (see chapter 18). Krueger's arrival nearly coincided with the eruption of the debt crisis. A crucial element in the management of the debt strategy by what George Soros would label as "the collective of lenders," was image management. Critical to the construction of image was the appearance of control, which has always been an essential prop to maintaining financial confidence. From the inception of the crisis, the Bank, anxious to avoid upsetting the delicate balancing act being orchestrated by this collective, especially in light of the strong uncertainty of the nature of the crisis and potent risks to the global financial system, imposed a tight control over internal analysis of the debt issue. A fear that the institution would be unable to separate any internal debate from its external message—understandable in an institution where internal debates were increasingly leaked as a routine matter—led to a stifling of debate on the subject within the institution. In early 1987, Benjamin King, called back from retirement to serve as acting vice president for research following Krueger's departure, found "a virtual taboo on any criticism of the Baker plan or suggestion that it wasn't working. This

92. For an early exposition of Sachs's position on the mutual benefits to debtors and creditors from debt relief under certain circumstances, see Jeffrey Sachs, "Managing the LDC Debt Crisis," Brookings Papers on Economic Activity, no. 2 (1986), pp. 397–440.

93. The editor's attempts to reassign to another part of the Bank were initially blocked until it became apparent that the ERS management had exceeded their authority. Leiserson joined the OED before leaving the Bank a few years later.

was, I think, the strongest suppression of free speech, by far, that I ever experienced in the Bank, which hitherto exercised little or no censorship."[94]

The Bank might have been better placed to provide leadership if it had been able to offer a rigorous intellectual analysis of the debt problem. That this did not occur was partly a result of a failure to strengthen the analytical capacity of the debt division, which in turn was a consequence of internal administrative turbulence in the ERS vice presidency. Although at one level it was simply one of those unpleasant things that all organizations periodically stumble into, drastic changes in management and personnel in the ERS vice presidency and the resulting rapid turnover in the Bank's research staff had significant effects on its research.

Censorship was applied, in particular, to the *World Debt Tables*, the Bank's annual publication analyzing the external debt of developing countries. The onset of the crisis greatly increased the document's visibility. A new (and initially modest) analytical introduction was added, which began to be viewed as an official institutional statement by the Bank on the debt issue. Drafts now had to be cleared by the Bank's senior management. More important, they were also reviewed by key G-5 members and the IMF, a move that compromised the independence of the analysis. This piece always contained scattered comments to the effect that there were problems, particularly for African countries, but they were very carefully worded. While Bank staff fumed at the asymmetry between the Fund's heavy-handed vetting of the *Debt Tables* statement and the Bank's scant opportunities to review Fund statements, it simply reflected the fact that the IMF was, without question, the senior partner on debt management.[95]

A notable exception was a conference entitled "International Debt and the Developing Countries," organized by the Bank's Research Department in mid-1984. The overview of the proceedings, published a year later, noted that the discussions had been "sobering," an acknowledgment of many serious unresolved problems: "Many participants agreed with the notion that some form of debt relief (in effect, forgiveness) may now be necessary. This viewpoint is rather new for market-oriented professional economists."[96] This was the farthest the Research Department would travel on this particular road until 1987.

The *World Debt Tables*, of course, were only a small part of the activities undertaken by the research complex to understand the nature of, and propose solutions to, the economic predicament that many developing countries now found

---

94. Benjamin King, personal correspondence, May 23, 1995.

95. For instance, although the Fund insisted on a few weeks of leeway to give their input to Bank drafts before anything was put out, corresponding materials from the IMF were typically received a day or two before they were presented to the Fund's Board or to its managing director.

96. Gordon W. Smith and John T. Cuddington, *International Debt and the Developing Countries* (World Bank, 1985), p. 17.

themselves in. The intellectual focus of the new group in the Research Department was on inappropriate policies in developing countries, an assessment that came to be broadly equated with any government intervention in markets. While major new research initiatives were launched, their emphasis, especially in the case of four large cross-country comparative projects, was on developing-country policies. Although observers both within the Bank and outside perceived the Research Department's messages as often simplistic and their tone strident, on two issues in particular—a drastic rethinking of the role of the state and trade liberalization—its overall thrust presaged the direction the Bank's borrowers would move toward in the ensuing years.

But relatively few resources were directed toward analysis of the major assumptions underlying the debt strategy as well as the policies of developed countries relevant to the debt problem, for example, taxation or regulatory policies relating to flight capital. There were exceptions: OECD trade policies and their effects on developing-country exports were given good attention. And analyses of OECD macroeconomic policies were commissioned in connection with *World Development Report 1985*, subtitled "International Capital and Economic Development." But that report, as released, was very restrained in this regard. In any case, whether by default or by design, the Bank's intellectual stance fortuitously dovetailed with the principal message of the overall debt management strategy: debt relief was unwise; it would simply postpone adjustment and make matters worse for the countries in the long run by eliminating any future access to international capital markets. Instead, belt tightening together with export-led growth should take care of the problem. That there was a problem was evident in a note by the Bank's senior vice president for operations, Ernest Stern, to his new president, Barber Conable, soon after the latter's arrival: "the public intellectual leadership [of the Bank] *has* been lacking [over the past five years]."[97]

Matters changed rapidly in 1987. As noted in the following section, the Bank's research complex became veritably fecund on the debt issue, a role further strengthened by the arrival of Stanley Fischer.[98] According to Fischer, however, the institution continued to be subject to pressures from its principal shareholders (particularly the United States, but also Germany and the United Kingdom).[99] Since debt, like devaluation, is an issue associated with expectations that can be

97. Memorandum, Ernest Stern to Barber B. Conable, "Organizational Issues," September 2, 1986.

98. A staff member reporting on a meeting of the G-10 to discuss the Bank's role in the debt crisis recorded that "the US delegate asserted that the . . . Bank already has 'too much uncontrolled internal activism' in this regard, manifested in . . . 'papers which turn up' that go well beyond what is supported by either senior management or the Board." Memorandum, Fred Levy to Moeen A. Qureshi, David Hopper, and Ernest Stern, July 20, 1988.

99. Letter, Stanley Fischer to Nicholas Stern, May 19, 1992.

self-fulfilling, creditor countries insisted that the Bank not raise controversial issues, especially debt relief, and downplay its skepticism regarding the viability of the official strategy.

A different issue arising from the Bank's analysis of the debt crisis concerns the processes it uses to gather and generate knowledge (these issues are examined further in chapter 12 of volume 2). Anyone interested in the intellectual history of the debt crisis would be struck by the degree to which the intellectual debate was dominated by voices from the United States, in contrast to the virtual absence of voices from the countries bearing the brunt of the crisis. This was also the case with the Bank. Conferences and symposia organized by the Bank on the debt crisis rarely included contributors from the debtor countries.[100]

The Bank's defense in this regard (and not just in the case of the debt crisis) is that it was simply looking for the best researchers to examine this complex problem, and the affected countries simply did not have that talent. This rationale, reinforced by reasons of administrative convenience, even if accepted at face value, cast doubt on the Bank's accomplishments in helping develop indigenous analytical capability over previous decades. But it is perhaps also true that the "client" for many Bank research staff has tended to be the North American academic research community. The dominance of economists in the Bank, and their strong links with the U.S. academic community, made it that much more difficult for other sources of ideas and intellectual discourse that were not part of this "loop" to be heard in this club.

Be that as it may, during the early years of the crisis, the periodic publicly disseminated formulations of the latest "consensus" on the debt crisis by the Bank (and its Bretton Woods twin), served largely to rationalize the political interests of the major shareholders, especially the United States, and by extension, of the commercial banks. Consensus is more easily achieved among self-selected groups sharing a common intellectual discourse. And the process of arriving at a consensus can serve a legitimizing role, however inadvertent the exclusionary mechanisms.

Phase II, 1985–88: Muddling On

In October 1985, the new secretary of the U.S. Treasury, James Baker III, unveiled a set of proposals that addressed the debt crisis focusing particularly on fifteen severely indebted middle-income countries.[101] The proposals—which would shortly metamorphose into a "plan" under a barrage of media coverage—called for

---

100. For instance, one organized in April 1984 and the other in January 1989.

101. The countries were Argentina, Bolivia, Brazil, Chile, Colombia, Côte d'Ivoire, Ecuador, Mexico, Morocco, Nigeria, Peru, Philippines, Uruguay, Venezuela, and Yugoslavia. The "Baker-15" soon became the "Baker-17" with the inclusion of Costa Rica and Jamaica.

"net new lending [by the commercial banks] in the range of $20 billion for the next three years."[102] For the first time since the inception of the crisis, the U.S. Treasury acknowledged that the Multilateral Development Banks (MDBs) needed "to be brought into the debt strategy in a stronger way."[103] In particular, Baker recognized that there was "ample room to expand the World Bank's fast-disbursing lending," so that the World Bank and the IDB could "increase their disbursements to principal debtors by roughly 50 percent from the current annual level of nearly $6 billion."[104]

Baker's gambit—reflecting the haste with which the proposals were formulated with apparently no consultations outside the U.S. government—reflected a growing perception that the "buying time" strategy was again sputtering. Between 1982 and 1985, net transfer of financial resources from Latin America had amounted to a debilitating 5.3 percent of GDP.[105] Per capita national income had declined by 10 percent since 1981. The faint glimmer of recovery and turnaround, prompted by the dramatic change in the current account between 1982 and 1984, had begun to fade. Crucially, the risks seemed foremost in Mexico. By the end of 1984, Mexico's stabilization program began to run off track, and by mid-1985 it fell out of compliance with the IMF. The three-year Extended Fund Facility signed with the IMF in 1982 had called for a budget deficit of 3.5 percent of GDP by 1985 and projected output growth at 6 percent; the actual deficit in 1985 was close to 10 percent, and growth was just 2.6 percent.[106] The devastating earthquake in September 1985 and the collapse of oil prices shortly thereafter, meant that at least for Mexico, the earlier strategy had well and truly run aground. Meanwhile, in July 1985, the new president of Peru, Alan Garcia, announced at his inauguration ceremonies—attended by the new secretary of the Treasury, James Baker—that Peru would unilaterally limit its debt-service payments to a ceiling of 10 percent of export receipts. With talk of contagion in the air, Baker's proposals held a twin significance: a concession in the official U.S. stance, acknowledging that mere belt tightening was not the answer—that growth was necessary for these countries to regain creditworthiness; and a sign to the world at large that someone was in charge and something was being done.[107] The

102. "Statement of the Honorable James A. Baker III, Secretary of the Treasury of the United States, before the Joint Annual Meeting of the International Monetary Fund and the World Bank, October 8, 1985, Seoul, South Korea." Reprinted in Pedro-Pablo Kuczynski, *Latin American Debt* (Johns Hopkins University Press, 1988), p. 103.

103. Ibid.

104. Ibid.

105. By way of comparison, the war reparations imposed on France during 1872–75 amounted to 5.6 percent of GDP; and those imposed on Germany between 1925 and 1932 amounted to 2.5 percent of GDP. See Andrés Bianchi, Robert Devlin, and Joseph Ramos, "The Adjustment Process in Latin America 1981–1986," paper prepared for World Bank-IMF Symposium on Growth-Oriented Adjustment Programs, Washington D.C., February 25–27, 1987, table 9.

106. Nora Lustig, *Mexico: The Remaking of an Economy* (Brookings, 1992), table 2-3.

107. According to Hobart Rowen, en route to Seoul, a National Security Council staffer confided to him: "There's not much there [in the Baker Plan], it's only an effort to buy time."

initiative represented a skillful effort by a politician adept at conveying a sense of control and rekindling hopes that the matter would soon be resolved. But fundamentally, Baker's proposals remained grounded in the view that the crisis was a liquidity problem.

The role granted to the Bank by the initiative came as a surprise to the institution. Barely three months had elapsed since the U.S. Treasury had argued: "At the present time we see no need for a GCI. On the basis of current information it is not clear to us how the Bank can increase its lending programs significantly at this time, without weakening lending standards or displacing alternative sources of finance in creditworthy countries."[108] A month before the Seoul meetings, the Bank's management, increasingly troubled by the almost capricious disposition of the U.S. Treasury, had convinced John Whitehead, then deputy secretary of state, to make a case for the Bank to Baker.[109] In addition, the Bank conveyed a note to Baker through the Bretton Woods Committee, emphasizing that the Bank's lending program was at its maximum level given the "rigid interpretation of existing policies. . . . *What is needed at Seoul is a clear political endorsement of an expansion in IBRD lending.*"[110] To this end, the note added that the United States would have to reassure other major shareholders that it would endorse a GCI in the near future. The U.S. Treasury consulted the Bank only forty-eight hours before Baker went public, and then, too, only on the narrow issue of the choice of the fifteen countries that Baker included in his proposals.[111]

Baker's proposals, which envisaged that the multilateral development banks in general, and the World Bank in particular, would play a more important role (but with the IMF continuing to play the "central role"), were more than simply a

---

Rowen, *Self Inflicted Wounds: From LBJ's Guns and Butter to Reagan's Voodoo Economics* (Times Books, 1994), p. 293.

108. Untitled note circulated to members of Congress from Bruce Thompson, assistant secretary (Legislative Affairs), U.S. Treasury, June 11, 1985.

109. The Bank's management had maintained cordial relations with Whitehead since 1980 when Goldman Sachs, which he then headed, had been added to its U.S. underwriting group.

110. "Aide Memoire," attachment to note from Moeen A. Qureshi to A. W. Clausen, September 19, 1985. The Bretton Woods Committee, a nonprofit American organization, was established in 1984 to serve as an unofficial educational and lobbying group for the IFIs.

111. A less commented upon aspect of Baker's Seoul proposals was his debt initiative for low-income countries. During a discussion of the use of Trust Fund reflows at a meeting of the IMF's Board (on September 13, 1985), the United States tabled a proposal on the use of these funds that went "well beyond" the Fund's proposals. Hitherto, the low-income countries had been regarded as much more the Bank's bailiwick. But here, too, the Bank was not even consulted, as Stern's discomfiture indicated: "It is, of course, regrettable that the U.S. would table a proposal involving the Bank in a major way without any prior consultation that I am aware of." Memorandum, Ernest Stern to the Managing Committee, "U.S. Proposal for an IMF/Bank Program to Promote Economic Adjustment," OPS/MC85-53, September 16, 1985. The only consultation had been with the G-6 and China.

Table 11-4. *Debt-Related Capital Flows to Latin America, 1978–93*
Annual averages, billions of U.S. dollars

Flows and transfers[a]	Prelude, 1978–81	Beginning through Baker, 1982–85	Baker through Brady, 1986–89	Post-Brady, 1990–93
Net flows				
World Bank	1.0	1.8	1.7	0.7
IMF	(0.1)	3.1	(0.4)	(1.0)
Official (excluding World Bank, IMF)	2.6	0.4	3.1	3.7
Private (publicly guaranteed)	15.6	11.8	1.4	1.0
Private (nonguaranteed)	7.4	(0.5)	(2.4)	7.2
Net transfers				
World Bank	0.4	0.8	(0.3)	(2.1)
IMF	(0.2)	2.6	(1.6)	(2.2)
Official (excluding World Bank, IMF)	1.6	(0.8)	1.6	0.7
Private (publicly guaranteed)	6.4	(6.0)	(15.3)	(7.9)
Private (nonguaranteed)	3.1	(7.7)	(6.1)	5.0

Source: World Bank, *World Debt Tables*, 1991 (CD-ROM version) and 1994.

a. Net flows on debt are disbursements minus amortization. Net transfers are net flows minus interest payments.

recognition of the need to shift gears from debt servicing through the compression of domestic demand (the standard IMF stabilization tool) to augmenting debt-servicing capacity by way of growth. As the figures in table 11-4 indicate, with the IMF's resources now exhausted and the commercial banks increasingly reluctant to expand net lending, the employment of MDB resources for debt-related "gap-filling" had become a financial reality.

The modest loosening of the reins by the U.S. Treasury foreshadowed a large increase in structural adjustment lending by the Bank, first to the SILICs and subsequently to the SIMICs. The staff was informed that "we foresee no difficulty in substantially expanding our lending program for those countries on the list, and indeed for others, where we can reach agreement on an acceptable multi-year adjustment program."[112] Country studies prepared in late 1985 argued that it was feasible to bring about rapid changes in policy which would have a sufficiently swift impact on output growth and export expansion to resolve the debt problem. But when the results were presented at a Board seminar, the optimistic prognosis and the realism in the Baker numbers was contested. The executive director representing one of the constituencies with Latin American members, demonstrated

112. Memorandum, Ernest Stern to operational vice presidents, "The Baker Proposal," November 5, 1985, p. 2.

that under equally plausible, but different, assumptions, the numbers simply did not add up: "If we are intellectually honest . . . we must admit that permanent debt relief must be part of a solution, and . . . we should not be afraid to say so."[113]

But in a financial crisis, as in war, truth is the first casualty. In hindsight, these studies proved to be "extremely optimistic."[114] Adjustment lending commitments in 1986 to Latin America tripled to $2 billion (about 40 percent of total Bank loan commitments to the region) from the average during 1983–85. Adjustment lending flows in 1986 represented a tenth of all international flows to the region, a significant jump over previous years.[115]

Although the Baker proposals caused the Bank's profile in the debt crisis to rise, the institution already was intensely involved in several SIMICs on the debt issue. Earlier, Jamaica had been an exception to Latin America's norm of the IMF playing the lead role among external promoters of macroeconomic reform. In Jamaica's case the Bank had shared the stage with the Fund and U.S. bilateral aid in supporting a major structural adjustment lending program. Despite Jamaica's enjoying the highest per capita lending by the Bank to any Latin American country during the first half of the 1980s, its external public debt as a fraction of GDP tripled, as did its debt-service ratio, even while actual policy reform was anemic.[116] As Krueger notes, politics intervened:

> Officials at the multilaterals recognized the inadequacy of Jamaican fiscal policy reforms and were reluctant to proceed with lending. . . . But these officials could not suspend lending easily because of U.S. pressure to support the new administration of Mr. Seaga. Despite U.S. rhetoric supporting policy reform in developing countries, Washington's enthusiasm for a change of government outweighed any balanced assessment of the actual policy mix in Jamaica.[117]

An interesting case was presented by Colombia, where the Bank's involvement helped forestall a debt crisis. Although Colombia had abstained from the borrow-

113. Statement by Kenneth Coates (executive director representing Argentina, Bolivia, Chile, Paraguay, Peru, and Uruguay) at Board seminar, "The Debt Problem and Growth," EDS86-1, February 21, 1986.

114. David Knox, interview with the authors, May 21, 1992. This view was echoed by another staff member involved with these studies who felt that they were rather impractical in that "we made these grossly over-optimistic assumptions." Nicholas Hope, interview with the authors, September 30, 1992.

115. In contrast, during 1983–85, adjustment lending disbursements to Latin America (about $700 million annually) were less than 2 percent of total disbursements to the region. Figures are from World Bank, "Report on Adjustment Lending II: Policies for the Recovery Growth," March 1990, annex tables 5.2–5.4.

116. World Bank, "Program Performance Audit Report: Jamaica, SALS II and III and Overview of SALs I–III," OED Report 8018, August 11, 1989, fig. 1, p. xviii.

117. Anne O. Krueger, *Economic Policies at Cross-Purposes: The United States and Developing Countries* (Brookings, 1993), p. 158. The fiscal deficit under the radical Manley regime averaged 13 percent of GNP during 1974–79; that under the conservative Seaga regime averaged 17.5 percent during 1980–85. Ibid., table 7-6.

ing binge of the 1970s, it, too, fell victim to the contagion effect that swept across the region after 1982. Even the country's short-term trade lines were in jeopardy. The historically strained relations between the IMF and Colombia led to a creative approach by all parties concerned: Colombia undertook macroeconomic reforms, with World Bank assistance, and the IMF agreed to monitor the program and give the arrangement its seal of good housekeeping, despite the absence of a standby. The Bank's annual lending to Colombia more than doubled in the period 1984–86 relative to the previous three years. The money, together with the World Bank's monitoring of Colombia's program, helped persuade commercial banks to voluntarily restore trade lines canceled earlier.[118]

But it was Mexico that became the test case for the Bank's involvement in the Baker strategy (see also volume 2, chapter 3). In the early years of the crisis, the Bank had been quietly working with the Mexican authorities, as and when its help was sought in technical analysis of various proposals being put forward by the commercial banks. An important policy breakthrough—on interest rates—was achieved in 1984.[119] Following Baker, the institution's role rapidly escalated. In April 1986 the Bank achieved a further breakthrough in its policy dialogue with Mexico with a half billion dollar trade policy adjustment loan that indelibly altered Mexico's trade policy stance. Overall lending volumes and the share of quick-disbursement operations rose rapidly. The dialogue between Bank officials and their Mexican counterparts became increasingly intense and frequent. Monthly exchanges between Ernest Stern and Gustavo Petricioli, the new secretary of finance and public credit, would painstakingly cover outstanding issues on each loan, both under preparation as well as those being implemented—identifying the bottlenecks and the steps required to reach resolution; and the exchanges would determine who would take responsibility for what steps and on what schedule—to expedite loan effectiveness and disbursements.[120] The Bank was faced with a tough balancing act between remaining firm on the policy conditionalities of its loans, on the one hand, and ensuring a flow of financial resources, on the other.[121] In the Mexican case, that balance was quite successful, at least until the end of the decade.

Outside Latin America for a time the immediate prognosis also appeared promising in Nigeria, where the Bank's lending sharply increased. In Yugoslavia,

118. Colombia secured a $1.5 billion financing package of short-term trade lines and $1 billion in medium-term credits from commercial banks. See also Colombia case study in chapter 10.

119. An umbrella agreement called GIRA (General Interest Rate Agreement) sharply reduced the level and range of interest rate subsidies across key economic sectors.

120. Petricioli had replaced Silva-Herzog in June 1986.

121. A senior World Bank staff member recalls a luncheon conversation with a U.S. Treasury official at the time when, over soup, the latter's stance was all: "We want you to be tough on conditionality." By the time coffee arrived, he had shifted completely to "How much will you be able to disburse this year?"

lending declined, owing to the country's unwillingness to proceed with any mean-ingful reforms. The case of the largest debtor, Brazil, is examined later.

In the final analysis, the Baker initiative did achieve some of its objectives. The mere recognition that belt-tightening per se was not the answer and growth was necessary for the indebted countries to regain creditworthiness was regarded as an important shift in the official U.S. position: it bought more time for the commercial banks, allowing them to strengthen their balance sheets. But perhaps its principal strength was psychological. By throwing sands of reassurance to the world at large that someone was in charge and something was being done, it checked the rising political tide that threatened to weaken the embankments of the debt management strategy. But, for the most part, Baker's proposals achieved little for the debtor countries. Indeed, it may well have prolonged the crisis. And the Bank's initial spurt of lending also proved short-lived. The reasons for both are examined in the next section.

Diagnostic Issues

With the Fund taking the lead in the early years of the crisis, short-term stabilization through demand management was the dominant policy goal. This was understandable, because of both mounting macroeconomic instability and the Fund's objective to avoid any breakdown in debt-service payments. As a result, however, the conflict between stabilization and growth objectives was seriously underestimated. The priority placed on servicing external debt put unprecedented demands on domestic savings, crowding out domestic investment. The resulting sharp decline in domestic investment dragged growth down with it.

The Baker initiative, recognizing that stagflationary conditions were seriously undermining debtor countries' capacity to service debt, put growth back on the agenda. The principal plank of the Bank's post-Baker strategy was that by judicious lending, focused on strengthening exports, it could help restore growth and im-prove the balance of payments, thereby helping the countries to work their way out of the debt crisis. To this end, "acceptable" programs were now required to incorporate policy changes that would:

> include the role of the private sector, the public investment program, the incentive framework (including prices, subsidies, price control mechanism, taxation and related matters), the relative openness of the economy in terms of its import regime and its export promotion efforts and the policy regarding the operation of existing public enter-prises both in terms of their burden on the budget and in terms of the inefficiency umbrella for private enterprises.[122]

By now the Bank, like many other Washington-based analysts, had become firmly convinced that the roots of the crisis lay in the quality of economic manage-

---

122. Memorandum, Stern to operational vice presidents, November 5, 1985.

ment of its borrowers. Whatever the relative weight of other causes, economic management in its borrowers (and non-borrowing shareholders, for that matter) had clearly been inadequate, in some instances wretched. Postmortems on the debt crisis by the Bank and Fund made the case that the protracted nature of the crisis stripped bare the depth of problems that had been masked by recourse to external borrowings. But the more valid this argument was, the more questionable was the belief that a measure of austerity and balance of payments relief would produce rapid recovery. One would expect that the deeper the hole, the more would be the time and effort required to pull out of it. As noted earlier, internally doubts were being cast on a central tenet of the Bank's strategy: that a quick transformation could be achieved, in particular, through export-led growth.

A large body of Bank studies had challenged the dogma of "export pessimism." By convincingly pointing to the East Asia experience, these studies had made a strong case for the considerable opportunities existing in export-led growth. But the fervor with which the Bank preached this idea led it to become overoptimistic about the supply response to "stroke-of-pen" changes in exchange rates, as well as government regulations and price liberalization. Measures necessary to ensure sustained increases in exports such as industrial restructuring or searching for product and market niches, would take much longer to put in place. But crucially, the investment response continued to be tepid, hemmed in by the twin roadblocks of economic uncertainty and fiscal pressures.

By the end of 1986, as the Baker initiative appeared increasingly moribund for the debtor countries, it was evident that its core intellectual premise—that the crisis was a liquidity problem—was fundamentally flawed. But the failure highlighted a broader issue: the understanding of the problem—its many dimensions and interlinkages—was much weaker than had been acknowledged. The haste to carry out reforms had led to an underappreciation of the fact that solutions frequently create their own problems. These might be different and perhaps more tractable but nonetheless ensured that the convergence to a sustainable growth path and restoration of economic well-being would take much longer. Devaluations usually made for healthier trade balances but had adverse effects on fiscal deficits, yielding inflation that undid the effects of the devaluation. The reasons for, and effects of, the large declines in production, in particular, were poorly understood. Thus, despite cutting expenditures, fiscal deficits would remain higher than had been forecast, as government revenues declined even faster as GDP fell and interest rates rose. Rapidly liberalizing the financial sector might lead to immediate and appreciable efficiency gains. But bank examiners, trained accountants, and a working regulatory system do not appear as fast as needed; and as experience with financial sector liberalization would demonstrate, there were quite mundane, but still sound, reasons, why haste often made waste.[123] The long period of economic

123. This had already been evident from the failures of the "Southern-Cone" experiments at the beginning of the 1980s.

and political uncertainty meant that changes in economic policy notwithstanding, capital flight remained important. In order to stem capital flight and rein in aggregate demand, governments were forced to increase interest rates sharply. But the resulting inimical effects on growth could undermine the larger program, exacerbating problems in the banking sector as well as those of indebted firms.[124] Not only did the adverse effects on growth ricochet onto government revenues, but with a growing domestic debt, higher interest rates adversely affected the fiscal deficit as well.[125] The fiscal cost of high inflation via the Tanzi effect (revenues lagging behind rising inflation-driven expenditures) was also a matter of serious concern.

The early reform efforts of the Bank focused on changing government policies, particularly with regard to the trade regime. Gradually, however, as the dominant threads in the Bank's reform efforts coalesced around a fundamental rethinking of the role of the state, the initial efforts at changing government policies expanded to encompass a more ambitious agenda: from deregulation to civil service reforms, from the reform of state-owned enterprises to privatization. The underlying thrust of the changes was both to reduce and to transform the role of the state and state institutions. These efforts were propelled by a complex amalgam of forces: shifting ideological and intellectual currents; intra-institutional dynamics; and pressures from the large shareholders. But to a considerable extent, the Bank was pushing against doors that already were being wrenched open by the economic collapse engendered by the debt crisis, reflecting changing economic thinking in many of the countries themselves.

Financial Impediments

The resource targets in the Baker initiative were extremely modest in relation to the magnitude of the problem.[126] Whereas net transfers from Latin America for this period were of the order of $90 billion, the targets for new lending by the commer-

---

124. The Brazilian financial sector provided a notable exception: Bank income was buoyed by substantial arbitrage profits arising from a complex indexation scheme for financial assets.

125. With rising real interest rates and falling asset prices, asset price deflation, and overindebtedness (the latter a result of prior expectations of growth and of current and future wealth) can feed on each other in a debt deflationary spiral, further imperiling economic activity. The classic explanation of such boom-and-bust economies goes back to Irving Fisher, "The Debt-Deflation Theory of the Great Depression," 1933, cited in Stephanie Flanders, "History Lesson," *Financial Times* (London), June 19, 1995, p. 21.

126. One of the most acerbic critics of the adverse effects of inadequate external assistance during financial emergencies has been Sachs. See, for instance, Jeffrey Sachs "Life in the Economic Emergency Room," in John Williamson, ed., *The Political Economy of Reform* (Washington, D.C.: Institute for International Economics, 1994), pp. 501–24.

Figure 11-2. *Net Debt-Related Flows and Transfers to SIMICs, 1980–88*
Percent

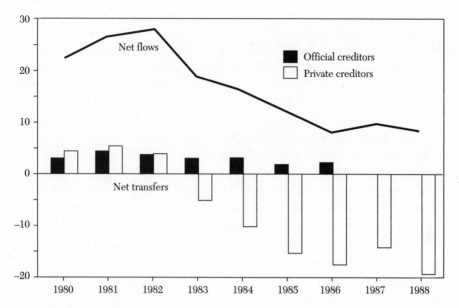

Source: *World Debt Tables*, 1988–89.

cial banks ($7 billion annually for three years) represented an interest refinancing ratio of just 25 percent.[127] In the end, even these modest flows were not forthcoming. While the multilaterals achieved the targets set for them, accounting for half of total net flows, commercial bank lending fell far short of expectations. As against the Baker targets of $20 billion, the commercial banks reportedly provided $4 billion between 1986 and 1988.[128] Furthermore, the resources forthcoming from the other public sector sources, the bilaterals and the IMF, were also meager. The result, as figure 11-2 indicates, was a further financial hemorrhaging in the SIMICs.

The disappointing performance of the Baker initiative on the financial front was perhaps unsurprising given its essential public relations purpose.[129] However, this

127. Ishrat Husain and Ishac Diwan, "Introduction," in Husain and Diwan, eds., *Dealing with the Debt Crisis* (World Bank, 1989), p. 4.

128. There is some dispute on whether the effort by the commercial banks was more substantial than what the above figures indicate (for instance, on how to treat arrears and repayments for debt-buyback schemes). See ibid., esp. table 11-1.

129. A contrasting perspective is Harold James, who notes in his semi-official history of the IMF, that "the flows to the Baker Plan countries were *somewhat lower* than envisaged by [Secretary Baker]. . . . [T]hey amounted to $28.6 billion rather than the $40 billion that might have been provided." James, *International Monetary Cooperation Since Bretton Woods* (Oxford University Press, 1996), p. 397. Emphasis added. According to World Bank

consequence was also due in part to the fact that the commonality of interests that had held the creditors together was rapidly fading. European banks had obtained generous tax breaks in making loan loss provisions and (except for the U.K. banks) had almost fully reserved for their developing-country loans. Moreover, the dollar's depreciation had driven down the dollar-denominated developing-country debt to a small fraction of the portfolio of European and Japanese banks. With the growth of a secondary market in discounted developing-country debt, small and regional U.S. banks had begun to exit. But perhaps epitomizing the lack of confidence in the Baker strategy was Citibank's announcement in May 1987 that it was adding $3 billion (25 percent of its total developing-country loans) to its bad-debt reserves.

The lack of an enforcement mechanism compounded the problem of fraying common creditor interests. Whereas in the earlier period the IMF and the U.S. Federal Reserve Board could promote "concerted" lending by tying Fund resources to additional lending from the commercial banks, the principal actors now saw a significant shift in their bargaining strengths. By 1985 the commercial banks were in a much healthier financial position while the Fund was facing large negative flows from Latin America.

Unfortunately, the official strategy did not alter to accommodate the new reality. By continuing to make their lending dependent on some resources forthcoming from the commercial banks, which (understandably) now demanded that their loans be serviced as a condition of participation, the Fund and the Bank lost leverage and willy-nilly became debt collectors for the commercial banks. Although the IMF's later refusal to acknowledge this role was understandable, there can be little doubt on this score.[130] Given its central role in the crisis, as Karin Lissakers, later U.S. executive director at the IMF, put it, "The IMF was in a sense, therefore, the creditor community's enforcer."[131] This view was echoed by Jacques Polak, the former research director and subsequently the Dutch executive director at the IMF:

> In the second half of the 1980s, however, commercial banks began to exploit this [linkage] approach. No longer afraid of becoming the victims of a generalized debt crisis, the banks began to realize that they could insist on favorable terms for themselves by blocking a country's access to Fund credit (and to other credit linked to a Fund arrangement). The Fund was thus pushed increasingly into being used by the commercial banks in the collection of their debts.[132]

---

figures, net flows to the "Baker-17" countries amounted to $21.7 billion during 1986–88; those to the heavily indebted middle-income countries (the country coverage was somewhat different) amounted to $26.1 billion during the same period. See *World Debt Tables, 1989–90*, tables 4, I.3.

130. See James Boughton, "The IMF and the Latin American Debt Crisis: Seven Common Criticisms," IMF paper on policy analysis and assessment, PPAA/94/23, October 1994.

131. Lissakers, *Banks, Borrowers and the Establishment*, p. 201.

132. Jacques Polak, *The Changing Nature of IMF Conditionality*, Princeton University Essays in International Finance 184 (September 1991), p. 15.

For its part, the World Bank's insistence that debtor countries remain "current on MLT [medium- and long-term] interest payments" to the commercial banks to retain access to Bank lending, served a similar purpose. A new, but still restrictive, policy on lending into arrears was formulated in 1986.[133] However, at the end of 1987 an internal Bank "Debt Task Force" suggested that the Bank's practice of making its loans contingent upon a "satisfactory" financing plan, thereby emphasizing agreement with the creditors, had resulted "in some circumstances [in] financing packages that were not consistent with the restoration of growth and credit-worthiness." The Bank, the task force argued, "should not support inadequately financed programs, nor, on the other hand, should it allow its lending to be blocked by the inability or unwillingness of other lenders to accept reasonable financial burdens. In appropriate cases, it should be prepared to accept the accumulation of financial arrears to other creditors as a source of financial relief."[134]

The Debt Task Force's stance on lending "into a situation of non-consensual arrears" was opposed by several of the Bank's senior managers, concerned by its repercussions on "the level of discipline of the payment system on which the Bank ultimately depends. The maintenance of contractual obligations represents in this context a fundamental point."[135] In fact, as shown in chapter 15, this view was not new to the Bank. During its first decade and a half, the Bank had adopted a similarly firm stance on external debt settlement, arguing that this was key to the institution's original purpose of restoring international capital flows. Since it took complex and, to some extent subjective, judgments to assess how much of a borrowing country's assemblage of arrears was "reasonable," the Bank now decided to restrict lending into arrears to cases involving a partial moratorium by an impoverished country that compressed domestic consumption under an agreed adjustment program.[136] In reality, strong aversion by the major shareholders ruled out the larger debtors from this interpretation.

Undoubtedly, this prudence stemmed from internal assessments emphasizing the escalating financial risks facing the institution and its limited room to maneuver. Lending ceilings arising from the Bank's capital constraints have already been noted. When Baker's proposals were announced, Bank staff informed management that the institution's "sustainable level of lending was . . . about $13.5 billion, which would be breached in FY87 under current lending plans."[137] At the same time, the Bank's portfolio risks were rising. The institution had already begun experiencing arrears problems, beginning with Nicaragua in 1984. Now, as the Bank prepared to ratchet up its lending to the high-risk countries, it began to worry about the

133. World Bank, Operational Manual Statement, OMS 1-28, 1986.

134. Memorandum, Jean Baneth, chairman, Debt Task Force, to Barber B. Conable, "Report on the Debt Problems of Highly Indebted Middle-Income Countries," December 17, 1987.

135. World Bank, Minutes of the Policy Committee of January 27, 1988.

136. Ibid.

137. World Bank, minutes of Managing Committee meeting of October 31, 1985, p. 1.

implications for its own credit ratings. Increasingly it looked for a clear signal from the United States that a GCI was in the works. Such an indication would lead the ratings agencies to take a more relaxed view, even though it might be a few years before the GCI was actually subscribed.

Yet, a year after Baker's speech, the signals emanating from the United States again seemed to suggest that, contrary to earlier indications, it did not want to enter into serious discussions on a GCI.[138] The United States announced that the Bank would have to place greater emphasis on "quality lending" and more "demand analysis" before it would consider a GCI. Other members objected that the United States was backing out of the "deal" implicit in Baker's proposals; namely, that the SIMICs would implement major policy changes and maintain debt service in exchange for, besides a modest increase in commercial bank exposure, U.S. support of increased lending by the Bank—which necessarily meant backing a GCI. The decline of the dollar in 1986–88 further limited the IBRD's capacity to increase lending. Eventually, as discussed in chapter 16, this decline, by reducing the Bank's headroom, would inject greater urgency to a capital increase. But meanwhile, the dollar's decline tightened the fetters on Bank lending.

The United States, however, not only opposed any capital increase but it blocked efforts by the Bank's management to liberalize repayment terms for the heavily indebted middle-income countries. The terms on IBRD loans had been hardened in 1977 (see chapter 15), and in 1986 the Bank sought a permanent liberalization of terms for low-income countries and a temporary one for the middle-income countries. The Bank's Managing Committee, having decided that U.S. support was "critical," sounded the U.S. Treasury but was turned down.[139] A modified version, calling for selective terms liberalization, did not find a consensus in the Board.[140] Liberalization of loan repayment terms would have to wait until mid-1987, when an agreement on the GCI was finally reached.

Attempts by the Bank to mobilize commercial bank resources through its guarantee umbrella also had little success. The possibility of gaining added leverage through the

138. Memorandum, D. Joseph Wood to Barber B. Conable, "Timing of GCI," September 19, 1986.

139. Following a conversation with James Conrow, deputy assistant secretary, Senior Vice President Qureshi reported that "Mr. Conrow had stated that both he and Secretary Baker would oppose terms liberalization on the grounds that it was unnecessary." World Bank, minutes of the Managing Committee, March 3 and March 17, 1986, p. 4. The appointment of Conrow had been unfortunate for the Bank. According to William Stanton (a former Republican member of Congress from Ohio and adviser to Conable), during the 1970s, Conrow, as Representative Bill Young's chief of staff, had shown "total ideological opposition to the Bank. . . . He was totally, ideologically opposed to IDA. He told me his personal goal for IDA was zero." Memorandum, William Stanton to A. W. Clausen, "Meeting with Secretary James Baker," July 22, 1985.

140. IBRD, "Selective Liberalization to IBRD Repayment Terms on New Loans," R86-70, March 18, 1986.

institution's guarantees had led to a protracted debate within the institution. The Bank's general counsel had initially raised the possibility of an interpretation of the Articles such that guarantees would count for less than an equivalent loan. Such an interpretation had been strongly opposed by the treasurer, who argued that this would have a detrimental effect on the Bank's credit standing in financial markets.[141]

The rare exception was a partial guarantee operation in Chile.[142] Although the amount itself was small, it was an important element in putting together a total rescue package of almost $6 billion in rescheduling and more than $1 billion in new money for Chile. Some regard the flow of funds stimulated by this operation as a turning point for Chile. The operation, however, drew fierce opposition from both within the Bank and major shareholders, especially the United States. A larger, and even more controversial, guarantee operation was one in Mexico. Despite the excitement surrounding Baker's announcements, Mexico and the commercial banks had struggled to reach a new agreement for almost a year. The agreement, involving a commitment of $7 billion by the commercial banks, included the Bank's participation in its largest ever partial guarantee operation, up to $750 million. The negotiations between Mexico and the commercial banks had been so contentious and the agreement was so financially tight that the Bank had little choice but to acquiesce in its participation. While the Bank's management put a brave face to strong criticism by its Board,[143] in fact it had been an unwilling participant and shortly thereafter it decided not to participate in such transactions in the future.[144]

In the end the Bank's attempts at catalyzing commercial bank financial flows failed to materialize because the net benefits to the borrower were low and commercial banks were looking for greater security than that available under the Bank's instruments.[145] Per se the Bank's cofinancing instruments provided little

141. The Bank's Treasury argued that since guarantees represent an irrevocable obligation for the Bank, it must be fully covered by the Bank's capital by the time it becomes callable. On that basis, capital had to be allocated gradually against outstanding guarantee commitments from the time they were signed; hence little or no leverage would be gained through the use of guarantees.

142. The partial guarantee cofinancing instrument—used by the Bank to guarantee the later maturities of a loan made by commercial banks—covered up to $150 million of principal against commercial bank cofinancing of $350 million.

143. See IBRD/IDA/IFC, "Summary of Discussions at the Meeting of the Executive Directors of the Bank and IDA, October 3, 1986," SD86-59, October 20, 1986.

144. Irritated by the Fund's "unfortunate disregard for the inter-linkages in [our] decision-making," the Bank made it clear to the Fund that it would "not participate in the financing of such a facility, either directly through the provision of a guarantee, or through any other cofinancing mechanism." Memorandum, Ernest Stern to Richard D. Erb, "Contingency Financing Issues," October 20, 1986. At the time the Fund was considering a similar "growth facility" for the Philippines.

145. Since commercial bank loans (for which the guarantee was provided) were on harder terms, the additionality provided by a guarantee was limited since the country lost the present value equivalent (about 20 percent in Mexico's case) of the guarantee amount in net Bank disbursements.

additional security beyond that associated with a good project. Guarantee instruments that would attract the commercial banks would have shifted the risk to the Bank: all loans guaranteed by the Bank increased its exposure and not that of the lender. In other cases, the commercial banks' desire for cross-default agreements and provisions that would share payments between themselves and the Bank ran counter to the Bank's wariness regarding provisions that could undermine its operational flexibility in the event of rescheduling.[146] Attempts at forming a new affiliate—MIGA—which could have been the best mechanism for the Bank to become more venturesome about issuing guarantees, bore fruit only in 1988, too late to be useful for this purpose. Instead, the Bank's stance, as summarized for incoming President Barber Conable, continued to be that "the commercial banks [sic] greatest comfort comes through a Bank-supported program of structural reform designed to promote sustainable growth and enhanced creditworthiness."[147]

The growing impact of the debt crisis on the Bank's own portfolio further constricted the institution's room to maneuver as the decade wore on. Nicaragua had already slipped into nonaccrual status, and in 1986 debt-servicing problems had spread to two of the Bank's medium-sized borrowers: Peru and Romania. Unlike the position of Nicaragua, which simply did not have the resources to maintain its debt service to the Bank, Peru's position was based as much on an unwillingness as an inability to pay.

By spring 1986, Peru's interest arrears, both to commercial banks as well as to the IMF, were mounting. The Peruvian president, Alan Garcia, had been denouncing both the Fund and the commercial banks. With two new loans ready to be presented to the Board, the Bank found itself in a perilous position.[148] Peru's public posture on its debt obligations, the impending possibility of the country being declared ineligible to use IMF resources, and its declining creditworthiness all led the Bank to question whether it should proceed with new loans and continue to increase its net exposure. The Bank surmised that it had three options in the matter: suspend disbursements by invoking the country's IMF ineligibility (there was no legal basis for this and there were precedents of the Bank continuing to disburse to countries declared ineligible by the IMF, e.g., Sudan and Guyana); regardless of Peru's status with the IMF, suspend disbursements owing to Peru's lack of creditworthiness, as perceived by the Bank itself (the legal basis for such action was dubious); or proceed to disburse already signed loans but desist from signing already negotiated ones and thereby minimize the growth of outstanding loans, to the extent feasible. The Bank's

146. Indeed, this was borne out during Mexico's 1989 Brady restructuring, when the Bank's 1986 partial guarantee operation complicated the negotiations.

147. Briefing materials prepared by Operations Policy Staff, "Highlights of Current Issues in Operations," for Barber B. Conable, April 1986, p. 2.

148. At the end of February 1986, the IBRD's outstanding loans to Peru stood at $716 million. Gross disbursements ($130 million in 1985), were expected to rise slightly to $142 million in 1986, with expected amortization payments of $55 million.

management was only too aware that all three options were unattractive: not suspending disbursements would increase the financial risks to the institution, but doing so would be interpreted "in Latin America and perhaps more generally . . . as a political act in response to our major shareholders and a step in aligning ourselves with the commercial banks" who were strongly pressing the Bank to stop disbursements.[149] The Bank chose the third option. In reprisal, Peru stopped servicing its IBRD debt and soon emerged as the Bank's largest borrower in nonaccrual status.

The spillover of the debt crisis to the Bank's portfolio caused the proportion of the portfolio in the "high-risk" category to rise by more than 60 percent between fiscal 1982 and fiscal 1988, from 39 percent to 64 percent. Arrears and nonaccruals rose as well, and the country exposure guidelines were being exceeded in more and more countries.[150] Aggravating the situation was the impact of the dollar's depreciation, which reduced IBRD net flows by a third, owing to the currency composition of IBRD loans (see chapter 16). The Bank's net flows to the highly indebted countries rose by 12 percent annually between fiscal 1985 and 1987. The rate of increase of the outstanding debt, however, was three times as much: 36 percent a year.[151] Such large and unanticipated increases in debt-servicing obligations to the Bank, at a time of extreme financial stringency, aggravated already tense relations between the Bank and several borrowers. Consequently the Bank's management was wary of any proposal (such as a decision to lend into an underfunded situation) that could imperil its preferred creditor status.

The criticism by the Bank's Board of the Mexico guarantee operation exemplified the difficulties facing the institution. Attempts to break the conventional operational mold raised fears about a shift in burden sharing and charges of "bailing out the banks." But given the rising volume and share of Bank and other official-creditor funds in declining overall net flows, this was indubitably happening in any case, as an internal task force on debt pointed out,

> Particularly, in countries where [the Bank] is heavily engaged in adjustment lending the resources it provides and the policy improvements it promotes have in recent years served mainly to finance debt service to other creditors. . . . By putting a large share of its loans into countries with severely impaired development prospects and debt servicing ability, financing debt service to other creditors, the Bank is also compromising the value of its portfolio, and ultimately its own creditworthiness.[152]

149. Memorandum, Ernest Stern to A. W. Clausen, "Bank Strategy towards Peru," March 24, 1986.

150. The share of the portfolio in countries exceeding both the "share of exports" and "share of debt service" exposure guidelines had doubled between fiscal 1985 and fiscal 1988 (from 12.5 to 25 percent). World Bank, "1988 Country Risk Management and Portfolio Review," Risk Management and Financial Policy Department, June 13, 1988.

151. Ibid., para. 3.4, table 3.2.

152. Memorandum, Jean Baneth to members of the Policy Committee, "Interim Report on Debt Problems of Middle-Income Countries," July 31, 1987, para. 6.

Table 11-5. *Real Debt of Developing Countries with Debt-Servicing Difficulties, 1982–92*
Billions of 1982 U.S. dollars

Year	To commercial banks	To official creditors	Share of official creditors in total
1982	278	115	29.3
1984	286	143	33.3
1986	278	187	40.2
1988	254	232	47.7
1990	222	251	53.1
1992	200	252	55.7

Source: Michael Dooley (1994), "A Retrospective on the Debt Crisis," paper prepared for the Fiftieth Anniversary of Essays in International Finance, Princeton University, table 2.

A subsequent retrospective on the debt crisis concluded that, just as governments had privatized debt in the 1970s their actions (or inactions) achieved the opposite effect in the 1980s. By 1988, even before the Brady proposals were announced, a substantial transference of risk from commercial to official creditors had already occurred (table 11-5).

For the Bank, as with any other financial institution, fungibility implied that part of the increase in its lending was to refinance its own loans. The financial predicament facing its borrowers meant that, in most cases, for the Bank not to have done so would have been less than responsible, to both the particular borrower and itself. A quarter century earlier (1964), when the Bank had resumed lending to Brazil after a hiatus of five years, the country was faced with a debt problem. At that time the Bank's management had quite matter-of-factly informed its Board that the new loans "for suitable projects [were] in the amount necessary to offset the net repayments of principal . . . on the Bank's existing loans to Brazil over the period 1965 through 1970."[153] Although now, as in the earlier case, the implicit reality was well recognized, the systemic nature of the current problem meant that, in contrast to earlier years, *officially* the Bank's management could no longer be as forthright. Any allusions to "refinancing," an otherwise common feature of banking, were now downplayed.

The Bank's financial limitations were exacerbated by the difficulties debtor countries experienced in reaching agreement with the Fund, as well as by the frequent unraveling of Fund programs. Since the Bank's adjustment-oriented (and quick-disbursing) lending was linked to Fund programs, its pace of disbursements began to lag further. However, proceeding in the absence of Fund-certified macroeconomic programs, as the Argentina episode would underline, amplified the

153. IBRD, "Report and Recommendation of the President to the Executive Directors on the Proposed Loans to the Central Electrica de Furnas, S.A. and Usinas Electricas do Paranapanema, S.A. in Brazil," P-421, February 17, 1965, p. 1.

Bank's political and financial risks. In seeking cover from these risks, the institution was perceived to be becalmed, even as its indebted borrowers were weathering stormier seas, a contrast that heightened the Bank's public relations problems.[154]

Trudging toward Debt Relief

The year 1986 was a poor one for countries caught in the grip of the debt crisis. With output stagnating, debt indicators worsened in sixteen of seventeen "Baker" countries. By the end of the year the Latin America region of the Bank began to question seriously the viability of the Baker strategy, recognizing that it had been "very, very optimistic, on two points: first, the speed with which governments could be expected to introduce the policy changes that we were talking about, and also the speed with which those policy changes could begin to produce results."[155]

Knox expressed his skepticism of the Baker Plan first at a retreat of the senior staff of the operations complex in mid-1986, and later at another retreat with the senior staff of the Western Hemisphere Department of the Fund. But when he suggested that the two institutions ought to start thinking in terms of debt reduction, the reaction in both institutions, as he later put it, "was one of horror."[156]

In March 1987 the Bank's senior vice president for finance, Moeen Qureshi, met with financial institutions in New York. His assessment, which he claimed was widely shared by the financial community in New York, was that

> the situation of the heavily indebted countries . . . is not getting any better; indeed it is getting worse. . . . The truth is that there is not only a debtor crisis but also a "creditor" crisis . . . there is no concerted approach or decision-making capability on the part of the commercial banks. The *machinery and the process for debt negotiations does not work and cannot work* in its present form.[157]

Qureshi's reading was that the Fund had relinquished its early leadership, having lost its political leverage in key developing countries. With the United States paralyzed by not wanting to be perceived as either "bailing out" the banks or the developing countries, Qureshi argued that the "only institution therefore that can and must now take leadership is the World Bank."[158] To varying extents, influential voices from within financial markets themselves increasingly questioned the prevailing official credo, recognizing both the inevitability and the need for debt relief.[159]

---

154. Typical of the tenor of the media coverage was Hobart Rowen, "World Bank's Fumbling the Ball on Debt Crisis," *Washington Post,* January 31, 1988, pp. K1, K8.

155. David Knox, interview with the authors, May 21, 1992, p. 6.

156. Ibid.

157. Memorandum, Moeen A. Qureshi to Barber B. Conable, "Visit to New York, March 26–27," March 28, 1987, pp. 1–2.

158. Ibid., p. 3.

159. Henry Kaufman (Salomon Brothers), "Debt Relief for Developing Countries in a Volatile World," 1987; David Lomax (National Westminster Bank), "The Debt Situation—

Shortly after his arrival in July 1986, the Bank's new president, Barber Conable, had set up a task force, under the chairmanship of Jean Baneth, to reexamine the debt problems of the middle-income countries. The report, in July 1987, concluded that "despite extremely optimistic assumptions about the quality of economic management in these countries, their prospects are bleak," and "despite substantial policy reform efforts by the debtor countries, the adjustment has occurred at the expense of growth. . . . [The Baker initiative has] not been succeeding in restoring growth to middle-income countries." To persist with this strategy, the report warned, entailed "high risks, and promises little visible payoff. The Bank should publicly state this view soon."[160] The report concluded that for these countries to simultaneously grow and reduce their debt burden, substantial financial relief was imperative.[161]

Underpinning the strong position taken by the task force was a growing realization that temporary alleviation of the debt-service burden while necessary, was not sufficient to renew economic growth; the large debt overhang posed a key obstacle. However, the report immediately ran into strong opposition from Moeen Qureshi, now the new operations chief, who, while concurring that the existing strategy "had not worked," regarded the suggested approach as "not practical; it appeared as an encouragement to default."[162] Qureshi, who only a few months ago had advocated a more vigorous approach by the Bank, in his new role now pressed for a more cautious stance, based on a voluntary, "market-based" approach. With the exception of Bolivia,[163] the subject of debt relief remained taboo in the Bank's public discourse.

Meanwhile in mid-1987, amidst a debt moratorium on its commercial bank debts, the largest debtor, Brazil, presented a debt plan wherein Brazil would obtain refinancing on "60 percent of the interest coming due on its commercial bank debt, while paying the banks the remaining 40 percent; on debt to the multilateral

---

The Next Stage," July 16, 1987; and the proposals by Shearson-Lehman/American Express, Herrhausen (CEO of Deutsche Bank), and De Carmoy (CEO of Midland Bank International) all envisaged debt relief through the creation of some sort of new financial entity. Cited in a memorandum, Alexander Shakow to Jean Baneth, "Recent Debt Proposals," December 10, 1987.

160. Memorandum, Jean Baneth to members of the Policy Committee, "Interim Report on Debt Problems of Middle-Income Countries," July 31, 1987, pp. 1, 2, 3.

161. For a group of eight countries (for which detailed analyses were done), the report estimated that debt relief of about a quarter of the face value of the debt was required. These estimates varied by country, from a high of 70 percent for Bolivia to zero for Colombia. It may be noted that these estimates were in almost all cases less than prevailing market discounts. The aggregate relief (24 percent) was also in line with what the commercial banks, led by Citibank, had begun to provision on their developing-country debt.

162. World Bank, "Minutes of Policy Committee Meeting of August 5, 1987," August 11, 1987.

163. World Bank, "Updating Country Economic Memorandum on Bolivia," Report 6455-BO, December 15, 1986, para. 91.

institutions and the Paris Club, Brazil would maintain an even cash flow."[164] Following conversations with some investment banks, Brazil's finance minister, Carlos Bresser Pereira, also floated the idea of converting the Brazilian debt to bonds, priced at a discount to the face value of the debt, later expanding this to include voluntary debt conversion bonds without any explicit link to the secondary market value.[165] The approach would, however, require a guarantee from a multilateral institution, and he suggested that the Bank play this role.

Bresser Pereira's proposals were summarily rejected by U.S. Treasury Secretary James Baker, although its principal elements—delinking negotiations with the commercial banks from those with multilateral institutions; debt securitization with guarantees from multilateral institutions—were analogous to those floated by Baker's successor, Nicholas Brady, nearly two years later.[166] The United States, seconded by the multilaterals, continued to insist that there could be no compromise on full interest payments by the debtor countries.[167] But the worries engendered by the "radical" nature of the Brazilian plan enabled the U.S. Treasury to persuade the commercial banks to reach rapid agreements with other debtor countries on terms as favorable as those granted a few months earlier to Mexico, which the banks had been unwilling to do until then.

At the 1987 annual meetings, speaking on behalf of the Latin American countries, Bresser Pereira again argued that the prevailing strategy was not working: the debtor countries could not both service their debt fully as well as implement the needed policy reforms. His criticisms were dismissed by Baker, who insisted that his two-year-old debt strategy "remains the only viable, mutually acceptable approach to debt problems."[168] The "market-menu" approach was slightly enlarged, with particular emphasis on debt-equity swaps. However, debt-

164. Luiz Carlos Bresser Pereira, "Brazil," in John Williamson, ed., *The Political Economy of Policy Reform* (Washington D.C.: Institute for International Economics, 1994), p. 345.

165. According to Bresser Pereira's account, Brazilian debt at the time was trading at a market discount of about 40 percent. His proposals envisaged converting the Brazilian debt to bonds priced at a discount of about 30 percent. The technical details of the securitization plan were worked out by First Boston, Inc., and S. G. Warburg.

166. Bresser Pereira, "Brazil." See also, Alexander Nicoll, "Quick Interim Loan on the Cards," *Financial Times* (London), September 10, 1987, p. 5.

167. The position was in contrast to the statesmanship on the same issue shown four decades earlier. Discussing the clause in the Anglo-U.S. loan agreement which would postpone the payment of interest in any year in which Britain found itself facing dollar imbalances, U.S. President Harry S Truman said, "It is not to our advantage to press for payment of interest when payment is impossible, and thus force default and a crumbling of international relations," as reported in "50 Years Ago," *Financial Times* (London), January 31, 1996, p. 13. The position of the United Kingdom on this issue during the 1980s did not reflect its own experiences although its postwar circumstances were certainly exceptional.

168. Samantha Sparks, "Finance: Latin America Calls for New Debt Plan," Inter Press Service, September 30, 1987.

equity swaps fizzled out after showing initial promise, as concerns arose about their inflationary effects.[169]

An exception to the lackluster outcomes of debt-equity swaps was Chile. Through the decade the country was an outlier in the region, although portrayed as the median case in several analyses. It had already undergone a wrenching transformation for more than a decade under a strong authoritarian government. The economic experiments and resulting mess at the beginning of the decade were largely of its own doing, as would be the efforts to resolve these problems. The Bank had little influence, in part because its lending was quite limited in the first half of the decade. Lending jumped sevenfold in the second half and provided a financial cushion for Chile's transformation, which remained, however, internally driven.[170]

As noted earlier, just a few months earlier an internal analysis by the Bank had come to the same pessimistic conclusions as Bresser Pereira. However, its reception within the Bank had been lukewarm, in part because of the turf battles and the deep schisms created by the 1987 reorganization. The institutional chaos engendered by the reorganization (see chapter 18) had already stymied any new initiatives from the Bank in the first year of Conable's presidency. A new study, deploying substantial resources, was launched in August 1987, this time drawing from all parts of the Bank. The financial and legal implications of dozens of debt proposals were examined in great detail. But once again the conclusions were bleak: *"There is a consensus that the current debt workout strategy is in serious danger of failing soon, and visibly, for lack of adequate net financing to support it."*[171]

The task force made two major recommendations. The first called for the Bank (together with the Fund) to take the initiative toward organizing central management of sovereign debt. With the exception of the Bank's general counsel, the proposal was rejected by the Bank's senior team management as a political nonstarter.[172] The second recommendation, that it should be prepared to lend into arrears, also proved contentious. Though not rejected outright, it was subject to quite restrictive conditions.

Management caution was underscored when, following a retreat of senior management, Conable noted to his senior managers, "The consensus of our discus-

169. Debt-equity swaps only reduce a country's liabilities if the swap occurs at a discount to the face value of the debt: the risk-adjusted value of the required payments on equity is the same as on debt. Governments could finance such an exchange either through internal borrowings (adding to an already expensive internal debt) or by printing money with its inflationary consequences.

170. From an annual $49 million in 1980–84 to $342 in 1985–89.

171. Memorandum, Baneth to Conable, December 17, 1987.

172. See memorandum, Ibrahim Shihata to W. David Hopper, "Towards Central Management of the Debt Problem on a Country-by-Country Basis," October 13, 1987. A recent formulation on similar lines is Jeffrey J. Sachs, "Do We Need an International Lender of Last Resort?" Frank D. Graham Lecture, Princeton University, April 20, 1995.

sions [on debt management] appeared to be to 'muddle on', i.e. flexibly to adjust the full range of debt management techniques to specific country situations. . . . For instance, it is obvious that for some countries, some forms of debt relief may become inevitable. The Bank, however, must worry about precedent."[173] Conable's decision with regard to the Bank's role reflected his position that the Bank should play a low-key but well-informed role, rather than be placed front and center in the debt strategy.[174] A hint of his approach had been evident in his senior appointments at the time of the reorganization, when he had turned down the request by the treasurer, Eugene Rotberg, to report directly to Conable, who had offered Rotberg the position of the Bank's "debt czar."[175] Rotberg's ebullient personality and reputation in financial markets meant that such an appointment, for better or worse, would inevitably have given the institution a significantly higher profile on the debt issue. Instead, Conable sought out Stanley Fischer, a professor of economics at the Massachusetts Institute of Technology and a widely respected authority on this subject, as vice president of research. Conable was well aware of Fischer's position that time had run out on the "muddle-through" approach. Fischer believed that while this had been the right strategy in the past, "the time for debt relief ha[d] arrived."[176] Although Fischer's appointment would resuscitate the institution's intellectual credibility, the degree of freedom, as Fischer candidly acknowledged later, remained severely circumscribed:

> The record shows that frank and open debate does not take place in official and banking circles. It was clear . . . to many much earlier, that growth in the debtor countries would not return without debt relief. . . . But [for the official agencies] to propose . . . an alternative would have required agreement among the major shareholders. . . . So long as the United States was not free to move, the IFIs [international financial institutions] were not willing to speak—though to be sure the repeated emphasis on debt reduction, with "voluntary, market-based" added sotto voce by the heads of the World Bank and IMF, was signaling their conclusion that it was time to move on.[177]

Throughout 1987–88, the Bank continued to analyze the debt issue intensely. Now the activist role was played by the research complex (with the operations management adopting a more cautious stance), as it pointedly questioned the

173. Memorandum, Barber B. Conable to Senior Management Council, "Senior Management Retreat—Follow Up," October 29, 1987.

174. For instance, in a president's report to the Board on progress on the debt front, staff conclusions of "limited progress achieved so far," were dropped in order to give the impression that the institution was "totally unambiguous" in its support of the Baker initiative.

175. In interviews with the authors, Conable (May 8, 1991) and Rotberg (November 2, 1990) disagreed on whether this was the reason for Rotberg's resignation. Conable felt that he could not have added another U.S. national to his senior management team.

176. Stanley Fischer, "Sharing the Burden of the International Debt Crisis," *American Economic Review, Papers and Proceedings* (May 1987), p. 165.

177. Stanley Fischer, "Foreword," in Husain and Diwan, *Dealing with the Debt Crisis*, p. v.

viability of the status quo, in particular, of the concerted lending–new money approach. There were repeated calls warning against further extensions of Bank credit to beleaguered borrowers in cases of underfunded programs. Thus in the case of Argentina Fischer argued, "it is difficult to see how Argentina can emerge from its current situation without obtaining debt relief at some point. . . . If we take the view that there is no viable financing plan for Argentina that does not involve debt relief, we should not disburse our money in a way that postpones debt relief without bringing a long-term solution closer."[178]

Such diagnoses, however, had little effect on the institution's official stance. The Bank's management was unwilling to take any steps that might jeopardize its brittle relationship with its major shareholders, especially the largest. Demonstrating remarkable public caution,[179] the institution decided to "adopt a reactive, ex post stance, on a case by case basis, as the need arises and appropriate country policies warrant," a position reflected in the series of reports on the crisis.[180]

Although the U.S. role was crucial in shaping the Bank's position in this matter, it must be emphasized that many commentators both within and outside the Bank, while deeply troubled by the plight facing debtor countries, were nonetheless worried about the broader ramifications of debt relief. For one, there was a point of principle: the borrowings represented contractual obligations and abrogating them unilaterally raised serious doubts about debtor countries' future access to international capital markets. The Bank necessarily had to weigh carefully the trade-offs between the benefits of debt reduction and the debilitating effects of a potentially long-term loss of market access for the affected countries.

But there was an additional element influencing the calculus of decisionmaking. Throughout its history, the Bank had always taken a tough line on the need for a negotiated settlement on external contractual obligations, whether the problem was bond defaults or nationalization of external investments (see chapters 2, 14, and 15). Although the Bank had become more tolerant during the 1970s, as an institution set up for the express purpose of greasing the wheels of international

178. Memorandum, Stanley Fischer to Barber B. Conable, "Argentina," September 2, 1988.

179. A note from Fischer to Conable (on debt) indicates the sensitivity of the issue for the Bank's management, "I have asked the Task Force to work discreetly. . . . Please let me know whether you want us to hide the study." Memorandum, Stanley Fischer to Barber B. Conable, "Internal Debt Study," May 2, 1988. In a similar vein, the draft *World Development Report 1988* had a sentence on the need for concessional debt relief, but it was dropped in the published version. Johannes Linn, interview with the authors, October 1, 1992.

180. World Bank, "World Bank Operational Strategy in the Heavily Indebted Middle Income Countries," R88-58, March 8, 1988; "World Bank Operational Strategy in the Heavily Indebted Middle Income Countries: Review of Recent Developments," R89-21, February 17, 1989. In contrast, in a paper prepared for the President's Council before the Berlin annual meetings (World Bank, "The Evolving Debt Crisis: Summary," September 1988), most options reviewed involved some form of debt relief.

finance, and itself dependent on international financial markets, this conviction remained firmly ingrained in its ethos.

Relatedly, the precedent effects of debt relief for a market-funded financial intermediary like the IBRD and the single largest creditor to developing countries, weighed heavily. The Bank's policies with regard to rescheduling its own loans also placed it in an awkward situation. However justified the rationale (which is examined in chapters 15 and 16), there can be little doubt that an institution that insists on its preferred creditor status remaining sacrosanct, while calling on others (the bilaterals and the commercial banks) to be more forthcoming, loses some of its credibility.

A different, but also difficult problem, was posed by the equity implications of debt relief. Proposals that argued for relating debt write-downs to the strength of a country's adjustment effort left unresolved the problem of those countries that had managed their economies well enough to avoid such a debt restructuring despite large external debts. Related to this was a much cited "moral hazard" problem. Debt forgiveness, it was argued, would merely provide further incentives to bad behavior. The argument had considerable validity in the early years, as it would have impeded the slow process of convincing borrower governments of the need for structural reform. Yet after the mid-1980s, this objection increasingly ran hollow. It is not difficult to distinguish between a country's willingness to pay and its ability to pay. There can be no dispute that the political controllers of many countries led (and if history is any guide, will continue to take) their countries to economic and political collapse. But that they would do so in future merely to avoid fully repaying external creditors, stretched credulity.

The case for debt relief was further undermined by the irksome issue of capital flight. As Onno Ruding, the Dutch minister of finance put it, "It is very hard to convince a European taxpayer to put money into an economy whose own taxpayers have taken all their money out."[181] However, as the decade wore on it became apparent that capital flight reflected both economic policies and economic uncertainty. While debtor countries had made substantial economic adjustment efforts, the debt stock itself emerged as a major source of economic uncertainty and capital flight.[182]

The case for debt relief was also affected by intellectual perceptions of the problem. In previous years, the focus had been on the need to provide short- to medium-term cash-flow relief. For instance, Hermann Abs, the architect of the 1953 German debt deal, as well as the successful restructuring of Indonesia's debt in the late 1960s, maintained that he had "always considered concessions on

181. Quoted in "Briefing for Washington," *The Economist Financial Report*, April 14, 1988, p. 2.

182. Indeed, if this was the principal constraint, debt reduction could have been made contingent to debtor countries' efforts to rein in capital flight.

interest payment as most important for successful debt settlement."[183] The Bank's thinking had been on analogous lines. Thus in 1986, Stern, in reacting to Conable's request for his views on a debt reduction plan proposed by Senator Bill Bradley, maintained that the feasibility of workout programs "will not, in the medium-term be made any easier by debt forgiveness. On the contrary, these programs require new capital. It is *not* essential that total debt decline in the near term, what *is* essential is that the *debt service burden* must decline."[184]

A recognition of the adverse effects of debt "overhang" was an important step in understanding the linkage between debt and growth. To the extent that a highly indebted country improved its economic performance, a large share of the benefits accrued to the creditors rather than the debtor country. Thus debt overhang acted as a tax on increases in current and future income, inhibiting investment and, consequently, growth. This was recognized by creditors, increasing their skepticism of the sustainability of adjustment programs, thereby creating a vicious circle in which negative expectations fed on themselves.

The inertia in 1988 was not due to any lacuna in analysis, but to a lack of political will. With little progress, the challenge facing the G-7 in their periodic meetings was to try to seem purposeful while doing little. The lag between internal staff consensus and shareholder approval largely reflected the obduracy of the major shareholders. Although Baker's departure made it less awkward to question the prevailing strategy officially, impending U.S. presidential elections meant that any new initiative would have to wait.

In October 1988 the United States felt compelled to extend a $3.5 billion credit line to Mexico, as a drop in oil prices led to severe liquidity problems; and with interest rates again rising, (LIBOR rose from about 7 percent in 1986–87, to 8.7 percent in 1988–89), the debtors, as Fischer pointed out, appeared "much like Sisyphus who was condemned forever to push a rock up a hill in Hades, only to have it roll down again as he reached the top."[185] Fewer and fewer voices continued to believe in the viability of the existing approach.[186] With Bush's election, the deck was clear for a new initiative.

183. Letter, Hermann J. Abs to Mike Faber, October 17, 1988. Through "some 'nibbling,'" Abs had achieved reductions on arrears of interest amounting to nearly 90 percent, on Germany's interwar debt, at the 1953 London Accord.

184. Memorandum, Ernest Stern to Barber B. Conable, July 14, 1986, p. 2.

185. Stanley Fischer, "Debt Progress Needs Open Trade," *Journal of Commerce*, November 7, 1988, p. 14A. Fischer was arguing that since "trade and debt are inextricably linked," progress on debt required greater trade openness in the North.

186. In the fall of 1988 an informal group consisting of representatives of commercial banks, debtor countries, the IMF, and the World Bank concluded that debt forgiveness was inevitable. "Bankers See Need for Third World Debt Relief," *Financial Times* (London), September 8, 1988, p. 4. J. P. Morgan, one of Wall Street's most respected financial institutions, came to a similar conclusion in "LDC Debt: a Critical Appraisal," *World Financial Markets* (December 30, 1988), pp. 1–2. To be sure, this was not a universal

Phase III: Winding Down

In March 1989, in a speech to the Bretton Woods Committee, U.S. Treasury Secretary Nicholas Brady put forward certain "suggestions" to resolve the debt crisis. His proposals included two key departures from the past: official support for debt reduction, underpinned by support from official creditors; and delinking IFI lending from commercial bank lending. Any debt reduction would, however, have to be negotiated on a voluntary basis and would be contingent on appropriate debtor country economic policies.[187] The breakthrough had been to admit that the debt overhang required reduction. Commercial banks were not about to forgive debts outright; they needed to be persuaded to accept some substitute: for example, paper of market-reduced face value but with guaranteed interest, or, alternatively, of nominal face value with reduced interest.

The shift in the U.S. position reflected a realization that the major governments simply did not have the will to coerce or entice the main protagonists to come to agreement. The change in tack implied greater financial risks to the IFIs, although the change in exposure had been occurring in any case (table 11-5). At the same time, without an early resolution, the IFIs were potentially faced with even graver risks.

The official antecedents of Secretary Brady's proposals could be traced to June 1988, when Japan proposed a debt initiative at the Toronto G-7 summit. Toyoo Gyohten, former Japanese vice minister of finance, would later recall: "To our great disappointment there were strong objections from the other G-7 countries, particularly the United States, the United Kingdom, and Germany, on the ground that the increased involvement of public institutions, either multilateral or national, would produce a serious transfer of risk from the private to the public sector."[188] The proposal—known as the Miyazawa proposal—was again aired at the Berlin meetings (reflected in guarded language in the communique of the Interim Committee) and, along with French President François Mitterand's proposals for the low-income countries, served as precursors to the Brady "Plan."

Though debt relief faced a host of impediments, a dearth of proposals, as noted earlier, was not one of them. All, however, failed in varying degrees to resolve

---

opinion. For instance, Cline argued that "recent growth stagnation [in major debtor countries] has been caused primarily by internal economic distortions (high fiscal deficits and inflation), not the debt burden." Consequently, his prescription was more of the same: "The basic international debt strategy remains valid, but intensified policy efforts are necessary." William Cline, "The Baker Plan: Progress, Shortcomings, and Future," World Bank, Policy, Planning, and Research Working Papers, WPS 250, August 1989.

187. In March 1989, a bolder proposal than Brady's was put forward by the chairman of Deutsche Bank, Herrhausen, who argued for *concerted* debt relief for highly indebted countries.

188. Paul A. Volcker and Toyoo Gyohten, *Changing Fortunes: The World's Money and the Threat to American Leadership* (Times Books, 1992), p. 223.

satisfactorily three principal problems. The first was to find an appropriate basis on which to price the debt to be bought from existing creditors, while minimizing the protests that the creditor governments were "bailing out" the banks. The second was to formulate debt-relief criteria. Relief based on per capita income would have little effect on the SIMICs, whereas one based on market evaluation of a country's debt would tend to reward previously profligate behavior. Relief based on negotiations similar to bankruptcy proceedings appeared to be the most logical course of action. But organizing such proceedings would first require an unprecedented degree of centralized management of debt, which few of the affected parties were willing to consider. The third problem was by far the most difficult to resolve: how to finance and distribute the costs of debt relief. The reluctance of creditor governments to provide debt relief on official debt, had made it virtually impossible for them to lean on private creditors to accede to nonofficial debt reduction.[189] The Brady Plan would essentially shift the burden of risk from commercial banks to IFIs, and indirectly from commercial bank shareholders to a combination of governments and bond markets (the latter in the case of the Multilateral Development Banks).

Two market operations served as the operational progenitors of the Brady initiative. The first, designed by J. P. Morgan in December 1987, had intended to retire $20 billion of Mexican debt by inviting banks to tender loans competitively (with those offering the highest discounts being offered the bonds), in exchange for securities with principal backed by U.S. zero-coupon Treasury bonds held by Mexico. The unenthusiastic response to the scheme[190] led the Bank of America to devise a somewhat similar proposal in the spring of 1988, but with an added proviso of credit enhancement by the World Bank through interest guarantees.[191] The modalities of the scheme were worked out jointly by the two institutions, with the debtor country chosen being Costa Rica.[192] Although Costa Rica had reached an impasse with its creditors, its debt was relatively small in absolute terms and creditor governments were favorably disposed toward it.

But the idea of interest guarantees—indeed any guarantees—met with a "very hostile" reception by the G-7 at the April 1988 Development Committee meetings,

189. In part this was because a substantial fraction of the official debt to middle-income countries was held by export credit agencies, which, like their commercial bank counterparts, feared being decapitalized.

190. Less than 20 percent of the debt was retired, at an average discount of 33 percent. In these schemes the zero-coupon bonds have a nominal value at maturity equal to the face value of the secured debt.

191. Memorandum, Moeen A. Qureshi to Barber B. Conable, "Bank of America Debt Restructuring Proposal," April 7, 1988.

192. At the time, Bank of America chaired Costa Rica's Bank Advisory Committee. The fact that Bank of America's chairman, A. W. Clausen, had recently served as the World Bank's president, undoubtedly created a favorable atmosphere for collaboration.

concerned with the precedent for large debtors.[193] The possibility of restructuring the guarantees through the Bank's new affiliate, MIGA, was also disallowed. An alternative proposal for the Bank to solicit other donors for a contingent interest-maintenance fund to guarantee the transaction, administering the scheme as a trust account, fell apart following opposition by the U.S. Treasury, which feared that this was a thinly disguised debt-forgiveness venture.[194]

U.S. blessing to greater IFI involvement in the debt strategy came amid mounting acrimony between the Bretton Woods institutions. Energized by its battle cry of "No more Argentinas," the IMF had been pressing virtually to eliminate an independent role for the Bank on macroeconomic issues through a new concordat on Bank-Fund collaboration. The forum through which it was making its case was the G-10, whose deputies had been meeting since April 1988 to plot a course on the role of the Bank and Fund in the debt strategy.[195]

In the Bank's view, the draft paper on Bank-Fund collaboration prepared by the Fund for the G-10 deputies went "well beyond previous discussions and agreements on Bank-Fund collaboration."[196] Concerned "about the existence and content of the paper," the Bank mounted an intensive educational and lobbying effort targeting the G-10 deputies, executive directors, and other G-10 officials. Presenting the Bank's case to the deputies, Stanley Fischer remarked: "We cannot help but be struck by a certain asymmetry in the treatment of the two institutions."[197] Responding to the draft report's characterization of the IMF "as the linchpin of the international debt strategy," Fischer wryly noted that "if an axle has only one linchpin, a wheel will fall off at the other end" and urged the deputies to recognize that the international debt strategy required "at least two linchpins."[198]

193. Memorandum, Ernest Stern to Barber B. Conable, "Costa Rica Debt Reduction Scheme," April 29, 1988.

194. Memorandum, David R. Bock to Moeen A. Qureshi, "Costa Rica: Request for Agreement to Proceed," July 22, 1988; memorandum, Moeen A. Qureshi to Barber B. Conable, "Costa Rica," July 22, 1988. Jeffrey Sachs, in testimony before the House Banking Committee on January 5, 1989, saw "in country after country Citicorp as being the leader in stopping any compromise on any of these issues . . . Citicorp is the very bank that is blocking such an agreement with Costa Rica right now." Citibank denied the charge.

195. The IMF has a permanent observer status at G-10 deputies meetings and provides the secretariat for the group. It was therefore not surprising that Fischer observed: "There is no question that the G-10 and others have a very pro-Fund view." Memorandum, Stanley Fischer to Barber B. Conable, "Preliminary Report on G-10 Deputies Meeting," January 31, 1989, para. 12. The IMF's superior status (to the Bank) has been even more obvious at the Paris Club.

196. Letter, Barber B. Conable to Michel Camdessus, January 23, 1989.

197. "Statement by the World Bank on the Draft of chapter 3" concerning the study by G-10 Deputies, "The Role of the Fund and the Bank in the Debt Strategy," delivered at a meeting of the deputies in Paris, January 27, 1989, by Stanley Fischer, vice president and chief economist, p. 6. Contained in memorandum, Stanley Fischer to Barber B. Conable, "Preliminary Report on G-10 Deputies Meeting, 1.27.89," January 31, 1989.

198. Ibid., p. 8.

The intense lobbying effort by the Bank paid off to some extent, although it did not overcome the greater trust placed in the IMF by the G-10.[199] While the new concordat represented a modus vivendi, the immediate task—to get the Brady initiative off the ground—compelled the two institutions to work together. A Joint Debt Task Force was established, and a more collaborative relationship ensued.

The extensive homework that had already been done within the Bank was evident by the speed with which it (as well as the Fund), formulated its guidelines for debt relief following Brady's speech. It was one thing to have a conceptual acceptance, but putting in viable operational criteria required a firm analytical base.[200] The Bank's initial prognosis on the viability of the Brady proposals was pessimistic. It appeared as if the projected debt reductions—between 10 to 20 percent of the debt stock, with debt-service reduction of between ½ and 1 percent of GNP—would be inadequate to move the countries rapidly out of their beleaguered status. Unless growth rebounded with sufficient robustness, the debtor countries' ability to service their remaining debt would be again impaired. Since the credit enhancements integral to the debt deals would transform the structure of the remaining debt, the specter of renewed debt-servicing problems implied a significant escalation in risks facing preferred creditors, and to the Bank. The disquiet was evident in a note sent to the Bank's president:

> The Brady Plan was formulated as an attempt to tilt the playing field in favor of the debtors and away from the banks. It may end up as a plan that shifts the balance marginally in favor of the debtors at great cost to the IFIs and at little cost to the banks. Further, the cost for the Bank will in the long run likely exceed that for the Fund, which will hope to have its money back (probably indirectly our money) before we do.[201]

The Bank's apprehensions had a strong basis, given the U.S. Treasury's interpretation of the proposals as requiring "a need on the part of the official institutions to live with more uncertainty and financing risk. He [Dallara] argued . . . the fact that the programs are tight and somewhat inflexible is putting additional pressure on the countries to adjust and manage in a more disciplined fashion."[202]

Although the resources of the IFIs were modest in relation to the debt burden, they were substantial in the context of their own resources, and especially of incremental funds. Two events eased the risks facing the Bank. The recently

199. For more details, see chapter 10 and volume 2, chapter 11.

200. These included country eligibility criteria and financial allocation guidelines, adequacy of financial packages and sequencing of funds, modalities and degree of debt relief and their appropriateness to different country situations, types of conditionality to ensure that policy changes and debt relief went hand in hand, availability of official financial backing, and tax and regulatory changes to facilitate commercial bank participation in debt relief.

201. Memorandum, Stanley Fischer to Barber B. Conable, May 22 1989.

202. Office memorandum, David R. Bock, "Meeting with U.S. Treasury on the Brady Progress Review," March 29, 1990, p. 2.

concluded GCI (its largest ever), considerably enhanced the institution's risk-bearing capacity. And, the conclusion by the Bank's legal counsel that any IBRD lending for debt reduction–related purposes meet well-defined "materiality criteria," in accord with the institution's Articles, also moderated risk.

The use of Bank resources—financing and/or negative pledge waivers—to support debt and debt-service reduction (DSR) operations for heavily indebted countries was approved in May 1989 (the IMF approved a similar program at the same time).[203] The approval, coming after two days of deliberations (and four hundred pages of transcripts) by the Bank's Executive Board, was a milestone for the institution.

Although the relative benefits of interest reduction versus reduction in the debt stock vary with country circumstances, the guidelines segregated the Bank's financial support for these purposes, reflecting its shareholders' views.[204] The U.S Treasury, which first favored debt buybacks (a position espoused by the Europeans as well), shifted its position to stressing interest reduction as it became clear that debt relief through reduction of face value, but at market interest rates, would require large upfront resources.[205] The rigidity of the initial guidelines was a constraint on the Bank's DSR operations, for example, with the Philippines. The guidelines were later relaxed (in 1992).

The test case for Brady, as with all previous official debt initiatives since the onset of the crisis, was Mexico. The negotiations almost collapsed at an early stage owing to the intransigence of the commercial banks, led by Bankers Trust (which was also one of the most exposed banks). Pressure from the U.S. Treasury, which

203. IBRD, "Operational Guidelines and Procedures for Use of IBRD Resources to Support Debt and Debt Service Reductions," R89-104, May 22, 1989. The operations were drawn from a menu of four principal instruments: new money, usually in the form of bonds coupled with the conversion of some existing claims from loans into bonds; buybacks, entailing prepayment at a discount; discount bonds, involving a conversion of existing claims into new claims with a discounted face value, longer maturities, and market interest rates; and par bonds, including front-loaded interest reduction bonds.

204. Set-aside funds, drawn from the existing lending program (up to 25 percent of a country's adjustment lending program; 10 percent in those countries where the Bank was concentrating only on investment lending), would be used to support principal reduction operations; any additional resources for DSR operations (of up to 15 percent of the Bank's overall lending program to the country) could be used for interest support only in connection with debt or debt-service reduction. A three-year lending period was assumed for these operations.

205. A detailed analysis of the pros and cons of interest reduction versus debt buybacks can be found in World Bank, "Analytic Issues in Debt Reduction," draft, April 21, 1989. Interest reduction offered several advantages for the Bank: larger, short-term cash flow savings for the debtor countries per dollar of Bank resources; and, via the longer duration of support provided, potentially greater policy leverage. On the other hand, buybacks reduced the Bank's entanglement, were politically advantageous in the debtor countries, and reduced the country's vulnerability to interest rate shifts.

was heavily engaged in the Mexico Brady operation, was instrumental in bringing around the commercial banks.[206] Further problems arose because of the unexpectedly tough posture adopted by Japan, which had been penciled in as by far the largest bilateral source of finance for Brady operations.[207]

Six months after Brady's speech, Mexico and the commercial banks reached an agreement in principle to cover $49 billion of Mexico's $69 billion foreign bank debt. Most (90 percent) of the "menu" of choices would reduce the commercial banks' stock of debt. As some observers predicted, few of the creditor banks chose the "new money" option.[208] The settlement was underpinned by $7 billion of official resources for credit enhancement, with funds from IBRD and cofinancing from Japan ($2 billion each) as the largest sources.[209] For the most part, the Bank stayed clear of the negotiations between Mexico and the commercial banks. Its intervention, which came after Mexico had already agreed to most of the points made by the commercial banks, succeeded in adding a modest contingency facility and eliminating the use of bearer bonds.

The relatively small direct role played by the Bank in the negotiations of the Mexican Brady deal can be understood in the context of Secretary Brady's injunction that the debt workouts be negotiated in the market, with the Bretton Woods institutions encouraging but not managing them. Bank staff analysis suggested that the workout process could be strengthened through greater "official support for well structured bargaining positions of debtor countries with strong adjustment programs."[210] However, Bank management was aware that the more entangled it became, both in the negotiations between debtor countries and commercial banks, as well as in the financing (through increased lending and even more through

206. Memorandum, David R. Bock to Barber B. Conable through Moeen A. Qureshi, "Mexico—Update on Discussions with Commercial Banks," June 5, 1989.

207. Memorandum, S. Shahid Husain to files, "Mexico—Debt Reduction Program," August 11, 1989. The Japanese stance, reflecting its newfound international confidence, was explained thus by a senior Japanese staff member at the Bank: "Privately, many Japanese complain that the U.S. Administration does not use its own money, but that it puts pressure on other donors to accede to one-sided requests from U.S. commercial banks." Memorandum, Koji Kashiwaya to Barber B. Conable, "Mexico: Debt Reduction—Credit Enhancement," August 14, 1989.

208. William Dale, former deputy manager of the IMF, was quoted as saying David Mulford and Charles Dallara, the purported designers of the Brady Plan in the U.S. Treasury, "must have had 'holes in their heads'" since banks do not offer fresh money to the same clients for which old loans are being marked down. Robert S. England, "No Banking on Brady," *National Review*, March 19, 1990, p. 41.

209. The Bank provided $750 million in set-aside funds and $950 million for interest coverage. Much of the money came from three adjustment loans (of $0.5 billion apiece) approved in June 1989; $22 billion of debt was exchanged for fixed-rate (6.25 percent) bonds of the same face value and another $20 billion of debt was exchanged for floating rate bonds at 35 percent discount to face value.

210. World Bank, "Analytic Issues in Debt Adjustment," p. 11.

guarantees), the greater the reduction in debt service the country was likely to receive, but the greater the risk to the Bank.

Board discussions reflected the same dilemma; the issue was a contentious one. Most developed-country executive directors stressed the importance of an "arm's-length" posture for the Bank, while their developing-country counterparts leaned toward a more "pro-active" role. The stance was an interesting revelation of where the two sides felt that the Bank staff's technical analysis (and perhaps sympathies) lay. In the end it was decided that the Bank should play what could be termed an "actively passive" role: the institution should not be a party to the negotiations, but it would take an active interest and provide technical analysis on request. As a result, the Bank's management felt that, "if it were not for the very firm view of most of our major shareholders that we should wait for the results of the negotiations and then apply our enhancements, we could surely have achieved much larger discounts in the recent negotiations."[211]

Through the following year, staff repeatedly expressed its frustration with the institution's operational stance, arguing that the Bank was being placed in potentially untenable positions.[212] As a result, the Bank's management decided to be more forceful in negotiations in articulating the institution's position regarding adequate financing and mechanisms to ensure growth. It also decided to extend the focus from commercial bank debt to official debt. But the Bank was once again inhibited from doing so, following "strong reservations" expressed by the U.S. Treasury, regarding the attempts by the Bank (and Fund) to become more directly involved in the negotiations.[213]

Contrary to most expectations, however, the Mexico Brady deal was the high-water mark of the Bank's participation in the Brady initiative as the crisis began to wilt. In 1989 the Bank had anticipated that the amount of additional resources allocated by the Bank to debt and debt-service operations "should not be more than $6 billion for the . . . three years FY90–92."[214] In fact only $1.44 billion was committed in "additional lending." In some cases (Mexico, Philippines, Venezuela, and Uruguay) the Bank provided financial support, whereas in others (Costa Rica and Nigeria), its role was restricted to providing waivers to its negative pledge clause. In still other cases (Chile, Brazil, and Peru), agreements were reached without any Bank participation.

The Latin American debt crisis seemed to end almost anticlimactically. There was no final denouement to the crisis, just a fading away as the protagonists reconciled, worn out by their struggle. The waning of the crisis, like its waxing, was

211. Letter, Ernest Stern to David Knox, July 30, 1990, pp. 1–2.

212. Minutes of the President's Council meeting, "Review of Progress Under the Brady Initiative," March 22, 1990; minutes of the President's Council, June 25, 1990.

213. Office memorandum from David Bock, "Meeting with U.S. Treasury on the Brady Progress Review," March 29, 1990.

214. IBRD, "Chairman's Summing Up," SecM89-692, June 1, 1989, p. 2.

Table 11-6. *Latin America: Economic Performance and Capital Flows, 1975–94*
Average annual percent change, unless otherwise noted

Indicator	1975–82	1983–89	1990–94
Real GDP	4.2	2.0	2.9
Per capita GDP	1.6	–0.1	0.9
Consumer prices	47.0	150.0	216.6
Saving[a]	20.8	19.2	17.7
Investment[b]	24.3	20.2	20.5
Current account balance	–3.5	–1.0	–2.7
Total net capital inflows ($U.S. billions)	26.3[b]	–16.6	40.1

Sources: World Economic Outlook, May 1995; "International Capital Markets: Developments, Prospects, and Policy Issues," August 1995.

a. Percentage of GDP.

b. Figures are for 1977–82.

partly due to unexpected interest rate shifts. These alone brought debt-servicing savings in excess of $11 billion annually, relative to projections. This amounted to double the net savings on external resource payments projected as a result of lending operations in support of the Brady initiative. What Volcker taketh, Greenspan giveth.[215] But even this liquidity relief was of secondary importance. The principal benefits were the restoration of confidence and the improvement of the investment climate for private investors, reflecting in part the drastic restructuring of economic policies over the decade, in which the Bank had played an important role. As confidence translated into sharp declines in real domestic interest rates (in Mexico's case, average real interest rates fell from about 30 percent in 1989 to 8.4 percent in 1990), the costs of servicing swollen *domestic* debt, whose budgetary burdens exceeded that of servicing the external debt, also declined.

As capital inflows surged—now not from commercial banks but from capital markets (pension funds and the like)—borne on the wings of returning flight capital, Mexico's chief debt negotiator and now undersecretary of finance, asserted, "For us Mexicans the [debt] crisis is over."[216] Indeed, the turnaround in capital flows to Latin America—about $57 billion a year between 1983–89 and 1990–94 (see table 11-6)—was astounding, especially in light of the pervasive gloom at the end of the 1980s.

215. Estimates are based on net savings on external resource payments projected at $4 billion to $6 billion per year. "The Brady Initiative: Issues for the World Bank," March 30, 1989, para. 18. Evaluations of the Mexican Brady deal had been based on interest rate assumptions of average LIBOR of 9.2 percent between 1989 and 1994 (S. van Wijnbergen to Moeen Qureshi, May 3, 1989) against actual LIBOR of 6 percent. "Global Economic Prospects and the Developing Countries," 1995, table 13. It had been estimated that interest rate changes of 100 basis points affected interest payments of the HIMICs by about $3.5 billion. Husain and Diwan, *Dealing with the Debt Crisis,* p. 6.

216. "Angel Gurria: 'For us Mexicans the Crisis Is Over,'" *Financial Times* (London), July 30, 1992, p. 5.

As the figures in table 11-6 also indicate, the turnaround in the real economy was more gradual. Yet the swing in confidence was anything but moderate. The gradualness of the changes in the real economy should perhaps not be surprising; a patient just released from the hospital rarely sprints away, at least not for long. The herdlike euphoria was most marked in the case of Mexico. The North American Free-Trade Agreement, membership in the OECD, and the *Economist* magazine, waxing eloquent that Mexican President Carlos Salinas "has a claim to be hailed as one of the great men of the 20th century," all exemplified Mexico's golden-boy status as perhaps no other country (with the exception perhaps of Chile).[217] Although internal Bank staff assessments did raise concerns about several issues that were later identified as important causal variables in Mexico's new crisis, regional management chose to downplay these concerns.[218] Indeed, a World Bank publication surveying Latin American reforms proclaimed that "consultants and academics are analyzing the Chilean and Mexican experiences to learn first hand how these countries, which only a few years ago seemed hopeless, are becoming increasingly attractive for international business. . . . [T]he reform process is mature and appears consolidated."[219]

The Bank's optimism with regard to Chile was well founded. But in Mexico, growth continued to be anemic: 2.5 percent per annum between 1990 and 1994 as against the Bank's projections of 4 percent in 1991 for the same period.[220] In almost any other country such limited growth, despite large capital inflows, would have invited a closer and more public questioning by the Bretton Woods institutions. But the web of Mexican "success" had ensnared its creators.

In order to ensure that the numerous changes in economic policies and institutional arrangements being put into place by adjustment programs did result in greater stability (a fundamental requirement for growth), measures to buttress credibility were implanted. Thus wrestling down inflation to lower levels became the motive for fixed exchange rate regimes. In the original script, flexible and market-based exchange rates figure prominently. Then, with the emphasis on external adjustment, overvalued currencies were seen as the root cause of a variety

217. Cited in Matthew Cooper, "Carlos, We Hardly Knew Ye," *Washington Post*, January 21, 1996, p. C3.

218. The Bank's warnings on real currency appreciation were, for instance, much more tenacious in the case of the CFA Zone countries. Of course, exchange rate issues are primarily the Fund's bailiwick. In Mexico's case, Bank staff had also made veiled warnings on the fiscal situation and the health of the financial system.

219. World Bank, *Latin America and the Caribbean a Decade after the Debt Crisis* (September 1993), p. 6. The report was written by the Bank's chief economist for Latin America, Sebastian Edwards. Mexico was similarly hailed as the prototype "successful post crisis adjuster" by the IMF. See Boughton, "The IMF and the Latin American Debt Crisis," p. 7.

220. The estimates are in World Bank, "Mexico in Transition: Towards a New Role for the Public Sector," Report 8770-ME, May 22, 1991, table G-2, p. 148.

of problems, from trade imbalances to capital flight. But as initial stabilization measures and efforts to service debt pushed up inflation, over time inflation replaced the current account as the major focus of attention. A credible anchor was seen as a sine qua non to curb inflationary expectations. And the anchor used—a fixed exchange rate or modest crawling peg—did succeed in rapidly reducing inflation. Yet the measure, almost by definition, inadvertently began to subvert the core philosophical rationale of "structural adjustment": which was to make economic structures of developing countries more flexible as to equip them with greater resilience to cope with increasing volatility in the global environment. Gradually, as real currency values again appreciated, the clouds of current account deficits again began to gather, and then, almost as sharply as the original crisis, lightning struck. In December 1994, the past became the prologue for a new crisis in Mexico.

Private capital had arrived like a shoal of fish to the coral reef that Mexican officials, in close conjunction with the Bretton Woods institutions, had crafted. But rapidly in early 1995, with one flick of the communal tail, the shoal was off. As Mexico struggled in 1995 with its worst recession in sixty years, accolades turned to brickbats, and the finger-pointing began. Ivy League suffixes that had so recently graced senior Mexican officials, suddenly became less visible.[221]

The rapidity and scale of the response to the 1995 Mexico crisis, in stark contrast to what occurred in the 1980s, underlined both what had been learned from the earlier episode and its limitations. A possible systemic crisis was nipped in the bud. But such extraordinary resources would scarcely be forthcoming for virtually any other country, and especially not in the event of a systemic crisis. The moral hazard inherent in the rescue undermined the case for self-regulation by international financial markets through risk-sharing. For Mexico itself, the results were decidedly mixed. Although the rescue ensured that it would not be faced with prolonged uncertainty with regard to external financial packages, this could not be said of Mexico's economic prospects, at the time of writing. If Mexico had sought to manage its new financial crisis through a bankruptcy-type procedure, would its citizens have been better or worse off than they were on the path it undertook? The new orthodoxy maintained that any break in meeting external financial obligations would have such detrimental long-term effects in the country's renewed access to international financial markets that almost any price was worth paying. Yet, in the absence of a serious examination of alternatives and costs, it appeared to be as much a matter of dogma as the outcome of hard analysis.

The new Mexican crisis also raised troubling questions about how an economy whose structural reforms were so recently touted as "broad and deep" (in the words of the World Bank report already quoted) could be once again faced, in

---

221. James Carville, a political consultant to the Democratic Party, put it well when he posed the rhetorical question, "Do you think if Salinas went to Auburn instead of Harvard he would have gotten the same press?" Quoted in Cooper, "Carlos, We Hardly Knew Ye," p. C3.

the words of Mexico's Finance Minister Ortiz, with "an adjustment of staggering proportions"? Why, despite the momentous structural changes, had the country not become more resilient to economic shocks, the fundamental rationale for structural adjustment? Were the policy mistakes of the Mexican authorities in 1994 so flawed as to drag Mexico into its deepest recession in nearly six decades? Or were they symptomatic of the fragile foundations of a hitherto impressive structure?

These are questions to be addressed by a future history. For the purposes of this chapter, two issues arise. One is that the legacy of the inflexible structure of external debt in countries with Brady bond–supported restructurings may prove quite messy in the event that any of these countries is confronted with a financial crisis in the near future.[222] The other is that, despite the Mexican example, the fundamental changes in the characteristics of private capital flows in the 1990s (in comparison with those in previous decades) are likely to prove more robust in the long run. These changes have led to more diversified sources of finance with equity investors, money market funds, bondholders, and foreign direct investment flows far exceeding commercial bank flows (table 11-7). Systemic risks are consequently less; and, especially in the case of foreign direct investment, these flows have relatively greater risk-sharing characteristics.

Some of the issues discussed in this chapter can be better fleshed out through a case study. Brazil, though certainly not "representative," illustrates well the complexities in the Bank's relationship with a large borrower in this turbulent period and highlights the limited room for maneuver when political instability intrudes.

An Illustration: Brazil

At the outset of the debt crisis, Brazil appeared comparatively well placed to weather the crisis. Notwithstanding the corrosion inflicted by some of the excesses of the 1970s, its economic moorings seemed sound. Its economy had grown by a remarkable 9 percent a year from 1965–80.[223] It had survived the first oil shock by implementing heterodox policies, with significant expansion of state-led investments in tradables financed by large external borrowings, a competitive exchange rate, and tight exchange controls. As inflation rose, indexation became increasingly common. Partly for these reasons—in contrast to the situation in many middle-

222. The total stock of long-term commercial bank debt of developing countries rose from $20 to $283 billion between 1970 to 1982. Subsequently, as commercial bank lending declined and bond financing grew, the total stock of developing country bond issues outstanding rose from $19 billion in 1980 to $224 billion in 1993.

223. World Bank, *World Development Report 1991*, table 2. However, John Williamson, in a personal communication, contends that growth was about 7.5 percent during this period (the discrepancy being due to serious anomalies in Brazil's growth in 1965, as recorded in the International Financial Statistics).

Table 11-7. *Latin America: Debt Indicators, 1979–94*
Period averages[a]

Indicator	1979–82	1983–86	1987–90	1991–94
External debt (billions of U.S. dollars)	266	385	432	523
Components of debt stock (percent)				
IMF credits	1	3	4	3
Short-term	27	12	13	19
Long-term	72	84	83	79
Private nonguaranteed	19	15	7	9
Public, publicly guaranteed	54	69	77	70
Multilateral	6	8	12	12
Bilateral	7	8	12	19
Commercial banks	32	43	39	15
Other private	9	10	14	24
Total debt service (billions of U.S. dollars)	49	49	48	54
Components of debt service (percent)				
IMF repurchases and charges	1	3	9	8
Short-term	14	12	6	7
Long-term	85	85	85	84
Private nonguaranteed	27	21	14	19
Public, publicly guaranteed	58	64	70	66
Multilateral	4	8	15	21
Bilateral	5	6	7	11
Commercial banks	40	39	32	9
Other private	9	11	15	25

Source: World Bank, *World Debt Tables*.
a. Numbers may not add up because of rounding.

income countries where external borrowings financed massive capital flight—Brazil's debts had been incurred largely to finance current account deficits.[224]

Yet these attributes of economic success masked deep underlying problems. As was the case in many other countries, easy access to private capital and the consequent rapid buildup of external debt had left the economy increasingly vulnerable to interest rate shocks. The failure to redress acute equity schisms during the boom years would greatly increase the difficulties of building the needed political consensus to carry out requisite fiscal reforms. These issues became prominent when Brazil, despite its stronger economic moorings, was also swept away by the powerful undertow of retreating private capital.

224. The ratio of capital flight to the increase in external debt in the period 1978–82 is estimated to have ranged from 50 to 100 percent for Argentina, Mexico, and Venezuela. In the case of Brazil it was of the order of 10 percent. Estimates from Miguel A. Rodríguez, "Consequences of Capital Flight for Latin American Debtor Countries," in Donald Lessard and John Williamson, *Capital Flight and Third World Debt* (Washington D.C.: Institute for International Economics, 1987), table 6.1, p. 130.

Brazil's macroeconomic picture during the 1980s was marked by several features: negligible primary fiscal deficits but substantial operational fiscal deficits;[225] steadily increasing inflation;[226] sharp cutbacks in investment (the share of investment in GDP declined from 30 percent in the late 1970s to 21 percent in the late 1980s); substantial trade surpluses (averaging nearly 8 billion per year in the 1980s) and a current account roughly in balance after 1984;[227] and an external debt, though the largest in absolute size, less than that of many other highly indebted middle-income countries (Brazil's debt-service indicators peaked by the mid-1980s).

After the onset of the crisis, the Bank's role in Brazil consisted largely of an expansion in its project lending, an increase in its share of project costs to accelerate disbursements, and some quick-disbursing policy-based credit operations designed to accelerate agricultural and industrial exports. As a result, 1983 disbursements ($1.2 billion) were double those of the previous year. Lending commitments in the fiscal period 1983–86 (averaging $1.55 billion) were more than double those of the previous four-year period (the increase was less marked on a calendar-year basis, as indicated in table 11-8). But as evident from table 11-8, despite the significant increase in lending, and though Brazil was its largest borrower, the Bank's financial role was quite limited.

In 1985 Brazil underwent a major political transition when, after twenty-one years, a new democratic government came to power. But the administration was plagued by weak political leadership, following the death of the president-elect, Tancredo Neves. Nevertheless, with record trade surpluses and a smart revival of growth (6.9 percent between 1984 and 1986, after the 1981–83 recession, when it declined by 2.4 percent per year), as the Bank's 1985 Brazil Country Program Paper noted, the economic environment appeared "more promising" than at any time since the beginning of the decade.[228] Consequently, the Bank decided to

---

225. The operational deficit averaged nearly 5 percent over the decade, reflecting the budgetary impact of real interest payments. The high inflationary environment of Brazil meant that through this period the nominal deficit, representing the net borrowing requirements of the government, was an inappropriate measure of the fiscal deficit, due to the large inflationary component of interest payments. A more appropriate measure was the "operational" deficit, which applied a "monetary correction" to the nominal deficit by deducting the size of interest payments needed to maintain the real value of the principal. However, the real fiscal effect under the government's control was the "primary" deficit—the operational deficit less real interest payments.

226. Monthly inflation increased from 6 percent in 1981–82 to 10 percent in 1983–84 to 15 percent in 1987 and 27 percent in 1989.

227. The current account moved from a deficit of $14 billion in 1982 to a small surplus of $0.6 billion in 1984, principally because of a $13 billion surplus in the trade account. Although this was partly due to a jump in exports, a sharp decrease in imports (58 percent of the decrease was accounted by declining oil imports, both because of the decline in oil prices and the increase of domestic energy substitutes) played a significant role.

228. World Bank, Country Program Paper, "Brazil," May 13, 1985, para. 1.

Table 11-8. *World Bank Lending to Brazil, 1979–90*
Annual averages

Lending	1979–82	1983–86	1987–90
Billions of U.S. dollars			
Commitments	0.9	1.4	1.0
Disbursements	0.4	1.2	0.9
Net flows	0.3	0.8	(0.1)
Net transfers	0.1	0.4	(0.8)
Disbursements as percentage of			
GNP	0.2	0.6	0.2
Imports	1.2	4.0	2.5
Gross domestic investment	0.7	3.0	1.0
Total government expenditures	0.8	2.2	n.a.
Net flows as percentage of			
GNP	0.1	0.4	(0.0)
Imports	0.8	2.7	(0.3)
Gross domestic investment	0.5	2.0	(0.1)
Total government expenditures	0.6	1.5	n.a.

Source: World Bank data.
n.a. Not available.

expand both the size of the lending program as well as the share of quick-disbursing operations to increase Brazil's portfolio share from about 8 percent to 13–14 percent, as long as an adequate reform program was forthcoming.[229] Although this would breach an important internal financial prudence ratio (10 percent to its largest borrower), it was felt that Brazil's size justified such an expansion. With internal financial projections forecasting the onset of negative net transfers to Brazil as early as 1987, financial risk management with regard to its largest borrower emerged as an increasing concern for the Bank.[230]

Unfortunately, Brazil's recovery proved transient. Soon thereafter, the economy entered into a prolonged crisis of stagflation. Influenced by the lackluster outcomes of ongoing IMF stabilization programs, the new economic team that took over in 1985 decided to avoid an IMF program.[231] Instead, it launched an innovative, but ultimately unsuccessful, "heterodox shock" program (called the Cruzado Plan) in

229. Minutes of September 23, 1985 meeting of Managing Committee, November 8, 1985. See section "Brazil CPP."

230. Memorandum, Shinji Asanuma to Moeen A. Qureshi, "Brazil—Portfolio Exposure," April 23, 1984.

231. Of all the financial rescue packages assembled under IMF sponsorship in the fall of 1982, Brazil's program was one of the least successful. An EFF agreement with the Fund fell through after failing to meet the first-quarter targets. It was renegotiated in late 1983 and followed by a large devaluation. However, growing unpopularity led the military regime to pursue populist macroeconomic policies. Rapid monetary expansion at the end of 1984 again led to a suspension of the 1983–85 EFF in early 1985.

February 1986. This was the first in a series of stabilization programs with hetero-dox elements that were launched over the next few years.[232] The reasons for their failure are complex, but a core problem was the government's inability to tackle public sector deficits and the use of monetary expansion to finance them. To some extent, underlying this inability was an unwillingness born of a strong belief that some deficit was desirable. As was the case with many orthodox programs, it is unclear to what extent the failure of the heterodox shock programs in Brazil and elsewhere in Latin America (in contrast, say, to the relative success achieved in Israel) can be attributed to different policies or to very different levels of external resources available.[233]

Brazil's poor relations with the IMF led it to cultivate more cordial relations with the Bank. Its request to the Bank in 1986 to increase its annual borrowing to $2 billion met a favorable response, contingent, however, on the usual caveat that the country adopt "an appropriate medium-term policy framework."[234] But the internal economic and political turbulence in Brazil was soon reflected in the Bank-Brazil relationship. Loan disbursements began to slow as the pace of loan processing faltered, in part as a consequence of internecine conflicts between the finance and planning ministries on Brazil's investment priorities. The price freezes that the heterodox plans deemed essential to break inflationary expectations came into conflict with the price liberalization goals of the Bank's loans for agriculture and power. Disagreements on interest subsidies delayed processing of new quick-disbursing agriculture credit loans.

Of Brazil's external creditors in 1986, only the Bank had a positive cash flow. As the Cruzado Plan rapidly unraveled with inflation touching four figures and Brazil found itself facing an impasse in its negotiations with its commercial creditors, it announced in February 1987 that it would suspend interest payments to the commercial banks for an indefinite period, though payments on trade credits would be maintained. With little recourse to external resources—Brazil continued to eschew a standby agreement with the IMF—it financed the overwhelming part of the government deficit through local borrowings. The resulting increase in the government's domestic debt undermined stabilization efforts.[235] Despite the urgent

232. The Cruzado Plan was followed by the Macroeconomic Control or "Bresser Plan" in June 1987; the "Summer Plan" of January 1989; Collor I (March 1990) and Collor II (February 1991); and the "Real Plan" launched in December 1993.

233. See, for instance, Eliana Cardoso, "From Inertia to Megainflation: Brazil in the 1980s," in Michael Bruno and others, eds., *Lessons of Economic Stabilization and Its Aftermath* (MIT Press, 1991), pp. 143–77.

234. Memorandum, Roberto Gonzalez Cofino for the record, "Mr. Conable's Visit to Brazil," December 19, 1986.

235. The share of credit to the government in total credit increased continuously over the decade (from 19 percent in 1980 to 34 percent in 1984 to 45 percent in 1988). Both the size and composition of the domestic debt (which included large intergovernmental and banking sector components) rendered traditional tools of monetary policy increasingly ineffective.

need to execute a stabilization program, the Bank recognized that the institution "could not do much to induce the Government to take the necessary steps, other than continuing its dialogue."[236]

But with the interest moratorium, the Bank's lending to Brazil began to come under pressure. Already a large agricultural sector loan had been put on hold at the urging of the U.S. Treasury, anxious that adverse reactions from congressional agricultural lobbies not spill over to an impending IDA replenishment and concerned as well by the absence of a link between the Bank loan and Paris Club payments by Brazil.[237] This time, since most of the scheduled loans were projects that did not depend on the current macroeconomic framework, and "were very high priority [projects] under any set of circumstances," the pressures were considerably deflected.[238]

By mid-1987, major changes had taken place both in the Bank's management and in Brazil's economic team. In June Brazil's new finance minister, Carlos Bresser Pereira, announced a new heterodox stabilization program (dubbed the "Bresser Plan") aimed at macroeconomic policy reform.[239] Bank officials raved about the

---

With highly liquid, indexed government bonds a close substitute for money proper and included in Brazil's broad-money supply aggregates (M_4), increased interest rates had a perverse effect: they increased the operational deficit and the quantity of money. An interesting discussion of some of these issues is provided in World Bank, "Brazil—Economic Stabilization with Structural Reforms," Report 8371-BR, January 1991.

236. Memorandum, Vinod Dubey, director CPD, to files, "Brazil—Medium Term Growth Strategy: Minutes of the OPC Meeting of February 12, 1987," March 5, 1987.

237. Memorandum, Ernest Stern to A. W. Clausen, "Brazil," May 29, 1986.

238. Five of eight projects scheduled (two rural development projects in northeastern Brazil, a livestock disease control project, a skills development project, and an industrial control project) went ahead as scheduled. Three other projects, all in infrastructure, did not. See memorandum, Ernest Stern to Barber B. Conable, "Brazil," April 6, 1987. During this period the IFC, together with Merrill Lynch and First Boston, had worked on developing a $100 million "Brazil Fund." As required by its Charter, the IFC needed to obtain a "no objection certificate" from the fund's host governments, in this case, Brazil and the United States, since the fund had a New York listing. Objections from the U.S. Treasury, stemming from Brazil's debt stance, forced the IFC to forgo $2 million in fees. The fund was, however, launched successfully by the two private investment banks. "Whose Loans Are They Anyway?" *Economist Financial Report*, May 12, 1988, p. 1. This was only the second time in the IFC's history when a government had formally objected in this manner. See IBRD/IDA/IFC, "Summary of Discussions at the Meeting of the Executive Directors of the Bank and IDA, and the Board of Directors of IFC, December 22, 1987," SD 87-73, February 10, 1988.

239. The Bresser Plan was similar to the Cruzado Plan in imposing a wage-price freeze but unlike its predecessor, which had resorted to freezing the nominal exchange rate (without any devaluation), it devalued the exchange rate and adopted a crawling peg exchange rate regime. Although it intended to focus on fiscal reforms, while renegotiating Brazil's external debt in the context of the moratorium on interest payments to private creditors, it, too, met its Waterloo on the fiscal front.

"significant change in attitude on economic policy matters [in the new economic team in Brazil]. . . . At no time in the recent past has the government been so willing and ready to work closely with the Bank."[240] As part of a graduated response, the Bank moved toward approval of a $500 million quick-disbursing power sector loan.[241] The loan, an adjustment operation, had been under preparation for some time, and Conable had indicated to the Brazilians that it would go through provided appropriate tariff actions were met.[242] These were now largely in place. Although there were worries about the short-term time horizon of the Bresser Plan, particularly the absence of an exit strategy once the wage-price freezes were lifted, the macroeconomic measures were seen to be a significant move in the right direction.

The negotiations of this loan were illustrative of the complex intertwining of issues and institutions. Since the planned loan was an adjustment operation, the Bank could only move with the concurrence of the IMF regarding Brazil's macro-economic framework. A crucial element in the debt strategy of the Bresser Plan was its attempt to delink Brazil's negotiations with the commercial banks from those with the IMF. While the Brazilian finance minister was prepared to negotiate a standby with the IMF, he had informed the Fund's managing director that he *first* wished to complete negotiations with the commercial banks and then proceed with an agreement with the IMF.[243] Concurrently, the Brazilian team wanted the Bank to vet its economic program, hoping to leverage a positive assessment into an increase in Bank lending as well as to enhance its negotiating position with the commercial banks.

Quite early in the crisis the Bank had begun to link loan commitments to evidence of "substantial completion" of agreements between the debtor countries and the IMF, the commercial banks, and the Paris Club. Now the possibility of delinkage presented the Bank with a historic opportunity, as well as grave risks. Even if the Bank did have the requisite macroeconomic expertise (a matter of some dispute), to become almost the sole lender in a country as large as Brazil entailed serious financial risks. But even more important were the political risks. As Stern put it to Conable, the proposed delinkage "has long-term systemic implications, since the influence of the Fund and, indeed, ours, rests on this linkage."[244] The Bank's processing of a balance of payments loan during an interest payments

240. Memorandum, S. Shahid Husain to Barber B Conable through Moeen A. Qureshi, "The Bank's Approach to Brazil," June 30, 1987, pp. 1–2.
241. Memorandum, Moeen A. Qureshi to members of the Policy Committee, "Brazil—Power Project," July 23, 1987.
242. Memorandum, Roberto Gonzalez Cofino for the record, "Mr. Conable's Meeting with Brazil's Finance Minister, Mr. Dilson Funaro," March 10, 1987.
243. Memorandum, Moeen A. Qureshi to Barber B. Conable, "Brazil Power Loan: Conversations with Mr. Camdessus," July 24, 1987. For an account of the Brazilian position see, Luiz Carlos Bresser Pereira, "Brazil," in John Williamson, ed., *The Political Economy of Policy Reform* (Washington D.C.: Institute for International Economics, 1994), pp. 333–54.
244. Memorandum, Ernest Stern to Barber B. Conable, July 24, 1987.

moratorium, Stern went on to argue, would "be seen by the commercial banks as a strong endorsement of the Brazilian position. Since Brazil is holding interest payments hostage for the negotiations, our condoning Brazil's strategy is likely to have seriously adverse repercussion in our relations with commercial banks."[245]

The Fund had been informed of Brazil's strategy by the Brazilian finance minister and of the proposed Bank loan by Moeen Qureshi, the Bank's new senior vice president for operations. Although Michel Camdessus, managing director of the Fund, had stated that he doubted the commercial banks would agree to negotiate in the absence of a Fund agreement, he had acceded to Brazil's request that it be allowed to test the waters. At the same time, he apparently concurred with the Bank's decision to proceed with the power loan and, indeed, stated that the Bank could tell the Brazilians the loan was being made "'with the full understanding of the Fund.'"[246]

Shortly thereafter, the Fund took the Bank to task, arguing that by "readily accepting Brazil's own fiscal target, the Bank [was] sending a signal, at a particularly delicate time in the debt strategy, that it is less demanding than the Fund."[247] But by sending copies of this exchange to the U.S. Treasury, the Fund itself was sending a signal about institutional turf. It made the Bank look permissive in contrast to the tougher Fund, an approach also favored by the U.S. Treasury. Moreover, by playing out their battles in front of the U.S. Treasury, both institutions, inadvertently, further circumscribed their autonomy, providing the Treasury with an opening to play the two institutions off against each other.[248] This would be evident in the Argentina episode a year later (see chapter 10).

The dispute with the Fund now forced the Bank to inform the Brazilians that for any future policy-based lending to take place, not only would there have to be agreement on appropriate sector-level policies and a satisfactory medium-term macroeconomic program, but the Bank would also need to "be assured that there was satisfactory progress towards agreement with the IMF, the commercial banks and other creditors on an overall financing package."[249] The new stance was, however, rendered moot by events within Brazil. The Brazilian government asked the Bank to postpone consideration of the power sector loan while it assessed the implications of its latest stabilization plan on the power sector.

Meanwhile Bresser Pereira floated his debt proposals (discussed in an earlier section), an important element of which was a call for the multilaterals, including the

245. Ibid.

246. Memorandum, Qureshi to Conable, July 24, 1987, p. 2; quotation in original.

247. Memorandum, Richard D. Erb to Moeen A. Qureshi, "Brazil: The Second Power Sector Loan," August 11, 1987. The Fund was concerned that given external financing constraints and the public investment targets set by the Brazilian authorities, there would be little room for the increase in the private investment necessary to achieve the growth objectives, unless the operational fiscal deficit target of 3.5 percent was reduced.

248. Copies of all the interchanges were sent to David Mulford and James Conrow of the U.S. Treasury.

249. Memorandum, Moeen A. Qureshi to David Mulford, "Brazil: The Second Power Sector Loan," August 6, 1987.

Bank, to maintain "an even cash flow."[250] This proposition met with strong opposition within the Bank. Although the Bank's management was prepared to give the matter sympathetic consideration given the country's predicament, especially if there was visible progress on the macroeconomic front, it was not prepared to accept positive cash flow as a matter of principle. Rather, the Bank decided that in the absence of progress on the macroeconomic front, it would restrict its lending to investment operations in a few sectors, so as to maintain zero net disbursements (in reality, net disbursements averaged negative $100 million annually between 1987 and 1990). The latter objective was viewed "as an approach for maintaining the Bank's lending capability in Brazil while facilitating a dialogue and it was also to be viewed as an element of prudent risk management."[251]

However, the Bresser Plan soon collapsed, a victim of political vacillation on the fiscal front. A new economic team took over and terminated the interest moratorium. In mid-1988 Brazil concluded a MYRA with the commercial banks, together with a standby agreement with the IMF and a rescheduling agreement with the Paris Club.[252] Later disbursements of the new money facility were linked, through a parallel cofinancing agreement with the Bank, with the aforementioned $500 million IBRD power sector loan (as well as $450 million in Japanese cofinancing).[253]

But once again the power loan stalled. With inflation at an annualized 1000 percent, the macroeconomic program again looked dubious, and with it the chances of a favorable assessment from the IMF. Sector conditions unraveled following major administrative changes in Brazil that brought the hitherto separate nuclear power program within this sector. The Bank now felt compelled to address and add nuclear power loan conditions to ensure a credible adjustment loan in this sector, further delaying the loan and the drawdown of the linked money. Willy-nilly, a strong link had been drawn between the nuclear power issue and commercial bank disbursements. Facing a second consecutive year of negative net transfers in 1988, and with so much riding on one loan, the Bank began to be concerned that internal pressures in Brazil could again lead to a moratorium, and that this time the Bank would be included as well.[254]

250. Bresser Pereira, "Brazil," p. 345.

251. World Bank, Operations Committee, "Minutes of the Operations Committee to Consider Brazil-Country Strategy Paper Held on March 16, 1988," March 25, 1988, p. 4.

252. The package with commercial banks, signed in October 1988, restructured approximately $82 billion of Brazilian debt, the largest restructuring ever. The package included exit bonds worth $1 billion.

253. The financing package amounted to $5.2 billion with a $4.2 billion first tranch. The commercial banks had wanted Bank guarantees: either a partial Bank guarantee, as in the 1986 Mexico operation (on late maturities of a cofinancing facility), or a contingent take-out facility. By this time the Bank, supported by the U.S. Treasury, had become wary of guarantees, worried that they might entangle it in reschedulings.

254. Memorandum, Armene M. Choksi to Barber B. Conable through Moeen A. Qureshi, "Brazil— The Macroeconomic Situation and the Second Power Sector: Outstanding Issues," November 8, 1988.

The Bank had expected to lend $800 million in adjustment operations and a further $1.6 billion in investment operations in fiscal 1989. While policy disagreements and macroeconomic disequilibria led to the abrogation of adjustment operations, the decline in investment loan commitments (to less than a billion dollars), was largely due to internal factors in Brazil. The fiscal 1989 lending program had to be reconstructed three times as political changes in Brazil altered investment priorities.[255] As a result, not only did new commitments decline, but disbursements on existing ongoing projects dropped by nearly a third below the Bank's normal disbursement profile because of a lack of counterpart funds. Undisbursed commitments reached record levels even as net disbursements turned negative for the first time in a quarter century.

Whatever the reasons, as net transfers by Brazil to the Bank climbed in 1987 and again in 1988, the Bank began receiving increasingly negative media coverage in Brazil. Under these circumstances the stalled power sector loan became a charged symbol in the Bank's relations with Brazil. In an effort to break the impasse, the power sector loan was allowed to die. In its place a quick-disbursing $325 million Environmental Reform and Energy Conservation loan, a transmutation of the earlier loan, was now proposed.[256] However, the sharp discrepancy between the time frame for disbursement (six months) and the proposed actions (many of which were of an institutional nature which would require years to implement) raised serious misgiving among the Bank's senior management regarding the suitability of the loan instrument for the objectives at hand. More important, the critics felt that the Bank should not proceed with a SECAL, since as Stanley Fischer, strongly supported by Stern, argued, there "cannot be a clearer case of an inadequate macroeconomic framework," in Brazil's case.[257] By this time, the "Summer Plan," launched earlier in the year, was facing collapse in the face of severe credibility problems. Not only had previous wage-price freeze plans failed, but with elections looming it was apparent that firm action on the fiscal front was unlikely in the near future.

255. Responsibility for World Bank operations was transferred from the Finance Ministry to the Ministry of Planning. A new constitution devolved several federal functions to states and municipalities, which meant that for investment loans the Bank now had to negotiate with different government entities. At the same time federal-state disagreements about the states' capacity to borrow delayed disbursements on existing Bank loans, due to lack of counterpart funds. All these factors considerably delayed securing internal agreements among the various branches of government.

256. The loan was to be disbursed in two tranches over six months. It addressed environmental issues associated with electricity generation and was not a broad environmental loan as suggested by the title.

257. Memorandum, Stanley Fischer to Barber B. Conable, May 5, 1989. Fischer argued that Brazil had been holding down the exchange rate to rein in inflation. The exchange rate would in due course become progressively overvalued forcing a sharp devaluation, at which point inflation would jump.

In their defense, the Bank's operations managers argued that even though the macroeconomic situation continued to be fragile, the need for flexibility outweighed macroeconomic objections, since Brazil had basically met the sectoral conditions. The loan in question had dragged on for more than two years and had become "the symbol of [the Bank's] relationship with Brazil which had deteriorated significantly—since we were seen as being inflexible and interfering in their domestic affairs."[258] But with the Bank still nursing the wounds of the Argentina episode, and the institution's role in the recently announced Brady proposals as yet unclear, Conable decided against proceeding with the loan. Instead, the financial objectives were partly met through two credit operations approved in May 1989.[259] The frequency with which Brazil had formulated stabilization plans and failed to implement them, led the Bank to limit its lending to those sectors that were relatively unaffected by macroeconomic policies: environment, agriculture, and social sectors.

In March 1990 the freshly installed Collor administration launched yet another economic plan, "Brazil Novo." The plan achieved some of its structural reform objectives, especially on trade policy and domestic deregulation, but like its predecessors soon began to founder on the stabilization front. As the economy slipped into its worst recession since 1981 (GDP would decline by 4 percent in 1990) and the balance of payments worsened, Brazil again began to run up arrears to commercial banks.

Although Brazil had reached an agreement in principle with the IMF for a $2 billion standby in September, the condition for approval (by the Fund's Board) was that Brazil reenter negotiations with the commercial banks and commit to regular payments to them. In late 1990, with payments by Brazil to the World Bank becoming frequently overdue, Brazil's chief debt negotiator went on record stating that if the IMF did not soon approve a standby agreement, the country would be unable to repay creditors other than the IMF.[260] In the event Brazil's proposals—based on a position that its payments would expressly take into account the country's severe fiscal constraints—were rejected by the commercial banks and, as a result, the IMF indefinitely postponed Board discussions of Brazil's standby program.[261]

258. Memorandum, S. Shahid Husain to Barber B. Conable, "Brazil—Proposed Environmental Reform and Energy Conservation Loan," April 22, 1989, p. 1.

259. An agricultural credit loan for $300 million (BR2971), which disbursed $227 million in fiscal 1990; and an agroindustrial credit loan (BR2960) for $300 million, which disbursed $138 million in fiscal 1990. Thus 60 percent of the $600 million dollars was disbursed over the next fiscal year.

260. Memorandum, S. Shahid Husain to Barber B. Conable, "Brazil—Visit of Mr. Ibrahim Eris, President of the Brazilian Central Bank," October 22, 1990.

261. The Brazilian proposals entailed transforming its outstanding medium- and long-term debt (approximately $60 billion including fully capitalized arrears) into bonds with

At this point, David Mulford of the U.S. Treasury asked the Bank's management to withdraw two project loans for Brazil scheduled for Board discussion two weeks later.[262] The basis for such action was U.S. concern regarding "Brazil's apparent lack of seriousness in its negotiations with the commercial banks. He [Mulford] did not want our lending to be a signal that we would continue to lend into arrears when there is an unwillingness to have good faith negotiations."[263] At the Inter-American Development Bank —where the U.S. executive director has the option of asking for a deferment of a loan for two months—a loan scheduled for November 2 was withdrawn.

The Bank's management argued that at a time of large net transfers to the Bank, and a country relationship made more vexing by problems related to environmental issues, delaying these routine projects would only serve to inflame Brazilian political attitudes on debt and seriously risked provoking Brazil to stop servicing its IBRD debt.[264] If Brazil went into protracted arrears to the Bank, the financial ramifications for the Bank would be extremely serious: the institution was faced with provisioning 1 percent of the affected portfolio per month, or about $1 billion a year, plus an annual income loss of about $650 million in foregone interest income, roughly twice its projected net income. Mulford was informed by the Bank's management that they "could not take administrative action which could have such consequences. If shareholders felt that, contrary to our advice, these routine operations should not be approved, then this should be on the basis of a full discussion of the likely consequences, since it involves substantial risks to shareholders' capital."[265] The position of the Bank's management was clear: the financial risks were potentially so large that management would be abdicating its fiduciary responsibility if it were to accommodate the G-7 position simply on the basis of an informal request.

---

maturities of forty-five years. The commercial banks in turn first wanted to strike a deal on arrears and impending interest payments before discussing any restructuring of the debt stock. Paralleling its external stance, the government's severe fiscal position would lead to an implicit default on its domestic debt, as a result of unannounced reductions in the indexed inflation compensation on its domestic debt. See Evan Tanner, "Balancing the Budget with Implicit Domestic Default: The Case of Brazil in the 1980s," World Development, vol. 22, no. 1 (January 1994), pp. 85–98.

262. The two loans were a Science Research and Training loan for $150 million and a Private Sector Finance loan for $300 million. The former was expected to disburse over six years, the latter over four years, with 50 percent over eighteen months.

263. Memorandum, Ernest Stern to Barber B. Conable, "Status Report on Brazil Loans as of November 3, 1990," November 3, 1990, p. 1.

264. The IBRD's outstanding portfolio in Brazil at the end of fiscal 1990 (June 30, 1990) was $8.1 billion, representing 9.22 percent of its portfolio. Net transfers were minus $724 million. By September 30, 1990, Brazil had $190 million in payments overdue by more than thirty days.

265. Memorandum, Stern to Conable, November 3, 1990, p. 1, reporting on his conversation with David Mulford.

Members were within their rights to ask for postponement, but the Board was the proper forum, so responsibility would be clear and transparent.[266]

A few days later the U.S. executive director called a meeting of the G-7 executive directors to press his country's case. The U.S. position met with strong backing from Japan and some support from the United Kingdom, while the other members regarded the approach as undesirable. A final decision was deferred pending a meeting of the G-7 deputies in Rome a week later. By then the Bank's management had persuaded the United Kingdom to join Germany in supporting its position, while Canada and Italy were undecided. France joined the United States and Japan in taking a hard-line position, but soon softened its stance, following quiet diplomacy by the Fund's managing director, who concurred with the Bank's management that the risks involved in Mulford's strategy were out of proportion to any benefits.[267] The vehemence of the negative Japanese views regarding Brazil's debt stance caught the Bank's management by surprise. This reflected the broader Japanese view on debt wherein, as the principal source of new bilateral funds, it was amenable to providing additional resources but was unwilling to countenance rescheduling and forgiveness, a position not unlike that of the Bank with respect to its own debt.

The sustained efforts by the Bank's management finally led the G-7 not to oppose the loans but to make strong statements at the Board meeting to send an adequate message to Brazil.[268] The Board discussions were sharply polarized. The almost perfunctory manner in which the Board had been informed through these two loans of a major restructuring of the Bank's portfolio did not help matters. The clear demarcation between the G-7 group and other members of the Board was evident in testy exchanges, attesting to the very different national interests and philosophical views on how to resolve the debt crisis. The G-7 position was that the Board could not ignore the impasse that existed between Brazil and its external creditors; indeed, that it was obliged to deal with Brazil's relationship with external capital markets. The G-7 argued that a concern for country creditworthiness obligated the Bank to exercise greater financial prudence through nonlending for three reasons: external debt problems signaled underlying economic problems; unsettled disputes would reduce the prospects of other sources of capital, increas-

266. Around this time, the Bank Group, strongly urged by the same shareholders, was vigorously espousing the importance of attributes such as "transparency" and "participation" for its lending stance.

267. Memorandum, Ernest Stern to Barber B. Conable, "Brazil—Further Update," November 6, 1990.

268. In the end the loans were postponed by two weeks. Despite media reports that this was due to pressure by the G-7 ("Brazil Loans Are Blocked," *New York Times,* November 19, 1990; "Putting the Squeeze on Brazil," *Journal of Commerce,* November 26, 1990, p. 8A), in reality the reason was Brazil's overdues, which had crossed the point wherein the Bank, as per its rules, could take new loans to its Board. In turn, the delays by Brazil were due to bureaucratic glitches at its end, rather than an unwillingness to service its loans on time.

ing the Bank's risks; and the Bank had to worry about the implications of the creditworthiness of its borrowers for its own market standing, in the interest of all its members.

The developing countries countered that the G-7 stance was a cover for parochial financial interests. Coming on the heels of the hiatus in Bank lending to China following Tiananmen Square, again at the instructions of the G-7, developing countries worried about the growing political interference in the Bank. Such pressures, they argued, would lose the trust and confidence of its developing country members.

At one level, the G-7's attempt to instruct the Bank's president not to propose a loan to the Board until a certain requirement was met—in this case, that Brazil should reach a settlement with the commercial banks—was contrary to the institution's Articles and bylaws.[269] More important for this discussion, it ran counter to discussions on debt reduction that had been held just a few months earlier, following the Brady proposals when the G-7, fearing an activist approach by Bank staff and management, had insisted that the Bank should not insert itself in negotiations between a member and commercial banks.

But with the debt crisis already ebbing, these battles subsided. Brazil eventually reached an agreement in principle with its commercial bank advisory committee on a Brady-type deal in July 1992, without the participation of the multilaterals.[270]

Comments and Conclusion

> "I have come for advice."
> "That is easily got."
> "And help."
> "That is not always so easy."
>
> —Arthur Conan Doyle, "The Five Orange Pips"

Borrowers, lenders, national regulators, and international dispensers of seals of approval—all share blame for the crisis. The dangers of overborrowing, while apparent later with the benefit of hindsight, were severely underestimated at the time. The heaviest costs, however, were borne by those with the least capacity to bear them: ordinary citizens of the debtor countries. Along with notably better

---

269. Under the institution's bylaws, the president prepares the agenda. While executive directors can ask for a postponement and vote against a loan, the president cannot be instructed not to present a loan to the Board.

270. The agreement, executed in April 1994, covered $59 billion of Brazil's total external debt of $139 billion and led to a reduction of $3.6 billion in the face value of its debt. Since almost half of Brazil's debt (mostly interest arrears) was rescheduled and not covered, the resulting debt reduction (estimated as equivalent to 19 percent of the eligible debt in net present value terms) was lower than in most other cases.

borrower policies, these costs could have been avoided in the event of initial debt forgiveness or substantial new long-term financial flows. Neither was provided since in practice both amounted to an indirect call on the resources of the commercial banks' parent countries.

For some, the precipitous decline in economic fortunes of the debtor countries meant that the 1980s were a "lost decade, development in reverse."[271] Yet the calamity also cleared the thickets of previous economic policies and economic institutions—in particular, the degree of government involvement in economic activity—and thereby allowed new space for major changes in economic policies. As a result, others (including the Bank), argue that faster growth will ensue, which will more than make up for the costs of the debt setback. If that transpires, the 1980s may represent a more complex picture of *reculer pour mieux sauter.*

Rarely in the Bank's history has national power been projected on the Bank on such a scale and intensity as was the case in the management of the debt crisis. The Bank's major owners, the G-7, responded to what they saw at first as a financial emergency and later as an opportunity for exercising policy influence, by, in effect, managing Fund and Bank policies toward the debtor countries.

Notwithstanding differing interpretations of the outcome, it would, however, be erroneous to reduce the course of the debt crisis to a simple deterministic variable, namely, the power exercised by major owners. The course was riddled with numerous idiosyncratic sandbanks which, aligned differently, could well have channeled events differently.

GLOBAL ECONOMIC VARIABLES. Despite the confidence with which financial programs and debt initiatives were put forth, their relative success was strongly predicated on key economic variables—interest rates, commodity prices, and exchange rates—which were quite unpredictable. If the Baker initiative had been followed by the lower global interest rates that prevailed after the Brady initiative, or vice versa, the results would have been quite different, as would be history's judgment.

THE COMMERCIAL BANKS. Walter Wriston, chairman and chief executive officer of Citicorp between 1970 and 1984, is reported to have remarked that "bankers are in the business of managing risk. Pure and simple, that is the business of banking."[272] The commercial banks scarcely lived up to Wriston's dictum before the eruption of the crisis. Subsequently, their real estate lending binge demonstrated a continuation of the practice of lending first and repenting later. But in case of their loans to developing countries, the overall record shows that the commercial banks did not have much grounds to repent. They managed their risks

271. For instance, Hans W. Singer, "The 1980s: A Lost Decade—Development in Reverse," in Hans W. Singer and Soumitra Sharma, eds., *Growth and External Debt Management* (St. Martin's Press, 1989), pp. 46–56.

272. "A Comedy of Errors," *Economist,* April 10, 1993; "Survey of International Banking," p. 3.

well by transferring them to the borrowers and official creditors.[273] To that extent, they did vindicate Wriston's adage.

THE ROLE OF THE UNITED STATES. As its largest shareholder, and with significant national interests at stake, the United States played a fundamental role in the Bank's management of the crisis. The fact that the United States could, and did, exercise a degree of control far in excess of its shareholding, was due to its perception that national interests were at stake and the low profile adopted by other large shareholders. The last, in turn, stemmed from a reluctance to strain bilateral ties as well as considerable empathy with the U.S. position.

As happens in a crisis, management devolved on a small group of individuals. Initially located at the Federal Reserve Board, the IMF, and the commercial bank advisory committees, by the mid-1980s the locus of decisionmaking had gravitated to a tiny, fervid group at the U.S. Treasury. The dogmatic zeal exerted by the Bank's largest shareholder was unprecedented in the institution's history.

THE DEBTOR COUNTRIES. The eccentricities of domestic politics in the debtor countries were another unpredictable factor, as demonstrated by the Brazil case study. While Chile and Colombia were notable exceptions, the rest plunged into economic chaos, which was both cause and consequence of political instability. Conversely, the electoral success and subsequent actions of political leaders in Argentina, Peru, and Venezuela at the end of the 1980s was also quite unforeseen.

At a more systemic level, one of the puzzling aspects of the debt crisis, especially over 1983–87, was why Latin American governments were such well-behaved, extremely cautious debtors, despite the extraordinary burden of repayment. Jesus Silva-Herzog, one of the principals in the crisis (in his capacity as Mexico's finance minister) and a key voice in Mexico's decision not to default, would later regret that decision as a "historical mistake."[274] Following his retirement, David Knox, the Bank's vice president for Latin America, made a case for *responsible* default by the debtor countries, and its acceptance by the international community, conditioned on strong debtor country performance. Knox argued that as a last resort, "if they played their cards correctly Latin American debtors would in fact have very considerable power to default partially or wholly."[275] Knox's judgment, termed "heretical" by the media,[276] received a surprising endorsement from Stern: "I accept the

273. See Jeffrey Sachs and Harry Huizinga, "U.S. Commercial Banks and the Developing-Country Debt Crisis," *Brookings Papers on Economic Activity*, vol. 2 (1987), pp. 555–606; Daniel Cohen, "The Debt Crisis: A Postmortem," *NBER Macroeconomics Annual 1992*, pp. 64–114; Michael P. Dooley, "A Retrospective on the Debt Crisis," paper prepared for the Fiftieth Anniversary of Essays in International Finance, Princeton University, 1994.

274. Jesús Silva-Herzog, interview with the authors, July 20, 1995.

275. David Knox, *Latin American Debt: Facing Facts* (Oxford, England: Oxford International Institute, 1990), p. 49.

276. See, for instance, *The Independent* (U.K.), "Heretical Approach to Third World Debt," April 17, 1990, p. 19. In fact, the media latched on to just one small aspect of an

proposition that the debtors have been too supine. . . . If debtors had been willing to play a role, or had been encouraged to, the legal framework would not have turned out to be such a [straitjacket]. And the participating banks would not have lost as much by earlier action as they have in the long run."[277] If these observations are valid, the debtor countries' actions require some explanation.

For one, the importance of image—and the need to maintain it—cannot be underestimated. For debtor-country finance officials, most especially in the early years, the debt crisis was first a matter of maintaining their "credit," in the sense of creditworthiness, thereby to retain access to international capital markets. That objective was incompatible with a debtors cartel.

Later attempts by the Latin American countries to organize themselves—in mid-1985 at Cartagena and again in late 1988 when the presidents of Brazil, Mexico, Argentina, Peru, Colombia, Uruguay, and Venezuela formed the Rio Club (a forum to discuss and coordinate their debt policies)—were halfhearted and too little and too late. The difficulties were, in part, due to the absence of a tradition of regional cooperation in Latin America, in addition to the fact that there were major debtors outside the region. Although economic trends were similar across the region, the growth-trough recessions, especially of the major debtors, were usually out of phase. Historically, because of its size, Brazil usually plowed its own furrow, while Chile's ideological inclinations kept it aloof. Furthermore, a key debtor—Mexico—was clearly uninterested, recognizing that its importance to the United States would ensure that it would (and did) get preferential treatment from the creditor community. Coordination was also made difficult by the rapid turnover of key officials in debtor countries. (The average finance minister's tenure during this period was less than fifteen months.)[278] And for many central bank and finance ministry officials, the domestic conflicts, as they battled with their presidents, colleagues in other ministries, and legislatures to come to grips with their country's fiscal problems, often overshadowed their external difficulties.

A potent combination of hope and fear played an important role. By periodically, and incrementally, putting in additional elements—reschedulings, MYRAs, MDB lending, market-menu options—the managers of the debt crisis put a lid on the stirrings of debt rebellions. Concurrently, decision makers in the borrowing countries convinced themselves of the credibility of the underlying threats, especially attachments and embargoes, from their creditors. Neither his-

---

extremely nuanced analysis. Knox's preferred option called for "workouts" that would combine major policy reforms with whatever mix of additional external finance and debt relief that would enable the reforms to work and be reasonably politically palatable.

277. Letter, Ernest Stern to David Knox, July 30, 1990, p. 7.

278. Excluding Mexico, Colombia, and Chile, the average tenure drops below twelve months. Moises Naim, "Latin America's Journey to the Market: From Macroeconomic Shocks to Institutional Therapy," April 1994, mimeo.

tory nor international law provided much basis for these fears.[279] Stern, for one, argued that the debtors "and the creditors, have been too awed by the lawyers and the fear of action by the free riders. I have always been very dubious about the possibility of law suits—either against other creditors or against the country."[280] As the Bank itself would later note, the outward orientation strategy emphasized by it and the Fund "strengthened the bargaining power of the banks by making the default penalties (partly related to trade) greater."[281]

The debtors' inability to organize themselves was reinforced by the creditor community's insistence on a case-by-case approach to the problem. After the announcement of the Baker proposals, the U.S. Treasury developed an even stronger aversion to overarching schemes, then being put out in droves. In theory, the case-by-case approach to the crisis offered the promise of a more equitable approach among countries. Both the sources of their predicament and the internal adjustment efforts being made could be more clearly identified. In practice it also allowed creditors to take up a divide-and-rule strategy. Collective action on the creditor side was justified as rational and efficient; that by borrowers was regarded as irresponsible, if not provocative.

There were other factors as well. For one, the crisis empowered a new generation of "technocrats" who used the fiscal pressures engendered by the crisis to persuade their politicians of the need for domestic reforms. Second, as Carlos Diaz-Alejandro had suggested, the reluctance to act stemmed from the phenomenon of "public debt and private assets." Even as national external debt soared, capital flight increasingly placed private assets in overseas havens, in the very banks that held national debt. Latin American elites were unlikely to countenance any scheme entailing default that would place their private assets at risk.

Furthermore, on those occasions when debtor countries did go into arrears, they invariably did so from a position of extreme weakness. Instead of first putting in place suitable domestic policies and then reducing debt service, a buildup of

279. The limited options available to creditors in the event of sovereign default was pointed out by Anatole Kaletsky, *The Costs of Default* (New York: Twentieth Century Fund, 1985). The historical experience is also reviewed by Peter H. Lindert and Peter J. Morton, "How Sovereign Debt Has Worked," in Jeffrey D. Sachs, ed., *Developing Country Debt and Economic Performance*, vol. 1 (University of Chicago Press, 1989), pp. 39–106. According to Benjamin Cohen, there is "limited, not to say dubious, basis in law for the usual list of legal sanctions threatened by creditors against recalcitrant debtors." Cohen, "Developing Country Debt: A Middle Way," Essays in International Finance 173, Princeton University, May 1989, p. 13. Barry Eichengreen and Richard Portes concluded that countries that defaulted in the 1930s "did not have inferior capital market access after World War II." Eichengreen and Portes, "Dealing with Debt: The 1930s and the 1980s," in Husain and Diwan, *Dealing with the Debt Crisis*, p. 70.

280. Letter, Stern to Knox, July 30, 1990. Indeed the only unequivocal winner in this crisis was the legal community.

281. Husain and Diwan, *Dealing with the Debt Crisis*, p. 5.

arrears was rarely a matter of policy; it was a matter of necessity for governments critically strapped for cash. In 1985 Alan Garcia came to power in Peru and announced a ceiling on external debt service (of 10 percent of exports). At the time, the country's reserves were equivalent to almost a year's imports. By simply building up arrears, large debtors can have access to substantial resources. An internal study by the Bank at the time concluded that if Peru used the resources freed in this way for investments to strengthen the economy, it could not merely get away with it but could do quite well.[282] But as events turned out, Garcia ran through his war chest of reserves by maintaining a grossly overvalued exchange rate and boosting domestic consumption. His flagrant mismanagement of Peru's economy provided an exemplary case for bankers to drive home their point on the evils that befall a country that goes for unilateral debt reduction: the resources saved are squandered, leaving the country worse off. David Knox recalls that when this point was made by London bankers, he said, "You know, you bankers really ought to erect a statue to Alain García because he has done you immense service because he has persuaded the world that reneging on debt doesn't pay."[283]

Although there can be no doubt that Garcia's egregious mistakes ran Peru aground, this was hardly an inevitable course. There were clear alternatives that could have resulted in a very different situation. The smaller countries were to prove more successful in setting unilateral limits on debt repayments. Shortly thereafter (in late 1986) Ecuador and Costa Rica unobtrusively set unilateral limits, without the posturing and bravado that had characterized Garcia's stance.[284]

THE ROLE OF THE BRETTON WOODS INSTITUTIONS. In examining the role that the Bretton Woods institutions were made to play in the debt crisis, one must ask whether it is sometimes better to do nothing than to do just a little. The market failure that was intrinsic to the debt crisis required potent central coordination to compel both debtors and creditors into a rapid settlement. An alternative course might have been to adopt a laissez-faire, hands-off attitude, leaving the commercial banks and debtors to sort it out among themselves. This course might have led to a quicker settlement, although it might also have pushed the global economy into uncharted waters. In the event, both alternatives were rejected for a strategy best described as "bumping down the staircase."[285]

The involvement of the Bretton Woods institutions in the debt crisis undoubtedly boosted their prominence in the international order. Their salience, however, was the result of the more political role that they played in the crisis relative to earlier years. Multilateral institutions have frequently provided political cover for their members. The Bretton Woods institutions have frequently served as scape-

282. David Knox, interview with the authors, May 21, 1992.

283. Ibid., p. 11.

284. The "conciliatory default" (a term coined by Kaletsky) strategy was also used in the eighties by Zimbabwe on its debts to South Africa.

285. Senior U.S. Treasury official, interview with the authors.

goats for political elites in developing countries (see chapter 12 on Sub-Saharan Africa). In the case of the debt crisis, they acted as instruments of their major shareholders in several ways.[286] First, their lending—and nonlending—decisions considerably strengthened the creditors' cartel. Second, their analytical voice provided a rationale for debt servicing and belt-tightening. And third, they withheld information that could have led to better informed decisionmaking, a point underlined by Stanley Fischer:

> The US squelched research on this [debt] issue during the mid-'80s. One of my reasons for going to the Bank was that I believed the debt issue was about to come to a head. . . . We had to keep the research quiet, because the institution was under political orders (not only from the US, also the Germans, and the Brits) not to raise issues of debt relief.[287]

Fischer's comments reflect the predicament of multilateral institutions caught between competing interests of various constituencies: in this case, the major shareholders, international financial markets, and the debtor countries. With debt, like the exchange rate, expectations can be self-fulfilling. As Fischer pointed out, "the reasons for creditor country skittishness are clear."[288] Critics focusing on a particular issue frequently overlook the constraints posed by the wide range of interests and responsibilities of the institution.

Could the Bank have taken a more independent, and consequently more confrontational, approach with regard to its major shareholders? Although the debt crisis was *the* most important issue for the affected countries, the Bank's management was tussling with the United States on several other fronts as well, from budgetary issues to operational policies on energy lending and the role of the private sector. But perhaps most important, it was tussling with the deep predicament facing the severely indebted low-income countries, especially in Sub-Saharan Africa. There, the need to secure IDA replenishments hung perennially like the sword of Damocles. The financial caution displayed by the Bank was partly imposed on it, but it was also strongly influenced by internal perceptions of prudent risk management in the inter-

286. A defense of the Fund's role in the debt crisis by the Fund's official historian does not discuss this point, confining itself to the Fund's role in helping the banks and the indebted countries. James Boughton, "The IMF and the Latin American Debt Crisis: Seven Common Criticisms," IMF, PPAA/94/23, October 1994. Similarly, Harold James, in his history of the international monetary system (commissioned by the Fund), concluded of the Fund's role as producing an "outcome that was generally desirable, and whose beneficiaries included the banks as well as the debtor nations." James, *International Monetary Cooperation since Bretton Woods*, p. 408. Before her appointment as U.S. executive director to the IMF, Karin Lissakers put it more candidly: placing a "political organization," like the IMF between creditors and debtors, "raises the question of 'Which way will its biases go?'" Quoted in Sikarene Wilder, "Loans to Third World to Be More Politicized by Mexican Debt Pact," *Wall Street Journal*, October 10, 1984.

287. Letter, Stanley Fischer to Nicholas Stern, May 19, 1992, p. 4.

288. Ibid.

ests of a wider constituency: bondholders and shareholders, but also a conviction that a financially weakened IBRD was not in the best interests of the borrowers.

Though all institutions face external constraints, some transcend their constraints more effectively than others. Were the Bank's external constraints so binding that it could have done little else, or were there factors internal to the institution that also affected its role? The question is a difficult one.

In the early years of the crisis, in addition to the aforementioned shareholder pressures, administrative upheavals and research priorities restricted the Bank's research work on debt. Internal bureaucratic politics exacerbated this problem, a point emphasized by Percy Mistry, a senior adviser and confidant to Qureshi in those years: "Internecine bureaucratic conflict— . . . a syndrome that was to plague the Bank throughout the 1980s—severely compromised the institution's capacity. . . . The Bank's senior-most managers were unable to think and act collectively in the interest of the institution or its borrowers. . . . The Bank's President failed to wield a fractious management group into an effective team."[289]

In part, this underlined the institution's handicap that arose from weak presidential leadership. Though in the early years the Bank's views were largely in agreement with those of the managers of the crisis, differences emerged but were contained in what, by the late 1980s, was becoming an attitude of genuflection to the wishes of the major shareholders. Thus, at a meeting of the President's Council to discuss yet another paper reviewing the debt strategy, a mere month before Brady's announcement, the minutes noted,

> Mr. Conable had . . . agreed with [the paper's] non-advocacy presentation. . . . Mr. Bock noted that the G-7 had stated that the MDBs could not be used for debt reduction and that they should avoid actions which would result in a transfer of risk to [themselves]. It would therefore be counterproductive for this paper to take an aggressive stand, declaring for example, that the [Baker] new money process was dead and to push specific debt reduction schemes.[290]

The argument was misleading. Not only had the prevailing strategy been transferring financial risk to the IFIs for some years in any case, but it was hardly a given that additional IFI lending in parallel with commercial bank debt reduction would increase the IFIs' risks. But it also raised a more fundamental point regarding the interpretation of "nonadvocacy" by the Bank as presenting views that were in concurrence with a select group of shareholders. In any bargaining situation with an asymmetry in power, a neutral stance will, in practice, favor the stronger party. By this time, as noted earlier, staff analysis had repeatedly, and with increasing vigor, questioned the viability of the prevailing strategy. In not sharing staff analyses

289. Percy S. Mistry, "The World Bank's Role in the Debt Crisis Affecting the Highly Indebted Countries," paper prepared for the G-24, 1989, para. 2.04. See also chapter 18.

290. World Bank, minutes of President's Council meeting, "Review of the Debt Strategy," February 15, 1989, p. 2.

with a wider audience, the Bank's management was, in effect, supporting G-7 rationalizations.

These weaknesses had led the institution early in the crisis to accede to pressure by a select few countries to vet ostensibly independent analysis like that provided by the *World Debt Tables*. The early intrusion on its analytical independence explains in part why, even after the fears of global financial stability ebbed, the Bank consciously shied away from going public with its doubts. Contrary to what some critics have suggested, the Bank had very little room to *prescribe* solutions to the crisis, given the extremely strong views of its shareholders on this front. However, there was no reason why the Bank could not have carried out a more honest analysis and made it available to all parties concerned. Although systemic financial risks precluded such a role in the early years, after 1985 this argument held little water. In retrospect, and especially in light of its large in-house analytical capacity, the Bank's diagnosis of the debt crisis in the early years was not one of the institution's finer moments. In reacting only to overt signals from the United States, the institution boxed itself into a studiously cautious official position, making it more difficult for it to persuade its major shareholders to be more open to alternate strategies, thereby contributing to the delays in the resolution of the crisis.

In the absence of transparency in the production and dissemination of information and analysis, decisionmaking is likely to be skewed. In recent years the Bank has been calling for greater transparency in decisionmaking in developing countries as well as for greater participation by those most affected by these decisions. But these principles were not applied to all of the institution's own shareholders during the debt crisis, with the result that certain interests were favored over others.

In two respects, however, the Bank's role in the debt crisis was simply a more visible strand of two threads that have run through the institution's history. The Bank has always acted as provider of balance of payments support. During this period, this function became more prominent. A second thread laid bare by the crisis is the inherent conflict between two purposes of the Bank. At one level its purpose is to promote international capital flows, which requires it to take measures to boost financial confidence. At another level, it has defined itself as, and is expected to play the role of, a multilateral, disinterested, technical development authority. But the truth that may result from playing the latter role true to form can be inimical to the boosterism that is inherent in securing financial confidence. In the long run there may not be any such conflict, but the long run is often a succession of shorter runs.

The debt crisis was a tremendous setback for the affected countries. It brought into relief the vulnerability of countries to overreliance on foreign borrowings and the inadequacy of international financial management. More pointedly, the crisis also highlighted the limitations of the Bretton Woods institutions in a world whose financial and political landscape had changed dramatically since their establishment.

TWELVE

The Weakness of Strength: The Challenge of Sub-Saharan Africa

Yes, my friend, allow me once more to commend the international life. Without it, who could ever bear the burden of governing these days? After all, where is one to look for recognition and understanding if not in the far away world, in foreign countries.
—Ryszard Kapuscinski, *The Emperor: Downfall of an Autocrat*

WITH TWO exceptions, this volume does not have regionally focused chapters. Geographical proximity lulls an observer into overestimating shared traits while underplaying diversity. To an extent, all Bank–country relationships are sui generis, and a historical account of the Bank's relations with a region risks oversimplification.

In the case of Sub-Saharan Africa, its size and number of political entities, social groups, languages, institutions, and ecological zones make it anything but homogeneous. The name itself is not quite accurate, for in Bank parlance it has included a wide swathe of the Sahara (about 5 million square kilometers in Burkina Faso, Chad, Mali, Mauritania, Niger, and Sudan) and, until the early-1990s, excluded South Africa.[1]

Yet the region is distinctive in the number of countries whose economic performance, broadly defined, has been a matter of deep concern to the global community, especially since the mid-1970s. The plight of these countries is not simply

---

1. Even among the Bretton Woods institutions there are differences in coverage. IMF data on "Africa" excludes Djibouti, Mauritania, Somalia, and Sudan, which are under its Middle Eastern Department. These differences of definition make it difficult to compare aggregations of regional data.

one of income or poverty. Indeed, by several criteria, the extent of poverty in South Asia in the early 1990s greatly exceeded that in Sub-Saharan Africa, and South Asia's average income was also about a fifth lower.[2] But in Sub-Saharan Africa social structures for material progress tend to be woefully weak, and since the mid-1970s the *directions* of income and poverty change have been down. Per capita income, for example, declined by more than 1 percent a year despite substantial external financial flows, and the prognosis into the early part of the next millennium remains bleak.[3]

The scale and scope of the Bank's engagement in Sub-Saharan Africa over the past twenty-five years has been substantially different from that elsewhere. For one thing, Africa is the only operational region for which, from the early 1980s onward, the Bank regularly undertook regionwide analysis. This chapter supplements what has been said about poverty, agriculture, rural development, and adjustment lending in the region in chapters 5–7 and 8–10.[4] Two important caveats should be mentioned. One is that our account is based heavily on World Bank documentation. Second, the data used in this chapter should be treated with caution. Debates on the region's many developmental problems have been frequently obfuscated by the use (and abuse) of data of dubious quality, a subject that is addressed later in the chapter.

Testing the Waters: The Early Decades

Africa's modern political map reflects the landgrabbing of the European colonial powers (Britain, Belgium, France, Germany, Italy, Spain, and Portugal) that was

2. According to World Bank figures, the number of poor (defined as population living below US$1 a day) in South Asia in 1993 was 515 million as against 219 million in Sub-Saharan Africa. The head-count index (percentage of population who are poor) was 43 and 39 in the two regions, which meant that the number of poor in South Asia was almost as large as the entire population of Sub-Saharan Africa. However, according to another measure—the poverty gap index, which measures the depth of poverty (as measured by the difference between the poverty line and the mean income of the poor, expressed as a ratio of the poverty line)—the figures for Sub-Saharan Africa (15.3 percent) are worse than those of South Asia (12.6 percent). World Bank (1996), *Poverty Reduction and the World Bank: Progress and Challenges in the 1990s*, table 1.2. Excluding South Africa, GNP per capita in Sub-Saharan Africa in 1994 was about $400 as compared with $320 in South Asia. World Bank, *World Development Report 1996*, table 1, pp. 188–89. However, real incomes on a purchasing power parity basis appeared approximately equivalent.

3. However, broader conceptualizations of human welfare, such as the UNDP's "human development index," appeared to have improved over the same period, albeit at a painfully small pace. UNDP, *Human Development Report, 1996* (Oxford University Press, 1996), tables 1.3, 1.4.

4. Three essays in volume 2 also deal with the Bank's engagement with the region: chapter 4 examines its relations with Côte d'Ivoire, chapter 5 its interactions with other external actors, and chapter 9 its projects in East Africa.

ratified by the Congress of Berlin (1885–86). The resulting boundaries bore little relationship to indigenous societies or polities, many of which had small populations and were landlocked.[5] The new jurisdictions became defined by the European languages spoken in them and the secondary education taught, which in turn produced the new elites who staffed independence movements and became, in the process, jealous defenders of the sovereignty of the new jurisdictions. Despite their artificial origin and political instability, juridically the new states proved to be remarkably stable.[6]

Colonialism had been widespread in the late nineteenth century and the first half of the twentieth century. But the African colonial experience was unique in the intensity and swiftness of competition among the continental powers. The pernicious effects of Africa's colonial experience and the suddenness of its entry into the "modern" world cast a long shadow.[7] The very form of government inherent in these nation-states, based as it was on European models and assumptions, was both alien to and in many respects unsuited to Africa. Compounding the problem was the decolonization process, which in most cases left the region with the formal structures of modern states but without the necessary foundations. Africa's predicament—and the Bank's role therein—cannot be understood without some idea of the nature of the state, with its all-embracing pretensions to authority, and the weak sense of nationhood in most countries in the region.[8]

A decade after the Bank opened for business, just two of its sixty members were Sub-Saharan African countries: Ethiopia and South Africa.[9] Africa was included in the department responsible for the metropolitan countries (called the Europe, Africa, and Australasia Department), since its colonial status meant that loans to the region could be made only if guaranteed by the colonial power. Nevertheless, the region accounted for as much as a tenth of Bank (then only IBRD) lending. These loans, which served to alleviate the dollar shortages of the European colonial powers, were largely directed to colonial interests, especially mining, either through direct investments or indirect assistance, as in the development of the

5. About half of the forty-eight states had populations less than 5 million. Fifteen of the forty-eight are landlocked: Botswana, Burkina Faso, Burundi, Central African Republic, Chad, Lesotho, Malawi, Mali, Niger, Rwanda, Swaziland, Uganda, Zambia, Zimbabwe, and Ethiopia, which became landlocked after the secession of Eritrea.

6. The breakup of Ethiopia, which led to the formation of Eritrea, is the only exception.

7. Crawford Young, *The African Colonial State in Comparative Perspective* (Yale University Press, 1994).

8. For the Bank's view of the historical evolution of the institution's role in Sub-Saharan Africa, see Ishrat Husain, "The Challenge of Africa," paper published as part of the series "The Evolving Role of the World Bank" (1994). A broad overview of the region's external economic relations is Paul Collier, "Africa's External Economic Relations: 1960–90," *African Affairs*, vol. 90 (July 1991), pp. 339–56.

9. Three countries in continental Africa, including Egypt. Edward S. Mason and Robert E. Asher, *The World Bank since Bretton Woods* (Brookings, 1973), table 4-1, p. 65.

transport infrastructure related to mining.[10] By the end of fiscal 1958, four-fifths of Bank lending to the region was going to South Africa, the Federation of Rhodesia and Nyasaland, and the Belgian Congo. With African countries lacking indigenous capability to prepare projects that met Bank lending criteria, projects were developed largely by expatriates.

The other location of the Bank's first foray into Africa had been Ethiopia, in 1950. The country was an exception in Africa, having escaped (except for a brief interlude in the 1930s to early 1940s) the depredations of European imperialism. Its relative isolation, however, did not mean that it was necessarily better placed to march up the "road to Huddersfield," James Morris's metaphor for industrialization and development in his travelogue on the World Bank's workings in 1963:

> Socially and politically, Ethiopia is sadly stunted: one of the most archaic of all the dizzily variegated states that can boast membership of the Bank. . . . The constitution, in principle impeccable, is in practice half meaningless. . . . From top to bottom of this nation you may recognize the European Middle Ages, from the semi-divine nature of the kingship to the social structure of the countryside, whose pattern of great man, tenant, and serf is almost precisely the shape of European feudalism seven or eight centuries ago.[11]

The Bank found lending to Ethiopia tough going. Early lending (averaging under $3 million a year during the 1950s) was directed at developing a rudimentary transport and communications infrastructure. Under a roads project, a highways authority was set up to plan and build a network of trunk roads in a country where virtually none existed. But instead, construction was repeatedly diverted to meet the emperor's whims: from palace parking lots to approach roads to princely retreats. Racked by protracted disputes, a telecommunications project took an inordinate time to get off the ground. But a decade (and three more loans) later, the country's telecommunications institutional foundations appeared to be taking root. Although committed to private ownership of development banks (that is, development finance companies, DFCs) in its early years, the Bank was forced by objective circumstances to set up a government-owned DFC because of the absence of a private sector alternative. (This proved to be the World Bank's first such venture, and the only public sector one it would finance until 1968.) Of the DFCs established at the time by the Bank, the performance of this one was the weakest, in large part because of Ethiopia's lack of a commercial culture, rather than political factors per se.

---

10. Roger Chaufournier, interview, World Bank Oral History Program, July 22, 1986. Roger Chaufournier served as vice president for the West Africa region for most of the 1970s.

11. James Morris, *The Road to Huddersfield: A Journey to Five Continents* (New York: Pantheon Books, 1963), p. 93. See also chapter 3 of this volume.

The situation created a dilemma for the Bank:

The World Bank is not terribly proud of its achievements in Ethiopia, its first African client, and the Ethiopians are not always complimentary about the World Bank. It has been a tiresome honeymoon. In particular, it has demonstrated how *long* it takes to shift a nation's gears, what an agonizingly muddled process the adjustment can be and how expensive a commodity is time. . . . Basically, and paradoxically, this is because the pace is too fast. Nobody has much choice in the timing of history, but it would really be better for everyone if the motion of the Ethiopian body politic could be retarded, to allow its several limbs to move in time. The demands of the coherent Ethiopians cannot long be denied, and it is in fact they who dictate the progress of the State; but the fact remains that while at one end of the national spectrum a handful of sophisticated young Ethiopians is perfectly able to manage a bank, run a factory, or fly a supersonic jet, at the other end most of the populace scarcely understands the meaning of money.[12]

Notwithstanding this fundamental disjuncture, there was little alternative but to press on:

As distasteful and maddening as the process is, even in Ethiopia the World Bank has no choice. If the momentum of change is not maintained, a whole generation will go sour. Already, because the pressure of political enlightenment demands more security for the Throne, schools have actually been closed down to save money for guns: many more such backslidings, political, social, or economic, could lead to catastrophe. At best, Ethiopia might go Communist, as her young intellectuals turn to the political philosophy that seems to offer the speediest prospect of change. At worst, this ancient State, addled by frustration and disillusionment, might degenerate into squalid and fissiparous anarchy, faction against faction, province against province, civil against military, as Shakespeare's violent noblemen squabbled long ago.[13]

These words were prescient not just about Ethiopia, but also about the problem the Bank would face throughout the region. With the institutions of the Ethiopian state scarcely distinguishable from the ruling regime, and with power so thoroughly centralized in the personage of the emperor, the Bank had little room to maneuver. Equally problematic, the country's political and social institutions were alien to the Bank's culture and experience.

As decolonization progressed, the Bank set up a new Africa department in 1961.[14] The number of African members increased from two to eight between 1957 and 1962, and then leaped to thirty-four by 1967. The appearance of the IDA, the push by the Woods Bank into agriculture, and the large expansion in staff and administrative spending (see chapter 4), all worked to propel the Bank into a greater involvement with the region. The number of reports on the region in the

12. Ibid., pp. 103–4.
13. Ibid., pp. 106–7.
14. The department was initially headed by Pierre Moussa, who was succeeded by Abdel Galal El Emary (a former finance minister of Egypt) in 1965.

1960s quadrupled over those of the previous decade. The earlier work of the general survey missions to Nigeria (1953), Italian Somaliland (1956), Tanganyika (1959), Uganda (1960), and Kenya (1961)—which had assembled a wealth of information on these countries—was supplemented by a landmark report on the region's agriculture.[15] Together with a long monograph on the region's economy by Andrew Kamarck, then director of its Economic Department, the two studies underpinned the Bank's analysis and knowledge of the region.[16]

A more practical addition to the institution's knowledge base of the region came with the establishment of the Agricultural Development Service in East Africa, drawing from former agricultural officers of the British colonial service.[17] Their field knowledge was supplemented by their familiarity with local languages, an asset whose value the Bank would severely underestimate over the years. The Anglo-Saxon Bank was faced with an acute language problem in West Africa, where the working language of government officials and the elite was French, while there were hardly any French-speaking economists in the Bank. Thus, despite the up-surge in analytical work and the degree of involvement it would soon get into, the Bank—and indeed scholars outside the Bank—had limited understanding of Afri-can institutions and society.

Lending was slow to take off. With the departure of the colonial powers, the absence of their guarantees raised creditworthiness concerns. Although this prob-lem was somewhat allayed by the availability of IDA loans, the absence of country knowledge and especially of local capacity to come up with fundable projects was soon apparent. As a result, lending continued to be dominated by "enclave" projects, which had lower financial risks and relied on foreign parties to do much of the project design work. To alleviate the problem, the Bank for the first time established regional missions—one in Nairobi for East Africa and the other in Abidjan for West Africa—to help identify and develop projects for Bank financing.

The general mood regarding the region's prospects was infected by post-independence euphoria. But even then, as the following story illustrates, the Bank's relationship with the countries of the region had a different timbre from that in most other parts of the world. In 1965 a Bank mission consisting of an engineer and two young professionals (one on his first-ever mission and the other on his second) went to Malawi to appraise a roads project. The road was supposed to go to the border of Zambia, and not so coincidentally it went by President Hastings Banda's

15. John C. de Wilde and others, *Experiences with Agricultural Development in Tropical Africa*, 2 vols. (Johns Hopkins University Press, 1967). The general survey missions and their reports are discussed in Mason and Asher, *World Bank since Bretton Woods*, p. 302.

16. Andrew M. Kamarck, *The Economics of African Development* (Praeger, 1967).

17. Although selected by the Bank, they were available for secondment for agricultural projects within the region on a reimbursable basis. The Bank assured them of employment between project assignments.

private farm as well. The team found that the project lacked merit but had to convey the message personally to the president himself. Recalling the incident four decades later, one of the young professionals related that the engineer did not have the stomach "to see the old man and say nix on this project," which left the two young professionals to handle the task. He described the scene:

> So [we] marched in to see the president, who is on this little platform, so he can look down on us, and we are sitting there to announce the results of our appraisal. So I give him the whole thing about how at present we can't get a positive rate of return, and the project is at least ten years off. The President grips the arms of his throne, staggers to his feet and reaches out toward me like he hasn't taken a breath for a while, topples off this pedestal toward me, and I think, "Oh my God, they are going to take us out and shoot us." . . . We had to be extracted from the room. . . I found this to be very heady stuff and to be working in Africa with these emergent countries in these very difficult situations was really something that I felt I wanted to do.[18]

The incident was symptomatic of several themes that would underlie the Bank's involvement with Africa. The fact that neophyte Bank staff members had access to the heads of government was bound to be "heady" and unique to this region. The degree of micromanagement exercised by Banda and much of the new leadership in Africa may not have been unique to the region, but when coupled with the fragility of the institutions there it would prove profoundly damaging. And, Edward (Kim) Jaycox, the young professional who narrated the anecdote, would have ample opportunity to fulfill his wish.

Optimism was fueled in part by a Bank report's observations that economic growth in the Congo, the Rhodesias, Kenya, and Gabon was "among the highest in the world."[19] Indeed, overall growth in the region was on par with that in Asia, the other low-income region of the world. The optimism was also a reaction to the prevailing mood of despair about Asia's prospects, driven by the carnage in Indonesia and Indochina, insurgencies and ethnic riots in Malaysia, and the gloom surrounding the economic problems of the Bank's largest borrower, India. Although China was not a member, news of the devastation being wrought by the Cultural Revolution was seeping out. Even Korea was then regarded as barely able to walk, let alone run.

Yet confidence was tempered. With growth rates of about 10 percent a year, one of the world's fastest growing countries in the 1950s had been Liberia. Nevertheless, the country was said to be achieving "growth without development," in view of the lack of linkages with foreign investment of the enclave type (in this case, the large rubber plantations of Firestone).[20] In the 1960s, despite its strong orientation

18. Edward Jaycox, World Bank Oral History Program, February 23, 1995.
19. Kamarck, *Economics of African Development,* p. 17.
20. Robert W. Clower and others, *Growth without Development: An Economic Survey of Liberia* (Northwestern University Press, 1966).

toward the private sector and foreign investors, the Bank was unhappy with the results of Liberia's "open door" policy, which at the time had resulted in "a massive inflow of foreign capital for iron ore mining." The Bank feared that the inflows were leading the country into a "very difficult financial situation."[21] The flows had come principally through supplier credits, which in the Bank's opinion were inherently undermining sound borrowings and debt management, as well as its own leverage. Concerned that such policies were placing Liberia's prosperity "on narrow foundations" (iron ore and rubber), while doing little to alleviate the sharp divisions between the descendants of American-Liberian settlers (who ruled the country) and the indigenous population in the majority, Bank lending was quite limited in the 1960s.[22]

The country that seemed to herald the future was Ghana, the first African country to win independence. In a region where pitiful investments in education had been one of the most baneful legacies of colonialism, Ghana had one of the better human resource endowments. It had a large sterling balance (as a result of wartime commodity price booms, its sterling balances exceeded those of India) and a healthy economy. Within a decade, under Kwame Nkrumah, Ghana became the archetype of a leadership determined to use the state as a vehicle to build the nation, but even more, to build itself. In practice, the leadership ended up by using the state in a way that undermined both. As Ghana's endowments leached away, they served as a harsh reminder of the costs of poor strategic choices by a country's political leadership.

The upheavals in Ghana, coming closely on the heels of the Congo crisis, were soon followed by the Biafran crisis in Nigeria. A spate of coups in the mid-1960s proved a bellwether of the state in Africa. The principal (and legally the only) interlocutor of the Bank in a member country was already showing unhealthy characteristics. Writing of his country's machinations in the region, René Dumont, the noted French Africanist, fulminated that the new African governing elites were behaving no better than their colonial predecessors. They appeared intent, he said, in particular through their indifference to the wealth-creating potential of the peasantry, to create "a modern version of Louis XVI's court."[23] Bank staff cautioned:

21. IBRD, "The Economy of Liberia," R63-101, September 4, 1963. The "open door" policy allowed "a generous initial period of exemption from certain taxes in order that the investor might quickly recover a part of his investment" as well as "unrestricted repatriation of profits." Ibid., para. 9.

22. Bank lending to Liberia during the 1960s was just $8 million. One reason, as McNamara later explained in a meeting with Liberia's finance minister, was that "Liberia . . . had exhibited such inability to overcome the deep divisions which existed among the various population groups there. The Bank . . . had therefore in the past hesitated to proceed with Bank lending." Memorandum, Leif Christoffersen for the record, "Liberia—Mr. McNamara's Meeting with Finance Minister Stephen Tolbert on April 3, 1972," April 5, 1972.

23. René Dumont, *False Start in Africa*, trans. Phyllis Nautsoff (Praeger, 1969), p. 32. Originally published in 1962 as *L'Afrique noire est mal partie*.

The very important role of the government in African economies notwithstanding, most economic activities take place *outside* the public sector. Economic growth in Africa can to some extent be measured by the shrinkage of the public sector's importance. . . . [I]t is, therefore, of prime importance for governments to maintain policies that encourage private investment. It helps greatly, too, if a government provides the environment for growth: honest and efficient housekeeping of its own affairs and finances, political and legal security for private investors and producers.[24]

But the increasing role of government in economic life in the region was also a response to an unpleasant reality of postindependence Africa: the Asian and European communities were dominating business life. In examining the economies of East Africa, the Bank had few illusions of the implications of this reality:

The fact that income and wealth is still so much associated with color—brown or white in this case—is inevitably a source of discontent and a potential threat to political stability. . . . An urgent requirement for the future is to reconcile the need for a continued contribution of the Asian and European communities to the development of the economy with the need for giving Africans a greater share in the commerce and industry of each of the countries.[25]

Africa's leadership was already looking for ways to develop indigenous managerial cadres rapidly. Though it had yet to embark upon a spate of nationalizations and expropriations, it was busy scouting alternative routes, such as cooperatives (as in Tanzania) and parastatal enterprises. While concurring that both routes were valid alternatives to nurture scarce indigenous managerial talent, the Bank maintained that none of the East African countries could "afford to do without the qualities of individual initiative and responsibility that often emerge from the development of private business. It is therefore essential that Africans be enabled to become businessmen and entrepreneurs in growing numbers. . . . It must be expected, too, that progress will be slow in overcoming the many handicaps from which Africans still suffer in establishing and developing competitive business enterprises of their own."[26]

Through the ensuing decades Africa would be in the chronic predicament of having limited indigenous technical and managerial cadres. Yet, as we note later, in their haste to escape the problem, all parties—African governments and external interveners—would adopt solutions that kept it festering for decades to come.

Since most Sub-Saharan African countries were late in becoming members of the Bank, the institution's profile in the region was low in its first quarter century.

---

24. Andrew M. Kamarck, *The Economics of African Development*, 2d ed., rev. (Praeger), pp. 272–73.

25. World Bank, "East Africa," R67-148, September 13, 1967, para. 86. Peter Bauer's work on West Africa had earlier highlighted the important economic role played by traders (of Asian and Middle-East descent) in that region. Peter P. Bauer, *West African Trade: A Study of Competition, Oligopoly and Monopoly in a Changing Economy* (London: Routledge and Kegan Paul, 1963).

26. World Bank, "East Africa," para. 89.

Instead the Bank was preoccupied with Asia, followed closely by Latin America. The bilateral aid agencies of the former colonial powers had better expertise and greater resources and were the region's dominant external actors at the time. In fact the Bank had some notoriety in the region for lending to Portugal and South Africa. Although it rebuffed the criticism the United Nations gave it on this count, it quietly reduced the maturities of its loans to South Africa and shortly thereafter ceased lending operations to the two countries.[27]

Plunging In: The McNamara Years

Shortly after Robert McNamara's arrival at the Bank in April 1968, he announced a plan to double Bank lending over the next five years. The new president proposed to give a greater institutional focus to Africa by splitting the Africa department into two—an East Africa department, which would continue to be headed by El Emary, and a West Africa department, with Roger Chaufournier at its helm.[28] This change, plus the significant increase in overall Bank lending, led to a quadrupling of Bank lending in the first half of the 1970s compared with the level of the previous decade.

Despite his initial preoccupation with Asia, McNamara soon began focusing on Africa. Following a long visit to East Africa in early 1970, McNamara returned less than sanguine about the region's prospects. His private notes reveal the nature of his concerns. Thus on Tanzania:

> With 5% of secondary age children in school today, how will it deal with the other 95% three decades from now? . . . The orientation of the students and faculty of the University was typified by the fact that the law school has 300 students and the agricultural school, recently started, 30. The agricultural school, 10 years from now, is expected to have an enrollment of 300. The only question asked by the chairman of the student body was whether we would finance such "advanced types of instruction" as "pilot training."[29]

27. For the record, although many developing countries voted against these loans at the Bank's Board, numerous others (especially the Latin American countries) did not. All the OECD countries voted in favor of the loans. A good account of the episode can be found in Mason and Asher, *World Bank since Bretton Woods*, pp. 587–91. Lending to Portugal resumed in 1976. However, the Bank continued to be ritualistically denounced by the UN Decolonization Committee for more than a decade and half, apparently because the two countries retained procurement privileges on bidding on Bank projects. In the same period the Bank continued to court South Africa to make an IDA contribution. Not surprisingly, however small South Africa's contributions, this move was never condemned.

28. While Chaufournier would continue in that capacity through the end of the 1970s, the East Africa department witnessed frequent turnover. El Emary barely lasted a year in his new job. He was succeeded as director of the East Africa region by Michael Lejeune. Following the 1972 reorganization, the position of director was upgraded to vice president, with Bernard Bell in that position. Bell was succeeded by Shahid Husain in 1974, who gave way to Willi Wapenhans in 1977.

29. Robert McNamara, "Random Thoughts," notes, January 1970.

On Uganda:

> The Ministers were an unimpressive group: ill-informed, long on complaints and generalities, and short on practical plans and action. Rarely did they disclose or admit their own deficiencies. For every problem they came back to one cause: a failure of the Bank. . . . Their behavior illustrated that socialization, while acceptable philosophically, imposes severe penalties, as an alternative to private enterprise, if it substitutes civil servants, with little sense of economics, for shrewd, aggressive, Asian entrepreneurs. . . . It was sad to leave Uganda, a potentially rich agricultural land, with such a feeling of despair over the incompetence of the government and the future of the country—a feeling more than confirmed . . . by Mackenzie who said that the government was not only incompetent but shot through with corruption.

On Kenya:

> The leadership of the economic and political institutions depends on expatriates to a far greater degree than I had realized . . . and yet Africanization is a political necessity . . . a combination of circumstances that may lead to disastrous results. The current census is showing Kenya's population problem to be worse than they anticipated (probably 3.4% per year).[30]

In the same trip to East Africa, McNamara visited Ethiopia, where he pressed the emperor to do more in the areas of agriculture and education. A year later (in late 1971), the Bank mounted a survey of the agricultural sector in Ethiopia. The report's findings underlined the severe constraints to rapid agricultural development and to Bank operations because of the lack of trained manpower, research and extension services, credit, and marketing and transport. However, the writers of the report were "most concerned about the land reform problem, . . . the one constraint on which, because of the acute domestic political problems, it is very difficult for outsiders to have effective influence."[31] The report confirmed, wrote McNamara to Haile Selassie, that the "slow rate of progress in agriculture is likely to persist until improvements in the tenure system are made, and it recognizes the great difficulties faced in solving this fundamental impediment to Ethiopian social and economic progress. All of us appreciate that in a matter of such high national importance your personal support and leadership are the main hope for achieving the needed changes."[32]

The government also resisted Bank suggestions that it reorient education investments toward practical agriculture training. Citing serious social and political

---

30. Ibid.

31. Memorandum, Michael L. Lejeune to Robert S. McNamara, "Ethiopia—Courtesy Call by the Ethiopian Ambassador to the United States," June 26, 1972, para. 6.

32. Letter, Robert S. McNamara to His Imperial Majesty, Haile Selassie I, November 1, 1972. The Agriculture Sector Survey, in three volumes, was the most comprehensive analysis of the country's pivotal rural sector. Its twenty-three annexes cover a range of issues, from specific crops to research and extension to rural health and nutrition to marketing and roads. "Agriculture Sector Survey," Report PA-143a, January 15, 1973. Annex 12, on land tenure, was a blunt and bleak assessment of the convoluted nature of land tenure in the country.

pressures, it instead persuaded the Bank to approve an investment project aimed at secondary education in rural areas. But time had finally run out. The trappings of "modernity" had set the barrel fermenting. Haile Selassie was ousted in a military coup in 1974. Another coup occurred in Uganda, barely a year after McNamara's trip there, and confirmed his fears that "the combination of tribalism, population explosion, rising expectations . . . and accelerating Africanization" would ensure "an unstable political foundation for economic development during the next decade."

Following his trip, McNamara and his advisers began to map out the Bank's strategy for East Africa. Greater attention would be given to agricultural credit, irrigation, education (including curricular reform and postprimary training), village industries, and DFC operations. These decisions were to be formalized through the launching of the rural development strategy in Nairobi in 1973 (see chapters 5 and 8). For the moment, however, the Bank would take a wait-and-see attitude toward Ujamma (village-resettlement schemes), which it felt were "without much substance." A similar caution seemed to prevail with regard to support for regionalization efforts through the East African community, which "appeared extremely fragile as it was apparent there was a conflict between regional and national interests in East Africa."[33]

After McNamara's visit to West Africa later that year, the Bank decided to recruit more French-speaking technical specialists and devote extra budgetary resources to landlocked states. But the most visible consequence of the trip was the Bank's decision to join hands with the World Health Organization in combating river blindness.[34] The Onchocerciasis Control Program was to prove one of the Bank's outstanding efforts at alleviating human suffering.

Following the East and West Africa trips of 1970–71, the Bank struggled to define its modus operandi in the region. William Clark, vice president for external affairs and a close confidant of McNamara, wrote a memo summarizing the region's special problems. There is, he said, "an extreme touchiness about sovereignty in most [African countries] and a strong suspicion that economic advice is for the benefit of the metropolitan country rather than the ex-colony." In their attempt to free themselves from metropolitan control, many countries in the region had been buying "economic snake bite oil from quacks." The difficulties were compounded "above all [by] a terrible shortage of skilled, trained experts below the ministerial level."[35] And the "greatest difficulty" facing the Bank in helping African countries, Clark argued, was "to gain their trust."

33. Memorandum for the record, "Meeting in Mr. McNamara's Office on Points Arising from His Visit to East Africa, January 20, 1970," March 5, 1970.

34. Memorandum for the record, "Meeting on Ideas Resulting from Mr. McNamara's Trip to West Africa," March 14, 1972.

35. Memorandum, William Clark to Robert S. McNamara, "Our African Trips," May 24, 1971.

But how was the Bank to instill and nurture trust? As the decade unfolded, the core premise in this strategy, notwithstanding private doubts of staff and management, was to give broad benefit of doubt to the country's own policies, as long as the leadership's goals appeared pro-developmental, while rapidly expanding the Bank's commitment to these countries. To demonstrate this commitment, the Bank multiplied administrative resources and field offices in the region and stepped up analytical work (the number of Bank reports on Africa quintupled from the levels a decade earlier).[36] But the most singular expression of this strategy was the change in lending.

Average Bank loan commitments to Sub-Saharan Africa increased eightfold between the 1960s and the 1970s (table 12-1). Real increases were more modest—about threefold—while the number of loans rose more than fourfold.[37] However, both Africa's share in Bank lending and the Bank's share in external flows to Africa barely changed over the 1970s.[38] The thrust of Bank lending to Africa was directed toward agriculture (about a third of all lending), particularly following McNamara's Nairobi speech in 1973 (see chapters 6 and 8). Loans for agriculture and rural development, many of them packaged as integrated rural development projects, together with transportation (a quarter), and lending for other infrastructure-related loans, accounted for 70 percent of all lending in this period. Education lending formed about half of social lending, with water and sanitation and urban lending forming the remainder.

There was virtually no lending for stand-alone population and health projects, although components were included in rural development projects. The Bank's attempts to place population on the agenda of Africa countries were, for the most part, strongly rebuffed. Opponents argued that restricting population growth would throttle the growth of already small markets, there was plenty of unoccupied land, a "young" population was more dynamic, and religious beliefs precluded "family planning." The Bank's own policies did not help matters in that the subject was treated as a population "control" issue rather than as part of broader health, gender, and poverty concerns. Only by the end of the decade did the institution decide to lend for health (chapter 5), allowing population issues to be addressed through maternal health and child care projects.

Rapid population growth implied higher dependency ratios and greater demand for social services. But demographic momentum also had important implications

36. In 1968 the Bank had six field offices, two of which were in Africa (regional missions in Abidjan and Nairobi). By 1980 the number had climbed to twenty-seven. Fifteen of the twenty-one new field offices were established in Africa. Most, however, served in a "facilitating" capacity.

37. The increases are less striking if one compares changes between 1969–70 and 1979–80, which amounted to a fourfold increase in nominal terms and somewhat more than double in real terms. The increase in the number of loans was more modest: from forty-five to seventy-three over the same period.

38. Bank lending to Africa rose from 12 percent of total lending in the 1960s to 14 percent in the 1970s (it would nudge upward to 15 percent in the 1980s).

Table 12-1. *World Bank Lending Commitments to Africa, Fiscal 1951–95*
Percent unless otherwise indicated[a]

Commitment	FY 51–59	FY 60–69	FY 70–79	FY 80–89	FY 90–95
Sector					
Agriculture	0	15	31	24	16
Finance and industry	0	1	8	12	11
Infrastructure[b]	87	69	39	22	18
Social[c]	0	8	16	16	29
Other[d]	13	8	7	26	26
Lending instrument					
Adjustment[e]	7	0	3	29	37
Sector investment and maintenance	11	11	16	22	10
Specific investment	82	86	72	37	46
Other[f]	0	3	9	12	7
Annual average					
Nominal commitments ($U.S. billions)	0.1	0.1	0.8	2.3	3.2
Real commitments (1995 $U.S. billions)	0.4	0.6	1.7	3.2	3.5
Number of loans	2.6	14	63.1	87.5	85

Source: World Bank (LCI database).
a. Numbers may not add up because of rounding.
b. Transportation, telecommunication, electricity.
c. Education, environment, population, water, sanitation, urban development.
d. Mining, multisector, oil and gas, public sector management, sector unclassified, tourism.
e. Sector adjustment, structural adjustment.
f. Emergency recovery, financial intermediation, technical assistance.

for what lay ahead. When coupled with even more rapid rates of urbanization (about two to three times faster than population growth rates), partly the result of economic policy choices, it led to urban political activism that was fueled by a burgeoning, poorly educated labor force with few employment prospects, a situation that weak governments contemplating major policy changes could ignore only at their peril.[39]

The Bank's relations were closest to countries in East Africa. Kenya, Tanzania, and Zambia accounted for nearly a quarter of all lending, and Ethiopia and Sudan for another tenth. Côte d'Ivoire and Cameroon were the largest borrowers in Francophone Africa, together accounting for slightly more than a tenth of Bank lending. Nigeria, which accounted for a quarter of the regional population and borrowed little in the first half of the 1970s, sprinted ahead to emerge, by the end of that decade, as the largest borrower in absolute terms (it received approximately

39. On the other hand, it is argued that greater urbanization may well dilute the power of ethnic and family ties that have been as baneful to "rational" economic decisionmaking.

14 percent of lending to the region). These eight countries together accounted for about 60 percent of all Bank lending to the region. The Bank did not begin lending to several African countries until the late 1970s and after. Lending to Comoros and Guinea-Bissau commenced in 1979, Zimbabwe in 1981 (after the break in 1965), Djibouti in 1982, Mozambique and São Tomé and Principe in 1985, Angola in 1991 and Eritrea in 1993. As of the end of fiscal year 1996, the thirty-year lending hiatus to South Africa continued.

The Bank was fairly comfortable with the macroeconomic policies of Côte d'Ivoire, Kenya, Mauritius, and Malawi. This accounts for the high volume of operations in Côte d'Ivoire (see volume 2, chapter 4) and Kenya (see chapter 6). High levels of lending in several other cases—most notably Liberia, Senegal, Tanzania, and Zambia—reflected the Bank's (and especially McNamara's) confidence in their leadership's goals even though the institution privately harbored doubts about the instruments and capacity to implement these goals. Thus after meeting President William Tolbert of Liberia, McNamara noted,

> The needs and plans of his government far exceeded the available resources and therefore it was essential that priorities be established; for example should agriculture continue to receive only 2% of the government expenditure while the University was planning to relocate at a cost of $36 million. . . . No acceptable development plan could be financed without additional public savings [which] would require a much tighter control of government expenditures, as well as additional revenue.[40]

Despite his reservations about Liberia's economic policies, McNamara was convinced that President Tolbert was "obviously a deeply religious man, truly concerned with the development of his people." Lending to Liberia soared from $34 million in the first half of the 1970s to $133 million in the second half.

In the Bank's opinion, the disjunction between means and ends was sharpest in Senegal, Tanzania, and Zambia. In Léopold Senghor, Julius Nyerere, and Kenneth Kaunda, the Bank faced charismatic leaders who offered a humanistic vision of African socialism and who were reputed for their personal integrity. For all that, their vision foundered on the hard rocks of impracticality and naive assumptions about human behavior. Throughout the 1970s, the Bank strongly supported the development strategies of all three through its lending. Then in the 1980s, like a disillusioned suitor, the Bank performed an abrupt about-face.

In his first meeting with Kaunda in 1972, McNamara warned that his country's development plan, while "well conceived was totally unrealistic in its relationship to available funds. It was essential that the investment program be cut and that current expenditures be squeezed as well."[41] Despite the Bank's misgivings, lending to Zambia escalated in the first half of the 1970s, driven by the difficulties

40. Robert S. McNamara, "Notes of Meeting with President Tolbert," January 18, 1973.
41. Robert S. McNamara, "Notes of Meeting with President Kaunda of Zambia," November 16, 1972.

caused by the Rhodesian problem. About half the funding was for hydroelectric power. The limited focus on agriculture and education also reflected the Zambian government's priorities. In 1975, in a meeting with President Kaunda, McNamara expressed the Bank's unhappiness with the country's priorities:

> His concern [was] that the whole economy was living off copper, with little effort to improve the employment opportunities and production in the rural sector, where the mass of the people still lived. The severe dualism which this gave rise to could have the seeds of future political and economic trouble. He was particularly concerned with growing food imports, while other claims on copper earnings were increasing. . . . Policies such as investment allocations, prices of agricultural products and allocation of administrative and managerial resources were still not geared to the welfare of the mass of the Zambian people. There was a heavy bias towards the urban population.[42]

As a result, in the second half of the 1970s the lending program was cut to less than half the earlier levels. Neither the previous increase in lending nor the later pruning of lending had much effect on core policies of the government. For Zambia, an extended period of economic decline was just beginning. An internal review would later note that "the outpouring of loans to Zambia from 1965 to 1976, when most of the disastrous policies were being generated, took place despite the fact that they were well understood by 1974, were at least partially understood by 1971 and should have been broadly understood even earlier."[43]

The problems of Zambia and of the Bank in Zambia, the review observed, had their roots in the "obsessively programmatic approach of the Bank, especially in Africa, which gave its clients little incentive to respect macroeconomic (or even microeconomic) critiques, and led the Bank into incautious project lending."[44] The repercussions of the programmatic approach would be abundantly clear in retrospect, as later Bank reports documented. But the question of how significantly the Bank could have affected borrower policies in the four cases mentioned can be docketed for later discussion.

Despite the perception of an overtly aggressive approach to lending by the McNamara Bank, the reality was that it was running faster than before within a system that was moving even faster than the Bank. Between 1970 and 1980 the Bank's share in Sub-Saharan Africa's outstanding long-term debt *declined* from 13.5 percent to 10.5 percent; its share of debt service dropped even faster—from 9.5 percent to 5.5 percent—partly because the share of IDA in its lending grew. Even so, IDA's share in Official Development Assistance to the region changed

42. Memorandum, S. Shahid Husain for the record, "Meeting with President Kaunda of Zambia," April 21, 1975.

43. Benjamin King, "From Dutch Disease to Dutch Auction: A Retrospective Review of the Zambian Structural Adjustment Program," 1988, para. 106.

44. Ibid.

little over the period, ranging between 6 and 7 percent through the 1970s. If Sub-Saharan Africa's short-term debt is included, the relative drop in Bank lending was even sharper.

AFRO-MARXIST STATES. During the period a number of Bank borrowers in the region harbored avowed Afro-Marxist regimes: Guinea (since independence in 1958), the (French) Congo (since 1967), Benin (1974), Madagascar (1975), and Ethiopia (1977). However, these countries had little industry to speak of and no industrial labor force, the supposed vanguard of proletarian revolution in classic Marxist thought. Although the population consisted mainly of the peasantry, any possibility of a Maoist variation was precluded by policies that heavily exploited the rural sector. What emerged was a self-styled Marxism of the political-administrative class, whose rhetorical enemy was imperialism more than capitalism. In general, the more bitter the colonial experience, the more radical the nationalism of the regime. This formulation of Marxism also served as a useful ideological tool for differentiating incumbent regimes from their predecessors.

The Bank was pragmatic enough to recognize that these regimes were eclectic in their ideological interpretations and policy practice. With lending an important goal, the Bank chose practical considerations such as the country's ability to organize and execute projects over ideology as the principal determinant of lending levels. Hence political instability, coupled with financial considerations—creditworthiness in the case of IBRD borrowers, and the limited resources of IDA in the case of IDA borrowers— were the more common constraining factors in restricting Bank lending.

Lending to Ethiopia declined sharply in the last half of the 1970s (to one-third of the real levels in the first half of the decade). Although the Ethiopian government claimed that the regime's Marxist ideology was the principal reason behind this drop, lending initially fell because of the chaotic political situation that prevailed between 1975 and 1977. The Ethiopian government's failure to initiate a process to provide compensation for its nationalizations in 1975 became the main stumbling block, and lending ceased until the issue was resolved at the end of 1980. During the 1980s the Bank emerged as one of the principal lenders to that country, even though Ethiopia had switched to the Soviet Union as its superpower patron in 1977.

There was no discernible change in lending to Benin, while lending to Madagascar, which witnessed an ostensibly Marxist regime climb to power in 1975, increased by more than 50 percent (in real terms) between the first and second half of the 1970s. An interesting case was Guinea, which received little Bank assistance in the 1970s. Like Ethiopia, Guinea was convinced that the Bank was "opposed to lending in socialist countries," though Sékou Touré's patently unpleasant blend of political repression and economic mismanagement were the real reasons.[45] When Sékou Touré decided to change course following an uprising by the market women

45. Memorandum, Roger Chaufournier to Robert S. McNamara, "Guinea—Briefing Paper," September 7, 1973, p. 2.

in 1977, McNamara quickly followed up with a visit to the country. Even then, the approach was gradual compared with what was in store—lending in the 1970s averaged $5 million a year, just 10 percent the level in the 1980s.

Although the Bank limited the size and scope of its lending in these countries, it maintained some sort of lending program in most of them, despite serious misgivings about their economic policies. The scope of lending was limited to three basic areas: enclave projects in mining; agriculture and rural development; and some support for basic economic and social infrastructure, principally roads, public utilities, and education.

DESPOTIC STATES. If the principal mechanism for building trust was boosting lending, an underlying dilemma remained unresolved: the steps to building trust presupposed that the Bank and a country's leadership shared common objectives, and, more fundamentally, that the goals of a country's leadership went beyond survival and self-aggrandizement. In some cases, there was little doubt even quite early on that both policies and leadership commitment were highly dubious. Barely a year after Idi Amin came to power in Uganda, the Bank politely cautioned Uganda's finance minister:

> The fundamental problem [is] the growth of expenditure by the government to a level which cannot be sustained without serious consequences for Uganda's domestic economy and balance of payments. . . . [T]he central problems which have to be dealt with are the long-run level of government expenditure as a whole, the priorities as between development and non-development expenditure and the mobilization of domestic resources.[46]

In 1973, the Bank extended a $2 million IDA credit to Equatorial Guinea for a highway project, recognizing that it was a "rather desperate attempt to find something to do in a new member country where the conditions for any effective action seemed very unpromising." Two years later Burke Knapp reported to McNamara: "The prospects for accomplishing anything with this project are extremely dim. . . . [I]n the face of Government's total lack of cooperation on the project, it is clear that institution building would be nil."[47] The egregious actions of the leadership led the Bank to cut off lending to the Central African Republic in 1972–79, Equatorial Guinea in 1972–83, and Uganda in 1971–80.

Although there was little ambiguity about the leaders' corruption in the above cases, in many others the picture was less clear—at least at the time. President Siaka Stevens of Sierra Leone was cautioned early on regarding "the dangers inherent in the failure to take prompt and wholehearted corrective actions to reverse the disturbing developments in both fiscal and debt management."[48]

46. Letter, J. Burke Knapp to E. B. Wakhweya, Ugandan minister for finance, February 11, 1972.

47. Memorandum, J. Burke Knapp to Robert S. McNamara, "Equatorial Guinea," June 24, 1975.

48. Letter, J. Burke Knapp to President Stevens, n.d., 1972, p. 2.

Publicly, the report to the Board was more circumspect, noting several developments that seemed to demonstrate that the government was taking corrective policy measures. The posture was understandable, since public berating is a dubious mechanism for bridging untrusting waters. By the mid-1970s, however, the country was faced with a deteriorating financial situation: its debt service arrears were mounting; revenue had fallen well short of budgetary expectations, while current expenditures galloped ahead; and wages and salaries were absorbing 90 percent of government revenues. Bank staff reported that "senior civil servants recognize that the situation is desperate, but neither they nor the Vice President, who is also Finance Minister, are able to control the President, who must be held primarily responsible for the economy."[49] Yet Bank lending doubled every five years after Stevens took power in 1971 until his resignation in 1985. By then the country's economy had plummeted, and its institutions were crumbling. Stevens's rule was a disaster for his country, and the Bank's support decidedly ill-advised.

The Bank was more resolute in Zaire, at least in the 1970s. Despite its size and geopolitical importance, the country had been one of the least prepared and had faced one of the most chaotic transitions to independence in Africa. It matched a paranoia toward foreigners—well founded, given the extensive interests of Belgium, France, and the United States—with a virtual absence of any technocratic cadres. Above all, the country would be saddled for more than three decades by what amounted to little more than a kleptocracy. Early on the Bank's resident representative in the Congo (Kinshasa) noted that "the administration is fragile, and the few competent Congolese civil servants are fully stretched. . . . The Congo government has come to recognize the importance of sound development policies, but remains substantially ignorant as to what they are."[50] In hindsight it would become apparent that the government in the Congo (renamed Zaire in 1971 before reverting to Congo in 1997) was more wily than ignorant. IDA lending to Zaire had been much less than what a country of its size and poverty could have obtained, largely because of the country's inability to prepare projects for Bank financing. Following a visit by McNamara in 1972, the Bank's resident mission was greatly expanded to help develop projects for Bank financing; a planning advisory team was attached to the executive to help "the Presidency [bring] about a major change in the country's dismal economic performance." Two years later, the mission leader wrapped up his effort at technical assistance, one of the largest by the Bank in Africa at the time, and concluded that "the authoritarian and leader-oriented nature of the regime, the political climate,

49. Memorandum, E. Peter Wright to J. Burke Knapp, acting regional vice president, Western Africa, "Sierra Leone," December 31, 1975, p. 2. According to the note, the president had increased salaries without consulting the finance minister and had been "most responsive to the peddlers of suppliers' credits, and [had] entered into a number of dubious deals against the advice of his officials."

50. Memorandum, A. G. El Emary to Hugh R. Ripman, "Resident Representative in Congo (Kinshasa)," September 19, 1969, paras. 2, 5.

the deteriorating economic and financial condition of the country and the personalities of key people," rendered such assistance moot.[51]

Mobutu Sese Seko had fine-tuned the art of playing up to external actors. Periodically the Bank would issue stern warnings and threaten dire action, at which point Mobutu would promptly assure the Bank that he would do everything they asked of him.[52] Alternatively, when this strategy began to falter, Mobutu tried bluster. In 1976, when McNamara dispatched a strong note to Mobutu warning him the Bank would withdraw from Zaire unless corrective actions were taken, Mobutu countered with a protest accusing the staff member who hand-delivered the message of "abusive" behavior.[53] Soon thereafter a staff member's family was attacked in a crude attempt at intimidation. But the Bank's gradual reduction of lending had little effect, as commercial banks and government-insured bilateral export credits bankrolled the regime.

In 1978 the Bank together with the International Monetary Fund sent teams of experts to take over key financial positions in the country's core financial institutions: the finance ministry, the central bank, the debt administration office, the planning office, and even the customs office. This action came at the behest of Western governments (those of the United States, France, and Belgium), worried by the political crisis that followed the insurgency in Shaba province, the failure of two stabilization plans, and a prospective debt default on Zaire's commercial bank loans.[54] These attempts failed, and by 1979 the Country Program Paper for Zaire concluded that the lending program for fiscal 1980–84 would "be kept to the minimum possible" for maintaining a presence in Zaire. The resident mission would be reduced, as would analytical work on the country.[55] Less than three years later, lured by Mobutu's guile and promises of reform and by pressures from the United States, France, and Belgium, the Bank embarked on an ambitious structural adjustment lending program to Zaire.

RESOURCE-RICH COUNTRIES. If the Bank's lending push was deemed an essential ingredient to building trust, this effort was often undermined by the availability of alternate sources of funds. Commodity windfalls were the most insidious. In a 1970 comment on a back-to-office report from an economic mission to Nigeria, Knapp stated: "The figures for the prospective oil revenues in Nigeria

51. Richard M. Westebbe, "Report on UNDP/IBRD Planning Assistance Project in Zaire," March 22, 1976, paras. 9, 2.

52. Memorandum, Michael H. Wiehen for the records, "Zaire—Meeting of Finance Minister Bofossa with Mr. McNamara," September 16, 1975.

53. Letter, Robert S. McNamara to His Excellency Mobutu Sese Seko, July 12, 1976.

54. A revealing account of this episode can be found in Thomas Callaghy, "Restructuring Zaire's Debt, 1979–1982," in Thomas J. Biersteker, ed., *Dealing with Debt: International Financial Negotiations and Adjustment Bargaining* (Boulder, Colo.: Westview Press, 1993), pp. 107–31.

55. World Bank, East Africa region, "Country Program Paper, Zaire: Postscript," July 16, 1979.

are certainly impressive. I gather that this has created a certain euphoria and, as is often true in these cases, new riches may lead to over-spending."[56] Until 1975 lending to Nigeria (measured on a commitment basis) had to be offset by Nigerian loans to the Bank. With the government having set ambitious targets for its third national development plan, most public sector agencies were unwilling to submit their projects to the appraisal and international competitive bidding procedures required for Bank projects. About the only sector in which the Bank could be active was agriculture. A drastic turnaround in Nigeria's resource position by 1976 led it to ask the Bank for a substantially augmented lending program: about half a billion dollars a year, a figure the Bank made clear was "highly unrealistic."[57] Moreover, with Nigeria arranging a $1 billion commercial bank borrowing, it was unclear "what advantages Nigeria sees in borrowing from the Bank with 'conditions'" when it had "access to 'unconditional' loans."[58] As events transpired, the conditions in Bank lending were modest. In agriculture, a sector that the Bank and Nigeria agreed offered the most value added for Bank lending,[59] their failure to agree to issues of immediate importance to the sector—fertilizer distribution and agriculture credit—clipped the rate of growth. Broader economic policies germane to the long-term health of the agriculture sector, such as pricing and exchange rate policies, were discussed but were not part of the conditions related to lending in the sector.[60]

In the early 1970s, Gabon, a country with one of Sub-Saharan Africa's highest incomes and an economy based on oil and mineral resources (manganese, uranium, and iron ore), approached the Bank for the financing of a railroad to an iron ore mine. The Bank's analysis revealed that under the expected traffic projections the railway line only made sense if the mine was developed, and even then just barely. The government wanted to build the line not only to the mine but to the south of the country, seeing it (rather than the alternative—roads) as an instrument for physically unifying the country. Attempts by the Bank to dissuade the offer of supplier credit were rebuffed by the financier: "The project [was] a political imperative. . . . [I]t was a situation comparable to the Concorde and . . . FED

56. Memorandum, J. Burke Knapp to Robert S. McNamara, "Nigeria—Back-to-Office Report of Economic Mission," June 19, 1970.

57. World Bank, "Nigeria: Topics for Discussion," topics for Mr. McNamara's discussions with Nigerian authorities, November 1977, para. 9. Lending in the five-year fiscal period 1977 to 1981 was actually about a third of this level.

58. Ibid., annex 2, "Nigeria: Issues, Objectives and Strategies for an Expanded Bank Lending Program," para. 16, 1977.

59. In the sixteen years to 1974, Nigeria had borrowed about $623 million from the Bank, of which just two loans (about 4 percent of lending) were for agriculture. In the six years between fiscal 1975 and 1980, the Bank made seventeen loans for agriculture for $415 million (52 percent of lending).

60. Memorandum, A. David Knox to Robert S. McNamara, "Nigeria—Background Brief for Your Meeting with Alhaji Gusau, Federal Minister of Agriculture," October 7, 1980.

[European Development Fund, or Fonds Européen de Développement] simply had to recognize this."[61] While aware of wide-ranging French interests in the country, the Bank could not have known the extent of the relationship between Omar Bongo, the president of Gabon, and the French presidency. Bongo had been personally auditioned for his job by Jacques Foccart, who as overseer of French interests in Africa had earned the sobriquet "Monsieur Afrique."[62] With ample oil and forestry revenues at its disposal, Gabon did not take kindly to the perceived slight by the Bank. There were just two small loans to Gabon in the 1970s,[63] and lending did not resume until 1988, when a decline in the country's economic fortunes led to an adjustment loan.

Though more limited in scale, windfalls in commodities outside of oil—phosphates (Senegal, Togo); cocoa and coffee (Cameroon, Côte D'Ivoire, Ghana); coffee (Kenya, Tanzania); uranium (Niger); copper (Zaire, Zambia)—nonetheless created an illusory sense of financial well-being. The adverse effects of commodity windfalls were exacerbated by the flood of commercial funds that flowed in. Repeatedly the Bank attempted to persuade countries of the OECD to curb their insurance cover for supplier credits. Not only were the projects poor investment decisions and an important source of corruption, but they would leave a mountain of debt. The Bank's pleas fell on deaf ears. The same governments that adopted a lofty attitude regarding "governance" in the 1990s were actively engaged in political and rent-seeking activities whose consequences were pernicious in the extreme. But in the global equation of power, "accountability" is not a particularly symmetric variable.

RESOURCE-POOR COUNTRIES. A different dilemma arose in the Sahelian countries, which had vast landlocked spaces and few resources. Although some problems, such as those arising from Niger's uranium boom in the late 1970s and political unrest in Chad and Mauritania, were similar to those in other countries in the region, the general outlook for the Sahel seemed much bleaker than that for other countries in the region. The Sahelian drought of 1973–74 had had a harsh impact, but the attendant relief efforts were mismanaged and thus exacerbated the political instability in a number of countries (Ethiopia, Mali, Niger). It also illustrated in a tragic manner the absence of suitable technical packages adapted to Sahelian agroclimatic zones. While constructive programs were being pursued by the combination of eight Sahelian countries and bilateral donors in the so-called Club du Sahel from 1974 onward, some bilaterals promoted large, high-cost irrigation schemes for which the recipient countries were ill prepared but that offered plum contracts to aid suppliers. The Bank initially held back but then joined.

61. Memorandum, J. Burke Knapp to files, "Discussion with FED officials—Gabon Railway Project," March 20, 1973.

62. Jacques Foccart, *Foccart Parle: Entretiens avec Phillipe Gaillard* (Paris: Fayard, Jeune Afrique, 1995).

63. One for $9.5 million in 1973 and another for $5 million in 1975.

Mauritania was a case in point. The Bank had first ventured into Mauritania in 1960, financing an "enclave" iron ore mining project, which more than forty-five years later would remain the principal commercial enterprise in the country. In the mid-1960s, at the request of the government, it sent a fifteen-member mission to the country. Economic activity was largely pastoral, severely circumscribed by the harsh physical realities of the country. The country's physical features were such, one staff member recalls, that it was "essentially a sandbox." Working closely with the president, the Bank set about formulating a strategy on various sectors that became the basis of a four-year plan for the country.[64] The report was well received by the government of Mauritania (and earned George Woods a medal from the country), but the Bank's lending program in the country remained minimal, confined to a few road and livestock projects.[65]

In a briefing paper for McNamara, Roger Chaufournier, the vice president for West Africa, laid out the problem:

> Mauritania represents an extreme case of a dual economy. Mining provided 75 percent of the country's export earnings and 25 percent of its tax revenues. However, this sector has remained a foreign-owned enclave industry with transfers abroad accounting for over half of total value added, limited employment . . . and little secondary effects on the traditional sector of the economy. . . . Stepping up the pace and broadening the base of Mauritania's development will at best be a lengthy and difficult process.[66]

The Bank, Chaufournier continued, had found "opportunities to develop economically viable projects in Mauritania [to be] limited. Accordingly, the competition among the various external donors, including the [People's] Republic of China, for the few available projects is keen."[67] Beyond roads and livestock, there appeared to be some irrigation possibilities along the Senegal River—the Gorgol agriculture project—but initial studies were unpromising, pointing to high capital costs.

In late 1974 Mauritania nationalized MIFERMA, the iron ore company so central to its macroeconomic fortunes. The Sahelian drought of the mid-1970s had put agriculture and food security high on the policy agenda. Attempts at developing

64. "Each time we would come to a sector with a draft conclusions and options, I would take the person involved and go see the President who was very closely involved in this work. . . . We would discuss it with him: what would go, what wouldn't go, and what his views were. Before we wrote anything, we already knew the boundaries within which policy could move." Richard Westebbe, interview, World Bank Oral History Program, January 25, 1988, p. 12. IBRD, "Mauritania: Guidelines for a Four-Year Development Program," November 1968.

65. Until 1971, the Bank lent $76 million for just three projects, dominated by the $66 million loan to the iron ore mine in 1960. Between 1971 and 1981, the Bank made a further ten loans for $120 million, $60 million of which was for the iron ore enterprise.

66. Memorandum, Roger Chaufournier to Robert S. McNamara, "Mauritania: Briefing Paper—Ambassador El Hassen's Visit," May 24, 1972, pp. 1–2.

67. Ibid., p. 2.

a rural development project in the southeastern part of the country based on rain-fed cultivation were abandoned, after it was concluded that agroclimatic conditions were adverse. Yet by 1975 it became evident that the Bank would participate in the Gorgol irrigation project.[68]

Five years later, in a rare occurrence, the irrigation project, now ready for final approval, was put for discussion to the President's Council since it posed a special set of questions. The ex-ante rate of return was 5.5 percent, substantially below the 10 percent norm sought of all projects. The discussants were cognizant of the need to balance an important point of principle with the fact that the Bank could not seem to come up with alternatives for the country. It was argued that if the Bank rejected the project, funds from other donors would be lost.[69] It was also argued that the project had a large "sunk political cost." Some said this was an "infant country" that had not previously benefited from large investments. McNamara was less than enthusiastic about the project: "In his view the world was putting too much money in the Sahel"—but fearing that rejecting the project would give the impression that the Bank could do nothing about the country, management let the project go ahead anyway.[70]

When the project was presented to the Board several months later—now showing a rate of return of 7 percent, still less than the 10 percent norm—it was approved without discussion. Projections had shown that after the project's completion the annual operational costs alone would be greater than the combined per capita income of the project beneficiaries. In the end even these benefits were not realized: the rate of return after completion was less than 3 percent, while the country's debt had increased by $100 million.[71]

Attempts at Regional Integration

Regional integration has for long been seen as the best way to skirt the obstacles posed by the small size of many of Sub-Saharan Africa's economies.[72] Although

68. Memorandum, Roger Chaufournier to Robert S. McNamara, "Mauritania," January 16, 1975.

69. Ninety-five percent of the total project costs of $93 million were to be funded by soft credits from external sources. IDA's share was 16 percent. IDA, "Mauritania: Gorgol Irrigation Project," IDA/R80-131, August 27, 1980. Between the mid-1970s and the early-1990s, net ODA as a share of Mauritanian GDP averaged 25 percent. For the Sahelian countries (Burkina Faso, Chad, Mali, Mauritania, and Niger), the average was 18.5 percent, with Burkina Faso, at 14 percent, being the lowest. World Bank, *African Development Indicators* (World Bank, 1996), table 12-5.

70. President's Council meeting of February 25, 1980.

71. It should be noted, however, that some years later the Bank opposed the West Africa Manantali dam—with potential benefits to Mali, Mauritania, and Senegal—on cost grounds. The project went ahead anyway as a showcase of German foreign aid. At the time of writing its economic benefits appear questionable.

72. Of forty-eight Sub-Saharan countries, one (Nigeria) is a giant with a population exceeding 100 million; only one other (Ethiopia) has a population exceeding 50 million. Ten

colonialism had left Africa with fragmented and artificial nation-states, its legacy also included a few institutions of regional scope. For one thing, the countries of Francophone Africa were grouped into two monetary unions, and a de facto customs union linked Kenya, Tanganyika (with the merger of Zanzibar into Tanganyika, the United Republic of Tanzania was the successor state), and Uganda. Besides having common service organizations in transport and communications, as well as a large number of "General Fund" services (including customs, statistics, and air traffic control), the three countries also shared a currency board (which effectively controlled fiscal and monetary policy), and a uniform trade regime.[73]

An early Bank mission to the region considered "this 'East African' approach to common problems . . . valuable," arguing that it was "highly desirable that future development should follow rather than struggle against the pattern set by economic geography."[74] But with independence the currency board was soon abolished, and with it the common monetary union. Each country developed its own currency and independent trade regime. The creation of the East African Community (EAC) in 1967 (through the Treaty for East African Cooperation), attempted to reestablish fraying cooperation. It formalized the de facto customs union that had existed between the countries for nearly five decades, as well as the continuation of the established common service organizations and many of the "General Fund" services.[75] A new financial institution, the East African Development ment Bank (EADB), was created to promote equitable industrial development.

Consequently, well into the 1960s, the Bank's approach to East Africa had a strong regional focus, both in its economic reports and in its lending. Beginning with a loan for railways and harbors in 1955, the Bank extended ten loans (amounting to almost a quarter billion dollars) to East African institutions for the expansion and modernization of transport and communication infrastructure and to the EADB.

Shortly after the EAC was created, however, the cooperative atmosphere soured. Political strains arising from the accession of Idi Amin in Uganda in 1971 and increasing differences in economic philosophy between Tanzania and Kenya were compounded by the severe budgetary and balance of payments problems

---

are ministates, with populations of a million or less, and thirteen others are small, with populations in the range of 1 to 5 million. The remaining twenty-three countries had populations ranging from 5 to 50 million.

73. The operations of the East Africa Currency Board also covered Zanzibar, British Somaliland, and the Aden Protectorate.

74. IBRD, *The Economic Development of Tanganyika* (Johns Hopkins University Press, 1961), p. 33.

75. To achieve a greater balance in industrial development and interarea trade flows, the treaty also permitted transfer taxes to be imposed by countries with a deficit in interarea trade of manufactured goods. In practice this meant that Uganda and Tanzania taxed imports from Kenya and that Tanzania taxed some imports from Uganda. See World Bank, "East African Community," R77-312, December 29, 1977.

experienced by all three countries. Imposition of exchange controls and import restrictions inhibited the operations of the Common Market. The authority of the Community institutions began to diminish. Once the parties failed to agree on arrangements for the transfer of funds between the regional offices and the service headquarters of the EAC corporations, their operations grew steadily shakier, and by the mid-1970s the Community had for all practical purposes become defunct.

The EAC's difficulties began to affect the Bank's lending and except for a second line of credit to the EADB in March 1976, Bank commitments ceased in 1973. Particularly troublesome for the Bank were the Community's mounting delays in meeting debt-servicing obligations to the Bank. The three countries had provided joint and several guarantees on the loans underlying their commitment to the "common cause" of the EAC. In 1976, with Uganda in dire financial straits and the Community's default an imminent prospect, the Bank first sought recourse from the other guarantor states. It was soon clear that the state of relations among them made this politically impossible. But with arrears mounting the Bank faced an equally intractable problem: it could not simply ignore a default by joint or several guarantors without suspending its lending and disbursements.

An interim arrangement was first worked out by Purviz Damry, the Bank's secretary in 1976. At the 1977 Annual Meeting, following protracted negotiations, a mediator was appointed to achieve a final settlement on the distribution of debts and assets of the EAC.[76] The process, originally anticipated to take a year, took more than six.[77]

Even as regional cooperation efforts were faltering in East Africa, developments in West Africa appeared more positive.[78] A more expansive mood found its way into Bank lending. Bolstered by the prevalent view that economic integration in West Africa was the only hope for large-scale industrial development in that region, the Bank made a particularly ambitious loan for a regional industrial project to produce clinker for cement production in Togo, Côte d'Ivoire, and Ghana. The project, one

76. The mediator was Victor Umbricht, a diplomat and former head of the Swiss Treasury. His account of the mediation effort is detailed in Victor H. Umbricht, *Multilateral Mediation: Practical Experiences and Lessons* (Boston: Martinus Nijhoff, 1989).

77. Under the "Damry" formula, the servicing of the debts of each of the corporations of the EAC was divided in proportion to the member country's actual holdings of the fixed assets of that corporation. Under the final settlement (signed in May 1984), the net assets and long-term liabilities of the defunct EAC were distributed among Kenya, Tanzania, and Uganda in the ratio of 42 percent, 32 percent, and 26 percent, respectively. World Bank, "East African Community—Proposed Settlement of Division of Outstanding Debt and Apportionment of Bank Loans," R84-125, May 14, 1984.

78. A regional development bank—the Banque Ouest-Africaine de Developpement (BOAD)—was set up within the framework of the West African Monetary Union (Union Monétaire Ouest-Africaine). And in 1975, the creation of the Economic Community of West African States (ECOWAS) was the first formal union between countries of Francophone and Anglophone West Africa.

of the largest industrial investments in that part of the world, did not have strong financial or economic justification but was perceived to have substantial intangible benefits.[79] It was hoped that the high financial costs would have positive externalities by laying the foundations of a regional economic and commercial institution that would serve as a precursor for planning and executing regional projects.

In the event, the plant shut down after barely four years of intermittent operation. The resulting debt servicing on a $317 million investment (the Bank's share being $60 million) meant that "instead of . . . goodwill to promote future cooperation, [the project] brought about recrimination and mutual distrust," as the practical difficulty of enforcing transnational arrangements when buffeted by economic recession and lower cost alternatives, became apparent.[80] Although at one level the project's failure was largely the result of a poor understanding of cement markets and the economics of clinker and cement production, it also underlined the danger of taking at face value the rhetoric of international solidarity and cooperation.

Even in better-conceived projects, regional components performed poorly. Loans to the Banque Ouest Africaine Développement (BOAD), serving the member countries of the monetary zone of the Union Monétaire Ouest-Africaine, mandated that at least half the credits were to finance regional projects (defined as projects accruing to more than one state). But in practice few such projects could be identified. Commenting on these loans, the Bank's Operations Evaluation Department later noted, "A lesson which goes beyond [this project] is that regional and sub-regional projects, involving more than one country are scarce and difficult to realize in West Africa."[81] They required a commitment from borrowing members, the report noted, that was simply not there in practice.[82]

These experiences and their repercussions on the Bank and borrowers, considerably cooled the Bank's ardor for lending for projects of a multinational and

79. The ex-ante financial rate of return was just 8 percent, and the economic rate of return barely 10 percent. IBRD, "Togo/Ivory Coast/Ghana Appraisal of CIMAO Regional Clinker Project," Report 1071-A, June 14, 1976.

80. World Bank, OED Project Performance Audit Report 7328, SecM 38-0821, June 23, 1988, p. 5.

81. Project Completion Report 11466, SecM93-0012, December 22, 1992, para. 126. The only other lending to projects of a regional nature was to railways: the Regie des Chemis de fer Abidjan-Niger (RAN), a railway system operated jointly by Côte d'Ivoire and Burkina Faso; and railway projects in Senegal and Mali, which attempted to link the two systems. Once again, the record was poor.

82. A recent study on the African Development Bank found that despite an explicit commitment to the issue since its inception, that institution's experience was equally discouraging. Lending for multinational projects amounted to just 2.4 percent of total commitments between 1982 and 1986 (against a target of 10 percent) and less than 1 percent in the early 1990s. The authors note, the "lofty pronouncements of African leaders have not been translated into commensurate action." E. Philip English and Harris M. Mule, *The African Development Bank* (Boulder, Colo.: Lynne Rienner, 1996), p. 151.

regional nature. Even in its analytical work the institution concentrated on indirect instruments like trade integration.

The Legacy of the 1970s

As the 1970s drew to a close, two trends—obscure at the time—converged that together would have a profound impact on the Bank's relationship with Africa in the next decade. In its first quarter-century the Bank was a modest partner in the aid effort in Africa, especially in Francophone Africa. But by the end of the 1970s, in the realm of economic development, the Bank had emerged as the dominant external actor in Africa. Its share in lending had not grown, and in Francophone Africa France was still preeminent, but the Bank had become the leading aid coordinator, analyst, and source of technical assistance. Where once bilateral aid agencies would have assisted the Bank in projects, the roles were now almost reversed.

Another trend was the growing gulf between the ambition and reach of the state apparatus in most countries and their limited administrative, managerial, and institutional capabilities. The fabric of the state began disintegrating, although this pattern was masked by relatively favorable exogenous circumstances (especially with respect to the 1980s). The new decade would not be as forgiving.

The convergence of these trends coincided with a change in presidents, both at the Bank and in its most important shareholder. These changes in leadership affected the degree of change, but not its direction. That had already been established at the turn of the decade.

Crossing the Rubicon

At the end of the 1970s, external commentators, as well as internal analysis and feedback from the operations complex, began painting a disquieting picture of trends in Sub-Saharan Africa. The oil-importing countries of the region had been hit hard by the external shocks in the decade: income losses due to adverse terms-of-trade movements and the decline in export volumes due to the slowdown of world trade averaged 4.4 percent of GNP during 1974–78. Although external flows to the region had jumped substantially, additional net external financing had offset three-fourths of these losses for the group as a whole, but just 37 percent in the case of low-income countries.[83]

The first oil shock, while benefiting the few SSA oil exporters (Congo, Gabon, Nigeria), had had only a modestly adverse direct impact on the majority of SSA

---

83. Bela Balassa, "Policy Responses to External Shocks in Sub-Saharan African Countries, 1973–78," World Bank Development Research Department Discussion Paper 42, November 18, 1982.

countries.[84] However, the indirect impact, through much higher prices for non-oil imports and sharp hikes in freight rates, was much more substantial. Rapid increases and wide fluctuations in the prices of key commodity exports inflated internal expectations and external perceptions of creditworthiness. The latter, combined with the liquidity of the international capital market, made it possible for borrowings to grow much faster than the region's economies. Few countries in the region developed adequate policy measures to accompany or follow the commodity booms. Virtually no country managed to pursue contracyclical policies, riding the terms-of-trade escalator, first down, then up.[85]

On the operations side, the zeal and excitement that had characterized the McNamara Bank through the mid-1970s was waning. An OED review of rural development projects that had been approved before the heyday of "new style" projects following McNamara's Nairobi speech painted a somber picture. The average rate of return on the eighteen projects reviewed appeared satisfactory, although substantially below appraisal estimates. But these results masked the fact that the satisfactory results were principally due to price movements, in the wake of soaring commodity prices in the mid-1970s. Less than a quarter of the projects had met the production targets expected of them.[86] By early 1981 the agriculture and rural development portfolio was faced with a "variety of problems," the principal culprit being "managerial" problems in the context of a deeper malaise in the "broader environment" and the "political/administrative structure." Lending programs were cut, in part in response to a growing conviction in the Bank that many African countries were unwilling to face important policy issues.[87] The 1979 *World Development Report* painted a pessimistic outlook for Sub-Saharan Africa, which intensified to "most disturbing" in the following year for fear that "average incomes would actually be lower in 1990 than [in] 1980."[88] The briefings for incoming president A. W. Clausen in early 1981 were filled with anxiety about the region's prospects. West Africa, they said, was rife with "political instability" and "the outlook appears distinctly grimmer and an atmosphere of disillusionment and

84. Oil imports were less than 10 percent of imports to begin with, and since these countries imported refined products whose prices rose less than half the price of crude oil, the overall impact was moderate.

85. The negative consequences of the failure to restrain government expenditures following favorable terms of trade and other revenue developments was emphasized by David Wheeler, "Sources of Stagnation in Sub-Saharan Africa," *World Development*, vol. 12, no. 1 (January 1984), pp. 1–23. David Bevan and others, *Controlled Open Economies: A Neoclassical Approach to Structuralism* (Oxford University Press, 1990), give a good analysis of the effects of the coffee boom in the second half of the 1970s on Kenya and Tanzania.

86. World Bank, "Rural Development Projects: A Retrospective View of Bank Experience in Sub-Saharan Africa," OED Report 2242, October 13, 1978.

87. Memorandum for the record, "Meeting on Regional Lending Programs FY1979 with Regional Vice Presidents and Mr. Baum, May 1, 8, and 17, 1979." President's Council meeting, September 24, 1979.

88. World Bank, *World Development Report 1980,* table 2.1, p. 6.

often outright pessimism pervades official and private circles, inside and outside the countries of the Region. This, essentially, is because of what happened during the seventies. . . . While causes for reasonable expectations have been noted, it should not be excluded that in the coming years, mounting social and political turmoil or financing chaos will create impossible operating conditions in a number of countries." As for East Africa, its prospects for the 1980s were equally bleak. The "diagnosis suggests that the development problems of Eastern Africa are complex and solutions to some aspects are largely a function of time (e.g., integrating diverse cultural and ethnic groups into a cohesive national identity and gaining political and institutional maturity). The Bank is not equipped to contribute much to this process."[89]

What the Bank could do, the briefings argued, was help stimulate and support policy reform by African governments, and help mobilize—and improve the effectiveness of—external assistance. There was some ground for reasonable optimism, in that there appeared to be "a sense of urgency" among some governments regarding "policy and institutional reforms." If there was one country that epitomized the Bank's disillusionment with the past, the break from it, and a preview of the future, it was Tanzania.

Tanzania: The End of the Romance

The Bank's involvement with Tanzania had begun with a large survey mission in 1959–60 whose report was a landmark analysis of the country's economy and influenced Tanzanian development strategies in the 1960s.[90] This report placed high priority on agriculture and in view of a paucity of private alternatives argued that the government could play a significant role in developing Tanzanian peasant agriculture. Recognizing that economic power was concentrated in the hands of non-Africans, the strategy put "the responsibility for development in the locus of political power rather than in traditional institutions controlled by economic powerful groups."[91]

Following Nyerere's Arusha Declaration in 1967, Tanzanian policies became much more radical and the Bank became more a follower than a leader. The reach of the state was extended through progressive nationalization of banking, commerce, industry, and land. Nyerere pressed on with the Ujamma strategy, but with the peasantry considerably less enamored than the leadership about its purported benefits, the pace was slow.[92] Because the peasantry was still reluctant to recognize the errors of its ways, the scheme took on a mandatory nature in 1974.

---

89. World Bank, "Western Africa: Profile and Prospects," pp. 4, 7, 18; and "East Africa Region: Overview," pp. 1, 9, briefings prepared for incoming president, A. W. Clausen, n.d.

90. IBRD, *Economic Development of Tanganyika.*

91. World Bank, "Tanzania: World Bank Tanzania Relations, 1961–1987," OED Report 8329, January 16, 1990, para. 4.09.

92. The World Bank had played an important role in earlier settlement schemes in Tanzania, indeed, urging the government to build more of them. However, the Ujamma

As noted earlier, the overt support for Tanzania notwithstanding, the Bank was concerned about Tanzania's economic performance from the early 1970s.[93] Subsequently, through 1976, it set its reservations aside and emerged as an enthusiastic supporter of Tanzania's development strategy. Lending grew rapidly, from $53 million in the 1960s to $96 million between 1970 and 1973, and then jumped to $315 million between 1974 and 1977. Like many other observers, the Bank had been caught up in "the cult of Tanzaphilia," stemming in part from the general probity of the country's leadership and the egalitarian ethical foundations of its professed ideology. These beliefs, particularly their translation to a focus on rural development, paralleled those of the McNamara Bank, then in its heyday of poverty lending (see chapters 6 and 8). While these values would fray under the pressures of the economic hardships of the 1980s, another trait would prove longer lasting, although the country would reap its benefits only gradually: Tanzania was unusual in the degree to which its leadership succeeded in nation building in a region where leaders have been prone to manipulate ethnic rivalries to advance their personal agendas.

The coffee boom in 1976–77 masked the economic problems in the country. In 1977 after Julius Nyerere himself publicly questioned parastatal performance on the tenth anniversary of the Arusha Declaration, the Bank followed suit, but in a low-key manner. Before this period the Bank was reticent in its criticisms of parastatal performance in Tanzania, which was even less than the generally low levels in other countries in Africa. There had been some concern regarding compensation for the nationalizations that followed the Arusha Declaration, but even that move was prompted by the United Kingdom, whose nationals had assets at stake. The relationship with Tanzania had been cemented by the unusual personal rapport between McNamara and Nyerere. Added to this, as the Bank's OED would later note in its review of Bank-Tanzania relations, was the fact that "until 1977, the increasing lending targets for Africa, and the unstable political situation making for low eligibility in a number of countries meant that there was 'pressure to lend' to Tanzania."[94]

The romance began to sour after a critical report in 1977, which argued that "the current temporary easing of balance of payments" provided the opportunity to address three major areas of long-term concern: agriculture production, domestic resource mobilization, and export performance.[95] However, in the next few years,

---

strategy was distinct from traditional settlement schemes in its efforts to organize them on a more *communal* basis.

93. Thus in the discussion of the CPP for Tanzania in 1972, "the President expressed concern over Tanzania's relatively weak economic performance in recent years and its limited export prospects for the immediate future," and cut back the proposed lending program. World Bank, "Tanzania—Country Program Paper: Postscript," April 10, 1972, para. 78.

94. World Bank, "Tanzania: World Bank Tanzania Relations," para. 4.31.

95. Memorandum, Mahbub ul Haq to Robert S. McNamara, "Tanzania CPP: Major Policy Issues," January 30, 1978.

even as the Bank's disillusionment with Tanzanian policies escalated, so did lending (from $315 million during 1974–77 to $485 million during 1978–81). In part, this was a response to the worsening economic situation. But also, with other donors increasing support for the country, the Bank convinced itself that it had to increase its lending if it was to have any hope of leverage in the country. Only at the turn of the decade did the Bank change course, whereupon it did an abrupt about-face.

Between 1978 and 1981, as relations cooled, negotiations over a program loan became increasingly convoluted over increasing conditions the Bank placed on policy reforms. The Bank's new toughness was timed unfortunately, as Tanzania was still reeling from the second oil shock, the war with Uganda, and a sharp decline in coffee prices. In a theme that would echo across the region in the ensuing years, the Bank argued that the external shocks had exacerbated the country's problems, not caused them, citing as evidence the decline in the volume of exports, which fell by a third between 1966 and 1979.

Understandably, the agricultural sector drew the most attention. The Bank had invested heavily in that sector during the decade and it was evident that performance was poor.[96] With Tanzania largely reliant on agricultural exports, it was essential, the Bank argued, to reverse the decline in agriculture in order to check the increasing balance of payments deficit. To this end it pressed the government to reexamine its agricultural policies for smallholder agriculture, with regard to production incentives (especially pricing policies on export crops), and parastatal efficiency in support services (inputs, extension, and transport). The Bank had earlier supported the supplementing of several crop cooperatives by marketing boards and helped create parastatals (in livestock, sugar, tobacco, and tea). Now, as evidence mounted that these parastatals were not only failing to deliver the requisite services to smallholders but in addition were becoming a growing financial burden on the exchequer, the Bank sought to reverse course.

Attempts at reform were stymied by Nyerere's adamant hostility to an IMF program prescribing fiscal austerity, devaluation, and decontrol of prices.[97] Strong ideological differences were compounded by the apparent "paternalistic and condescending" manners of a visiting IMF mission.[98] With Tanzanian arrears to the

96. By 1991 the Bank's OED had evaluated twenty-two agricultural and rural development projects made to Tanzania in the 1970s. Just three were deemed satisfactory, and only one had a rate of return greater than at appraisal. Thirteen had a negative rate of return.

97. During this period, when the IMF was pressing Tanzania to devalue, one of the authors of this study who had just become the governor of the central bank of Peru, was contemplating a gradual devaluation of the peso. He recalls being strongly advised by a senior IMF staff member against any such move on the grounds that "real devaluation" was not possible. To allay his doubts, a fresh Chicago Ph.D. was trotted out who went on to "prove econometrically" this supposed new doctrine on exchange rates. Views on the benefits of a fixed exchange rate regime also differed in the early 1990s, between Argentina and Mexico, on the one hand, and Francophone Africa, on the other.

98. Memorandum, IMF, office of the managing director, to files, "Visit of the Ambassador of Tanzania," January 7, 1980. In retrospect, however, the ambassador's complaint that the

Bank mounting, staff urged McNamara to discuss "the current very serious situation of Tanzania" with the finance minister and the president. McNamara traveled to Tanzania in January 1980. With the Bank asking "for policy changes essentially identical to those of the IMF," relations were at a low ebb.[99]

In an attempt to break the impasse, at McNamara's initiative an independent advisory group was formed to help achieve a consensus on needed reforms.[100] The advisory group's efforts ended in failure, largely because of the Tanzanian government's failure to act with sufficient vigor on the exchange rate. But the extensive discussions on the speed of change, the relative emphasis on demand restraint versus supply-side measures, and social protection measures helped lay the seeds of future changes.

As Tanzania's economic fortunes plummeted, so did Bank lending (from $485 million in 1978–81 to $201 million in 1982–85), as it increasingly linked lending to major policy reforms.[101] In late 1981, the new Bank president, A. W. Clausen, informed Nyerere that an agreement with the IMF was a precondition to Bank adjustment lending. Even disbursements on committed loans ceased for a while because of overdue service payments by Tanzania, and this situation led to a peevish exchange between the Bank and Tanzania.[102] The very warmth of the earlier relationship contributed to the fractiousness, in that the Tanzanian leadership, faced with its worst crisis, viewed the Bank's actions as a betrayal by a close friend. The Bank for its part regarded the Tanzanian leadership as beset by ideology and unwilling to face up to the crisis that had befallen the country.

The Berg Report

Through the 1970s, the common interests of African countries, as expressed in their periodic meetings with McNamara, focused on the volume of lending and

---

IMF mission had "assumed that the President himself was either ignorant or ill-advised," would not stand the test of time.

99. "Topics for Discussion," briefing note prepared for McNamara, January 7, 1980. There were, however, disagreements within the Bank. Ul Haq, for instance, argued that "given the socialist structure of Tanzania, the pricing mechanism may have a more limited role to play than in some other developing countries." Memorandum, Mahbub ul Haq to Robert S. McNamara, "Tanzania CPP: Major Policy Issues," January 9, 1980.

100. The group included E. Michanek, former head of CIDA, and Cranford Pratt and Gerald Helleiner, both of the University of Toronto. In organizing the group, the Bank made a rare gesture, a testimony to the relationship between McNamara and Nyerere. An earlier exception was a mission of "three wise men" to India in 1960 to assess its third plan. Mason and Asher, World Bank since Bretton Woods, p. 677.

101. World Bank Country Program Paper, "Tanzania: Postscript," January 6, 1982.

102. Memorandum, Willi Wappenhans to Ernest Stern, "Tanzania—Overdue Service Payments," September 17, 1982; memorandum, Jochen Kraske to files, "Meeting with President Nyerere," October 19, 1982.

distribution of concessional resources, employment of Africans in the Bank, and the representation of African countries on the Bank's Board.[103] In early 1979 the African contact group (formed in 1978) had its first meeting with McNamara and put forward a similar agenda.[104] The economic situation in the region was not brought up, but in a later 1979 meeting the African governors of the World Bank asked the institution to undertake a special study of the region's needs and possibilities for renewing and accelerating its development. The Bank agreed. The result, issued in August 1981, was a report called "Accelerated Development in Sub-Saharan Africa: An Agenda for Action," popularly known as the Berg Report (after the report's coordinator, Elliot Berg; see also chapters 8 and 9).

The report's central messages, as summarized in a memo from Stern to McNamara, formed the essential elements of the Bank's thinking on Africa for the rest of the decade. In analyzing the "extraordinary depth of [Africa's] economic crisis . . . and the relatively poor prospects for the future," the report was

> very clear that a major set of reasons relates to the domestic policies followed in many African countries which have provided an inadequate incentive for agricultural growth; strongly discouraged the private sector from making the contribution it is capable of; placed an undue burden on government and the public sector in the face of limited administrative and managerial talent; and have spent an undue share of their investments on low priority projects.[105]

Three other contributing factors were held to have "compounded" these internal problems. First, the external situation, including petroleum prices and slow growth in industrialized countries. However, the external environment was deemed to have affected all developing countries; consequently, "changes in the terms of trade were not a major cause of the economic crisis prior to 1978." Second were factors specific to Africa, "such as prolonged adverse climatic conditions, an unusual amount of civil and military strife leading both to direct expenditures and to large-scale refugee movements." And third were donor policies, "which have supported domestic strategies which were inappropriate, which have financed budgetary expenditures without adequate planning of long-term consequences, which have promoted projects which are inappropriate, and which often have provided advice

103. Memorandum, Robert S. McNamara to the governors of the African Group Countries, "Reply to Your Memorandum Delivered at the 1974 Annual Meetings," February 13, 1975; McNamara, memorandum for the record, "Meeting with African Executive Directors and Alternates," January 26, 1977; McNamara, memorandum for the record, "Second Meeting with the African Executive Directors," September 7, 1977.

104. Memorandum, Roger Chaufournier for the record, "Meeting with the African Contact Group, January 23, 1979," March 9, 1979. The African contact group was led by Marcel Yondo, minister of finance of Cameroon.

105. Memorandum, Ernest Stern to Robert S. McNamara, "African Study," April 23, 1981.

which exacerbates specific problems, such as the creation of additional public sector enterprises or adding generally to governmental responsibility."[106]

The report, Stern informed McNamara, argued that while "a substantial improvement in the prospects for growth and development in Africa was possible," it would require African "governments individually coming to grips with the distortions of price and resources allocation and the operational responsibility assigned to the public sector and making necessary changes." This would have to be underpinned by "substantially increased aid flows," plus "significant changes in donor policies to make aid flows more responsive to African needs, including more emphasis on training, administration, transfer of technology, and supplementing government revenues." Consequently much better coordination among donors was required and the Bank should be prepared "to take a lead in assisting governments to undertake the changes indicated on the one hand and to raise the resources and strengthen donor coordination on the other."[107]

The Berg study framed a dialogue between universal and regional assessors that would continue through the 1980s. Assigning primary responsibility for Africa's predicament to weak or flawed domestic policies, it shifted the Bank's focal engagement with the region from the specific and secular to the conceptual and policy level. The Bank's analysis of African economies was in contrast to the central message of the Organization of African Unity's "Lagos Plan of Action," which had preceded it by a year and which placed the onus of Africa's predicament largely on malignant external forces. For that reason, as well as the general apathy toward the African regional multilaterals in Washington, the Lagos Plan had little impact.[108] While the two reports indeed held contrasting views of the roots of Africa's crisis, the differences were less in the analysis per se than in the rhetorical battles that ensued. The latter, garnished with generous side orders of self-interest, ideological proclivities, and limited knowledge, would mark the two extremes of the debate. And in any case, as Nyerere pointed out, the Berg Report "challenged the regrettable tendency in Africa to act as if the origin of our own problems affected the necessity for us to undertake the task of dealing with them."[109]

In the late summer of 1981, even before the Berg Report was formally presented, the staff was thinking of ways to "sell" it to those to whom it was being addressed. The receptions the report received in a variety of fora in the early months of 1982—a meeting of the Development Assistance Committee, an Arab/OPEC meeting, pronouncements of the European Economic Community and United Nations Development Program, a conference of the United Nations

106. Ibid.
107. Ibid.
108. These included the UN's Economic Commission for Africa (ECA) and the Organization for African Unity (OAU) in Addis Ababa, and the African Development Bank (AfDB) in Abidjan.
109. Letter, Julius K. Nyerere to A. W. Clausen, July 26, 1982.

Children's Fund—were unexpectedly negative.[110] Although the African governors
of the Bank and Fund at their meeting in Dakar in March 1982 appeared to
recognize that the report contributed to the implementation of the Lagos Plan of
Action, African development and planning ministers attending a conference of
the Economic Commission for Africa in Tripoli at the end of April were very
hostile to the Berg Report, declaring it to be "in fundamental contradiction with
the political, economic and social aspirations of Africa." The Bank, struggling to
cajole donor governments (particularly the United States) to increase contributions to IDA on the basis of the increased needs for Africa, took this contradictory stance to heart. Notwithstanding its strained relations with Tanzania, the
Bank sought Nyerere's assistance to ensure that the OAU summit later that year
would give "consistent signals . . . on the African position not only to the Bank,
but to the international community at large."[111] The Berg Report had urged the
international donor community to double ODA (defined as net disbursements) by
the end of the decade. Nyerere suggested that these levels were unlikely to be
reached:

> Quite apart from the inevitable influence of the different political and technical environ-
> ment of the two meetings, it [was] perhaps not surprising that the Development Mini-
> sters meeting of ECA . . . should react with what amounts to a scream of frustration. . . .
> But mixed signals—however frustrating—are no monopoly of Africa, as can be seen by a
> most cursory glance at the communiques issued after such Summit Meetings at Ottawa,
> Versailles, Cancun and Paris—to say nothing of the stream of messages which come out
> from other offices in Washington D.C.![112]

There were many substantive criticisms of the Berg Report's analysis and its
recommended agenda for action, principally that its emphasis on policies reflected
a monodimensional view of the problem. The criticisms also reflected a perception
that the report was a foil to the Lagos Plan, and a leading edge of a "neoliberal"
agenda. A decade and a half later, many of its most trenchant complaints—especial-

110. See memorandum, Colin Bruce and Rene Springuel to Luis de Azcarate, Ravi
Gulhati, Pierre Landell-Mills, and Stanley Please, "Development Policies in Sub-Saharan
Africa: Our Mission to Ethiopia, Kenya, Malagasy, Tanzania and Zimbabwe," February 18,
1982.

111. Letter, A. W. Clausen to His Excellency, Julius K. Nyerere, June 21, 1982.

112. Letter, Nyerere to Clausen, July 26, 1982. The Berg Report had called for a
"substantial" increase in net disbursements of ODA—from $4.9 billion in 1980 to $17.8 billion in 1990 (a doubling in real terms)—to accompany major policy reforms by African
countries so as to ensure reasonable economic growth (2 percent per capita). Later Bank
data showed that the Berg Report had seriously underestimated net ODA in 1980: the 1980
figures were raised to $7.5 billion. Net ODA to Sub-Saharan Africa in 1990 was $17.35 billion (*African Development Indicators*, 1996, table 12-1). However, aggregate net resource
flows to Sub-Saharan Africa barely changed, increasing from $15.1 billion in 1980 to
$17.1 billion in 1990 (*World Debt Tables, 1996*).

ly those related to the pathology of the state in Africa—would appear quite tame by comparison with what the Bank (and other donors) would be saying. But at the time, the report broke a taboo: never before had the Bank been as publicly critical of such a large group of borrowers. The Bank was caught off guard by the broad-ranging hostility the study provoked in the very countries it thought it was trying to help, unconscious that few things infuriate people as much as new and sudden demands that hit many simultaneously and represent a break with accepted norms.

Somewhat chastened, the Bank asked two outsiders to gauge African percep-tions of the World Bank.[113] The study found that African perceptions were less than laudatory. Official Africans had mixed feelings about Bank-funded technical assis-tance, the complaints being concentrated in ministries of agriculture. Bank-led interdonor coordination was poor (which was not surprising since almost no one wanted to be coordinated). Bank officials engaged in the dialogue "usually tend to be young, junior and inexperienced" people who "'bully' African technocrats."[114] A poor understanding and neglect of local institutions was exacerbated by the crea-tion of "unnecessary parallel institutions which squander precious managerial resources." The Bank frequently imposed "unnecessarily numerous conditions [and] research studies" and was "obsessed with imposing the need for technical consultants and technical experts." The OED was too negative. SALs were on the right (nonproject) track but were too all-encompassing, diffuse, and given to clumsy implementation. And the Africans complained that the Bank recruited few Africans. This assessment was at least partly shared within the Bank. Returning from a visit to Kenya, at the time one of the Bank's most highly regarded borrowers in the region, Stern questioned the institution's ground-level diplomatic style and skills:

> As I mentioned in my letter, I was impressed during my visit with the mutual cooperation and self-help attitude of the Kenyans. I suggested that our efforts are likely to be most successful if we approach our own efforts in the same spirit, and I urged you to guide your staff in this direction. I mentioned this because I was concerned that too many of our staff in Kenya, whether because they are products of the British-style education system or of the British colonial service, or whether it is merely the state of mind, reflect attitudes in private, and to local staff, which did not seem to me conducive to achieving that objective. These sensitivities will need to be given special consideration in future recruiting for RMEA [Regional Mission in East Africa] assignments. It will take a special effort on the part of everyone to ensure that the Kenyans we work with regard us as co-workers who share the same goals, and not as a privileged foreign elite.[115]

113. Anthony Hughes and Dunston Wai. The latter subsequently joined the Bank. The authors' conclusions drew upon a selection of seven African countries and an assortment of donor country development agencies.

114. "Summary of African Perceptions of the World Bank," annex memorandum, David Knox to senior WAN staff, "Perceptions of the World Bank in Sub-Saharan Africa," Decem-ber 20, 1983.

115. Letter, Ernest Stern to David Loos, director RMEA, November 8, 1982.

These assessments helped galvanize the Bank into redoubled action. Although the Latin American debt crisis was of greater financial and political import to the Bank's major shareholders (see Chapter 11), in the ensuing years Africa became increasingly central to the Bank's concerns.[116]

The Storm Breaks (1980–87)

As the crisis in Sub-Saharan Africa deepened, so did the Bank's involvement. The degree of the Bank's commitment to Sub-Saharan Africa during this period was unprecedented for the region, for that matter, for any region in any period. The institution's attention steadily widened, from project- and sector-level issues to macropolicies, and, beyond that, to core issues of governance and the state.

By the mid-1980s, the Bank had emerged as the preeminent external economic actor in Sub-Saharan Africa. Although perhaps not intending to, the multilaterals, through greater involvement in the region, hastened the end of the heyday of bilateral aid agencies in the development business. By turning to multilateral institutions the donors could both ensure resource flows and exercise some leverage, while at the same time retaining the ability to distance themselves and criticize the institutions if events took a turn for the worse. For the Bank, this preeminence was an undoubted boon. But this gain, partly sought by the Bank and partly thrust upon it, proved to be somewhat of a Trojan horse. More than any other task the Bank had undertaken, its engagement in Sub-Saharan Africa sapped the institution's self-confidence. The journey to seek out the source of Africa's problems began with an intrepid flourish. But as the years rolled by, behind its public confidence were substantial internal doubts fed by a mixture of frustration and bafflement as expectations were repeatedly thwarted. Disappointment turned into irritation at the seeming recalcitrance of the clients to partake of its wisdom. This view, which was increasingly shared by other donors, gradually led the Bank to adopt a burgeoning conditionality agenda, from economic to social and political issues, and within economic issues to ever more detailed micro-level conditionality.

The problems of the Bank in Africa stemmed in part from an incompatibility between fundamental traits the institution brought to the region and the nature of Sub-Saharan Africa's problems. Throughout its history the Bank had been much more successful as a wholesaler than as a retailer, more effective in countries with governments that were themselves effective. Paradoxically, in these countries the Bank was less "needed." Conversely, where it was most needed—in weak states with limited capacity—it was forced to take on retail functions while grappling with obdurate problems of a fundamental political and organizational nature, issues in

116. In these years the Bank's senior managers frequently stressed that Sub-Saharan Africa had become the institution's center of attention and would have its highest priority.

abundance in Sub-Saharan Africa. Although critics of the Bank were quick to point to its shortcomings, they were also unable to point to other external actors who were doing a superior job on a noticeable scale. Invariably the same critics that censured the Bank for its alleged wrongdoing were the ones that called upon the Bank to do more.

The African states faced their own paradox: they needed the Bank more even as they wanted it less. Numerous borrowers would learn that dancing with an elephant poses the risk of being bruised; despite the best of motives, the risk rose with the degree of asymmetry in partners' capabilities. But many others would learn to dance quite nimbly, adopting a deferential dialectic that scrupulously observed form. For some, aware that it represented the only mechanism to influence the conduct of more powerful actors, it was the deference of the weak. For others, aware both of the constraints that would militate against strong sanctions and of the sundry possibilities of subverting the substance of many an agreement, it was a calculated deference of the shrewd.

Constraints

By the early 1980s past actions (and inactions) had left SSA decision makers with little room to maneuver. The situation was now made even worse by natural misfortunes and structural constraints.

POPULATION GROWTH. One such miscalculation for which Sub-Saharan Africa would pay a heavy price was the nonchalance with which the region's leadership brushed aside the need to grapple with the implications of rapid population growth. Between 1965 and 1990, Sub-Saharan Africa's population doubled, from a quarter billion to a half billion (under reasonably favorable projections, it was expected to double again, to a billion people, in the next twenty-five years). During the 1970s, despite McNamara's personal preoccupation with the issue, the Bank's efforts in this direction were almost completely stymied both by the region's leaders and by its own emphasis on narrow supply-side measures. The determinants of population growth are complex. But the reality remained that the inaction regarding the demographic momentum that had been building up in Africa since the 1950s would prove to be one of the singular—and, for all practical purposes by the 1970s, autonomous—factors impeding the region's fortunes.

THE NATURE OF THE STATE AND SOCIETY IN SUB-SAHARAN AFRICA. "Are there 'states' in Africa?"[117] This perplexing question is said to be at the heart of the region's problems. Many observers have questioned the sturdiness of African national governments and their relatedness to their popular, especially their rural,

117. Brian Van Arkadie, "The State and Economic Change in Africa," Ha-Joon Chang and Robert Rowthorn, eds., *The Role of the State in Economic Change* (Oxford: Clarendon Press, 1995), pp. 187–211.

constituencies. The artificiality of many of Africa's states, a weak sense of nation-hood, and their institutional fragility have all contributed to the region's travails. The colonial era formed the states, but before the long and arduous consolidation could really get under way, the structures crumbled under the onerous load put on them. Civil and military strife, leading to high levels of security-related expendi-tures and large-scale refugee movements, further weakened the prospects for development.

The paradox of the state in Africa was that its ostensible omnipotence coexisted with the reality of its fundamental weakness. The Bank would adopt the view that the state's gross overextension in the economic sphere was the principal cause of the region's dwindling economic fortunes, which ultimately came back to enfeeble the state itself. This view, widely held both within the Bank and outside, gingerly sidestepped a deeper question: whether the problem was rooted in the societal foundations on which the superstructure of the state had been built.

Many African countries emerged from colonialism with highly differentiated societies having limited internal coherence and weak social formations. The "debility of political mediation" revealed "the disjunction of society itself," and the resulting social struggle resulted in a profound disjuncture between the power of the state to inflict violence and its power to mobilize broad sections of society to advance societal goals.[118] The ingredients that make up the connective tissue of a society have always been somewhat enigmatic. If "social" capital (an elusive con-cept at best) is what holds it together, then the social foundations of the state in Sub-Saharan Africa were fragile to begin with. As Jerry Rawlings, president of Ghana, put it:

> People talk about capitalism as one mode of development and communism or socialism as another mode, but at least they're both on the move, using different paths. They have something in common, namely a certain level of social integrity, a certain national character, a demand for accountability. All of which is missing in most of the third world. But without it, your capitalism or your socialism, or whatever it is, isn't going to work.[119]

In the absence of social legitimacy, it had initially seemed logical for the dominant actors in Sub-Saharan Africa to view the state as the cement of society, and thereby gain legitimacy. But the colonial and postcolonial attempts at state formation compromised the indigenous political order. Institutions set in place often exacerbated ethnic rivalries, imbuing them with new methods and resources. Societal fragmentation meant that political parties lacked nuclei, other than regional or ethnic loyalties, around which to form. The alternative—authoritarian

---

118. Jean-Francois Bayart, *The State in Africa: The Politics of the Belly* (London: Longman, 1993), p. 8.

119. Quoted in Richard Jeffries, "Ghana: The Political Economy of Personal Rule," in Donal B. C. O'Brien, John Dunn, and Richard Rathbone, eds., *Contemporary West African States* (Cambridge University Press, 1989), p. 87.

structures that used state patronage to create clientelism as the binding agent—failed even more miserably. Rejecting capitalism as an alien entity, many SSA states plunged into an equally alien socialism, centralizing power and reaping its ascribed privileges. Rather than being a means to an end, the state seemed to become an end in itself. Normally sympathetic observers of the region lamented that the very idea of statehood as conceived by Europeans and transplanted to Africa was alien and that the "most distinctively African contribution to human history could be said to have been precisely the civilized art of living fairly peaceably together *not* in states."[120] Thus it is not surprising that some observers concluded the "curse of the nation state" had "fastened a deadweight of discouragement to every real chance of civility."[121]

The weakness of Sub-Saharan Africa's states, in particular its national governments, posed difficult, and in some cases, insurmountable, challenges for the Bank.[122] By the early 1990s, the continued lackluster performance of many of Sub-Saharan Africa's economies and mounting criticism by Africans of the role of their governments prompted the Bank to seek alternatives to national governments.[123] But a troubling underlying question remained: whether a multilateral institution that had been designed to work with, and through, nation-states and whose comparative advantage had been its engagement with national governments was an appropriate mechanism to serve as the principal external interlocutor for the region?

THE ROLE OF EXTERNAL POWERS. The external world intruded more heavily in Sub-Saharan Africa than in any other region. This reflected the weakness of SSA states, which allowed external actors, both national and multilateral, to intervene with relative ease. In some cases the die was cast by the manner in which the colonial powers withdrew in the 1970s. Portugal, for instance, refused to recognize the nationalism of the independence movements of its SSA colonies (Angola and Mozambique, Guinea-Bissau and Cape Verde) and this in effect condemned them to abjure reformist options. For most of the period, governing circles in the United

120. John Lonsdale, "States and Social Processes in Africa: A Histographical Survey," *African Studies Review*, vol. 14, nos. 2–3 (June–September 1981), p. 139.

121. Basil Davidson, *The Search for Africa: History, Culture, Politics* (New York: Times Books, 1994), p. 250. This view, of the "tragic" encounter between African and Western concepts of statehood, is also emphasized by Christopher Clapham, *Africa and the International System: The Politics of State Survival* (Cambridge University Press, 1996).

122. For an extreme case, Equatorial Guinea, see Robert Klitgaard, *Tropical Gangsters* (Basic Books, 1990).

123. This view was expressed repeatedly to Bank staff by African interlocutors in the consultation process leading to the study, World Bank, *Sub-Saharan Africa: From Crisis to Sustainable Growth: A Long-Term Perspective Study* (World Bank, 1989). For an acerbic African critique of the state in Africa see, Jonathan H. Frimpong-Ansah, *The Vampire State in Africa: The Political Economy of Decline in Ghana* (Trenton, N.J.: Africa World Press, 1992).

States and the United Kingdom looked the other way as South Africa subverted their own cherished beliefs on governance. Joined at the other end by the Soviet Union, external powers "participated" in Africa more fully during the cold war in the 1980s, a participation that would prove crippling to many of the region's countries.[124] While Angola, Mozambique, and the Horn of Africa bore the direct brunt of its ravages, its indirect effects were felt almost as severely in countries such as Liberia, Guinea, and Zaire.

Although the cold war was one of the most pernicious external influences, other forces rivaled for that dubious distinction. In a region where political influence and votes in multilateral fora were frequently up for sale, there was never a shortage of official courtiers. Arab countries and Israel courted SSA countries for their votes in the United Nations on Middle East issues, with activities ranging from Israel supplying Samuel Doe with his bodyguards or Idi Amin with supplies, to the Arab countries financing the Nimeri regime in Sudan. China and Taiwan played financial ping-pong diplomacy as they courted African countries for political recognition (or de-recognition). Then there were commercial interests masquerading as aid, which in some cases also served as a convenient conduit for political funding in the home country, as was Italy's case in Ethiopia and Somalia, and Belgium's in Zaire.[125] Even the Vatican was not above looking the other way.[126] On the other hand, good intentions alone were not sufficient to stave off disastrous effects, as the Nordic countries discovered in Tanzania. It could hardly be more poignant that a country whose leadership was so committed to the idea of self-reliance, a philosophy that attracted donors in droves, had become a prime example of external dependency by the 1980s. Perhaps more than any other country, France in its former colonies symbolized the ambiguity of the relationship between external powers and Sub-Saharan Africa. Significant commercial interests, as well as political and security reasons, were yoked to a powerful cultural imperative. Thus, although France was

124. A good account of the cold war in Africa may be found in Zaki Laïdi, *The Superpowers and Africa: The Constraints of a Rivalry, 1960–90,* trans. Patricia Baudoin (University of Chicago Press, 1990).

125. Wolfgang Achtner, "The Italian Connection: How Rome Helped Ruin Somalia," *Washington Post,* January 24, 1993, p. C3. According to Achtner, "Control over the aid and development projects was shared by all the political parties in exactly the same way that all jobs in the vast public and semi-public sector were divided up. Ethiopia . . . was awarded to the Christian Democrats. The Socialist Party got Somalia." In 1987–88, Italian ODA to Somalia (about $200 million) amounted to more than 20 percent of Somalia's GDP.

126. The Basilica of Our Lady of the Peace at Yamoussoukro is estimated to have cost between $100 and $300 million. Houphouët-Boigny insisted that he had paid for the church from his own pocket; if so, it was deeper than his country's treasury. The church, construction of which began in 1986, just when Côte d'Ivoire's economy began a protracted downward spiral, was given to the Roman Catholic Church and consecrated by the Pope in September 1990. John Stackhouse, "Vatican Outpost a Despot's Monument," *Globe and Mail* (Toronto), March 30, 1996, p. A1.

one of the most ardent champions of Africa in global fora, as well as one of its principal sources of foreign aid, it could as easily countenance a Jean Bédel Bokassa on the grounds that he was, after all, "a very pro-French military man."[127]

The relationship between some of Africa's leaders and their foreign patrons was cogently captured in a description of the relations between Jonas Savimbi of Angola and his U.S. and apartheid-era South African patrons: "He had courage and persistence, but his greatest talent was that of the shoeshine artist, who could buff the toecaps of his foreign patrons to such brilliance that all they saw when they peered down at his labors was a quickening image of their own glory."[128]

Such delusions of glory would seem quixotic in retrospect, were their effects not so tragic. Perhaps the most detrimental long-term impact of the intertwining of baneful external influences and shoddy domestic leadership was felt by the region's flimsy institutions. The cold war and other external meddling would wreak substantially greater havoc on Africa's frail body politic than elsewhere. The inherent asymmetry between the effort it takes to build institutions and the ease with which they can be wrecked would be apparent even when propitious circumstances were regained.

COMMODITIES AND TERMS OF TRADE. The constraints imposed by the divergence between expectations and possibilities were exposed by the volatility of commodity prices (figure 12-1). The region was almost completely dependent on commodities for exports.[129] Such high concentration on just a few commodities meant that commodity price trends were crucial to the region's fortunes. Non-oil commodity prices declined by 1.5 percent annually between 1974 and 1980, and even more steeply in the next decade: 5.4 percent between 1981 and 1990. Although there was a modest recovery in the first half of the 1990s (about 1.2 percent a year between 1991 and 1995), this recovery was likely to be short lived.[130] In retrospect it would appear that it was the favorable terms of trade in the 1970s rather than the rapid decline thereafter that was the exception. The spike in prices had created expectations and altered habits in ways that the new decade could not support.

Through the 1980s and into the early 1990s, the Bank maintained that the commodity price shocks afflicting Sub-Saharan Africa were not exceptional (in

127. Jacques Foccart, the architect of French policies in Africa, quoted in Peter J. Schraeder, "From Berlin 1884 to 1989: Foreign Assistance and French, American, and Japanese Competition in Francophone Africa," *Journal of Modern Africa Studies*, vol. 33, no. 4 (1995), p. 545.

128. Jeremy Harding, *The Fate of Africa: Trial by Fire* (Simon and Schuster, 1993).

129. The share of manufactures in Sub-Saharan Africa's exports was about 8 percent in 1981–83. World Bank, *Global Economic Prospects and the Developing Countries* (World Bank, 1996), table A2-2, p. 72.

130. Non-oil commodity prices were projected to decline by about 1.6 percent during 1996–2005. World Bank, *Global Economic Prospects*. A long-term analysis of commodity prices can be found in Eduardo Borensztein and others, "The Behavior of Non-Oil Commodity Prices," IMF Occasional Paper 112, 1994.

Figure 12-1. *Indices of Commodity Prices*
1990 US$

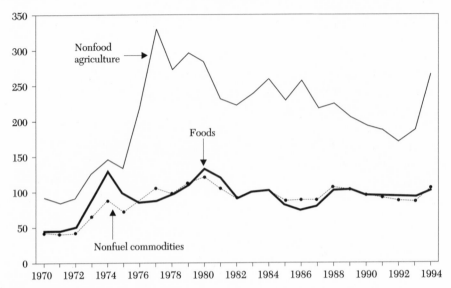

Source: World Bank data.

comparison with the shocks in other regions) and in any case were significantly offset by external resource flows. But others argued that the negative consequences of commodity price shocks went beyond the short term, because uncertainties in the duration and extent of such shocks rendered policy responses ineffective.[131]

CLIMATIC CHANGES. From the 1960s onward, rainfall in Sub-Saharan Africa decreased, particularly in a large swathe of the Sahel. This climatic change, which has extended into the 1990s, posed "one of the greatest climatological puzzles of the twentieth century."[132] Recurrent droughts not only ravaged economies heavily dependent on pastoral and agricultural activities, but they also channeled scarce resources into short-term relief activities, away from longer-term concerns.

DATA. An important factor accounting for the fractiousness of debates on Sub-Saharan Africa was the poor quality of data underlying the national accounts of countries in the region. The point can be illustrated by divergent estimates of GDP

131. See Angus S. Deaton, "Commodity Prices, Stabilization and Growth in Africa," Princeton University, Research Program in Development Studies, Discussion Paper 166, 1992.

132. F. Alayne Street-Perrot and R. Alan Perrot, "Abrupt Climate Fluctuations in the Tropics: The Influence of the Atlantic Ocean Circulation," *Nature,* vol. 343 (February 15, 1990), p. 607. Also M. Hulme, "Rainfall Changes in Africa: 1931–60 to 1961–90," *International Journal of Climatology,* vol. 12 (1992), pp. 685–99.

growth (annual averages) for the Sahelian countries over the decade 1960–70. These estimates come from seven sources. The smallest span between the highest and the lowest estimates was 23 percent, in the case of Mauritania. For Burkina Faso, there was a sixfold difference; for Chad, it was elevenfold; and for Mali, thirteenfold.[133]

Data problems afflicted every aspect of the African situation. Accurate demographic data, such as the size and growth rate of the population, existed in no more than a few African countries. Social statistics, such as those relating to literacy, school enrollment ratios, and poverty levels, were beset with substantial margins of error. And in the field of economic statistics, basic economic series such as GDP and resource flows were frequently lacking.[134] Data that were important to external agencies (foreign aid, balance of payments, external debt) were more reliable. But even here, as in the World Bank's external debt statistics, data on debt stock for a particular year published in reports two years apart commonly varied by a quarter. Even trade statistics, which had previously been seen as reliable, were found severely wanting.[135] National accounts and price statistics were even worse.

The weakness of African data was due to a variety of factors: the large share of the subsistence sector in these economies, poorly staffed and underbudgeted statistical offices, and misreporting or even false reporting.[136] In some cases, such as Nigeria, political sensitivities precluded undertaking a census. Throughout the 1980s, statistical offices with low political backing suffered disproportionately from budget cuts, and this, too, had an adverse impact on the quality of Sub-Saharan statistics. There were also technical difficulties, such as arose in measuring per capita incomes when exchange rates were being changed frequently.[137]

During the 1970s research and data collection and dissemination became an increasingly important facet of the Bank's activities. But data gathering is an

133. World Bank, "Technical Notes," in *Accelerated Development in Sub-Saharan Africa: An Agenda for Action* (World Bank, 1981), p. 187.

134. Ramesh Chander, "Information Systems and Basic Statistics in Sub-Saharan Africa: A Review and Strategy for Improvement," World Bank Discussion Paper 73, 1990.

135. For a painstaking analysis of the issue, see Alexander J. Yeats, "On the Accuracy of African Observations: Do Sub-Saharan Trade Statistics Mean Anything?" *World Bank Economic Review*, vol. 4, no. 2 (May 1990), pp. 135–56.

136. Thus the Bank's OED report on Bank-Tanzania relations noted, "Tanzania is unusual, even for a developing country, in that there is a general shortage of reliable statistical information, and an almost complete lack of statistics on crop acreages. . . . ([F]urthermore) the District Agricultural Development Officers usually fake data, particularly hectarages and yields." World Bank, "Tanzania: World Bank Tanzania Relations," p. 2, n. 1.

137. Fischer's comments illustrated the problem: "I was . . . puzzled about the figure of GNP per capita used in the policy framework paper ($536) because it differs so greatly from our own Atlas figure ($290)." Memorandum, Stanley Fischer to S. Shahid Husain, "Zambia: PFP," August 15, 1989.

arduous task. And in the World Bank, as indeed more widely, incentives in economic research were heavily biased toward creating models or advancing the latest policy, while the grinding work of data quality control received little recognition.[138] A 1982 report, *Organization of Bank Statistics*, observed that "the present system as a whole lacks integrity."[139]

At the end of the decade the Bank's statistical adviser highlighted the problem revealed in Bank reports: between 1981 and 1986 there was a gap of about 60 percent between the IMF's estimates of the GDP of Zaire and those of the Bank; consumption data showed the share spent on motorcars in Rwanda, Cameroon, and Ethiopia (4 percent) to be equivalent to that in Australia, the United Kingdom, and West Germany. Furthermore, GNP per capita growth rates were shown for countries for which underlying GNP data did not exist; and share of agriculture in GDP was reported for countries for which GDP estimates were not available.[140]

The Bank's management had traditionally taken the view that statistics were "important—and better statistics are useful. But they are a) not the central problem in Africa, in any sense and b) *not* in our area of comparative advantage."[141] Collecting and collating data from primary sources and developing statistical systems for its members were supposed to be the responsibility of the UN system, not of the Bank.[142] Yet, while they had to depend largely on secondary sources, Bank staff were necessarily collecting data for operational purposes, often in an ad hoc

138. T. N. Srinivasan, for one, puts it bluntly: "Publications of international agencies, such as the *Human Development Report* [of the UNDP] and *World Development Indicators* of the World Bank, give a misleading, if not altogether false, impression of the reliability, comprehensiveness of coverage, comparability and recency of the data, and fail to warn the unwary users of the serious deficiencies in the data." Srinivasan, "Data Base for Development Analysis: An Overview," *Journal of Development Economics,* vol. 44, no. 1 (June 1994), p. 4. Similarly, Jerzy Rozanski and Alexander Yeats observe that weakness in the data notwithstanding, there is "no indication that users are generally aware of the limitations and discrepancies in the basic data on which they rely." Rozanski and Yeats, "On the (In)accuracy of Economic Observations: An Assessment of Trends in the Reliability of International Trade Statistics," *Journal of Development Economics,* vol. 44, no. 1 (June 1994), p. 126.

139. The report's working group was chaired by Benjamin King, the former director of the Bank's Development Economics Department.

140. Ramesh Chander, "Quality of Bank Data," draft, May 18, 1989, and annex 1, "Vagaries of Bank statistics." For Zaire, data are in constant 1980 prices (millions of Zaire) as reported in the 1987 IFS and *World Tables*. Data on the structures of consumption are from *World Development Indicators 1988,* table 6. The GNP growth rate anomalies relate to data reported in the 1988 *World Bank Atlas*. In 1987 the share of agriculture was reported for twelve countries for which no GDP data estimate existed.

141. Memorandum, Ernest Stern to Jean Baneth, "African Statistical Development," August 4, 1983.

142. The exceptions were data on debt, and data gathered from the Living Standards Measurement Surveys and Social Dimensions of Adjustment, both of which were introduced in the 1980s.

fashion. The problem was certainly widespread, but it was most acute in Sub-Saharan Africa. A workshop on research priorities relating to Sub-Saharan Africa in 1984 stressed the need for a substantial investment in data improvement, but the question of the division of labor between the Bank, the country, and other institutions was not resolved. In any case, the Bank argued, although its SSA data were weak, its basic analysis was robust enough to withstand such uncertainty. Yet the precision of numbers in Bank reports on the region and the confidence of prescriptions, especially in the 1980s, belied the uncertainty of the underlying data, and of the effects of policy changes.[143] One observer was constantly "amazed" at the nonchalant way in which the Bank handled data: "The current situation can only be explained in terms of political economy: the economics staff continued to produce the data it wanted, while the operational staff maintained full freedom on the data it used. The net result was a de facto segmentation of the 'market for data' in the Bank."[144]

At the end of the decade, the Bank began to devote greater attention to the issue.[145] Technical assistance in the area increased, and the Bank even made some loans specifically for statistical development (in Nigeria and Uganda). In 1989 the Bank, together with the UNDP, initiated a publication series devoted to data, *African Economic and Financial Data,* which evolved into the biennial *African Development Indicators,* the single most comprehensive source of data on the continent. Yet even here the coverage reflected, albeit indirectly, the pressures and interests connected with multilateral institutions. Even by the mid-1990s, data on public enterprises, a subject on which the Bank had waxed eloquent over the preceding decade and a half, were sparse, whereas data on environmental indicators, a relatively newer concern for the Bank, were much more extensive. Data, their quality and control, would play an important role in constructing shibboleths and (mis)informing debates.

143. In the case of Tanzania, although official data recorded exports increasing moderately from about 9 percent of GDP in the prereform period (1981–85) to about 14 percent in the reform period (1986–90), "adjusted" data showed a jump from about 10 percent to 27 percent of GDP; while official data had gross domestic savings drastically reducing from 10 to 1 percent of GDP, adjusted data showed a moderate increase from less than 11 percent to more than 13 percent of GDP between the 1981–85 and 1986–90. Nisha Agarwal and others, "Structural Adjustment, Economic Performance, and Aid Dependency in Tanzania," World Bank Policy Research Working Paper, WPS 1204, October 1993, table 1. The "adjusted" numbers were based on the authors' identification of three major problems in Tanzania's macroeconomic data: flawed compilation of national accounts, underrecording of foreign aid, and underrecording of exports.

144. Memorandum, Enzo Grilli to Ramesh Chander, April 19, 1989.

145. Ramesh Chander, "Building Statistical Capabilities: A Role for the Bank," June 12, 1989.

The Advent of Adjustment Lending

In earlier years there were two strongly contrasting views about the reasons for Sub-Saharan Africa's problems. The Bank view, as stated in the Berg Report, emphasized the internal roots of the crisis, particularly incorrect government policies. The prescription followed from the diagnosis: restructure the incentive regime of African economies by letting the market, rather than overextended or underskilled governments, determine prices—be it for foreign exchange, money (interest rates), or agricultural inputs and outputs. The African view, as encapsulated in the ECA's Lagos Plan of Action, was that stagnation was due primarily to external causes (terms of trade, weather, civil strife) and structural variables, factors that were beyond their control. In calling attention to force majeure causes, they pressed the international community for substantially augmented resources to see them through what at the time appeared to be a slump.

The initial focus was on stabilization, with the IMF as the principal external actor. But the short duration and hard terms of the IMF's response was fundamentally ill-suited for a problem so complex and requiring a much longer-term solution. By mid-1982 it was already apparent that Sub-Saharan Africa was facing a far more serious crisis than had been thought and that the prospects for recovery were gloomier than the Berg Report had predicted. Exports continued to stagnate and the terms of trade to decline. The experience of the previous two to three years had led to "increasing skepticism regarding the modalities and the feasibility of rapid recovery and adjustment."[146] Key financial assumptions—terms of trade, private flows, costs of servicing commercial debt—were all going in the wrong direction, and their cumulative effect drastically undercut the financial assumptions of the 1981 strategy. The mood of the 1983 report, "Sub-Saharan Africa: Progress Report on Development Prospects and Programs," was considerably less sanguine regarding the pace of recovery, concluding that the continuing economic crisis was "overwhelmingly a production crisis"; consequently "increased external assistance was critical."

Internally, the Bank geared itself for a more forceful and sustained effort in several ways. The risks entailed in such a strategy were evident:

> We must recognize that the role and reputation of the Bank Group is at stake in Africa. To be frank, the Bank has stuck its "neck out a mile" in Africa. We have said publicly on many occasions that we are giving Africa the highest priority among development problems in the world. We have been telling Africa how to reform, sometimes in terms of great detail. Now a significant number of these African countries are beginning to follow the Bank's advice. If these programs fail, for whatever reasons, our policies will be seen widely to have failed, the ideas themselves will be set back for a long time in Africa and elsewhere.[147]

146. World Bank, "Suggested Agenda for IMF-IBRD Consultations on Sub-Saharan Africa," EANVP, June 14, 1982.

147. World Bank, "Eastern and Southern Africa Region: Fact Sheet," briefings prepared for incoming President Barber Conable by the operations complex, Eastern and Southern Africa region, April 23, 1986, p. 5.

In quantitative terms, the SSA region already had the largest share of staff and budgetary resources, which now increased further. Through this period the Bank devoted one-third of its regional staff resources to Africa, even though its share of lending volumes was less than a sixth of total lending (the ratio was similar at the International Finance Corporation).[148] One of the most visible expressions of the Bank's attention to the region, beginning with the 1981 Berg Report, was a series of special pan-regional reports issued nearly every second year.[149] The number of reports on Africa doubled over the levels of the previous decade. The Executive Board, especially the representatives of Western Europe and Canada, also pushed for a stronger Bank commitment in Africa. Thus in July 1983 Dutch Executive Director van Dam, in the course of an alarmed review of the position of Sub-Saharan Africa, remarked, "We have recognized Africa as a priority area; we should make available the best of our staff to deal with Africa's problems."[150]

All manner of special World Bank events and programs rained on Sub-Saharan Africa from the mid-1980s onward. The Economic Development Institute re-allocated its resources, greatly stepping up its Africa work.[151] By the mid-1980s, the region accounted for half of all EDI efforts. EDI's links with local institutions increased (from five in 1984 to twenty in 1987), as did the number and range of policy seminars and exchange programs on various aspects of adjustment for senior officials and politicians. Under a new Program of Special Technical Assistance, Bank staff members were seconded to development agencies in low-income mem-

148. By the size of its administrative budget, the Bank's Africa region was larger than any regional development bank. In its administrative and operational arrangements for the region, the Bank fluctuated between a single regional arrangement (before 1972, and again between 1987 and 1995) and two separate regions (between 1972 and 1987 and again from 1995), one comprising West Africa and the other East and Southern Africa. In the early 1980s, as regionwide initiatives were launched, the need to better coordinate Africa-wide matters led to the establishment of a Special Office for African Affairs, in the office of the senior vice president for operations. Although it created some vertical tension between operations-central and the two regional vice presidencies, its dominant effect was to dramatize front-office engagement in the Africa cause.

149. World Bank, *Accelerated Development in Sub-Saharan Africa: An Agenda for Action* (1981); *Sub-Saharan Africa: Progress Report on Development Prospects and Programs* (1983); *Toward Sustained Development in Sub-Saharan Africa, A Joint Program of Action* (1984); *Financing Adjustment with Growth in Sub-Saharan Africa, 1986–90* (1986); *Sub-Saharan Africa: From Crisis to Sustainable Growth: A Long-Term Perspective Study* (1989); *Adjustment in Africa: Reforms, Results, and the Road Ahead* (1994); *A Continent in Transition: Sub-Saharan Africa in the Mid-1990s* (1995). Dozens of sector-specific reports were also produced in this period.

150. World Bank, "Committee of the Whole Meeting—July 26, 1983: Statement by Mr. Van Dam . . . ," EDS83-5, July 27, 1983, p. 3.

151. This change in direction followed up on the recommendations of a task force chaired by Shahid Husain. See World Bank, "The Future of the Economic Development Institute," Report 4441, April 8, 1983.

ber countries, again mostly to African countries.[152] There was a major, elaborately staffed effort to rethink and enlarge the Bank's Africa-related research. Along with the aforementioned special reports, there were clusters of special seminars and multitudes of special program initiatives: a Special Facility for Sub-Saharan Africa, an African Capacity Building Initiative, a Special Program for African Agricultural Research, an IFC Fund for Small and Medium-Sized Enterprises for Sub-Saharan Africa, an African Enterprise Fund, an Enterprise Support Service, an African Project Development Facility and NGO Outreach Program, and a Cross-Border Initiative. In 1988, under Kim Jaycox's leadership, the Bank formed a special African advisory council, composed of distinguished African journalists, scholars, and other leaders who met to advise the institution semiannually.

A succession of external shocks and continued deterioration of the external climate led the Bank to reduce somewhat its emphasis on the internal roots of the crisis. While African governments were seeing "the need for policy changes" to turn back the "legacy of 20 years of largely inappropriate policies," recovery was said to be hampered "by the lack of external capital."[153] By 1984, after a second year of drought in much of the continent, the Bank found "the crisis was so acute that corrective action could not await further analysis of issues." Yet, while "the success of the proposed action programs depended first and foremost on the political will of Africa governments,"[154] the 1986 report emphasized external shortfalls:

> Growth and equity programs already under way are foundering because of inadequate donor funding, which is often inappropriate in form and timing. . . . In the absence of adequate financial support, structural reforms cannot be achieved with growth. Adjustment through further economic contraction is not a feasible alternative in a continent where per capita income levels are no higher than they were twenty years ago. In the past, the Bank has argued that resource availability is only one element in addressing Africa's development; the political will of African leaders, essential to effectively utilize both domestic and foreign resources, is also critical. But there is now growing evidence that many African countries are exercising this political will. Their commitment and efforts must be matched by the political will of the donor community to increase the resources available to implement growth-oriented adjustment programs.[155]

In late 1983 the Bank began to play a much more aggressive role in mobilizing resources, especially by augmenting its aid coordination role. Initially, at least, it

152. In 1987, twenty-three Bank staff members were serving as resident advisers to African governments and institutions to assist in macroeconomic and sectoral policy analysis, development planning, and debt management.

153. Memorandum, Ernest Stern to A. W. Clausen, "Special Action Program for Africa," December 20, 1983.

154. World Bank, "Toward Sustained Development: A Joint Program of Action for Sub-Saharan Africa, Summary of Discussion of the Committee of the Whole Meeting," SecM84-808, September 18, 1984.

155. Memorandum, A. W. Clausen to Executive Directors, "Financing Adjustment with Growth in Sub-Saharan Africa, 1986–90," February 21, 1986.

was cautious on this score because of uncertainty as to its "mandate": "For instance, does this mandate include a role in decisions on how to handle the burden of existing debt? How far can we go in 'disciplining' donors who insist on low priority projects of commercial or purely political interest? Do the donor countries see 'aid coordination' primarily as a way to get the Bank to put pressure on countries for reforms, or also as a vehicle for ensuring that adequate resources are available to support these reforms and ensure they do not fail?"[156]

Its reservations notwithstanding, the Bank's coordination role grew steadily. During 1980–82, only five African consultative groups that the Bank chaired were meeting on a regular basis (every twelve to eighteen months). By 1987 this figure had climbed to sixteen. The number of sector meetings also increased substantially. In 1986 sector meetings were held in twelve countries. In most cases the Bank took the lead in helping the African governments organize these meetings and prepare the necessary documentation. Since only interested donors participated in specific sector meetings, it was hoped that donors could reach a consensus concerning the sector strategy and investment priorities, the required institutional and policy changes, and mobilization of the necessary resources.[157]

Its increased coordination role soon made the Bank the pivotal player in resource mobilization, giving it a leverage unmatched in any other region. Sub-Saharan Africa gained a growing share in IDA funding, which increased from less than a quarter in IDA 5 to nearly half in IDA 8 before receding to about 40 percent in the mid-1990s (figure 12-2). With the region emerging as the largest beneficiary of the Bank's concessional facilities, the average terms of overall Bank lending softened noticeably.

Hamstrung by the U.S. decision to curb contributions to IDA 7, the Bank launched a Joint Program of Action in August 1984 (the "joint" in the title referred to a closer collaboration between African governments and institutions, bilateral and multilateral donors, and the World Bank, which would provide fast-disbursing financing). The institution then rapidly built on the success of this initiative by organizing a special donor meeting in January 1985 that led to the creation of a new concessional lending instrument, the Special Facility for Africa (SFA).[158] The SFA, which became operational in July 1985, provided $2 billion in additional support to IDA-eligible countries in Africa over three years.[159] Eligible countries were those that undertook a program

156. World Bank, "Eastern and Southern Africa Region: Fact Sheet," April 23, 1986, p. 5.

157. For instance, Senegal's first CG meeting in December 1984 was rapidly followed by a series of sector meetings: telecommunications, 1984; energy, 1985; agriculture, 1986; water supply, 1986; and industry, fishing, and tourism sector in 1987.

158. The meetings were chaired by Abdlatif Al-Hamad, former finance minister of Kuwait, and Mr. Lagayette, deputy governor of the Bank of France.

159. Two-thirds of the direct contributions of $1,200 million came from France, Italy, the Netherlands, and the IBRD (in the form of a $150 million transfer from net income). Another $790 million (almost 40 percent from Japan, with Germany and the United Kingdom as the other principal contributors) was provided in the form of special joint financing used in support of operations undertaken by the facility. Memorandum, Barber B. Conable to the executive directors, "Special Facility for Sub-Saharan Africa: Termination," IDA/R89-101, July 17, 1989.

Figure 12-2. *IDA Commitments to Sub-Saharan Africa*
Billions of 1995 U.S. $ (annual averages)

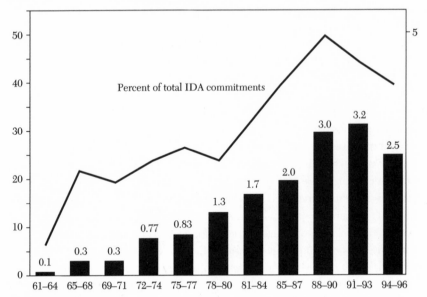

Source: World Bank data.
Note: Based on loan commitments.

of policy reforms, including structural and institutional improvements. Nearly 40 percent of these resources went to four countries: Ghana, Madagascar, Malawi, and Zaire. At the time, all four countries appeared to be taking significant steps to break from the past. By the early 1990s, only Ghana could be said to be have done so.

The Agenda

At the heart of the Bank's agenda was the desire to reshape the role of the state in Africa, giving greater scope to markets and the private sector. A pervasive distrust of markets and of the price mechanism imbued the intellectual climate of the region. The Bank became increasingly engaged in nudging domestic political processes to alter economic policies. Although conditionality was an important tool in this regard, it was less potent than initially expected in the absence of well-grounded supporting beliefs.

The Bank focused on three broad areas: the structure of incentives, institutional reform, and the balance between public and private sectors. An effort was made to reorient incentives through more liberal trade policies and pricing reforms in exchange and interest rates, agriculture, and utilities. The strategy was to shift the onus of price setting from governments to markets by liberalizing markets.[160] In addition, governmental reform focused on the budget, especially the size and composition of budgetary expenditure, the civil service, and public enterprises. Institutional reform, seen as a necessary complement to macroeconomic reform, received less attention in practice.

Reforms in the external sector focused on trade policies and the exchange rate. Numerically, conditions relating to such reforms were less than the Bankwide average for other borrowers, and retrogression was more frequent.[161] Although initially the Bank and the IMF were faulted for their apparent singlemindedness on exchange rate policies, there came to be little doubt about the severe damage overvalued exchange rates had inflicted.[162] One glaring effect was that domestic alternatives were eschewed for seemingly cheaper foreign substitutes in agriculture, the most important sector for production and employment. Even the nominally nontradable construction sector used substantial imported inputs. Overvalued exchange rates also undermined importsubstitution strategies, which then had to be maintained by high rates of protection. With tax bases that had become highly dependent on international trade, an overvaluation of the real exchange rate undermined tax revenue and the attainment of fiscal balance and, as in the case of the CFA-franc zone, put an onerous burden of adjustment on unsustainable deflationary policies.[163] Given the degree of deterioration in terms of trade that SSA countries would face, there was a strong case for the Bank's emphasis on exchange rates. In its eagerness to show its poverty-friendly face, however, the Bank oversold the pro-agriculture and pro-poor aspects of devaluation, whose effects, while substantial for farmers engaged in the production of export crops, was quite limited for subsistence farmers.

Trade policy reform programs in Sub-Saharan Africa were also promoted at a slower pace than in other regions. An overemphasis on tariff measures, especially in the early years—at the expense of exchange controls, import licensing, and direct or indirect export taxes—meant that the anti-export bias in the region's economies

160. The Bank's vocabulary began to change as well. In the early 1980s, the Bank called for "liberalizing" markets in "developing" countries. A decade later, "developing" countries had been transformed to "emerging markets"; and markets themselves were no longer to be "liberalized" but rather "unleashed."

161. John Nash, "Implementation of Trade Reform in Sub-Saharan Africa: How Much Heat and How Much Light," World Bank Policy Research Working Paper 1218, November 1993.

162. It should be emphasized that at the time many members of the G-30 believed then that the real effective exchange rate could not be changed at all, a view also strongly held in the IMF. Peter B. Kenen and Clare Pack, "Exchange Rates, Domestic Prices and the Adjustment Process," Group of Thirty, Occasional Paper 1, 1980.

163. Vito Tanzi, "The Impact of Macroeconomic Policies on the Level of Taxation in Developing Countries," *IMF Staff Papers*, vol. 36 (1989), pp. 633–56.

did not show dramatic changes.[164] The Bank's reform agenda in the external sector was later criticized for tending to deindustrialize Africa. Although there was some truth in this belief for certain countries and sectors, the slow pace of change in the external sector per se cast doubts on the strength of the linkage.[165] Still, the inability to stem the decline of the industrial sector in Sub-Saharan Africa was an undoubted weakness of the structural adjustment agenda.[166]

Even so, pushing through changes in the external sector was much simpler than initiating more direct reforms affecting the state. Such difficulties were exacerbated by the often superficial research base on which diagnoses were based. Despite the significant increase in the priority accorded to Africa in Bank operations in the 1970s, as well as the rapid expansion of institution-wide research activities, the latter effort had largely bypassed Africa, with some exceptions notably in the cases of Côte d'Ivoire, Kenya, Nigeria, and Tanzania. The paucity of research and of local capacity in the region would seem to have been ample reason to attract a disproportionate amount of the Bank's considerable research strengths. The reality was the reverse, in large part because of the dissonance between the professional incentives for the Bank's research staff and the more practical research requirements of the region.[167]

The perception in the early 1980s that there were "too many government employees who get paid too much" in Africa illustrated the problem.[168] The notion

164. There were several reasons for this. First, there were revenue concerns. In general (mainly because of overvalued exchange rates), trade liberalization did not affect trade-related tax revenues except in the countries with a fixed exchange rate. Second, tariff reforms were undermined by the growth of donor-financed imports, which were exempt from tariffs. Third, the indirect taxation effects of parastatal marketing monopolies meant that a different set of changes were required, which were a much more demanding affair.

165. Faezeh Foroutan, "Trade Reform in Ten Sub-Saharan African countries," World Bank Policy Research Working Paper 1222, November 1993. According to one estimate, in the early 1980s, the average *effective* tariff in fixed-exchange-rate countries in Sub-Saharan Africa was 22 percent, substantially higher than in the variable-rate countries (15 percent). By the end of the decade, it had dropped in the former case to 20 percent and increased to 18 percent in the latter. The record of trade reforms was well analyzed in World Bank, *Adjustment Africa: Reforms, Results and the Road Ahead* (World Bank, 1994).

166. Sanjaya Lall, "Structural Adjustment and African Industry," *World Development*, vol. 23, no. 12 (December 1995), pp. 2019–31.

167. As Ravi Gulhati, chief economist for the East Africa region pointed out at a seminar on Africa research in October 1984, sophisticated methodologies favored by the research staff, which "while they can win scholastic awards or prestigious publications, may not be appropriate for Africa." Gulhati, "Research on Africa: A User's Perspective," October 1984, attachment to memorandum from Gulhati, "Eastern Seminar on Africa Research," October 17, 1984.

168. David L. Lindauer and Barbara Nunberg, "Introduction: Pay and Employment Reform of the Civil Service," in David Lindauer and Barbara Nunberg, eds., *Rehabilitating Government: Pay and Employment Reform in Africa* (World Bank, 1994).

that "African wages were too high" contributed to the "urban bias" thesis. More careful analysis would later reveal that, at least in much of Anglophone Africa, urban-rural wage differentials had peaked in the early 1970s, and even then the perceived gap had been "almost certainly exaggerated."[169] Over the next two decades, the differential between urban and rural wages was reduced even further. The wage data on which the Bank's perceptions (as well as those of other observers) of the early 1980s were based dated back to the mid-1970s. Even as of the mid-1990s, data on wages and unemployment in Sub-Saharan Africa were so infrequently available and what was available was generally of such dubious quality that easy generalizations were simply unwarranted.[170]

By the mid-1980s the Bank had become more aware that wage realities were more complex.[171] Although the quantum of public sector employment, its quality, and its motivational impulses posed a grave problem, inflation had long eroded the real wages of government employees in most countries outside Francophone Africa.[172] The decline in real wages and wage compression severely undermined bureaucratic morale. As discrepancies between government salaries and those of parastatals, the private sector, or donor-supported consultancies increased, there was a steady outflow of already scarce talent from government offices, especially at senior levels. However, at least in the early 1980s, an exaggerated idea of the extent of the urban-rural wage gap may have led the Bank and Fund to be too hasty in trying to achieve a market-determined exchange rate, since its inflationary effects cut deeply into the urban real wage.

The condition of state finances was another chronic concern. As seen from table 12-2, the degree of fiscal imbalance at the turn of the decade was such that the need for deep fiscal cuts was not in doubt. Countries used a variety of ways to circumvent budgetary gaps—allowing domestic and external arrears to build up, drawing on the credit of parafiscal agencies (commodity stabilization funds), and raiding the resources of foreign exchange earning parastatals. Despite much brouhaha on cutting back government expenditures, both overall government

169. Dipak Muzumdar, "Wages in Africa," Africa chief economist's office, February 1994.

170. For instance, 1995 World Bank data on the distribution of wage and non-wage employment in different sectors of the economy cover only fourteen SSA countries. In only four cases were the data less than a decade old. World Bank, "Workers in an Integrating World," *World Development Report 1995*.

171. David L. Lindauer, Oey Astra Meesook, and Parita Suebsaen, "Government Wage Policy in Africa: Summary of Findings and Policy Issues," CPD Discussion Paper 1986-24, April 1986.

172. This reflected differences between countries with a fixed exchange rate and those with variable rates. By one estimate, the wage bill as a fraction of GDP rose by 10 percent in fixed-rate countries in Sub-Saharan Africa but declined by about 15 percent in variable-rate countries during the 1980s. Karim Nashashibi and Stefania Bazzoni, "Exchange Rate Strategies and Fiscal Performance in Sub-Saharan Africa," *IMF Staff Papers*, vol. 41, no. 1 (March 1994), table 6, pp. 110–11.

Table 12-2. *Sub-Saharan Africa: Fiscal Balance, 1975 to Early 1990s*
Percentage of GDP, annual average

Composition[a]	1975–79	1980–85	1985–89	1990–MR[b]
Including grants	–10.6	–6.9	–5.9	–6.5
	(–6.2)	(–5.4)	(–6.1)	(–5.7)
Excluding grants	–11.2	–7.7	–7.5	–8.3
	(–7.4)	(–6.8)	(–8.3)	(–8.0)

Source: *African Development Indicators,* 1994, 1996, tables 7.1, 7.2.
a. Figures in parentheses are minus Nigeria.
b. Most recent year available in *African Development Indicators,* 1996.

expenditures and current expenditures barely budged during the 1980s.[173] This meant that as interest costs rose the burden fell on capital expenditures. Later, interest costs were stabilized by being capitalized; this, however, led to a rapid escalation of the debt overhang.

With resources severely constrained and the region's already large dependence on external resources growing, the Bank directed its efforts at raising domestic resources and improving allocative efficiency. The region had low savings rates, even though beginning from the 1960s tax-to-GDP ratios grew rapidly. By the end of the 1970s, the average tax effort in the region was comparable to that in other regions; but, because of the region's low incomes, it represented a greater burden on taxpayers.[174] By the mid-1980s, the Bank began to give more serious attention to tax reform—moving away from the heavy dependence on trade and domestic production taxes to a greater focus on domestic consumption and the restructuring of investment incentives.[175] This in turn required more sophisticated institutional structures, which would take time to evolve. It was therefore imperative to look more closely at possible improvements in government activities with taxlike effects such as pricing of state-owned enterprises, marketing board operations, and quantitative restrictions on trade.

The extent to which the Bank and IMF's drive for fiscal discipline through loan conditionality bit into much needed social expenditures with adverse impacts on

173. In their sample of twenty-eight SSA countries, Nashashibi and Bazzoni found that public expenditures "remained remarkably steady at about 28 percent of GDP between 1980 and 1991." Ibid., p. 108.

174. Zmarak Shalizi, Vasant P. Gandhi, and Jaber Ehdaie, "Patterns of Taxation in Sub-Saharan Africa: Trends in 'Tax Effort' and Composition during the Period 1966–81," CPD Discussion Paper 1985-48, January 1985. By 1979 tax revenue in Sub-Saharan Africa was 17.0 percent of GDP compared with 12.4 in South Asia, 16.8 in East Asia, and 17.9 in Latin America.

175. Zmarak Shalizi and Lyn Squire, "Tax Policy in Sub-Saharan Africa: A Framework for Analysis," World Bank, Policy and Research Series 2, 1988.

the poor would be a bone of contention between the Bank and its critics. Public expenditure data had been an important domain of Bank economic and sector work, although from country to country the data had varied in detail, scope, frequency, and coverage. This effort now became more systematic. Internal analysis of the pattern of expenditure reductions in the 1970s had shown that capital expenditures were more vulnerable than recurrent expenditures: social and general administration expenditures were most protected, those on infrastructure were least protected, and the "productive sectors" were in the middle. The pattern of expenditure cuts followed political reality: sectors that were more wage- and salary-intensive and therefore incurred the highest social costs to political elites suffered the least cuts.[176] Beginning with analysis of recurrent nonwage outlays, budget subsidies, and public employment and wages, the scope and depth of public expenditure reviews gradually increased.[177] But it was only in the early 1990s that public expenditure reviews became an important tool in the Bank's country assistance strategy. In part, this was due to difficulties in developing yardsticks to judge the level and pattern of spending, especially with regard to minimum recurrent costs in key sectors or the appropriate division between investment and maintenance.

In parallel, Bank staff began to steer public investment reviews toward donor-supported "white-elephant" projects. Its efforts at donor coordination were sorely tested when it attempted to curb these projects, a thankless, underappreciated task. Although investment priorities could well differ in certain cases, for the most part "donors" resented having their commercial or political interests blocked. It was not simply a matter of scarce financial resources being frittered way; scarce managerial talent and outlays on recurrent costs were being drawn into projects of dubious priority.

The projects typically entailed construction: roads, government buildings, OAU centers, and dams. Classrooms for buildings and universities abounded, but many of those built remained empty for lack of staff funds. While developed country executive directors were urging the Bank to monitor country investment and expenditure programs, their bilateral aid programs, which were driven by different concerns, frequently worked at cross-purposes.[178] Since these projects were in-

---

176. N. L. Hicks and A. Kubisch, "The Effects of Expenditure Reduction in Developing Countries," November 1983, cited in Tariq Husain, "Public Expenditure Adjustments," draft, May 15, 1984, p. 1.

177. Memorandum, Willi Wappenhans to Eastern Africa region staff, "EAN Management Memorandum No. 19: Work on Public Expenditure," June 27, 1984.

178. The Bank's files contain many examples: a paved road to link two small regional capitals, crossing some 550 kilometers of semidesert with little economic potential (loan amortization started before the road was completed and debt service and amortization for the loan exceeded the country's entire road budget); a 1,150-kilometer road built in a Sahelian country joining the capital with a small regional center that was no closer than 100 kilometers from the few viable agricultural areas; a large dam in Senegal; a port in

Table 12-3. *Trends in Sub-Saharan Agriculture, 1975 to the Early 1990s*[a]
Average annual percentage growth

Category	1975–79	1980–85	1985–89	1990–MR[b]
Agriculture	0.4	1.0	3.6	0.6
Food per capita	–2.2	–2.0	0.7	–2.2

Source: *African Development Indicators*, 1994–95 and 1996, tables 8-2 and 8-5.
a. The region suffered from major droughts during 1982–84 and in 1992.
b. Most recent date (circa 1993).

variably contract-intensive, with rich possibilities for political featherbedding, many officials in borrowing governments were not enthusiastic about them, either. For donors, their later sanctimoniousness on "governance" issues glossed over their own role in this matter. The intensity with which many Western nongovernmental organizations criticized the environmental implications of the Bank work was in sharp contrast to their passivity when it came to abysmal capital-intensive projects, many promoted by their own countries, that merely laid to waste a country's economy but not its ecology, at least as directly. Rivers of red ink running through a country's budget may well endanger the country's health. But in the new era, they simply did not excite the passions the way endangered species did.

Public enterprise reform, a centerpiece of state reform, was comparatively tepid. In its early years it focused mainly on raising tariffs or prices of publicly provided goods and services to reflect their economic value more closely. To reform enterprises, rather than eliminate or privatize them, was the credo. Because the agenda focused on agriculture, parastatal reform initially largely concerned agricultural parastatals.

AGRICULTURE AND THE RURAL ECONOMY. Policies designed to pull SSA agriculture out of its stagnation (table 12-3) had been a mainstay of the Berg Report. By this time there was substantial evidence that African farmers faced exceedingly high levels of taxation, not only direct (export taxes, producer prices, and agricultural inputs), but especially indirect (overvalued exchange rates and trade policies). State

---

Comoros; a hotel in Togo; a new port in Sudan (instead of improving existing facilities), being pressed by the Federal Republic of Germany. See letter, Ernest Stern to Eberhard Kurth, Germany's executive director, October 10, 1984. In the case of a cement plant in Niger, Japan and France tried to "outbid" the other in what seems to have been a patently uneconomic venture. When the Bank tried to persuade them to desist, each "leaked" information on how bad the other country's proposal was. In Uganda, in reaction to the Bank's attempts to eliminate a Spanish-financed airport from the country's investment program, the Bank was denied access to Spain's capital markets. Such projects were not confined to the traditional donors. In Niger, the Bank attempted to convince China to desist from building a stadium in Niamey, arguing "that while the construction of a stadium can serve many useful purposes . . . I would hope it would be possible to allocate the resources . . . to other high priority activities in Niger." Memorandum, Ernest Stern to Naijiong Xu, China's executive director, "Stadium Project in Niger," November 2, 1984.

control over rural markets had created opportunities for bureaucratic rents, which gradually became the driving force behind agricultural policies whose effects had been to emasculate Africa's rural economies.[179] Removing or at least sharply reducing them, "getting the markets to work," was expected to produce the desired supply response. Consequently price reforms, especially those affecting agricultural export commodities, emerged as the principal plank of the Bank's agricultural agenda.

At the time, however, little was known about the *relative* responsiveness of SSA agriculture to price incentives. As detailed in chapter 8, the official single-minded-ness with which the Bank was pushing price liberalization as the panacea was strongly questioned by many of its agricultural technical staff.[180] Although the Bank's 1970s agriculture and rural development strategy in Sub-Saharan Africa had unraveled, it had helped stimulate broader social science research on agricultural development in Africa.[181] The research was, however, confined to a few Anglo-phone countries, and its priorities reflected donors' concerns. More important, few African researchers were involved and the results had only limited dissemination, especially in Africa. By the mid-1980s, it was also clear that the Bank's research in Africa was dominated by social scientists with poor understanding of the tech-nological issues in this area.[182] Thus it is not surprising that the Bank emphasized price variables in African agriculture to the exclusion of almost everything else.

The other pillar of the Bank's strategy—agricultural commodity exports—also drew some criticism. The Bank urged countries in the region to shift their agricul-tural policies away from their "obsession" with food self-sufficiency to non-food export crops on the basis of comparative advantage. Entities like the Economic Commission for Africa (a strong proponent of food self-sufficiency) contended that the strategy exposed the region to an "adding up" problem.[183] The Bank countered

179. The classic exposition of this thesis was Robert H. Bates, *Markets and States in Tropical Africa: The Political Basis of Agricultural Policies* (University of California Press, 1981).

180. Thus the OED report on Bank-Tanzania relations cites evidence showing that in 1981 "Bank staff have no firm analytical framework for determining required price increases for each crop." The OED report states that again in 1981, internal complaints were voiced that, "in absence of farm budget surveys and data on cross supply elasticities, Bank staff have no analytical base for determining required price increases for each crop." World Bank, "Tanzania: World Bank Tanzania Relations," para. 7.65.

181. Just how little empirical work existed can be gauged by the fact that there was no reference to Africa in the influential work by Theodore W. Schultz, *Transforming Traditional Agriculture* (Yale University Press, 1964).

182. Carl Eicher, "Agricultural Research for African Development: Problems and Pri-orities for 1985–2000," paper prepared for a World Bank conference on research priorities for Sub-Saharan Africa, Bellagio, February 25–March 1, 1985.

183. The problem (also known as the "the fallacy of composition") refers to a negative impact of a simultaneous expansion of output of commodities facing a relatively inelastic world demand. Under certain conditions, declines in terms of trade would be so acute that export revenues and real incomes would actually fall, despite increases in output.

that export revenues were down not so much because of a decline in the terms of trade as because of reduced export volumes, brought about by excess production elsewhere (Africa's share in global non-oil, primary commodities exports declined from 7.3 percent in 1970 to 2.7 percent in 1990).[184] In reality, the Bank had long recognized the problem in the case of beverage crops, and for this reason had curtailed direct lending for tea in 1973 and coffee and cocoa in 1982 to ensure that the investments it supported did not impose penalties on other exporters. On the other hand, it effectively promoted such commodity exports through structural adjustment loans. These contradictions notwithstanding, the prices of beverage crops continued to decline and world output to increase, largely because of investments in countries that could obtain funds from other sources. The realization that the Bank was a minor player in beverage markets led it to rethink its lending policies on beverage crops in 1995.[185]

Some who supported the Berg Report's criticism of Africa's antirural predilections at the same time vehemently opposed its emphasis on the production of (non-food) export crops. On the basis of simple static comparative advantage, the countries should have exported cash crops and imported food. But the "border prices" used in such analysis often ignored or downplayed both the reality that this often purely theoretical "world price" had been distorted by large OECD subsidies[186] and the often greater costs (relative to border prices) incurred in getting food to interior areas because of severe infrastructural constraints, as well as the food security risks posed to weak states arising from any significant dependence on external food supplies.[187] The greater volatility of non-food agricultural commodity prices relative to food prices (figure 12-1) also meant that the strategy further exposed the very countries that needed to be protected from risk. For all the lessons of East Asia the Bank was espousing, it did not take to heart that food

184. Ishrat Husain, "Trade, Aid and Investment in Sub-Saharan Africa," paper presented at the Royal African Society Conference on Africa, St. Catherine's College, Oxford, March 21–23, 1993.

185. World Bank, "The Bank Group's Policy On Beverage Crops: A Reassessment," R95-184, November 6, 1995.

186. The assumption of the tradability of food crops in the African case is examined by Christopher L. Delgado, "Why Domestic Food Prices Matter to Growth Strategy in Semi-Open West African Agriculture," *Journal of African Economies*, vol. 1, no. 3 (November 1992), pp. 446–71.

187. The magnitude of costs posed by Africa's meager infrastructure is illustrated by a UNDP official's claim that "the cost of providing one meal—usually a fistful of corn—for a refugee in a camp in, say, Sudan: the expense of transporting this fistful of corn, its storage and the service that gets it to a refugee is higher than the price of a dinner at the most expensive restaurant in Paris." Quoted in Ryszard Kapuscinski, "Startled in the Dark," *Granta*, vol. 48 (Summer 1994), p. 211. For a thoughtful analysis, see Jean-Philippe Platteau, "Sub-Saharan Africa: The Crucial Role of (Infra)Structural Constraints," *Cahiers de la Faculté des Sciences Economiques et Sociales de Namur*, Serie Recherche 128, 1993/6, August 1993.

self-sufficiency had been a core element of the political strategy of countries in that region; there are aspects of governability that transcend narrow conceptions of comparative advantage. Severe droughts and accompanying famines in the Horn of Africa forced the Bank's hand, and from the mid-1980s it began to address food security concerns more directly.[188]

Although at the rhetorical level the Bank's approach to the region's rural economy appeared to have a narrow focus, in practice this was much less so. The large existing agricultural project portfolio had a significant inertial effect. These projects involved parastatals, many of which had been built up by the Bank itself. Consequently, despite the apparent inefficiency of the agricultural parastatals, the Bank sought for a long time to improve them rather than eliminate them. Rhetoric notwithstanding, its efforts to eliminate the monopoly powers of agricultural parastatals, especially those engaged in marketing and trade-related activities, were not as indiscriminate as its critics alleged. Even in Ghana, a country in which the Bank's role loomed large, major agricultural parastatals continued to play some role well into the 1990s.[189]

From about the mid-1980s, the Bank gradually shifted back to a more expansive view of the problems of rural Sub-Saharan Africa, modifying its earlier position that constraints to growth stemmed principally from "inadequate motivation rather than from inadequate technology."[190] The Bank's research complex initiated an ambitious comparative study in 1984—"Managing Agricultural Development in Africa (MADIA)"—to examine the sources of agricultural growth in the region and the relative effects of domestic policies, the external environment, and donor assistance.[191] The emphasis on prices and markets did not diminish, but rather the agenda devoted greater attention to non-price variables affecting agricultural supply. The shift to the variables that affect *aggregate* agricultural supply defused the food-export crops debate to some extent, since in any case farmers make their own decisions and, pricing apart, in reality governments lack control over the choice of crops at the farm level.

As part of this shift, the Bank established a Special African Agricultural Research (SPAAR) program in 1984 as a mechanism for coordinating donor efforts so

---

188. On a related issue, food aid, the Bank took the position that despite the best of intentions, the "ample supplies of food on highly concessional terms, has been a major element in the growing dependence of Africa on imported food grains. . . . It would be a grave mistake to repeat that type of intervention." Memorandum, A. W. Clausen to Ferdinand van Dam, "Sub-Saharan Africa," February 14, 1984.

189. According to a recent OED assessment, it was only toward the end of the 1980s that the Bank's AgSECALs reflected a decisive shift toward market orientation in agricultural reform programs. World Bank, "Reforming Agriculture: The World Bank Goes to Market," OED Report 15883, 1996.

190. World Bank, *Accelerated Development in Sub-Saharan Africa*, p. 55.

191. The study focused on Cameroon, Nigeria, and Senegal in West Africa and Kenya, Malawi, and Tanzania in East Africa. Its results were published in a series of working papers and in Uma Lele, ed., *Aid to African Agriculture—Lessons from Two Decades of Donor's Experience* (Johns Hopkins University Press, 1991). Also see chapter 8 in this volume.

as to strengthen national agricultural research systems in the region. During the 1960s and 1970s, agricultural research inputs in Sub-Saharan Africa (expenditures and staff relative to the value of agricultural production) had increased four to five times, and the ratios were comparable to other regions. But, together with the four research institutes of the Consultative Group on International Research located within the region, these inputs had limited impact because the national research programs were themselves weak. The SPAAR initiative sought to improve matters by developing a project information system, organizing regional networks, instituting mechanisms to assess promising technologies, and preparing guidelines for the reinforcement of national research capabilities. In this regard it sought to supplement the work of the International Service for Agricultural Research (ISNAR), one of the CGIAR institutes, which paid considerable attention to Africa.

The next logical step was to put a much stronger effort into extension. But many within and outside the Bank expressed concern about the degree to which it pursued the model chosen: the Training and Visit system, guided by its creator, Daniel Benor (see chapter 8). Bank agriculture veterans complained that the T&V extension model had become a "religion" in the Bank.[192] There was also a sense that young Bank staff, often with little agricultural field experience, advocated T&V as if nothing else mattered and dismissed past achievements and alternatives. In contrast, Bank management was much more enthusiastic, not only because of T&V's established track record (especially in South Asia) but also because of its simplicity, which was highly attractive in a region where administrative complexity was the bane of good intentions. But perhaps most important, Benor's leadership injected the program with an enthusiasm that boosted morale in a region that much needed it.

Simultaneously, the Bank made greater efforts to better understand the microstructure of rural markets: the insecurity of land tenure resulting from a weakening of traditional communal land systems, problems of inputs and rural infrastructure, informal credit markets, and distribution and storage networks. Three initiatives were particularly notable. Against a background of widespread concern about the critical situation in the water resources sector in Africa, the Bank initiated an ambitious long-term project designed to prepare an inventory of Sub-Saharan Africa's water resources.[193] The severe and endemic problems in rural

192. The complaints were several: it was creating yet another government bureaucracy with high recurrent costs, whose medium-term budgetary implications were bound to crowd out other, and perhaps more pressing, needs such as a lack of research packages: an overreliance on peripatetic field workers as the conduits of information.

193. The "hydrological assessment" initiative involving forty-two countries aimed at putting together a continent-wide database on groundwater and surface water resources. There were no central depositories for water plans with a number of the few studies that existed still with the former colonial powers. This study began by first assembling the status of data collection and processing and subsequently developed programs for the rehabilitation and improvement of hydrometric systems.

transport led to creative initiatives in road maintenance and intermediate forms of transport to bridge the wide gulf between truck transport and head loads. And third, the Bank started paying substantial attention to the impact of growing population pressures on the region's fragile environment.[194]

Entering the 1990s, the institution drastically cut back lending through public sector rural credit, input supplies, and processing and marketing. Instead the Bank emphasized nationwide programs supported by investment credits for particular subsectors. So far, the changes in the Bank's agricultural agenda do not seem to have had a noticeable effect on Sub-Saharan Africa. Although lags are only to be expected (even in the absence of shocks arising from political instability), the goal of doubling agricultural growth rates to 4–5 percent annually continues to be daunting. In the absence of agricultural gains of this magnitude, a satisfactory economic outlook for the region would be unlikely to materialize.

The Operational Landscape

Bank operations in Sub-Saharan Africa in this period did not play out as expected. Despite the large increase in the staffing of the Bank's Africa operations, the region retained a certain Cinderella image. Thus in April 1985, three months after the Special Office for African Affairs (SOA) opened its doors, its supporters were disappointed to see it "still struggling to obtain adequate staff and budgetary and logistical support."[195] In part this was due to the personnel practices of the Bank, in that staff assignments reflected the preferences of staff member, rather than operational needs. Consequently, notwithstanding outstanding individual work at all levels, the aggregate staffing quality in the Africa region was less than the Bank-wide average. For a while in the 1980s, when there were strong signals from the Bank's hierarchy indicating that Africa was an institutional priority, service in and on Africa caught on rapidly within the institution. But this was not sustained. Some staff departed in frustration, feeling that they could achieve little in what was perceived to be a very difficult field environment, while others moved to new professionally rewarding challenges—be it the environment or private sector or East Europe. The region's work had a more than average dependence on consultants, and staffing was uneven; in places and at times it seemed callow.

194. Norman Borlaug, the "father" of the Green Revolution, has argued that "World Bank fear of green political pressure in Washington became the single biggest obstacle to feeding Africa," quoted in Gregg Easterbrook, "Forgotten Benefactor of Humanity," *Atlantic Monthly*, January 1997, p. 80. Borlaug traces the effects of these lobbies through their opposition to the use of inorganic fertilizers. The effects of environmental lobbies on the World Bank is examined in chapter 13 in volume 2.

195. Memorandum, Pierre Landell-Mills to M. Ismail Serageldin, "Special Office for African Affairs: Objectives," April 22, 1985.

The Bank's project portfolio also began facing increasing difficulties. During the 1970s the institution had built up a large portfolio of agricultural and rural development projects in Sub-Saharan Africa (see chapter 8). Many of these had been based on commodity price projections that were now being invalidated. In other sectors, project implementation began to falter as cash-flow problems in the region mounted and counterpart funds dried up. Disbursement procedures were relaxed by seeking increasing recourse to revolving funds. The Bank had already established a project preparation facility in 1976 (used primarily by African countries), which provided advances on future Bank operations to help complete the project preparation process, provide initial institutional support to project agencies, and facilitate future project implementation. The resources of this facility were first supplemented in the late 1970s when the Bank increased lending for free-standing technical assistance projects.[196] This facility was further supplemented in 1985 by the Special Project Preparation Facility, which provided grants that would allow governments in Sub-Saharan Africa to hire personnel (mostly expatriates) to help prepare both investment and adjustment programs presented to aid coordination meetings.

For its part, the IFC, together with the UNDP and the African Development Bank, established an analogous facility for the private sector—the African Project Development Facility—to help African entrepreneurs prepare medium-sized private sector projects. The IFC, again with financial support from the United Nations Development Program, also made some efforts at developing a program of advisory work in Africa to help member countries attract foreign direct investment. An African management services company was instituted to provide qualified and experienced management services to selected public and private sector enterprises in Africa and to train African managers. But despite the number of such initiatives, their magnitude and effects were modest.

Even as initiatives for Sub-Saharan Africa mushroomed, a growing gulf emerged between the key operational assumptions of the Bank and its modus operandi in the region. Traditionally, the Bank held borrowers responsible for preparing operations suitable for financing. Borrowers were meant to be responsible for implementing projects. Hence supervision was limited to broad monitoring and midcourse correction and occasional intervention. Here, as well as in project preparation, the weakness of the borrowers and deteriorating conditions meant that the line between assisting borrowers and undermining borrower responsibility and commitment was tenuous. The project preparation facility and the special facility had been created to help bolster the countries' abilities to prepare projects, especially in Africa. In reality these facilities transposed borrower responsibility

---

196. Thirty-eight technical assistance loans and credits totaling US$290 million were made to Africa in 1982–86. At the end of 1985, free-standing technical assistance operations were under implementation in thirty African countries.

into a legalistic nicety, since, with the crisis intensifying, swiftness in project preparation took center stage.[197] The traditional concept of enforcing borrower project responsibility eroded. Lending documents meant to bind borrowers to actions deemed essential for project success were not compatible with environments with a high degree of instability, since key assumptions changed during implementation.

Furthermore, project supervision had to bear a greater burden, as the significance of broader policy issues beyond the purview of the project or borrowing agency—such as funding shortages, broad managerial issues, the economic environment—increased. The small size of most SSA countries meant that the Bank undertook fewer operations per country, which in turn meant there were fewer opportunities to "piggy back" on previous operations.

The successive droughts in 1983–84 and the specter of famine, fostered by the acuteness of the cash-flow problems facing dozens of African governments, intensified pressures for short-term crisis management.[198] Normally, the latter was the domain of the IMF, but by now reflows to the IMF were an important part of the equation.

At the beginning of the 1980s, despite the publicity attached to the Berg Report, the IMF had been the principal source of external finance in Sub-Saharan Africa, having plunged into the region with uncharacteristic enthusiasm, even as the IBRD drastically cut lending for creditworthiness reasons.[199] Although publicly arguing that this apparent anomaly merely represented the differing mandates of the two institutions and not disagreements between the institutions' assessments of long-term creditworthiness, Bank officials privately grew anxious that the institution

197. Memorandum, J. C. Peter Richardson to S. Shahid Husain, "Are World Bank Processes Suited to the Needs of Sub-Saharan Africa?" January 9, 1985.

198. The FAO had caught on earlier to the magnitude of the crisis and the precariousness of food supplies. An internal Bank analysis commented that the Bank's weak response, "in terms of credible action programs" was "striking [and] has become a serious concern to us." West Africa Regional Office, "Economic and Sector Work Program FY84–86," February 1984, p. 1.

199. The flood of writings around the 1980 annual meetings suggest that at the time the Fund was struggling to maintain a role for itself, which explains its hasty foray into Africa. Its angst was short lived after the debt crisis burst open less than two years later. Some examples: Paul Fabra, "Developing Nations Seek Overhaul of IMF and World Bank," *Times* (London) Europe supplement, October 7, 1980, p. 4; Jurek Martin, Peter Riddell, and Nicholas Colchester, "IMF Tortoise in a Fast Changing World," *Financial Times* (London), September 29, 1980, p. 15; Canute James and David Tonge, "Developing Countries Prepare to Vent Discontent with IMF," *Financial Times* (London), August 22, 1980, p. 4; Harvey D. Shapiro, "IMF's Identity Crisis," *Institutional Investor,* September 1980, p. [97]–120; James Lewis, "How Jacques de Larosiere Is Caught in a Crossfire," *Euromoney,* October 1980, pp. 62–71; David Blake, "Where Is the IMF Heading?" *Financial Times* (London), October 2, 1980, p. 21.

Table 12-4. *Net Transfers of Bretton Woods Institutions to Sub-Saharan Africa,*
1980–95
Billions of U.S. dollars

Institution	1980–83	1984–87[a]	1988–91[a]	1992–95[a]
IMF	4.39	(3.22)	(1.99)	(1.20)
World Bank	2.83	4.70	3.93	1.52

Source: *World Debt Tables, 1996.* IMF data for 1995 are provisional.
a. Figures in parentheses are negative numbers.

would end up being the IMF's bagman. The IMF's facilities virtually ensured that,
of the two institutions, it would be the first to get in and the first to get out. With
the region's economies continuing to worsen, the Bank sought greater consultations
and coordination with the IMF: "The purpose of such an informal meeting would
be to consider whether the tools, approaches, and concepts we are using are
appropriate, whether there are other approaches we might explore, and whether
we are making the most effective possible use of the complementarities of the
capacities of both institutions in this difficult setting."[200]

In 1983, the IMF disbursed nearly $3 billion to Sub-Saharan Africa. Since 1980,
the IMF's exposure had increased dramatically, and the shorter terms of the IMF's
facilities meant that reflows to the IMF were now due. But the economic turnaround had failed to transpire (an internal IMF analysis noted at the time that the
results of twenty-six programs in Africa had been unsatisfactory). This abrupt reversal
of flows from the IMF, along with the depth and intensity of the crisis, meant that the
Bank's earlier cautious approach began to unravel. Thus we see Stern warning of
problems in countries such as Equatorial Guinea and Chad where "we are . . . being
pressured to prepare structural adjustment loans in support of SAF [Structural
Adjustment Facility] financing in the absence of the country meeting our normal
criteria for adjustment lending."[201] The Bank filled the breach in the balance of
payments with an increase in quick-disbursing adjustment loans (table 12-4). Adjustment lending had been formulated to achieve two objectives besides transferring flexible resources: changing policies and reforming institutions. The urgency
of the financial needs weakened the latter two objectives, particularly the last.

Adjustment lending as a percentage of total World Bank lending to the region
jumped from 13 percent ($0.9 billion) in 1980–83 to 36 percent ($3.3 billion) in
1984–87. These flows helped stave off financial pressures on the IMF until it
inaugurated its Structural Adjustment and Enhanced Structural Adjustment
facilities in 1986 and 1987, respectively. The Bank regarded the SAF with mixed
feelings. On the one hand, the fact that "despite much high sounding rhetoric, [the

200. Memorandum, Ernest Stern to William B. Dale, "Africa," June 24, 1982.
201. Memorandum, Ernest Stern to Barber B. Conable, "Lunch—October 30, 1986,"
October 29, 1986.

SAF] has as its principal objective to get the IMF repaid by substituting longer term money for the current outstanding IMF resources" would reduce the diversion of Bank resources to repay the Fund. On the other hand, the Bank worried that the SAF would carry lower performance criteria: "The Fund is prepared to proceed with SAF programs even where their standbys have failed. . . . We do not feel secure that in the absence of standby agreements there will be adequate support on the stabilization side to protect our investment in structural adjustment lending."[202] There was good reason for such fears—the Bank was observing a high correlation between the failure of its structural adjustment lending and the failure of countries to comply with IMF standby agreements. To the IMF's credit, it took the initiative to come to its own rescue by shifting its lending to these countries from short-term loans on hard terms to long-term loans on soft terms through its SAF and ESAF. Yet these moves were merely buying time by changing the structure and terms of SSA debt. In the end they would delay, but not resolve, this mounting problem.

As noted in chapter 10, when SALs were introduced they were aimed at medium-income countries that had the institutional wherewithal to undertake such changes and whose economic structures had some resemblance to the SAL analytical framework. In Sub-Saharan Africa adjustment efforts were undertaken in economies with features that, though present in many developing countries, were present to a much greater degree: small industrial sectors, with tiny manufacturing sectors; a large share of agriculture, particularly peasant agriculture; high degrees of trade openness as measured by trade-to-GDP ratios; severely underdeveloped and oligopolistic capital and product markets; weak human resources and entrepreneurial skills; segmented labor markets; large parallel markets; and large capital flight of both human and financial capital. In turn these facts were both the cause and consequence of the pervasive institutional weakness in Africa.

The structural constraints would have normally implied lower supply elasticities. But these characteristics, when coupled with severe problems on data quality, introduced a far greater element of uncertainty in the policy results of traditional macroeconomic policy prescriptions. Ordinarily this would have been expected to introduce a greater circumspection in setting performance targets. But that did not occur. In the early years, Senior Vice President Ernest Stern firmly turned down numerous SAL proposals by the Africa regional vice presidents, arguing that they were faddish and ill-conceived. But the intensification of the crisis in Africa in 1983 led to an upsurge in adjustment lending, especially sector adjustment lending programs (of the thirty-four SECALs over the period fiscal 1979–85, half were to Sub-Saharan Africa). With many African countries unable or unwilling to implement economy-wide SALs and balance of payments pressures mounting, SECALs

202. Ibid. The SAF was financed from reflows from the Trust Fund created by the sale of IMF gold in the mid-1970s.

with their narrower sector focus seemed to represent a viable middle path. But the efficacy of balance of payments loans in the absence of a viable macro framework would continue to be a concern within the Bank.

The acceptability of early SALs proved illusory. The Bank had in fact been quite surprised at the demand for SALs from seemingly unlikely candidates with centrally planned economies such as Guinea-Bissau and the Congo. Wilfred Thalwitz, the program's director for West Africa, reported at an EDI seminar that leaders were candidly saying they would wait to come to the Bank until they ran out of cash. "It is a Faustian bargain," he said; "sign your soul for cash; no sense of how one will repay."[203] Vice President Jaycox spoke of the problems being encountered: "demoralized" bureaucracies; the IMF "over-exposed and unlikely to be paid-back"; governments unwilling to discuss the "sensitive issues of ethnicity," fearful "that the Asian minority could capture new economic opportunities."[204] In 1986 in-house correspondence drew attention to the political underpinnings of the problem:

> I fear that current Bank dogma not withstanding, poor development prospects for Africa are not uniquely due to economic mismanagement. . . . [P]erhaps we can catch a glimpse of the situation if we understand that with (a) increasing population pressures (b) a small base of educated or trained manpower (and thus high wages) (c) French and English educated elites having the power to protect their own living standards, and (d) declining living standards imposed by reductions in terms of trade or export demand, we have all the prerequisites for economic management which satisfies power relationships but which is dysfunctional for the economy as a whole, and the question becomes one of how to break the insidious logic of the system.
>
> . . . The real question then becomes: to what extent do we try to substitute ourselves for national planning agencies, and to what extent should we? That is, of course, the direction we're ultimately going, particularly with policy-based lending, and perhaps we should think a bit about the longer implications of what we are doing, since, as we are increasingly recognizing, we can't really "teleguide" these things from Washington.[205]

The acute problems suffered by the very small and poor SSA countries can be illustrated by a vignette relating to São Tomé and Principe, a tiny island country that had followed an ostensible Marxist strategy since its independence from Portuguese rule in 1975. São Tomé and Principe decided to steer a different course in the mid-1980s and for the first time approached the Bank for loans. By this time food aid accounted for about half its imports, despite a fertile agroclimate. Cocoa plantations, a major basis of the economy, had been so rundown that production had declined to a quarter of the levels of a decade earlier. The labor force had moved out of agriculture into government employment, mostly as clerks. To cover

203. Memorandum, Lisa Pachter to Alex Shakow, "The Political Economy of Sub-Saharan Africa, EDI Conference, December 3–5, 1986," December 8, 1986, p. 4.

204. Ibid., pp. 1–2.

205. Memorandum, Michel Palein to Xavier de la Renaudière, "Draft Zero, 1986 Sub-Sahara Africa Report," January 6, 1986.

its bills the government had been relying on central bank borrowings. A Bank economist later recalled his visit:

> When we got there we understood immediately that the problem was somewhat like Guinea Bissau. If you were to conduct a full reform, change the exchange rates, bring under control all the sources of overvaluation, you had to bring goods into the economy. The President told me before December of 1986, "Yes, I have Christmas coming. You may not realize this, but this country is really not part of Africa. We have been under 450 years of Portuguese control and our consumption patterns are those of Portugal. If I don't get $2 million worth of cheese, wine and other food by December, I'm not going to survive." Indeed he had to get money to do that. . . . To get the goods in the market in time, we used an unused line of credit which hadn't been used for general repairs and maintenance. We made available a $2 million advance out of that credit to enable the government to place immediate orders for the goods.[206]

In return the Bank obtained a wide array of macroeconomic reforms in such areas as the exchange rate, public finance, and credit policies as well as in the crucial cocoa sector. São Tomé and Principe's precipitous decline was checked, but a decade later its long-term economic prospects seemed equally bleak.

Adjusting to Adjustment: 1987–94

By the mid-1980s, the Bank had established itself as the preeminent external actor in Sub-Saharan Africa. This role was further consolidated around 1987 because of two factors. First, the institution's Africa push had acquired a de facto and symbolic leader. Edward (Kim) Jaycox was one of the rising younger executives of the institution. Before the Bank's 1986–87 reorganization, he was vice president of one of the two African regions. After serving as chairman of the reorganization's steering committee, he was made vice president for the single, recombined, Sub-Saharan Africa region. The 1987 reorganization moved the locus of bureaucratic power of the Bank's operations to regional vice presidents and directors. Jaycox (along with Shahid Husain in Latin America) proceeded to invest unflagging activism in the role. Second, shortly thereafter (in 1988) the Bank negotiated the Special Program of Assistance for Africa (SPA), establishing for the first time a focal point for coordinating the balance of payments portion of external assistance to Sub-Saharan Africa undertaken by all major official donors. The Bank served as chairman of the SPA with the bilateral donors providing the bulk of the financing.

These years saw a peaking of adjustment lending to Sub-Saharan Africa (slightly less than 40 percent of all lending to the region). For a time there appeared to be a breakthrough in Sub-Saharan Africa's largest country, Nigeria. Following the collapse of oil prices in 1986, the Nigerian economy appeared to be on the verge of

206. Richard Westebbe, interview, World Bank Oral History Program, January 25, 1988.

collapse (export earnings fell from $26 billion in 1980 to $12 billion in 1985 to just $6.4 billion in 1986). The IMF being politically persona non grata, the Babangida government's "IMF plebiscite" was a skillful homegrown solution. By rejecting the IMF's advice publicly and quietly implementing its principal components, it appeared to offer an optimal solution. The Bank supported the Nigerian program with two adjustment loans totaling nearly a billion dollars and with substantial consultations and dialogue. The institution took the lead in pressing for devaluation and reduced oil subsidies (the latter were a chronic bone of contention). Clausen and Stern raised the issue of devaluation directly in a meeting with the Nigerian minister of finance in February 1984. The issue was again raised with a visiting Nigerian delegation in September 1984. At first the Nigerians demurred, charging that the Bank simply wanted to increase the amount of counterpart funds for its loans so as to speed up its own projects. After General Babangida arrived in August 1985 (to replace General Buhari), with direct devaluation appearing highly sensitive, the Bank—with the IMF's concurrence—supported a SAL that substantially expanded the second-tier market for foreign exchange. The initiative was "a politically acceptable way of getting a major move and of gathering information about market-clearing rates."[207] The Bank persevered and shortly thereafter Nigeria devalued.

For a time the economy appeared to be responding well. GDP, which fell by 1.7 percent a year between 1980 and 1986, rebounded with a growth of 4.7 percent a year between 1986 and 1992. Yet by 1990 the Bank and Nigeria were at odds over the government's public expenditures, particularly its investments in a few large capital-intensive projects. In particular, the million-ton Ajaokuta steel complex became the main "stumbling block" on a budgetary and financial policy loan in late 1990.[208] As Nigeria's political leadership changed, so did its economic priorities. The Bank had honed its political skills in Nigeria and gradually came to understand the interrelationships between economic policies and political realities: the rhetoric of national sovereignty as a cover for regional ethnic rivalries; and the exigency with which successive governments almost as a matter of faith abandoned previous governments' projects, leaving the economic landscape littered with half-complete projects. But that knowledge was of little help when domestic power struggles played themselves out. Nigeria's fortunes had gone tragically awry, a victim of its political leadership's own follies.[209]

207. Memorandum, Wilfred Thalwitz to Ernest Stern, March 7, 1986.

208. By the end of 1989 an estimated $3 billion had already been spent on the complex, but a further $2 billion was needed for completion. In September 1989 a memorandum of understanding was reached limiting further expenditures on the project to $45 million per year which the Bank wanted to provide for working capital and spare parts for a Delta mill then operating well below capacity. This did not happen, the Nigerian position being that so much money had been spent that a "final push" would see the project through.

209. For a devastating Nigerian view, see Wole Soyinka, *The Open Sore of a Continent: A Personal Narrative of the Nigerian Crisis* (Oxford University Press, 1996).

In another large SSA country, Sudan—where arrears to the IMF had developed in 1985 and the country was declared ineligible for IMF funds in February 1986— the Bank continued to lend for a small "core program" of about $60 million a year. Arrears to the IMF and the civil war in the South became major concerns of the donors, and the Bank had to take them into account. But it persevered, organizing a special donors' meeting for an emergency flood reconstruction program in December 1988. Civil strife increasingly dogged Bank operations, and the government of Sudan was informed that "in the absence of significant progress toward achieving peace, it would become increasingly difficult to continue to mobilize the level of assistance that Sudan requires."[210] As the civil war intensified, the Bank decided "not to go ahead with Board presentation in view of the deterioration in the peace process and the probable reversal of the progress made in flood relief."[211] But the link of lending to progress on the peace process sat uneasily among staff who felt that "unless we take action soon, the Bank's credibility as a non-political technical organization will be seriously damaged."[212] The country's international political stance, especially its opposition to the Gulf coalition in 1991, led the Bank to disengage from Sudan. The country went into nonaccrual status in 1994.[213]

In Liberia, Sergeant Doe took over in a coup in 1980 (and in quick succession became General Doe, Commander-in-chief Doe, then His Excellency President General Dr. Doe). Despite manifest evidence of the sordid nature of his regime, Liberia emerged as one of the largest recipients of U.S. aid in Africa.[214] In late 1987 the Bank decided to close its resident mission in Liberia, as well as nine ongoing projects there, in an effort to send a strong signal to the Doe regime. But the damage had been done, and the country imploded, becoming one of the first of the new post–cold war era's failed states.

The institution was more tolerant of Mobutu's Zaire. A potent mix of cold war interests of the United States and the commercial interests of Belgium and France meant that despite an outstanding and long-established track record of kleptocracy, Zaire remained one of the largest aid recipients in Sub-Saharan Africa during the 1980s. Thus when the Bank was pressing Mobutu to denationalize Gecamines (the vast copper mine), Stern reported to Clausen: "There are, however, strong vested

210. Letter, Barber B. Conable to Al Sadiq El-Mahdi, prime minister of Sudan, December 8, 1988.

211. Memorandum, E. V. K. Jaycox to Moeen A. Qureshi, "Sudan—Emergency Flood Reconstruction Project," January 3, 1989, p. 2.

212. Memorandum, Callisto E. Madavo to Barber B. Conable, "Sudan—Emergency Flood Reconstruction Project," February 2, 1989, p. 2.

213. Although IBRD's exposure (principal outstanding) in Sudan was just $6 million, IDA's exposure was $1.25 billion; $63 million of principal and charges were due at the end of fiscal 1996.

214. In a personal communication to the authors, a former senior U.S. official engaged with Africa linked the increase in U.S. assistance to the fear of being blamed for "losing" Liberia (the United States had significant investments in communications intelligence infrastructure in the country) as Doe cannily flirted with Libya and Cuba.

interests in the present structure, particularly on the part of Belgium. You may therefore hear from Mr. de Groote about this."[215] As noted earlier, Bank lending to Zaire had leveled off in the latter half of the 1970s. With McNamara's departure, however, the Bank paralleled the support from other donors by sharply increasing lending: from about $30 million a year during 1976–81 to $87 million between 1982 and 1985 and then to $128 million between 1986 and 1989.[216] External pressure alone, however, cannot explain the Bank's stance. Many external observers of Zaire, especially in U.S. circles, reluctantly accepted the "Mobutu or chaos" argument; however detestable Mobutu's actions, he was the only person who had the guile to hold the country together. The repercussions of a collapsing Zaire—the third largest by population in Sub-Saharan Africa and the largest country in the continent by land area, bordering nine other states that were themselves quite weak as well—could not be easily dismissed.

But the Bank's culture and processes were important as well. Given Zaire's importance, successive managers attempted to demonstrate that their actions had finally succeeded in turning the country around. Repeatedly these attempts failed, but since managers often changed, any "learning" was periodically truncated. A few measures of perseverance, together with a pinch of ambition and a dollop of self-delusion, served to satisfy an Executive Board that was only too prepared to hold its nose until it "discovered" governance at the end of the decade. The Bank remained financially engaged with the country much past what prudent judgment may have warranted. For some in the Bank, the fact that most lending was IDA credits, posing little financial risk to the institution, intensified the lack of discipline. In November 1993, Zaire went into nonaccrual status with $97 million of IBRD loans and $1.4 billion of IDA credits outstanding. At the time of writing Zaire's economic and political prospects were so bleak that there was little doubt that sooner or later the Bank would have to find some way to write off these sums.

By the late 1980s there was a growing sense that the pendulum had swung too far with regard to the institution's macroeconomic focus, especially in Sub-Saharan Africa, and that the emphasis of adjustment lending needed to be reevaluated. Somewhat ironically, a voice of caution on the dangers of going overboard with adjustment lending was the Bank's new chief economist, Stanley Fischer, who frequently challenged the Africa region on its penchant for quick-disbursing loans,

215. Memorandum, Ernest Stern to A. W. Clausen, March 4, 1982. Jacques de Groote served as Belgium's executive director at the IMF and World Bank for more than a decade. His connections with Mobutu were highlighted in Edward T. Pound, *Wall Street Journal*, "IMF, World Bank Aide Has Dealings Hinting at Conflict of Interest," December 28, 1990, pp. 2, 31.

216. During the latter half of the 1980s (1986–90), in absolute terms, Zaire was the sixth largest recipient of net ODA from DAC donors (after Ethiopia, Kenya, Senegal, Sudan, and Tanzania), receiving almost double that of Ghana. World Bank, *African Development Indicators 1994–95*, table 12-2, p. 316.

arguing, "We have to take a serious look at the question of whether our policies are focusing too much on stabilization and too little on growth."[217] Referring to Kenya, he asked why the region "want[ed] to move quickly with adjustment lending while the Kenyan government prefer[red] a slow pace of reform."[218] His uneasiness was shared by others in the Bank who worried that both SSA borrowers and the Bank had become addicted to adjustment lending in Sub-Saharan Africa. If the earlier rationale for the SAL instrument was the mismatch between broad policy objectives and the then primary instrument of investment lending, there was now a perception that in Sub-Saharan Africa adjustment lending was being used to finance operations that were better suited to investment lending:

> Two operations, the Malawi agricultural SECAL and the Senegal SAL IV raise concerns about potential addiction to quick disbursing lending. Each of the two countries have had several adjustment operations and the continued use of this instrument raises questions. In the Malawi SECAL, the main purpose of the operation was to improve the productivity of the smallholder farmers. It is not clear that the adjustment loan was the appropriate instrument to address this long term problem. Although there are important policy issues which the operation seeks to address (land-rent regulations, tobacco legislation and fertilizer subsidization), investment-type operations may be more appropriate to support a research program for high yielding seeds, a critical element in the improvement of smallholder productivity. In addition, this operation was not drawn from a clearly articulated sector strategy to which the government was committed.[219]

> The Senegal SAL IV raises the issue of government commitment and ownership of the adjustment program. This is the seventh adjustment operation the Bank has undertaken in that country. Yet government commitment to policy reform continues to be weak and it is perhaps weaker now than for prior operations. The Region explained that government commitment was improving but that this was motivated primarily by Senegal's need for quick disbursing assistance! After six adjustment operations ownership of the adjustment program still does not exist.[220]

The problem was particularly acute in Francophone Africa, where as a "consequence of the current exchange rate situation," Fischer argued, the region was "doing far too much adjustment lending relative to project lending, in both Senegal and Mali. This feature of our lending is damaging long-term growth, as is the monetary squeeze that is needed to try to maintain the

217. Memorandum, Stanley Fischer to John Holsen, Johannes Linn, and others, "Renewal of Growth," August 6, 1989. Fischer's reactions followed a review of programs for Tanzania, Malawi, Bolivia, Sri Lanka, and Côte d'Ivoire. For three of these five, the programs foresaw "negative growth of per capita consumption through 1997."

218. Memorandum, Chakwuma Obidegwu to files, "Post-OC Note: Kenya," June 27, 1990, concerning Operations Committee meeting to discuss the Kenya CSP and export development and an ASECAL, June 1990.

219. Memorandum, Robert Liebenthal to Stanley Fischer through Alexander Shakow, "Operations Committee Business—June-August 1989," October 20, 1989, para. 2.

220. Ibid., para. 3.

parity."[221] The uneasiness with the deus ex machina character of adjustment lending was shared by others within the Bank:

> Lately there has been some uneasiness that many CSPs are focusing too narrowly on macroeconomic issues without paying sufficient attention to broader questions of development strategy.... This is not to deny the crucial importance of macroeconomic adjustment for the Congo at the present juncture. It is simply to say that there are other issues of developmental significance for the Congo in the medium-term that also merit close attention.[222]

Francophone Africa may have also been an extreme case because of a particularly active senior manager (the country director) whose fondness for SALs earned him the nickname "Dial-a-SAL." For the region as a whole, the emphasis on adjustment lending made it appear that these loans were bearing practically the entire burden of policy change in a country. But it was the quick-disbursing nature of this instrument in view of continuing balance of payments difficulties, rather than the policy aspects per se, that was often the driving motive.

A Changing Agenda

In 1986 the Bank, recognizing the need to look beyond the medium term for stimulating growth in Africa, began work on such a study. In addition to having a longer time horizon, this study—known as the Long-Term Perspective Study (LTPS)—differed markedly from the Bank's earlier reports on the region in the process by which it was formulated. A protracted and staff-intensive interactive process with African leaders, institutions, and donors marked a conscious attempt at consensus building in the diagnosis of problems and possible solutions.[223] In part, this shift was guided by private apprehensions, as indicated in a note from Jaycox: "All of us working or interested in the future of Africa are concerned to the point of alarm about the longer-term prospects for Africa, even assuming that Africa and we are able to come through the processes of structural adjustment successfully."[224]

---

221. Memorandum, Stanley Fischer to Barber Conable, "Senegal and Mali CSPs," October 20, 1989. In a separate note to Conable, Fischer noted that "Because of both IDA and serious adjustment efforts that appear to be under way in Senegal..., I believe we have no choice but to continue with adjustment lending at the present. But we should figure out a way to reach an agreement with the Senegalese and the French that we will sharply reduce the share of rapidly disbursing lending within the next three years." The reference to IDA draws attention to the linkage between French support for the IDA replenishment and Bank lending in Francophone Africa.

222. Memorandum, Alexander Shakow to M. Ismail Serageldin, "Congo: Initiating Memorandum for a CSP," October 5, 1989.

223. A good account of the process may be found in Ramgopal Agarwala and Pushpa N. Schwartz with Jean Ponchamni, "Sub-Saharan Africa: A Long-Term Perspective Study," paper prepared for World Bank Workshop on Participatory Development, May 17–20, 1994.

224. Memorandum, Edward V. K. Jaycox to Barber B. Conable, "Meeting with Mr. McNamara re CG for Africa on Long-Term Issues Urgently Requiring Attention Now,"

Further, senior management in the Bank became increasingly concerned with the broader risks posed to the institution arising from its high profile in the region. These concerns led the Bank to take the lead (with the help of the Dutch) in forming a "Global Coalition" for Sub-Saharan Africa, which was seen as "a way to increase the level of consensus [with donors and African intellectuals] and reduce the Bank's risk and profile."[225] The forum, however, proved less successful at consensus building than was hoped as other multilaterals (and some bilaterals) complained that they were being cast as cheerleaders for the Bank.

In the process of formulating the LTPS, two messages were hammered home by many African participants: an insistence that the Bank deal frontally with issues of "governance" in Africa, including styles of government and corruption—topics hitherto avoided by the Bank, at least in any explicit way—and renewed emphasis on regional integration. The Bank soon applied itself to both issues.

REFORMING THE STATE. By the mid-1980s, the battle cry of less government had a qualifier: less but better government. The need to shore up public sector administrative capacity was addressed by efforts aimed at containing the size and improving the performance of the core civil service. Early on, these efforts focused on shorter-term emergency steps to reform employment and pay policies by focusing on cost containment and rationalization of remuneration. Various technical tools—removal of "ghost" workers, wage freezes, enforcement of retirement age (or early retirement), elimination of guaranteed entry into the civil service—were deployed. Although quantitative retrenchment targets were often set, for the most part the politically contentious issue of retrenchment by dismissing civil service members was not pressed with much vigor by the Bank. Cost containment was gradually supplemented by efforts to rationalize remuneration packages—monetizing remuneration, rationalizing wage discrepancies, and wage decompression.[226] By the end of the decade, the efforts had further broadened to include improvements in management capacity, an issue subsumed under the broader rubric of "capacity building."

Civil service reform was one facet of the Bank's (and donor community's) efforts at "institution building," an area that had always been a prominent aspect of the

---

October 21, 1988. Jaycox identified the problems facing Africa at the "juncture of four areas of concern: the rate of demographic increase, the pace of 'modernization' of small-holder agriculture, the resulting environmental impact, and, finally the capacity of Africans to understand and manage these forces and the macro-economic forces that drive, aggravate, and could alleviate these very negative trends."

225. World Bank, "Minutes of the President's Council Meeting—March 12, 1990," March 14, 1990.

226. Between 1981 and 1991 civil service reform featured in fifty-five (about two-thirds) of the adjustment loans and about 60 percent of the technical assistance loans to Sub-Saharan Africa. A good account of these measures can be found in Barbara Nunberg and John R. Nellis, "Civil Service Reform and the World Bank," World Bank, PRE Working Paper 422, May 1990.

Bank's operations. An endemic frustration was the fact that despite seemingly endless efforts, public institutions not only failed to deepen their roots but frequently regressed. What makes institutions tick is an amorphous area to begin with, and an understanding of public bureaucracies was not the Bank's strongest suit. In part, the discipline of public administration ranked low in the intellectual hierarchy in the "development" field, and the Bank was no exception. More than any other part of the Bank's activities, it was an area where one would assume that experience would be especially prized. Notwithstanding endless incantations about "institution building" in reports and analysis, the internal organizational culture of the Bank was inimical to individuals with deep-rooted external experience. Moreover, institution building is an activity with a long gestation period, much too long to be accommodated within the budgetary, bureaucratic, and political cycles of most donors. Even if all these factors were favorable, ground realities were not. Political imperatives apart, "traditional" factors—concerning, for example, ethnicity and kinship—proved more resilient in Africa than anticipated.

In the early part of the decade, two major internal reviews, one of technical assistance in Africa and the other on institutional development, were sharply critical of Bank efforts.[227] But the emergency-like atmosphere led the Bank and other donors to seek institution-building quick fixes by invoking large doses of "technical assistance," the basic ingredients of which were studies, reports, and the training of local staff and expatriate personnel attached to sundry government offices. The cost effectiveness of such assistance was repeatedly questioned.[228] In a stinging critique in 1993, Vice President Jaycox assailed the heavy costs of technical assistance and the paucity of results. But the Bank and other donors had only themselves to blame: they had made studies and reports central elements of "institution building."

The views of the African governments on the virtues of prolonged temporary technical assistance were sharply at odds with those of external agencies. Many officials in Africa regarded technical assistance as an employment program for expatriates. Experts came and went, rarely speaking the local language and with little understanding of local conditions. As a result, the technical assisters rarely developed the trust that comes with continuity or overcame problems of competence.[229]

227. World Bank, "Report on Technical Assistance in Sub-Sahara Africa, 1982"; World Bank, Operations Evaluation Department, "The World Bank Institutional Development in Africa: A Review of World Bank Project Experience," 2 vols., May 17, 1984.

228. An often-cited UNDP study concluded that the cost of technical assistance for Tanzania in 1988 amounted to around $300 million, of which $200 million went to salaries, while the total cost of the Tanzanian civil service was about $100 million. Elliot J. Berg, coordinator, Rethinking Technical Cooperation: Reforms for Capacity Building in Africa (New York: UNDP, 1993).

229. According to one source, sensing the potential for work in state corporations, McKinsey, a prestigious management consultancy company, used Tanzania as a "training

Externally aided projects were invariably designed in ways that ensured that the receiving country required external help to make them work. The Bank's projects typically outweighed local capacity enough to require a high level of imported technical and managerial competence. Shouldered aside, recipient countries lost interest. The poor outcomes were consequently not too surprising.

In response, the Bank made "capacity building" part of the lexicon, and it and other donors took several initiatives in this direction. The EDI, together with the UNDP and the International Labor Organization, sought to strengthen African management development institutes and linked up with the African Development Bank (AfDB) and the International Fund for Agricultural Development to strengthen the operational management of agricultural projects. An Africa Capacity Building Institute (ACBI), launched with the UNDP and the AfDB in 1990, was set up to create a fund to be used to build regional and national institutes to enhance the indigenous capacity for economic and policy analysis. The initiative met with teething troubles, mainly because of poor and heavy-handed leadership.[230]

A different tack adopted by the Bank to address "governance"-related issues while retaining its technocratic mandate entailed detailed public expenditure reviews (PERs). The large share of external resources in government budgets and mounting criticism of the social sector impact of adjustment programs heightened interest in such reviews. PERs grew rapidly at the turn of the decade because of the demands of the Special Program of Assistance for Africa. As nonwage operations, maintenance expenditures, and issues such as military expenditures came under greater scrutiny, conditionalities on social sector spending in adjustment loans increased rapidly (from 7 percent of adjustment operations in the early 1980s to about a third of all adjustment operations). PERs emerged as one of the institution's main analytical instruments supporting its poverty-alleviation efforts.[231] However, while the conceptual basis of much of this work was reasonably well founded on intrasectoral issues, the empirical justification on the intersectoral allocations was weaker.[232]

---

ground" for staff used in developed country contracts: "Their last big Tanzanian contract was for 'decentralization.' . . . Their work was eventually terminated when it became apparent that it was potentially never-ending." Andrew Coulson, *Tanzania: A Political Economy* (Oxford: Clarendon Press, 1982), p. 345, n. 14.

230. In contrast, the AERC—Africa Economic Research Consortia—launched by the IDRC to develop and nurture local policy and analytical capability, was much more successful. A good account is Jeffrey S. Fine, "The AERC Experience: An Essay on Research and Higher Education in Sub-Saharan Africa," October 1995.

231. The PER-poverty reduction nexus was strengthened following the Social Summit in Copenhagen in 1995 which called for (among other recommendations) the Bretton Woods institutions to ensure budgetary transparency and accountability in the use of public resources in order to increase the quality and effectiveness of social expenditures.

232. The relationship between public expenditures and economic growth is quite complex, and the often strong conclusions implied by the degree of lending conditionalities were questionable. Thus with respect to the allocation of government spending, "all of the

Although a seemingly simple concept, PERs required substantial effort and skill. Given their weak capacity, PERs were done mostly by Bank staff or consultants made available to the country (Ghana was a notable exception; the country assumed responsibility after a few rounds of these reviews). As an auditing exercise, the informational content of a sound analysis of public expenditures was important in and of itself, both for budget management and, if put in the public domain, to guide public debate on the issue. Yet, there was the risk that PERs might emerge as the latest "magic bullet" on the poverty front as loan conditions based on PERs, such as those on health expenditures, began to reach down to the level of composition and budget management processes, including ceilings on wage expenditures, floors on medicines, and share of drugs. The dilemma between one set of laudable objectives and another, "ownership" of the programs, remained.

Some Bank staff had long worried that their analysis had little to say about "the cultural and social environment in which economic policy and management decisions are being framed in Africa."[233] Commenting on the 1983 report, "Sub-Saharan Africa: Progress Report on Development Prospects and Programs," a senior adviser and veteran Africa staffer argued that "the major cause of the crisis is political and not economic and is caused by self seeking, corrupt, politicians and senior civil servants who really don't care or are not allowed to care about development and their people."[234]

The Bank had for the most part adhered to its constitutional proscription on taking political considerations into account in its lending decisions. In the late 1970s, when the Carter administration had put pressure on the Bank to take human rights into consideration, the institution made a distinction between economic rights and civil rights, arguing that both its mandate and comparative advantage lay in the former (chapters 9 and 18). However, the prolonged nature of the economic crisis and the lack of response to conventional therapeutic measures in Sub-Saharan Africa, as well as a donor community emboldened by the demise of the cold war, rendered this distinction increasingly tenuous, as the Kenyan case illustrates.

Under Jomo Kenyatta's leadership during the 1970s, Kenya had established a solid track record, partly because of the competence of its senior bureaucracy (see

---

standard candidates for productive expenditure—capital, transport, and communication, health, and education—had either a negative or insignificant relationship with economic growth." Shantayanan Devarajan, Vinaya Swaroop, and Heng-fu Zhou, "The Composition of Public Expenditure and Economic Growth," *Journal of Monetary Economics*, vol. 37 (April 1996), p. 338. The problem has been compounded by severe deficiencies in the data. Internal Bank reviews have cautioned that many public expenditure reviews lack even basic data on functional and economic composition of expenditures, major programs, private sector provision, and so on, required for informed decisionmaking.

233. Memorandum, Ravi Gulhati to Stanley Please, "Africa Report: Draft I," July 6, 1984.

234. Memorandum, Alexander Storrar (senior adviser) to Stanley Please, July 12, 1983.

chapter 6). Despite being one of the first off the starting blocks in availing itself of the Bank's SALs, its economic performance deteriorated, and by the mid-1980s the early attempts at reform had ground to a halt.[235] However, the "halo" factor from earlier years persisted, strengthened by the even weaker economic performance of other SSA countries.[236] During the discussion of the Kenya Country Strategy Paper and two SALs in 1990, concerns were expressed regarding "the worsening corruption, the concentration of political power and arbitrariness in government, and increased political intolerance and abuse of human rights." Even so, the government appeared to have "demonstrated the capacity to manage change,"and the Bank felt that the "current troubling situation will be brought under control and thus there is no need for the Bank to prepare to react to it."[237]

The strategy did not make much headway, although few viable alternatives presented themselves, as the infighting among President Daniel Arap Moi's political foes revealed. The situation in Kenya made a particular impression on the Bank's resident representative, Peter Eigen, who resigned and formed an international NGO ("Transparency International"), which by the mid-1990s had helped place corruption on the international agenda.

In November 1990, at a Consultative Group meeting for Kenya chaired by the World Bank, donors took the unprecedented step of linking aid to Kenya to economic *and political reform*. The event was a milestone in establishing that "governance" issues should be on the agenda of donors and the international financial institutions. Corruption, military expenditures, human rights, and democracy, hitherto regarded as being outside the explicit purview of the Bank, emerged as an acceptable part of its agenda, especially in Sub-Saharan Africa. While the pressure principally emanated from the major shareholders, it was not restricted to them.[238] By the early 1990s, Kenya faced growing pressures from the donor community who, together with the Bank and IMF, pressed President Moi to hold multiparty elections. When held, the elections were marred by charges of irregularities, which led to a freezing of donor funds. Other erstwhile East African favorites, Malawi and Tanzania, also came under increasing pressure from the

---

235. Thus in 1996 Stern noted, "I thought we were suitably diplomatic in our overall assessment on the pace of adjustment, since the sectoral discussions clearly showed failure to follow through in many important areas and little progress in others. The pace of adjustment is not independent of its success. Moving 'in the right direction' too slowly will not reach the desired results later; it is unlikely to reach them at all." Memorandum, Ernest Stern to Jochen Kraske, "Kenya—CEM," May 27, 1986.

236. For example, this view is articulated by Paul Mosley, "How to Confront the World Bank and Get Away with It: A Case Study of Kenya, 1980–87," in Chris Milnes and A. J. Rayner, eds., *Policy Adjustment in Africa* (Macmillan, 1992), pp. 99–131.

237. Operations Committee minutes of meeting to discuss the Kenya CSP and export development and an ASECAL, June 1990.

238. The ECA, for instance, called for a reduction of military expenditures in 1989.

donors on governance grounds, and they, too, experienced reductions and a block-age of funds.

The demise of the cold war, tightening donor budgets, and mounting frustration at the limited results that donor assistance had produced contributed to putting "governance" issues at the center of the development agenda in Sub-Saharan Africa. It is not yet clear to what extent the Bank has taken to heart the claim of Lynda Chalker, the British minister for Overseas Development in 1991 that "Western money can buy good government."[239] It will not be surprising if this does happen. What will be surprising is if it can be made good.

REGIONAL INTEGRATION REDUX. In response to the malaise of the African states and a desperation born of continued economic difficulties, by the late 1980s there was increasing clamor for an intellectually familiar limited response: economic integration. However artificial, the boundaries of African states were a reality. Without challenging the shapes or identities of the cooperating states, contiguous groups of states could band together for specified joint ventures. The best known was trade; the cooperators could adopt a more open, if not a thoroughly common, market. They also could go for multistate projects, especially of the infrastructural kind, or even, if the spirit of amity luxuriantly blossomed, they could consider a pattern of complementary industrial development.[240]

As noted earlier, however, the Bank's experience with Sub-Saharan African economic integration had been quite negative. As a financial institution whose loans have to be guaranteed by sovereign nations, the Bank found defaults on such loans by one country hugely problematic. If anything, the increasing political fragility and mounting portfolio problems during this period were bound to make the institution even more chary. For most of the 1980s, the Bank showed little interest in the issue. Nevertheless, the conventional wisdom was that the Bank should promote integration. This view was repeatedly expressed by African inter-locutors during the LTPS study, and the demand by then had become a fixture with African governments. The Africa regional department sought to respond by developing two regional loans: one in support of regional trade and investment in the Preferential Trade Area of Eastern and Southern Africa (PTA) and the other to the central African customs union (UDEAC) of six countries (Cameroon, Congo, Gabon, Central African Republic, Chad, and Equatorial Guinea). The first loan was to facilitate cross-border private investment, while the second was to promote

239. Quoted in Oliver Furley, "Introduction: Africa: The Habit of Conflict," in Furley, ed., *Conflict in Africa* (London: Tauris Academic Studies, 1995), p. 15.

240. Four forms of integration (in increasing degree) may be distinguished: free-trade areas that eliminate trade barriers between their members; customs unions that adopt a common external tariff in addition to enjoying duty-free access to members' markets; common markets that extend the customs union to freeing the movement of capital and labor between members; and economic unions that aspire to coordinate members' economic policies.

complementary fiscal and other structural adjustment reforms that would collectively supplement the national reforms of the member countries.

By 1990, the regional loans had been under preparation for at least three years, with the Bank discussing them with the respective recipient regional-agency staffs and their member governments, as well as with other concerned multilaterals, namely, the IMF, the European Community, UNDP, and the African Development Bank.

However, there was also a good deal of lingering skepticism in the World Bank about the fruitfulness of African economic integration as a Bank objective. It was frequently remarked that integration's track record had been repeatedly poor, not only in Africa but also in several Latin American experiments. In late January 1990, a month before the Bank was to meet with the multilaterals just mentioned, Enzo Grilli, later Italy's executive director at the Bank and subsequently at the IMF, wrote a forceful memorandum to Moeen Qureshi questioning the regional-integration push. Grilli's skepticism reflected a strong theoretical critique that trade blocs merely led to trade diversion rather than trade creation. Moreover, in the particular case the production benefits of integration tended to be small and uncertain; and the "equitable distribution of costs and benefits of regional cooperation is particularly tricky."[241]

There would be other skeptical voices.[242] For instance, there were important practical problems, such as how macroeconomic conditionality would work with integration in practice. The idea that the Bank would not disburse unless all six countries had met the tranch conditions was not plausible, particularly if the loan was part of any one country's financing plans.[243] The push led by regional management met with skepticism from other parts of the Bank, in part because of a record of overpromising by this team. Eventually the idea was dropped, and in its place a project to promote private cross-border investment was approved. Whereas regional economic integration was still designated as one of the Bank's priority goals in Africa, the region's actual integration agenda remained quite limited.

At the end of the 1980s it was estimated that Sub-Saharan Africa as a whole had more than two hundred multilateral institutions, many of them established for the ostensible purpose of promoting some aspect of regional integration. As of the mid-1990s, five regional groupings existed in the East and Southern Africa regions whose overlapping memberships and objectives were the source of considerable confusion.[244] In reality, with the exception of monetary union in the Francophone countries, the

---

241. Memorandum, Enzo R. Grilli to Moeen A. Qureshi, "Regional Integration and Regional SALs," January 22, 1990, para. 9.

242. Memorandum, Sarath Rajapatirana to Christian Poortman, April 17, 1990.

243. Memorandum, Stanley Fischer to M. Ismail Serageldin, "Regional SAL for UDEAC-BEAC Countries," January 13, 1990.

244. They include the Southern Africa Customs Union (SACU), the Common Monetary Area (CMA), the Southern African Development Community (SADC), the Common Market for Eastern and Southern Africa (COMESA), and the Cross-Border Initiative (CBI).

principal forces leading to regional integration have come from the informal channels of trade, capital flows, and labor migration. A region whose leadership has been notably recalcitrant in sharing power broadly within their own countries was unlikely in practice to be strongly committed to ceding power to extraterritorial jurisdictions.

Dominance and Image

During the 1970s, the easy availability of external resources—commodity booms, commercial loans, foreign aid—helped to erode both economic discipline and the Bank's leverage. Further reducing the Bank's leverage were forces internal to the Bank: the "McNamara lending factor," so to speak. In the new decade, the situation changed drastically and with it, the Bank's leverage with respect to the countries of the region. For one, the region's economic plight had worsened. Second, the Bank's lending increased sharply, in absolute but even more in relative terms. And finally, its coordination role was considerably strengthened.

That coordination was required was not an issue.[245] But the Bank's relative strengths meant coordination could very easily turn into domination. This became especially apparent when the institution assumed a pivotal role in financial coordination with the creation of the SPA, a much needed mechanism for institutionalizing donor coordination. Although the mechanism considerably enhanced the institution's leverage on borrowers (blocking a tranch release stopped the flow of cofinancing resources as well as the Bank's own resources), the IMF still retained the official gatekeeper role in most cases. The IMF was the senior partner in the policy framework papers (PFP), jointly prepared by the staff of the two institutions for countries undergoing adjustment programs. The "most important area of disagreement" between the two institutions was "the quantitative macro-economic framework," with Bank staff regarding the IMF's scenarios as "insufficiently growth-oriented."[246] The differences reflected the Fund's preoccupation with the size of the fiscal deficit and the level of external debt and the Bank's stronger concern with growth, as well as its more optimistic assumptions concerning the prospects of external financing. These differences spilled over into contentious debates on specific budgetary items, especially the size of the public investment program, the civil service wage bill, and the level of recurrent expenditures on material and supplies, with the Bank adopting a more relaxed stance than the IMF.

But it was its dominance of the intellectual discourse that solidified the Bank's preeminent role. Despite much publicized skirmishes with the UN Economic Commission for Africa, other multilaterals, even the IMF, were simply not in the same league as the Bank in terms of the sheer volume of analysis on the continent.

---

245. In a country as small as Burkina Faso, there were about 50 bilateral and multilateral donors with about 2,000 projects; and about 180 NGOs with another 2,400-odd projects.

246. Memorandum, Moeen A. Qureshi to Barber B. Conable, "Bank-Fund Differences on Country Strategies in Africa," March 21, 1989.

The bilaterals (with the exception of France and the Nordic countries) were in retreat, and notwithstanding some spirited action by a small academic community, by the early 1990s the Bank was claiming to be "involved in 90 percent of the analytical research on Africa."[247] Whatever the basis of this unsupported figure, such dominance raised uneasy questions about the realism of the macroeconomic projections and validity of underlying data submitted in the context of loan documentation. An internal memo was revealing in this regard:

> The choice of assumptions is critical in this context. . . . Since the objective of policy reform is to adjust the structure of the economy, data from the "structurally unadjusted" past is much less relevant for adjustment lending than for investment lending. Hence, the task managers for adjustment operations have much more latitude in their choice of assumptions. In the absence of a rigorous analytic framework that can quantify the results of policy reforms, a lot depends upon the discretion of the task manager. No matter that, in any particular country, the ICOR has never been less than 6 in the past. If there is to be a policy reform package that includes streamlining the public investment program and beefing up the local capital market, a point or two may be shaved-off the ICOR on that account. Or, if there is to be an adjustment of real interest rates from negative to positive, the marginal savings rate may be increased a few percentage points and, maybe, the ICOR reduced another half point or so to reflect "efficiency gains." Similar modifications may be made to import elasticities, export growth rates and so forth depending on the specifics of the policy reforms contemplated. Plug all these assumptions into the RMSM and you will get a rate of GDP growth that is constrained only by the imagination of the task manager and the requirements of the lending program.[248]

Yet the leverage provided by the Bank's dominance of both financial and intellectual resources rang hollow in many instances; leverage translated most easily to policy rhetoric, less so to policy adoption and still less to policy implementation. Leverage was also undermined by practical constraints such as the need to protect its portfolio (in Côte d'Ivoire), the need to demonstrate the credibility of its policy advice (in Ghana), and the need to exhaust a given volume of resources in a finite amount of time. The donors' insistence on a floor for Sub-Saharan Africa in IDA helped further rigidify the allocation system and reduce the Bank's leverage substantially: "If pressures to move us in that direction are not resisted, we will end up throwing money at Africa's real problems—as has been done in the past by the international community—with the inevitable result that structural change will not

247. World Bank, "Regional Briefing: Africa—February 3, 1993, Presentation by Mr. Jaycox," SecM93-181, February 18, 1993. p. 2.

248. Memorandum, Frank Earwaker to Robert Liebenthal, December 12, 1989, para. 5. RMSM refers to the macroeconomic consistency model used by the Bank. Another problem was that "there is absolutely no record in the project documents of the assumptions on which the projections are based." Memorandum, Frank Earwaker to Stanley Fischer, "Central African Republic: Comparability of Projections Made for the Frist SAC and for the Second SAC," April 10, 1990.

be institutionalized.[249] More often than its critics would have it, the Bank would give its borrowers the benefit of the doubt. In some cases this was an objective assessment that recognized the need for flexibility warranted by new analysis or a change in circumstances. In others ambitious managers and staff anxious to appear to be "doing" something undermined leverage. But it was not just that "leverage" was an elusive concept; it was also delusive, especially in the many countries where state capacity was so weak. The option of simply pulling out was exercised rarely and with a great deal of reluctance.

The period from 1980 onward witnessed economic decline in most of Sub-Saharan Africa and of unprecedented power being wielded by the Bretton Woods institutions. A corresponding sharp increase in vocal criticism of the Bank contributed to a growing "image problem" for the institution. A recurrent reproach of the Bank was that its policy prescriptions were highly standardized and unsuited to African realities. The search for the right "formula" for development has of course hardly been peculiar to the Bank, but its perceived intellectual leadership made it the most visible target. Furthermore critics often seized upon its intellectual pronouncements, which in the early 1980s had a distinct ideological edge. In reality, the Bank's operational approach, as distinct from its pronouncements, was not as uniform as its critics alleged and was shaped, to varying extents, by opportunities and constraints in individual countries. The operational caution was more evident early on in the decade, as Ernest Stern's thinking at the time indicated: "There . . . remains some question in my mind as to whether it is desirable to try and put out detailed guidance in an area where we ourselves are groping for the right approach or whether it would not be better, having laid down the policy, to await initiatives from the countries and the regions, stimulated of course by our own analysis of requirements."[250] But as the decade wore on, operational prerogatives drove oversimplification. Most borrowers had little internal capacity or financial alternatives to challenge the prescriptions. Others, more interested in emergency cash injections than in seriously implementing the paper agreements, signed on without much regard to the implications.

Some of the criticism from within Sub-Saharan Africa can be ascribed to the Bank's policy prescriptions, which disrupted existing cozy relationships that favored certain elites and interest groups. The thrust of Bank policy and lending stance in the 1980s uncovered some unpleasant realities in developing countries as a whole, not simply in Africa: realities of power, privilege, and plenty enjoyed by the few amidst widespread penury. Prospective changes in the status quo that threatened to alter the structure of power and privilege were bound to be fiercely resisted. And since many of the elites who felt threatened were the very ones who had access to

249. Memorandum, Ernest Stern to Shinji Asanuma, "Review of Country Lending Programs, FY 86–89," December 23, 1985.

250. Memorandum, Ernest Stern to Robert S. McNamara, "Lending for Structural Adjustment," January 31, 1980.

media to voice their views, the external perception was undoubtedly overplayed. This was evident in the Bank's approach on governance issues that were first brought to light by the LTPS at the urging of African intellectuals who were forthright about their own leadership's role in their nations' travails.

Criticisms of the Bank also stemmed from the fact that it was increasingly identified with the IMF, an equivalence that sat uneasily among Bank staff:

> Based on . . . discussions with government officials my personal observation is that our close and at times almost inseparable association and identification with the Fund may be creating some "image" problem for ourselves. Till recently, the Bank was treated relatively more favorably by the policy makers and opinion-makers in Africa, but this appears to be at stake. A number of specific factors may be eroding the goodwill and capital we have built up over time in Africa: the joint Policy Framework Paper (PFP) written mainly by the Fund staff; the primacy of the IMF in the discussions of the macroeconomic issues; and the Bank's support for adjustment only if the Fund program is on track. . . . Perhaps it may be impractical to ask for some "distancing" from the Fund but a renewed emphasis on our traditional role may not be out of place.[251]

Nonetheless, the reasons underlying the hostility toward the Bretton Woods institutions went much beyond the simple self-interest of threatened elites. In many cases it reflected genuine doubts about the appropriateness of their prescriptions, especially since the economic turnaround was much weaker than promised. The anger could also be traced to the perceived double standards of "accountability" being applied by the donor community. The borrowers were being told to institute major changes, many of which were risky both personally for their leaders and for the economies; then they were lectured on the need for accountability in their governance. Prescriptions zigzagged as one fad after another was deemed invalid and the next took its place. Meanwhile, the advisers making those demands faced no personal risk, and the institutions they represented were subject to little accountability, at either the institutional or personal level (nor for that matter were shareholders or external NGOs who pushed their own agendas). These realities contributed to a strong sense of indignation and resentment among the borrowers.

It was also evident that the Bank's "style" in Sub-Saharan Africa was different from that in other regions, even in countries that were as weak as many of those in Sub-Saharan Africa. On something as mundane as the 18 percent currencies in the

---

251. Memorandum, Ishrat Husain to Stanley Fischer, "Problems of Transition in the Structural Adjustment Programs," January 31, 1990, para. 13. The impact of the image was not merely on the dialogue. In March 1991 following the overthrow of President Moussa Traore in Mali, "the popular conception that they [Bank and Fund] were themselves complicit in the corrupt dealings of their clients, [was] expressed dramatically in Mali, where the local offices of the World Bank were attacked by angry crowds, while the IMF was sometimes referred to (by its French initials FMI) as *Famille Moussa et Intimes* ('Moussa Traore's Family and Friends')." Ernest Harsch, "Accumulators and Democrats: Challenging State Corruption in Africa," *Journal of Modern African Studies,* vol. 31, no. 1 (March 1993), p. 40.

IBRD's capital (see chapter 14), the Bank insisted on using the subscriptions of African countries to meet its own administrative expenses (rather than import precious foreign exchange to meet these expenses) in those countries. On the other hand, when China flatly refused to allow the Bank to do so, the Bank quietly overlooked it for more than a decade. These currencies had a maintenance-of-value clause, which meant that as SSA countries devalued their currencies, they had to pay twice. Even worse, these countries were not even IBRD borrowers but were still subject to such inequities. Bank staff and reports would tread much more cautiously with regard to a Brazil, China, India, or Russia than almost any SSA country.

The Bank's "image" problem made it more difficult for the institution to use less visible channels of influence. Although not discernible from the outside throughout the 1980s, this wide-ranging criticism of the Bank led to considerable hand-wringing within the Bank's management, who were somewhat baffled that their substantial efforts and good intentions were being so misinterpreted. At one level, there was a worry that the criticism would undermine the case for a larger IDA replenishment, already under stress from the often shrill critiques emanating from the environmental lobby. But more fundamentally, there were growing worries that the hostility toward the Bank was corroding the trust essential for a successful relationship with a borrower. Of all developing-country officials, African authorities tended to be the most sensitive to perceived slights. The Bank, as noted, had not always put its most seasoned or diplomatic foot forward in its representation in Africa. Relations between the Bank and ECA would have been almost comic had they not been so costly. When Elliot Berg went to Addis Ababa for comments on his 1981 report, senior officers would not receive him. Through the decade, relations between the Bank and ECA were decidedly lukewarm. In early 1989 they worsened following the publication of the Bank's *Africa's Adjustment and Growth in the 1980s* report (in collaboration with the UNDP). President Conable of the Bank quickly brought together the two parties—along with senior personnel from UNICEF, AfDB, UNDP, the EC, and IMF—in a "reconciliation meeting" in May 1989.[252]

Although the Bank was not prepared to make major changes in policy messages, it did take several steps to counter perceptions of arrogance. A council of African advisers was established in 1988. The LTPS was formulated through a wide-ranging consultative process both within and outside Africa. On a wide range of issues—poverty, roads, and water—the Bank either established or strengthened networks of African officials and intellectuals, donors, and NGOs, drawing upon them for analysis and strategy formulation or simply as a forum to exchange views among various participants.[253] EDI seminars and media events were also used to

252. "Joint Statement on Africa's Long-Term Development," May 10, 1989.

253. A mid-1990s Africa region task force on poverty reduction drew upon the advice of a group of distinguished Africans (called the "Oslo group," since it had been formed at the initiative of the Norwegian government).

establish stronger communication with middle-level officials and other sensitive opinionmakers in SSA countries.

These activities gradually began to move the Bank back toward its erstwhile emphasis on rehabilitating physical infrastructure while sustaining its more recent stress on the social sectors. In any case, quite apart from problems of image, the limited private sector response to the decade-long changes led the Bank to focus more strongly on microeconomic analysis: sectoral issues, investment priorities, institutional changes, regulatory changes, and privatization. The limitations of improvements in the macroeconomic-policy-stance lesson had been most evident from the Ghanaian experience, the country in which the Bank and donors had been most active through the 1980s. Although, as discussed in chapter 10, the turnaround in the economy had been impressive, the feeble response of the private sector remained a matter of concern.

Francophone Africa

Of all the external powers in Africa, France shared to a unique degree cultural, political, and economic interaction with its former African colonies.[254] When the winds of decolonization had been sweeping through Sub-Saharan Africa in the late 1950s, in Francophone Africa two stark alternatives presented themselves: Sékou Touré's seemingly heroic call that he would "prefer freedom in poverty to opulence in servitude" and, in Côte d'Ivoire, Houphouët-Boigny's opposition to the "mystique of independence" and a preference for a strong fraternal association with France. Two decades later, Côte d'Ivoire appeared to have had the best of it.

Although the Bank's involvement in the rest of Sub-Saharan Africa grew during the 1970s, in Francophone Africa it continued to play second fiddle to France, which regarded the institution with some suspicion, both as a potential competitor and possible Trojan horse for projecting U.S. influence into the region. During the 1980s, as the Bank's role increased, relations between France and the Bank alternated between cooperation and a deep animosity. France, along with other continental European powers, regarded the Bank's fervent conversion to markets and the private sector as an Anglo-Saxon ideological mind-set. Bank staff on their part regarded many of the objections from France as a cover for maintaining its hegemony over the region. France, they felt, had little interest in the Bank group other than how much IDA was directed toward Francophone countries. Views differed in areas as diverse as agricultural extension systems and trade reform. French interests affected reforms especially in the largest Francophone countries: Cameroon, Côte d'Ivoire, and Senegal. By the early 1990s while the Bank, the

254. A large literature has examined the French power in Africa. A good summary is Guy Martin, "Continuity and Change in Franco-African Relations," *Journal of Modern African Studies,* vol. 33, no. 1 (March 1995), pp. 1–20.

IMF, and even the Caisse Française de Développement (CFD) were severely critical of Cameroon's policies, the country became the largest recipient of French Official Development Assistance. In Rwanda, Mitterand's solid support of President Juvenal Habyarimana despite his association with the massacre of the Tutsi people in October 1990, meant that the Bank's hands-off policy mattered little. French interests similarly affected reforms in Togo.[255]

These differences came to a head over the issue of devaluation of the CFA franc, the mainstay of France's financial umbrella over the region. At the center of the controversy was Côte d'Ivoire, the crown jewel of French interests in the region and one of the most successful SSA countries until the mid-1980s.[256] Although the overvaluation of the CFA franc also affected the Bank's operations in other countries in the zone, the Bank's strategy was to attempt to resolve the issue by focusing on Côte d'Ivoire:[257]

> The Côte d'Ivoire has the largest total trade and is the most influential country in the CFA franc zone, and its economic and political stability is a major preoccupation of France. Although most of the other countries in the CFA Zone have also experienced a substantial loss of competitiveness since 1986, the Côte d'Ivoire will be the key player on exchange rate reform because of its leadership position in BCEAO, which has recently been the more dynamic of the Zone's two central banks. Failure to induce fundamental policy change in the RCI would either condemn most of the CFA zone countries to low growth and excessive dependence on external assistance for the foreseeable future or lead to the break up of one or both of the monetary unions.[258]

Côte d'Ivoire merits further discussion because of its pivotal role in the region. At the beginning of the 1980s, its situation was similar to that of many Latin American countries. Strong growth in the previous decade had led the government to become overconfident, as was manifest in a commercial borrowing binge. As the external environment deteriorated, the country faced a growing debt problem. The

255. A report in November 1992 by the CFD was apparently severely critical of French involvement, "citing criticism ('much harsher than this report') from the new generation of Africans which will take over leadership positions and 'judges severely the help we have given to its seniors.'" "France I: Democracy Tastes Sour," *Africa Confidential*, vol. 34, no. 5 (March 5, 1993), p. 5. See Serge Michailof, ed., *La France et l'Afrique: vade-mecum pour un nouveau voyage* (Paris: Editions Karthala, 1993). Michailof was the CFD director in Dakar.

256. For an Ivorian perspective on relations between the Bank and Cote d'Ivoire, see volume 2, chapter 4.

257. Thus in a note to Conable, Fischer, referring to a SAL to the Central African Republic, cautioned: "The main issue was once again the CFA franc. It is very difficult to discuss rational policies in the presence of so overvalued an exchange rate. And it is also difficult for PRE to discuss such operations when we insist—rightly—that an adequate macroeconomic framework is a necessary condition for adjustment lending." Memorandum, Stanley Fischer to Barber B. Conable, April 7, 1990. Cameroon and Senegal were other important examples.

258. World Bank, "Côte d'Ivoire: Structural Adjustment Program: Initiating Memoranda," June 13, 1991, pp. 4–5.

Bank's program of structural adjustment began with two SALs—one in 1981 and the second in 1983—in parallel with an IMF program: an Extended Fund Facility in 1981 and two standby agreements in 1984 and 1986. A later OED evaluation would report: "It was clear to Bank staff involved in both cases that there was lack of commitment and 'ownership' right from the beginning of the loans concerned."[259] Therefore it was not surprising that little structural change resulted, but it was masked for two reasons, both exogenous: commodity prices continued to be buoyant; the dollar's strength resulted in an effective devaluation of the CFA franc and boosted the competitiveness of exports.

Following the Plaza accord of 1985, a sharp depreciation of the dollar led to a strengthening of the CFA franc. Simultaneously, the prices of coffee and cocoa, Côte d'Ivoire's principal exports, tumbled, and caused large imbalances in the budget and the balance of payments. The Bank's recommended strategy focused on increasing agricultural production and exports, and it pressed Côte d'Ivoire to cut producer prices, in light of sharply falling international prices. However, the president, Houphouët-Boigny, adamantly refused, confident that history was on his side; prices had fallen many times earlier and each time they had rebounded.

A third SAL was initiated in 1986, emphasizing reductions in recurrent expenditures, but the Ivorian government continued its questionable investments.[260] Yet, as with the earlier SAL, tranch releases were approved despite a spotty record on compliance with conditionality, either because "non-economic factors may have been given considerable weight and/or country relations concerns were seen as paramount."[261]

In May 1987, with external prospects continuing to deteriorate, Côte d'Ivoire suspended external debt-service payments. Within the Bank, as the dust of the 1987 reorganization began to settle, the new director decided to change tack; he proposed a series of SECALs, beginning with an Agriculture SECAL (AgSECAL) aimed at reducing the relative price of cocoa (with respect to coffee) paid to producers. The government, however, remained "fundamentally opposed" to this change, as well as to any reductions in the civil service wage bill. Ignoring the checkered past of the three previous SALs, the initiating memorandum for the AgSECAL called attention to the country's "five years of courageous adjustment efforts" and attributed the setbacks in 1987 to "reasons totally beyond its [that is, the country's] control."[262] Concluding that "the Government's excellent track

259. World Bank, "Effectiveness of SAL Supervision and Monitoring," OED Report 9711, June 26, 1991, para. 39.

260. These included extravagant expenditures on the grand basilica and an agriculture school (ENSA), both in Yamoussoukro.

261. Portfolio Management Task Force, "Supervision of Policy Based Loans," Working Paper C, 1992, p. 53.

262. These included "a substantial drop in export prices of cocoa and coffee; a sharp appreciation of the CFA franc against the US dollar; and a decline in the international demand for Ivorian coffee." Memorandum, Christian Poortman to Moeen A. Qureshi, "Côte D'Ivoire: Revised Update of Economic Situation and Bank Strategy," October 21, 1987, with attachment, "Republic of Côte d'Ivoire: Update of Economic Situation and Bank Strategy," para. 3.

record in pursuing reforms and respecting its debt commitments is well established," the memorandum called for "strong external support."[263] In addition, an ESAL (Energy SECAL) was initiated.

The proposal met with widespread skepticism from other parts of the Bank. The financial policy and risk management vice presidency worried about the implications for the IBRD portfolio. Arguing that the adjustment scenario envisaged in SAL III was "no longer valid," D. C. Rao, in a highly critical review, called for "a thorough reassessment of the Bank's assistance strategy."[264] The uneasiness again surfaced a few months later when Rao "urge[d] the operations committee to ask the Region to present a more complete and better documented review of the Bank assistance strategy . . . before proceeding much further with the processing of the two adjustment operations now being proposed."[265] Vice President Joseph Wood warned that the proposed strategy was "excessively risky for the Bank," especially since the country "so far has demonstrated only modest results (in terms of efficiency gains) from 5 years of adjustment efforts."[266] The skepticism was echoed from the research complex. Alex Shakow cautioned his senior vice president, David Hopper, that it was "alarming that, after 3 SALs, the Côte d'Ivoire now has to embark on a recovery program." In particular he questioned why SECALs had been chosen at this stage when the adjustment issues were still macroeconomic (particularly fiscal and exchange rate issues).

With the "first-best" policy instrument of devaluation ruled out, the question of how to adjust relative prices between tradable and nontradable goods became increasingly pressing. As part of the third SAL, the Bank attempted to pursue a "second-best" strategy (in substitution for a devaluation) of import tariffs cum export subsidies. The sophisticated administrative capacity that this would entail—from information gathering to processing and enforcement—and the effects of smuggling, given the porous borders of the country, were glossed over. The entire exercise proved futile, a case of technical sophistication overwhelming administrative realities.

By 1989, the course of events escalated tensions among the Bank, the IMF, France, and Côte d'Ivoire. These issues centered around concerns with arrears, the risk of Côte d'Ivoire going into nonaccrual status, and the parity of the CFA franc. With the Africa region of the Bank preparing to place three SECALs (agriculture, energy, and water) to the Board for approval, strong objections were raised once again from other quarters of the institution. The vice president of the finance and

263. Ibid., para. 34.

264. Memorandum, D. C. Rao to M. Ismail Serageldin, "Côte d'Ivoire—Creditworthiness," September 18, 1987.

265. Memorandum, D. C. Rao to Vinod Dubey, "Côte d'Ivoire—Bank Assistance Strategy," November 16, 1987, para. 12.

266. Memorandum, D. Joseph Wood to Moeen A. Qureshi, "Côte d'Ivoire—Bank Assistance Strategy," December 9, 1987.

risk policy department refused to sign three statutory committee reports on the proposed loans (suggesting instead an investment loan or two), believing that the institution did not have "a viable basis for IBRD lending" to the country.[267] Indeed, "the major issue identified by the region, the OC [Operations Committee] and the PC [Policy Committee] is the present lack of credibility of the Government's medium-term macroeconomic framework, due to the critical need for an exchange rate devaluation, while there is no consensus with the Fund and the French government that a devaluation be undertaken."[268] Within the Bank two views on adjustment lending had emerged. In contrast to the views of the development economics vice presidency, the Africa region argued that the absence of a suitable macroeconomic environment should not a priori rule out adjustment lending. Indeed, SECALs were seen as a practical alternative of ensuring that at least some movement towards policy change was taking place while ensuring crucial balance of payments support.

As the Bank's senior management struggled with the issue of the three SECALs, Conable was advised that though a short-term program had been put in place,

> nevertheless, there is also agreement among the staff that it would be a gross mis-representation to our Board to pretend that Cote d'Ivoire has developed a Medium-term Program of economic adjustment. Cote d'Ivoire's creditworthiness presents a major issue for the Bank and it will be seen by other countries (including Egypt) as another example that the Bank will, if put under sufficient political pressure, provide adjustment lending in the absence of a Medium-term Program.[269]

Anxious about Côte d'Ivoire's arrears, the Bank was increasingly looking to "the possibility of using the French loan to clear up arrears until about December 1, thus giving the government some breathing room."[270] France's pivotal role in filling the gap, together with its potential contributions in a forthcoming IDA replenishment, enhanced its influence. Although dubious about the economic merits of the loans, managers in the finance complex cautioned that "we should, if at all possible, avoid a confrontation with France prior to the conclusion of the IDA negotiations,"[271] which prompted Stern to warn Conable, "By now, we have all been contacted by various levels of the French Government. There is no doubt that they take the matter very seriously and that it has the potential of adversely affecting a wide range of relations."[272]

267. Memorandum, D. Joseph Wood to Ernest Stern, "Côte d'Ivoire," August 24, 1989.

268. Memorandum, Kevin Cleaver to Moeen A. Qureshi, "Côte D'Ivoire—Agriculture Sector Adjustment Operation (ASAL)," September 15, 1989, para. 6.

269. "Your Meeting with Mr. Camdessus," undated and unsigned memo to Barber B. Conable, in President Conable's Côte d'Ivoire country file.

270. Memorandum, M. Ismail Serageldin through Moeen A. Qureshi to Barber B. Conable, "Côte d'Ivoire—Meeting with Mr. Moise Koumoué Koffi, Minister of Budget," September 18, 1989, para. 4.

271. Memorandum, D. Joseph Wood to Ernest Stern, August 24, 1989.

272. Memorandum, Ernest Stern to Barber B. Conable, September 27, 1989.

The IMF approved a standby in November 1989 and the Bank approved the set of three SECALs (agriculture and energy in October and December 1989 and a water-SECAL in June 1990). Despite reasonable progress on the latter two SECALs, the overall macroeconomic situation continued to deteriorate. A joint Bank-Fund mission in February 1990 already concluded that "the program was off-track" and recommended cuts in budgetary current expenditures, including public sector wages. The ensuing social and political unrest led the government hurriedly to announce compensating measures. The initial plan that had been agreed between the IMF, donors, and the Bank in October 1989 called for a two-stage reform process: first, a stabilization program redressing the fiscal deficit; and, second, medium-term issues of competitiveness and wages. "However, in December 1989, we and the IMF prevailed upon the government to accelerate the schedule and collapse the two stages into one. They did, and it misfired. The political situation got out of hand with government authority fast disintegrating."[273]

In mid-April, Houphouët-Boigny appointed Allassane Ouattara, chairman of BCEAO and former head of the IMF's Africa department, to take charge of the adjustment program.[274] Ouattara's reputation ensured that a "new Letter of Intent will be initialed by the IMF and Mr. Ouattara on May 10. This, in turn, will prompt the French government to release the first tranche of its SAL in the equivalent amount of $75 million. It would be used to clear up Cote d'Ivoire's arrears vis-à-vis the Bank, which have now reached $78 million."[275] By June 1990 the IMF had approved a new enhanced program, but the arrears situation was again precarious and this limited the scope of action by the Bank. Progress on implementing conditionalities on the adjustment loans was slower than expected, with the result that disbursements from the Bank and cofinancers fell substantially below projections. Other sources of money also did not materialize, and by November, with the country again in arrears ($87 million), the Bank asked France to provide bridge financing for about FF 800 million until the expected disbursement of other loans came through. The Bank's anxiety was understandable. Upon pressing Côte d'Ivoire's officials about the repeated nature of late payments to the Bank and threatening to suspend disbursements, the officials "informally related the servicing of IBRD debt with the size and timing of IBRD disbursements."[276] With internal analysis projecting continued economic stagnation in the near future, the issue of debt servicing remained at center stage.

273. Memorandum, Moeen A. Qureshi to Barber B. Conable, "Côte d'Ivoire: Next Steps," June 5, 1990, para. 2.
274. The Banque centrale des Etats de l'Afrique de l'Ouest (BCEAO) is the common central bank of the seven member countries of the West African Monetary Union, the common currency of which is the franc de la Communauté financière d'Afrique.
275. Memorandum, Pierre Landell-Mills to Barber B. Conable, "Côte d'Ivoire . . . ," May 9, 1990.
276. World Bank, "Country: Côte d'Ivoire," briefing for Barber B. Conable, September 19, 1990.

By this time there was a growing consensus within the Bank that adjustment through deflation would simply not work. The Operations Committee concluded that "there were no prospects for a medium-term recovery of Côte d'Ivoire without a real devaluation . . . within the foreseeable future, i.e. the next 18 months. . . . This strategy clearly puts the issue of devaluation at the core of the Bank's decisions concerning lending after the interim phase. Resolution of this issue would require extremely sensitive discussions with France at the highest level."[277]

Given the preeminence of the IMF in exchange rate issues, the question of devaluation would become a sore point between the Bretton Woods institutions.[278] Because the parity of the CFA franc concerned all members of the monetary zone, a devaluation was a complex and difficult matter. Although all countries in the zone were by now suffering from the effects of overvaluation, the degree varied among countries. The CFA franc zone had been a bulwark of monetary stability in a region where stability was a rarity. Some feared that a devaluation would simply spark inflation, wipe out the gains, and force the country into a flexible—and unstable— exchange rate regime. The monetary relationship between the CFA franc and the French franc meant that any decision to devalue first had to have the blessing of France, as the guarantor of convertibility. All thirteen countries of Africa's CFA zone and the two central banks had to be consulted. Moreover, effective im- plementation of a devaluation and the necessary package of accompanying measures simultaneously in thirteen independent countries would pose a major challenge. For such a devaluation to have a reasonable probability of success, the preparatory work had to be done by a handful of key players. The work needed to be shrouded in secrecy and completed swiftly, since, in a fixed-exchange rate regime, talk of devaluation would result in capital flight and make the prospects of devaluation self-fulfilling. Bank staff had been examining the challenges facing the CFA zone since the mid-1980s, but any ideas about changing the exchange rate regime were quietly dropped under instructions from senior management.[279] In 1989 a decision was taken to examine the many interrelated issues that would affect a successful realignment of the CFA zone and restore competitiveness while retaining monetary stability.[280] By mid-1991, following extensive analysis, Bank

277. Minutes of the Operations Committee to consider "Republic of Côte d'Ivoire— Agriculture Sector Adjustment Loan," held on August 29, 1989, p. 2.

278. In the 1980s the Bank frequently crossed into the IMF's domain on exchange rate issues (see volume 2, chapter 11). The rationale, as Stern explained in the case of Zimbabwe, was "our concern to strengthen Zimbabwe's competitive position in the export market has also led us to focus on the two elements which are principally in the Fund's domain: the exchange rate and the size of the budget deficit." Memorandum, Ernest Stern to Richard Erb, "Zimbabwe—Discussions with Government on Policy Reform," June 27, 1986.

279. Kathie L. Krumm, "Adjustment in the Franc Zone: Focus on the Real Exchange Rate," Report CPD 8707, April 1987.

280. The sensitivity was so acute that the project was even given a code name—"Project Z"—the letter "Z" implying that this was the "last option."

staff recommended a one-time real depreciation of "40 percent in foreign currency terms (or 67 percent in CFA terms)."[281]

Ministers from France periodically warned the Bank that "this was an important 'dossier' for France, economically and politically."[282] At a meeting of the ministers of the franc zone in Ouagadougou at this time, the French minister of finance confirmed France's belief that a parity change of the CFA franc was not an issue and in a letter to Conable expressed his "deep concern" that despite the actions of the Ivorian government in restructuring the administration and efforts on the fiscal side, the Bank was not putting in place fast-disbursing loans during fiscal 1991. France's strong views were also shaped by a growing intellectual conviction against devaluation arising from the idea of the "franc fort" in the context of European monetary union. Furthermore, quite apart from French interests, devaluation was adamantly opposed by much of Francophone Africa's elite, which stood to lose their relatively lavish import-intensive lifestyle in the event of a devaluation.

In late 1990 Ouattara was appointed prime minister. About the same time the Bank appointed Michael Gillette the new director of the Francophone countries. Gillette traveled to Côte d'Ivoire in January 1991 and warned Ouattara that it would no longer be possible for the Bank to condone further tranch releases unless tranch-release conditions were met. In return he promised that the Bank would commit itself to a new set of three adjustment loans conditioned on a medium-term framework explicitly addressing the competitiveness of the economy. But the government's response, when it came two months later, did not credibly address the overvaluation of the exchange rate. In the absence of a nominal exchange rate adjustment, the Bank concluded that "unless massive wage and budget cuts were introduced, which may not be politically and socially feasible, chances for restoring growth and competitiveness were slim."[283]

Meanwhile, the earlier SECALs had been progressing reasonably well, with the exception of the AgSECAL, the third tranch of which had stalled since three critical conditions were outstanding.[284] The reasons seemed evident to the Bank: "So far as we can tell, the Government's reluctance to fulfill these three conditions stems principally from political considerations. These agricultural institutions were

281. World Bank, "External Adjustment in the CFA Zone: Issues and Options," August 12, 1991, para. 6.

282. Memorandum, Jean-Louis Sarbib to Edward Jaycox, through Edwin Lim, "Meeting between Mr. Qureshi and the French Minister of Cooperation [Ms. Edwige Aviceh]." August 23, 1991.

283. Memorandum, Franz Kaps to files, May 7, 1991, para. 8, citing document submitted to Ouattara and K. Kablan Duncan (minister of economy).

284. These conditions related to a reform of the agriculture credit Bank (BNDA), the stabilization fund (CAISSTAB), and the price equalization fund (Caisse de Perequation). Performing loans in the BNDA amounted to some CFAF 5 billion out of a total portfolio of CFAF 75 billion.

in the past the principal sources of guaranteed rents as well as the origin of enormous non-budgetized funds used by the political leadership."[285]

The third tranch of the AgSAL was released in early June. At the same time a joint Bank-IMF mission to the country was unable to reach agreement with the government on either a stabilization program or a medium-term framework. At the end of the month (June 1991), Ouattara visited Washington. A briefing prepared for Conable noted that "as Mr. Ouattara knows very well, the Bank cannot envisage providing any more quick disbursing assistance without an agreed medium-term framework for adjustment. This discussion has been going on for three years, frankly without significant progress—the credibility of both Bank and the Fund is on the line on the issue of real adjustment in the franc zone countries." Conable was asked to seek assurances from Ouattara "on the precise extent of the adjustment needed in the Real Effective Exchange Rate [and to] suggest [that] Mr. Ouattara write all this [various assurances concerning exchange rate, time period over which depreciation would occur, and precise trigger points] in a letter to you which will be kept strictly confidential."[286]

Institutional leverage was, however, undermined by the IMF's refusal to act on the issue. Periodically the IMF would approve a one-year stabilization program with assurances that things were just about to get better.[287] Its repeated lack of success did not deter the Fund from concluding further agreements. Given the Fund's continued inaction on the exchange rate issue and strong protests by France, the Bank maintained a facade of avoiding any direct mention of the subject by couching its approach to the Ivorians in terms of "competitiveness." The country would have to adjust its cost structure of tradables and nontradables to become competitive. And, there were only two alternatives: reduce the cost structure in the modern sectors by a direct assault on wage levels in the public sector (which was a leader for the modern sectors), to be followed by changes in the modern private sector or, second, change the exchange rate parity.

Nonetheless, the Bank began preparing another set of three quick-disbursing policy loans to restructure the financial sector, support programs for the human resources sector, and address competitiveness and regulatory issues. The fact that a quick-disbursing instrument was being used to address one of the most difficult long-term issues—human resource development—demonstrated the extent to which balance of payments imperatives were in the driver's seat. The three new SECALs were ready in June 1991,[288] but their presentation to the Operations

285. Memorandum, Michael J. Gillette to Barber B. Conable, "Côte d'Ivoire—Visit of Ivorian Minister of Agriculture," April 5, 1991, para. 9.

286. The Bank was pushing between 30 and 35 percent. World Bank, "Côte d'Ivoire: Talking Points for Meeting with Mr. Ouattara," June 28, 1996.

287. Michael Gillette, interview with the authors, December 29, 1992.

288. The initial program called for $330 million for the three SECALs. This was raised to $450 million to "maintain a positive net transfer position during the critical first two years of

Committee was delayed as arrears once again forced the Bank to suspend disbursements.[289] At a tense OC meeting the region argued that the country now had a medium-term framework obliging it to take some fairly draconian steps in developing its future. In return the Bank would provide official liquidity at this juncture so that the Ivorians did not fall behind in their debt-service obligations to the Bank, while at the same time trying to make policy adjustments in the context of the medium-term framework. However, disbursement conditions on the second tranche were to be linked to a resolution of the "competitiveness" issue. Staff analysis estimated that this would require a devaluation of at least 30–35 percent, which they were confident was virtually impossible to achieve in the time frame through internal compression. The precipitous decline of the country's economy had one silver lining (real per capita GNP declined by 25 percent between 1986 and 1990): it was declared IDA eligible at the end of June.[290] Objections from the finance complex that the country was not creditworthy and posed unacceptable financial risks to the Bank were overcome by front-loading the operations with IDA—in short, IDA funds were put at risk to pull the IBRD's chestnuts out of the fire.[291] These restraints proved effective in limiting the Bank's financial exposure. Another two years would pass before the devaluation would occur. The second tranches of the three loans amounting to $250 million were withheld. At the time of devaluation IDA credits were substituted for the unreleased IBRD loan tranches.

At the time, however, Gillette's adamant stance had ruffled many feathers. Strained relations with France on the CFA issue came to a head in 1991–92, when Stern, in a note to the files, stated: "Let us be clear that there will be *no* reference (direct, indirect, implied, hinted) to this [CFA franc] issue by us in any IDA-related document or in any of our discussions with *any* delegation or official."[292] One consequence was that Gillette, who had been strongly pressing the CFA devaluation issue, was removed from his position in May 1992 under pressure from France,

---

its implementation until the economy responds to the adjustment measures and is able to start servicing its restructured external debt." Letter, Barber B. Conable to Pierre Bérégovy, Minister of State, Economy, Finance, and Budget, May 9, 1991, unofficial translation, p. 8.

289. Overdue service payments totaled approximately US$34 million. IBRD/IDA, Memorandum from the vice president and secretary, "Côte d'Ivoire: Suspension of Disbursements," SecM91-944, IDA/SecM91-285, July 22, 1991.

290. At France's urging, Stern had asked the country department to examine the country's eligibility for IDA. The analysis found that per capita GNP in 1990 stood at $720 (using the Atlas methodology) or $728 (current exchange rate method), "slightly below" the IDA eligibility cutoff of US $740.

291. The $200 million financial sector adjustment loan was approved in October 1991. The $100 million competitiveness and regulatory reform loan and the human resources development adjustment loan were both approved in December.

292. Memorandum, Ernest Stern to files, "France—Discussions on January 11, 1992," January 14, 1992; emphasis in original.

a rare instance in which a senior Bank manager was asked to step down.[293] Once again the Bank was caught in the complex web of IDA replenishment negotiations. France's contribution to IDA 8, IDA 9, and IDA 10 totaled 2.54 billion SDR. IDA lending to the CFA countries in the same period totaled 3.66 billion SDR.

Gillette claimed that the Bank was never really able to engage the French Treasury in any meaningful discussion of a long-term framework or the competitiveness in the franc zone. The French Treasury forbade its staff to discuss the issues, even informally. But fixed parity had served the region well for many decades, imposing a monetary discipline that countries in other parts of the region could only envy. Even within the Bank, some were concerned that too much was being made of the benefits of devaluation as a panacea for the country's problems. Returning from a visit to the country, Ishrat Husain, the Africa region's chief economist, noted in late 1991:

> I was struck by the little progress that has been made in IVC [Côte d'Ivoire] in liberalizing factor and goods markets. The rigidities in the labor market in the hiring and firing of workers, in the access and availability of capital, excessive taxes and tariffs, fees of various kinds on almost all type of private sector transactions and pervasive price controls in the economy were something which I had not registered fully. Perhaps I had focussed too narrowly on the exchange rate issue. I agree with the Minister of Finance that, unless these rigidities are eliminated, the response to exchange rate changes is likely to be muted as the transmission mechanism from relative price changes to corresponding changes in investment and output decision would be muted.[294]

The CFA parity issue in general and Côte d'Ivoire in particular also became a sore point in the Bank's relations with the IMF, which described it as an "Argentina in reverse"[295]:

> The IMF is now preparing an interim 12 month stabilization program to cover the period from mid-1991 to mid-1992. . . . Without a viable medium term framework in which to place its program, the Fund may have to aim at extremely large increases in revenues, which, in view of the 15 percent decline in revenues since 1988, are unlikely to be achievable in the face of a continuing decline in GDP and imports. . . . An indication of the Fund's commitment to this program is that its own net exposure in the Côte d'Ivoire would actually decline during the program period as repayments to the IMF would be larger than new drawings.[296]

293. Michael Gillette, interview with the authors, December 29, 1992, p. 14.

294. Memorandum, Ishrat Husain to Edward Jaycox, "Mission to Nigeria and Côte d'Ivoire—November 4–12, 1991," para. 20.

295. "Your Meeting with Mr. Camdessus," undated and unsigned memorandum to Barber B. Conable, in President Conable's Côte d'Ivoire country file. The reference was to the 1988 confrontation between the Bank and the IMF on lending to Argentina. See volume 2, chapter 11.

296. World Bank, "Côte d'Ivoire: Structural Adjustment Program," p. 3.

The subject was raised between Conable and Michel Camdessus in one of their periodic meetings, without any resolution.[297] Camdessus informed Conable (as relayed by Lawrence Summers who had become chief economist of the Bank), that "the Fund did not need any more assurances from the Ivorians, that they were prepared to trust Ouattara and support him now because of his political difficulties."[298] Quite apart from political factors, the IMF's predilection for anti-inflation policies (which could involve a fixed exchange rate as "nominal anchor") would have made it more supportive of the fixed CFA than the World Bank. It justified its stance by maintaining that the real effective exchange rates in the region were only slightly overvalued (less than 10 percent), in contrast to the Bank's substantially higher estimates (between 20 and 40 percent).[299]

A year after the approval of the SECALs, progress had been achieved on a number of reform conditions. However, there was no resolution of the competitiveness issue. The Bank refused to budge on the second tranch release of all three loans despite continuing pressures from both the country and France. In August 1992, in a meeting of the heads of Francophone African countries, there were indications that the leaders would agree to a devaluation. However, pending elections in Cameroon served as an excuse to postpone the decision.

Following Gillette's dismissal, the Ivorians continued to press for a waiver of the second tranch conditions through the French alternate executive director by questioning the legal nature of the "competitiveness conditionality" relating to the release of the second tranch of all three SECALs.[300] At the annual meetings in 1992, Jaycox's remarks to the Ivorian delegation revealed the impasse that had been reached:

297. Memorandum, Sven Sandstrom to Michael J. Gillette. "RE: Camdessus Lunch," July 27, 1991.

298. Memorandum, Michael J. Gillette to Franz Kaps, "RCI," July 30, 1991.

299. James M. Boughton, "The CFA Franc Zone: Currency Union and Monetary Standard," IMF Research Department, Working Paper WP/91/133, December 1991. IMF, "External Adjustment in the CFA Franc Zone: Issues and Options," 1991. For Côte d'Ivoire, however, the report estimated that the figure was "substantially higher." Four years later another IMF report estimated that "by 1990–91, the two largest economies in the franc zone, Côte d'Ivoire and Cameroon, incurred the highest real appreciation (36 percent and 32 percent, respectively)." Nashashibi and Bazzoni, "Exchange Rate Strategies," p. 101.

300. The government had submitted to the Bank a document entitled "Medium-term Framework (MTF) for Economic and Financial Policies, 1991–1995." Para. 32 of the MTF stated: "The Government will restore the competitiveness of the economy in accord with agreed indicators before requesting the release of the second tranche of any of the sector adjustment loans currently under preparation in support of this medium-term framework. The Government will hold periodic reviews on this issue with the World Bank and the IMF to assure consistency in its program. Similarly, when presenting its respective letters requesting Bank assistance to sector policies, the government stated each time [that] . . . the Program will be implemented in the context of the Medium-Term Framework." Memorandum, Franz Kaps to Edward Jaycox, "RCI—Meeting with French Alternate ED," September 14, 1992.

Mr. Jaycox . . . noted that, despite having made remarkable efforts in the area of internal adjustment, RCI had lost about 30 percent of its GNP over the last few years and it appeared to him that the Government was at the end of the road. In response, the Minister acknowledged that the UMOA [West African Monetary Union] heads of state had decided against a parity change and opted for renewed efforts in internal adjustment. . . . Mr. Jaycox commented that neither the Bank nor the IMF had any new ideas on how to resolve the competitiveness issue. Reducing the civil service force does not suffice; rather there was a need for substantial nominal salary cuts—in the order of 30 percent or more. He asked the Minister whether he thought that such a dramatic move was possible; a much smaller salary cut had been tried two and a half years ago but had failed.[301]

If the Bank regarded its "marge de manoeuvre" as "rather limited" without a resolution of major macro issues, French officials were deeply unhappy at what they perceived as the Bank's dogmatic position on devaluation despite France's servicing of Côte d'Ivoire's debt service to the Bank: "'Ces discussions vont durablement affecter nos relations avec la Banque.'"[302]

But the continued economic travails of Francophone Africa and the mounting financial costs to France meant that it was only a matter of time before devaluation occurred. When France had earlier given up its veto rights in the two regional central banks, it had established ceilings for annual increases in credits to member governments. However, state enterprises were excluded, which proved to be a severe problem. For about five years there had been widespread public speculation on the devaluation of the CFA franc. Economic decline was exacerbated by the large capital flight that had ensued, and this increased pressures for a devaluation. With France committed to meeting the Maastricht criteria for the European Monetary Union (EMU), the strong link between the French franc and the Deutsche mark meant that, to a degree, Francophone Africa's economic fortunes would be yoked to the Bundesbank's policies. During 1993 France quietly began to lay the technical and political groundwork for the devaluation. By late 1993 devaluation awaited growing behind-the-scenes pressures to overcome the strong resistance of Senegal and elections in Gabon at the end of the year. The death of Houphouët Boigny in December 1993 removed a major symbolic resistance, and in January 1994 the CFA franc was devalued to 50 percent (of its previous value in French francs).

In the immediate aftermath of the devaluation, Côte d'Ivoire's fears of monetary instability proved unfounded; growth was robust, although the results were more muted for other members of the zone. Unlike other countries in Sub-Saharan Africa, Côte d'Ivoire, because of its rigidity to the CFA, had forced both the Bank and the Francophone countries of the region to come to grips with microlevel

301. Memorandum, Franz Kaps to files, "Côte d'Ivoire—Meeting with Government Delegation," September 23, 1992.

302. Memorandum, Franz Kaps, "RCI—Mr. Lafourcade's Meeting with French Ambassador [to Côte d'Ivoire]," October 30, 1992.

impediments that saddled the economies with inefficiencies. The growth response, once devaluation came, was in large part a reflection of the brush clearing that such prior efforts had accomplished.

The issues were never as stark as Bank partisans of devaluation made them out to be. During the same period the Bank was taking a much softer line on devaluation in Mexico and the reverse position—*against* devaluation in Argentina and Peru—despite mounting evidence of overvaluation in those countries (chapter 11). As noted earlier, even the Bank's chief economist was concerned about the frequency and intensity with which the policy prescription of devaluation was invoked without a careful evaluation of the negatives. Sub-Saharan Africa, with a preponderance of small countries in desperate financial straits and limited institutional capacity, was poorly equipped to resist the Bank's policy advice, which in some instances was propounded like the laws of nature. In the case of Côte d'Ivoire and the CFA zone, France intervened with a passion rare for a major power toward impoverished countries. In some cases, as in the Bank's indiscriminate approach to the region's agricultural parastatals or agriculture extension systems, France's opposition played a moderating role. But in the case of the CFA franc, its intervention backfired, prolonging the region's problems.

Financial Resource Constraints and Debt

To an unexpected degree, Sub-Saharan Africa's economic fortunes in the 1980s and the World Bank's involvement with them revolved around the problem of external debt. The problem was "unexpected," not because it was not acute for the region, but because Africa's borrowing abroad had, in absolute terms, been far less than Latin America's and consequently posed nothing like the same threats to the global financial system. Moreover, unlike in Latin America, in Africa the bulk of indebtedness was to official lenders, who as a group were quicker than private banks to agree to debt adjustments and, to begin with, had done much of their lending to Sub-Saharan Africa on concessional terms. Yet debt was indeed writ large in the SSA-World Bank relationship in this period.

Like other developing regions, Sub-Saharan Africa had responded to the shocks of the 1970s by increasing its reliance on external resources. This increase was funded mainly by an expansion of long-term loans from official and private sources—the latter largely underwritten by export credit agencies. Between 1973 and 1983 Sub-Saharan Africa's debt grew sixfold, with the volume of official lending lagging loans from private creditors. After the second oil shock, SSA countries tried to bridge widening payments gaps with a burst of relatively short-term external borrowing, mostly from the IMF or commercial sources. As their financial condition worsened, private flows dried up and official concessional flows stepped into the breach. By the mid-1980s, the debt issue had become intertwined with the levels of output and exports.[303]

Compared with Latin America, Africa experienced less dispute over solvency. As early as 1984, an internal Bank paper argued that if the international community was sincerely committed to Africa's development, it was tempting to tell creditors simply: "Debt to Africa is lost."[304] But the report cited several reasons why the reality had to be glossed over: the importance of preferred creditors (the multilateral institutions) in this debt; the weak financial position of creditor governmental and quasi-governmental institutions, especially their export insurance agencies; the need to maintain a modicum of access to commercial finance; and creditor country concerns about spill-over effects to Latin America, where their financial stakes were much higher.

As Sub-Saharan Africa's financial crisis intensified in the mid-1980s, various proposals were mooted by the international community to alleviate the region's debt burden: an IMF gold sales program, rescheduling multilateral debt, the creation of a debt-relief facility partly backed by World Bank capital; and a special (non-quota) allocation of SDRs to be used to service multilateral debt.[305] In a 1986 report, "Financing Adjustment with Growth in Sub-Saharan Africa," the Bank analyzed the gravity of the debt problem and the possible impact of various solutions then being floated. The report singled out a number of countries that, given their debt burden and export prospects, were unlikely to grow out of this problem within the next decade. A year later an internal analysis concluded that many countries face "a severe cash flow problem,"[306] which arose "in large part because a high proportion of debt service must be paid to preferred creditors."[307]

During the first half of 1987 Bank staff held informal discussions with selected donor countries (both within an outside the context of the Paris Club) regarding

303. See Charles Humphreys and John Underwood, "The External Debt Difficulties of Low-Income Africa," in Ishrat Husain and Ishac Diwan, eds., *Dealing with the Debt Crisis* (World Bank, 1989), chap. 3.

304. World Bank, "Notes on the Debt and Prospects of Sub-Saharan Africa," prepared for Colloquium on International Debt and the Developing Countries, July 25–27, 1984, Harper's Ferry, W. Va.

305. The last from the European Union, the so-called "Delors initiative" in 1987.

306. World Bank, "Alternative Rescheduling Scenarios for Debt of the Poorest African Countries," May 12, 1987, p. 3. The analysis based on twenty-two countries undertaking major reforms was that "[B]ased on all known sources of additional aid flows (including IDA-8), basic commodity trade prospects, and current approaches to the debt issue, per capita income growth prospects for this group are marginal and per capita consumption prospects are negative." Twelve of twenty-two countries with major debt problems were in Sub-Saharan Africa: The Gambia, Madagascar, Mali, Mauritania, Niger, Senegal, Sierra Leone, Somalia, Tanzania, Togo, Zaire, and Zambia. Other poor countries outside Africa included Haiti and Nepal.

307. World Bank, "Current Bank Work on African Debt Issues," May 22, 1987, p. 2.

the possibility of providing special debt relief to twelve to fifteen countries in the region. The G-10, meeting on Africa's debt problem in Paris, was unwilling to act on reductions in interest rates, choosing instead to extend grace periods and maturities, and provide additional concessional assistance. In the absence of robust growth, this implied recurrent reschedulings by the Paris Club and the capitalizing of interest payments. The IMF was pressing for an enlargement of the SAF. With arrears to the IMF projected at SDR 1.3 billion at the end of 1987, members concluded (as recorded in a Bank staff's back-to-office report) that "because the main need is to preserve the monetary character of the IMF, the Managing Director would be opposed to gold sales (because reserves would be needed in the 1990s) and to further SDR allocations (because there is, in his view, not the support among the members)."[308]

In contrast, Germany felt that the IMF "should contribute some resources to the SAF enhancement through gold sales." Although a decade later these views would virtually reverse, the end result at the time was the creation of the ESAF. In addition creditor governments addressed the cash flow problems of SSA countries through the Special Program for Assistance to Africa, launched in 1988.

The SPA added an extra $1 billion in disbursements to Sub-Saharan Africa and was seen as a way "to compensate for the delay in obtaining interest rate relief through the Paris Club."[309] The creation of the ESAF stemmed the IMF's arrears problem. Beginning with IDA 7, where the allocation for Africa was supplemented by a Special Fund for Africa, the region's share steadily increased (see figure 12-2). In addition, Africa was the principal beneficiary of an expanded Lome convention. And at the initiative of the Nordic countries, the Bank added a fifth dimension to its debt initiative, through which donors provided additional financial assistance specifically for the repayment of outstanding IBRD debt of IDA-eligible countries (low-income, debt-distressed countries undergoing adjustment). The succession of initiatives brought additional breathing room and, with projected economic recovery, it was hoped that the problem would be contained. The G-7's caution and solidarity continued until the resolution of the Latin American debt crisis at the end of the 1980s.

Bank operational staff were keenly aware of the tension between the goals of short-term financial and budgetary stabilization and debt reimbursement, and of long-term development. As noted below, the picture was complicated by the contradictory signals of the adverse effects of large (and growing) debt stocks while actual debt service was more moderate. But the salience of the debt issue was more than just about numbers. Limited government capacity in African debtor countries meant that the transaction costs of repeated reschedulings imposed a particularly

308. C. Humphreys, "Draft Note, Summary of the Discussion at the G-10 Meeting on African Debt Problems, Paris, July 10, 1987," July 20, 1987, pp. 1, 3.

309. Memorandum, Sven Sandstrom to Moeen A. Qureshi, "Paris Meeting," December 7, 1987.

onerous burden.[310] If the rapid growth in Bank lending undermined quality in the 1970s, the integrity of lending in the 1980s was undercut by the need to maintain debt servicing as short-term cash-flow prerogatives overrode long-term concerns. This led to an almost irreconcilable paradox: a shared view across the political spectrum about the long-term nature of Africa's economic problems, but an operational focus repeatedly buffeted by the acuteness of a balance of payments problem that constantly forced the institution to cope with short-term concerns. Since official debt, including multilateral debt, was a very large fraction of African debt, the issue of forestalling defaults to the Bank and other "preferred creditors" became endemic. It perpetuated a recurring crisis-like atmosphere that forced a short-term focus on cash-flow management.

The institutional peculiarities of IDA, with steadily rising floors on Sub-Saharan Africa's share in IDA, the need to exhaust these resources within three years, and the de facto use of resource transfers for debt servicing all combined to undermine the integrity of IDA lending. The cases of Cameroon and Zambia are illustrative. As with other countries in Francophone Africa, Cameroon's economic and financial health grew increasingly desperate by the end of the 1980s. In September 1992 the Bank ceased disbursements on ongoing projects, pending clearance of arrears. A last-minute payment of arrears by France prevented Cameroon from sliding into nonaccrual status. By year end, overdue payments had again climbed to $80 million, and the Bank once again froze all disbursements to Cameroon. In January 1993 France granted a special loan of $109 million of which $73 million was passed to the World Bank only hours before Cameroon would have been declared by the Bank to be in nonaccrual status.[311] Once more the money proved to be little more than a Band-Aid. Two months later, the Bank suspended disbursements to Cameroon because of mounting arrears. The following year, after the devaluation of the CFA franc, lending resumed with a series of adjustment credits (Cameroon's economic decline having rendered it IDA-eligible). When these loans were presented to the Bank's Board, some executive directors questioned the "realism" of the projections but

310. This was one of the arguments of Gerald K. Helleiner, "The IMF, the World Bank and Africa's Adjustment and External Debt Problems: An Unofficial View." *World Development*, vol. 20, no. 6 (June 1992), pp. 779–92. The Bank's viewpoint was provided by Ishrat Husain, "A Comment on the IMF, the World Bank and Africa's Adjustment and External Debt Problems: An Unofficial View," *World Development*, vol. 21, no. 12 (December 1993), pp. 2055–58. Tony Killick estimated that the number of negotiations related to IMF and World Bank programs, debt relief, and bilateral aid undertaken by African governments between 1980 and 1992 was about *eight thousand*. Killick, "Enhancing the Cost-effectiveness of Africa's Negotiations with Its Creditors," in UNCTAD, *International Monetary and Financial Issues for the 1990s*, vol. 3 (New York, 1993), pp. 1–27.

311. According to news media reports at the time, "Financial experts in Yaounde wonder, however, if France will come to the rescue once more in April, when Cameroon is expected to have again accumulated arrears of about $80 million to the Bank." World Bank, *Development News—Daily Summary*, January 19, 1993, p. 2.

were told that it was they who lacked realism if they wanted the institutions's loans to be serviced. The financial relationship between the Bank and Cameroon had now become such that the Bank was locked into adjustment lending in the medium term to ensure a sufficiently large volume of quick-disbursing loans.

The "ritual dances of debt" were even more pronounced in the case of Zambia, which had seen its economy decline since the mid-1970s. Cautious attempts at economic reform since the early 1980s had had limited payoffs for both internal and external reasons (the political inability to adjust to changing realities, the collapse of copper prices, and drought), and the program was abandoned in early 1987. Soon thereafter (August 1987) Zambia went into arrears and slid into non-accrual with the World Bank. In Zambia, as in several other instances, optimistic commodity price projections that never materialized led to underfunded Bank-Fund programs, which soon collapsed.[312] The decline in its per capita income and lack of creditworthiness made Zambia IDA-eligible and by mid-1990 the Bank was considering a series of IDA-financed adjustment loans, which would be preceded by a bridge loan to clear Zambia's IBRD arrears. In turn the proceeds of the IDA loans would repay the bridge loan. On the one hand, the operation reflected the Bank's flexibility and its wide-ranging attempts to bring back on board countries that had slipped out of its financial safety net. Yet, as Stanley Fischer commented in the case of lending to Zambia, this flexibility also led to skewed analysis:

> The macroeconomic projections are not credible. The program starts with major fiscal and monetary contractions. Yet we project positive growth for 1990. That is unlikely to happen. We would be better off levelling with the Zambians than giving them a rosy scenario that does not work out. Another way of putting the issue is that the external funding that is projected is insufficient to justify the predicted growth rates, and that we have misled the donors by suggesting their contributions are sufficient to enable Zambia to begin growing this year and enter vigorous growth next year. While considerations such as the messages we give the Zambians and donors are no doubt important, the basic objection is that we should in any case provide sensible predictions that we believe.[313]

But massaged projections were not enough to yield a plausible scenario for Zambia. IDA allocation criteria had to be bent to give the country an IDA alloca-

---

312. Thus in the case of Zambia, actual prices of copper in 1982 and 1983 were about 55 percent of IMF forecasts in 1981; prices in 1984 and 1985 were about 57 percent of forecasts in 1983. With copper accounting for nearly 95 percent of Zambia's exports, the highly inaccurate forecasts ensured that the program had little chance of success. Joshua Greene, "A Review of IMF-Supported Adjustment Programs in Zambia, 1976–1984," 1986, p. 18, table 10.

313. Arithmetically, this growth rate was projected on the basis of assumptions that investment would increase by more than 8 percent of GNP between 1989 and 1990, even while monetary policy was being tightened. This, as Fischer pointed out, was not plausible. Memorandum, Stanley Fischer to Wilfred Thalwitz and Moeen A. Qureshi, "Zambia: Economic Recovery Credit IM," August 27, 1990, p. 1.

tion that on a per capita basis was equal to that of the best-performing country.[314] The need to clear arrears took precedence over actions crucial for long-term success (namely changes in the regulatory regime for private sector activity and the overall incentive regime, including exchange rates). Disbursements were heavily front loaded even though a failure would leave the Bank with even less room for maneuver in the future, especially given the limited availability of IDA resources. Following the clearance of arrears by Zambia in 1990 (see chapter 16), nearly 70 percent of the $1.1 billion lending commitments between fiscal 1990 and 1995 were in the form of adjustment loans. At the time of writing, Zambia's economic recovery faced a long haul.

In cases like Zambia's, the Bank was in a tight corner. Once a country went into arrears and formal nonaccrual, the institution's ability to act was severely circumscribed. Time and again the Bank was faced with a difficult choice: it could put in more rapidly disbursing money to forestall nonaccrual, but at the cost of appearing to underwrite regimes that were not reform-minded. In cases such as Liberia, Somalia, Sudan, and Zaire, once a country fell into nonaccrual status there was little doubt that matters would go from bad to worse.

Debates on SSA debt were confused by several factors. First, financial flows tied to long-term debt were less than a third of net resource flows by the mid-1980s, and about a fifth by the end of the decade. Flows that did not create debt, as either private or official grants, were the principal mode of financial flows to Sub-Saharan Africa by the mid-1980s. Second, although the stock of debt as well as debt service due grew alarmingly large by the late 1980s, the debt service actually paid was relatively moderate. Third, the share owed multilateral creditors grew steadily, from about 13 percent in 1980 to 30 percent of outstanding long-term debt by the end of 1995 (with the Bank group alone accounting for about 20 percent). Growing multilateral flows in this period, as well as their increasingly concessional character, had been seen as a sine qua non for enabling the countries in the region to climb out of the crisis. But with the expected recovery of SSA economies failing to transpire, the growth in the volume and share of nonreschedulable multilateral debt began to be seen as part of the problem rather than the solution. Between 1980 and 1994 Sub-Saharan Africa's debt grew from $58 to $165 billion, despite debt forgiveness exceeding $15 billion. Yet, net disbursements during this period totaled just $72 billion, which meant that more than a third of the growth of the region's debt stock was due to interest arrears, interest capitalized, and cross-currency valuations. Between 1988 and 1994 just 46 percent of the growth of Sub-Saharan Africa's debt stock could be accounted for by additional net disbursements.

314. There is a certain unfortunate irony that bad performance is in a sense rewarded with more concessional money. On the other hand, it would be farfetched to make the case that a country would deliberately underperform simply to get access to what really is a limited amount of concessional assistance.

Table 12-5. *Financial Flows to Sub-Saharan Africa, 1970–94*
Annual averages, billions of U.S. dollars

Flow	1970	1980	1984–87	1988–91	1992–94
Aggregate net flows	1.7	15.1	11.1	16.6	16.7
(of which World Bank)	0.1	0.7	1.6	1.8	1.9
Percentage Bank	6.3	4.6	14.4	10.8	11.4
Aggregate net transfers	0.4	7.6	5.9	7.6	7.8
(of which World Bank)	0.1	0.5	1.2	1.0	1.0
Percentage Bank	18.1	5.9	19.3	13.0	13.1
Real 1995 U.S. dollars					
Aggregate net flows[a]	6.5	26.0	15.1	19.4	17.6
Aggregate net transfers[b]	1.6	13.1	8.0	8.9	8.3

Sources: World Bank, *World Debt Tables.*
a. Aggregate net flows = net flows on long-term debt + official grants + FDI + net IMF purchases.
b. Aggregate net transfers = aggregate net flows – interest on long-term debt – profits on FDI.

At the same time, the resources appeared to be too little, given the steep decline in terms of trade and indigence of many countries. The optimal balance would be a perennial tension. Throughout the period the magnitude of external flows to the region posed a vexing paradox. By any reasonable criterion of needs, the money was modest, with real aggregate net transfers remaining unchanged since the early 1980s (table 12-5).

Although levels of ODA to Sub-Saharan Africa increased, the large increase in the ODA to GDP ratio (about 12 percent by 1994) was only partly the result of this increase (table 12-6). Steep currency depreciation meant that in most countries, despite positive GDP growth (between 1.5 and 2 percent), GDP measured in dollars fell.[315] A different measure, ODA as a share of imports, which is less prone to exchange rate–driven measurement problems, varied between 25 and 30 percent from the mid-1980s onward. On closer examination, however, the net figures here too were much less, with much of ODA probably driven into "off-shore" expenditures, especially on expatriate salaries and "technical assistance."

Even then the question of foreign aid dependency remained a perennial problem. There were questions whether the greater flows financed investment or consumption. Based on net ODA figures in table 12-6, by the early 1990s net ODA as a share of recipient countries' investment was greater than 100 percent in twenty-one countries (and for seventeen had been since the mid-1980s).[316] In many

315. The size of the informal economy in Sub-Saharan Africa, which probably grew during this period, may well have led to GDP being underestimated, in which case the ODA/GDP ratio would be even lower, although since the underreporting of output was a continuing affair, the relative decline in the ratio would not have been much different from that reported.

316. World Bank, *African Development Indicators 1995–96*, tables 12-8 and 2-12.

Table 12-6. *Net ODA versus Net Official Flows, Selected Years*
Annual averages, billions of U.S. dollars

Item	1980	1984–87	1988–91	1992–94
Net ODA	7.4	9.7	15.2	17.2
Net disbursements of official concessional long-term loans + net official transfers	5.1	7.7	11.1	11.0
GDP	214.4	177.6	174.0	161.7
Imports	43.6	29.0	34.3	38.3

Source: *African Development Indicators*, 1994–95 and 1996, tables 2-5, 5-2, 5-6, 6-1, 6-5, 12-1.

cases there were troubling implications of relatively large volumes of aid and external financing whose seemingly large share of GDP (and, by extension, of consumption, investment, and government expenditures) had important implications for macroeconomic management, especially Dutch disease effects on the exchange rate and effects on economic incentives. Perhaps most worrying was a sense that the multitudes of donors and external NGOs were sapping borrowers of their initiative for self-help.

Beginning with the "Toronto terms" in June 1988, a succession of initiatives was launched to reduce the burden of official debt, each successive initiative extending the concessionality of debt relief.[317] Despite official support for the buyback of commercial bank debt, the cancellation of a part of ODA debt, restructuring of pre–cutoff date bilateral debt, and the provision of new concessional financing, the unsustainable high debt overhang persisted. Although each of these official initiatives trumpeted large debt forgiveness, the exclusion of several major categories of debt meant that actual debt reduction was substantially less.

Calls for multilateral debt to be included in debt rescheduling and/or reduction mounted. In 1994, the Bank in its *World Debt Tables*, argued that "while multilateral institutions must continue to make an important contribution to the resolution of the SILIC [severely indebted low-income countries] debt problem, the rescheduling of multilateral loans or the write-off of debt (or the use of reserves or loan loss provisions for reduction purposes) as suggested by some, would entail costs to all multilateral borrowers that would far outweigh any benefits to a few."[318] A few months later the Bank would unveil just such an initiative.

A major impediment to debt reduction was the "moral hazard" problem. The debt burden, so the reasoning went, was an outcome of poor policies. Forgiving debt meant rewarding profligacy and, especially for multilateral institutions, raised

317. The Toronto terms were followed by London terms ("enhanced Toronto terms") at the end of 1991 and the "Naples" terms, initiated in December 1994. Conditions were per capita GNP cutoffs ($500) and debt-to-export ratios of more than 350 percent on a net present value basis.

318. World Bank, *World Debt Tables 1994–95*, pp 45–46. Of the forty SILICs so categorized by the Bank in 1995, thirty-three were in Sub-Saharan Africa.

issues of fairness across borrowers. Such arguments, while undoubtedly partly valid, were incomplete. For one thing, as in so many of these cases, the profligacy was that of the region's ruling classes. But the burden of paying the price fell on ordinary citizens. In theory this asymmetry could have been resolved to a degree if, for instance, overseas accounts of nationals of a severely indebted poor country seeking debt write-offs were subject to examination and seizure. If media reports were to be believed, Mobutu's private accounts alone could reduce Zaire's external debt substantially. But such ideas would have been regarded as heresy in both creditor and debtor countries. It was not just the effort required but the awkwardness that such moves would have entailed, namely an acknowledgment that private financial institutions in many Western countries as well as other "offshore" havens had been instrumental in safeguarding ill-gotten gains.

There was also the uncomfortable reality that moral hazard arguments were invoked only with regard to borrower behavior. Multilateral debt forgiveness when at least some of the debt was due to political pressure by the major powers or the personal agendas of staff, without any repercussions for either, also had potential for moral hazard. For the Bank, any debt reduction would have to be paid for directly or indirectly from net income. This meant that debt forgiveness would partly be paid for by IBRD borrowers. For years, many of these borrowers had privately expressed skepticism regarding some of this lending. However, in the belief that what goes around comes around, none had ever gone on record against such lending. Now the chickens had come home to roost. Having shared the responsibility for decisionmaking as shareholders, it was perhaps proper that IBRD borrowers share the financial implications of their silence.

Outcomes?

There was a great debate at the end of the 1980s over whether structural adjustment "worked" in Africa. As indicated in chapter 10, the World Bank in an apologist mode tended to overclaim, but so did the Economic Commission for Africa and other critics negatively. With Sub-Saharan Africa's economic turnaround proving elusive, these debates became increasingly contentious as the 1980s wore on. In early 1989 the Bank, collaborating with UNDP, issued a report, *Africa's Adjustment and Growth in the 1980s*, which suggested that adjustment was working in Africa. In Stanley Fischer's view, the answer was "probably not": the report's properly hedged conclusions, he said, implied caution against relying on this one analysis. A number of its assumptions about which countries were strong adjusters, the impacts of external shocks, and so on, were judgmental. "There is no evidence that these judgements were made badly, but other judgements could have been made."[319]

319. Memorandum, Stanley Fischer to Barber B. Conable, "African Adjustment," May 8, 1989.

However, Kim Jaycox's flat introductory statement to the document that "recovery has begun" inflamed ECA, which had not reviewed the draft. ECA issued a sharp rebuttal.[320] Similarly, another Bank report comparing performance of SPA countries and non-SPA countries appeared to show dramatic results in the former, but those results were the result of Nigeria's being in the non-SPA group. Without Nigeria "the comparisons would look very different."[321]

Still, as Stanley Fischer emphasized, debates on structural adjustment should not deflect attention from "the overriding fact that there is no alternative to adjustment—the resources to continue without adjusting are simply not there [in Africa]."[322] When a country's balance of payments was badly and stubbornly out of line, beyond the coping capacity of available transfers and foreign investments, the only solution was to effect fiscal and other policy adjustments that would bridge the gap. Good alternatives were not available. But if adjustment was inevitable, the meaningful issue was the degree to which governments could reduce the costs or increase the benefits of particular measures. The pain of adjustment could be eased by external assistance. But in some cases the adjustment-or-not debate concealed the perverse role of aid in reducing the need to adjust.

In reality, weak evidence (in the sense of the quality of data and a bewildering array of definitional ambiguities), when added to the sheer number of variables, meant that the rush to judgment was too often premature.[323] A principal objective of adjustment lending had been to restore the region's macroeconomic fundamentals so as to ensure financial sustainability. But as table 12-7a indicates, two key variables, domestic savings and investment, were not restored.[324] If anything, they worsened. For many critics the Bank had emasculated the state in Sub-Saharan Africa. Again as seen from table 12-7b, at the aggregate level key economic indicators of government involvement in an economy showed little change. Although government expenditure dropped from the levels of the late 1970s, if

320. Mosley and Weeks scored ECA's data analysis somewhat higher on points, but both sides, they found, overargued their cases. Paul Mosley and John Weeks, "Has Recovery Begun? Africa's Adjustment in the 1980s Revisited," *World Development,* vol. 21, no. 10 (October 1993), pp. 1583–1606.

321. Memorandum, Stanley Fischer to Stephen O'Brien, "Paper on Second Phase of the Special Program of Assistance," April 2, 1990.

322. Memorandum, Stanley Fischer to Barber Conable, May 8, 1989.

323. Tony Killick's extensive analysis of the impact of IMF programs illustrates the ambiguities and difficulties in drawing strong conclusions while emphasizing that reality is much less dramatic than either the IMF or its critics have painted. See Tony Killick, *IMF Programmes in Developing Countries: Design and Impact* (London: Routledge and Overseas Development Institute, 1995).

324. Disaggregated data would obviously be more illuminating. However, the discussion that follows is meant to raise some questions rather than arrive at answers. These figures (which exclude South Africa) do not change appreciably if Nigeria is excluded.

Table 12-7a. *SSA National Accounts, 1975–93*
Percentage of GDP

Item	1975–79	1980–85	1985–89	1990–93
Consumption	80.0	85.3	86.5	87.0
Investment	23.7	17.5	16.0	17.0
Domestic savings	20.0	14.7	13.6	13.8
National savings	17.7	9.3	9.0	8.8
Net ODA	5.4	7.2	8.9	12.7

Source: *African Development Indicators,* 1994, 1996, tables 2-6, 2-8, 2-12, 2-13, 12-5. Data exclude South Africa.

Table 12-7b. *SSA Government Finance, 1975–94*
Percentage of GDP

Item	1975–79	1980–85	1985–89	1990–94
Consumption	14.7	15.4	14.9	15.7
Deficit/surplus (including grants)	–10.6	–6.9	–5.9	–6.5
Deficit/surplus (excluding grants)	–11.2	–7.7	–7.5	–8.3
Revenue (excluding grants)	19.4	18.3	17.3	17.9
Expenditures (of which)	30.2	26.0	24.8	26.1
Wages and salaries	13.2	19.0	24.1	28.0
Subsidies and current transfers	n.a.	13.6	n.a.	n.a.
Capital	n.a.	34.8	24.9	22.3

Source: *African Development Indicators,* 1994, 1996, tables 2-7, 7-1, 7-2, 7-4, 7-6, 7-14, 7-18, 7-19. Data exclude South Africa.

n.a. Not available.

Nigeria is excluded, there was little change for two decades. Current expenditures remained constant and overall government expenditures barely budged as well.[325] This meant that as interest costs rose the burden fell on capital expenditures. Later interest costs were stabilized by being capitalized, but this in turn led to a rapid escalation of the debt overhang. Wages and salaries as a fraction of government expenditure actually increased (although here the increase was principally in the countries with a fixed exchange rate; declines were observed in countries with a variable rate). Military expenditure in Sub-Saharan Africa rose between 1986 and 1990 in comparison with the period 1972–85 (from 3.1 percent of GDP to 3.4 percent).[326] Although the trend reversed in the early 1990s, the increase in the 1980s was remarkable, given the seeming salience of external leverage.

Both total revenue and tax revenues increased in countries with a variable exchange rate, although trade-related tax revenues did not change despite trade

325. This view is corroborated by Nashashibi and Bazzoni, "Exchange Rate Strategies."
326. Malcolm D. Knight, Norman Loayza, and Delano Villanueva, *The Peace Dividend: Military Spending Cuts and Economic Growth* (World Bank/IMF, 1996).

liberalization. In fact, in the fixed-rate countries total and tax revenues declined mainly as a result of large declines in trade taxes, which were traced to overvalued exchange rates. Trade liberalization simplified complex procedures and controls but did not have a material impact on the average *effective* tariff. In the early 1980s, the average effective tariff averaged 22 percent in fixed-rate countries and 15 percent in the variable-rate countries. By the end of the decade, it had dropped to 20 percent in the former case and increased to 18 percent in the latter. One reason that this occurred was the simultaneous exchange rate adjustments, one of the most successfully implemented elements of the reforms.

More than anything else, it was the task of reviving production that appeared Herculean. The stifling effects of state economic intervention were universally acknowledged. But standard prescriptions of deregulation did not seem to affect matters greatly. A suspicion of ethnic minorities' and foreigners' roles had contributed to a broad distrust of markets, fueled by the weakness of indigenous business classes and entrepreneurship.[327] In marked contrast to Southeast Asian states, which built upon the tremendous entrepreneurial capabilities of their Chinese ethnic minorities, SSA states pursued policies of Africanization as an instrument of ethnic patronage for state leaders to such extremes that they effectively emasculated the potent entrepreneurial capacity of their minorities.[328]

The Bank group found few viable direct operational mechanisms to advance private sector activity. An ostensibly vibrant informal sector appeared to offer a viable option, but there was little understanding of just how to promote it.[329] The IFC's pattern of investments was bipolar. At one end were initiatives to nurture domestic entrepreneurship. The Africa Enterprise Fund was established to promote very small projects, but with decidedly lukewarm results. At the other end were large resource extraction projects, the only ones that seemed to attract foreign capital and entrepreneurs. These projects undoubtedly brought large investments, but their enclave nature meant that they had few linkages with the rest of the economy. More worrisome, as was the case with the IFC's decision to push for a large mining investment in Sierra Leone in the late 1980s,

---

327. The point is emphasized by Thandika Mkandawire, "The Political Economy of Privatisation in Africa," in Giovanni Andrea Cornia and Gerald K. Helleiner, eds., *From Adjustment to Development in Africa: Conflict, Controversy, Convergence, Consensus?* (St. Martin's Press, 1994), pp. 192–216.

328. For the Kenyan case, see David Himbara, "The Failed Africanization of Commerce and Industry in Kenya," *World Development*, vol. 22, no. 3 (March 1994), pp. 469–82.

329. In the 1990s, the Bank began a more systematic analysis of the informal sector in Africa as well as enterprise-level constraints in the manufacturing sector. See Leila Webster and Peter Fidler, eds., "The Informal Sector and Microfinance Institutions in West Africa" (World Bank, 1996); and the publications of the Regional Program on Enterprise Development by the Bank's Africa Technical Department.

the Corporation did not ponder whether such investments would simply provide rents to dubious regimes.[330] The fact remained that as long as SSA elites retained a deep suspicion of market forces, market liberalization would be grudging and modest.

Outcomes were also muted on two key elements of state reform: state-owned enterprises and civil service reform. Public enterprise reforms during the 1980s focused largely on physical and financial rehabilitation rather than divestiture. It was only when more than a decade of effort had shown such inadequate results that the Bank moved more aggressively into privatization, and its approach became more sophisticated than the often poorly designed privatization programs of the 1980s.[331] Ostensibly the Bank's leverage in Sub-Saharan Africa was substantially greater than in Latin America; yet the fact that the pace of privatization was much less was a warning flag on the real limits of the Bank's leverage. The political reluctance of Sub-Saharan Africa slowed the spread of privatization; at the same time, the weakness of market institutions limited its benefits.

Critics (both within and outside) attacked the Bank's focus on growth.[332] If the Bank was careless and selective in its use of data, its critics were hardly less so. For many, the simple correlation of Sub-Saharan Africa's economic decline with Bank adjustment programs was sufficient to warrant causality. UNICEF's *Adjustment with a Human Face* was a case in point. As noted in chapters 7 and 10, the concerns raised by this work were a timely and much needed reminder that, with all the attention on policies, structures, reforms, and conditionalities, the essential subject—human welfare—had received short shrift. Nonetheless, the report's analytical foundations were themselves problematic. Ghanaian officials pointed out that data for a case study in their country were gathered at the end of a long drought and consequently did not separate the effects of adjustment from the effects of the drought, but their protests were ignored.[333] The outcry that resulted from the work led the Bank to put together an expensive poverty-alleviation program (PAMSCAD), with little ownership by Ghanaian authorities. An intrinsic weakness of such targeted programs was that they required good administrative capacity, which, as the failure of the rural development projects in the 1970s had painfully demonstrated, was unrealistic in Sub-Saharan Africa. Still, programs like PAMSCAD served a purpose in supplying political grease to quiet squeaky wheels. Kaunda's refrain to Jaycox—"How do I sell to my people the concept that the program has made them

330. Memorandum, Sir William Ryrie to Barber B. Conable, "Sierra Leone—Koidu Kimberlite Project," July 3, 1989. The purported benefits of the project were in stark contrast to the realities of Sierra Leone as painted in William Reno, *Corruption and State Politics in Sierra Leone* (Cambridge University Press, 1995).

331. World Bank, "World Bank Assistance to Privatization in Developing Countries," OED Report 13273, August 19, 1994.

332. See, for instance, World Bank, "Taking Action for Poverty Reduction in Sub-Saharan Africa: Report of an African Region Task Force," Report 15575-AFR, May 1, 1996.

333. Joseph Abbey, interview with the authors, Cartagena (Colombia), April 19, 1994.

less miserable than they would have been without it?"—had made the Bank sensitive to the political reality that it had to "buttress and bolster reform programs" in order to handle the downside costs.

Another response to the UNICEF report was the SDA program, established in collaboration with the UNDP. Instead of attempting to adapt the existing Living Standards Measurement Study program, the SDA created a large parallel bureaucratic apparatus, reflecting the agenda of donors and researchers, while also attempting to shore up public relations. Such efforts diverted limited local data-gathering and -processing capabilities to handle donor-supported projects that could bring in money to cash-strapped organizations at the cost of the painstaking and incremental efforts at building statistical offices. Unfortunately, here too an early review of the program that bluntly pointed out this reality was pummeled by the Bank and UNDP, which attacked the messenger instead of the message.[334]

The neglect of the "human" dimension was also emphasized by the UNDP's Human Development Report which emerged as an influential critic of the Bank. Ironically, Sub-Saharan Africa's growth was its Achilles heel—its performance on the "Human Development Index" (HDI) in the 1980s was relatively more positive, seemingly better than either the 1960s or 1970s.[335] However, since less than a third of African countries had any census or survey on literacy in the 1980s, these numbers must be treated carefully. The Bank had stressed without much backing that structural adjustment was in general poor friendly (see chapters 7 and 10), while critics assailed it as inimical to the poor, especially its advocacy of cuts in government expenditures. Subsequent analysis did not appear to support the latter view, at least in an aggregate sense, although again strong conclusions were unwarranted.[336] These debates did not confront the fundamental reality that while economic growth may or may not help the poor, economic decline almost never does.

During the 1980s Bank lending for social sectors in Sub-Saharan Africa remained broadly unchanged. Lending for education declined from about 11 percent

334. The review ran to 110 pages; the Bank's response to 50 pages. The review team was headed by Enrique Lerdau, who had left the Bank following the 1987 reorganization. Lerdau had been one of the most highly respected senior operational managers of the Bank for nearly two decades. The Bank attacked the review on the grounds that Lerdau harbored a "grudge" against the institution as a result of the 1987 reorganization.

335. According to figures in the 1996 Human Development Report, Sub-Saharan Africa's Human Development Index increased from 0.201 in 1960 to 0.257 in 1970; it climbed to 0.312 in 1980 and further to 0.379 in 1990. Aside from the general difficulties in interpreting index numbers, these estimates should be interpreted with considerable caution in view of the poor quality of the underlying data.

336. David L. Sahn, Paul Dorosh, and Stephen Younger, "Exchange Rate, Fiscal and Agricultural Policies in Africa: Does Adjustment Hurt the Poor?" World Development, vol. 24, no. 4 (April 1996), pp. 719–47. For a dissenting view, see Alessandro Pio, "The Social Impact of Adjustment in Africa," in Cornia and Helleiner, eds., From Adjustment to Development in Africa, pp. 298–314.

of all lending to the region in the early 1970s to about 6 percent in the 1980s but there was an offsetting increase in lending for health.[337] Nevertheless, the Bank remained the largest source of external finance for education in Africa after France in this period, and the largest in primary education.[338]

For a variety of reasons the Bank began to emphasize social sector lending by the end of the 1980s (see chapter 7). Its stance toward primary education merits attention. Through the 1980s, the Bank advocated with increasing vigor that education outlays be shifted from higher education to primary education, to boost literacy levels. By the late 1980s, the institution had become almost dogmatic about the importance of primary education, arguing that investments in primary education (especially girls' education) had the highest rates of return. The success of East Asia was also laid to such investments. At the same time, the Bank strongly pushed for a restructuring of expenditure patterns within the education sector. To address the problem of inadequate non-salary inputs in the primary education sector, the Bank proposed that high teachers' salaries should be curbed— on the basis of data that were seven years out of date. Inflation had already been shaving teachers' real wages.[339] Given that the paucity of trained manpower was one of the most critical scarcities in Africa and had led to a continuing and insidious dependence on expatriate technical assistance, the implications of withdrawing resources from higher education were underplayed. The problems were exacerbated by the economic and political policies of SSA states that had cost the region dearly in a loss of its most precious resource: human capital, which had fled to other countries.

In emphasizing East Asia's achievements in primary education, the Bank did not dwell on the reality that East Asia had done so through its own efforts. Primary education seemed an area ideally suited for self-help. The Bank, however, decided to undertake direct lending. Foreign financing accounted for about two-thirds of the Bank's primary education projects in Sub-Saharan Africa in the 1990s.[340] These expenditures, undoubtedly padded to move greater foreign exchange, included the paraphernalia (studies, consultants, training, and vehicles) that seemed to demonstrate how good intentions could undermine basic tenets of self-help.[341]

The oversophistication in social sector lending was symptomatic of a Bank-wide problem. As criticisms of the institution's lending record mounted, particularly

337. World Bank, "The World Bank's Role in Human Resource Development: A Statistical Overview with Special Reference to Sub-Saharan Africa," OED Report 10811, June 26, 1992.

338. Only Sweden and UNICEF allocated a larger share of their lending for education to Africa for primary education. In the early 1980s, 83 percent of Bank funding for education was devoted to capital expenditures.

339. Memorandum, Ravi Gulhati to Xavier de la Renaudière, "Critique of Sub-Saharan Africa Report, 1986: Zero Draft," January 6, 1986.

340. Based on seven primary education projects between 1990 and 1995.

341. World Bank, "Republic of Zambia: Education Rehabilitation Project," Staff Appraisal Report (SAR) 10843-ZA, September 22, 1992; "Federal Republic of Nigeria: Primary

following the release of the Wapenhans Report in 1992, the Bank responded in the classic manner of a bureaucracy under siege: it became ever more meticulous, elaborate, and detailed in the design of its loans. Every virtuous goal of development was sought in the project design stage, with well-intentioned pressures from the Nordic countries as well as other countries (Canada, Germany, the United States, after 1992) making matters worse. There was little recognition that the best could well be the enemy of the good; that indeed expecting very high average rates of project performance was naive. In the end, such projects rolled out Rolls-Royces where Model-Ts would have served. Long-term sustainability of such projects was improbable, and they did little to enhance self-reliance. Governments have committed to primary education without the help of tens of millions of dollars of studies, analysis, and vehicles. The Bank had only to examine the much touted East Asian model to underscore that reality.[342] Indeed, if primary education was such a basic need, surely a basic function of the government was to provide it. And if governments could not discharge such a basic responsibility on their own accord, what else could they do? There could be no doubt of the importance of primary education, and the Bank's bully pulpit role was laudable. Yet egged on by a belief and pressures that wherever it saw important issues, meticulously engineered Bank lending was needed, the institution did not seek recourse to alternatives such as adjusting its overall lending volumes to some agreed-upon government effort and borrower self-help.

The Bank's 1994 *Adjustment in Africa* report concluded that the fruits of adjustment had not yet been borne in Africa, but that this was not due to faulty diagnosis of policy reforms advocated in adjustment lending. Rather, it was the inadequate and half-hearted adoption of reforms that was the problem: "The analysis supports the foregoing conclusion: changes in macroeconomic policies have a positive and statistically significant effect on growth."[343] The assessment ruffled feathers. In fact, the results were very sensitive to two observations that the report neglected to point out.[344] It was also at some odds with an IMF study, which

---

Education Project," SAR 8714-UNI, November 21, 1990; "Angola: First Education Project," SAR 10338-ANG, May 1992; "Republic of Chad: Basic Education Project (Education 5)," SAR 11680-CD, March 2, 1993; "Rwanda: First Education Sector Project," SAR 9136-RW, March 2, 1991; "Republic of Uganda: Primary Education and Teacher Development Project," SAR 10320-UG, March 1, 1993; "Cape Verde: Basic Education and Training Project," SAR 13568-CV, December 17, 1994.

342. Nearly 60 percent of expenditures in the Bank's social sector projects in Africa (population, health, and nutrition) during 1970–90 were foreign exchange.

343. World Bank, *Adjustment in Africa: Reforms, Results, and the Road Ahead* (World Bank, 1994), p. 139.

344. The regression coefficient (1.91 with a *t*-statistic of 2.88) was crucially dependent on one observation, Cameroon. Dropping that, the slope is just 1.31, and the *t*-statistic 2.24. "If Rwanda is also dropped from the sample, the slope coefficient falls to 1.14 and is no longer significantly different from zero." Howard White and Joke Luttik, "The Countrywide Effects of Aid," World Bank, Policy Research Working Paper 1337, 1994, p. 19.

Table 12-8. *Number of Adjustment Loans to Sub-Saharan Africa, 1981–95*

Number of loans	0	1	2	3	4	5	6	8	9	10	12	13	14	15	16	22
Number of countries	11	4	6	7	6	1	2	1	1	2	1	2	1	1	1	1

Source: World Bank Financial Database.

in examining growth, savings, and private investment performance in the region in the period 1986–92, concluded that "inappropriate macroeconomic policies were the *second* largest contributing factor to the poor growth performance of Sub-Saharan African countries as a group, . . . after the impact of rapid population growth rates and unfavorable weather."[345]

There was considerable evidence that many policy reforms had indeed not been implemented. But that equally raised questions regarding the Bank's actions. Through successive SALs in a host of SSA countries (table 12-8), as well as tranche releases of individual SALs, Bank staff had repeatedly emphasized that reforms were being implemented: otherwise there would have been little basis on which to mount additional SALs and little to countenance the release of tranches.

There are several conflicting interpretations of the political effects of structural adjustment. On the one hand, many (especially in the 1980s) argued that structural adjustment was a conservative "anti-statist" agenda, designed to emasculate the state. On the other hand, if, as some have argued, the dominant groups holding power in Sub-Saharan Africa have lived off the income they derive from their position as intermediaries for the international system, then the reality that the Bank strongly supported the two principal sources of such intermediation—international aid and commerce—implied that structural adjustment was perhaps a profoundly conservative undertaking.[346] In a different vein, while visible indicators of economic change and reform appeared to have changed little, the intellectual milieu and terms of debate changed radically. It was a measure of the psychological distance traveled that, a decade after the Berg Report, Bank critiques of the state in Sub-Saharan Africa—which, if anything, were more scathing—caused barely a ripple. When C. Y. Amoako, one of the principal authors of the Berg Report, became head of Economic Commission for Africa, it was symbolic of the distance that both the Bank and African countries had traveled on that most difficult of roads: the bumpy path of ideas. The Bank—through countless analyses, papers and reports, meetings, seminars, and discussions with African officials and intellectuals, bilateral donors, multilateral agencies, and academics outside Africa—had shaped views on African development, but these interactions, in turn, also shaped and

345. Michael Hadjimichael and others, "Effects of Macroeconomic Stability on Growth, Savings, and Investment in Sub-Saharan Africa: An Empirical Investigation," IMF Working Paper WP/94/98, August 1994, emphasis added, p. 86.

346. Bayart, *The State in Africa*, p. 25.

changed the Bank's views. But it is too soon to tell whether and to what extent this relatively greater consensus would affect Sub-Saharan Africa's future.[347]

Concluding Remarks

In the space of two decades, from the early 1970s to the early 1990s, Sub-Saharan Africa went from being a region of lesser concern for the Bank—albeit one in which the institution, by the default of most other pro-development actors, played a major role—to one of open, nagging, and unresolved anxiety. During the 1970s the institution placed considerable trust in Africa's leaders. Time and again, it gave them the benefit of the doubt, while focusing its energies at the micro, project, level. The outcomes were unsatisfactory. In the 1980s, while the institution mounted a prodigious effort in Sub-Saharan Africa with a zeal reminiscent of the McNamara era, it made an abrupt about-turn, both in its processes and focus, insisting on formal ex-ante conditionality and fixing its sights at the macropolicy level. The results were not markedly different. Africa remained a puzzle with more than a few missing pieces. Time and again, the Bank grasped at new concepts of what these missing pieces could be, only to be tripped up by elusive hazards of implementation.

By the early 1990s new global changes were putting their mark on the Bank's relations with the region. Even as the Bank was proclaiming that "Sub-Saharan Africa will remain at the center of its attention in the 1990s," events in East Europe and the end of the cold war coincided with growing donor fatigue with regard to Sub-Saharan Africa.[348] Anxious that traditional donors were shifting their attention to East Europe and Central Asia, and that support for Africa could be waning, the Bank, with other partners, crafted the Global Coalition for Africa (GCA)—a consensus-building forum of African governments, the United Nations, the Bretton Woods institutions, and donor countries—which first met in 1991. The GCA initiative attempted to provide a forum to achieve a greater consensus with other donors and African intellectuals. But the GCA also represented a tactical shift by the Bank (begun with the LTPS) to "achieve a higher degree of shared responsibility to reduce the risk to the Bank of [its] high profile."[349] The shift toward greater open-mindedness within the Bank also reflected the insecurity of being a Pied Piper whose lead seemed not to be panning out.

Squeezed between the needs of East Europe and donor fatigue, Sub-Saharan Africa's share in the Bank's budgetary allocations and IDA fell, as did the volume of

347. See, for instance, Cornia and Helleiner, *From Adjustment to Development in Africa.*

348. Moeen A. Qureshi, "The World Bank in the 1990's," draft article prepared for publication in *Harvard International Review,* November 21, 1990, p. 5.

349. Minutes of the President's Council meeting—March 12, 1990, "Sub-Saharan Africa—Global Coalition," March 14, 1990.

ODA directed to the region. The magnitude of effort directed by the international community (and the Bank) to Bosnia in comparison with a Liberia or a Rwanda, despite the much more acute human tragedy in the latter, reflected new political priorities.

At the time of writing there appeared to be two contradictory currents in the Bank's engagement with Sub-Saharan Africa. On the one hand, the Bank was exercising leadership in moving substantial elements of Sub-Saharan Africa and the international community to a consensus on the economic strategy for the region, underpinned by a resurgence of sound technical work—ranging from water resources to road transport, public expenditures, agriculture, and the environment—which had few equals in its quality. On the other hand, the pressures to show quick results were also leading the Bank into areas and issues where it had historically little competence or comparative advantage, a consequence of changing fashions and pressures from donor governments, Western NGOs, and activist sections of its staff.

Although there seemed to be some reason to believe that the worst was behind for many countries in the region, the prognosis appeared dismal in other cases where the state had for all practical purposes ceased to exist. Still, the remarkable turnaround in Uganda, an early case of a seemingly failed state, offered hopeful possibilities of rebirth nurtured by strong domestic leadership and external support. The cautious attitude of two potential clients for the Bank—Eritrea and post-apartheid South Africa—signaled a new wariness regarding external assistance arising from the region's experience in the 1980s. Though financially enfeebled, newly independent Eritrea chose to move slowly to avail itself of external assistance as it struggled to define its own priorities. Similarly, the Bank's hopes—and heavy investment in preparatory work—that a post-apartheid South Africa would be a major borrower were thwarted when that country also proved to be a reluctant borrower. Instead, South Africa's substantially greater financial and bureaucratic capacity led the Bank into engaging the country in a sophisticated dialogue and advisory relationship. The process appeared to bring out the best of the Bank's strengths, with constructive outcomes for the client.

More generally, the countries of Sub-Saharan Africa, and in particular its elites, had to come to terms with the contradictions and harsh realities of their own actions. Given the already relatively high levels of external funds, there was an increasing incoherence between their calls for greater international assistance, on the one hand, and their mounting protests against external interference and their rhetoric of self-reliance, on the other. The resurgence of external private flows almost completely bypassed Sub-Saharan Africa; the region's problem was not too much but too little exploitation by multinational corporations. Nor could the region simply ascribe its problems to a lack of voice in major multilateral institutions: the travails of the African-controlled Africa Development Bank did little to buttress that case.

These contradictions were symbolic of a deeper failure, that of the region's leadership, which had neglected to provide the essential ingredient only they could supply, and in the absence of which external efforts were doomed to flounder, namely, political stability. General Olusegun Obasanjo, former Nigerian head of state, castigated his fellow African leaders for being "interested in little more than survival and the accumulation and perpetuation of power [with] policies far removed from social needs and developmental relevance."[350] Notwithstanding the often complex underlying rationale, in the end it was results that mattered. And the results, for much of Sub-Saharan Africa, had been such as to leave them exposed four-odd decades after independence. Their weakness meant, as Nelson Mandela argued in a speech to his fellow heads of states at an OAU summit, "in the end we were held up as the outstanding example of the beneficiaries of charity. . . . On our knees because history, society and nature had defeated us, we could be nothing but beggars."[351]

It was therefore not surprising that Africa received both the fruits and the burden of flagging charity: resources with heavier moralistic and intellectual baggage. The donor community and the Bank increasingly applied to Sub-Saharan Africa a different standard than would have been unacceptable elsewhere. "The vision of economies operating with undistorted commodity markets and freely flowing capital, with just social policies that deliver social services in an equitable manner, officiated by a multiparty political system, innocent of corruption and pure of purpose," one observer noted, was "an attractive Utopia, but not particularly realistic."[352]

Issues of governance were undoubtedly fundamental to Sub-Saharan Africa's predicament as well as to its future. Both the need for, and the difficulties of, ensuring that political institutions in Sub-Saharan Africa be more effective actors in economic development could hardly be underestimated.[353] But the nostrums proposed—"accountability," "transparency," "participation," and "civil society"— bore little resemblance to either Bank advice or country practice in East Asia. Bank reports and donor countries steered clear of pushing the latest morally galvanized "magic bullet" on East Asia, even as they argued for its sine qua non character in Africa. But then Africa was on its knees and dependent on the Bank and donors, whereas the other was a self-confident, economically vibrant region representing large potential markets for the Bank's Part I shareholders.

350. Statement by Olusegun Obasanjo, chairman, Africa Leadership Forum, "The Impact of Changes in East Europe on Africa," April 1990.

351. Nelson Mandela, "African Renaissance," adapted from a speech given to the OAU meeting of heads of state, June 1994. Reproduced in *Granta*, vol. 48 (Summer 1994), p. 253.

352. Brian Van Arkadie, "Economic Strategy and Structural Adjustment in Tanzania," in Leila Frischtak and Izak Atiyas, eds., *Governance, Leadership and Communication: Building Constituencies for Economic Reform* (World Bank, 1994), p. 127.

353. An excellent summary of the issues is E. Gyimah-Boadi and Nicholas van de Walle, "The Politics of Economic Renewal in Africa," in Benno Ndulu, Nicholas van de Walle, and contributors, *Agenda for Africa's Economic Renewal*, ODC Policy Perspectives 21 (New Brunswick, N.J.: Transaction Publishers, 1996), pp. 211–39.

Undoubtedly there was a double standard. Yet, it also reflected the very different magnitude of the problem in Sub-Saharan Africa in relation to other Bank borrowers, as well as growing donor financial fatigue and exasperation at the lack of results. There was less reflection on the gyrations of donor concerns, reflected in the Bank's actions, which were intrinsically time-inconsistent. During the negotiations of IDA 9 in the late 1980s, at the insistence of the United States, the donors had put private sector development at the top of the Bank's priorities. By the mid-1990s, concerns about private sector development had become overshadowed by "social development," the donors' new fashion du jour. Capacity building and institution building, including market institutions, were inherently long-term processes, requiring a patience and horizon in Sub-Saharan Africa that would be even longer than in many other parts of the world. Yet the variables driving the Bank and other donors—changing donor fads, annual lending targets, annual OED evaluations, annual aid budgetary allocations, three-year PFPs, three-year IDA replenishments, frequent Board member and staff and managerial rotations—all added up to short operational horizons.

In one respect, the Bank committed the very error that it saw as the root of the region's problems: like the SSA state, it manifested a marked inability to judge institutional limitations. Though it correctly saw institutional weakness as the heart of the region's predicament, it overestimated its own ability to help in such matters. Technical assistance projects, whose larger aim had always been capacity building, had the worst performance record of any sector of Bank lending, even though they had seldom ventured into issues that were explicitly political. As the Bank prepared to become even more deeply involved in social policy issues at the time of writing, its hubris was troubling.

Although many observers criticized the Bank for its arrogance toward weak SSA counterparts, its actions seemed as much a result of earnestness and overzealousness. Bank staff may well have found the process of dealing with African leaders "heady stuff" (in Kim Jaycox's vivid characterization). Indeed, often they were naive in their belief in the power of formal contractual obligations to set things right. In any event, it severely underestimated the proficiency with which politicians could subvert the best-laid plans. Consequently, it was not surprising that in many cases it was the Bank, and not SSA countries, that was outmaneuvered.

The Bank's engagement with Sub-Saharan Africa had other important implications for the institution. Despite its periodic reporting, the meager results contributed to a growing self-doubt. Desperate to obtain additional resources for Sub-Saharan Africa, the Bank accepted donor conditions on IDA replenishments that soon affected the Bank group as whole. The proliferation of performance targets was accompanied by an expansion in the range, detail, and explicitness of conditions. Fewer, more modest, and looser targets, longer time horizons, and a willingness to walk away would perhaps have constituted a more appropriate response. But short-leashed, unwavering interventionism was the institutional choice, driven to a considerable extent by donors. The need to garner IDA re-plenishments and maintain donor interest in Sub-Saharan Africa also led to over-selling. Thus at a meeting of the Council of African Advisers, "Mr. Jaycox . . . noted that Afro-pessimism had negative psychological consequences and could become a self-fulfilling prophecy, which should therefore be avoided. We have no alternative but to be optimistic—realistic always—but positive in our efforts."[354] Even in the best of circumstances the Bank's money, advice, and conditions could not guaran-tee outcomes. The "necessary" optimism required to bring donors on board almost necessarily ensured "failure."

The Bank's quasi-monopolistic role in a struggling region made the institution an easy scapegoat for observers looking for someone to blame. The burden of leadership seldom meets universal acclaim, and the owners of multilateral institu-tions are particularly adept at shifting blame to multilaterals when the terrain gets rough, as the United Nations would learn in Somalia and Bosnia, and the Bretton Woods institutions in Sub-Saharan Africa. It must be emphasized that the Bank's policy prescriptions and operational stances were all approved—more or less unan-imously—by the Bank's owners, exercising their prerogatives through the executive directors. Even more, as was the case with the instructions of the IDA deputies in the context of IDA replenishments, many were imposed on the institution by some of its major shareholders, for a variety of reasons. The record on this is unam-biguous. Consequently, to whatever extent the Bank "failed" in Sub-Saharan Africa, it was the wider Bank—its management, Board and, above all, major shareholders —that did so.

At this writing the likely process of SSA economic recovery appeared to be proceeding at an implausibly slow, prolonged pace, with the human tragedy in some parts heartrending. "Realistic" projections of SSA economic prospects, with concessional transfers to Africa declining absolutely as well as relatively, had real per capita incomes barely inching ahead, falling farther and farther behind income and welfare growth in the other regions of the world. Yet, just four decades ago, the prognosis for Asia was equally pessimistic. Given the record reviewed in this chapter, it might be better for the region in the long run if the Bank and other external actors heeded T. E. Lawrence's admonition: "Rather let them do it imper-fectly, than try to do it perfectly yourself. For it is their country, their war, and your time is short."

354. Office of the vice president, Africa region, World Bank, "Salient Points of the Eighth Meeting of the Council of African Advisers, September 17–19, 1991," p. 7.

THIRTEEN

The International Finance Corporation

Jonas Haralz

AFTER THE United States had decided to support the establishment of the International Finance Corporation, the *Economist* announced the event under the caption "To IBRD—a Son (IFC)." In an article in *Bank Notes,* Shirley Boskey, describing the IFC proposal, raised the question, why a son rather than a daughter?[1] After all, she wrote, the IFC had already displayed certain traits popularly supposed to be feminine. It had kept people waiting since at least 1951, when it had first been publicly proposed in a report to the president of the United States. It would be engaged principally in spending money: its capital of $75 million to $100 million, as well as retained earnings. And it had already changed its mind in at least one respect: originally intended to concentrate on equity investments, it was now to refrain from holding capital stock in the enterprises it helped to finance.

A Child Is Born

Whether properly referred to as a "he" or a "she," there seemed no doubt that the IFC's childhood would be brief and that it would be earning its living at an early age. Moreover, it may be added to Shirley Boskey's reflections: whatever the

---

1. Shirley Boskey, "The International Finance Corporation," *Bank Notes,* vol. 9, no. 4 (April 1955), pp. 3–5. Boskey was at this time a member of the Technical Assistance and Liaison Staff, the Bank unit that, together with the Office of the General Counsel, had been engaged primarily in the preparation of the IFC proposal. *Bank Notes* was a Bank in-house organ and forerunner of *Bank's World.*

gender, there could be no doubt about the parentage. The idea of an International Finance Corporation, dedicated to furthering economic development through the growth of productive private enterprise, was formed into a concrete proposal in the World Bank and would never have become reality without the Bank's perseverance.

In a statement presented at an informal discussion during the annual meetings of the Bretton Woods institutions in Istanbul on September 15, 1955, Robert L. Garner, the vice president of the Bank and future first president of the IFC, reviewed the reasons why establishing the IFC had been necessary. The aim of economic development was the increased production of goods and services, with its consequent effect on living standards. Public funds and efforts would have to provide many of the necessary elements for development, especially in the field of education, health, and other basic services. But the essential ingredients for effective performance—entrepreneurship, venture capital, technology, trained labor force, and management—could best be obtained, and even only be obtained, from private enterprise. Yet the mechanism for encouraging productive private enterprise was not readily at hand. The Bank was hamstrung by the requirement for government guarantees and its inability to provide venture capital. While public investment in power, transport, and other utilities, supported by the Bank, had opened up opportunities for private initiative and effort, the flow of private capital to take advantage of these opportunities had been disappointingly small. It was to increase that flow, by helping to remove or lower some of the barriers obstructing it, that the International Finance Corporation was being created.

How would the IFC go about its task, Garner went on to ask. The Charter wisely described this only in broad outline, leaving the detail to be filled in on the basis of actual experience. There were nonetheless important features of the Charter which would shape the fundamental character of the institution. First, the IFC could use its resources only in association with private investors, and it was hard to foresee a situation in which the private participants should not put up the major share of the capital. Second, though a government interest in the enterprise would not necessarily preclude an IFC investment, the test would be whether or not the enterprise was essentially private in character. Third, the IFC was not to undertake any financing for which, in its opinion, sufficient private capital could be obtained on reasonable terms. On the contrary, a principal function of the IFC would be to bring together potential investors and entrepreneurs. A fourth restriction was that the IFC would not assume responsibility for managing any enterprise in which it had invested. It would seek to protect itself through a judicious choice of partners, rather than through involvement in operations. Finally, although the IFC would not be permitted to own capital stock, its investment authority would be cast in terms broad enough to permit it to operate as a provider of venture capital. It would relate financial returns to risks through participation in profits and revolve its funds by selling its investments to private investors, whenever that could be done on satisfactory terms.

These provisions would be well adapted, Garner believed, to enable the IFC to play its intended role not merely as a supplier of capital but as a catalytic agent to stimulate investments. Many enterprises had held back from international investment because of lack of resources to investigate opportunities abroad or because of fear to embark alone into unfamiliar terrain where they might not receive fair treatment. In the last analysis, the IFC's success would have to be measured not so much by the amount and profitability of its own investments as by the amount of additional investment it stimulated from other sources. In this connection, it was worth emphasizing that the IFC would necessarily pay close attention to the general climate for private investment in the countries in which it operated. In time, because of its international cooperative character, the IFC might come to be regarded as an objective and informed agency whose advice on private investment problems was freely sought and seriously attended. Thus contributing to a constructive change of attitude to the whole problem of private capital movements, the benefits of the IFC would extend far beyond the effects of its immediate investment activities.

Ancestry

The perceived need of directly promoting private investment, which eventually led to the establishment of the IFC, was being articulated even before the Bretton Woods Conference. Within the U.S. delegation, the State Department proposed that the Bank should be permitted to lend without the guarantee of host governments. This approach had to yield, however, to the more cautious view of the Treasury, requiring guarantees in all cases. At the conference itself, a proposal to relax the demand for guarantees was turned down during a committee debate. Furthermore, within the U.S. delegation, there was support for equity participation by the Bank. The issue was not pursued, however, because of different views within the delegation, as well as opposition from other delegations, and in particular from Lord Keynes. So, at Bretton Woods the aversion to mixing operations of public institutions with private enterprise, together with the spirit of caution, carried the day.[2]

As its Articles were finally formulated, the Bank was to promote private foreign investment by means of guarantees or participation in loans and to supplement private investment with its own funds, when private capital was not available on reasonable terms.[3] It soon became clear, however, that while the Bank could readily operate in fields like infrastructure, largely dominated by public institutions, the requirement of government guarantees and the inability to invest in equity would obstruct financing of the private sector and the promotion of private capital flows.

2. See Bronislaw E. Matecki, *Establishment of the International Finance Corporation and United States Policy: A Case Study in International Organization* (Praeger, 1957).
3. IBRD, *Articles of Agreement*, art. I (ii).

A memorandum of early 1949 describes how the Bank, after appraising the need of industrial investments in a developing country, found itself lacking the tools to promote that investment either from within the country or from the outside.[4] The memorandum went on to suggest a two-stage program in order to deal with this situation. In the first stage, the Bank would establish a Development Services Department, which, among other things, would seek to interest private enterprises in investigating, organizing, financing, and managing projects in developing countries. As a second stage, an International Development Corporation could be established as a subsidiary of the Bank and be empowered to invest funds in development projects without government guarantee, principally as equity. It would normally seek to associate itself with both local and foreign investors and would as a matter of policy favor the sale of its holdings to local investors after a period of successful operations. In general, its activities might be patterned after those of the U.K. Colonial Development Corporation, established in 1948. After further consideration within the Bank and, presumably, some outside consultation, the Proposal for an International Development Corporation appeared in an advanced form in a memorandum of March 1950.[5]

This design of an IFC-type organization became the basis for the deliberations of Bank management with outside parties. These were first and foremost U.S. government agencies, as the major part of the funds required had to come from the United States. Following up the developmental aspects of his inaugural address, President Harry S Truman asked the International Development Advisory Board, headed by Nelson Rockefeller, to consider "with maximum dispatch and effectiveness the broad objectives and policies of the Point Four program."[6] This assignment was given on November 24, 1950, two weeks before a national emergency was proclaimed in the United States on account of the Korean War.

The Advisory Board acted with the speed requested and transmitted their report, "Partners in Progress," to President Truman already in March 1951.[7] The report recommended a new International Development Association, supplementing international lending activities by financing public works in developing countries on a grant basis. Moreover, it proposed the creation of an International Finance Corporation, as an affiliate of the World Bank, with authority to make

4. Memorandum, Richard H. Demuth to John McCloy and Robert Garner, "Organization of the Bank in Relation to Its Development Activities," February 11, 1949.

5. Memorandum, Richard H. Demuth, "Proposal for an International Development Corporation: A Suggested Application of the Point IV Policy," March 16, 1950.

6. Letter, Harry S Truman to Nelson Rockefeller, chairman of the International Development Advisory Board, November 24, 1950. Included in appendix A of IDAB, "Partners in Progress," pp. 89–90. This Board had been established under the Act for International Development (Public Law 535, Title IV, sec. 409) for the purpose of advising and consulting with the president on the program carried out under the law.

7. International Development Advisory Board, "Partners in Progress: A Report to the President by the International Development Advisory Board," March 1951.

loans, without government guarantees, to private enterprises and to participate in equity investments together with private investors. The latter proposal had resulted from close and largely informal contacts of members of the Advisory Board with representatives of World Bank management, especially Robert Garner and Richard Demuth. It followed the outline previously drawn up within the Bank in all respects, except that it explicitly excluded equity investments from carrying voting rights. This emphasized the view that the Corporation should not become involved with enterprise management, an issue on which the Advisory Board held strong views.[8]

The "Partners in Progress" report received much attention, but its recommendations had anything but smooth sailing in U.S. government agencies, in business circles of the United States and other investing countries, and in the international community, as represented by the United Nations. In fact, almost four years passed before the U.S. secretary of the Treasury approved the "Partners in Progress" recommendation on the IFC, though in a substantially changed form, thus opening the way for its final acceptance. The IDA proposal had to follow an even longer and more tortuous path. The delay was obviously influenced by the shift in U.S. administrations in the beginning of 1953, but skepticism and direct antagonism to both the IDA and the IFC recommendations was widespread and deeply rooted in all the fora concerned.

The U.S. government agencies most strongly opposed to the IFC proposal were the Treasury Department, the Federal Reserve System, and the Eximbank. Their view was that public participation in the ownership of private enterprises ran counter to the free enterprise system and would tend to undermine that system. It was, moreover, contended that if public international support was required for equity investments in developing countries, these investments were probably not economically justified in any case. There were concerns about the proliferation of international bureaucracies and the eventual weakening of the discipline imposed on borrowers by the World Bank and the Eximbank. Budgetary considerations also played their role, as the U.S. share of the proposed $400 million capital of the new organization would have amounted to as much as $150 million. Other U.S. government agencies, in particular the Department of State, as well as the Department of Commerce, were in favor of the proposal, but less vigorous in their views than the opponents.

Looming behind the official U.S. attitude was the belief that business circles in the United States, as well as in other industrial countries, were strongly opposed to the IFC proposal. This impression may have been exaggerated under the impact of the forceful and persistent antagonism of the National Foreign Trade Council, a U.S. organization broadly representative of companies active in the field of foreign trade. An informal survey by the World Bank of the investment communities in the

8. See Matecki, *Establishment of the International Finance Corporation*, pp. 71–74.

principal investing countries, as well as a meeting of bankers and businessmen convened during the Bank's Annual Meeting in Mexico City in 1952, revealed both strong opposition and a measure of interest in the proposal.[9] The opponents contended that the problem for private investment in developing countries was not the lack of capital but the absence of an appropriate investment climate, the creation of which the activities of an IFC-type organization were more likely to delay than to promote. Nevertheless, the Bank reported that a considerable, perhaps preponderant, group of private investors would seek to avail themselves of the eventual services of the Corporation. Later on, business views became more positive, perhaps reflecting the increasing confidence in the World Bank. In May of 1955, after the approval of the proposal by the U.S. administration, Robert Garner was able to report great interest in the IFC among businesspeople, as well as growing support and even enthusiasm.[10] At the congressional hearings held that summer, the National Foreign Trade Council was the only organization opposing the establishment of the IFC.

At the United Nations, intense deliberations on economic development issues had been going on since 1946 under the auspices of the Economic and Social Council. The concern had, however, been primarily with public rather than private international financing of development and had centered around the proposal for a United Nations Economic Development Administration (UNEDA), intended to supplement World Bank activities by financing development projects unable to yield commercial results. In May 1951, almost immediately after the appearance of the "Partners in Progress" proposals, a Group of Experts appointed by the UN Secretary General expressed a full and unqualified support for the recommendation of an International Development Association. The group's support for the establishment of an International Finance Corporation was, on the other hand, limited to an exploration of possibilities. This reflected the primary interest of developing countries in public financing, combined with reservations about international private financing.

The requested exploration of the IFC proposal was undertaken by the World Bank, which during the following years submitted three reports on the IFC proposal to the United Nations.[11] These reports, together with statements by the Bank's president, Eugene R. Black, both before the United Nations and at the Bank's annual meetings, helped keep the IFC proposal afloat and provided it with identity and stature separate from the International Development Authority. In its

9. IBRD, "Report on the Proposal for an International Finance Corporation," April 1952.

10. Matecki, *Establishment of the International Finance Corporation*, p. 89.

11. IBRD, "Report on the Proposal for an International Finance Corporation," R-584/2, April 1952; IBRD, "Report on the Status of the Proposal for an International Finance Corporation," R-688/1, May 1953; IBRD, "Second Report on the Status of the Proposal for an International Finance Corporation," R-793, June 3, 1954.

last report to the United Nations (the Second Status Report of June 1954), the Bank made the proposal considerably more palatable to the capital-exporting countries by stating specifically that IFC operations could begin with as low a paid-in capital as $50–100 million, with further expansion in sight when its capability and the need for its services had been demonstrated.

It was, nevertheless, public international financing that continued to be the focus of interest at the United Nations, now in the form of a Special United Nations Fund for Economic Development (SUNFED).[12] The discussion on this proposal became intensive at the eighteenth ECOSOC session in the summer of 1954, where the developing countries solidly and strongly supported the immediate establishment of SUNFED and, less vigorously, that of the IFC. The ranks of the industrial countries were divided on the issues, and the United States was on the defensive but still unyielding in its opposition.[13]

Pressures for action were also accumulating in specific parts of the developing world. In Latin America, an Inter-American Development Bank for Industrial, Agricultural, and Mining Development as well as a scheme for the support of commodity prices was being proposed by the Economic Commission for Latin America under the leadership of Raúl Prebisch. These proposals, together with the SUNFED proposal, were to be discussed at an Inter-American Economic Conference in Rio de Janeiro on November 22, 1954. At the same time, urgent pleas for more active development assistance in Asia, including an Asian Marshall Plan being promoted by the prime minister of Japan, were being addressed to the economically more advanced countries, especially to the United States. The USSR and its satellites were using the opportunity to offer developing countries long-term exchange contracts for their products.[14]

At the World Bank Annual Meeting in late September 1954, demands of developing countries for increased financial aid were both universal and more vocal than before. It was after that meeting that Eugene Black, having maintained close contact on the issue with U.S. authorities over the previous years, took a new initiative. After talks with Treasury officials, he submitted what come to be known as the Black Plan. In a letter of October 20, 1954, he restated his belief that the Corporation would be more effective if it had power to make equity investments.[15] If there were an insuperable opposition to this in principle, however, he believed that the utilization of debentures with income and conversion features could

12. "Report on a Special United Nations Fund for Economic Development," prepared by a committee appointed by the Secretary General and presented to the 16th ECOSOC session, 1953.

13. Matecki, *Establishment of the International Finance Corporation,* p. 119.

14. Ibid., pp. 120–24.

15. Letter, Eugene R. Black to W. Randolph Burgess, undersecretary of the Treasury for Monetary Affairs, October 20, 1954 (drafted by Davidson Sommers, World Bank general counsel).

achieve sufficient flexibility for successful operations. Another element of the plan, not specifically mentioned in the letter, was the reduction of paid-in capital from $400 to $100 million, previously suggested in the Bank's report to the United Nations.

Without further ado, Secretary George M. Humphrey accepted the plan and announced on November 11, 1954, less than two weeks before the Rio conference, that the U.S. administration would ask Congress for approval to participate in a proposed International Finance Corporation, organized as an affiliate to the World Bank. The authorized capital would be $100 million, out of which the United States would provide $35 million. The Corporation would operate in the area of venture capital. Without directly providing equity financing, it would be empowered to issue securities, bearing interest only if earned, and convertible into stock when purchased by private investors. The operations of the Corporation would necessarily have to be experimental, and their measure of success would be in the stimulation of the international movement of private funds. When subsequently submitting the proposal to Congress, President Dwight D. Eisenhower gave it strong support.[16] On December 4, the U.K. government announced that it had been led by the revised American position to reconsider its original attitude. A week later, a resolution for the establishment of the IFC was unanimously adopted by the UN General Assembly, and the World Bank was asked to draft statutes for the Corporation.

Traits of Character

The purpose and character of the International Finance Corporation, as it was perceived at the time, were carefully spelled out in the process of drafting and deliberating its Articles. By intention, the Charter was, however, left with a degree of flexibility for accommodating lessons of experience and changes of circumstances. Outright amendments of the Articles have been made on two occasions, first to make the holding of equity possible and, later, to permit borrowing from the Bank within specified limits. Otherwise, the original Charter has proven sufficiently flexible to allow for an evolution of concepts, policies, and operations. Much of the description and analysis of the following review of the IFC's history focuses on this process.

What do the Articles themselves, as well as reports, statements, and records of discussion from the time of foundation, say about the views prevailing at the outset? How did the founders regard such main characteristics of the institution as its relationship with the Bank, its role as investor, its promotional activities, its choice of domestic and foreign partners, its attitude toward publicly owned

---

16. Dwight D. Eisenhower, "Message from the President of the United States Urging Enactment of Legislation Permitting the United States to Join with the Other Free Nations in Organizing an International Finance Corporation," House Document no. 152, 84th Cong., 1st sess., May 2, 1955.

enterprises, and its efforts to improve the investment climate? And, equally important, what were the intentions regarding the Corporation's funding and profitability and the understanding of its developmental character?

RELATIONS WITH THE BANK. The affiliation with the Bank was believed to be essential. Without it, the IFC would not be able to carry out its functions. But this affiliation needed to be of a complex nature, at the same time firm and somewhat distant. It needed to mitigate the fears of private investors of unfair treatment by governments and to alleviate their apprehension about associating themselves with public funds. This complexity was perhaps the most important consideration for establishing the IFC as a separate corporation rather than as a department of the Bank. There were other significant reasons, however, such as the reluctance to open up the Bank's Articles of Agreement for revision, and the different nature of procedures and staffing required for operations with the private as opposed to the public sector. Financial separation was strongly emphasized, not least in order to prevent the higher risk of the IFC operations from affecting the creditworthiness of the Bank. But, in spite of their different identities, the two organizations would be striving toward the same goals, and their affiliation would facilitate coordination and avoid conflicts. The joint utilization of administrative, economic, engineering, and legal services would be convenient and would save on costs.

The particular method of affiliation was considered less significant than the affiliation itself. Earlier, it had been proposed that the Bank should hold all the voting shares of the Corporation, obtained at nominal value from the member governments, which provided the capital. It had even been contemplated that Bank officials might form the Board of Directors of the Corporation.[17] According to the Articles of Agreement, however, the affiliation was ensured by making the governors and executive directors of the Bank ex officio governors and directors of the Corporation, and by making the president of the Bank ex officio chairman of the Board of Directors of the Corporation. Moreover, the president of the Corporation was to be appointed by the Board of Directors on the recommendation of the chairman, in effect leaving the choice of the IFC's highest official to the president of the Bank.[18]

17. See IADB, "Partners in Progress," and memorandum from Demuth, March 16, 1950.

18. The three World Bank affiliates, IDA, IFC, and MIGA, are organized as entities separate and distinct from the Bank. Their Articles of Agreement do not, however, provide for the same relationship with the Bank in all three cases. IDA and the IFC have ex officio the same governors and executive directors as the Bank, whereas in MIGA this is not the case. Again, in IDA and the IFC the president of the Bank is ex officio the chairman of their boards, but this is not stipulated for MIGA. In the case of IDA, the president of the Bank is ex officio the Association's president, whereas in the IFC and MIGA the president is appointed by the Board of Directors on the recommendation of the chairman. In reality, the president of the Bank has been both chairman of the Board and president in all three

THE ROLE AS INVESTOR. The aim of the IFC was to help establish and expand sound private enterprises in developing countries. In order to do this, it would have to act as a venture investor cooperating with private investors. It was equity capital, ready to assume risks as well as expecting to participate in gains, that was needed in developing countries much more than loan capital with fixed interest and maturities. This was the concept from the beginning, which the initial exclusion from holding stock did not change. Loan capital had its place and could be provided by the IFC if necessary, especially in connection with equity investments. But the Corporation's attitude and approach were meant to be those of an equity investor who was helpful in initial stages and subsequently withdrew when the going became easier and a satisfactory selling price could be obtained for the investment.

Linked to this view, from early on, was the conviction that it would be unwise for a public institution like the IFC to assume management responsibilities in private enterprises. This attitude was emphasized by the "Partners in Progress" report and achieved its extreme expression in the exclusion of shareholdings, at the insistence of the U.S. Treasury. After experience had demonstrated the need for straight equity investments, the attitude toward management responsibility remained the same, as was clearly expressed in the amended Articles.

PROMOTIONAL ACTIVITIES. That the IFC should have a promotional attitude was taken for granted from the beginning. Promotional activities could be of more than one kind, however. They could be of a relatively passive character, when the initiative lay with private investors and the role of the IFC was to provide contact with other investors, a measure of knowledge regarding technical or local conditions, or a degree of assurance regarding official behavior. They could also be of a more active character, with the IFC bringing forward a project idea initiated by itself or received by it in an incipient state. In those cases, however, it would need to find private investors to work with, who could take over the project and make it their own, so that IFC participation would remain within its statutory and customary limits. It appears that this second, more active promotional role was from the beginning conceived as a possible and even an attractive mode for the IFC's

---

affiliates, except for the IFC during 1956–61, when there was a separate president. In all of the affiliates, the presidents are the chiefs of the operational staff, according to the charters, as is the case in the Bank itself. However, in the IFC, since 1961, and in MIGA the president has in effect delegated this function to an executive vice president, operating with a staff distinct from the Bank's staff, except for some joint services. In IDA, on the other hand, there is no executive vice president and no separate staff. These differences in organization are rooted in the dissimilar objectives of the affiliates. Both the IFC and MIGA were intended to operate with the private sector without host-government guarantee, while the Bank and IDA were to work primarily with the public sector, and with the private sector only on the basis of government guarantees, although this was not specifically required in IDA's Charter. A certain distance from the Bank, consequently, became a characteristic of the IFC and MIGA, even more pronounced for the latter than the former.

operations. It was realized, however, that this role would be highly difficult to implement, and it was the first, or more passive one, that was expected to prevail.

DOMESTIC AND FOREIGN PARTNERS. According to the Articles of Agreement, the IFC was to implement its purpose by bringing together investment opportunities, domestic and foreign capital, and experienced management.[19] This did not discriminate between domestic and foreign partnership. Going back to the earliest proposals and following the argumentation thenceforth, it becomes clear, however, that there were highly limited expectations for the availability of private domestic capital and the capability of domestic entrepreneurs in developing countries. The main contribution of the Corporation was therefore expected to be in the promotion of foreign investment, with the cooperation of foreign and domestic capital considered highly desirable. This notion traced its origin to the Bank's Articles of Agreement, which stated that one of its purposes was "to promote private foreign investment," an assignment the Bank had found that it had no adequate tools to implement.[20] The perception at the time was that private foreign investment was not significantly recovering after the war and that developing countries were thus being deprived of much needed capital, and, even more important, of the technical and managerial knowledge that ordinarily went with direct foreign investment.

PUBLICLY OWNED ENTERPRISES. The Bank's management, as well as the leading shareholders of the IFC, held clear-cut views regarding private versus public enterprises. Private enterprise was the only efficient way to produce agricultural and industrial goods as well as to provide commercial and financial services. The purpose of the IFC was to promote that kind of enterprise, which would exclude the support of publicly owned enterprises. The complication, however, was that most developing countries had formed government-owned entities to act as substitutes in the absence of private enterprise or to work with and to promote private entrepreneurship. The door had therefore to be left slightly ajar. This was done by stating in the Charter that a government or other public interest in a productive private enterprise "shall not necessarily preclude the Corporation from making an investment therein."[21] In the first IFC policy statement, a phrase from an earlier draft of the Articles emphasized that the enterprises in which the IFC invested had to be "essentially private in character."[22]

IMPROVEMENT OF THE INVESTMENT CLIMATE. The early supporters of the IFC were keenly aware of the essential importance of a favorable climate for

19. IFC, *Articles of Agreement*, art. I.

20. IBRD, *Articles of Agreement*, art. I (ii).

21. IFC, *Articles of Agreement*, art. III, sec. 1. For a detailed description of how the wording of Article III, Section 1 came about, see the section "The Attitude toward Publicly Owned Enterprises" in this chapter.

22. IFC, "Statement of Operating Policies," IFC/56/R-22/1, July 31, 1956, p. 1. Approved by the Board of Directors on July 30, 1956.

private investment. They saw the improvement of this climate as a major purpose of the IFC, which, as described in the Articles, was "to help create conditions conducive to the flow of capital, domestic and foreign, into productive investment in member countries."[23] In the documents and discussions related to the IFC's establishment, this aspect of its operations is not mentioned much, however, nor is it made clear how the IFC was expected to implement this part of its agenda. Nevertheless, it was understood that the IFC would have special opportunities for taking up issues arising from its own operations and for acquiring knowledge of the nature of conflicts between governments and investors and of the best way to reconcile them.[24] In a speech to the United Nations Economic and Social Council in April 1955, Eugene Black expressed the hope that the IFC would be able to help improve the investment climate and encourage government policies favoring private investment.[25] Robert Garner saw the benefits of this extending far beyond the effects of immediate investment activities.[26] Moreover, in hearings before the U.S. Congress, an administration representative stated that an improvement of the investment climate was nothing less than the principal objective of the IFC.[27]

FUNDING. In its early stages, the IFC had no access to funding except from its member governments. To the extent that the Corporation was to engage in venture investments, borrowed funds could not be utilized, and this kind of investment was intended to be the mainstay of its operations. To the extent that borrowed funds might appropriately be used for lending operations, such funds were not accessible for the Corporation itself, as it lacked financial strength as well as reputation in the markets. Support from the World Bank, through guarantees or direct lending, was on the other hand considered problematic at a time when the Bank was establishing its own creditworthiness. Moreover, neither guarantees nor loans could be extended by the Bank without an amendment to its Articles. The IFC's operations were consequently confined within the limits of its small original capital, with the uncertain prospect of a capital replenishment at some future time, in case this was deemed justified and practicable by its major shareholders.

PROFITABILITY OF IFC. The Articles of Agreement made it clear that the Corporation was to undertake its financing on terms and conditions normally obtained by private investors, taking into account the risks involved. The invest-

---

23. IFC, *Articles of Agreement*, art. I (iii).

24. IBRD, "Report on the Proposal for an International Finance Corporation," April 1952, p. 15.

25. Eugene R. Black, speech to the 19th Session of ECOSOC (Economic and Social Council of the United Nations), April 7, 1955.

26. Robert L. Garner, vice president, "Informal Discussion: International Finance Corporation," statement to the Board of Governors, Istanbul, September 15, 1955.

27. IBRD, secretary's memorandum, 1-257, June 6, 1955, concerning the testimony of Samuel Waugh, assistant secretary of state for economic affairs, at hearings before the International Finance Subcommittee of the Senate Banking and Currency Committee.

ments were then to be sold when that could be done on satisfactory terms.[28] There was, in other words, to be no element of subsidy in the financing. That the Corporation was expected to be profitable was also clear from the stipulations regarding dividends.[29] Moreover, a protagonist of private enterprise could hardly be expected to operate otherwise than on a profitable basis. But the level of profits would depend on how much was spent on the preparation and promotion of projects as well as on efforts to improve the investment climate. It would also depend on the extent to which the Corporation allied itself with more venturesome investors and thus assumed higher risks. Conceivably, this could imply profits in an interval between what was normal for a private investment company down to what was required to maintain the real value of the paid-in capital intact. In the first case, the Corporation would be operating like a private investment company, except that through its position as a public institution, affiliated with the Bank, it would be lowering the political risks associated with investment, thus attracting additional investors. In the second case, it would be using all the returns from its capital for the promotion of individual projects, for provisions against losses from high-risk investments, or for the improvement of general business conditions. Where the IFC was to place itself in this interval between full commercial returns on its capital and the bare maintenance of its real value was not considered during the time of establishment. In fact, it did not come up within the institution, at least not in a formal way, until many years later.

THE DEVELOPMENTAL CHARACTER. That the purpose of the IFC was the same as that of the Bank, namely, to further economic development, was clearly stated in Article I of its Charter. The founders saw this developmental character principally in terms of the promotion of private enterprise as such. Well-run, profitable, private businesses were urgently needed in developing countries. Even by helping to get only a few of them going, the IFC would be making an important contribution to development, as these examples would be followed by others. There were, however, two significant qualifications to this view, which were expressed in the Charter itself. In the first place, the IFC's participation had to be essential for the realization of a project; in the second place, the enterprise supported had to be productive in nature, and it had to contribute to the development of the country.

The first qualification was expressed by the stipulation that the IFC should not "undertake any financing for which in its opinion sufficient private capital could be obtained on reasonable terms."[30] It was further clarified and supported by the requirement that financial terms and conditions should be determined with an eye to the terms and conditions normally obtained by private investors. Moreover, the

28. IFC, *Articles of Agreement,* art. III, secs. 3 (v) and (vi).
29. IFC, *Articles of Agreement,* art. IV, sec. 12.
30. IFC, *Articles of Agreement,* art. III, sec. 3 (i).

Corporation was required to revolve its funds by selling its investments whenever this could be done on satisfactory terms.[31] These requirements implied that the enterprises in which the IFC invested had to be of normal profitability, or have the prospect of acquiring such profitability within a reasonable period of time. The IFC was thus neither to substitute for nor to compete with other investors. Instead, it was to use its special position as a public institution to introduce investors into little known territory. It was to be a supporter of private enterprise that could bring investors and entrepreneurs together and help to realize projects that otherwise would not have come about. These characteristics were strongly emphasized during the preparatory and early operational phases of the Corporation, at the same time that concerns were being expressed about the practical difficulties in fulfilling them. Substantial as these difficulties might be, it was, however, only to the extent they could be overcome that the IFC could render its developmental contribution.

The second qualification was less straightforward than the first. It was expressed in the Charter by the use of the word "productive" to qualify "private enterprise" and by the condition that these "productive private enterprises" should "contribute to the development" of member countries. Little attention was devoted to this qualification in reports preceding the establishment of the Corporation. The same was true of the first Statement of Operating Policies of 1956.[32] That statement specified that investments would not be made in social projects, such as housing, hospitals, and schools, and not, "normally," in basic public utilities. After stating, in accordance with the Articles, that the operations of supported enterprises had to be "productive in character" and "contribute to the development of the economy," it proceeded to present three investment criteria by which the IFC's decisions would largely be influenced. These were the extent to which private capital would be brought in through the IFC's participation, the profitability of the investment, and its contribution to a diversification of the Corporation's portfolio. It would, consequently, appear that, in the IFC's early stages, enterprises were considered "productive" and "contributing to the development of the economy" largely, if not exclusively, to the extent that they were profitable as well as capable of mobilizing private capital. Contrary to what later became the case, a significant discord between profitability and developmental character was hardly perceived in the IFC's early years.

ESTABLISHMENT. On April 11, 1955, after discussions by its Board of Directors over a period of two months, the World Bank published the Articles of Agreement of the International Finance Corporation as approved by the Bank Board for submission to member countries. The signing of individual governments followed in due course, but at a slow pace, with Canada, India, and the United

31. IFC, *Articles of Agreement*, art. III, sec. 3 (v) and (vi).
32. IFC, "Statement of Operating Policies."

Kingdom signing in October of 1955. In that same month an ad hoc committee was set up within the Bank to plan and coordinate the preparatory work for the initiation of the IFC's operations. In December 1955, the United States accepted the Articles, and on July 20, 1956, the IFC's Charter came into force when France and Germany signed, which brought capital subscriptions up to the required level of $78 million.

Finally, on July 24, 1956, the IFC was formally constituted and Robert L. Garner appointed as its president. Other principal positions were filled by John G. Beevor, vice president; Richard H. Demuth, assistant to the president; and Davidson Sommers, general counsel. The last two retained positions at the Bank simultaneously. The International Finance Corporation, a progeny of the World Bank, whether a son or a daughter, was up. But would it run?

Early Years, 1956–69

The first years of the IFC brought disappointment, even deep disappointment, to its supporters. It would, of course, have been unreasonable to expect rapid expansion and success of a new institution entering an unfamiliar field, provided with only small capital, and hampered by numerous restrictions imposed by its founders. But even when this was taken into account, the record of the IFC's first years appeared to be poor, so poor, indeed, as to raise legitimate questions about the justification for its existence.

Faltering Steps, 1956–61

After five years of operation, at the end of fiscal year 1961, the IFC's Board had approved investments of $44 million, an average of less than $10 million per year.[33] During that year, approvals had in fact been only $5 million, after having reached $18 million in the previous year. Forty-five projects had been endorsed in eighteen countries, concentrated in Latin America. Only about one-fourth of the capital and reserves of $107 million were tied up in these investments, as several of them had not yet come to implementation and a few had been sold. The major part of the capital remained in U.S. government obligations, the returns from which had so far provided the Corporation with most of its income. Out of thirty-two investments that had become effective and not been sold, thirteen were operating profitably and ten with losses, half of them being in serious trouble. The remaining ones were in too early a stage of operations to ascertain their condition.[34] The Corporation

33. Throughout this chapter, statistical information refers to fiscal years. The stretch of fiscal years is from July of the previous calendar year to the following June. Fiscal 1961 thus covers the period from July 1960 to June 1961.

34. Eugene R. Black, president, statement to the IFC Board of Directors, IFC/R61-51, October 17, 1961.

itself had returned a modest average profit of 2 percent of net worth, just about enough to maintain the value of its capital intact.

There were several reasons for the slow beginnings of the IFC. The two most commonly mentioned, both at that time and later on, were the restrictions on equity holdings and the small size of the initial capital: that is to say, the two concessions the World Bank had offered to the U.S. Treasury in 1954 in order to obtain its support for the IFC's establishment. Important as these reasons undoubtedly were, there are other aspects to the issue, as is indicated by the slow growth of the IFC even after these obstacles had been removed. In fact, the demand for the services the IFC offered was not as large as had been expected. The world was somewhat different from what the initiators had believed.

The promotion of foreign direct investment had originally been considered a major field of operations for the IFC. The large companies, mainly engaged in such investment, were, however, operating on a scale vastly exceeding the IFC's capacity. Smaller companies that the IFC could recruit as partners in foreign investment had, on the other hand, little inducement to go abroad at times of high domestic prosperity in the capital-exporting countries and growing economic nationalism in developing countries. As a result, partnership with foreign investors, although not unimportant, played a lesser role than had been expected.

As for domestic private partners, they were also difficult to attract. The IFC lacked local contacts and knowledge, in large part because of its centralized location in Washington.And it found, in general, that the need was greatest for equity capital, which it could not provide. Prospective investors also had little knowledge of the IFC, and the products it was offering—loans with profit-sharing and convertibility features added to fixed maturities and interests—were not an attractive amalgam. Loans from national export-financing institutions, as well as suppliers' credits, although of shorter duration, might appear just as advantageous, besides being easier to obtain. The denomination of IFC loans in U.S. dollars, contrary to what would have been the case with equity investments, was an additional and, apparently, strong deterrent. Moreover, the environment in most developing countries lacked the competitive conditions that would have induced firms to expand and search for partnership, especially when the firms were tightly held by families or other small groups concerned with protecting enterprise control.

The management and staff of the IFC soon became painfully aware of these conditions. There was an almost frantic search for a more appropriate tailoring of instruments, and proposals were formulated urging a more activist approach. Upon his departure from the Corporation in 1960, the assistant director of investments, John C. Evans, who had come to the IFC from a Wall Street firm, wrote a confidential memorandum to Robert Garner describing the institution as a lender operating at the lower edge of long-term lending while expecting investment returns. What the IFC needed to become, however, was an investment institution offering straight equity, or, given the present Charter, "equity notes" of long-term duration with only a nominal rate of interest, intended to be held for at least four or five years. These instruments could then, eventually, be combined with long-term loans. More responsibility had to be given to the investment officers, who had to be well trained and venture oriented. Limits of exposure needed to be greatly extended and the capital, which had been provided for a pilot experiment, quickly employed with the aim of justifying replenishment.[35]

The World Bank was likewise concerned about the IFC. One of Robert Garner's closest associates during his years at the Bank, S. Raymond Cope, offered him his thoughts on the future of the IFC in a personal note of October 1960. He stated that the IFC had disappointed its warmest supporters, had done much less business than expected, and had difficulties in finding investments that, while not being too risky, were sufficiently remunerative. Whether justified or not, complaints were being voiced about the severity of investment terms, the complicated form of agreements, and the time required for negotiations. Contemplating the character of the IFC, Raymond Cope emphasized that it could not be run as a private corporation: "It should be business-like, it should be efficient, and it can legitimately have profit making as one of its objectives. But it is inescapably a creature of its member governments and must act in accordance with broad objectives which are those of its members as a whole."[36] The IFC's main task must be to help others invest rather than to find profitable investments for itself. It should consequently be concerned with investment conditions rather than with individual investments and widen its activities by taking up underwriting, working closely with local financial institutions, and helping to develop domestic capital markets. In order to do this, close cooperation between the IFC and the Bank would be required, and industrial financing ought to be a joint undertaking of the two institutions.

In the midst of disparate forces and conflicting advice, Robert Garner basically stuck to the policy of caution that he had adopted from the beginning. He was unwilling to aim at a speedy employment of IFC capital without a reasonable prospect of replenishment. He avoided substantial and risky exposures that might endanger the future of the institution, and he sought to secure that future through an ample margin of profit. He was by no means unresponsive to new ideas, however. In a presentation to the Board in late 1960, he described three new fields of action for the IFC: investments in development finance companies (DFCs), actively being considered in Latin America; the preparation and promotion of new ventures, principally in Africa and Southeast Asia; and, finally, the influencing of governments for the improvement of business conditions.[37] Most important, how-

35. Memorandum, John C. Evans to Robert L. Garner, August 15, 1960.

36. Memorandum, S. Raymond Cope to Robert L. Garner, "Thoughts on the Future of the IFC," October 12, 1960, with a personal letter dated October 21, 1960, IFC Policy File no. 30, "Operating Policies and Procedures," vol. 2.

37. Referred to in memorandum, Robert L. Garner to T. Graydon Upton, assistant secretary of the Treasury, "Notes Regarding IFC's Operations," December 1, 1960.

ever, both he and Eugene Black had by early 1960 become convinced of the necessity of amending the IFC's Charter in order to permit it to invest in straight equity. This view was propounded in Garner's address to the Annual Meeting of 1960.

The reasons behind this conviction, as well as the future course envisaged for the IFC, were elaborated by Eugene Black about a year later in a letter to Senator William Fulbright at the time the amendment was being considered in the U.S. Congress.[38] Black explained that the original proposal for the IFC had been developed by the World Bank's management in order to obtain power to do what the Bank could not do: lend without government guarantees and invest in equity. The objection to the equity feature by the then secretary of the Treasury, George Humphrey, had been considered fatal. Subsequently, the Bank convinced itself that the IFC operations need not be unduly restricted by the exclusion of straight equity. Experience, however, had proved otherwise, and he now believed that an amendment to the Charter was vital if the IFC was to be able to do its job. The IFC was an investment institution, seeking to provide venture capital on commercial terms and to encourage investment by private businessmen in productive enterprises, soundly conceived and carefully investigated. But the IFC had not been able to meet the hopes of its creators because it was prohibited from using the main tool of investors, capital stock. It had instead been forced into a complicated pattern of finance that was open to the suspicion of seeking both the protection of a creditor and the rewards of a stockholder and that lacked a legal basis in many countries. By being able to invest in capital stock, the IFC would be able to strengthen the capital structure of enterprises, encourage investors to take stock, share in risks and profits in a traditional manner, and negotiate investments in simple and acceptable forms. It would also be able to use options and convertibility more efficiently and enter the field of underwriting. This change would not imply, however, that all the IFC's investments would be in equity. A substantial part would be in loans and in combined equity and loans. Furthermore, Black emphasized that as before there should be no participation in enterprise management.

The proposed change in the Charter was not opposed by the outgoing Eisenhower administration and had an easy acceptance by the incoming Kennedy one. It also received a favorable reception in the U.S. Congress, although some senators raised the same kind of objections put forward in 1954, and it was well received by other member countries. The change came into effect on September 1, 1961.

The Charter amendment replaced the convoluted Section 2 of Article III, stipulating what kind of investments the IFC could and could not do, by a simple sentence: "The Corporation may make investments of its funds in such form or

38. Letter, Eugene R. Black to Senator W. Fulbright, chairman, U.S. Senate Committee on Foreign Relations, August 3, 1961. (Original draft prepared by J. G. Beevor, vice president of IFC.)

forms as it may deem appropriate in the circumstances." Moreover, in order to emphasize that the Corporation would refrain from management responsibilities, a phrase was added to Section 3 (iv) of Article III stating that it should not exercise voting rights in enterprises in which it had invested for any purpose within the scope of managerial control.

A New Beginning, 1961–62

On October 15, 1961, soon after the amendment to the Articles had become effective, Robert Garner retired and Eugene Black took over as president of the IFC, remaining at the same time the chairman of its Board. A new post of executive vice president was assumed by Martin M. Rosen, who had come from the World Bank a few months earlier to serve in this position. This top-management structure has been retained ever since, although the relationship between presidents and executive vice presidents has varied in accordance with the views and personalities of these officials.

There were two main reasons for establishing the new structure. In the first place, it was essential to create confidence in the institution, and what better way to do so than to lend it more of the prestige that the World Bank, and Eugene Black himself, had acquired. In the second place, the IFC had during its first five years become more remote from the Bank than had at first been intended. This could be explained by the understandable tendency of a new institution to assert its independence. It was, however, in part due to Robert Garner's posture. After nine years in the second place in an international institution, he was not inclined to share his new position with his former superior, Eugene Black.[39] Hence moves were made to establish the IFC's identity in staff recruitment, personnel policies, and legal services, and, in general, to increase the distance between the management and staff of the two institutions. The joint presidency was intended to check this tendency and bring about the harmonious relationship that had originally been envisaged.

In a comprehensive statement to the Board on October 17, 1961, Eugene Black gave his views on the position of the IFC. While briefly presenting the record of the first five years, he did not dwell on its deficiencies, focusing instead on the future opportunities opened up by the amendment of the Articles. Largely adhering to previous understandings of the IFC's role and procedures, he advocated somewhat greater flexibility in the type of investments, which would lead toward larger projects than before; a greater variety in instruments of equity, quasi equity, and credit; and support for agriculture and services in addition to manufacturing industry. Three fields were mentioned as especially suitable for IFC emphasis:

39. Within the Bank and the IFC, it was interpreted as a sign of this that in the first five annual reports of the IFC Black's name did not appear as chairman of the Board, although all the other members of the Board representing member countries were listed.

development banks, promotional activities, and underwriting. Development banks, or development finance companies, were expected to be of major importance to the IFC, but since the Bank, too, had become active in this field, activities here called for close cooperation between the two institutions. Promotional activities for new and important projects, which otherwise would not come about, were justified in some countries, although such activities would be expensive and difficult. Underwriting could now become a major field of operations, either as direct underwriting or as standby agreements, when the IFC was able to hold straight equity as well as different kinds of credit instruments. Indicating a desire to establish closer relations than before with the private investment community, Black said he had engaged George D. Woods, chairman of the First Boston Corporation, as an informal adviser to review the IFC's present portfolio and hoped to engage other advisers of similar background.

Early in 1962 a Department of Development Bank Services was established within the IFC and made responsible for financial and technical assistance to industrial development banks for both the IFC and the Bank. That same year, IFC studies on the possibilities of promoting particular industries were initiated in two countries, Iran and Venezuela, and a major underwriting operation was launched for the benefit of a Mexican steel company. An advisory panel of five distinguished investment bankers was established. During the following years, further important steps were taken to follow up the initiatives indicated in Eugene Black's statement. He did not stay with the IFC for more than about a year, however, for he retired at the end of 1962. The next president and chairman of the Board, George Woods, soon had new signals to give to the Corporation, and the executive vice president, Martin Rosen, was also making his own imprint as the decade proceeded.

An Industrial Initiative, 1963–65

When George Woods took over the presidency at the beginning of 1963, the World Bank had an established position in financial markets and a reputation as a careful and experienced lender and adviser in the field of infrastructure. Woods believed that the time had come to employ the Bank's strength in new ventures and soon presented his ideas to the Board.[40]

As he saw it, the more obvious and easily manageable infrastructure requirements of developing countries were by now being met, to a large extent through the Bank's efforts. The Bank should now diversify its activities and move into new fields, particularly into agricultural modernization, soundly based industrial growth, and widespread education and training. An obstacle to becoming more involved with industrial development, however, was the need for host-government

---

40. Memorandum from President George Woods to Board's Financial Policy Committee, "Bank Financial Policy," FPC63-8, July 18, 1963.

guarantees, although this requirement had not prevented the Bank from making a significant contribution in this field. As much as 16 percent of its total lending up to June 30, 1963, had aimed at industrial development, provided to a large extent through development banks and directed toward small and medium-sized industries. The time had now come to provide support to pioneering manufacturing industries that could make developing countries less dependent on extractive industries and agricultural products. The long-term loans needed to make such projects attractive for investors were of an individual size and total volume that exceeded the capacity of the IFC and local development banks. Such loans would consequently have to come from the World Bank itself, after a necessary change of its Articles of Agreement. In coordination with the IFC, Bank lending would only be applied when the amount was higher than the IFC's investment limits. When appropriate, it could also be combined with IFC equity investment. Commercial interest rates would be charged, which would exceed the normal rate of the Bank, and in order to protect the Bank's credit rating, the total amount of nonguaranteed lending would not exceed the Bank's accumulated surplus and reserves. Concurrently with this lending activity, the Bank would substantially strengthen its technical assistance in the industrial field, mainly for the support of development banks, industrial estates, and project feasibility studies.

The Board conducted intensive discussions on all the president's proposals during the summer of 1963. At the annual meetings of that year they were presented in the president's address. They were not favorably received. Although some executive directors responded positively, the prevailing view was that private industrial development did not need such strong support, and that it could make inroads on other activities of the Bank. Many were also opposed to weakening host-government guarantees. A number of directors believed that industrial promotion ought to be conducted primarily by the IFC rather than by the Bank.[41]

The reaction to his proposal convinced George Woods that the IFC might be a better channel for increased industrial activity than the Bank itself. The IFC's capital was very limited, however, and a large part was already invested or committed. The issue then became how best to augment the IFC's financial resources: by a capital increase, by borrowing in the market, or by a transfer of resources from the Bank. The first two alternatives, which became important later on, were ruled out because they were not considered feasible in the prevailing circumstances. The preferred choice, the utilization of Bank resources, presented substantial technical hurdles, and it was not until August 1964, after intensive deliberation within the Bank's management and its Board, that the final proposals were approved by the Board.[42]

41. Minutes of meetings of the Financial Policy Committee on July 30, August 1, and September 17, 1963, FPC63-11, FPC63-12, and FPC63-15.

42. IFC, "Bank Loans to IFC," R64-98 and IFC/R64-26, July 24, 1964, considered at Board meeting of August 3, 1964. Subsequently amended and becoming R64-98/1 and

The Board expressed some sympathy for a direct IFC capital increase, as well as for IFC borrowing in the market. In the management's view, however, a general capital increase would be ill-timed in view of the pending IDA replenishment, and offers for a special capital contribution were not forthcoming. The sale of IFC bonds without the Bank's guarantee was not deemed practicable and, with the Bank's guarantee, was likely to lower the acceptance of the Bank's own bonds.

The remaining alternative was that the Bank should lend to the IFC. This could, according to legal opinion, be done without changing the charter of either institution by establishing a Trust Fund to which the Bank would transfer a portion of its current income as a grant, and then the Fund would make loans to the IFC.[43] It was, however, considered more appropriate to authorize the lending in the Bank's Charter, to place a limit on the amount, and to incorporate that same limitation in the IFC's Charter as well.[44]

The agreed limit was an aggregate amount of debt, incurred by the Corporation from any source, of four times its subscribed capital and surplus, implying a leverage of 4:1. This was at the time considered equal to about $400 million, based on the IFC's subscribed capital of $100 million and the absence of any debt from other sources.[45] Two main considerations appear to have entered into the decision to set the limit at this level. In the first place, this was in line with the rules the Bank had established in dealing with development banks, and it was considered appropriate that the IFC should not receive more favorable treatment than these banks. In the second place, this limit would keep the lending to the IFC well within the amount of the Bank's supplementary reserves, thus clearly demonstrating that it was using neither borrowed funds nor paid-in capital for nonguaranteed lending to the IFC.

The amendments to the Articles were confined to the lending authorization and its limits and did not include any guidance regarding interest rates, maturities, or other terms. The intention was, however, that the loans to the IFC would carry the same interest rates and be subject to the same terms as other Bank loans, especially loans to development banks. On the other hand, the IFC would be free to set its relending rates and other terms in accordance with its own general policy.[46]

As it was not prudent to invest borrowed funds in equity, access to Bank resources could not enhance the IFC's capacity for equity investment. It was the

---

IFC/R64-26/1, dated August 4 and considered at Board meeting of August 6, 1964. The amendment concerned the incorporation of borrowing limits into the IFC Charter in addition to lending limits in the Bank Charter.

43. Aron Broches and R. B. J. Richards, aide memoire, April 10, 1964.

44. IBRD, *Articles of Agreement*, art. III, sec. 6; IFC, *Articles of Agreement*, art. III, sec. 6 (i), last clause.

45. In accordance with the amended Articles, the limit would, strictly speaking, have been $480 million as there was an accumulated surplus of $20 million.

46. Memorandum, "Minutes of IBRD Senior Staff Meeting, SSM/M/64-22, June 19, 1964." The meeting took place June 11, 1964.

declared intention of the president and the executive vice president, however, that borrowing should eventually cover all credits granted by the IFC, also those dating from previous years. This would leave the entire amount of the IFC's capital and surplus free for equity investments, which was considered important in view of the prevailing belief that there was greater need for equity investments than for loans.[47]

By the time the Board approved the amendments to the Articles of Agreement of both institutions on August 6, 1964, the member countries had reached a general consensus. The amendments were subsequently ratified and entered into force on December 17, 1965, when the required number of votes had been received. The first loan agreement between the World Bank and the IFC, providing conditions close to those the Bank applied to loans to development banks, was concluded in October 1966.

What had begun as an initiative to center industrial activities in the Bank, supported by the IFC, had thus ended in placing the main responsibility with the IFC and calling on the Bank to provide the financial support. The shift would be followed by organizational rearrangements. Development-bank operations were already constituted in the IFC, where Bank loans as well as the IFC equity investments were processed. In March of 1965, a further step was taken. In order to organize the support for industrial development effectively, the appraisal and supervision of industrial projects were moved to the IFC. The existing Industry Division of the Projects Department was divided in two, and the industry personnel moved to the IFC while the water supply section remained with the Bank. The IFC would thus, in the case of industry, perform the services that in other sectors were performed by the Projects Department. This was the same arrangement that, after some contention, had been adopted for development banks three years earlier.

By now the IFC had the potential to play an important role in industrial development because of the technical capacity it had achieved. Beginning in its first years, and progressing strongly under Martin Rosen's leadership, the IFC had strived to acquire high technical competence. Arriving at the IFC as a chemical engineer in 1966, Makarand Dehejia, later one of the Corporation's most experienced technicians, encountered a dedicated staff that looked upon itself as a pioneer of industrialization in developing countries. Their approach was that of a venture investor, with close and continued hands-on relations with the client, rather than that of a creditor.[48] Martin Rosen was highly exacting in his demands from the staff, to which he gave the example of his own excellence. His attitude has been likened to that of a Swiss watchmaker who places emphasis on every detail and closely supervises their assembly to ensure they properly fit together.[49]

47. Statement by George Woods at Board meeting of July 7, 1964. Memorandum, "Bank and IFC Financial Policy," FPC64-14, IFC/FPC64-2, July 15, 1964.

48. Makarand Dehejia, interview with the author, May 15, 1995.

49. Ladislaus von Hoffmann, interview with the author, May 17, 1995.

On this basis of new financial strength, appropriate organization, and technical competence, both Martin Rosen and George Woods had high hopes for the IFC's contribution to industrial development. In a magazine article, Rosen described the prospects for enabling the IFC to participate in large, capital-intensive projects and to make substantial financial contributions, thus becoming a significant factor in meeting the financial needs of private enterprises in developing countries.[50] George Woods went further than this: he believed the "IFC, with its vastly increased resources, might turn out to be a catalyst of exceedingly great value between very large corporations in Western Europe, Canada and the United States, and the developing countries."[51] In presenting the recommendations for amendment of the Articles of Agreement to the Board of Governors in Tokyo in 1964, he stated that the IFC, with increased resources, could make much larger commitments in individual transactions than before, and that such new dimensions of the IFC's activities would contribute greatly to the development process of member countries.[52]

The IFC in the 1960s: An Overview

By the mid-1960s, the two main obstacles to the IFC's early activities had been removed: first the exclusion of equity holdings, in 1961, and, subsequently, the shortage of funds, in 1965. The result was not a dramatic expansion of operations, but rather a measured rate of growth. Annual investment approvals rose from an average of less than $10 million a year in the IFC's first five years, 1957–61, to just below $40 million a year in the five-year period 1965–69. The average project size more than tripled at the same time, from $5 to $18 million, and the IFC average project participation increased from $1 million to almost $3 million. However, the Bank was not called on to provide funds at an early stage, as expected, and the first drawing on the loan agreed in 1966 did not take place until 1970. In the meantime, the Bank loan agreement had served as a backstop for increased commitments. The prospect of major operations with multinational companies, envisaged by George Woods and Martin Rosen in the mid-1960s, had materialized to little more than a modest extent by the time they left office in 1968 and 1969, respectively. Nevertheless, by 1970, the annual level of investment approvals passed the $100 million mark, in the neighborhood of which it remained until 1974.

Compared with the level of operations of the Bank, and with the increase in that level, the IFC's activities continued to appear rather insignificant, and its management and staff were under pressure to explain the relevance of the institution. This

50. Martin M. Rosen, "IFC: Its Policies and Operation," article prepared for *European Business Review*, September 1965.

51. Memorandum, "Bank and IFC Financial Policy."

52. George D. Woods, annual address, 1964 annual meetings of the Boards of Governors, Tokyo, September 7–11, 1964.

was done by referring to the total amount of funds the Corporation was able to attract to private investment as a more appropriate basis of judgment than the investment of its own funds. Moreover, the IFC had by now assumed responsibility for the preparation and supervision of all industrial projects of the Bank Group, and its activities were clearly affecting the investment climate in some developing countries. Most important of all, it was quality that mattered rather than quantity, a ground on which the IFC increasingly felt that it was standing firmly as the 1960s proceeded.

A 1963 memorandum of the Corporation's general counsel, R. B. J. Richards, posed the question directly: "Why does not IFC do more business?"[53] After initially stating that the IFC in fact did more business than it was usually credited for and that its significance, in any case, could not be evaluated by numbers, he went on to explain the constraints under which the IFC operated both because of its Charter and of its self-imposed policies. He asserted that although there were few ready-made investment opportunities in developing countries, there was no real shortage of investment capital, as good projects were able to obtain financing. The IFC was consequently left with special situations. He then suggested that the IFC ought to be more active in promotions, based on country economic surveys, and that it should seek to become a clearinghouse for investment opportunities and a depository of expertise in technology, finance, and legal matters relating to such opportunities.

Indeed, in the 1960s as a whole, the IFC was progressing on a rather broad front and on a firm basis. Furthermore, it was moving very much in accordance with the intentions of its founders. The originally perceived role of the IFC as a venture investor could now be more freely pursued. As a consequence, equity investments soared, exceeding one-half of total approved investments in 1963 and 1964. Thereafter, the proportion declined to one-third for the remainder of the decade. Even more important than the proportion, however, was the fact that lending was not looked upon as an independent instrument but as part of a total investment package that included equity. This was a policy rule, frequently referred to and apparently followed in most cases. Straight lending was an exception, and the annual report for 1966/67 stated that no project approved during that year was without an equity feature. A venture investment attitude permeated the organization. The IFC grew proud of the expertise it could contribute to prepare projects that were technically outstanding, financially sound, and commercially viable, and thus attractive to other investors. Frequently, the role of adviser had to be assumed over an extended time, as well as that of a supporter when trouble emerged. This led in due course to Board representation in some companies, especially in DFCs. Client satisfaction became another hallmark for the Corporation.

53. Memorandum, R. B. J. Richards to files, "Thoughts on a Recurrent Theme. Why Does Not IFC Do More Business?" September 12, 1963.

Attractive as this mode of operation was, and as much as it conformed with the original goals of the IFC, it was not suited to an expanding number of customers. The approach was an outgrowth of the management style of Martin Rosen, who wanted to give his close attention to every case. Instead of being a resource for broad industrial development in many countries, the IFC was becoming what Rosen described as a "special situations institution." This was not what most of its member countries wanted the IFC to be, nor what George Woods essentially had intended.

Attentive as the IFC was to meticulous project preparation, it did not do much to promote projects conceived within the organization or brought to it at an incipient stage. There were studies of the feasibility of certain industries in particular countries and of the development of individual projects from the bottom up. However, the Corporation found it most productive to work with established companies and with projects that had gone through a substantial degree of preparation.

In addition to becoming an experienced venture capital investor, the IFC was in the 1960s increasingly successful in attracting additional investors and funds to the projects it supported. Underwritings and syndications became an important part of its activities, as evidenced by the more rapid expansion of its gross investments than of the net investments financed from its own funds. It was also able to accelerate the sale of previous investments and thus revolve its capital more rapidly. The catalytic effects, measured as the ratio between the investment of other equity investors and lenders and the IFC's own net investment, were as high as 7:1 during the years 1962 to 1969, which is about as high as they ever became. The funds thus attracted came by and large from outside the host countries. Free to invest in equity and ready to participate in larger projects than before, the IFC had more success in working with foreign investors than during its first years. As had been the intention of the IFC's founders, joint ventures between foreign and local investors became the favored mode of operations. In the three fiscal years 1967–69, there were nineteen such ventures out of thirty-one principal projects with which the IFC was associated. Recording this, the 1969 annual report went on to say that, apart from exceptions based on special conditions, multinational companies would continue to be the IFC's typical mode of investment.[54] In cases where a local partner was not immediately available, it became the IFC's policy to reserve some of its shares for sale to such partners at an early opportunity.[55]

In its emphasis on foreign investment, the IFC was going against a trend in its member countries, which became pronounced in the late 1960s, and even more so in the 1970s. Restrictions and regulations were the order of the day, rather than the improvement of the investment climate that the IFC was expected to support

54. IFC, *Annual Report, 1969*, p. 6.
55. IFC, "General Policies," draft February 24, 1966, approved by the Board December 29, 1966.

according to its Charter and policy. All the same, the IFC was able to carry out studies for such improvements and help with their implementation in some countries, notably in Indonesia in 1968–69. In line with its overall responsibility for industrial development, this kind of activity was considered to be in the domain of the IFC rather than that of the Bank.

As it grew more flexible, the IFC extended its operations to new sectors, such as agriculture, agribusiness, and tourism. But the major part of its investments during the 1960s, apart from development banks, was in capital and intermediate goods industries such as iron and steel, nonferrous metals, timber, pulp and paper, building materials, and, to an increasing degree, fertilizer. These industries accounted for more than 60 percent of IFC investments from its own funds in 1962–69, and the IFC's emphasis on them can be attributed to a view of their pivotal role in economic development.[56] These industries were also suitable for the IFC because of their relatively large size, the potential for the transfer of technology, and attractiveness for foreign investors. They were also the ones governments were usually most interested in promoting and about which the IFC was rapidly acquiring special knowledge. After the introduction of the new breeds of cereal grains requiring greater use of fertilizer, George Woods took a keen interest in bringing fertilizer industries to developing countries, in particular India and Pakistan.

The promotion and financing of development banks was a field of great activity for the IFC in the 1960s. From 1962, when the IFC became responsible for Bank Group relations with these companies, until 1969, this kind of investment represented 16 percent of IFC investments. The number of projects, twenty-five in all, was higher than in any other category. The investments were mainly in equity and frequently were supplemented with substantial loans from the World Bank, appraised and supervised by the IFC. The development banks, which the IFC and the World Bank supported, were essentially privately owned, without exception deemed to be under private control, and exclusively devoted to the financing of private investment. As originally seen by the Bank, the merit of development banks was the possibility of reaching through to small and medium-sized enterprises and avoiding the government guarantee problem, for the retail loans did not have to be guaranteed. When the IFC became able to invest in equity, lending and equity investment could be combined. This offered new opportunities to channel technical assistance through the banks, and to use them as clearinghouses for investment opportunities, as mobilizers of local and foreign capital, and as promoters of capital markets. In the case of development banks, the IFC soon made an exemption to the practice of not accepting seats on a company board. In effect, it saw development banks as national replicas of itself, pursuing the same aims with similar means. During the 1960s the IFC regarded them as a principal instrument for its

56. See IFC, "Statement of Operational Policy," July 30, 1956, and Black, statement to the Board of Directors, October 17, 1961.

activities and an important conduit for its own and the Bank's investment. Early examples of success among these banks were seen in India, Pakistan, Iran, and Morocco.[57]

As operations expanded, the IFC's net income increased and its financial position grew stronger. By 1969 most of its income derived from its own operations, substantially from dividends and profit participation. Although at a modest level of 3.5 percent of capital during 1962 to 1969, net income stayed above the average U.S. rate of inflation of 2.5 percent per year. At the end of fiscal year 1969, accumulated retained earnings were close to $50 million, or almost one-half of the paid-in capital. This was considered an accomplishment for an institution that had been struggling to achieve profitability.

Toward the end of the 1960s it thus appeared that the IFC had recovered from its inauspicious beginnings and emerged as a well-established institution set on a steady course. Its technical capacity had become recognized, its financial position strengthened, and it had been given the lead in the Bank Group's efforts for industrial development. It could be argued, however, that these accomplishments had been achieved to the detriment of greater expansion, stronger promotional efforts, and a larger developmental impact. Indeed, the sequel followed a different track than might have been expected. Powerful influences from the outside world and an internal change of leadership would shift the IFC, together with the entire World Bank Group, in a new direction before the 1960s were over.

Emphasis on Development, the 1970s

When Robert S. McNamara took over the leadership of the World Bank Group in April 1968, the mission of industrial development assigned to the IFC by his predecessor must have appeared out of proportion to the strength of the carrier. Including retained earnings, the IFC's capital was only $150 million, the volume of its own operations barely reached $100 million a year, and, at about 160, its staff was less than one-tenth of that of the Bank. Even so, the Corporation had been charged with the preparation, appraisal, and supervision of all Bank Group projects in the field of industrial development, which appeared to be gaining in importance as the needs for infrastructure became better satisfied. In this endeavor it was dependent on the Bank for funds as well as manifold services.

Although this arrangement looked like an anomaly, there was a valid reason for it. In the early years of the World Bank and the IFC, industry was considered the domain of private enterprise and something that public institutions like the Bank should deal with only at arm's length. Hence the IFC was established as a separate entity. As the need for support became greater in its field of action, the obvious

57. See R. B. J. Richards, William Diamond, and Robert B. Glynn, "International Finance Corporation," April 26, 1963.

solution was to try to strengthen its financial and operational capacity, as compared with that of the Bank. This was the road chosen by George Woods after meeting resistance to the idea of helping the Bank itself better to deal with private enterprise through a revision of the government guarantee requirement.

The new president saw things differently, however. And the times had changed. Mixed economies had become the order of the day in the industrialized world, and most developing countries had turned to government leadership in almost every field of activity. McNamara himself did not regard public or private ownership as a central concern. As long as enterprises were being led by competent managers and enjoying a reasonable degree of autonomy under market discipline, it did not matter whether their owners were private or public. Development, leading to the alleviation of poverty, was the overwhelming objective of the Bank Group. Whether that objective was sought along the pathways of private enterprise or government initiative was a matter of national and political preference; and, for the time being at least, this preference was mainly in one direction.

From this point of view, the Bank itself was the appropriate instrument for industrial action, and not the IFC. With its large capital, trusted position in financial markets, numerous and capable staff, and intimate relations with governments, it would be able to do much more in a shorter time than the IFC could do, even with a strengthening of its resources. Accordingly, a shift in responsibilities was in order.

The path marked out for the IFC for the following decade was thus much narrower than the one it had begun to travel during the 1960s. It was also a somewhat different path in that now the aim was to pursue economic development rather than the profitability of the enterprises supported. That distinction had not been given much prominence during the Corporation's early years, as development and profitability were on the whole expected to go together. There had, however, always been a dissenting view, primarily represented by the developing member countries. This view was now gaining support among industrialized countries and was expressed in the Report of the Commission on International Development, headed by Lester B. Pearson.[58] Most important, this view was shared by the new president of the Bank and the IFC. McNamara's reorientation led in the following years to significant changes in almost every aspect of the IFC's policies and practices compared with those that had prevailed in the Corporation's early years.

The Transfer of the DFC Department

As a first step toward a reorientation of the Bank Group's industrial policy and a restructuring of its implementation, the Development Finance Companies De-

---

58. Lester B. Pearson, *Partners in Development: Report of the Commission on International Development* (Praeger, 1969), esp. pp. 114–15.

partment was transferred from the IFC to the Bank in November 1968. This department had been established within the IFC early in 1962 and was responsible for dealing with DFCs for both the IFC and the Bank.[59] Originally limited to promotion, technical assistance, and policy guidance, the department had within a year become responsible for all operations with DFCs, including supervision. By the time the department was transferred to the Bank in late 1968, it had participated in the organization or restructuring of twelve DFCs and prepared a total of thirty-four Bank loans as well as nineteen IFC investments. In fiscal 1968 its operations had accounted for 17 percent of Bank and IDA lending during that year, and an even higher proportion of IFC investments. By this time the portfolio administered by the department amounted to more than $600 million invested in twenty-seven companies. In eleven of them, the IFC was represented on the boards. The department's staff totaled thirty-seven, which was more than 20 percent of IFC's total staff.[60]

In a July 1968 report to McNamara, the director of the department, William Diamond, reviewed its operations and analyzed its functions and structure.[61] Significant frictions, said the report, were inherent in the running of a large program of Bank lending from within the IFC. Also, further complications might result from an increased scale of Bank lending to DFCs and possible changes in Bank Group policies in this field. Nevertheless, the report saw significant advantages in retaining the relationship with the IFC, both with regard to the DFC operations themselves and the IFC's overall operations. In conclusion, it pointed out that the purpose of operations with DFCs had not been simply to retail Bank resources but to stimulate private investment and create capital markets. This had united the objectives of the Bank and the IFC and justified placing the DFC function in the IFC. If the purpose were to change, and, in particular, if government finance companies were to be used as agencies for state enterprises, there would be less reason to have this function in the IFC.

The president opted for a shift, saying that it would facilitate an expansion of operations, streamline procedures, and permit the IFC to concentrate on direct financing.[62] The department was transferred as a whole, with its functions, organizational structure, and management unchanged, and it was placed directly under the Bank's president, thereby avoiding the intermediation of a vice president. (It was the only operational department with such status.) Following the

59. Although DFCs had been dealt with in the Bank since 1952, they had not been the task of a specialized department; the work was essentially handled by the staff of the Industry Division of the Technical Operations Department.

60. William Diamond, "The Work of the Development Finance Companies Department," Report to Robert S. McNamara, July 25, 1968.

61. Ibid.

62. Robert S. McNamara, Administrative Circular, "Transfer of Development Finance Companies Department," October 31, 1968, effective as of November 1, 1968.

transfer, there were no changes in objectives or policies for a number of years. The operational memoranda issued in December 1970 and March 1971 followed that of March 1968 in emphasizing private investment. The DFCs supported by the Bank were to engage primarily in financing private enterprises, and only in exceptional cases were parts of the proceeds of Bank loans to be used for state enterprises. Moreover, the Bank was not to give assistance to DFCs unless one of the country's aims was to encourage private investment and the investment climate was conducive to private enterprise.

It was not until 1976 that the emphasis on private investment disappeared from operational statements. By then the DFC Department had been reduced to a core unit, and loan operations had been dispersed among area departments in conformity with the 1972 reorganization. In an Operational Manual Statement of September 1976, which formally remained in force until 1992, private enterprises, state-owned enterprises, and mixtures of the two had become equally acceptable as clients of Bank-supported DFCs. In addition, the encouragement of private enterprise had been replaced by the contribution to government development objectives as a criterion for Bank financing of DFCs.[63]

The transfer of the DFC Department greatly weakened the IFC's ability to employ intermediary financing as a major policy instrument. The IFC now moved from the center to the periphery of the Bank Group's industrial activities, reflecting the movement away from the encouragement of private enterprise to the support of state-owned enterprises.

A Review of Industrial Policies

In early 1969, a few months after the transfer of the DFC Department, the Bank Group initiated a broad review of its industrial policies, apparently at the request of McNamara, for his own orientation. This review was carried out by an outside consultant, William S. Gaud, who had recently been an administrator of USAID, together with Richard Demuth, now the director of the Bank's Development Services Department. Their report, dated May 6, 1969, was not presented to the Board and may not have had a wide circulation among Bank and IFC management and staff.[64] Its conclusions and recommendations were, however, reflected in a number of policy and organizational decisions of the following months and years. What also lends the report special relevance is that one of its authors was soon to

63. World Bank/IDA, "Operational Memorandum: Development Finance Companies," 5.11, March 29, 1968; World Bank/IDA, "Operational Memorandum," 5.20, December 31, 1970; World Bank/IDA, "Operational Memorandum," 2.64, March 31, 1971; World Bank, "Operational Memorandum: Development Finance Companies," 3.73, September 1976.

64. William S. Gaud, consultant, and Richard H. Demuth, "The Role of the Bank Group in Supporting Industrial Growth," World Bank, Development Services Department, May 6, 1969.

become the first IFC executive vice president appointed by McNamara and that the other had been a leading promoter of the Corporation in its early stages.

The report was critical of the low volume of the IFC's operations and recommended a number of steps for their expansion. It maintained that the "IFC still regarded itself more as a 'special situations investment company' than as a development agency."[65] It urged the IFC to place greater emphasis on institution building, that is, on financial intermediaries and capital markets, promotion activities, and flexibility in investment policies, especially in the granting of straight loans. It also recommended that the average size of commitments be increased even further than it had been so far, with smaller investments left to intermediaries. In order to accomplish this, the senior professional staff needed to be both enlarged and given greater authority than before.

These remarks signaled a shift away from both the concept of the Corporation and the style of management developed during the years of Woods and Rosen. Instead of the small institution, cultivating outstanding workmanship and promoting enterprise through examples of technical and financial quality, the report envisaged a larger institution with a broader perspective, no less concerned with volume than with content, more with overall development impact than with individual project results. The financial profitability versus development issue, soon to be given center stage by the Pearson Report, was presented as follows: "Unlike a conventional investment company which is interested primarily in profits, the IFC's primary interest is in development. Its loan policies should be flexible and its outlook imaginative. It should not be afraid to experiment. In principle, it should be prepared to do whatever needs to be done to get a sound enterprise moving."[66] In keeping with the view that profitability should not be the primary criterion for decisionmaking, the report maintained that the ability to sell mature investments should not be a major element of the IFC's policy and that straight loans ought to become an important IFC instrument.[67]

Turning to the Bank's industrial policy and practices, the report strongly advocated a leading role for the Bank itself: "If the Bank Group is to give effective support to industrial development it cannot leave the whole job to the IFC. Indeed, the IFC's Articles characterize its role as supplementing the activities of the Bank."[68] The Bank had, according to the report, fallen short in providing the required leadership because industry lent itself less to planning and control than sectors like agriculture and transport. This had led the Bank to take a reactive attitude, receiving industrial proposals rather than examining industrial needs and conducting a pragmatic follow-up. The Bank, it continued, had until recently locked itself out of a large area of industrial activity by holding firmly to the view

65. Ibid., p. 3.
66. Ibid., p. 10.
67. Ibid., pp. 7–10.
68. Ibid., p. 13.

that industry was the province of private enterprise and that state-owned industrial enterprises were to be excluded from Bank financing. The subordination of industry had led to a scattering of responsibilities for industrial development throughout the Bank Group, in sharp contrast to other sectors.[69]

According to the report, the time had now come for the Bank to embark upon a comprehensive program to support industrial growth. Industrial-sector reviews needed to be instituted and advice, guidance, and technical assistance on industrial policies given to governments. Assistance should be provided to identify and prepare industrial projects, eventually to be followed up by helping to find appropriate managers. Together with financing, this kind of assistance should be provided to sound industrial projects in the public as well as in the private sector.

In order to implement this industrial policy, the report recommended, an Industry Projects Department should be established within the Bank, having the same functions and position as other project departments within the organization. The DFC Department could occupy a parallel position, and the recently established Industrialization Division of the Economic Department could be retained as a research and policy unit. Appropriate coordination among these Bank entities, as well as with the IFC, would be ensured by an Industry Coordination Committee.

In October 1969, an Industrial Projects Department was established in the Bank, broadly along the lines proposed in the Gaud-Demuth report. The IFC's involvement in the Bank's industrial lending was thereby ended. A Coordination Committee on Industrialization was set up in December 1969, with representatives of the Industrial Projects Department, the Development Finance Companies Department, the Economic Department's Industrialization Division, and the IFC.

The Recommendations of the Pearson Commission

The Commission on International Development, headed by Lester B. Pearson, had been proposed by George Woods in 1967, and was instituted by McNamara a year later. Its report, presented in September 1969, was published under the title "Partners in Development." Its recommendations, thirty-three in number, received the immediate and intensive attention of the World Bank's management. On McNamara's initiative, detailed responses were prepared for each of them and presented to the Board.

In a departure from current political trends, the Commission strongly supported the role of private capital in economic development and devoted a chapter to private foreign investment and the policies appropriate to stimulate that investment. It recognized the important role that the IFC and other organizations with

---

69. The report does not mention that in March 1965, George Woods had moved the appraisal and supervision of all industrial projects to the IFC, whether they were to be financed by the Bank or the IFC. This had been done precisely in order to unify support for industrial development more effectively, as had been the case concerning financial companies when the DFC Department was established within the IFC in 1962.

links to the private sector could play in identifying projects and promoting invest-ment. At the same time, it criticized the IFC for not paying sufficient attention to government policies, for overemphasizing profitability as an investment criterion, and for not taking project initiatives. Its criticisms and recommendations regarding the IFC were, on the whole, accepted by McNamara and the Board and thus became an important point of departure for the IFC's reorientation in the 1970s.

The central issue raised by the Commission regarding the IFC was the extent to which its policies should be reoriented to emphasize the development effect of its investments and not just their profitability. In the analysis of the relevant recom-mendation in McNamara's memorandum to the executive directors, it was pointed out that, as recognized by the Commission and stated in the IFC's Articles, profitability was an essential investment criterion for an institution that wanted to encourage private enterprise and to revolve its funds by selling its investments.[70] Nevertheless, it was agreed that developmental significance should be given a more prominent place in the IFC's investment decisions than it had been given so far. This shift in emphasis was, according to the memorandum, already reflected in a recent revision of operational policies that had been submitted to the Board. It would be further strengthened by the appointment of an economic adviser within the IFC and by benefits resulting from the work of the new Industrial Projects Department of the Bank, which would complement the work of the IFC.

This acceptance of the Commission's view became the springboard for a num-ber of initiatives in a developmental direction. It is not certain, however, that the Commission had such broad implications in mind. Its remarks were made with a view to emphasizing the need for sound advice on government policies, advice that it believed the IFC had neither been able nor willing to provide. Taking policies as given, the IFC had been led by profit considerations to invest in projects that had marginally, if at all, contributed to economic development. This was, in particular, the case in sectors subsidized by very high effective tariff protection. The Com-mission's remarks could thus be interpreted as meaning that development and profitability clashed because of market distortions, created by government policies. In that case, a reconciliation would be brought about when the distortions had been corrected. In the ensuing reorientation of the IFC's policies, however, the view prevailed that, when deciding on its investments, the IFC had to have further criteria in mind besides profitability, whatever market conditions might be.

The other main IFC issue raised by the Commission concerned project iden-tification and investment promotion, in which it believed the Corporation should become more active. In his response to this recommendation, the president stated that the Commission was correct in its view that the IFC in the past had been

70. Memorandum to the executive directors, "Pearson Commission Recommendations Relating to the World Bank Group," R69-232, December 11, 1969; "Pearson Commission Recommendation No. 7 Concerning IFC Policies."

content to leave project initiatives to other investors.[71] There were, however, plans under way to change this, which the Commission had not taken fully into account. These plans, presented to the IFC Board in July 1968, implied that the IFC might, in some instances, assume responsibility for implementing a project from its inception. This could not be done, however, without employing special staff in locating investment opportunities on the spot.[72]

A further recommendation of the Commission, regarding industrial and foreign investment policy advice, was also of substantial relevance to the IFC. The Commission maintained that the World Bank, as well as other international institutions, should expand their activities in this field. Moreover, such activities could in the future be fully transferred to the IFC, when the Corporation had been able to achieve the proposed reorientation toward a more developmental and promotional approach. The president responded positively to the call for greater advisory activities, although he envisaged this primarily as an assignment for the Bank itself: specifically, for the area departments, the Industrialization Division of the Economic Department, and the new Industrial Projects Department, which would be concerned with general industrialization policy, including the establishment of priorities for industrial development. The advisory role of the IFC would be limited to the private sector, perceived as only a part of the industrial sector, and, more particularly, to the flow of foreign private capital.[73]

The Issue of Protection

The question as to whether the IFC should finance highly protected industries had arisen at an early stage of its existence. In 1959 Leonard B. Rist, the director of the Bank's Economic Department, had considered the issue in a memorandum.[74] His approach was pragmatic and flexible. He said that the degree of protection enjoyed by an enterprise applying for IFC financing ought to be compared with the protection of similar products in industrialized countries as well as with the general level of protection prevailing in the host country. If protection was out of line with either one or both of these standards, it should be investigated whether the industry carried direct or indirect benefits to the country that might justify an unusually high level of protection.

71. Memorandum to the executive directors, "Pearson Commission Recommendation No. 9 Concerning IFC Project Identification and Investment Promotion Work," December 11, 1969.

72. The president's response did not mention that active promotion had, indeed, been IFC policy from the very beginning, and that its implementation had met with major difficulties, which, as it turned out, continued to afflict similar efforts in years to come.

73. Memorandum to the executive directors, "Pearson Commission Recommendation No. 10 Concerning Advice on Industrial and Foreign Investment Policies," December 11, 1969.

74. Memorandum, Leonard B. Rist, "Industrial Protection and IFC," March 9, 1959.

The conclusions of this memorandum do not appear in IFC operational statements from this time. Clearly, in its early years the IFC paid little attention to tariff protection, or, for that matter, to other forms of market distortions. It was not the IFC's mission to seek to influence general economic policies, and protectionist policies were accepted as legitimate instruments of industrialization. Government policies were thus taken for granted and believed likely to remain in place during the five to fifteen years of IFC investments. This was the reality to which entrepreneurs, and consequently the IFC, had to adapt.[75]

By the late 1960s the views on protectionism were shifting away from benevolent acceptance to a more critical attitude. Several trade studies, especially one carried out in the World Bank by a team headed by Bela Balassa, had called attention to the substantial economic and social costs attached to heavy reliance on protection.[76] As early as August 1968, McNamara had stated his intention not to present to the Board projects that required "undue protection." Then in December 1970 the Bank Group established internal procedures requiring special review and justification for projects with nominal protection in excess of 25 percent.[77] In the meantime, the Pearson Commission had singled out the lack of attention to highly effective tariff protection as a major shortcoming of the IFC.

It fell to the newly appointed executive vice president, William Gaud, and his economic adviser, Moeen Qureshi, to institute in the early 1970s IFC policies for taking account of protection.[78] The first step was to recruit economic staff to the Corporation, capable of economic analysis of investment proposals, with due regard to the industrial sector studies increasingly being completed in the Bank itself. Although tariff protection was the issue that gave rise to this initiative, the approach led to a consideration of market distortions in general and to attempts at an overall economic project appraisal. This was done by introducing, beginning in 1971, the calculation of an economic rate of return (ERR) in addition to the traditional financial rate of return (FRR). The ERR was the rate equalizing the present value of total economic costs and benefits over the life of the project. Because external economies that were difficult to measure were not included in the calculation, the ERR could also be interpreted as a measure of what the financial return would be under undistorted market conditions.[79]

This was a major revision of policy, and at first it was not well received by IFC staff. Later, however, it came to be regarded as a useful safeguard against risks

75. Ladislaus von Hoffmann, interview with the author, May 17, 1995.

76. Bela Balassa and others, *The Structure of Protection in Developing Countries* (Johns Hopkins University Press, 1971).

77. IFC, "Policy on Industrial Protection," IFC/SecM72-21, July 21, 1972, p. 2.

78. Qureshi had served as an economist with the IMF before being appointed economic adviser in the IFC in 1970. He became vice president in 1975 and executive vice president in 1977.

79. IFC, "Policy on Industrial Protection," p. 6.

related to shifts in government policies.[80] Well aware of views in developing countries as well as among its own staff, IFC management was careful to implement the policy only gradually. Thus in 1972 the 25 percent nominal protection rule was still in effect, and the industrial protection policy paper stated that the IFC would not refuse to finance highly protected industries provided that the projects themselves appeared "to be sound from an economic and financial standpoint."[81]

Development Orientation

Toward the end of 1969, immediately after the appearance of the Pearson Commission Report and the establishment of the Industrial Projects Department, McNamara presented his first General Policies statement to the IFC Board.[82] Contrary to what had been done previously, this statement assigned equal positions to profitability and development. While the 1956 Statement of Operations had said that supported enterprises had to "contribute to the development of the economy," it had, in effect, specified profitability, together with the ability to attract additional private capital, as the essential criteria for investment. According to the new statement, while profitability was "essential," economic benefit to the country was "equally essential." The 1967 operational booklet had said: "IFC's activities are similar in many respects to those of a private investment banker."[83] In the 1970 version this sentence was retained, with the significant addition that, inasmuch as the IFC's objective was to promote economic development, "its investments must do more than meet the test of the market."[84]

In his first talk to the IFC staff in early 1970, the new executive vice president, Gaud, stated that the impression had been created that the IFC had overplayed profitability at the expense of development.[85] Whether or not this had been true in the past was irrelevant, but it should not become true in the future. Subsequently, a confirmation of the policy shift was included in McNamara's address to the Annual Meeting in Copenhagen in September 1970. This was the only substantive remark he ever made about the IFC in his official speeches. He said that he fully agreed with the viewpoint expressed, for example, by the Pearson Commission, "that the policies of the International Finance Corporation should be reoriented to give greater emphasis to the development implications of its investments, and

80. Ladislaus von Hoffmann, interview with the author, May 17, 1995.
81. IFC, "Policy on Industrial Protection," p. 3.
82. This statement eventually became the IFC *General Policies* booklet of 1970. It was introduced to the Board in a memorandum of November 26, 1969, detailing all significant changes from the previous 1967 version. The statement was subsequently approved by the Board on December 16, 1969.
83. IFC, "IFC General Policies, Draft," IFC/SecM66-38, November 25, 1966, p. 1.
84. IFC, *General Policies,* January 1970, p. 4.
85. William S. Gaud, talk to the IFC staff, January 22, 1970.

should not simply stress their profitability."[86] In this reorientation, McNamara and Gaud had full and strong support of the IFC Board, with which they consulted extensively on several occasions.

To place development rhetorically at the side of profitability was one thing. To sort out the consequences of that move was another and more difficult matter, with which the IFC was deeply engaged throughout the 1970s and early 1980s. To an extent, it is still an unsettled issue. A door had, indeed, been opened wide.

One implication of this change in attitude was that the effects of protection would now need to be taken into account, as the Pearson Commission had specifically mentioned. As explained earlier in the chapter, this was dealt with by introducing an economic rate of return. In essence a modification of profitability calculations, the economic rate of return gradually became an additional instrument of investment appraisals. Taking general developmental characteristics into account was another issue. The operational policy statement of 1970 attempted to present examples of how this could be done, and how the IFC thus could do more than meet the market test. These examples were contributions to higher national income, greater foreign exchange earnings, increased employment, improved labor and management skills, higher productivity, more ample supply of essential goods and services, and the acquisition of technological and scientific knowledge. Such diverse and vague criteria could obviously not be worked into quantitative investment appraisals, and in the next operational statement the listing was not repeated. They could, however, be taken into account in a qualitative way, and be used in addition to established criteria of economic and financial returns in rating industries and projects.[87]

A more radical way of introducing development implications was to lower the standard of project profitability. This standard had in effect been set at the level of the market by stipulating the potential sale of investments. Its lowering would imply that sales would no longer be an important objective of the Corporation. This was, indeed, what Gaud and Demuth had advocated in their report and what Gaud had again emphasized in his talk to the staff in early 1970. That this was not far from McNamara's own view can be gauged from his concluding remarks at a Board seminar in 1974: "The closer IFC moves to being a commercial enterprise, the less capable it will be to perform developmental functions."[88] No change in the policy of investment sales was, however, incorporated in operational statements.

86. "To the Board of Governors, Copenhagen, Denmark, September 21, 1970," *The McNamara Years at the World Bank: Major Policy Addresses of Robert S. McNamara, 1968–1981* (Johns Hopkins University Press, 1981), p. 115.

87. For example, in response to questions raised at a Board seminar on IFC policies and practices held July 2, 1974, the staff explained that projects yielding returns below 8–10 percent would only be accepted if they yielded important external economies. Memorandum, Ladislaus von Hoffmann to the Board, April 18, 1975.

88. IFC secretary's department, "Salient Points on IFC Policies and Practices," July 10, 1984. Conclusions of chairman, Seminar on IFC Policies and Practice, July 2, 1974.

An expansion of investment volume, greater sectoral diversification, more emphasis on promotional activities, an enhanced level of operations in less advanced countries (especially smaller and poorer countries), and, on the whole, an assumption of higher risks, were considered parts of a developmental orientation. To this was eventually added coordination with government development goals and a special regard for the role the public sector was playing in industrial development in many countries. All these considerations were bound to lead to significant changes in operational policies, which came to be expressed in policy statements and comments during the years 1970–78. Changes thus emerged in such areas as relative focus on equity and loan investments, promotional activities, the choice of domestic and foreign partners, and relations with publicly owned enterprises—all of which aimed to bring IFC operations into a more developmental position than before.[89]

Equity Investment and Lending

One of the objectives of Executive Vice President Gaud was to achieve greater flexibility in the forms of investment. In his view there was an unfulfilled demand for loan capital in developing countries that the IFC ought to attempt to meet without tying itself to equity investments.[90]

After equity investments had become possible for the IFC in 1961, loans were only to be granted in combination with equity or quasi-equity investments. Later on, loans not connected with equity, so-called straight loans, were accepted as exceptional. The 1969 policy revision still considered the combination of equity and lending the normal procedure, although straight loans were no longer regarded as exceptional. Moreover, when granted, such loans were to be secured by commercial bank guarantees or charged with higher interest rates than loans combined with equity. This was a compromise between Gaud's emphasis on flexibility and the traditional IFC view of the Corporation as an equity investor. As early as 1973, however, full flexibility had been introduced. Henceforth, the IFC was to be "flexible in its terms and make its investments in such forms as may be appropriate in the particular situation."[91]

The new IFC leadership leaned away from equity because it had its eye fixed on larger volume and greater industrial and geographical diversity of operations. It perceived a large unfulfilled demand for loans without equity connection in most developing countries. The IFC's previous management had, it was believed, been reluctant to try to meet this demand as the loans, in order to compensate for the

89. Numerical data relating to changes in operational direction are presented and discussed in the section, "IFC Operations in the 1970s."

90. "Interviews: William S. Gaud of the International Finance Corporation," *Finance and Development,* no. 1 (March 1970), pp. 12–18.

91. IFC, *General Policies,* August 1973, pp. 3–4.

risk involved and be marketable, would carry interest rates higher than the Board would accept. Such considerations would have to be set aside if the IFC was to evolve from a "special situations investment company" to a development agency, advancing into new types of industry and into countries that it had not operated in before.[92]

There was yet another reason behind the new policy. For the sake of prudence, the IFC was unwilling to hold equity investments in excess of its paid-in capital and retained earnings. A continued increase in equity investments would have made a capital replenishment necessary in the early 1970s. Although that increase could have remained small, it might not have been easily obtained from member governments given the prevailing views of development priorities. Neither was it an urgent concern for the Bank Group leadership, so long as lending operations could proceed on the basis of the IFC's borrowing from the Bank, a source that was only beginning to be tapped in 1970.

No less important than the shift in policy were the external conditions taking hold in the early 1970s. As inflation outstripped interest rates, borrowing became more attractive for enterprises than equity financing. Moreover, as the influx of oil money impelled commercial banks to expand lending to developing countries, opportunities opened up for the IFC to support and participate in that lending. But whether driven by internal shifts in policy or by radical changes in external conditions, the IFC's mode of operations moved decisively from equity investment to straight loans. The venture investor mentality of the early years waned and a commercial banking attitude took hold.[93]

Foreign and Domestic Partnership

The IFC also shifted its emphasis in the area of foreign and domestic partnerships. Originally, either one of these partnerships was acceptable, while their combination was welcomed. By 1967 investments were, "generally," not to be made without local participation. But because it was recognized that such participation would not always be immediately forthcoming, the IFC could reserve shares for future domestic disposal. In the 1969 policy revision, the position of domestic participation was further strengthened by eliminating the word "generally." The guidelines now stated unequivocally that "IFC will invest in a venture only if there is provision for local participation." However, the possibility of reserving shares, in case such participation was not available at the time, remained the same as before.[94]

---

92. Gaud and Demuth, "The Role of the Bank Group," pp. 3, 7–10. The new management also had a special interest in making loans to private organizations formed by a number of financial and other concerns in industrial countries, such as ADELA, operating in Latin America; PICA, operating in Asia; and SIFIDA, in Africa.

93. For a discussion of the IFC as an equity investor, see memorandum, Barber B. Conable to the Board of Directors, "IFC Equity Policies," IFC/R87-150, October 21, 1987.

94. IFC, "Statement of Operating Policies"; and IFC, *General Policies* booklets 1967 and 1970.

These gradual and modest shifts in policy guidelines disguise an even sharper adjustment in operational practice. In the early years of the IFC, the promotion of foreign private investment was a major objective of the Corporation, and only limited prospects were seen for domestic investments without foreign support. As late as 1969, joint ventures between private foreign and domestic investors were seen as the IFC's preferred mode of operations.[95] A few years later, the management was assuring the Board that joint operations with foreign companies were not a major component of the IFC's agenda.

In a Board seminar discussion of July 1974, a number of directors, from both developed and developing countries, urged the IFC to remember at all times that a greater emphasis on development went hand in hand with a strong desire for greater national control of ownership and management of industrial and mining enterprises.[96] In response to these views, the staff explained that the IFC was more willing than other institutions to support domestically owned and controlled enterprises.[97]

Almost three years after this, in January 1977, during a major Board discussion connected with the then ongoing IFC capital increase, a director from a developed country expressed regrets over the image the IFC had acquired as an institution, not of development, but of assistance to multinational companies for their penetration into the developing world. Another director, also from a developed country, referring to the ongoing work on multinational companies in the United Nations, stated that the IFC needed to observe the recommendations of UN bodies and assist developing countries in their efforts to achieve economic independence. Responding to these remarks, the executive vice president, Ladislaus von Hoffmann, explained that, on the whole, the IFC had little to do with large multinational companies, which neither required the IFC's assistance nor had a liking for its procedures.[98] In an internal discussion at a meeting of Bank department directors a few days later, held on the occasion of his departure from the IFC, von Hoffmann, in a somewhat resigned tone, expressed his feeling that the IFC's emphasis had to be on domestic private investment, as foreign private investment was stagnating and being discouraged in many countries.[99]

95. IFC, *Annual Report, 1969,* p. 6. "While there have been, and there will be, exceptions dictated by individual needs of particular projects, the joint venture, multinational company will continue to be the development enterprise into which IFC typically puts its resources."

96. IFC, secretary's department, "Salient Points of IFC Policies and Practices," July 10, 1974, summary of Board discussion of July 2, 1974.

97. These replies to questions not fully answered orally during the meeting were not presented until almost a year later, April 18, 1975.

98. Transcript of Board discussion of the paper "IFC Activities," IFC/R76-70, December 2, 1976.

99. Notes of World Bank department directors' meeting, January 17, 1977. IFC Policy File no. 30, "Operating Policies and Procedures," vol. 2.

It is a further striking indication of the change in views on foreign investment that during the 1970s there was a discussion within the IFC and with the Board regarding the IFC's eventual assistance in transferring foreign assets in developing countries to local ownership.[100] Given the climate in many developing countries, the IFC's management believed it might be justified in assisting such transfers, especially in the form of underwriting, if they fulfilled general IFC criteria and appeared likely to contribute to the country's development. The Board reacted cautiously, but on the whole positively, to this tentative proposal. There were, however, doubts about whether such transactions, not aiming at new investment, were in agreement with the IFC's Articles, and no transactions were performed, with one exception, a case in which new shares were issued in addition to those transferred.[101]

In less than ten years, the IFC had thus moved from a position of strongly promoting foreign private investment to strongly supporting domestic control. It again took less than ten years for the world and the Corporation to move to another position, more akin to the original trait.

Promotional Activities

Approved in the immediate wake of the Pearson Commission Report, the 1969 operational policy guidelines came out in full favor of promotional activities.[102] Included in such activities were project identification and promotion, support of DFCs and of capital markets, increased attention in developed countries to investment in developing ones, and, finally, advice and counsel for the growth of the private sector. Nothing of this was new, but the emphasis was more prominent than before. Of particular importance was a paragraph not found in previous pamphlets. Titled "Project Identification and Promotion," it argued that the IFC could take responsibility for developing a project from its conception through feasibility, detailed engineering and marketing studies, to the identification of partners and the putting together of a financial plan. This was the kind of active project promotion envisaged for the IFC from the beginning but seldom realized in practice. It was now to become a more prominent feature of the IFC's agenda than before, as William Gaud further emphasized in his first talk to the staff in January 1970.

There was a difference not only in emphasis but also in substance between the new leadership's approach to promotion and that of its predecessors. The Woods-

100. According to McNamara's "To Do" list of May 25, 1968, this was already being considered for Latin America at that time.

101. See memorandum, Peter Calderón to José E. Camacho, "IFC Financing of Equity Investment," October 16, 1984. This memo gives a general review of the issue. The specific case mentioned was a Bata shoe company in Cameroon, 1975.

102. Appearing as the 1970 *General Policy* booklet, these guidelines were discussed and approved by the Board on December 16, 1969.

Rosen concept of the IFC promotion had primarily been one of bringing together domestic and foreign partners in relatively large and complicated deals, where the IFC's technical and financial expertise could be an essential component. In line with the developmental ideas of the times and the aversion to foreign investment, the approach of the 1970s was geared toward smaller projects and less advanced countries, not least in Africa, with an even greater role than before for the IFC and less dependence on foreign partners.

An early step taken to implement the promotional plans was to establish a Capital Markets Department in March 1971, a move that eventually proved to be of profound importance. Acting for the entire World Bank Group, this department was to assist developing member countries in improving their capital and money markets. It was, in particular, to help to build private capital market institutions that would contribute to the growth of domestic savings and to their efficient integration through market mechanisms.[103]

Active project promotion moved less rapidly. During an extensive two-day Board discussion in February 1973, the Board urged greater promotional activities, while acknowledging the increased financial burden this would entail.[104] In his subsequent response, President McNamara stressed the progress that had been made since 1968 in widening the IFC geographical coverage and giving greater attention to project promotion and development of capital markets.[105] Even greater emphasis would be given to the promotion of new enterprises in the future. Because this was difficult and expensive, early results could not be expected. McNamara then announced the formation of a special promotional unit of four professionals, which would help operating departments develop new business and be directly responsible to the executive vice president. A similar measure had been recommended in the Gaud-Demuth report of 1969. Called the Office of Industrial Promotion, it was transformed in 1975 into an Investment Promotion and Special Projects Department under a new director.[106]

These efforts on behalf of active project promotion ran into serious difficulties, which, in their turn, occasioned repeated organizational rearrangements and a turnover of personnel. One problem was that they clashed with the structure of the Corporation, which was based primarily on regional responsibility. Another was that persons with the appropriate inclination and experience for this kind of work were difficult to find. After all, this was quite different from ordinary banking. Most important, it was not easy for a centralized international organization to locate and nurture projects of various kinds in a number of countries.

103. IFC, *Annual Report, 1971.*

104. The discussion was based on a memorandum from the president to the Board on operation policy, December 19, 1972, IFC/R72-62. Discussed by the Board on February 22 and 27, 1973. Discussion summarized in memorandum to the directors, n.d.

105. Memorandum from the president to the directors (n.d., but likely from April 1973), in answer to their comments during the discussion on February 22 and 27, 1973.

106. IFC, *Annual Report,* various issues.

In his reply to the comments of directors at the IFC's Board discussion in January 1977, Executive Vice President von Hoffmann explained these difficulties at length.[107] Perhaps, he said, there was a lack of appreciation for what it really meant to get these things done. The IFC was devoting a good deal of resources to the subject, but it would be a disservice to the countries concerned to establish unrealistic targets. In his presentation to the internal meeting of Bank directors a few days later, von Hoffmann returned to the same subject and expressed doubts about whether the IFC had an appropriate role in active project promotion as the private sector was often quicker in perceiving new opportunities than the IFC.[108] The Corporation's essential role might therefore be to identify and promote appropriate sector policies and, on the basis of such policies, to seek to engage investors. "The lack of investment was not so much due to a lack of perception of opportunities as the consequence of detrimental government policies."

By the time of these meetings, von Hoffmann had already resigned from the IFC in order to take up a position in the private sector. His successor, Moeen Qureshi, who had been the IFC's first economic adviser and subsequently served as vice president to von Hoffmann, decided to make a renewed effort on behalf of active promotion. He abolished the previous department and moved its promotional functions to the economic adviser, who, as director of a new Development Department, was to be in charge of economic issues, project promotion, and policy advice to member governments.

The Attitude toward Publicly Owned Enterprises

The position of the IFC's founders regarding publicly owned enterprises, described earlier, remained largely in force until the late 1960s. The subsequent evolution of the IFC's views on this subject cannot be fully understood without some knowledge of how the relevant provisions of the Charter originally came about.[109] The draft IFC Articles, presented to the Board of the World Bank in early 1955, provided that a government or other public interest in a productive enterprise "shall not preclude the Corporation from making an investment therein if, in the opinion of the Corporation, such enterprise is essentially private in character." During the Board's first discussion of the proposal, a question was raised about the meaning of "essentially private in character." Seeking to avoid an argument over a thorny issue, the British executive director, Viscount Harcourt, suggested that the qualification should be left out, thus ending the section with the word "therein." Sensing how radically this would change the substance of the section, Eugene Black, who was chairing the meeting, declared that he could only agree to this if the word "necessarily" was placed in front of "preclude." This was accepted by the

107. This meeting was mentioned in note 98.
108. This meeting was mentioned in note 99.
109. IFC, *Articles of Agreement,* art. III, sec. 1.

Board, and the sentence came to read: "The existence of a government or other public interest in such an enterprise [that is, a productive private enterprise] shall not necessarily preclude the Corporation from making an investment therein."[110]

Some members of the Board, in particular those representing Latin America, South Africa, and Yugoslavia, were concerned that this wording might prevent the IFC from supporting government initiatives designed to assist private enterprise or to compensate for its insufficiency. During subsequent Board discussions, a rewording of the section was consequently suggested, aiming in particular at getting rid of the word "necessarily." Eugene Black was unyielding, however. He believed that government initiatives of the kind these directors had in mind should be supported by the Bank and not by the IFC: "That is what the Bank is for." Moreover, it was of great importance to maintain the understanding that the IFC was not set up to help government institutions: "That's not the idea of it. The idea of it is to try to encourage and improve the flow of private capital." Leaving out the word "necessarily" would be "a very serious thing."[111] Receiving strong support from the U.S., British, and German executive directors, in particular, Black's view prevailed, without a formal vote being taken.[112]

For almost fifteen years, or until the end of the 1960s, the IFC's operational policies maintained the position originally adopted by the Board. Involvement with partly owned government enterprises was avoided. When exceptions were made, the enterprise had to be privately controlled and operated, with government ownership not exceeding 25 percent. As before, however, other views were represented on the Board, and policies in developed and developing countries alike were moving toward a more active role for governments in industrial development. This led to some softening of the original stance in the 1969 revision of the General Policies Booklet, which included a statement, following the "not necessarily preclude" formula, explaining: "Each case will be examined in the light of such factors as the extent of government ownership and control, the nature of the enterprise, its developmental importance, and the possibility of increasing the extent of private ownership in the future."[113] Even before this, the level of permissible government participation had been lifted from 25 to 49 percent.

An acceptance of government majority ownership in the IFC-supported enterprises was soon to follow. In 1971 the Corporation's general counsel came to the conclusion that Yugoslavia's so-called cooperative enterprises could, under the conditions prevailing in that country, be regarded as being equivalent to private enterprises and thus be eligible for IFC support.[114] During the Board's major policy

110. Bank Board discussion, February 11, 1955.
111. Memorandum, R. B. J. Richards to legal files, "Articles of Agreement, History of Article III, Section 1," December 8, 1966.
112. Bank Board discussions, March 31 and April 5, 1955.
113. IFC, "General Policies," revisions attached to a memorandum to the Board of Directors, IFC/R69-52, November 28, 1969.
114. Memorandum, R. B. J. Richards, general counsel, "Financing by IFC Enterprises in Yugoslavia," June 9, 1971.

discussion of February 1973, strong demands were made for an open-minded attitude toward public enterprises. It was even maintained that, if necessary to achieve this aim, a revision of the Corporation's Articles should not be excluded. Reaching out to government-owned enterprises was believed to be the most effective way to expand the IFC's activities, and valid reasons were not seen for the IFC to refuse to invest in largely or wholly government-owned enterprises elsewhere, as long as it could operate in Yugoslavia. The nature of management and control, and the degree of orientation toward the private sector, should be the decisive consideration rather than the form of ownership. One speaker went so far as to state that in many countries, if private capital had any role at all, it lay in association with government capital.[115]

In a memorandum to the Board before these discussions, McNamara had not proposed any change in the policy of withholding the IFC's support from enterprises with majority government interests.[116] He had further stated that the IFC was frequently urged to extend financing to such enterprises but was prevented from doing this by its Articles. After the meetings, in a written response to the directors, he took a different position.[117] He stated that several directors had expressed a strong desire for the IFC to assist enterprises in which governments had a large or majority interest and had, furthermore, maintained that the elements of private management, freedom from government control, and safeguards for business efficiency were more important than percentages of ownership. He agreed that the IFC should be open-minded in this regard, and that majority government ownership should not, of itself, be a bar to IFC investment. This should be determined case by case, and Article III, Section 1 of the IFC's statutes provided sufficient latitude in this regard.

The new General Policy Booklet, presented for the Board's approval in June 1973, stated simply that "government participation in an enterprise" would not necessarily preclude IFC's investment, instead of saying, as previously, that "government ownership of a minority interest in an enterprise" would not do this. It further stated that the IFC was "prepared to support 'mixed enterprises,' i.e. joint ventures between private enterprise and government,"[118] a gesture that had not been extended before.

This decision of 1973 was an important milestone in the evolution of the IFC's attitude toward publicly owned enterprises. But it was not the end of the journey. At the Board's seminar discussion a year later, directors of developing countries again strongly maintained that the IFC's reluctance to deal with partly or wholly

115. Discussions of the Board, February 22 and 27, 1973, as summarized in memorandum to the directors, n.d.

116. Memorandum to the directors, "Operating Policies," IFC/R72-62, December 19, 1972.

117. See note 105.

118. IFC, *General Policies*, August 1973, p. 2.

government owned enterprises was an important reason for the sluggish increase in its operations.[119] They further maintained that the IFC should be able to go along with the well-defined trend to increase national control and government participation in key sectors of the economy. Responding to this, the U.S. representative said that there was no need for the IFC to lend assistance to what were essentially government operations.

The issue came up once more in connection with the capital increase in 1976–77. In the policy paper prepared on that occasion, McNamara reiterated that majority ownership by the government was certainly not, of itself, a bar to IFC investment.[120] In two respects he then went further than this. First, he said, there was no formal reason why the IFC should not use a governmental body as an agent for making funds available to the private sector.[121] Second, it was possible to envision circumstances in which the IFC might serve a useful function in support of the private sector by assisting enterprises wholly owned and controlled by the government with a view to early divestiture of a part or all of the government holdings to private interests.

On the second of those two issues, McNamara did not have the support of his general counsel. In a statement to the Board, R. B. J. Richards gave his support to operations with wholly owned DFCs without taking up the issue of nonfinancial public enterprises.[122] On that subject he had, however, presented rather firm views in an internal memorandum a few days earlier. Stating that such an interpretation of the Articles was not "absolutely impossible," it could in his view command little credibility or respect: "One may define a sheep as including a wolf in sheep's clothing but few will believe that such a wolf is a sheep."[123]

In the Board, the views of the directors followed a similar pattern as before, with directors from developing countries and European developed countries taking a firm stand in favor of operations with publicly owned enterprises. One of the latter even went so far as to say that development orientation should imply the elimination of the distinction between public and private types of companies. During the discussion, however, McNamara did not recommend support of wholly government-owned companies, other than for DFC intermediation, and there was no decision of the Board on this score. Notably, the U.S. and Canadian representatives recorded their dissenting views. The U.S. alternate executive director said he understood the case for the IFC's willingness to invest in enterprises predominantly owned by the government and accepted the need for flexibility in this regard but

119. July 2, 1974.

120. Memorandum, Robert S. McNamara to the directors, "IFC's Activities," IFC/R76-70, December 2, 1976. Considered by the Board at a meeting of January 6, 1977.

121. This appears to have been accepted even earlier. See W. S. Gaud and R. B. J. Richards, "Investment by IFC in Mixed Governmental and Private Enterprises," draft of August 20, 1974.

122. Discussion, January 6, 1977.

123. Memorandum, R. B. J. Richards, general counsel, "Can IFC Invest in a Wholly Owned Government Enterprise?" December 29, 1976.

believed it was of utmost importance to insist that operations strictly observe business principles. The IFC should not give support to activities that were likely to expand government at the expense of the private sector.

Without a formal position being taken, flexibility continued to increase with regard to wholly government owned enterprises. In 1978, Executive Vice President Qureshi proposed to McNamara that fully government-owned DFCs should become eligible for IFC equity investment and technical assistance.[124] His justification was that in many African countries there was no other option for IFC operations than institutions of this kind. This was followed up with equity investments in government-owned DFCs in at least three African countries.

At the end of 1980, an internal memorandum of the Legal Department stated that a good case could be made for the IFC to invest wherever its presence served to promote or preserve the private sector.[125] Such a role could justify a partnership with a wholly government-owned enterprise, in particular circumstances and under certain conditions. The views expressed in this memorandum appear, however, to have received a negative response within the department. Two months later, the general counsel, José Camacho, in a memorandum to all IFC lawyers warned against the complications that might arise from investments in enterprises in which governments had, or were likely to have, a controlling interest, directly or indirectly.[126] The lawyers were asked to bring any proposed investments in such companies to his attention at an early stage. The tide had begun to turn.

At his departure from the IFC in early 1977, Ladislaus von Hoffmann made some thoughtful observations about the evolution of IFC views on its role with regard to publicly owned enterprises. He said that "IFC's operating dogma had evolved along with the realities of life"[127] and that the IFC now realized that in some countries it was essential to work with government-owned enterprises in order to fulfill the IFC's mandate for mobilizing capital for developing countries. In retrospect, eighteen years later, he believed, however, that the watering down of the private-public distinction had, perhaps, been the IFC's greatest mistake.[128]

Financial Aspects

The reorientation of the IFC's operations toward developmental goals was bound to have financial consequences for the Corporation. Most of the measures

124. Memorandum, Moeen A. Qureshi to Robert S. McNamara, "Africa: Investments in Publicly Owned DFCs," March 8, 1978.

125. Memorandum, Peter Calderón to José E. Camacho, "Evolution of the Concept of 'Private Enterprise' and IFC's Investment Authority," November 7, 1980 (updated January 19, 1981).

126. Memorandum, José Comacho, general counsel, to all IFC lawyers, "Government Control in Project Companies," March 10, 1981.

127. World Bank department directors' meeting, January 17, 1977, p. 4.

128. Ladislaus von Hoffmann, interview with the author, May 17, 1995.

taken for reorientation involved higher operational costs, greater risks or lesser returns than would have resulted from previous policies. This applied, in particular, to increased promotional activities as well as to greater sectoral and geographical diversity. The reduced emphasis on equity investments as compared with lending and on the partnership with multinational companies in favor of domestic investors was likely to lead to similar results.

The financial source most immediately available to the Corporation in support of the new policies was the return from its own capital. The small original capital had, however, not been increased since the IFC's establishment. Moreover, the modest yields of 3 to 4 percent earned in the 1960s did not leave much leeway either for growth or for developmental activities. The policy reorientation of the early 1970s was consequently tempered by declarations of financial caution. In particular, management stressed that promotional activities were bound to be costly and that the scope for the assumption of high risks was very limited. In his response to comments made by directors during the discussions of the IFC's operational policies in February 1973, McNamara explicitly stated that the IFC had to cover its expenses, make reasonable provisions for risks, and earn a return on its capital.[129] How high a return ought to be aimed at was not indicated, however.

A few years later, in early 1977, McNamara, together with the departing Executive Vice President von Hoffmann, returned to the subject of the Corporation's capital yields. In that connection, McNamara remarked: "Three and a half percent per year. What multinational company earns that? Either we are inefficient compared with multinational companies or we are doing something different than MNCs. I think it is the latter."[130] What the IFC was doing differently, was helping with policy design and project preparation as well as engaging in promotional activities and participating in low-yielding projects that private investors were not willing to undertake. During this same Board discussion, von Hoffmann estimated that the IFC was devoting 25–30 percent of its staff resources to lesser developed and smaller countries that represented no more than 10 percent of the population of the member countries eligible for investment.[131]

The IFC could raise the financial support for its developmental activities in several ways. First, it could aim at a lesser return on its own capital. In effect, this

129. The policy approved by the Board in July 1968 and confirmed at this time, February 1973, set the rule that costs incurred in promotional activities should be capitalized as part of IFC investment in the projects if such investment proceeded but otherwise should be charged to the budget. The management was authorized to incur such costs within a limit of $250,000 potential charge to the budget and a maximum of $50,000 for any single project. "IFC Business Promotion Activities," dated December 15, 1972, and appearing as an appendix to the memorandum from the president to the directors, "Operating Policies," IFC/R72-62, December 19, 1972. See also the memorandum from the president to the directors regarding discussion on February 22 and 27, 1973, referred to in note 105.

130. Transcript of Board discussion, January 6, 1977.

131. See note 98.

was happening during the 1970s as the nominal rate of return for the years 1970 to 1979 remained at about 4–5 percent while the annual rate of inflation in the United States had more than doubled, from 2–3 percent in the 1960s to about 7 percent in the 1970s. The IFC was thus using up its capital to a significant extent, which may, however, have been an unintended result from the sudden rise in inflation as much as a consequence of the greater emphasis on developmental policies.

Second, the IFC could seek financial support for developmental activities from the Bank. This was, in fact, recommended for technical assistance purposes by some directors and is an issue that has surfaced time and again. It was not accepted by the Bank/IFC management, however, except for the Bank's contribution to the IFC's Capital Markets Department.[132] Indirectly, this nevertheless took place through the transfer of industrial policy advice from the IFC to the Bank, which was strongly pursued by McNamara.[133]

Third, the IFC could seek a significant capital replenishment from its owners, which was the natural course to take in view of the small capital originally provided. Such an increase had been seriously considered in the 1960s but was abandoned in favor of borrowing from the Bank. That solution had not, however, given the IFC the benefit of increased free capital. A few years into the 1970s, the limit of borrowing from the Bank, amounting to four times capital and reserves, was being approached and the constraints on equity investments, which could not exceed total capital, were being increasingly felt.

A significant capital increase was thus becoming a necessity both for the continued expansion of lending operations and the maintenance of equity investments, as well as for the support of the developmental orientation. When von Hoffmann became executive vice president, in September 1974, he took this matter up with McNamara, who agreed to a tentative exploration of the attitude of the U.S. Treasury, which would be crucial for the outcome.[134] A rather ironic constellation of circumstances produced a more speedy and generous result for the IFC than the initiators had dared to hope. Just as in 1954, the United States was under pressure for increased contributions to development financing; and now another Republican administration preferred to channel that financing to private enterprises rather than to governments and public agencies. The U.S. Treasury, therefore, proved to be favorably disposed toward a rather large contribution to an IFC capital increase, establishing a base for an overall increase of a substantial magnitude. At the same time, most of the other industrial countries as well as the developing countries themselves, had become much more favorably inclined to the IFC than at an earlier stage because of its developmental reorientation and, in particular, its more

132. Amounting (at least until 1984) to 25 percent of the department's staff budget. Memorandum, "IFC Five-Year Program FY85–89/Capital Increase—Questions and Answers," IFC/SecM84-18, March 22, 1984.

133. See review of Board discussion of January 6, 1977, referred to in note 98.

134. Ladislaus von Hoffmann, interview with the author, May 17, 1995.

beneficent attitude toward publicly owned enterprises. Although based on different motives, there was, consequently, a broad support for a major capital increase for the IFC. The sailing was not entirely smooth, however. Some objections were raised by the United Kingdom, then under a Labour government, and by France, but were soon overcome with support from the U.S. Treasury. The result, finally approved in November 1977, was a capital replenishment of $480 million, lifting the IFC's paid-in capital to a total of $650 million, which was expected to be sufficient for the Corporation for a ten-year period of expansion.

A Dual Strategy

Although capital replenishment had thus opened up wider financial avenues for development orientation, further means to this end continued to be sought. In fact, the directors representing France and the United Kingdom, the two countries that had shown some reluctance toward the capital increase, offered ideas about how the profitability of the Corporation could be maintained at the same time that developmental objectives were pursued. Such efforts came to be known as a "dual strategy" and were adopted to a significant extent in the IFC's operations in the late 1970s and early 1980s.

In July 1974 the Board had carried on extensive and freewheeling discussions on IFC policies and practices. They centered largely on the development-profitability dilemma.[135] During this discussion, the French director advocated what he called a "proportional principle." In accordance with its objectives, he maintained, the IFC had to engage partly in profit operations and partly in development operations. It should obtain its resources accordingly, borrowing from the market for the first and receiving subsidized resources from the Bank for the second. Somewhat later, during the Board's policy discussion of January 1977, which was related to the capital increase, the British executive director expressed similar views.[136] The IFC would have to accept low returns from a number of its investments, in fulfillment of its development objective. This could, however, be compensated by higher returns from other projects. A cross-subsidization in favor of the smaller and poorer countries would thus be brought about, although he said he was using the word "subsidy" with hesitation.

During these two Board discussions, IFC management made no mention of the "dual strategy." Nor was it referred to in general policy statements. It was presented, however, in the IFC's first Five-Year Program for the fiscal years 1979 to 1983, under the title of "Financing Mix."[137] The program stated that the Cor-

135. See note 96.
136. See note 98.
137. IFC, "IFC Five-Year Program: FY79–83," IFC/R78-18, March 27, 1978. See, in particular, pp. 10 and 36. In the 1980 updating of this program, IFC, "IFC Five Year Program: FY81–85," this policy, said to have been adopted in 1978, was confirmed and the term "dual strategy" applied. IFC/R86-55, June 2, 1980, p. 4.

poration sought to serve all of its developing-country members, but that it was "imperative" for its financial viability that promotional costs, technical assistance, and participation in smaller and riskier investments be balanced by returns from relatively large, less risky, and more remunerative investments. This approach to meeting the costs of a large number of small investments in less developed countries from the returns of a smaller number of large transactions in more advanced countries was deemed to be "a critical feature" of the strategy of the Five-Year Program. When William Ryrie arrived as executive vice president in 1984, he found it an important characteristic of the IFC's policy.[138]

IFC Operations in the 1970s

The new developmental orientation instituted at the end of the 1960s and the beginning of the 1970s had profound effects upon the IFC's operations in subsequent years. The number of operations increased sharply, while their average size remained the same. All the expansion took place in lending, while equity investment stagnated. Sectoral diversity became somewhat greater as investments in consumer goods expanded, while at the same time the IFC's role in financial intermediation diminished. Activities were extended to many more countries than before, while overall regional distribution remained largely the same. Participation with foreign direct investors declined and investment in partly owned government enterprises became common. Domestic majority ownership—private, public, or mixed—evolved as the prevailing norm. The impact of specific promotional activities was modest, while efforts to improve business environments were for the most part limited to conditions and institutions relating to capital markets.

The expansion of operations did not proceed at a regular pace, but rather in leaps, shaped by administrative changes, the availability of funding, and external conditions. There were sharp increases in fiscal years 1969 and 1970, in response to the preparatory activities of previous years. Then, with the introduction of new policies and organizational changes, the operational level came to a standstill for a time. This evoked criticism from the Board and was followed by a sharp leap in 1974. Then came another standstill. This time, capital shortage was a limiting factor and, after the substantial capital increase of November 1977, operations increased sharply from 1978 to 1980. Over the decade as a whole, from 1969 to 1980, the average annual increase of the IFC's approved investments for its own account, adjusted for price increases, was 10 percent.[139] Expressed in 1994 prices, investments approved in 1980 amounted to $715 million, which was almost triple the 1969 approvals of $260 million.

138. Sir William Ryrie, interview, World Bank Oral History Program, August 10, 1993, pp. 33–34.
139. During the 1960s, or from 1960/61 to 1969, the increase had been as much as 20 percent a year, albeit from a very low base.

This increase in operations was based entirely on their number, which grew from twenty in 1969 to fifty-three in 1980. This was a different pattern of expansion from that in the 1960s, when a higher level of operations was derived partly from a greater number of projects, but even more from their larger average size. The amount of the IFC's investment per project was, in 1994 prices, $12 million for the years 1970 to 1979, and the average project size $90 million, practically the same figures as for the years 1966 to 1969. This standstill in investment and project sizes resulted from the decline in financial sector activities balancing the increase in consumer goods industries, both of small project size. The average size may also have been kept down by the Bank's increased industrial activities, which diverted larger projects, for example, in the fertilizer industry, from the IFC to the Bank.

Another characteristic of the operational growth of the 1970s was its exclusive dependence upon lending and, to a minor extent, quasi equity, principally in the form of subordinated loans. The IFC's approved investments in equity, adjusted for price increases, were considerably lower in 1980 than they had been in 1969. As an annual price-adjusted average, they were also lower in 1970–79 than in 1966–69. By 1980 equity amounted to 10 percent of the IFC's approved investments for its own account, quasi equity to 9 percent and loans to 81 percent. In 1969 the corresponding figures had been 35 percent for equity, zero for quasi equity, and 65 percent for loans. A shift in the relative importance of equity investments and lending was, as already stated, one of the principal aims of the new policy orientation of the 1970s. It was also a consequence of the opportunities for lending created by the growth of the Euromarkets. It went farther, however, than the IFC's management considered desirable, and in the late 1970s an increase in equity investments once more became an expressed policy goal.[140]

As before, the majority of the IFC's investments in the 1970s went to industries producing capital and intermediate goods. In spite of the declared goal of greater diversification and more attention to small-scale enterprises, these industries maintained a position of 63 percent of the value of approved investments for the IFC's own account in 1970–79 compared with 61 percent in 1962–69. At the end of the decade, in 1979, their proportion was even as high as 70 percent, compared with 60 percent in 1969. Within this group, fertilizers had a sharp decline, in amount as well as in relative terms. Increased diversification was, on the other hand, evidenced in greater investments in consumer goods industries such as textiles, food and agribusiness, and general manufacturing, which increased their share from 14 percent of the value of investments for the IFC's own account in 1962–69 to 24 percent in 1970–79. Tourism remained a small and unchanged proportion, and a special effort for investments in energy and mining toward the end of the 1970s did not produce results until later. The counterpart to the increase in consumer goods industries was a sharp decline in financial sector investments from 16 percent of the total

140. IFC, "IFC Five-Year Program: FY79–83."

in 1962–69 to 8 percent in 1970–79. This was a consequence of the transfer of the responsibility for DFC operations to the Bank, which was only partly compensated by the activities of the Capital Markets Department, established in 1971.[141]

The IFC in its early years had not been able to operate on a regular basis in more than a few of its member countries. In 1960–64, the average number of countries per year receiving approvals had been 9, increasing to 12 in 1965–69. By 1970–74, this number had risen to 18, and by 1975–79 to 25. At the end of the 1970s, the number was slightly more than 30 a year, rising to about 40 during the 1980s.

The concentration of IFC investments in a small number of countries has long been the subject of critical comment. Up to 1975, no more than ten countries received about 90 percent of the value of approved investments every year. At that time, this proportion moved to about 80 percent for the ten highest countries, and 90 percent for the fifteen highest. It remained at that level until the early 1990s, when it moved further down. Between 1965 and 1984 the countries most frequently included in the group of ten highest were the following, in order of frequency: Brazil, Turkey, Mexico, the Philippines, Yugoslavia, Argentina, and India. Looking at the portfolio instead of annual approvals, there have been substantial variations in the position of individual countries. Comparing the years 1969 and 1980, only three countries were among the ten with the highest investments in both years: Brazil, India, and the Philippines.

Another way of looking at geographical diversity is to consider the distribution among the five regions into which the IFC has grouped its operations. This distribution has been by and large stable throughout the lifetime of the Corporation, with 10 percent of the value of annual approvals going to Sub-Saharan Africa, another 10 percent to the Middle East and North Africa, 15 percent to Europe, 25 percent to Asia, and 40 percent to Latin America and the Caribbean. The stability has prevailed in the face of policies aimed at increasing geographical diversity, thus reflecting basic conditions in the regions themselves. In Europe, the stability is due to the fact that Central and Eastern European countries have replaced more industrialized Western European countries in recent years.[142]

One of the principal aims of the reorientation of the 1970s was to extend operations to the smaller and poorer members of the Corporation and, in particular, to expand operations in Sub-Saharan Africa. Already in the 1960s, significant investment efforts were made in such African countries as Ethiopia, Mauritania, Senegal, Sudan, Tanzania, and Uganda, as well as in such Latin American and Caribbean countries as El Salvador, Honduras, Nicaragua, and Jamaica. Expansion efforts were now redoubled and strongly heralded by the Corporation. They did not lead to any breakthrough in Africa, however. As a matter of fact, the share of that region

141. See the table in note 216.

142. See the table in note 217. This pattern is reflected in the 1994 portfolio of the Corporation, which has broadly the same distribution.

in overall approvals, though small, was higher during the mid-1960s (1964–67) than it was in the 1970s. Nevertheless, during the second half of the 1970s, the share of Sub-Saharan Africa moved up to and past 10 percent of total approvals.

No consistent statistical material is available regarding foreign and domestic participation in IFC-supported enterprises. In annual reports, policy papers, and statements of the Board, figures on this matter are occasionally presented in order to make or emphasize a point. Thus, in the 1960s the prevalence of foreign participation is demonstrated, whereas in the 1970s the preponderance of domestic participation is emphasized. Although comparative statistics are lacking, there is nevertheless ample evidence to indicate that the policy reorientation of the 1970s led to greater domestic participation in IFC operations and a diminishing role for multinational companies. The 1969 Annual Report had stated that more than 60 percent of the principal development enterprises with which the IFC had been associated in the past three years were joint venture, multinational companies.[143] In early 1977, on the other hand, Executive Vice President von Hoffmann reported to the Board that in recent years there had been a surge in domestic investments in the IFC's portfolio, and that joint ventures were by now only a minor part of new investments instead of being a large majority, as in previous years.[144] Two years later, the 1979 Annual Report stated that almost all privately owned enterprises supported that year by the IFC had domestic majority ownership.[145] That report also made it clear, however, that in more than half of these enterprises there had been some foreign participation, involving in most cases technical assistance and the supply of technology in addition to capital.

As in the case of foreign and domestic participation, there is no consistent information on IFC investments in enterprises partly or wholly owned by governments. Reviewing the IFC's evolution over twenty years, the 1976 Annual Report stated that only a marginal increase in government ownership of enterprises supported by the IFC had taken place during the previous five years.[146] On the other hand, information presented in annual reports for the years 1978–84 as well as in the Five-Year Programs for 1979–83 and 1981–85 indicates an increasing penetration of the policy concerning publicly owned companies introduced in the early 1970s.[147] This is, furthermore, strongly confirmed by a survey prepared by the IFC in 1987.[148] By the end of June of that year, 46 percent of the IFC's investment

143. IFC, *Annual Report, 1969,* p. 6.

144. IFC, "IFC's Activities." See also note 98.

145. IFC, *Annual Report, 1979,* p. 13.

146. IFC, *Annual Report, 1976,* p. 6.

147. The FY81–85 program, prepared in 1980, states that more than one-fifth of projects undertaken in fiscal 1979 had a majority public ownership and more than one-half had some degree of such ownership. IFC, "IFC Five-Year Program: FY81–85," p. 4.

148. IFC, "Government Ownership in Companies in Which IFC Invests," IFC/SecM87-141, July 29, 1987.

portfolio, by numbers rather than amounts, was in companies with some government participation; of this group, 12 percent had majority and 34 percent minority participation. Even at this time, the investment pattern had not changed appreciably, as 41 percent of the approvals of the three fiscal years 1985–87 had been in such companies, 8 percent with majority and 33 percent with minority government interest. Fully government-owned DFCs were accepted as intermediaries after 1973 and equity investments were made in some of them from 1978. Investments in wholly owned government enterprises, other than DFCs, were never formally approved as policy, although such investments were considered in some cases and made in at least one company.[149]

Statistical information regarding promotional activities is even less available than data on foreign and domestic participation and investment in government-owned enterprises. During the 1970s, annual reports began to present investments in new companies as an indication of the results of such activities. In fact, however, there is little to go by except impressions of management and staff members, expressed on various occasions. All such statements indicate limited results for the promotion of projects from the beginning or from a very early stage, except for the financial sector. The repeated reshuffling of promotional activities within the Corporation points in the same direction. This is further illuminated in a report from Moeen Qureshi to McNamara soon after the former took over as executive vice president in 1977. He said the IFC's objective was to promote growth in the small and least-developed member countries, and he was dissatisfied that no breakthrough could be seen in these promotional efforts. New and more innovative instruments and ways of operating were needed to assist local institutions and enterprises in these countries.[150]

The Reorientation: An Overview

The IFC's reorientation over the 1970s originated from the outside and was brought into the organization by Robert McNamara and the executive vice president he appointed, William Gaud. The firm sense of purpose and instrumentality that the Corporation had developed in the 1960s gave way in the 1970s to new attitudes and approaches gaining prevalence in the world at large. This could only be accomplished over a period of time in an institution where the management and staff essentially remained the same as before. To begin with, the reorientation was largely on the surface, while former ways prevailed underneath. The strong expansion of operations and the movement toward somewhat greater sectoral and geographical diversity did not take place overnight. The policies regarding relations with foreign and domestic investors and with government-owned enterprises

149. The MABE of Greece, an asbestos producer.
150. Memorandum, Moeen A. Qureshi to Robert S. McNamara, "IFC Operating Program for FY78—First Quarterly Review," July 19, 1977.

changed only gradually. Efforts to strengthen promotional activities remained more or less separated from the mainstream of operations. The major immediate shift was the decline in equity investments as compared with lending.

During his term, William Gaud directed his attention principally to policy issues, while actual operations were being carried on by the existing experienced staff. Ladislaus von Hoffmann, who as vice president was Gaud's deputy and subsequently succeeded him, had been brought up in the institution and was in many ways similar to Martin Rosen. Over time, however, the weight of new staff began to make itself felt, in particular that of Economic Adviser Moeen Qureshi and the economists he brought with him. At the same time, the views of the old-timers began to adjust to what was perceived to be the new reality. Toward the end of the decade, when Qureshi had succeeded von Hoffmann as executive vice president, the institution was no longer what it had been ten years earlier. Its purpose had broadened, its means of implementation had expanded, and its volume of operations had multiplied. It had, in essence, become a supporter of industrial development, in line with the World Bank's overall direction, rather than a promoter of the private sector.

Though the reorientation was influenced by external conditions, McNamara was the powerful force behind it. Views on his attitude toward the Corporation have differed, however. William Ryrie, who was a member of the Board during part of McNamara's presidency and subsequently became the IFC's executive vice president in the mid-1980s, is critical of the move to expand the Bank's financing of industry, whether private or government owned, and of the transfer of DFC financing to the Bank. In his view, this tended to marginalize the IFC, which with greater support, more capital, and larger staff, could have become the Bank Group's main instrument for industrial development.[151] On the other hand, Moeen Qureshi, who served as executive vice president under McNamara for four years (1977–80), points to the strong expansion of the Corporation's activities during that period, which could not have happened without McNamara's encouragement and support. He, moreover, explicitly denies that McNamara diminished the role or the prospects of the IFC.[152]

These views need not be altogether contradictory. Upon his arrival, McNamara believed that the Bank Group had failed to play a significant role in the industrialization of developing countries.[153] He was not ready to assign this role to the IFC both because of its small size and its mandated support of the private sector and foreign private investment. But once a decision had been taken in favor of the Bank as the principal instrument, McNamara could support the IFC within the limited framework to which it had been assigned. He took particular interest in remodeling its policies during the years 1969 to 1974, began early to plan for an

151. Sir William S. Ryrie, interview with Richard Webb and Devesh Kapur, December 12, 1990.

152. Moeen A. Qureshi, interview with John Lewis, Richard Webb, and Devesh Kapur, April 5, 1991.

153. See, for example, McNamara's "To Do" list, May 25, 1968, item 93.

expansion of its operations, and promoted an increase in its capital when that became necessary for both expansion and developmental orientation in the mid-1970s.[154] On the other hand, the issues closest to McNamara's heart—poverty alleviation, social development, and equity—could not effectively be pursued through the IFC. In his official speeches he only once commented on the IFC and never mentioned the private sector, as if that sector, to which the IFC from the beginning had been dedicated, had no role to play in the development process. McNamara's first choice of an executive vice president from the outside reflected the perceived need for reorientation, while the two subsequent choices of insiders indicated a reliance on the Corporation's own strength and maturity. With Moeen Qureshi an executive vice president as of early 1977, with the capital increase accomplished, and the policy reorientation completed, the path was set for the IFC's further evolution in the direction McNamara had wanted.

In 1978, looking to the future in its first Five-Year Program, the IFC's management saw a world very much like the one that had been evolving since the late 1960s.[155] Governments would have the leading role in economic development, and domestic control of foreign investment would be required. In this world, the IFC would have a purpose in dealing, on behalf of the World Bank Group, with cases in which a commercial approach was appropriate, typically but not exclusively in the "private" and "mixed" sectors of the economies. The agenda of the Corporation would remain much the same as it had been during the 1970s: a significant expansion of activities, a wider geographical range, a broader sectoral spectrum. Flexibility and openness would reign in the relations with "mixed" enterprises as well as with wholly government-owned entities as channels for support to the private sector. The role of a mutually acceptable third party in the sensitive relations between governments and the private sector, in particular as regarded foreign investors, would be increasingly assumed. In giving emphasis to support for smaller and poorer countries, a more active promotional role would emerge, entailing project identification and development and a higher level of technical assistance. In addition, a close and continuing dialogue with member governments was envisaged regarding their broader economic and social objectives and the support of the IFC's operations for the realization of these objectives. In meeting this agenda of expanded and broader operations, the Corporation was expected to maintain a sound financial position, partly with the help of the dual strategy.

Profitability as a Development Objective, 1981–94

At first, the view of economic conditions and the IFC's prospects presented in the Five-Year Program of 1978 was substantiated. Despite weaknesses and un-

154. See, for example, McNamara's "To Do" list, August 2, 1969, item 44.
155. See IFC, "IFC Five-Year Program: FY79–83," esp. pp. 1–9.

certainties in the world economy, developing countries were maintaining much of the economic momentum they had achieved in the 1970s. Their borrowings in the Euromarkets reached new heights in 1979, at maturities and spreads more favorable than before. The IFC's volume of operations expanded during the first two years of the program, 1979 and 1980, at an exceptional rate, at the same time that the number of countries served by the Corporation moved to a higher level.[156] A 1980 updating of the program affirmed the objectives of the original program and predicted that the achievements of the first two years would be exceeded.[157] At the same time, it was acknowledged that the program was operating in the context of unusually severe constraints and uncertainties in the world economy. In particular, rising energy prices had made structural adjustments essential, and the IFC needed to consider its role in that connection.

What took place in subsequent years was an accommodation to external circumstances that was no less profound than the one that had occurred in the 1970s. The shift happened in a different manner, however. In the early 1970s a new direction had been dictated from above and subsequently amalgamated into the institution. Ten years later, no new direction was specifically laid out. In fact, the existing objectives and policies were at first restated and emphasized. Under the influence of changing conditions and perceptions, however, operating practices were transformed as increasing doubts arose within the organization about the course that had been followed and the results it had been leading to. By 1985, when the Corporation had come under new leadership, it was undergoing an explicit shift in objectives and policies.

The emphasis now was on profitability as a development objective, both for the enterprises the IFC supported and for the finances of the Corporation itself. During the 1970s, a number of objectives, deemed to be crucial for development, had been accorded as much standing as profitability. This elevation of objectives had weakened the quality of investments, it was now said, and had eroded the financial strength of the IFC itself. Although not discarded, these other objectives were to be given a distinctly secondary position. The principal developmental objective of the Corporation would henceforth be the establishment and operation of profitable private enterprises, for which the IFC's support was essential. In order to achieve this objective, the IFC would have to further its own financial strength. Instead of pursuing profitability and development as distinct objectives, the IFC would pursue them as one.

IFC in the Early 1980s

The economic conditions of the early 1980s—high interest rates and exchange rate turbulence, stagnation, and decline in many developing countries—severely

156. The annual rate of increase in IFC's net investment approvals was more than 25 percent in real terms from 1978 to 1980, and the number of countries receiving investments reached about fifty a year, compared with twenty to thirty a few years earlier.

157. IFC, "IFC Five-Year Program: FY81–85."

affected the operations of the IFC. High interest rates curtailed loan demand, while exchange rate instability and depressed economic conditions obstructed equity investments. At the same time that new investments were held back, the vulnerability of previous investments was brought to light. During the years 1981 to 1984, the real value of the IFC's new investments contracted, and none of the specific goals of sectoral and regional distribution and promotional activities established by the Five-Year Program was closely approached. In the same period, provisions against losses on former investments tripled.

During these times of external adversities and internal dilemmas, the IFC did not have the good fortune of steadfast leadership. In July 1979 McNamara had decided that he required Moeen Qureshi's services in the Bank as senior vice president for finance. Since no successor was appointed as the IFC's executive vice president, Qureshi had to serve in two positions until January 1, 1981. As a consequence, the conduct of operations fell increasingly to the Corporation's two vice presidents, Judhvir Parmar and Gordon McClure, the former responsible for Europe, Asia, and Africa, and the latter for Latin America. A third vice president, James Kearns, was brought in from the Bank to be in charge of finance and planning, but stayed with the IFC for less than a year. The successor to Qureshi that McNamara eventually appointed was Hans A. Wuttke, a high official of Germany's powerful Dresdner Bank. However he failed to earn the support of the IFC's Board and its staff and resigned at mid-tenure, in April 1984. His successor, Sir William Ryrie, appointed by A. W. Clausen, who had become president of the Bank and the IFC in 1981, could not assume his new position until October of 1984. The IFC was thus left without a full-time or a fully effective executive vice president for more than five years.

The number of the IFC's operations, which had reached a level of fifty-three in 1980, remained practically unchanged from 1981 to 1984. At the same time, the average investment per project of approved financing for the IFC's own account declined from $13.5 million in 1980 to $11 million in the years 1981 to 1984 (in 1994 prices). This decline of almost 20 percent in the approved value of investments was accompanied by an even greater decline in actual commitments and disbursements. The bulk of the investments remained in loans. Instead of increasing in value, as the five-year plan had intended, new equity investments were now lower, in real terms, than they had been in the 1960s. There was some gain in the IFC's activities in relation to private capital flows to developing countries, which had diminished sharply. But at a level of 2.4 percent of these flows in 1980 to 1984, IFC investments remained quantitatively insignificant.

Sectoral distribution of investments changed little in the early 1980s, with capital and intermediate goods industries taking up three-fifths of the value and consumer goods industries, including tourism, accounting for one-fifth. The financial sector regained the relative position it had maintained in the 1960s, with investments in capital markets almost replacing those in DFCs. Although the drive for energy investments had yielded some results, they were much more modest than intended.[158]

Unlike sectoral distribution, regional distribution changed significantly in the early 1980s, principally as a result of external conditions. The economic downturn was much less severe in Asia than in the other continents. As a result, the IFC's Asian investments increased in real terms by 6 percent a year, and their relative share in approved investments shot up. Europe, the Middle East and North Africa, and the Latin American–Caribbean areas all declined. Sub-Saharan Africa, which during the 1970s had become a special target for IFC investment, had won a sharp increase in approvals from 1975 to 1980, rising from three investments a year to eleven, and almost tripling investment value in constant prices, lifting its relative share to 12 percent. This rise continued in the early 1980s, but principally because of the decline on the other continents, except Asia. Between 1980 and 1984, the number of African investments only increased from eleven to fifteen per year, and their real value rose but 2 percent a year.

Promotional activities had been placed in the forefront of the Five-Year Programs. Initiatives for eliminating economic bottlenecks, tapping unexploited resources, supplying critical consumer goods, and developing new industries were at the top of the agenda. More staff was to be employed for promotion, policy advice, and supervision. In fact, however, promotional activities did not assume a prominent position. They became largely confined to two specialized departments, Capital Markets and Development. In the early 1980s the former was engaged in policy advice and institutional support while introducing new types of financial activities, in particular, leasing. The Development Department, established in 1978, was beginning to render advisory services relating to foreign direct investment. It was actively promoting shrimp farming and the poultry industry in various countries. A Caribbean Project Development Facility was established in 1981 in cooperation with other international and regional institutions, and a similar facility was being prepared for Africa; it later became an important instrument for the IFC's operations in that continent.

There was no renewal of the intensive discussion of the 1970s concerning publicly owned enterprises and foreign investment. The policies established on these issues remained in force, but their implementation changed in accordance with the transformation of outside opinion. Instead of being apologetic about its role as a promoter of the private sector, the Corporation was now looking toward the opportunities this role presented. The 1982 Annual Report stated that the IFC had been "established as a catalyst for private investment and in the present uncertain environment this role takes on perhaps even more significance than in

158. See note 215.

the past."[159] In 1984 the new Five-Year Program for 1985 to 1989 stated that "governments have become more aware of the benefits of policies which encourage private sector activity and are finding that such incentives need not compromise the attainment of other social objectives." In the case of the IFC itself, the program took the unqualified position that "IFC's role is to assist private sector development."[160]

The IFC's policies on investments in mixed private and public sector enterprises were reviewed in 1984.[161] As presented in a memorandum to the Board by President A. W. Clausen, the review confirmed the policies that had evolved during the 1970s, according to which majority ownership by government was not, of itself, a bar to IFC investment. Compared with the 1970s, however, the emphasis had shifted from flexibility to restraint. Even in countries with less than an enthusiastic attitude toward the private sector, the IFC's role was to seek to preserve and promote this sector, and involvement with mixed enterprises was perceived to be a means to promote the private sector's long-term interests.[162] As early as 1982, it was envisaged that the IFC would assist in the privatization of parastatal companies.[163]

As the view of foreign direct investment in developing countries began to shift its emphasis from domestic control to development opportunities, the IFC's attitude followed suit. The 1982 Annual Report drew renewed attention to the IFC's "traditional role of mobilizing foreign risk capital flows for developing countries."[164] And in the 1984 Five-Year Program, the expansion of foreign investment was included in the first of its four main objectives.[165] Formally, however, the policy remained the same as in the 1970s; that is to say, the IFC would only invest in a venture if there was a provision for local participation. It was not until 1988 that the position had returned to the pre-1969 view that full foreign ownership could be accepted if no local shareholder could be found.[166]

What increasingly attracted the attention of IFC management in the early 1980s was the condition of the portfolio and the overall financial position of the Corporation. Write-offs increased substantially in 1981 and the growth in arrears was noted in 1982.[167] As a consequence, specific reserves were raised in 1982, from 3.2 percent to 4.6 percent of the disbursed and outstanding portfolio. Thereafter they were raised every year until 1987, when they reached 9 percent. By June 30, 1985, it was concluded that 18 percent of the mature portfolio, that is, investments more

159. IFC, *Annual Report, 1982*, p. 15.

160. Memorandum, A. W. Clausen to the Board of Directors, "IFC's Five-Year Program: FY85–89 and Increase in Capital," IFC/R84-10, February 3, 1984, pp. 4, 6.

161. Memorandum to the Board of Directors, "IFC Investments in Mixed Private and Public Sector Enterprises—An Overview," IFC/R84-2, January 11, 1984.

162. Memorandum to the Board, January 11, 1984, paras. 15 and 16, p. 8.

163. IFC, "IFC Five-Year Program, FY84–88," IFC/R82-96, October 29, 1982, p. 55.

164. IFC, *Annual Report, 1982*, p. 15.

165. Memorandum, Clausen to the Board, February 3, 1984, p. 9.

166. IFC, "IFC Operating Practices and Policies, Guidelines for IFC Staff," July 1988, p. 4.

167. IFC, *Annual Report, 1981 and 1982*.

than three years old, were experiencing serious problems, and an additional 32 percent of the investments were performing below hoped-for levels. The other half of the investments were considered sound and performing satisfactorily.[168] As would be expected, equity investments had a much higher proportion of problems (40 percent) than did loans (14 percent). In order to give greater attention to inadequately performing investments, they were in early 1984 removed from the jurisdiction of the investment departments and placed in a newly established unit, which devoted itself to cases requiring "intensive care."

Not surprisingly, deteriorating economic conditions in developing countries had affected the IFC's portfolio. The question now was whether adequate provisions had been made for this eventuality, and what could be done to nurse investments back to health in spite of continued economic difficulties. A more intriguing issue was the degree to which the problems stemmed from deficiencies in the IFC's own procedures and supervision. The common view in the IFC was that general economic conditions bore the main responsibility for the state of the portfolio. Some also believed that internal deficiencies were partly to blame. With the drive for expansion, a new attitude had developed within the Corporation: careful processing of projects and their subsequent supervision were not as highly valued as before. Furthermore, the attempts to expand investments in less advanced countries and to enter new sectors of operations were believed to have lowered the quality of the portfolio.[169] These views led to stricter investment discipline and, later on, to organizational changes.

Deteriorating external conditions affected not only the IFC's portfolio. They also had a direct impact on its net income, through the increased cost of funds, reduction in dividends received, and lower capital gains from sales of investments. These effects were imposed on a net income that was less than robust. In the five-year period 1980 to 1984, the IFC's net income was reduced to an annual average of 3.9 percent of capital and reserves, as compared with 4.8 percent in 1975 to 1979. Indeed, taking the rate of inflation into account, the IFC, having barely maintained its capital intact from 1968 to 1972, from then on experienced a steady erosion of its net assets.[170] This became even more disconcerting when the Cor-

168. IFC, "Briefing Book" for President Barber B. Conable, April 4, 1986, p. 19.

169. Ryrie, Oral History, August 10, 1993; and Ryrie, interview with the author, October 12, 1995.

170.

	1960–67	1968–72	1973–85	1986–90	1991–94
IFC's net income as a percentage of capital and reserves (annual averages)	2.84	4.69	4.14	8.02	7.80
U.S. consumer price index, percent increase (annual averages)	1.71	4.62	7.58	3.97	3.21

The net income percentages refer to fiscal years, while the CPI refers to calendar years.

poration was faced with the prospect of significant losses on its portfolio. These considerations eventually resulted in a number of financial measures. The immediate reaction, however, was to raise the issue of a new capital increase as early as 1982, several years before the time that had been envisaged in 1977, and just when the IFC's activities were stagnating.

The Capital Increase of 1985

The proposal for a substantial capital increase, presented to the Board by Executive Vice President Wuttke in October 1982, projected an important role for the IFC in the revival of economic growth in developing countries in the years ahead.[171] When the immediate crisis lifted, it suggested, developing countries would be in great need of new capital and at the same time would view the private sector more positively than before. As the private sector affiliate of the Bank, the IFC was expected to assume an increasingly prominent role "as a mobilizer of private equity and debt capital, as a source of project preparation services, and as a supplier of high quality policy and technical assistance for private sector development."[172] The capital increase was required to back up an expansion of activities and, in particular, to make possible an increase in equity investments and to support the costs of project preparation, advice, and technical assistance beyond the levels that would be accepted by private institutions.

The proposal was for additional capital of $750 million, more than doubling the existing $650 million, to be paid in over a period of five years. This would permit an 11 percent annual increase in the real value of the IFC's investments for its own account during the Five-Year Program period of fiscal 1984–88, and a 5 percent increase per year in the five following years. Apart from the new emphasis on private sector development, the program's orientation was similar to that of the Five-Year Program of 1978 (fiscal 1979–83). The emphasis was on equity investments; greenfield projects, especially in smaller and poorer countries; and ventures in new sectors, in particular oil and gas exploration. A major addition was planned for staff devoted to special promotion, policy, and technical assistance.

In fact, it was not the projected expansion as such that made the capital increase necessary, but rather the combination of expansion, continued emphasis on developmental expenditures, and a weak net income position. At this time (at the end of fiscal year 1982), the Corporation's ratio of debt to capital was less than 1:1, far below the limit established by its Articles, which was 4:1. It would have been possible almost to double the portfolio on the basis of increased borrowing without exceeding a leverage of 2.5:1, the norm adopted by the IFC's management. This would, however, have brought the finances of the Corporation into an intolerable

171. IFC, "IFC Five-Year Program: FY84–88."
172. Ibid., p. 6.

position as the spread on borrowed funds was at a level of 2.0 to 2.25 percent, while administrative costs, before provisions, were at a level of about 3 percent of disbursed and outstanding portfolio, a ratio that had increased significantly since the 1970s.[173] As the costs associated with developmental activities were estimated at one-third of administrative costs, such activities would have had to be more or less eliminated in order to obtain a balance on borrowed funds.[174] Another possibility, hardly realistic in the existing circumstances, would have been a significant increase in lending charges. The solution proposed by the program was consequently a large capital increase. This would make it possible to retain, and even to increase, developmental expenditures, expand equity investments, and, at the same time, maintain net income at the approximate level of inflation, thus avoiding a continued erosion of the Corporation's capital.[175]

The program was discussed at a Board seminar in December 1982, which was followed up by technical notes and further seminar discussions. It received support of a general nature at the meeting of the Development Committee and the IMF–World Bank annual meetings of September 1983. On that basis, in February 1984 President Clausen presented the Board with a revised program, which, after further discussion and some changes, was approved by the Board in June 1984.[176] The principal change was a reduction of the capital increase, from the proposed $750 million to $650 million, which implied a doubling of the existing capital. In this form, the capital increase obtained the approval of the Board of Governors in December 1985.

The revised program was essentially a somewhat reduced and streamlined version of the original 1982 program. The projected expansion of investments was 7 percent per year in real value. The emphasis on promoting economic development through support for the private sector, including foreign investment, had been sharpened, and the main initiatives were now limited to four: financial market development, corporate restructuring, investment in Sub-Saharan Africa, and energy exploration and development. Also somewhat more emphasis was placed on maintaining an acceptable minimum level of net income. The support of all the Corporation's owners had been obtained on the basis of a combination of private sector promotion, on the one hand, and the retention of most of the developmental intentions of the previous decade, on the other.

Reorganization

In July 1984, in the immediate wake of the Board of Directors' approval of the capital increase, President A. W. Clausen appointed a successor to Hans Wuttke.

173. Ibid., p. 74.
174. Ibid., para. 1.13, p. 5.
175. Ibid., para. 11.14, p. 77.
176. Memorandum, Clausen to the Board, February 3, 1984, together with Annex Volume, IFC/R84-10/1, of the same date. Also, memorandum, A. W. Clausen to the Board of Directors, "IFC's Increase in Capital," IFC/R84-10/2, May 31, 1984.

For a while, he had considered moving Moeen Qureshi back to his former position in the IFC, giving him at the same time the responsibility for the Bank's industrial and DFC operations. Such a move would have aimed at coordinating Bank and IFC activities in the private sector, as George Woods had attempted to do in the 1960s and later was sought by different means in the 1990s. Although agreeable to Qureshi himself, this idea was not realized.[177] Instead, the appointment went to Sir William S. Ryrie, a high-level British civil servant, who had been executive director of the IMF, the World Bank, and the IFC in the 1970s. This move was not well received by the IFC's largest shareholder, the United States, which believed that a person with strong private sector experience would be the appropriate choice, especially at a time when the private sector was assuming a more prominent role than before in economic development.[178] But the decision was that of President Clausen alone, as acknowledged by the Treasury in a press release. Subsequently, using the occasion of declaring his support as U.S. governor for the capital increase, Secretary Donald Regan congratulated Ryrie on his appointment and expressed his appreciation of the IFC.[179]

Upon his arrival in October 1984, Ryrie found the Corporation in disarray after being without an executive vice president for six months. Operations had been declining, portfolio problems were emerging, morale was low. On the other hand, the capital increase had been approved by the Board of Directors and the plans for its use had been spelled out in a five-year program. Depression and debt problems in developing countries, together with a turn toward appreciation of the private sector, created new opportunities for an expansion of the IFC's operations, in the wake of IMF–World Bank structural adjustment efforts. It was essential to act quickly in order to consolidate the institution and get it moving on the right track. The means Ryrie chose to achieve this was a reorganization, carried out within three months of his arrival, and a drive toward the IFC's market borrowing, initiated at the same time. The first of these actions is discussed in this section, and the second in the following one.

As a small institution, the IFC had not paid much attention to its administrative organization. It had been operating through regional investment departments, supported by a rather strong Engineering Department and, after 1971, an increasingly important Economic Department. The small size of the institution had promoted a form of micromanagement wherein the executive vice president and the one or two vice presidents considered every project together with department

177. Moeen A. Qureshi, interview with the author, January 22, 1996.

178. The preferred choice of the U.S. Treasury was Carlos Rodriguez Pastor, a banker who had been a high official of the Wells Fargo Bank and subsequently minister of finance of Peru.

179. U.S. Department of the Treasury, "Treasury News," press release, July 13, 1984. Letter, Donald Regan, secretary of the Treasury, to Sir William S. Ryrie, December 11, 1984.

directors.[180] These procedures remained essentially unchanged when the annually approved projects increased from about twenty in the early 1970s to about sixty in the mid-1980s. Wuttke had attempted to come to terms with administrative problems by increasing the number of vice presidents from three to six, without changing the basic pattern of organization. This move, however, weakened the position of the department directors, reduced the authority of the executive vice president, and tempted the regional vice presidents to seek reciprocal support in their decisionmaking.

Ryrie's solution was to go in the opposite direction from the one taken by his predecessor.[181] He, in effect, requested the resignation of three of the vice presidents and reorganized the Corporation according to what he called a "matrix system," implying institution-wide responsibilities at the top, while the regional structure of investment departments was retained below. On the operational side, this left three vice presidents, together with the executive vice president, in the leadership. One vice president was responsible for all new investments, another for the existing investment portfolio, and the third for finances and general policy and planning.[182] The advantages of this new setup were twofold. First, the vice presidents would be able to concentrate on the total of the IFC's activity in each of the three areas in which the most apparent weaknesses had developed in the early 1980s, that is, in the preparation of investments, the care of the portfolio, and management of the financial position of the Corporation itself. Second, it strengthened the position of the directors of the regional investment departments, who now worked directly under central management, as well as the position of the executive vice president himself, who had become the leader of a small operational management group of altogether four people.

Market Borrowing

It had long been an IFC ambition to borrow from the market without support from the World Bank. The fear, however, had always been that this would imply higher interest rates than the Bank could obtain and would obstruct the Bank's own marketing. In the mid-1980s a number of circumstances combined to make the IFC's market borrowing feasible. First, the Corporation had become much larger, and it was scheduled to grow fast in the years to come. Second, its financial position was being greatly strengthened by the new capital increase. Third, through its

180. Ryrie, Oral History, August 10, 1993, p. 6.
181. Ibid., p. 27.
182. This organization did not come fully into effect until 1987. During 1985 and 1986, one vice president was in charge of new investments, the second was in charge of portfolio and financial management, and the third in charge of corporate affairs and development, including capital markets. Besides these three operational vice presidents, the general counsel and the director of the Engineering Department had the positions of vice president.

investment operations, in particular underwritings and syndications, the IFC had become well known and respected in international financial markets. All this made market borrowing much more likely to succeed than before.[183]

By this time, the IFC's borrowing arrangements with the Bank were no longer modeled on the Bank's operations with DFCs, as they had been in the beginning. Since 1971, the Bank had in effect acted as a treasury manager for the IFC, mobilizing capital for its benefit on an actual cost basis.[184] Funds were provided both in U.S. dollars and other currencies, basically at fixed interest rates, and were drawn by the IFC according to its needs, with the required liquidity held by the Bank. These arrangements, originally highly favorable to the IFC, were becoming difficult to manage in times of turbulent interest and foreign exchange rates and were creating increasing friction between the two institutions. As an investor, the IFC found itself more compelled than the Bank to adjust to customer needs and to market trends. This applied in particular to the introduction of variable interest rates and derivative instruments. Moreover, as a much smaller institution, the IFC could make use of pockets of capital supply that were not of interest to the Bank. Also, under conditions of an inverted interest rate structure, prevailing in the first half of the 1980s, the IFC would gain by holding and investing its own liquidity.

Consequently, there were strong reasons for the IFC to strive for market borrowing, at least to some significant degree. To the Bank's financial managers, concerned about the Bank's marketing position, such activities by the small affiliate still looked like a nuisance. This view shifted, however, when the Bank began to run into headroom problems for its borrowing and its capital increase was seriously delayed, at the same time that the IFC had been able to increase its capital. The issue then became to seek an optimal leverage for the capital of both institutions, independently.

Some borrowing from sources other than the World Bank had been projected in the fiscal 1985–89 program, which formed the basis for the capital increase.[185] As soon as William Ryrie took over the position of executive vice president in October 1984, he was introduced to the subject by Richard Frank, who was then the IFC's director of financial management and planning. According to Ryrie's own account, he found the idea highly appealing and bold, since the IFC's financial position was not strong at the time, and the papers issued would not be backed by the Bank.[186]

183. This section is in part based on the author's interviews with Sir William S. Ryrie, October 12, 1995; Richard H. Frank, October 25, 1995; and Vasant H. Karmarkar, November 6, 1995.

184. Memorandum, Aron Broches, "Bank Loans to IFC," May 1982. This memorandum gives a full account of the lending-borrowing relations of the two institutions in the 1960s and 1970s.

185. Memorandum, Clausen to the Board, February 3, 1984, para. 5.03, p. 26.

186. Sir William Ryrie, *First World, Third World* (New York: St. Martin's Press, 1995), pp. 157–58; Ryrie, Oral History, August 10, 1993, p. 37.

The IFC thus decided to make a modest start with some privately placed bonds, and as early as December 1984 the Board of Directors authorized the raising of funds directly from international capital markets. The IFC's Annual Report for fiscal 1985 describes the decision as a move to improve the matching of the Corporation's capital and operational needs, as well as to expand the financing available to the IFC. Subsequently, $100 million was raised on the Eurodollar market and DM 90 million in Germany, at highly satisfactory terms. Nevertheless, the larger part of required loan funds was still to be raised from the Bank.[187]

Once successful placements had been made, it became attractive to shift the major part of borrowing to the markets. The IFC's financial staff, under the leadership of Richard Frank, strongly advocated this course, and before long the Bank itself encouraged this course of action. It drew particular support from Ernest Stern, when he had become senior vice president for finance. The syndicating banks, with which the IFC cooperated, were also eager to utilize existing opportunities fully. By fiscal year 1987, the IFC's borrowing was largely in the financial markets, and it was relying on the Bank mainly for the funding of small amounts in diverse currencies, for which it would not be worthwhile to go to the markets. Nevertheless, a new funding agreement with the Bank was concluded in 1988, to enable the IFC to align the rates and maturity structures of its borrowings from the Bank more closely with the loans it made to its clients.[188]

A further logical step was to shift from private to public placements. Unless this was done, the liquidity of the IFC's bonds would be limited, and this in turn would affect their pricing. To do this, a rating process was necessary, and it was completed in 1989, when the IFC received triple-A ratings from both Moody's and Standard & Poor's. The first public issue, of US$200 million, was launched in June 1989. It was followed a month later by a second issue in Japan.

The financial liberation of the IFC from the Bank had thus been completed. But to what extent was it a reality, and to what extent an illusion? And, if it was a reality, had the IFC then in effect moved from the friendly discipline of an affiliated institution to the harsher one of the international financial markets?

In the process of obtaining a high rating and introducing its own public issues, the IFC had certainly benefited from its relation with the Bank. But the principal strength of the IFC was not its relationship with the Bank as such, but rather the fact that, like the Bank, it was a public institution, owned by countries all over the world, including the major industrial powers, which were bound to have a strong sense of responsibility for the institution. In one respect, the IFC had a stronger position than the Bank: all its capital was paid in, instead of being a commitment to meet certain contingencies, as was the case for most of the Bank's capital. By a statement in the bond documents themselves, it had been made clear that the Bank

187. IFC, *Annual Report, 1985*, pp. 5–6.
188. IFC, *Annual Report, 1988*, p. 18.

had no responsibility for the IFC's bonds. The rating companies had also gone to great lengths to delve into the IFC's financial position and operations; and they had established a number of benchmarks that the IFC would have to observe in order to maintain its rating. Thus there were strong reasons to believe that the IFC's rating and acceptance in financial markets were essentially based on its own identity and behavior, although the Bank's high reputation in the markets would have been a significant support, especially in the beginning. This was the belief of the IFC's management at the time, and it is even more strongly felt today.

In order to obtain a triple-A rating, the IFC had to accept obligations regarding its debt-to-equity ratio, its level of liquidity, and its ratio of equity investments to capital. The policies corresponding to these obligations were approved by the Board of Directors in 1989.[189] The first obligation restricted the amount of debt to 2.5 times the capital (2.5:1) instead of the four times (4:1) stipulated by the Articles of Agreement in 1965, when borrowing from the Bank had been authorized. This was not a greater restriction than the IFC had wanted to impose, and at the end of fiscal 1989 this ratio was in fact only 1.4:1. The liquidity policy was to maintain a level of liquidity at all times, including undrawn borrowing commitments from the World Bank, sufficient to cover 65 percent of the next three years' estimated net cash requirements.[190] This did, in fact, not go any further than the IFC's matched funding policy, which required the Corporation to have liquid resources sufficient to fund all approved but undisbursed investments. As for the equity-capital ratio, the obligation was that the portfolio of equity investments, together with that of quasi equity, would not exceed capital and reserves, while straight equity would not exceed one-half of that amount. This was a restriction from previous practice, as the IFC's own benchmark had been that straight equity, rather than straight and quasi equity, should remain within the limits of capital, in effect regarding quasi equity as a type of loan. By this time, however, the use of quasi equity, principally in the form of subordinated loans, had increased substantially, and the risks of this type of investment had, within the IFC, begun to be regarded as close to those of equity.[191]

On the whole, the IFC considered the restrictions imposed on its financial conduct by the rating process similar to its own previous practice, or to practices that would soon have been adopted in any case. In one respect, the IFC was going even farther than the rating agencies had requested. A policy of provisioning against eventual losses had been introduced by the IFC in 1974, establishing

189. Memorandum, Barber B. Conable to the Board of Directors, "Rating of IFC's Debt Securities and Proposed Financial Policies," IFC/R89-37, April 17, 1989. See also IFC, *Annual Report, 1989*, p. 21.

190. At the time of the rating, an assurance was provided by the Bank, in accordance with an approval of its Board, regarding the availability of undrawn borrowing commitments for liquidity purposes. See memorandum, Conable to Board, April 17, 1989, para. 18, p. 6.

191. Vasant H. Karmarkar, interview with the author, November 6, 1995.

provisions of both a specific and a general nature. The specific provisions were determined through reviews of the portfolio conducted twice every year. The general provisions were intended to cover risks from "immature" investments, that is, those that could not yet be subjected to review and were set at about 2 percent of the disbursements of loans during the previous three years, and at 15 percent of equity disbursements. After a thorough review of provisioning practice, the IFC in 1989 adopted a more rigorous policy for general provisioning, which had not been stipulated by the rating agencies.[192] According to the new policy, which was further amended in 1992, general provisions would take into consideration unidentified risks of the entire portfolio, instead of only those of immature investments.[193] These unidentified risks were related to the concentration of investments in single projects, sectors, and countries. To a large extent they were of a political rather than a commercial nature. The new policy resulted in more than a doubling of general loss reserves from 1988 to 1991, from 2.2 percent of portfolio to 5.0 percent.

In the second half of the 1980s, the IFC was thus moving into substantially more rigorous financial policies than it had followed before. This was certainly related to the adoption of market borrowing. More important, however, it was based on the view that financial policies in the 1970s and early 1980s had not been adequate and had surfaced in portfolio problems and a net income insufficient to maintain the value of the capital. This needed to be corrected under all circumstances. In this context, market borrowing was seen as an instrument of external discipline, and thus a protection against a recurrence of previous weaknesses.

A Mid-Term Course Correction

With the increase in capital secured, its administration strengthened, and the full access to financial markets coming into place, the IFC was prepared for a large and sustained expansion of its activities. However, the directions for this expansion, decided upon in 1984 under the strong influence of previous policies, soon came to be considered out of tune with prevailing prospects. This occasioned a course correction in 1987, at the mid-term of the fiscal 1985–89 Five-Year Program, a move thoroughly prepared for by a major study and supported by the Board after an extensive discussion in March 1987.[194]

The Mid-Term Review was concerned with the interpretation of the IFC's developmental role, the quality of its investments, and the special initiatives it was

192. Memorandum to the Board of Directors, "Review of IFC Policy and Procedures for Determining the Reserve against Losses," IFC/R89-2, January 3, 1989.

193. Memorandum to the Board of Directors, "Review of IFC Policy and Procedures for Determining the Reserve against Losses," IFC/R92-34, March 10, 1992.

194. IFC, "Five-Year Program Mid-Term Review," IFC/R87-12, February 5, 1987; IFC, "Summary of Discussion of the Board of Directors of IFC, and the Executive Directors of the Bank and IDA, March 3, 1987," SD87-12/1, May 8, 1987.

taking. Above all, it was concerned with the financial position of the Corporation itself. The Review linked the IFC unequivocally to a market-based private sector: "IFC's role is to promote economic development through market-based activities in support of the private sector. . . . Only by succeeding in a market environment can the enterprises generate development benefits for the country." Furthermore, in order to fulfill its role, the "IFC must not only promote profitable projects, but also remain profitable itself." While not seeking to maximize profit, it needed to strengthen its net income, and thus help to protect itself against adversities. Rather than being in conflict with the IFC's developmental role, this was a basis for that role.[195]

The Review maintained that, broadly speaking, the program envisaged in the original 1985–89 Five-Year Program continued to be justified. This included substantial growth in projects and investment volumes, an increase in equity and quasi-equity investments, greater sector diversification, and wide geographic coverage. It also included special attention to the four areas of high priority: financial markets and institutions, corporate restructuring, private enterprise in Sub-Saharan Africa, and energy exploration and development. However, modifications in practices and priorities were required.

In lending, greater emphasis needed to be given to investment volume and somewhat less to the number of projects, resulting in an increase in the average size of investments. At the same time, variable interest rates and pricing changes were required to reduce cancellations and prepayments, while closer portfolio supervision would help to improve loan portfolio performance. In equity investments, greater use of quasi-equity instruments would expand the portfolio and ensure its yields, while early sales of investments could augment the Corporation's capacity to support new ventures. With respect to the four priority initiatives of the program, two of them needed to be accelerated and two modified and rephased. The financial markets and institutional development initiative was proving to be of singular importance in helping to develop financial markets and promote their international linking. The need for the corporate restructuring initiative was greater than anticipated. On the other hand, the Sub-Saharan Africa initiative could not attain the expected volume, because of the scarcity of large projects in the region. The number of investments could be maintained, however, if services were set up to assist investment preparation and management training.[196] Finally, the energy exploration and development initiative needed to be recast and rephased in response to market conditions following the decline in oil prices.

---

195. IFC, "Five-Year Program Mid-Term Review," p. 19. See in particular the section "Objectives, IFC's Role," pp. 19–20.

196. This referred to the African Project Development Facility and the African Management Services Company, launched in 1986. Later, these initiatives were followed by the African Enterprise Fund (AEF) and the Enterprise Support Service for Africa, in 1989 and 1995, respectively.

The efforts to improve net income emphasized liability management, higher productivity, and the introduction of business plans. Through market borrowing, funds would be raised on favorable terms, corresponding to investment needs. Operational procedures would be streamlined, staff growth curbed, and the management of expenses tightened. Business plans would make each department responsible for its contribution to the Corporation's financial outcome and for balancing activities and diversifying risks. The objective was to achieve an average return on net worth of between 4 and 5 percent, thus maintaining the real value of the IFC's capital.

The Board of Directors considered the Mid-Term Review at a meeting on March 3, 1987.[197] No comments were made regarding the strong market and private sector orientation of the Review. This was a remarkable turnaround from the Board discussions of the 1970s, and even those earlier, when attitudes toward publicly owned enterprises and foreign direct investment had been the principal— and emotional—topics. This time the debate revolved around the question of the IFC's profitability versus its developmental role. Some said it was appropriate for the IFC to seek a strong financial position in order better to fulfill its development mandate, others that the IFC's concern for its financial position, although legitimate, was apt to impair its developmental role. In following years, this remained a principal issue within the Board, between Board and management, and among the staff.

Contributing to Development

The IFC had always had mixed feelings about furthering development through the promotion of profitable enterprises. Although in the early years of the IFC's operations, a significant discord between the aspects of profitability and development had not been perceived by the Corporation's leaders, some doubts had lingered. As described in a previous section, the view that emphasized development and made it equal with profitability had gained primacy at the end of the 1960s.[198] Now, in the second half of the 1980s, a new course of unification was being set, akin to that of the early years. Nevertheless, many remained uneasy, within the IFC itself, on its Board, and among the public. In what way and to what extent was the IFC in fact developmental? From 1989 to 1994, the IFC sought to come to grips with this question in a series of reports on its contribution to development, one of which was published as a companion piece to its Annual Report of 1992.[199]

197. IFC, "Summary of Discussions," May 8, 1987.
198. See the section "Emphasis on Development" in this chapter.
199. IFC, "The Development Impact of IFC Operations," IFC/R89-36, April 13, 1989; IFC, "Development Impact of IFC Operations: 1990," IFC/SecM90-119, August 13, 1990;

First, the reports affirmed that the projects in which the IFC invested were, indeed, profitable. Second, they sought to demonstrate that the projects were beneficial to the economy of the host countries. Third, they explained the nature of the IFC's assistance to the projects and asserted the extent to which it was essential, and therefore developmental. Finally, they reviewed a number of IFC activities, apart from investments, that had impacts on development.

The affirmation of profitability was based on assessments of a significant number of IFC investments both immediately after they had become operative and, for some of them, following several years of operation.[200] The two assessments did not differ much, and, according to the 1994 paper, the median FRR for 292 projects was 11.0 percent. There were substantial differences among sectors, with highs of 18 percent in mining and 16 percent in iron and steel, and lows of 7 percent in food and agribusiness as well as tourism. Regional rates ranged from a median of 13 percent in Asia and Latin America to 9 percent in Sub-Saharan Africa. From a comparison of the results of IFC investments and those of developing-country affiliates of U.S. firms for the year 1986, the 1989 report concluded that they were similar, and that the IFC had thus achieved financial returns at par with purely commercial operations.[201]

The assessments next compared the financial rates of return with estimated economic rates of return, using the same sources as before. The IFC had begun calculating ERRs in 1971 owing to concerns about investments in highly protected industries and this had gradually become a routine part of project appraisals.[202] The estimates of ERRs replaced the prices of inputs and outputs of the FRR calculations with prices expected to prevail under largely undistorted market conditions.

IFC, "IFC's Contribution to Development: 1992," IFC/R92-16, February 4, 1992; IFC, "IFC's Contribution to Development: 1994," IFC/R94-164, June 21, 1994. The 1989 report was also published as IFC, "The Development Contribution of IFC Operations," Economic Department Discussion Paper 5. The 1992 report appeared, in a somewhat edited form, as IFC, "Contributing to Development," ISBN-0-8213-2195-1, companion piece to the IFC's *Annual Report, 1992.*

200. The assessments were based on two sources: Investment Assessment Reports (IARs), prepared at the time of project completion and initiation of operations; and reports of the Operations Evaluations Unit (OEU), covering several years of actual operations. In the first case, financial rates of return and economic rates of return, calculated at the project appraisal, were reestimated on the basis of actual rather than expected project cost and with due regard to major changes in other assumptions. In the second case, ex-post rates of return were calculated. Substantial differences were not found in results from the two sources. The development contribution papers covered 110 projects in 1989, 200 in 1990, 232 in 1992, and 292 in 1994. One-quarter of the cases had been reviewed by OEU in 1992, and three-quarters came from IARs, which had covered about one-third of the projects completed during that year.

201. IFC, "The Development Impact of IFC Operations," IFC/R89-36, April 13, 1989, p. 9.

202. See the section "The Issue of Protection" in this chapter.

Thus an attempt was made to eliminate the effects of taxes, tariffs, and subsidies, as well as skewed exchange rates and nontariff barriers. On the other hand, the estimates did not attempt to revise labor costs in the light of prevailing unemployment, and benefits accruing and costs borne outside the project were seldom taken into account.[203] On the whole, the calculation of ERRs aimed not to arrive at a comprehensive economic impact, but to determine whether the project achieved an acceptable economic return.

The comparison of ERRs and FRRs revealed a close proximity, with the ERRs being slightly higher. Thus, in the 1994 assessment, which found the two rates to be even closer than they were for previous years, the median ERR for 292 investment projects was 11.3 percent, compared with an FRR of 11.0 percent.[204] There were significant differences, however, in some industrial sectors. For chemicals and petrochemicals, food and agribusiness, iron and steel, and nonferrous metals, FRRs were somewhat higher than ERRs, indicating net protective effects. The opposite was the case in cement and construction materials, as well as in tourism. According to the 1992 analysis, 80 percent of 232 projects had made a positive contribution to the economy, and almost 60 percent had generated real economic rates of return of 10 percent or more.

The papers thus concluded that average economic returns of the IFC's investment projects were quite high and that the Corporation had, on the whole, been able to avoid investments that exploited distorted economic conditions. In the case of substantial foreign ownership, however, the economic benefits might accrue more to the foreign owner than to the host country. Conscious of this possibility, the IFC introduced a modified rate of return to be employed under such conditions, known as the return to the domestic economy (RDE). Calculated only ex-ante, at project appraisal, this rate was intended to give occasion to financial rearrangements, if it turned out to be significantly lower than the standard ERR and the FRR.[205]

Although not included in the ERR calculations, external economies were frequently referred to as proof of a developmental impact over and above project profitability. Often these economies were based on demonstration. A successful investment incited action by other investors, and the introduction of new technology or a marketing achievement opened the road for other firms. Then there were backward and forward linkages, when investments created conditions for other projects in the chain of production and distribution. The utilization by other firms of a project's investment in human and physical resources was also common. This included training of personnel and the provision of service facilities and infrastruc-

203. According to Moeen Qureshi, substantial environmental diseconomies were given attention. Qureshi, interview, January 22, 1996,

204. Comparable figures from the 1992 report were 11.5 and 11.0, and from the 1990 report 13.3 and 11.9, respectively.

205. See IFC, "IFC's Contribution to Development: 1992," annex, p. 33.

ture. The IFC's investments presented many examples of this kind, which were described in the development contribution papers. A question the papers did not specifically address was whether external economies played a role in the IFC's project selection, which they would not have played in the decisions of private investors.

After establishing that the IFC's projects were, on the whole, profitable to their owners as well as economically beneficial to their host countries, the papers proceeded to demonstrate how the IFC could achieve a developmental impact over and above what a private investor would have accomplished. For this purpose, the 1992 report formalized three guiding principles for the IFC's activities, which have since been reiterated in a number of IFC publications. They were named the business principle, the catalytic principle, and the principle of special contribution.[206] All of them had their roots in the Corporation's Articles, and none of them had, in general terms, ever been disputed, although from time to time they were given different interpretations, especially the business principle.

THE BUSINESS PRINCIPLE. The business principle implied that the IFC should not merely finance the private sector but should act as its partner, sharing investment risks under market discipline. It consequently had to aim at profitability, just as the private sector did, but that aim should not necessarily be seen as conflicting with development. In essence, the IFC's role was "to combine the object of profitability with that of development." More specifically, "IFC's contribution to development is to be found in successful (that is, profitable) companies of all types and sizes, which owe their success to a significant extent to IFC's participation and support."[207] Several corollaries were seen as following from this principle. First, in order to participate successfully with private partners, the IFC had to have a record of profitability both for its investments and for itself as an institution. Second, companies in which the IFC invested ought not to rely on market distortions for their profitability, as this would be in conflict with the development objective. Third, the "dual strategy" of the late 1970s and early 1980s should not be implemented by balancing highly profitable investments, where the IFC's participation might not be needed, against unprofitable investments, which ought not to be made in the first place.[208] On the other hand, investments in larger enterprises with low processing costs could be balanced against investments in smaller, profitable, enterprises, involving relatively high processing costs.

---

206. This is the order in which the three principles are presented in the 1994 contribution paper. In the 1992 paper, which is the one mainly followed in the present presentation, the catalytic principle is placed first, the business principle second. The same order is followed in an up-front section of IFC's *Annual Report, 1995*, titled "Contributing to Development." In a more recent IFC publication, "Collaboration with Private International Financial Institutions" (November 1995), the business principle is referred to as the business partnership principle, and the principle of special contribution as the principle of non-displacement.

207. IFC, "Contributing to Development," p. 3.

208. See the section "A Dual Strategy" in this chapter.

THE CATALYTIC PRINCIPLE. According to the catalytic principle, the IFC should strongly seek to bring in investing partners and limit its own participation to the minimum required to secure satisfactory financing from private, risk-taking sources. This mobilization could take the form of cofinancing, whereby the IFC's participation encourages other investors to provide funding, whether in loans or equity. But it could also take the form of syndication, wherein the IFC would sell participation in its loans, and of underwriting security issues. In the financing of projects, the IFC should always assume a minority role so that the bulk of funding, as well as the leadership and management responsibility, would lie with private parties.

THE PRINCIPLE OF SPECIAL CONTRIBUTION. The principle of special contribution concerned the participation in investments that would not have been made, or not have become equally profitable and economically beneficial, without the IFC's assistance. It was derived from the specification in the Articles that the Corporation should "not undertake any financing for which in its opinion sufficient private capital could be obtained on reasonable terms."[209] This nondisplacement provision implied that the IFC's participation had to supplement rather than supplant the role of market operators. In view of the IFC's character as a public institution, the special contribution could reduce the risks of its partners so that projects that otherwise would not proceed, could go forward. The contribution could, broadly, be supplied in three different ways. First, owned by governments from all over the world and closely related to the World Bank, the IFC faced lower country risks resulting from political and economic conditions than a private investor. Through its participation in a project, it could transfer this risk reduction to other investors, furnishing comfort without issuing a formal guarantee. Second, supported by its stock of public capital, the IFC could reduce the risks of other participants by providing loans and equity for longer terms than the market was prepared to accept. Third, again relying on its public capital and going further than a private investor would do, the IFC could use its expertise, experience, and local knowledge to help structure the project, technically, legally, and financially, in a way that reduced the risks of the investment, whether country or project risks, and increased the economic returns.

In summary, the papers suggested that the IFC's contribution to development consisted of profitable investments that were economically beneficial for the host country and would not have come about, or not have yielded the same benefits, without the IFC's help. An additional contribution was then found in the IFC's support of policies and institutions promoting the development of the private sector. The requirement that the IFC should make a development contribution implied a greater discernment in the IFC's selection of investments than in that of private investors. This had not been felt strongly so long as profitability and

209. IFC, *Articles of Agreement*, art. III, sec. 3 (1).

economic benefits were largely considered identical. When that was no longer the case, beginning at the end of the 1960s, a number of other criteria had been brought into the assessment that tended to encumber the IFC's operations as an investor in private enterprises. By the late 1980s and early 1990s, with market-based methods and market discipline coming to the fore, profitability and economic benefits were again largely seen as coinciding. The stipulations remained, however, that the IFC's participation should be essential for the investment to succeed and their development contribution in most cases enhanced by external benefits. While the development contribution papers demonstrated the IFC's prerequisites for its task and presented examples of accomplishment, they could not ascertain that the IFC, as a rule, was meeting the stipulation of essentiality, nor that it was paying substantial attention to external economic benefits in its investment choices.

Essentiality

A basic tenet of the IFC has always been that the essentiality of its participation needed to be taken into account in every investment decision, not necessarily in the way that the project would not have come about without the IFC's presence, but at least in the way that it would become significantly more viable with the IFC's support.[210] This was also an issue of great interest to the IFC's Board. Nevertheless, some within and outside the Corporation continued to doubt whether the IFC's participation had been required in several or even many of its investments.

Essentiality is seldom easy to establish, and it may shift during the preparation of a project. The desire to increase the volume of operations and improve profitability will point the institution toward investments requiring easy appraisal and promising relatively safe returns. The reliable countries, the well-known companies and the trusted collaborators might thus be chosen, even when they could have done without the IFC's support.

In the early 1970s, when concerns arose about the reconciling of profitability and development, economists and economic calculations were inserted into the appraisal process as a means to ensure attention to development contributions. This led eventually, in the late 1970s, to the creation of a rather strongly staffed and positioned Development Department, which was entrusted with calculating ERRs; evaluating the development impact, including the essentiality of IFC participation; and initiating promotional efforts. Ten years later, the need for this supervisory role was not felt to be as strong as before. Profitability had again taken the position of primary development objective. The calculation of ERRs was by now commonplace, while its significance had been somewhat reduced by the progress of economic liberalization. Active promotion had become an even more doubtful proposition than before in economies that were more and more market oriented.

210. Ryrie, interview, October 12, 1995.

Furthermore, a rapid expansion of activities and a strengthening of the Corporation's financial position had become primary goals.

In these circumstances, the position of the Development Department began to be considered a hindrance to operational efficiency. Following the lead of the Bank's 1987 reorganization, the IFC in 1988 moved most of its economists to the investment departments, leaving only a core Economic Department. In their new locations, the economists were expected to carry out much of the previous development supervision. Separated one from another in departments of an orientation different from the one they represented, their influence was bound to be limited. At higher levels, there was no specific authority to raise developmental issues with operating department directors, whether essentiality or external economic benefits.

The preparation of the four contribution papers was in itself a sign of the uneasiness that still surrounded the development issue in the late 1980s and early 1990s. The Board continued to raise questions. Within the IFC, in a sample survey of investment officers' opinions in 1994, only a few of those questioned believed that developmental impact was a consideration in project selection, while a majority thought that it should be.[211] In the view of William Ryrie: "Many of the IFC's staff could legitimately be criticised for being interested solely in concluding transactions and showing insufficient awareness of the wider development role."[212] Most recently, the IFC in November 1995 issued comprehensive guidelines about its relationship with private international financial institutions, where the principle of special contribution, now called the principle of nondisplacement, was strongly emphasized.[213] Thus the IFC continued its search for an appropriate combination of profitability and developmental impact.

IFC's Operations, 1985–94

The strong expansion of the IFC's operations, beginning in 1985, took place in two phases, one lasting from 1985 through 1990, and the other from 1992 onward. During the first phase, investment approvals for the IFC's own account increased by an average of 22 percent a year in constant prices, which was similar to the increase of the 1960s, but on a much lower basis. Then came a year of standstill, 1991, when expansion had to be halted because of the delay in the new capital increase. After that increase had been obtained, expansion continued, this time at the more moderate pace of slightly more than 13 percent a year from 1992 through 1994. This expansion, combined with the contraction in private capital flows to developing countries, lifted the IFC's gross investments to about 5 percent of total

211. Carried out by the Economic Department.

212. Ryrie, *First World, Third World,* p. 146.

213. IFC, "Collaboration with Private International Financial Institutions: Practices and Policies," November 1995.

private capital flows to these countries in 1985 to 1991, almost twice the previous level.

As had been the case in the 1970s, the expansion was principally based on an increase in the number of projects, from 56 in 1984 to 231 in 1994, while the average size of the IFC's net investment for its own account rose only moderately, or from $9.1 million in 1984 to $10.6 million in 1994, calculated in 1994 prices.[214]

The most striking characteristic of the two phases of expansion, 1985 to 1990 and 1992 to 1994, is the sectoral redistribution of investments. Previously that distribution had changed very little, with capital and intermediate-goods industries retaining their leading role and the proclaimed efforts at sectoral diversification and breakthrough into new activities seemingly having little impact. This time, the growth was primarily concentrated in three sectors: capital markets and financial services, energy, and infrastructure. During the two phases combined, the growth of these three fastest-expanding sectors was twice the rate of the traditional industrial sectors. This became most pronounced in later years, and in 1994 one-half of approved investments for the IFC's own account were in the three as compared with about 20 percent in the early 1980s and 10 percent in the 1970s.[215]

The remarkable progress of financial sector investments resulted obviously in part from the worldwide trend toward liberalization of capital movements and financial sector reform. It was also related to the IFC's own strong efforts in this area, through the working of the Capital Markets Department, beginning in 1971 and becoming especially prominent in the mid-1980s. Energy investments, mainly directed to oil and gas development and later on to exploration, came to be emphasized after the second oil crisis at the end of the 1970s. They did not acquire real significance, however, until the late 1980s. Infrastructure investments had previously been negligible but came on strongly in the early 1990s, reaching as

214. The figures for 1994 are affected by the introduction of the African Enterprise Fund in 1989, which includes a significant number of projects of a very small average size (about $0.6 million IFC net investment per project). Excluding the AEF investments, the figures for 1994 would be 198 projects with an average IFC investment of $12.3 million.

215.

Sectoral Composition of Investments
IFC net, percentage of total amounts approved

Sector	1962–69	1970–79	1980–84	1985–89	1990–94	1994
Capital and intermediate goods industries	61.3	63.4	62.5	46.4	37.7	34.0
Consumer goods industries (including tourism)	16.3	26.1	17.5	20.3	18.9	15.2
Financial sector	15.8	8.1	15.2	20.2	23.4	28.6
Energy	2.5	2.0	4.3	8.7	9.3	7.0
Infrastructure	4.2	0.4	0.5	4.3	10.8	15.3
Total	100.0	100.0	100.0	100.0	100.0	100.0

much as 15 percent of total IFC approvals for its own account in 1994, with an even higher share in pipeline projects. With a strong trend toward private participation in infrastructure investments, the opportunities in this field greatly exceeded the IFC's capacity.

The expansion of the IFC's investments differed widely among regions, principally influenced by prevailing economic conditions. In the 1985 to 1990 growth phase, most of the expansion took place in Latin America, where commercial bank credits had largely been discontinued at that time. During the most recent growth phase, 1991 to 1994, expansion was most rapid in the Middle East and North Africa, now also including Central Asia, and in Europe, where the impact of new member countries was strongly felt.[216]

Already in the 1978 Five-Year Program, the objective was to increase the share of equity investments in the IFC's activities. This could not be realized in the early 1980s, because of exchange rate turbulence and depressed economic conditions. In 1980–84, at 15 percent of total approved investments, equity investments, including quasi equity, were at a lower level than ever before. Their revival remained a goal, however, which began to be realized after 1988. For the years 1990 to 1994, total equity investments reached an average of 23 percent of approvals, and as much as 29 percent in 1994. The increase was to a large extent the result of the expansion of financial sector and infrastructure investments, where the IFC's use of equity was considerably more common than in other fields.[217]

The operations of the IFC during the ten-year period 1985–94 did not follow the lines drawn up in 1984, nor were they in close accordance with the mid-term correction of 1987. They were shaped to a large extent by conditions which

216.

Regional Distribution of Investment Approvals
Financing for IFC's own account (percent)

Region	1962–69	1970–74	1975–80	1981–84	1985–90	1991–94
Sub-Saharan Africa	9.3	5.5	12.2	16.4	11.0	10.6
Asia	27.5	22.7	18.5	24.8	22.2	26.1
Europe	5.4	25.9	17.5	13.1	12.8	16.8
Middle East and North Africa	21.5	9.0	13.7	10.8	7.5	12.6
Latin America and the Caribbean	36.3	36.9	38.1	34.9	46.5	33.9
Total	100.0	100.0	100.0	100.0	100.0	100.0

217.

Equity Investments in Relation to Total Approved Investments
Percent

Investment	1966–69	1970–79	1980–84	1985–89	1990–94	1994
Straight equity	33.4	14.0	9.5	9.7	15.8	23.0
Total equity	33.4	19.0	14.7	16.5	23.2	29.1

originally had not been foreseen but were later successfully seized upon. The opportunities for expansion proved to be much greater than expected in 1985 to 1990 and to exceed the limits imposed by capital availability after 1991. The sectoral distribution of investments changed radically, for the first time in the IFC's history, while the regional distribution remained close to what it had always been. The planned increase in equity investments did not take place except as a result of the shift in sectoral distribution. The view expressed by the IFC staff in the discussion of the 1987 Mid-Term Review, that the IFC could not fully plan its activities, but had to be responsive to changing market opportunities, was realized in fact.[218]

A New Capital Increase

As the 1980s ended, the IFC saw an increase in its capital resources as an urgent need. Developing countries were turning toward the private sector as the driving force of development and socialist countries were entering a process of economic transition. Foreign private investors, in particular commercial banks, remained hesitant, however, after the experience of the debt crisis. The need and demand for the IFC's services appeared greater than ever. But without an increase in capital, the Corporation's growth would have to be contained within a few percentage points per year, in contrast to the annual expansion of more than 20 percent in the late 1980s. Otherwise, the established ratios of debt to capital, and of equity portfolio to capital, would soon be exceeded. And without the continued blending of borrowed funds with free capital, the developmental objectives of resource mobilization, project improvement, and balanced regional distribution of investments could not be achieved.

The timing of this capital increase, originally intended to be agreed upon in 1990, was not the most opportune, however. The Bank itself had just gone through a rather painful process of capital increase. An expansion of the resources of the IMF was under way, and so was an IDA replenishment. Regional development banks were obtaining more capital, and a new institution of that kind, the European Bank for Reconstruction and Development (EBRD), was in the making. Most important, the U.S. Treasury was engaged in a major effort to promote and reorient the Bank Group's activities for private sector development. Although an IFC capital increase could appropriately be seen as a part of such an effort, the U.S. Treasury, to the dismay of most of the Bank Group members, was not prepared to accept it without an agreement on overall private sector policies. As a result, the IFC's capital increase was held up for more than a year until an agreement was reached between the U.S. Treasury and Bank President Barber Conable and was

218. IBRD, "Summary of Discussions at the Meeting of the Board of Directors of IFC, and the Executive Directors of the Bank and IDA, March 3, 1987," SD87-12/1, May 8, 1987, para. 27, p. 5.

confirmed by the Bank's and the IFC's Board at the end of June 1991. Specifying a number of measures for strengthening the Bank Group's private sector policies, the agreement confirmed the importance of these policies within the context of the Bank's established objectives of poverty alleviation, human resources development, and environmental protection. The subsequent approval of a capital increase by the IFC's Board of Governors followed in May 1992.

In planning papers explaining the need for a capital increase of $1.3 billion, a doubling of the previous stock, the IFC emphasized its efforts for the overall stimulation and support for private investment, foreign as well as domestic.[219] First among the areas singled out for particular IFC attention was mobilization through loan syndication and underwriting, to which was added the sale of securitized loans, an innovation for the IFC. In general, the encouragement of portfolio investment in developing countries, equity as well as bonds, was seen as a field of great promise, tapping the huge pool of savings of industrialized countries for emerging markets. This led in the following years to IFC initiatives for establishing and supporting country and emerging market funds and for assuming joint-lead management for numerous securities issues.

Another facet of the mobilization effort was the development of domestic capital markets by helping to strengthen the framework for such markets as well as to establish and support local financial institutions. This was a continuation of previous efforts that had gathered strength in the 1980s. Related to this was a renewed emphasis on increasing the share of equity and quasi equity in the IFC's portfolio.

An evolving need was seen for the support of privatization and the restructuring of corporations. In particular, it was stated that private investment in developing countries would increasingly be directed to basic industries, including infrastructure, which had previously been dominated by the public sector. The Corporation's involvement, even by financing only a small part of the total investment, could help such projects to be soundly structured, thus reducing risks, increasing returns, and attracting private investors. What the IFC's management had in mind were mainly basic manufacturing industries. After the Board had expressed some caution regarding the IFC's role in the transfer to the private sector of such industries, or in new initiatives in this field, the emphasis shifted to infrastructure, which, indeed, became the most rapidly expanding part of the IFC's activities in the first half of the 1990s.[220]

219. IFC, "IFC in the 1990s and Need for a Capital Increase," IFC/SecM90-43, March 23, 1990; IFC, "IFC Capital Increase: Discussion Paper," IFC/R91-26, February 21, 1991, and IFC/R91-26/1, March 12, 1991; memorandum, Barber B. Conable to the Board, "IFC Capital Increase," IFC/R91-79, May 29, 1991. See also IFC, "FY 92–94 Growth Strategies and FY92 Business Plan and Budget Framework," IFC/R91-23, February 12, 1991.

220. IFC, "IFC Capital Increase: Discussion Paper," February 21, 1991, para. 57; memorandum, Conable to Board, May 29, 1991, para. 17; IFC, "Summary of Discussion at the Meeting of the Board of Directors of IFC, March 5, 1991," IFC/SD91-7, April 23, 1991, pp. 4–5.

The IFC thus sought to respond to market developments, where it could play an important role in a process of financial and structural transition. But the traditional emphasis on small enterprises and less advanced countries was not neglected. The needs of small and medium-sized enterprises (SMEs) was to be met principally by the use of financial intermediaries, as it had been before. This time, however, the IFC's assistance was to have a market basis and be rendered through private intermediaries that would be able to survive in an increasingly competitive financial environment. The respective roles of the IFC and the Bank in intermediary lending were established in policy guidelines that gave the IFC a leading position in countries where financial sector reform was not a major objective.[221]

With respect to less advanced countries, the preparatory papers argued, a capital increase was required to enhance IFC activities in such areas as Sub-Saharan Africa and the Middle East, while seizing opportunities offered in Asia and Latin America and supporting economic transition in Eastern Europe. To a degree, assistance to less advanced countries and countries in economic transition was to be delivered through specially targeted programs, such as the African Project Development Facility, the African Enterprise Fund, and Business Advisory Services in Eastern Europe.

Financial strictness was a condition of the 1992 capital increase. For the first time, financial returns of the Corporation were required to exceed the rate of inflation. The IFC's management initially proposed a 6 percent return on net worth, with the prospect of achieving a return of 8 percent within ten years. In deference to the U.S. Treasury view that the return should be set as high as 8–10 percent, this proposal was subsequently lifted to 7 percent for 1992–96 and 8 percent thereafter.[222] In order to support these higher returns, the IFC would have to recover the cost of extensive appraisal and special efforts on projects by charging market-based fees. Through higher efficiency, administrative costs were to decline from 3 percent of portfolio to 2.3 percent within a few years. Returns on equity investments were expected to be substantially above past experience, while borrowing costs, based on the Corporation's financial strength, would remain as much as 25 basis points below LIBOR. Indeed, management held out the possibility, in favorable circumstances, of a return on net worth of between 8 and 10 percent. If realized, such additional profits would be redeployed to help increase the IFC's investment capacity.[223]

The U.S. Treasury demand for higher returns on IFC capital was in part directed toward limiting promotional and developmental expenditures that might be considered excessive. But it was also based on the view that the IFC had not

221. IFC, "World Bank Policies Guiding Financial Sector Operations," R91-80, IDA/R91-53, IFC/R91-62, April 26, 1991. See in particular para. 34, p. 15.

222. See IFC, "Summary of Discussion at the Meeting of the Board of Directors of IFC, March 14, 1991," IFC/SD91-8, April 23, 1991, para. 24.

223. Memorandum, Conable to Board, May 29, 1991, pp. 10–11.

been efficient enough either in employing its capital or containing its administrative costs. As a public institution, with recourse to government funds for capital replenishment, the IFC had not exercised the same financial rigor as an enterprise operating under market discipline. Therefore higher returns could, to an extent, be achieved without curtailing the developmental impact that public money was intended to provide.

Not unexpectedly, IFC management had a somewhat different view. It agreed that higher returns than previously achieved were necessary to ensure the Corporation's financial health and its standing in the financial markets. Beyond this, however, and beyond some limited increase in efficiency, higher returns would infringe upon the IFC's development objective. Management believed that there was no consensus in support of this among the Corporation's owners.[224] The final capital increase paper stated that it would "strive for the highest possible income that can be achieved by means which would be fully consistent with the IFC's developmental mandate and with an appropriate regional distribution of investments."[225] In essence, this position was confirmed by the Board in its final discussion of the capital increase on June 20, 1991.[226]

This thorough deliberation of the IFC's appropriate return on its net worth, of related financial policies, and of the consequent impact upon developmental activities resulted in somewhat of an impasse. Given the conflicting views on these subjects, any other outcome would hardly have been possible. Nevertheless, it had been established that a substantial part of the yields of IFC capital, instead of being used directly for developmental expenditures, should be used to strengthen its financial position and expand its investment capacity. To this end, the Board set a tentative goal of 8 percent of the Corporation's net worth, which in fact was achieved during the years 1991–94.[227]

As approved by the Board of Directors at the end of June 1991, the capital increase was $1.0 billion, instead of the $1.3 billion originally proposed. In spite of this reduction, the IFC was able during the next few years to expand at an annual rate slightly above the 12 percent originally aimed at on the basis of the higher capital increase. However, the reluctance of shareholders to replenish capital prompted IFC management to seek ways to avoid further capital increases for at least another decade. The new target for return on capital was helpful in this respect. But in order to maintain the annual rate of growth at the 12–13 percent that IFC management considered appropriate, the Corporation's leverage—that is, its use of borrowed funds as compared with capital—would have to be lifted above the level of 2.5:1, determined by the IFC's own practice and its commitment to

224. IFC, "Summary of IFC Board Discussion, March 14, 1991," para. 33.
225. Memorandum, Conable to Board, May 29, 1991, para. 45.
226. Memorandum, "Board of Directors' Meeting, June 20, 1991: IFC Capital Increase," statement of Mr. Conable, chairman, IFC/SecM91-90, June 28, 1991, p. 2, last paragraph.
227. See the table in note 171.

rating agencies. This was done, while maintaining the triple-A rating, through the adoption in 1994 of a risk-weighing system concordant with the rules of the Basle Committee, which were being assumed in banking supervision throughout the world.[228] While not exceeding the IFC's statutory leverage of 4:1, this system was expected to permit the desired growth of 12–13 percent a year throughout the 1990s.[229]

The base for stable expansion thus established made it possible for the IFC to become a significant supporter of the globalization of financial markets, the transition from public to private sector activities, and the advance of the least-developed economies. To a significant extent, however, the main element of the base was no longer the provision of free capital from shareholders, as it had been for the largest part of the IFC's existence, but the building up of capital within the organization itself and its employment under well-established rules of prudence.

IFC-Bank Cooperation

During the capital increase debate, the relationship of the IFC and the Bank became a more prominent issue than it had been for a long time. After George Woods had given the responsibility for intermediary lending and industrial policy to the IFC in the 1960s and McNamara had subsequently moved it back to the Bank, scant attention had been devoted to this relationship. The IFC had, on the whole, conducted its transactions without explicitly coordinating them with the Bank's general policies and country strategies, and its advisory activities had been largely confined to areas that at the time were of limited interest to the Bank, such as private foreign investment and capital markets. Even in the financial sector, where both institutions were heavily engaged, there had been little cooperation.[230] The Bank had tended to regard the IFC and its operations as irrelevant to its own activities, while the IFC had been satisfied to remain outside the Bank's sphere of attention. This did not change in the 1980s, in spite of A. W. Clausen's decision to bring the IFC's executive vice president into the President's Council. On the contrary, partly as a consequence of its own market borrowing and increased financial strength, the IFC at this time was intentionally moving away from the Bank.

228. Given the name of "capital adequacy policy," this system stipulated a capital level of 30 percent against weighted exposures, as compared with a minimum of 8 percent for commercial banks according to the Basle rules, and a customary level of 10–14 percent for highly creditworthy banks and 20–30 percent for specialized institutions.

229. IFC, "Review of IFC's Financial Policies," IFC/R93-33/1, April 16, 1993; IFC, "IFC's Capital Adequacy," IFC/R94-58, March 25, 1994.

230. A striking indication of this was the Bank's "Report of the Task Force on Financial Sector Operations" of August 1, 1989, R89-163. This major policy report gave no account of IFC's experience in financial sector operations, nor did it assign IFC a position in relation to the Bank's future financial sector operations.

With private sector development achieving prominence as an objective for the Bank Group as a whole and with the IFC expanding operations in sectors such as infrastructure and intermediary financing, where the Bank had previously dominated, the traditional attitude could not be sustained. Better coordination and greater cooperation within the Bank Group were evidently called for, and this was strongly supported by the Bank's and the IFC's Board, as well as being high on the U.S. Treasury list of private sector actions.[231] Consequently, the report that formed the basis for the June 20, 1991, debate on private sector policies contained a section on staff guidelines for cooperation, which in effect were confirmed by the Board.[232]

According to the guidelines, the Bank's strength for supporting private sector development was in the fields of macroeconomic and sectoral policies and the shaping of institutional environment, including the framework for privatization, as well as in the financing of social and physical infrastructure. The IFC's strength lay in direct transactions with the private sector, in institution building for capital markets, and in advisory work for foreign investment policies and privatization. To achieve greater cooperation between the two institutions, the IFC was to become a contributor and participant in the Bank's country strategy process with regard to private sector development. In part, this would take place through the preparation of Private Sector Assessments for specific countries under the auspices of the Bank's country departments and the IFC's investment departments. A central coordinating unit would be established in the IFC to assist in the coordination, but no similar setup was considered necessary in the Bank.[233]

The Bank was expected to take the lead in financial sector reforms, while calling upon the relevant IFC expertise regarding the regulatory environment, the introduction of financial instruments, and the development of capital markets. For the most part, direct lending to the private sector would be left to the IFC, except in large-scale operations. The preference in financing private sector investments was to be first, private financing without either IFC or Bank support; second, IFC market-based financing; and third, Bank financing with government guarantee. Lending through financial intermediaries, including lending for the benefit of small and medium-sized enterprises, was to be left to the IFC, except where it was closely related to financial sector reform.[234]

231. Secretary Nicholas F. Brady, statement to the Development Committee, September 24, 1990.

232. IFC, "Private Sector Development: Strengthening the Bank Group Effort," R91-79, IDA/R91-52, IFC/R91-60, April 26, 1991, annex 2; memorandum, "Board of Director's Meeting, June 28, 1991."

233. This unit was called the "Private Sector Strategies Unit." It later became part of the Corporate Planning Department, to which other functions were also assigned.

234. Guidelines for financial sector operations were contained in a paper: IFC, "World Bank Policies Guiding Financial Sector Operations."

The staffs of the two institutions received the plans for closer cooperation and coordination with mixed feelings. On the IFC side, there were, as always, concerns about the ability to maintain its views and working procedures in association with a larger and more powerful institution with an ambience different from its own. In the Bank, people were reluctant to hand over, or to share, fields of operations and had doubts about the IFC's relevance and capabilities. At the same time, there was an understanding on both sides of the need for cooperation in conditions greatly different from before. The preparation of Private Sector Assessments was soon initiated, and later expanded to more countries than originally intended. Cooperation in the setting of country strategies and the delivery of services was established. The results were considered beneficial in both institutions, although the IFC remained apprehensive about possible Bank dominance.

In order to make better use of the opportunities that the capital increase had provided, the IFC carried out a reorganization that came into effect on July 1, 1992. The aim was to enhance the IFC's capabilities by bringing together technical and financial specialists in crucial fields. This broke with the regional principle of organization, which had prevailed from the beginning, by dividing operations among four sectoral investment departments and five regional departments. Characterized by its author, Executive Vice President Ryrie, as the most radical reorganization ever made in the IFC, it was expected to gain in specialization what it lost in straightforward responsibility.[235] Two of the new sectoral departments covered areas where Bank operations had previously been predominant: infrastructure and oil, gas, and mining. The two other departments were in charge of chemical industry and agribusiness. Paradoxically, the only area in which operations had always been run on a sectoral basis, capital markets, was now turned over to the regional departments. This was justified by the large number of operations as well as by divergent financial conditions in client countries. An unintended consequence of the reorganization, except for capital markets, was to complicate the nascent cooperation with the Bank, where operations were as before conducted on a strictly regional basis.[236]

---

235. Sir William S. Ryrie, interview, World Bank Oral History Program, September 17, 1993, pp. 1–5.

236. The four new sectoral departments were infrastructure (electric power, telecommunications, and transportation); oil, gas, and mining; chemicals, petrochemicals, and fertilizers; and agribusiness. They became responsible for investments in their respective fields in cooperation with their regional counterparts. Investments in other sectors, such as general manufacturing, textiles, and tourism, remained with the regional departments, which also assumed responsibility for investments in capital markets under the overall coordination of a core Capital Markets Department. The number of regional departments was reduced from eight to five: Asia, except for Central Asia; Europe, including Russia; Latin America and the Caribbean; the Middle East and North Africa, including Central Asia; and Sub-Saharan Africa. As a part of the reorganization, the regional departments were specifically entrusted with formulating and implementing an overall strategy in their respective regions.

At the end of calendar year 1992, the Bank carried out a major reorganization of its own, which implicitly recognized the need for more concentrated action for private sector development than Bank management had earlier accepted. A new vice presidency was established for finance and private sector development, together with two other vice presidencies, for human resources development and environmentally sustainable development. The mandate of these new units was to provide expert services in their respective fields for the support of the Bank's country departments, which retained both country and project authority. The Bank's program for the use of guarantees as complements to loans was then upgraded in 1994.[237] Conducted under a vice presidency for cofinancing and financial advisory services, this program was specifically directed toward the support of private investments in infrastructure, where the IFC by now was strongly engaged, as was another Bank affiliate, the Multinational Investment Guarantee Agency (MIGA).

Thus in the mid-1990s the Bank was emphasizing its private sector activities to a greater extent than had been anticipated during the debate of 1991. For this purpose it had created new units within its organization and brought new instruments into use. At the same time, the IFC was expanding its operations in the Bank's previous domains of infrastructure and the financial sector more rapidly than had been foreseen, and the new affiliate, MIGA, also engaged in private sector operations, was coming into its own. The measures for cooperation and coordination within the Bank Group initiated in 1991 were consequently proving inadequate. When restructuring the top management of the Bank in 1995, James Wolfensohn, the new president taking over from Lewis Preston, reacted to this situation by giving one of the Bank's five managing directors the responsibility for the overall coordination of the Bank Group's strategies and activities for private sector development. It was one more approach in a series of efforts to bring about an orderly pursuit of common goals of institutions owned by the same members and sharing the same Board and president.

An Overview, 1956–94

During its first five years of operation, the IFC approved investments amounting to about $10 million per year. It took almost ten more years, until 1970, for annual approvals to reach $100 million.[238] Indeed, the IFC in its early years was a laggard and was so perceived by itself as well as by others. But its owners never intended the IFC to be fast moving. They considered its existence to be experimen-

---

237. Memorandum, Lewis Preston to the Executive Directors, "Mainstreaming of Guarantees as an Operational Tool of the World Bank," R94-145, July 14, 1994. Discussed by the World Bank Board on September 8, 1994.

238. In 1994 prices, these figures would be $45 million and $400 million, respectively.

tal and had different views about its role. Some questioned the ability of a public institution to promote private enterprise, while others disputed the emphasis given to the private sector. Expected to work through encouragement and demonstration rather than the force of financial resources, the IFC was endowed with a minimal amount of capital and restricted by stipulations that experience soon revealed to be impractical.

After its Articles had been amended to allow it to hold straight equity and to obtain additional resources by borrowing from the Bank, the IFC had a spurt of growth in excess of 20 percent annually for the seven years 1962–69. Since then the growth of investment approvals, in real values, has averaged about 10 percent a year. Some years, expansion was held back by inadequate resources, whereas in other years it was spurred by capital injections, administered in 1977, 1985, and 1992. In the early 1980s there was a backsliding, occasioned by recession and debt crisis and aggravated by internal policy and management problems. By 1994 annual approvals had reached a value of $2.5 billion.

Additional capital resources have not been easily forthcoming from the IFC's owners, its member countries. There have been strong competing claims from the Bank itself, from IDA, from regional development banks, from the many agencies of the United Nations, and from bilateral aid. And there have always been national budget stringencies. Furthermore, divergent views of the objectives of profitability and development and of the position of the public and private sectors have complicated the process of replenishment. The largest shareholder, the United States, while a strong supporter of the IFC as a promoter of profitable private enterprise, has been less than satisfied with the Bank Group's overall private sector policies, as well as with the IFC's own financial performance. By contrast, many of the other members have tended to emphasize the IFC's role as an overall development institution and to discount the need for the profitability of the Corporation itself.

In the wake of the 1985 capital increase, the IFC sought to bolster its financial independence by initiating market borrowing in its own name. This led to more rigorous financial policies, making possible a triple-A rating and public placement of bonds. Further policy adjustments, adopted after the 1992 capital replenishment, sought to support the IFC's growth more strongly from internal sources, thus reducing the need for recourse to its owners.

At its establishment, the IFC was perceived as a venture investor, working with private investors. But it was not considered appropriate for a public institution to assume management responsibilities, and the IFC was barred from holding straight equity. Because this limitation proved to be a serious obstacle to operations, it was soon removed by a change in the Articles. Management responsibility remained precluded, however, although the IFC exercised an advisory function through board representation in some companies, especially financial companies. Following the amendment, equity became the fulcrum of the IFC's operations from 1962 to 1969, by itself or supported by loans. In the early 1970s this direction of operations was said to be preventing the Corporation from reaching a greater number of countries and enterprises and was shifted toward lending, unconnected with equity investments. Stimulated by low interest rates, this became the IFC's principal mode of operation, with the result that its mind-set came to resemble that of a commercial banker more than that of a venture investor. In due course, the shift was believed to have gone too far and to have become a restraint to the IFC's developmental role. Efforts to increase the share of equity investments were not successful, however, in the adverse economic climate of the 1980s. Not until the 1990s did equity investments have a strong recovery, connected with the expansion of financial sector and infrastructure operations.

From the beginning, the IFC was expected to act as a catalyst, bringing together investment opportunities, domestic and foreign capital, and experienced management. In consequence, the IFC kept its own share at a low level compared with the level of other participants. An early rule was that the IFC's financing should not exceed one-third of that supplied by other investors. Later the IFC considered it desirable to aim at mobilizing from other sources six times the capital it provided itself. This has been the average over the Corporation's lifetime, when the very first years are excluded.

The additional capital associated with the IFC's investments was expected to come from both domestic and foreign sources. Preferably, the IFC was to be instrumental in bringing the two together. Over time, however, the view of the position of domestic and foreign participation has shifted back and forth. First, it was believed that the availability of domestic capital and the proficiency of domestic entrepreneurs were highly limited, and that consequently the IFC needed to be closely allied with foreign investors. Later on, during the 1970s, domestic control of enterprises became a priority and the importance of foreign participation was sharply downgraded. This was, in due course, followed by a renewed emphasis on foreign investment and, in particular, on joint domestic and foreign ventures.

That the IFC should be ready to go farther than a private investment bank in seeking to make projects viable through technical, financial, and legal preparation was always taken for granted. For this purpose, the Corporation could legitimately use a substantial part of the return from the capital provided free of charge by its members. At the same time, views differed about how much of an entrepreneurial role ought to be assumed. Should the IFC limit itself to projects that were already far advanced, or should it take up project concepts at an early stage and seek to develop them further? Should it even promote its own ideas and procure partners for their implementation? Such active promotion was considered a possibility in the IFC's early years, although it was not put to practice except in the case of financial institutions. In the 1970s, however, activism, endorsed by the Pearson Commission, became a policy priority and remained so for almost twenty years. A special staff group was organized for its implementation and soon changed into a department. When that attempt yielded disappointing results, a new and stronger

Development Department was formed in the late 1970s with active promotion as one of its principal purposes.

The general view within the IFC is that active promotion has not been successful, except in the financial field, where the IFC had special expertise to offer. Opinions differ, however, as to its merits. Some say that project ideas cannot be successfully nurtured in an institution like the IFC: entrepreneurs are to be found in the field, and that is where conceptions have to develop. Others believe that, in the absence of active promotion, the IFC will be drawn to projects in which its participation is not essential, and that activism will yield satisfactory results if it is properly pursued with full backing from top management. By the late 1980s, the more restrictive view of promotion, always favored by the rank and file of investment officers, had decisively gained the upper hand. This stemmed from the greatly increased reliance on markets, as well as from disappointing results. But it was also related to the rigorous financial policies adopted by the IFC, which left less scope for promotional expenditures than before. As somewhat of a substitute for active promotion, targeted programs for project development and management support were introduced, the high costs of which were partly financed from outside sources.

Related to the issue of promotion was that of project size. By spreading its activities to many small projects, the IFC might conceivably have a greater impact on development than by concentrating its efforts, even if the latter meant larger overall volume. On the other hand, it was realized that foreign investors would find small projects less attractive than larger ones, and that small projects were expensive to promote, appraise, and supervise. In the 1960s, the trend was toward investing in larger projects, which were more attractive for foreign investors. In the 1970s and early 1980s, the emphasis was on smaller projects, which were more suitable for domestic entrepreneurs. Later on, large projects were viewed favorably as a means to reduce administrative costs. Despite these varying policy preferences, the average size of projects, and of the IFC's net contribution to them, remained by and large constant. Since the early 1960s, the average size of the IFC's projects has been in the range of $70–$90 million, in 1994 prices, and its own net contribution has remained at $10–$13 million. Indeed, despite intentions to the contrary, the IFC has never found a way to deal with small projects. Attempts to use intermediaries for this purpose were aborted when the responsibility for DFCs was moved to the Bank. And the later use of special programs targeted toward small enterprises has suffered from centralization and high costs.

At an early stage, the IFC's investments came to be directed primarily toward manufacturing industries producing capital and intermediate goods. These industries included cement and construction materials, chemicals and petrochemicals, fertilizers, industrial equipment and machinery, iron and steel, mining, nonferrous metals, and timber, pulp, and paper. From the early 1960s to the mid-1980s these industries constantly absorbed somewhat more than 60 percent of the IFC's investments. In these industries, standard technologies were as a rule available and the interest of foreign investors was present. Perceived as the basis for industrialization, they were well received by developing countries. Adding to their attraction was the expertise soon acquired by the IFC itself. Later, the promotion of consumer goods industries, such as food and agribusiness, general manufactures and textiles, as well as tourism, became a part of the drive for greater developmental impact. Their share in the IFC's annually approved investments increased to more than 25 percent during the 1970s. Influenced by disappointing results, it subsequently declined again to below 20 percent, where it had been before.

A major change in sectoral patterns came with the rapid advance of investments in financial enterprises, energy, and infrastructure, which taken together increased from 10 percent of approved net investments in the 1970s to 40 percent in the early 1990s. Investments in Development Finance Companies (DFCs), important in the 1960s, had fallen off when the responsibility for relations with these enterprises was transferred to the Bank in 1968. Efforts to revive financial sector operations through the establishment of a Capital Markets Department began to bear fruit in the early 1980s and subsequently were strongly stimulated by the worldwide move toward the opening and development of financial markets. Energy investments, particularly in oil and gas exploration, which were placed on the IFC's agenda at the time of the second oil crisis, did not become substantial until the late 1980s. Infrastructure investments, which had been shunned by the IFC as belonging to the public domain, suddenly became a major field of activity after 1990, when private participation in this sector began to be solicited in many developing countries and the IFC responded strongly to the opportunity.

Some questions have been raised about the distribution of IFC investments among countries. Mandated to finance viable enterprises, the IFC was drawn toward the relatively few countries in which business conditions were favorable and the participation of foreign private investors was forthcoming. In order to counteract this tendency, special efforts have been made now and again to reach less advanced regions and countries, and a disproportionate share of promotional expenditures has been devoted to this purpose. As a result, the IFC's reach has increased substantially over time. The concentration of investment approvals, as measured by the share of the ten countries with highest amounts each year, has moved from 90 percent before 1975 to 70–80 percent thereafter, until coming down to 65 percent in 1991–94.

If the IFC's investments in less advanced countries were to be successful, however, improved business conditions had to go hand in hand with the investments. This was recognized by the IFC's Articles, and the IFC's first president, Robert Garner, considered this task more crucial than investments. By itself, however, the IFC lacked both the stature and the resources to take on an overall policy advisory role. For that purpose, Bank-IFC cooperation was essential, combining, on the one hand, the Bank's standing with governments and its ample resources, and, on the other hand, the IFC's knowledge of the private sector and its operational flexibility. This cooperation came about in relation to DFCs in the 1960s, and it might have been extended to a wider field if the IFC had maintained the leading role in industrial development given to it by George Woods. This was not to be, however, as responsibility for both DFC relations and industrial development was transferred to the Bank by Robert McNamara, who at the same time rejected the Pearson Commission's recommendation that eventually the IFC should be given the lead in seeking to improve business environment.

Thus the IFC did not assume the policy role for private sector development originally envisaged, and the Bank did not, after the 1960s, seek to utilize the IFC's capability in this area. In particular fields, however, especially capital markets and foreign direct investment, the IFC made important contributions to the improvement of business conditions. To this, privatization and private participation in infrastructure were later added. With the Bank assuming private sector development as a major mandate in the early 1990s, the issue of utilizing the IFC's experience and determining its role in the process gained renewed attention. Modest in character, the new policies called for cooperation and clarification in the relationship, with some shifts in responsibilities and changes in organization in both institutions, extending to the appointment of a Bank Group coordinator for private sector issues in 1995.

Twice during its forty years the IFC has fundamentally shifted course. During the first decade and a half of its existence, it proceeded along the lines laid out by its founders. It saw the fulfillment of its development objective first and foremost in the creation and expansion of profitable private enterprise. It believed that bringing foreign investors into developing countries was of primary importance, preferably, but not necessarily, in cooperation with domestic entrepreneurs. In its view, the appropriate role of government was to stimulate the development of the private sector without taking part in the process of production and trade. In its relations with the Bank, it sought to keep a distance, while at the same time taking on the responsibility for joint operations in DFC and industrial operations.

Spurred by outside influences, which were brought into the organization by a new leadership, all this changed in the late 1960s and early 1970s. Overall economic development became the primary objective, in place of the creation of profitable private enterprise. The calculation of economic rates of return was introduced as a corrective to financial returns. Promotion of foreign direct investment became dependent on domestic control. Partnership with governments became acceptable, even in enterprises owned in the majority by the state. With the Bank assuming the leading role in DFC and industrial operations, the IFC, while substantially expanding its activities, became a marginal partner in the Bank's pursuit of industrial development in which no clear distinction was drawn between the public and the private domain.

In the mid-1980s the IFC reversed course, principally in response to an overall trend in world affairs, but also in reaction to the Corporation's own experience. The creation and expansion of profitable private enterprise came again to be regarded as a primary development objective. The promotion of foreign direct investment became once more a high priority, without necessarily being linked to domestic partnership. Investment in enterprises partly owned by governments came to be avoided, although not totally excluded. Support for the development of capital markets and for privatization and private participation in infrastructure were placed prominently on the agenda. At the same time, measures were taken to improve the Corporation's portfolio, weakened during the economic disturbances of the early 1980s, to enhance the level of provisions against doubtful investments and to increase the rate of return on capital.

Buoyed by the resurgence of private enterprise in developing countries, and with new sectors and regions opening up for its activities, the demand for the IFC's investments and services was stronger in the early 1990s than ever before. The divergent attitudes toward foreign direct investment and public ownership of enterprises, which had divided its membership and confused its policies, were no longer at issue. The view that the creation of profitable private enterprise was the Corporation's principal development objective was on the whole unchallenged. With a strong financial position and its own market borrowing firmly established, a basis for robust growth of operations was secured for years ahead. In a way, the IFC had for the first time come into its own.

Even so, some of the early ambiguities remained. These were mainly questions about the essentiality of its support, the extent of its promotional activities, and its relations with the Bank. With the opening up of financial markets and the sharply increased flow of private capital to developing countries, it became more problematic than before to discern where the IFC's investments and services were needed in order to make projects more viable than they otherwise would have been. With strict aims for financial returns, the scope for promotional activities became more limited, yet the need for such services in less advanced countries was still great. With the promotion of private sector policies moving high up on the Bank's agenda, with the IFC expanding into fields that had been more or less a Bank preserve, and with MIGA assuming a significant role as private investment guarantor, the need for both cooperation and clarity of demarcation within the Bank Group became even greater than before. At the same time, in view of the growth in the IFC's size, financial strength, and self-confidence and the attention being devoted to its special field, the relationship was bound to achieve a greater degree of parity than in earlier times.

THE BANK IN THE
WORLD BANK

CHAPTERS 14–16

THE NEXT four chapters turn from the Bank's operational activities, the principal subject matter of this history, to the financing of its varied and large developmental effort. The discussion is divided into two parts. Chapters 14 to 16 provide a chronological account of the finances of the International Bank for Reconstruction and Development: how it has funded its activities, managed risk, and structured its loans and what role it has played in global financial flows. Chapter 17 focuses on the International Development Association. The following comments are an introduction to the first of these parts.

Of the many official and multinational agencies that were spawned in the creative, hopeful, internationalist atmosphere of the postwar years, none, with the exception of the International Monetary Fund, achieved the financial and operational expansion, growth of influence, or degree of autonomy enjoyed by the Bank during the subsequent half century. This exceptional performance was due mainly to the unique arrangements made for financing the Bank.

Under these arrangements, the Bank's level of activity was to depend largely on its ability to borrow rather than on budgetary transfers from governments. Admittedly, the Bank's lending did carry *some* fiscal cost to its member governments: a small fraction of its lending was financed out of paid-in capital subscriptions; in addition, members took on a contingent liability by guaranteeing all Bank lending. However, contingent liabilities turned out to be comparatively painless, as far as budgetary decisions were concerned, because the perceived risk became increasingly negligible. As chapters 14 to 16 explain, governments did at times leash in the Bank by withholding or delaying their agreement to take on larger contingent liabilities—through the subscription of additional unpaid, "callable" capital—but these checks did not significantly affect the rapid and almost continuous growth of the institution over several decades.

More was involved in the Bank's rapid financial growth than fiscal independence. Though the fiscal cost was minimal, the full guarantee on loans by members became a powerful argument for the Bank's ability to borrow at the lowest market rates available. Moreover, its governmental clientele proved quite safe, in part because of the "cooperative" element involved in Bank membership, which strengthened its image. Also, the ability to borrow cheaply together with a near absence of competition as a long-term lender (of untied funds), made it easy for the Bank to generate annual surpluses. Since dividends were not distributed, these surpluses, even after deductions for substantial levels of development activity, allowed the institution to continually increase its equity and future surpluses.

Of these various elements of the IBRD's financial success, some were given to the institution in its Charter, and some were the result of later decisions and management abilities. Easily the most significant of the post–Bretton Woods decisions was the one that permitted the Bank to become a direct lender rather than, as the Charter had envisaged, a guarantor for private investments.

The direct lender role was backed by the U.S. government's guarantee, which was crucial to establishing and anchoring the Bank's market standing in its first two decades. Gradually, this standing was bolstered by the guarantees of other shareholders of the Organization for Economic Cooperation and Development. A growing confidence in the Bank's financial health and management, quite apart from shareholder guarantees, strengthened the Bank's market reputation, despite the significant shift in Bank lending from OECD members to other countries. An important factor in this accomplishment is the Bank's access to a parallel pool of resources, namely that of IDA.

Paid-in capital played a small—and diminishing—role in Bank lending. Established with an initial capital of $10 billion, of which 20 percent was paid in (nine-tenths in local currency) and the rest callable, the IBRD experienced three general capital increases, in 1959, 1979, and 1989, with a steady decline in the paid-in portion to 10, 7.5, and 3 percent, respectively. The long hiatus between the 1959 and 1979 capital increases resulted in a steady erosion in the real value of its capital during the 1970s. Although subscribed capital subsequently recovered, paid-in capital is today even less in real terms than it was four decades ago. Nonetheless, through its leveraging the IBRD has been able to commit almost a quarter of a trillion dollars in long-term development finance in its first half century with total paid-in capital contributions of less than $11 billion. The Bank achieved this remarkable leveraging by applying the sovereign credit of its rich shareholders —in the form of their capital guarantees of about $90 billion—to market borrowings, $110 billion of which remained outstanding as of 1995.

With modest paid-in capital to start, and severely limited additions over time, the Bank from early on relied on borrowing as its principal source of loanable resources. By the late 1970s, retained earnings formed a larger fraction of loanable resources than paid-in capital, and today they are almost double paid-in capital. With the institution's financial maturation, its cash flows changed significantly. Lending grew most rapidly in the 1970s, but then changed little in subsequent years. Correspondingly, loan repayments became an increasingly important source of funds and by the mid-1990s were on par with borrowings in this regard.

The Bank's borrowings—how they came about, where and how it borrowed and at what cost—are a central topic of chapters 14 to 16. Borrowings grew rapidly in the Bank's first decade, and then again at the end of the 1950s, but they leveled off in the following years. Borrowing and lending soared during the 1970s, under Robert McNamara. The pace continued through the next decade but slackened considerably thereafter. The decline in net borrowings was much sharper, with new borrowings serving principally to roll over existing borrowings. In tandem with the upheavals in financial markets, major changes occurred in the structure of Bank borrowings: in currencies, instruments, and sources. Diversification—not only among currencies, instruments, and markets but also between markets and government borrowings—was both an indispensable tool and a goal in its own right. Borrowing innovations helped the institution become a premier global borrower.

Despite its considerable visibility, however, the Bank has remained primarily a "niche player" in intermediating international capital flows. It enjoyed a virtual monopoly on multilateral lending in the 1950s, but once the regional development banks got into gear, the Bank could no longer dominate the scene. Despite the large growth in its lending and borrowings during the 1970s, the institution barely kept pace with the overall growth of financial intermediation that occurred in that hectic decade. And even when the Bank's role increased with the onset of the debt crisis, as private capital fled the developing countries, the renewed burst of private lending reduced the Bank's financial role to a minor one by the end of the decade. In 1994, for the first time since the Bank was established, even net flows (gross disbursements less amortization) turned negative.

Another issue addressed in these chapters concerns the implications arising from the need to maintain favorable market perceptions of the institution's governance. The Bank's success in this respect helped shield it—and in due course other multilateral banks, which replicated the model—from the vagaries of political pressures to a much greater extent than other multilateral institutions and explains much about the power it acquired, its degree of political autonomy, and the largesse of its administrative budget.

The finance story of the IBRD begins in chapter 14 with the design of the Bank's financial structure at Bretton Woods, the laying of the foundations, particularly under Presidents John McCloy and Eugene Black, and the period of consolidation under George Woods. Chapter 15 focuses on the rapid expansion of the Bank under McNamara at a time of great volatility and change in financial markets. This achievement was all the more exceptional in that it occurred despite little change in the Bank's capital. Chapter 16 follows the Bank through the turbulent 1980s and the early 1990s, to see how it managed its exposure to a range of financial risks, from funding risks to loan portfolio risks arising from the debt crisis.

FOURTEEN

The Evolution of the World Bank as a Financial Institution

THIS CHAPTER turns to the World Bank's first three decades, to see how it developed as a financial instituion. The financial blueprints of the Bank, conceived at Bretton Woods and codified in the Bank's Articles, anchored the initial design of its financial structure and policies and their subsequent evolution. At the same time, the Bank's first three presidents, in particular John McCloy and Eugene Black, laid its financial foundations by winning over a skeptical U.S. financial community, convinced that the institution would either wilt under the first blast of another depression or fall prey to the machinations of Washington politicians. But the Bank confounded its most severe early skeptics by gaining the imprimatur of an "AAA" rating. The early period from the late 1940s to the end of the 1950s was also the heyday of the "dollar bank," when the U.S. government's capital contributions and U.S. financial markets were singularly dominant in the financial resources of the Bank, although by the end of the period, the internalization of the Bank's resources had become discernible. Then came the 1960s, a decade that began with considerable promise but that soon found the Bank facing its most serious challenges to date arising from exogenous changes in markets and clientele.

Drawing the Blueprints

In the interwar years international finance exhibited two sharply divergent trends. The first half of this period (the 1920s) was characterized by a liberal trend sparked by the resurrection of the gold standard and the dominance of international finance by private capital and bankers from the "City" in London and New York. International lending, or development related financing as it was later termed, was largely bond based. The international monetary order, in turn, was governed by the troika of the Bank of England, the Federal Reserve Bank of New York, and the Morgans.

By the end of the decade, the international system had been severely shaken by complex financial and real factors, including the U.S. stock market crash of 1929.[1] The subsequent global economic crisis led to large-scale international bond defaults, and these in turn severely undermined confidence in earlier convictions concerning the inherent virtues of a liberal financial order and the prevailing institutional arrangements. The international lending boom and subsequent bust would leave deep scars that would heal gradually, only for the cycle to be repeated. The U.S. Senate Committee on Banking and Currency had found "the record of the activities of investment bankers in the flotation of foreign securities . . . one of the most scandalous chapters in the history of American investment banking. The sale of these foreign issues was characterized by practices and abuses which were violative of the most elementary principles of business ethics."[2]

However, the opprobrium heaped on U.S. bankers in the 1930s was also linked to the sordid saga of their domestic lending, with the result that the domestic experience of U.S. banks "was seared almost as deeply into their [bankers'] ultra-conservative subconscious."[3] The ensuing distrust of private financiers led governments to deepen domestic and international controls, which, while always present in some form and fashion, now became immensely more stringent and comprehensive. Financial controls came to be seen as an essential and legitimate instrument of national economic strategies. The advent of another global conflict and the need for participating states to mobilize capital, strongly reinforced the conviction that it was necessary for governments to control finance.[4]

Meanwhile, the economic convulsions of the early 1930s also sharply altered the American political landscape. In his election campaign, Franklin Roosevelt had severely attacked the New York financial community (particularly the House of Morgan) for causing the nation's economic woes. Roosevelt, in turn, was seen as having betrayed his own class, and his subsequent launching of the New Deal added to the bitterness.[5] The emergence of the U.S. Treasury, under Secretary

1. A classic rendition of the story may be found in Charles P. Kindleberger, *The World in Depression, 1929–1939* (University of California Press, 1986), especially chapter 14, "An Explanation of the 1929 Depression."

2. John T. Madden, Marcus Nadler, and Harry C. Sauvain, *America's Experience as a Creditor Nation* (Prentice-Hall, 1937), p. 205.

3. James Grant, *Money of the Mind: Borrowing and Lending in America from the Civil War to Michael Milken* (Farrar Straus Giroux, 1992), p. 249.

4. For a superior historical analysis, see Eric Helleiner, *States and the Reemergence of Global Finance: from Bretton Woods to the 1990s* (Cornell University Press, 1994).

5. When Hitler's finance minister Hjalmar Schacht went to Washington in 1933 to warn Roosevelt that Germany might be unable to service $2 billion in debt held by American investors, Roosevelt reportedly exclaimed, "Serves the Wall Street bankers right!" His advisers then convinced him of the potential damage of his jest, and Schacht was informed the next day of

Henry Morgenthau, Jr., as a center of New Deal radicalism, would ensure a persistent antagonism between the Democratic New Dealers at the U.S. Treasury and the Republican Wall Street financial community, which would continue even into the Truman era.[6] In due course, the Treasury would use the opportunity presented by the need for postwar planning to expand its struggle with domestic bankers from the national to the international sphere. Together with their British counterparts at Bretton Woods, the Treasury mandarins would seek to "make finance the servant, not the master, of human desires—in the international no less than in the domestic sphere."[7]

Harry White's initial proposals (of March 1942) for a "Bank for Reconstruction and Development of the United and Associated Nations," set out the proposed institution's "prime task and justification" to "supply capital at rates of interest low enough with a period of repayment long enough to give the borrowing country reasonable hope of being able to repay the loan."[8] White's initial designs for the proposed institution were highly ambitious in scope. It would, in some measure, serve as a world central bank performing for member governments the same services that a central bank performs for commercial banks under its national jurisdiction (and that later would be performed to a degree by the Bank for International Settlements). Its loans would be made in part in the currency of the borrowing country, and in part in its own (non-interest-bearing) notes, which it would issue and which would be backed by gold. Its investments would have an anticyclical character. In addition to long-term loans, it would supply short-term capital to facilitate international trade as well as participate in commodity price stabilization. It could act as agent or correspondent for member governments and their central banks, and act as trustee, registrar, or agent in connection with any loans it was associated with. It could also make loans or participate in loans to other multilateral agencies, provided that a majority of the members of these agencies were also members of the Bank. The institutional design also incorporated elements of venture capital. The Bank would encourage private capital by sharing risks through participation in equity investments (up to 10 percent of its paid-in capital) and supplement it by capital from its own account.[9]

Between White's first drafts and the first published version of the plans of the World Bank in November 1943, the scope of the institution narrowed considerably.

Roosevelt's deep concerns. Ron Chernow, *The House of Morgan: An American Banking Dynasty and the Rise of Modern Finance* (New York: Atlantic Monthly Press, 1990), p. 395.

6. In the 1948 presidential campaign, Truman described his opposition (the Republican Party) "as blood suckers with offices in Wall Street." As quoted by Kevin Phillips, "The Unnerving Precedents," *Washington Post*, January 8, 1995, p. C2.

7. Richard N. Gardner, *Sterling-Dollar Diplomacy in Current Perspective: The Origins of Our International Economic Order* (Columbia University Press, 1980), p. 76.

8. Ibid., p. 85. For a full discussion of the early drafts, see Robert Oliver, "Early Plans for a World Bank," Princeton Studies in International Finance 29, September 1971; and Henry Bitterman, "Negotiating History of the Bank" (World Bank, 1967), processed.

9. The proposal was carried forward in all subsequent drafts before being finally expunged at Bretton Woods at the insistence of the United States. Oliver, "Early Plans for a World Bank," p. 46.

The earlier plan for a single institution with wide-ranging functions was dropped. The central banking features were incorporated into the design of the International Monetary Fund, which emerged as the principal focus of the ensuing deliberations. Only some of the investment-lending ideas present in the original White proposal were retained for the World Bank.

These changes occurred for several reasons. To begin with, there was the increasing influence of more conservative leaders recruited from finance and industry into the Roosevelt administration during the war; the forthright opposition of Winthrop Aldrich, the chairman of Chase who, unlike most of his Wall Street colleagues, had been a supporter of the New Deal, was another important reason. White, who fancied himself a keen observer of the political landscape, may also have been anticipating legislative difficulties following the success of the Republican Party in the fall 1942 elections. Those functions of the Bank that seemed to usurp the functions of existing (principally private) institutions were quietly dropped. The United Kingdom was virtually absent from the discussions on the Bank until the publication of the November 1943 draft; from the beginning the United Kingdom did not expect to borrow from the Bank. At the same time, acutely aware of its perilous financial situation, the United Kingdom was principally concerned with minimizing its financial liability to the institution. For all these reasons, "when, on the eve of Bretton Woods, the negotiators finally focused on the Bank, they were in a conservative mood."[10]

The amount of the Bank's initial capital—$10 billion—was the working figure from White's first draft, who had arrived at this figure backwards, so to speak. Notwithstanding Keynes's declaration that there was "no foundation whatever for the idea that the object of the proposals [was] to make the United States the milch cow of the world," White was fully aware that an important segment of U.S. opinion would view the proposals in precisely this light.[11] After estimating that the U.S. share of the Bank's capital would be about one-fourth (based on relative national incomes and international trade), he reckoned that the U.S. Congress could, at most, be induced to contribute $2.5 billion; hence the Bank's capitalization of $10 billion.[12] However, the initial drafts called for one-half of this to be paid in, with nontransferable shares of limited liability, and the remaining callable at the Bank's discretion.[13] At the Atlantic City conference, the British proposed that only 20 percent of the capital be paid in, of which not more than 20 percent would be in gold. Furthermore, while the American proposal had contemplated additional periodic calls on the subscribed capital to cover direct Bank loans, with the remainder to back securities or guarantees, the United Kingdom viewed the paid-in portion as a

10. Gardner, *Sterling-Dollar Diplomacy*, p. xxii.

11. Quoted in Oliver, "Early Plans for a World Bank," p. 11.

12. Robert W. Oliver, *International Economic Co-operation and the World Bank* (London: Macmillan, 1975), p. 112, n. 28.

13. Gardner, *Sterling-Dollar Diplomacy*, p. 74.

one-time contribution.[14] The paid-in portion was eventually set at 20 percent, of which 2 percent was to be paid in gold or U.S. dollars and the remaining 18 percent in local currency.

It may have seemed somewhat anomalous for the British to insist on a capital structure that relied largely on callable capital rather than paid in-capital, especially given Keynes's admonishment of financial institutions with precisely such a structure. Several decades earlier Keynes had served as member of a Royal Commission on "Indian Currency and Finance." In that capacity, while commenting on Indian banks, he observed: "These banks have discovered that there is, or may be, a useful ambiguity in the public mind between nominal capital and paid-up capital, and that nothing is cheaper than to increase the former."[15]

Keynes had gone on to castigate such "comic opera" banks whose "Gilbertian characteristics [were] calculated to bring the name and profession of banking into disrepute."[16] Yet in 1944, financial prudence had to give way to political and fiscal realities. In part the outcome reflected a delicate balance between the United Kingdom's competing interests in wanting to preserve a large share in the Bank's capital while keenly aware that its dire financial situation precluded large financial commitments. But the mechanism was also an ingenious solution to share risks jointly and severally among member nations corresponding to their capacity to bear risk, while recognizing that the bulk of actual resources would come from one market. Even so, the insistence by the British and European governments-in-exile at the Atlantic City conference that the Bank adopt conservative financial policies may be construed as indicative of their desire to compensate for a financial structure resembling "comic opera" banks.

One example of financial conservativeness was the insistence by the British and the European governments-in-exile at Atlantic City that the Bank's lending power be limited to its subscribed capital.[17] Although the desire to boost the overall level of activity of the new institution pushed for higher lending ceilings, considerations of limiting potential liabilities on the unpaid portion of capital, as well as concerns about adverse market reactions of what would amount to partial guarantees by the members if the IBRD's market liabilities exceeded 100 percent of capital and reserves, made for a counterbalancing caution. The U.S. draft at Bretton Woods, drawing on the practice of other financial institutions, had suggested that the amount of loans and investments of the Bank be limited to 200–300 percent of the its capital and surplus. Keynes had argued that a liability exceeding 100 percent

14. Bitterman, "Negotiating History of the Bank," p. 39.

15. Quoted in Walter Eltis, "Keynes on Third World Bank Failures," *Central Banking*, vol. 4, no. 1 (Summer 1993), pp. 40–42.

16. Ibid., p. 41.

17. Edward M. Bernstein, quoted in Stanley W. Black, *A Levite among the Priests: Edward M. Bernstein and the Origins of the Bretton Woods System* (Boulder, Colo.: Westview Press, 1991), p. 42.

imposed a moral commitment on countries to make good on their commitments. The issue excited unusually strong opinions, particularly from the Dutch, who insisted that it be limited to 75 percent of unpaid subscriptions (that is, 60 percent of total capital). The United States lowered its position to 150 percent. A compromise was reached in the drafting committee when the chairman proposed splitting the difference—reducing the U.S. position by a third and adding a third to the Dutch proposal.[18] The compromise was aided by the general belief, reflecting the confident tenor of the time, that the lending constraint could simply be relaxed at a later date by increasing the authorized capital. This was the genesis of a much debated issue in the Bank in later years: the 1:1 gearing ratio.[19]

Once agreement was reached on the Bank's capital structure, it was evident that whereas membership in the Bank offered borrowing advantages, membership in the Fund seemingly imposed a code of conduct on exchange rate policy. Moreover, in the Fund there was a direct relationship between a country's drawing rights and its contribution to the institution's capital. There was no such correlation in the Bank. Indeed, a larger share in its capital imposed both greater current and contingent liabilities without any corresponding financial benefits. To ensure that countries would not free ride and join the Bank while remaining unwilling to shoulder the responsibility and the inconvenience entailed in joining the Fund, membership in the Bank was made contingent to membership in the Fund.[20] In addition, the capital share in the Bank was linked to Fund quotas to ensure that countries accepted contingent liabilities in the Bank comparable to benefits of large quotas in the Fund. In stark contrast to the positions adopted in future capital increases of the IBRD, when countries would fiercely bargain for the privilege of a larger capital share, at the time the proposal faced strong opposition from many developing countries, particularly those from Latin America, while most of the sterling-area countries accepted the equivalence. The impasse was eventually broken by U.S. willingness, along with that of Canada and China, to accept a larger subscription in the Bank.[21]

A further point of contention was whether the Bank would principally guarantee private flows or lend directly on its own account. It was evident at the time that, in

18. Aron Broches, interview, World Bank Oral History Program, July 11, 1961. Broches was part of the Dutch delegation at Bretton Woods and later served as the Bank's general counsel.

19. IBRD, *Articles of Agreement*, art. IV, sec. 1(a). The "gearing ratio" is the ratio of capital plus reserves to loans outstanding and disbursed.

20. Furthermore, it was argued that the success of the Bank depended on currency stability and maintenance of balance of payments equilibrium, which were necessary obligations under the Fund's Articles.

21. The initial U.S. subscription in the Bank's capital was $3,175 million, compared with $2,750 million in the Fund. The subscriptions of the larger Latin American countries were reduced to 70 percent of their Fund quota; those of the smaller Latin American countries were further reduced to 40 percent.

the immediate postwar period, the United States would be the principal, if not the sole, source of capital. Several European nations recognizing that they would be considered more creditworthy by a discerning market, favored the guarantee approach to direct loans and, in the case of direct loans, country-specific interest rates, corresponding to rates on guaranteed loans. Countries that had not defaulted on prewar loans (Norway, for example) felt particularly strongly that uniform interest rates on loans would discriminate against them. The view of the Bank as a financial cooperative with equitable lending rates, however, eventually prevailed.

The emphasis in the Bank's Articles that its principal role would be to guarantee private flows—thereby assuming that private capital flows would be forthcoming in considerable amounts—rather than lend on its own account, appears at first glance to be at odds to the proposition of limited international capital flows, underlying the construction of the Bretton Woods regime, as institutionalized in the IMF.[22] However, the deep skepticism shared by both British and American negotiators with regard to the prospects of international long-term capital flows reemerging in sufficient volume did not extend to short-term flows. Both parties held firm views that the twin goals of a liberal trading order and stable exchange rate regime required the reigning in of "destabilizing" short-term private capital movements.[23]

As is often the case, these early decisions on the financial structure of the Bank would have significant effects on the institution. The consequences for the Bank's lending policies are discussed in detail in chapters 2–4. In effect, the direct U.S. capital contributions to the institution were its only usable resources. In view of the modest size of these resources, the preponderance of the Bank's resources would have to be raised in financial markets, which at the time meant the U.S. market. It was therefore essential that the Bank's president be a U.S. national, to help bolster confidence in the institution on Wall Street and thereby establish its credit rating in the only market that mattered.[24] The financial structure entailed only an initial upfront outlay. Further direct calls on member government treasuries would be extremely small over the next three decades (table 14-1). In contrast, the IMF obtained its funds almost entirely from governments. This was one reason why in the first few decades after Bretton Woods, the central banks and finance ministries of the larger shareholders would be more keenly interested in the Fund's governance and management, while the Bank remained less visible on their radar

22. IBRD, *Articles of Agreement,* art. I (ii).

23. As Robert Solomon would later put it, "More broadly, it is evident that the architects of the IMF and World Bank did not expect private capital movements to be of substantial magnitude in the system they were creating." Robert Solomon, "Looking Back," *Central Banking,* vol. 5, no. 1 (Summer 1994), p. 40.

24. In turn, this led to the unspoken agreement that a European would head the IMF, a tradition that has continued to this date. At the time, the Fund was preoccupied with the problem of weak European currencies and the feeling was that a European would be more suitable to cure the monetary ills of Europe.

Table 14-1. *IBRD Leverage: Paid-In Capital Subscriptions and Loans Outstanding, 1949–95*[a]

Billions of U.S. dollars

Year	Total paid-in		U.S. paid-in		Loans outstanding	
	Nominal	Real[b]	Nominal	Real[b]	Nominal	Real[b]
1949	1.7	9.2	0.6	3.3	0.6	3.4
1959	1.9	11.3	0.6	3.8	2.3	14.0
1969	2.3	9.6	0.6	2.7	5.0	20.8
1979	3.7	6.5	0.8	1.5	17.4	30.7
1989	8.6	10.2	1.6	1.9	77.9	92.5
1995	10.9	10.9	2.0	2.0	123.5	123.5

Source: *World Bank Annual Report*, various years.

a. Paid-in capital figures for 1979 were calculated on an SDR basis and with a dollar-SDR rate of 1.20635. Loans outstanding exclude loans approved but not yet effective and undisbursed balance of effective loans.

b. 1995 U.S. dollars, based on IBRD commitment deflators.

screens.[25] Partly for this reason the Bank's management would enjoy greater autonomy than their Fund counterparts.

The deep antipathy between the U.S. Treasury and U.S. financial markets continued through Bretton Woods. Wall Street was not invited to Bretton Woods.[26] This was hardly surprising given Morgenthau's injunction that the Bretton Woods institutions should reflect the "instrumentalities of sovereign governments and not of private financial interests."[27] When Morgenthau resoundingly proclaimed at the concluding session of the Bretton Woods conference that the Bank's lending would "drive . . . the usurious money lenders from the temple of international finance," the object of his scorn was hardly in doubt.[28]

Yet, as noted above, despite Morgenthau's bravado, substantial modifications had already been made to the design of the Bank, largely a concession to Wall Street and a conservative Congress.[29] These changes, however, did not mollify Wall Street. Its reaction to the Bretton Woods proposals continued to be relentlessly

25. Needless to say, the very different roles of the two institutions in their first quarter-century was the major reason behind the asymmetrical attention.

26. The one banker who was part of the U.S. delegation, Edward Brown, came from the First National Bank of Chicago.

27. Morgenthau, quoted in Gardner, *Sterling-Dollar Diplomacy*, p. 76.

28. "Address of the Honorable Henry Morgenthau, President of the Conference, at the Closing Plenary Session," July 22, 1944. Reprinted in *Proceedings and Documents of the United Nations Monetary and Financial Conference, Bretton Woods, New Hampshire July 1–22, 1994*, vol. 2 (GPO, 1948), p. 1227.

29. Even the language used to draft the Articles at Bretton Woods kept Wall Street in mind. Edward Bernstein, White's deputy, recounts how during the initial negotiations between the United States and the United Kingdom in 1943, Keynes agreed to accept White's revised plan but wanted to rewrite it in "bancor." Bernstein questioned Keynes why, if he accepted the plan, he wanted to rewrite it. Keynes replied, "Because your plan is

hostile. With the Bretton Woods agreements requiring congressional ratification, Wall Street aggressively stepped up its opposition. A premier New York bank, the Guarantee Trust Company, called the plans "dangerous," claiming that they would "substitute fallible human judgment and discretion for the impersonal action of the markets."[30] The American Bankers Association wrote a series of pamphlets opposing the agreements. Although the Association's ire was directed principally at the Fund, this was a tactical maneuver to avoid being seen as obstructionist to both institutions.[31] The financial press was equally acerbic, labeling the whole Bretton Woods idea a boondoggle and giveaway program.[32] The agreements were also attacked in the U.S. Congress by politicians espousing traditionalist and isolationist views. Senator Taft, a Republican from Ohio who spearheaded the attacks, declared the proposals were going to be "pouring money down a rat hole," a phrase that would assume hallowed status in the conservative American lexicon on foreign aid.[33]

The tussle between the U.S. Treasury and Wall Street soon spilled over into several key decisions that would have major consequences for the Bank. Morgenthau's primary objective as secretary of the Treasury was "to move the financial center of the world from London and Wall Street to the United States Treasury."[34] Anxious to insulate the two institutions from the "politics of Congress," the British, joined by a number of other delegations, sought to situate the institutions in New York.[35] But Fred Vinson, Morgenthau's successor as secretary of the Treasury, adamantly argued that they should be located in Washington, because the two institutions were not "just two more financial institutions." This decision "in the eyes of the U.S. delegation symbolized a transfer of control of international finance from Wall Street to Washington."[36] The decision further confirmed the close national (and particularly American) governmental control of the institutions,

---

written in Cherokee," whereupon Bernstein rejoindered, "The reason it is in Cherokee is because we need the support of the braves of Wall Street and this is the language they understand." Bernstein, quoted in Black, A Levite among the Priests, p. 39.

30. Quoted in Gardner, Sterling-Dollar Diplomacy, p. 98. Sadly, over the next decade Guarantee Trust would itself fall victim to "fallible human judgement," having become "fat, sleepy, dowdy" (Chernow, The House of Morgan, p. 532), and in 1959 it merged with J. P. Morgan.

31. See Ansel Luxford, interview, World Bank Oral History Program, July 1961, p. 24. Luxford joined the Bank from the U.S. Treasury and later served as its assistant and associate general counsel.

32. William L. Bennett, "The World Bank and the Investment Market," draft typescript, March 6, 1969, p. 1.

33. Quoted in Gardner, Sterling-Dollar Diplomacy, p. 130. The IMF was the specific target of attack in this case.

34. Letter, Henry Morgenthau, Jr., to President Harry S Truman, quoted in Gardner, Sterling-Dollar Diplomacy, p. 76.

35. Ibid., p. 258.

36. Edward S. Mason and Robert E. Asher, The World Bank since Bretton Woods (Brookings, 1973), 38.

rather than the autonomy Keynes had sought for them. In the long run it ensured that the Bank would have to steer a perilous course between the Scylla of an inquisitive and ever-brooding Congress and the Charbydis of financial markets.

Following ratification, the Bank struggled to become a functioning institution.[37] By the first Annual Meeting in 1946, the Bank's usable resources were confined to the 2 percent capital subscribed in gold by all members and the 18 percent paid-in share of the United States. The U.S. contribution alone, $635 million, formed almost the entire loanable resources of the Bank. As table 14-1 indicates, in real terms (constant 1995 dollars), this initial U.S. contribution to the Bank's capital was substantially greater in 1949 than in 1995, nearly half a century later! While total paid-in capital increased more than 6-fold over this period, in real terms it increased by less than 20 percent. Since initially a large proportion of the non-U.S. capital contributions were not convertible, "usable capital" in real terms actually declined. Meanwhile the IBRD's outstanding loans increased 36-fold (175-fold in nominal terms). History has provided few examples of such an outstanding leveraging of resources and influence.

Yet, despite the institution's severely limited resources, expectations of Bank lending were much exaggerated. In a transmittal letter to Congress, Truman proclaimed: "It is expected that the International Bank will begin lending operations in the latter half of 1946 and that during the calendar year 1947 the International Bank will assume the primary responsibility for meeting the world's international capital requirements that cannot be met by private investors on their own account and risk."[38]

At this time, however, the Bank barely existed as an institution and its first president, Eugene Meyer, had just assumed office. Truman's first choice for president, Lewis Douglas, then president of the Mutual Life Insurance Company of New York, withdrew from consideration after Morgenthau (no longer Treasury secretary) assailed Douglas's connections "with big business and Wall Street, his tie-ins with international financiers, and his general point of view."[39] His replacement, Eugene Meyer, publisher of the *Washington Post,* was well respected in Wall Street from his earlier incarnation as head of a successful investment banking house.

During Meyer's tenure, the Bank worked with the U.S. Treasury in initiating legislation at the federal and state level (beginning with the all-important New York state) in seeking approval for investors to buy IBRD securities. Meyer made the rounds of the financial community, and although his personal relations with them were cordial, this "did not presage the slightest interest on the part of the financial community in buying Bank securities."[40] In any case, Meyer did not get the

37. The story of the early years is elaborated in ibid., chap. 2.
38. Gardner, *Sterling-Dollar Diplomacy,* p. 291. The exaggerated claims were no doubt motivated by the need to generate enthusiasm for the passage of the required bills.
39. Mason and Asher, *World Bank since Bretton Woods,* p. 41.
40. Ibid, p. 44.

Table 14-2. *The Financial Community Antecedents of World Bank Presidents*

President	Tenure	Before arrival
Meyer	June 1946–December 1946	Investment banker on Wall Street (Eugene Meyer and Company) before World War I
McCloy	March 1947–June 1949	Counsel to Chase National Bank (later Chase Manhattan)
Black	July 1949–December 1962	Senior vice president at Chase National Bank
Woods	January 1963–March 1968	President, First Boston
McNamara	April 1968–June 1981	None
Clausen	July 1981–June 1986	Chairman, chief executive officer, Bank of America
Conable	July 1986–August 1991	U.S. Congress, House Banking Committee
Preston	September 1991–May 1995	Chairman, J. P. Morgan & Co.

Sources: Edward S. Mason and Robert E. Asher, *The World Bank since Bretton Woods* (Brookings, 1973); Ron Chernow, *The House of Morgan: An American Banking Dynasty and the Rise of Modern Finance* (New York: Atlantic Monthly Press, 1990).

opportunity to test the markets. Frustrated with endemic battles with his Board, particularly with Emilio Collado (the U.S. executive director and the last major connection with the activist Treasury New Dealers in the Bank), Meyer resigned six months after his appointment.

After several false starts, John McCloy was persuaded to become the Bank's second president. With the arrival of the Wall Street trio of McCloy as president, Black as U.S. executive director, and Garner as vice president (and unofficial general manager) in March 1947, and the parallel departure of Collado, the last traces of the New Dealers in the Bank were expunged. Wall Street had triumphed. McCloy's appointment was seen as a Wall Street coup d'état and established a precedent whereby all future presidents of the World Bank, with two exceptions, would have strong credentials in the U.S. financial community (see table 14-2).

Laying the Financial Foundations: 1947–59

The new management regime was remarkably representative of the "self-selected aristocracy of lawyers, bankers, corporate chiefs, and government officials [the quintessential] representatives of the old American Establishment."[41]

41. Kai Bird, *The Chairman: John F. McCloy—The Making of the American Establishment* (Simon and Schuster, 1992), p. 14. The various business and personal networks of the Bank's early leadership are detailed in Philip Burch, *Elites in American History*, vol. 3: *The New Deal to the Carter Administration* (Holmes and Meier, 1980), pp. 93–95, 118–19.

The New Management Team

Like its only other significant competitor, the "City" in London, at the time Wall Street was characterized by a web of interlocking business and social relationships. John McCloy joined the Rockefeller family's law firm of Milbank, Tweed, Hadley and McCloy in Wall Street in early 1946.[42] He had been recommended to Harry Truman by the chairman of Chase National Bank, Winthrop Aldrich. Chase, a Rockefeller bank, was Milbank, Tweed's most important client. McCloy had served on the International Advisory Committee of Chase, along with Eugene Black, then a senior vice president of the Chase Bank. In his case too, Aldrich had suggested that he go down to Washington to become U.S. executive director. Robert Garner was previously treasurer of the Guaranty Trust Company (later Morgan Guaranty) and at the time was financial vice president and director of General Foods Corporation. A fourth member of the team, E. Fleetwood Dunstan, senior vice president at Banker's Trust in charge of its bond issues, became the Bank's first marketing director. The new regime also found some kindred spirits in the fledgling institution. The Bank's legal counsel, Chester McLain, who had been running the Bank in the interim, had been a partner of McCloy's at the law firm of Cravath, Swaine and Moore. Two recently recruited senior staff—Treasurer Daniel Crena de Iongh, and Leonard Rist, the head of the Economic Department—were distinguished European bankers.[43]

The new regime would serve as midwife to an institution that was almost stillborn. It rapidly set about establishing the institution on "sound" lines. Foremost of its tasks was establishing the Bank's credit in Wall Street and instituting the financial terms and structure of its loans.

Early Attempts at Raising Resources

From the outset, the Bank's lending capacity was severely circumscribed by its limited paid-in capital.[44] By the end of its first year, the Bank had $727 million available from its capital subscriptions, the overwhelming fraction of which was the U.S. contribution of $635 million.[45] The growing clamor for funds from its members had made it abundantly clear that the institution had to rapidly seek recourse to market borrowings. Shortly after its arrival, the Bank's new management team concluded that its most important task was to swiftly establish a market for the institution's obligations in the United States.

42. Ironically, McCloy was also the brother-in-law of Lewis Douglas, whose candidature for the Bank's presidency Morgenthau had done much to torpedo.

43. Both Crena de Iongh and Rist had served briefly as alternative executive directors in the Bank and Fund for Holland and France, respectively. Rist had earlier worked for Morgan et Compagnie in Paris.

44. This section is based in part on Henry J. Bitterman, "Early Bank Bond Issues," draft typescript, November 29, 1966.

45. This was about one-twentieth of the $13 billion outlay of the Marshall Plan.

The psychology of international lending has long been strongly cyclical, alternating between periods of overbrimming euphoria and unreserved suspicion of foreign lending. Whereas a century ago Dickens had penned Ebenezer Scrooge's nightmare of his secure British investments being transformed into default-prone U.S. securities, the shoe was now on the other foot, with U.S. investors having prospective nightmares. Following the bond defaults of the 1930s, confidence was once again in the trough phase; the mere word "international" rankled deep on Wall Street. At the end of 1945, nearly 46 percent ($2 billion) of dollar-denominated outstanding bonds were in default with sovereign bond issues accounting for more than two-thirds of the defaults.[46] But despite widespread defaults, actual yields had "more than compensated British investors and nearly compensated U.S. investors for interruptions to debt service and write-downs of principal."[47] Market psychology is essentially a matter of perception, however; and, to put it mildly, perceptions were not favorable for international lending.

Another major problem confronting the Bank was that its securities were not eligible for investment by various financial intermediaries in the all-important U.S. market. The institution being sui generis, its bonds were neither fish nor fowl. The U.S. securities market was then governed by a welter of legislation. Separate statutes applied to various classes of institutional investors, at both the federal and the state level. The Bank's bonds could not be traded in the government segment of the market since the IBRD was not a government nor an agency of the United States. But neither could its bonds be traded on corporate desks, as it was not a utility or a business corporation.

The U.S. government was quite conscious of the Bank's dilemma. Upon ratification of the Bank's Articles (and even before the inaugural meeting at Savannah in March 1946), the National Advisory Council (NAC) and the Securities and Exchange Commission (SEC) began a series of exploratory meetings with representatives of commercial and investment bankers and insurance companies. The U.S. executive director, Emilio Collado, took the lead in the legislative campaign

---

46. As of the end of 1945, 87 percent of European bonds outstanding, 60 percent of Latin American bonds, and 56 percent of Far Eastern bonds were in default. Among the sixteen Latin American countries, only one (Guatemala) was not in default. Of the twenty European borrowers, only three (France, Finland, and Ireland) were in full service, and in the Far East and Africa, only Australia and Liberia were in good standing. James R. Greene, "Government Borrowing in the International Financial Markets," in William H. Baughn and Donald R. Mandich, *The International Banking Handbook* (Homewood, Ill.: Dow Jones-Irwin, 1983), p. 151.

47. Barry Eichengreen, "Historical Research on International Lending and Debt," *Journal of Economic Perspectives*, vol. 5 (Spring 1991), p. 154. According to Eichengreen, the realized returns of interwar loans (based on an analysis of more than 200 dollar bonds and 125 sterling bonds) was 5 percent on sterling issues compared with yields of just above 4 percent on consoles and 4 percent on overseas dollar issues, only "slightly below Treasury bond yields."

and, in March 1946, achieved the first notable success with the passage of legislation in New York authorizing investment by savings banks in that state. Bankers
themselves became interested and in February 1946 the Investment Bankers
Association of America established a "foreign investment committee" to examine
the unique issues posed by IBRD bonds.[48]

Within a month the Bank established a Marketing Department in New York City at
the Federal Reserve Bank of New York. The campaign to launch the Bank's first bond
issue was waged on several fronts. An opinion from the U.S. attorney general was
furnished to convince skeptical investors that the United States was liable for its share of
the callable capital regardless of the actions of other governments and that such an action
did not require any further legislative appropriations. IBRD bonds were, therefore, as
good as the obligations of the Treasury itself, although legally they were not obligations of
any government. The U.S. comptroller of currency was also persuaded to make an
exception, in the case of the IBRD, to its policy of not issuing an "eligible" list of securities.

The nature of SEC registration requirements posed a more difficult problem. In
accordance with SEC regulations, the exempt securities market (largely Treasury,
state and local bonds) was distinct from the corporate securities market. The Bank
wanted to cast its net wide and sell its bonds through both classes of dealers, but
could only do so if its securities were either added to the exempt list—which
required congressional action—or if the SEC granted it specific exemptions. The
former was ruled out both because of time constraints and because, in seeking
ratification of the Bretton Woods Agreements Act, the Treasury had assured Congress that the Bank's securities would be subject to the normal safeguards of U.S.
securities legislation. Consequently, the Bank sought—and obtained—selective
exemptions from the SEC. Notwithstanding the exemptions, the SEC viewed the
selling procedure of the first bond issue as contrary to the provisions of the
Securities Act.[49] The Bank disagreed. Fortunately, the SEC did not pass a formal
ruling and the NAC worked with the Bank in helping to pass enabling legislation in
Congress in 1949 making Bank bonds "exempt security," and thereby allowing
commercial banks to buy the Bank's bonds for investment.[50]

The legislative battle was much more protracted at the state level. Each state
had its own laws governing the scope of investments of state-chartered institutions.
State by state the Bank sought the support of state banking and insurance commis-

48. Among the members of the group were Eugene Black, E. F. Dunstan, Harold Stanley
(of Morgan Stanley), and representatives of First Boston.

49. Specifically, the SEC felt that communications between the Bank and the securities
dealers before registration constituted an offering of the bonds, which was a violation of the
Securities Act. The precise nature of the problem is examined in Louis Loss, *Securities
Regulation* (Boston: Little, Brown, 1951), pp. 351–55.

50. "Exempt securities" included the direct obligations of the IBRD, securities
fully guaranteed by it, or the guarantees by the Bank (but not the underlying
obligation, to cover the case of partial guarantees). At that time commercial banks
could only deal in government or municipal bonds; they were prohibited from
dealing in all other bonds.

sioners for requisite administrative and legislative changes to make its bonds legal investments for insurance companies, savings banks, and pension funds. Then, as now, legislatures attempted to attach conditionalities. "In one state, a puzzled Irish politician listened to Black in private for 45 minutes and finally said, 'Mr. Black, I haven't the faintest idea what you're talking about. But you look like an honest man; and I'll help put through a bill to make your bonds legal for investment in this State on one condition—that you never lend a (blankety-blank) nickel to Britain.'"[51] It would take more than a decade before most U.S. states would pass the appropriate legislation.

A parallel campaign vigorously targeted the investment community. In Eugene Black, the Bank had availed itself of a bond salesman with a redoubtable reputation.[52] There were numerous speeches and meetings with bankers, lawyers, insurance company executives, regulatory agencies, and the like, before the Bank's first issue, for $250 million, was launched, four months after McCloy's arrival.[53] The bond issue was described as a "nine-day wonder" with more than 1,700 firms subscribing. The issue was oversubscribed—aided considerably by a higher interest rate and generous commissions—but went so quickly to a premium that many dealers sold out rapidly. For this reason, as well as a weakening in the bond market, the bonds soon dropped sharply to well below par.

The first bond issue held two principal lessons for the Bank. First, it was clear from the discussions with the principal players in the U.S. market that the dollar capacity of the borrowing market was limited to the U.S. portion of the callable capital. And second, the Bank realized that establishing its bonds would take a much more protracted effort. Echoing the song by George Cohan, "You won't do any business if you haven't got a band; the folks expect a street parade and uniforms so grand," the Bank's senior management incessantly hit the financial trail, twirling their batons and striking up a lively forward march. Concurrently, it became customary for the Bank to invite members of the investment community to spend a few days in Washington. A Public Relations Department (later Information Department) was quickly geared up to serve Black's firm belief that the Bank needed a publications effort specifically directed at the financial community for the sale of its bonds. Thereafter the Bank's Treasury Department would serve as perhaps its most effective marketing and public relations campaigner.[54]

51. Quoted in "Profile of a President," *Bank Notes,* vol. 13, nos. 7–8 (July–August 1959), p. 4.

52. Black's skills as a bond salesman had been honed in the 1920s, when, as a volunteer in the big Victory Loan Drive after World War I, he loaded a big truck with surplus guns and helmets, some wounded veterans, and stumped all over Georgia. The state of Georgia surpassed its bond quota. In 1933 he had joined the Chase National Bank in New York as a vice president, eventually becoming a senior vice president in charge of its multibillion dollar investment portfolio.

53. Of this amount, $150 million was in 3 percent, twenty-five-year bonds, and $100 million in 2.25 percent, ten-year bonds. In real dollars, this was one of the largest bond issues by the Bank until the launching of the global bond in 1989.

54. The relative success of the campaign can be gauged by Black's appearance on the cover of *Time* and *Newsweek.* Even conservative financial publications such as *Fortune* ran

In tandem with the institution's efforts to establish a market for its bonds, the Bank put into place certain policies in order to enhance its credibility in the bond markets. An important component was its insistence that prospective borrowers settle their prewar bond defaults. To be sure, this insistence was partly ideological; the Bank qua bank shared the religious sanctions of the banking order against defaults. However, there was an important practical rationale. The Bank felt that it was important not only to help the borrowing countries reestablish their credit but also essential to establish the struggling institution's credit rating on Wall Street. This was underscored when, contemplating the first loan application from Chile, Black received a phone call from "one of the important banks in New York which said that [the Bank was] about to make a loan to Chile, and if we did make it they presumed that we would write the loan off to 10 cents on the dollar (the then market price of Chilean bonds)."[55] The Bank's management felt that it could hardly expect to successfully sell its bonds to a community whose investors held unpaid liabilities of the same country to which it was making a loan, without ensuring that the prospective borrower was at a minimum making efforts to settle its debts. The borrowers, on the other hand, were not kindly disposed to what they perceived as the Bank's role as Wall Street bill collectors. While in Chile's case the Bank approved two loans the day after Chile reached a settlement with its foreign shareholders, the issue would bubble up periodically during the 1950s and 1960s, casting an unpleasant pall over the relationship between the Bank and several of its newer members. Although the issue faded away in the 1970s, it would erupt in a more systemic manner in the 1980s.

Other safeguards attached to its loan conditions were designed to cover the Bank against credit and transfer risks. Under the general rubric of country creditworthiness, a country's macroeconomic policies were closely examined (see chapter 3), even if assessing creditworthiness was (and remains) frequently an educated guess. Loan agreements initially contained a "consultation clause," requiring, among other things, prior notification of proposals to contract additional external debt, thus allowing the Bank to express its views on the proposed transaction. However, two countries, the United Kingdom (during negotiations for a loan to the Colonial Development Corporation) and France, were completely unprepared to give prior notice to the Bank before incurring external debt. Recognizing that the United Kingdom and France would not give in, and that it had little choice but to extend the same exception to other borrowers, in 1951 the Bank accepted its legal counsel's recommendation that the provision be eliminated from future loan agreements.[56]

---

gushing stories on the Bank. This was also partly the result of Black's personal preferences. He was essentially an external affairs president who left the day-to-day running of the Bank to his general manager, Bob Garner.

55. Eugene R. Black, interview, World Bank Oral History Program, August 6, 1961, p. 6.

56. Memorandum, Davidson Sommers to Eugene R. Black, May 22, 1951. Not surprisingly, the change was vigorously opposed by the Bank's treasurer.

Another legal safeguard that the Bank put into its loan agreements was the negative pledge clause, whereby the borrower would pledge not to give physical security to any other lender (then used extensively in connection with unsecured bond issues).[57] Although the principal stated purpose of the clause was to ensure a preferred creditor status for the Bank by reducing transfer risks, in reality the clause would principally serve to burnish the Bank's image in capital markets. In the event, the clause had an important serendipitous effect. The Bank used the negative pledge clause as a justification to get debt-related data arguing that it needed to monitor data on new borrowings in order to have security in equal measure with other lenders. This led the Bank to gather information on public and publicly guaranteed debt and was the genesis of the Bank's role as the primary source of data on developing-country debt, the only data for which it is the original source.

In trying to sell its bonds, the IBRD initially (between 1947 and 1952) experimented with several marketing operations. The first issue was sold by agency operations (under which the distributors get a commission but have no other obligations). Subsequently, the Bank experimented with competitive bidding which raised funds on more favorable terms. The aggressive pricing, however, had adverse effects in that the underwriter (Halsey Stuart & Co., a Chicago firm) was unable to unload the bonds. At that point, the Bank reverted to an agency system, simultaneously switching to smaller issues and using, in turn, principal firms. However, the second agency bond issue was "rather unsuccessful," and the bonds had to be sold at a discount.[58] In analyzing the failure, the Bank concluded that "there was a lack of knowledge of the Bank as well as a growing sentiment in the United States against foreign lending."[59] In addition, it was clear that despite the immense effort that had gone into marketing, the investor base for the Bank's bonds remained narrow. Beginning with a $50 million issue in May 1952, the Bank switched from agency to "negotiated underwriting."[60]

---

57. There were some exceptional instances when instead the Bank sought a lien for its loan. For instance, a shipping loan to the Netherlands in 1949 was secured by a lien on the ships. A more contentious case was an irrigation loan to Iraq in 1950 (loan no. 85). Not only was the Bank's own loan secured by an assignment of oil royalties, but at the Bank's insistence the local project costs were also thus secured. At the Board discussion it became clear that realistically the conditions were unenforceable. The Bank could hardly go off seizing ships carrying oil, in the event of a default. Shortly thereafter the Board approved a resolution stating: "As a general principle the Bank does not seek or accept liens on specific revenues or assets as security for loans to member governments." IBRD, "Bank's Policy on Security for Loans to Member Governments," Resolution 145, M-208, June 26, 1950.

58. IBRD, "Seventh Annual Meeting," R-628, August 18, 1952. It appeared that many banks and sellers in the selling group had subscribed to the issue ($100 million 3¼ percent thirty-year bonds of 1951 due 1981) hoping that prices would immediately rise rather than stimulate interest in the bonds among the investing community.

59. IBRD, minutes of the Financial Policy Committee, FPC/M/53, January 10, 1952.

60. Another option, private placements (for instance, with the large insurance companies), was not attempted until much later.

In choosing an optimal marketing arrangement, the Bank was faced with trading off the short-term price advantages of competitive bidding for long-term benefits of the relationships offered by marketing operations, wherein the underwriting syndicates would have incentives to establish and maintain markets in Bank bonds.[61] Finally, after consultations with principal dealers in 1952, the Bank settled on negotiated underwriting, with Morgan Stanley and First Boston as its two underwriters: the former because of its reputation as a wholesaling house and links with Europe (through Morgan Grenfell), and the latter because of its established retail system. By agreeing to be a comanager, Morgan Stanley made a rare exception to its then iron rule of always being sole manager on issues with its name standing alone at the top of the tombstones.[62] The Bank's move met with considerable heartburn. Although most underwriters who were initially upset later joined the syndicate, several stayed away.[63]

Even as the new underwriting arrangement gave the Bank greater confidence in its ability to raise funds, the government sector of the U.S. bond market declined following certain actions by the Federal Reserve. The renewed difficulties in selling its bonds compelled the Bank to modify its liquidity policy from a conservative full-cash coverage against commitments to an estimated one year's loan disbursements.[64] Shortly thereafter, it launched a short-term (two-year) bonds-and-notes program, aimed largely at the central banks of member governments. The IBRD's attempts to "pedestalize" its (dollar) bonds, by persuading governments to buy them as part of their reserves, was quite successful, and by the end of the decade this program had emerged as a fairly stable, albeit modest, source of Bank funds.

Over the rest of the 1950s (indeed, for most of its history) the Bank attempted to broaden its investor base. In the United States, state and local pension funds were particular targets. Its forays outside the United States also came fairly early. Already by 1952, "more than $125 million of its total outstanding obligations of $535 million were held outside the US."[65] The gradual broadening of borrowings

61. The 1 percent commission for the negotiated underwritings was twice that for agency-type operations, at a time when U.S. government yields were 2.5 percent. IBRD, minutes of the Financial Policy Committee, FPC/M/53, January 10, 1952.

62. Chernow, *The House of Morgan*, p. 517. In the parlance of financial markets, tombstones are advertisements that announce a credit that has been arranged or a bond issue made. Chernow remarks that the opportunity to be "banker to the world's bank, [was] a big enough honor to satisfy even the most swollen Morgan ego" (p. 518).

63. There were two notable holdouts: Halsey Stuart & Co., the Chicago firm that had won the mandate for the Bank's first issue by competitive bidding and lost a considerable sum in the process; and C. J. Devine, then the largest government bond house (it later merged with Merrill Lynch), which had done "a Horatius at the bridge and made a market in the [Bank's first bond] issue, and lost a packet in the process." Both were understandably unhappy that their previous efforts had gone unrecognized. Bennett, "The World Bank and the Investment Market," p. 7.

64. IBRD, "Liquidity Policy," FPC/15, October 20, 1952.

65. IBRD, *Seventh Annual Report, 1951–1952*, pp. 37–38.

continued and in September 1954 the Bank sold its first dollar bond issue ($50 million) entirely abroad. Major constraints to non-U.S. borrowings including capital controls still in effect, small size of the markets, and higher interest rates (about a 1 percent premium in an era of fixed exchange rates) did not discourage the Bank from seeking to borrow in these markets. Diversification limited saturating the U.S. market and thereby reduced the Bank's borrowing costs in the United States. A higher initial cost was a price to be paid to build up a market in its own paper. In some cases, borrowers faced with an acute dollar shortage were finding it difficult to repay Bank loans disbursed in dollars. Diversifying the currency of borrowing allowed the Bank to furnish its borrowers with a nondollar currency. Furthermore, a conscious decision was made to establish the impression that the Bank was international, more than just a dollar bank which got its money either through the U.S. government or the U.S. market.

The Bank's first nondollar issue was a private placement with the BIS in 1948 in the amount of 17 million Swiss francs. In 1951, Switzerland—which did not become a member until four decades later—gave IBRD bonds a favorable tax status. Through most of the 1950s Switzerland remained the most important nondollar market, even though individual issues were small and tightly controlled. The first public nondollar borrowing operation was a 5 million sterling offering in London in May 1950. However, stringent capital controls in the United Kingdom meant that this market was never of consequence for the Bank.[66] Other currencies of modest significance to the Bank's borrowings in this period were the Canadian dollar, the Dutch guilder, and the Belgian franc.[67]

By the end of the decade, an important new market was opening up in the Federal Republic of Germany. The Bank had already been engaged in short-term borrowings, principally dollars, from the Deutsche Bundesbank. The first public issue in Germany (DM200 million in fifteen-year, 5 percent bonds) in 1959 was also the largest nondollar issue by the Bank thus far. The issue was sold by a syndicate of more than seventy German banks, with the Deutsche Bank as the principal manager and the Dresdner Bank as comanager. Given the traditional *macht der banken* that has characterized German financial markets, the choice of banks was understandable.[68]

66. The syndicate was led by Baring Brothers & Co. According to Mason and Asher, *World Bank since Bretton Woods* (p. 139), the Bank's suggestion that the prospectus carry "a full description of the borrowing institution . . . was waved aside [by Baring], with the assurance that the name of Baring was all that was needed." The venerable name of Baring would unfortunately not be enough to save that institution itself in 1995.

67. More detailed data are available from Mason and Asher, *World Bank since Bretton Woods,* table F-2, pp. 858–59.

68. Hermann Abs, the then chairman of Deutsche Bank, later intersected with the World Bank in other ways as well. He was one of "the three wise men" the Bank sent to India and Pakistan in 1960 and was later instrumental in helping arrange the Indonesian debt settlement.

Another element in the Bank's strategy to mobilize nondollar resources was to persuade member governments to release for disbursements the 18 percent local currency portion of their capital subscription. Constant public exhortations by management and subtle pressure—in several cases the Bank informally linked its loans to the country releasing its 18 percent contribution—led many European shareholders to release their local currency subscriptions. The paid-in 18 percent capital subscription was also the principal source of the Bank's operating profits since it basically broke even on the margins between its lending and borrowing rates.

Although the financial implications of the 18 percent local currency portion of capital subscriptions were small for the Bank by the end of the 1950s, the issue had considerable nuisance value and raised interesting questions of equity for a multilateral institution. This was particularly the case after the United States unilaterally forced the Bank to adopt the 1972 SDR as the unit of account rather than the SDR itself (see chapter 15). A "maintenance of value" clause meant that many developing countries that released their 18 percent funds were forced to pay twice as their currencies depreciated. The Articles enjoined the Bank to seek a country's approval before using its 18 percent currencies for lending, which was interpreted to mean that for any other purpose the country's permission was not required. The Bank used these currencies often for administrative purposes in the country concerned, but only in the weaker (especially African) countries—which were not even IBRD borrowers to begin with—while deferring to the wishes of strong borrowers like China, which simply refused permission.

In addition to relying on equity capital and bonds the IBRD, from early on, tapped resources from loan sales—selling a portion of the borrower's obligations from its own portfolio. These loan sales served a dual purpose. In addition to raising more resources for the Bank, they helped in reestablishing the country's credit. The first guaranteed sales of Bank loans were those to the Netherlands shipping industry in 1948; the first nonguaranteed sale of a Bank loan was the Luxembourg loan of 1950. From time to time, the Bank coordinated its lending with private placements by institutional investors, which resulted in joint participations. The first loan with joint private placement by the borrower was a $50 million loan to South Africa, together with $30 million from eight U.S. commercial banks. Occasionally, the Bank linked its loans to public issues by the borrowing countries, often a prelude to the country graduating, as it were, to a more independent status. Thus the Bank made a $10 million loan to Belgium in 1957 in tandem with a $30 million Belgium bond issue in the United States. In the following two years this technique was used in operations in Austria, Denmark, the Federation of Rhodesia and Nyasaland, Italy, Japan, and the Union of South Africa, all countries with good market creditworthiness.

In contrast to its energetic role in ensuring participation and sales of its loans, the Bank quite early balked at getting more deeply involved with loan guarantees.[69] Essentially, the Bank felt the markets might view its bonds, with their implicit government guarantees through their liability on uncalled capital, with greater equanimity than individual government securities guaranteed by the Bank, even though these carried the same contingent liability of member governments. In financial markets the Bank's guarantees competed with its own borrowings. From the borrowers' point of view, guarantees would not only have been more expensive than direct Bank loans (because they entailed two credit risks) but also did not contribute to additional resource flows: the Bank interpreted its Articles to mean that the full value of the guarantees had to be provisioned against its lending capacity. Moreover, the Bank was jealously husbanding its own market ratings and felt that, despite its guarantee, the market would differentially price the paper of borrowers with different credit risk, leading to adverse affects on its own paper. Furthermore, as the OECD borrowers dropped away, market interest in guarantees also waned. Another important, albeit unstated, reason may explain the Bank's qualms on this issue. A greater use of guarantees would have surely circumscribed the Bank's role in the detailed supervision of projects that the Bank had set as its model and, perhaps, even its influence in project and sector-related policies.[70]

Through the decade the Bank gradually reduced its reliance on government monies (table 14-3). By 1954, usable paid-in capital had already dipped to less than 50 percent of its loanable funds, and by the end of the decade, borrowings emerged as the Bank's single largest source of funds. A similar transformation occurred in the geographical origin of funds. The U.S. share fell from almost 90 percent in 1949, to about 40 percent in 1959. However, the U.S. dollar continued to dominate the currency structure of funded debt, accounting for nearly 85 percent of funded debt by the end of the decade.

Loan Policies and Procedures

Concurrent with its attempts to raise resources, the Bank was striving to lay the groundwork for its lending procedures and policies. The concern with financial markets and, relatedly, a strong sense of fiduciary responsibility, had important implications for the Bank's organization and operating procedures. In an important early innovation, the Bank put into place a simple procedural device for administering its loans. After consulting with several New York banks (notably the New York Trust Company), it implemented a system whereby, with respect to disbursements, a Bank loan was tantamount to an enormous letter of credit that

69. The reasons for this are spelled out in Mason and Asher, *World Bank since Bretton Woods,* p. 107.

70. A recent interpretation argues that the Bank decided to go in for direct lending rather than guarantees so that it "could develop greater independence from financial markets in determining the projects to be financed and the terms of the loans that it provided to its borrowers." On the contrary, as documented in chapter 2, the Bank's management

Table 14-3. *Financing the Bank: The Early Years*
Cumulative totals in billions of U.S. dollars

Finances	1949	1954	1959[a]
Total resources	1.0	1.9	4.5
Net borrowings	0.3	0.8	1.9
Sale of loans	0.03	0.1	0.6
Usable subscriptions	0.7	0.9	1.5
Repayments of principal	. . .	0.02	0.3
Income from operations	0.02	0.1	0.3
Source of funds			
Obtained within United States	0.9	1.2	1.8[b]
Outside United States	0.1	0.7	2.8[b]
Currency composition of			
borrowings			
U.S. dollars	0.3	0.7	1.6
Other	. . .	0.1	0.3

Source: J. H. Williams, "International Bank for Reconstruction and Development" (1967), table 6; IBRD, Annual Reports; SecM64-258, November 4, 1964.

a. Includes delayed deliveries in U.S. dollars and undrawn notes in Deutsche marks.

b. Estimates.

could be drawn upon against documentary evidence of expenditures. A system of careful end-use supervision of projects was established, and, until 1952 (when the first of its periodic reorganizations occurred), the supervision of projects was the responsibility of the Treasury Department. As a result, in the institution's early years, the Treasury Department was one of the largest administrative units within the Bank.

The Articles of the Bank allowed for full flexibility in setting lending rates.[71] An early decision delinked lending rates from the risk characteristics of a borrowing country. Lending rates would, however, vary with the maturity and currency of individual loans, reflecting the underlying borrowing costs. Until 1964, lending rates were fixed at 1.25 percent above the estimated cost of borrowings. This markup included the statutory commission fixed by the Articles at 1 percent for a decade as a way to build up liquid reserves.[72]

From early 1948 to the end of 1956, medium-term borrowing costs were lower than long-term costs, and interest rates on Bank loans reflected this difference. For instance, in the first half of 1953, Bank loans carried seven different rates (ranging

---

deliberately sought greater dependence on financial markets so as to gain autonomy from Washington. And this had a significant effect on the character of its lending. Michael Gavin and Dani Rodrik, "The World Bank in Historical Perspective," *American Economic Review Papers and Proceedings*, vol. 85 (May 1995), p. 330.

71. IBRD, *Articles of Agreement*, art. III, sec. 4, requires only that the "rate of interest be reasonable and appropriate to the project."

72. Ibid., art. IV, sec. 4(a).

from 4⅛ percent to 4⅞ percent).[73] After 1956, the difference between medium- and long-term borrowing costs by and large disappeared and the Bank moved to two "standard" lending rates: loans with long-term maturities (sixteen years or longer) and loans of less than sixteen years.[74] Two years later, when the devaluation of the French franc led to earnings losses, the practice was reviewed. However, the Bank decided to continue with its practice of basing lending rates on borrowing costs, without consideration to income risk and currency management.[75]

The amortization and grace periods of the early loans were project-, not country-specific. Two loans to Chile approved in 1949 are illustrative. One, for hydroelectric power, had a 20-year maturity and 5-year grace period, while the other, for agricultural equipment, had a 6.5-year maturity and a 2-year grace period. The Bank was also conscious of the fact that it "cannot be indifferent to the currencies in which they [its borrowers] incur obligations"[76] and sought to provide the borrower with its choice of currency. Not surprisingly, given the dollar shortages at the time, this largely meant dollar lending. But quite early on (as in the loan to the Netherlands in 1948 in Swiss francs) single-currency nondollar loans were available if the borrower's circumstances so warranted. Early Bank loans were by and large in dollars, principally because of the market availability and borrowers' requirements of dollars.

If there was an underlying principle to the terms of Bank loans, it was that the loans "should as far as practical conform to 'market' standards."[77] There were three major reasons for this: "First, it protects lenders from 'unfair' competition from the Bank. Second, it gets borrowers accustomed to conventional lending terms so that they adjust their financial practices to conditions they would meet if in due course they were to borrow on their own credit. Thirdly, it has advantages to the Bank as an institution." Indeed, the Bank's reputation as a prudent financial institution benefited from "not only its own financing, but also the more intangible considera- tion of the general 'appearance' of its lending."[78]

Longer amortization periods, for instance, could leave the Bank exposed to accusations of "borrowing short and lending long."[79] But when all is said and done,

73. Although the principle of cost-plus pricing for lending rates was established early on, the precise definition of borrowing costs, as well as the extent and basis of the relative markup would change over time. There were many technical questions: should the markup be applied to market borrowing costs or average cost of funds (including equity)? Were the market borrowing costs to be based on some period average, and if so, what period? Should the markup include a commitment fee based on undisbursed amounts? Answers to these questions varied over time.

74. IBRD, "Memorandum: Interest Rates on Bank Loans," FPC-37, May 2, 1956.

75. World Bank, "Non-dollar Currency Earnings," R58-70, June 27, 1958.

76. IBRD, *Fifth Annual Report, 1949–50*, p. 14.

77. S. R. Cope, "Terms of Bank Loans," August 26, 1963, processed. At the time Cope was the director of operations for Europe.

78. Ibid., paras. 16, 45.

79. Ibid., para. 14.

the Bank clearly occupied a unique niche in the market for long-term loans. For many Bank borrowers, a market for loans with long amortization and grace periods simply did not exist. For those who did have access to the New York market (European borrowers and Australia, Japan, and New Zealand), their public issues carried maturities between five and twenty years and interest rates of 4½ to 6 percent. Although these terms were comparable to those of Bank loans, these countries would in addition have to pay commissions at the level of 2½ percent of the principal amount.[80]

The Road to AAA

Even as the Bank was establishing its reputation over the 1950s, its management was aware that its competitive advantage was due in part to its capacity to borrow money relatively cheaply from financial markets and in part to the fact that "easy money" was not readily available to its prospective borrowers. The Bank's capacity to borrow depended on the quality of its bond ratings, which explained why it would act in a manner that would seem to pay inordinate attention to Wall Street. The reason for the lack of easy money was more exogenous, although the Bank would attempt to be persuasive in that regard, too.

Years later, the Bank would look back and thus rationalize its success in financial markets in the 1950s: "As the success of its operations became apparent, financial markets lent the Bank increasing sums and finally in 1959 gave it top credit rating."[81] There was little doubt as to the "success" of operations in a financial sense. Good relations with borrowers and the scrupulousness with which they served their financial obligations helped. Moreover, as indicated in chapter 3, investors' confidence in the IBRD was bolstered by the "image" of Bank lending: the deliberate, conservative manner with which it went about appraisal and supervision of loans. Long lags between project approvals, completion, and actual outcomes meant that the "success" of individual projects was not a factor in perceptions of the institution in capital markets. Indeed, the virtually inverse correlation in the 1980s between the narrowing yields between the Bank's borrowings and comparators, on the one hand, and declining project performance ratings, on the other, underscored that reality. The reasons for the receptivity of U.S. markets, said Black, were more prosaic: "the United States Government guarantee . . . ; the fact that the United States Government must approve every dollar issue by the Bank; the often expressed interest of the United States Government in making a success of the institution; and the fact that the Bank is operating at a substantial net profit."[82]

80. Samuel L. Hayes III and Philip M. Hubbard, *Investment Banking* (Harvard Business School Press, 1990), p. 31.

81. K. Sarwar Lateef, ed., *The Evolving Role of the World Bank: Helping Meet the Challenge of Development* (World Bank, 1994), p. 19.

82. Letter, Eugene R. Black to Maple T. Harl, chairman FDIC, January 29, 1951, p. 1.

From their first issue, the Bank's bonds had been rated "A" by Fitch Investors' Service and Standard & Poor's. Moody's, which at the time had a policy of not rating bonds and securities of financial institutions, was persuaded to make an exception in the case of the Bank, and also proceeded to give the Bank's bonds an "A" rating. Although the move upward to "AA" followed shortly thereafter, in 1951, investors continued to demand higher bond yields, in relation to other AA corporate yields, through much of the 1950s.

The move to AAA proved much more difficult, however. Time and again, the Bank was frustrated with the attitude of the ratings agencies. Even the normally unflappable Black remarked that the unwillingness of Moody's stemmed from "a disposition to be ultra-conservative on anything labeled 'international.'"[83] By the mid-1950s, the Bank was pressing the ratings agencies to be more explicit in what they would require on the part of the Bank to qualify for AAA, only to be turned away with murmurs of concern about the long-range political and economic prospects for the world. The real reason seemed to be closer to Black's earlier suspicion of an enduring prejudice among some board members of the agencies who had "acquired strong inhibitions against international or foreign situations."[84] Gradually the Bank chipped away at these residual reservations through a sustained campaign of quiet persuasion, only to be informed in mid-1958 that its ratings were in jeopardy because its outstanding obligations were approaching the U.S. share of the callable capital.

Responding to these fears raised by the ratings agencies, the Bank rapidly mobilized its first capital increase. At the New Delhi annual meetings in 1958, the governor for the United States proposed a doubling of the Bank's capital. The increase sailed through with a minimum of fuss, principally because of the strong backing by the institution's largest shareholder and because it did not entail any increase in paid-in capital: the entire amount of the additional subscriptions was left subject to call. On September 15, 1959, the Bank's authorized capital was increased from $10 billion to $21 billion.[85] Shortly thereafter S&P and Moody's upgraded the Bank's ratings to AAA.

The Bank found it more difficult to contain what it regarded as "easy money" from other sources of capital. In these early years it firmly believed that "in the long run, international capital . . . can provide only a minor part of the capital needed for development."[86] And, to the extent that recourse was sought to international capital, "foreign development financing should preferably be derived mainly from private sources."[87] Thus, although the Bank was enthusiastic in seeking out private

83. Ibid., p. 2.

84. Memorandum, William L. Bennett to Harold N. Graves, "Talks with Rating and Investment Advisory Services . . . ," October 21, 1955, p. 2.

85. The total was increased by $1 billion to allow for additional allotments to new members.

86. IBRD, *Fourth Annual Report, 1948–1949*, p. 14.

87. Ibid., p. 13.

participation in its loans, its attitude toward official funds—which at the time meant U.S. agencies—was unreservedly hostile. There was little of the later ardor on the supposed "catalytic" effects of its loans. Rather, it was much more concerned about the "danger that other lending may 'freewheel' on the Bank's loans."[88] With unhappy recollections of international lending still fresh in their minds, the Bank's management, which had a strong representation of former bankers, was concerned that even "a slight improvement in the financial situation of a country makes the country borrowing-happy and stimulates lending operations," which could lead to an unsustainable buildup of debt.[89]

Fearing that in an international lending equivalent of Gresham's law its efforts to ensure "sound" lending would be undermined by less careful lending, the Bank aggressively sought to control other sources of lending. When asked if the "Bank would be even more successful if it was the only lending institution, so that a country wouldn't get bailed out so to speak, by other agencies," Black replied in the affirmative.[90] For these reasons, despite their close relationships with the U.S. administration, both McCloy and Black lobbied vigorously against the Eximbank. The Bank's position, as outlined in an eighteen-page memorandum from McCloy to U.S. President Truman, was not that it opposed U.S. aid flows, only that "such additional assistance be in the form of grants, rather than in the form of illusory loans."[91] Although the Bank succeeded in blocking Eximbank loans (which were about 1 percent cheaper) in several cases, this was not sufficient. When Eisenhower took office, Black furiously lobbied for the liquidation of the Eximbank and nearly succeeded.[92] In the latter half of the 1950s, Bank officials turned their attention to short-term export credits, time and again warning against the problems such credits posed for the borrowers.

While it need hardly be added that the Bank's efforts were largely, as Black himself admitted, "futile," the very fact that both McCloy and Black could have even seriously considered that the Bank could displace or forestall all other official lending, made the Bank appear to be living in a kind of never-never land. Other organizations were understandably averse to take the purity of the Bank's motives at face value. Given the thrusts of bilateral, particularly U.S., foreign policy in those years, the Bank's resource transfer functions were relatively modest, less than 5 percent of total capital flows to developing countries in the mid-1950s.

It was understandable that the Bank's efforts in this regard did not endear the institution to all its constituencies. By the end of the decade, the countries in Latin America banded together to persuade the United States, now worried about the

88. Memorandum, D. Crena de Iongh to Eugene R. Black, "Consultation Covenant in Loan and Guarantee Agreements," SLC/O/332, June 4, 1951.

89. Ibid., p. 1. The specific reference in this case was to Mexico.

90. Black, Oral History, August 6, 1961, p. 35.

91. Bird, *The Chairman*, p. 299.

92. Turhan Tirana, "The Export-Import Bank of the United States," p. 401.

region following Castro's success, to back an alternate financial intermediary that would be more amenable to their wishes. The formation of the IDB would be "at once a tribute and a rebuke to the World Bank."[93]

For the Bank's management, the institution's growing market dependence had proven to be a useful political shield whose rhetorical value was at least as important as the undebatable reality.[94] In the early days, when McCloy was trying to sell the Bank's bonds, investors would state that although they liked him personally, they feared what could happen if after he left "some damn politician" was put in there. McCloy would have to repeatedly reassure them that he would ensure that would not be the case. Similarly, Black in his last years of office in responding to an interviewer on the question of his successor, assured his interviewer that "if they tried to put some politician in there, nobody would buy the bonds. They [the Bank] wouldn't have any money."[95] It would be a mark of the distance the Bank had traveled when a quarter century later the fears of the Bank's early presidents would come to pass—without a hiccup from the financial markets.

As McCloy and Black's statements illustrate, the presumed reactions of financial markets straddle a considerable swamp of uncertainty. This uncertainty contributed to the institution's risk averseness but also without a doubt enhanced Bank management's operational autonomy vis-à-vis its shareholders. The Bank would go on to become many things to many people, but its fundamental structure as a "sound" parastatal financial institution, increasingly based on market funds, would remain unaltered.

Financial Consolidation: 1960–68

At the turn of the decade the Bank was beginning to face a substantial change in its environment. With decolonization in full swing, there was a rapid increase in the institution's membership. The extremely modest economic capacity of its newer members would have major implications for the World Bank group. During the five years of Woods's presidency, the Bank's membership expanded by a third, whereas its total subscribed capital increased by only 10 percent, and "usable" paid-in capital increased at an even lower rate. This limited the Bank's access to free equity funds. The low creditworthiness of many of the newer members would necessarily limit the growth of the IBRD and gradually shift the institution's financial center of

93. Mason and Asher, *World Bank since Bretton Woods*, p. 578.

94. Garner, in his characteristically blunt manner, cogently summarized the issue when asked, "Do you feel that it was a fortunate thing that the Bank was substantially dependent upon the bond market for its funds, that this helped to make the Bank sound?" "Yes . . . it's been a useful thing. It's also been a very useful argument, to tell the people why the Bank must pay attention to financial opinion and judgments." Robert Garner, interview, World Bank Oral History Program, July 19, 1961, pp. 44–45. For a more extensive treatment of the issue, see chapter 3 in this book.

95. Black, Oral History, August 6, 1961, p. 51.

gravity away from the IBRD. This period also marks the emergence of Germany as the principal market for the Bank's borrowings.

Lending to the industrialized countries having peaked, major shifts were occurring in the institution's clientele. In Latin America the Bank faced competition from the IDB, which was both more congenial in its operating style and more flexible in its lending conditionalities. Furthermore, thanks to Castro, the region now had substantially enhanced access to resources at concessional terms, principally from the IDB's Fund for Special Operations and the Alliance for Progress. With the battlefields of the cold war shifting to developing countries, this pattern was being replicated in Asia and parts of the Middle East. But borrowers in the Bank's Middle East and South Asia region faced severe lending ceilings owing to creditworthiness concerns, which now posed a difficult problem for the Bank.[96]

Managing Portfolio Risk

The achievement of AAA rating for its bonds had been a milestone in the Bank's quest for financial respectability. But even as it was gaining this accolade, the pressing problem was not so much the availability of finance but borrower creditworthiness. Between 1955 and 1958 the foreign debt of low-income countries had increased by 60 percent, and the Bank began to face the reality of a severely circumscribed "absorptive capacity" in the form of limited creditworthiness of these borrowers as well as many of the newly joining members.[97] Simultaneously, the Bank's lending was moving away from the richer countries of Europe. Consequently, between the mid-1950s and early 1960s, the credit risks facing the Bank increased sharply as the quality of its portfolio deteriorated visibly (table 14-4).

The Bank's credit concerns were especially directed to its portfolio in South Asia, and, in particular, its largest borrower, India. Since the late 1950s, the Bank had become very much aware of India's balance of payments problems. A report on the Indian economy in mid-1958 began with the sobering assessment: "India is in the grips of a foreign exchange crisis."[98] At that point the IBRD held 28 percent of India's external public debt. In turn, India accounted for 13 percent of the IBRD's loan portfolio.[99] The Bank undertook several steps to address the situation.

96. Memorandum, Escott Reid to Richard Demuth, "Bank Financial Policy," May 10, 1963.

97. Dragaslov Avramovic and Ravi Gulhati, *Debt Servicing Problems of Low-Income Countries* (Johns Hopkins University Press, 1960). The study was one of the early comprehensive in-house analyses of developing-country debt by the Bank.

98. IBRD, "Current Economic Position and Prospects of India," Report AS-68a, R58-82, July 28, 1958, p. iii.

99. Ibid., p. 41. It should be noted that the figures cited in the report differ from those in the *Annual Report 1958*. According to the latter, India's share of the IBRD portfolio was 10.5 percent.

Table 14-4. *Proportion of the IBRD Loan Portfolio Outstanding to Borrowers in Various Risk Categories, 1955–75*
Percentage share of the portfolio at the end of fiscal year

Category	1955	1959	1963	1967	1971	1975
I (virtually no risk)	66.0	51.1	37.8	34.2	27.5	29.4
II (some risk)	26.4	28.2	34.9	45.8	52.4	55.1
III (some risk of default requiring concessional rescheduling)	7.6	20.7	27.3	20.0	20.1	15.5

Source: Loan Portfolio Analysis Unit, Third Progress Report, December 1975, annex 5.

It began to sharply reduce its exposure to India. IBRD disbursements, which accounted for nearly 42 percent of disbursements from all foreign loans to India in the three years ending March 31, 1959, were projected to decline to just over 8 percent in the following two years, both because of an increase in contribution by others and a slowing down of the IBRD's own disbursements.[100] Responding to a request from the government of India in September 1958 the Bank, in association with the United States and the United Kingdom, convened the Aid-India Consortium. And, at about the same time, Black dropped his decade-long objections to IDA.

The circumstances surrounding the genesis of IDA, its effects on the World Bank group and its role in promoting development are examined in detail in chapters 17 and 18. The discussion here will be confined to the effects of IDA on the financial aspects of the IBRD. While the discussions on IDA were in high gear, Black despatched his general counsel, Davidson Sommers, to New York to talk to the Bank's underwriters. Black and Woods (then chairman of First Boston, one of the two managing underwriters of IBRD bonds) both shared the feeling that "soft-lending" was not a reputable activity for any respectable lending institution.

The argument almost immediately won Woods, and the markets, over. Much later an elaborate internal analysis of the IBRD's loan portfolio acknowledged that the decline in the portfolio share of the most risky category of borrowers, between the end of the 1950s and the mid-1970s, could be explained as "presumably resulting from the introduction of IDA."[101] As table 14-4 indicates, the decline of the riskiness of the IBRD's portfolio after 1963 coincided with a substitution of IDA for IBRD lending in several large countries, particularly India and Pakistan.

100. IBRD, "Recent Economic Developments and Current Prospects of India," Report As-71a, SecM59-40, February 20, 1959, appx. 2, p. 18. The trend is similar if grants are included, in which case the IBRD's share was projected to decline from 34 percent to 7.6 percent.

101. World Bank, Programming and Budgeting Department, "Loan Portfolio Analysis Unit: Third Progress Report," December 31, 1975, p. 6.

Although IDA's finances have always been distinct from those of the Bank (except for IBRD transferring a fraction of its net income to IDA) there can be little doubt that from the very beginning IDA played an important role in allaying creditworthiness concerns with respect to IBRD lending. In IDA's early years, however, potential investors and the public at large found it difficult to distinguish between the two. As a result, the Bank's finance staff were once again obliged to aggressively hit the campaign trail, to educate the investment community regarding the differences between the two.

Rethinking Financial Policies

Somewhat paradoxically, even as it concluded that there was an increased need for "soft credit," the IBRD itself was faced with an embarrassment of riches.[102] Under Black, the Bank's senior management would periodically gather informally at occasions that came to be known as "lost weekends." At the last such meeting under Black, which Woods attended, the discussions centered on what steps the Bank might take to curb the growth of its rapidly expanding reserves.[103] With the institution's net income increasing "at an almost indecent rate," there was concern that if the Bank did not take immediate steps to deal with the issue, external pressures might force it to take precipitous action.[104] The decisions taken to deal with this issue would set off a chain of events that would substantially alter the trajectory of the Bank group. The Bank's increased financial strength would seep into recommendations calling for a bolder lending stance and thereby attempt to offset the growing affluence of the Bank with the chronic penury of IDA.

Black retired from the Bank in 1962 and was succeeded by George Woods. As chairman of First Boston, Woods had impeccable credentials in the financial community. He had been involved with the Council of Foreign Bondholders and was regarded as tough on defaulting debtors. First Boston had been one of the two lead underwriters of IBRD bonds since 1951 and Woods and the Bank knew each other well. In addition to being familiar with the Bank's finances and its market, he had led important lending missions for the institution. Although both Black and Woods hailed from the Wall Street financial community, there was an important difference in their backgrounds. As a universally regarded bond salesman par excellence, Black's experience had been almost exclusively on the funding side of

102. See, for instance, IDA, "The Need for an Increased 'Soft Credit' Component in Development Aid," IDA/FPC 62-4, December 17, 1962.

103. Harold N. Graves, interview, World Bank Oral History Program II, July 24, 1985, pp. 22–23.

104. Mason and Asher, *World Bank since Bretton Woods*, p. 407. According to Mason and Asher, the immediate concern seemed to be (once again) a restive U.S. Congress, which was eyeing the Bank's profits as a possible source for financing the UN's perennial budget problems. See ibid., pp. 120–21.

the balance sheet. Woods, on the other hand, came from the investment side. At First Boston he made the final decision as to which securities the firm would underwrite (that is, commit itself to buy). The different experiences of the two presidents, coupled with the structural changes in the Bank's environment and its own development, would lead to a different set of institutional priorities over the 1960s.

The Bank's steadily growing net income and reserves need some explanation. The Articles had mandated that for the first ten years of its operations the Bank was to levy a commission fixed by the Articles at 1 percent in its first decade of operations as a way to build up liquid reserves.[105] The commission—and its allocation to a "Special Reserve"—had been perceived as a device to strengthen the credit of the Bank and, relatedly, the security of its bonds. However, its origins belie its principal purpose. The idea came from the British, who had been anxious throughout not to commit to any obligations requiring substantial contributions in the future. Keynes had argued that the Bank "should aim at so conducting its business that there would be a good hope of the pool of commissions being sufficient by itself to carry it most of the way."[106]

In the first few years of its operations, the Bank's net income was simply allocated to surplus. The policy was changed in 1950, following Poland's withdrawal from the Bank.[107] Net income was now allocated to a reserve, called a supplemental reserve, against losses on loans and guarantees made by the Bank.[108] This policy has been maintained since then. The issue was reexamined in mid-1955, preceding the expiration of the mandatory ten-year period of the 1 percent commission. In the end a divided Board agreed to continue with the commission following management's recommendation of possible "unfavorable reaction in the market" if the status quo was not maintained.[109] Barely a year later, the reserves appeared to have built up sufficiently for Black to recommend a dividend.[110] To ward off

105. IBRD, *Articles of Agreement*, art. IV, sec. 4(a).

106. Quoted in K. Varvaressos, "Criticisms against the Bank and Suggestions for Their Refutation," April 11, 1950, p. 87, processed.

107. Poland's withdrawal had created an anomalous situation. As per the Bank's Articles (VI, sec. 4), the repurchase price of the shares of a withdrawing member were to be based on the book value of its shares, and consequently a withdrawing member was entitled to its proportionate share in the surplus and net income of the Bank. It had been understood that given the institution's fledgling status, the surplus and net income were to be used for the Bank's purposes. IBRD, "Establishment of Reserve against Losses on Loans and Guarantees," R-357, July 25, 1950.

108. IBRD Resolution 55, "Transfer of Surplus to Reserve against Losses on Loans and Guarantees Made by the Bank; Action Taken by Executive Directors Establishing Such Reserve," September 14, 1950. The Special Reserves, as required by the Articles, had to be kept in liquid form to be available only for meeting the Bank's obligations. The supplemental reserves were a bookkeeping account, used as part of the Bank's operating capital.

109. IBRD, "Financial Policy Committee—Notice of Meeting," FPC/33, June 27, 1955.

110. Two percent of the average amount of 18 percent capital outstanding on loans during the year and 2 percent on the (2 percent) subscribed capital. IBRD, "Charges on Bank Loans and Allocation of Net Income," R-1023, December 6, 1956, para. 11.

opposition Black soon added a sweetener of reduced commission charges (by ¼ percent) along with the payment of a dividend.[111] The issue proved sufficiently divisive for the matter to be diplomatically deferred. While it was discussed sporadically, the matter stood there until now.

The allocation of net income would be a matter of continuing debate within the institution over nearly four decades. Why was this the case? The IBRD's equity, the "free" money available to the institution, can increase either through fresh injection of paid-in capital or additions to reserves. In practice, the cost of additions to paid-in capital is borne largely by the larger, nonborrowing shareholders. Reserves, on the other hand, can only increase from successive annual allocations from net income, which in turn depend partly on loan charges, the cost of which is borne by the borrowers and partly on income generated by the Bank's liquid portfolio. Insofar as higher levels of reserves imply a better financial health of the institution, it benefits all members. Furthermore, high reserves also benefit the borrowers in the long term by reducing the Bank's overall cost of funds, and therefore lending charges. But borrowing countries would contend that higher borrowing costs shifted the burden to current borrowers. Moreover, they argued, in pushing for higher reserves the larger shareholders were seeking to reduce both their own contingent liabilities (the non-paid-in part of subscribed capital) and future injections of paid-in capital. Effectively, this implied that the strong link between power (institutional control through larger voting shares) and financial burden was being weakened.

Compounding the problem was the lack of a firm yardstick for an appropriate level of reserves. Time and again the Bank's management would argue that reserves serve to provide an assurance to the markets, "but since this is a psychological matter, it cannot readily be given precise quantitative expression."[112] After building up its reserves over the 1950s and early 1960s, the reserves to loans ratio gradually peaked at 23.4 percent in 1965 before declining over the next two decades (see figure 15-1).

The interrelated issues of loan charges, reserves, and uses of net income were laid out in a staff paper on the Bank's financial policy.[113] Management's proposals to address these issues outlined several options including a reduction of loan charges,

111. IBRD, background memorandum for Financial Policy Committee meeting, FPC57-40, January 11, 1957.

112. IBRD, "Principal Considerations Affecting Conclusions as to Appropriate Levels of Bank Reserves," R57-39, June 4, 1957, p. 11. Woods similarly stated that "the question [of the adequacy or inadequacy of the reserves] was not susceptible of a mathematical determination. It was a question of judgement." IBRD, "Memorandum of Meeting of Bank Financial Policy Committee," FPC63-7, para. 17. It may be noted that at the time, although the reserve ratios of the IDB were lower than the Bank's, its bonds too were rated AAA. The difference was that the IDB had assured the bond markets that its dollar debt would not exceed the liability of the United States.

113. IBRD, "The Bank's Financial Policy," FPC63-5, January 31, 1963.

transfers to IDA, payment of dividend, or the continued buildup of reserves.[114] The paper deserves some attention since the basic issues analyzed have, to varying extents, persisted ever since.

Management was averse to reducing loan charges for several reasons:[115]

—A small reduction would have limited immediate effect on the growth of reserves.

—Too large a reduction would blunt the Bank's efforts to get the higher income borrowers to go to the market, given that the Bank's charges were already low in relation to relevant market comparators.[116]

—Relatedly, lower charges would also make it more difficult for the Bank to sell portions of its loans to private borrowers.

—The reductions would make no difference to the Bank's less creditworthy borrowers, a rapidly growing category.

—Any substantial reduction would adversely affect the Bank's market image as an institution run on sound lines. This might make the Bank's bonds less acceptable.

Woods accepted that a transfer to IDA would be "the most effective and tidy way of assuring that some part of the Bank's income . . . will continue to be used for economic development." However, his personal preferences were unequivocal: "I feel strongly that there should be no direct transfer of Bank earnings to IDA. . . . [S]uch transfers would have a serious adverse effect on the standing and reputation of the Bank."[117] Clearly, Woods was not worried about the financial costs to the Bank and possible adverse implications on the Bank's reserves given that instead he "favored the recommendation for a dividend payment in the amount of $50 million," having satisfied himself that the Bank could do so "without impairing its financial soundness or its reputation for conservatism in the financial and business community."[118] Several reasons were advanced against such a step:

—IDA's Articles (Article VI, Section 6) provided that it should not borrow from or lend to the Bank. Thus, although they did not expressly prohibit such an action, any transfer "would therefore violate the spirit, even though not the letter, of the Articles."[119]

114. Another alternative, giving the borrowers an annual rebate on loans outstanding, was not considered because a significant fraction of the benefits would accrue to past industrial-country borrowers.

115. IBRD, "The Bank's Financial Policy," FPC63-5, January 31, 1963. Quotations on the following pages are from this document, unless otherwise noted.

116. It does not appear that the Bank ever seriously contemplated the argument that the Bank could conceivably, at least in some cases, use its marginal competitive position to drive down market rates. Understandably, the Bank's management was, and has continued to be, extremely reluctant to see this as an objective of Bank lending.

117. "Financial Policy Committees of Bank and IDA, Joint Meeting," introductory statement by the president, Bank/FPC63-1, IDA/FPC63-2, January 15, 1963, p. 2.

118. Ibid., p. 3.

119. IBRD, "Bank Financial Policy," pp. 16–19.

—"A direct transfer would run counter to the representations made to the market at the time IDA was established and in its early days. . . . [A]part from any question of good faith, the transfer might appear objectionable to the market, as an indication that the Bank intended to engage in 'giveaways.'"[120]

—Another problem was that some members of IBRD were not members of IDA. Was it fair to transfer any portion of earnings to an institution, even an affiliated institution, to which some Bank members did not belong?

—The Articles had contemplated only two options for allocating net income other than reserves: a reduction of loan charges or a dividend. "If the Bank's members wish to dispose of profits in a way not contemplated (even if not actually prohibited) by the Articles, the Articles themselves should be amended to authorize that action, and the action should not be taken in the absence of an amendment."[121]

There was no mention of another, more prickly, reason. A transfer to IDA could also create conflict among the borrowing members. The middle-income borrowers (at the time, principally Latin American countries) were mainly interested in having loan charges reduced since they would derive little benefit either from transfers to IDA or from a dividend payment.

Even at this early stage of IDA, the replenishment problem had already begun to hover over the Bank's management. Given the Bank's worries on the resources available for IDA, Woods's arguments against a transfer to IDA may appear puzzling. In reality, Woods was hoping that the payment of a considerable dividend would reap substantial goodwill for development assistance in conservative political and financial circles, which in turn would parlay into greater resources for development assistance overall.

Woods's initial set of proposals met a wary reception, with the consensus in the Board clearly against dividends. Woods then promised a more thorough examination of the interrelated financial issues. Over the next few months, during spring 1963, a succession of drafts was prepared by Richard Demuth, then director of Development Services and an outstanding "ideas" man. Woods now saw an opportunity to make his mark on the institution's lending side, just as his predecessor Black had done on the borrowings side. Overriding the objections of several of his senior staff, a new set of proposals was tabled several months later.[122]

—The supplemental reserve was to be frozen, while continuing the 1 percent commission for allocation to the Special Reserve. Instead a new "earned surplus" account was to be created.

—The idea of dividends was dropped, Woods having been convinced that "such action may impair the Bank's reputation as a developmental institution."

120. Ibid.
121. Ibid.
122. IBRD, "Bank Financial Policy," FPC63-8, July 18, 1963.

—Woods reiterated his opposition to any transfer to IDA and his conviction that it "would adversely affect the Bank's standing in the financial community."

—An early loan instrument was resuscitated in a new form called "maintenance import loans," or program loans. New loan instruments offering longer periods of grace and amortizations were proposed, as were modest reductions on loan charges.

—The most important proposals concerned major changes in the lending focus of the Bank, including loans for agriculture, education, and technical assistance (see chapter 4). One of these is important here: Woods proposed that the Bank's Articles be amended to allow for lending to private industrial enterprises without full government guarantees.

Before the Board could hold its discussions, Woods fell seriously ill. His senior managers made it clear to him that he had to compromise on two important aspects of his proposals to ensure Board approval. The Board was unhappy with Woods's refusal to transfer IBRD profits to IDA and also opposed his proposal that the Bank's Articles be amended to allow the Bank to extend long-term loans to private industrial enterprise without full government guarantees.[123] The latter issue was neatly finessed. During the course of informal consultations, it was suggested that the same objective could be met by channeling Bank funds through the IFC for lending on the lines of its DFC loans.[124] The Bank's reputation as a borrower now being firmly established, it could use its borrowing capacity on behalf of the IFC, thus augmenting the IFC's meager resources. The Articles of the IBRD and the IFC were accordingly amended in December 1965 to allow the Bank to lend up to four times the unimpaired capital and surplus of the IFC.[125]

Over the course of the following year, Woods retreated from his original stance. Concurring with the Board's preference, he recommended a transfer of $50 million from the IBRD's net income to IDA, beginning with fiscal 1964, attributing the shift in his position to the reassurances he had received from the financial community.[126] The passage of time undoubtedly made it easier for the financial community to overlook Black's assurance, given at IDA's creation, that there would be "no leaks from the Bank to IDA." It is likely that the problems afflicting the IDA replenishment acted as a persuasive lever. At the same time, the set-aside to the Special Reserve was discontinued, and all income from loan charges was treated as net income.

The Brakes on Financial Intermediation

Having decided to pay much greater attention to the lending initiatives of the Bank, Woods created a new vice presidency for finance and delegated many

123. Letter, Burke Knapp to George Woods, August 3, 1963.
124. IBRD, "Bank/IFC Financial Policy," Bank/FPC64-6, IFC/FPC64-1, June 15, 1964.
125. For the Bank, this was the first of its only two amendments to date. The amendment to the IFC's Articles was its second.
126. IBRD, "Bank and IDA Financial Policy," Bank/FPC64-5, June 5, 1964.

financial policy issues to his new vice president, Siem Aldewereld. But the institution's comfort in its financial security would be short-lived. The financial context was beginning to change perceptibly. With the problems of the dollar beginning to mount, it was a matter of time before the echoes would be heard in a still predominantly "dollar bank."

The pressures on the dollar had begun a few years earlier when foreign-held dollars began to exceed U.S. gold reserves and touched off the first gold crisis in October 1960. The U.S. government gradually took successive steps to curb capital outflows and reduce the pressures on the dollar. An Interest Equalization Tax (IET), imposed in July 1963, added an effective 1 percent tax on foreign borrowers classified as developed countries (twenty-two in all) in U.S. capital markets. These measures were extended, in early 1965, to cover bank loans. "Voluntary" restraints were requested of foreign lending by U.S. banks and corporations. As the pressures on the dollar continued unabated, the IET rate was increased to 1.5 percent in 1967. Beginning in 1968, controls were also imposed on dollars raised by U.S. corporations to finance foreign direct investment in industrialized countries.

In parallel with the increasing capital controls in the United States, there were significant developments in financial instruments and in other capital markets. With the creation of the negotiable certificate of deposit (popularly known as CDs), by Citibank in 1961, the seeds of a future revolution in the financial intermediation were being planted. Just a few months earlier, nine Western European countries had accepted Article 8 obligations of the IMF, rendering their currencies convertible. And in June 1963, responding to the new opportunities created by U.S. capital controls, S. G. Warburg & Co. (a British merchant banking firm) lead-managed a $15 million issue by Autostrade (an Italian state highway authority), helping launch the Eurobond market.

During this period (1963–68), IBRD lending commitments barely changed, as a consequence of the phasing out of lending to the industrialized countries and the declining creditworthiness of many of its other borrowers. The rapid increase in new membership did little to halt this trend. In 1963, and again in 1964, net borrowings turned negative as the Bank—awash in liquidity because of lower-than-anticipated disbursements, a high volume of loan sales ($1 billion from 1959 to 1963), and large net earnings—attempted to reduce its liquidity. However, loan sales declined dramatically after the passage of the IET. Although the IET exempted participations in Bank bonds, the Bank decided to respect the rationale behind the IET and as a matter of policy decided not to sell to U.S. investors loans made to any of the IET-designated countries.[127] For this reason, as well as higher yields on competing securities, loan sales steadily declined over the next four years, from $273 million in 1963 to $67 million in 1967.[128]

127. World Bank, *Annual Report 1963–1964*, pp. 16–17.
128. Loan sales during 1963–67 were about 40 percent of the levels in 1959–63.

Table 14-5. *Effect of IBRD Operations on U.S. Balance of Payments*
Millions of U.S. dollars

Account	Through FY 1963	FY 1964–68
Current account[a]	2,567	911
Capital account		
Assets[b]	2,071	155
Liabilities[c]	0	680
Balance of capital account	–2,071	525
Net change	496	1,436
Memo: U.S. balance of payments deficit	–1,940[d]	–4,290

Sources: World Bank data.

a. Includes procurement of goods (specifically identified as originating in the United States plus the same proportion of procurement not identifiable by country of origin); interest payments to U.S. bondholders living in the United States; interest to loan holders; administrative expenses incurred in U.S. dollars in the United States, including the issuance cost of bonds; investment income.

b. U.S. payments of 1 percent subscription; U.S. payments of 9 percent subscription; net IBRD bond sales (bonds sold for delayed delivery are included in the year in which settlement was made); net IBRD loan sales.

c. During this period all investments had maturities over one year (figures exclude Euro-deposits).

d. 1963 data. Source: Paul Volcker and Toyoo Gyohten, *Changing Fortunes* (Times Books, 1992), p. 363.

Aided by low inflation, the first half of the decade was a period of relative stability in bond markets. Long-term yields began to rise in the United States from the middle of 1965 responding to loose fiscal and tightening monetary policy. In Europe long-term interest rates had begun to increase a year earlier, fueled by a rising demand for funds and reduced U.S. capital exports. A 6¼ percent Canadian dollar issue in November 1966 was the highest offering yield on any Bank issue to date. But the most important issues affecting the Bank's financing were the developments in U.S. capital markets.

Facing growing balance of payments deficits, the U.S. Treasury adopted a tough stance to curb capital outflows from the United States. Convinced that the operations of the Bank group were adding to U.S. deficits, the U.S. Treasury sought to clamp down on the two possible sources: Bank borrowings in the United States and U.S. contributions to IDA. But contrary to the U.S. Treasury's perceptions, the Bank's operations, rather than being a drain, were having a favorable effect on the U.S. balance of payments (see table 14-5).

For the first time since its inception, the Bank began to face the threat of being shut out of its largest market. In May 1964 the senior staff was informed that U.S. balance of payments problems precluded the Bank from going ahead with a planned bond offering in the U.S. market. Following a short respite in 1965, the Bank was again denied permission to borrow in the U.S. market the following year. Unlike Black, Woods had less clout with the U.S. administration, and the United States had less latitude to accommodate the Bank. Poor personal relations between Woods and Henry Fowler, the then Treasury secretary, did not help matters.[129] The sharply reduced access to U.S. markets was unprecedented for the Bank. Fearing that it would be unable to meet its obligations to its borrowers, it began to limit the growth of IBRD lending. Actual loan commitments began to lag even while project identification and preparation continued apace.

The restrictions on access to U.S. capital markets further pushed the Bank to diversify its borrowings. Of the thirty-four bonds issued during the years Woods served as president, nineteen were dollar denominated, eight in deutsche marks, three each in Canadian dollars and Swiss francs, and one in Swedish kronor, the first such borrowing in that currency. The Canadian dollar borrowings (one each in 1965, 1966, and 1967, for a total of $65 million) marked the Bank's return to the Canadian market after a decade. The overall volume of borrowings, however, grew quite modestly to just over $2 billion gross, $0.7 billion net, in marked contrast to a rapid growth of the rest of the institution's activities (see table 15-1).

A less visible consequence of the restrictions placed on the Bank in U.S. capital markets was the change in the Bank's investments of its increasing liquidity. Through its first quarter century the Bank was a conservative and passive investor, partly because of the state of financial markets in those years. Initially, with the dollar as its sole currency holding, the IBRD invested only in bonds, notes, and other obligations of the United States.[130] As its borrowings gradually expanded, the Bank broadened its investment authority to include holdings of the currency of any country in "bonds, notes and other obligations of such country."[131] In both cases, the maturities of these obligations were not to exceed five years. But from time to time exceptions were made to this policy. In 1960 investments were broadened to six-month time deposits with selected banks in the United States and Canada. The initial limit of $100 million was gradually raised to $500 million by 1965 and $700 million in 1969. In 1966 the Bank began to invest in U.S. government agency obligations, although formal authorization from the Board was not sought until 1969.[132]

Although this diversification into agency obligations partly reflected higher yields relative to Treasury bills and notes, the institution had little choice, given its undertakings to the U.S. government that all funds derived from dollar borrowings in U.S. markets would be invested in such a manner that it would not have any adverse impact on the U.S. balance of payments. To comply with those assurances,

129. According to one staffer, Woods's feelings regarding Fowler were "unprintable." William Bennett, interview, World Bank Oral History Program, January 20, 1988, p. 17. The Bank's general counsel at the time also agreed that "Woods had very bad relations with Henry Fowler." Aron Broches, interview, World Bank Oral History Program, November 7, 1985, p. 24.

130. IBRD, Resolution 63, M-99, July 23, 1947.

131. IBRD, Resolution 181, M-216, March 22, 1951.

132. IBRD, "Investment of Bank Funds in United States Government Agency Securities," R69-186, September 10, 1969.

these investments had to have an original maturity exceeding one year, for the simple reason that U.S. government practice did not record investments of one year or less as offsetting inflow of funds for balance of payments statistics. For this reason the Board approved that the proceeds of the $200 million issue in January 1965 "should be placed with commercial banks . . . for a period of not less than thirteen months, thus increasing the funds held by the Bank in this form from $300 million to $500 million."[133] This committed the Bank in 1969 to hold at least $1 billion in investments with a maturity exceeding one year.

Heretofore, the Bank had always maintained that its lending was demand-constrained; in particular, there was a dearth of viable projects as part of a well-conceived development program. Now it had to plan for a possible supply constraint due to a limited access to funds. In fact, on occasions the shadow cast by the paucity of loanable resources, due to capital market constraints, led the Bank to delay the consideration of new loan applications and even seriously consider the possibility of suspending further loan operations.[134]

It had already, in 1965, introduced a higher "market eligible" rate, for its more creditworthy borrowers, who had been targeted by the IET.[135] Since the IET increased the cost of foreign borrowing in U.S. capital markets, the Bank feared that countries such as Japan and Italy, which it had been trying to wean away from its loans, would revert to further borrowings from the IBRD. A higher interest rate would also make it easier to sell these loans to the market. The introduction of a differential interest rate among its borrowers was noteworthy in another regard. From the beginning the IBRD had eschewed, by not charging a risk premium for the less creditworthy borrowers, strict financial criteria in its loan charges. It now went a small step further by charging, in effect, a small negative risk premium.

This change in the Bank's loan policies was adamantly, and understandably, opposed by the countries affected. The Bank tried to make amends by examining alternate mechanisms to help the affected borrowers meet their capital require-ments. One proposal called for the Bank to assume an underwriting role wherein the Bank would warehouse bond issues from these countries—in other words, it would buy them on its own account, keep them on tap, and, as market interest grew, make them available to the market. In the end, this did not occur, probably because it amounted to an indirect form of lending, bypassing the "productive purposes" test mandated by the Articles.

The Bank also now began to get more involved in proposals that sought to increase resource flows to developing countries. The most prominent of these, such

133. IBRD, "Minutes of Meeting of the Executive Directors of the Bank," M65-1, January 28, 1965, para. 9.
134. See memoranda, J. Burke Knapp to George Woods, untitled, January 20, 1967; and "Bank Lending Program for the Rest of This Fiscal Year," February 3, 1967.
135. IBRD, "Market Eligible Loans," R65-9, January 25, 1965.

as the Horowitz proposal and the supplementary financing facility, sought to augment IDA resources.[136] In the end, these proposals, as well as other variants, did not amount to much. For the most part, the amount of concessional resources was a politically fixed reservoir. New schemes would at best amount to new taps to the existing reservoir. They might change the rate of flow for a short time, as well its sources and sinks but would have little effect on the overall volume of resources.

An interesting proposal to augment nonconcessional resources was put forth by Luis Machado, the executive director representing a group of Latin American countries. The "Machado proposal," as it came to be called, in a novel twist on the Bank's guarantee capacity, proposed that the Bank guarantee government bond issues in local currency with a maintenance of value clause. This proposal sought to address two problems plaguing the countries in Machado's constituency: to provide a means of raising local noninflationary finance and a financial asset that would be attractive enough to rein in flight capital.

Bank staff analysis effectively threw cold water on the proposal. Acceptance of the proposal would amount to "a confession of defeat in designing and implementing a comprehensive and well-designed fiscal and monetary policy. . . . What would be the advantages in terms of additional opportunities for the Bank to influence internal policies of member countries?"[137] There could be a moral hazard in that governments might deliberately force the invocation of guarantees to get free foreign exchange; the Bank would be guaranteeing one set of financial assets but what would be the effects on other nonguaranteed financial assets, such as time deposits? And while value-indexed bonds had been used in more developed countries (most notably in Finland, France, and Israel), even there the experience had been mixed. Little weight seems to have been attached to a potentially valuable by-product: the opportunity to develop local capital markets in government debt instruments. The proposal was perhaps too early for its time and was quietly dropped.

---

136. The "Horowitz" proposal, named after its proponent, then governor of the Central Bank of Israel, was an interest subsidy fund. It would resurface a decade later, in a somewhat modified form, as the "Third Window." The idea of the supplementary financing facility originated with the United Nations Conference on Trade and Development, where it had been proposed by Sweden and the United Kingdom in 1964. The proposal envisaged that the Bank, under certain circumstances, might guarantee the funds necessary to finance the imports of a country even if the country's exports declined—as long as the Bank had the authority to make recommendations about the fiscal and monetary policy of the country. The scheme was seen as not directly apropos to development and more in the realm of the IMF, whose vehement opposition to the scheme was in no small way responsible for burying the proposal.

137. IBRD, Economic staff, "Comments on Dr. Machado's Proposal," August 26, 1963.

Arrears and Rescheduling

The creditworthiness problems facing several of the Bank's borrowers meant that sooner or later the Bank would be faced with an arrears problem.[138] In 1965 the Bank made two loans to Brazil after a hiatus of six years, with the explicit purpose of offsetting the maturities due on earlier loans.[139] During the 1950s and 1960s the Bank also rescheduled loans on project considerations on several occasions, when delays in project implementation had occurred. This option was followed by the Bank in the 1950s with Paraguay and Haiti, in 1963 with Lebanon, and in 1964 with two coal loans to Chile.[140] More notably, in Haiti's case the Bank had rescheduled loan repayments on balance of payments grounds on two separate occasions.[141] But in all these cases the amounts were relatively small and raised few questions. A very different situation presented itself in the period 1966–68 in the case of India.

As detailed in chapter 9, India's economic and debt problems steadily worsened in the mid-1960s. The country's debt-service ratio had doubled from 1960 to 1965, and in early 1966 India formally asked the Bank to take the lead in arranging a rescheduling of its debt-service payments. While the Bank embarked on a major policy reform attempt in India, it also took several steps in the context of the Aid-India Consortium to mitigate India's debt problem. The first response was an additional $50 million IDA program credit, "approximately the amount of principal payments due to the Bank in 1966/67."[142]

---

138. This section has drawn heavily on two excellent memoranda from the Legal Department: office memorandum, Antonia Macedo to Patrick Heininger, "Rescheduling of Bank Loans," June 30, 1981; and office memorandum, Ibrahim Shihata to Moeen A. Qureshi, "Legally Acceptable Options to Deal with Default Possibilities," LEG/MC84-19, September 13, 1984.

139. IBRD, "Report and Recommendation of the President to the Executive Directors on the Proposed Loans to Central Electrica de Furnas, S.A., and Usinas Electricas do Paranapanema, S.A., in Brazil," P-421, R65-26, February 17, 1965.

140. Paraguay, loan no. 0055, approved December 6, 1951; Haiti, loan no. 0141, approved May 4, 1956; Lebanon, loan no. 129, approved August 25, 1955; Chile, loan nos. 0171 and 0172, approved July 18, 1957.

141. In December 1963, because of Haiti's difficult foreign exchange situation brought on by severe hurricane damage to its export crops, the Bank agreed that service payments due in January 1964 would consist of interest only. The Bank also agreed to reschedule repayment of the $1.6 million of principal still outstanding to run from July 1, 1964, through July 1, 1971, thereby reducing annual service payments by one-half to about $260,000 per year. In January 1968, because of acute foreign exchange stringency and the discouraging outlook for Haiti's exports, the Bank postponed repayment of two-thirds of the principal due on January 1, 1968, and July 1, 1968, and to an extension of the amortization period by one year to include the above payments. See memorandum from the president, "Haiti: Request for Revision of Amortization Schedule of Loan," 141-HA, R68-4, January 5, 1968.

142. B. R. Bell, "India's Request for Deferment of 1966/67 Debt Service Payments: Further Background Note," IND 66-3, March 31, 1966, para. 10.

As the severity of India's debt problem became clear, it was apparent that the Bank, as the largest creditor due total debt service over the next five years, would have to do more.[143] In a meeting called to examine solutions to India's debt-servicing problems, Burke Knapp reminded the group that "an effort had been made to design one or more fast-disbursing loans to India in order to offset the approximately $77 million," in loan service payments due the Bank by India over the following year, but "it now appeared impossible to find and process sufficient rapid-disbursing loans to meet the situation."[144] An interim arrangement was urgently needed pending a long-term settlement of India's external debt.

In July 1967, anticipating a solution to the Indian debt-servicing problem, Woods proposed that the Bank offset the receipt of approximately $50 million in principal payments due during that fiscal year, by depositing an equivalent amount in a special non-interest-bearing account with the Reserve Bank of India (India's central bank), with no restrictions on its use.[145] India was negotiating with other creditors and Woods, in order to persuade other creditors to reschedule, offered to reschedule the Bank's own loans. However, Woods sprang the proposal on the Board without prior notification, informing it that "Counsel advises me that no formal action is required by the Executive Directors in this connection."[146] The action angered some members of the Board, who saw it as a disguised rescheduling and insisted on an opinion from the legal counsel regarding the legality of the proposed deposit. After the counsel opined in the president's favor, the arrangement was approved with one important modification:[147] interest would be charged at a rate equal to the average rate earned by the Bank from its liquid investments (that is, excluding loans).[148] Consciously or otherwise, an equivalence had been drawn between the Bank's largest capital contributor and its largest borrower. In both cases the institution used its large, liquid investment portfolio to provide it with greater operational flexibility when the two countries were facing severe balance of payments problems.

143. The Bank's share of total service payments due 1966–71 was 25 percent. Other large creditors were the United States (22 percent), Germany and the United Kingdom (each 15 percent), and Japan (13 percent). IBRD, "India: Debt Relief," IND 66-13, October 24, 1966, table 6.

144. Memorandum, Robert Cavanaugh to files, "Loans to India," April 21, 1967. Cavanaugh was then the treasurer of the Bank.

145. IBRD, "Statement by Chairman on India's Debt Servicing Problem," SecM67-183, July 11, 1967; and IBRD, "India's Debt Servicing Problem," R67-115, July 20, 1967.

146. IBRD, "Statement by Chairman on India's Debt Servicing Problem," SecM67-183, p. 2.

147. Lester Nurick, deputy general counsel, "Statement Regarding Legality of Proposed Deposit with Reserve Bank of India," SecM67-194, July 24, 1967. See also Nurick, "Notes Regarding Legality of Proposed Indian Deposit," draft memorandum dated July 17, 1967.

148. See Resolution 67-38, SM67-23, IDA/M67-19, July 25, 1967. France voted against the resolution.

In July 1967 the Bank appointed Guillaume Guindey as special consultant to assist on India's debt settlement.[149] His report, submitted in January 1968, proposed that members of the consortium provide debt relief in the amount of $300 million for the next three fiscal years, in order to reduce the burden of debt-service charges to approximately 20 percent of India's expected export earnings. In recognizing the Bank's position as "preferred creditor," it was agreed that its contribution be in the form of postponement of repayment of principal, with interest charged at rates specified in the applicable loan agreements on the postponed amounts. Since this imposed a lighter burden on the Bank in relation to other creditors, the Bank was to provide a larger amount of the debt relief than called for by the basic formula (10 percent).[150] At the Bank's insistence, it was acknowledged by the consultant and consortium, that the manner of its contribution must be somehow different from that of other creditors. Guindey had noted in his report that "the fact that the bulk of the resources of the Bank derive from its borrowing operations, clearly limits its freedom of action . . . therefore . . . the Bank is not able to provide its contribution in a form which would be equal in quality to the contributions of the country members."[151] Because of its position as "preferred or privileged" creditor, the Bank agreed to charge interest on any postponed amounts despite the "anomaly caused by increasing debt service charges through debt relief."[152]

According to Bank staff, the proposed Indian rescheduling, as recommended by the Guindey report, could be distinguished from previous international debt rescheduling exercises in three important ways, which stemmed from the nature of the debt problem itself: the fact that the Bank was a major creditor of the country involved; the country had not overindulged in short-term supplier credits; and "there [was] no question of a default or inability of the debtor country to meet its obligations."[153]

The executive directors' major concern over the proposed Indian rescheduling was the nature of the precedent that Bank participation would create.[154] The president informed the executive directors that the "only precedent being estab-

149. Guindey had served as director general of the BIS and, at the time, was chairman of the Caisse Centrale pour la Cooperation Economique.

150. See Guillaume Guindey, "Report," January 18, 1968, attachment to IBRD, "India's Debt Servicing Problem," R68-21, February 1, 1968. The president's report recommended that the Bank "postpone for each of the four Indian fiscal years beginning April 1, 1967, an amount of $15 million of principal repayments falling due on selected loans from the Government of India." IBRD, "India—Participation in Indian Debt Relief Action," R68-39, March 8, 1968, para. 7.

151. Guindey, "Report," pp. 14–15.

152. First draft of statement by Mr. Woods to the executive directors on February 23, 1968 (David A. Dunn, February 15, 1968), quoted in memorandum, Macedo to Heininger, June 30, 1981, p. 4.

153. Ibid., pp. 4–5.

154. See memorandum, Macedo to Heininger, June 30, 1981, p. 5.

lished is if a similar situation arises in the future we are not going to try to avoid it."
He described the situation as "extraordinary," "rare and unusual," and "if it comes
up in the future—must be examined on their merits." Noting that originally he took
the position that the World Bank should not participate in debt reschedulings,
Woods informed the executive directors:

> In view of the particular set of facts presented by the India situation I had a change of
> heart and if we, officers of the Bank and Executive Directors, do not take the position of
> enlightened creditors recognizing severe problems that this debtor had and take steps
> forward to meet problems we will do ourselves more damage than we may do if our
> subsequent Annual Reports show with respect to $10 million or $15 million of the
> servicing due to us, we have extended it for 10 years. The precedent of recognizing a
> financial problem, of stepping out to meet it and in taking that step to meet it with the aid
> of the best qualified talent we can hire in the world, is a very good one.[155]

A divided Board eventually approved the president's proposal.[156] The divisions
in the Board did not reflect objections to the proposed rescheduling per se but
rather arose from the management's reluctance to invoke its Articles as a basis of
rescheduling on this occasion as well as in the previous cases.[157] Several directors, citing
Article IV, Section 4(c), expressed the view that such action could be taken only after
India had applied for relief, which was not the case. In addition, it was not clearly
established that as serious as India's problem may have been, this was a case of acute
foreign exchange stringency that made it exceedingly difficult for India to service its
debt to the Bank. Woods felt that there was no need for insisting on an application from
India and bluntly told the Board that, unless the general counsel advised him
otherwise, he would not subject India to "the indignity of a pauper's oath." Woods's
opinion reflected the Area Department's strong objection to authorization of the
action under Article IV, Section 4(c),[158] since they considered that reliance on that
provision would imply India's inability to pay its debts, which was not the case.[159]

The general counsel, who was not present at the meeting, later submitted a
memorandum on the relevance of Article IV, Section 4(c) to the proposed rescheduling.[160] In his memorandum, Aron Broches argued that Section 4(c) did not
apply in the Indian case, since no application for relief had been made, and that in any
event the rescheduling could be undertaken under the Bank's general powers to adjust

155. Ibid., p. 5.
156. IBRD/IDA, "Minutes of Meeting of the Executive Directors of the Bank and IDA,"
SM68-14, IDA/M68-11, March 19, 1968.
157. See IBRD, "India—Proposed Participation in Indian Debt Relief Action,"
president's memorandum, R68-21, February 1, 1968.
158. IRD, *Articles of Agreement*, art. IV, sec. 4(c) authorizes relaxation of conditions of
payment on Bank loans when a member "suffers from an acute exchange stringency, so that the
service of any loans contracted by that member . . . cannot be provided in the stipulated manner."
159. See memorandum from Macedo to Heininger, June 30, 1981, p. 6.
160. See IBRD, "India—Participation in Indian Debt Relief Action," president's
memorandum, R68-39, March 8, 1968.

loan terms. He added, however, that should, contrary to his view, Section 4(c) be held to apply, this would not create any problem since the proposed rescheduling was consistent with the limits of the debt relief defined by the section.[161] A number of directors disagreed. One director, insisting that the section should apply, maintained that earlier contacts between the Bank and the Indian government constituted a formal application. Another contended that the section did not require an application and that the Bank could act on its own motion if the requirements of the section were met. He thereby requested that the minutes should show that in approving the rescheduling the Board was acting under Article IV, Section 4(c).

In the end, the minutes recorded that the "Executive Directors, noting that their action had been taken in the light of Article IV, Section 4(c) of the Bank's Articles of Agreement, agreed that within the next few months they should further discuss the legal and policy implications of that provision."[162] Such discussions never occurred.[163]

The Indian rescheduling was regarded as "unique" at the time, with the Bank having concluded that, on balance, the advantages of participation in this case outweighed the disadvantages. There does not seem to be any indication that the action, taken in conjunction with the Bank's major shareholders, resulted in any adverse reaction in the capital markets toward Bank bond issues. As circumstances and the balance of the Bank's interests changed in the early 1970s, it was made clear to India that Bank lending was to be conditional on the understanding that the Bank would not participate in any rescheduling.[164]

Conclusion

At the end of the 1950s, the Bank appeared to have overcome almost all of the financial hurdles that had confronted the institution in its formative years. Its capital had been doubled, its bonds had been upgraded to AAA, its reserves and net income were healthy and rapidly growing and, with the addition of IDA, it had at

161. Thus confirming another general counsel's observation that "the language of the section (Article IV, Section 4(a)) *like so many other provisions of the Articles, is ambiguous.*" IBRD, "Article V, Section 4(a), of the Articles of Agreement," R57-4, January 8, 1957, p. 1. Emphasis added.

162. Minutes of meeting, March 19, 1968, p. 4. See also memorandum, Macedo to Heininger, June 30, 1981, p. 6. Only two executive directors agreed with the general counsel's opinion, four were not sure, and five disagreed.

163. "In a dissenting opinion circulated by one executive director shortly after the meeting, it was pointed out, among other things, that a difficult balance of payments situation was a general problem, not particularly related to a Bank loan and that the inclusion of a special provision (Article IV, Section 4(c)) stipulating the conditions under which the Bank may act in view of a country's balance of payments situation would appear superfluous and unnecessary if the General Counsel's interpretation was accepted." Memorandum, Macedo to Heininger, June 30, 1981, p. 6, fn. 26.

164. Ibid.

its disposal a substantial pool of concessional resources. Both its incumbent president and the president-in-waiting had the full confidence of financial markets. Last, but hardly least, the institution's image in financial markets was excellent, as indicated by the opening paragraph of Standard & Poor's *Bond Selector:*

> Under excellent management, the World Bank has achieved the highest reputation for constructive action in international affairs, ranging even beyond the principal function of facilitating investment for productive purposes in member countries. Good earnings have resulted in the accumulation of large reserves and there is every indication that the Bank will continue to achieve favorable results.[165]

For a while, in the early 1960s, the Bank's new boldness reflected the institution's confidence in its financial health. Yet, over the remainder of the Woods presidency (1965–68), it was the limitations in the institution's access to financial resources and not a lack of vision that reined in its growth. The problems of the first IDA replenishment were a harbinger of what would almost become a ritualistic bloodletting with each IDA replenishment. And for reasons that were largely exogenous to the institution, the IBRD found itself cornered by its continued dependence on U.S. capital markets. With financial constraints boxing in the institution, the sitting president, increasingly embattled, could do little but ride out the storm. The lesson seemed clear: the institution's access to financial resources was crucial to its ambitions. It was a lesson the new president marked well.

---

165. "International Bank for Reconstruction and Development," *Bond Selector; Canadian-Foreign* (a publication of Standard & Poor's), December 15, 1960, p. 1000.

FIFTEEN

Riding the Credit Boom

The parable of the talents is a parable about power—about financial power—and it illuminates the great truth that all power is given us to be used, not to be wrapped in a napkin against risk.

—Robert McNamara, 1968[1]

WHEN Robert McNamara became the fifth president of the World Bank on April 1, 1968, he took over an institution that was financially solid, albeit perhaps stolid. The institution's financial environment was perceptibly changing as the locus of global savings and balance of payments surpluses shifted and new centers of capital began to emerge. The sedate world of banking was beginning to stir with the appearance of novel financial instruments. Bankers, hitherto preoccupied with asset management, now began to pay increasing attention to liability management.

Any president would have been forced to respond to these exogenous changes. But a new president, determined to sharply increase the scope and scale of the Bank's lending, could not achieve his objective by simply responding to exogenous changes in global financial trends. With the financial world revving up from the sedate pace of country driving to the more contentious pace of city driving, the new driver would have to constantly remaneuver the institution to stay ahead of the pack.

The financial story of the McNamara Bank has two distinct phases. Almost immediately after his arrival McNamara announced a doubling of Bank lending

---

1. Robert S. McNamara, "To the Board of Governors, Washington, D.C., September 30, 1968," in McNamara, *The McNamara Years at the World Bank: Major Policy Addresses of Robert S. McNamara 1968–1981* (Johns Hopkins University Press, 1981), p. 7.

over the next five years—fiscal 1969–73—which forms the first phase. During much of this period, however, persisting balance of payments problems in the United States restricted the IBRD's ability to tap its principal market, compelling it to seek out new markets. The Bank proved adept at mustering the resources, by gradually diversifying both its sources of borrowings—initially from Germany and increasingly from Japan—and the structure of its borrowings in its principal markets.

. The second phase, from 1974 to 1981, was precipitated by the first oil shock. The Bank responded by shifting track and striving to tap a new source of funds, from the Organization of Petroleum Exporting Countries. Borrowings from OPEC in the mid-1970s, however, proved to be a short interlude. The Bank again switched its borrowings, first to the U.S., German, and Swiss markets in 1976–77. Subsequently (1978–81), while the German and Swiss markets retained their importance as sources for Bank borrowings, the Bank almost completely withdrew from the U.S. market, shifting instead to Japan. Finally, at the end of the period, the Bank began tapping an entirely new market source: the Eurobond market. In comparison with its earlier history, this period witnessed much greater annual variance in the structure of Bank borrowings, between markets and official sources and within particular markets and official sources. The strategy unfolded partly as a response to the evolving nature of financial markets. As OECD countries relaxed capital controls, opportunities in nondollar markets grew. And as financial markets expanded, the Bank had less reason to rely on official borrowings.

Although the second half of the McNamara presidency witnessed a "coming of age" of the Bank as a borrower—"by 1975, the Bank had firmly established itself as one of the world's largest non-sovereign borrowers"[2]—by the mid-1970s, the institution was forced by capital constraints to rein in the rapid rise in its lending. In seeking to lift this constraint, the Bank was now compelled to rethink its financial policies. For much of the latter half of the 1970s the Bank struggled to augment its *financial capacity* to lend, as it sought to persuade its largest shareholder to accede to a capital increase and to arrive at a consensus among all shareholders on the terms of such an increase.

But the financial story of the McNamara Bank is more than a story of successful financial intermediation. It is also a search for institutional autonomy. His predecessor's travails had sensitized McNamara to a notable weakness in the institution's room for autonomy: the need to seek the consent of the country in whose market or in whose currency the IBRD could borrow. He, together with his treasurer, Eugene Rotberg, engineered an aggressive strategy for diversifying borrowings—in terms of countries, markets, instruments, terms, maturities—which, on the one hand, raised additional resources and, on the other, vastly broadened the markets and currencies of borrowings. At the same time, the strategy substantially augmented the institution's liquid resources, thus ensuring that the IBRD

2. Percy Mistry, "The World Bank's Role as a Borrower," draft, 1989, p. 209.

could now, to a greater extent, stay out of particular markets, whether for financial or for political reasons.

Cranking up the Borrowing Machine: 1968–73

Less than two months after taking over as president, Robert McNamara wrote out a set of detailed notes to himself. This "list of projects" would serve as a tactical road map as he set out in transforming the institution. A month later, he also had the basic blueprints of his first five-year lending program in place.[3] And with respect to the financial aspects of the institution, he laid out two basic goals for himself and the Bank: The first was to broaden the sources and instruments of IBRD financing, in particular, those outside the U.S.:

> Lay out in detail a borrowing schedule by country for each of the next five years, paying particular emphasis to Kuwait, Saudi Arabia and Libya.
>
> Develop new sources of financing: try to increase the holdings of the Bank's securities by the Central Banks. Break into the European pension trust market (we are now obtaining these funds only in Sweden); obtain approximately $50 million per year from Kuwait (the head of the Kuwaiti Fund is young, educated at California and HBS, and close to Rosen [then executive vice president of the International Finance Corporation]). See the Foreign Minister, who is a brother of the King and former Finance Minister, when he comes to the UN in September; arrange through Carli for annual sale of approximately $80 million of Bank bonds in the Italian market. Discuss with the Swiss Central Bank a FY69 Bank borrowing program of approximately $45–50 million.[4]

The second was to seek mechanisms to protect the Bank against funding risks:

> In the event the U.S. Government refuses permission for large borrowing for FY 69, develop a plan for standby credit with commercial banks.
>
> In the event that risks or high costs in the capital markets make it impossible or undesirable to borrow all of the funds required for the Bank's lending program, consider whether additional funds could be obtained by requesting member governments to pay in a portion of the subscribed but unpaid capital. A portion of such subscriptions perhaps could be scheduled for payment to the Bank over a period of years in local currency. It might be agreed that the additional payments would be used only for "conditional" financing.[5]

To achieve these goals, McNamara prepared to deploy his well-honed political skills, reminding himself to "develop strong personal relations with the governors of

3. Years later he commented on this early, headlong rush: "It's a little like being an architect. The most important contribution an architect can make is in his first 90 minutes, or 90 days. It's that first look, that first vision." Paul Hendrickson, "McNamara: The Jangling Riddles of a Man in Perpetual Motion," pt. 1 of 3, *Washington Post,* May 8, 1984, p. C4.

4. From Robert McNamara's notes, May 25, 1968, pp. 2, 5.

5. Ibid., p. 3.

central banks and the key governors of the World Bank. Write them a note every now and then thanking them for their assistance."[6]

Over the next few years, McNamara periodically drew up new lists constantly trying to ferret out new pockets of savings that the Bank could intermediate. These ranged from initiating reviews of the world's capital markets and the channels and instruments most appropriate for the Bank to tap these markets to meeting Chicago bankers, improving the "liquidity" clause of the IBRD's two-year Central Bank notes to make them more attractive to central banks, and repeatedly reminding himself to "develop strong personal relations with the Governors of Central Banks and the key Governors of the World Bank."[7]

McNamara had good reason to keep in mind that with respect to the Bank's borrowings, he had to assiduously cultivate a constituency other than financial markets. In the previous five-year period, more than 50 percent of the Bank's gross borrowings had emanated from the central banks and governments of member governments, principally in the form of their subscriptions to the Bank's two-year central bank offerings. Over the next five years, even while the Bank's gross borrowings would increase to $6.8 billion from $2.3 billion in the previous five-year period, the share of central banks and governments would climb to 60 percent. At a time when financial instruments had a limited range, the IBRD's debt instruments offered a welcome diversification and yield pickup for central banks. The fact that their governments were also shareholders of the institution undoubtedly facilitated matters.

The need to cultivate central banks and other governments was underscored by the continued tenuousness of the Bank's access to the U.S. market. Faced with continued pressures on the dollar, in January 1968 President Johnson announced further capital controls. U.S. corporations could no longer raise dollars for investment abroad in developed countries. As noted earlier, in 1964 the United States had imposed borrowing restrictions on the Bank to contain its capital outflows. The Bank had continued to borrow with the proviso that the proceeds would be invested in U.S. dollar funds, in interest-bearing time deposits, and U.S. government and agency obligations. McNamara rapidly reached a similar understanding with the United States after his arrival. The Bank would be allowed to launch a $250 million issue in the U.S. market subject to two conditions: it would "'lock up' through FY '70 in medium-term securities whatever it borrow[ed] in the United States in FY '69"; and "would use its 'best efforts' to increase non-US borrowing to 50 percent of total borrowing."[8] Under these assurances to the U.S. government, the Bank in 1969 committed to "hold approximately $1 billion in investments over

6. Ibid., p. 5.

7. See Robert McNamara, "List of Projects," April 21, 1969, p. 4. See also August 2, 1969; January 29, 1971; October 23, 1971; December 1, 1972.

8. Robert McNamara, "Memorandum of Conversation with Secretary of Treasury Fowler," July 17, 1968.

one year (excluding U.S. Treasury notes or bonds) through at least June 30, 1970."[9] Agency securities were not released to the market, but held to maturity and the proceeds reinvested.

Shortly after his arrival, McNamara made the rounds of financial markets, traveling to New York several times in his first few months, as well as to Frankfurt and Zurich. One of his first acts was to challenge the existing underwriting arrangements under which Morgan Stanley and First Boston had served as the Bank's only underwriters in the U.S. market since 1952. The arrangement was in tune with the general climate of "relationship banking" that characterized investment banking at the time, wherein client relationships were all important and there was little price competition. Given George Woods's antecedents from this community, it was not surprising that he had not questioned the arrangement. McNamara regarded the existing underwriting arrangements as a little too cozy. Furthermore, in the course of his discussions he had become aware that the secondary market for the Bank's bonds was fairly thin. Consequently, he made an early decision to add Salomon Brothers to the Bank's underwriters, because of the firm's acknowledged strengths in this area. Although both Morgan Stanley and First Boston protested against the addition, they could do little but go along;[10] the Bank was too important a client, and McNamara too strong a president for them to have acted otherwise.

According to one participant, the payoffs were apparent in McNamara's first deal after taking over as president:

> McNamara was an imposing and intimidating kind of client, and in this case he didn't like our price recommendation. And Larry Parker, who was negotiating for us [Morgan Stanley] said, "Well I've got to go and consult my partners," and he got up to leave. Then John Gutfreund [of Salomon Brothers] said, in a whimsical way, "Well, I guess I'll have to go and consult my partner, too." Then he paused and said: "Well, she's always said yes to whatever I want to do. I guess we'll go along." It's putting a hell of a lot of pressure on the other guy when John in effect says, in a cute fashion, "I'll do what you want, McNamara, and we'll make First Boston and Morgan Stanley follow it."[11]

At his first Annual Meeting speech, McNamara announced that "the Bank Group should during the next five years lend twice as much as during the past five

9. IBRD, "Investment of Bank Funds in United States Government Securities," R69-186, September 10, 1969, p. 2. Investment limits in time deposits which had been initially set at $150 million in 1958, had been gradually raised to $700 million in 1969, and were further raised to $1,200 million in 1972.

10. According to McNamara, First Boston threatened to quit if other underwriters were brought in, but recanted when McNamara instead threatened to fire them. Robert McNamara, interview with the authors, May 16, 1990. The lead management group in the U.S. dollar domestic market was further expanded in 1980 with the addition of Goldman Sachs and Merrill Lynch. Shearson Lehman joined in 1988.

11. Institutional Investor, *The Way It Was: An Oral History of Twenty Years of Finance* (New York: Institutional Investor, 1987), p. 43.

years."[12] Several months later, in an address to the Bond Club in New York in May 1969, McNamara announced that the Bank would increase its net borrowings to $600 million a year, which equaled 1 percent of long-term funds raised in the capital markets of industrialized countries and was sufficient to sustain both a doubling of the Bank's lending over the next five years as well as a substantial increase in the liquidity that had been drawn down in the previous years.[13]

The seemingly radical tone of his inaugural Annual Meeting speech, with its strong criticism of past development strategies (see chapter 5), did not go over well with the financial community. The influential German weekly *Die Zeit* characterized his speech as "simple, impressive and naive."[14] The *New York Times*, commenting on the three major groups likely to provide McNamara with "stiff resistance" in switching to the new course, put the first as "the relatively small number of men who make the market for its bonds."[15] For the new president, it was clear where the nub of his problem lay.

Remarkably, at the same time that McNamara was announcing a doubling in the Bank's lending over the next five years, one of the most prominent commercial bankers announced a 15 percent earnings growth target for *his* institution—in other words, a doubling of earnings over the next five years. While McNamara's objectives for the World Bank were very different from those of Walter Wriston for Citibank, both shared a common ambition in seeking the rapid growth of their institutions. But initially, at least, the markets appeared less willing to accommodate McNamara's ambitions.

The Bank's first issue following the speech—"a goddamn measly" SF 80 million (then $18.6 million)—was a failure, with almost half of the issue remaining in the hands of the underwriting group of the big three Swiss banking troika.[16] Later folklore—including the Swiss underwriters—blamed the failure on McNamara's radical speech. The financially prudent Swiss banking community may well have regarded McNamara's declaration in his Annual Meeting speech that he did not "believe that the utter avoidance of risks is the path of prudence or wisdom" as

12. McNamara, "Speech to the Board of Governors, Washington, D.C., September 30, 1968," p. 6.

13. Robert S. McNamara, "Address to Bond Club, New York, May 14, 1969," in McNamara, *The McNamara Years at the World Bank*, pp. 53–66. This was triple the net borrowings in the previous five years. In reality the Bank's net borrowings averaged $781 million over the period fiscal 1969–73.

14. *Die Zeit*, October 4, 1968. It later expressed "regret about the insipid comment on McNamara's speech" in a letter from Theo Sommer to William Clark, October 10, 1968.

15. The other two obstacles were Congress, "especially the Senate Foreign Relations Committee," which held the key to an impending IDA replenishment, and developing-country politicians, "who must be made to realize that investment in education and agriculture can make greater contributions to economic growth than outsized steel mills." *New York Times*, October 1, 1968.

16. Robert S. McNamara, interview with the authors, May 16, 1990.

somewhat ill-advised. However, notwithstanding the claim by the managing partner of a Zurich private bank that "it was no surprise that the issue flopped after the speech of McNamara outlining the social aims of the bank's new lending policies,"[17] the "plain fact was that the Swiss banks responsible for the issue had misjudged the market. The criticism of World Bank policies which had found their way into the press seemed due as much as anything to feelings of pique on the part of some Swiss bankers."[18]

Following the failure of the bond issue, the Bank's treasurer, Cavanaugh, resigned. He had been convinced all along that the Bank simply could not raise resources on the scale that McNamara had in mind. McNamara in turn wanted someone who shared his bullish vision for the Bank. And he rapidly found a kindred spirit in a new treasurer, Eugene Rotberg, who would later be eulogized as "The-Man-Who-Raised-$100 billion" in his two decades at the World Bank.

At the time, Rotberg was an associate director at the Securities and Exchange Commission. He and his colleagues at the SEC had acquired prominence through their involvement in efforts to open up Wall Street to competition by restricting the highly anticompetitive practices of the securities markets.[19] The U.S. presidential election campaign in the fall of 1968 had convinced Rotberg to look for a new job. By his own admission his "knowledge of the bond market was *de minimis*" and he shared with many others at the SEC a "somewhat cynical attitude toward the role of financial intermediaries, particularly their perceived importance to an economy or society."[20] This did not faze McNamara. Whatever it was about Rotberg—his

17. "World Bank's Sale of New-Bond Issue Assailed by Swiss," *New York Times,* December 9, 1968, p. L71.

18. Memorandum, Dennis Rickett to files, "Dr. Stopper's Visit with Mr. McNamara," April 18, 1969. At the time Stopper was the president of the Swiss National Bank. To try to set the record straight the Swiss National Bank analyzed the causes behind the poor performance of this issue. Apparently in pricing the issue, too much weight was attached to domestic Swiss rates and too little to international rates, in particular the relationship between the Swiss and German markets. The sixteen-year bonds carrying a 5¼ percent coupon were issued at 99 percent, for an effective yield of 5.303 percent. Just two months earlier the Bank had sold DM400 million of twelve-year bonds carrying a 6½ percent coupon at par, with a prospective deutsche mark revaluation around the corner. "Swiss Miss," *Economist,* November 9, 1968, p. 86.

19. Rotberg had earlier served as chief counsel in the Office of Policy Research at the SEC and coauthored a landmark "Special Study of Securities Markets," which launched a tortuous, decade-long, process of opening the U.S. securities industry to effective competition. See Joel Seligman, *The Transformation of Wall Street: A History of the Securities and Exchange Commission and Modern Corporate Finance* (Houghton Mifflin, 1982), pp. 388–405.

20. Eugene H. Rotberg, interview, World Bank Oral History Program, April 22, 1994, pp. 4–5. When asked by McNamara what he thought of investment bankers, Rotberg recalls having stated, "Well, I'm trying to put most of them in jail for violations of the Sherman Act, or to prevent them from engaging in practices like price-fixing." And as for commercial bankers, they were "people who wore white buck shoes on little boats around Long Island Sound and holding martinis in the summertime." Ibid., pp. 8–9.

candor, strong sense of public service, or his sangfroid—McNamara offered him the job as the Bank's treasurer, saying, "It beats the hell out of selling automobiles."[21]

Both McNamara and Rotberg knew little about banking, although McNamara was certainly knowledgeable about corporate finance, having served as controller of the Ford Motor Company. He would later claim to have retained two lessons from his bank management professor at Harvard Business School: First, "Always set up a reserve for a risk you know not where." And second, "There's nothing you can't buy or sell at a price."[22] For his part, Rotberg had developed an outstanding institutional knowledge of Wall Street firms and how they really operated. Their ignorance of banking was probably just as well. With major changes in financial markets in the offing, a neophyte had an advantage in not being particularly burdened by the old ways of doing things. But, perhaps more than anything else, both shared a trait that would resonate with the psychology of financial markets. If there is one truism about financial markets, it is that they are all about confidence. And confidence was one quality that the Bank's new president and treasurer possessed in magnificent abundance.

At the time, McNamara's single-minded concern with financing the Bank by rapidly expanding its borrowing program appeared to face formidable obstacles. He could hardly have been aware that an era—the postwar "golden age" during which the richer nations had witnessed an unparalleled era of economic growth and financial stability—was coming to a close. In November 1968 enormous capital flows into Germany (principally from France and the United Kingdom) sent international currency markets into turmoil. Market volatility would markedly increase over the next five years. The collapse of Penn Central in the United States in 1970, the suspension of dollar convertibility a year later, the move to floating exchange rates, the oil shock in 1973, the collapse of Franklin National Bank in the United States and the Herstatt Bank in Germany in 1974, would all keep financial markets on edge. Yet amidst all the tumult, new opportunities would present themselves as policy decisions and technological advances would radically transform global financial markets and the scope and instruments of financial intermediation.

The Bank's bonds occupied a small segment of domestic capital markets, that reserved for foreign (that is, nonresident) borrowers. Over the 1960s, its share of public issues in the United States and Germany (its largest markets) had been about 0.4 percent.[23] Its access to these markets was often affected by government interventions in the pursuit of domestic policy objectives. When countries faced

---

21. Ibid., p. 9.

22. McNamara, interview with the authors, May 16, 1990.

23. IBRD, "IBRD Financial Operations, FY74–78," R71-276, December 15, 1971, pp. 23–25.

rising balance of payments surpluses, they would attempt to stimulate access to foreign borrowers, hoping that the resulting capital outflows would reduce the pressures on appreciation of the domestic currency.[24] The reverse position—curtailment of borrower access to reduce (it can never totally prevent) capital outflows—was normally associated with weak balance of payment positions and concomitant efforts to reduce downward pressures on the domestic currency. The continued pressures on the dollar, along with large capital inflows into Germany in 1968–69, and Japan's emergence as a net creditor in 1969, for the first time since World War II, were harbingers of the shifts in the Bank's borrowings.[25]

The Bank's access problems in the U.S. market were amplified by a severe bear market in the sort of long-term, fixed-interest-rate bonds that had been the staple of its borrowings. The U.S. bond market had been in decline for more than two decades. In May 1968, *Institutional Investor* magazine in a cover story entitled "Can the bond market survive?" lamented: "There is a nagging suspicion that bonds as they have existed in the past are something of an anachronism as a modern investment vehicle."[26] When the Bank first went to the bond market in 1947, interest rates for fixed-rate, long-term bonds, were 2.5 percent. A decade later, in 1956, they climbed to 3.5 percent, and soon jumped to 4.5 percent in 1959. By 1966, interest rates had again climbed, now to 5.5 percent. In March 1969, the New York Telephone Company, an AAA borrower, issued forty-year bonds bearing 7½ percent coupons. By the end of the year, similarly regarded borrowers were paying 9 percent. The secular increase in bond rates meant that bond investors had suffered significant losses over the previous quarter century. Major institutional investors in bonds, such as university endowments and pension funds, began to move out of bonds into financial instruments with shorter maturities, more equity features, and new short-term investment vehicles, such as floating rate notes.

Following a $250 million issue in September 1968, the Bank stayed away from the U.S. market for the next two years, fearing that the "softness" of that market made the success of an issue unpredictable. Responding to the changing asset preferences of major purchases of its bonds in U.S. markets, the IBRD introduced

24. In those years the proceeds of nonresident borrowings in a domestic capital market were usually converted by the borrower into U.S. dollars, the principal international settlement and trade currency. Large purchases of U.S. dollars could thus affect the exchange rate of the currency being sold since in bear markets they amplified prevailing downward pressures, while in bull markets they reduced pressures toward a currency revaluation.

25. Lawrence Krause and Sueo Sekiguchi, "Japan and the World Economy," in Hugh Patrick and Henry Rosovsky, eds., *Asia's New Giant: How the Japanese Economy Works* (Brookings, 1976), pp. 441–42.

26. John F. Lyons, "Can the Bond Market Survive," *The Institutional Investor*, vol. 3 (May 1969), p. 34.

borrowings in the intermediate-term market (original maturities of five years or less), on which the U.S. government drew heavily.[27] Although, at the time, nearly a third of the Bank's funded debt was already of intermediate maturity, this debt was entirely held by public institutions, mainly central banks. Prior to this change, the Bank's public issues were almost exclusively long-term obligations with maturities of ten to thirty years. Despite the introduction of the new instrument, it is interesting to note that the Bank stayed away from the U.S. market for six of the thirteen years of the McNamara presidency, continuing a trend begun under Woods.[28]

From fiscal 1969 to 1973, the Bank's gross and net borrowings almost tripled and quadrupled, respectively, in relation to those of the previous five years (table 15-1). Borrowings from central banks and official sources had emerged as an important source of IBRD funding since the mid-1960s and continued to remain so until the late 1970s (tables 15-1 and 15-2). There was a significant change in the country distribution of borrowings with the U.S. share dropping markedly (16 percent). Japan emerged as the largest source of net borrowings during this period (27 percent), although Germany held the largest share of the Bank's outstanding debt (29 percent), which reflects the sizable balance of payments surpluses in those two countries. Switzerland, whose importance grew markedly over the 1970s, was a modest market in these early years. The other notable change occurred in borrowings in Saudi Arabia, Kuwait, and Libya, which together accounted for 5 percent of net borrowings.[29]

Public borrowings in other markets were minor. In several cases, in the late 1960s and early 1970s, these borrowings were not undertaken for volume or price reasons, but because they were useful in making the Bank's case with the U.S. authorities, that it was attempting to make all efforts to go to other markets. It borrowed in the United Kingdom in 1971, after a lapse of twelve years, and in France and Canada in 1972.[30] In all three cases, the Bank abstained from further borrowings over the rest of the decade. While the Bank did make a few public offerings in the smaller European countries over the 1970s, many of them were regular subscribers to the Bank's two-year central bank issues.[31]

Changes in the currency composition of the Bank's debt mirrored the shifts in markets (table 15-2). The dollar's decline in the funded share of the Bank (from 74 percent in 1969 to 39 percent in 1973), would be reflected in lower nominal borrowing costs, larger borrowing volumes, and increased institutional autonomy.

27. IBRD, "IBRD Borrowing in Intermediate Term Market," R70-203, October 28, 1970.

28. The years were 1970, 1973–74, 1979–81. In the Woods era, the Bank had abstained from the U.S. market in 1963–64 and 1966.

29. IBRD, "Revision of IBRD/IDA Program, FY74–78," R74-115, June 4, 1974, p. 34.

30. The 150 million Euro-franc borrowing was arranged by six banks headed by Lazard Frères and a syndicate of about sixty banks.

31. These included Austria, Belgium, Denmark, and Italy.

Table 15-1. *Evolution of World Bank Borrowings, 1964–81*
$U.S. millions, annual averages

Type of borrowing	1964–68[a]	1969–73	1974–77	1978–81
Volume				
Gross borrowings	490	1,359	3,474	4,741
Net borrowings	201	781	2,315	2,534
Borrowings outstanding (end of period)	3,524	8,882	18,478	27,798
Sources				
Medium- and long-term borrowing				
Total markets	234	617	1,777	3,166
Public offerings	n.a.	n.a.	1,194	1,565
Private offerings	n.a.	n.a.	584	1,602
Central banks and governments	255	742	1,655	1,558
Short-term borrowing[b]	...	...	42	17
Maturity structure (years)				
Annual borrowings	8.9	7.1	n.a.	n.a.
Borrowings outstanding	8.2	8.5	n.a.	6.05
Loans outstanding	10.1	10.5	n.a.	9.71
Bond issues[c]				
World Bank	738	1,440	3,710	4,470
International organizations	1,068	2,139	6,473	8,370
Developing countries[d]	260	473	1,930	4,117
Total	4,564	8,289	26,341	40,326

Sources: World Bank Annual Reports; IBRD treasurer's office; Eugene Rotberg, *The World Bank: A Financial Appraisal* (1981). Note on average lives of lending and borrowings, prepared for World Bank management meetings with U.S. Treasury, ca. 1976.
  a. 1965–68 annual average for bond issues.
  b. Total of outstanding debt with maturity of one year or less.
  c. Calendar year annual average.
  d. Excluding Israel.
  n.a. Not available.

Table 15-2. *Evolution of World Bank Borrowings: Classification of Outstanding Debt, 1968–81*
End-of-period percentages

Classification	1968	1973	1977	1981
By source of borrowing				
Central banks and government accounts	30	47	35	27[a]
Other	70	53	65	73[a]
By country				
United States	41	27	28	17
Germany	22	29	24	23
Japan	...	16	9	16
Switzerland	6	5	8	15
Other	31	23	31	29
By currency composition of funded debt				
U.S. dollar	74	39	50	34
Deutsche mark	13	29	24	25
Yen	...	16	9	17
Swiss franc	6	5	9	18
Other	7	11	8	6

Sources: World Bank Annual Reports; IBRD Secretary's Report R71-276, p. 20; Rotberg, *The World Bank*.
  a. 1980 figure.

The shift would, however, come at a cost, less visible at the time. The Bank's loans were expressed in dollars, but loan disbursements—and corresponding repayment obligations—were increasingly in appreciating currencies (the deutsche mark and the yen).[32] Since the entire currency risk was borne by borrowers, the real financial costs of these loans would be much higher than the attractive nominal interest rates. The Bank and its borrowers faced a dilemma, although it did not appear so at the time. In an era of a depreciating dollar, a dollar World Bank was financially increasingly attractive. But that was at cross-purposes with the political imperatives of the Bank's management and most of its members, restive with the dominance of the United States.

Despite the tremendous increase in the volume of IBRD borrowings over the entire period (1968–81), the institution's share in the medium- and long-term segment of global financial intermediation—the international bond market—actually declined (from 16 percent before McNamara's arrival to 11 percent at the end of the 1970s). There can be little doubt that the rising tide of financial intermediation in the latter half of the 1970s lifted many boats with it, including the Bank.

The new markets in which the IBRD was now venturing were in different stages of liberalization with the central banks and monetary authorities carefully guarding access to these markets. Each had its distinctive institutional aspects, which posed different problems for the Bank. The institution's experience in three of the more important markets—Germany, Japan, and Switzerland—is examined next.

Borrowings in Germany

The Bank's borrowings in Germany had begun in 1957, with official borrowing from the Bundesbank. A series of private placements in U.S. dollars, and subsequently in deutsche marks, were started at the time. These were refinanced as each original borrowing matured, effectively giving the Bank access to long-term funds. The first public issue, lead-managed by the Deutsche Bank, had been launched in 1959. Of the Bank's principal markets, the deutsche mark market was the only one in which a sole-lead-manager arrangement (with Deutsche Bank as the lead manager) would prevail into the 1990s.

At the time, nonresident borrower access to the German bond market was regulated by the Capital Markets Subcommittee of the Bundesbank.[33] By mandating that all foreign deutsche mark issues be managed and underwritten by German banks, the Bundesbank's control over these borrowings was ensured. The arrangements between the World Bank and the Bundesbank were largely in the form of

32. The Bank paid for contracts under a project in the currency billed by the supplier, converting the currency of disbursement into the currency needed to pay the bills. The U.S. dollar equivalent of the currency disbursed was deducted from the U.S. dollar face value of the loan until the loan was fully disbursed.

33. As part of its market liberalization moves, the Bundesbank abolished this committee in the mid-1980s.

verbal gentlemen's agreements. Although there were no specific quantitative ceilings on the Bank's deutsche mark borrowings, the Bundesbank required the Bank to clear all proposed deutsche mark borrowings, whether or not transacted in Germany, and whether through bond issues, private placements, or loans. The only impediment placed by the Bundesbank on the Bank's deutsche mark borrowings was its refusal to grant the Bank permission to borrow deutsche marks from central banks/official sources other than OPEC, stemming from a concern in those days that the deutsche mark should not become a reserve currency.[34]

Immediately following McNamara's arrival, the mutual interests of the Bank and Germany for an expansion of the Bank's borrowings were almost thwarted by idiosyncratic personal factors. The then German minister of economics, Karl Schiller, was unhappy with the "impolite handling" of his proposal to have Otto Donner nominated to the Pearson Commission.[35] Schiller also let it be known that if the purported invitation of the German government to hold the 1970 annual meetings in Berlin was not taken up, his government would suffer a loss of face.[36] Furthermore, Schiller sought to make a linkage between Bank borrowings in German capital markets and appointment of a German Vice President in the World Bank.[37] McNamara refused and, though just a few months earlier the Bank was being asked to raise its borrowings in Germany, Schiller began expressing concern over the impact of large IBRD issues on German interest rates.[38]

However, matters were duly sorted out and the Bank's borrowings dramatically escalated in Germany, both through private placements with the Bundesbank and market offerings. A new source of savings was tapped in Germany—the savings bank network. Although medium- and long-term capital market conditions were also deteriorating in Europe, in tandem with U.S. market conditions (the Bank was borrowing deutsche marks at 6 percent and yen at 7.14 percent), the Bank found it worthwhile to borrow because, as Rotberg put it, "even at an 8% rate, the proceeds could be profitably placed, at present, in time deposits in the United States, where the rate on 12–15 month deposits was 10%."[39]

34. The principal source of such borrowings was the Saudi Arabian Monetary Agency.

35. Memorandum, J. W. Strobl to William Clark, "Notes on Bank-German Relations," February 5, 1969, p. 1. Apparently the Bank did not have a say in the selection of the panel members of the Pearson Commission. Lester Pearson had instead opted for Wilfred Guth, then chairman of Deutsche Bank.

36. Memorandum, Siem Alderwereld to Robert S. McNamara, "Discussion with Karl Schiller, Minister of Economics, FRG," October 3, 1968. On being informed of this position of the German government by William Clark, Fritz Caspari (then Willy Brandt's chef de cabinet) was reportedly "deeply shocked" since Brandt himself "was very skeptical of involving Berlin in the affairs of an international but Western organization such as IBRD."

37. His candidate being Wilhelm Hanemann, deputy assistant secretary in the German Economics Ministry. See also IBRD, minutes of President's Council, April 7, 1969.

38. Memorandum, Robert S. McNamara to Siem Aldewereld, December 9, 1968.

39. SSM/M/69-25, August 19, 1969. There is no mention in these minutes of possible exchange rate risks. This issue is taken up later in the chapter.

The fact that the IBRD was an important and prestigious client and that many financial institutions would have liked to have its business meant that in Germany, as elsewhere, the choice of underwriting institutions or the composition of underwriting syndicates, posed delicate judgments for the Bank. In 1968 and 1969 the IBRD placed, in four operations, a total of DM 950 million with the Westdeutsche Landesbank (WLG) and Deutsche Girozentrale-Deutsche Kommunalbank (DGZ).[40] Subsequently, facing a decline in liquidity and increased domestic demands for private placements, the WLG appealed to McNamara personally to allow the savings banks to play a more important role in the IBRD's public issue syndicate, then lead-managed by Deutsche Bank. Fearing that the official German establishment and the Bank's finance complex were too closely linked to the Deutsche Bank, the president of WLG paid a confidential visit to Washington in late 1971 to press his institution's case, bypassing the German executive director and even the Bank's own finance complex. Although McNamara did not change the issuing syndicate, he used the leverage provided by the prospective competitive offer from WLG to pressure Deutsche Bank to reduce issuing costs.

Borrowings in Japan

The rapid growth of the Bank's borrowings in Japan was in part happenstance. In 1969 Japan had, for the first time, emerged as a net creditor since the war. With a ballooning balance of payments surplus, Japan, like Germany, was seeking mechanisms to limit the surplus and thereby mitigate upward pressures on the yen.[41] Following the revisions of its quotas in the IMF, Japan emerged as the fifth largest shareholder in the Bank in 1970. Another factor influencing the Japanese decision to allow the Bank to borrow there was a sense of gratitude for the "the great contribution toward the development of the Japanese economy" made by the World Bank (Japan had recently graduated from Bank lending in 1965).[42] This set the pattern for the financial relationship between the Bank and Japan in succeeding years: Japan's burgeoning trade surpluses, its attempt to recycle them, partly to maintain harmony with its trading partners (particularly the United States) and partly for reasons related to the politics of "burden-sharing," and the relationship of these complex factors to Japan's financial contributions to the World Bank.

40. IBRD, *World Bank Annual Report, 1969*, pp. 26–27. At the time the WLG was the largest German bank, with deposits exceeding four times that of the Deutsche Bank. The WLG belonged to a group of regional banking institutions called "Landesbanken" (state banks) or "Girozentralen" (clearing banks). These institutions have served as the central banks for the German public savings banks as well as manage the liquid reserves of the savings banks.

41. At the time, 360 to the dollar.

42. IBRD, *World Bank International Development Association*, Annual Report (World Bank, 1970), p. 35.

In the first phase, in late 1969, Japan prepaid some of its loans to the Bank ($160 million). But Japan's surpluses were too large to be disposed of in such a manner. Shortly thereafter, the World Bank began to borrow directly from the Bank of Japan, beginning with a special issue of $100 million in early 1970.

This led to the beginning of the second phase, in 1970, with the opening of the Tokyo office of the Bank following Japan's emergence as one of the institution's five largest shareholders. When McNamara took the decision he was advised by his senior managers to restrict the office's role. In particular, the Bank's then vice president for finance, Siem Aldewereld, did not want any financial functions to be vested in the proposed office. And, most were strongly opposed to appointing a Japanese national to head the office, feeling that such a person "is bound to be 'their' man more than 'our' man."[43] But McNamara, who from the very beginning was convinced of Japan's importance as a potential source of funds for the Bank, recognized the political advantages to be gained and overruled his managers. Given the structural characteristics of Japanese financial markets at the time, which were under the strong regulatory grip of the Ministry of Finance, his move was to prove politically astute. The Tokyo office, unique among other Bank offices, was to be headed by a national of the country, seconded by the Ministry of Finance.[44] Its responsibilities were principally to raise funds in Japanese capital markets, although this gradually broadened to encompass operations related to joint and parallel cofinancing. Consequently, unlike any other office of the Bank outside its headquarters, it was administratively located under the Bank's finance complex.

At the time, capital markets in Japan were rudimentary and heavily regulated. Savings were largely placed in fixed-term bank savings accounts. The government and public institutions sold bonds to the banks, which held them in their portfolio until maturity.[45] The banks could, however, use government bonds as collateral for borrowings from the Bank of Japan. The Bank's first public issue in Japan was eased by the Asian Development Bank's (ADB) breakthrough, which in December 1970 became the first foreign borrower to float yen-denominated bonds (called *samurai* bonds) in Japan.[46] The ADB's task was facilitated by Japan's close links with the ADB, both as its largest shareholder (together with the United States) and the fact of the ADB's president being a former senior bureaucrat with the Ministry of

43. Memorandum, H. R. Ripman to Robert S. McNamara, "IBRD Office in Tokyo," November 5, 1969, p. 2. Ripman attributed the quotation to Burke Knapp.

44. The arrangement has continued to this day, although not without some reservations in several quarters of the Bank.

45. At the time more than a third of government bonds in Japan were bought by individuals, compared with less than 5 percent in the United States.

46. To accommodate the ADB issue, the Ministry of Finance had to modify or grant waivers on a host of regulations. See James Horne, *Japan's Financial Markets: Conflict and Consensus in Policymaking* (Sydney: George Allen and Unwin, 1985), p. 174.

Finance. The ADB issue, while officially a public issue, was closer to a private placement. The Bank's issue (at 11 billion yen, an order of magnitude larger than most bond issues in Japan at the time) was perhaps the first true public issue. For the government of Japan, which at the time was cautiously beginning to liberalize its capital markets, multilateral borrowers were a helpful mechanism in the early stages of the development of the domestic bond market. Local banks were encouraged to participate in bond issues of the multilateral development banks by making these issues eligible for use as collateral. In turn, the World Bank issues performed a useful function as price leaders in the Japanese market.

From the very beginning the Bank settled into a pattern of rotating the lead management for its domestic yen public issues among the big four Japanese securities firms (Nomura, Daiwa, Yamaichi, and Nikko), an arrangement that would later be extended to its Euroyen public issues.[47] In addition to learning how to handle the structural issues unique to the Japanese financial markets, the Bank had to adapt to a different negotiating style. Rotberg would later recollect one of the first IBRD borrowings in Japan:

> I had been told that in negotiating transactions in Japan there's a lot of ritual, that everything's very formal. I knew the cost of borrowing was going to end up at about 7 percent, and I didn't want to spend two months drinking tea until we got down to that point. I started off the meeting by saying: "Look, I know we're going to end up at 7 percent—that's already been decided by our betters, the Ministry of Finance. So let's just shake hands, say you've been delightful, and that's it." There was this impassive response: "Come back tomorrow." The next day, I come back and I'm told: "We've heard very much what you said; we know you don't want to negotiate or bargain. We know you believe that rates are arbitrarily set in Japan and we respect that. We can assure you that it's a fair price. The cost is 12 percent." I said "Fine, we can pay 4 percent." Two weeks later, after a lot of tea, we ended up at 7 percent.[48]

On the whole, the Bank's relations with Japan in the McNamara years were quite warm, ensuring the institution privileged access to Japanese capital markets. To an extent, the McNamara Bank was drawing upon the reservoir of goodwill the Bank had established for itself in the previous lending phase of the relationship. The Bank's contributions were still fresh in the minds of the concerned Japanese officials, several of whom had been active participants in Bank-funded projects.[49] At the same time, the Bank was undoubtedly served well by McNamara and Rotberg's astute cultivation of senior Japanese officials.

47. In mid-1991, the Bank temporarily suspended Nomura and Nikko from primary business for behavior "not up to the standards [the Bank] expect[s] of our financial partners." Letter, Ernest Stern to Lew Preston, September 5, 1991.

48. Eugene H. Rotberg in *The Way It Was: An Oral History of Twenty Years of Finance: 1967–1987,* compiled by the editors of *Institutional Investor* (New York: William Morrow, 1988), p. 243.

49. For instance, Finance Minister (and later Prime Minister) Fukuda had participated in loans from the Bank in 1957, a fact that he chose to share with McNamara twenty-one years later. Memorandum for the record, "Meeting with Prime Minister Fukuda," Tokyo, June 8, 1978.

To be sure, there were differences. The Ministry of Finance was always wary of the potential risks of large issues. It insisted that the Bank export the proceeds of its borrowings as rapidly as possible, as well as keep yen out on loan as long as possible. It also restricted the Bank's liquidity investments in yen and, toward the latter half of the McNamara regime, began to express uneasiness about what it perceived to be the Bank's overly aggressive management of its liquidity portfolio. There were other nonfinancial concerns as well (see chapter 18).[50]

However, unlike Germany, the Bank's borrowings in Japan had a greater annual variance, as they closely tracked the country's balance of payments fortunes. While Japan accounted for 27 percent of borrowings in 1969–73, its share was less than 15 percent during 1974–81, as it struggled with balance of payments problems following the oil shock. The Bank stayed away from the Japanese capital market for four years (August 1973 to July 1977), partly because the market was closed to nonresidents from the end of 1973 to mid-1975, but principally because interest rates were too high.

Borrowings in Switzerland

Switzerland was an unusual context for the Bank's borrowings because it was the only country with a major capital market that was not a member of the Bank. Switzerland was also unique in that it became a member of the regional development banks much before it joined the World Bank.[51]

Before the oil shock (1968–73), Switzerland was a relatively modest market for the Bank, which found borrowings in Germany and Japan more attractive. As in the U.S. and Japanese markets, the Bank used a rotational arrangement in Switzerland, with its public issues lead-managed alternately by the Swiss "Big Three": Union Bank of Switzerland, Swiss Bank Corporation, and Crédit Suisse. The arrangement reflected the reality of the Swiss franc market. Its strong cartel nature left the Bank with little choice (the Big Three captured nearly three-quarters of all public issues).

The Swiss market was not one of McNamara's favorites. He never quite forgave the Swiss bankers for the way they had handled his first bond offering. Thereafter, as he would state later, he made sure that he talked with them "with his hands in his pockets."[52] He was also puzzled by the Swiss market's pricing mechanism.[53] What annoyed McNamara the most about the Swiss market was his perception of price

50. Japan was perennially concerned with the volume of Bank (and especially IDA) lending to Southeast and East Asia and the low representation of Japanese staff in the Bank.

51. If Switzerland could have become a member of the Bank alone, without joining the IMF, it would have done so from quite early on. As it was, Switzerland and Brunei were the only countries where the insistence at Bretton Woods that a country had to join the IMF before it became a member of the Bank mattered.

52. McNamara, interview with the authors, May 16, 1990.

53. For instance, the continued large gap between public and privately placed issues seemed odd, given that arbitrage would be expected to gradually close the gap over time.

gouging by Swiss underwriters, whose commissions were by far the highest the Bank paid in any market.[54] At the time it was customary in Switzerland to allow several weeks between the printing of the prospectus (which included the price) and the offer to the public. Swiss underwriters therefore claimed that, in pricing an issue, they had to add a risk premium against price movements in the interim period. The Bank found little merit in this argument given the controls exercised over the market. The Swiss bankers, on the other hand, regarded McNamara's moralistic stance as irrelevant to business transactions.

The failure of an IDA referendum in Switzerland in 1976 did little to improve Bank management's views on Switzerland. At the end of the decade, McNamara paid a visit to Switzerland and, in a meeting with senior Swiss officials, vented his frustrations, calling the Swiss aid effort a "disgrace," asserting that the country had been enjoying a "free ride" by remaining eligible for procurement from the Bank Group, and that "Switzerland would be less of a nation if it did not become a member."[55]

What was less recognized was that the Bank, too, had been enjoying a free ride as a result of Switzerland's nonmembership. For the Swiss authorities were unique among the Bank's principal markets in not bringing nonfinancial issues into market-access considerations. But frustrations notwithstanding, the Swiss market grew increasingly important for the Bank after the first oil shock, particularly during 1978–81. The Swiss franc market was attractive both because it did not have significant capacity limitations or unpredictable access constraints for creditworthy nonresident issuers, although the Swiss National Bank maintained strict market control.[56] Like Germany and Holland, Switzerland periodically determined the "appropriate" aggregate volume of capital exports to modulate capital flows and exchange rate pressures.

Borrowings from Official Sources

Borrowings from central banks formed an important source of funds for the Bank and furthered the idea of the Bank as a credit cooperative. These borrowings, in the form of two-year bonds, had begun in 1956 and accounted for 20 percent of

54. In 1971, the fee was 3¼ percent. Senior staff meeting, SSM/M/71-19, June 30, 1971.

55. Memorandum for the record on a meeting with senior Swiss officials, December 17, 1980, pp. 1–2.

56. At the time, all foreign borrowings in Switzerland of SF 10 million or more, and bank loans with maturities of more than one year arranged for nonresidents, were subject to formal Swiss National Bank authorization. Payments of principal and interest had to be made in Switzerland in Swiss francs. Private placements were also subject to the Swiss National Bank's approval with a range from SF 20 million to 200 million. However, the World Bank was exempt from observing this ceiling.

all borrowings between 1964–68. In the early 1970s, total holdings by central banks in the Bank's two-year bond issues accounted for 0.5–0.7 percent of total gross reserves of the Bank's member countries, with central banks of developing countries accounting for 50–60 percent (about 1–1.5 percent of their reserves).[57] For the Bank, the benefits were more than just financial. There was a sound strategic reason as well, as the Bank nudged the central banks to become "more intimately [involved] in the Bank's affairs."[58] Cultivating close relations with governments and central banks meant that the governments would themselves approach the Bank when conditions were favorable, if there was a sudden increase in liquidity. In turn, the central banks of the member countries derived advantages of being able to place their liquidity into an institution where they had a stake. In the 1980s another reason would become important. During the debt crisis, the Bank's short-term central bank offerings would provide a safe haven to the central banks of several countries whose commercial debts were in default and who were avoiding placing their liquid assets in foreign banks fearful of legal action (see chapter 11).

The Liquidity Buildup

As noted earlier, from the very beginning McNamara was determined to build up the Bank's liquidity. One of his early "to do" lists emphasized the need to "analyze the probability that prohibitions on Bank borrowing in one or more of the major markets will be offset by increased access of the Bank to other markets." The principal justification for high liquidity was of course its safety-net aspect, in the eventuality that the Bank was unable to borrow as planned. This concern was heightened in McNamara's early years, owing to the large and increasing amounts the Bank was planning to borrow and the considerable uncertainty surrounding its borrowing plans. Underlying the uncertainty were the Bank's Articles of Agreement, which required the Bank to obtain the country's permission to borrow in its markets and currencies. In smaller markets, this access continued to be weighed on an issue-by-issue basis. In larger markets, access was renegotiated on an annual basis. The Bank tried to persuade governments to agree to extend access to their markets for three years at a time, but to no avail.

Periodically, the Bank was shut out of major markets at short notice. In July 1972 McNamara reported that the United States had denied the Bank permission to raise a $200 million bond issue, "in order to show Western Europe and Japan that it will not be a major capital exporter, no matter what the channel."[59] In early 1973 the United States expressed reluctance to back an increase in the Bank's two-year

57. During the 1970s, the largest subscribers for these two-year U.S. dollar issues were Saudi Arabia, Libya, and Italy.

58. Senior staff meeting, SSM/M/69-24, August 14, 1969.

59. Minutes of the President's Council, July 31, 1972.

central bank bond issues,[60] and again in 1974, refused permission for the Bank to issue $250 million in bonds.[61] Both Japan and Germany denied the Bank access to their markets in the aftermath of the oil shock. And in most other countries, domestic capital markets continued to remain closed to external borrowers.

The high levels of liquidity can be traced to other important factors as well.[62] Contrary to normal expectations of a carrying cost of liquidity, high levels of liquidity began to be justified for their high investment yields. The preferred access to capital markets and the protection afforded by its Articles precluding it from taking any currency risk, led the Bank to aggressively play with arbitrage possibilities.[63] Thus quite early Rotberg announced that "funds which the Bank had recently borrowed at 8 percent had been placed at rates as high as 10¼ percent."[64] In reality, while the former represented the average cost of borrowings in various currencies, the latter referred to U.S. dollars. With the yield curve remaining mostly negative in these years, except for one short period (in 1971, when the yield curve reverted to a positive slope as short-term rates fell from 10½ percent to 4⅝ percent), the Bank claimed to make substantial returns on its liquid investments, enough for it to justify large negative spreads in its loans. In essence, the liquidity pool was heavily weighted with dollars; and borrowers received loans with lower interest rates, but since the Bank disbursed hard, low-interest currencies, they also faced considerable exchange rate risks.

If high levels of liquidity served as an insurance against market-access risks, they also helped the Bank's management ensure greater institutional autonomy. The link between these two elements was later recognized by an executive director for the United States:

> Because the bank is required to obtain the permission of each country's authorities for its frequent borrowings, denial of permission has traditionally been a useful and discreet technique for major sponsor control. But the ability of the bank to now borrow in sizable amounts in a variety of major currencies, *as well as its acquisition of a large liquidity reserve* . . . has also served to reduce U.S. (and other sponsor) leverage.[65]

60. Minutes of the President's Council, March 5, 1973.

61. Minutes of the President's Council, February 4, 1974.

62. Liquidity levels, which were maintained at 50 percent of the following three years' borrowing requirements, were reduced to 40 percent in 1973. See IBRD, "IBRD Financial Policies," R73-55, March 27, 1973. It was clear from staff discussions that the assumptions underlying the previous policy were subjective. See IBRD/IDA, senior staff meeting, SSM/M/71-10, April 6, 1971.

63. "It would pay the Bank to borrow dollars in the United States, or borrow other currencies and to conserve its dollars if those dollars could be retained in its liquid portfolio." IBRD/IDA, senor staff minutes, SSM/M/70-4, February 2, 1970, p. 2.

64. Senior staff meeting, SSM/M69-33, November 10, 1969.

65. James Burnham, "Understanding the World Bank: A Dispassionate Analysis," in Doug Bandow and Ian Vasquez, eds., *Perpetuating Poverty: The World Bank, the IMF, and the Developing World* (Washington D.C.: Cato Institute, 1994), p. 78. Emphasis added. James Burnham was U.S. executive director for the Bank from 1982–85.

The Oil Crisis and Its Aftermath

During the first five years of the McNamara presidency the Bank underwent a dramatic transformation. Staffing levels, lending and borrowing volumes, number of projects and project objectives, studies and analysis, and rhetoric had all expanded at rapid rates. The institution had committed itself to more projects and to lending more money to the lower-income countries in five years than in the previous twenty-three years combined.

The key element underpinning McNamara's vision for the Bank and its role as a global institution was financial resources. In his first five years, lending commitments of the IBRD had more than doubled (from $4.3 billion between 1964 and 1968 to $8.9 billion between 1969 and 1973), while borrowings had expanded even more rapidly (from $2.5 billion to $6.8 billion). The greater financial capacity of the IBRD was paralleled by more than commensurate increases in the resources of IDA: its lending had tripled, to $3.9 billion, in relation to the earlier period, although the IFC's growth had been somewhat more sedate (chapter 13).[66]

The successful accomplishment of the bold, and what many had then regarded as rash, financial targets set in 1968 gave McNamara the confidence to set even more audacious goals for the Bank for the following five years (fiscal 1974–78). At the Bank's Annual General Meeting at Nairobi in September 1973, he outlined a significant shift in the qualitative focus of the Bank's goals and strategy. The proposed shift, in which poverty alleviation in its borrowing countries would now occupy center stage in the Bank's operations, would be backed, McNamara promised, by another near doubling of Bank group lending, from $13 billion to $22 billion. With inflation looming large, however, he underlined that real growth in lending would be a more modest 40 percent.

Barely a month after the Nairobi speech, OPEC announced a 70 percent increase in oil prices. By December 1973 a near quadrupling of oil prices (in dollar terms) would render moot many of the basic financial assumptions underlying McNamara's speech. The year had already begun on an uncertain note. Following the second devaluation of the dollar in February 1973, the major currencies of the world had been allowed to float. Further changes in financial markets would follow the February 1974 termination of capital controls in the United States (by removing the Interest Equalization Tax in place for more than a decade), a relaxation of the same in Germany, and an international banking crisis in mid-1974 following the collapse of Franklin National Bank in the United States and Herstatt Bank in Germany. But for the most part, these changes would be overshadowed by the radical transformation of global financial imbalances, in particular, the rapidly

66. Total financial commitments of the IBRD, IDA, and IFC, in current prices, was $5.8 billion in the period 1964–68 and $13.4 billion in the period 1969–73, a doubling in real terms.

escalating current account surpluses of the OPEC countries. Up to that point, the McNamara Bank had played its financial cards rather shrewdly in tracking the shifts in global savings, and in planning its borrowings accordingly. But the suddenness of the oil shock meant that the institution was pressed into a new, more reactive phase.

The effects of the oil shock on the Bank's members was immediate. The most important sources of the Bank's borrowings in the previous five years, Japan and Germany, faced large current account deficits which effectively closed their capital markets to the Bank. And the United States refused to permit the Bank to issue $250 million bonds in January 1974.[67] The hiatus in borrowings in Japan would last for three years and in Germany for eighteen months. The Bank would then have to assiduously cultivate a new market: the OPEC countries. As oil importers, many of the Bank's borrowers faced enormous new balance of payments pressures. In order to assist these countries, the Bank attempted to increase its lending but faced several major hurdles. Its capacity to increase lending would be reined in by the statutory confines posed by its limited capital. And, to the extent that it could significantly increase lending, the very reasons for doing so—the deteriorating external environment facing these countries—also called attention to the reduced creditworthiness of these countries, and therefore to the health of its loan portfolio. The resulting concern for the Bank's own standing in financial markets was amplified by the steady decline in some of the institution's principal financial indicators, forcing it to reexamine its financial policies.

Diversifying Borrowings: The Case of OPEC Countries

In early 1974 it appeared that the Bank had little choice but to seek new borrowings from the OPEC countries, whose burgeoning current account surpluses appeared to offer a ready source to tap into. Following the quadrupling of oil prices in December 1973, the Bank's research complex, under Hollis Chenery's leadership, undertook an extensive analysis of the effects of oil price increases.[68] Armed with early results on the adverse effects of the oil price increase on developing countries, senior staff traveled to major OPEC countries, particularly Iran, Kuwait, and Saudi Arabia and the OPEC headquarters in Vienna, to share their findings. Their conversations revealed that OPEC was quite unaware of the drastic resource implications of the oil price hikes for oil-importing developing countries. The Bank attempted to channel this sympathy into increased resources for the IBRD through greater borrowings and IDA contributions from OPEC.

67. Minutes of the President's Council, February 4, 1974.
68. "Implications of Increased Petroleum Prices since the Beginning of 1974," SecM74-25, January 1974; "Additional External Capital Requirements of Developing Countries—Interim Report," R74-43, March 5, 1974; "Prospects for the Developing Countries," Report 477, July 8, 1974.

Before the oil price increase of 1973, the IBRD's borrowings in OPEC countries had been principally through their participation in its central bank offerings. Indeed, as noted earlier, borrowing from these countries had been on McNamara's agenda from the very beginning. The first direct borrowing transactions in Saudi Arabia, with the Saudi Arabian Monetary Agency (SAMA), were in 1968 for US$30 million. This was followed by a series of uninterrupted subscriptions by SAMA to the Bank's two-year central bank issues for US$20 million per fiscal year. Borrowings in Kuwait totaled KD 130 million (US$304 million) between 1968 and 1973, and in Libya they totaled LD 40 million (US$129 million) in 1970 and 1973.

Following the oil shock, Bank borrowings from OPEC countries jumped dramatically, accounting for a third of all Bank borrowings in the period fiscal 1974–76.[69] In 1974 a number of major borrowing operations were conducted in Iran, Nigeria, Saudi Arabia, and Venezuela.[70] At the same time, OPEC countries more than doubled their subscriptions to the IBRD's two-year central bank issues. These countries were an important partner of the Bank in cofinancing projects amounting to nearly $3 billion between 1974 and 1981. Of this amount, the Saudi Fund for Development and the Kuwait Fund for Arab Economic Development accounted for $900 million and $850 million, respectively.

In turn, at the request of several OPEC countries, the Bank maintained technical assistance missions to help them in their investment decisions.[71] The Bank's management also actively canvassed for a larger capital share for OPEC members in the Bank in the 1976 selective capital increase. During this period, the quinquennial review of IMF quotas was under way, and OPEC's share was expected to increase from 5 to 10 percent. Although reviews of shares in the Bank's capital were normally based on parallelism with the Fund, in discussions with major OPEC countries McNamara offered to try to negotiate an increase in the OPEC countries' share to nearly 15 percent, which, given the record of the extreme difficulties in changing relative voting power in the IBRD, was quite an extraordinary offer.[72]

Yet, despite the early flurry of borrowings, OPEC proved to be a disappointing source of funds for the Bank, accounting for about 8 percent of all borrowings from

69. In the eighteen months following the oil shock, nearly 80 percent ($2.2 billion) of the Bank's net borrowings of $2.8 billion was raised from OPEC countries.

70. Two dollar borrowings from the government of Iran for US$350 million; a US$240 million borrowing from the government of Nigeria; two private placements of SRL 500 (US$141) million and US$750 million with SAMA; a US$400 million and Bs 430 (US$100) million loan from the Venezuela Investment Fund. Other borrowing operations included a Dh 300 (US$76) million borrowing from the UAE, and a US$30 million loan from Oman.

71. While the effort was most pronounced in Saudi Arabia, the Bank also provided small amounts of technical assistance to Kuwait, the United Arab Emirates, and Libya. The countries paid for much of this assistance.

72. Memorandum, Saad El-Fishawy for the record, "Saudi Arabia: Mr. McNamara's visit," April 7, 1975.

1977 to 1981. Although there was a modest recovery between 1982 and 1984 (nearly 12 percent of borrowings), borrowings from OPEC countries declined steadily thereafter. Between 1974 and 1981 capital contributions to the Bank Group (borrowings, IDA replenishments, and Third Window contributions) accounted for just 1.4 percent of OPEC's current account surplus. The combined share of the Bretton Woods institutions, about 2 percent, was little better.[73] This was in contrast to the much more generous disposition of OPEC toward oil-importing developing countries: the flow of funds to developing countries from OPEC accounted for 13 percent (excluding the IMF and the World Bank) of OPEC's current account surplus during this period.[74] But the principal channels of OPEC funds for developing countries remained either bilateral or new multilaterals such as the International Fund for Agricultural Development, where they hoped to exercise greater influence. Although OPEC recycled large amounts of capital flows to developing countries, clearly the World Bank was not a preferred option. Why was this the case?

IRAN. Initially, Iran appeared to offer the first major breakthrough for tapping OPEC capital surpluses. At the Shah's initiative, the president of the World Bank and the managing director of the IMF met with him in Tehran in February 1974.[75] The Shah proposed an equivalent of the Marshall Plan for the developing countries, with financing to be split equally between OPEC and the industrialized countries. While the fund would be jointly managed by the Bank and the IMF, its governance would be split three ways between the industrialized countries, OPEC, and developing countries.[76] The Shah's proposal met with a frosty reception from Saudi Arabia and an even more dismissive reaction by the United States. The Bank then concentrated on raising resources from OPEC through the more traditional channels of IBRD borrowings and IDA contributions.

Even though the Shah's proposal was a nonstarter, the Bank and Iran reached an understanding that Iran would cease to be a net borrower from the Bank. The

---

73. The figures are taken from Jahangir Amuzegar, "Oil Exporters' Economic Development in an Interdependent World," IMF Occasional Paper 18, April 1983, pp. 62–63, tables 27, 28.

74. Ibid., p. 63. Indeed, some of the OPEC countries, such as Kuwait and Saudi Arabia, had by far the highest share of ODA to GNP during this period.

75. According to Munir Benjenk, the Bank's vice president for the region at the time, the Shah was briefed on the resource implications for the developing countries by his prime minister who, in turn, had been given a detailed briefing by Munir Benjenk. Munir Benjenk, interview with the authors, March 2, 1995. See also Margaret de Vries, *The International Monetary Fund, 1972–78: Cooperation on Trial*, vol. 1: *Narrative Analysis* (International Monetary Fund, 1985), p. 317. According to one source, the size of the proposed fund was $3 billion. Anthony Sampson, *The Money Lenders* (London: Hodder and Stoughton, 1981), p. 266.

76. The proposed governance structure was analogous to that of IFAD as well as the "Energy Affiliate" (proposed by the Bank at the end of the decade).

government of Iran would loan $200 million to the Bank with a further $150 million loan in October 1974 to offset three loans made by the Bank to Iran in May 1974 totaling $148 million. However, the last two loans (totaling $52.5 million) made by the Bank to Iran later that year were not offset because of significant differences in the interpretation of the offset agreement. The Iranians claimed that offset should be based on disbursements (since their loans to the Bank disbursed immediately), whereas the Bank took the position that the offset should be based on commitments (since its own loans disbursed much more slowly). A major dispute over the Bank's lending operations in Iran (see chapter 9) further queered the pitch, and Iran refused to participate in IDA 5 and contribute to the Third Window. Relations appeared to thaw following meetings in early 1977, but the political upheavals in Iran that began in late 1977 put an end to any further borrowing possibilities.

SAUDI ARABIA. Borrowing terms were a hurdle early in negotiations with Saudi Arabia. An office memorandum of a meeting with Anwar Ali, governor of SAMA, records that "Mr. McNamara said he found it difficult to explain that the Bank would have to borrow for lending to poor countries at a rate higher than the IMF which was principally concerned with the problems of the rich countries."[77] However, later in the year, aided by the diplomacy of Mohammad Shoaib, McNamara reached an agreement with Anwar Ali that future borrowings would "be set on market terms (at the level of U.S. Agency securities of comparable maturity), but of course at a level no higher than paid by the IMF for funds borrowed from OPEC countries for re-lending to developing nations."[78] Agreement was reached on a $750 million loan from SAMA (the largest ever by the Bank). Unfortunately, Anwar Ali died shortly thereafter, and "market terms" proved to be a more ambiguous concept than was realized at the time. In June 1975 the Bank was looking to borrow $1.2 billion from Saudi Arabia. Within a few months this had been reduced to $600 million, and by the end of the year borrowings accounted for only $215 million. With the exception of 1976 (when it was just over $300 million), Bank borrowings from SAMA averaged less than $100 million a year between 1977 and 1981. SAMA felt that on direct loan transactions it should receive the market yield as well as the benefit of the full commissions which the Bank would have paid on

---

77. Memorandum, I. P. M. Cargill to files, "Visit of Mr. Anwar Ali, the Governor of the Saudian Monetary Fund in Jeddah," May 3, 1974. At about the same time, SAMA had agreed to lend SDR 1 billion in Saudi riyals for the IMF's oil facility (nearly a third of the total) at 7 percent. De Vries, *International Monetary Fund,* pp. 326, 346–47. The only Saudi riyal borrowing by the Bank in fiscal 1975 (SRL 500 million, or $141 million) was 8 percent ten-year bonds.

78. Memorandum of conversation between Anwar Ali and Robert S. McNamara, October 23, 1974. Shoaib, who had just retired as vice president in the Bank, had close personal ties to Anwar Ali from Pakistan when Shoaib had been finance minister and Anwar Ali had served in Pakistan's central bank.

private placements. SAMA also believed that it could get substantial reallowances from the Bank's underwriters and therefore could do better in the market than by dealing directly with the Bank. By contrast, Bank staff felt that they had been able to persuade other central banks, such as Bundesbank and the Bank of Japan, to buy IBRD securities at prevailing market rates without having to share the commissions with them, and the Bank could not act differently with SAMA.[79]

KUWAIT. The principal obstacles to borrowings in Kuwait were the choice of currencies and of underwriters. Kuwait desired the Bank to borrow in Kuwaiti dinars. The principal interlocutor of the Bank in Kuwait, Abdlatif Al-Hamad (then director-general of the Kuwait Fund), explained that dinar borrowings would provide a hedge against a depreciating dollar and help Kuwait to "internationalize" the currency as a medium of exchange. The Bank argued that the value of the dinar was not set by market forces and it could not be internationalized so long as the currency was unavailable as a short-maturity money market instrument or as a vehicle for international settlement of transactions. Moreover, borrowers were not keen to use a currency that was not used in international trade.

When the Bank demurred on borrowing in dinars (preferring U.S. dollars), the Kuwaitis insisted that the pricing be comparable to yields they could obtain in subscribing to "topclass" borrowers in the Eurobond market. The Bank, however, rejected any equivalence with "topclass" borrowers in Eurobond markets, arguing that was not a relevant benchmark.[80] Instead it initially suggested pricing based on a spread over U.S. bonds or alternatively equivalent to U.S. agency offerings, and when this was not accepted, it proposed yields approximately equivalent to the secondary market for its bonds.

Another bone of contention was the Kuwaiti government's insistence that the Bank deal through various Kuwaiti institutions, such as the Kuwait Investment Company (KIC) and Kuwait Foreign Trading and Investment Company (KFTIC), rather than in the form of direct placements with the government or with the Kuwait Central Bank. The Kuwaiti authorities believed that such an arrangement would be helpful in developing their domestic capital market. The Bank did make some public offerings in Kuwaiti dinars through KIC but objected to undertaking private placements through Kuwaiti institutions, arguing that the institutions were being used essentially as a channel for placing government funds. In turn, Kuwait interpreted this as a lack of desire on the Bank's part to work with Kuwaiti financial institutions.

VENEZUELA. Venezuela was the only other large potential source of borrowings. The Bank borrowed $500 million in 1974 from the Venezuelan Investment

---

79. Frictions with SAMA appear to have been compounded by the narrower concerns of SAMA's advisers (from Morgan Stanley, Robert Flemings and Company, Union Bank of Switzerland, and White Weld and Barings) on rates, maturity, and liquidity.

80. Eurobonds were, in general, more expensive than bond issues by foreign sovereign borrowers in domestic markets. The Bank stayed away from the Eurobond market until 1980.

Fund. Like Saudi Arabia and Kuwait, Venezuela insisted that part of the borrowing (in this case 20 percent) be in bolivars.[81] The Venezuelans had initially insisted on earmarking their contribution to the Bank for lending to Latin America but were persuaded otherwise after receiving assurances from the Bank's management that the Bank intended to substantially increase its lending to Latin America. In return the Bank agreed to establish a resident office in Caracas and agreed to provide Venezuela nonreimbursable technical assistance.[82] Yet within three years a planned $200 million bond issue failed to materialize, the Bank suspended its nonreimbursable technical assistance program (following a Board decision on the matter), and closed its Caracas office. These decisions were not received kindly, and the Venezuelan finance minister complained to McNamara that the "decision of the Bank's Management would seem to confirm the strong anti–Third World attitude of some Bank officials."[83] While ruffled feathers were smoothed, there were no further significant Bank borrowings from Venezuela.

Relations with OPEC: A Missed Opportunity?

In retrospect, the thwarted expectations of the IBRD in intermediating OPEC funds to developing countries were the result of a complex amalgam of factors. In the first place, IBRD debt instruments were somewhat unattractive given the marked preference for short-term liquid assets in OPEC investment portfolios: the bulk of OPEC investments were held in money market investments. Second, nonfinancial considerations were not important enough to tip the balance since the major OPEC countries may well have felt that the Bank—like so many other agencies and countries following the oil shock—was always asking for something, be it IDA, Third Window, capital subscriptions, cofinancing, or borrowings, while OPEC influence on basic policy matters concerning the Bank remained marginal.

Third, though more nebulous, there is reason to believe that the Bank was inattentive to its diplomatic style and negotiation skills.[84] Although McNamara took strong personal interest in courting the OPEC countries almost immediately after his arrival, the principal interlocutor for the Bank was its new vice president for finance, Peter Cargill, who had succeeded Siem Aldewereld in 1974. Cargill's imperial style (he had been in the elite Indian civil service in British India) was not the ideal fit for a situation where the Bank was soliciting funds. Furthermore, the organizational separation of that part of the Bank that had something to offer (its

81. The Bank wanted at most 5–10 percent of the borrowings to be in bolivars. The Bank accepted the Venezuelan position on the condition that future borrowings would be in dollars. Over the next decade, annual borrowings from Venezuela averaged less than $7 million.

82. Memorandum, Adalbert Krieger to Robert S. McNamara, "Briefing for the Meeting with the Venezuelan Delegation," June 12, 1974, and attached aide memoire.

83. Letter, Hector Hurtado to Robert S. McNamara, June 22, 1977.

84. Martijn Paijmans, interview with the authors, March 28, 1996.

technical assistance, housed in the operations complex), from the group negotiating its funding requirements, was not helpful in this particular milieu.

Finally, the Bank-OPEC relationship was also afflicted by the reverberations of OPEC's ostensible challenge to the status quo in global economic and political power, which was also echoed in other multilateral institutions. Through much of 1974–75, the United States viewed the rise in the price of oil as a threat to its political leadership and battled hard to roll back oil prices.[85] However, the Bank refused to endorse the U.S. position that rolling back oil prices would best serve the developing countries. Instead, in analyzing the consequences of the oil price increase on its members, it accepted the increases as a given. Such a stance had not endeared the Bank to its largest shareholder, which initially opposed any attempt aimed at providing large *official* balance of payments assistance to oil-importing developing countries, regarding such efforts as undermining its attempts to persuade these countries to put pressure on OPEC to roll back oil prices.[86] Subsequently, the United States also voiced strong opposition to any Bank lending to OPEC members.[87] The Bank contended that though several OPEC members had a capital surplus, they nonetheless wanted to avail themselves of the Bank's technical assistance and devised "offset" arrangements with countries such as Nigeria and Iran, whereby its borrowings from these countries corresponded to equivalent amounts of lending by the Bank at comparable terms.[88] This arrange-

85. A record of a meeting between McNamara and George Shultz, then Secretary of the treasury, notes, "Mr. Shultz appeared to think that if a sufficiently firm attitude were adopted by the oil-consuming countries, some reduction in the present prices could be secured." Memorandum, Denis Rickett for the record, "Discussions with Part I Countries: United States," January 28, 1974, p. 2.

86. The United States had opposed the formation of the IMF's Oil Facility, but Bill Dale, who was in the chair at the time, having just vacated the job as U.S. executive director at the IMF, ruled that this was not an issue on which the United States had veto power. John Williamson, personal communication. Total funding for the IMF's 1974 and 1975 Oil Facility amounted to $6.9 billion, of which OPEC contributed nearly $5 billion. The Fund had approached the Bank for a 500 million SDR loan for the facility. The Bank, however, declined on the grounds that its primary responsibility was to the developing countries. More than half of the drawings under the Oil Facility were made by OECD countries, particularly Italy and the United Kingdom. A separate Subsidy Account (totaling SDR 101 million) helped developing countries defray their interest costs on drawings from the Oil Facility. De Vries, *International Monetary Fund*, pp. 346–47, 352–55.

87. Memorandum, Rickett for the record, January 28, 1974. A later press report on the U.S. opposition to Bank lending to oil-producing countries quoted a "senior Treasury official" as stating, "What's wrong with taking a millionaire off welfare?" The target of this particular move was apparently Nigeria. "Money, Mysticism and Saving the World," *Washingtonian Magazine*, March 1975, p. 100.

88. An alternative arrangement—repurchase by the country's central bank either directly through the IBRD's loan portfolio or participation agreements on new loans—was considered, but not implemented. This arrangement, referred to as the "Thailand Formula," was based on a precedent set in the case of Thailand whereby the Bank's loans had been purchased by the country's central bank, in the period that Thailand was receiving large amounts of dollars from the expenditures of U.S. military forces.

ment was also opposed by the United States on the grounds that an OPEC country's loans to the Bank essentially entailed a transfer from the holdings of U.S. Treasury bills to Bank bond holdings and therefore did not burden the country's reserves, while it still received additional loans from the Bank.[89] However, quite rapidly, the Bank itself became increasingly reluctant to countenance offset arrangements as it began to face lending ceilings. Offset arrangements, it was argued, "crowded out" other borrowers since they inflated both the asset and liability side of the balance sheet.

A further problem arose from the heightened sensitivities that surround issues and countries in the Middle East. Articles in the U.S. media and the pro-Israeli lobby in the U.S. Congress attacked the Bank on the grounds that an "actual or potential reorientation of Bank policy seeking larger contributions from certain Arab OPEC nations could involve the Bank with the anti-Israeli activities promoted by these countries."[90] Later, the Bank was attacked for precisely the opposite bias.

At the end of the decade, following the second oil shock, the Bank's new vice president for Finance, Moeen Qureshi, attempted to inject greater warmth into the lukewarm relationship and held a series of meetings over the latter half of 1979 with both Kuwait and Saudi Arabia. However, an unexpected problem emerged on the eve of the 1979 annual meetings when Kuwait, Saudi Arabia, and other Arab countries objected to certain articles with an anti-Arab bias that had been reproduced in the press clippings routinely circulated to senior staff and executive directors for information by the Bank's External Relations Department.[91] Although the press clippings were for internal informational purposes, some executive directors circulated them to their home governments. Qureshi later reported to his new president, A. W. Clausen: "Al-Hamad informed me that both Al-Ateeqi and he were severely criticized at a meeting of the Arab League for supporting an institution which disseminated such anti-Arab propaganda."[92] Another sore point was the absence of any Arab representation in senior positions in the Bank.[93]

89. See IBRD, minutes of President's Council, December 9, 1974, and December 16, 1974. The United States was more favorably inclined to a buyback operation, even though there appeared to be little difference.

90. Letter, Representative David Obey to Robert S. McNamara, August 19, 1975. At the time Obey was a member of the Appropriations Committee in the U.S. Congress, which controlled appropriations for IDA. It is interesting that Obey, like many other members of the U.S. Congress, would choose to bring up issues directly with the president of the Bank rather than through the U.S. Treasury and the U.S. executive director's office, the official representative of the country in the Bank's Board.

91. Memorandum, Attila Karaosmanoglu for the record, "Mr. McNamara's Meeting with H. E. Sheikh Mohammed Abalkhalil, Minister of Finance and National Economy, Saudi Arabia," October 5, 1979.

92. Memorandum, Moeen A. Qureshi to A. W. Clausen, "Relations with Arab Countries," July 7, 1981. At the time, Al-Ateeqi was finance minister and Abdlatif Al-Hamad, head of the Kuwait Fund.

93. Various possibilities were considered for a vacancy opening up for a vice president for the West Africa region, as well as the possibility of a new vice presidency for handling all IDA negotiations, but for various reasons these attempts did not bear fruit for another couple of years.

But the renewed diplomacy by the Bank appeared to be bearing fruit when, in the spring of 1980, the Bank reached an understanding with the Ministry of Finance and National Economy and the governor of SAMA that SAMA would lend from $700 million to $1 billion to the Bank. The money was to be raised partly through direct borrowings and partly through public offerings.[94] The first large borrowing under this initiative was a placement of DM 200 million in July 1980. Shortly thereafter, a four-currency transaction for a total of $400 million was negotiated with SAMA but remained unsigned because of the "PLO issue." The Saudis and other Arab countries were furious at what they perceived as the partisan handling of the attendance of the Palestine Liberation Organization (PLO) at the 1980 Annual General Meeting by the managements of the Bretton Woods institutions. Saudi Arabia also delayed signing a $400 million loan agreement in the fiscal 1981 program.[95] While there was more than a hint of gamesmanship in the manner in which the Bretton Woods institutions handled this issue, there can be no doubt that with the IDA replenishment and the General Capital Increase languishing in the U.S. Congress, the Bank had no room to maneuver. As was the case with the decision to cease lending to Vietnam a year earlier, in balancing issues of principle with the interests of the institution and its broader membership, reliance on government funds tipped the balance.

Finally, it is interesting to speculate on whether, even if the Bank's efforts had been more successful, it would have mattered in a substantial way. Although the Bank's cost of funds are likely to have been lower, even if the Bank had conducted its *entire* gross borrowings (during the period 1974–81) in the OPEC countries, it would have accounted for just 7.5 percent of OPEC's current account surplus. For all its seeming salience, the Bank's very modest financial stature on the global stage is frequently forgotten. The availability of financial resources notwithstanding, the size of the Bank's subscribed capital was the fundamental constraint to its financial intermediation role. And, as discussed later, by 1975 the Bank's lending was subject to ceilings not because of borrowing constraints, but because of its limited authorized capital. The selective capital increase in 1976 and the 1979 GCI

94. The finance minister was Sheikh Mohamed Abalkhalil and the governor of SAMA, Abdul Aziz Al-Quraishi.

95. From briefing paper titled "Arab Countries," prepared for incoming President Clausen, n.d. (circa spring 1981). Although publicly the Arab countries had stopped lending to the Bank, in early 1981 SAMA relented, somewhat agreeing to lend to the Bank, but only through market purchases that would ensure anonymity. The Libyan Central Bank also conducted a "'silent' placement in Dutch guilders, despite the existence of the lending embargo." But large direct operations were ruled out. The PLO issue also delayed the SDR 8 billion ($10 billion) loan by Saudi Arabia to the IMF. The interest rate on that loan—the terms of which were eventually agreed to in February 1981 after nearly a year of negotiations—was the weighted average of rates on five-year government securities in the five SDR currencies. Suzanne Wittebort, "Saudi Arabia's New Clout at the IMF," *Institutional Investor,* September 1981, pp. 141–50.

reduced this lending constraint; by 1977 the Bank was again able to meet its borrowing requirements in the German, Japanese, and Swiss markets and consequently appears to have been less willing to accommodate special arrangements for the OPEC countries.

In retrospect, the "privatization" of the $433 billion OPEC current account surplus between 1974 and 1981 and the resulting easy access to funds from commercial banks reduced demand pressures from borrowers for IBRD funds, and correspondingly the institutions leverage as well (chapter 10). The small share (about 2 percent) of the Bretton Woods institutions in recycling this surplus would be an important factor in the debt crisis of the next decade.

Impact on Lending

As indicated earlier, the Bank's analysis in the aftermath of the oil shock offered a gloomy prognosis regarding the balance of payments deficits of developing countries. To assist its members, the Bank now proposed a sharp increase in its planned lending program (see table 15-3), although the higher figures also reflected higher inflation. IBRD lending, which had almost doubled in the two years following McNamara's arrival (averaging about $800 million in fiscal 1967–68 and $1.5 billion in fiscal 1969–70), plateaued around $2 billion over the next three years (fiscal 1971–73). Following the first oil shock there was a significant jump in lending, which more than doubled in the next two years (fiscal 1973–75), the most rapid increase since the 1950s (or since). Lending projections were substantially revised but even by early 1975, however, financial constraints began to put a brake on the rapid expansion.

At a meeting called to review the Brazil CPP and the lending program for fiscal 1976–80, McNamara decided to overrule the region's recommendation and cut the lending program to $3 billion (as against the $3.45 billion proposed by the region).

Table 15-3. *IBRD Planned Borrowings and Lending, Fiscal 1969–78*[a]
Billions of U.S. dollars

Borrowing/lending	Actual, 1969–73	Projected, end-1971	Projected, end-1974	Actual, 1974–78
Commitments	8.9[b]	14.0	22.1	22.4[c]
Gross disbursements	4.7	9.8	12.5	11.4
Net disbursements	2.9	6.7	9.2	8.4
Borrowings	6.8	11.3	13.9	17.5

Sources: For end-1971 projections: IBRD, "The Scale of IBRD Financial Operations, FY74–78," R71-276, December 15, 1971. For actual 1969–73 and mid-1974 projections: IBRD, "Revision of IBRD/IDA Program, FY74–78," R74-115, June 4, 1974. For actual 1974–78: "Review of World Bank Group Financial and Operating Programs and FY80 Administrative Budgets," R79-111, May 14, 1979.

a. Lending figures do not include loans to the IFC or to developed countries.

b. Memo (1995 U.S.$): 32.

c. Memo (1995 U.S.$): 54.

Table 15-4. *Net Resource Receipts of Developing Countries, 1970–79*
Billions of U.S. dollars

Source	1970–74	Percent	1975–79	Percent
World Bank	5.8	4.6	16.6	5.0
IBRD	3.4	2.7	10.7	3.2
Other multilateral	8.5	6.7	24.0	7.2
Bilateral	40.9	32.3	84.9	25.4
Private	32.8	25.9	92.6	27.7
Export credits	13.9	11.0	48.7	14.6
FDI	17.1	13.5	52.5	15.7
Other	7.8	6.2	15.1	4.5
Total	126.8	100.0	334.4	100.0

Source: OECD, *Development Cooperation*, 1980.

"The main reason Mr. McNamara gave for not approving the proposed increase, was that IBRD funds were now limited. He was also concerned at the high relation between interest and charges on IBRD loans to Brazil and the Bank's net income."[96] McNamara went on to elaborate that with the IBRD rapidly approaching its statutory lending limit, if the proposed program for Brazil were approved, it would mean that funds for other countries would have to be cut.[97] And, although Brazil's debt-service ratio was low, the interest payment on IBRD debt was projected to exceed 100 percent of the Bank's net income. "'This is hell' he exclaimed."[98]

The restraints posed by the Bank's limited capital would be moderately relaxed, first by a selective capital increase in 1976, and more substantially by the general capital increase of 1979 (discussed later). Although this reduced the rate of expansion in IBRD lending, it still doubled during the next six years (fiscal 1975–81), and on a much larger base.

The Bank's rapid growth in the 1970s must however be kept in context. In fact, as the figures in table 15-4 illustrate, despite all the brouhaha on the growth in World Bank lending over the decade, its role in net resource transfer scarcely changed in relative terms. The need to recycle OPEC surpluses had led to a dramatic growth in global financial intermediation. The rising tide of financial intermediation bore all manner of seemingly well-laden boats to the developing-

96. Memorandum, George Zaidan to John H. Adler, "Meeting of the Review Group: Brazil," May 30, 1975, p. 2.

97. Under Article III, Section 3 of IBRD, *Articles of Agreement of the International Bank for Reconstruction and Development*, amended effective February 16, 1989, "The total amount outstanding of guarantees, participations in loans, and direct loans made by the Bank shall not be increased at any time if, by such increase, the total would exceed one hundred percent of the unimpaired subscribed capital, reserves, and surplus of the Bank" (p. A-I-4).

98. Memorandum, Zaidan to Adler, May 30, 1975, p. 4.

Table 15-5. *Brazil: Cost of Funds from IBRD and Commercial Sources*[a]
Annual averages

Year	IBRD	All commercial sources		
		Total	Financial institutions	
			Total	Commercial banks
1974–75	7.75	7.95	8.3	9.2
1976–78	8.7	6.9	7.1	7.4
1979–82	9.15	13.0	14.0	14.9

Source: D. R. Weigel, "The Cost Competitiveness of the Bank: A Progress Report," May 14, 1984.

a. Cost was calculated as interest paid divided by average outstanding. Loans from commercial sources include government-guaranteed export credits, suppliers credits, and loans from commercial banks. The different maturity structures, disbursement profiles, and currencies of disbursement make it difficult to strictly compare IBRD loans with those from commercial sources. The figures should be treated as illustrative only.

country shores. The most striking galleons bore the insignia of commercial banks whose loans, despite interest charges that were higher than alternative sources, grew dramatically during the latter half of the 1970s.

The enormous supply of cheaper money from alternate sources through the decade meant that, in the aggregate, the supply push of the McNamara Bank notwithstanding, the institution would have had little leverage in the non-IDA eligible countries in any realistic range of alternate scenarios. Not only was the Bank's share rather small but, in the case of several middle-income countries, for a period its lending rates were higher than alternatives. This was despite the fact that through much of the 1970s the Bank attempted to isolate borrowers from its rising average cost of funds by reducing the lending rate spread.[99]

The figures in table 15-5 are illustrative. Although the average cost of commercial bank loans to Brazil was consistently above the cost of all funds from financial institutions (which includes government-guaranteed export credits) and above the cost from all private sources (including suppliers credits), the fact that these loans disbursed quickly with few questions asked made them much more attractive. During the period 1976–78, the average cost of funds from commercial banks was lower than the cost of funds from the IBRD. Beginning in 1979 the cost of funds obtained by Brazil from commercial banks increased rapidly in relation to the cost of IBRD loans. The relationship between the cost of IBRD and private-source loans was similar in other middle-income countries such as Korea and Colombia. In Brazil's case, however, lending constraints arose as much out of portfolio reasons as higher financial and transaction costs.

In addition to expanding lending on its own account, the Bank, along with the international community, searched for ways to alleviate the short-term balance of

99. Calculated as the difference between the interest paid on average outstanding loans and the interest paid by the Bank in relation to total funds mobilized (both equity and borrowing). This spread fell from about 260 basis points in fiscal 1970 to 120 basis points in fiscal 1978.

payments problems of many lower-income developing countries. Although levels of Official Development Assistance increased considerably, which in the Bank's case boosted the resources of IDA (see chapter 17), they were still quite constrained. Proposals abounded to augment these resources, but few came to fruition.[100] On its part, the IBRD sought to expand lending through two mechanisms: the "Third Window" and cofinancing.

THIRD WINDOW. The Third Window mobilized donor grant contributions to an interest subsidy fund. By defraying interest subsidies on loans at terms intermediate between those of the Bank's standard loans and of IDA development credits, the Third Window allowed the Bank to expand its self-imposed ceilings on lending to less creditworthy borrowers. Negotiations for an Intermediate Financing Facility, or Third Window, began in early 1975, and agreement was soon reached on a fund that would allow the Bank to lend an additional $1 billion for one year, to begin as early as possible in fiscal 1976.[101] In the end the resources committed to the Third Window were modest ($154 million) of which OECD members contributed 60 percent and OPEC countries 40 percent, allowing additional lending of $700 million over two years (fiscal 1976–77).[102]

COFINANCING. Another not-so-new idea that was given a fresh lease on life was cofinancing. The number of IBRD/IDA cofinancing projects rose from about thirty-eight a year in the early 1970s to nearly ninety a year by the end of the decade. Their value rose even faster, from about $1.2 billion to $4.0 billion over the same period.[103] Official sources accounted for the principal source of cofinancing (60 percent), with export credits and commercial banks accounting for the remainder. OPEC countries were the most important source of official cofinancing during the mid-1970s. As these countries developed the capabilities of their own agencies, they began to lend more on their own account, and by the end of the decade Japan emerged as an important source.

Although the Bank had been in the business of cofinancing with official (bilateral and multilateral) agencies, in 1975 it launched cofinancing operations with commercial banks whereby both parties entered into separate lending agreements with borrowers. The commercial loan was on market terms. The arrange-

100. The IMF's Oil Facility and the IFAD were the most visible multilateral successes. Some other proposals that were mooted but failed to take off were the SDR "link proposal" floated by the G-24; Kissinger's proposal for an international resource bank for non-oil mineral lending, driven by his conviction that the Western alliance faced a looming shortage of strategic minerals; and UNCTAD's proposal for an "International Bank for Debt Redemption."

101. Essentially, the fund would support lending equal to the present value of the interest subsidy over the life of the corresponding loans. The amount was roughly 5 percent of the amount of the loans for every 1 percent reduction of interest below the IBRD's standard lending rate. To this end, the fund paid the IBRD semiannually an amount equal to 4 percent per year of the outstanding amounts of principal on intermediate-term loans.

102. IBRD, "Summary of Third Window Operations," SecM77-573, July 12, 1977.

103. IBRD, "World Bank Cofinancing," R80-22, February 19, 1980, p. 2.

ments included optional cross-default clauses and a memorandum of agreement signed by the IBRD and the agent for the commercial banks providing for exchange of information on the project and on the borrower's ability to service the debt.[104] In reaction to these changes, commercial bank cofinancing jumped to about a fifth of all cofinancing. But at the end of the decade, as debt-service problems emerged, the Bank decided to put the brakes on commercial cofinancing because of the fear of being caught up in possible rescheduling (see chapter 11).

During this period, officially the Bank would regularly drum up its enthusiasm for cofinancing. Internally, however, the ardor was more muted for several reasons. Cofinancing always had dual objectives: to add to resources and introduce borrowers to capital markets. Although the annual volume of cofinancing was not inconsequential—equivalent to 15 percent of total Bank lending in the early 1970s and about 35 percent at the end of the decade—staff was skeptical about the extent to which cofinancing resulted in additional resource flows to the developing countries. Whatever the effectiveness of cofinancing in linking borrowers with private capital, in general, it was both expensive in terms of staff time and a volatile source of finance.[105] Poor internal incentives—managers were given little credit for arranging cofinancing despite the additional efforts required—and mixed signals from management (Cargill, for instance, was severely critical of the program), added to institutional ambivalence on cofinancing.[106]

In any case, the Third Window and cofinancing were at best sideshows, the main event being the Bank's own lending program. The revised increased IBRD lending program would precipitate the need for a capital increase, given the statutory limits on the Bank's lending. Furthermore, a necessary corollary to the mid-1974 decision to substantially increase the Bank's lending program was that there would have to be a parallel increase in the Bank's borrowings.[107] But the increased financial load proposed by the new lending program, coming on top of five expansionary years, now kindled a sense of disquiet. Was the Bank's financial health sufficiently robust to absorb the increased risks posed by the new environment? What were these risks, and how appropriate were the Bank's financial policies to handle these risks? How was all this going to play out in the financial market's perceptions of the Bank? And how was it going to affect the Bank's borrowings prospects?

104. In addition, the IBRD would frequently perform certain administrative services for the commercial banks, such as acting as "billing agent."

105. At the time it was estimated that cofinancing increased a project's staff costs by 5–10 percent during appraisal and 20 percent during supervision.

106. A record of a meeting of the Bank's senior management notes that staff was "becoming bored with the Bank's cofinancing attempts." IBRD, memorandum for the record, "Meeting on Cofinancing," March 2, 1978. Present were McNamara, Knapp, and Cargill.

107. Although, given the lags between loan commitments and loan disbursements, planned increases in borrowings were less than those for lending commitments. See table 15-3.

Table 15-6. *World Bank Cost of Funds, Fiscal 1970–82*

Fiscal year	Average cost of borrowing outstanding (percent)	Average cost of total funds (percent)	Differential due to free equity (basis points)
1970	5.59	2.83	276
1972	6.34	3.59	275
1974	6.62	4.46	216
1976	7.32	5.62	170
1978	7.45	6.09	136
1980	7.28	6.00	128
1982	8.15	6.74	141

Source: Weigel, "The Cost Competitiveness of the Bank."

Effects on Financial Health

Even before the oil shock, the rapid growth of the Bank during the period 1968–73 had caused some anxiety among the Bank's major shareholders. There was a feeling in some quarters that the Bank's rapid expansion was placing undue stress on quantitative targets at the expense of quality. Others felt uneasy about the financial operations of the institution. Some wondered whether the rapid buildup of borrowings, concurrent with declining "traditional" financial ratios, was financially prudent. Although few disputed Bank management's position that such conventional banking criteria were of "no more than limited applicability to the Bank," some nervously observed that the *trends* were indicating a continuous decline since McNamara's arrival (table 15-6 and figure 15-1). Between 1966/67 and 1974/75, two key ratios—the reserves to loans outstanding and the usable equity to loans outstanding—had fallen from 25 to 18 percent and from 61 to 41 percent, respectively.

From time to time, the major shareholders also expressed concern about the declining trend in the institution's financial ratios, stemming from the negative spread between the Bank's borrowing and lending rates.[108] As noted earlier, the Bank had reformulated its lending rate policy in 1967 in response to increases in market interest rates in the 1960s. The new policy, reflecting months of debate and compromise in the Executive Board, had set the Bank's lending rate "as low as is compatible with the maintenance of the Bank's ability to raise . . . the funds it needs."[109] In order to maintain this ability, it was agreed that the Bank would pay due regard to such factors as the adequacy of its reserves, the interest coverage ratio, and earnings trends. The Bank's financial position would be reviewed annually (or more frequently, if necessary) by the

108. For instance, quite early in McNamara's tenure, the finance minister of France, Valéry Giscard d'Estaing, raised the issue with McNamara who felt that "while this might become a problem, he did not think there was one at present. . . . The situation would have to be watched closely but he thought that the real test was the level of the Bank's earnings." IBRD, memorandum for the record, "France," October 4, 1971.

109. IBRD, "Policy Re: Standard Interest Rate," R67-182/1, December 27, 1967, p. 1.

Figure 15-1. *IBRD, Income Adequacy Financial Ratios, 1948–95*
Percent

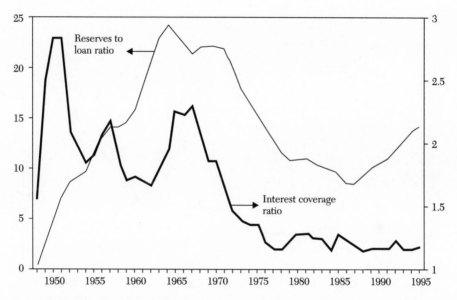

Source: World Bank, Financial Operations Department.

Figure 15-2. *IBRD Subscribed Capital, 1946–95*
Three-year moving averages; billions of U.S. dollars

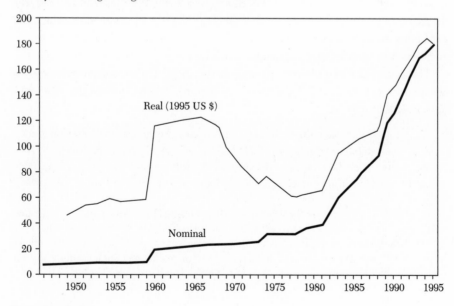

Source: Annual reports.

Figure 15-3. *IBRD Paid-In Capital, 1946–95*
Three-year moving averages; billions of U.S. dollars

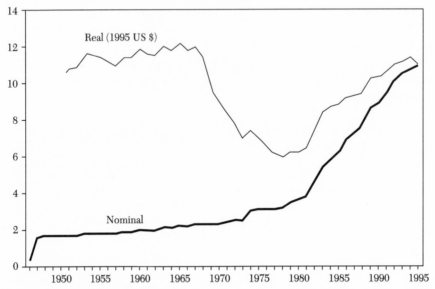

Source: Annual reports.

Board, which would then determine an appropriate spread between the cost of borrowing and the lending rate.[110] However, soon after McNamara's arrival, with interest rates continuing to rise, the Bank's management recommended that the lending rate remain unchanged for that year, and that the increased borrowing costs not be passed on to its borrowers.[111] This implied, for the first time, a negative spread between the Bank's lending rate and its borrowing costs.[112]

The emergence of a negative lending spread in the IBRD's loan operations was deemed to have limited repercussions on its borrowing operations. For the markets, as Knapp stressed,

> the guarantee portion of the IBRD capital has been and continues to be a decisive factor in the marketability and rating of IBRD bonds. . . . The only questions which our New York underwriters have raised in recent years at virtually every "due diligence" meeting on the occasion of new issues, pertain to the prospects for the regular and prompt

110. Borrowing costs were the weighted average of actual borrowing costs and estimated borrowing costs over the next six months. The spread was initially fixed at ⅜ percent.

111. Board records reveal that the recommendation was approved without any completely dissenting voice. The misgivings reflected concerns on market reactions, given the institution's intention to aggressively expand lending. IBRD, "The Bank's Lending Rate," R69-225, December 2, 1969.

112. It must be emphasized that the spread between the Bank's *total* cost of funds and its lending rate continued to be positive.

servicing of IBRD loans, and to the level of net income in absolute amounts and in relation to interest payments on our bonds.[113]

In 1972, as market interest rates continued to climb, the Bank reviewed its lending rate policies and decided to delink lending rates from current borrowing costs, since, "contrary to concern expressed by some, the 'negative spread' [had] not adversely affected the Bank's standing as a borrower in the financial markets of the world."[114] After admitting that it "was extremely difficult to determine and measure the specific factors which bear on the judgment of people who evaluate, market, and buy IBRD bonds," the report concluded that as far as the lending rate was concerned "the only major quantifiable factors to which great weight must be given are changes or prospective changes in the level of net income."[115] Instead, the review recommended that the lending rate be determined on the basis of a broad judgment of the Bank's ability to raise the funds it needed, and the effects thereon of the lending rate and the income it was projected to generate.

The following year, as the Bank's conventional financial indicators continued to deteriorate, the institution initiated a major review of its financial policies.[116] There was broad agreement that the "Bank had to achieve a 'delicate balance' between its role as a development institution and its role as a market-based institution, commanding confidence as a consequence of *prudent* financial management."[117] However, there was little consensus on what constituted "prudent" financial management, or on the relative importance of the "discipline" of traditional financial ratios. Although net income was now enshrined as the principal indicator of financial soundness, judgments still had to be made on the adequacy of net income as a buffer in relation to other financial variables: the size and maturity composition of the Bank's liquid holdings, the riskiness of the loan portfolio, and the interest rate risks facing the Bank.

As the Bank prepared to ratchet up lending further following the oil shock, its financial health raised new concerns. The U.S. executive director, Charles Sethness, sent a personal note to McNamara expressing his apprehension about the institution's capacity to bear financial risk, in view of the declining financial ratios

113. Memorandum, J. Burke Knapp to Robert E. Wieczorowski, U.S. executive director, January 11, 1972, pp. 1–2.

114. IBRD, "IBRD Lending Rate," R72-178, June 29, 1972, para. 7a. The "marginal spread," that is, the difference between the cost of new borrowings and the lending rate on new loans, was negative from fiscal 1968–74, with the exception of fiscal 1973. The "average spread," defined as the difference between the average cost of the Bank's outstanding debt and its average return on disbursed loans, was negative from fiscal 1970 to 1974.

115. Ibid., para. 8. The paper also downplayed the importance of conventional financial ratios such as the interest coverage ratio or the rate of return on equity, maintaining that markets appeared to hold a rather "detached view" on such ratios.

116. IBRD, "IBRD Financial Policies," R73-55, March 28, 1973.

117. IBRD, "Summaries of Discussions at Meetings of the Executive Directors of the Bank and IDA, April 24 and 26, 1973," SD73-19, May 11, 1973, para. 4. Emphasis added.

and increasing risk exposure following the oil shock.[118] Sethness urged McNamara to increase lending rates and restrain the growth in the lending program. Sethness's concerns, particularly those regarding the Bank's financial health and the widening spreads between the cost of the Bank's new borrowings and loans, were shared in part among the Bank's management and were reflected in the June 1974 paper to the Board that proposed increases in the lending program.[119] The paper called attention to the fact that the oil shock had pushed up the Bank's borrowing costs and administrative expenses, in part because of higher inflation. These two changes threatened a key indicator of the Bank's financial health: its net income prospects.

But the projected net income problem was more than just the result of rapid inflation. The long lead time required to translate new lending rates into income and the declining ratio of equity capital in lending were two additional factors.[120] To address these adverse developments and protect the Bank's net income, McNamara proposed increasing its lending rate. To underline the seriousness of the situation, he also proposed that "transfers of IBRD net income to IDA in subsequent years should be deferred, at least until other measures are taken to improve the Bank's underlying capital position."[121] While the lending rate was increased (from 7.25 percent to 8 percent), the president's recommendation for suspending transfers to IDA was, with a few exceptions, strongly opposed by the Board. McNamara used that opportunity to propose initiating informal discussions with member countries on the form, size, and timing of a capital increase.

Concurrently, steps were initiated to address the increased riskiness of the institution's loan portfolio arising from the worsening economic circumstances of many of its borrowers. Although the Bank had long since established systems for assessing economic performance and prospects for individual countries, it did not have any systematic procedure for assessing the risks of its loan portfolio, both in toto and in individual countries, and the implications of such risks for the institution's own portfolio. It then established a Loan Portfolio Analysis Unit, organizationally located under the vice president of finance.[122]

118. Memorandum, Charles Sethness, "Proposals Reflecting My Very Strong Personal Concern over Bank's Projected Financial Operations," March 1, 1974.

119. For instance, Chenery noted that the real rate on Bank loans had fallen from 5 percent to 2–3 percent by early 1974. He urged McNamara to increase the lending rates, arguing that in the changed circumstances the present rate was too low to provide an adequate surplus over expenses. Memorandum, Hollis Chenery to Robert S. McNamara, "Revised Lending Program for FY 1974–78," April 23, 1974.

120. Memorandum, Hollis Chenery to Robert S. McNamara, "Review of Financial Policies," October 23, 1974. The asymmetry in disbursement profiles between the Bank's borrowing and loans means that rising borrowing costs adversely affect net income even if accompanied by commensurate increases in lending rates. Of course, the reverse is true if interest rates are falling.

121. IBRD, "Revision of IBRD/IDA Program, FY74–FY78," R74-115, June 4, 1974, para. 119.

122. Memorandum, James Kearns to Robert S. McNamara, "Creditworthiness," July 19, 1974.

The influence of the new unit was evident in the next financial policy paper at the end of 1974. The recommendations of the paper veered toward a relatively more conservative philosophy, as it analyzed the adequacy of the Bank's capital in relation to its risk-carrying capacity. The lending rate was further increased, and the Bank, now for the first time, recognized the need for specific reserve targets to "ensure that the reasonable risk of potential losses on loans is adequately covered by the Bank's equity capital."[123] A year later these net income objectives were reformulated in terms of a target for the interest coverage ratio and related to the Bank's reserve requirements.[124]

Although the Bank had always emphasized to investors the security offered both by its reserves and its callable capital, around this period the Bank gradually began to shift its stance and place increasingly greater emphasis on its highly liquid reserves as the principal security for investors. There was growing recognition that for the Bank to ever seek recourse to its callable capital was effectively a doomsday option. As the Canadian executive director put it: "Management and the Board should think about callable capital as a Christian thinks about heaven, that it is a nice idea but no one wants to go there because the price of admission is death."[125]

Since McNamara's arrival, the Bank's lending had increased rapidly: 20 percent in nominal terms and 10 percent in real terms between fiscal 1969/70 and fiscal 1976/77. However, its capital—both paid-in and subscribed—had remained essentially unchanged in nominal terms, while suffering a steep erosion in real terms (figures 15-2 and 15-3).

As a result, increases in the equity base had not been commensurate with the escalating financial operations of the Bank. An internal analysis of the Bank's exposure to income risks from loans, either due to risk of rescheduling of loans or a temporary hiatus in debt-service payments, concluded that the Bank's ability to withstand income risks had not kept up with the growth of its lending operations.[126]

The report's conclusions were particularly worrisome, since the Bank was poised for another big spurt in lending to respond to the balance of payments predicament facing many of its members. There was growing recognition that the Bank's equity base would have to be strengthened to support the planned expansion. But any increase in equity could only occur by some combination of additions to paid-in capital (through a capital increase) and an increase in net income retained in the Bank's business (that is, as reserves). Net income, in turn, was a function of lending terms, but only with a lag. And, while lending rates could always be increased, there

123. IBRD, "Review of IBRD/IDA Program and Financial Policies," R74-256, December 12, 1974, para. 37, p. 16.

124. IBRD, "Review of IBRD Capital Structure," R75-215, November 5, 1975.

125. Statement by Canadian executive director, Claude Isbister, at a meeting to discuss IBRD financial policies, IBRD, "IBRD Financial Policies," EDS73–14, April 27, 1973.

126. Memorandum, I. P. M. Cargill to Robert S. McNamara, "Loan Portfolio Analysis Unit—Second Progress Report," September 17, 1975.

was a fine line between the Bank's financial objectives and its development objectives. At the same time, it was becoming clear that in the absence of a capital increase the proposed expansion in Bank lending following the oil shock would stall in the near future owing to statutory limitations. A capital increase would therefore kill two birds with one stone: the paid-in portion would strengthen the Bank's equity base; the callable portion would enhance its capacity to lend. It would of course, place additional resource demands on the institution's shareholders, especially its larger shareholders.

Capital Increases

As the Bank's management now prepared its case for a capital increase, it encountered serious difficulties. The capital increase paper, originally scheduled for Board discussion in mid-1975, was postponed to the end of the year because it had become clear that U.S. support would not be forthcoming. Although U.S. objections had far greater weight, they were not the only ones being voiced. Both Japan and Germany were urging financial caution and a restrained increase in the size of the Bank's capital. In the face of this opposition, Bank management revised its strategy. The capital increase would be undertaken in two stages: an initial selective capital increase (SCI), in parallel with the quinquennial review of quotas in the IMF, followed thereafter by a GCI.[127]

The Selective Capital Increase of 1976

The U.S. position, which was key to securing a capital increase, was articulated by Treasury Secretary Bill Simon and Undersecretary for Monetary Affairs Edward Yeo. Simon's attitude toward the Bank had already soured when, in his earlier capacity as energy "czar" following the oil shock, the Bank had refrained from providing intellectual support for the U.S. position that oil prices should be rolled back. He had watched with considerable unhappiness the unhealthy appetite for autonomy that the Bank's president seemed to have. The veto power of the United States on a capital increase provided an opportunity to press the U.S. Treasury's case.

The discussions between a small group of Bank and Treasury officials unfolded over several months in early 1976. The U.S. Treasury's initial reaction was that the needs of developing countries were exaggerated, and that, in any case, private finance could do a better job. But the early ideological skirmishes soon gave way to more substantial issues. The Treasury's position that a deterioration in the quality of the Bank's balance sheet had eroded because

127. IBRD, "Review of IBRD Capital Structure," R75-215, November 5, 1975. The SCI's linkage with the IMF's quota increase followed past practice.

equity had risen slowly in relation to other assets and liabilities, was not disputed. But there were sharp disagreements on the effects of this erosion and the remedial measures to curb further erosion.

In fiscal 1970, the IBRD's average cost of borrowed funds outstanding was 5.59 percent, while the average cost of total funds, including equity, was only 2.83 percent (table 15-6). Thus, availability of (free) equity capital cut the cost of funds in half. The rapid expansion of the Bank since McNamara's arrival increased borrowings in relation to usable equity. This factor, coupled with the rising costs of borrowing in the 1970s, served to reduce both the absolute and relative impact of free equity on the Bank's cost of funds. Most of this decline in the contribution of free equity had occurred by fiscal 1978. It was stemmed after that because of capital increases that provided a welcome infusion of fresh equity and expanding reserves arising out of increasing net income, in turn the result of changes in financial policies and robust yields on the Bank's liquidity investment portfolio.

The U.S. Treasury's case for the need to stem the decline in the Bank's financial indicators was built on the widening spreads between Bank bonds and U.S. Treasury issues in the 1970s, in relation to the 1960s. According to the Treasury's analysis, the villain of the piece was the IBRD's policy on loan terms, which led the institution to operate at a negative spread. Although there was no doubt about the declining financial ratios of the Bank and widening spreads, proceeding from correlation to causality was a leap of faith.[128] As already mentioned, the Bank's own analysis professed agnosticism on what variables really drove investors to hold IBRD bonds. The Bank's treasurer, Eugene Rotberg, reported back to McNamara, following one of his innumerable meetings with the financial community: "There was *no* expressed concern about our net income, our reserves, our debt-equity ratio, the types of loans we make, nor any of the other matters we recently have been preoccupied about."[129]

Rotberg then went on to list the real reasons that underpinned investors' faith in the Bank's securities. These were explained to investors in private meetings, "since they go to the political/financial nature of the Bank and the relationships between the Bank and its various constituencies":[130]

> The uncalled subscriptions outside the United States are "made good," as a practical matter, by our borrowings in these same countries.
>
> There need be no drain on the foreign exchange reserves of member countries should there be an uncalled capital subscription if we have bonds outstanding in that country's currency.

128. For instance, during this period, the spreads of ATT bonds against U.S. Treasury bonds also widened. ATT bonds were a standard AAA corporate comparator used by both the U.S. Treasury and the World Bank.

129. Memorandum, Eugene H. Rotberg to Robert S. McNamara, "Meetings with Institutional Investors: Boston, February 11, 1976," February 12, 1976, p. 2.

130. Ibid.

The political pressures in any member country would be to honor an uncalled capital subscription since such obligation in fact was for the benefit of their own financial institutions and bondholders—not for the benefit of developing countries.

Therefore, the diversification of our borrowings not only provided us with increased resources but also, as a practical matter, assured the viability of the uncalled capital.

There was a coincidence of interest between the bondholder and the large capital subscribing member countries. This has the effect of increasing the probability of our access to markets. Governments realize that it is preferable, politically and financially, for the Bank to have access to markets to meet our cash flow requirements rather than calling on unpaid capital.

The Bank would stop disbursing if there were debt renunciation. I also argued that it would seriously jeopardize the extension of IDA credits for IDA-eligible countries. IDA subsidizes the Bank, not vice versa, despite the $100 million transfer—and also subsidizes the commercial bank exposure to IDA-eligible countries.[131]

Rotberg's understanding of investor behavior failed to persuade the U.S. Treasury to alter its position. It dug in its heels, insisting that the Bank implement three principal changes in its financial operations before the United States would countenance a capital increase.

1. *The lending program.* Treasury officials argued that annual commitments should be "below an amount in nominal terms," so as "not [to] require a capital increase beyond the proposed selective increase until members agree on such an increase."[132] This position reflected U.S. concerns that the rapid expansion in lending would soon effectively force the hand of shareholders to accede to a capital increase. Otherwise the Bank would be obliged to cut back new lending so abruptly as to be disruptive. The Bank's Articles had defined the lending limit in terms of disbursements and not commitments. In an expanding Bank, disbursements lagged commitments substantially. Consequently, when the Bank approached its "lending" limit, it was in fact approaching its disbursement limit, with many approved but not fully disbursed loans on its books. Compliance with contractual obligations to borrowers—and to the Articles—was only possible if a capital increase was approved.

In an early meeting, McNamara promised Simon that the Bank would limit its lending program such that these fears would not come to pass. A new concept—the sustainable level of lending (SLL)—was now devised to indicate the maximum volume of annual IBRD loan commitments that could, under certain assumptions, be sustained indefinitely without causing disbursed and outstanding loans to ex-

---

131. Ibid., pp. 1–2.

132. In operational terms, this was translated into a maximum lending program of $5 billion with the selective capital increase and $6.1 billion if the Bank hardened its lending terms. The U.S. Treasury positions are extracted from "Proposed Policy Elements," p. 1, an undated, unsigned statement received by the Bank from Undersecretary Yeo on February 27, 1976. This is referred to in a memorandum from I. P. M. Cargill to U.S. executive director Charles Cooper, "Lending Rate Formula—United States Proposal," April 5, 1976.

ceed the limit established in the Articles of Agreement.[133] The SLL did not place a rigid ceiling on the IBRD's level of annual commitments but served principally as an approximate indicator of when decisions on new capital were required. The concept of the SLL would henceforth become the norm for all future discussions among the Bank's shareholders on capital increases.

2. *Financial policies.* The Treasury proposal called for changes in financial policies to "assure it of sufficient income and additions to reserves to increase its risk-taking capacity pari passu with the amount of loans outstanding and with changes in riskiness of outstanding loans." To this end, the Treasury insisted that the Bank establish a formula-based lending rate.[134] The objectives of the formula would be to, first, free bank income from "built-in subsidy to ordinary capital lending." Second, it would create a "semi-automatic system, which does not normally require Board approval for rate changes once its rules are established. Lending rate changes then become to a much greater degree technical questions and to a far lesser one matters of political controversy." The Treasury also insisted that the proposed formula should ensure a faster translation of borrowing costs to lending rates and additions to reserves.

3. *Transfers to IDA.* In the interim, the Treasury urged a postponement of transfers to IDA for two years to improve the Bank's equity position.

The essential thrust of the Treasury's stance—eliminating subsidies of the lending rate through income from capital—highlighted the crux of the dispute.[135] Whether the Bank ought to pursue a policy of charging borrowers the "full cost" of lending operations was as much a political question as a financial one, whose answer depended largely on the willingness of the major shareholders to provide concessional development finance. The U.S. position was that the burden of strengthening the equity base be shifted to the borrowers through a hardening of the Bank's lending terms.

Several months of fractious exchanges between the U.S. Treasury and the Bank followed. After one such meeting, the Bank's finance vice president reported to McNamara: "I . . . am baffled to understand who benefitted from the discussions

133. The SLL focuses on the longer-term capital adequacy of the institution. The SLL is calculated by: (a) estimating the growth over the years of the statutory lending limit, defined as the total of unimpaired subscribed capital, general and special reserves, and surplus; and (b) projecting the loans disbursed and outstanding that will result from constraining future commitments and ensuring that they do not exceed the projected statutory limit at any time. An alternative measure is the "headroom," which is more relevant than the SLL if one is concerned with near-term capital adequacy. This issue is taken up again later in the chapter.

134. It is perhaps more accurate to say that the insistence on a formula-based lending rate was due to Edward Yeo. In his previous incarnation in Chicago banking, Yeo had been a strong advocate of formula-based lending rates.

135. The Treasury proposal stated: "The eventual income effect of this policy and formula would be that the annual Bank earnings would approach a sum equal to equity times the average borrowing rate." Memorandum, Cargill to Cooper, April 5, 1976, annex 2.

that took place between us and the Treasury."[136] An understanding was finally reached whereby the United States agreed to allow an SCI and an increase in the Bank's lending program, up to a ceiling of $5.8 billion, in return for a "formula" approach to the lending rate and a hardening of loan terms. Although the developing countries were indignant—they were being asked to accept harder loan terms as part of a package to enlist the support of the United States without any assurance of future U.S. support for a GCI—they had little choice. The proposal was eventually approved by the Board, whose votes on the issue fell along a sharp North-South line (nine members approved, six opposed and four abstained).

As a consequence, the terms of new loans carried several important modifications.[137] Loan terms were hardened; terms were differentiated by three country groups to distribute the hardening of terms broadly, in line with country debt-servicing capacities.[138] For the most part, this three-tier repayment structure has been maintained ever since, although the country composition of the groups has varied with changing country per capita incomes.

Although the decision to harden the repayment terms of Bank loans was initially taken in the face of capital constraints on lending that emerged before the 1979 GCI, subsequent relaxation of terms was precluded by a worsening in the financial environment surrounding the Bank. Formula-based lending was introduced in fiscal 1977. A specific markup (of 50 basis points) over marginal borrowing costs was reintroduced, and lending rates were revised quarterly.[139] Because interest rates also had become more volatile, this led to frequent changes in the Bank's

---

136. Memorandum, I. P. M. Cargill to Robert S. McNamara, "Capital Increase," March 27, 1976.

137. The principal changes were: (a) the repayment method was shifted from an annuity, which provides for a level schedule of debt-service payments after the expiration of the grace period, to a system of equal payments of principal (EPP), under which the likely pattern of payments of principal plus interest peaks immediately upon the expiry of the grace period and declines thereafter; (b) grace periods and maturities were reduced (on average to 3.8 and 19 years respectively, from an average of 4.5 years grace period and 21 years final maturity in FY72-76); and (c) repayment terms were differentiated by country, whereas previously they had been set on the basis of project considerations. See IBRD, "Grace Periods and Final Maturities on FY77 Bank Loans," R76-206, August 9, 1976. The average grace period was subsequently corrected on a technical basis to 4.1 years. See IBRD, "Grace Periods and Final Maturities on IBRD Loans in FY78 and FY79," R78-180, July 21, 1978.

138. Flexibility was provided to allow differentiation of terms on project grounds within the prescribed country averages, for instance, trading off a longer grace period against a shorter maturity period or balancing a loan with "softer" terms against one with harder terms. The guidelines also provide room for exceptions in the case of smaller countries, where there were too few loans to permit such averaging, provided that Bank-wide averages were maintained. These considerations are described in IBRD, "Amortization of FY77 Bank Loans," SecM76-672, September 27, 1976.

139. The borrowing cost was "normalized" by applying a complex formula that adjusted the Bank's actual borrowings undertaken during the prior quarter to an average life of eight

lending rate.[140] In order to provide some year-to-year stability in lending rates, the Bank again revised the policy in 1979, when it decided to set lending rates 50 basis points over its long-term average borrowing costs.

When the dust had settled, the Bank management's original proposal to increase the Bank's capital had been whittled down from $30 billion to $8.44 billion. As events turned out, management had staged a tactical retreat. During the course of negotiations for the SCI, McNamara set up a task force to examine the future role of the World Bank. The task force's work would lay the groundwork for a much larger capital increase: a $40 billion (GCI) in 1979.[141] But for the moment, the compromise resulted in a hardening of the Bank's loan terms while moderately strengthening its capital.

In retrospect, these events were noteworthy in several respects. Despite an initial focus on the interest rate risks facing the Bank, the opportunity to come to grips with two principal elements underlying the Bank's financial risks was allowed to slip by. First, the Bank was lending long term at fixed interest rates; given the long disbursement profiles of its loans, with annual loan commitments steadily expanding, and undisbursed and unfunded commitments steadily rising, the institution's exposure to interest rate mismatch between its assets and liabilities mounted. And second, although there was at least some discussion on the interest rate risks facing the Bank, in the protracted discussions and position papers on the "subsidy" element of Bank lending, the real cost of Bank lending, taking into account the exchange rate risks borne by the borrowers, was left unaddressed. Finally, the *process* established an unhappy precedent. For the first time, a shareholder had, unilaterally, explicitly linked efforts to augment the Bank's financial resources to institutional policy changes, and had prevailed. It was a lesson that would not go unnoticed among the institution's other major shareholders.

---

years, defined as the "norm." The "normalized" borrowing cost was reviewed each quarter and took into account the maturity and amount of debt issued and, if needed, a proxy cost of borrowing. If there was no long-term borrowing with an average life of twelve years during the preceding quarter, the Bank included a market-based index of long-term U.S. dollar borrowing cost to compute the "normalized" cost. At the time the policy was introduced, the market-based index used was the quarterly average of the Salomon Brothers's index of new AAA utility bonds with an assumed average life of twenty-five years.

140. The policy resulted in increased lending rate volatility over the period of 1977–79 (lending rates fluctuated between 7.45 percent and 8.90 percent during that period; during the same period the yield on U.S. medium-term government bonds went from 6.69 percent in 1977 to 9.71 percent in 1979). The Bank's actual borrowing costs were at 7.55 percent in the first quarter of 1977 and 8.07 percent in the third quarter of 1979 but fluctuated widely between these two years, reaching as low as 4.95 percent in the second quarter of 1979. Unlike commercial loans, however, the Bank's lending rates continued to be fixed for the full maturities of the loans, shielding its borrowers from interest rate volatility.

141. IBRD, "Future Role of the World Bank and Its Associated Capital Requirements," R77-18, February 1, 1977.

The 1979 General Capital Increase

While the SCI of 1976 was under way, McNamara initiated staff analysis on a general capital increase. As noted earlier, the GCI of 1959 had gone practically unnoticed and faced few political problems, largely because of forceful support by the United States, whereas now efforts to increase the Bank's capital aroused considerable discord. Henceforth, the Bank's management had to be much more savvy regarding the timing and scale of a capital increase. Unlike previous capital increases, which had taken place when the IBRD was practically the only game in town, now other multilateral funding initiatives had to be taken into account, including those for the non-IBRD parts of the Bank, IDA, and the IFC (and later MIGA). In proposing the scale of a capital increase, the Bank's management had to weigh the trade-offs between asking for a large increase (and risking failure) or reducing the scale and achieving a quick approval but then having to go back to the shareholders more frequently. Although it was obviously important to get as high a fraction of paid-in capital (its "free money"), this again had to be balanced against possible liberalization in the terms of payment to improve the chances of shareholder approval.[142] And casting an increasingly dark shadow were fundamental issues of institutional governance. As countries jostled to improve or retain their shareholdings, allocation of voting rights and seats on the Board became inextricably tied to the financial aspects of a capital increase.

Despite the 1976 SCI, the IBRD continued to "fac[e] a ceiling on Bank lending and, hence, an allocation problem."[143] The allocation problem was to be the genesis of another divisive debate, that related to "graduation" policies. The United States argued that a capital increase could be postponed and/or reduced in scale, if middle-income borrowers, particularly in Latin America, were "graduated" out of IBRD lending. In these debates both management and the Bank's membership were split on whether the criteria for Bank lending to middle-income countries should be based on their access to capital markets or level of income.[144] The Bank's management proposed reducing the volume of lending as countries moved up the income scale. Tensions continued until, with the onset of the debt crisis, the issue became moot.

Following on the work of the "Future Role of the World Bank" task force, the Bank's management recommended a doubling of the institution's capital, that is, an

142. For a given amount of paid-in capital, there was also a trade-off between a lower paid-in portion and a higher total increase.

143. Memorandum for the record, "Policy Review Committee on IBRD Policy vis-a-vis Higher-Income Countries," February 4, 1977.

144. At this time the IDB had established nominal lending ceilings in Mexico, Brazil, and Argentina of $250 million a year per country. The Bank's management argued that the acceptance of these ceilings at the IDB weakened their case in the Bank. Memorandum for the record, "Meeting on Graduation of Higher-Income Countries," January 10, 1979.

increase of $40 billion, to carry out its mandate in the next decade.[145] Cognizant of the hostile climate, it even considered a dividend option to build support. However, with a new U.S. administration, matters appeared more hopeful for a while. The United States was now more supportive of the Bank's expansion plans and agreed to support a capital increase that could support an increase in lending in real terms of 5 percent per year. The honeymoon was short-lived, however, and the United States soon made its support conditional on sufficient progress being made on five issues before making a formal commitment: policy leverage with recipient countries, human rights, salaries, travel, and accountability. The list was quickly pared down to two: human rights and staff compensation. After McNamara objected that it was an "untenable position to let action on the capital increase hang on the salaries issue,"[146] the United States agreed to support in the interim a $6.8 billion lending program for fiscal 1979.[147]

While negotiations were continuing, a new problem emerged. What unit of value would be used for the valuation of the Bank's capital? Under the Bank's Articles, its capital stock, the size of the Bank's capital, payments to be made by members on account of their subscriptions, maintenance of value of paid-in capital, and calculation of the lending limit were all linked to the 1944 dollar.[148] Bank members had two fundamental obligations to the institution with respect to their subscription to capital stock after the initial payment for it. One was to maintain the value of the part of the paid-in portion of their subscription held by the Bank in terms of the "United States dollars of the weight and fineness in effect on July 1, 1944" (so-called 1944 dollars).The second was to respond to calls, if and when made, up to the amount of the callable portions of their subscriptions, also valued in terms of the 1944 dollar.[149]

Following the devaluations of the U.S. dollar in 1972 and 1973, the United States adjusted its obligations to the Bank accordingly by making a maintenance of value payment (on the basis of the last par value of the U.S. dollar established in

145. Commenting on the reactions to the proposed increase, William Clark (then vice president for external relations), would later note in his diary, "Talk about $40 billion causes vertigo (unless weapons system)."

146. IBRD, memorandum for the record, "Meeting with Messrs. Solomon and Bergsten, U.S. Treasury, on IBRD Capital Increase," January 31, 1978, p. 3.

147. IBRD, memorandum for the record, "Meeting on U.S. Treasury's Position on IBRD Capital Increase," February 1, 1978, p. 1.

148. IBRD, *Articles of Agreement of the International Bank for Reconstruction and Development,* art. II, sec. 2(a). This same unit of value, the 1944 dollar ("United States dollars of the weight and fineness in effect of July 1, 1944"), was the basis for the determination of the amounts payable by members on account of the paid-in and callable portions of the Bank's capital pursuant to Sections 5 and 7 of Article II, and for determining the obligations of members, or the Bank, on account of maintenance of value pursuant to Section 9 of Article II.

149. Members accept this obligation when they subscribe to shares.

1973 wherein one 1944 dollar was equivalent to 1.20635 current U.S. dollars) and appropriating the amount necessary for this purpose to meet any calls on the uncalled portion of its subscription. However, as the form of the proposed Second Amendment to the IMF's Articles of Agreement began to emerge in 1974, the question of the valuation of the Bank's capital also arose. The difference between the unit of value and the current U.S. dollar was more than just a matter of conceptual significance: it also had financial consequences.[150]

In 1976 the Bank's general counsel, Aron Broches, took the position that after the effectiveness of the Second Amendment, references in the Bank's Articles to the 1944 dollar should be understood to refer to the SDR as valued under the Fund's Articles; a draft interpretation of the Bank's Articles to this effect was circulated to the executive directors.[151] The executive directors took no action on the question, principally because the United States did not accept the proposition that the SDR could be substituted for the 1944 dollar by interpretation.

As a result of the Second Amendment to the Articles of Agreement of the IMF, which became effective on April 1, 1978, the term "United States dollar of the weight and fineness in effect on July 1, 1944" became obsolete, since, with the disappearance of par values, it was no longer possible to translate that term into any currency, the U.S. dollar or any other.[152] In early 1978, when it became clear that the Second Amendment to the IMF's Articles would soon become effective, the general counsel submitted a legal opinion concluding that upon the coming into effect of the Second Amendment the term "United States dollar of the weight and fineness in effect on July 1, 1944" must be understood as referring to special drawing rights as valued under the Fund Articles, on the basis that one 1944 dollar equals one SDR.[153] In that opinion he also considered, but rejected as a legal matter, an alternative interpretation to the effect that this term should be read as

---

150. This section draws upon: IBRD, "Minutes of Meeting Held on February 28, 1979," JAC/M79-1, March 19, 1979; and "Valuation of IBRD Capital, Opinion of the Vice President and General Counsel," Ibrahim Shihata, December 15, 1983. A detailed analysis of the issue may be found in Ibrahim Shihata, "The Standard of Value of the Bank's Capital after the Demise of the Gold Standard," in *The World Bank in a Changing World*, vol. 2 (The Hague: Martinus Nijhoff, 1995), pp. 71–126.

151. IBRD, memorandum to the executive directors, "Valuation of the Bank's Capital," SecM76-423, June 8, 1976.

152. The Second Amendment abolished par values and the official price of gold and defined the unit of value of the SDR no longer in terms of gold, but as the sum of specified quantities of specified currencies, commonly known as the basket. In some respects, the Second Amendment did no more than sanction a situation which had existed de facto for several years. Specifically, the basket was adopted by the Fund as early as 1974 when the general floating of currencies had made par values almost irrelevant.

153. IBRD, memorandum to the executive directors, "Valuation of the Bank's Capital," SecM78-251, March 29, 1978.

meaning 1.20635 U.S. dollars, that is, the last par value of the U.S. dollar. The Asian Development Bank's general counsel also came to an identical conclusion.

After the Second Amendment became effective, on April 1, 1978, the Joint Audit Committee of the Board had to consider its consequences for the presentation of the Bank's annual financial statements for the year ended June 30, 1978. The balance sheet for that year (and subsequently through 1986) shows the capital of the Bank expressed in SDRs translated into dollars valued at the market exchange rate on the balance sheet date.[154] Reference was made to the problem created by the entry into force of the Second Amendment and the conclusion reached by general counsel in his legal opinion. However, a note was added to the effect that the general counsel had also stated that the executive directors in the exercise of their statutory power under Article IX could conclude that the 1944 dollar would be taken to mean 1.20635 current dollars.[155]

But how could the executive directors arrive at a conclusion that had been rejected as a legal matter? The general counsel rationalized:

> In acting under Article IX, the Executive Directors are exercising the statutory powers of interpretation in which they are not bound by strict rules of law. The Executive Directors would presumably wish to receive the advice of the Bank's General Counsel but, faced with alternative possible interpretations, they would not be bound by his advice, except, in my view, if he were to advise them that adoption by them of one of the alternatives would constitute an abuse of the interpretation power. But in this case that issue does not arise. While it is my opinion that as a legal matter the reference to the 1944 dollar must be read as referring to the SDR, I could not say that an interpretation by the Executive Directors under which the 1944 dollar would be taken to mean 1.20635 current U.S. dollars *was so completely devoid of foundation* as to constitute an abuse of the interpretation power.[156]

The loophole suggested by the above opinion was necessary to accommodate the U.S. stance on the issue. The U.S. Treasury was adamant on maintaining the status quo, fearing that while adoption of the SDR would not be a problem for congressional appropriations, it would lead to authorization difficulties from a Congress wary of any open-ended authorization. The executive branch, weary of its

154. The balance sheet further shows under "Other Assets" and "Liabilities," an item entitled "Notional amounts required to maintain value of currency holdings," which represents the amounts that would be due if maintenance of value were settled on the SDR basis.

155. The executive directors' statutory power refers to their power to interpret the Bank's Articles. Article IX provides that any question of interpretation of the provisions of the agreement arising between any member and the Bank or between any members of the Bank shall be submitted to the executive directors for their decision.

156. Statement by the general counsel to the Joint Audit Committee, February 28, 1979. Emphasis added. The general counsel further argued: "In making this statement I am taking account of the fact that what is at stake is essentially a definition of the mutual rights and obligations of members and that in such a matter the members of the Bank should have considerable latitude." Ibid.

continuing battles with Congress on funding multilateral institutions, under-standably did not want to carry another cross for the Bank. For the United States, the issue was clearly less a financial issue and more a political one. Fred Bergsten, negotiating for the United States, proposed as a pragmatic matter to continue with the status quo, arguing that "the Bank had been living in sin already for years."[157] But the continuation of the status quo implied that the United States, alone of any Bank member, would be relieved of maintenance of value (MOV) obligations. Extending it to all other members would favor countries with depreciating curren-cies and penalize those with appreciating currencies. Furthermore, the absence of a standard of value (SOV) provision made it difficult for the Bank to inform its bondholders of the value of its capital.

As negotiations dragged on, the Bank began to plan for a contingency-reduced lending program.[158] The key obstacle now became reconciling opposing German and U.S. views. Germany opposed the U.S. stance on the SOV and, contrary to the U.S. position of 5 percent paid-in, insisted on the paid-in capital share being retained at 10 percent, as it associated a low paid-in portion with financial irresponsibility.

With active support from the Dutch and the British, a consensus was gradually arrived at. The paid-in portion was now reduced to 7.5 percent, which was higher, however, than the U.S. recommended level of 5 percent. The obstacle posed by the SOV issue was skirted by the time-honored bureaucratic solution of deferring the matter. Thus the members would be informed of the general counsel's opinion that the Bank move away from the 1944 dollar to the SDR; but since member govern-ments were in disagreement, insofar as it resulted in any new obligations with respect to MOV, such a step should only be made by amendment to the Articles. And, since the United States exercised veto power on any amendments to the Articles, face was temporarily saved on all sides.[159]

The Bank's Board finally approved the GCI resolution in June 1979. There was, however, one further hurdle to cross. A capital increase requires a vote by the Board of Governors of the Bank. As per the Bank's Articles, there are two require-ments for adoption of a capital increase resolution: for purposes of a quorum, replies from governors representing at least two-thirds of the voting power; and for approval, a three-fourth majority of the total voting power. The U.S had informally made it clear that it could not introduce the necessary legislation until after the 1980 election. Since the U.S share was 23 percent, the Bank's management had to pull all stops with all other members to cast their vote in order to render the capital increase effective in January 1980.[160]

157. IBRD, memorandum for the record, "Meeting on Valuation of the Bank Capital," March 24 and 27, 1978.

158. IBRD, memorandum for the record, "Meeting on IBRD Capital Increase," October 27, 1978.

159. The other major divisive issue—allocation of voting rights and seats on the Board—is discussed in chapter 18.

160. IBRD, "IBRD General Capital Increase," R80-3, January 4, 1980.

The need for compromises to come to an agreement on the GCI was undoubtedly aided by external factors, in particular the second oil shock at the end of 1978. Higher inflation, plans for expanded energy lending, the prospective move into structural adjustment lending, and China's looming membership—all strengthened the case for a GCI. Yet there can be little doubt that the steady perseverance of Bank management, particularly of McNamara, was the key to both the size and the timing of the capital increase. McNamara wanted to go further, to increase the Bank's lending capacity, and briefly toyed with the idea of changing the IBRD's gearing ratio (from 1:1 to 1:2). Strong opposition by Rotberg, who made it clear that the markets would not take kindly to such a change, laid the idea to rest. Instead the Bank examined the possibility of creating a subsidiary—an Energy Affiliate—that could obtain substantial OPEC resources through the use of short-term facilities. The ill-fated saga of the Energy Affiliate is examined in chapter 16.

Debt Rescheduling: A Hardening Stance

In November 1975, as the IBRD was preparing for its largest bond offering in the U.S. market, the Bank's prospectus mentioned that "the Bank follows a *policy* of not taking part in debt rescheduling agreements."[161] This statement, which appeared to alter the Bank's position on the subject as stated in its earlier prospectuses, was subsequently enshrined in all future bond prospectuses. Since McNamara's arrival, the Bank's practice on the subject of rescheduling its own loans would have been strongly suggestive of such a policy. Indeed, the general tenor of the discussions in the Bank's Board in the preceding years, indicates that the Board would, in general, have been prepared "to acquiesce or accept that strong opposition to Bank participation in debt rescheduling was the position of the President and the Bank Staff."[162] But it was also true that at no stage did the president ever specifically recommend that the Board adopt a resolution on debt rescheduling, nor did the Board ever approve of such a *policy*.[163]

The first prospectus issued by the Bank contained detailed references to the Articles, including a reference to Article IV, Section 4(c) "as providing that the

161. Ibrahim F. I. Shihata, "Treatment of Bank Borrowers in Cases of 'Acute Exchange Stringencies' and 'Default,'" legal memorandum on Article IV, Sections 4(c) and 7(a) of the IBRD Articles of Agreement, January 2, 1985, p. 15. Emphasis added. The statement followed a paragraph commenting on the recent strains on non-oil-producing developing countries. This was the first prospectus to be issued in the new format. There does not appear to be any discussion on the statement's inclusion, or the basis for it, anywhere in the Bank's files.

162. Memorandum, Antonia M. Macedo to Patrick Heininger, "Rescheduling of Bank Loans," June 30, 1981, p. 2.

163. The evolution of the Bank's position on participation in debt rescheduling and, in particular, the changes in the language in the Bank's prospectuses draws heavily from two sources: ibid., and Shihata, "Treatment of Bank Borrowers."

Bank might in the circumstances defined in the Section in its discretion accept service payments in local currency."[164] No reference was made, however, to the members' right to apply for relaxation of loan terms in certain circumstances.[165] Nevertheless, it was generally understood in the Bank that such a right existed, with a corresponding obligation on the Bank to give serious consideration to such an application if made.[166]

The Bank's second prospectus, issued in 1950 after the Bank's securities were exempted from the U.S. Securities Act of 1933, was silent on the possibility of adjustment of loan terms. It mentioned only that the policies and procedures indicated in the prospectus were subject to change, to the extent permitted under the Articles.[167] It was only in 1951 that the Bank, as a result of comments by the staff of the U.S. Securities and Exchange Commission (SEC),[168] stated for the first time in a prospectus that it "may also relax or modify contract requirements, reduce charges or otherwise waive rights under existing loan agreements, as may be appropriate in relation to changing Bank policies or as may appear advisable because of the economic situation of particular borrowers or guarantors."[169]

The language of the February 1950 prospectus, which in fact exceeded the scope of Article IV, Section 4(c), and seemed to state the implied general power of the Bank to adjust loan terms, was repeated with minor changes in all U.S. prospectuses until 1960. No reference was made in these prospectuses to the few cases of extension of amortization schedules made in the 1950s. In 1960, the Bank, after a two-year absence from the U.S. market, issued a new prospectus that contained no reference to the Bank's power to relax or modify loan terms, referring only to the fact that "within the scope permitted by the Articles, [the Bank's] policies must necessarily be developed and adjusted in the light of experience and changing conditions."[170] This new attitude was probably influenced by the discussion of the IDA Articles in the Financial Policy Committee of the Bank's Board and by the doubling of the Bank's authorized capital which, according to Aron Broches, made it "not difficult to persuade the underwriters to accept the deletion of most of the old language."[171] Subsequent prospectuses used this new language. Again no

164. Aron Broches, "IBRD Article IV, Section 4(c) and 7(a), IDA Article V, Section 3, Modification of Terms in Loans and Credits," January 1982, p. 9.

165. According to Aron Broches, the first general counsel of the Bank (Chester A. McLain) considered the provision of Article IV, Section 4(c) potentially "dangerous." Ibid., p. 9.

166. See ibid., pp. 8–9, where he adds that the Bank "may not decline [the application] on the simple ground that it is entitled to insist on punctual performance of the loan agreement and to declare a default."

167. Ibid., p. 10.

168. Ibid., p. 10.

169. Ibid.

170. Ibid., p. 14.

171. Ibid.

mention was made in the prospectuses of several reschedulings in the decade in the case of Haiti and Chile. Only the rescheduling of loans to India in 1968 was mentioned in the U.S. prospectus of that year, perhaps because of its size and because of the protracted debates in the Bank's Board on the issue.

The debates surrounding the India debt rescheduling were so heated that the question of the Bank's participation in the rescheduling of the external public debt of member countries was put on hold following McNamara's arrival. But it could hardly be avoided altogether and during the period 1970–75 it resurfaced periodically in connection with Board discussions of various reports on aspects of the Bank's financial policy.[172]

At the end of the 1960s, the debt problems of low-income countries cast a pall of pessimism over other development prospects. Many commentators were even predicting that the Second Development Decade (DD II) would in reality turn out to be the Decade of Defaults. It was in this gloomy atmosphere that McNamara announced at the 1970 Copenhagen Annual Meeting that the Bank would undertake a major study on the "debt problem." The study was transmitted to the Board of Governors in 1971 as a staff report, however, since the Board had insisted on the disclaimer that "the views expressed in the paper were those of the staff and did not purport to represent the views of the Executive Directors of the Bank or the Governments which appointed or elected them."[173] The reason was that the report had stated: "Since the Bank's direct participation in debt rescheduling would have an adverse effect on both the volume and cost of capital available to it, such action is not planned in the future."[174] When an executive director questioned this statement in light of the Articles of Agreement, McNamara indicated that "he would prefer not to make formal reference to the Articles."[175]

---

172. Meeting of April 20, 1971, to discuss IBRD, "Bank Liquidity Policy," R71-64, March 31, 1971; meetings of August 5 and 10, 1971, to discuss Staff Study on "External Debt of Developing Countries," R71-178, 178/1, July 14, 1971; meetings of April 24 and 26, 1973, on "Review of IBRD Financial Policies," R73-55, March 27, 1973; meeting of March 19, 1974, on IBRD, "Additional External Capital Requirements of Developing Countries," R74-43, March 5, 1974; meeting of July 30, 1974, during discussion of "Review of IBRD/IDA Program, FY74–78," R74-115/IDA 74-42, June 4, 1974; meeting of June 18, 1974, discussing approval of a loan and credit to India; meeting of January 21, 1975, on "Review of IBRD/IDA Program and Financial Policies," R74-256, December 11, 1974.

173. Transmittal letter from the president to individual governors, August 16, 1971. Edward S. Mason and Robert E. Asher, *The World Bank since Bretton Woods* (Brookings, 1973), p. 226, quote the statement as the Bank's position, adding, however, that the staff study was "approved" by the executive directors.

174. IBRD, "External Debt of Developing Countries," para. 24, p. 11. See also "Proceeding of Meeting of Executive Directors, August 10, 1971"; IBRD, "Summaries of Discussions at Meetings of the Executive Directors of the Bank and IDA, August 10, 1971," SD71-29, August 25, 1971; "Minutes of Meeting of the Executive Directors of the Bank and IDA Held in the Board Room on August 10, 1971, at 10:00 a.m.," M71-37, August 13, 1971.

175. See IBRD, "Summaries of Discussions. . . ," SD71-29, August 25, 1971.

The staff position was reiterated in different fora and reflected concerns that for a financial intermediary gearing up to rapidly expand its lending—and borrowings—to compromise on its "preferred creditor" status would adversely affect the cost and volume of market borrowings. A paper on the Bank's liquidity policy, while pointing to the increasing risk of debt default or rescheduling because of "high levels of debt service" plaguing its borrowers, nevertheless stressed that reschedulings should exclude the Bank. The paper admitted that although direct effects of any rescheduling would "be temporary and not great in amount, it could substantially reduce the Bank's ability to place new bond issues in the capital markets and therefore should not be accepted."[176]

Understandably, the hardening of its position on the rescheduling of its debt was partly a matter of external posturing. The Bank made it clear that under these circumstances it was prepared to

> assist in the alleviation of a country's debt service burden through the provision of new loans on appropriate terms. This procedure was used to assist Brazil when that country experienced debt servicing difficulties in 1964. The Bank Group has considerable flexibility in setting maturity and grace periods on its loans, and will use such flexibility in appropriate ways to assist countries in debt servicing difficulties. It will thereby reduce the burden of relief to be shared by other creditors.[177]

Two episodes now gave some flesh to the Bank's practice. Following the division of Pakistan and formation of Bangladesh in 1971, the Bank faced what then seemed a unique situation. How were the obligations of the undivided country to be divided between the two nations? While the allocation seemed simple enough in the case of specific investment projects, by virtue of geographical location, it was much more difficult to make judgments in the case of balance of payments program loans. The negotiations lasted almost four years before an agreement was reached: Bangladesh would accept liability for projects "visibly located" in the country.[178] At the time, one executive director asked whether the consolidation of loans and credits to Bangladesh in 1975 amounted in fact to a form of rescheduling. McNamara replied: "Yes, [it is a form of rescheduling]. . . . It is the first time there has been a rescheduling since the Indian rescheduling of '68. . . . But, of course, the circumstances here of a country dividing are really quite unique."[179]

176. IBRD, "Bank Liquidity Policy," R71-64, March 31, 1971, para. 15, p. 4.

177. IBRD, "The External Debt of Developing Countries," SecM71-407, August 18, 1971, para. 135, p. 50.

178. Bangladesh assumed liability of about 84 percent of the amount the Bank Group originally asked it to assume. The IBRD loans were incorporated into a new IBRD loan with a term of thirty years, including ten years of grace, with an interest rate computed as an average of the rates of the old loans (the grant element was estimated at 33 percent). The IDA credits were similarly consolidated into a new loan at standard IDA terms. IBRD, "Bangladesh—Proposed Consolidation Loan and Credit," R75-24, January 24, 1975.

179. IBRD, "Proceedings of Meeting, February 11, 1975," p. 179.

When asked for confirmation that this "unique" case would not be a precedent for the future, McNamara stated that he hoped "we will never face another country dividing. If we do, we may have to consider this a precedent."[180] And indeed, in 1996, the case of Bangladesh would serve as a precedent for the consolidation and rescheduling of loans to Bosnia and Herzegovina.

Chile appeared to present a more "normal" case. In November 1970 Salvador Allende took over as president, and during his tenure the Bank did not lend to Chile. The reason cited was the Chilean government's failure to make "reasonable progress toward a reasonable settlement" on the expropriation of assets of U.S. copper companies and Chile's reduced creditworthiness due to increasing macro-economic instability.[181] The financial aspects of this story deserve attention here.

Chile's balance of payments steadily deteriorated in 1971 and it sought a re-scheduling of its debt. In a private conversation with Burke Knapp, the U.S. executive director, Robert E. Wieczorowski, reported on a meeting of the National Advisory Council (NAC) staff to discuss U.S. policy toward rescheduling of Chilean debts at which "there was a very strong feeling at the meeting that the World Bank should participate in the rescheduling." Apparently the Eximbank in particular had stressed that "if the World Bank had to participate in reschedulings, it would give us [the World Bank] an incentive to be a 'prudent' lender."[182] The United States had raised the question of the Bank's participation in debt rescheduling not only in reference to Chile but as a broad policy matter.

The Bank's management strongly opposed any such move. In replying to Wieczorow-ski's request for Bank participation in debt rescheduling, Knapp raised the stakes:

> There is no question that the adverse effects of rescheduling debt service payments due to the Bank would be pronounced, not only in this country but also abroad. . . . If, contrary to our views, member governments should take the position that the IBRD should participate in reschedulings, it would be essential for us to discuss with them what measures they would be prepared to take to restore the damage to the Bank's financial position and to its ability to borrow in the capital markets which would result from such action.[183]

With the Bank refusing to make new loans to Chile on the grounds of poor creditworthiness and poor disbursement of existing loans, net transfers to Chile turned negative in 1972.[184] Faced with the prospect of no new loans from the Bank and a rapidly deteriorating economy, Chile stopped servicing its Bank debts at the end of 1972, even as it continued to service its debt to the IDB. As its arrears

180. Ibid., pp. 179–80.

181. Memorandum, Richard Dosik to files, "Chile—Mr. Knapp's Meeting with Delega-tion," October 4, 1971.

182. Memorandum, Knapp to McNamara, January 6, 1972.

183. Ibid.

184. Of the three loans made in 1970, $17.9 million of $19.3 million remained undis-bursed more than three years later. See IBRD, "Chile Technical Assistance Project," R73-223, September 7, 1973, annex 2, p. 1.

mounted (they reached $8.4 million in the first six months of 1973), Chile and the Bank reached a modus vivendi in mid-1973. Chile agreed to resume payments and liquidate its arrears by the end of the year. In return, the president proposed to the Board that the Bank fund "certain payments of interest during construction on two loans for projects in Chile which are still in course of disbursement. . . . This proposal . . . would provide $8.3 million toward covering Chile's debt service to the Bank during the calendar years 1973 and 1974."[185] In addition the Bank agreed to make a small technical assistance loan. However, a month later, before the proposals could even be approved by the Board, Allende was deposed in a military coup.

Another factor contributing to the Bank's increasing skittishness on rescheduling was its declining financial ratios: "We are confident that the financial community . . . will recognize that the decline in the interest coverage ratio is not a sign of a deteriorating financial situation, as long as substantial absolute levels of income and liquidity are maintained and *as long as the Bank does not participate in debt reschedulings of its borrowers and is not affected by defaults.*"[186]

Following the oil shock, the deteriorating economic circumstances of its borrowers added to the Bank's nervousness about this issue. In trying to balance increased lending with creditworthiness concerns, the Bank began to seek assurances from marginally creditworthy borrowers that the "Bank would not be requested to participate in future debt reschedulings."[187] The *Economist* ran an article stating that "officials at the World Bank now admit that there is a risk of some of its borrowers being forced to reschedule their debt repayments." Citing Cyprus and Chile as the two most worrisome, the magazine went on to state: "The World Bank is obviously anxious that the bond markets, where it raises its money, should not draw wrong conclusions from the fact that it is doing a loan quality exercise."[188] Shortly thereafter an internal review concluded that "the ratio of income-at-risk to net income increases threefold over the next decade. This suggests that as the risks [themselves] are growing only modestly in relation to the growth of IBRD business,

185. IBRD, "Chile: Agreement for the Resumption of Payments to the Bank and IDA," R73-200, August 7, 1973.

186. IBRD, "IBRD Financial Policies," R73-55, March 28, 1973, para. 14, p. 6. Emphasis added.

187. This particular reference was to India. Given the ceilings on IDA, McNamara was looking for ways to increase IBRD loans to that country, particularly for fertilizer plants to reduce fertilizer imports. Worried about India's creditworthiness, however, he proposed that if IBRD were to resume lending to India, "this could possibly be connected to a declaration on the part of India that the Bank would not be requested to participate in future debt reschedulings." Memorandum for the record, "Meeting to Discuss India's Lending Program," April 22, 1974. See also McNamara's personal annotations on office memorandum by Mervyn Weiner to Robert McNamara, "India—Your Meeting This Afternoon," October 4, 1974.

188. "Defaulters?" *Economist,* February 22, 1975, p. 95.

the ability to withstand risks is not growing correspondingly."[189] Two months later, the Bank changed the language in its bond prospectus.

The apparent hardening in the Bank's position on the rescheduling of its own debt was a particularly interesting aspect of the difficulties facing the Bank and built-in institutional imperatives that would necessarily constrain its room to maneuver on the debt issue in general. At the time, however, the Bank chose to balance its accommodating stance on expanding lending and relatively moderate increases in lending terms with a tougher posture on rescheduling its own debt. Whatever the overall welfare implications of such a stance, the shift would serve the institution well during the next decade by deflecting pressures to reschedule its own loans.

Raising Financial Resources

With only limited borrowing success in OPEC countries, raising funds to fuel the continued expansion in lending, while minimizing costs, continued to be challenging. Loan sales, moderately important in earlier years, dwindled to insignificance. The need to further boost borrowings to meet escalating funding requirements meant that institutional focus was principally directed to volume concerns, with less attention to cost considerations, especially those affecting the system as a whole.

Loan Sales

In contrast to previous decades, the 1970s saw loan sales plummet, especially during the mid-1970s. In comparison with borrowings, loan sales were now quite trivial as a source of Bank funding (table 15-7). There were several reasons for the decline.

At the beginning of the decade the Bank had established four criteria for selling portions of Bank loans: to replenish the Bank's loanable resources, to help bring its borrowers to capital markets, "to promote private foreign investment," and "to save money for borrowers by selling portions of a loan at rates less than the loan rate."[190] Market interest rates increased over much of the period, and the Bank's lending rates lagged behind these rates. With the Bank unprepared to sell its loans at discount (which would result in a capital loss on the books), the loans held little attraction for investors. The adoption of the quarterly adjusted lending rate formula in fiscal 1977 mitigated this problem. The increased volatility in interest rates

189. Memorandum, Cargill to McNamara, "Loan Portfolio Analysis Unit," September 17, 1975. The report had concentrated on income risks facing the Bank from loans either due to risk of rescheduling of loans or a temporary hiatus in debt-service payments.

190. Operational Policy Memorandum 3.40, March 31, 1971.

Table 15-7. *Loan Sales, Fiscal 1960–77*

| Fiscal year | Annual average (U.S.$ millions) | Percentage share | | Loan sales/total borrowings in period (percent) |
		Participation	Portfolio sales	
1960–63	259	15	85	66.3
1970–73	80	55	45	5.7
1974–77	62	27	73	1.9

Source: Memorandum, H. C. Hittmair to Raymond Goodman, August 17, 1977.

created a different problem. Commercial banks, which accounted for more than half of the Bank's loan sales, had shifted to floating rates on asset and liability management and were reluctant to invest in fixed rate financial assets, particularly for participation with maturities of more than five years. In addition, in view of the creditworthiness problems facing many of the Bank's borrowers, the absence of Bank guarantees may have diminished the market's perceptions of the quality of paper, although given the lending binge that the commercial banks were themselves indulging in, this appears unlikely. Loan sales picked up modestly after the mid-1970s, as investors sought to acquire maturities in strong currencies for speculative purposes or for hedging against liabilities in such currencies.

Perhaps the most important reason that the Bank's Finance complex had "turned bearish on the subject of Bank loan sales" had to do with income concerns.[191] Loan sales were likely to result in a (book) financial loss for the Bank and were therefore justified only if there were other overriding advantages. Since loan sales were a substitute for Bank borrowings, the financial test to be applied was the cost of borrowing funds (in a particular currency and maturity) relative to the realized returns in selling from the loan portfolio. As Finance Vice President Peter Cargill explained to McNamara, "As a practical matter, the cost of borrowing for the Bank should at all times be lower than the market levels required to sell loan certificates, with limited liquidity, without a Bank guarantee. It is therefore unlikely that sales from portfolio would continue."[192] Cargill's proposal that the Bank's relevant staff Operational Directive (OD 3.40) be amended to incorporate stringent financial tests for loan sales effectively terminated loan participation in 1977.

Borrowings

In 1974, following the first oil shock, existing financial assets suffered substantial book losses. This would mark the beginning of revolutionary changes in financial

191. Memorandum, Raymond Goodman to J. Burke Knapp and Ernest Stern, September 21, 1977.

192. Memorandum, I. P. M. Cargill to Robert S. McNamara, December 28, 1977, p. 2.

instruments and markets.[193] Through most of the 1970s the yield curve in the U.S. market featured a negative slope, to the point that this inversion practically became the "norm." The effects of the "Volcker shock" at the end of the 1970s only compounded the impact on the U.S. capital market of inverted yield curves.[194] Investors began to modify their asset preferences accordingly, veering noticeably toward short-term, high-yielding assets. This increasing bias toward more liquid assets was reflected in market innovations, in particular the phenomenal growth in money market assets. As financial markets shifted toward shorter maturity, variable-yield instruments, bond markets languished in the United States.

At the end of 1974 the Bank's underwriters had expressed the view that the Bank could raise up to $2 billion priced closely to U.S. agencies, in the U.S. market.[195] And indeed the U.S. market was the largest source of Bank borrowings between fiscal 1976 and 1978, accounting for nearly 30 percent of all borrowings.[196] However, higher interest rates in the U.S. market for fixed-rate, long-term funds and the availability of funding from alternate low-cost sources meant that the U.S. market, despite being the largest and most versatile capital market in the world, became a relatively minor source of funding over the rest of the decade. In fact, the Bank stayed away entirely from the U.S. market between fiscal 1979 and 1981.[197]

In 1981, although interest rates prevailing in the United States were even higher, market and capacity constraints in its other low-cost markets and access uncertainty forced the Bank to return to the U.S. market. The Bank's absence from the U.S. market had been costly in that investors had once again to be educated about its activities and its bonds.[198] Cognizant of the problem, the Bank decided in

193. The year 1974 saw the worst bear market in common stocks since the great crash of 1929, with prices dropping nearly 40 percent over their levels two years before. Inflation-adjusted stock prices were at the levels prevailing two decades earlier. These losses spilled over into the bond markets, which suffered a 35 percent loss of purchasing power. Peter Bernstein, *Capital Ideas—The Improbable Origins of Modern Wall Street* (Free Press, 1992).

194. On October 6, 1979, Paul Volcker, the new chairman of the board of governors of the Federal Reserve System, announced that the Fed would henceforth target money supply instead of interest rates in controlling the availability of credit in the United States. As a result interest rates in the United States became much more volatile.

195. This view was expressed by John Gutfreund of Salomon Brothers. See memorandum, Eugene H. Rotberg to files, December 16, 1974.

196. Because of the size of the U.S. market, the Bank was a minor player in terms of overall volume. Even in 1975—the peak year for the Bank in the U.S. market in this period when the Bank's issues constituted 26 percent of foreign bond issuances—it accounted for 4 percent of total private sector borrowing and a mere 1 percent of total gross borrowing.

197. The United States seldom engaged in access constraints during this period, in contrast to the 1960s. There were exceptions. In 1980 it withheld approval for a deutsche mark Bank issue in New York on grounds that the issue would provide negative signals to the foreign exchange market.

198. For instance, when the Bank was planning to return to the U.S. market in 1981, John Whitehead, who then headed Goldman Sachs, asserted that knowledge of the Bank had

1980 to enlarge its management group by including Merrill Lynch and Goldman Sachs.[199]

The three most important markets for the Bank between fiscal 1977 and 1981 were Germany, Japan, and Switzerland, which accounted for 29 percent, 17 percent, and 15 percent of all borrowings, respectively. Borrowings from private sources (that is, excluding "special" placements and central bank loans) in the German capital market were the largest single source of Bank funding. In each of these markets the Bank was the most important nonresident borrower. However, for reasons discussed in chapter 16, the Bank stayed away from the burgeoning Eurobond market in the 1970s (an exception was a Euroyen issue in August 1977, for $75 million equivalent).

The Cost of Borrowing

Although there is little doubt about the Bank's success in rapidly increasing its borrowings over the 1970s, there is less certainty about the relative cost of its borrowings. This is perhaps not surprising, since McNamara's main objective was to "maximize the flow of resources and to consider spreads only as secondary as long as these margins remained within reasonable limits."[200] Still, it is not too clear why, with the exception of Japan, secondary market yields on Bank bonds (relative to yields on government bonds) increased in the Bank's principal borrowing markets—Germany, Switzerland, and the United States—during the period 1973–81 (table 15-8).[201]

"dissipated" owing to its absence since July 1977. Investors had to be reeducated again and if the Bank was thinking of raising $2 billion to $3 billion per year from the U.S. market, "it could not afford selectivity as to rates and markets." Memorandum for the record, "Meeting with Mr. Whitehead, Goldman Sachs," February 26, 1980.

199. Merrill Lynch's chief executive officer, Donald Regan, had for several years been lobbying the Bank arguing the case for his firm's inclusion to the Bank's three managing underwriters (see, for instance, memorandum for the record, "Meeting with Mr. Donald T. Regan, Chairman and Chief Executive Officer of Merrill Lynch and Co., Inc., April 27, 1978"). The Bank's treasurer had not been persuaded of the merits of Merrill Lynch's case. It was perhaps fortunate that the Bank nonetheless added Merrill Lynch to its managing underwriters in 1980. The supplicant-master relationship would soon reverse following the appointment of Donald Regan as Treasury secretary in the new Republican administration.

200. Memorandum for the record, "Meeting with Mr. Whitehead, Goldman Sachs," February 26, 1980.

201. Memorandum, J. Rolfo and S. Rajasingham to Eugene Rotberg, Hans Hittmair, and Hugo Schielke, "Yields on IBRD Bonds in the Secondary Market; A Comparison with Government Bonds in the US, German, Swiss, and Japanese Markets," May 4, 1982. The paper compared yields on IBRD bonds with yields on government bonds (Treasury issues in the United States; issues of the Bundesrepublik, Bundesbahn, and Bundespost in Germany; issues of the Confederation in Switzerland; and government bonds in Japan) of similar characteristics in domestic bond markets where the Bank had a sizable amount of bonds

Table 15-8. *Average Spreads of Bank Bonds Relative to Government Bonds, 1973 and 1981*[a]

Country	1973		1981	
	Yield	Spread	Yield	Spread
Japan	7.74	100	8.62	10
Germany	8.57	–137	10.00	–40
Switzerland	5.44	–60	5.48	138
United States	6.80	50	13.50	100

Source: Memorandum, J. Rolfo and S. Rajasingham to Eugene Rotberg, Hans Hittmair, and Hugo Schielke, May 4, 1982.

a. The spread is the amount by which the average yield on the Bank bonds is above the average yield on the government bonds. A negative spread would mean that Bank bonds are, on average, yielding less than comparable government bonds.

There was considerable variation within the period. In the United States, despite the overall increase in both measures, an examination of the end-of-month spreads and corresponding yields did not indicate any strong correlation between the size of spreads and movements in the interest rate level. In the German market, although Bank bonds were at a negative spread for most of the period (owing to the absence of a withholding tax on World Bank bonds for nonresidents), spreads in general increased as government interest rates dropped and declined again as government yields rose. Spreads in the Swiss capital market showed the largest increase over the period. Only in Japan were spreads higher during the earlier part of the period than in the later part, although there were considerable fluctuations in spreads within those periods.

The Bank's treasurer would later adduce several reasons for the higher spreads on Bank bonds during this period:[202] restrictions on various institutional investors as to how much paper of international organizations they could hold; the fact that the Bank did not engage in open market activities to support its own bonds; and the limited liquidity of Bank paper.[203] However, these factors do not explain the *in-*

---

outstanding during the period January 1973 to December 1981. The results were based on end-of-month market quotations on outstanding issues in each of the four markets. For purposes of comparison, a sector with a maturity range of four to ten years was defined. Within this sector, the average yields (on a semiannual basis) were calculated as well as average coupons and average maturities to provide some perspective to the comparison. In addition, the average yield of government securities maturing in less than a year was included for comparison with the medium-term average yields.

202. Eugene H. Rotberg, World Bank Oral History Program, April 22, 1994.

203. This was one reason cited by the governor of SAMA, Anwar Ali, in 1974. Commenting on the Bank's largest bond issue at the time ($750 million), the *New York Times* stated: "Trust fund and pension fund managers, however assert that the market for World Bank securities is not liquid enough, and some hesitate to buy its bonds for that reason." "World Bank Back in U.S. Debt market," *New York Times*, December 10, 1975, pp. 73, 77.

crease in spreads. While the Bank's intermittent presence in the U.S. market in the 1970s may have reduced the liquidity of its paper, in other markets, such as that of Switzerland, the widening spreads seemed connected with too frequent issues (and too much Bank paper).

A contributing factor in the U.S. market may have been the Bank's decision, in the early 1970s, to drop commercial banks from its underwriting syndicate, on the grounds that they appeared to add little to the placement of its paper. However, the presence of commercial banks was a feature of the government market, since only government securities (and those of the IBRD) were excluded from the provisions of Glass-Steagall. As a result, the Bank's paper apparently migrated from government trading desks to so-called Yankee desks, a subsector of the U.S. corporate market that includes mainly foreign and supranational issues. It is likely that the psychological element of this shift alone widened spreads by more than a few basis points. In 1989, when the Bank's bonds once again traded on government rather than corporate desks, following its first "global bond" issue, spreads in the Bank's bonds declined markedly (see chapter 16).

The Turn of the Decade and the End of the McNamara Era

By 1980 Robert McNamara had spent twelve years as president of the World Bank. During this period the institution had flourished and had emerged as a much more prominent global institution. From the beginning, McNamara had been convinced that if the Bank was to harbor global ambitions, its financial intermediation role had to increase tremendously. At the same time, he was conscious that the requirement that the Bank seek ex-ante approval of the countries and currencies in which it wanted to borrow was a potential constraint to institutional autonomy. Thus began the McNamara-Rotberg road show, paralleled only by the McCloy-Black-Garner road show in the early years of the Bank. Their strategy had been to consciously diversify countries, markets, and sources of borrowings, even paying a premium (in terms of higher borrowing costs) to establish the Bank's presence. With diversified sources, the Bank could more easily ride out political storms arising out of political pressures on its lending operations. But an equally important element of their strategy was a conscious attempt to build up debt and consequently interest groups in different markets. If pressure was put by a major shareholder on an issue that could imperil the financial health of the institution, counterpressure could be brought through these new interests that now had a stake in the financial health of the institution.

The financial underpinnings of McNamara's ambitions for the Bank had meant that McNamara, perhaps more than any president since his time, took a strong personal interest in the financial operations of the institution, particularly the development of new markets and pricing of new issues. He had largely persuaded the institution's major shareholders to go along with his ambitious plans for the institution. And before his departure he had engineered the largest ever capital increase in the Bank's history, thus providing the Bank with the financial capacity to ratchet up lending even further in the new decade.

Yet the very financial success of the 1970s also laid the seeds of several problems that would confront the Bank in the new decade. In late 1980, as the Bank was drawing up plans for its borrowings over the following five years (fiscal 1982–86), its newly appointed senior vice president for finance, Moeen Qureshi, painted a somber picture regarding the Bank's financial prospects.

> There has been a major deterioration in the structure and depth of long-term capital markets [and] the Bank faces great uncertainty with respect to future access and costs in its traditional markets. . . . [I]t is not possible today to indicate, reasonably and prudently, that an expanded IBRD lending program [can] be funded in the markets at costs that would preserve IBRD's reputation as an effective and efficient development financing intermediary. . . . [T]he financial risks for the Bank, implied by our existing lending procedures have increased greatly in the current capital markets environment. An IBRD lending program of $90–95 billion during FY82–86 without any change in existing procedures could escalate these risks to insupportable levels. The most important financial risk facing the Bank under current market conditions arises from the long time lag between commitments and disbursements.[204]

Qureshi was referring to the Bank's enormous interest rate exposure arising from its contractual obligation of funding $30 billion of undisbursed loans at fixed interest rates averaging around 8 percent, even while market interest rates were touching 15 percent. In addition to dealing with the problem of funding outstanding commitments on low-interest loans, it had to find ways to fund new loans and price new commitments as it was planning a sharp increase in its lending program, with the entry of China and new lending initiatives planned for energy and structural adjustment lending.

The decision by Japan and Germany to limit the Bank's access to their capital markets during the rest of the fiscal year (1981) and the unresolved row with Arab members over the PLO issue created yet another obstacle. The Bank had no option but to substantially increase expensive dollar borrowings both from U.S. domestic sources and from Euromarkets, despite a potentially dramatic impact on the cost of funded debt, in order to meet its funding needs.[205] With borrowed funds now

204. Memorandum, Moeen A. Qureshi to members of the Finance Committee, "FY82–86 Borrowing Program," November 17, 1980, pp. 1–3.

205. An internal report on the Bank's funding access reported at the time: "The Bundesbank's recent decision on the payout of a SAMA private placement is a particularly worrying development. It indicates that the German monetary authorities are becoming increasingly ruthless, and that the imperative of curbing the external payment deficit is being given total priority over all other considerations. As a result, the Bank will have to rely increasingly on borrowing other currencies, including the more costly US dollars, both from domestic and offshore sources." World Bank, Financial Studies Division, *Recent Developments in Foreign and International Bond Markets, and Implications Thereof for IBRD Funding*," December 2, 1981, paras. 77, 79.

accounting for nearly two-thirds of the IBRD's cash receipts, and market borrowings accounting for more than two-thirds of total borrowings, the Bank was limited in its options.[206]

The fact that the Bank now found itself boxed in and having to face up to more expensive borrowings because of changes in the currency mix of its funding was strongly related to the lagged effects of past funding strategies. Although its privileged position had resulted in considerable nominal cost savings for its borrowers at the time, the Bank was confronting a substantial amount of unfunded commitments that had to be funded at current market rates. These commitments had been priced in line with borrowing costs that were now unattainable under soaring interest rates.

In addition, the Bank, along with many other financial institutions at the time, faced income risks arising from the health of its loan portfolio. By mid-1978 internal concerns were being raised about mounting arrears on commercial bank debts in some of the Bank's clients. Following a major analysis of the health of the IBRD's loan portfolio, the Bank's finance vice president, Peter Cargill, warned that there had been a "marked deterioration in the quality of the portfolio since end 1975 . . . [raising] several issues which require urgent attention. . . . [T]he increased riskiness in the loan portfolio has not been matched by a compensating increase in our capacity to bear risks."[207]

Although nearly four years had elapsed since the Bank began to methodically examine its portfolio, it was clear that the impact had been quite limited. The reasons were unsurprisingly prosaic: "a diffusion of responsibilities, a lack of orderly procedures and an inability or unwillingness to link operational decisions to the results of creditworthiness evaluations."[208] The problem was symptomatic of the perpetual struggle between loan and credit departments that all financial institutions face. It also partly reflected the difficulties of operationalizing country risk analysis. The subject of "country risk" had emerged as a hot issue in the 1970s, as major commercial banks engaged in a frenzy of international lending. In many cases fancy quantitative tools prevailed over country knowledge. Notwithstanding such analysis, in most cases, as Volcker admitted of similar problems at the U.S. Federal Reserve Board, "it did little to slow lending. The whole process was deliberately nuanced, apparently too nuanced for bank examiners in the field to manage or banks to respond effectively."[209]

206. Market borrowings accounted for 67 percent of total borrowings in the period fiscal 1977–81 as against 45 percent in fiscal 1969–73.

207. Memorandum, I. P. M. Cargill to Robert S. McNamara, "Riskiness in IBRD's Loan Portfolio," October 25, 1978.

208. Memorandum, K. Georg Gabriel to I. P. M. Cargill, "Issues Arising from an Evaluation of the Riskiness in IBRD's Loan Portfolio," October 18, 1978.

209. Paul A. Volcker and Toyoo Gyohten, *Changing Fortunes: The World's Money and the Threat to American Leadership* (Times Books, 1992), p. 196. Such sentiments were

Cognizant of the multiple risks facing the Bank, Qureshi's note had made clear that the institution's borrowing plans "would, in my view, entail changes in our financing procedures and operations which seem far too drastic and risky for the Bank's role and reputation, and the implications of which we have not yet fully considered."[210] Barely a year earlier, the Bank had been quite dismissive about borrowing in Euromarkets but within the year had been forced to change tack. Likewise, Qureshi's call for caution before making "drastic and risky" choices was now somewhat moot. For the Bank, making such changes was no longer a question of if, but when.

---

widespread. Robert Slighton (then chief economist of Chase) was quoted as saying, on the subject of country risk analysis, "You'd be impressed by how much they knew, but appalled by the difficulty of transferring that knowledge into policies for loans." Quoted in Sampson, *The Money Lenders,* p. 256.

210. Memorandum, Qureshi to members of Finance Committee, November 17, 1980.

SIXTEEN

Coping with Financial Turbulence

THE ONSET of the 1980s found the Bank a dramatically transformed financial institution. This transformation had resulted from a congruence of three forces: the striking increase in global financial intermediation during the 1970s, a supportive political climate, and personality factors in the shape of the institution's leadership. Although the period had been marked by hitherto unprecedented economic and financial upheavals, the institution had, for the most part, attempted to shield its borrowers from the turbulence of the period. In the process, however, the Bank itself became exposed to much greater financial risks. The most important thread running through the finance story of the 1980s was the institution's struggle to manage its exposure to a succession of risks that had little precedent. At stake was the institution's financial health, and in turn, its standing as a successful financial intermediary.

The Bank's paramount concern in the first half of the decade was how to deal with market risks, especially those associated with interest rate mismatches and funding. Later in the decade, the Bank was exposed to credit risks arising from the declining health of the Bank's loan portfolio. The latter, in turn, were the outcome of one of the deepest crises ever simultaneously afflicting the Bank's borrowers: the international debt crisis of the 1980s. That crisis profoundly affected the Bank's African and Latin American borrowers. However, the nature and magnitude of the crisis, as well as the Bank's role, were quite distinct in the two regions. The issues arising from the complex intertwining of the debt crisis with structural reforms within the Bank's borrowers, are examined in chapters 10 and 11. This chapter concentrates on the fallout from the debt crisis on the IBRD's financial situation as it simultaneously struggled to find the financial resources to help its borrowers while seeking to limit the risks on its own financial well-being.

Bank lending during this period increased moderately between 1982 and 1985, and then steadily through the rest of the decade. Thereafter it stagnated even in nominal terms. Lending in real terms remained essentially unchanged through this period. The Bank made several attempts to augment its lending through institutional innovations, but with little success. By the end of the decade, however, it had regained control over its financial risks, following a near doubling of its capital, a newly expanded membership, and its emergence as one the cheapest global borrowers. Indeed, the Bank appeared poised for a major expansion in its lending. Yet no such expansion occurred. That paradox is one of the final concerns of this chapter.

The Nature of the IBRD's Financial Risks

Managing risk is the fundamental business of banking. The travails of many international banks through much of the 1980s put into context the difficulties in getting a grip on this complex issue. To understand the nature of these risks, one must begin with the Bank's balance sheet. On one side, as in any financial intermediary, are the Bank's assets: these consists of its loans outstanding and (liquid) investments. On the liability side are its borrowings and its equity, comprising its usable capital and reserves (retained earnings).[1] The Bank's usable capital in turn comes from the paid-in portion of its capital, while its reserves are built through annual allocations from net income.[2]

IBRD Balance Sheet

Investments	Borrowings
Loans	Capital
	Reserves

Assets   =   Equity + Liabilities

The nature of the IBRD's financial risks and their relative significance has varied over time, under the influence of external events as well as internal policies and practices (table 16-1).

1. Strictly speaking, the IBRD's balance sheet also includes items classified as "other receivables" (on the asset side) and "other liabilities" (on the liability side), of which amounts receivable and payable for currency swaps are the most significant. Their exclusion here does not affect the tenor of the argument.

2. Owing to the nonconvertibility of some members' 18 percent capital contributions, the Bank's usable capital is less than its paid-in capital.

Table 16-1. *Principal Financial Risks to the IBRD, 1950s to Early 1990s*

Type of risk and balance sheet variables affected	1950s	1960s	1970s	Early to mid-1980s	Late 1980s to early 1990s
Currency mismatch	▄				▄
Interest rate mismatch (borrowings, loans, investments)				▄▄▄	
Funding access (borrowings)		▄	▄	▄▄▄	
Investment (investments)				▄▄▄	
Loan credit (loans)				▄▄▄▄▄	
Reserves to loans ratio (reserves, loans)					▄
Residual interest mismatch (loans, investments, borrowings, capital, reserves)					▄

Source: World Bank, Investments Department, "The Changing Face of IBRD Financial Risks: Historical Overview," n.d., processed.

The Bank faced a *currency mismatch* risk in its early years owing to the possibility of currency mismatch between assets and liabilities in the balance sheet. The Articles had already ensured that the Bank's operations should be structured so as to minimize its currency exposure risk.[3] By matching borrowing obligations in any one currency with assets in the same currency, either by holding or by lending the proceeds of its borrowings in the same currencies in which they were borrowed, this particular form of currency mismatch risk to the Bank was essentially eliminated.[4] A different, and unusual, currency risk facing the IBRD—one that entailed a risk to its function but not to its capital—arose out of the mismatch between the currency composition of its assets and the standard of value of its capital. As noted in chapter 15, this risk to its "headroom" arose because the Bank's capital—and thus its total lending capacity—was fixed in dollars and became apparent in the 1970s when the dollar depreciated against other major currencies after the breakdown of the Bretton Woods system in 1971. Although exchange rate changes left the IBRD's capital (and lending limit) unchanged, the nondollar loans in its portfolio rose in value, reducing the allowable margin for new loans. This had little operational significance at the time but would pose a considerable headache to the institution during the period 1986 to 1988.

3. Article IV, Section 4(b)(ii) requires that in the case of loans made out of borrowings, the total amount outstanding and payable to the Bank in any one currency shall at no time exceed the total of Bank borrowings in that currency.

4. Relatively small currency risks remained when the Bank agreed in 1950 to drop the requirement that earnings on 18 percent currencies be automatically converted to dollars. In 1957 the Bank suffered its first loss on nondollar earnings following the devaluation of the French franc. This aspect of currency risks to the Bank in its early years is examined in IBRD, "Losses Due to Currency Devaluation," R68-47, March 1968.

The risk of an *interest rate mismatch* refers to the possibility that the Bank might commit to lend at one rate set according to the cost of borrowing at the time of commitment, and then find, when it came time to disburse the funds, that the cost of borrowing had changed. Unlike commercial bank loans, the Bank's loans disbursed over a long period of time (six to seven years). Since the loan changes were fixed at commitment, it effectively delinked the cost of funding from the loan's interest rate. The interest rate mismatch risk was low as long as market interest rate volatility was low. Unfortunately, this was not the case during much of the 1970s and 1980s.

Under the Bank's Articles, the institution requires the consent of the country whose currency and in whose market it borrows. As a result, the Bank faces *funding* risks arising from the possibility that access might be denied when it needs to borrow in a particular currency or market. Access restrictions could occur either for political reasons or because of domestic economic problems in a particular market. In addition, access to borrowings can be imperilled by market developments, as when financial markets are in turmoil and/or due to rapid structural changes in the specific market segments of its borrowings.

Investment risks pertain to the Bank's investments of its portfolio of liquid assets. These may arise either because of adverse interest rate movements or because of credit risks posed by the issuer of assets. The risk to the Bank's investment portfolio due to interest rate movements was particularly apparent in the first half of the 1980s. The *credit* risk on the institution's loan portfolio is the standard risk faced by any financial institution when the borrower is unable to service its debt and consequently falls into arrears, nonaccrual, and possibly default. The Bank had been faced with this risk intermittently over the first four decades of its history. However, the problem was of an entirely different magnitude from the early 1980s onward.

The Bank has also faced three other risks: the *reserves to loans ratio* risk arising out of the differing currency composition in the two; and a *residual interest rate* mismatch risk due to the differing interest rate characteristics of the institution's liquid investment portfolio and its borrowings. In terms of the overall risks faced by the Bank, however, these risks have been considerably less significant than the risks enumerated above. Finally, in parallel with all organizations that stepped into the brave new world of finance that emerged in the 1980s, the Bank faced significantly greater *operations* risks emanating from inadequate control systems. As table 16-1 indicates, although the Bank faced different risks at different periods in its history, the 1980s were unprecedented in the combination and intensity of the Bank's risk exposure. The nature of these risks and the Bank's attempts to cope with them form the principal theme of this chapter.

Funding and Interest Rate Risks

As noted in the conclusion of chapter 15, by the fall of 1980 the Bank's senior management had become quite uneasy as the implications of the financial risks facing the institution began to sink in. A year later, Qureshi was reporting to his new president, "Our situation is coming under increasing financial strain."[5] The Bank was experiencing an unprecedented confluence of interest rate, maturity mismatch, and market access risks.

According to an internal staff analysis of the Bank's borrowing prospects at the time, there was still ample potential for medium- and long-term fixed-rate funding in amounts commensurate with the Bank's anticipated requirements, but it was "equally evident that, in order to fill its anticipated funding needs, the Bank [would] have to include an increasingly larger proportion of U.S. dollar denominated debt, both from U.S. domestic sources and from the euromarkets. This, in turn, [would] have a dramatic impact on the Bank's average cost of funded debt."[6]

The cost impact of being forced to borrow more U.S. dollars raised a number of fundamental issues and, as the paper noted, was a consequence of "the current impact of past funding strategies." Uncertainty, financial crises, and currency upheavals notwithstanding, throughout the 1970s the Bank had been able to switch markets whenever necessary, and to line up alternative sources of medium- and long-term fixed-rate funds when access to certain markets was constrained or undesirable. The Bank used its flexibility, as a matter of explicit strategy, to minimize *nominal* costs of funding. The Bank could do this because it could pass on the full cross-currency risk of its funding to its own borrowers.

Corporate treasurers, by contrast, *had to* adopt a flexible borrowing strategy during the same period and, in the case of large multinational corporations, displayed considerable skill in adapting to "uncertainty" in the international financial environment of the 1970s. They often switched from long-term to short-term funding, and from single-currency to multicurrency borrowing, mostly in offshore markets. In doing so, corporate treasurers were able to enlarge their funding capability and enhance the potential for domestic and international expansion. They also introduced greater risk (for example, cross-currency risk, "maturity mismatching," and interest rate variability) in their funding. Thus, in the private sector, flexibility and its concomitant risks were the necessary cost of sustained expansion. The IBRD's borrowings strategy and financial policies, on the other hand, meant that

---

5. Memorandum, Moeen A. Qureshi to A. W. Clausen, September 14, 1981.

6. Memorandum, Eugene Versluysen to D. J. Wood, P. Mistry, and K. Ikram, "Recent Developments in Foreign and International Bond Markets, and Implications Thereof for IBRD Funding," December 3, 1981, p. 1.

Table 16-2. *Interest Rate Mismatch Risks, 1979–82*

Fiscal year	Average interest rate on undisbursed loans (percent)	Average cost of new borrowings (percent)	Volume of undisbursed commitments (U.S.$ billions)
1979	7.96	6.22	16.3
1980	7.88	8.24	18.1
1981	8.10	9.61	21.6
1982	8.75	11.19	25.0

Source: Note from S. Ben Hui, FRSFP, to Devesh Kapur, May 19, 1995; World Bank, *Annual Reports*, 1979 to 1982, summary statement of loans.

although its privileged position has resulted in considerable nominal cost savings for its borrowers at the time, it now leaves *a substantial amount of unfunded commitments that had been priced in line with borrowing costs that are now unattainable.* Yet, these commitments will have to be funded at current market rates, in the light of a new currency-mix. There is a dual problem. First, how to fund outstanding commitments on low-interest loans. Secondly, how to fund new loans and price new commitments. Given that these problems are intrinsically different, it is unlikely that a single solution would be suitable for both.[7]

The Bank fixed the lending rate at the time of loan commitment for the entire maturity of the loan. The loans were not fully funded at the time of commitment. Commitments had rapidly increased during the 1970s, from $1.7 billion in fiscal 1970 to $7.6 billion fiscal 1980. But undisbursed loans rose even more rapidly (from $2.9 billion to $18.1 billion in the same period) owing to the nature of the Bank's business and procedures, as projects gradually got going. Overoptimistic disbursement forecasts and implementation problems in many borrowers exacerbated the buildup of undisbursed loans.

As a result of this so-called lag risk, the Bank now found itself exposed to having to fund loans at rates that were substantially higher than what the loans were committed to earn.[8] Between 1979 and 1982, the spread between the interest rate on undisbursed loans and the marginal cost of borrowings declined from 174 basis points to *negative* 244 basis points (table 16-2). Furthermore, the Bank's loan portfolio had, on the average, a longer maturity than its outstanding borrowings. Both the lag risk and the maturity mismatch risk were important sources of the Bank's income problems.

The sharp increase in interest rates had not only caused an unprecedented increase in the Bank's borrowing costs but also reduced the Bank's borrowing flexibility in major capital markets by squeezing long-term bond markets. This was

7. Ibid.
8. Memorandum from the president, "Review of IBRD Income Prospects and Policies," R81-304, November 20, 1981, para. 39.

particularly apparent in the U.S. market. Between fiscal 1976 and fiscal 1982, U.S. Treasury bill rates rose from 4.99 percent to 11.07 percent, peaking at 14.70 in 1981. The Bank's borrowing costs rose from 7.87 percent to 11 percent during the same period.

The Bank also faced considerable uncertainties with regard to market access in some of its principal markets. As the largest nonresident issuer, its share of borrowings were near the official and prudent financial limits in several major capital markets. Japanese authorities asked the Bank to stay away from their capital markets in the last few months of fiscal 1981. The constraints were even stronger in Germany, the largest single source of Bank funding over the fiscal 1977–81 period. As the country's external accounts deteriorated, the Capital Markets Subcommittee of the Bundesbank (the regulator of nonresident borrowers to the German bond market) closed the German bond market to all foreign borrowers, including the Bank, from the end of May to mid-June 1981.[9] IBRD deutsche mark issues were, for the first time, subjected to a total embargo during the "issue pause" of early 1981.[10] The Bank was also requested (by the Bundesbank) to "take it easy" in future borrowings, and to concentrate such borrowings in public issues.[11] The Bundesbank also asked the Bank to defer a deutsche mark placement with the Saudi Arabian Monetary Agency arguing that the Bank was "crowding out" other deutsche mark borrowers—including the German government—by tapping offshore sources of deutsche marks.

Consequently, the Bank had to turn to other markets, in particular, the more costly U.S. dollar market, out of necessity rather than by choice. Although the United States was the largest and most versatile capital market in the world, the Bank had completely stayed away from this market from fiscal 1979 to 1981, an absence explained by the Bank's pursuit of low nominal cost funding and the sufficient availability of funding from low-cost sources. The switch back to U.S. market funding reflected real and anticipated access and capacity constraints in other markets.

With the dollar market, the problem was not access constraints. Whereas in some markets the claim that the Bank's borrowings "crowded out" other borrowers may have been justified, this was never the case in the U.S. market

9. The German current account had moved into deficit in the spring of 1979 after three decades of consistently large surpluses. The deficit in 1980 reached US$16 billion, making West Germany the principal deficit country in OECD. Between the end of 1979 and February 1981 the deutsche mark fell in value against the U.S. dollar by 23 percent, depreciating strongly against the yen and pound sterling, although it remained fairly stable against other European Monetary System currencies.

10. Traditionally, the Bank had been exempted during "issue pauses."

11. Loans and "special placements" are, generally, direct drains on the capital account of the balance of payments because they are funded domestically. IBRD deutsche mark bonds, on the contrary, having traditionally attracted nonresident investors, did not affect the capital account.

where the Bank's borrowings had always been inconsequential in overall volume terms.[12] And, at least initially, the new U.S. administration did not engage in access constraints, being ideologically opposed to interfering in financial markets in this manner.[13]

Along with the new U.S. administration, the Bank's financial staff worried about what it perceived as an anti-Bank psychosis in some sectors of Wall Street, spurred by tirades from sections of the financial press (principally *Barron's* and the *Wall Street Journal*). Despite their AAA rating, IBRD bonds tended to attract terms comparable to those of AA industrial and A utilities, thereby increasing the absolute—and relative—cost of U.S. debt. "Spreads" between Bank bonds and comparable U.S. Treasury debt had been volatile, reaching (and sometimes exceeding) 100 basis points (1 percent).[14]

Instead, the major problem confronting the Bank in the U.S. market was the limited availability of fixed-rate, long-term funds at prices the Bank (and other preferred borrowers) could afford. Negative (or inverted) yield curves had led to sizable contractions of bond markets in the United States.[15] Investor behavior had evolved accordingly with a pronounced propensity toward short-term, high-yielding assets. Investors' changing asset preferences and increasing bias toward more liquid assets were reflected in the phenomenal growth in money market assets. The liquidity afforded depositors the funds necessary for investment in short-term, highly liquid assets. The trend toward shorter-maturity, variable-yield instruments led to a shrinkage in the medium- and long-term U.S. bond market.[16]

Several steps were now proposed to bolster the institution's financial situation. The Bank approached its larger shareholders to accelerate their subscriptions to

12. In 1975, a peak year for IBRD borrowings in the United States, when the Bank's borrowings constituted 26 percent of foreign bond issuances, they accounted for 4 percent of total private sector borrowing but just 1 percent of total gross borrowing. The large share of the IBRD's liquid portfolio placed in U.S. markets meant that net claims on U.S. capital markets were substantially lower. World Bank, Financial Studies Division, Financial Policy and Analysis Department, "Recent Developments in Foreign and International Bond Markets, and Implications Thereof for IBRD Funding," December 2, 1981, para. 112.

13. An exception to this rule was the withholding of approval in 1982 for a deutsche mark Bank issue in New York on the grounds that it would provide negative signals to the foreign exchange market.

14. The spreads were generally larger when market rates declined.

15. Throughout most of the 1970s, the yield curve in the U.S. market featured a negative slope, to the point that this inversion practically become the "norm."

16. Between 1976 and 1981, the value of long-term, fixed-yield instruments declined from $39 billion to $27 billion and their share from 13 percent to 6½ percent. Similarly in the Eurodollar market, between 1975 and 1980, the share of fixed-rate bonds fell from 86 percent of the total market size to 64 percent. Mirroring the fall in the fixed-rate sector was the growth in floating rate notes (bonds with a coupon adjusted periodically in line with the movement in short-term interest rates).

the newly approved General Capital Increase. However by early 1981, a year after the beginning of the subscription period for the GCI, only half of what the Bank had expected to come in as lendable resources had been received. A decision by the United States to stretch out its subscription over a six-year period triggered a go-slow response from France, Japan, and Germany on releasing local currency portions of their capital subscriptions.

But it was clear that early access to shareholder capital would only be a temporary palliative, and not an answer, to the larger risks facing the Bank. Major initiatives involving changes in loan policies and innovations in borrowings were launched to cope with the risks posed by the unfunded $25 billion debt overhang. But risk, like energy, is never destroyed—its burden is simply shifted. The next few sections examine these issues.

Changes in Loan Policies

It was evident to the Bank's management that funding these undisbursed commitments at prevailing market interest rates without raising lending rates would substantially reduce net income and, thereby, the growth of reserves. An acceleration in the continuing steady decline in the reserves to loans ratio (see figure 15-1) would send negative signals to markets, raising the cost of borrowings. As the Bank's Managing Committee discussed the implications of substantial increases in the IBRD's lending rates, managers from the operations and policy complexes worried that the changes would result in the Bank moving more in the direction of a commercial bank than a development institution. Operations managers were worried about a prospective loss of business since "if borrowers have good market access and little need for technical assistance, [they] won't accept our high interest rates and burden of conditionality."[17]

The lending rate policy guidelines approved in 1979 provided for a 50-basis-point spread (0.5 percent) above the cost of borrowing (weighted by amount and maturity for the twelve months centered on the date of review). That policy had stipulated that management could recommend a different spread if required. As dollar interest rates soared, exceeding 16 percent, and the Bank's borrowing costs touched 11 percent, an automatic application of the lending rate would have resulted in an increase of 165 basis points in the June 1981 review. Instead, rates were increased by 1 percent and by a further 1 percent in September. In two years, lending rates had increased by 3.45 percent, the most rapid increase in the Bank's history.[18]

17. IBRD Managing Committee, "Summary of Discussion and Committee Actions," meeting of October 26, 1981, p. 3. The worries were particularly about "countries such as Brazil and Mexico since the Bank cannot borrow more than about ¼ percent better than commercial banks."

18. IBRD, "Review of Lending Rate," R81-157, June 10, 1981. Memorandum from the President, "Review of IBRD Income Prospects and Policies," R81-304, November 20, 1981.

However, increases in lending rates impact net income with a lag. Although a commitment fee of 0.75 percent was already in place, the deterioration of the Bank's short-term income prospects due to the overhang of undisbursed loans was sufficiently alarming to persuade the Board to approve a front-end fee. In early 1982, the Board, slightly modifying management's recommendations, approved a 1½ percent front-end fee on all new IBRD loans while leaving the lending rate and commitment fee unchanged (at 11.60 percent and ¾ percent, respectively).[19] As a result of these changes, the nominal grant element of IBRD loans dropped from about 14 percent in 1974–78 to minus 2 percent during 1980–84.[20] Eventually these policies overshot their target in that realized net income would be substantially greater than forecast. In part, this was due to the lock-in feature of the high fixed-interest loans of fiscal 1980–82, which contributed substantially to profits in the 1980s.[21] Later in the decade, as the IBRD's financial position strengthened and loan charges were eased (the front-end fee was lowered twice in 1984 before being eliminated in early 1985), the grant element on IBRD loans increased to 10 percent during 1986–90.

Although these changes would improve immediate net income prospects, they did not deal with the two fundamental risks facing the Bank: funding and interest rate risks. These were addressed by implementing two basic changes in the way the Bank had borrowed and lent money: engaging in short-term or variable-rate borrowings on a large enough scale that they could provide a significant source of funding; and moving to variable-rate loans on the lending side. The Bank recognized that these changes "represent[ed] fundamental departures from the financial structure and policies that have guided World Bank operations since the founding of the Bank, and are expected to have significant effects on the Bank's borrowers."[22]

19. Memorandum from the president, R81-304, November 20, 1981; "Minutes of Meeting of the Executive Directors of the Bank and IDA of January 5, 1982"; and memorandum from the president, "IBRD Lending Rate and Other Loan Charges," R82-101, April 13, 1982, para. 4. Management had recommended an increase in the commitment fee to 1 percent, a front-end fee of 1 percent and a lending rate of 11.85 percent, or an increase of 25 basis points above the existing rate. The Board justified its decision to increase the front-end fee as a quick way to improve net income and the interest coverage ratio. The decision to maintain the lending rate at 11.60 percent was explained by the decrease in the Bank's borrowing cost which had declined by 107 basis points from the time the Board paper was prepared in November and when it was reviewed by the Board in December.

20. Michel Vangeas, "IBRD Lending and Other Flows: A Question of Competition, Background Note," March 18, 1992. The grant element is a measure of the concessionality of a loan and is calculated as the difference between the present value of the future debt service payments expressed as a percentage of the face value of a loan. The above numbers are based on a discount rate of 10 percent.

21. In fact even as financial policies were being changed to augment net income, the Managing Committee, confronted with a higher than expected net income, noted that, "$601 million was a very high figure to report as net income for FY82," IBRD Managing Committee, "Minutes of July 2, 1982, Meeting."

22. "Memorandum on Reasons for a Change in IBRD Borrowing and Lending Rate Policies," May 4, 1982, para. 2.

The Bank's move to a variable-interest rate lending rate system was only partly driven by the need to moderate its exposure to interest rate risk (and hence provide greater stability to its net income). Equally important was the need to alleviate funding risks that had arisen by the shrinkage of the IBRD's traditional sources of medium- and long-term fixed-rate borrowing and to go where the money was: in short-term and variable-rate instruments. The much greater interest rate risks inherent in such borrowings meant that the Bank had to change its lending rate policies.[23] An additional reason for initiating the short-term variable interest rate borrowing program was to invest these funds in "broadly matching maturities thereby locking in the positive spread existing between the various short-term markets. The operations and investing would be self-contained and profitable."[24]

While the variable lending rate system would shift the interest rate risk to borrowers, the pooling system ensured that changes in the lending rate would occur only gradually. Stability in the lending rate was considered a desirable characteristic in the financing of development projects. The pool-based variable lending rate system was instituted at the beginning of fiscal 1983. Under the new policy, all new loans would pay 50 basis points over the average cost of the qualified borrowings, defined as the outstanding borrowings issued since June 30, 1982.[25]

Innovations in Borrowings

At the turn of the decade the Bank had already reached a crossroads of sorts in its funding strategy. Even without the scare of 1981, the institution would have had to adapt to the major structural changes that had occurred in international capital markets over the previous decade. The funding problems in the Japanese, German, and Swiss markets in 1981 would, in retrospect, prove to be a blessing in disguise. If necessity is the mother of invention, Bank staff, faced with serious funding problems, became very inventive. In fact, over the decade from the currency swap operation in September 1981 to the global bond in 1989, the Bank's innovativeness in its borrowing operations was an achievement that won the institution plaudits from a broad cross section of market observers. Its "enormous contribution to the development of the international capital markets, identifying and opening new

23. Indeed, the Board paper argued that "the *first* reason to change the Bank's lending rate policy is to accommodate the new types of borrowing." Memorandum from the president, "Proposed Changes in IBRD Borrowing Practices and Lending Rate Policies," R82-182, June 3, 1982, para. 3.01. Emphasis added.

24. Memorandum, Eugene Rotberg to members of the Finance Committee, "U.S. Market-Variable Rate Borrowing Program," March 24, 1981, p. 10. The countries whose currencies were to be used may well have demurred if they perceived that the borrowings were largely for interest arbitrage purposes.

25. The lending rate was to be recalculated and announced every January 1 and July 1, becoming effective in the subsequent semester. IBRD/IDA, "Minutes of Meetings of the Executive Directors of the Bank and IDA," M82-40, IDA/M82-39, July 14, 1982; and IBRD, "Proposed Changes in IBRD Borrowing Practices and Lending Rate Policy," R82-182, June 3, 1982.

sectors, and sponsoring innovative concepts" would earn it the accolade the "Borrower of the Decade."[26]

International financial markets at the beginning of the 1980s were composed of two distinct segments: banking markets and bond markets. The principal segments of international bond markets were the fixed-rate Eurobond market, the floating-rate note market, and the foreign bond markets, the last being the foreign segments of domestic bond markets. As a result of the macroeconomic shocks of the 1970s— much higher levels of inflation and interest rates as well as increased volatility of both exchange and interest rates—several major financial market trends had emerged, which would now accelerate: internationalization, integration, expansion, mobility, and an explosion in the techniques and instruments of financial inter-mediation, which began to erode erstwhile sharp distinctions between inter-national banking and bond markets.

The rapid mobility of funds meant that the Bank had to be much more agile in locating and tapping new sources of funds. The principal element in the transfor-mation of financial intermediation was the shift from fixed to floating rate instru-ments, transferring risk from creditors to borrowers. Investors were reluctant to incur large capital losses on fixed-rate instruments when interest rates moved upwards. Conversely, borrowers were increasingly chary of locking in high nominal rates. As a result, banking market intermediation became more important relative to bond markets and, within bond markets, a shift to floating rate notes, and analogous instruments, was occurring. The shrinking pool of long-term, fixed-rate bond markets was particularly apparent in the high-inflation economies of the United States and the United Kingdom. By contrast, in Germany the authorities actively discouraged the growth of floating rate instruments, fearing that it may institutionalize inflation. However, in Germany, as well as in Swiss and Japanese markets, changing investor sentiment was manifested in shortened maturities of fixed-rate instruments in the long-term bond market.

Faced with severe pressures in raising resources through traditional financial instruments, the Bank introduced a succession of new borrowing instruments: currency option bonds, currency swaps, and a short-term borrowing program introduced in autumn 1982.[27] Following this, there were borrowings at variable interest rates, interest rate swaps, and new instruments for borrowing from mone-tary authorities; an ECU borrowing in late 1983; floating rate notes in early 1984; and serial zero coupon bonds in 1985.[28] These changes met with a less than

26. "World Bank: A Decade of Market Patronage," *International Financing Review, 1980–1989: Review of the Decade* (London: IFR, 1989), p. 33.

27. Currency option bonds allow the investor to link the value of principal and interest to more than one currency. The Bank first used this technique in a seven-year dollar/SF–linked issue in April 1982.

28. Floating rate notes are hybrid financial instruments combining the characteristics of a money market instrument (repricing over a spread over a short-term rate) with a medium- to long-term maturity, the key characteristic of a traditional bond.

enthusiastic reception in German financial circles, which, like their Swiss counterparts, had already regarded the introduction of adjustment lending with some wariness and now regarded the Bank's increasing recourse to short-term and floating rate borrowing instruments, as well as excessive dependence on nondollar markets, as inappropriate to the institution's mandate.[29]

In parallel with other financial institutions with a large Latin American exposure (including the IDB), spreads of IBRD issues over Treasury instruments of comparable maturity widened in the immediate aftermath of the Mexican crisis. By early 1983, however, the markets' move to quality led to a strengthening of the IBRD bonds (the Bank achieved its lowest spreads over the past twenty-five years in a two-tranch bond issue for $400 million in February 1983). Throughout the 1980s, the Bank did quite well on its liabilities side, even as it continued to struggle on the asset side of its balance sheet as the fallout from the debt crisis intensified, in part because other financial intermediaries were in such poor shape.

During the first half of the decade the Bank's dollar borrowings faced unexpected funding problems as a result of its indifferent relations with the U.S. Treasury, a state of affairs that would prevail over much of the decade. Increasingly, the U.S. Treasury extended its battles on the Bank's lending policies into actions that impaired the Bank's financial maneuverability. The strong opposition of the United States to the Bank's energy policy, in particular, its lending for hydrocarbon projects led David Mulford to warn the Bank that "since we had consistently ignored their wishes, they were reviewing whether the Bank should continue to have access to the capital markets."[30] In 1982 the Board had authorized a new short-term borrowing program under which the Bank would issue discount notes. The program was authorized following an assurance by the U.S. Treasury that the authority would be valid for *at least* ten years, after which consent could be revoked, but only after twelve months' notice. At the time, the U.S. executive director, James Burnham, had stated that "his authorities believed very much in the concept of open capital markets . . . and he hoped that their example had been noted by others."[31] Burnham now informed the Bank's treasurer that the United States was prepared to give authorization for such issuance only with the proviso that the authority could be revoked at any time on twelve months' notice. The "short-leash" was an about-face to the understandings reached in the Board. The Bank's financial staff had brought in these new instruments assuring the Board that there was no market risk on the funding of short-term paper.

> It would be an anomaly if a funding risk would occur not because of [the institution's] credit standing but rather because the U.S. Treasury, for political reasons, saw fit to

29. See the section, "The Financing of the International Monetary Fund and Multilateral Development Banks," in *Monthly Report* of the Deutsche Bundesbank, September 1983, p. 43.

30. Memorandum, Ernest Stern to Tom Clausen, "Meeting at the U.S. Treasury with Assistant Secretary Mulford," April 6, 1984.

31. IBRD/IDA/IFC, "Summaries of Discussions," SD82-46/1, September 22, 1982.

deny us access to refinancing. . . . Jim [Burnham] confirmed . . . that if the Bank did not change some of its basic policies, specifically oil and gas lending, that the U.S. Treasury was prepared to take some drastic steps of which this was the first shot. He confirmed that he intended to use this new approach as a vehicle to make known their displeasure.[32]

Eugene Rotberg further feared that if management did not compromise, "the U.S. Treasury, Mulford in particular, will simply conclude that if that didn't work, perhaps something more severe will."[33] And indeed Rotberg's fears came true when, a month later, Mulford informed the Bank that "in light of market conditions we will be unable to respond affirmatively to the full amount of the U.S. dollar borrowings implied by the program. I, therefore, suggest that you revise downward substantially your planned program of U.S. dollar borrowings."[34]

The proposed borrowing program of $4,467 million for fiscal 1985 was cut by $700 million after protracted discussions in order to obtain U.S. support for the borrowing resolutions for the fiscal 1985 lending program at the Board meeting. But just before the meeting, the U.S. executive director asked for a deferment claiming that Mulford and Beryl Sprinkel had not had time to focus on the issue. Several days later, apparently on Sprinkel's instructions, the United States agreed to support the borrowing program, but only if it were further reduced by $900 million. Again, management felt that it had little option and Moeen Qureshi recommended that "we go ahead and accept whatever we can get out of the U.S. at this time. I do not believe we shall gain anything letting this issue fester further."[35] The Board was told that "at this point, we do not know whether or how those dollars will be replaced. The income and lending rate effects are uncertain."[36] Ceilings on the size of the Bank's dollar borrowing operations continued. Thus, of the $9 billion borrowing program for fiscal 1987, the Bank could borrow only $1.9 billion in public markets (that is, U.S. and Eurodollar market) and only $1 billion in the U.S. domestic market.[37] The ceilings imposed a financial cost as they implied a departure from optimal borrowing strategies.

Meanwhile, the structure of the Bank's dollar borrowings changed substantially during the first half of the 1980s with the Bank steadily expanding its dollar

32. Memorandum, Eugene H. Rotberg to A. W. Clausen and Moeen A. Qureshi, "Increase of $250 Million Discount Notes," May 29, 1984, p. 1.

33. Ibid., p. 2.

34. Letter, David Mulford, assistant secretary, U.S. Department of The Treasury (International Affairs), to Moeen A. Qureshi, June 25, 1984.

35. Memorandum, Moeen A. Qureshi to A. W. Clausen, July 16, 1984, p. 2.

36. Statement by Mr. Rotberg to executive directors, "FY85 U.S. Dollar Borrowings," SecM84-720, August 3, 1984, p. 2.

37. Memorandum, Moeen A. Qureshi to Barber B. Conable, "Lunch with Goldman Sachs," March 6, 1987.

borrowings in Euromarkets for cost reasons.[38] The share of U.S. dollars borrowed in the U.S. market dropped markedly—from 62 percent in 1975–79 to 26 percent in 1980–84, even as dollar borrowings doubled between the two periods. Even as the Bank stayed away from the U.S. market, major changes were occurring in the U.S. fixed-income securities market. Competition changed dramatically, both because of significantly larger U.S. Treasury offerings (a result of large budget deficits) and an explosion in the variety of financial products available to investors. Increased interest rate volatility raised the level of trading activity in institutional portfolios, and with it the liquidity premium on fixed-income securities. By the mid-1980s, the Bank had become an insignificant borrower in the U.S. market.

EUROBOND BORROWINGS. The institution's entry into the Eurobond market marked its first major foray to diversify its borrowings.[39] This market had rapidly expanded over the period 1974–77; after a sharp falloff in new offerings in 1978 the market regained some of its buoyancy thereafter. The Eurobond market was inherently different from all domestic markets for foreign bonds, being, by definition, a free, unregulated market where trends—both in the demand and supply of funds—were the direct reflection of underlying shifts in the international economy, rather than of administrative fiat. Nevertheless, at the time, national authorities of some major countries could, and did, indirectly control the flow of Euroissues denominated in their national currencies. For instance, Switzerland had placed a complete embargo on Swiss franc–denominated issues outside Switzerland; and in the case of Euro–deutsche mark issues, the Bundesbank insisted that they be managed by a German bank.

The absence of capacity constraints (for borrowers enjoying the Bank's credit rating) suggested that the Eurobond market would be a gradually increasing source of funding. A problem in this market was that shifts in investor preferences, and international bond and currency arbitrage in general, strongly influenced the currency composition of the new issues market at any one time. With costs fluctuating in line with domestic market rates for each currency, the availability of funds would have to take precedence over the Bank's preferred currency-cost profile.

Despite the rapid expansion of the Eurobond market during the 1970s, the Bank stayed away from this market (with the exception of a $75 million equivalent Euroyen borrowing in 1977). Dollar interest rates were relatively high, especially from the late 1970s onward, and the Eurodollar bond market was consequently not a particularly cheap form of financing. As for other currencies, it was usually cheaper to borrow in the national market of the currency being borrowed. How-

38. On comparable transactions, Eurodollar deals were consistently 15–30 basis points cheaper than dollar borrowings in the U.S. market. Memorandum, Kenneth G. Lay to Donald Roth, "U.S. Dollar Borrowings," January 13, 1988.

39. The Eurobond market is the market for bonds sold internationally and outside the jurisdiction of any single national authority.

ever, the reluctance to test the Euromarkets also reflected the Bank treasurer's uneasiness about the lack of transparency in the Eurobond market.

The Bank first entered the Eurodollar market in June 1980, raising $500 million in the Eurodollar sector in a two-tranch issue, and followed it with a further offering of $500 million in July 1981. The circumstances of the first Eurodollar operation, in which the Bank chose Paribas over its traditional European manager Deutsche Bank, vividly illustrated both the relationships and stature that Rotberg had built for himself and the institution over the previous decade. As recounted by Pierre Haas, then chairman of Paribas,

> [My colleague] called me . . . at 8.30 p.m. to tell me, "The market has moved, and I think we can do the World Bank in Europe cheaper than in the States." Two minutes later I called Gene Rotberg, and there was silence: He couldn't believe what I said. Now, he knew me, and he knew I was incapable of giving him a cut rate just to get a deal. . . . Then he was very pensive, the way he is on the telephone, and said, "All right, let me think about it." . . . Then the next night . . . I was called out, and Gene says, "You have the deal if you can stick to that rate. I'll give you till tomorrow." . . .
>
> So then, to come back to trust, I knew that for him this deal was as important as it was for us, because it was the first time the World Bank borrowed dollars outside the U.S., which was something the board of directors was not very keen on. So what was at stake was his reputation and his job, and my reputation and the reputation of our bank with him. Gene trusted that we could deliver. [As] a good treasurer [he] knew well the personality of each of the firms and of each of the operators.[40]

Over the course of the next few Eurodollar issues, the Bank settled on Deutsche Bank as the book-running lead manager with CSFB as colead and another dozen or so banks as comanagers.

SWAPS. The attractiveness of the Euromarkets was evident when, in August, $290 million was raised in two tranches and the proceeds were switched into Swiss francs and deutsche marks in a swap operation with IBM. A similar operation took place in September involving the issuance of two tranches of Eurodollar bonds totalling $330 million, and swapped into Swiss francs and deutsche marks.

The currency swap with IBM turned out to be a landmark operation, enhancing the arbitrage opportunities available to the Bank. At the time, the Bank faced dollar interest rates of about 17 percent and Swiss franc and deutsche mark rates at 8 and 12 percent, respectively. Bank staff felt that it was better to disburse the low nominal currencies rather than the high-interest-rate dollar. However, the Bank's Deutsche mark and Swiss franc borrowings had already exceeded the limits set by the authorities of these countries. Moreover, there were indications that the Swiss market was beginning to suffer from indigestion from the large volume of the Bank's borrowings in that market. At the same time, IBM, which had borrowed

40. Pierre Haas, former chairman, Paribas International, quoted in *The Way It Was: An Oral History of Twenty Years of Finance* (New York: Institutional Investor, 1987), p. 279.

deutsche marks and Swiss francs, currencies that had since depreciated, was keen to sell them to realize a healthy book profit. The two institutions decided to swap their currency obligations. Under the arrangement, the World Bank borrowed dollars at 17 percent; IBM agreed to pay the interest and amortization on this dollar loan to the World Bank; in exchange the World Bank took on IBM's Swiss franc and deutsche mark obligations, paying interest and amortization to IBM.

Although not the first such transaction, the market stature enjoyed by the two participants gave the technique a stamp of respectability and accelerated the establishment of the currency swap market. As was to be the case with many other innovations in the Bank's borrowings instruments in the 1980s, the Bank's standing in financial markets paid handsome dividends. Market operators, keenly aware of the legitimacy granted to a new financial product if utilized by the Bank, bombarded the institution with new ideas.[41]

For the World Bank, currency swaps ameliorated interest costs. The Bank's early swap operations were predominantly dollar/Swiss franc until the Swiss National Bank placed some restrictions. Gradually the Bank extended its swap operations into longer maturities and a broader range of currencies. In fiscal 1985, swaps were broadened into interest rate and cross-currency interest rate swaps. Initially it appears that in several cases, swaps were undertaken without much consideration between the timing of the borrowing and the timing of the swap. Later swaps were only undertaken when a minimum of 30 basis points of savings in relation to direct borrowings could be realized.

Swaps provided the Bank with high arbitrage possibilities because of preferential access in highly regulated markets, particularly in Western Europe. In the Italian market, for instance, Italian tax arbitrage provided the Bank with considerable savings after it obtained tax-exempt status for its lira bonds in 1986. The Bank issued floating rate notes aimed at Italian investors and swapped them into fixed-interest-rate U.S. dollar borrowings taking advantage of historically low-interest-rate swaps. In addition to the Italian lira, the principal vehicle currencies for swaps were the Australian dollar and the Canadian dollar in the first half of the decade and the Finnish markka and the Spanish peseta in the second half.[42] The process of deregulation in these markets meant that the arbitrage opportunities also declined. In addition to arbitrage pos-

41. According to Jessica Einhorn, a member of the team that helped devise the first swap, Peter Gottsegen, then in charge of World Bank relations at Salomon Brothers, first suggested the opportunity. "The Winning Ways of Jessica Einhorn," *Euromoney*, June 1995, p. 45. Bank insiders credit Lester Seigel, a former physicist, with putting together the technical parameters of the operation.

42. The Bank also undertook modest borrowings in the smaller European markets, including the Austrian schilling market (for the first time in 1980), the Belgian capital market in 1984, the Danish kroner market in 1985, and a Norwegian kroner borrowing in 1982. In almost every case the Bank would swap the respective net proceeds of these issues into another currency (usually Swiss francs).

sibilities, diversification of borrowings was also justified by a "market presence" argument: broadly construed to include continuity of relationships with a shareholder and the investment community in that country and an insurance against funding and market-access risks.

Swaps had two additional implications for the Bank. They brought with them a new concern in risk management owing to the credit risk arising out of swap counterparties risk. If such a risk ever materialized, it would be passed through to the borrowers. Consequently the Bank initially maintained a policy of limiting its swap activities to AAA-rated companies. A swap insurance program was instituted in 1986 but proved largely inconsequential. More important, swaps increased the Bank's reliance on hard currencies and exacerbated the exchange rate risks faced by borrowers.

SHORT-TERM BORROWINGS. In mid-1982, following the changes in the Bank's borrowing and lending policies, the Bank initiated a short-term and variable-rate borrowing program with an initial ceiling of $1.5 billion. The move met with considerable uneasiness among Board members worried about the prudence of an institution lending long while borrowing short. The short-term borrowings program initially focused on establishing a discount note program in the U.S. market, the least expensive and most liquid source of U.S. dollar funds.[43] Consent was obtained from the U.S. Treasury for the Bank to refinance and roll over these notes for a period of not less than ten years, with a one-year termination notice. The first discount notes were sold in September 1982 and the $1.5 billion ceiling was reached within a month. By 1984 the program had been expanded to $2.5 billion.

In tandem with the market-based short-term borrowings the Bank also embarked on a new facility designed to attract official funds. A new "Central Bank Facility" was created (it began operations in January 1984 with an initial ceiling of $750 million) as a device to expand borrowings from central banks. This complemented the long-established two-year central bank issues, which tapped the foreign exchange reserves of the institution's member central banks. The latter had become a permanent source of funds for the Bank, being largely refinanced as each original borrowing matured, and for long had allowed the Bank to use long-term funds at intermediate-term costs.[44] However, the share of official reserves invested directly in World Bank securities had eroded from 3 percent in the mid-1970s to less than 2 percent by the end of 1982. The Central Bank

43. At the time, the size of the short-term paper market in the United States was estimated at about $660 billion, which was more than one-third of total marketable debt in the United States. See "Technical Note on IBRD Short-Term Borrowing Program," June 30, 1982.

44. In the early 1980s they were being offered at 25 basis points above comparable Treasury securities. The largest subscribers to the Bank's two-year issues for U.S. dollars had been Libya, Saudi Arabia, and Italy.

Facility was created to reverse this trend and was a one-year dollar deposit facility with interest rates based on a spread over one-year Treasury bill rates and adjusted monthly. The facility had two features that were particularly attractive to developing-country central banks: its high liquidity (a provision of withdrawal of deposits on two days' notice before maturity without penalty); and anonymity, with the identities of the central banks not shared even with the Bank's executive directors. Although the latter aspect was particularly important to those central banks concerned with keeping their reserves out of the gaze of their country's creditors, its aggregate size was too small to be of much significance in this regard.

COLTS. The dollar's decline in mid-1985 led many in the Bank to believe that the demand for dollar-based securities from nondollar-based investors in Europe and Japan would also decline. Concerned with this development, the Bank set to redress the imbalance in its dollar borrowings between the U.S. and Euromarkets and in 1986 launched a new program called COLTS (Continuously Offered Long-Term Securities). By offering three- to thirty-year paper, with the investor free to chose any maturity within this period, the COLTS program was a particularly innovative attempt to adapt the structural features of the short-term commercial-paper market to the long-term bond market.[45] Using U.S. Treasury securities as its benchmark, the COLTS program gave the Bank flexibility to direct demand to the maturities it preferred at any point in time by offering the paper in that maturity at a higher spread over comparable Treasury paper.

The COLTS program, sales of which were limited to North American investors, was developed with the specific objective of getting the maximum sales force and investor exposure for each dollar borrowed. It was designed to help the Bank widen its sales force away from the bulge bracket securities firms to include those of mini-institutional and retail sales forces of the smaller securities firms scattered across the U.S. market.[46] Direct contact across a much wider investor cross section was also seen as a way to bolster political support for an institution that was politically embattled and that by this time was facing adverse name recognition and public relations problems. However, it did not last long and never raised large volumes of funds, as it was soon overtaken by another borrowing innovation: global bonds.

BORROWINGS IN NONTRADITIONAL MARKETS. Although the IBRD was a minor player in the three largest markets (during the period 1981 to 1983, its borrowing was less than 1 percent of total gross bond issues in the United States, Japan, and Germany), its share was much larger in the narrower set of foreign

45. Commercial paper is IOUs with any maturities (usually not longer than a year) that are traded daily through dealers. Bonds are securities bearing a fixed coupon and a stated maturity that are first sold to underwriters, who in turn distribute them to investors.

46. The COLTS program initially employed Goldman Sachs, Merrill Lynch, Shearson Lehman, and Salomon Brothers as agents. After the first year, First Boston and Morgan Stanley were added to the group, while Salomon Brothers was dropped because of poor performance.

borrowers—6 percent in the United States, 15 percent in Germany, and 25 percent in Japan. It was therefore important, for political reasons even more than financial reasons, that the Bank extend its efforts to tap new markets. Although many of the countries to which the Bank now turned had regularly participated in the Bank's official borrowings, the capital markets of most countries of the OECD (other than the G-3 and Switzerland) had been closed to external borrowers, particularly after the 1973 oil crisis. As they sought to cautiously liberalize their capital markets, however, acceptance of an IBRD borrowing operation was a safe way to test the waters.

A surprisingly robust source for IBRD borrowings in the first half of the 1980s was the Dutch guilder, in both the domestic market and the Euro–Dutch guilder sector, accounting for more than 5 percent of gross borrowings between fiscal 1982 and fiscal 1987. The Bank reentered the Canadian capital markets in fiscal 1984, after an absence of a dozen years. In August 1984, the Bank became the first issuer of Canadian dollar paper in the Asian dollar market. In November 1984 and again in January 1985, the Bank launched its first non-U.S. floating rate notes (FRNs) and the longest maturities achieved by the Bank by placing two Can$100 million ninety-nine-year FRNs with a limited group of institutional investors in the domestic market.[47] In addition, the Canadian dollar emerged as the second most important currency vehicle for swaps.

After the Bank's first and only issue in the Euro–French franc market in 1972, the Bank entered the French domestic market in 1985 with a modest FF 1 billion (US$107 million) bond issue. This issue, which was swapped into Swiss francs at attractive savings, was the culmination of a yearlong series of negotiations between the Bank and the French Treasury, which led the authorities to exempt IBRD bonds from France's 10 percent withholding tax (the Bank was the only borrower in the French market, other than the French government, to be exempted from the tax requirement). However, the French Treasury's sensitivity to yield comparisons that could place French government bonds in an unfavorable light led it to intervene in the pricing of Bank bonds. Ultimately, it insisted that the Bank's bonds be priced at a yield 5 basis points above the "market" yield recommended by the issue's management group. The French market would, however, be marginal to the Bank.

In the dollar market the Bank followed up on the success of the COLTS program by placing increased emphasis on individual research and marketing calls on many of the largest pools of capital in the U.S. market. The COLTS program signified a tactical shift in the Bank's borrowing strategy which, at least since the 1960s, had relied principally on dealers, to inform itself of investors preferences. However, a structural shift in financial markets, with dealers increasingly involved

---

47. These borrowings, which were priced at a spread over ninety-one-day government Treasury bills, increased the average life of the fiscal 1985 borrowing program by about two years.

in trading on their own account, meant that it was difficult to distinguish between dealers' own preferences and the claims made on behalf of end investors. Beginning with the COLTS program, the Bank shifted tack on market research, placing a considerably greater weight on direct contact with investors to better assess their needs.[48] The results were changes in product design that ran counter to the then conventional "market" wisdom. The most well-known outcome of this modified approach was the "global bond."

GLOBAL BOND. Around 1987, several staff in the Bank's Treasury Department became convinced that structural impediments in the fixed-income securities market were preventing the institution from achieving the quality of yields that its financial situation warranted.[49] In the beginning of 1988 work began on designing a product to remedy this situation and over the next eighteen months, the Bank developed a new method of distributing and trading securities that came to be known as "global bonds."[50] Overcoming considerable skepticism from underwriters, Bank staff began to doggedly address the many technical barriers to the creation of a global financial instrument: differing underwriting conventions and fees; varying systems of organization of investment dealers businesses; incompatibility of clearance and settlement systems across markets.

In designing the global bond, the approach was to incorporate in a single instrument features that major participants in the international markets valued in fixed-income securities. For Euromarket investors, this meant structuring the issue so as to assure active trading on London Eurobond desks, Euro-clear or Cedel clearing and settlement, and the same tax treatment as the Bank's seasoned Eurodollar bonds (non-U.S. source income and an absence of withholding, backup withholding, information reporting, or certification of non-U.S. ownership). Since the much larger size of individual global bonds meant that the Bank would be entering the markets less frequently, new interest rate hedging mechanisms were also put into place.[51]

At the same time, the instrument sought to provide Euromarket investors with the backstop of U.S. domestic market demand—by improving the bonds' potential appeal to investors in the United States. Taking full advantage of the Bank's leverage in such a high-profile deal, and one that would signal the Bank's choice of

48. An informed review of this subject can be found in "Improving Bond Offerings for Institutional Investors: Review and Outlook," attachment II, in IBRD, "Funding Operations Report: First Quarter FY92," R91-229, October 22, 1991.

49. Memorandum, Kenneth G. Lay to Donald Roth, "U.S. Dollar Borrowings," January 13, 1988.

50. Kenneth G. Lay, "Mobilizing Private Savings for Development: IBRD and the Capital Markets" (World Bank, 1994), p. 16. Initially, this instrument was termed "universal bond."

51. This meant that borrowing costs would reflect interest rates prevailing only a few days in a year, rather than be spread out more evenly over the year, as in the case with several medium-size issues. Deferred and anticipatory rate-setting agreements were used to separate the timing of the issues from the setting of the rates and to average out the cost of funds.

the "international bulge bracket"[52] for U.S. dollar securities, the Bank's new treasurer, Donald Roth,[53] insisted to the underwriters for the first global bond issue that the price of admission to the syndicate was to trade the IBRD's paper on the "agency" desk, rather than the higher-cost "Yankee" desk.[54] One by one all the major players agreed. Global bonds were traded in the United States in the agency market, included in the agency classification in bond indexes, and more widely accepted in the general "repo" collateral markets.[55]

The first global bond—a $1.5 billion ten-year maturity offering—launched simultaneously in New York, London, and Tokyo in September 1989, was widely acknowledged as a landmark deal, both for the Bank and in the annals of global financial integration. Its success put to a rest skeptics who had doubted European investor interest in registered bearer bonds (their reputed unalterable preference was for nonbearer bonds). Its yield-spread performance, trading, and liquidity were a significant improvement to existing Bank paper. Although the second global bond had mixed results, the instrument was soon extended to the deutsche mark and yen and emerged as the major source of IBRD borrowings, accounting for nearly two-thirds of IBRD borrowings in 1994. In using the cheaper funds from global bonds to refinance some of its preglobal issues, the Bank also lowered its overall cost of funds.

The idea inherent in the global bond—bridging segmented domestic and offshore markets, and better product design through extensive direct contact with investors— was extended to other products. In 1990 the Bank developed a prototype for small-scale global distributions aimed at different market segments by issuing New Zealand dollar notes, that resulted in both significant cost savings as well as obtained a much

52. The "bulge bracket" refers to the five or six largest U.S. investment houses. The "international bulge bracket" is an extension of the concept to the largest dozen or so international lead underwriters. There is intense jockeying among investment houses to be included in the bulge bracket, based on the presumed signaling effect on their placement power in a specific market segment.

53. Donald Roth served as Bank treasurer from 1988 through early 1992. Before joining the Bank he had been chairman of Merrill Lynch Private Capital.

54. Until the early 1970s the Bank's paper used to trade on the "agency" desk of U.S. security houses, those dealing with securities issued by a U.S. federal agency. At that time, a decision was taken to exclude commercial banks from the IBRD's underwriting syndicate on the well-founded view that they contributed little to the placement of its paper. However, the presence of commercial banks was a feature characteristic of the government securities market, the only segment of the market open to commercial banks under Glass-Steagall regulations. For reasons that are not altogether clear, following the exclusion of the commercial banks from the IBRD's underwriting syndicate, IBRD securities migrated to so-called Yankee desks, a higher-cost subsector of the U.S. corporate market that includes mostly foreign and supranational issues.

55. Repo (or repurchase) collateral markets refers to the arrangement by financial institutions to borrow short-term (usually one day) money by transferring specified securities to the lender with the agreement that they will buy them back.

larger volume of funds in that currency. Nevertheless, gains from a "benchmark" Swiss franc issue launched in 1991 were more modest.[56]

BORROWINGS IN THE 1990S. By the early-1990s, the funding risks for the Bank had dropped to an all-time low. Consent requirements (mandated by the Bank's Articles), had been gradually relaxed by the members where the Bank's principal markets are located. Even in the big three markets, the leash given the IBRD was much longer.[57] Indeed, if anything, the pressures were in the opposite direction, with several countries pressing the Bank to increase borrowings in their markets. Earlier procedures whereby the Bank had to bring each individual borrowing to its Board as well as seek permission from the country or currency of borrowing, was clearly unworkable in an era where market conditions change in minutes. Cognizant of this reality since 1990, the Bank's Board was presented with an annual borrowing plan, with quarterly updating, instead of the earlier issue-by-issue approach. To be sure, there still were occasional hiccups. In 1991, for instance, Spain closed its markets to the Bank and also threatened to withdraw from the Global Environment Facility after a mandate had been awarded, upset by an operational decision by the Bank in Uganda.[58]

The Bank also emerged as the cheapest global borrower bar the G-3 Treasuries with its borrowings serving as benchmarks for other large borrowers (see figure 16-1), the culmination of a long and painstaking process, and clinched by the advent of the global bond at the turn of the decade.

But, as of the mid-1990s, for a variety of reasons, the portents for the Bank's borrowings appear less bright than the impressive performance of previous years. First, having achieved borrowing costs so near those of the G-3 Treasuries, the institution's scope for any marked improvement was both much less, as well as much more difficult. The rapid diffusion of financial innovations also meant that

56. In part this was due to the cozy oligopolistic market structures prevailing in the Swiss market. The big three—Swiss Bank Corporation (SBC), Union Bank of Switzerland (UBS), and Credit Suisse (CS)—strongly disagreed among themselves on the merits of the issue, with SBC in favor, while UBS and CS complained about the performance of the bonds (tightly priced, no justification for liquidity premium, difficult to place, and so on).

57. These requirements are somewhat of an anachronism, as became evident when the Bank sought to borrow in European currency units (ECUs) in the mid-1980s. This prompted debates on whether the ECU was a currency or a unit of account and if the former, was the Bank then required to seek permission from all members of the European Community?

58. Apparently, following a Public Investment Review in Uganda, the Bank had reached an agreement on investment priorities. Shortly thereafter the Bank learned that Uganda had agreed to an airport project with a Spanish firm that was backed by national export guarantees. Arguing that the project was of dubious merit given the precarious state of the economy, the Bank threatened to withhold its support for a transport sector loan. The Ugandan government withdrew from the project. Angered by the Bank's role the Spanish government—already unhappy with Spain's low share in Bank procurement—denied Bank access to peseta borrowings. Tracy Corrigan, "World Bank and IFC Barred from Spanish Bond Market," *Financial Times*, January 28, 1992, p. 27.

Figure 16-1. *Relative Spreads: IBRD minus AAA Financials in U.S. Dollar Markets*

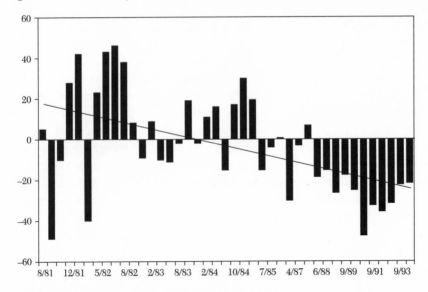

Source: World Bank, Risk Management and Financial Policy Department.

the advantages accruing from specific financial innovations were short lived. Thus, although the advent of the global bond allowed the Bank to capture a 5- to 10-basis-point advantage with respect to other similarly placed institutions, as markets evolved this dropped rapidly to between 2 and 5 basis points.

Second, structural changes in global capital markets were weakening some of the reasons underlying the Bank's past borrowings' success. In previous years the Bank's success as a borrower was undoubtedly aided by the fact that its securities, like those of other supranational borrowers, occupied a special position in each domestic market equivalent to that of domestic government or government-guaranteed issuers. This last, however, occurred only after sustained representation by the Bank that granting such access was mutually beneficial. For the Bank, it would help reduce funding costs by accessing a broader investor base in its primary market offerings. For countries beginning to liberalize their capital markets, an IBRD borrowing was an important first step in securing their authorities' confidence on the prudence of such a step. Thus the Bank's treasury operations facilitated capital market liberalization, an interesting sidelight to its other objectives. As countries began to cautiously liberalize their capital markets, the Bank was often the first foreign borrower allowed in their markets, a measure of the institution's reputation and a certain trust in an institution which the countries were also part owners of. In this role the Bank helped develop specific segments of financial markets, increase underwriting competition (for instance in Switzerland), and establish benchmarks for other borrowers.

Over the 1980s, however, capital market liberalization in the countries where the Bank's borrowings had been concentrated meant that the traditional arbitrage advantages that accrued to the Bank shrank. At the time of writing, the Bank had not accessed the large new pools of savings emerging in East Asia in noteworthy advantageous ways. Unlike many other governments that gave the Bank preferential access in the initial stages of liberalizing their capital markets, Singapore authorities were not particularly interested in the Bank in this regard. Taiwan was ruled out because of Chinese sensitivities.[59] And the Asian Development Bank nosed out the Bank to the post in the Republic of Korea, as the country cautiously began opening its capital markets.

In 1989 the Hong Kong government for the first time permitted nonresident issues of Hong Kong dollar debt. The Hong Kong and U.K. authorities pressed the Bank to increase borrowings, arguing that a borrower of the Bank's quality would send a clear confidence in the Hong Kong market and its future under Chinese leadership. In particular, borrowings with maturities beyond 1997 would underlay confidence in Hong Kong's long-term prospects. At first, despite the inclinations of its Treasury Department, the Bank demurred, based on a long-standing principle of not borrowing in those markets where it continued to be a lender (reflecting Hong Kong's status as part of China in 1997, a borrower). Eventually the Bank did borrow in the Hong Kong market, but ensured that its borrowing maturities were within the colony's reversion date to China. Subsequently, it decided to consider borrowing in countries that had not graduated from its lending, as long as viable opportunities existed and the country was willing.

In previous years, as a borrower, the Bank enjoyed an important advantage over its competitors that had allowed it to stay ahead of the pack: it was the largest nonsovereign borrower in many markets and the largest supranational borrower in most markets. Size when added to savvy is a powerful combination and in prior years had served the Bank well.

Since the mid-1980s, however, the Bank's role as a financial intermediary— intermediating financial flows from capital-rich to capital-poor countries—has waned (see page 1108). Even in nominal dollars, borrowings were essentially unchanged from 1983 to 1991 at about $10 billion. A moderate increase in 1992–93 was again followed by a decline in 1994–95. In fact, net borrowings (gross borrowings minus debt retirement) have been negative since 1987 supporting the contention of those who have argued that the Bank has been on a financial "treadmill" in recent years—its borrowings being used to "'churn' its own debt [rather] than to expand net resource flows to its borrowers."[60] This state of affairs mirrors the Bank's

59. The Asian Development Bank, however, has borrowed in Taiwan, which is a member of that institution.

60. Percy S. Mistry, "The World Bank's Role as a Borrower," report to Group of Twenty-Four, UNCTAD Secretariat, Geneva, January 1991, p. 16. Exchange rate effects and refinancings confuse the picture (refinancings were particularly important in the late 1980s owing to a large volume of yen refinancing). The IBRD's borrowings outstanding increased

low net disbursements on its lending side (averaging less than half a billion dollars a year between 1994 and 1996).

The shrinkage of the Bank in the financial dimension is particularly manifest in changes in relative size. Ranked twenty-seven among global banks in 1984 (measured by assets), by 1995 it ranked sixty-eight (table 16-15). In 1993–94, for the first time the European Investment Bank edged out the Bank as the largest supranational borrower. Erstwhile successful borrowing programs such as COLTS declined, squeezed between the sizable borrowings raised by global bonds and unchanging overall borrowing volumes. The market consensus on the Bank's new financial product innovations—such as the structured note program—were not as laudatory as previous innovations.[61] Furthermore, as per market perceptions, by the early 1990s other supranational borrowers had caught up with the Bank having also developed strong borrowing programs.[62]

The Currency Variable

Previous chapters have discussed the financial terms of Bank loans, particularly interest rates and timing elements: maturity, grace period, and disbursement speed. This section examines another, less familiar, feature of the Bank's loans: their currency composition, and the role of the Bank's liquidity.

From its founding, the Bank followed the practice, laid down in its Articles, of adopting a currency-neutral stance on its loans by requiring that all loan-service payments be made in the currency loaned, although this is not necessarily required by the Articles in all cases.[63] Typical Bank loans were multicurrency loans but

---

from $79.5 billion to $111.7 billion (implying an increase of $32.2 billion in net borrowings) between 1987 and 1995, principally because of the larger dollar value of nondollar borrowings (yen and the DEM group). However, on an annual cash flow basis net borrowings (gross borrowings minus debt retirement) over the same period were minus $1.3 billion.

61. See, for instance, Aline van Duyn, "Do Investors Need the World Bank?" *Euromoney*, March 1995, p. 10. Structured securities are combinations of bonds and embedded derivatives that link the principal and/or coupon payments to one or more indices such as exchange rates and interest rates. These transactions are tailored to quite specific investor niches.

62. *Euromoney*, for instance, ranked the Inter-American Development Bank, as the best supranational borrower in 1994. "Best Supranational Borrower: Inter-American Development Bank," *Euromoney*, June 1995, p. 80.

63. The Articles mandate that interest, principal, and other charges for loans made from the Bank's own funds (paid-in capital, reserves, and surplus) must be paid in the currency loaned (Article IV, Section 4(b)(i)). For loans made out of borrowed funds, the Articles only specify that the total amount outstanding and payable in a specific currency under all such loans cannot exceed the total amount of the outstanding borrowings made by the Bank and payable in the same currency (Article IV, Section 4(b)(ii)). In reality the Bank's Articles contain several provisions dealing with the use and exchange of currencies (and related

because the loans were not fully funded at the time of commitment, the standard loan agreement stated the amount of the loan in terms of the U.S. dollar equivalent. Under loan agreements, borrowers are obligated to pay interest and principal in the currencies actually used for disbursement to them. However, borrowers had little control over the currencies disbursed *or* over the sequence of recall of currencies. The Bank had the right to use for disbursement on any loan any of the currencies it had available and to specify the currencies in which each amortization payment was made (up to the total amount of each currency used for disbursement and outstanding under the loan). The borrower would know the currency composition of a loan only when disbursements were completed. More, it did not control the order in which the Bank asked for repayment. Neither the borrower nor the Bank could foresee the currency composition of the loan at any time during the repayment period. The Bank retained control of the order of repayment of currencies, and since the Bank itself did not know what currencies it would need until just before the maturities fell due, borrowers had no control over the currency exposure of their loans. As a matter of course, the Bank would recall high-interest currencies first (subject to currency-specific cash flow constraints).[64]

This system had been instituted under largely fixed exchange rates and with the dollar as the predominant currency of disbursement. Both assumptions gradually eroded, first, as the Bank began to diversify its borrowings, and, second, with the breakdown of the Bretton Woods regime in the early 1970s, as a result of which exchange rate volatility increased rapidly (table 16-3).

In effect, the currency regime of the Bank's loans had the characteristics of a lottery. Not only did it expose the Bank's borrowers to increased risks, but the resulting wide variance in the effective costs of IBRD loans across borrowers was anomalous for an institution that prided itself on being a cooperative financial institution, whose financial policies ensured equity across borrowers.[65] Although

---

issues of subscriptions and maintenance of value). These stipulations are complex, and the criteria on currency holdings on capital, borrowed funds, and earnings vary. Some, like the differences between "2 percent currency" and "18 percent currency" of capital subscriptions, are an anachronism reflecting the specific currency regime at the time of drafting (and serve little purpose other than a nuisance value). See memorandum of the Legal Department, "Legal and Policy Restrictions on the Borrowing, Use and Conversion of Currencies by the Bank," March 10, 1988.

64. "As a general rule, the currencies which are recalled from loans are those required for debt service and after this need has been satisfied, those that provided the highest yield on investment. These in turn tend to be soft currencies which results in the pool of currencies outstanding on loans being weighted more heavily with hard currencies." Report to the Joint Audit Committee, "Allocation of Currencies among Borrowers," JAC 77-20, August 24, 1977, para. 12.

65. A briefing to the Joint Audit Committee of the Board noted that "the degree of unevenness depends largely on how much the exchange rates between currencies disbursed by the Bank vary. How serious a problem this might be cannot be predicted with any

Table 16-3. *Relative Volatility of Nominal Exchange Rates among G-3 Currencies, 1960–94*

	Standard deviation of monthly percentage change			
Exchange rate	1960–71	1972–80	1981–90	1991–94
Deutsche mark–dollar	0.82	3.43	3.39	4.04
Yen–dollar	0.80	3.06	3.52	2.55
Deutsche mark–yen	1.08	3.21	2.68	3.22

Source: Peter B. Kenen, ed., *Managing the World Economy: Fifty Years after Bretton Woods* (Washington, D.C.: Institute for International Economics, 1994), p. 246.

the inequity was first recognized in the mid-1970s, for reasons that are not apparent the Bank moved somewhat leisurely and examined the issue in detail only toward the end of the decade. At that time the Board was informed that exchange rate movements had for the most part increased the debt-service obligations of the Bank's borrowers in terms of both the borrowers' own national currencies and the U.S. dollar, the currency by which the Bank's loan commitments are measured. However, these exchange rate changes have not only increased the effective cost of borrowing from the Bank for the borrowers as a group, they have also accentuated differences in exchange rate effects on individual borrowers that have always been part of Bank operations.[66]

To remedy this problem the Bank sought to put into place a currency pooling system, an accounting device designed to redistribute the exchange risk more evenly among borrowers.[67] Under this system, all amounts disbursed on all currency pool loans were recorded in a pool and amounts recalled for payment deleted from the pool. Each loan was, therefore, equivalent to a multicurrency loan composed of a proportional share of the currencies outstanding.[68] Two other options—changes in the Bank's currency allocation practices and introduction of currency-specific interest rates—were rejected.[69] It would take another two-and-one-half years before the recommendation to convert to a currency pooling system came into effect in 1980.

---

confidence." See memorandum, K. Georg Gabriel to Joint Audit Committee, "IBRD—Allocation of Currencies among Borrowers," JAC 76-3, February 17, 1976, p. 12.

66. IBRD, "Distribution of Exchange Rate Risks Among Borrowers," R78-259, November 30, 1978, p. 1.

67. The description of the currency pooling system draws heavily from Pierre Yourougou, "IBRD Loan Charges and Related Policies from 1946 to 1990," June 23, 1992.

68. The currency pooling system was analogous to a mutual fund. While individual loans were disbursed in different currencies, they shared the same currency composition as any other one in the pool, regardless of the currencies disbursed or recalled on that loan. On any given day, the set of currencies a borrower owed on a loan was not a function of disbursements or recalls on that loan but rather of the accumulated sum of all prior disbursements net of all prior recalls on all loans with outstanding balances in the pooling system on that day.

69. The concept of currency-specific interest rates would be resuscitated a decade later in the form of single-currency loans.

The currency pooling system equalized the currency risk among the borrowers, but it did not alter the currency risk for the group. The Bank continued to disburse and recall the currencies which fitted its funding, debt servicing, and investment priorities. The loan pool currency composition, therefore, changed over time and, as before, borrowers were not in a position to anticipate the currency mix and could not manage their foreign exchange risk even if they wished to do so. Furthermore, for a given borrower, the fit between the pool's currency basket and its own needs was happenstance.

The currency pooling system was an elegant solution to a difficult problem. But it had one problem: few understood it. With borrowers' liabilities changing daily as a result both of exchange rate changes and movements within the currency pool, the exchange risk became entangled with the lending rate "in a way that [made] measuring and managing exchange risk difficult (from the borrower's point of view)."[70] Its complexity meant that for all practical purposes it was opaque not only to the Bank's borrowers but also to the institution's own operations staff. Only a handful of Bank staff understood the basis of the system, its long-term impact on effective costs, and how it distributed risk. As for the borrowers, even in the mid-1990s, fifteen years after it was instituted, a Bank report assessing the progress of the pilot Single Currency Loan program concluded that "many borrowers did not fully understand the terms of their existing currency pool loans."[71]

For long the Bank's currency choices were driven principally by considerations of market access (to ensure borrowing volumes) and nominal costs, i.e., interest rates. Over the 1970s another rationale emerged: currency choices that maximized returns from the Bank's liquid investments. Although Bank management did, at one stage, state that its currency policies "reflect[ed] the financial policy governing the Bank's *liquid assets*," this argument does not appear to have been openly articulated later.[72] Thus currencies of borrowing were driven by market considerations and by the Bank treasury's liquid investment priorities. Borrowers' preferences were a residual factor. The Bank would periodically defend its currency policies on the grounds that a "change in this policy would not be to the borrowers' long term advantage because any deterioration in the Bank's financial performance will eventually require higher interest rates on loans."[73] In order to understand the linkages between the Bank's currency policies and its liquid investments, it is necessary to examine the Bank's liquidity and investment policies.

70. Memorandum, Barbara N. Opper to Moeen A. Qureshi, "Responses to Your Questions on the Loan Charges," March 20, 1987, para. 3.
71. IBRD, "Review of the Single Currency Loan Pilot Program and Proposed Expansion," R95-91, May 11, 1995, para. 14.
72. IBRD, "Allocation of Currencies among Borrowers," para. 12. Emphasis added.
73. Ibid.

Liquid Investments

Following on the rapid growth of the Bank's liquid portfolio in the 1970s (see chapter 15), by the latter half of the decade it had grown large enough for the institution to emerge as an important market player. The large size of the institution's portfolio and active portfolio management received increasing—and almost uniformly laudatory—attention from the financial press.[74] The Bank's acumen in managing its portfolio was widely admired among market observers. The key to this feature was the apparent high returns on the liquid portfolio, a result of the active management of its portfolio that commenced after the first oil shock.[75] During the period 1974–78, while the Bank's investment holdings more than doubled (from $3.7 billion to $8.7 billion), the turnover of its portfolio increased eighteenfold (to nearly $90 billion a year).[76] By the mid-1980s, when the investment portfolio increased to about $20 billion, the Bank, on average, turned over its portfolio every two days: this amounted to more than $3 trillion a year. By the end of the decade, the Investments Department was managing a total liquid portfolio of $24 billion. Approximately two-thirds of this portfolio was invested in money markets (markets for short-term and variable-rate instruments) and the rest in bond markets (encompassing fixed-rate instruments of longer maturities). The money market portion, largely invested in commercial bank deposits, was characterized by large daily transaction volumes. In contrast its bond market investments were turned over at a more sedate pace and relative to the money market portfolio carried greater interest rate risk, but less credit risk. These characteristics of the Bank's investment portfolio implied volatile yields broadly in line with short-term interest rates.

Through most of this period, the contribution of the Investments Department to the Bank was considerable. While it did well to weather most financial shocks, the relative performance of the liquid portfolio during this period is difficult to judge. The Bank's Investments Department uses benchmarks to monitor performance. However, there are many legitimate ways to construct benchmarks and one can

---

74. For a sampling, see "The World Bank's Aggressive Cash Strategy," *Business Week*, May 1, 1978, p. 87; C. Frederic Weigold, "Systemized Risk, Rate of Return Guide Huge World Bank Portfolio," *American Banker*, May 9, 1978, p. 1; Clyde H. Farnsworth, "How the World Bank Manages Its Money," *New York Times*, December 2, 1979, p. F3; Kenneth H. Bacon, "World Bank Treasurer Rotberg Strives for Flexibility on $9.7 Billion Portfolio," *Wall Street Journal*, September 23, 1980, p. 6; Daniel Hertzberg, "Specialized Breed of Trader Manages World Bank's Huge Pool of Assets," *Wall Street Journal*, March 30, 1981, p. 25; Arlene Hershman, "World Bank: Doing Well by Doing Good," *Dun's Business Month* (U.S.), February 1984, p. 48; Ben Weberman, "Smart Answers to Dumb Questions," *Forbes*, May 19, 1986, p. 110; and John M. Berry, "World Bank Is a Global Bellwether: Huge Investment Portfolio Sways Financial Markets," *International Herald Tribune*, July 22, 1986.

75. Occasionally when markets go topsy-turvy (as during the Gulf War in 1991), the Bank resorts to a fallback passive investment strategy.

76. The Bank's principal investments are, of course, its loans. In this section, however, "investments" will refer to the institution's liquid portfolio.

exceed benchmarks and still underperform the market or underperform the benchmark and yet beat the market.[77]

In 1978, then vice president for finance, Peter Cargill, engaged James Van Horne of Stanford University to review the investment activities of the World Bank. Van Horne soon realized that the question of investment management was inextricably linked to the issue of the size of the Bank's liquidity holdings. His study concluded that there were "positive and significant costs to maintaining liquidity" and that these costs were "best approximated by the difference in new borrowing costs and the return on new investments *on a currency-by-currency basis* as opposed to an overall basis."[78] In light of these costs, Van Horne argued that "the level of liquidity [was] too high" and recommended reducing it from 40 percent of three-year borrowings to 30 percent. Finally, commenting on the performance of the investment portfolio, Van Horne found that the data *"do not demonstrate* that the active investment management strategy employed resulted in excess returns being earned on a risk-adjusted return basis. By the same token, the [B]ank earned a fully satisfactory return, again on a risk-adjusted return basis."[79] Looking back, he would later recall that he had been "somewhat 'gentle'" in his remarks. "Nonetheless, there was no evidence of significant value added and no justification for the large liquidity."[80]

But the implications of the Van Horne study were downplayed by the Bank. As we have seen earlier, between fiscal 1978 and 1980, the Bank chose to stay out of the U.S. dollar market (except for a $750 million loan floated in July 1977) and met virtually its entire borrowing need in the three "hard currencies"—the deutsche mark, the Swiss franc, and the yen—in that order of importance. The primary reason for the shift in currencies borrowed was justified on the grounds that "the nominal cost advantages resulting from borrowing in the three hard currencies rather than in U.S. dollars appeared to offset the potential costs of the foreign exchange risk involved."[81]

In 1980 Moeen Qureshi became the new senior vice president of finance. Keenly aware of the increased financial risks facing the Bank, Qureshi invited Jacques Polak, the highly respected research director of the International Monetary Fund for nearly a quarter century, who had just retired, to examine the currency structure of the Bank's borrowings and its liquid portfolio.

77. The problem is compounded by the fact that "market performance" (at a comparable twelve-month duration used by the Bank) is a more elusive concept than may first appear. As late as 1988, the Investments Department lacked adequate benchmarks for its nondollar portfolio.

78. James C. Van Horne, "Review of World Bank Liquidity and Investment Policies," unpublished paper, July 13, 1978, p. 1. At the time the author was a professor of finance at Stanford Business School.

79. Ibid., para. 3.

80. James C. Van Horne, personal communication, July 14, 1995.

81. IBRD, Treasurer's Department, "Cost of IBRD Borrowings," SecM80-120, February 20, 1980, p. 1/2.

Polak argued that if interest rate differentials among major capital markets were indicative of future exchange rate changes, the Bank could be indifferent, from a cost point of view, whether it borrowed in one currency or another; savings in interest on loans expressed in "strong currencies" as compared with loans expressed in U.S. dollars could be expected to be roughly offset by the higher cost of making interest and amortization payments in the appreciating currency. But, according to Polak, international capital markets were characterized by large and persistent deviations from interest rate/exchange rate parity conditions so that the effective cost, on interest and exchange rate changes combined, of borrowing in one currency could differ substantially from that of borrowing in another currency.[82]

Polak's analysis provided little support for the choice made by the Bank to concentrate its borrowings over the previous three fiscal years (fiscal 1978–80) in the so-called strong currencies and to forego borrowing in U.S. dollars beginning in July 1977. On the contrary, he found that, as a result of this policy, the Bank had incurred a substantially higher effective cost of borrowing than if it had made maximum use of the U.S. dollar market.

Polak followed up his analysis on the Bank's choice of currencies of borrowing with an analysis of the Bank's liquidity investments. In a strong critique, he argued:

> It appears to be widely accepted in this institution that the net cost of the Bank's maintaining a substantial portfolio of liquid assets is zero, or probably negative, and that the Bank is therefore not faced with the need to weigh the cost of maintaining a particular amount of liquid assets against the benefits expected from this liquidity. . . .
>
> If the cost of the Bank's liquidity has been far from negative over the past five years, why does this not appear anywhere in the Bank's books? The basic answer to this question is that the Bank's finances are so structured as to keep the net results of almost all the Bank's financial decisions from appearing as Bank profits or losses. The Bank's borrowing costs are passed on to its debtors, with a margin to cover its overhead. The Bank assumes no open exchange risk on the currencies it borrows; that risk is covered either by investment in the same currency or by lending in the same currency. By these financial arrangements, the two economically linked components—interest rates and exchange rates—of the Bank's investment decisions are severed.[83]

Polak's evaluation met, not surprisingly, with a hostile reaction by Bank treasury staff who countered that Polak's analysis "confuse[d]: Accounting costs and real costs; Book yields and financial returns; Marginal analysis and average analysis; Some of the parts and the sum of the parts of a system; Stocks and flows; data;

---

82. Jacques J. Polak, "Which Currencies Should the Bank Borrow?" October 24, 1980. An extensive literature has examined the evidence on foreign exchange market efficiency. A useful survey can be found in Mark P. Taylor, "The Economics of Exchange Rates," *Journal of Economic Literature*, vol. 33 (March 1995), pp. 13–47.

83. Memorandum, Jacques Polak, "The Cost of the Bank's Holdings of Liquid Assets," December 4, 1980, pp. 1, 8. Also Jacques Polak, "Performance of the Investment Portfolio," December 4, 1980.

dates," and "ignore[d]: Market capacity in different currencies; Effect on lending rate policy; Risk; LDC Central bank assets and liabilities; Market value of Bank debt; Market value of Bank commitments; Value of liquidity in selling bonds; Problem of distribution for system gains and losses."[84]

Polak's analysis had indeed ignored the restrictions (timing and volume) under which the Bank could borrow in any market, which, as noted earlier, constrained the Bank's room to maneuver. Yet the essence of Polak's argument, that the benefits of the Bank's policies in this area were "internal, the costs external," was not seriously challenged. With Polak returning to the IMF, now as an executive director, the debate was abruptly truncated and the underlying philosophy remained unchanged.

One reason why the Van Horne–Polak critique had little impact was that it came at a most inopportune moment for the Bank. The market risks the Bank was facing just then had arisen out of the large interest rate mismatch between its undisbursed commitments and its new borrowing costs and were undoubtedly the most acute in the institution's history. The Bank's net income was under severe pressure, as the average lending rate spread continued to decline. The pressures were partly abated by the 1979 GCI, which raised the equity base. The Bank also realized a high return on its liquid asset portfolio by taking advantage of an inverted yield curve. As an internal analysis later reported,

> The Bank took advantage of interest rate differentials among currencies, and borrowed an increasing proportion of low nominal cost currencies. It disbursed those currencies to borrowers, while investing high nominal cost currencies in the liquid asset portfolio. As a result, borrowers paid a higher *effective* spread (i.e. the difference between the average return on loans and the average cost of the currencies actually disbursed).[85]

The strategy of disbursing low nominal cost currencies (primarily deutsche mark, Swiss franc, and Japanese yen) initially favored borrowers. Although international interest rates soared, IBRD borrowers were favored by lower interest rates (figure 16-2).[86]

This strategy further allowed the Bank to hoard its dollars in its liquid asset portfolio whose higher returns boosted net income. To the extent this translated into increased transfers to reserves it strengthened the Bank's equity. It is likely that the Bank's borrowing costs were also trimmed both because higher liquidity gave the Bank greater funding flexibility in volatile markets and also because of a

84. Memorandum, Philip Spray and Hugo Schielke to Eugene H. Rotberg, "Cost of Holding Liquid Assets," December 31, 1980. Also, memorandum, Eugene Rotberg to Jacques Polak, "Analysis of Funding and Investment Policy," December 11, 1980.

85. D. R. Weigel, "The Cost Competitiveness of the Bank: A Progress Report," May 14, 1984, p. 3, processed.

86. This was also partly a result of the currency pooling system which reduced volatility in IBRD lending rates. As a result the IBRD's pool-based lending rate lags behind the market both on the upside and on the downside. For borrowers with market access, when interest rates dropped, pool rates were relatively more expensive.

Figure 16-2. *IBRD Lending Rate and LIBOR, 1971–95*
Percent

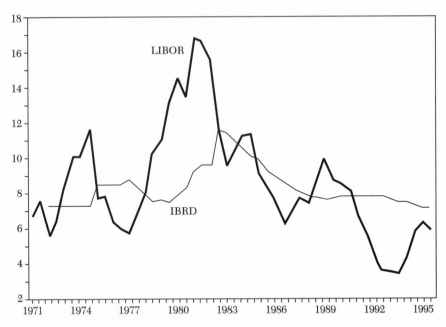

Source: IMF, *International Financial Statistics; World Economic Outlook.*

signaling effect since markets demand higher spreads to compensate for perceptions of financial weakness, as would have been indicated by declining net income.
Moreover, since the currencies received by borrowers continued to depreciate
relative to the dollar, the initial effective costs were even lower.

In doing so, however, the Bank traded off the prospect of an immediate increased return on the liquid asset portfolio plus the short-run cost reduction to
borrowers against the *possibility* of later increased costs to borrowers if the currencies disbursed were to appreciate sufficiently to offset the interest rate differentials.
This strategy allowed the Bank to offset the risks resulting from the combined
adverse effects of past financial policies and adverse market conditions, namely, the
rise in the average cost of funds and the effects of the decline in the share of free
equity on the average cost of funds. The risks were transferred to borrowers in the
form of increased currency risks, by disbursing low nominal cost currencies and
preferentially recalling high nominal ones (basically dollars).

The dollar share of currencies disbursed by the Bank is given in table 16-4. Two
alternate measures of developing-country currency preferences are shown for
comparison: the currency structure of developing-country debt in the case of
liabilities and of developing-country reserves for assets.[87] Discrepancies between

87. In general, the currency composition of reserves is influenced by a country's exchange
rate arrangements, its trade flows with reserve country currencies, and the currency of

Table 16-4. *Developing-Country Currency Preferences and IBRD Disbursements, 1971–93*[a]

Percentage share of U.S. dollars

Years	Liabilities: Long-term debt	Assets: Foreign exchange reserves	IBRD net disbursements
1971–75	50	64	30
1977–80	52	64	7
1981–85	60	64	5
1986–89	50	60	58
1990–93	46	62	104[b]

Source: Currency structure of developing-country debt: World Bank, *World Debt Tables*. Currency structure of foreign exchange reserves: IMF, *International Financial Statistics*. Data on currency structure of IBRD disbursements and recalls are from currency reports supplied by comptrollers.

a. Figures on long-term debt are based on the calendar year. Foreign exchange reserves are end-of-year figures. Net disbursements are based on the fiscal years basis. Net disbursement data for 1971–75 are approximate.

b. The figure exceeds 100 percent because of large negative net disbursements in other currencies.

the Bank's currency choices and those of developing countries is particularly marked over the period 1977 to 1985.

In 1985, the Bank had several opportunities to mitigate the risks posed by this practice. Early in the year, the Bank's treasurer publicly pointed to the potential for borrowers to realize substantial savings on future debt repayments denominated in deutsche mark, Swiss franc, and yen by restructuring the currency structure of their debt obligations. Eugene Rotberg estimated that the savings could amount to as much as $6 billion, just on the $31 billion the Bank had disbursed in these currencies to its borrowers over the last seven years.[88]

As a practical matter, at the time very few developing countries could have availed themselves of Rotberg's advice. The pall cast by the debt crisis meant that commercial bank dollar-denominated loans were difficult to obtain. And, even at the end of the decade, for developing-country borrowers, hedging was available only on short-term maturities and there was very limited liquidity in these markets, especially beyond six months' maturity.

---

denomination of its debt-service payments. See Michael P. Dooley, José S. Lizondo, and Donald K. Mathieson, "The Currency Composition of Foreign Exchange Reserves," IMF Working Paper, WP/88/61, July 1988.

88. According to the story carried by wire services, Rotberg stated that if the countries expected "that the strong U.S. dollar will eventually weaken and the other major currencies will appreciate from their currently depressed levels, this may be the time for them to use their dollar reserves or even seek commercial bank dollar-denominated loans to buy West German marks or other foreign currencies at favorable exchange rates and then hold such assets for eventual repayment of outstanding World Bank loans." "Rotberg Says Third World Overlooking Possibilities for Big Savings on Debt Repayments," as reported in World Bank, "Development News—Daily Summary," January 25, 1985.

Could the Bank itself have acted more forcefully on Rotberg's prognostications? Any speculation should be mindful of the unusual and unexpected behavior of the dollar in that period and the consequent large room for errors. But the Bank's own currency choices for its borrowers clearly did not reflect its public concerns and an internal proposal to restructure the currency composition of the asset side of the balance sheet by disbursing some dollars from the liquid portfolio and replacing them with deutsche mark/yen recalled from the loan currency pool failed to take off.[89] Moreover, at an advisory level, a request by China for technical assistance on asset-liability management, to help the Bank's borrowers deal with the risks posed by these issues, met a negative response among the Bank's management. The failure to respond was in part due to turf rivalry between the operations complex (which normally handled technical assistance to borrowers) and the finance complex (which had the expertise on this matter), a dispute that Clausen did not resolve.

Later, Rotberg reflected that it was "difficult even now to know precisely why Bank management did not press harder for a total restructuring of the liabilities of the Bank and/or its borrowers when the U.S. dollar was strong in 1985."[90] Although Rotberg's bottom line, that "there was simply no drive/incentive—or informed experience—on the part of financial staff, the senior management, or the countries themselves to engage in hedging operations or change the structure of the Bank's balance sheet," is largely correct, it is also likely that it was difficult for the finance complex's senior management to free itself of the money illusion associated with investing in high nominal rate currencies.

IMPLICATIONS. The sharp decline of the dollar led to a rapid increase in the effective cost of IBRD loans, even while nominal costs remained practically unchanged (table 16-5).[91] An important rationale underlying the Bank's financial polices—the desire to shield its borrowers from interest rate volatility—was seriously undermined.

Relatedly, the currency management policies of the Bank greatly inflated the borrowers' liabilities to the institution, in dollar terms. This effect has been particularly pronounced in the decade 1986–95, sharply reversing the gains of the

89. According to World Bank data, in fiscal 1985 the World Bank disbursed $8.7 billion, less than *20 percent* in dollars. On the other hand, of the $3 billion in repayments, it recalled more than *50 percent* in dollars.

90. Eugene H. Rotberg, "The Financial Operations of the World Bank," background paper prepared for the Bretton Woods Commission, 1994, p. 213.

91. Although the figures on internal rate of return in table 16-5 are based on exchange rates prevailing in that period, given the effective life of the loans and exchange rates prevailing since (1988–95), the results would remain broadly unchanged. According to Bank data, a disbursement of US$100 equivalent at the start of the currency pool in fiscal 1981 resulted in a borrower's obligation of US$163 equivalent at the end of June 1995. World Bank, *Annual Financial Report,* 1995.

Table 16-5. *Effective Cost of All Fully Disbursed IBRD Loans, 1985–88*[a]

	Valuation dates			
Cost	June 30, 1985	June 30, 1986	June 30, 1987	December 31, 1988
Geometric mean				
1. Based on coupon rates[b]	8.35	8.34	8.35	8.35
2. Realized cost to date[c]	6.80	6.90	7.63	9.03
Internal rate of return				
3. Realized and unrealized cost to date[d]	3.42	9.03	11.98	12.69

Source: World Bank, FRS, October 1988.

a. Effective cost of fully disbursed IBRD loans incorporating the movement of exchange rates but excluding the effect of commitment fees and the front-end fees. Uses U.S. dollars as the numeraire, based on data extracted from the Bank's Financial Database. The data consist of all loans effective after June 30, 1976.

b. Based on geometric average of the quarterly average lending rates of the aggregate set of loans. The quarterly lending rates are calculated as an arithmetic average of the lending rates weighted by historical U.S. dollars outstanding.

c. Realized effective cost to date incorporating the effect of exchange rate movements based on the geometric average of the annual realized book yield of fully disbursed IBRD loans.

d. Effective cost of fully disbursed IBRD loans, including realized and unrealized valuation changes as measured by the internal rate of return. This measure assumes that the outstanding amounts for each loan are repaid at the same exchange rates as prevailed on the valuation date.

early 1980s (table 16-6).[92] Despite the new currency management policies put into place in 1989 (discussed later), the dollar-equivalent liabilities continued to balloon relative to the Bank's net disbursements, in part due to the overhang effects of earlier loans. Of course this does not necessarily mean that the borrowers were subject to that much foreign exchange exposure, because the U.S. dollar may not be the relevant numeraire currency for measuring their exposure. New currency policies introduced at the end of the decade fixed the currency pool (at one U.S. dollar for every 125 yen for every 2 deutsche mark group), making it much more transparent and, consequently, easier to manage.

The sharp increase in the dollar value of loans outstanding also increased the Bank's risks. Between the end of 1984 and the end of 1987, the Bank's exposure rose by 76 percent, significantly increasing its credit risks. Furthermore, the practice of allowing very different currency compositions in the accounts that made up

92. In addition to net disbursements, IBRD exposure is also affected by loan sales and prepayments, both of which reduce its exposure. Neither has played much significance in the Bank's history except for the 1950s, when loan sales were significant (see chapter 15) and the late 1980s when prepayments totaled $5 billion and loan sales amounted to another $1 billion. During the 1980s, their combined effects reduced IBRD exposure by less than 10 percent. Exchange rate changes, on the other hand, increased IBRD exposure by nearly 30 percent. See World Bank, Risk Management and Financial Policy Department, "Key Factors Affecting IBRD Exposure, FY81–91," table 3.1, in "1991 Country Risk Management and Portfolio Review," vol. 1, main report, June 24, 1991, p. 41.

Table 16-6. *IBRD: Net Disbursements and Changes in Loans Outstanding,*
1947–95

Billions of U.S. dollars

Time period	Net disbursements	Change in loans outstanding[a]
1947–68	7.3	5.2
1969–80	16.6	21.5
1981–95	52.3	96.8
1981–85	24.7	14.7
1986–90	21.2	47.7
1991–95	6.4	34.4
Total (1947–95)	76.3	123.5

Source: World Bank data.

a. Loans outstanding exclude loans approved but not effective and undisbursed balance of effective loans.

the Bank's main prudential ratios had also made it more difficult to manage these ratios (in particular the reserve targets).

It had not been necessary to base the pool on all borrowings, including those that supported the IBRD's liquidity. The underlying rationale was the sense that the Bank was a cooperative and that, since no dividends were paid, the benefits of high investment income—which by increasing reserves would reduce costs by enhancing creditworthiness or lower spreads as well as enhance lending capacity— would be shared with the borrowers.

But implementing the idea of a cooperative was another matter altogether. Intertemporal inequities soon became evident, since some countries graduated while in other cases borrowing levels fluctuated for various reasons. Then, too, the actual borrowers were not always the countries as sovereign borrowers, but agencies, corporations, and banks within the member countries. To them, the interest to be paid was relevant, since it was not recycled into benefits in which they shared. Development banks sometimes had to absorb part of the costs of Bank loans to buffer their borrowers from the interest (and currency) risk of the pool compared with other available sources of finance.

But perhaps worst, the virtuous cycle was not as self-contained as suggested. As net income grew and became more stable, so did pressures to use it for activities that brought few benefits to the IBRD's borrowers. The Bank found it difficult to stave off pressures from major shareholders to use net income for causes that were in their political interests. Contributions to IDA became a regular feature, with the amounts increasing in later years. Grant financing for various purposes was proposed, including funding for a subset of the membership, and was not always resisted successfully. And although reserves and provisions were an important component of prudential financial management, the debate about the level of both was often fueled by the concern that increasing them was not reflected in better pricing for borrowed funds, which (in later years) were close to sovereigns. And finally, administrative costs, financed out of income, expanded without serious concerns for many years, even though it was not always clear that the additional services bought were what the Bank borrowers would have wanted in quite that volume or the social dirigisme that the Bank began to indulge in.

It is difficult to arrive at a precise bottom line on the financial implications of the Bank's currency policies over the last two-and-a-half-odd decades. But there can be little ambiguity that the incidence of risk fell on that part of the system that had the least financial comparative advantage to bear it. If risk had been managed in the interest of the system as a whole (i.e., the Bank and the borrowers), and not just the Bank, it is likely that the overall costs to the system would have been lower.

In retrospect, several reasons can be advanced to explain why the risks posed by the currencies of lending were allowed to fester for so long. The Bank had matured under a stable exchange rate regime. Currency risk was relatively less important simply because exchange rate volatility was less (see table 16-3). There was also little pressure from borrowers, whose preoccupation was largely with interest rates and timing elements (maturity, grace period) of loans as the principal measures of the cost of Bank loans.[93] Furthermore, given the unpredictability of exchange rates, there was an underlying belief that, in the long run, it would all wash out. However, the long-run trend (at least since the breakdown of the Bretton Woods regime until the mid-1990s) saw the dollar depreciate against other major reserve currencies. The fact that the Bank's Articles shielded the institution from currency risks also led to a somewhat blasé attitude—reenforced by the quasi-monopoly position enjoyed by the Bank in many LDCs during much of the 1980s. In allowing the United States to use bureaucratic trivialities to veto common sense, the Bank succumbed to U.S. pressures to disallow the SDR as the unit of value of the Bank's capital. This meant that IBRD loans continued to be denominated in dollars rather than SDRs, which, as a weighted basket of currencies, would have been less risky. Finally, the underlying attitude that what was good for the Bank was good for its borrowers revealed a certain hubris in the institution. Although valid to a substantial extent, there are limits to the argument which the institution would have done well to recognize.

---

93. Whether this reflected "money illusion"—a failure to distinguish between monetary and real variables—is a matter of conjecture. For an argument on the pervasiveness of money illusion see, Eldar Shafir, Amos Tversky, and Peter Diamond, "On Money Illusion," MIT Department of Economics working paper, August 1994.

Credit Risk

By the mid-1980s the IBRD had weathered the worst of "market" risks, that is, risks arising from adverse movements of interest rates and exchange rates. But as awareness grew that the debt crisis was going to be a long and difficult affair, it became apparent that the principal risk now confronting the Bank was "credit" risks—the risks to its loan portfolio. With commercial banks withdrawing, limited bilateral resources, and the deteriorating economic health of many of its borrowers, it was only a matter of time before serious arrears emerged—and the Bank's credit risks escalated. The institution's founders had mandated that the IBRD be the lender of last resort, but it was an open point on how the institution could balance the risks associated with that role.

Portfolio Deterioration

The first case was Nicaragua in 1984. After the overthrow of Anastasio Somoza, the Bank supported the new Sandinista regime with a series of IBRD and IDA loans between 1980 and 1981.[94] Lending subsequently ceased because of the government's economic policies, which aggravated the problems created by the U.S.-supported Contras.[95] The Bank succeeded in avoiding arrears in payments until the middle of 1984 by restructuring an industrial rehabilitation loan to provide foreign exchange to cover debt service payments to the Bank. When that loan was fully disbursed and the total undisbursed amount of Bank loans to Nicaragua totalled only $2.4 million, of which $1.3 million was already committed, the Nicaraguan government stopped servicing its debt to the Bank.[96] The Bank sought to buy time and obtain payment of all arrears in excess of 180 days to stave off nonaccrual status. To this end it enlisted the Mexican finance minister, Jesús Silva-Herzog, to try to persuade Nicaragua to continue to service its obligations.[97]

---

94. Three IBRD loans totaling $70 million and two IDA loans for $37 million were made.

95. On the question of the politics of the Bank's posture toward Nicaragua, David Knox, then vice president for Latin America, had this to say: "I think that the answer to your question, on whether the Bank's response would have been more sympathetic had the political circumstances been different, has to be yes and no. One of my nightmares was what we would do were the Nicaraguans to start putting in place policies that we could support. I feared that political pressure, and not only from the U.S., would be so great as to prevent us from helping the country. As it turned out, the question never arose during my term of office. The Nicaraguans persisted in policies that were self-destructive, and that despite the advice we gave them." Letter, A. David Knox to Devesh Kapur, April 1, 1993.

96. Memorandum, A. David Knox to Ernest Stern, "Nicaragua: Provisions for Probable Losses," June 4, 1986.

97. A payment of $2 million to the World Bank before December 1 would "buy" three months before arrears in excess of 180 days would occur, and an additional payment of

These steps did not succeed and, for the first time in its history, the Bank placed a member country in nonaccrual status in December 1984.[98] In turn, the Nicaraguan government, exercising its rights under the Bank's Articles, asked for a rescheduling of its obligations to the Bank or acceptance of payments in local currency. However, as noted in chapter 15, the Bank had hardened its stance on rescheduling during the 1970s. The rationale for this policy was that it was not in the interest of the membership as a whole for the Bank to reschedule loans. Among the reasons advanced were the adverse effects on access to borrowed funds and their cost; the reduced creditworthiness of the Bank and its implications on the risk to shareholder capital; and the equity implications among borrowers, as it implied an increase in the cross-subsidy of the weaker credits by the stronger ones.

The flip side of this policy, as an internal memo argued, was that the Bank would assist its borrowers in financial difficulties,

> by maintaining a flow of resources "voluntarily" and that it will adapt the terms of its new lending (i.e. change the blend) in order to provide the debt service relief needed. In other words, the no-rescheduling policy can be made to stick with the borrowers and other lenders because [the Bank maintains] an ongoing relationship with the borrower and is rarely in the position envisaged in the Articles of Agreement of having made one or a few loans that are resulting in a negative net transfer.[99]

But, the memo continued, the situation in Nicaragua "does not fit the 'model' outlined above." The Bank had stopped lending on performance grounds and faced negative net transfers, a position that it normally sought "to avoid as a general rule."[100]

Differences within senior management emerged as regards the Bank's posture to the Nicaraguan request. Both the operations and finance complexes did not want to make an exception of Nicaragua to the de facto no-rescheduling policy. In

---

$7 million by February 1 would buy another three months. These minimum payments were only a "holding action" and would not have lifted the suspension of disbursements. In addition Silva-Herzog promised to try to get Nicaragua a credit of $2 million (through oil shipments or by marginally increasing imports from Nicaragua) as well as to persuade Venezuela, Colombia, and Spain to join Mexico to provide a loan of $2 million to Nicaragua to make the minimum payments to the Bank. Memorandum, Rainer Steckhan and Heinz Vergin to Ernest Stern and Moeen A. Qureshi, "Nicaraguan Arrears—Visit with Finance Minister Silva-Herzog of Mexico," November 1, 1984.

98. Nonaccrual status implies that interest and charges accrued but not paid are deducted from the Bank's income. IBRD policy places in nonaccrual status all loans made to or guaranteed by a member of the IBRD if principal, interest, or other charges with respect to any such loan are overdue by more than six months, unless management determines that the overdue amount will be collected in the near future. In addition, if development credits by IDA to a member government are placed in nonaccrual status, all IBRD loans to that government are also placed in nonaccrual status.

99. Memorandum, David Bock to Moeen A. Qureshi, December 27, 1984. At the time Bock was director of the Financial Policy and Analysis Department.

100. Ibid.

contrast, the Bank's general counsel maintained that the Articles mandated the Bank take a more open stance. A legal memorandum argued:

> The Bank's declared policy of non-participation in rescheduling agreements has not been applied as an absolute and inflexible prohibition. . . . Given such flexibility, an amply motivated and adequately flexible general policy against participation in rescheduling agreements cannot be properly described, under the circumstances in which it was adopted, as against the Bank's Articles. Such a policy cannot, however, prevail over the Articles' requirements. If a member requests relaxation of payment terms under either of the provisions analyzed in this paper, he is entitled to a fair hearing. The Bank must consider the request in the light of all the considerations provided for and described above, recognizing that if the borrower is indeed unable to service the loan, the alternative to the adjustment of the terms of the loan would be the borrower's default. It has the right to relax the loan terms, but is under no obligation to exercise this right.[101]

The memorandum further argued that the Bank could indeed "consider relaxing the payment terms for those members who, for no particular fault on their part, experience acute foreign exchange difficulties which make them unable to service their future payment obligations as originally agreed." However, it was apparent that opening the doors to one borrower could soon open a can of worms and jeopardize the overall interests of the institution's members as a group. It was also clear that the Bank's posture was

> a reasonably hard line, one that we may be able to get away with in the Nicaraguan case. Certainly we will win the PR battle in the financial markets and in the U.S. European opinion will be very divided and there is a fairly high risk that brinkmanship of this sort will unite rather than divide the LDCs. . . . The main difficulty with this approach, however, is that it is good only for the small countries where our exposure can be written off without major impact on income. We could not sustain this position in a medium-sized country and although commercial practice is to use leverage in the situations where you have it, we need to be very sensitive to the general policy issues since all borrowers are members and their sense of "ownership" is one of the reasons we have a preferred creditor position.[102]

The apprehensions of senior Bank officials that the tough posture towards Nicaragua would be difficult to replicate in the case of a large debtor was soon tested in the case of Romania. The country had been an active borrower from the Bank since 1974 but, following a severe liquidity crisis in 1981, had stopped borrowing from the Bank in May 1982. The Ceaucescu regime took draconian measures to reduce debt through current account surpluses obtained by import restraint and export generation. As a result, the country's debt fell rapidly from

101. Ibrahim F. I. Shihata, "Treatment of Bank Borrowers in Cases of 'Acute Exchange Stringencies' and 'Default.'" Legal memorandum on Article IV, Sections 4(c) and 7(a) of the IBRD Articles of Agreement, January 2, 1985, para. 28, p. 24.

102. Memorandum, Bock to Qureshi, December 27, 1984.

$10.5 billion in 1981 to $5.9 billion in 1986. Romania was, in a sense, a "model" debtor, at least from the creditors' point of view. However, even Ceaucescu's maniacal policies were overwhelmed by two consecutive severe winters in 1985 and 1986 and the country again faced a severe liquidity crisis.

Relations between the Bank and Romania were already strained on a range of issues from policy to procurement, and Bank staff had little faith in the possibility of any major change. However, since Romania was not interested in borrowing further from the Bank, the concerns of Bank staff were moot. Beginning in early 1986, Romanian officials were aggrieved that even while their country had stopped borrowing from the Bank and net flows were negative in 1985, its dollar-denominated IBRD debt actually grew and began to build up arrears with the Bank.[103]

With IBRD exposure in Romania at $1.8 billion, equal to 3 percent of IBRD's loan portfolio, the Bank had good reasons to be extremely nervous. The Romanians had disavowed any intention of further borrowing, and the Bank's preferred creditor status looked anything but. The share of IBRD in Romania's outstanding debt had risen from 11 percent in 1981 to about a third in 1986. Net disbursements and net transfers were strongly negative and undisbursed balances totalled only $5.5 million. Even as Romania's arrears to the Bank were mounting, it continued to pay its other creditors: it was paying the commercial banks, although negotiating a rescheduling; it was also paying the Fund. It even favored IBRD's cofinanciers by allowing them to stand aside in planned reschedulings.

It was clear to Bank officials that it had "to negotiate a solution to this problem from an exceedingly weak financial bargaining position."[104] It decided, pending clearance of arrears, to undertake one operation per year (amounting to $150 million to 200 million), since "a continued policy of no lending could put that [portfolio] at serious risk."[105]

But the problem for the Bank was that Romania was simply not interested in another Bank loan. By the end of July 1986 Romania's arrears amounted to $115 million and it appeared that by October 1 the Bank would have to place its Romanian portfolio in nonaccrual status.[106] On August 1, another middle-sized borrower—Peru—went into nonaccrual status. At the beginning of the year the Bank had decided to cease lending to Peru on creditworthiness grounds as well as Peru's posture toward its commercial creditors.[107] Facing negative net transfers,

103. Between 1985 and 1987, IBRD net flows (or net disbursements) to Romania were negative $0.5 billion. In the same period Romania's debt outstanding to the IBRD grew by $0.4 billion.

104. Memorandum, Heinz Vergin to Moeen A. Qureshi, "Romania Arrears," June 17, 1986, p. 2.

105. Memorandum, Ernest Stern to Barber B. Conable, "Romania," August 15, 1986.

106. As per the Bank's policy, payments overdue by sixty days were classified as arrears. All loans to a borrower in arrears by more than six months were classified as nonaccrual.

107. The Peruvian case was intertwined with the Bank's position in the debt crisis and is addressed further in chapter 11.

Peru, in turn, decided to cease servicing Bank debt. Consequently, the Bank was more than keen to avoid having Romania's $1.9 billion portfolio meet the same fate.

Through the next two years Romania repeatedly incurred large arrears to the Bank. In mid-1987, following an appeal from Barber Conable to Nicolae Ceauces-cu, Wilfred Thalwitz, then vice president for the region, was dispatched to Romania.[108] The discussion made it clear that Ceaucescu was personally laying down the policy, and that he was determined to seek a bilateral solution to the problem of what he regarded as a highly inequitable treatment of Romania by the Bank. Romanian officials charged that the Bank, in its loans to Romania, had deliberately starved the currency pool of dollars and not recalled currencies pro rata with respect to currencies disbursed. Bank calculations showed that Romania had not been singled out by the Bank.[109] But at the end of the year the key Romanian officials negotiating with the Bank were fired or demoted, payments were again suspended and, for the first time, Romanian officials publicly denounced the Bank.[110] The Bank was back at square one, and negotiations had to begin all over again.

An agreement with Romania was finally reached in May 1988 whereby the Bank, which had been resisting Romania's demands for a bilateral deal, now agreed to one. Romania would prepay the entire $2 billion of outstanding IBRD debt over a relatively short period of time and would not borrow any further from the Bank. A one-time exception was granted to Romania: it could choose the (convertible) currencies of prepayment; a fixed interest rate would be charged equal to the prevailing short-term market rate for each currency on the date of the agreement. By March 1989 Romania repaid its entire balance to the Bank.

In retrospect, the Bank had escaped by a whisker. In 1986 the institution was quite vulnerable to a $2 billion default (the size of Romania's outstanding debt to

108. Letter, Barber B. Conable to Nicolae Ceaucescu, president of Romania, July 30, 1987.

109. On the one hand, internal analysis supported Romania's contention that it "indeed owe[d] far more Swiss francs and Deutsche marks—and fewer yen and especially fewer dollars—than [were] outstanding on all other non-pooled Bank loans." Memorandum, Barbara N. Opper to Ernest Stern, "Currency Composition of Romania's Nonpool Loans," July 31, 1987. Another internal analysis, comparing financial costs of the thirty-three loans to Romania with comparators (loans to other countries made within three months of a Romanian loan), however, revealed that the cost of Romania's borrowings from the Bank was lower than the costs of comparators' borrowings ($71 million in present value terms). "The Financial Cost of Loans to Romania in Comparison with the Average Cost of Comparator Loans," September 16, 1987. The fact that Romania had not taken advantage of the opportunity to convert $811 million of undisbursed nonpool loan amounts to the currency pool when it was established in 1980, confused the picture.

110. A few months later in a statement circulated to its Board, the Bank was accused of using exchange rate fluctuations "as means of plundering and impoverishing developing countries." "Romania's Views and Proposals, by President Nicolae Ceaucescu, for a Global Solution to the Problems of External Debt and Excessive Interest Rates." Submitted to the Board of the World Bank, April 12, 1988.

Table 16-7. *IBRD Nonaccruals, Fiscal 1985–95*

	1985	1987	1989	1991	1993	1995
Number of countries in nonaccrual status	1	4	9	8	7	7
Total nonaccrual debt (U.S.$ billions)	0.1	0.8	3.8	2.5	2.5	2.6
Net impact of nonaccruals on net income (U.S.$ millions)[a]	15	117	621	777	413	168

Source: World Bank, *Annual Report,* various years; IBRD, "Allocation of FY95 Net Income and Plan for FY96," R95-143, July 14, 1995, table 2, annex 4.

a. Sum of interest and fees not accrued and loan loss provisions minus reversal of nonaccruals.

the Bank). Ceaucescu's decision to abjure global financial interlinkages and the absence of any undisbursed Bank commitments meant that the institution was essentially at the mercy of a capricious leader. His decision to turn around and repay the Bank (when he could have easily done the opposite) will remain an enigma. Although the Bank could breathe a sigh of relief, for the Romanians the price was steep. The country's repayments to the Bank averaged 2.5 percent of GNP during 1988–89, at a time when its economy was already in dire straits.

Beginning with Nicaragua, over the next decade, loans to seventeen countries were placed in nonaccrual status at various times. Ten cleared their arrears to the Bank, but seven others remained in nonaccrual status as of 1995.[111] The percentage of the portfolio in nonaccrual status rose rapidly in the late 1980s, peaking at 4.1 percent in June 1989 before gradually declining to 2.1 percent at the end of fiscal 1995. The impact of nonaccruals on the IBRD's net income was quite significant (table 16-7).

The sustained nature and magnitude of the arrears problem that began in the mid-1980s was historically unprecedented. As per internal assessments, the riskiness of the IBRD portfolio sharply escalated over the latter half of the 1980s. It stabilized in the first half of the 1990s but did not reverse course (table 16-8).[112] The abeyance of the debt crisis did not lead to a reduction in the Bank's overall credit risks, in part because of increased lending to the transition economies in East

111. The ten countries were the Congo, Guatemala, Guyana, Honduras, Nicaragua, Panama, Peru, Sierra Leone, the former Yugoslav Republic of Macedonia, and Zambia. As of 1995, seven countries remained in nonaccrual status: Bosnia-Herzegovina, Iraq, Liberia, Sudan, Syria, Federal Republic of Yugoslavia, and Zaire.

112. However, portfolio risk increased in 1995, owing to the economic crisis in Mexico, the Bank's largest borrower. The portfolio risk analysis is based on a variety of exposure indicators. These include the share of each borrower in the Bank's loan portfolio as well as exposure indicators within a country, that is, with the share of the IBRD and other preferred creditors in the borrower's total external debt and debt service. In the late 1980s to early 1990s there was some fine-tuning on the risk categories and their relative weight in lending decisions. Nevertheless, as in all cases of risk analysis, the assignment of risk ratings retains a considerable amount of subjectivity.

Table 16-8. *Degree of Risk of IBRD Loan Portfolio, Selected Fiscal Years*[a]
Portfolio distribution, percent

Risk category	1980	1985	1990	1992	1994
Low	71.4	40.5	37.1	30.3	30.0
Medium	20.0	53.5	31.7	46.0	44.7
Severe	7.9	2.6	26.2	18.9	18.8
IDA only	0.7	3.1	1.2	2.7	4.3
Nonaccrual	0.0	0.3	3.3	2.1	2.2
Portfolio score (0–100)	37	53	59	60	59

Source: World Bank data.

a. In assessing its portfolio risk, the Bank places each borrowing country in one of seven risk categories. The overall index assigns a weight of zero to countries in the lowest risk category, a weight of twenty to those in the next risk category, and so on up to a weight of 100 to those in the highest risk category, which includes borrowers in nonaccrual.

Europe and the countries of the former Soviet Union. An additional factor was the increased inflexibility in the debt structure (and therefore of debt service) of many of its borrowers. As a result of the debt reduction deals of the late 1980s, both the share of preferred creditors and of nonreschedulable bonds increased sharply (see chapter 11). In 1985, thirteen countries, representing 18 percent of the Bank's portfolio, exceeded the preferred creditor exposure guideline (preferred creditor debt service to public debt service to be within 35 percent); a decade later (1994), thirty-one countries representing about half of the portfolio exceeded this guideline. On the other hand, another exposure indicator (IBRD debt service to exports) showed significant improvement in the 1990s.

In addition to the growth of arrears from countries in nonaccrual status, the Bank had also faced a sharp growth of payment arrears over thirty days. In an attempt to improve payment performance, new arrears policies were put into effect from mid-1991. The new policies had both a carrot and stick element to them. The carrot was a waiver of a part of interest charges on a year-by-year basis, depending on the Bank's financial health and net income. The stick was much tighter payment deadlines and penalties attached to these deadlines.[113]

The rapid growth of arrears to the Bank during the 1980s strained the bedrock principle underlying the IBRD's financial health: its preferred creditor status.[114] The concept began to wear thin during this period, due to negative net flows and the growing share of inflexible debt and of course due to the economic crisis gripping these countries. In general, however, the Bank's borrowers continued to give it priority in servicing their external debt obligations. No doubt this was largely

113. For instance, if repayments are overdue by thirty days, new loan submissions to the Board are delayed. Overdue payments greater than sixty days now result in a suspension of all disbursements to the country.

114. An analysis of this subject can be found in Jeremy Bulow and Kenneth Rogoff, "Is the World Bank a Preferred Creditor?" draft typescript, 1991.

motivated by the countries' desire to keep their access to Bank funds alive. However, this would not explain the behavior of countries such as Afghanistan, Lebanon, and Iran which continued to service Bank debt throughout the 1980s despite negative net flows and poor prospects of a resumption of Bank lending.[115] Peer pressure from other borrowers (and fellow developing countries) and a vague sense of the Bank as a cooperative perhaps partly explain this behavior.

The Response

The growth of arrears and the persistence of the headroom problem inevitably had several consequences. As detailed later, several financial policies that had remained largely unchanged over previous decades were modified. Country creditworthiness reviews became more careful and sophisticated. To a certain extent these reports compensated for what was generally regarded as a long-standing decline in the quality of creditworthiness analysis at the individual country level. In its early years, driven by the need to build up and protect its credit rating, the Bank perforce could not take its preferred creditor status for granted. Creditworthiness analysis was taken seriously reflecting the conservative banking psychology of the era.

But over time, as the institution grew more secure with regard to its credit rating and its preferred creditor status, creditworthiness analysis at the Country Assistance Strategy level (as manifest in Country Program Papers and Country Strategy Papers) had declined as the lending machine and perceived internal incentives to lend ratcheted up in the 1970s. Perhaps aware of this inevitability, McNamara had created a centralized Loan Portfolio Analysis Unit located in the finance complex (chapter 15).

Yet, the integration of portfolio risk analysis with country assistance strategy was less than happy. There were inevitable conflicts between the creditworthiness analysis unit which would understandably err on caution, while the operations departments would equally inevitably err on greater lending. The "creative tension" envisaged by McNamara worked to an extent but the long intervals between successive "Country Risk Management and Portfolio Review" (three years), considerably reduced its effectiveness. The issue had also not exercised the Board much either. Beginning in 1982, the review became an annual exercise. These reports were (understandably) tightly held and emerged over the decade as an important tool for managerial decisionmaking on country lending volumes. Unfortunately, in the latter half of the decade their usefulness was impaired by questions of process—in particular, turf battles between the operations and finance complexes. Following the 1987 reorganization, a specific Risk Management Depart-

115. In turn the Bank has had an unblemished record in servicing its own obligations on schedule despite major political upheavals: to Iran in 1980–81; and Kuwait in 1990–91.

ment was created and by the end of the decade CSPs incorporated a greater awareness of risk management concerns. By the early 1990s, the institution's systems and processes of risk management appeared to have become more robust.[116]

Improved analysis notwithstanding, the Bank struggled with various options as it attempted to reconcile the difficult trade-offs involved in improving the health of its loan portfolio: relaxing conditionality on quick-disbursing structural adjustment loans; relaxing creditworthiness assessments; utilizing IDA to maintain lending and net disbursement. As Stern noted to Qureshi, "None of these are very attractive options but their unattractiveness ought to be assessed against the possibility of defaults to the Bank. . . . I, personally, do not consider any of them desirable but agree that they must be judged against similarly undesirable ramifications for our financial standing if we incur defaults."[117] The institution's response was complicated by pressures engendered by its declining headroom (discussed later) which was raising concerns among its underwriters. An internal review of the Bank's loan portfolio in 1987 painted a somber picture: the Bank now had a high-risk portfolio and its vulnerability to debt-servicing difficulties had increased substantially. Amidst the tumult of the 1987 reorganization, the two senior vice presidents jointly warned Conable of the Bank's predicament: while the immediate crisis had been precipitated by exchange rate movements, the deterioration had been long coming, the cumulative effect of the path that the institution had been traversing since the beginning of the decade, and stemmed from three factors:[118]

—The IBRD's share in its borrowers' total debt service had increased sharply, partly because of increased IBRD lending and partly because of exchange rate changes. Since 1980, the debt service (owed to the Bank) to exports ratio had (on average) tripled in the Baker list of countries and had quadrupled in developing countries as a whole.

—IBRD net transfers were turning negative for an increasing number of countries. A country facing a liquidity squeeze would be logically tempted to first pay those creditors with whom it had prospects of a favorable net transfer position.

—Its prudential financial ratios had declined significantly. If borrowers accounting for just 6 percent of its portfolio fell into arrears, it would wipe out net income.

Various strategies were considered, but reducing IBRD exposure to the severely indebted middle-income countries was rejected, as it would both undercut the adjustment efforts under way and potentially precipitate the very debt-servicing

116. The need for strong central risk management systems was apparent in 1994 in the case of Mexico. In the spring of that year, the region argued for higher lending limits to Mexico basing its case on the country's good economic performance. This did not occur because of strong resistance from the Country Risk Management Division, whose stance was vindicated at the end of the year.

117. Memorandum, Stern to Qureshi, March 21, 1984, p. 2.

118. Memorandum, Moeen A. Qureshi and Ernest Stern to Barber B. Conable, "Creditworthiness Review," April 8, 1987.

problems the institution was seeking to avoid. Another alternative, increasing the share of fast-disbursing loans to avoid negative net transfer, met a wary reception: the "option of using quick disbursing assistance to manage debt service profile is already being used to the limit in many cases."[119] Any further increases would lead to severe volatility in future disbursements and even greater pressures down the line.

International Development Association

A useful aid in alleviating the arrears problem was the Bank's access to IDA. Between 1980 and 1994, twenty-two severely indebted low-income countries had simultaneous negative IBRD net transfers and positive IDA net transfers.[120] The economic decline of several borrowers with sizable IBRD debt—Côte d'Ivoire, Egypt, Honduras, Nigeria—made them IDA-eligible, because of declining per capita income and reduced creditworthiness.[121]

IDA's potential role in helping IBRD's creditworthiness had been recognized, of course, well before IDA's creation and proved particularly helpful to the IBRD in South Asia in the 1960s and early 1970s (see chapter 15).[122] The Bank's former treasurer, Eugene Rotberg, when asked if the Bank's creditors saw "IDA as a means to bail out the Bank," replied,

> I hope so. . . . What would inexorably happen if there were no IDA is that, one way or another, the Bank would try to find a way to lend to countries at, say, three percent below market. Indeed the EBRD is now discovering that a lot of the ex-Soviet states are not credit-worthy . . . yet that institution is under pressure to lend [to] those countries. That's what happens to institutions. IDA doesn't "bail out" the Bank. It's more of a safety valve to permit economic and financial support to countries which are not credit-worthy but, if it were not available, would probably get some Bank lending at the margin and, in so doing, I believe jeopardize the financial credibility of the Bank.[123]

119. Financial Policy Committee, "Minutes of Meeting of March 19, 1987," April 3, 1987.

120. The countries were (in alphabetical order) Cameroon, the Congo, Côte d'Ivoire, Ethiopia, Ghana, Guinea, Guyana, Honduras, Kenya, Liberia, Madagascar, Mauritania, Nicaragua, Nigeria, Senegal, Sierra Leone, Sudan, Tanzania, Togo, Uganda, Zaire, and Zambia. In many of these countries IDA net transfers to the countries exceeded net transfers to IBRD by these countries in almost all years. World Bank, *World Debt Tables, 1996.*

121. The dollar per capita income criteria for IDA eligibility and the sensitivity of dollar per capita income to exchange rate effects, have meant that "correct" per capita income figures were somewhat subjective.

122. IBRD, office memorandum drafted by Ben King and others for, and at the behest of, Richard Demuth, "Examinations of a Proposal for Administration of an International Development Fund by the Bank," November 1, 1950. See chapter 17 for further details.

123. Eugene Rotberg, interview, World Bank Oral History Program, April 22, 1994, p. 31.

Adjustment Lending: Solution or Problem?

The introduction of fast-disbursing structural adjustment lending at the beginning of the decade had already increased the financial risks to the Bank, causing some major shareholders (Japan and Germany, in particular) to express their reservations with regard to such lending. In fact the Bank had long presented its project lending as giving it greater financial protection. Thus Qureshi and Rotberg made the case in public that "unlike some bilateral lending institutions and most commercial banks, it takes the World Bank five or six years to disburse the funds. . . . Failure of a country to service debts at the World Bank would jeopardize not only new lending but also disbursement on already-committed loans. That is the guts of project lending."[124]

In contrast to project lending, however, in cases where the Bank decided to support a country's adjustment efforts with a series of SALs, its exposure would rise rapidly. Adjustment lending had a double or nothing element to it. If the adjustment program was successful, by the time the repayments to the Bank were due the country's balance of payments problems would have turned around and alternative (market) sources of financing would be available. On the other hand, this entailed a "deceleration" risk emerging in the medium term, especially if reforms failed to turn the economy around. As the commercial banks had learnt, the longer the foot was placed on the accelerator, the greater the exposure when it was taken off. Although portfolio risks could be contained by staff assurances that, "to the extent there is policy slippage [on SALs], lending will be concomitantly lower," there were few foolproof safeguards against "risks that policy slippage will occur after Bank exposure has already risen, as was the case in the 1980s."[125] And to add to the complexities of decisionmaking, a seemingly cautious project lending approach posed its own risks, since an absence of economic reforms was likely to worsen a country's economic and financial problems—and thereby its ability to service Bank loans. But adjustment lending was not the only bow in the Bank's quiver to make quick disbursing loans. Other, less visible, lending modes such as financial intermediary loans, alleviated the burden carried by adjustment loans.[126]

124. Kenneth N. Gilpin, "Talking Business with Qureshi and Rotberg of the World Bank," *New York Times,* July 19, 1983, p. D2.

125. IBRD, "Review of Adequacy of Loan Loss Provisions and Reserves," R93-73, April 22, 1993, p. 5. One of the principal recommendations of RAL I (Review of Adjustment Lending) had been that "limits on overall amounts of adjustment lending should be established on portfolio quality grounds; these limits should be different for IDA and IBRD." Minutes of Operations Committee to consider *Adjustment Lending Policy Paper,* July 11, 1988.

126. "Although formal structural adjustment and program lending has not exceeded 10 percent, this is a very limited indicator. As you know, many policy-based, quick-disbursing operations, are not counted in this total as a matter of convention. This is true, for instance, of the fertilizer import loan for Nigeria, the export development loans for Jamaica, Brazil and Mexico, or rehabilitation credits for Ghana. Operations of this sort account for 20–25 per-

Understandably, the effects of adjustment lending on the Bank's financial health became a matter of extreme sensitivity within the institution. In early 1990, an article in the *Washington Post* based on an interview with Stanley Fischer (the ostensible subject of which had been the Multi-Fibre Agreement) stated that the Bank was contemplating a gradual phasing out of adjustment lending, in part out of fear that the institution's creditworthiness was being harmed by adjustment lending.[127] Fischer's statement caused jitters in the Bank's finance complex, always sensitive about any fallout on the institution's credit rating, although Fischer had not said anything specific on the subject. As he later stated, he "should have made the positive case for adjustment lending as helping protect our portfolio and improve our credit rating, rather than not discussing the issue when it was mentioned by a journalist," implying that it was his silence that tipped the interviewer's hand.[128] But Fischer also challenged Stern, "Your denial that the Bank's concern over the level of adjustment lending might even be related to our credit rating is puzzling." While Stern only admitted to the "special risks posed by the possibility of abrupt changes in flows" (and thereby pointing to the need for "careful management of fast-disbursing lending"), Fischer was more blunt:

> Certainly there are more, and more important, reasons than the risks you refer to for making that change—not least a concern that long-term dependence on such lending may blunt members' adjustment efforts. I would have thought though that anything that creates risks in our relationships with borrowers would at the margin affect our credit rating.[129]

Although the debate reflected less the reality of the portfolio than the need to maintain a common front to the outside, by this time the Bank had already decided to reduce IBRD adjustment lending. The 1990 medium-term budget planning framework postulated a decline in IBRD adjustment lending to 20 percent in 1991–93 from a high of 26 percent during 1987–90.[130] The move received a frosty reception from the United States, however, which interpreted it as a sign of the Bank's lukewarm support for the Brady debt strategy (see chapter 11).[131]

---

cent of our total operations in the past two years." Letter, A. W. Clausen to Jacques Delors, minister of economy, finance, and budget, April 24, 1984, p. 4.

127. Hobart Rowen, "World Bank to Make Fewer Quick Loans to the Third World," *Washington Post*, March 15, 1990, p. A29.

128. Memorandum, Stanley Fischer to Ernest Stern, March 16, 1990.

129. Ibid.

130. In reality adjustment lending loan commitments during 1991–93 were somewhat higher (23 percent) due to lending to East Europe. See table 10-1a.

131. "He [Mr. Coady, U.S. executive director] expected to receive a strong reaction in the morning. In this connection, he cited the problems that the Treasury is presently encountering with our supposed shift of policy away from adjustment lending, which the Treasury interprets as being non-supportive of the debt strategy." Memorandum from David Bock, "Meeting with Mr. Coady on Brady Progress Review," March 22, 1990.

Workout Processes for IBRD Arrears and Nonaccruals

Toward the end of the 1980s, the Bank began taking steps to assist members in nonaccrual status by mobilizing sufficient Bank and non-Bank resources. Such a policy had to balance three objectives: helping the country become current to the Bank and thereby regain access to the Bank's resources, protecting the Bank's position and image in financial markets, and appropriate burden sharing among the creditors. The policy (approved in May 1991), akin to the IMF's "rights accumulation" policy, allowed the Bank to process loans during a preclearance performance period (although no Bank loans can be signed, declared effective, or disbursed before arrears clearance).[132] To be eligible for assistance under this policy, a country had to undertake an adjustment program in agreement with the Bank; undertake a stabilization program, endorsed and monitored by the IMF and, if necessary, supported by an IMF program; establish a viable medium-term financing plan that would include the clearance of arrears to all IFIs; and make current debt-service payments falling due during the performance period.

Concurrently, the Bank would carefully craft a "bridge" loan from bilateral and commercial sources. Since no one was going to bridge on an unapproved loan, loan approval was needed before the clearance of arrears. The loan signature (needed to make it effective) was conditioned on arrears clearance. On a specific date, the bridge loan would be extended to the country to clear its arrears to the Bank and, in turn, disbursements from the Bank's loans would repay the creditors of the bridge loan. In practice this meant that a series of complex financial transactions would have to be completed in a matter of hours.[133] Although in effect the Bank was advancing the money to clear arrears to itself, the policy was a pragmatic accommodation to the procedural complexities of a multiparty package.

In the absence of debt forgiveness, the policy adopted was the only workable solution to a problem aggravated by the growing fraction of inflexible (principally multilateral) debt. As a consequence, arrears and their clearance increased stresses with other multilateral creditors, particularly the IMF. In 1989, concerned about the erosion of the IMF's de facto preferred creditor status (payments were being made to other creditors even as arrears were being accumulated with the Fund), the Fund attempted to formalize this status (at the time its arrears were more than three times that of the Bank).[134] The Bank questioned the wisdom of such a move since this would have led to all the MDBs wanting comparable treatment, thereby making it more difficult to resolve the arrears problem. While the IMF withdrew

132. Memorandum from the president to the executive directors, "Additional Support for Workout Programs in Countries with Protracted Arrears," R91-70, April 11, 1991.

133. The bridge loan to Zambia to help clear its arrears was extended for seventy-two *minutes.*

134. Memorandum, Michel Camdessus to Ernest Stern, "Preferred Creditor Status," February 17, 1989.

the proposal in response to the Bank's concerns, the issue brought into salience the problems arising from the transformation of debt from private creditors to public creditors that had occurred over the 1980s.

Later, as arrears clearance procedures were developed, in cases where the Bank's arrears were cleared before the IMF, and those of the Fund were to be cleared under the IMF's "Rights Approach Program," the Bank began to come under pressure from donors asking it to provide incremental balance of payments support so as to ensure that the debtor countries in question remained current with obligations to the IMF.

There were disputes within the Bank group as well. A case in question was a proposed IFC loan for a large mining project in Sierra Leone, a country that was in nonaccrual status at the time. On the basis of the IFC's claims on the large benefits from the project, the Bank's management argued that if the benefits were so large and the IFC's involvement so crucial, that should be used as leverage to get the country to pay off its arrears.[135] What conclusion would a debtor country draw if two arms of the institution were not acting to mutually reenforce the pressures on the country to pay? Moreover, the Bank's management was looking for a quid pro quo from the IFC in lieu of the fact that in earlier decades, in cases of expropriations of IFC-financed projects, Bank lending had been linked to a satisfactory resolution of that issue. Eventually it was decided that in cases of countries in nonaccrual to the Bank, the IFC would only lend to an entity to safeguard IFC's interest or where workout programs were sufficiently advanced.

By 1994 this policy had been successful in clearing arrears to the Bank for seven countries.[136] However, the first attempt at a workout program in this fashion—Zambia in April 1991—rapidly went off the rails. By the end of the year Zambia was again in nonaccrual status and the process had to be restarted in January 1992. In contrast with the Zambian program, the new policy proved much more successful in the case of Peru. Although Peru's arrears to the Bank were the largest of any country, its ability to repay was extremely limited in early 1991.[137] Unlike Zambia, Peru was not IDA-eligible. It was therefore essential that the Bank obtain a bridge loan extended over a longer time frame, to ease the need for the Bank to make unusually large new disbursements immediately after arrears clearance to avoid appearances of refinancing arrears. Bridge finance from donors (largely from

135. The IFC claimed that the project with an investment of $70 million would generate a billion dollars of exports (over a period of fifteen years) and would not proceed without the IFC's involvement. Memorandum, Sir William Ryrie to Barber B. Conable, "Sierra Leone—Koidu Kimberlite Project," July 3, 1989.

136. The Congo, Guatemala, Nicaragua, Panama, Peru, Sierra Leone, and the former Yugoslav Republic of Macedonia.

137. The issue of Peru's arrears clearance was first discussed among various parties at the IDB Annual Meeting in Japan in April 1991. At that time, per capita income in Peru had already declined by a third over the preceding three years.

Japan) in conjunction with an IMF Rights Accumulation Program credit of SDR 610 million and three Bank SALs totaling $1 billion cleared arrears to the two institutions. Unlike Zambia, a reversal of capital flight appears to have aided the more successful Peruvian effort.

The Zambian arrears clearance process occurred by allocating IDA resources to the country that was equal to the per capita allocation of the best-performing IDA country. While on the one hand IDA donors had been stressing the link between IDA allocations to country performance, the process distorted IDA allocations with IDA resources being diverted from good performers to cover Bank arrears. Other prominent examples included Guyana and Honduras.

Another step, at the urging of the Nordic countries, was the creation of a new facility called the "Fifth Dimension." Through this facility the Bank, together with bilaterals, provided additional resources (on IDA terms) to assist IDA countries that were ineligible for loans on IBRD terms (that is, "IDA-only" countries) but had outstanding IBRD debt prior to the creation of the program (September 1988). To actually receive a supplemental credit from the Fifth Dimension program, the countries had to be current on servicing IBRD and IDA debt and have in place an acceptable adjustment program. These resources ($1.1 billion between fiscal 1989 and 1995), culled from IDA reflows, were allocated annually in proportion to a country's interest payments on its IBRD debt.[138]

In the late 1980s, as the economies of many countries in the CFA Zone declined, IBRD debt servicing was essentially maintained by financial flows to those countries by France. However, following an assurance by France in 1989 that it would not allow arrears to develop, the Bank continued with IBRD lending despite serious reservations among staff about creditworthiness and fundamental economic management issues centered around the devaluation of the CFA franc. This simply delayed the date of reckoning, worsening the problem. As a result of the devaluation of the CFA franc in January 1994, as well as plummeting economic fortunes, several countries in the region became IDA-eligible, aiding IBRD repayments. France did keep its word: its IDA contributions were in line with the IBRD debt servicing of the CFA Zone countries.

Despite these various initiatives, by the mid-1990s some critics began asking whether for many "highly indebted low income countries" much of the lending— overwhelmingly official—was simply keeping up appearances of debt servicing, and thus whether the enterprise had become a "surreal money go-round." During the 1980s the multilaterals had sharply increased lending to these countries, largely in Sub-Saharan Africa. When the economic turnaround failed to materialize in the expected time frame, the countries and their creditors were confronted with the consequences of a worsening debt overhang, and with it the difficulties posed by

138. Allocations from the Fifth Dimension have covered more than 90 percent of the eligible countries' IBRD interest payments.

the mounting share of inflexible multilateral debt.[139] A comprehensive solution to the debt problem of highly indebted poor countries was seen as vital, not only for the affected countries but also to boost the integrity of development lending.[140] For any such proposal to succeed, debt write-offs would not only have to be steep but necessarily conditioned on country performance. It would also mean that creditors would lose the political benefits of the short-term leash provided by rescheduling ad infinitum. At the time of writing the international community was debating a plan floated by the World Bank to address this complex problem (see chapter 12).[141]

Operations Risk

As the complexity and size of the Bank's financial operations expanded, particularly from the late 1970s onward, operations risks grew as well. However, upgrading of institutional financial control systems lagged. Beginning in the late 1980s, the Bank began to regear its financial control systems when it became apparent that internal controls had been lax with noncompliance on established policies. A credit risk unit was moved from the Investments Department to the treasurer's office to ensure better compliance. New guidelines were formulated, and its investment authority was modified in 1989 to allow greater flexibility in the management of its liquid assets. A further revamping of internal controls began in the mid-1990s, following the arrival of a new controller.

Still, the probity underlying the Bank's financial operations has been a striking institutional trait over the past fifty years, and one that is frequently overlooked. For a portfolio as substantial and as actively traded as the Bank's large and manifold

139. As of the end of 1994, about two-thirds of outstanding debt was bilateral and 21 percent multilateral (including IMF). However, the latter's share in debt servicing was considerably higher due to their preferred creditor status, about 40 percent.

140. As of the end of 1994, under realistic assumptions, between thirty and forty countries had an unsustainably high debt burden in the mid-1990s. Given the limited consensus on criteria, time horizons, and assumptions of economic prospects, judgements are subjective. Mathew Martin, "A Multilateral Debt Facility—Global and National," in *International Monetary and Financial Issues for the 1990s*, vol. 8 (United Nations, 1997).

141. The World Bank's proposal called for a write-off on bilateral debt (up to 90 percent) and the creation of an arm's-length debt facility that would, under quite careful conditions, in effect, write off multilateral debt. There were difficult questions with regard to fundamental questions of fairness, moral hazard, and "burden sharing" between the bilaterals and the multilaterals. There were also sharp differences on how to fund the IMF's share of the debt relief operation, although it was assumed that the Bank's financial contribution would come from its net income or surplus. Furthermore, it was unclear if the demanding qualifying criteria, designed to discourage "moral hazard," were too stringent to be realistic; if so, in attempting to contain current repercussions, the problem could likely worsen down the road.

security offerings and considerable volumes of disbursements on its loan operations, this probity was a testament to institutional culture and a carefully nurtured
atmosphere of public service.

Changes in Financial Policies

The increased financial risks facing the Bank and its borrowers, and the fact that the
context in which the Bank's financial policies had been designed had fundamentally
altered, pushed the Bank to undertake major changes in its financial policies.

CURRENCY MANAGEMENT. By the time of the Plaza accord in September
1985, the dollar share of the Bank's outstanding loans was less than a quarter.[142] As
the dollar declined, the Bank began to receive complaints from its borrowers.
During the 1986 annual meetings a number of delegations, particularly from Asia,
raised the question of the costs of Bank loans. This concern led countries with the
financial wherewithal, such as Korea, to prepay. In other cases, rather than go through
the inconvenience of prepayments, they began to curb their borrowings. But it was the
scare given by Romania, and Ceaucescu's brinkmanship in threatening default on
Romania's debt servicing to the Bank over this issue, that put the Bank on notice.

The Romanian episode accelerated changes in several key aspects of the Bank's
financial policies that were already under way. Although the effects of these
policies were identified by several staff in the finance complex in the mid-1980s, it
took time to overcome internal inertia. Work on a major review of currency
management commenced in 1987, and led to several key changes in the Bank's
approach to currency management in 1989.[143] The result of these changes was to
reduce the volatility of the effective cost of Bank lending. Borrowers would henceforth pay only for the currencies they actually received and the currency mix of
disbursements (and hence, payment obligations) would now be sufficiently stable
to render it a hedgeable product. And, for the first time the cost of carry of liquidity
was made transparent.

The new lending rate formula excluded the costs of debt funding the liquid
portfolio. A targeted currency pool was introduced, making the currencies of
disbursement much more transparent.[144] Instead of lumping all costs, the risks and
costs of a loan product were now restricted to and paid for by the borrower who had

---

142. On September 22, 1985, following a meeting of the G-5 finance ministers at the Plaza
Hotel in New York, the G-5 publicly announced that the dollar was too strong, no longer
reflecting "fundamental economic conditions" and called for "orderly appreciation" of other
currencies against the dollar. Paul A. Volcker and Toyoo Gyohten, *Changing Fortunes: The
World's Money and the Threat to American Leadership* (Times Books, 1992), p. 357.

143. IBRD, "Review of IBRD Currency Management," R88-232, October 19, 1988.

144. The currency pool ratio was fixed with the target ratios for the currencies in the pool
being 1 U.S. dollar for every 125-yen and 2-deutsche-mark equivalent (including deutsche

the product. The currency composition of reserves was also gradually brought in line with that of loans.

The decision to adjust the currency mix of Bank lending had obvious implications on the currency mix of Bank borrowings. An unexpected complication arose. Through most of the decade the Japanese market had been one of the most important markets for the Bank. In the latter half of the 1980s financial contributions from Japan came to be closely tied with the geopolitics of "burden sharing." Various recycling plans of Japan's surpluses were announced and IBRD borrowings in the Tokyo capital market were included in these figures.[145] However, in 1988, in light of planned changes in its currency management policies, the World Bank's optimal borrowing strategy called for a reduction in its yen (and the deutsche mark group) borrowings. This led to considerable tension between Ministry of Finance officials and the Bank. Having been one of the Bank's strongest backers when the institution needed access to Japanese financial markets, as well as the largest cofinancier of Bank operations by far, Japanese officials felt let down now that they in turn needed the Bank to borrow to meet their publicly promised recycling targets. An apparently undiplomatic intervention by Mulford aggravated the problem, precipitating a sharp Japanese reaction, and obliged the Bank to beat a diplomatic retreat.[146] Although during this period the Bank appears to have borrowed more in yen than its optimal borrowing strategy called for, the Bank's yen-funding program reflected a carefully deliberated balance between short-term cost minimization and long-term relationship management.

Another step was a long-belated introduction of currency choice to borrowers in the form of single-currency loans in 1993. An opportunity to offer its borrowers a choice of currencies in which to denominate their loans had presented itself in the late 1980s when the Bank undertook major changes in its currency management policies. The option was rejected on the grounds that,

> offering borrowers a choice presupposes the Bank's ability to modify its borrowing program rapidly to reflect the composition of borrower's demands. While market access is not currently a pressing problem, there may well be occasions in the future when we might meet shareholder resistance to sharp expansion or contraction of the Bank's borrowing in their market. . . . Second, it is very doubtful whether all borrowers would willingly abide by their currency choices if they turn out to be wrong ones.[147]

---

marks, Swiss francs, and Dutch guilders), such that the target currencies comprised at least 90 percent of the pool value.

145. In 1987 Japan announced a $65 billion capital recycling program for 1987–92.

146. According to the Japanese version, Mulford "told Mr. Gyohten that Mr. Stern, with Mr. Roth, visited him recently and said to him that Japan was forcing the Bank to borrow 25 percent in Yen." Memorandum, Mitsukazu Ishikawa, executive director for Japan, to Ernest Stern, July 5, 1988. In his reply Stern disputed this version.

147. Memorandum, Ernest Stern to members of the President's Council, "Review of IBRD Currency Management," October 6, 1988.

While the first argument reflected Bank management's caution stemming from its experience over the decade, the second was less persuasive. After all the borrowers had abided with the considerable risks arising from the absence of choice.

The Bank cautiously responded in 1993 with a pilot program for LIBOR-based single-currency loans (SCL), providing its borrowers with a choice of loan terms for the first time since the 1950s.[148] The initial targets of the SCL were financial intermediaries.[149] Subsequently, in mid-1995, the program was considerably expanded, following extended consultations with borrowers. Borrower eligibility was relaxed (up to half a country's annual lending program or $100 million, whichever was greater); currency choice was widened (to any currency in which the Bank could appropriately fund itself); and a fixed-interest-rate option was added.[150] The continuance of ceilings (albeit, less restrictive) reflected the strategic concerns of the Bank. Since the demand for single-currency loans was heavily skewed toward U.S. dollars, it placed the institution in relying more heavily on one shareholder for meeting its obligations, although the United States allayed these concerns by considerably relaxing consent requirements on IBRD borrowings.

PROVISIONING. The growth of loan arrears and nonaccruals forced the Bank to reengineer its policy that hitherto had been to charge loan losses against income. Such a policy, if implemented, would have implied that a serious default would result in an abrupt decline in income. The establishment of a loan loss reserve through provisioning against income was first considered in mid-1983. Such a step, it was hoped, would provide protection from a sudden impairment of income. However, concerns were raised that establishing a loan loss reserve could be misinterpreted by markets, thereby adversely affecting the Bank's rating, as well as giving borrowers a mistaken impression that the Bank was prepared to absorb loan losses. The proponents of the "self-fulfilling prophesy" arguments prevailed, and the proposal was rejected. Instead, a small tinkering in Bank policy was made so that loan loss could be written off against the $293 million Special Reserve.[151]

The first loan provisions were approved in June 1986, specifically for loans to Nicaragua. Two years later a single consolidated loan loss provision applicable to the entire nonaccrual portfolio was established.[152] Estimates of the consolidated

---

148. IBRD, "A Proposal to Introduce Single Currency Loans," R93-5, January 15, 1993. The two-year pilot program was limited to $3 billion in new commitments and five currency choices: U.S. dollars, deutsche marks, French francs, Japanese yen, and pounds sterling.

149. These institutions onlend in a single currency and bear the interest and exchange rate risk (or else the government does). A single-currency loan considerably simplifies their business.

150. IBRD, "Review of the Single Currency Loan Program and Proposed Expansion," R95-91, May 11, 1995.

151. This reserve had been established by the Articles and was frozen in 1964.

152. The lump sum covered only countries in nonaccrual status and was calculated annually on the basis of an assessment of collectibility risk in the near and longer term. The lump sum was increased each month by 1 percent of the total debt outstanding of countries

Table 16-9. *IBRD: Debt, Equity, and Reserves, 1955–95*
Annual averages

Years	Equity (U.S.$ billions)	Reserves and surplus (as percentage of equity)	Usable capital (as percentage of equity)	Equity/debt
1955–56	1.1	19	81	1.29
1968–69	3.2	44	56	0.86
1981–82	6.3	58	42	0.21
1994–95	25.5	69	31	0.24

Source: World Bank, *Annual Report*, various years.

provision were now based on the Bank's assessment of the near-term and longer-term collectibility of arrears in each nonaccrual country. In 1991 these were extended to cover not only those countries already in nonaccrual status but also those with a high probability of accumulating protracted arrears. At the same time, it was decided that provisions should be set as a percent of loans outstanding and disbursed, and the net present value of callable guarantees.[153]

Another major change was a drive to more prudential financial ratios, in particular, by raising its level of reserves. The Bank's reserves serve two principal, and related, roles: guarding against credit risks, and retaining the confidence of financial markets. After building up its reserves over the 1950s and early 1960s, the reserves to loans ratio gradually eroded from 23.4 percent in 1965 to a low of 8.5 percent in 1986 (see figure 15-1). One reason for the decline of the actual reserves to loans ratio below the 10–11 percent target, despite large annual additions to reserves, was that the reserves to loans ratio has been vulnerable to exchange rates and to factors affecting net income. Because the U.S. dollar had a greater weight in reserves than in loans, the depreciation of the dollar since 1985 contributed to erode the ratio. At the same time, net income also fell below target as loans in nonaccrual status increased.

Concurrently the Bank's portfolio risks had increased substantially during this period. To offset these increased risks, the Bank had to increase its equity to enhance its risk-bearing capacity. However, the cost of doing so was now increasingly spread among all shareholders, as equity was fortified principally by additions to reserves, which in turn was bolstered by transfers from net income. Paid-in capital, the principal direct financial contribution by the Bank's nonborrowing members, as a share of equity has continued to decline over the last three decades—a trend that looks likely to continue in the future (table 16-9).

_____

in nonaccrual status in order to prevent having to fund a large increase in provisions at the end of the fiscal year.

153. The rate, originally set at 2.5 percent, was increased to 3 percent in 1993. The level of provisions was adjusted monthly according to the change in the value of the overall IBRD portfolio.

NEGATIVE PLEDGE CLAUSE. Underpinning the Bank's preferred creditor status was the negative pledge clause in Bank loan agreements which assured the Bank equal treatment with other creditors.[154] Consequently the Bank had entertained few requests for granting waivers to its negative pledge clause and had addressed them on an ad hoc basis. In addition, and separate from its interest in containing its financial risks, the Bank had always regarded securitized foreign lending with concern, believing that it was likely to lower discipline in project selection by both debtors and creditors.

A change in policy was first prompted in 1990 by the Bank's participation in the debt and debt-service reduction operation for Mexico, which could not go forward without the waiver of the Bank's negative pledge, since the creditors would receive bonds as collateral to the reduced debt. It would have been contradictory for the Bank to finance a debt-reduction operation involving the establishment of a collateral and simultaneously to refuse to waive the negative pledge clause. Following the Mexican case, the Bank adopted a general policy of participating in Brady-type debt and debt-service reduction operations and waived its negative pledge clause in such operations, both where it participated directly in the financing but also where it was not involved in financing.

As proposals for financing countries of the former Soviet Union began to surface in 1992, pressures emerged, notably from the export credit agencies (ECAs) of the major industrialized countries, for establishing escrow accounts in Russia and other former Soviet states, to help secure external financing. The ECAs first sought the Fund's acquiescence (if not approval) in the establishment of escrow accounts and subsequently began to press the Bank to modify its negative pledge policy.

The IMF, in line with its objectives, was concerned about the adverse effects of escrow-backed financing on the implementation of macroeconomic and structural policies.[155] But the Bretton Woods institutions were also concerned that such arrangements could also reduce their leverage which, after all, was based on the ability to deliver external financial assistance in return for policy changes. A situation whereby a country desperate for foreign exchange could avail itself of such resources by encouraging securitized lending without necessarily changing its policies, was inimical to the two institutions' leverage on policy reform. Furthermore, there was the danger of proliferation, both within the debtor country and in other countries, through spillover effects. There were concerns that if some lenders were given the waiver to establish escrow accounts, others might also insist that escrow accounts be established as guarantees for their own loans.

154. The negative pledge clause in the General Conditions in the Bank's loan agreements requires a borrower who creates any lien on public assets for the benefit of other creditors to equally and ratably secure the Bank's loan as well.

155. Since escrow accounts lead to a segmentation of a country's reserves, they hamper the country's efforts to manage its foreign exchange as well as undermining the development of a broad-based foreign exchange market.

On the other hand, there was also a strong case for modifying the clause. Economic assets in the countries of the former Soviet Union were almost entirely in the public sector; the transition to a market economy required a rapid increase in the role of the private sector. However, until privatization of existing assets made progress and was supplemented by new private investment, most economically important assets would fall under the purview of the negative pledge clause as soon as the Bank signed its first loan with the government. Escrow accounts were a normal commercial practice and without the added measure of security and protection for their arrangements, private lenders would be unwilling to lend to the governments concerned. But if the governments did provide the additional protection, that would run counter to their negative pledge in their loan agreements with the Bank.

The balance was tilted by political considerations.[156] The Bank had been lending to China for more than a decade and was initiating a lending program for Vietnam. In neither case was there any evidence that foreign private investment had been held back because of the lack of a waiver in the negative pledge clause. Although there was a wide consensus that the changes under way in the countries of the former Soviet Union, especially Russia, required a forceful external response, the financial commitments were woefully inadequate. For the new Clinton administration, caught between its strong desire to increase aid to Russia and strident domestic opposition to any increase in foreign aid, loans through the U.S. Export-Import Bank to underwrite sales for Russian oil and gas projects represented a way out of the dilemma. The dollar figures of such credits would be visibly impressive, while not requiring any approval from Congress. The credits would be secured by offshore escrow accounts into which Russian oil and gas producers would channel hard-currency earnings rather than the alternative of Russian sovereign guarantees of repayment.

It was apparent to the Bank's management that any change in the negative pledge formula that would be meaningful to the countries of the former Soviet Union would have to be discriminatory to other Bank borrowers if the financial risks to the institution were to be contained. Economically important assets were publicly held in all the Bank's borrowers. Their degree varied and consequently any cutoff point would necessarily be seen as arbitrary. On the other hand, expanding coverage to ensure equity would increase the financial risks to the Bank to unacceptable levels.

156. As the following note from the Dutch executive director indicates, the consultation process reflected these pressures. "Notwithstanding the fact that, according to the *New York Times*, the U.S. Import-Export Bank, in advance of Board consideration, has already received personal assurances from 'key members' of the Board (whose voting power cannot be ascertained) on their support for granting general waivers on the Negative Pledge clause, I thought it might still be of interest to convey my views on the above mentioned subject." Memorandum, Eveline Herfkens to Lewis Preston, "IBRD's Negative Pledge Policy with Respect to Lending for Investment Projects (Doc R92-214)," December 29, 1992.

The initial reformulation of the negative pledge policy, submitted to the Board in late 1992, contained several "damage control" clauses carefully crafted to limit the risks to the Bank. First, the eligibility criteria for waivers was made contingent on a "program of structural change, including satisfactory macroeconomic policies."[157] Second, waivers would only be granted to "special purpose entities" (SPEs), separate enterprises established as borrowers to account for the new loans and incremental output resultant thereof, an arrangement designed to insure that existing production was not used to pay off the loans.

Furthermore, the management's proposals sought to exclude waivers to direct lending (as opposed to guarantees) by export credit agencies, despite strong representations from Japan. While the U.S. Export-Import Bank's proposals only involved its guarantees on commercial bank credits, the Japan Export-Import Bank usually made direct loans rather than guarantees. The Bank's management attempted to persuade Japan to accept this formulation, but without success. While the original paper to the Board included only guarantees, the Japanese executive director insisted on tabling an amendment, which was accepted by the Board, overriding management's position.

However, the restrictions proved too onerous, and the Bank found itself unable to issue any waivers. The countries that had been the object of the waivers had been unable to establish programs of macroeconomic stabilization as defined in an IMF program. The SPEs proved operationally infeasible. Finally in December 1993, a further relaxation in policy was approved with the country eligibility criteria limited to the country's "making progress on privatization."[158] The SPE concept, so ardently defended just a few months earlier, was now dropped.

An important reason for the changes was peer pressure by a sister institution. As management put it to the Board, "The EBRD has decided on a waiver policy considerably more flexible than ours. Obviously, we are not bound by that—but it does create major confusion for private investors, since the difference in policy, supported by the same shareholders, cannot be explained by differences in the structure of the two institutions."[159] Of course, the two MDBs did not have the "same shareholders," but they did have the same shareholders that mattered. Their different policies reflected, in part, the fact that the executive directors of the same

157. "IBRD's Negative Pledge Policy with Respect to Lending for Investment Projects," R92-214, November 25, 1992, para. 9.

158. IBRD, "Modification to IBRD's Negative Pledge Policy with Respect to Lending for Investment Projects," R93-199, November 29, 1993, para. 6. The new policy permitted waivers for export-earning projects in countries where 75 percent or more of the income-producing assets were public. The liens were limited to eighteen months of debt service; the lender would have to be a private entity (or 51 percent in the case of cofinancing with an official agency) and the loans would have to have a maturity of at least five years.

159. Ernest Stern, "Statement to the Board on Modification to the IBRD's Negative Pledge Policy with Respect to Lending for Investment Projects," SecM93-1272, December 14, 1993.

shareholders in the two institutions received their instructions from different ministries.

The first waivers granted were for Russia and Uzbekistan. All waivers granted to countries in transition (in contrast to waivers related to debt-related operations) had built-in triggers designed to protect the Bank's interests. In the end, the contentiousness surrounding the negative pledge waivers proved to be much ado about little. Empirical support linking external private investment to the Bank's decision to modify its negative pledge clause—relative to a host of other variables—remains nonexistent.

NET INCOME. In addition to building up reserves, the Bank's net income has served two further purposes: an adequate level and trend of net income demonstrates soundness to the financial markets, the major source of the funds loaned by the Bank; net income remaining after allocation to reserves has been used at shareholders' discretion for broad development objectives, of which the principal one has been annual transfers to IDA (a practice begun by George Woods in 1964).

As noted in the earlier discussion on the Bank's currency policies, there was a pervasive belief that the institution's liquid portfolio was a net moneymaker for the institution, in fact, the principal source of its net income.[160] Even as changes in currency management were under way, the Bank's liquidity policy was revised in 1987, raising liquidity from 40 percent to 45 percent of the next three years' net cash requirements. At the time, it was argued that "the principal objective of liquidity policy is to guard against the possibility of unforeseen variations in the Bank's cash flows, the most important of which is the possibility of an interruption in borrowings."[161] Market conditions were perceived to be "more serious now than in recent years" and the "risk of temporary erosion of investor confidence" had altered significantly: prudence called for a higher level of liquidity. Possible financial costs due to a carrying cost of liquidity were not discussed.[162]

Since then, a number of changes have occurred that appear to have raised questions about the Bank's continued high liquidity. Market access risks for the Bank have declined sharply. The changes in financial policies enumerated earlier

---

160. Thus Percy Mistry (formerly a senior adviser in the Bank's Finance complex during much of the 1980s) vigorously argues that "maintaining liquidity at higher levels than is actually necessary in present market conditions" (common to all MDBs) reflects the MDBs' "vested interest in retaining and strengthening their roles as *financial arbitrageurs*" since these investments are an important "profit centre" for the institutions. Percy S. Mistry, *Multilateral Development Banks: An Assessment of Their Financial Structures, Policies and Practices* (The Hague: FONDAD), p. 237.

161. IBRD, "Review of IBRD Liquidity Policy," R87-290, December 21, 1987, para. 15. In reality the change was marginal: liquidity had averaged 44 percent over the previous decade (1978–87). The liquidity ratio was thereafter specified a range of 45–50 percent, since deviations in disbursements from plans made it hard to manage a precise figure.

162. Ibid., paras. 19–20.

Table 16-10. *IBRD: Components of Return on Assets, 1981–95*
As a percentage of average earning assets

Component	1981–85	1986–90	1991–95
Interest spread on loans and investments	0.48	0.62	0.48
Interest spread earned on loans[a]	–0.01	0.81	0.76
Interest spread earned on investments[a]	1.82	–0.17	–0.98
Contribution of reserves, capital, and surplus	1.03	1.12	1.40
Commitment fee, other income, front-end fee	0.93	0.29	0.10
Less:			
Administrative expenses	0.77	0.57	0.63
Loan loss provision	0.00	0.24	0.29
Return on earning assets	1.67	1.22	1.05

Source: IBRD, "Allocation of FY95 Net Income and Plan for FY96," R95-143, July 14, 1996.

a. Based on average cost of debt weighted by the currency composition of loans and investments, respectively.

sharply reduced the susceptibility of the Bank to market risks. Several borrowing innovations, particularly the advent of the global bond in 1989, cut the Bank's intermediation costs to an all-time low. In short, in the early 1990s the Bank's funding risks clearly were substantially lower than in the previous decade.

Since the Bank's borrowings are primarily medium and long term, and its liquidity investments are short term, with yield curves typically upward sloping, under normal circumstances it costs the Bank money to carry liquidity, as is the case with any institution.[163] This was probably why, when Lewis Preston arrived at the Bank in 1991, the "high" level of liquidity was one of the key financial issues that he asked to be briefed on.[164] During the period 1981 to 1985 the net spread earned from the Bank's liquid portfolio was 1.8 percent. A decade later (1991–95), it was –0.98 percent and is projected to be even more negative over the next three years (table 16-10). No doubt, the high liquidity carried by the Bank is based on a judgment, always difficult, balancing the costs-of-carry with market risks and reduced borrowing costs. But this judgment perhaps also reflects a certain inertia, force of habit, and a continued strong belief in the exceptional value added by its Investments Department (as both Van Horne and Polak pointed out years ago).[165]

Not surprisingly, the allocation of net income has been a contentious issue among the institution's shareholders. It has been a political issue with fault lines running along both the North-South fault line and splits among the borrowing

163. The "cost-of-carry" is the incremental cost of borrowings at the present time, as opposed to borrowing sometime in the future, factored for the returns earned in investing the additional liquid assets.

164. "Briefing for Mr. Preston, Finance Issues," April 12, 1991.

165. Before his departure in 1995, the Bank's managing director, Ernest Stern, concurred with this assessment. Ernest Stern, interview with John Lewis, Richard Webb, and Devesh Kapur, January 5, 1995.

countries. In the former case, the major shareholders have understandably pushed for higher reserves both to reduce their risk of contingent liabilities and to reduce paid-in capital increases in any future capital replenishments. Borrowers, more interested in reducing their borrowing costs, have instead pushed for reduced levels of net income. But borrowers have also been divided, with some (especially Brazil and other Latin American countries, increasingly joined by other IBRD-only borrowers) insisting that net income be used to lower loan charges rather than supplement IDA, to which they lack recourse. Higher loan charges to provide for adequate provisions for nonaccruals also exposed cracks in the Bank's self-image as a financial cooperative, since the burden was largely shouldered by one group—the borrowers who had continued to service their Bank debt in a timely way.

In 1974 the Bank's Governors agreed that net income could be allocated on grant basis and this would be equivalent to formal distribution.[166] In 1987 (and again in 1988), as concerns on reserves adequacy mounted (with the declining reserves to outstanding loans ratio) Bank management, for the first time since 1974, recommended that no net income be transferred to IDA. Subsequently (in fiscal 1991), the executive directors approved a framework to guide the annual process of net income allocation giving first priority to reach a targeted reserves-to-loans ratio (which was gradually raised to 14.25 percent by 1995); the second priority was placed on reducing borrower costs by prefunding waivers of loan interest charges up to 25 basis points for the following fiscal year.[167]

The framework also identified two other uses for the residual net income. One was to support high-priority development activities. The other was to accumulate funds temporarily in a "surplus account," adding to the institution's financial strength pending future use of these funds. Both were indicative of the changing nature of "burden sharing" in the funding of development activities.

The principal rationale for creating the surplus account was the uncertainty about the risk scenario and represented a balance between strongly divergent views within the Board on the level of reserves. The insistence by most of the G-7 shareholders for a larger level of reserves appeared to be prompted by two concerns. First, the G-7 have also been pressuring the Bank to lend more to Eastern Europe, particularly Russia, as well as to loosen its negative pledge clause to the same end. And second, the major shareholders' view, acknowledged by the Bank's management, is that achieving *any* paid-in capital in the next GCI would be extremely difficult. With this in mind, a surplus account (with a movable cap) could

166. While allocation to reserves is made by the executive directors and "noted with approval" by the Board of Governors, only the latter decides on the allocation or distribution of net income.

167. These interest charge waivers are provided to all borrowers which have serviced all of their loans within thirty days of their due dates during the prior six months. IBRD, "Medium-Term Outlook and Policy on Annual Allocation of Net Income," R90-193, September 21, 1990.

be seen as a device to squirrel away funds that could later be added to equity if the fear of an absence of additional paid-in capital in a future GCI were realized. At the same time, the surplus account, by adding to the institution's earnings capacity, also stemmed growing pressures on the institution's administrative budget.

The debates on the allocative priorities of net income also brought into relief long-simmering dissension on what should or should not be included or funded out of the administrative budget, given the inverse relationship between the size of the administrative budget and net income. The Bank began making grants from net income in 1964—for IDA. Until 1982, with an exception in fiscal 1972 and fiscal 1973, grants to other organizations were made through IDA. In fiscal 1982—at the urging of its auditors who argued that since grants were expenses made to organizations not affiliated with the Bank, grants began to be treated as a part of the cost of doing business and included under the administrative budget—the Bank ended up with two types of grants: one, called "special grants," are included in the administrative budget; and the other derive from net income.

Beginning with an annual allocation for international agriculture research (the CGIAR system) in 1971, the "special grants program" funded from the administrative budget steadily increased in scope and size over the next quarter century, although its funding remained concentrated on two broad areas: international agriculture (about two-thirds) and health (about a fifth).[168] The expansion of "special grants" has been countered by the major shareholders, who have been exerting political pressure to rein in the administrative budget (which was much more "visible") and allocate some of these expenditures below the line, that is, to fund worthy causes out of net income.

However, the Bank's auditors had insisted that transfers out of net income— equivalent to a dividend—be justified as benefiting the entire membership. The need for such a justification led several IBRD borrowers to question the basis for transfers from IBRD net income for IDA. Although they were persuaded to accept the interpretation, it was more difficult to justify including activities whose benefits accrued to a subset of the IBRD's membership. This was the case, for instance, with the Debt Reduction Facility for IDA-only countries, created in 1989, by way of transfers from net income.[169] The problem was finessed by some agile gymnastics, wherein it was agreed that IDA would "administer" the program. By the end of 1995 operations were completed in ten countries, with substantial benefits. The facility retired about $2.5 bil-

168. The criteria for the special grants program (SGP) emphasize multicountry benefits, multidonor support, and independence of the recipient institution from the Bank Group. By the early 1990s, funding for the SGP accounted for about 5 percent of the Bank's budget (between $60 million and $70 million).

169. The purpose of the facility was to help low-income countries restructure their commercial debt. The Bank committed $300 million between 1989 and 1998 for this facility by way of transfers from net income.

lion of commercial debt at an average buyback price of just 12.8 percent using less than $150 million of IBRD resources (and $192 million of cofinancing).[170]

In recent years, in rebuilding its reserves and surplus, the Bank has been reinvigorating itself as a sound financial institution. But these resources have also emerged as a tempting target to fund a range of worthy causes. The Bank began using part of its net income to fund humanitarian causes and, under pressure from the large shareholders, to fund activities in *nonmembers*.[171] Trust funds for technical assistance to the former Soviet Union, for investment activities in Gaza, and for jump-starting the reconstruction effort in Bosnia and Herzegovina without waiting for financial normalization and membership were three prominent examples.[172] And at the time of writing, a proposal for reducing multilateral debt in the highly indebted poor countries, funded in part by the Bank's net income and surplus, was gathering momentum.

Several of these cases represent foreign policy interests of some of the Bank's largest shareholders, rather than intrinsic merits of benefits to the institution's membership as a whole. Traditionally, the large shareholders would have funded their interests through direct claims on their budgetary resources, but in the strained fiscal environment of the 1990s, the cost would be borne by all of the Bank's members.[173] Although a framework for allocation of net income had been developed, it was apparent that with net income projected at about a billion and half dollars and a comfortable level of reserves, in the absence of a strategic vision for the use of net income beyond allocations to reserves and waivers of commitment fees, these resources are likely to be raided to fund ad hoc emergencies or to substitute for declining donor contributions to IDA.

Attempts at Increasing Leverage

The ceiling placed on IBRD lending at the beginning of the decade led to considerable work on alternatives to augment the IBRD's financial leverage. The

170. World Bank, *World Debt Tables, 1996,* table 2.6. The ten countries benefiting from the program were Niger, Mozambique, Guyana, Uganda, Bolivia, Sao Tomé and Principe, Zambia, Albania, Sierra Leone, and Nicaragua. The retirement of $1.1 billion of Nicaragua's commercial debt in December 1995 was the single largest operation.

171. Examples include grants to the World Food Program in 1984–85 to support relief efforts for the famine in Sub-Saharan Africa and in 1993 to fund relief operations in Rwanda.

172. The Bank committed $30 million for the G-7–mandated study on the former Soviet Union. It has committed $140 million to the Trust Fund for Gaza through 1995, funded by transfers from IBRD surplus earmarked for IDA; a $150 million Trust Fund for Bosnia-Herzegovina was created from the surplus account.

173. It could be argued that where the problem—and benefits—are clearly of a regional nature, regional multilateral institutions should bear the brunt of the burden. Only where regional multilateral institutions are weak, should global institutions fill the breach.

simplest option was a change in the IBRD's conservative gearing ratio. Since such a step would, in due course, have caused the Bank's outstanding debt to substantially exceed the callable capital of its "AAA" members, the move was staunchly opposed by the Bank's treasurer, who feared its consequences on the institution's ratings. Instead the institution directed its efforts at several other options to increase its financial leverage: an Energy Affiliate, a World Bank's Bank, cofinancing, and MIGA.

Energy Affiliate

The idea of an Energy Affiliate gathered steam after the second oil shock, amidst serious concerns about the energy prospects of non-oil producing developing countries. The proposal had strong backing from the Arab OPEC countries, Kuwait and Saudi Arabia in particular, as well as the Carter administration. In August 1980, the Bank's Executive Board recommended that the institution explore the establishment of such an affiliate. Discussions on the financing, organizational structure, and voting arrangements continued over the next year and a half.

The idea was to establish an institutional mechanism partly to aid the recycling process and partly to increase the Bank Group's lending capacity while both maintaining its financial integrity and limiting the burden on the larger shareholders. The Energy Affiliate was principally expected to tap the OPEC countries for funds and, in return, these countries would have enhanced voting rights in the affiliate. In general, the majority favored the idea of "floating shares" (emulating the practice at the IMF) with votes linked to financial contribution.[174] Developed and developing countries were to have equal voting rights with a residual share held by the Bank. It was expected that the affiliate would have a capital of $10 billion to $15 billion, of which 10 percent would be paid in. With a gearing ratio of 2.5 to 1, the affiliate was expected to lend $25 billion to $30 billion between 1982 and 1986.[175]

However, the arrival of the new U.S. administration doomed the proposal. Not only was the new team in the Treasury hostile to any further expansion of the World Bank, it adopted a strong ideological stance that truly attractive energy projects could always be satisfactorily implemented by the private sector without World Bank involvement. The proposal was finally buried at the Toronto Annual General Meetings in 1982, by which time global preoccupations had also radically shifted.

World Bank's Bank

The sharp reversal of capital flows that followed the onset of the debt crisis forced a reexamination of options that could potentially help the institution escape

---

174. Note by the chairman on meetings held on the Energy Affiliate, November 24, 1980, and February 2–3, 1981.

175. IBRD, "Expanded Energy Lending—Energy Affiliate," R81-78, April 15, 1981.

the constraints posed by lending ceilings. In early 1983, the Bank began to examine the possibility of setting up a separate financial vehicle called the "World Bank's Bank"—a wholly owned, highly leveraged subsidiary resembling a private commercial bank rather than a public agency, with an investment of about $500 million by the IBRD (at about $100 million to $150 million a year).[176] Legally it appeared possible for the IBRD to create a subsidiary that would require legislative action by only one government.[177] It was thought that such a subsidiary could act as a captive cofinancing wing of the Bank and raise up to $5 billion for financing Bank-approved projects and programs in the period 1985–87. The subsidiary would take a leadership role in assembling commercial bank syndicated credits, retaining as little for its own account as possible. The lending, focusing on larger borrowers, would be principally program-type lending. It would fund itself predominantly in Eurocurrency markets, essentially in the manner of a commercial bank, and would benefit from IBRD-provided means of comfort (for example, a liquidity backstop). It was conceived as an indirect means of leveraging the Bank's capital more effectively than could be achieved under the existing Articles.

Although it was generally felt that such a subsidiary would increase the Bank's financial leverage, it was recognized that this could not be a sufficient reason for the establishment of such an affiliate. The subsidiary would have to serve a genuine catalytic function by giving the institution additional flexibility both in resource mobilization (easier cofinancing through commercial banks, greater access to short-term markets) as well as in lending (lending without government guarantees, possibility of rescheduling, flexible procurement techniques).

Considerable work was done in developing this proposal through 1983. But the proposal raised numerous questions. Any transfer of the IBRD's net income for equity purposes would, of course, affect loan charges as well as transfers to IDA. The proposed "World Bank's Bank" could well pose risks to the IBRD through its guarantees of the subsidiary's borrowings, as well as loans to the subsidiary and the placement of IBRD liquidity in the subsidiary's paper. Even without the Bank acting as a formal "lender of last resort," the institution would obviously have to be heavily committed to ensuring that a major subsidiary did not fail.

By mid-1984 support for the proposal had all but died out. The major shareholders were less than enthusiastic, since the proposed structure of the Bank's Bank would have placed it at greater arm's length from their control. Borrowers were not uniformly enthusiastic, either. Those that did not expect to benefit from the subsidiary feared that it might substitute for the expansion of IBRD lending; there was also the fear that once established, it would serve as an argument for resisting further capital increases of the IBRD.

176. The concept was given shape in the finance complex (under Roberg and Bock) on the basis of a proposal by Pat Heininger (a member of the Bank's Legal Department).

177. The United Kingdom was the prime candidate.

Cofinancing

The rapid expansion of Bank lending in the 1970s was accompanied by a concomitant increase in cofinancing (see chapter 15). The bulk of this amount (nearly two-thirds) had been official cofinancing, mostly with bilateral donors (table 16-11). Most of the remainder had come from export credits (25 percent). Private cofinancing through commercial banks, while relatively modest during the 1970s (10 percent), surged at the turn of the decade, amounting to more than a fifth of all cofinancing.

The arrival of a new president appeared to presage a major expansion of the Bank's private cofinancing operations. As a former commercial banker, Tom Clausen came into the institution charged with enthusiasm on this front. With the onset of the debt crisis, as commercial banks scrambled to find greater comfort through guarantees, the Bank seemed poised to greatly expand its private cofinancing operations.

In 1983 the Bank introduced a new cofinancing technique: the "B-loan program." Under this program the Bank participated in the later maturities of a commercial loan to encourage banks to extend their own maturities and thereby achieve an overall lengthening of maturities. The largest such case of the B-loan facility was Hungary, which leveraged almost a billion dollars. In 1985, a $150 million partial guarantee operation in Chile against commercial cofinancing of $350 million was an important element in putting together a total rescue package of almost $6 billion in rescheduling, and over $1 billion in new money, for the country.[178] A large partial guarantee operation (up to $750 million) for Mexico in October 1986, while helping the country in reaching agreement with its commercial creditors did not find favor with the Board.

During this period, there was an extended and protracted debate within the Bank about the possibility of gaining added leverage on the institution's guarantees. The Bank's Legal Counsel had initially raised the possibility of an interpretation of the Articles such that guarantees would count for less than an equivalent loan. This interpretation was strongly opposed by the treasurer on the grounds that financial markets would react adversely to any such move. In the end it was decided that since guarantees represented an irrevocable obligation for the Bank, it must be fully covered by the Bank's capital by the time it becomes callable. On that basis, capital was to be allocated gradually against outstanding guarantee commitments from the time they were signed. Such a policy ensured that there was little leverage to be gained through the use of guarantees.

178. Another variation that was attempted was contingent obligations, with the Bank taking a contingent participation in the final maturity of a commercial loan designed with a fixed level of combined installments of floating interest and variable principal repayments. This was used, however, in only one small operation: a $3.3 million livestock loan to Paraguay in 1984.

Table 16-11. *Annual Average World Bank Sources of Cofinancing, 1973–94*
Billions of U.S. dollars

Fiscal period	Official		Export credits		Private		Total cofinance	Total IBRD/IDA lending	Percentage of total IBRD/IDA lending
	Total	Percent	Total	Percent	Total	Percent			
1973–79	1.3	64	0.5	25	0.2	11	1.9	6.5	30
1980–89	3.9	62	1.2	19	1.2	19	6.3	15.6	40
1990–94	7.9	71	1.9	18	1.3	11	11.1	21.2	51
Total	3.9	66	1.1	19	0.9	15	5.9	14.1	42

Source: IBRD, "A Review of Cofinancing at the World Bank," SecM94-214, March 1, 1994, annex A.
Notes: Figures are based on data available at the time of Board presentation, as adjusted by subsequent changes to the project financing plans when available.

It was therefore not surprising that for the most part the rhetoric of private cofinancing far exceeded actual achievements. The levels of private cofinancing increased relatively modestly over the next five years, although the figures may underestimate the drastic decline in commercial bank cofinancing over this period that would have occurred in the absence of the new cofinancing initiatives. For the creditworthy countries (of East Asia, for instance), there was little demand since these countries retained access to jumbo sovereign risk loans. The benefits were marginal relative to the costs of a loss of flexibility to the borrower and additional risk to the Bank. For countries that were not creditworthy, the security provided by cofinancing was insufficient to tempt commercial banks to expand their exposure. In the case of the severely indebted middle-income countries, where all commercial bank lending was concerted (that is, involuntary), there was little scope for cofinancing, which by definition was voluntary. Since the mechanics of involuntary lending required the banks to put up new money proportionate to their existing exposure, there was little possibility of banks increasing their voluntary exposure. The repeated rescheduling of commercial bank loans made the Bank chary of having its B-loans dragged into the process.

The commercial banks were looking for greater security than that available under the Bank's instruments. Per se, the Bank's cofinancing instruments provided little additional security beyond that associated with a good project. The commercial banks understandably wanted to shift the risk to the Bank. All loans guaranteed by the Bank increased its exposure and not that of the lender. The Bank also resisted the commercial banks' desire of cross-default agreements and provisions that would share payments between the Bank and commercial banks, arguing that such provisions would undermine its operational flexibility in the event of rescheduling. In 1989, as reschedulings and debt forgiveness on commercial debt rose, and as the risks to the Bank's own portfolio rose to unprecedented levels, the Bank decided to terminate its B-loan program in response to concerns that the "B-loan" program, by providing a broad range of protection to the financier, was exposing the Bank to unacceptable risks. In its place the Bank unveiled a new program: Expanded Cofinancing Operations (ECO) as part of its stepped-up efforts to work with private foreign capital in developing countries.

The limited results from private cofinancing notwithstanding, cofinancing as a percentage of IBRD/IDA lending rose from 30 percent in the 1970s to nearly 50 percent at the end of the 1980s. This growth was largely due to the increase in official cofinancing, as both bilateral and multilateral cofinancing rose markedly over the decade. The Program of Special Assistance (1983–84) for Sub-Saharan Africa was one example. The Bank especially began to rely on cofinancing to augment SAL resources, particularly with Japan and other MDBs.[179] The Special

179. Between 1981 and 1990, while IBRD/IDA lending increased by 75 percent from $12.4 billion to $20.7 billion, cofinancing increased nearly threefold (from $3.5 billion to $13 billion). Between 1981 and 1983 average annual cofinancing resources for adjustment

Joint Financing initiative under the Special Facility for Africa and subsequently the Special Program of Assistance for Africa represented a major shift in the way the Bank viewed and used official cofinancing. Cofinancing became an instrument of aid coordination rather than a simple augmentation of resources.

During the latter part of the decade, the regional development banks began to link an increasing fraction of their lending with the World Bank. The IDB joined in cofinancing World Bank adjustment lending operations after a new president assumed office in that institution in 1988. Measured as a fraction of its own lending, cofinancing with the World Bank was most important for the African Development Bank. Cofinancing with the Asian Development Bank was largely confined to large infrastructure projects in that region. Among bilaterals, a rapid expansion in cofinancing operations by Japan resulted in a surge in bilateral cofinancing. Increased Japanese cofinancing was part of the country's capital recycling plans following the Plaza accords and a recognition of the ease of disbursements by piggybacking onto Bank lending operations. During this period Japan was by far the largest bilateral cofinancier (it accounted for 46 percent of all bilateral cofinancing during 1983–93). Initially (from fiscal 1986), this was primarily nonconcessional (but untied) financing through the Export-Import Bank of Japan, but from 1988 there was a large increase in concessional cofinancing from the Overseas Economic Cooperation Fund.

Multinational Investment Guarantee Agency (MIGA)

Perceptions of noncommercial risks had long hampered the flow of FDI to developing countries. In the early 1960s the Bank was asked (by the OECD and again by UNCTAD) to examine ways to establish an international organization that would insure private foreign investment in developing countries against noncommercial risk. For more than a decade, the institution sought to find common ground among its members to establish an "international investment insurance agency." Finally, in 1973, frustrated by the lack of consensus on basic issues such as financial participation and voting arrangements, the Bank discontinued its effort.[180] Developing-country attitudes toward foreign direct investment had hardened, and there was little the institution could do to change that reality.

The initiative was revived by Clausen at the 1981 annual meetings, but again little progress occurred.[181] The initiative was then taken up by the new general counsel, Ibrahim Shihata, who had prior experience in this area.[182] Several years of exhaustive studies and discussions followed. Even then, when the Bank's Board

---

operations accounted for barely $27.2 million. By 1988–90 this figure had jumped to $2.85 billion (annual average), an almost hundredfold increase.

180. World Bank, "International Investment Insurance Agency," R73-9, January 11, 1973.

181. World Bank, "Multilateral Investment Insurance Agency," R82-225, July 14, 1982.

182. In his capacity as the general counsel of the Kuwait Fund for Arab Economic Development, Shihata had been instrumental in establishing an Arab agency to insure investment against noncommercial risks and promote investment from the richer Arab countries in the poorer ones.

Table 16-12. *MIGA's Guarantee Activities, Fiscal 1990–96*

	1990	1991	1992	1993	1994	1995	1996	Total
Number of guarantees	4	11	21	27	38	54	68	223
Maximum aggregate liability ($U.S. million)	132	59	313	374	372	672	862	2,784
Approximate amount of FDI facilitated ($U.S. billion)	1.0	0.9	1.0	1.9	1.3	2.5	6.6	15.2

Source: MIGA data.

finally approved the convention in September 1985 to establish a Multilateral Investment Guarantee Agency (MIGA), support was lukewarm, with several prominent countries (both major borrowers as well as G-7) abstaining.

The international convention establishing MIGA finally took effect in April 1988, too late to play any catalytic financial role in debt-distressed (middle-income) countries.[183] Still, its broad acceptance after decades of opposition by developing countries reflected their greater receptivity to equity finance, especially foreign direct investment, chastened by their experience with debt flows. Besides providing insurance for foreign investments in such ventures against noncommercial risks, MIGA undertook to provide technical and advisory services rendering advice to member states in the formulation and implementation of their policies toward foreign investments.[184]

MIGA's role was seen as complementing national and private insurers. Despite a slow start (in part, the result of lackluster leadership), as developing-country attitudes toward foreign direct investment underwent a sea change, the demand for MIGA's services soon spurted (table 16-12). It also reflected a broader shift in an increased demand for the Bank group's risk mitigation instruments, even as demand for its traditional lending instruments languished.

However, MIGA's activities were limited by its small initial capital stock (SDR 1 billion, of which just 10 percent was paid in) and a conservative approach to underwriting, held down by a low ceiling of contingent insurance liabilities to

183. MIGA was established as an international organization pursuant to an international treaty, similar to the Articles of Agreement of the IBRD. Its relationship with the World Bank is analogous to that of the IFC: it is an autonomous institution operating on its own account and within its own responsibility while maintaining a symbolic, but significant linkage with the Bank. The president of the Bank is ex officio the chairman of the Board and in this capacity nominates the person to be elected by MIGA's Board as its executive vice president (its chief executive officer). Details can be found in Ibrahim Shihata, *MIGA and Foreign Investment* (Martinus Nijhoff, 1988).

184. Immediately after operations began, MIGA concluded an agreement with the IFC converting the Foreign Investment Advisory Services (FIAS), which had been established by the IFC in 1986, into a joint facility supported equally by the IFC and MIGA. Although FIAS appeared to have performed well, MIGA withdrew from its relationship with FIAS in 1994 to conserve its limited resources.

capital.[185] By the mid-1990s, MIGA's rapid growth was already straining its underwriting capacity. Despite relaxing the risk-to-asset ratio (to 3.5:1), MIGA was running out of headroom to sustain further expansion in business. At the time of writing, although support for a MIGA capital increase was nearly unanimous, several large countries (the United States, France, and Germany) were balking at any capital increase that would require cash outlays from members, while being averse to any reduction in their shareholding. Instead it seemed likely that IBRD resources would be drawn upon to ease MIGA's financial constraints.

Capital Adequacy

With the onset of the debt crisis, the Bank's management became increasingly concerned with the constraints imposed by the ceilings on its lending. Stern advised Clausen to "brief the Secretary [George Shultz] *again* on the artificial limitation imposed on our annual lending volume."[186] As noted in chapter 15, in gaining support of the U.S. Treasury for the last capital increase the Bank had agreed that its annual volume of lending would be guided by the concept of a "sustainable level of lending"—a level of lending commitments that can be sustained indefinitely without requiring a further capital increase. The new team in the U.S. Treasury, however, now insisted that the SLL serve as an absolute limit rather than as a guide. But the technical underpinnings of the SLL concept made it quite sensitive to the dollar/SDR exchange rate. As the dollar appreciated between early 1982 and mid-1983 (the dollar/SDR rate having appreciated from 1.21 to 1.05), the SLL dropped by $1.8 billion, almost a fifth.[187] The simplest solution for increasing lending was, of course, a capital increase. Through much of the decade the institution would struggle to persuade its largest shareholder to accede to a capital increase.

Selective Capital Increase

While an IMF quota increase was in the works in 1981–82 (the eighth review of quotas), the Bank was planning a $20 billion SCI, following the long-established tradition of parallelism with the IMF. It was hoped that this could be followed up by a GCI in 1985.

185. Initially, the "risk-to-asset" ratio was set at 1.5:1, with a provision to be relaxed over time to 5:1 without amending the Convention.
186. Memorandum, Ernest Stern to A. W. Clausen, "Meeting with Secretary Schultz," August 3, 1983, para. 3. Emphasis added.
187. See "Briefing note for Mr. Clausen on the Selective Capital Increase," September 21, 1983. Contained in memorandum from Dale R. Weigel to Moeen A. Qureshi, September 21, 1983.

Although other members of the G-7 were open to the idea of a two-stage SCI—a small increase of $2.9 billion to modify relative rankings and a $16.8 billion increase with actual subscriptions to be folded into a subsequent GCI—the United States was adamantly opposed unless outstanding policy issues with it were first resolved. Furthermore, the United States argued that the proposed $20 billion increase "would give flexibility under the sustainable lending level policy and would expand the Bank's lending capacity," undermining its position on curbing any expansion of Bank lending.[188] The U.S. Treasury was also worried that a proposed quota increase of the IMF, already under attack in the U.S. Congress, would be further jeopardized if there was a push for a substantial SCI at this stage. Instead, the United States favored a much smaller SCI ($3 billion), scaled to accommodate selective increases for only those countries whose percentage share in total IMF quotas would increase as a result of the Eighth General Review of Quotas.

These anxieties prompted several G-7 countries to persuade management to withdraw a paper arguing the case for a $20 billion SCI, on the grounds that since the arguments were difficult to refute it would put undue pressure on them.[189] While Germany and the United Kingdom were supportive of management's position, they declined to challenge the United States.[190] Japan agreed to back the U.S. position after extracting a U.S. promise to support its efforts to secure the number-two ranking in the Bank.

In the end a compromise SCI of $8 billion was agreed upon in 1984, aided by the requirement of a three-fourths majority voting power for a capital increase which effectively gave both the G-7 and the developing countries an effective veto. It was accepted that a strict parallelism with the IMF would not be possible because that would have caused the U.S. share to drop below 20 percent (and therefore would have reduced its veto power) and altered the rankings among the G-7.

The "Headroom" Problem

The capital adequacy of the Bank has been measured in two principal ways. The "sustainable level of lending" is a long-term measure, while the Articles themselves impose another lending limit, requiring a measure of *near-term* capital adequacy.[191] This measure—termed "headroom"—is the difference between the Bank's statutory lending limit and the total amount outstanding of loans and callable guarantees.

188. Memorandum, Moeen A. Qureshi to A. W. Clausen, June 13, 1982.

189. Memorandum, Moeen A. Qureshi to A. W. Clausen, "Meeting with G-6 Directors after the Development Committee Agenda—The SCI Issue," July 1, 1983. It is unclear whether Canada or Italy was excluded from the "G-6" referred to above.

190. Memorandum, Qureshi to Clausen, June 13, 1983.

191. According to Article III, Section 3, "The total amount of guarantees, participations in loans and direct loans made by the Bank shall not be increased at any time, if by such increase the total would exceed one hundred percent of the unimpaired subscribed capital, reserves and surplus of the Bank."

During the early years of the Latin American debt crisis (chapter 11), the Bank's major shareholders, by insisting that the SLL be treated as a ceiling, had circumscribed the Bank's ability to respond to the debt crisis. By the mid-1980s, as the fortunes of many Latin American countries worsened, Bank management, borrowing countries, and some of the higher-income countries (notably the Nordic countries), pressed for a GCI to allow the Bank to boost its lending levels. Following the decline of the dollar after the Plaza accord in September 1985, however, more pressing financial considerations arose.

The Baker Plan officially sanctioned a greater role for the Bank in lending to higher-risk countries. This meant that the institution had to be more concerned about the prudence of its financial ratios. Over time, ratings agencies went from insisting that the Bank's outstanding debt be less than the U.S. share of callable capital for the institution to retain its AAA rating to accepting the callable capital share of industrialized countries as a group. By the end of the 1970s, they began also to accept the additional security provided by the Bank's large liquid assets. Given the currency structure of the Bank's borrowings, as the U.S. dollar declined, the dollar value of the Bank's outstanding debt grew rapidly in relation to the security provided by the callable capital. At the end of 1986, for the first time, the Bank's funded debt became equal to its callable capital and projections showed that in the absence of a capital increase, the callable capital of industrial countries would in a few years barely exceed 50 percent of funded debt.

On the other side of the balance sheet, the dollar's rapid decline had a dual impact on the Bank's dollar-denominated loan balances. Loan balances increase in two ways: through an increase in net disbursements and through exchange rate movements. In 1985, appreciating currencies (the deutsche mark, Dutch guilder, Swiss franc, and yen) represented nearly three-fourths of the currencies outstanding on the Bank's loans. Between September 1985 and September 1986, the IBRD's loan balances increased by $19 billion, of which nearly $15 billion was accounted for by exchange rate changes.[192] In the four-year period, 1984–87, net disbursements by the IBRD totaled $21.6 billion. In the same period the developing-country debt outstanding to the IBRD increased from $36.6 billion to $89.0 billion: an increase of $52.4 billion.[193]. Meanwhile the IBRD's statutory limit (subscribed capital plus reserves), being denominated in dollars, remained fixed.

With net disbursements running at about $5 billion a year and the dollar continuing to decline, the Bank's headroom declined precipitously. Projections in February 1987 showed that the headroom of $17 billion (42 percent of undisbursed loan balances) at the end of 1986 would whittle down to $7 billion by the end of

192. Memorandum, Joe Wood to Barber B. Conable, "Adequacy of Bank Capital," January 23, 1987.
193. World Bank, *World Debt Tables*.

June (15 percent of undisbursed loan balances) if nondollar currencies appreciated by another 10 percent. By the end of March the projections were more ominous: a further 10 percent depreciation of the dollar against major currencies would wipe out the Bank's remaining headroom altogether. A further decline of the dollar would push the Bank's outstanding loans over its statutory lending limit.

The Bank was now boxed into a nasty legal corner with loan contracts obliging the Bank to disburse and the Articles obliging the Bank not to disburse. This prompted the Bank's general counsel to warn that "the consequences of reaching a point where further disbursements would result in the Bank exceeding its lending limit would be extremely serious for the Bank, whether disbursements were to be continued or suspended."[194]

The sensitivity of the "headroom" to exchange rate changes had been made explicit in the Board discussions on the SLL. However, the results were presented on the basis of sensitivity tests of U.S. dollar/SDR between 1.1 and 1.3, in order not to appear as though it was trying to put pressure on the United States to act on the GCI through the use of "alarmist" projections.[195] By October 1987, the U.S.$/SDR had moved past 1.3, and in December it crossed 1.4.

The exchange rate sensitivity of the Bank's headroom was in turn related to a somewhat esoteric aspect of the Bank's capital structure: the standard of value of its capital. During the 1979 GCI discussions, the U.S. assistant secretary of the Treasury, Fred Bergsten, had made it clear that the United States could not, as a practical matter, accept the contingent liability consequent to an interpretation of the SDR as the unit of value (see chapter 15). Since the United States had placed this as a clear condition of its acceptance of a GCI, the matter had been resolved by the time-honored practice of shelving the issue.

When Clausen arrived, the Legal Department briefing noted that "one of the most troubling problems now facing the Bank is how its capital stock is to be valued."[196] The executive directors had not taken up the general counsel's advice to

194. Memorandum of the general counsel, "Capital Adequacy—Legal Aspects," April 1987, para. 17. Contained in a memorandum from Ibrahim F. I. Shihata to Moeen A. Quereshi, April 6, 1987. At the time the General Conditions on the Bank's loans permitted suspension of disbursements only for specified conditions, of which adherence to the provisions of the Articles was not one. Both the General Conditions as well as international law prevented the Bank from citing its own Articles as an independent reason for suspending its contractual obligations to disburse. In 1991, the Bank modified the General Conditions on its loans "to eliminate any doubt that, as an ultimate step, the Bank would adhere to its Articles even if this required a suspension of disbursements, partial or total." "Modification of the Bank's General Conditions with Respect to the Bank's Lending Limit," R91-51, March 8, 1991, para. 4.

195. Memorandum, Joe Wood to Barber B. Conable, "Adequacy of IBRD Capital," January 23, 1987.

196. IBRD, "Briefing Prepared for Mr. Clausen—The Legal Department," May 1, 1981, p. 21.

exercise their statutory power of interpretation and left the matter unresolved, a result of U.S. opposition. Since the United States was isolated on the issue, the outcome of bringing the matter for interpretation before the Board (which only required a simple vote to settle the matter) was a foregone conclusion. Consequently, the United States argued that any change could only come through an amendment of the Articles and not by interpretation, an understandable position since it exercised veto power to block any amendment.

Finally, a compromise of sorts was agreed to, and in October 1986 the executive directors adopted a formal interpretation under which the standard of value for the Bank's capital would be the SDR, but it would be fixed at its historical (1974) value of $1.20635, with the proviso that the adequacy of the Bank's capital under this standard would be kept under regular review. The arbitrariness of this interpretation—and it could hardly be termed anything but—was a necessary concession to political pragmatism.[197]

But shortly thereafter, the dollar's decline at the end of 1987 reduced the headroom to less than $7 billion; a further 8 percent depreciation would have wiped out the headroom. Once again the institution had to scramble to find ways to increase the statutory lending limit. Several options—loan sales to commercial banks, official agencies (in the form of participation certificates to central banks), and even to IDA; prepayments; bridge financing—were discarded as it became apparent that their effects would be small and costs potentially large.[198] Instead, a major effort was mounted to persuade countries to subscribe to allocated but as yet unsubscribed shares. Transfers from net income to IDA and special grants were reduced.[199] The resolution creating "membership shares"—these were created at the 1979 GCI to preserve the voting power of smaller countries, but because of U.S. insistence that the GCI not exceed $40 billion, were not used as a basis for lending—was amended, now allowing these shares to be used as a basis for lending. The combination of steps increased the Bank's headroom by $8 billion in 1987. Although limited, without these increases the Bank would have exhausted its headroom by the end of 1987.[200]

The only real solution was to add substantially to the capital base through a capital increase, which occurred shortly thereafter. A temporary strengthening of

197. The one country that doggedly challenged the interpretation was Algeria. The Algerian governor wanted the issue to be referred to the Bank's Governors but this did not transpire.

198. Under the proposal, IBRD participations up to $500 million would be sold to IDA, financed by IDA's investment holdings. The terms were such as to ensure that IDA's income and liquidity would be protected. See IBRD, "IDA purchase of IBRD loans," SecM88-541, IDA/SecM88-150, May 13, 1988.

199. With the exception of 1967, transfers from net income to IDA and special grants in the period 1987–89 (average of 6 percent of net income) were the lowest since the practice began under George Woods in 1964.

200. IBRD, "Options for Dealing with the Headroom Problem," SecM88-204, February 25, 1988, para. 9.

the dollar in early 1988 and prompt subscriptions to the 1988 GCI by a few major shareholders helped reduce the headroom risk.[201]

Renewed financial uncertainties prompted a reopening of the interpretation of the standard of value of the Bank's capital. A Board committee concluded that "while the Committee members, except one, believe that the SDR would be the appropriate standard of value, the Committee also feels that such a change in the standard of value should be the result of consensus among members of the institution."[202] The reality of the situation was succinctly put in a briefing for Conable prior to his meeting with Onno Ruding, the Dutch finance minister,

> He [Ruding] remains a strong advocate of using the SDR as a standard of value. The simple fact is, however, that this cannot be done without an amendment to the Articles, which the U.S. could, and will, block. . . No matter how much Mr. Ruding may dislike this reality (and he is hardly alone in this), all efforts to change this have been unsuccessful, and there is nothing further we can do.[203]

There the matter rests. Since then, the headroom risks have for the most part abated, as a result of the large size of the 1988 GCI, a more balanced basket of loan currencies, and a general stagnation of Bank lending and low net disbursements.

General Capital Increase

In mid-1984 the Bank launched a large exercise called the "Future Role of the World Bank," hoping that the process would create the consensus required for a capital increase. While an earlier (1977) "Future Role of the World Bank" exercise had almost exclusively focused on the rate of growth of commitments, now the impact of alternative disbursement rates and their consequences for overall net disbursements and net transfers became central to the determination of the institution's financing requirements.

The following year, after sounding out European shareholders, Qureshi reported back to his president that the only basis on which those countries would support a GCI "*at this time* will be the need for support for additional capital to accommodate a growing lending program. Our only hope of convincing them lies in demonstrating that within the next couple of years our program will significantly exceed the SLL."[204] But a drop in lending in 1985 appeared to raise questions about whether the capacity would be put to use. On the one hand, an expanding lending program was required to convince the major shareholders of the urgency of a

---

201. Japan, Germany, and the United Kingdom subscribed immediately. Most countries spread their subscription over the five-year subscription period.

202. IBRD, "Report of the Ad Hoc Committee on the Valuation of Bank Capital to the Executive Directors," R89-180, August 31, 1989, para. 21.

203. Memorandum, Ernest Stern to Barber B. Conable, July 13, 1989.

204. Memorandum, Moeen A. Qureshi to Tom Clausen, "Re: GCI Strategy," April 12, 1985, p. 1.

capital increase. On the other, if policy conditionality were taken even semi-seriously this could not occur in any predictable manner. The United States seized on this dilemma to voice its opposition to a capital increase arguing that "at the present time we see no need for a GCI. On the basis of current information it is not clear to us how the Bank can increase its lending program significantly at this time, without weakening lending standards or displacing alternative sources of finance in creditworthy countries."[205]

The scales were tipped, however, by the Bank's mounting financial risks. The shift to SALs had accelerated net disbursements than would otherwise have been the case, reducing the Bank's headroom, adding to the headroom risks posed by exchange rate changes. The impact of SALs on the financial structure of the Bank had been foreseen quite early on:

> Because SALs disburse more quickly than other forms of Bank lending, an increase in SAL lending would have a financial impact on Bank operations. Roughly speaking, each $100 million of SAL financed by the Bank will increase current year borrowing require-ments by about $80–100 million above the amount assumed on the basis of aggregated project disbursement profiles. An increase in SAL lending over present levels would also advance the date at which the sustainable level of IBRD lending [would be] reached.[206]

Thus even though, as part of the 1979 GCI agreement, an understanding had been reached that limited the Bank's annual lending commitments, the more rapid disbursement profile of SALs would put pressure on capital adequacy earlier than what was envisaged when the agreement was put into place. The deepening debt crisis both increased the demand for quick-disbursing operations and worsened the credit risks facing the Bank. Peru's confrontational posture on servicing Bank debt was exacerbated by the extreme unpredictability of whether Romania would go into nonaccrual status. There was also nervousness about the willingness of several other countries (Jamaica, Yugoslavia) to service Bank debt. Anxious about its financial vulnerability, the Bank pressed the United States to publicly signal its support for a GCI. Although there would be a lag of a few years before the GCI was actually subscribed, the fact that a GCI was in the works would lead the ratings agencies to take a more relaxed view of the Bank's finances.

The role given the Bank in the Baker Plan had raised hopes that the United States would be more forthcoming regarding a capital increase. Yet by the fall of 1986, signals emanating from the United States again seemed to suggest that it did not want to commence serious discussions on a GCI.[207] It now escalated its

205. From untitled note circulated to members of Congress from Bruce E. Thompson, assistant secretary (Legislative Affairs), U.S. Treasury, June 11, 1985, p. 6.

206. IBRD/IDA, "Structural Adjustment Lending: Progress Report," SecM82-314, April 8, 1982, p. 20.

207. Memorandum, D. Joseph Wood to Barber Conable, "Timing of the GCI," September 19, 1986.

demands for further "quality lending" and "demand analysis," a puzzling stance in light of the "deal" implicit in the Baker Plan: the SIMICs would undertake major policy reforms and continue with debt service and, along with a modest increase in commercial bank exposure, the United States would support increased lending by the Bank, which necessarily meant supporting a GCI.

Another stumbling block was Japan's insistence on a "harmonization" of its share in IDA with its IBRD shareholding. It was clear that an increase in Japan's share could essentially come only at the expense of the United States, if the voting share of other countries were to remain largely unchanged. The "deal" between the United States and Japan was a bilateral issue and was worked out between Mulford and Toyoo Gyohten in 1987. An important ingredient of this deal was an amendment to the Bank's Articles (only the second since inception) to maintain the U.S. veto.

One reason for the U.S. Treasury's reluctance to move on the GCI was not to rock the boat on getting IDA through Congress while maintaining a publicly uncommitted posture on the GCI, pending the 1988 presidential elections. Eventually the headroom problem forced the Treasury's hand. In mid-1987 it agreed to phase in discussions on the GCI but insisted on avoiding explicit consideration of size and timing until the annual meetings. Discussion on size ranged from $40 billion to $80 billion, with the paid-in component ranging from 0 to 7.5 percent. The Bank's management was prepared to trade in a lower paid-in portion in order to obtain a larger GCI. Finally in 1988, after protracted and contentious negotiations, the Bank's major shareholders approved a general capital increase of $74.8 billion, taking the Bank's authorized capital to $171.4 billion. However, citing increasing budget difficulties, the major shareholders insisted that the paid-in component be reduced to just 3.0 percent. By 1995, the Bank's authorized capital had further increased to $184 billion to accommodate new members, in particular Switzerland and the countries of the former Soviet Union.

Barely three years later, even as their fiscal problems worsened, the OECD countries accepted a 30 percent paid-in contribution to a new MDB: the European Bank for Reconstruction and Development (EBRD).[208] The very creation of the EBRD, the rapid agreement among the major OECD countries on a much larger budgetary outlay ($3.45 billion versus $2.25 billion in the case of the 1988 IBRD GCI) for an institution most of whose functions could potentially have been replicated by the IBRD at a smaller cash outlay, raised interesting questions on the relative priorities of the Bank's major shareholders, as well as the perceptions of the European shareholders concerning the Bank's relative effectiveness and governance (see chapter 18).

In retrospect, the 1988 GCI was a critical achievement by the Bank's management. Given the low net disbursement levels in the 1990s, the GCI provided the

208. The EBRD's subscribed capital was ECU 10 billion ($11.5 billion at the time).

institution with ample headroom, thereby reducing the potential political leverage inevitably involved in raising capital through appropriations for an extended period. It was another matter that this bequest would be severely underutilized in the 1990s.

The Prepayment Carousel

By the mid-1980s, as interest rates declined from their highs earlier in the decade, the Bank began to explore options for refinancing a part of its debt. Although a significant portion of its debt was prepayable in principle, almost all of this was yen-denominated debt totaling approximately $3.4 billion.[209] The Bank estimated that it could save nearly half a billion dollars (in present value terms) by refinancing these borrowings and any delays would cost it almost $6 million monthly. Japanese creditors, while not rejecting the Bank's moves, lobbied Japan's Ministry of Finance to press the Bank to cap the amounts to be prepaid. In response, the ministry petitioned the Bank to act "responsibly" by deferring or limiting prepayments so as not to disrupt the syndicated-loan market in Japan. The Bank was prepared to accept the Japanese position, but only on the condition that it received appropriate compensation in due course for the forgone savings.

In the difficult years of the early 1980s, the Japanese market had been singularly important for the Bank. Having supported the Bank strongly in those difficult years, Ministry of Finance officials were upset at the Bank's new position with its implications for substantial financial losses for Japanese investors. As negotiations dragged on, the Bank decided to speed up the pace by sending notice to prepay two issues. In retaliation, as reported by the Bank's Treasurer, the institution was "threatened with reduced access or a denial of access to the Japanese markets. In fact, the Japanese authorities have required that we place our next two yen operations on hold for the time being, pending an acceptable resolution of the prepayment issue."[210]

Staff analysis did not find these threats credible, in view of Japan's announced intention to increase recycling of its burgeoning current-account surplus. Furthermore, the staff was aware that, at the same time that the Japanese financial institutions were complaining about the Bank's lack of responsibility, they were themselves active prepayers of their own high-coupon debt in the dollar and Swiss franc markets. But on the other hand, as circumstances would have it, the Bank itself was protesting the actions of some of its borrowers (Korea and Thailand) who,

209. The amount was ¥530 billion at ¥155/US$1, which had been extended by syndicates of Japanese long-term credit banks, insurance companies, trust banks, and city banks.

210. Memorandum, Eugene H. Rotberg to Barber B. Conable, "Prepayment by IBRD of Yen Loans," January 27, 1987, para. 9.

faced with an identical situation as the Bank with its yen debt, began to prepay their higher-cost IBRD loans. To complete the circle, several of these borrowers could do so because of cheap Japanese bilateral credits that were now becoming available to them. At about the same time, the IBRD reached an agreement with the IFC allowing the latter to prepay $531 million of outstanding loans to the World Bank, the net effect of which was to add $37 million to the IFC's net income with a corresponding decline in the IBRD's.[211]

In addition to making prepayments on its yen debt, the Bank also issued prepayments on a number of other currencies, in particular on a number of Swiss franc issues. This action not only produced direct savings, but it cut down the supply of IBRD paper in the Swiss market, reducing the saturation premiums being paid by the IBRD in that market. The action was also aimed at reaping political benefits by alleviating Japanese concerns that the Bank was confining its prepayments to the yen market.[212]

Normally, the Bank encouraged prepayment of IBRD loans and accordingly waived a borrower's contractual obligation to pay a prepayment premium. By early 1988, however, it had become evident that loans carrying above-average fixed interest rates (in relation to the average rate on all IBRD loans to a country) were accounting for a disproportionate share of loan prepayments. Concerned with the adverse financial implications of selective prepayments to the Bank on other borrowers, the Bank put new policies into effect such that the premium was not waived for the portion of prepaid loans carrying above-country-average interest rates. An exception, however, was made for countries with a disproportionate share of IBRD's more expensive loans.[213]

Lending

Although the 1980 General Capital Increase doubled the IBRD's capacity to lend, this increase was based on projections of global economic prospects done in 1977. But following the second oil shock, the earlier assumptions were no longer valid. The Bank planned to respond to the new circumstances by increasing

211. Memorandum, Mooen A. Qureshi to Barber B. Conable, "Proposed Prepayment and Cancellation of IBRD Loans to IFC," March 5, 1987, p. 1. According to Qureshi, the IFC's request went "somewhat beyond the provisions of the Master Loan Agreement (MLA) that governs all IBRD loans to IFC." The IFC was "entitled, as a matter of right, to make a small part of [the] prepayment; another part could be justified by 'stretching' a little the existing agreements and understandings, and for the balance we would have to 'build' a case." Memorandum, Qureshi to Conable, March 6, 1987.

212. Memorandum, Elena Folkerts-Landau (through Rene Karsenti) to Jessica Einhorn, "Threshold Level of Savings Justifying Prepayment," March 24, 1989. The other currencies were issues in Austrian schillings, Belgian francs, and Kuwaiti dinars.

213. IBRD, "Waiver of the Prepayment Premium on IBRD Loans," R88-248, November 22, 1988.

Table 16-13. *Planned and Actual World Bank Lending, Fiscal 1982–86*

Lending	1982	1983	1984	1985	1986	Total (1982–86)
IBRD						
Planned (1981)	9.6	10.7	11.9	13.2	14.6	60.0
Actual	10.3	11.1	11.9	11.4	13.2	58.0
IDA						
Planned	4.1	4.7	5.0	5.3	5.6	24.7
Actual	2.7	3.3	3.6	3.0	3.1	15.8

Source: Budget documents.

lending for energy investments as well as making quick-disbursing structural adjustment lending for countries prepared to undertake significant policy reform. In the face of higher than anticipated inflation, it also sought to increase traditional project lending to preserve the earlier lending program in real terms. Furthermore, with China joining the Bank in 1980, lending to the largest country in the world had to be factored into the lending program.

When SALs were introduced, questions arose as to whether the new instrument would be at the expense of traditional lending or provide additional resources. Initially, it was assumed that SALs would be in the order of 5–7 percent of IBRD lending, "a small enough margin for us to be able to accommodate . . . without seriously raising the question of the impact of this lending on a further capital increase."[214] Within a year, however, incoming president Clausen was informed that "SAL operations for large countries such as India and Brazil cannot be accommodated unless the Bank's resources are significantly enlarged . . . [because] recently IBRD resources have been approaching statutory lending limits. In these circumstances, both IBRD and IDA resources are subject to rationing."[215] By the end of 1982, portfolio limits had been placed "on the four large countries—India, Brazil, China, and Indonesia."[216]

The 1981 (and 1982) budget memoranda envisaged a 1982–86 IBRD lending program of $60 billion and about $25 billion for IDA. As table 16-13 indicates, even though these levels of lending were planned before there was any indication of a prospective debt crisis, actual lending levels were even less than the planned figures. While this seems understandable in the case of IDA, which is exogenously

214. Memorandum from Ernst Stern to Robert S. McNamara, "Structural Adjustment Lending," March 17, 1980, p. 2.

215. IBRD, "Development Policy Staff: Brief for Mr. Clausen," May 21, 1981, appendix 2, pp. 15, 17. In fact, actual allocations for individual countries were further constrained by creditworthiness considerations at three levels: the borrower's overall creditworthiness for projected debt; IBRD debt service as a fraction of total debt service; and the borrower's share in the Bank's portfolio (p. 19).

216. Memorandum, Ernest Stern to members of the Managing Committee, "World Bank Program of Special Assistance to Member Countries, 1982–84," January 21, 1983.

Table 16-14. *Annual Average IBRD Lending, Fiscal 1981–95*
Billions of 1994 U.S. dollars

Lending	1981–85	1986–90	1991–95
Commitments	17.2	18.4	16.3
Gross disbursements	11.3	14.1	11.9
Net disbursements[a]	7.9	5.4	1.3
Net disbursements[b]	7.9	6.3	1.8
Net transfers	3.5	(2.2)	(6.6)

Source: IBRD, Annual Financial Reports.
a. Including prepayments.
b. Excluding prepayments.

determined, it is less obvious why IBRD lending fell short of planned levels in fiscal 1985–86, despite the obviously greater financial distress afflicting many of its borrowers.

In early 1983 management proposed a two-year "Special Action Program" to accelerate disbursements under existing and proposed loan commitments and to shift the structure of lending to quicker-disbursing "high priority operations."[217] Steps were taken to streamline disbursement procedures and expand the use of statements of expenditure and revolving funds. These special account advances resulted in increases of net disbursements of nearly a billion dollars between 1980 and 1984 and another $1.8 billion between 1985 and 1989.[218] Privately, however, management recognized that these increases were meager considering the magnitude of the problem.[219]

The most significant feature of Bank lending during the decade and a half (1980–95) was its stagnation (in inflation-adjusted terms). Bank commitments had tripled (in constant dollars) between 1973 and 1982. Over the next decade, commitments remained broadly constant, at around $16 billion to $18 billion (in 1994 dollars), and then declined moderately in real terms in 1994–95 (table 16-14). Bank lending was responsive to a degree to the economic shocks in many of its borrowers: to Latin America during the debt crisis (discussed in chapter 11) and again

217. IBRD, "World Bank Program of Special Assistance to Member Countries, 1983–84," R83-22, IDA/RBS-10, January 28, 1983.

218. The amounts advanced in each period were recovered in subsequent periods. Advances in the two periods totaled $1 billion and $5 billion, respectively. The Latin American region was the biggest beneficiary, accounting for nearly 40 percent of the special account advances. Constance Ely Hachana, "Special Account Advances and Recoveries by Region in 1980s," personal communication with the author, September 24, 1993.

219. The minutes of the January 24, 1983, meeting of the Managing Committee note that the discussion then turned to "how the SAP [Special Action Program] could best be publicized in a way that did not draw attention to the relatively low levels of net resource transfers involved." IBRD, "Minutes of January 24, 1983 Meeting," January 26, 1983.

in 1995; to South Asia in the early 1990s; to borrowers adversely affected by the Gulf crisis; and to East Europe and the countries of the former Soviet Union in the 1990s.[220]

As a financial contributor to developing-country investment and balance of payments, however, the Bank's financial intermediary role was disappointing. Gross disbursements increased moderately over the decade, but fell back to earlier (1981–85) levels in the first half of the 1990s. The decline was even sharper in net disbursements, with levels in the first half of the 1990s about a sixth of their levels a decade earlier (table 16-14).

The stagnation of IBRD lending in the 1980s occurred despite the emergence of two major new borrowers: China, from 1980, and India, which began to resort to large-scale IBRD borrowings as its IDA share was curtailed. External shocks clearly also increased the "demand" for the Bank's money, as alternative commercial sources dried up. This would manifest itself in a major structural shift in the composition of IBRD lending: a decline in investment lending (and even more of the number of investment projects), and a parallel increase in adjustment lending.

In 1991, as Lewis Preston prepared to take over as new president of the World Bank, a briefing note from the Bank's finance complex noted, "Constraints on effective demand for Bank funding not entirely clear," and advanced several hypotheses: the "impact of changing performance standards; impact of changing risk perceptions; reduced demand for borrowing by governments; poor business development."[221] In order to shed light on this puzzle, a major internal review was mounted to analyze the factors affecting IBRD lending in the 1980s. The review concluded that the stagnation of lending in that decade was principally due to demand factors, that is, to economic conditions in the Bank's borrowers.[222] First, after the "overborrowing" of the 1970s, a period of digestion was inevitable. The economic crisis afflicting many of the Bank's borrowers during the decade forced serious cuts in public investment, and therefore in the demand for the Bank's funds. The crisis also reduced the creditworthiness of these countries, forcing the Bank to become more cautious in its lending stance, as portfolio risks grew. Equally important, a more forceful stance by the Bank in regard to borrowers' policies affected both the supply and the demand for Bank loans.

On the other hand, the report linked the limited growth in demand for IBRD money in East Asia (other than in China, where until the mid-1980s it was limited by that government's policy of linking its IBRD borrowing to its IDA allocation),

220. During the Gulf crisis in 1990–91, the Bank mounted a resource mobilization effort for ten of the most seriously affected countries which had a limited short-term response capacity. Egypt and Jordan were the highest priority. Bangladesh, Pakistan, Sri Lanka, and Sudan were the next category and India, Morocco, Philippines, and Turkey were the third.

221. "Briefing for Mr. Preston, Finance Issues," April 12, 1991.

222. IBRD, "Factors Affecting IBRD Lending in the Eighties and Implications for the Nineties," SecM92-1096, August 6, 1992.

despite their booming economies, to the availability of cheaper alternatives, whether concessionary bilateral (chiefly the Overseas Economic Cooperation Fund) loans or private financing.[223] Countries such as Thailand became almost grudging in their willingness to "accept" Bank loans. At the turn of the decade, as some of these countries continued to display muted enthusiasm for its loans, the Bank tried to link its undertaking analytical work on these countries (which the countries were still keenly interested in) to a minimum borrowing program.

In essence the report's conclusions boiled down to saying that IBRD lending was constrained either because countries were not creditworthy or because they were too creditworthy, an explanation that did not satisfactorily resolve the puzzle. For instance, the report attached considerable weight to the decline in public investment in its borrowers and the resulting decline in the institution's investment lending. But the evidence for this assertion was weak. While the *share* of public investment (in GDP) had indeed declined during this period, its (nominal) *level* had actually risen, albeit modestly.[224] In any case, the very small proportion of public investment financed by the Bank, less than 5 percent, would not appear to warrant the weight attached in the report. Even if the Bank had simply increased its share by a couple of percentage points, a substantial increase in investment lending could have materialized.

In fact, between 1982 and 1988 the volume of Bank lending was checked by supply constraints as well. The rigid ceilings on the sustainable level of lending limit, set in place consequent to the 1979 GCI agreement and the "headroom problem," prevailing during 1986–88, meant that at least through 1988, the aggregate volume of IBRD lending would have changed little in any alternative scenario.[225]

As the Bank entered the 1990s, the situation appeared to change drastically. The Bank's financial *capacity* having been amply augmented by the 1989 GCI, its

223. While the nominal costs of the OECF loans were low (around 2.5 percent), their real costs were substantially higher since they were denominated in a rapidly appreciating currency (yen).

224. According to an IFC study, average public investment as a fraction of GDP (in a sample of forty-one developing countries, excluding China) declined from 8.8 percent during 1981–86, to 7.5 percent during 1987–92. GDP in the same period rose from $1,524 billion (in 1984) to $ 2,262 billion (1990 figures). Thus the level of public investment actually rose from $134 billion in 1984 to $170 billion in 1990 (although the time periods are not strictly comparable, they are indicative). Data from Robert Miller and Mariusz Sumlinski, "Trends in Private Investment in Developing Countries: Statistics for 1970–92," IFC Discussion Paper 20, 1994; World Bank, *World Development Report,* 1986, 1992.

225. An internal analysis done as part of the 1984 "Future Role of the World Bank" exercise found that the aggregate net disbursements projections were "rather sticky" over the next few years, falling in the range of $6 billion to $8 billion under a wide range of plausible assumptions. The declining trend in net disbursements over the next few years could only be reversed by an increase in fast-disbursing loans in the fraction of total lending.

Table 16-15. *Ranking of the World Bank among Global Banks, Selected Years*
By assets

Bank	1952	1960	1972	1984	1992	1995
IBRD	8	4	<10	27	40	68
IBRD + IDA	...	...	7	10	32	41

Source: World Bank, *Annual Report*, various years. 1952 and 1960: Philip H. Burch, *Elites in American History: The New Deal to the Carter Administration* (Holmes and Meier, 1980), pp. 72, 124; 1972, 1984, and 1992: *The Banker*, July 1985, p. 133; *The American Banker*, July 29, 1993, July 1996, pp. 143–44.

management exuded confidence that the institution was in an "excellent position" to expand its lending program, "as planned, to reach a commitment level of $20 billion in the early 90's."[226] The economic crisis confronting many of its borrowers was finally beginning to wane. A host of new lending opportunities, in the guise of the countries of East Europe and the former Soviet Union, Vietnam, and South Africa appeared at hand: there were twenty-three new or reactivating borrowers. And the financial costs on its loans appeared exceedingly attractive: a priori, a 25-basis-point markup on the borrowing costs of one the world's cheapest borrowers should be cheaper than a public issue in the same currency.[227] Although the SLL rose to almost $30 billion by 1995, Bank lending continued to stall at around $16 billion in the first half of the 1990s. Lending commitments during the three-year period fiscal 1993–95 ($48 billion) were only 70 percent of planned commitments ($68 billion). The stagnation was mirrored on the borrowings side. The decline in the Bank's financial intermediation role is apparent from figure 16-3. Consequently the IBRD's relative standing among global banks also seriously eroded (table 16-15).

Why was it that an institution that could borrow (and lend) long-term money at some of the cheapest rates, whose loans were presumed to have a substantial value added element through the quality of its advice and technical assistance, would face a stagnant demand even as private financial flows to developing countries showed a strong upward trend?

Several explanations may be advanced, none particularly satisfactory. An obvious external reason was the decline of "spread banking," the principal form of financial intermediation by the IBRD. This was manifest in structural shifts in borrower preferences and international financial flows from official to private flows and within private flows: a greater reliance on equity finance (either portfolio finance or FDI) relative to debt finance (the preferred vehicle for private flows in the 1970s). Furthermore, the decline of the public sector limited sovereign borrowing, and with it the demand for IBRD loans.

226. Draft opening statement by senior vice president, Finance, Ernest Stern to the Executive Board on fiscal 1989 results, July 17, 1989.

227. If the currency is the difference, long-term borrowings on a currency risk–adjusted basis are also unlikely to be cheaper (unless of course the countries have a full match between earnings and debt liabilities).

Figure 16-3a. *Relative Financial Intermediation Role of IBRD—*
International Bond Issues: IBRD Bond Issues as Share of
Percent; three-year moving averages

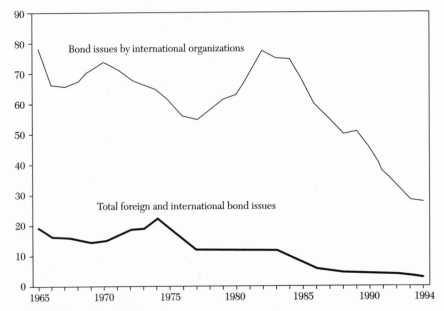

Source: World Bank *Annual Reports;* BIS *Annual Reports;* International Capital Markets, various issues.

Figure 16-3b. *Relative Financial Intermediation Role of IBRD—*
Net Debt-Related Flows to LDCs: IBRD Net Flows as Share of
Percent; three-year moving averages

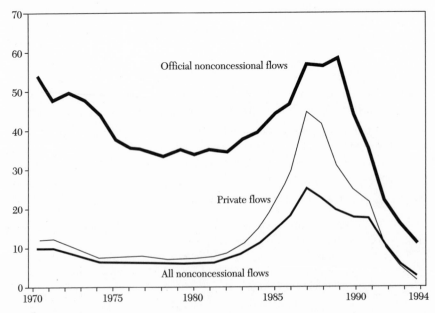

Source: *World Debt Tables.*

But important reasons internal to the Bank could be identified as well. One variable that did not appear to be a factor was administrative budget constraints.[228] There were some indications that the rise of structural adjustment lending "hollowed out" the Bank's project expertise, in particular that related to traditional investment projects, adversely affecting the institution's capacity to deliver such projects. The fact that the level of risk attached to the Bank's loan portfolio did not recede from its climb over the previous decade further inhibited lending.

Another factor was the Bank's financial product. Even though the institution had become increasingly innovative and venturesome with respect to its liability management, particularly its borrowings, it showed a curious lack of initiative on its asset side, namely its loans. The financial structure of Bank loans continued to be "plain vanilla," a stodginess that contrasted sharply with the burgeoning range and specificities that began to be available in financial markets. External observers remarked that "the Bank must act more like a bank, providing loans that are packaged in a way that serve borrowers' interest, not its own treasury's convenience."[229] The extremely competitive nature of the financial markets in which it borrowed, in contrast to the quasi-monopoly position it held during much of the 1980s in the markets in which it lent, may explain this. Perceptions of increased financial risks during the 1980s and an attrition of the Bank's banking and financial expertise may have also contributed to this state of affairs. Although, as noted earlier, the single-currency loan program unveiled in the early-1990s was a significant step in offering borrowers a wider choice in financial products, the range was still narrow, considering the array of financial products available in markets.

But perhaps the most important reason for the stagnating loan demand was the greater intrusiveness of the Bank, beyond narrow economic criteria. Borrowers wishing to avail themselves of Bank loans were thus faced with steadily increasing transaction costs. The lean harvest being reaped by the Bank in its lending may well be the inevitable long-term consequence of the succession of accommodations it made to pressures from interest groups, largely its major shareholders, endeavoring to retain short-term access to soft government funds (IDA, GEF). As a consequence, the Bank has become more risk-averse (or judicious, depending on the

228. The Bank's operational budget increased by 35 percent in real terms over the 1980s, whereas total lending (IBRD + IDA) increased by 19.5 percent. The number of lending operations actually fell by 8.5 percent. Between fiscal 1990 and 1994, budget expenditures again increased at an annual rate of 7 percent, while loan commitments declined by 2 percent annually.

229. Remarks by Lawrence Summers, undersecretary of the Treasury for International Affairs, before the Overseas Development Council, October 11, 1994. There is no record of Summers stressing this issue in his prior capacity as a vice president in the World Bank. Similar views have been expressed by other, normally prudent observers: "Increasingly, the real beneficiaries of the Bank's special status are its bondholders . . . [b]orrowers have already started to cancel World Bank loans because they can obtain better products on the markets." "Rejuvenating Fund and Bank," *Central Banking*, vol. 5, no. 1 (summer 1994), p. 26.

point of view) in what it lends for, particularly in the case of "hard" infrastructure investment projects.

There are, however, two important silver linings in the stagnation of lending. At the aggregate level, the phenomenon weakened the "money pushing" argument that became a favorite club to beat upon the Bank (although it does not eliminate the argument in individual cases). To an extent, as revealed by the criticisms of the Bank by certain shareholders on the slow pace of disbursements to Russia just before elections in that country, on lending the Bank is dammed if it does and dammed if it does not. These criticisms after all came from the same shareholders who have also been wont to criticize the institution for its "lending culture" and its attendant repercussions on project quality.

Moreover, a declining demand from borrowers (as in East Asia) could be welcome news to the Bank. If a country's access to capital markets provides it with its external capital requirements and the Bank is no longer needed, the Bank ought to congratulate itself on a job well done. How valid this proposition is for a majority of the Bank's borrowers is, however, moot.

Either way, in the absence of significant changes, at the time of writing IBRD lending was expected to remain constant in nominal terms (at about $16 billion) over the following decade. With rising repayments on existing loans, net flows were projected to remain essentially flat. In recent years, the Bank has attempted to make a virtue out of necessity, downplaying its financial intermediary role and recasting itself as a "knowledge intermediary." Through the Bank's history, however, institutional and policy advice have gone hand in hand with lending. The Bank has always delivered, in that sense, a "joint product." Delinking advice from lending will be a challenging goal.

Concluding Thoughts

In its first half century the Bank proved itself an outstanding example of financial leveraging, committing almost a quarter of a trillion dollars in long-term development finance, with total paid-in capital contributions of under $11 billion. The main explanation for this notable performance lies in the unique arrangements made for financing the Bank. In essence, the Bank's level of activity has depended largely on its ability to borrow rather than on budgetary transfers from governments. Admittedly, the Bank's lending did impose some fiscal cost to its member governments: a small fraction of its lending was financed out of paid-in capital subscriptions; and, in addition, members took on a contingent liability by guaranteeing all Bank lending. Contingent liabilities, however, are comparatively painless as budgetary decisions go, particularly when, as became increasingly the case with the Bank, the perceived risk seemed to be negligible.

An additional factor was an institutional structure that, at least in principle, was organized as a financial cooperative. The nonborrowing shareholders endowed the institution by direct cash contributions in the form of paid-in capital, but especially by assuming large contingent liabilities in the form of callable capital. The borrowers also contributed to capital, albeit in quite modest amounts. More important, for the most part they faithfully serviced their financial obligations, granting preferential treatment to the institution.

In practice, however, for the first two decades the only nonborrowing shareholder whose guarantees mattered was the United States. The institution certainly did not have the degree of democratic decisionmaking that could be associated with a cooperative. This reality, however, was not unhelpful to Bank management's cautious and skillful direction of borrowing and lending, which laid the foundation of a sound financial institution.

The Bank's initial paid-in capital helped jump-start the institution as a going concern. The callable capital plus cautious management ensured growth. Over the decades the institution's equity grew fairly steadily, partly through additions of paid-in capital but largely through additions to reserves out of its substantial net income. In effect, the Bank's equity has been tantamount to an endowment whose value is apparent when the institution's fortunes are today compared with a second pillar of the postwar multilateral system, the United Nations.

The financial story of the Bank had two major implications for the institution. One, its financial persona affected its lending stance in several ways. The early switch in roles, from a guarantor to a direct lender, coupled with its Articles' injunction to make loans to (or through) national governments, led the Bank to pay careful attention to issues of country creditworthiness to safeguard the financial integrity of its loans. It was via this road that the Bank began to address policy issues, principally of a type that were the operational commonsensical prerequisites of sound lending.

Though the Bank's financial and development personas have always been inextricably linked, there have been periods in which their coexistence has been more competitive than complementary. The tension between institutional policies and practices thought to advance pressing development objectives on the one hand, and the vital need to project the image and reality of financial probity on the other, has been a recurrent theme in the Bank's history, albeit of varying intensity. The Bank's financial traits have served both a lubricating and a braking function on its lending stance. This tension has been reflected on several fronts: the sectoral composition of lending in its early years, with the bias against "social" lending reflecting anxieties about the reactions of Wall Street; loan charges that have to balance its development mandate with the need to support a strong market standing; in some instances, forced lending to stem arrears but undermining policy leverage; in others, limiting the volume of lending because of portfolio concerns despite a perceived developmental rationale.

In its early years, when the institution was painstakingly building up its standing in financial markets, financial imperatives were paramount. As the Bank established its reputation for financial soundness, the demands of these imperatives ebbed, particularly in the 1970s, and the development persona began to dominate. Financial exigencies in the 1980s led to a reassertion of the Bank's financial persona, as the institution confronted a multitude of financial risks. At the close of the half-century mark, the Bank's exposure to a broad range of risks, be it market access or interest rate movements, was quite low. Credit risks, which continue to remain relatively high, constituted an exception.

A second implication of the Bank's finance story has been its effects on the institution's governance. As its financial strength grew and took firmer root, the cost of ownership fell: easier borrowings and comfortable equity reduced the need for additional paid-in capital; higher reserves and the track record on defaults diminished the risks to the callable part of subscribed capital. One consequence of that financial trend was that the influence that came with ownership became less expensive—indeed almost costless—and therefore more attractive. This reality has been manifest in the greater intensity of disputes that have grown up around even slight changes in capital share.

It is important to understand that the manner in which the Bank financed itself was fundamental in developing institutional autonomy. Although in its early days the institution owed its existence to the nurturing provided by the United States, even then the institution was apprehensive of the fickleness of state support. For this reason, President John McCloy had stressed that "the necessity of going to private investors for funds, in addition to keeping the bank's management in touch with financial markets also insures that its operations will be free of political influence."[230]

But if the institution gained political autonomy, its dependence on Wall Street also constrained its lending policies. By accepting IDA, the Bank loosened the sinews of Wall Street; but in due course IDA would gradually tie the institution to the priorities of governments through the Catherine wheel of periodic replenishments. The market-based autonomy that the IBRD gained for itself was slowly, but surely, eroded by the public monies that were the mainstay of IDA. Donor-government interference in Bank decisionmaking increased in the 1980s, a trend that was aggravated by the acceptance of other "free" money such as the Global Environmental Facility and other trust funds.

As a financier, belying its image, the Bank has always been a small player, a reality that its presidents have had few illusions about. The IBRD enjoyed a quasi-monopoly position in the long-term international capital markets of the 1950s and 1960s. Despite a dramatic increase in lending over the 1970s, its position eroded significantly due to profound changes in international capital markets; but it partially regained its position in the 1980s with the onset of the debt crisis.

230. *New York Times,* May 27, 1947.

By the mid-1990s, the Bank's financial health was robust and it enjoyed an enviable reputation in financial markets. Yet Bank borrowing and lending had stagnated due to a combination of factors: the resurgence of private capital flows in the 1990s, borrower preferences for equity finance (relative to debt finance), the steeper transaction costs that attached to Bank loans, and lending limits prompted by credit risk concerns. In fact, with projections of negligible net Bank lending over the next decade, the Bank's financial intermediary role appeared to have run aground. If the past is a guide, the Bank may well find that delinking money from advice is a tricky venture.

The ebbing of the Bank's financial intermediary role means that it has become a relatively smaller borrower and customer in financial markets. Consequently, its leverage with financial markets, an erstwhile strong political ally, is weakening. Market forces often play a useful disciplining role in curbing the power of states, in both national and multilateral contexts. Consequently, for the Bank, balancing institutional and financial autonomy will be challenging in the days ahead.

Appendix: IBRD Finances

Figure 16A-1. *IBRD Total Loanable Resources*
Billions of 1990 U.S. dollars

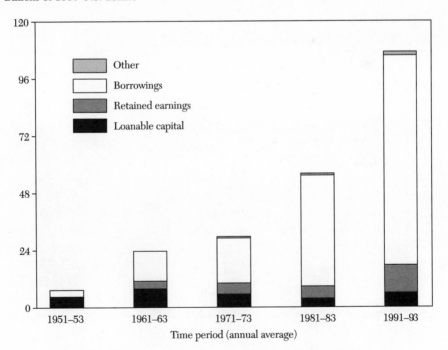

Source: IBRD's financial history data, prepared by Central and Operational Accounting Division, October 7, 1993.
Notes: "Loanable capital" includes paid-in capital, less net receivable. "Retained earnings" includes reserves and net income. "Other" includes net other assets and liabilities (for example, due to IDA) and accumulated provision for loan losses.

Figure 16A-2a. *IBRD Sources of Funds*
Millions of 1990 U.S. dollars

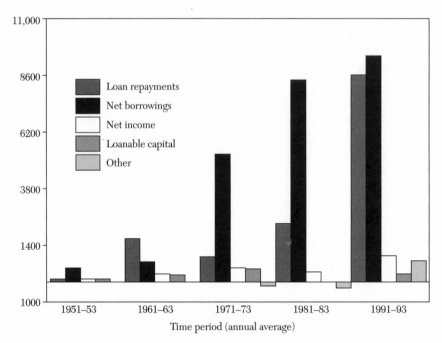

Time period (annual average)

Figure 16A-2b. *IBRD Applications of Funds*
Millions of 1990 U.S. dollars

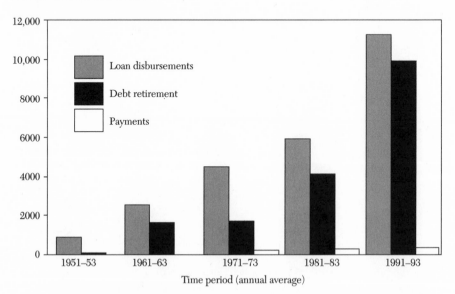

Time period (annual average)

Source: IBRD's financial history data, prepared by Central and Operational Accounting Division, October 7, 1993.
Notes: "Payments" includes payments to IDA, GEF, DRF, and TATF.

Figure 16A-3a. *Volume of IBRD Borrowings: Gross Borrowings,*
Fiscal Years 1950–95[a]
Billions of U.S. dollars; three-year moving averages

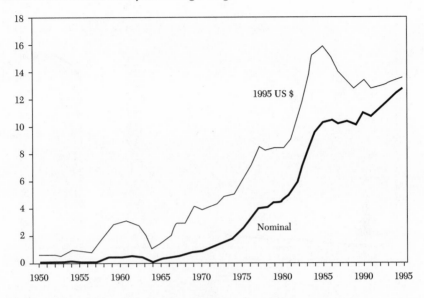

Figure 16A-3b. *Volume of IBRD Borrowings: New Borrowings,*
Fiscal Years 1960–94[b]
Billions of U.S. dollars; three-year moving averages

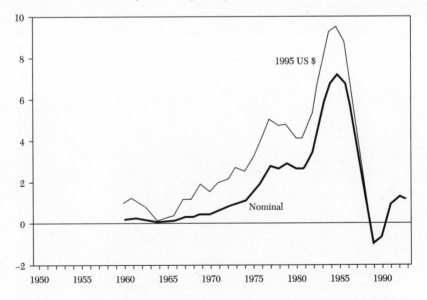

Sources: Gross borrowings: World Bank *Annual Reports,* various issues. Debt retirements: for FY1961–93, IBRD's financial history data, prepared by Central and Operational Accounting Division, October 7, 1993.
Notes: Medium- and long-term borrowings are at face value. After 1983, short-term borrowings are included.
a. Medium- and long-term borrowings after swaps.
b. Gross borrowings less debt retirement.

Figure 16A-4a. *Volume of IBRD Lending: Commitments, Fiscal Years 1950–95*[a]

Billions of U.S. dollars; three-year moving averages

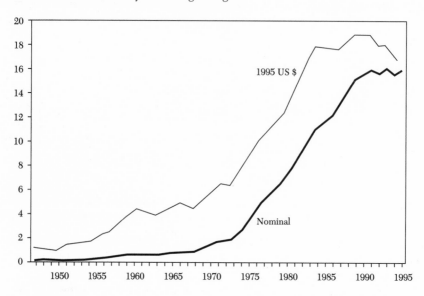

Figure 16A-4b. *Volume of IBRD Lending: Disbursements, Fiscal Years 1950–95*[b]

Billions of U.S. dollars; three-year moving averages

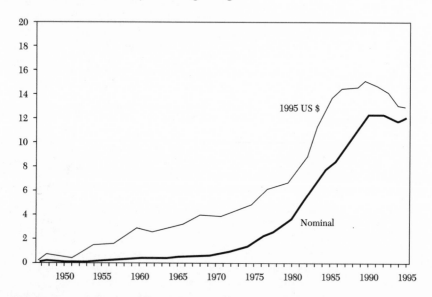

Sources: Commitments and disbursements: for FY1947–70, Edward S. Mason and Robert E. Asher, eds., *The World Bank since Bretton Woods* (Brookings, 1973), pp. 192, 832; for FY1971–95, World Bank annual reports.
Notes: IBRD disbursement deflator for disbursements, net flows and net transfers, and commitment deflator for commitments (FY1995 = 1). FY1949 disbursement and commitment deflators were used for 1947 and 1948.

Figure 16A-5a. *Volume of IBRD Lending: Net Flows, Fiscal Years 1950–95*[a]

Billions of U.S. dollars; three-year moving averages

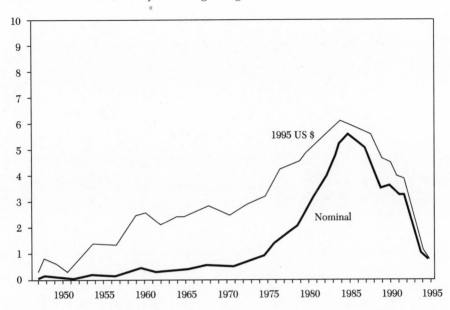

Figure 16A-5b. *Volume of IBRD Lending: Net Transfers, Fiscal Years 1950–95*[b]

Billions of U.S. dollars; three-year moving averages

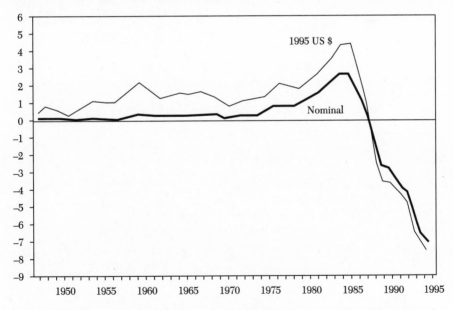

Source: Repayments: For FY1947–71, Mason and Asher, *World Bank since Bretton Woods*, p. 857; repayments data for FY1972–93 and interest payments for FY1947–93 are from IBRD's financial historical data, prepared by Central and Operational Accounting Division, October 7, 1993. Data for FY94 and FY95 are from annual reports.
a. Disbursements less repayments.
b. Net flows less interest payments.

SEVENTEEN

IDA: The Bank as a Dispenser of Concessional Aid

THERE IS much continuity in the World Bank story but also significant change. One of the major, transforming changes occurred in 1960, when a branch of concessional lending—of what would come to be called Official Development Assistance (ODA)—was grafted onto the institution's nonconcessional trunk. The International Development Association drew on radically different resources than the International Bank for Reconstruction and Development. The addition greatly broadened the Bank Group's clientele of borrowers and its scope for constructive work. As well, it altered the Bank's relationship with its members. But the effects ran in both directions: the choice of the Bank as mediator for the new government-to-government concessional transfers also heavily conditioned the brand of multilateral concessional lending that followed.

The Run-Up to IDA's Launching

What took shape in 1960 was a function both of the new program's organizational habitat and of ideas and forces that had been in play in the wider international arena for more than a decade.

The Bank as Host

As earlier chapters have indicated, before 1960 the World Bank had developed a distinct character that many interests in and around the institution greatly valued. Both staff and owners prided themselves on the Bank's professionalism and technical expertise. Although the staff spoke with an Anglo-American accent, it was drawn from a growing diversity of cultures and aspired to a transnational homogeneity in which national origin was a recessive characteristic. While the full-timers respected their accountability as agents of the Bank's members, they prized the measure of autonomy that was evolving, in part because of the funding mechanism with which the institution had been endowed, which early managements had worked hard to make operative.

The mechanism consisted of using owner governments' guarantees (rather than much of their taxpayers' money) to borrow in private money markets at better terms than those at which the Bank's borrowers could obtain on their own, with the proceeds then being passed along to the country borrowers with a modest markup and a good measure of guidance. This mixed public-private multilateral funding system was attractive to all the participating parties. It offered its borrowers a better deal than they could get by themselves. It offered private investors government-guaranteed returns at market rates. The Bank's principal owning and guaranteeing members got control over flows of funds and of the influence associated with them at the cost of comparatively small public appropriations. At the same time, although the commitments of faith and credit of owner governments were never perceived to be casual, the fact that they were not costly to taxpayers meant that governmental oversight—in particular, parliamentary oversight—of the Bank's uses of its borrowings could be less searching than if the funds had been drawn from national budgets.

Indeed, if the IBRD's borrowing-lending mechanism was used circumspectly and was not afflicted with untoward external shocks, its only deficiency was that its benefits were insufficiently available to the poorest countries, which were not creditworthy enough to help build a loan portfolio that would support the Bank's own creditworthiness. In the early 1950s Eugene Black saw this limitation as no great problem. According to Sir Arthur Lewis, when he and his fellow authors of the 1951 United Nations report, *Measures for the Economic Development of Under-Developed Countries,* went to see Black in early 1951, convinced that the Bank should move rapidly to an annual lending rate of at least $1 billion, Black was adamant that a pace of $400 million would be quite enough for some time.[1]

At the time Black seemed to have little sympathy for the demands then mounting for additional flows of multilateral resources to the poorer countries at *concessional*—that is, less than market (less than IBRD)—terms. But as the 1950s proceeded, two things would change. First, the Bank in general, and Black in particular, would become concerned about the way creditworthiness considerations were inhibiting the Bank's outreach to would-be borrowers. This became notably the case in the institution's dealings with its two most populous clients, India and Pakistan. Second, from the end of the 1940s proposals were being

---

1. Eugene R. Black, personal conversation with an author.

pressed for the establishment of a multilateral concessional assistance program under the auspices of a new agency to be established under the authority of the Economic and Social Council of the United Nations. Eugene Black and his colleagues thought that, whatever its intrinsic merits, if there were to be such a program, it might be better run by the World Bank.[2]

Design Issues for Multilateral Concessionality

Between 1949 and 1951 four official study exercises, two undertaken by the United Nations and two by the United States, defined four design choices that a decade later would have to be made in establishing IDA. In chronological sequence the four exercises were: UN Sub-Commission on Economic Development, V. K. R. V. Rao, chairman, March 1949; *Report on Foreign Economic Policies*, by Gordon Gray to U.S. President Truman, November 1950; *Partners in Progress*, report to President Truman by the U.S. International Development Advisory Board, Nelson Rockefeller, chairman, March 1951; and *Measures for the Economic Development of Under-Developed Countries*, report by the "UN experts" Alberto Baltra Cortes, D. R. Gadgil, George Hakim, W. Arthur Lewis, and Theodore W. Schultz, May 1951.

All four studies advocated the establishment of an ongoing program of concessional transfers under multilateral auspices. "Concessional" was not as sharply defined as it came to be at the end of the 1960s, but it meant softer than market terms that contained a considerable "grant element."[3] The design choices the studies addressed were purposes, scale, grants or soft loans, and location.

PURPOSES. There were two rationales for concessionality. First, whole economies might be too poor to service any or some of their external borrowing needs on commercial terms. Second, aside from such macro needs, countries might need help establishing systems and services that, although vital to development, did not quickly generate recoverable returns to the capital invested in them. Such was the

---

2. This was the view articulated at the time by Black's trusted aide, Richard Demuth. The proposed ECOSOC agency was the Special United Nations Fund for Economic Development (SUNFED). In 1963, in retrospect, Black told James Weaver that "the International Development Association was really an idea to offset the urge for SUNFED." James H. Weaver, *The International Development Association: A New Approach to Foreign Aid* (New York: Praeger, 1965), p. 28.

3. The reference is to the 1969 decision of OECD's Development Assistance Committee (DAC) that ODA must have a "grant element" of at least 25 percent, the grant element being the excess of a loan's face value over the sum of the present values of the repayments that the terms (interest rate, duration, grace period) of the loan will generate, present values being calculated at a "market" rate of interest assumed to be 10 percent. (Generally, a loan will not convey a grant element of over 25 percent if its maturity is less than ten years, unless its interest rate is well below 5 percent. An outright grant, of course, has a grant element of 100 percent.)

case with many infrastructural and social sector outlays. Of the four seminal studies, the 1949 Rao report leaned on the first rationale, the other three on the second. Yet there was some blurring of the two—as, indeed, there would be in IDA itself; and the span of non-self-liquidating activities that were advocated differed widely. For instance, in the cases of the two 1951 reports, the funding agenda of the Rockefeller report's "International Development Authority" was limited to public works, whereas the UN experts would have called on their "IDA" to support, along with rural public works, subsidized agricultural credit, public health and education, development-related research, development planning, and the improvement of plan implementation.

SCALE. Obviously a key design choice for any new aid program concerns the size of its assistance budget. Again the two 1951 reports established the limits proposed by the early documentation on pro-multilateral aid. At the low end, the Rockefeller group suggested that "IDA" receive an experimental contribution of $500 million. This would have been run down over several years, making for an average annual capacity to commit only a moderate fraction of $500 million. The "experts," on the other hand, would have had their "IDA" build fairly rapidly to an annual commitment of $3 billion, that is, to more than ten times the Rockefeller rate.

What was not obvious at the time was that over the decades to follow, volumes of aid flows would prove to be overwhelmingly supply driven. Only one of the four seminal documents (that of the experts) attempted a demand-side calculation of the *needs* for concessional transfers. The calculation was very crude, compared with the rest of the report's argumentation—but not inappropriately so, since never in the history of foreign aid have aggregative transnational estimates of aid needs been taken very seriously by groups of donors. Rather, the targets donors have set—and have or have not implemented—have been supply based; they have been political statements of donors' projected capacities to give aid.

Furthermore, legislated aid appropriations have invariably claimed very small fractions of the total public budgets of even the most generous donors. Frequently the appropriations are unpopular, and raising them is apt to be politically painful. But the level itself is subject to wide discretion; it does not encroach much on other accounts; and its height can be a matter of historical accident. Thus, once established, the size of an aid program acquires a certain inertia. The scale at which the real IDA-to-be would start was likely to have a lingering effect.

GRANTS OR SOFT LOANS? The early designers of multilateral concessional aid were aware that soft loans could be close substitutes for grants (in the most straightforward variety of soft loan, "softness" being imparted by lower-than-market interest rates or longer-than-market durations or grace periods). Three out of four of the seminal documents voted for grants rather than soft loans as their preferred concessional transfer vehicles. The 1949 Rao report suggested soft loans would be more salable politically. But the others thought grants would be simpler.

They reasoned that if a graduated array of concessionalities was desired, this could be achieved as well by directing two transfers, one hard and one soft, to the same purpose and blending the mix, as by tailoring the terms of a single loan.[4] The writers of the other reports also thought soft loans might cast a cloud over the creditworthiness of the institution issuing them or crowd out market-based loans of the IBRD sort. This was a view volunteered by the World Bank itself in 1951.[5]

Another retrospective aside may be useful. All of the early "designers" assumed that the concessional (grant or gift) money their multilateral intermediary would disburse, whether at full strength (grants) or somewhat diluted (soft loans), could only come from one main source: grants to the intermediary of tax monies by national governments. Although the products of a comprehensive transfer agency might be graded into several degrees of concessionality, their sources were bifurcated: either private funds at market rates or 100 percent governmental grants.[6] This would prove to be one of the defining constraints on the IDA experience. There would be repeated, largely failed, attempts to contrive supplements or substitutes for the parliamentary appropriations upon which nearly all concessionality depended.

In the end, however, as to the grants-versus-soft-loans choice, the V. K. R. V. Rao view prevailed. To many of the American legislators, editorialists, and interest-group leaders to whom the IDA initiative had to be sold in the 1950s, a grant was a giveaway, and a loan, however soft, was more businesslike. IDA's proponents accepted this preference.

LOCATION. The fourth dimension of choice in the pre-IDA documentation requires little elaboration. The reports typically divided along North-South lines. The UN documents, reflecting the preferences of the growing number of sovereign developing countries, as well as those of the Soviet bloc and of a few smaller Western nations (for example, the Nordic countries and the Netherlands) with a

---

4. Much later, in the "Third Window" proposal (see below), this issue would return to the IDA story.

5. Weaver, *The International Development Association*, p. 57.

6. Although the text is essentially right, it slides over two complications. First, a government *can* use borrowing from its private sector (not its central bank) as a noninflationary source of public finance that substitutes for taxation. By this means, private saving is channeled to public uses, and if total (private and public) investment does not exceed private saving plus the excess of taxes over current government expenditures by more than the growth in the economy's productive capacity, there should be no demand pull on the price level. This kind of governmental tax avoidance is costly; depending on the interest rate that domestic lenders have to be paid to part with their liquidity together with the pace of amortization, the charges for the government build up to some moderate premium over the taxes that would produce an equivalent stream of resources. But in the past some governments—Japan is an important example—have followed the pattern routinely, and when they do, this kind of debt funding is the equivalent of taxpayers' money in the dichotomy in the text; logically, it is just as appropriate a source as tax collections for grants to such multilateral intermediaries as IDA.

particular empathy for the developing countries, opted for a new agency reporting to ECOSOC. A formal proposal for the Special United Nations Fund for Economic Development was put into play in 1953.[7] At the same time, it was natural for the larger Western countries, which would be expected to provide most of the taxpayer funding for the new initiative, to shy away from a one-flag, one-vote location in favor of a Bretton Woods site where the program could be more readily controlled.

Unless they were interested in forestalling the whole idea, the real question for these proponents was whether the benefits of attaching a new soft lending program to the Bank would outweigh any risks posed to the character of the institution.

The Bank and the United States: IDA promotion in the 1950s

IDA-to-be had two ambivalent promoters during the 1950s: the World Bank itself, as personified by Eugene Black and his immediate staff; and elements in both the legislative and executive branches of the U.S. government. Both were hesitant, reluctant, and harbored mixed views of the matter. But by default they were the sponsors of Bretton Woods–style concessional transfers.

Although Black was at first cool to the idea of concessional multilateral transfers, his staff could see the operational advantages, if there were to be such a program, of affiliating it with the Bank. Such a location, they said in a November 1950 draft, would avoid duplication, permit more comprehensive planning, and make for greater leverage in behalf of appropriate economic policies.[8]

The striking thing about their November 1950 draft was its anticipation of the difficulties a nonconcessional-concessional linkage could pose: reduction in the Bank's autonomy; diminished standing in the private market, "which has never looked too kindly on 'give-away organizations'"; and the risk that the Bank would be

---

Second, when a sovereign state raises revenues via taxation, or by such an equivalent as royalties on state-owned mineral resources, those that it transfers to a multilateral do not *have* to be given; they can be lent. Indeed, member governments sometimes have made loans to the Bank Group to bridge temporary gaps in IDA funding. As IDA developed, however, virtually all bilateral inputs to the multilateral were in grant form, just as nearly all members did in fact finance such inputs by taxation. Thus the dichotomy the text poses—between private market money and concessional taxpayers' money—is the relevant one.

A further amendment is in order. Throughout its career the World Bank, to facilitate the management of its portfolio, has done a fair amount of short-term borrowing, in part from member governments or their central banks (see volume 2, chapter 10). The dichotomy in the text refers to the acquisition of funds (if borrowed, typically long-term) for transfer as long-term loans and credits.

7. United Nations Department of Economic Affairs, *Report on a Special United Nations Fund for Economic Development,* submitted by a committee appointed by the secretary-general, E/2381, March 18, 1953.

8. IBRD, office memorandum drafted by Benjamin King and others for, and at the behest of, Richard Demuth, "Examinations of a Proposal for Administration of an International Development Fund by the Bank," November 1, 1950.

accused, however unfairly, of allocating its concessional transfers in a way calculated to facilitate the servicing of IBRD loans—and therefore safeguarding the Bank's own creditworthiness.[9] In order to minimize these dangers, as well as any disturbance to the harmonious culture of the institution, the authors of the November 1950 paper proposed an arm's-length kind of linkage: What they called the International Development Fund would have its own board and, via a year-by-year renewable contract, retain the Bank as managing agent of the Fund.

Interestingly, precisely the same arm's-length scheme surfaced in U.S. documentation—via the Rockefeller report—a few months later. But the U.S. government also proved to be cool, on balance, to the idea of a Bank-affiliated IDA once the Eisenhower administration came to power in 1953. From the beginning of the new regime, however, there was a division within it that eventually, and in a somewhat roundabout way, would enlist the U.S. executive branch in the pro-IBRD/ IDA camp. The thoroughly conservative, isolationist, antigovernmental wing of the Republican Party, represented within the administration by George Humphrey, secretary of the Treasury, had little or no use for pro-development governmental interventions, therefore little for foreign aid, and none at all for multilateral assistance.

Juxtaposed, and circumspectly encouraged by the president, was the internationalist eastern-U.S. establishment that by the start of the 1950s had translated the cold war into an economic contest to be played out in the developing countries. Remarkably, this anticommunist, pro-development alliance drew leaders from both parties as well as from the corporate, trade union, academic, and journalistic worlds. The historian Blanche Wiesen Cook has captured the flavor of the movement and, in particular, spotlighted one of its defining moments: a "private" conference for a World Economic Plan that (with Eisenhower's quiet blessing) was convened by the Time-Life Corporation's C. D. Jackson at Princeton, New Jersey, on May 15–16, 1954.[10] For advance reading, Jackson sent participants five reports, including the Gray and Rockefeller reports already noted.[11] The two leaders of the new robust-aid school of development studies at the Massachusetts Institute of Technology, Max Millikan and Walt Rostow, wrote the interim report on the deliberations of the conference. It concluded, they recorded, that there should be "coordination . . . sufficient scale . . . and continuity" in the provision of resources for development.

What made the gathering particularly impressive, however, was the identity of the participants. Besides the aforementioned, they included Lloyd Berkner, presi-

---

9. "The Bank as administrator of the Development Fund might well have to justify its conduct in detail and to suffer embarrassing enquiry from politicians with special interests." Ibid.

10. Blanche Wiesen Cook, *The Declassified Eisenhower: A Divided Legacy* (Doubleday, 1981), pp. 301ff.

11. The others were the 1952 "Paley" report on raw materials policy, the 1953 "Bell" report on trade and tariffs, and the 1954 "Randall" report on foreign economic policy.

dent, Associated Universities, Inc.; Richard Bissell, Central Intelligence Agency; Robert Bowie, Department of State; Arthur Burns, chairman, Council of Economic Advisers; General Robert Cutler, White House special national security assistant; Allen Dulles; Arthur Flemming, director, Office of Defense Mobilization; Robert Garner, IBRD; Gabriel Hauge, White House economic specialist; David McDonald, president, United Steelworkers of America; John MacKenzie, Atomic Energy Commission; Thomas McKittrick, Chase National Bank; the ubiquitous Edward S. Mason; H. Chapman Rose, U.S. Treasury; Harold Stassen, director, Foreign Operations Administration (the U.S. bilateral aid agency); Abbott Washburn, United States Information Agency; and the scientist Jerome Wiesner of MIT.

It would be hard to have assembled a more thrusting set of establishmentarians—who included, it should be noted, the vice president of the World Bank. Quite clearly, although Secretary Humphrey would remain in stalwart opposition until he finally stepped down in 1957, the anticommunist, pro-development internationalists promised to prevail. Throughout the middle 1950s they had the secretary of state with them: although John Foster Dulles was a fiscal conservative, he was prepared to contest communism in any venue. Late in the Eisenhower years, when Dulles was replaced by Christian Herter, who was joined by Douglas Dillon as economic undersecretary, and Robert B. Anderson succeeded Humphrey at Treasury, the administration's tilt toward development assistance was even stronger.

But this did not automatically imply a pro-IDA tilt. Many of the development-assistance cabal had a predilection for bilateral aid—it was more manageable; it was easier to deploy it strategically and to tailor it to diplomatic needs. But here, as to the executive branch, is where the SUNFED factor became decisive. Among the growing UN delegations in New York in the 1950s the demand for the multilateral aid in the SUNFED mode did not subside; indeed, the Soviet Union was a particularly insistent supporter. Two Americans much respected by Eisenhower, Paul Hoffman and Henry Cabot Lodge, took up that cause, but Secretary Anderson and Eugene Black rejected it, being prepared to accept an IBRD-based IDA as, at minimum, a lesser evil.[12]

As the 1950s drew toward a close, other factors, too, were shaping what would become the IBRD and U.S. administration position. For one thing, it became increasingly apparent, especially to the Bank, that creditworthiness considerations were cutting the institution off from some of its major customers. The Bank's propensity for outreach—its ability to promote development—would be encountering a powerful constraint if it did not have a complementary concessional product line to go with its nonconcessional one. This became evident first in the cases of the subcontinental pair, India and Pakistan. In the late 1950s, halfway through its second five-year plan, India ran through the balance of the foreign

12. Cook, *Declassified Eisenhower,* pp. 314–15.

exchange reserves it had accumulated during World War II. It thereby became an urgent candidate for rescue by concessional transfers.

India itself became an active agent in the formation of pro-IBRD/IDA thinking. It established a group of gifted official pro-aid advocates in Washington. Recognizing that India would get larger transfers sooner from a Bank-based than from an ECOSOC-based concessional facility, the group became a resourceful pro–Bretton Woods lobby.[13]

In the final analysis, however, what triggered the IDA decision was somewhat bizarre, although it underscored how separated governmental powers are in the United States. A particular Democratic senator from Oklahoma, a former journalist named Mike Monroney, in the middle 1950s became seized with the needs of developing countries for soft loans, of the advantages of multilateral aid, and of the advantages of the World Bank as the dispenser of such aid. This facet of Monroney's career is best remembered by the degree to which he was lured by a chimera. At the time, the United States' PL 480 food aid was "sold" for local currencies that were blocked from most uses outside or inside the issuing country. Somewhat similarly, the new (1958) U.S. bilateral capital assistance program, the Development Loan Fund (DLF) gave dollar loans repayable in blocked local currency. Monroney's hope was that these tokens somehow could be converted into real resources that those owning them, for example, the United States, could loan to poor countries at concessional rates.[14]

But this was not the senator's only gambit; he was indeed interested in real aid to needy countries, whatever the financial vehicle, and he pressed his case with vigor. Sympathizing, Senator William Fulbright, chairman of the Senate Committee on Banking and Currency, appointed Monroney chairman of its Subcommittee on International Finance, thereby allowing the latter to convene hearings on his IDA proposal in March 1958. In late February 1958 Monroney announced his plan to introduce a Senate resolution supporting the establishment of the new intermediary, a proposition that Black at once said the Bank "should be willing to explore."[15]

---

13. Chief of the group was B. K. Nehru, cousin of the prime minister and senior civil servant, who later served as his country's regular ambassador to the United States and as governor of several Indian states including Kashmir. Other participants, posted to executive or alternative executive directorships in the Bank and Fund or counselorships in the embassy, included C. S. Krishnamoorthi, later the initial vice president of the Asian Development Bank, and I. G. Patel, later secretary of economic affairs and governor of the Reserve Bank of India, who has reminded us of the role of India's Washington team in the late 1950s.

14. Senator Monroney was not the only politician to be bemused by PL 480–blocked currencies. Ten years later executive office staff would have a hard job persuading President Lyndon B. Johnson that U.S.-owned blocked currencies were not entitlements to other countries' exports.

15. *New York Times*, February 24, 1958, p. 1. Cited in Edward S. Mason and Robert E. Asher, *The World Bank since Bretton Woods* (Brookings, 1973), p. 387. Monroney introduced his resolution the same day.

At this point the Eisenhower administration was still not quite on board for the IBRD-IDA connection. Earlier, the U.S. Treasury and the Bank both had been appalled by Senator Monroney's suggestion that a "second Bretton Woods Conference" be called to consider the creation of a concessional transfers facility. (Both had feared that all could come unstuck in a new, constitution-rewriting international conference.) Accordingly, the senator accepted the view that his goal could be achieved by a sense-of-the-Senate resolution that the United States should move within the Bank for the establishment of an IDA affiliate. His March hearings were supportive of such a resolution. Both public and congressional favor for the proposal mounted, and by late May the administration, led by Secretary Anderson and Undersecretary Dillon, had come around. The Monroney resolution, with some administration revisions, now read:

> Resolved, that recognizing the desirability of promoting a greater degree of international development by means of multilateral loans based on sound economic principles, it is the sense of the Senate that prompt study should be given by the National Advisory Council on International Monetary and Financial Problems with respect to the establishment of an International Development Association, as an affiliate of the International Bank for Reconstruction and Development.
>
> In order to achieve greater international trade, development, and economic well-being, such study should include consideration of the following objectives:
>
> (1) Providing a source of long-term loans available at a reasonable rate of interest and repayable in local currencies (or partly in local currencies) to supplement International Bank lending activities and thereby permit the prompt completion of worthwhile development projects which could not otherwise go forward.
>
> (2) Facilitating, in connection with such loans, the use of local and other foreign currencies, including those available to the United States through the sale of agricultural surpluses and through other programs.
>
> (3) Insuring that funds for international economic development can be made available by a process which would encourage multilateral contributions for this purpose.[16]

Before the end of July the preceding resolution won a handsome (62–25) majority in the Senate. Anderson and Dillon began consultations with other donor governments (the Germans still thought IDA "a wooly-headed idea")[17] and at the September annual Bank and Fund meetings (in New Delhi that year) the treasury secretary announced that the United States was seriously studying the proposal of a Bank-based IDA and hoped others would do the same.

Clearly, a number of elements had contributed to the U.S.-Bank collaboration on behalf of IDA during the 1950s. But personal factors often supply the finishing touches to such ventures. James Weaver was told in the 1960s, "The Treasury would have held

16. U.S. Senate Committee on Banking and Currency, *Report on the International Development Association*, 85th Cong., 2d sess., 1958, p. 6. Cited in Weaver, *The International Development Association*, pp. 87–88.

17. Weaver, *The International Development Association*, p. 90.

back on IDA until today unless Monroney had gotten all the publicity, the Senate Resolution, etc." At the same time, he heard, "Black gave a dinner for a bunch of Republicans and told them it was alright and they decided to support it."[18]

IDA's Early Years

In the United States the National Advisory Council on International Monetary and Financial Problems (NAC) studied the IDA proposal over the span of a year beginning in mid-1958 under the chairmanship of Secretary Anderson, who simultaneously was discussing the matter with his counterparts in other governments. At the end of July 1959, shortly before the NAC's final report to the Senate on the Monroney resolution, Anderson wrote President Black of the Bank saying that, sensing widespread agreement among the Bank's members, he recommended that in the upcoming Annual Meeting, the governors direct the executive directors to draw up Articles of Agreement for an International Development Association. Black forwarded Anderson's proposal to the other governors with a concurring covering letter; he included some U.S.-suggested guidelines for the charter-drafting exercise.[19]

Following debate, on October 1, 1959, the governors unanimously instructed the Bank's executive directors to formulate Articles of Agreement for IDA for submission to member governments, specifying in the Articles what level of contributions would bring the Association into being. Under Eugene Black's chairmanship the Board turned to forthwith; before the end of January 1960 it distributed Articles of Agreement to members for ratification, specifying the trigger level of subscriptions as $650 million. Subscriptions of that amount, including that of the United States, were reached on September 24, 1960, and IDA operations began with the inaugural meeting of its Board on November 8, 1960.[20]

---

18. Ibid., p. 88.

19. The proposed guidelines were as follows: (1) IDA's purpose was to promote the development of less developed members whose needs could not be met by the IBRD, by financing projects of high priority; (2) any member of the Bank could join IDA; (3) voting should be weighted by the capital subscribed; (4) authorized capital was $1 billion, to be paid half immediately, the balance over five years; (5) the United States would contribute about $320 million; (6) IDA's resources were to be "reconsidered" every five years; (7) subscriptions were to be partly in gold or convertible currencies, partly in own currencies; (8) 20 percent of each country's quota was to be freely disposable by IDA, which would have authority to suspend the obligation of the less developed countries to pay in convertible currency; (9) IDA should be enabled to borrow from member governments and other sources; (10) arrangements should be made for IDA to receive the currencies of one member from another member. National Advisory Council on International Monetary and Financial Problems, *Report on the Proposed International Development Association* (GPO, 1959). Reported in Weaver, *The International Development Association*, p. 93.

20. That is, with the Bank's Board acting as the Board of IDA.

The Articles: The Mechanics

It is useful to consider at two levels what was wrought in IDA's establishment in 1960. The mechanics of the new construct were quite straightforward. All member governments of the Bank, and (contrary to the wishes of some members, including the Nordic countries) no other governments, could join the new institution. Because of the different resource sources on which IDA, in contrast with IBRD, would depend, some members would be donors, others potential recipients, of IDA credits. It was thought appropriate formally to segregate the two groups into "Part I" and "Part II" countries—although at the outset these designations at the margin were rather arbitrary, governments had to agree to their designations, and countries could shift from one group to the other.

Contrary to the earlier American proposal, all members, according to the Charter negotiated, had to contribute some gold or convertible currencies. For Part II countries, however, the requirement applied to only 10 percent of their subscriptions; the balance could be in their own currencies. All subscriptions of Part I countries, on the other hand, had to be convertible. In all cases, contributions could be paid in installments over a period of five years. Over the objections of those Part I countries (notably the United Kingdom, Belgium, and the Netherlands) that felt their relative incomes had declined from those implied by their shares of Bank capital, it was decided that IDA subscriptions should be kept proportionate to IBRD subscriptions: they should amount to 5 percent of the latter as of the end of 1959. As to votes, each member was allocated five hundred plus one for each $5,000 of subscription. This gave the Part II countries a bit more voice than they had in Bank voting after the IBRD's capital increase of 1959.

The new institution had the same board and management as the institution to which it was affiliated. Despite the preferences of a number of its members, it was to make its capital transfers in the form of soft loans only, not grants, IDA being left free to decide the kind and degree of softness its credits would offer. Like the Bank, it was to make project lending its normal mode of operation, "projects" being defined with the same flexibility and being subject to the same "special-circumstances" exception as in the IBRD case. Finally, as to the sectoral and substantive span of IDA-eligible projects, funding could be provided to

> any project which is of high developmental priority, that is, which will make an important contribution to the development of the area or areas concerned, whether or not the project is revenue-producing or directly productive. Thus projects such as water supply, sanitation, pilot housing and the like are eligible for financing, although it is expected that a major part of the Association's financing is likely to be for projects of the type financed by the Bank.[21]

21. IBRD, *Articles of Agreement of the IDA and Accompanying Report of the Executive Directors of the IBRD* (January 26, 1960). Quoted in Mason and Asher, *World Bank since Bretton Woods*, p. 393.

Deeper Consequences of the IBRD-IDA Union

So much for the surface mechanics of IDA's addition to what came to be called the World Bank Group. Another among the aspects of IDA's establishment—namely, that at the outset the program's financial size was small—was as explicit as those just cited. But the significance of this fact lacked transparency; it is therefore included in the set of underlying consequences of the Bank-IDA merger discussed in this section.

SCALE. IDA started with a notional capital of $1 billion, and the initial subscriptions from Part I "donor" members provided only three-quarters of that amount. The $1 billion goal, after a good deal of intervening inflation, was only twice the rather paltry, public works–focused, fund Nelson Rockefeller had proposed nine years earlier. Several member governments, both Part I and Part II, argued hard for a bigger starting figure, but the United States, although the most active sponsor of the new program, felt it should start modestly. In its final months the Eisenhower administration held fast to the $1 billion ceiling.

For its part, the Bank (having moved far beyond President Black's notions of appropriate operating scale of a decade earlier) was troubled by the scantiness of the start-up funding. As Vice President Burke Knapp noted in an oral history interview in 1961, management worried about the formidable mismatch between the scarcities of IBRD and IDA funds relative to their respective demands. For the first time the institution would be facing a major allocative, that is, rationing, problem.[22]

At the September 1962 annual meetings Eugene Black already was making an insistent plea for a quantum increase in IDA funding. IDA's future, he said, was the central issue in the development scene. A normal and justified rate of expansion would cause it to commit $500 million in the current year and keep growing. If the Association was to "become a principal instrument for the development of the poorer countries, and not just a minor gesture of good will toward them—it will clearly require a very substantial addition to its resources."[23] Mason and Asher describe the negotiations (1961–64) of the initial replenishment of IDA as relatively "uneventful" compared with the typical turbulence of the replenishment exercises to follow. But if this peaceful drive for funds was good-natured, it was not generous. It produced only three years' worth of contributions averaging $250 million annually—*less than half* Black's target. Thus the Bank/IDA began to learn the hard lesson of ODA-funding momentum: thanks to its financially anemic beginning, IDA, where each replenishment was likely to be a major determinant of the next, seemed destined for a lean future.

THE SEAMLESS WEB. In 1960 friends of the IBRD were still nervous about the Bank's virtue being compromised by close association with a public charity.

---

22. J. Burke Knapp, interview, World Bank Oral History Program, pp. 31–32. Cited in Mason and Asher, *World Bank since Bretton Woods*, p. 396.

23. Cited in Weaver, *The International Development Association*, p. 157.

Thus, for example, the motive for having IDA acquire separate Articles of Agreement, and not be the subject simply of an amendment to the Bank's Articles, was to keep some distance between the two. Eugene Black's promise that prevented Bank profits from being transferred to IDA until he resigned had the same explanation.[24]

Nevertheless, the defining aspect of the Bank-IDA merger was its closeness. For most *operating* purposes, the two operations became as one. In their determination to capture the IDA idea away from SUNFED, both the Bank itself and most of its Part I members led by the United States, rather than just combining institutions, gave a second face to the same institution—but in a way that changed the original as well as the add-on.

The "seamless web" between the Bank and IDA, made unmistakable by their shared management, staff, and organizational structure, had a profound effect on the Bank. It massively increased the institution's borrowing clientele. As was evident in the way agriculture began to take hold as a Bank subject even in the late Black years, the addition of IDA drew the institution into a whole array of non-self-liquidating fields, including those of poverty alleviation and the social sectors. And once these new subjects developed standing and competence within the house, they became also the objects of IBRD lending. It is not too much to say that the Bank's whole McNamara era would have been unthinkable without the IDA add-on.

The merger had an equally profound impact on the multilateral concessional lending program. It immersed the latter thoroughly and fully in the Bank's operating culture. Not only did the same people manage and do the work of the nonconcessional and concessional programs: it was the same work. Over the years Bank practitioners have attested that IDA work has been done with the same care and prudence that has characterized IBRD operations. Project appraisal, negotiating, and supervising methodologies have been essentially the same, and typically they have been pursued with comparable rigor. Although sometimes differences in degree would be observed between the readiness of many "IDA countries" and many non-IDA countries for policy reforms, the policy-based lending regimes proposed for the two groups would not differ in kind. There can be no doubt that IDA's institutional texture is very different from what would have emerged in an ECOSOC setting. The proof of the Bank's successful assimilation of IDA is that the merger made no perceptible dent in the IBRD's creditworthiness. (Indeed, the irony would be that, decades later, IDA, on occasion, would become a *defender* of the senior institution's creditworthiness.)

HETERODOXIES AVOIDED. It suits the image of assimilation to note certain operational choices that its Charter allowed IDA that have not been taken up, arguably because they would not have suited good World Bank style. For one thing, reflecting vestiges of the Monroney advocacy, the Articles allow IDA both to

24. The policy was one George Woods overturned soon after assuming office.

operate in a DLF-style mode (dollar loans repayable in unconvertible local curren-cy) and to accept as resources from one donor the currencies of another member, *if* the latter agrees to such deployment. It is hard to imagine that the framers of the Charter believed the second of these options (invoking Monroney's aspirations for PL 480–blocked currencies) would have found any takers. In any event, IDA in practice has shunned both. Instead it quickly opted for orthodox soft loans, but with a high measure of concessionality (fifty-year term, ten years of grace; annual repayments of 1 percent of principal from the eleventh through the twentieth year, 3 percent thereafter; 0.75 percent service charge).

A second example of cultural conformity is that although the Articles deny IDA the option of making capital grants, they do, via some circumlocution, permit the Association to make technical assistance grants from member-contributed resour-ces. It appears that this is an option IDA never has used, although the cases of trust funds, of members' special contributions in excess of subscriptions, and of the Bank's funding of international research ventures out of IBRD profits blur the issue.

AUTONOMY/ACCOUNTABILITY TENSION. The assimilation of IDA into Bank style and practice gave it protective coloration against donor monitoring. The Bank had established a good measure of buffering against close, detailed member review. For example, it was firmly established in 1947 that all program proposals were initiated by management and never by the Board. The same procedural ground rules extended willy-nilly to IDA.

On the other hand, as emphasized earlier, the donor members of the Bank had an intense self-interest in the funding of IDA. They needed to hold IDA account-able—as they as governments were accountable—for its uses of their taxpayers' money. It was inevitable, therefore, in a Bank-housed IDA, for great tensions to build between the institution's appetite for autonomy and the demands of its Part I owners for accountability. Day to day the latter were repressed under Bank proce-dural norms. But the accountability demands were virtually bound to break loose during the recurrent replenishment exercises to which IDA was committed by its dependence on taxpayer inputs.

IDA as a Member of the Donor Community

With the formation of IDA, the World Bank became an aid agency. Within less than two decades it would become the world's leading, and most influential, single such provider of development assistance. But the Bank would continue to share the concessional transfers scene with a variety of other actors. Those governments that would be called the "traditional" bilateral donors launched their Development Assistance Committee at the Organization of Economic Cooperation and Develop-ment in Paris in the same 1960 birth year as IDA. What would become legions of nonofficial pro-development interveners into developing countries had just begun to proliferate in the early 1960s.

Figure 17-1. *IDA in the Context of ODA*

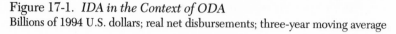

Billions of 1994 U.S. dollars; real net disbursements; three-year moving average

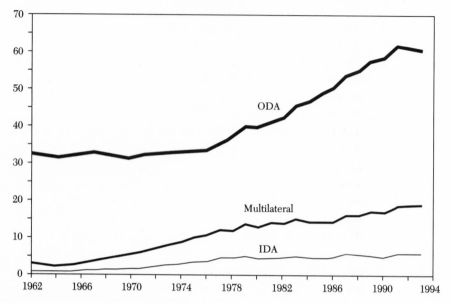

Source: OECD DAC reports, various years.

On the multilateral side, the regional development banks, each, early on, with a concessional loan affiliate or "window," were established in this sequence: the Inter-American Development Bank, 1959; the African Development Bank, 1963, which established the (concessional) African Development Fund in 1974; the Asian Development Bank, 1966 (beginning some concessional lending in 1968 and formalizing the Asian Development Fund in 1974); and the International Fund for Agricultural Development in 1977 (created at the initiative of Arab donors). Meanwhile an assortment of UN specialized agencies and components of the United Nations Secretariat had taken shape—among them the International Labor Organization; Food and Agriculture Organization; World Health Organization, United Nations Educational, Scientific, and Cultural Organization; United Nations Children's Fund; United Nations Development Program; and United Nations Fund for Population Activities (UNFPA)—all focused on or related to development and all transferring different types and amounts of resources on concessional terms.

Until 1976 the International Monetary Fund was not a concessional lender. But in that year this changed when, provided with the windfall that recently had occurred in the Fund's gold holdings and faced with developing-country demands triggered by the first oil shock, the IMF created a Trust Fund that made 2.9 billion

Figure 17-2. *Multilateral and IDA Flows as Percent of ODA*
Three-year moving average

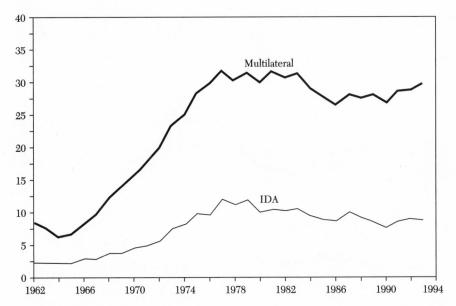

Source: OECD DAC annual reports, various years.

SDRs of concessional loans between 1976 and 1981. Partly by recycling reflows from this earlier Trust Fund lending and partly via fresh bilateral contributions, the IMF repeated its forays into concessional lending with a Structural Adjustment Facility in 1986 and an Extended Structural Adjustment Facility in 1987.

Figures 17-1 to 17-3 chart the dimensions of IDA in 1962–91 compared with total overseas development assistance and total multilateral ODA. In the early 1960s IDA was anything but a dominant concessional donor. From 1962 through 1968 IDA accounted for less than half the net disbursements of multilateral ODA, which itself amounted to less than 10 percent of total ODA. In 1969 the multilateral share of ODA shot up to 15 percent and began a climb that would characterize most of the 1970s. In 1970, when the multilateral share of ODA was 16.5 percent, IDA claimed a quarter of that amount, whereas the UN agencies, the soft window of the IDB and European Community (EC) assistance accounted for 32, 21, and 11 percent, respectively. Through most of the 1970s and since, however, IDA commitments have exceeded those of the UN agencies, as they have the ODA outlays of both the regional development banks and the EC. In 1990 dollars, IDA commitments reached peaks of more than $5.6 billion in 1978 and again in 1988. The former, however, was about 16 percent of global ODA, the latter, only 11 percent.

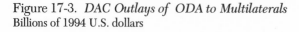

Figure 17-3. *DAC Outlays of ODA to Multilaterals*
Billions of 1994 U.S. dollars

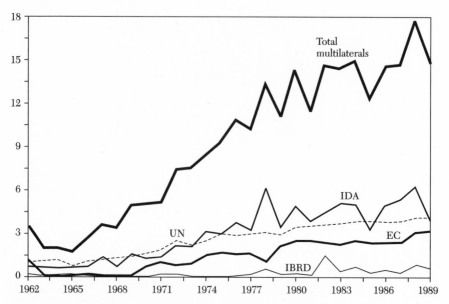

Source: OECD DAC annual reports, various years.

The Rest of the Chapter

The thoroughgoing merger of IDA and IBRD operations means it would be redundant to insert in this chapter separate discussions of the sectoral and functional topics examined elsewhere in the book, such as an IDA-specific treatment of the institution's work on agriculture and rural development. What belongs here are matters *peculiar* to IDA, and, of these, one subject—IDA replenishments—gives the chapter its chronological dimension.

By definition, IDA has placed a continuing draft on member governments' public revenues. But instead of being solicited annually, contributions have been gathered in multiyear, typically three-year, batches whose sequence has supplied the pulse to the IDA story. The record of the first ten IDA replenishments is examined. Their dates, totals, and principal contributors and sources are summarized in table 17-1.

A second distinctive IDA issue is that of the allocation of IDA credits among borrowing countries. From the time of the 1950 King-Demuth memo, it was recognized this would be a contentious issue for a multilateral distributing scarce concessional resources, and so it proved to be as soon as the Association became operative. What should be the subset of IDA-eligible developing countries, and should intercountry allocations be determined case by case, by formula, or in response to which criteria?

Table 17-1. IDA Replenishments by Country and Replenishment Period

Millions of real 1990 U.S. dollars (using beginning-year deflators)

Country	Initial (1961–64)	Percent of total	IDA1 (1965–68)	Percent of total	IDA2 (1969–71)	Percent of total	IDA3 (1972–74)	Percent of total	IDA4 (1975–77)	Percent of total	IDA5[a] (1978–80)	Percent of total	IDA6 (1981–84)	Percent of total	IDA7 (1985–87)	Percent of total	IDA8 (1988–90)	Percent of total	IDA9 (1991–93)	Percent of total	Total (1961–93)	Percent of total
Canada	194	5.0	203	5.6	280	5.9	410	6.2	550	6.1	735	5.8	1,012	4.9	610	4.5	615	4.7	674	4.8	5,285	5.2
France	272	7.0	302	8.3	363	7.6	410	6.2	508	5.6	678	5.4	1,154	5.5	1,050	7.7	898	6.9	1,078	7.6	6,713	6.6
Germany	272	7.0	354	9.8	437	9.2	640	9.6	1,032	11.4	1,376	10.9	2,634	12.6	1,508	11.1	1,469	11.2	1,630	11.5	11,351	11.1
Italy	93	2.4	146	4.0	180	3.8	265	4.0	364	4.0	486	3.8	823	3.9	763	5.6	749	5.7	759	5.4	4,628	4.5
Japan	173	4.4	201	5.5	248	5.2	394	5.9	993	11.0	1,300	10.3	3,374	16.2	2,532	18.6	2,783	21.3	2,944	20.1	14,940	14.6
Netherlands	143	3.7	80	2.2	109	2.3	185	2.8	266	3.0	370	2.8	666	3.2	552	4.1	540	4.1	468	3.3	3,379	3.3
Sweden	52	1.3	73	2.0	295	6.2	279	4.2	361	4.0	482	3.8	658	3.2	370	2.7	322	2.5	372	2.6	3,265	3.2
U.K.	674	17.3	471	13.0	580	12.2	851	12.7	1,002	11.1	1,339	10.6	2,079	10.0	916	6.7	841	6.4	950	6.7	9,702	9.5
U.S.	1,646	42.3	1,521	41.9	1,791	37.8	2,625	39.3	3,008	33.3	3,938	31.2	4,838	23.2	2,990	22.0	3,077	23.5	3,065	21.6	28,499	27.9
OPEC[b]	25	0.5	16	0.5	20	0.4	30	0.4	54	0.6	912	7.2	1,214	5.8	594	4.4	427	3.3	328	2.3	3,620	3.5
Total	3,543	91.2	3,368	92.8	4,303	90.7	6,088	91.2	8,138	90.2	11,615	92.1	18,452	88.4	11,884	87.5	11,721	89.6	12,269	86.5	91,382	89.3
Other[c]	344	8.8	263	7.2	441	9.3	587	8.8	889	9.8	998	7.9	2,414	11.6	1,698	12.5	1,368	10.4	1,917	13.5	10,917	10.7
Gross	3,887 (2,915)[d]	100.0	3,631 (2,723)[d]	100.0	4,744	100.0	6,675	100.0	9,026	100.0	12,613	100.0	20,866 (15,650)[d]	100.0	13,582	100.0	13,089	100.0	14,186	100.0	102,299	100.0

Growth rates

Replenishment period	Replenishment	Annual
Initial to IDA 1	-6.6	-1.7
IDA 1 to IDA 2	30.7	6.9
IDA 2 to IDA 3	40.7	12.1
IDA 3 to IDA 4	35.2	10.6
IDA 4 to IDA 5	39.7	11.8
IDA 5 to IDA 6	65.4	18.3
IDA 6 to IDA 7	-34.9	-10.2
IDA 7 to IDA 8	-3.6	-1.2
IDA 8 to IDA 9	8.4	2.7

Annual growth rates

Country	1961–93	1961–84	1965–74	1975–84	1981–93
Canada	4.2	8.6	10.5	10.7	-4.0
France	4.7	7.5	4.5	14.6	-0.7
Germany	6.1	12.0	8.8	16.9	-4.7
Italy	7.2	11.5	8.8	14.6	-0.8
Japan	9.9	16.0	10.1	22.6	-1.4
Netherlands	4.0	8.0	12.6	16.5	-3.5
Sweden	6.8	13.6	21.1	10.5	-5.6
U.K.	1.2	5.8	8.8	12.9	-7.5
U.S.	2.1	5.5	8.1	8.2	-4.5
OPEC[b]	9.0	21.4	8.8	67.9	-12.3
Total	4.2	8.6	8.8	14.6	-4.0
Other[c]	5.9	10.2	12.2	18.1	-2.3
Gross	4.4	8.8	9.1	15.0	-3.8

Source: IDA 10, "Burden Sharing," Discussion Paper no. 6, June 11, 1992.

a. Includes total basic and special contributions.
b. Saudi Arabia, Kuwait, United Arab Emirates.
c. Other, including Part II, country contributions, transfers from Bank profits, and IDA reflows.
d. Normalized to a three-year rate.

A third IDA-specific issue concerns the availability or not of other forms of soft money than appropriated grants from member governments. From the beginning of the new affiliate, both the scarcity of IDA resources and the inclination of the Association's Part I members to micromanage IDA's uses of their taxpayer resources drove Bank/IDA management to seek alternative sources of, or devices for stretching, concessional funds that would relax both the resource scarcity and the degree of donor intervention. This search for supplements to parliamentary purses and ways of relaxing their power has not been very fruitful so far, but the effort persists.

Replenishments

IDA's replenishment exercises have been times of anxiety and excitement, and they have had a rhythm. As noted, Eugene Black, and George Woods after him, deplored the thinness of the soft-loan affiliate's initial funding. Opting for a three- rather than five-year replenishment cycle, IDA donors managed to complete negotiations for "IDA 1" (as became the replenishment jargon) before the end of 1964.[25] But they were tightfisted, holding the scale of activity to the same $250 annual rate that the Association's start-up money had provided. George Woods elected for a quantum jump to $1 billion annually. The U.S. government gave him mixed signals. The new Treasury secretary, Henry Fowler, told Woods to raise his own money; the United States could not do it for him. Nominally, the administration supported his target (neither other donors nor leaders in Congress agreed), but the American administration wanted both to reduce its share of the total (from more than 40 percent to one-third) and, in effect to adopt source tying—limiting the U.S. contribution to the amount of IDA procurement from the United States. The other donors objected to Woods's extensive one-on-one caucusing with the United States. They roundly rejected the source-tying idea. The most Woods could manage was an "end-of-the-queue" arrangement for the Americans; he got only $400 million annually; and the U.S. Congress delayed even this so much that the exercise was not completed until long after the end of George Woods's term.

After this troubled round, replenishment settled into a three-year rhythm, until IDA 6, which was so difficult to negotiate that the outlay period (1981–84) was stretched to four years, again for U.S.-related reasons.

25. The nomenclature about IDA replenishments can be confusing. In table 17-1 the replenishment periods shown are those during which donor contributions negotiated during the years preceding were available for funding IDA credits. Thus, for example, "IDA 3" resources available for funding IDA credits during 1972–74 were negotiated in 1969–71. But among the Bank and its members most of the talk and conferring about IDA 3 occurred during the earlier period.

Table 17-2. *IDA Per Capita Commitments*
Real 1990 U.S. dollars; three-year averages

Country	1965–67	1975–77	1985–87	1991–1993
Giants[a]				
China[b]	. . .	. . .	0.53	0.81
India	1.58	1.78	0.99	1.30
Large/medium[c]				
Bangladesh	1.50	3.64	4.50	2.46
Ghana[d]	0.00	1.46	10.11	20.24
Pakistan	2.47	2.27	2.44	2.20
Tanzania	0.65	4.77	3.75	10.54
Mini[e]				
Guinea-Bissau[b]	. . .	. . .	15.26	8.25
Guyana[d]	0.00	3.36	7.84	30.62
Lesotho	6.60	6.09	5.77	10.12
Low-income countries	0.52	0.99	1.30	1.91

Source: IBRD/IDA annual reports, 1992 Sex and Age Distribution of World Population, 1992 World Debt Tables.
a. Above 0.5 billion population.
b. Lending to China did not begin until 1981 and to Guinea-Bissau, 1979.
c. Between 10 and 100 million population.
d. There was no lending to Ghana from 1962 to 1963 and to Guyana from 1961 to 1969.
e. Less than 2 million population.

Trends in IDA Funding

Tables 17-1 and 17-2 and figures 17-1 and 17-2 summarize IDA's money-raising and -granting experience. There was, obviously, a great deal of growth in total contributions during the Association's first three decades—total collections increased almost fivefold in real terms, or more than 4 percent annually. But there were two distinct phases: virtually *all* the overall growth was finished by the early 1980s. Real contributions to IDA were flat thereafter.

There was some fluctuation within each of these periods. Contributions to IDA 1 (on a per annum basis) lost some ground. But then began a surge that carried through and beyond the 1970s, peaking in a particularly troubled—but in the aggregate, high-yielding—IDA 6. The "other" category in table 17-1 that also peaked in IDA 6 includes contributions by such members of OECD's Development Assistance Committee (DAC) as Australia and Switzerland that the table does not list individually, by Part II members, and by the Bank/IDA institution itself out of IBRD profits and (later) IDA reflows.

Comparative Contributions

More of the macro story is apparent in the country columns of table 17-1. Two contributors, the United States and the United Kingdom, have had long-term programs of reducing their funding shares. But since, under the rules of the house, "regular" funding shares are tied to voting allotments, this meant that those seeking a relative reduction in their financial commitments have sought, at the same time, to minimize their loss of influence in the institution, and, of course, that those taking up larger financial shares have had opposite agendas with respect to Bank/ IDA governance.

Because the United States was IDA's principal founder, heaviest voter, provider of 42 percent of the initial funding, and host country, how the relative retreat in U.S. funding progressed has been a central theme of IDA's financial history. Over the period covered in table 17-1, the relative start-to-finish growth in U.S. con- tributions to IDA was only half that in total IDA funding. The outcome reflected a burden-sharing purpose but also ambivalence and episodic changes within the American executive branch, sharp conflicts between the executive branch and congress, efforts by other members of IDA to delay or compensate for the Ameri- can decline, and efforts by Bank management to mediate the process—along with the collateral claims and tensions that have arisen over institutional governance.

As often as not, the U.S. executive and legislative branches have collaborated (often adversarially) to delay IDA replenishments. Thus they managed to stretch the replenishments of both IDA 2 and IDA 6 to four-year exercises, and repeatedly, even when the United States (often having bargained down replenishment targets) has joined timely three-year commitments, it has failed to provide appropriations on schedule. Sometimes the threatened breakdowns in IDA operations were avoided by Bank management's willingness to operate with perilously low reserves (as in 1968). Frequently, other members provided offsets. Typically the others were reluctant to accept formal reductions in the U.S. share, or the United States hesitated to accept the contingent voting-rights adjustment. But commonly within a replenishment period, other donors have been willing to accelerate their con- tributions to compensate for American lags. (In an oral history, Irving Friedman, George Woods's chief economist, remarked that he was in the rather regular habit of phoning up the Dutch and the Canadians for such help.)[26] And in recent replenishments—indeed, in every one from IDA 6 through IDA 10—it became a near norm for other members to compensate for American delays by making "supplementary" contributions that did not carry voting implications.

Meanwhile, as table 17-1 shows, Britain was executing an even sharper with- drawal: from more than 17 percent of the initial funding to less than 7 percent of IDA 9. Its counterpart (with whom, also, some of the associated voting-share issues had to be adjusted) was Japan. Even if deterred by difficulties in obtaining in- creases in its voting share, Japanese funding of IDA rose radically in real terms to some eighteen times its initial level.

The combined British and Japanese shares increased from 23 to 24 percent of the total over the period of table 17-1, taking up some of the space vacated by the United States. More than a third of the latter was occupied by the table's group of

26. Irving Friedman, interview, World Bank Oral History Program, March 1974, p. 35.

named continental European countries plus Canada, which, although diverse, is not a bad composite for discussion purposes. Canada, the Netherlands, and Sweden, as comparatively strong supporters of the Bank/IDA, maintained their shares throughout. France, starting even with Germany, was content to let the latter run ahead, while Italy increased its contribution more than tenfold. The OPEC donors' contributions bulged in the sixth replenishment and remained substantial thereafter.

The balance of the vacated U.S. space was occupied by the table's "other" category, including, in addition to other donors and contributions of Bank profits, the beginnings of significant reflows from earlier IDA loans.

The Replenishments in Sequence

The first ten replenishments can be grouped for discussion as follows: IDA 1 and 2; IDA 3 through 5; IDA 6 and 7; IDA 8 through 10.

IDA 1 AND IDA 2. In IDA 1 the donors retreated a bit from their moderate initial level of contributions to the Bank's new concessional operations, and George Woods had four years rather than three years of trouble getting together the commitments for IDA 2. It has been argued that Woods's $1 billion per year target was excessively ambitious. On the other hand, he had few precedents to go by; his eminent predecessor had been demanding $500 million a year for IDA as early as 1962, indicating further increases to follow; the new president had been turned loose by U.S. Secretary Henry Fowler to raise his concessional funds unassisted; and he evidently thought he needed to go with a high asking figure to get an acceptable increase. As table 17-1 indicates, he in fact got a substantial increase and started the IDA 2–3 surge.

In the negotiations over IDA 2, the United States began what would become an almost unbroken sequence of special replenishment demands. During the Kennedy and Johnson administrations, for the first time since World War II, the country was greatly concerned about its negative balance of payments. In the face of other donors' protests, the United States argued that, instead of being tied, its contributions should be put at the back of the IDA 2 queue, in the hope that, by the time they were drawn, the American payments gap would be narrowed.

IDA 3 THROUGH 5. These were the vintage replenishments of the McNamara years, raised during 1969 through 1977, disbursed largely during 1972 through 1980. IDA's financial growth achieved and sustained a pace that did not persist long after the tenure of Robert McNamara. How much was it his personal achievement?

Events suggest that the IDA 3 rise was by no means entirely, probably not even mainly, a McNamara phenomenon. In terms of momentum, it was hooked to Woods's IDA 2. At the time of the adoption of the International Development Strategy for the Second Development Decade (September 1970), the case for development assistance was perhaps more widely and warmly agreed upon than at any time before or since, and this was not yet a McNamara consensus. McNamara had an important role in mounting the Pearson Commission, which contributed a consensus voice, but the Commission was not his creature. McNamara was scarcely a darling of the Nixon administration, and yet that administration was pro-aid, and, to boot, as advised by its Peterson Commission (reviewing the foreign aid question) it was pro-*multilateral* aid, as was Pearson.[27] Indeed, the desire to enlist other governments in sharing the foreign aid burden via the mechanism of multilateral assistance carried over from the Johnson to the Nixon administrations.

Thus, in tuning in quickly and insistently on the promotion of IDA contributions, as McNamara did as soon as he joined the Bank in April 1968, the new president was riding a wave already swelling. It is unclear how much he added to its IDA 3 height. But what does seem apparent is his considerable responsibility for sustaining IDA's money-raising momentum through the 1970s. (The later section "Replenishment Politics" discusses the nature and the intensity of the tactics McNamara used for pressing the IDA cause.) Arguably, the political environment was less conducive to IDA expansion than it had been at the beginning of the decade. During the second Nixon and the Ford administrations, McNamara's relations with the U.S. executive branch (for example, with Treasury Secretary William Simon) were more difficult than they have been with the earlier Nixon people; and (see volume 2, chapter 6, of this work) they were less congenial than might have been expected with the combined executive and legislative branches when President Jimmy Carter came to power in 1977. In the 1970s there were many more multilateral pro-development agencies competing for concessional resources than there had been in the 1960s. From 1974 onward, at the same time that the first oil shock rendered the developing countries more strident in their demands for development assistance and other concessions, the reaction of many "northern" policymakers to such demands was increasingly dyspeptic.

To a significant extent, however, the excesses of the "North-South dialogue" probably strengthened McNamara's IDA hand. He had committed his institution to an antipoverty, pro-equity course that resonated convincingly with all donors inclined toward such purposes. Yet under his leadership IDA's image remained nonideological; compared with the alternatives, it was seen as a professionally competent, well-managed instrumentality for public funds.

At the same time, the Bank was encountering growing difficulties in the 1970s in making its IDA case with the legislative branch of McNamara's own government. The fall and winter of 1973–74, coincident with the first oil shock, was a rough time for foreign aid in the United States. In October the bilateral aid bill was voted down in the House of Representatives and in January IDA 4 suffered the same fate. Both

27. The Presidential Task Force on International Developments headed by Rudolph Peterson, former head of the Bank of America, subsequent head of UNDP, reported in 1970.

measures were retrieved, but the experiences demonstrated the thinness of the support for development assistance in the Bank's largest donor member, as well as the extraordinary separation of executive and legislative powers in the United States, where aid-funding measures needed to clear both authorization and appropriation votes in both lower and upper houses. As had been the case right along, but now appeared more precarious, all of the appropriations implementing three-year IDA authorizations were one-year money bills requiring renewal each year. As fortification against the implicit risk, the U.S. delegation to the meetings of IDA deputies took to including, beginning with IDA 5, one or more members of Congress in the party.

IDA 6 AND IDA 7. No replenishment has a reputation for being more conflicted than IDA 6. It was prepared at the end of President McNamara's tenure. The world surrounding the Bank was in a period of politico-economic turmoil.[28] Within IDA's own orbit, severe burden-sharing strains, mainly between the United States (in particular, the U.S. Congress) and the rest, were inherited from IDA 5.

It was the new Reagan administration, however, that gave IDA 6 its image. To an unprecedented extent the new U.S. regime threatened to renege on the commitment of its predecessor. This forced IDA to add a fourth year to the replenishment period and grant the United States some familiar late-queuing advantage. And while other contributions were rising, the United States sharply reduced its fraction of IDA 6 to only 23 percent of the gross replenishment, compared with an IDA 5 share that had been eight percentage points higher.[29] This was the largest replenishment-to-replenishment drop in the relative American contribution in the whole IDA record.

Yet the new team in Washington only intensified, it did not change, the pattern of "U.S. retreat" that, quantitatively speaking, has been the abiding theme of the IDA story. Between IDA 4 and IDA 5 the American share already had dropped six percentage points—from 39 to 33 percent. The share remained in the 21–24 percent range in the four replenishments following.

Arguably, the low point in the relationship between the Bank and the United States as an IDA contributor was reached in IDA 7. Battered by the IDA 6 experience, the Bank sought only to maintain the new replenishment at the preceding real level. This suggested a target quickly scaled down by President A. W.

28. One can mention the second oil shock (1979), the subsequent interest rate shock, Iran hostages (1979), invasion of Afghanistan (1980), the accessions of Prime Minister Margaret Thatcher (1979) and President Ronald Reagan (1981), a commodities slump, and the imminent debt crisis of 1982.

29. By the fall of 1981 internal Bank memoranda acknowledged that "IDA faced a crisis"; there was a shortfall in fiscal 1982 commitment authority to the tune of $1.5 billion. The result was a sharp (43 percent) cut in the lending program for South Asia. Sub-Saharan Africa, with only an 11 percent reduction, was partly protected. International Development Association, "IDA Seventh Replenishment," IDA/RPL/83-16, September 13, 1983, para. 84.

Clausen from the $17–18 billion range to $16 billion. The Reagan administration announced that, on the contrary, it could not contribute more than 25 percent of a replenishment with country contributions valued at $9 billion overall, and the United States simply stonewalled; it forced its will on other donors, and Bank management had to patch together a Special Facility for Africa to accommodate the more generous propensities of the other donors.

IDA 8 THROUGH 10. The three following replenishments achieved similar quantitative results but were increasingly contentious. As noted earlier, IDA 8 negotiators found that a march had been stolen on the Bank by its near neighbor: with the SAF and ESAF, the Monetary Fund had renewed its role in concessional lending. The IDA 8 transaction also saw a U.S. push to harden the terms for IDA credits, maturities being reduced from fifty years to forty years for IDA-only borrowers and thirty-five years for (IBRD/IDA) "blend" countries. But these were not the distinguishing characteristics of the period, which was preoccupied, instead, with rivalries over member voting rights, impacted differences over inter-country allocations of credits, and (most of all) the increasing application of policy constraints on Bank/IDA management by members' IDA deputies.

Replenishment Politics

Presidents of the World Bank typically have met weekly with an in-group of their senior managers, one called the President's Council in Robert McNamara's time. One thing that upset McNamara when he met with that group his first day in office (April 1, 1968) was to discover that no senior person had a standing assignment (President Woods's recruit, former Senator Willis Robertson, was no longer present) to monitor events in the U.S. Congress bearing on the World Bank Group and, more particularly, on IDA replenishment. The gap was quickly closed. Since then Bank presidents have always had at their elbows one or another former member of Congress to follow issues on Capitol Hill, represent the Bank there, and facilitate Bank communications with pivotal U.S. legislators.

When one pages through the minutes of the President's Council (by whatever name), the amount of time the institution's assembled top management has allotted to IDA replenishments, more particularly, to their fortunes in the U.S. Congress, is striking. A year after McNamara's arrival, he received a memorandum from a member of the Bank's external relations staff who had lunch with the director and others of the staff of the House Committee on Banking and Currency (which dealt with legislation relating to the World Bank, the Fund, and other international financial institutions). It is worth quoting from Perry K. Sellon's memo at some length:

> When I asked [Paul Nelson] what really lay behind all the back-chat in Banking and Currency hearings on the need for better "communications" between the Bank and the Committee, we got quite an interesting outburst from Nelson which, together with what

we have been hearing on the Senate side, indicates a build-up of Capitol Hill pressures for greater congressional participation in the whole Bank-IDA activity.

. . . Nelson revealed that Felipe Herrera, Arnie Weiss and the IDB [Inter-American Development Bank] crew had thrown quite a party for the Banking and Currency Committee a week or so before our IDA hearing. [Congressman] Widnall and others were miffed that our Bank never sees fit to do likewise. Gene Black . . . used to take good care of congressmen and senators. George Woods never raised a finger.

. . . Nelson then . . . managed to convey the impression that such buttering up of the Committee was a useful exercise. [He said] that his committee was thoroughly aware of the way IDB is operated, the back-scratching that goes on there.

. . . [C]ertain congressmen deduce that something similar must be going on in our Bank. On Capitol Hill, it is known, according to Nelson, that a management survey (critical in tone) was made several years ago of our Bank's operations. These congressmen would like to see that survey. Nelson also mentioned the old demand that the General Accounting Office do an audit of this Bank.

Nelson . . . explained that there is considerable irritation on the Hill because we and other development banks come to Congress with international agreements already completely worked out and acceded to by U.S. officials before Congress gets a whack at them. He described Congress as being tired of being told by the Executive Branch simply to vote for or against a *fait accompli*. . . . [He] would not be surprised to hear demands that members of Congress be consulted about, or be included in, negotiations for the Third Replenishment of IDA.[30]

Obviously, there is no avoiding the focus on *American* replenishment politics. Not only has the U.S. government been close at hand and the largest contributor to IDA; it is almost unique in having two genuinely independent decisionmaking branches that always are in at least semiconflict and both of which need wooing. Moreover, for most of IDA's life, by being the reluctant, retreating, partner, the United States has had even greater leverage than its sheer size would suggest. Having the Congress as a constraint has further strengthened the hand of the U.S. administrations in bargaining with other members; and the habit the other members have had of prorating their contributions to those of the United States has strengthened the latter's leverage on the collective outcome. In short, while the United States by no means has been IDA's whole political story, it has been the protagonist around which other plots thickened.

STRUGGLES OVER SCALE AND SHARES. At this point one may speak of the Bank, in the person of its employees, as an actor, not simply an agent of its owners. As such, the institution usually has been biased toward larger rather than smaller IDA replenishments, and it has used various tactics to this end. Thus, in his first trip to Canada as president, McNamara advised the Canadian government not to lower the heat on the U.S. Congress by coming in with an extra input to the prolonged assembly of IDA 2 contributions before the November 1968 U.S. election—but

30. Memorandum, Perry K. Sellon to Robert S. McNamara via William Clark, "Congress, the IDA Bill, and the Third Replenishment," April 11, 1969.

then, please, to do so.[31] In mid-1972 McNamara held back on contributing Bank profits to IDA, again to keep the pressure on Congress, this time in behalf of IDA 4.[32]

Debates over how, and how ardently, to promote replenishment size sometimes have been heated *within* the Bank, the most prominent instance being in connection with IDA 7, negotiated during 1982–84. This time, as indicated earlier, the gap between the Bank's asking figure and the bottom of the range established by the United States was exceptionally large: $16 billion versus $9 billion. Moreover, there was tension between the two senior vice presidents. Ernest Stern, senior vice president for operations, did not think Moeen Qureshi, senior vice president for finance, and, in particular, Andre de Lattre, the venerable French civil servant who had been hired to assist Qureshi, were pressing hard enough for a high enough total. Their strategy and that of President Clausen was to negotiate the United States up to an aggregate number nearer the Bank's $16 billion than the American $9 billion. The Reagan Treasury played a cool hand. It got the mooted total whittled down to $12 billion, but then in December 1983, as time was beginning to run out, refused to consider more than the U.S. share of $9 billion. How was the difference to be made up? Qureshi favored, once again, a "supplemental" scheme wherein good-willed members would provide extra resources that would not have voting share implications but also could not be used for procurement in the United States. Stern demurred: members were tired of nondescript supplementals; go for a Special Fund for Africa. Clausen and Qureshi pushed their supplemental proposition all the way to the July 1984 G-7 meeting in Tokyo, where Germany and Japan, partly to minimize embarrassment to the United States, led its rejection. Finally, the Bank availed itself of the Special Fund for Africa alternative.

Japan, of course, was the main protagonist of voting shares realignment among IDA's Part I members. It mentioned its interest in more votes as early as 1972 to Burke Knapp when he visited Tokyo. It pressed the issue again in 1978, again during the 1983–84 struggle just sketched, and in 1986 it tranched its contribution to IDA 8, making the last one-third contingent upon obtaining increased shares of IDA and IBRD capital.

Bank management did not have an autonomous stake in these share negotiations. Its interest simply was in mediating the share issue to keep it from being disruptive; it argued, though, for what it saw as fair. The Japanese should get the increments of control they paid for. Management, however, took a strong stand on another dimension of the shares question: the allotments to Part II countries. When votes were being reallocated, as they were in 1970, it was natural for Part I members, who were busy either defending or trying to augment their allocations,

---

31. Memorandum, Robert S. McNamara for the record, September 9 and 10, 1968, concerning meetings held in Ottawa, September 4, 1968.
32. Minutes of President's Council meeting, July 10, 1972.

to look longingly at the shares of those members (many of them on the receiving end) who were not supplying the new resources. Here McNamara stonewalled. He flatly vetoed the proposal that Part II votes be reduced from 33 percent to 16 percent of the total. Part II countries, he insisted, must not significantly lose relative voting strength, and that, substantially, has remained the institutional position.[33]

BURDEN SHARING UNDER CONDITIONS OF EXCHANGE RATE UNCERTAINTY. It is ironic that IDA replenishments featured hard bargaining over comparative burdens, down to the first decimal place, when exchange rate volatility often, ex post, altered the ex-ante burdens materially. The problem became more pronounced following the breakdown of the world's fixed exchange rate regime in 1973. A maintenance of value (MOV) provision in the replenishment agreements reduced IDA's exposure to currency fluctuations through IDA 3. The United States then made the elimination of MOV provisions a condition of its joining IDA 4, thereby exposing the Association to exchange rate risks. Through IDA 5, IDA credits were denominated in dollars, as were repayment obligations. However, at this time the dollar appreciated sharply, reducing the dollar value of the non-U.S. donor contributions that IDA had not drawn down. The Association faced a cash loss exceeding $1 billion, which transfers from the IBRD and IDA reflows (that otherwise would have enhanced IDA's commitment authority) were used to cover.

Starting with IDA 6, the Association began denominating its credits in SDRs. Nevertheless, there was a potential currency mismatch between the SDR currency basket and the composition of donor contributions to IDA.[34]

LOBBYING. Over the years the Bank worked hard at lobbying its members in behalf of IDA. Starting with William Clark, whose arrival as the Bank's external relations specialist was contemporaneous with McNamara's, the institution ran extensive and comparatively effective programs of press and public relations. Bank presidents and senior executives found their way onto television talk shows. The presidents—especially McNamara and Conable, whose milieu it was—conducted active programs of arranged but informal encounters with American legislators. The presidents and senior officials were in frequent and recurrent contact with ministers and heads of those governments that were heavy subscribers to IDA.

The IDA 5 negotiation offered as nice a vignette as any of what a basketball fan would call a "full-court press" by Bank staff. The time and place were January 12, 1976, the president's office:

> Mr. Gerin-Lajoie had told Mr. McNamara privately in Jamaica that Canada was willing to take the lead in the forthcoming London meeting and support a $9 billion IDA replenishment. Mr. McNamara said he was willing to go to Canada whenever this would be

---

33. Minutes of President's Council meeting, February 16, 1970.

34. In IDA 5, the SDR was a twelve-currency basket with a composition reasonably close to donors' comparative inputs into IDA. But on January 1, 1981, the SDR moved to a five-currency basket, increasing the risk of mismatches with the composition of the IDA inputs.

considered most useful. Mr. King from the U.K. said that his Government had avoided a cut in its foreign aid program and was now in a better position to move ahead on IDA5. The U.K. would favor an increase in real terms. Mr. McNamara asked Mr. Diamond to work on Canada and the U.K. to obtain a strong statement at the London meeting. Mr. Diamond said that he was doing this and also wanted to include Norway and Kuwait in the group of leaders. Mr. Lubbers would approach the Norwegian Government. Mr. Cargill's visit to Kuwait had been postponed. The plan was now for Messrs. Cargill and Diamond to go to Kuwait before the London meeting. Mr. McNamara said that he was concerned that no OPEC ministers had been present in Jamaica. He had talked to Mr. Al-Hamad and expressed his concern, particularly with respect to the Bank's relationship with Saudi Arabia. Mr. Al-Hamad would visit Saudi Arabia and discuss the matter with the authorities and inform Mr. McNamara. Mr. Al-Hamad had said that a 10% share of OPEC in IDA5 was possible with a $100 million yearly contribution from Saudi Arabia and a $50 million contribution from Kuwait. Mr. McNamara said that the United States had no plan with respect to IDA5 and that staff work on the matter in the Treasury was clearly inadequate.

In a subsequent meeting on January 13 with Messrs. Goodman, Diamond and Merriam, Mr. McNamara requested Messrs. Diamond and Merriam to make a political study of required U.S. action with respect to IDA, including an analysis of IDA4 and a plan for IDA5. In particular Mr. Diamond should study future U.S. disbursements for IDA. Possibilities of using the U.S. portion of the restituted IMF gold for IDA contributions should also be studied. Finally, the one-year extension of IDA4, which had been mentioned by the United States, should be examined. Mr. Diamond said that the Deputies meeting after London would be held in Tokyo before the end of June. He would go to Japan before then. Mr. McNamara asked Mr. Diamond to talk to Mr. Soejima before seeing government officials in Japan and added that he was willing himself to go to Japan. The Germans should not be pressed at this stage. Mr. McNamara asked Messrs. Cargill, Diamond and Goodman to prepare a plan and strategy for the February meeting of Deputies, including required follow-up. He also asked Mr. Diamond to prepare a note on how governments' IDA commitments are transformed into payments, particularly the timing involved.[35]

Not infrequently management enlisted the heads or other representatives of some of the Bank's Part II governments to weigh in with Part I governments particularly receptive to their voices. Such was the case when, in 1975, Julius Nyerere of Tanzania was encouraged to persuade Olaf Palme, the Swedish prime minister, to lobby other Part I leaders on behalf of IDA 5. A particularly well-known and successful instance was when, in 1982, Indira Gandhi addressed Margaret Thatcher and was so effective that Mrs. Thatcher carried the cause to several of her G-7 counterparts. As a tally maintained in the finance complex revealed, the enlistment of such intervention was remarkably extensive and systematic in the case of IDA 7. Every operational subdivision of the Bank was pressed to rally its recipients to pro-IDA advocacy, and by April 1984 dozens of Part II heads of

35. Memorandum, Robert S. McNamara for the record, January 13, 1976.

governments and finance ministers had been encouraged, one by one, to press the IDA 7 case on a collection of (in some cases, as many as six) Part I counterparts.[36]

On one occasion, in 1982, when it felt the prospects for IDA 7 as well as the consummation of IDA 6 were threatened by the minimalist tendencies of the new Reagan administration, the Bank bent its full report-preparing capacities to the service of IDA advocacy. *IDA in Retrospect: The First Two Decades of the International Development Association* was produced in six months to the visual and editorial standard of a World Development Report. The authors had a tough assignment, namely, to put IDA's best foot forward without damaging the Bank's reputation for analytical quality and objectivity. They succeeded to a degree that was well received by most (Part I as well as Part II) member governments.

MEMBERS' LEVERAGING OF ISSUES. As emphasized, member governments are more accountable to their taxpayers for IDA's than for IBRD's use of resources. Singly or in subsets, they sought to tie strings to their replenishment contributions that, whether in behalf of itself or other members, the Bank's management resisted. Donor members had concerns about the direct impacts of IDA operations on their commercial well-being. Thus Canada more than once complained about not getting its fair share of IDA-financed procurement and speculated about source-tying its contributions. The United States, with the Congress the more vociferous branch, tried to stipulate that its contributions carry balance of payments protections, at least of the end-of-queue sort used in IDA 2.

More controversial, however, were members' attempts to use replenishment exercises to exert stronger-than-usual influence over IDA's lending programs. Some of these were collective efforts by most Part I members to gain more active programming roles. In particular, especially during the Bank's adjustment lending "era," Part I owner countries pressed to play a livelier role in reviewing and guiding programming at the *country,* and not just project or sectoral, level. But Bank management resisted the pressure; and the Board's conventions inhibited executive directors' demands.

"IDA deputies," however—those groups of officials from capitals who negotiated replenishments every three years and, unlike executive directors, unambiguously represented the governments that employed them—lacked similar inhibitions. IDAs 9 and 10 broke ice for the Board, stipulating a level of country-program involvement for the latter that seemed unlikely to recede. Collectively the deputies attached a growing list of conditions to their final determinations. In the case of IDA 9, for example, these included the demand that the Bank increase its collaboration with the IMF, provide for greater Board involvement in the release of SAL tranches, schedule annual country reviews, and undertake new environmental initiatives, leading to a revised Operational Directive on environmental procedures.

In IDA 10 the deputies went a step farther, prescribing that IDA was to maintain separate rising trends of both social sector and antipoverty programs.

36. Tabulation: status of IDA 7 campaign as of April 27, 1984.

Since such programs already claimed some 40 percent of IDA investment lending and 28 percent of all IDA outlays, these stipulations encroached severely on management's programmatic discretion.

The most dramatic leveraging of issues, however, was that by particular governments, and the most active of the latter (not surprisingly) was the United States. The United States, of course, did not confine its suggestion making to IDA-replenishment negotiations. But, with the Congress standing behind or reaching around it, the American administration was disposed to make its catalogue of demands not only insistent but comprehensive on replenishment occasions. In July 1973, for example, McNamara was told by the U.S. Treasury these were the stipulations under which the United States would join IDA 4: a ceiling of 33⅓ percent for the U.S. shares; aid to Indochina; an independent external audit of Bank operations; removal of the "maintenance of value" clause; a commitment that future IDA replenishments would be leveled off in real terms; restraints on the Bank's administrative budget; a reduction in the differences between Bank and U.S. government salaries; attention to the U.S. position on expropriation in Peru; and reconsideration of the Bank's position on rescheduling the servicing of its own debt.[37]

Some of the most visible single-issue pressures from the United States occurred during the Carter administration (1977–81). The administration's insistent effort to have the Bank factor political human rights into its lending criteria was not confined to, but spilled into, IDA replenishment negotiations. The most infamous intrusion from the viewpoint of other members involved the Congress. As President McNamara was boarding an airplane in 1979 he was told that if he did not then and there promise there would be no lending to Vietnam during the period of the replenishment, the IDA 6 bill faced imminent defeat. He authorized the sending of an immediate letter to the Congress so stating.[38] Subsequently he defended himself on the ground that there was no Vietnam business in the pipeline; quite aside from outside pressures, none was contemplated. But he was faulted procedurally: he should not have trespassed on the Board's prerogative to authorize loans; and he should have communicated formally only with a member's administration, not directly with its legislature.

But the United States was not the only member seeking to exert unilateral leverage during replenishment exercises. As noted, Japan pressed for, indeed tranched its subscription in behalf of, an increased voting share. Both Italy and

37. Minutes of President's Council meeting, July 2, 1973.

38. "Events of the past year have raised a very serious question about Vietnam's current commitment to a rational development policy. These questions were sufficiently fundamental to warrant a suspension of new lending to Viet Nam." Letter, Robert S. McNamara to Representative Clarence Long, November 1, 1979. McNamara signed the letter without consulting his senior staff. His Vietnam-related staff did not agree with the view expressed in the letter.

Japan linked contributions to more favorable personnel treatment for their nationals. France repeatedly demanded concessions for its clients and its policy preferences in West Africa—and won, thanks to the way a medium-size donor can hold a replenishment negotiation hostage.

By the early 1990s, if the replenishment process had not broken down, at least for the time being, it had seemed to go sour. Ernest Stern reported to the Board on IDA 10, "But the final agreement also can be seen as an unravelling of a system of collaborative multilateralism. . . . Burden-sharing has become the antithesis of collaboration."[39]

Intercountry Allocations to IDA Recipients

Because what is being distributed is mostly taxpayers' money, IDA lending has been inherently more interesting than IBRD lending to donor governments. The quantity of the former is inherently scarce, and the intercountry allocation of IDA credits has been more contentious, by far, than has been distribution of IBRD loans among country borrowers.

A Low-Income Country Ceiling

In the years before IDA there was debate over whether scarce multilateral concessional transfers should go, across the whole array of developing countries, to such needed non-self-liquidating activities as public inputs to agriculture, the social sectors, and intracountry poverty alleviation, or whether, on the other hand, they should be reserved for whole poor countries. The issue was put largely to rest in IDA's early days. The Association's Articles of Agreement did indeed authorize the new institution to finance non-self-liquidating activities, but in 1964 the Board, in a determination reaffirmed during the negotiations for IDA 2, decided that credits typically should be extended only to IDA's lower-income members.[40] In 1964 the (not unexceptional but effective) ceiling was set at $250 per capita, and that "IDA eligibility" marker, steadily adjusted upward for inflation, has remained in effect ever since. In fiscal year 1993 the figure was $1,235.[41]

But this eligibility ceiling clearly did not, by itself, constitute an allocative formula. There were not enough resources to meet all the demands of the IDA-eligible country group.

39. Ernest Stern, managing director, statement to the Board, December 22, 1992, SecM92-1579, pp. 1–2.

40. IDA, *IDA in Retrospect: The First Two Decades of the International Development Association* (Oxford University Press, 1982), pp. 7, 23.

41. Figure in 1991 U.S. dollars. Memorandum from the president, "Per Capita Income Guidelines for Operational Purposes," SecM92-1158, August 24, 1992.

Allocative Norms

IDA's overwhelming country allocation issue at the outset—and, in fact, in some senses even down to date—was India's share. In part because of the readiness of India's project and other claims, the share started off at 55 percent of the total. India and Pakistan together received 70 percent of early allocations. These, however, were thoroughly unsustainable figures, but not so much because they violated abstract norms. (Soon India's and Pakistan's *per capita* shares would fall, and ever after remain, below IDA country averages.) Rather, the absolute size of the early South Asian shares was too vulnerable to the competing claims of other Part II members and their Part I sponsors.

Although most members of IDA sought defensive support from allocative formulae from time to time, few wanted to be bound by them tightly. Similarly, Bank management and staff have resisted mechanistic allocations; they wished to retain a good measure of operational discretion in their use of resources. At the same time, all parties have recognized the advantage, almost the necessity, of having some allocative guidelines, and those that have been employed trace back to discussions in the summer of 1964. As these norms were explained to the recently arrived Robert McNamara by his deputy, Burke Knapp, in June 1968, they were the following: the recipient country had to be insufficiently creditworthy to obtain substitute credits elsewhere on serviceable terms; it had to show a record and promise of good economic performance; it had to have good projects at the ready; and its "stage of development" (that is, its aggregate level of poverty) had to warrant IDA assistance.[42]

There was a linear evolution of these norms. By the time of 1982's *IDA in Retrospect,* the same four criteria were cited, but now income per capita (that is, national poverty) came first and creditworthiness, second. It was pointed out that, although the two were closely connected, they could diverge. A poor country might nevertheless have strong external accounts. Thus, for example, Indonesia, although with an IDA-eligible per capita income level, tended not to qualify because of the abundance of its oil exports. Performance, listed third, was to be assessed in terms of macro indicators including growth and savings rates but also in terms of the quality of "administration and economic management," as well as "the speed and direction of change." (There was not yet specific reference to policy and market-oriented policy reform.) Governments were not to be penalized for matters beyond their control. Project readiness was fourth on the 1982 list; concern was expressed that the Bank and other interveners provide technical assistance in support of project preparation; but remaining constraints on absorptive capacity could not be disregarded.

Still of a piece with its past, IDA's later doctrine on country allocations was encapsulated in a 1989 document on the division of lending among IDA-eligible countries that emphasized performance considerations and provided some strik-

---

42. "Criteria for the Distribution of IDA Funds," June 19, 1968, in J. Burke Knapp files.

ingly precise estimates of what countries' entitlements in 1989 SDRs should be. Knowledgeable Bank staffers were to rate each country's performance as "high," "moderate," or "low" in each of three policy categories: short-run economic management (mainly of demand); long-run economic management (mainly supply-side restructuring); and the country's poverty-alleviation record as characterized by its delivery of social services, as well as reforms removing distortions from labor markets and from rural-urban terms of trade.[43]

According to the 1989 prospectus, a "moderate" overall performance would entitle countries in the 2–50 million population range to an annual normative IDA allocation of SDR 5.36 per capita; a "low performance" would yield only SDR 2.72, whereas a "high" performance would be good for SDR 8.75 per capita.[44] Thus at the end of the 1980s IDA's country allocation policy held itself out as performance-intensive. This is specifically the case in regard to the borrowing country's anti-poverty effort. The same 1989 document proposed that, if both short-term and long-term economic performance were estimated to be moderate, variance in the antipoverty category alone would yield this array of entitlements: for "high" poverty alleviation effort, SDR 6.30 per capita; for "moderate," SDR 5.36; and for "low" effort, SDR 4.49.

"Entitlements," of course, are not guarantees, and the Bank continued—necessarily, in terms of its procedures—only to approximate the indicated norms in its ongoing operations. But the guidelines might have considerable steering effect.

Bending the Norms to Accommodate Country Size: India, China, and the Ministates

Almost from the beginning, nations at the extremes of the population-size range of IDA-eligible countries have been treated as exceptions to the allocation norms. Evolving without much dissent, the ministate exception was formalized in the 1989 allocations document with the provision that countries of less than two million people typically would be entitled to higher than average IDA credits per capita, the rationale being that very small countries encounter significant diseconomies of small scale in their provision of public and social services.

All of the drama over the size issue, however, has been at the opposite end of the spectrum. For IDA's first twenty years, India was its only giant recipient. It was four times as populous as such other large IDA-eligible countries as Indonesia and prepartition Pakistan, and, despite South Asia's early head start in winning IDA allocations, the squeeze on India soon set in. It was feared that the giant, if treated proportionately, would soak up too much of the resource pool needed for the

---

43. World Bank, "Review of IDA Lending Allocation Criteria and Guidelines," October 1989, contained in memorandum, Alexander Shakow, SPRDR, and Heinz Vergin, OPNDR, to Moeen A. Qureshi, OPIVSV, October 27, 1989.

44. The significance of the population factor is addressed in the next subsection.

multiplicity of other claimants. By February 1968 Burke Knapp was writing, "I do take your point about India, which undoubtedly will continue to get a relatively low allocation in per capita terms, but I am afraid this will continue as a 'fact of life.'"[45] By the following month the decision to lower India's putative share of the IDA total to 40 percent (and Pakistan's to 12.5 percent) had become firm.[46]

The 40 percent norm for India stayed in place for a dozen years. The inclination of many donor as well as other recipient members to reduce it did not disappear, but management, supported by the United Kingdom and a few other Part I members, defended the norm on the grounds of fairness and of no worse than mixed reviews of Indian performance. India's status quo, however, was undermined at the start of the 1980s by the entry of the second Asian giant, the People's Republic of China, into the set of IDA claimants, just as the combined India-China share was becoming crowded by mounting concern over the urgency of Sub-Saharan Africa's IDA needs.

President McNamara in 1980–81 presided over carefully considered calculations of how, under circumstances where IDA 6 totals and projected allocations already were jelled, an IDA share for China that quickly became nontrivial could be incorporated into IDA's allocative design while minimizing the abruptness and severity of India's allocative decline.[47] But it was not possible to cushion the latter very much. Both inside and outside the Bank, geopolitical dynamics pushed for a rapid convergence of China's and India's shares, and this scenario was reinforced by the exceptionally positive working relationship the Bank established with China early on. Thus, crowded by Africa's claims, by 1989, in contrast with India's former 40 percent, the two giants wound up sharing a 30 percent slice of the IDA more or less equally. India, like China, received a good bit of IBRD money, but its "blend" had hardened remarkably within less than a decade.

One intriguing aspect of the India-China parity deserves brief mention. If the two countries were to get equal shares of a scarce resource reserved for low-income countries, it strengthened the case if China were as poor as India. In 1980, when, to be sure, the Bank had not yet been able to do any on-the-ground data work in China, its internal documentation estimated China's GNP per capita as being more

45. Letter, J. Burke Knapp to Geoffrey M. Wilson, deputy undersecretary, Ministry of Overseas Development (United Kingdom), February 15, 1968.

46. Many years later Burke Knapp recalled part of the rationale for the 40 percent ceiling: "The U.S. was putting up 40 percent of the funds. . . . The U.S. at that time might have had 60 percent of the GNP of the contributing countries, but . . . what was said was . . . 'it would be really improper for any country, whatever else might be said, to have to contribute more than 40 percent and, on the other hand, for any recipient country to receive more than 40 percent.'" J. Burke Knapp, interview by Devesh Kapur and Richard Webb, June 26, 1991, pp. 26–27.

47. Minutes of President's Council meetings, February 19, April 24, May 12, 1980; memorandum, Ernest Stern to S. Shahid Husain, "China—IDA Allocation," January 20, 1982.

than twice India's ($390 versus $150, both in 1976 dollars).[48] By the late 1980s, it amazed many analysts to find the per capita GNP figures for the two countries running neck and neck in the 1988 through 1991 *World Development Reports*, while, at the same time, China's output per head was generally reckoned to have been growing much faster than India's.

As chapter 10 indicates, some of this anomaly can be attributed to technical (exchange rate and socialist pricing) factors. But some senior Bank personnel— others firmly disagreed—joined many outsiders in seeing the statistical parity as having been politically motivated. By 1993 the Bank's conventional (exchange rates converted) estimates of GNP per capita for China and India had widened to $370 and $340, respectively.[49] Moreover, the Bank finally began to publish the alternative International Comparison Project (ICP) estimates of purchasing power of currencies (PPC) of incomes per capita in 1989 in the statistical annexes of the *World Development Report;* and when estimates for the two countries were first published in the 1992 edition, the appearance of India-China parity was shattered.[50]

Other Country Allocation Issues

The other great allocative shift in the 1980s was in favor of Sub-Saharan Africa (SSA). At the end of 1982 Ernest Stern raised his voice against regional allocative formulas. The difference between Sri Lanka and Kenya, he said, should not be a function of geography.[51] But events overwhelmed this view. At the time those proposing a regional focus on Sub-Saharan Africa mooted a 30 percent IDA share for the region. By 1989 the starkness and interconnectedness of the region's deteriorating plight had become compelling in the minds of the institution's managers, its Board, and the IDA deputies. The 1989 guidelines established a normative allocation of 45 percent for the region (with higher IDA per capita implications than those for other low-income countries, let alone for China and India).

Other issues arose from time to time around the fringes of the country allocation question. IDA-IBRD blends have been widely used for countries that are creditworthy enough to obtain some, but not enough, of their needed external funding on nonconcessional terms (or, in the giant country cases, where meeting all their

48. Memorandum, Paul V. Applegarth to Moeen A. Qureshi, February 14, 1980.

49. World Bank, *World Development Report 1993,* table 1.

50. For 1991 India's and China's comparative percentages of U.S. GNP per capita were estimated to have been 5.4 percent and 9.1 percent, respectively. A year later the comparable estimates were shown as 5.2 percent and 7.6 percent. World Bank, *World Development Report 1992,* table 30; and World Bank, *World Development Report 1993,* table 30. See technical notes.

51. Memorandum, Ernest Stern to Percy Mistry, "IDA Allocations Criteria," December 27, 1982.

IDA-worthy needs would dry up too much of the concessional resource pool). In IDA, compared with IBRD, decisions concerning "graduation," that is, complete withdrawal from access to the institution's funding, have been greatly facilitated by the maintenance of the well-known IDA ceiling. Graduation happens more or less automatically and nontraumatically.

Questions of the demotion, the retrogression, of previous graduates back into IDA recipient status have not been as easy. Such retreats were uncommon earlier but became more common in the 1980s. The Bank was reluctant to accept renewed claims on its scarce concessional resources, especially if this would reward poor performance. In the latter 1970s, for example, it rejected U.S. suggestions that the Philippines and Thailand be returned to IDA rolls.[52] On the other hand, there were instances—Nigeria in the late 1980s was such a case—in which better-off countries that have fallen onto hard times regained some IDA eligibility.[53] A few closely related cases have involved defensive (IBRD portfolio-protecting) considerations for the Bank. Indonesia in 1977 was one such case, in which it was decided that in part "because of our great concern regarding the mounting exposure of the Bank in Indonesia . . . at least $100 million a year out of our Indonesian program should be covered by IDA."[54] A similar consideration contributed to the return of the Côte d'Ivoire to partial IDA funding in the late 1980s. Zambia became a particularly obvious case in 1991.[55]

It enhances one's understanding of IDA country allocations practice to relate it to that of other aid donors. IDA's distributions of credits were more heavily concentrated on low-income countries than those of most bilateral and multilateral donors. In terms of the degree to which distributions *within* the low-income set have been driven by predetermined formulae or norms, IDA stands somewhere in the middle of the range. Some UN agency allocations have been quite rigidly formula-driven. Those of bilateral donors have been highly discretionary. IDA had its norms, and took them seriously, but was not bound by them.

A quotation from the minutes of a regular 1990 meeting of the President's Council, which was addressing the use of IDA for "debt workout" purposes, captures the range of Bank management's opinions about allocative flexibility.

52. Memorandum, J. Burke Knapp to Robert S. McNamara, "IDA Allocations for the Fifth Replenishment," May 27, 1977.

53. Minutes of President's Council meeting, September 14, 1988.

54. Memorandum, Knapp to McNamara, May 27, 1977

55. See chapter 12 and volume 2, chapter 5. In the Zambian case, the country had gone into arrears in 1987. A bridge loan from the United Kingdom and United States was arranged to clear the arrears to the IMF and the IBRD, and an IDA credit with "a high level of retroactive financing" (as Bank staff put it to the Board) was used to repay the bridge loan. After this episode, at the urging of the Nordic countries, an IDA Debt Reduction Facility, using IBRD profits, was created. Also the "Fifth Dimension" was established—for the payment of IBRD interest (not amortization)—for IDA-only countries. These initiatives are discussed under "Workout Processes for IBRD Arrears and Nonaccruals" in chapter 16.

Mr. Qureshi asked what the difference was between allocating normal IDA resources to a debt workout and the allocation of IBRD net income for this purpose. Mr. Stern said that the issue was compartmentalization. Mr. Fischer felt that there was an advantage to a separate IDA pot for debt workouts since it was hard to explain in these debt workout cases the large deviation from normal IDA allocation criteria and norms. Mr. Qureshi disagreed. He argued that the IDA did not have rigid norms. A 25 percent deviation from the norms was not considered unusual. For the SPA [Special Program of Assistance for Africa] countries it was impossible to allocate according to the norms. There was the need to deviate significantly from the norms in order to respond to the policy-based lending provided by other donors. Mr. Stern, however, felt that the norms were important. They, for example, provide a useful handle for IDA to use in cases where external pressures are placed on IDA to dramatically increase its lending and shoulder a disproportionate share of the burden. IDA needs to hold to its normal allocation criteria.[56]

Finally, although it had not been a formal criterion, de facto attention some-times has been given to complementing the actions of other donors. Such was the case when large U.S. aid to India suddenly stopped in 1972, as well as when the same country agreed, although it was poor enough to qualify, not to take money (hard or soft) from the Asian Development Bank for many years in order not to soak up too much of that new institution's resources.

Stretching and Augmenting IDA Resources

IDA credits are the Bank's concessional product. Efforts by the Bank's owners and managers to modify the product have had two objectives: to grade the degrees of concessionality the Bank's credits/loans provide to match better the spectrum of borrowing countries' needs for concessionality; to enlarge the volume of conces-sional resources available to IDA beyond that which donor member parliaments have been disposed to appropriate. In the overall sweep of things, the second appears to have been much the more important issue.

Multiple Brands versus Blends

IBRD and IDA draw from two radically different financial sources and pose sharply different terms to their borrowers. As awareness grew (it would have been hard to avoid) that developing countries, as to their creditworthiness, comparative poverty, and pro-development performance, did not fall into binary sets, the Bank and its mentors have wished to grade the concessional-nonconcessional packages offered to borrowing members into more than two categories.

The dominant solution that the Bank arrived at over the years was akin to the one that three of the four seminal 1949–51 reports on multilateral concessional

56. Minutes of the President's Council meeting, May 30, 1990, and Special Program for Africa (SPA).

assistance reached (see the subsection "Grants or Soft Loans?" early in the chapter). They thought a mixture of grants and nonconcessional loans was the best way to deliver the desired degree of concessionality to a borrower. Similarly the practice of those managing Bank country programs was to suit the *blend* of a country's IDA and IBRD borrowing to its characteristics (along with, especially in the case of the giants, the competing claims of other borrowers). "IDA eligibility" served to "entitle" the borrower to only *some* IDA money. How much of its total borrowing need it got in soft-money coin—whether it was a blend, at all, and, if so, how much of a blend—depended on the strength of its claim.

If this is the way the institution, more or less simply and successfully, coped with differentiation, then the contemplation or creation of a separate intermediate facility (for example, the so-called Third Window considered in the 1970s) interposed as to softness between IDA and IBRD must be seen as a temporary detour.

Nonparliamentary Augmentations of Concessional Flows

The thought of getting more soft money than donors seemed ready to provide entered the minds of the Bank's managers almost as soon as its soft-loan affiliate entered its doors. At least two early hypothetical strategies for doing so loomed up.

INTEREST RATE SUBSIDIES. Interest rate subsidies of the sort Governor David Horowitz of the Central Bank of Israel proposed to the initial United Nations Conference on Trade and Development (1964–65) were quickly the subject of a World Bank staff paper ("The Horowitz Proposal," 1965). The idea was to go to the market for capital but to provide it to poor countries at a subsidized rate with some benign agent—for example, donor governments—supplying the interest rate spread. At first blush it looked as if taxpayers' money used this way could generate a large multiple of the ODA it could fund directly. The difficulty: the donor's obligation to fund the rate spread persisted for the life of the loan. Thus if the latter were twenty years and a program of subsidized lending continued for twenty years, the ODA budget eventually would be dominated by a sandwich of annual subsidies twenty layers deep, and the aid program would have little current mobility. In principle the problem could be solved if the benign source would provide an endowment of capital sufficient to earn enough to cover the interest spread. But, for an enlarged ODA flow, that would require a one-shot capital input so massive as to be quite implausible politically. The conclusion (although the idea of interest subsidies would keep turning up in Bank discussions): interest subsidies are a feasible foreign assistance alternative only for loans of far shorter durations than IDA's.

THE SDR LINK. The idea of the SDR link was mooted when special drawing rights were first distributed as a new reserve currency in 1970. It was an interesting pro-development scheme: instead of being distributed in accordance with IMF quotas, this newly created international money would first go to developing countries from whom developed countries wanting the extra liquidity that the SDRs would afford, would have to buy it with a round of aid goods. Many "link" advocates, moreover, saw IDA in a pivotal role: instead of the SDRs going directly to the developing countries, IDA would receive the SDRs in the poor countries' behalf as a supplement to its donor funding and then subject these resources to its normal modes of distribution.

But the SDR link would also have some problems. It was feared that the development-promoting purpose would run away with the liquidity-modulating intention of the innovation and turn it into an engine of international inflation. For this and other reasons most of the principal donor governments rejected the link proposal. Furthermore, the SDRs came to have interest rates equivalent to short-term market rates attached to them. Therefore even if it could be provided that their accretion as a supplementary form of IDA funding always would be driven only by liquidity, not development, considerations, their interest rates would have to be subsidized if the SDRs were to be converted into concessional transfers. And that would invoke all of the problems of subsidizing interest on long-term instruments already discussed.

Thus these initial ideas came to very little as far as IDA supplementation was concerned. Remaining issues as to nonappropriated IDA resources can be divided along external-internal lines. On the one hand are there remaining possibilities for nonbudgetary/parliamentary *external* sources? On the other hand, what supplements to IDA funding can come from *within* the World Bank Group itself?

In 1985 the first question was tackled by a "Netherlands/Nordic Working Group" established to assist the Development Committee's Task Force on Concessional Flows to consider "nontraditional" (that is, "exotic," extrabudgetary) forms of aid. The setting was that these country members of the task force were reluctant to give up on these hopeful possibilities. At their own expense, therefore, they commissioned an able and seasoned set of specialists from inside and outside their governments to have a go at the subject. The group squeezed all the known alternatives—seabed royalties already were lost, the SDR link was a nonstarter, international taxes or checkoffs of domestic taxes had no early future—and came out, reluctantly, with a firm negative.

Two internal sources of IDA funding may be important in the future:

—Assignments of Bank income already have made important contributions to such favored uses as the CGIAR budget. The capacity will continue and be nontrivial but limited.

—Reflows from past IDA lending are, of course, rising and become available for direct IDA redeployment. The growing dimensions of this source suggest to those who value institutional autonomy that the happenstance that the original IDA design's choice of soft loans rather than grants as the concessional agency's principal product was a considerable blessing.

Conclusion

The IDA lessons are vivid. IDA has made the Bank what it is, in terms of scope of clientele and range of service. But the taxpayer source of IDA resources always has posed a threat to Bank autonomy. For a couple of decades the threat was staved off by the protective coloration of the seamless IBRD/IDA web and (in some measure) by gifted and energetic management. But after 1980—with the higher silhouette of adjustment lending, a pricklier United States, and scarcer resources all around—IDA's cushioning against dysfunctional intrusions was badly eroded.

EIGHTEEN

The Bank's Institutional Identity: Governance, Internal Management, External Relations

THE FOUNDERS of the World Bank created what turned out to be an enduring *institution* —which is to say, an organization of some staying power whose character could not be conveyed simply by adding up the functional elements. There was a corporate identity that, for the institution, was roughly comparable to what personality is to a person. The identity expressed itself both in internal characteristics and behaviors and external relations, and it evolved. It would be remiss not to try to capture the institutional story.

In its first fifty years the Bank grew enormously, provided a stage and context to some vivid personalities, and underwent several quite profound, sometimes abrupt changes of role and course. Yet, arguably, the most noteworthy feature of the institution was its continuity, the hardiness of a set of characteristics it acquired in its very early years. The elements of the identity that formed before the end of the 1940s constituted a kind of base upon which the character of the institution thereupon evolved sequentially. That evolution can be divided into periods, and those adopted for the purpose of this discussion are the presidencies: Black, Woods, McNamara, and the three following McNamara, stopping with Preston's last full year, not because presidents always have dominated institutional events but because their comings and goings set neutral milestones for the account.

The Formative Years: 1944 to 1949

The first thing to be said is that the institution started very small. When it opened for business in June 1946 it had only a handful of employees. At Bretton

Woods the Bank had been the also-ran. It was an unknown quantity, not lacking interest for such early and eminent appointees to its Executive Board as Pierre Mendes-France of France, Robert Bryce of Canada, and Luis Machado of Cuba. But, with a low, indistinct silhouette, the new Bank was too problematic to threaten anyone very much. Together with its funding arrangements, its inconspicuousness gave the institution an untrammelled opportunity, incrementally, to acquire scale and force.

Out of the Limelight

It was hard to find a president for the new Bank. After several others declined, Eugene Meyer, former investment banker and government official, current publisher of the *Washington Post,* signed on for the job in June 1946 at age seventy. Meyer made several formative decisions and did some important hiring. But immediately he got into a debilitating tug-of-war with Emilio Collado, the aggressive U.S. executive director, formerly of the State Department, over the comparative prerogatives of the Bank's management and Board. Meyer's appointment of Harold Smith, former U.S. budget director, as Bank vice president, did not work out to the liking of Meyer or others. The president abruptly resigned—in a scant six months—and the fledgling institution was thrown into an even deeper presidential appointment crisis that ended when John J. McCloy, New York lawyer and wartime Washington official, was persuaded to take the post in February 1947.[1]

McCloy's arrival was a major punctuation point. He won a concession from the Truman administration that, with Collado out, the U.S. executive director would be one agreeable to the Bank president.[2] The new president, consequently, brought a three-man team from New York: himself together with, as vice president, Robert Garner, long-time commercial banker and latterly vice president of General Foods, and, as U.S. executive director, Eugene Black, vice president of the Chase National Bank. Most important, before taking over, McCloy secured from the Bank Board a protocol whereunder henceforth all loan proposals would come from Bank management; the Board would be limited to reacting to management initiatives: "It was understood . . . that . . . the management would actually manage the institution and the directors would play the usual role of general supervision without interference in the conduct of the business."[3]

Two early circumstances had particular institutional consequences. "Reconstruction" (especially of war-torn Europe) was the first of the two purposes the

1. Sensing lack of support in the Board, Smith resigned when Meyer did, agreed to stay on as interim acting president but then died unexpectedly in January 1947.

2. For more detail on organizational matters in the Meyer and McCloy presidencies, see Edward S. Mason and Robert E. Asher, *The World Bank since Bretton Woods* (Brookings, 1973), chaps. 3, 4.

3. Richard Demuth, interview, World Bank Oral History Program, 1961, pp. 8–11.

institution's name suggested, and the Bank's initial (1947) lending did indeed consist of non–project reconstruction loans—to France, the Netherlands, Denmark, and Luxembourg. But it soon became apparent that reconstruction needs in Europe were quite beyond any scale the International Bank for Reconstruction and Development could reach quickly. The U.S. bilateral response was the Marshall Plan, proposed in June 1947. President McCloy was gracious and probably effective in the support he gave the Marshall Plan legislation, but he had little choice. Circumstances rubbed in the fact that the IBRD was still a quantitatively modest venture relative to the world's needs; the Bank acquired a certain air of detachment. It continued to make investment loans to governments of the future Organization for Economic Cooperation and Development for reconstruction purposes for some time. But such loans accounted for only a small fraction of ongoing official lending. By default, the situation forced the Bank quickly to concentrate on the "development" half of its declared mission. This was a cause of which the Bank staff's knowledge was modest, as was that of most other contemporary interveners.

The other institution-shaping factor was the funding mechanism with which the Bank was equipped. Unlike most other postwar multilaterals, the IBRD got an endowment of paid-in capital. This endowment grew with the institution, partly through the paid-in capital contribution of future capital increases, but more, through transfers to reserves from net income. Second, as early as the Meyer presidency it was decided that, instead of guaranteeing private loans to borrowing member countries, the Bank typically would lend to the latter directly, using resources that, with the help of members' guarantees, the Bank had borrowed in private financial markets.[4] Because the institution tended to lend as a monopolist—the individual borrower had few alternative suppliers of the loan types and terms the Bank offered—the Bank had the capacity to mark up its loan rates as needed. And the price inelasticity of the demand for its loans was exploited in another way: the Bank, especially since it did not need to strive for a profit with the same diligence as a private bank, could add the costs of extra vetting, extra analysis, and extra technical assistance into the body of a government's borrowing and still cover the enlarged total under markup pricing.[5]

4. At Bretton Woods the expectation was that the Bank guarantee would be the main mode of investment assistance. However, the private lenders preferred to lend to the Bank, new as it was; the borrowing governments preferred to borrow from the multilateral agency rather from private lenders/investors, especially in markets that were not yet ready again to accept developing-country bonds; and the Bank did not shrink from the more direct role.

5. The markup was not assured: sometimes (see chapter 16) interest rate and exchange rate leads and lags could leave the Bank at a disadvantage. But the *average* arrangement was appropriately and securely profitable to the institution. It should be further remarked that if the Bank had stuck to relying mainly on the guarantee mode of investment intervention, the "markup" pricing just described still might have been possible; fees would have been charged for guarantees, and demand for them presumably would have been inelastic. But the income-generating propensity of direct lending was transparent and straightforward. It enhanced the comfort zone around the Bank.

These financial birthmarks were long lasting.[6] In the first place, as is emphasized repeatedly in this work, they meant that the Bank's preemptive first task in the 1940s and 1950s was to earn a good credit rating in New York. This preoccupation was powerful in shaping the organization. The McCloy-Black team, as noted, all came, at least figuratively, from downtown New York. Insofar as the Bank displayed economic ideology and American political preferences, these tended to be those of New York financial circles. Harold Smith, a technocratic New Dealer, was gone, as was the State Department New Dealer, Collado. As between the two American cabinet departments rivaling for closeness to the Bank, John Snyder's Treasury won preference over State.

The two U.S. departments both had played parental roles. Treasury's Harry Dexter White wrote the American plan for the Bretton Woods institutions, but the secretary of state issued the invitations to the conference. Like the other early members of the Fund and Bank, the United States made its ministry of finance, that is, the Treasury, senior ministry for international financial purposes. This was settled in the U.S. Bretton Woods Agreements Act (signed just before President Franklin Roosevelt's death), which made the secretary of the Treasury chairman of a new National Advisory Council (other members: State, Commerce, Federal Reserve, Export-Import Bank) launched to oversee relations with the Bank and the Fund. Treasury was assigned to sustain the U.S. government's primary interface with the Bretton Woods institutions and to pursue the government's interests respecting them with the Congress. At the same time, State would continue to maintain a close watch on Fund and Bank affairs, especially as they affected particular foreign countries and regions.

The other consequence of the financing mode was quiet but profound. Incrementally during the 1940s and 1950s the small but growing new Bank discovered that the constraints on its administrative budget were soft and accommodating. The Bank made money; it more than could pay its own way. It could go first class, and hire and develop the quality to justify doing so. This is not to say the institution became profligate. A key staffer of the time recalls that Bank leaders worried a great deal about not becoming easy spenders.[7] Garner, the most conservative of the McCloy-Black team, was reputed to be a particular economizer, at least until he got his own (IFC) agency. And, although in the 1950s the Bank had the resources to start on its own the Economic Development Institute experiment that began in 1956, President Black ruled that EDI would not be launched unless it got financially substantial votes of confidence from the two American foundations (Ford and Rockefeller) evincing interest.[8]

6. The two degrees of financial freedom just noted—one from the earnings on the endowment, the other from rate markups—were due to be reinforced by a third once IDA got under way, since funders of that program were required to contribute to the institution's administrative budget.

7. Richard Demuth, interview with the authors, September 13, 1995.

8. J. Burke Knapp, interview with the authors, October 10, 1995.

Nevertheless, there is no question that the ability to incur higher rates of service-delivery charges than most other public agencies became a distinguishing characteristic of the World Bank. Per million dollars lent, it could employ more staff at higher average salaries, hire more consultants, commission more country studies, hold more seminars, issue more publications, and provide its functionaries better creature comforts.

Weighted Members

Straightaway at Bretton Woods it was decided that the distribution of control of the World Bank among member governments would be sharply different from the voting pattern—each flag with one vote—that would be adopted for the United Nations General Assembly a year later. Instead Bank members' votes were to be weighted, not by population (as is the case with the allocation of votes among the geographical components of many national assemblies) but by countries' comparative economic saliences. The formula for the Bank adopted at Bretton Woods essentially followed that chosen for the International Monetary Fund. In the year preceding the 1944 conference the U.S. Treasury had proposed a distribution based on countries' gold and dollar balances and the volume and variability of their international trade. The comparatively newfangled concept of national income was added to the mix, partly because of its intrinsic importance, partly because the gaps and uncertainties still surrounding such estimates left abundant room for political bargaining.[9]

The bargaining, using the American formula and a British counterpart as points of departure, that eventuated at Bretton Woods understated the gap between North and South that came to be conventionally recognized when serious national income estimates and country comparisons of such estimates based on the exchange rate became available a few years later. In the Bretton Woods allocation, those countries that would become the OECD got about 70 percent of the total quotas, whereas, under the statistical conventions that would prevail a decade or two hence, their 1947 figure was considerably higher.[10] On the other hand, if and when global national income accounting got around to general use of "purchasing power parity" (PPP) gross product estimates—a change that had not yet come fully to pass at the present writing—most North-South gaps would be narrowed, and a 70 percent share of the world's productive activity in 1947 would be much closer to the mark for the future OECD.

9. J. Keith Horsefield, ed., *The International Monetary Fund, 1945–65: Twenty Years of International Monetary Cooperation*, vol. 1, *Chronicle* (IMF, 1969), pp. 94–100.

10. The 1947 references in this paragraph are to subscribed members on June 30, 1947. There were forty-four, compared with the forty-five listed at Bretton Woods. From the earlier list the USSR had withdrawn and Australia, Haiti, Liberia, and New Zealand had not yet joined. Côte d'Ivoire, Lebanon, Syria, and Turkey had been added.

Some of the country estimates of comparative economic saliences contained within the Bretton Woods total were quite skewed. Thus, although the shares of IBRD stock allotted to China and India (6 percent and 4 percent of total stock) were plausibly high compared with those of other developing countries, the United Kingdom's share (14 percent) was grossly high compared with that of France (6 percent). However, in terms of future national income estimates based on the exchange rate, the founders got the United States' share of Bank stock about right. The United States (and this was the dominant fact about the distributing of institutional stock) was accorded 35 percent of the total—which, once such things were reckoned, would not be far off from the U.S. share of global product at the time.[11]

The founders of the Bank coupled this capital share with unique governing rights for the United States. The Articles provided that certain major changes— notably amendments of the Articles themselves—could be effected only by con- stitutional majorities of at least 80 percent. Only the United States had the 20 percent of the shares that qualified a single member to block such changes. The United States had so much more than this threshold that for many years there was generous space, as new members were added to the Bank, for paring the U.S. share without disturbing its veto.

The very decisiveness of the U.S. lead in the Bank's governance may have contributed administrative flexibility in the early years, especially as to hiring. Most other multilaterals tended to be caught in a stultifying web of national hiring quotas. In the Bank there was no apparent prospect that recruits from another country or country group would displace the U.S. lead in the institution. Thus there was little appetite for taking on the inefficiencies inherent in a system of formal national job entitlements. Instead the tendency—not invariant but typical—was to build a meritocracy that was less preoccupied than were many multilaterals with matters of nationality and region.

Members of the Club

The young Bank had a strong tendency to build a distinctive, self-reinforcing in-group. There was a fair national and occupational diversity in the early staff—

11. The founding developing-country members of the Bank seemed not to have thought the allocation of stock shares to the United States was excessive. On the contrary, Latin American members, because of the paid-in capital requirements that went with Bank (as opposed to Fund) voting shares, objected to the heights of their allocations. To accom- modate them, the United States accepted an extra percentage point or two of the stock. To fill out the details of quotas and shares allocations a bit more: membership in the IMF was a precondition for membership in the IBRD. Switzerland remained outside the Bank until 1992 because it objected to the disclosures that would attend joining the Fund. Australia and New Zealand had the same objection, but held out against joining only for a year or two at the start. San Marino was the only country that joined the Fund but not the Bank.

Americans, British, a surprising number of Dutch, bankers, lawyers, a few economists (more of the last would start coming in the 1950s). But from the beginning there was a heavy emphasis on quality: the Bank paid well and recruited well.

And, as just indicated, from early on there was a tilt in the staff toward homogeneity, toward a measure of denationalization. Staff and would-be recruits from the European continent, and from other regions than temperate North America, might well add, "Yes indeed—*Anglo-Saxon* denationalization." Such, certainly, was the case with language. The commitment to nothing but English as a working language (so unlike the United Nations) had consequences for the Bank and the Fund. It skewed employment access significantly, favoring South Asia over East Asia, for example, and, in Europe, applicants from the British Isles over those from the continent. Moreover, in the case of candidates who were not native English speakers, recruitment favored graduates of institutions, especially American and British, that taught in English. The Bank's English medium commitment also had something of an elitist result, although any common language requirement would have had a similar effect. In non-English-speaking societies as well as those, such as South Asia, where English was a prominent second language, fluency in the language tended to be correlated with preferred economic and social status.

The new Bank prided itself on having a different style and pace from the U.S. government whose Washington address it shared. We have spoken frequently about the Bank's extensive, albeit sometimes stressful, relations with its "twin," the Fund. And, of course, from its earliest years the Bank had close relationships with its borrowers. Similarly, it was not distant from the financial markets and institutions from which it wished to borrow, or from governments from which it sought permission to engage in such borrowing. But as to the rest of its external relations, the early Bank had a standoffish, arm's-length style, in part, no doubt, to avoid acquiring encumbering associations in the eyes of private financial institutions lending to it. From the beginning, such standoffishness was vividly the case with respect to the United Nations. In 1944 the Bank's Articles of Agreement required it to "give consideration to the views and recommendations" of competent international organizations.[12] And the 1945 UN Charter provided that the "various specialized agencies, established by intergovernmental agreement and having wide international responsibilities were to be brought into relationship with the United Nations" under the umbrella of the Economic and Social Council. The respective agencies were to negotiate relationship agreements with ECOSOC. Among other things, the Charter empowered the UN General Assembly to "examine the administrative budgets of . . . specialized agencies with a view to making recommendations to the agencies concerned."[13]

When the Bank's new executive directors first met in May 1946 they found awaiting them a letter from ECOSOC recognizing the Bank's identity as a special-

12. IBRD, *Articles of Agreement,* art. V, sec. 8.
13. United Nations, *Charter of the United Nations,* art. 17 (3).

ized agency and asking that the negotiation of the Bank–UN agreement be started. Other specialized agencies—the International Labor Organization and the Food and Agriculture Organization—had already entered into such agreements. But the Bank (management and Board) and the Monetary Fund—both with different financial sources than the other agencies—decided to stall. Prolonged negotiations ensued. Based on a draft whose author, Richard Demuth, later remarked was more a declaration of Bank independence from than cooperation with the United Nations, an agreement was finally and grudgingly approved by ECOSOC and the General Assembly in late 1947. The Bank meanwhile fell into an ongoing pattern of participating in ECOSOC's Administrative Committee on Coordination and sending observers to ECOSOC meetings, "putting up," a Bank representative to the UN later stated, "a mist of cooperation."[14]

One further note is worth including in this sketch of the institutional beginnings that occurred through the McCloy presidency. It teaches that an element of randomness has operated in Bank affairs since the beginning. One might suppose that a procedural mandate built into the very constitution of the institution would have a good chance of being implemented. Yet, although the Bank was instructed by the Articles to appoint a distinguished Advisory Council (it did) and meet with that body at least annually, the council met only twice, in 1948 and 1949. As the Articles had directed, the council included "representatives of banking, commercial, industrial, labor, and agricultural interests."[15] The meetings were contentious and inconclusive. "It was through this medium," say Mason and Asher, "that other specialized agencies of the UN system, which would be consulted in appointing members of the council, hoped to exercise some degree of influence on Bank policy."[16] But the hope was aborted; at this writing the third meeting of the council has yet to be called.

If John McCloy's arrival punctuated the early history, his departure, in May 1949, came sooner than expected. It suggested that, despite his solidifying effects, the Bank's prestige was still limited: McCloy, who had been restless to get on with his career, accepted posting as the U.S. high commissioner in Germany. Eugene Black began a presidency that would exceed 13 years.

The Years 1949 to 1962

The transfer of Bank leadership from John McCloy to Eugene Black was full of continuity; they had been virtual partners. Under its new president the institution

14. Mason and Asher, *World Bank since Bretton Woods*, pp. 54–59, provide a fuller account of these events. The statement is that of Donald Fowler, interview with the authors, November 13, 1992.

15. IBRD, *Articles of Agreement*, art. V, sec. 6.

16. Mason and Asher, *World Bank since Bretton Woods*, p. 32.

would have 13 years to grow moderately, entrenching already established traits. Yet the evolving experience was not uneventful. By 1959 the Bank would achieve its first great practical goal—an AAA credit rating with the leading financial evaluation agencies—and two major sets of experiences would be accruing, the one involving programs and personnel, the other (the principal governance issue for the 1950s bank) relations with the institution's largest owner.

Projects, Regions, and the 1952 Reorganization

As chapter 9 reports, there was a quiet explosion of project work and project emphasis in the World Bank between 1949 and 1960. The emphasis had been mandated by the Articles. Good project work became a proud specialty of the Bank. Capacity to do it was enhanced by the enlistment of field-seasoned technical specialists being released by the disestablishment of colonial governments under-way in Asia and starting in Africa. By sticking methodically to its project knitting, the Bank managed to stay above much national political turbulence, both in its industrialized members and in its borrowers.

In 1952 the Bank undertook its first major reorganization (others would follow in 1972 and 1987). There were several motivations. One was to devolve loan operations into a regional pattern. Such operations had been highly centralized—for one reason, to optimize the use of scarce technical and other specialists without letting them become regionally segregated. Also there had been pressure from the Executive Board. Once the latter had been faced down by President Mc-Cloy's assertion of management's initiatory prerogative, the Board had been at pains to demand that the Bank's transactions with its several clientele regions be evenhanded, and therefore centrally controlled. But now some pro-decentralization pressures were building. The sheer (mounting) size of the loan portfolio made such a case; more insistently, there was a perceived need for the Bank to give more weight and focus to countries—borrowing countries—as units for Bank decisionmaking. The 1952 reorganization distributed operations to three area departments (Asia and the Middle East; Europe, Africa, and Australasia; and the Western Hemisphere) and made countries the units of programming within each.

But then the reorganization included a measure—the launching of a new "Tech-nical Operations Department" (later renamed the "central projects department") —that proved that the lodestone of the design was attempted balance between the countries-areas side and the sectors-projects side of the Bank. As emphasized in chapter 9, there was a potential competition between these two that was due to become kinetic. But for now the effort was to do two things—build area depart-ments while, at the same time, creating a powerful *central* projects department to structure the Bank's surging projects work. In the minds of some of its designers, in short, the attempt was to achieve a marriage between the Bank's "diplomatic" and "technocratic" components that required them to share staff and line functions.[17] Each had some of both.

The 1952 treatment of economics as a Bank activity provides an interesting twist on the foregoing and is worth noting because of the privileged role economics work was due to play in the Bank's later development. Compared with the technical fields, economics got an inverted decision in 1952. There had *been* a central economics department, which now was mostly dispersed to the Bank's geographic (i.e., country and regional) units. Our coauthor Jonas Haralz (of chapter 13), who was a Bank economist at the time and was transferred to the Western Hemisphere Department, recalls this as a bounty for people like himself; they got to do "real" economics, mixing into real developmental decisions—unlike the rump central economics staff that remained after the 1952 reorganization. That staff continued to be headed by the statistician noneconomist, Leonard Rist, whom Black had hired as chief economist, and it continued for two years yet to include Paul Rosenstein-Rodan, the academic star among the early Bank's economists.[18] But as Haralz recalls it, these central economists in the 1950s wielded little influence compared with what country economists often were able to accomplish.

There is a distinction here that will remain important in Bank affairs. Haralz and his country economist colleagues were doing applied country analysis—using their professional tools and training to illuminate specific contemporary development and policy needs. The efforts of their counterpart central-staff economists to make cross-country diagnostic and policy-prescriptive analyses and models for the Bank's general edification got only a limited hearing in the 1950s. Later on central research economists would command more attention.

How Autocratic, and How Un-American?

Eugene Black's term provided full disclosure of the salience of the office of World Bank president. Once they are in place, the heads of multilateral agencies tend to have a good deal of discretion. In the case of the Bank, this had been evident already in John McCloy's time. As we saw in the matter of the Articles' mandate concerning an Advisory Council, the constraints that the constitutional law of the institution placed on management were not very rigid. The Articles required interpretation, and, short of unlikely appeals to the very governors of the

17. See the discussion in chapter 9. The characterizations were by John H. Williams (quoted by Mason and Asher, *World Bank since Bretton Woods*, p. 76), an astute early observer of the institution.

18. Rosenstein-Rodan, who was No. 2 to Rist, served seven years (1947 to 1954) before moving to the new development economics program at MIT. Many recognize Paul N. Rosenstein-Rodan, "Problems of Industrialization of Eastern and South-Eastern Europe," *Economic Journal*, vol. 53 (June–September 1943), pp. 202–11, as the first published paper of the new subdiscipline of development economics.

Bank, authoritative interpretations—for example, of how special "special" circumstances had to be to legitimize nonproject lending—were those of the institution's general counsels. Chester McLain and Davidson Sommers, the first two general counsels, like their successors, were very able chief lawyers. They were taken seriously by their colleagues and gave the organization valuable tactical and policy guidance. But their office was not accorded the capacity to block cherished moves (or non-moves) of the Bank establishment on constitutional grounds. The Articles were not very constraining.

What remained, if the Bank was not going to be run autocratically, was a strong resident Board. But thanks to what we can call the "McCloy coup," the Board, quite explicitly, was not strong. It was permitted no initiatives, and in response (it is quite generally agreed) the quality of its membership declined markedly during the 1950s. As a result, day-to-day governance of the Bank was indeed autocratic. But it was nearly always gracious. Although the Board was not able to put forward new initiatives, management recognized that, without broad consensus, the negative power of the Board could become a problem. Consequently, while the Board was kept on a short leash, it was treated with generous respect. The staff was valued, and most of the time President Black's last word was decisive.

In its external relations, the standoffishness that had characterized the initial years continued. The Bank minimized its identification with the United Nations. As both chapter 3 and chapter 17 on IDA recount, the desire to forestall the Special United Nations Fund for Economic Development, a major proposed capital grants program and agency, was a principal factor bringing Bank management around during the 1950s from opposing IDA to sponsoring it. Although Mason and Asher report growing cordiality between Eugene Black and Dag Hammarskjöld in the late 1950s, Bank–UN relations would not take a major forward step until George Woods.

Despite the World Bank's ideological leaning in the 1950s, it did little active fraternizing with foreign private profit-seeking firms trying to trade with or invest in developing countries, other than in mining—and the protocol was that the Bank was to relate to indigenous developing-country firms only through their governments.[19] What would later be called NGOs (nonprofit nongovernmental organizations) were less prevalent in the international development field than they would be in subsequent decades, and the Bank had little to do with them. It was well aware of the two trailbreaking American foundations, Rockefeller and Ford, that were engaging in pro-development operations in the 1950s, but until the mid-1960s, the institution's encounter with them was very limited. The foundations, in fact, probably are better classified with the development research community, in

19. In 1956, however, the International Finance Corporation (IFC) was launched as the first "affiliate" member of the World Bank Group. The subject of a separate chapter in this work, IFC has been frontally engaged with the Bank's relations with the private sector.

the universities and elsewhere, than with NGOs. But actually, despite Alec Cairncross and the EDI of which he was the first head, the Bank had comparatively little of the nexus with academic and research development-studies departments and institutes that would become so common in the 1970s and 1980s. This was less because of standoffishness than the fact that the nonofficial development studies community scarcely yet existed in the early 1950s. The analytical head start in the field belonged to such official entities as the Bank.

Eugene Black was jealous of the distinctiveness of his institution and its measure of independence. But he also was a realist. There were still very few bilateral donor agencies; the U.S. assistance agency was much the largest and in places, for example, postwar Korea, operated at a scale far beyond the Bank's capacity. The Bank and the U.S. agency, as also the French and British aid operations, stayed in reasonably close touch in the client areas they shared, and, in the case of the American agency, in Washington. Once the bilateral donors organized the Development Assistance Committee of OECD in 1960 for the purpose of exchanging information and coordinating aid policies, the Bank became a regular observer at and participant in DAC meetings.

During the Bank's early presidencies the need for interdonor aid coordination was less marked than later; there were fewer donors. But also the Bank, as a comparatively small and somewhat specialized donor, was not quickly seen by itself or others as the group's natural and pivotal coordinator. Gravitation in this direction began importantly (as a joint venture between the Bank and the United States) with the establishment of the India Aid Consortium in 1958, followed by a similar consortium for Pakistan two years later. At first these semiannual or annual gatherings served mainly to assess the recipient's need for foreign exchange and elicit pledges of assistance from participating donors. But increasingly the meetings would become fora for the review and evaluation of recipient policies and programs.

The 1950s Bank resisted direct out-of-channel member pressures on its decisions. It succumbed occasionally to various members—for example, in the 1950–52 period to U.K. interventions respecting both Iraq and Iran (see chapter 9). But its overriding—indeed, its defining—governance problem in the 1950s was its relationship with the United States. The relation was complex. At one level Black, for a true Southern gentleman, was downright raucous in his defense of turf against U.S. encroachment. Thus the rivalry with U.S. Export-Import Bank through much of the 1950s.[20] At the same time, there were substantive factors that went a long way toward harmonizing interactions with the largest donor. In terms of U.S. politics, during eight of Black's thirteen years the Washington administration that interacted with the Bank's conspicuously Republican-style team, was of an internationalist Republican persuasion.

20. Mason and Asher, *World Bank since Bretton Woods*, pp. 496–500.

In the same vein but more important, the Bank under Black and the United States were ideologically compatible. As a matter of its own convictions, not at the behest of the Eisenhower administration, the Bank was ambivalent about pushing the kind of national economic planning the new development economists were beginning to peddle; it was slow to get into softer social-sector activity, even agriculture; it was reluctant in its acceptance of the need for concessionality in international transfers; and it largely confined itself to infrastructure building because its preference for private sector over public sector industrialization was so strong.

To a fair extent, therefore, the Bank needed no philosophical brainwashing by the U.S. administration; they were twin souls. And yet Eugene Black, although on the one hand he hated to be a tame asset of his principal owner, on the other hand was a realist. The issue came to a head in a way of which little notice was taken.

The heading of this subsection is deceptive. The Bank was an international agency and therefore was supposed to be non-American, if not "un-American." But in the United States in the 1950s, "un-American" became a feared epithet, and the Bank's management concluded that it needed to knuckle under to demands of its country of residence. Concern about national loyalty in the American Congress and government in the early 1950s subjected U.S. nationals working for multilateral agencies, including the World Bank, to U.S. loyalty screenings and reviews. The U.S. demand came at the start of the Eisenhower administration in 1953. The message from John Foster Dulles was stern:

> Secretary Dulles has asked me [wrote his assistant secretary] to express to you the extreme importance he attaches to obtaining the full cooperation of all the heads of the Specialized Agencies of the United Nations in the administration of Executive Order No. 10422. He believes it is manifest that without this full cooperation the objectives of the Order cannot be achieved, and without such achievement, continued support of these Organizations by the United States cannot be assured.[21]

The Bank's Executive Board met immediately on the subject and, as management recommended, the Bank acquiesced—as did other multilaterals. In the Bank's case, Americans who got caught up in the procedure in more than a perfunctory way were defended by some of the institution's leaders, particularly, it is said, by Vice President Garner. And there were very few casualties. But the development was deeply dispiriting (it confounded illusions of autonomy). The remarkable thing is, the practice persisted. Quietly, routinely, the Bank's American new hires were subjected to U.S. loyalty clearance until, in 1986, the ruling of a 1984 case involving an American physician blocked from working for the World Health Organization was no longer contested by the government. The decision, by a U.S. circuit court, was that Executive Order 10422 had been unconstitutional on First Amendment grounds all along.[22]

21. Letter, John D. Hickerson, assistant secretary of state, to President Eugene Black, February 21, 1953.

22. *Ozonoff v. Berzak*, 744 F. 2nd 224 (First Circuit 1984). *Hinton v. Devine*, 633 F. Supp. 1023 (E.D.P.A. 1986) relied on the first case to hold Executive Order 10422 unconstitutional.

The Culture of the Early Bank

It is hard for the retrospective outsider to see the World Bank in 1962 as other than rather circumspect and rather remote. It is also hard to remember how *small* the great institution still was. In fiscal year 1962, the final one of the Black presidency, the Bank had a staff of 881 including 349 professionals. The U.S. Agency for International Development, also a Washington-based institution, employed a "regular" staff (other than 5,370 foreigners in the field) of 7,218, with 62 percent of them stationed abroad. The Bank's loan commitments that year, together with the start-up commitments of the new International Development Association's IDA credits, totaled $1.02 billion. USAID's commitments of grants and loans totaled $2.5 billion; the U.S. Export-Import Bank added another $1.9 billion of U.S. bilateral commitments.[23]

As said, the members of the smallish World Bank operation were an exclusive, merit-ridden, prudent, quite civil, and cerebral club. They did quite well a limited array of things the owners valued. The institution was literate in macropolicy issues but much less active than it would become. It already was exhibiting strong analytical and literary propensities, but more in the idiom of country studies than of disciplinary research.

Not all during the 1950s had been gray prudence. There had been flashes of great venturesomeness. Perhaps the most striking was the Indus Basin initiative discussed in chapter 8.[24] Another venture had been the launching of an Economic Development Institute with a much broader subject-matter sweep than the Bank's own operations had in 1956. The most powerful institution-shaping event during Mr. Black's tenure was the formation of IDA in 1960. But, as discussed in other chapters, the impacts and implications of this event were so central to the Woods incumbency that the subject is assigned to the next section.

The Years 1963 through Early 1968: The Bank Gets a Push

Superficially, George Woods looked like Eugene Black. He was another American banker from New York—a leading, highly successful one, appropriately (for the evolutionary stage the institution had now reached) oriented more toward the project-lending than the market-borrowing side of the World Bank's business. Woods had worked in and on India enough to be recognized as a de facto expert on

23. See *U.S. International Cooperation Administration Operation Reports,* 1962, 1963; *Export-Import Bank of Washington: Report to the Congress,* for the period ending June 30, 1963; World Bank, *Annual Report,* various issues; *The Bank Group Human Resources Strategy 1989 Update,* vol. 3, statistical appendix, table 8; Mason and Asher, *World Bank since Bretton Woods,* table 4-2, p. 67.

24. And more extensively by Harold Graves in Mason and Asher, *World Bank since Bretton Woods.*

that country.[25] Black not only knew him; Woods had done several critical pieces of work for the Bank and, particularly after the Bank president learned that such leading lights as Douglas Dillon and David Rockefeller were not available, became the successor Black preferred.

It is easy to exaggerate the contrasts between the two presidents—Black the patrician, Woods the self-made plebeian. It is true Woods was poor, from a single-parent family, was self-made, spoke with a Brooklyn accent, never went to college, and rose from seventeen-year-old office boy to become in 1951 at age fifty chairman of the First Boston Corporation, a powerful investment bank that was one of the World Bank's two designated underwriters. But Woods was no rank outsider to the culture of the Bank. In fact he had been a leading member of the New York financial establishment for a dozen years before he came to the World Bank.

Woods also had positive political credentials. He rated highly with the Kennedy administration, which earlier had tried to make him head of the United States' newly reconstituted bilateral aid agency, USAID—until the so-called Dixon-Yates embarrassment blocked the appointment.[26]

Woods brought a different or stepped-up set of substantive interests to the job. Whether or not his modest origins had anything to do with it, he was more devoted to development as a cause—to improving the lot of the poor countries—than had been characteristic of the IBRD. He was more interested than previous Bank management in poor-country agriculture and educational development. Notable among his substantive changes was his importation of his self-taught, obviously astute, interest in systemic macroeconomics. His thinking and interests were less project-bound than had been the World Bank norm.

A further difference between the two men was in personality and style. Woods was blunt-spoken, often acerbic. This was a shock coming after the gentility of Gene Black. It was much more like Robert Garner, but now the toughness was coming from the top of an organization that had featured internal good manners. Side-by-side organizations in fact vary greatly in their internal manners. Under Black the Bank had been one in which sharp interpersonal corners had been rounded; this was the style of the club. Woods came on as the unreconstructed U.S. Army major that he had been—thin skinned, given to frequent fits of temper, harsh (often before others) in his rebukes to colleagues.

Inherited Changes Woods Made His Own

As other chapters have detailed, IDA was a profoundly important turning for the Bank. In terms of perceived creditworthiness, the Bank's clientele had been shrinking. A whole new class of borrowers with weak commercial credit now (in 1960)

25. He helped set up the premier Bank-assisted development finance company (DFC) the Industrial Credit and Investment Corporation of India (ICICI).

26. See Robert W. Oliver, *George Woods and the World Bank* (Boulder, Colo.: Lynne Rienner, 1995).

was being added.[27] As Chapter 4 has described, the array of activities eligible for Bank/IDA funding was broadened; they no longer needed to be directly self-liquidating, and contributions to local costs became more acceptable.

The Woods administration embraced and advanced IDA's programmatic changes in agriculture, education, and elsewhere; the operations they supported ran down the original endowment and first replenishment of IDA funds more quickly than the Association's founders had expected; and exhorting members to produce a second replenishment proved to be the frustrating preoccupation of the second half of the Woods incumbency.

The second new input to the Bank's institutional character that Woods inherited was the YP (Young Professionals) Program. The scheme, which began as the Junior Professional Recruitment and Training Program and was renamed in 1966, was carefully prepared at the end of the Black presidency. The idea was, in the manner of such civil services as the British and Indian, to provide the Bank with a cadre of exceptionally bright and academically well and appropriately trained young professionals who would look toward long careers in the institution and "would be capable of growing into high positions in the Bank."[28] The program was shaped by a committee chaired by (then) Vice President Sir William Iliff in early 1962. Approved by the Board in June, the new venture was warmly welcomed by George Woods when he arrived in January 1963. Its governing committee and those who assisted it in choosing the first cohort included a number of noteworthy names in the Bank: William Howell, Peter Cargill, Richard Demuth, John de Wilde, Henry Fowler, Ray Goodman, Paul Hoffman, and Richard Van Wagenen, who was recruited from academia to administer the enterprise. Some of the first batch of appointees would become as famous in Bank annals as the committee members. Eleven of them were chosen from more than two hundred applicants: two from France and one each from Colombia, India, Turkey, the Philippines, Switzerland, Italy, Germany, the United Kingdom, and the United States. All were men. Five of the eleven had or were finishing Ph.D.s in economics and the other six had one or more master's degrees or other advanced credentials. Their disciplines, in addition to economics, included law and engineering.[29]

The formula worked as intended. Future YP classes would be even more selective than the first, but the baptismal group fulfilled expectations. By the

27. Decolonization in Africa led to the expansion of Bank membership from 68 in 1961 to 102 in 1964.

28. The phrase is from the first brochure for the program, issued in February 1963.

29. In contrast with the initial class, the 164 young professionals recruited during 1991–95 had the following characteristics (in percentages): Part I nationality, 63, Part II nationality, 37; women, 47; men, 53; Ph.D.s, 59; MBAs, 18; MAs, 23 (including public affairs, policy, administration); field of economics, 58; field of finance, 21; other fields, 21. In the category of country of awarding institution, the United States accounted for 62 percent; the United Kingdom for 15 percent; and others for 23 percent.

twenty-year mark seven of the eleven would still be with the Bank, and two of them would become vice presidents. As will be noted, however, problems lurked in the formula that were not appreciated at the outset.

Openings, Outreachings

As a newcomer, George Woods was less inwardly turned than his predecessors to the Bank institution. Although the YPs were due to become the Bank's classic "company men," they were high-quality fresh blood at the time of arrival, and one can surmise that Woods welcomed the fact that four of eleven came from borrowing countries. Woods also was given to fresh hirings at high levels from outside the Bank. One was Bernard Bell, found to head the controversial Bell Mission to India, discussed in our agriculture and "policy" chapters. Bell had been a senior official of the U.S. Export-Import Bank at the time Eugene Black was doing battle with that organization. Woods not only hired Bell, he kept him after the Indian exercise, stockpiling the recruit, as it were, for Robert McNamara to make him central to a new departure in Indonesia (see chapter 9). After Bernard Bell discovered Sir John Crawford to lead the agriculture end of the India study, Crawford became another Woods import (see chapter 8). Although he did not actually join the Bank, he was a shaper of Bank agricultural, and agricultural research, doctrine in the latter 1960s under both Presidents Woods and McNamara.

Woods's choice of the veteran Dutch minister, Bank staffer, and then executive director, Pieter Lieftinck, to head a great study of West Pakistan water issues in the 1960s has been discussed in chapter 8. The appointment was not quite from outside the Bank, but in terms of normal personnel procedures, it was unexpected. A more notable senior appointment from outside was that of Mohammad Shoaib in 1965 as the Bank's first vice president from a developing country. Shoaib, a former Bank executive director, had been holding the finance portfolio in Pakistan. Very important, to implement Woods's intended upgrading of macroeconomics, Irving Friedman was brought across from the Monetary Fund to serve as the Bank's chief economist.

This receptiveness to outsiders, moreover, was not just selective. Relatively speaking, under George Woods the World Bank staff experienced its peak growth. The ratio of newly arrived outsiders to insiders rose faster than during any other presidential term. The Bank opened its doors.

Finally, President Woods had little of Eugene Black's standoffishness in relations with the United Nations. He gave a forthcoming speech at the formative conference of the United Nations Conference on Trade and Development in Geneva in 1964. He welcomed collaborations with UN agencies that would marry the latter's technical expertise to the Bank's resources. Such arrangements were formalized with both the United Nations Educational, Scientific, and Cultural Organization and the Food and Agriculture Organization during fiscal year 1964.

As discussed in chapter 9, it was under Woods that the Bank's Latin American region reached out to wield influence on borrowing countries' macropolicy choices. The instruments under Gerald Alter's directorship of the Western Hemisphere Department were marshaled sets of project loans conveying macroeconomic policy recommendations. At the same time, the Bell Mission and its linkage to non–project lending in India had much the same intent (see chapter 9).

"The Decade of Economics"

Such later vice presidents and chief economists as Hollis Chenery, Anne Krue-ger, and Stanley Fischer might have been bemused if and when they heard that Burke Knapp called the 1960s "the 'economic' phase of the Bank's work"[30]—the field was more prominent during their terms. However, going back to the distinc-tion made for the 1950s between workaday country economics and central-staff research and modeling, the 1960s were a period in which George Woods was determined to beef up the institution's level of central macroeconomic analysis. Country economics remained important in all the Bank's regional operating units, and the new crops of YPs in terms of education were economics-oriented. But the president gave a boost to Bank-wide and clientele-wide macroanalysis by recruiting Irving Friedman as chief economist from the IMF together with Andrew Kamarck as director of a reconstituted Economic Department; Woods encouraged them to build the central economics staff.

Friedman, who was an able but brittle man, overreached. Despite Woods's backing, he failed to win for the Economics Committee status equal to the Technical Operations Department in clearing loan proposals—and in the process became a butt of staff ridicule. (He became a target for McNamara's sparing new broom when the new president arrived.) Doing Woods's bidding, Friedman also had a substantive failure: the Bank's members refused to adopt a so-called supplementary finance scheme (first advanced by the British at the initial UNCTAD conference at Geneva in 1964) for augmenting official transfers when developing countries ran into heavy weather cyclically.

The donors were not forthcoming. Meanwhile, however, Friedman, Kamarck, and their colleagues broke some ground for the wider swathe macroeconomics would cut in Bank work in later decades. For his part, Woods was embarked on learning a very practical and painful macroeconomic lesson—about the reluctance of aid donors to base their decisions on analyses that estimated recipients' resource needs (rather than the resource supplies donors were disposed to offer). The first IDA replenishment had been at an annual rate of $250 million. With Friedman's help in estimating recipient needs and IDA's appropriate share thereof, Woods concluded that the second IDA replenishment should be at an annual rate not less than $1 billion—and set out to implement that target.

30. J. Burke Knapp, interview, World Bank Oral History Program, October 16 and 29, 1981.

IDA's Early Strains on the Institution

For Woods IDA was a deceptive phenomenon. He saw it as the centerpiece of the job he was taking on, and its launching, albeit at modest scale, had featured U.S. sponsorship. The first funding had been run down faster than expected, and in his first year the new president watched members without great difficulty pledge their first replenishment of the program—for the next three years at an annual rate, as just remarked, of $250 million. But by his third year IDA funding turned into a continuing nightmare.

Certain complicating factors were inherent. Compared with their vetting of IBRD finance, member governments were far more jealous of the taxpayers' money they were asked to contribute to IDA. Further, as the largest contributor, the United States had an ongoing bent toward diminishing its relative burden. Further yet, by the time the second replenishment was being negotiated there was also a sharp current-events edge to the U.S. position: for the first time postwar the United States was shaken by a balance of payments problem, which made it allergic to untied transfers, like those of Bank/IDA, whose resulting U.S. exports might not keep pace with the transfers. The issue was compounded by the fact that, as noted, Woods was driven to seek a greatly expanded IDA. He sought an amount three or four times what appeared to be in view.

Finally, the problem had procedural and personal aspects. By April 1965 Douglas Dillon, friend of development transfers, was gone from the U.S. Treasury. His replacement, Henry ("Joe") Fowler, had a lower reading of the development priority—a fact that contributed to the poor chemistry between him and George Woods. Fowler demanded that, henceforward, the Bank/IDA do its own money raising.

Woods's tactical response to the assignment was unfortunate. He tried to deal with the donors one at a time, thereby maximizing suspicions of inequities. He was encouraged by his staff to propose a fail-safe arrangement for the U.S. payments balance: the adjusted U.S. contribution would not exceed IDA procurement from the United States. When this scheme was vehemently rejected by other members, an end-of-the-queue arrangement for the United States (see chapter 17) was substituted. In the end, with the second replenishment negotiation stretching out beyond the end of the Woods term, its designed annual rate was whittled down to $400 million.

The Quality of Leadership, and the Succession

What failed in the Woods presidency, basically, was effective governance. President Woods had a far more contentious relationship with the Bank's Board than Eugene Black had had. Board meetings not infrequently were combative. A few members, such as the Netherlands' sturdy veteran Lieftinck, welcomed the rough-and-tumble debate. But most did not. The allegiance to the president of the Bank's growing staff was mixed. Woods was ineffective in interacting with the U.S. Congress. His diplomacy with member governments frequently misfired. And for a man who retrospectively can be credited with a great vision for the Bank and a number of bold innovations, Woods was widely perceived to have a sour personality. Bad health may have been a factor. In the summer of his first year at the Bank, Woods almost died of an aneurism, and (although he would in fact live into his and the century's eighties) he seemed quite mindful of his mortality at times thereafter.

It is questionable whether George Woods, already sixty-two when he came to the World Bank, ever aspired to a second term, but certainly he set aside any such ambition before he was far into the IDA replenishment battle. On March 23, 1967, Woods addressed to the executive directors of IBRD, IDA, and IFC an extraordinary two-page document that had the appearance of a hasty last will and testament, setting out "my suggestion as to an interim management measure" if "I should suddenly become unable to express my views to you." The president would have had the Bank temporarily run by a three-man "Management Committee" (Burke Knapp, chairman; Shoaib; and Siem Alderweld). He dwelt longest in this short document on the governance of IFC under emergency circumstances. But then at the end he wrote: "Candidates I would suggest, to be researched and considered for the post of President of IBRD/IDA and Chairman of IFC, assuming he is to be a United States citizen, are: J. Richardson Dilworth (Rockefeller Brothers), Orville Freeman (Secretary of Agriculture), Kermit Gordon (Brookings Institute), and Robert McNamara (Secretary of Defense)."

By the fall of 1967, Woods's preference had narrowed to Secretary McNamara, with whom he had been meeting occasionally. Others in the decision-advising group, including Secretary Fowler and Livingston Merchant, the U.S. executive director, continued to consider such other names as Douglas Dillon and David Bell, former head of USAID. But Woods plumped for McNamara, as (more importantly) did President Johnson. With McNamara accepting, Johnson announced his nomination on November 30, 1967. McNamara would assume his duties the following April, picking up one of Woods's last initiatives, namely, the latter's proposal that a "grand assize" of development experts and political leaders be appointed to assess the world's policy needs for carrying forward developing-country development. The result was the Pearson Commission that McNamara set in motion.

The McNamara Years: 1968 to 1981

The World Bank had few mass staff meetings during the McNamara presidency. Indeed, one might have joined the Bank as a professional in the early or middle 1970s and scarcely seen the man at the top for years on end. He circulated through the institution's offices very little; he did not eat in its cafeterias or executive dining room; he even avoided the elevators, climbing the eleven flights to his office most days of his incumbency. He flew economy class and pressed the practice on a reluctant staff, not simply to accommodate critics but as an expression of his own taste and priorities.[31]

A Midlevel Perspective

So what would a new recruit have made of his institution in those days? He would have perceived, perhaps first, that it was growing. He might have learned at once that the Bank's country membership was multiplying. Between 1965 and 1975, IBRD membership grew from 102 to 125, while IDA membership increased from 94 to 114. The number of Part II countries in IDA increased from 76 to 93 during the period; Part I, from 18 to 21. But the stronger sense would have been of the growth of staff numbers. Professional staff increased from 752 to 2,552 during the thirteen years of the McNamara presidency. Annual YP cohorts, which as we have seen began with eleven in 1963, ran as high as thirty-four in the 1970s.

The staff was becoming more diverse in at least two ways. The number of women in professional and managerial positions rose rapidly, with the numbers from Part II countries increased from 14 percent to 35 percent in the same period.[32] At the same time, the focus of the interdisciplinary distribution that had emerged during the Black and Woods presidencies intensified. A considerable number of technical, legal, and public relations appointments continued to be made, and staff rolls started having a scattering of other-than-economics social scientists. But the dominance of economics, finance, and business-studies backgrounds was even more pronounced than during the Woods years. The economists, moreover, were in two distinct sets, although individuals often migrated from one to the other. There was a research staff larger and more serious than in previous periods, dedicated, somewhat like a university faculty, to the development of new knowledge. The researchers were meant to have spillover effects on Bank operations, but, in addition to truth-seeking for its own sake, their primary mission was to enhance the Bank's image outside the institution. Second and more numerous, "practicing" economists, mostly in the Bank's regional bureaus, engaged heavily in the "economic and sector work" (ESW) that became the analytical mainstay of the intensity with which the institution conducted its lending operations.

Almost certainly, the new recruit in the 1970s would have been impressed by the competence of the colleagues he joined. They were well trained, mainly were diligent, were of high average capacity, self-confident in their operations, and quite

31. Purviz Damry, interview with the authors, June 27, 1991.

32. Memorandum, H. R. Ripman to Robert S. McNamara, "Bank Staff Nationality Distribution," May 22, 1969. See also World Bank, *Review of World Bank Financial and Operating Programs and FY 88 Budget,* June 15, 1987, annex 6.10, p. 3.

typically had the denationalized homogeneity that had been developing in the Bank's earlier periods. Staff members had a strong, rather proud, sense of craftsmanship about their work.

There was a second (dollar) element, of course, to the 1970s growth: programs, lending, and funding all were strongly on the rise. Between 1965 and 1970, average Bank commitments were $1.5 billion and average disbursements were $1.0 billion; between 1975 and 1980, average commitments rose to $8.2 billion and average disbursements were $4.2 billion.

The new recruit would have perceived an endemic tension: the institution's signals and incentives, as well as its resources, emphatically promoted expansion. But the rhetoric and mores of the institution as strongly urged no slackening of operating—in particular, project—quality.

A new hire to the Bank in the early 1970s might have been surprised to find that she or he had joined a developmental department store. Previously the institution had been quite specialized; mainly it had done knowledgeable and seasoned infrastructure lending. George Woods had presided over a spreading of the lending portfolio into agriculture and education. But now the Bank was assembling an enhanced, administratively complex mode of agriculture and rural development lending, it had a focus on population, it was further into education, it had or was getting environment, nutrition, urban, and industry programs, and it would be trying to take on energy in a big way. At the end of the decade, having got into, it was getting out of tourism; and it largely shied away from health programs during the 1970s. But with its acquisition of the mantle of the world's leading development promotion agency, the Bank seemed to feel a responsibility, instead of lingering over comparative advantage considerations, to deal with nearly all aspects of development.

A middle-level recruit in the 1970s would have joined a staff that was an amalgam of vintages. As a group, the old hands were more wary of the new looks the new president had brought, but all vintages fell into an established mode of great operating prudence. Operationally, the Bank acted risk-averse, although in part, arguably, because it was entering riskier lines of lending. In any event, indubitably, it was paper-bound. The number of its reports grew from an annual average of 101 in the 1950s to 204 in the 1960s to 715 in the 1970s. It chewed things over to a fare-thee-well. The first paperwork on individual project-exploring missions was reviewed and edited by a series of supervisors, one after the other, all the way up to the vice presidential chairman of the Loan Committee—and then each of the whole series of further papers on the same project went through the same drill. Bank decisionmaking was prolix. Individual memoranda and reports were detailed and long.[33] Parallel clearances proliferated. And so did reviews of

33. On October 14, 1977, as vice president, South Asia, Ernest Stern addressed his division chiefs and loan officers: "I have . . . urged you to exercise control over the size of appraisal reports. . . . [M]y exhortations have fallen on infertile ground. The latest example is

previous decisions, and composite reviews of previous reviews. The reviews peaked in the Operations Evaluation Department (OED) that began as the Operations Evaluation Unit (OEU) in 1970; but this did not forestall major ad hoc evaluations by operating and analytic staff units.

While the whole phenomenon of assessing, cross-checking, and second-guessing can be attributed in good part to an institutional bent towards prudence, it was facilitated by the pervasiveness of the soft-budget constraint earlier discussed. As long as there was capacity further to check and cross-check the checkers—and at length, not cryptically—there was a Parkinsonian tendency to claim the resources available for doing so. But there were other factors at work besides sheer bureaucratic propensities. The decision process put a premium on the quality and fullness of official documentation. The institution had adopted the practice of carrying each individual loan (as opposed to batches or categories of loans) to the Executive Board for approval. Within the Bank the ability to sail loans past the Board smoothly thus became a mark of success.[34] In turn, this put a premium on the clarity and meticulous thoroughness of documentation. Another Board-related factor may have been in play. It will be remembered that the McCloy- and Black-diminished Board had gotten fractious in George Woods's time. McNamara is remembered by some of his senior officers as encouraging the policy, in order to quiet the Board, of keeping it swamped with reading.[35]

McNamara himself was a reader. One of his personal assistants recalls giving advice to a colleague inquiring about ways to elicit favorable reactions from the president, "The way to get to McNamara is to write it on a piece of paper, not to talk to him. He reads faster than people can talk."[36] The premium on staff writing also got raised by a personnel assessment process that emphasized current rather than past assignments and whose elements were not all precisely or reliably quantified. Project results often were not easily measured, especially before participating personnel had been transferred to other assignments. This put a heavy responsibility on the staffer who wanted to be appreciated to write up a good case ex ante and, if the self-appraisal was challenged, to write a still better one the next time around.

The recruit in the 1970s would have joined an institution that was still notably headquarters-centered. The reorganization of 1972, having dispersed most central

---

the appraisal report for the Calcutta Urban Development project which runs 275 pages. . . . Effective immediately, I will no longer accept . . . any staff appraisal report, the principal text of which exceeds 50 pages or the total length of which, including annexes exceeds 100." Other veterans have topped Stern's figures, saying that the average size of country economic and sector reports in their day ran to 300–400 pages.

34. The Board never—and, at this writing, still has not—rejected a loan; but management did sometimes have to withdraw loans from consideration to avoid such an outcome.

35. Documents to the Board averaged less than 300 annually in the 1950s. The number rose to 510 in the 1960s and jumped to 1,140 in the 1970s.

36. Four former McNamara executive assistants, interview with the authors, September 29, 1992.

project staff personnel to regional subdivisions, putting them, along with country and multicountry departments, under the command of regional vice presidents, had effected a measure of administrative decentralization. But, geographically, the great majority of Bank analysis and preliminary as well as final decisionmaking was done in Washington, and a large part of the life of operational staff consisted of out-and-back missions whose time in-country was calibrated in weeks rather than years. Those on mission, albeit knowledgeable and, as to the country in question, becoming more so, were received by borrowing country counterparts who perceived them as temporary visitors. At this point, Indonesia and, to a lesser extent, India were exceptions to this pattern (see chapter 9), and in many other countries the Bank had mission-servicing residential offices. But, overall, it was one of the more headquarters-centered development assistance agencies.

There was a related point a recruit would have appreciated quickly. Compared with other organizations with an international outreach—for example, ministries of external affairs—the Bank had evolved the preference that its staff, for the most part, not become geographically typecast. To start with, there was a strong tilt in operations against having headquarters-based nationals of borrowing countries work specifically on their own countries. But, further, it was the custom to move individual officers quite frequently from one geographic assignment to another. The effect, in terms of the expertise wanted in Bank operations, was to give familiarity with universal institutional policies and norms precedence over knowledge of country.[37]

Finally, one can speculate on the harmonics about the (little-articulated) style of the place that our hypothetical recruit might have picked up after her or his 1970s arrival. The Bank was distinctive. It saw itself as sharply differentiated from the United States and indeed other governments. It did not share space and mandates easily with other, notably the New York, Geneva, and Rome, United Nations multilaterals. It was moving self-reliantly away from its limited partnerships with FAO and UNESCO. Although close to, it was very distinct from the International Monetary Fund, which it saw as monolithic and rigid—compared with the limited but valued spaciousness for pluralistic thoughts and analyses in the Bank. The Bank was proud of its mission and (however critical) proud of its leader in the 1970s. It had the world-class No. 1 that staff thought it deserved.

View from the Twelfth Floor

Robert McNamara managed by leading, and part of his leadership was systems-based. As he had done at Ford and the Pentagon, he prescribed comparatively complex decisionmaking formats and procedures for the institution that were

---

37. It is at least interesting that the same distinction commonly is made between economics and the other social sciences: region-specific political scientists and sociologists are more common than region-specializing economists.

quantitative and time-bound. On arrival he instructed units to set forth five-year operational plans. Programming and budgeting were formalized and precisely scheduled. Country Program Papers (CPPs) became a regularized mechanism for relating the totality of Bank interventions in a borrowing country to a review of the latter's needs, performance, and prospects.

It was wrong, however, to mistake McNamara's quantitative vocabulary for his total message. Substantively, his span of attention was extremely wide, but he led by projecting a fairly small set of emphatic themes. Perhaps the strongest was expansion, on the principle that the world needed much more of what he believed the World Bank was meant to do. In retrospect particularly, the president's most celebrated theme was poverty reduction, with an emphasis more on absolute poverty than redistribution. There were much more specific foci as smallholder agriculture, checking population growth, nutrition, and urban development. Central principles—for example, the proposition that equity could be promoted without loss of growth or efficiency—were pursued with an intensity and conviction that were not easily displaced. Some themes, however, were nudged from center stage by later arrivals.

Theme projection became a major art form in the Bank. Presidential speeches —especially the president's speech at the annual Bank-Fund meeting—were the most prominent vehicles. The subjects, emphases, and content of such statements, eventually involving large groups of the staff, began to be plotted nine or ten months before the event. The September 1973 Nairobi speech, bringing promotion of smallholder agriculture to the antipoverty cause, was the most famous, but it was only the most memorable member of a long series.

McNamara was a complex and, in a sense, compartmentalized person. He arrived, as remarked, a dedicated promoter, not only of poverty reduction, but of efficiency and the nonsacrifice of project quality to program expansion. But—more striking—he was as intense and knowledgeable about the financial management of the Bank's borrowings as he was about the design and administration of its antipoverty and other lending. In his close supervision of IBRD bond marketing McNamara displayed some of his traits as a personnel manager.

The new president by no means wielded an indiscriminate new broom; mostly he employed the personnel he had been supplied. This was symbolized by Burke Knapp, who was the Bank's No. 2 when McNamara arrived and remained so for ten years, until he retired after three decades of Bank service. The new president, however, did fail to hit it off with a few senior staff members, easing them out in decisions that he and they arguably shared. Within a few years Richard Demuth and Gerald Alter became such cases, but the first was Robert W. Cavanaugh, the treasurer who embarrassed the institution and its new president by failing successfully to market a small September 1968 offering of IBRD bonds in Switzerland. As his replacement McNamara chose Eugene Rotberg, a lawyer at the U.S. Securities and Exchange Commission who lacked closely relevant bond-selling or underwriting experience. But he was an intellectual and personality match for the president, and by the 1980s, having become renowned for market wizardry, Rotberg would be something of an institution himself.

In a rapidly expanding bank, it was easy to leaven the scene with key recruits without much resort to dismissals. This was a major McNamara tactic. One of his inner-circle-to-be—William Clark, with British government and think-tank experience, selected by George Woods to head Bank public relations—arrived the same day McNamara did. A pivotal early appointment was that of Hollis Chenery, then at Harvard, as the Bank's chief economist. This helped lead to two other inner-circlers-to-be: Mahbub ul Haq, Pakistani economist and planner, and Ernest Stern, former deputy chief of the Pearson Commission staff and most recently USAID's chief programmer. Among the president's other, as it were, "personal" hires were his series of personal assistants (all of whom, whether by design or not, were non-Americans and went on to distinguished and productive careers in the Bank), Bernard Bell, already on board but lofted to a unique role in Indonesia, and Montague Yudelman, brought from OECD to head the institution's agricultural and rural development work.

In the course of his thirteen years, President McNamara found many more favorites among older and newly joining Bank staff members. He relied on such stars heavily, both to discharge increasingly responsible managerial assignments and for shared policy analysis and drafting. The president actively sought conceptual inputs from outside the Bank, drawing repeatedly on people such as Barbara Ward and Sir John Crawford as well as sponsoring formal high-level policy analysis exercises: first, the Pearson Commission, McNamara's implementation of George Woods's "grand assize" idea, and then, a decade later, the development-reviewing, North-South bridging commission McNamara helped initiate and shape under the chairmanship of former chancellor Willy Brandt.

The president was an indefatigable builder and wielder of influence in behalf of the Bank and the development cause. Within the institution he took great pains with one-on-one meetings with members of the Board. When Claude Isbister of Canada was an executive director, his regular private meetings with McNamara were an invaluable source of information about Board attitudes and intentions, a role that presidential staff contacts with other executive and alternate executive directors tried to play after Isbister left.[38] Other chapters including the preceding one on IDA have dwelled on the way the McNamara Bank hovered over its relations with OECD owner governments, most particularly the United States. Sometimes in Bank circles little significance is attached to the fact that McNamara, as a high U.S. official, had been visibly affiliated with the Democratic Party from 1960 on and remained so during his thirteen years at the Bank, during eight of which the opposing party held the U.S. presidency. The Bank was strenuously

38. Former presidential assistant Sven Burmester, interview with the authors, December 1995.

active in pursuing constructive relations with the U.S. government, while at the same time preserving a measure of autonomy from that government in its legislative as well as its executive (both Democratic and Republican) manifestations.

Influence was considerably a function of image. The image of the McNamara Bank, thanks to the president, was of a champion of the poor, a partisan of its Part II clients. McNamara himself related best to other charismatic leaders, whether of South or North: Julius Nyerere, Indira Gandhi, K. A. Suharto, Luis Echeverría, Helmut Schmidt. The story is told that when he first went to India and stayed in the president of India's palace in 1968, he hit it off famously with the temperamental Indira Gandhi but never got around to meeting with resident Bank staff. What kept the Bank president from appearing unrealistic or softheaded, however, were—aside from his own acumen—at least three things. First, McNamara's seconds in command, Burke Knapp, then Ernest Stern, while different from each other, supplied ballast against presidential whimsy. Second and broadly, as the presidency proceeded, the institution took on so much weight—its staff became so substantial—that it lost any capacity to appear flighty. Third, the Bank's image as a center of sober, first-class research inoculated it against the charge of misplaced emotionalism. Quite clearly, placing the imprimatur of Hollis Chenery's scholarly reputation on the Bank's analytical work from early in his tenure was one of the president's more telling moves.

Institutional Finer Print: Some Facets of the McNamara Years

The temper of the institution during a Bank presidency is defined in good part by the conjunction of lesser issues that occupy the calendar. At least seven facets of the McNamara years deserve noting: the Development Committee, relations with the regional development banks, the matter of China's joining the Bank, the Bank's posture in late rounds of the North-South dialogue, the low volume of interstate mediation in the Bank's work, slack that is said to have accumulated in the institution's internal administration, and the end of Burke Knapp's long tenure.

1. The "Development Committee"—officially the Joint Ministerial Committee of the Boards of Governors of the World Bank and the International Monetary Fund—was something of an accident. In 1974 (after the oil shock hit), the "Interim Committee" of the IMF was created to bridge to the time when a permanent small assembly of representative finance ministers from South and North had been established to monitor monetary and exchange rate policy. That body was never constituted; the Interim Committee became de facto permanent; and to avoid neglect of the Bank, a Development Committee also was established to keep watch on medium- and large-term (Bank-type) resource transfers to developing countries. In the Development Committee, the Bank had the lead, but both "twins" were involved. The two committees met at a time adjoining the Bank-Fund annual meetings and also at a half-yearly point in the spring.

Accidental or not, the Development Committee addressed a need widely felt by the middle 1970s. This concerned the number of country representatives who could effectively deliberate in a meeting. The Bank and Fund, like the UN General Assembly, were moving past the one-hundred-member mark. It was impossible for plenaries of this size to deliberate in any effective way without devolving into blocs of one kind or another. In the Bank and Fund the recognized need was for a small representative assembly of ministers analogous to the executive boards of two dozen or so directors (instead of the ten dozen or more in plenaries) which were meeting on a continuing basis.

But then, in the initial response to this intention, sheer logistics seemed to condemn the Development Committee to ineffectiveness.[39] Meeting time for the committee was confined to a single day every six months. Twenty-four ministers of finance, planning, or development assistance or their delegates were in attendance, each arriving with a prepared speech. Admitted observers from UN bodies, the regional banks, OECD, DAC, and other multilaterals were similarly prepared if time was available. There was virtually no opportunity for back-and-forth debate. Early in the committee's life it made a habit-forming decision that each Development Committee meeting should issue a communiqué. Hence before every meeting the committee secretariat prepared a draft that was tinkered with at a luncheon of principal delegates who settled the text for afternoon release. If the objective was genuine ministerial interchange, it would have been hard to contrive a more sterile procedure.[40]

Yet the Development Committee problem was more than logistical. President McNamara turned on the innovation. At the outset he had favored it, but then when the committee's first executive secretary, Sir Richard King, undertook to establish a Development Committee secretariat sufficiently independent to outclass OED's critical autonomy, the president lost interest aggressively; the Development Committee was confined to its own staff of rudimentary proportions, drawing personnel and other inputs as assigned by the Bank. By mid-1976 McNamara was telling the Board that the failure of the Development Committee was affecting both Bank and Fund reputations adversely, and other managers, notably Ernest Stern, were expressing similar views.[41]

---

39. Were it within the present scope, a similar case could be made about the Interim Committee.

40. The one exception to this logistical bleakness was the task force device with which the committee experimented during the late 1970s and early 1980s. Country members of the committee posted representatives to groups that considered particular issues at far greater length than the committee's own meetings allowed, and the task forces filed reports of some substance and interest. But the committee's use of the procedure lapsed for a decade following 1985.

41. Memorandum, Ernest Stern to Ernest Sturc, IMF, "Development Committee Board Discussion," July 14, 1976.

Defenders of the Development Committee objected that, had top management wished, its problems could have been fixed. For instance, efforts could have been made to secure a larger percentage of ministerial attendance at meetings. Possibly the meetings could have been lengthened; certainly they could have been differently ordered, with, for one thing, the communiqué exercise being eliminated or reduced. Some of this would be done early in the Wolfensohn presidency. For a long meanwhile, however, the Development Committee survived. Few of its supporters were devoted. But once it became a routine appurtenance, regularly chaired by a developing-country minister and with an image of friendliness to the third world, Bank managers believed the political costs of ending the committee outweighed the several costs, pecuniary and otherwise, of keeping it.

2. The World Bank's relations with the regional development banks were still rather ragged in the McNamara years. All of the regional banks except the European were in place by the early 1970s, but their early histories were neither uniform nor oriented in any formal way to the World Bank. If an ignorant person in the late 1980s happened onto the coexistence of the universal and regional development banks she or he might have imagined a system in which the regional banks were territorial spokes from a central institution, not unlike the relationship between the (regional) reserve banks and the Board of Governors in the U.S. Federal Reserve System. Such a guess would have been quite wrong. As to the three main regionals, the Inter-American Development Bank had been hustled together in 1959 almost in defiance of World Bank policies, particularly as to nonlending in such "soft" areas as education, agriculture, health, and planning; the African Development Bank (1964) was so preoccupied with the theme of Africa for the Africans that it was ill-structured to secure donor support; and the Asian Development Bank (1965) reflected tension between the two chief donors, Japan and the United States, in which the second acquiesced in a Japanese-led operation only when the United States needed diplomatic bolstering for its military venture in Indochina.

The World Bank did, in fact, play an active informal advisory role in the formation of the Asian Bank during the 1960s, and as the regional banks developed, a limited ad hoc division of labor (as to countries and sectors) evolved between that bank and the World Bank. But little linkage and no formal gradation of coverage or responsibility emerged within the MDB set—and, as the lead player, the World Bank during the 1970s showed few signs of such interest.

3. Joint reference to the Asian Bank and the World Bank points the way to a major institutional development of the McNamara incumbency: the launching of Bank membership for and operations in the People's Republic of China in 1980. The conspicuous contrast between the two banks was in their attendant treatment of the Republic of China/Taiwan. Taiwan had been an exceptionally constructive member of the Asian Bank, graduating gracefully from loan-recipient to donor status and supplying some outstanding personnel to the bank, especially in its

agricultural department. On the other hand, as of 1980, the Asian Bank's prospective relationship with the newly joined People's Republic of China promised to be somewhat attenuated: China would be expected to join India in forgoing the access to the bank's concessional resources that their incomes per capita would have indicated—the rationale for this forbearance being, simply, that these two giants were so large that they would soak up too much of the limited concessional resources of the regional institution if they insisted on a "poverty" share comparable to that of other members. The result was that the Asian Bank, with its nominal and quasi de facto Japanese leadership, refused to expel Taiwan from membership as a by-product of enrolling the People's Republic, and the latter, while protesting, accepted the outcome. The affront to China's sovereignty was less conspicuous than it would have been in the World Bank case.

The position in the World Bank was different. The Republic of China (the antecedent of Taiwan) had started off as a charter member, occupying the Bank's China slot. Therefore, when the People's Republic of China was ready to join, Taiwan had to be displaced from that slot. Moreover, it was President McNamara's final year. In terms of real politick, for completeness, the world's greatest development institution needed its largest developing country as a member, especially at a time when China already appeared to be entering a stage that was more receptive to the kinds of inputs the Bank offered.

McNamara was heavily engaged in setting the initial pattern of the World Bank's China involvements. For its part, China's demands on the World Bank were multiple and insistent. It was adamant about Taiwan; hiring of Taiwanese nationals, data on Taiwan, and Taiwan-related nomenclature all needed the approval of the People's Republic. IBRD lending to China was not to exceed the country's receipt of IDA credits. And Bank publications mapping or discussing Chinese borders in dispute with other countries required China's clearance.

4. In the later days of the North-South dialogue in the New International Economic Order (which, as noted, can be viewed as ending in the Cancun, twenty-one-country summit of October 1981) the World Bank kept its own counsel. Bank management parroted neither Part II nor Part I positions, having done its best, by inspiring the Willy Brandt Commission, to provide a bridge between them. The chances that the two blocs could accommodate their differences in the launching of a New Round of Global Negotiations in late 1980 were aborted, in good part, by the fallout of the second oil shock on OECD member governments. The "New Round" debated at the UN overlay a longer-booked exercise, that to draw up an International Development Strategy for the Third Development Decade (the 1980s), and it was in the latter that the Bank provided a perspective on the North-South debate that was comparatively conservative as to feasible goals. Thus of the various major projections of the developing-country average growth rates that should be targeted for the 1980s, the Bank's estimate—some 5.6 percent real growth per year—was the lowest. Analytically the Bank preserved its reputation for

sobriety. But, compared, for example, with the U.S. (Carter administration) delegations to the ongoing UN plenaries at the turn of the decade, Robert McNamara was careful not to make any strident attacks on Southern aspirations. The Bank avoided the main lines of fire.

5. An institutional facet that was largely missing in the McNamara period was that of the Bank as an international mediator. Nothing happened to evoke memories of the roles the World Bank had played in the 1950s with respect to the Indus River settlement or the Aswan High Dam.[42] From their files it is evident that one of the frustrations of the two people occupying the two top positions in the Bank at the end of the decade was their failure to find a formula to induce the governments of Bangladesh, Nepal, and India—more particularly, India—to let the Bank be an analytical and/or negotiating handmaiden to the solution of South Asia's "Eastern Waters" problem. The problem was how to use the river and groundwater storage system of the Ganges and Brahmaputra watersheds to the greatest advantage of the three countries. The Bank's would-be contribution foundered on Indian sovereignty.

Indeed, in the 1970s the Bank was more closely bounded by the nationhood of its borrowing clients than it had ever been before. This was evident in the institution's forced participation in the disestablishment of the East African Federation (Kenya, Tanzania, Uganda). Further efforts to encourage and/or deal with multi-country regions—in Africa and Latin America as well as in Asia—had little place or momentum within the institution and came essentially to nothing.

6. Another comment on the Bank's 1970s administrative experience was made vehemently both at the time and in a much later interview by the veteran staffer, Martijn Paijmans, who was chosen by Robert McNamara in early 1979 to become vice president in change of the institution's administrative, organizational planning, and personnel complex. The position was broadly that, at this relatively late date in his incumbency, the president felt that what Paijmans called the Bank's ignoble side—administrative services, housekeeping, personnel, and so on—needed shaping up and called on Paijmans, an apostle of order, system, and efficiency, to do it.

Paijmans was appalled at what he found. After three months he reported to McNamara: "I would say if only 25% of the analytical rigor we bring to bear on our line operational work had been applied to the administrative wing of this institution we would not face a number of issues that confront us today. . . . What has struck me most . . . is the extraordinary degree of freedom that has been given to managers and staff alike."[43] In a later memo Paijmans summarized the first year of his vice presidency: The impression was of "an unguided, uncontrolled and complacent share of the Bank's activity—an area of activity which is unnoticed and unrecognized when things go right but is immediately noticed when things go wrong."[44]

42. See chapter 8 in this book and Mason and Asher, *World Bank since Bretton Woods*, chap. 18.
43. Memorandum, Martijn Paijmans to Robert S. McNamara, July 5, 1979.
44. Memorandum, Martijn Paijmans to Robert S. McNamara, March 27, 1980.

The vice president pressed insistently for house rules that would regularize administrative practices. In particular, he persuaded his senior colleagues including the President's Council to adopt an extensive text setting forth guidelines for managers entitled "Managing People in the World Bank Group." One senses that, although McNamara had instigated the Paijmans operation, the latter was not in the forefront of the president's attention during his last year in office. Paijmans, from his side, became extremely critical of McNamara's alleged blind spot with respect to "ignoble" administrative issues.[45] The vice president was due to have a much closer fit with A. W. Clausen, who shared his set of management values.

7. Like other institutions, the World Bank has been knit together as much by particular individuals as by continuities of policy and process. No one person knit better or across more chapters of the history than Burke Knapp. When, finally, after nearly thirty years of service, his retirement time came in July 1978, Robert McNamara gave Knapp an appreciative send-off:

> Staff Announcement, June 26, 1978
>
> . . . No one on the staff who has had the good fortune to know Mr. Knapp over the years can possibly be unaware of the gigantic contribution he has made to the world of the Bank. But no one, perhaps, has been in a better position to appreciate that daily phenomenon during this past decade than I.
>
> His dedication, his careful judgement, his grasp of relevant detail, his ability to harmonize divergent views and bring them to a practical consensus, these traits have characterized his work ever since I have known him.
>
> Such traits are rare and valuable enough in themselves, but when they come complemented with a gentleness and quiet charm, an infectious sense of courtesy and good humor, and an unfailing attitude of fairness and consideration, they take on a very special worth.[46]

The Institution since 1981

Other chapters have emphasized the sea change the World Bank—and the world to which the World Bank related—underwent at about the time Robert McNamara was leaving the institution. What happened to the continuity of the Bank as it was making the transition? Under three one-term presidents, Clausen, Conable, and Preston, the changes were extensive. Yet the identity with which the Bank entered the 1980s was not dislodged. By the end of 1994, however, when the institution was past the excitement and turbulence of the early 1980s, it was arguably less of a force than it had been in the 1970s. Certainly it was exhibiting less self-confidence.

45. Martijn Paijmans, interview with the authors, March 1996.
46. Administrative circular, June 26, 1978.

Institutional Aspects of the "Bend in Events"

Although the World Bank had lost a leader, was having a hard job replenishing IDA, and was having its running room curbed by its largest owner, in some ways it was on a roll in the early 1980s. It was inaugurating structural and sectoral adjustment lending, the major new phase of policy-based lending discussed in chapters 9 and 10. The Bank emerged as the headquarters, the fountainhead—some half-jokingly said the Vatican—of neoorthodox development economics. Its was the most authoritative articulation of the longer-term side of the so-called Washington consensus (the IMF dominated the short run) concerning appropriate relations between states and markets, including international and interacting national economic policies.

In terms of commanding the public podium, one more McNamara decision, namely, to launch the *World Development Report* in 1978 as an annual forum of development policy observation and opinion, proved pivotal. For the official, think-tank, academic, and media segments of the development community, the annual *World Development Report* quickly became a centerpiece of policy debate. Moreover, the institution's research establishment was transformed to give "the new orthodoxy" a more cohesive voice. The 1970s had witnessed an extraordinary rise in both the volume and the range of the Bank's research output. This growth, directed by the vice president for research, Hollis Chenery, reflected one of McNamara's visions for the institution. By the mid-1970s, the Bank had become the preeminent player in development-related research. In his last years at the Bank, however, Chenery appeared to withdraw from the bureaucratic fray, largely confining himself to issues related to his own substantive interests. At his departure, the research complex was reorganized. An important policy-oriented component was shifted to the operations complex, the argument being that, with the Bank's new focus on macropolicy, operations needed to have stronger analytical expertise within its own organizational frame; but the job remained the most important economist's job in an economics-bent organization.

The selection of Chenery's successor had been dogged by controversy. The politico-ideological shift under way was reflected in both the selection of the new Bank president and, in turn, his choice of Anne Krueger as Chenery's successor. Internal management and personnel changes in the new economic research service (ERS) vice presidency rapidly ensued.[47] The new group in the research establishment regarded the former incumbents as deficient in appropriate technical economic skills and wedded to the "statist" ways of the past. It is hardly uncommon

47. Not only was there a rapid turnover (only eight of thirty-seven higher-level staff in the Development Research Department [DRD] remained there three years later), but staff from other Bank departments were reluctant to transfer to ERS. A staff memo (dated July 25, 1985) noted that over a period of two years, more than ten senior Bank staff turned down offers of managerial positions in ERS and that three division chief positions had remained vacant for almost two years.

for a new manager to try to shape his or her new subordinates in his or her own image, but the degree of such thought control in this instance, by new arrivals with utter confidence in their version of the truth, was unusual. The abrupt onset of intolerance for dissent contaminated the atmosphere for open intellectual inquiry on which good research depends.[48]

Between early 1983 and 1986, the Bank's Personnel Department informed the institution's senior managers that the Economics Department had adopted an "intelligence" system to detect staff divergences from establishment positions, that it was categorizing staff by schools of economic thought and openly favoring "loyalists," and that it was hiring staff on fixed-term contracts to render them more pliable. ERS, the personnel people said, increasingly was seen as a unit selling ideology instead of objective research. The situation might warrant senior management attention.[49]

A principal effect of the changes was to concentrate power in the front office of the research vice president, which expanded rapidly. Staff of the office began to exercise quasi-line functional controls, undermining the authority of two departmental directors. The change in style also led to conflicts with other parts of the Bank. A hitherto collegiate mode was replaced; the management of ERS "encouraged a hard and confrontational approach to staff, the underlying philosophy being that this would generate better results."[50] Although the change was most manifest in the ERS vice presidency, it was, as the Bank's ombudsman noted in his annual report, part of the broader institutional shift, reflecting a "disturbing trend for the Bank. . . . [E]stablished procedures and processes for resolving problems are not working. . . . The Bank is changing in style, tone, and culture, becoming an institution different from what it has been and what staff have known."[51]

Thus there was an inside-outside discrepancy. Externally in the early 1980s the Bank projected an image of authoritative, unequivocal analysis, but internally there were differences and doubts. Moreover, knowledge of the latter now seeped to knowledgeable constituencies outside the Bank, damaging the credibility of official Bank assertions, for example, about debt. At the same time, inside, awareness of the manner and scale of the overturn that had occurred in the Research Department arguably diminished the confidence with which Bank managers addressed

48. In 1985 a research paper series (called yellow-cover staff working papers) was discontinued by order of the operations complex following the publication of a paper that argued that the supply response of African agriculture to price reform alone would be inadequate, thus appearing to dilute the official stress on the importance of "getting the prices right."

49. The points are made in various internal memoranda from the Personnel and Management Department during 1983 to 1986. The thrust was summarized in "ERS Management Issues," July 25, 1985.

50. Memorandum, Personnel Management Department, September 18, 1986.

51. Memorandum, J. B. Hendry, ombudsman, to Martijn Paijmans, vice president, Personnel and Administration, "OMB Annual Report for FY86," July 21, 1986.

macro-policy issues. With President Clausen, Ernest Stern had presided over the formation of the institution's "Washington consensus" image. His candor, therefore, was striking when, soon after Barber Conable's arrival, Stern told him, "The public intellectual leadership [of the Bank] *has* been lacking [over the past five years]."[52]

On the one hand, the sharpness of the research switch had to be attributed to the Bank's president; he was in charge. On the other hand, President Clausen's rapport with the U.S. administration was decidedly lukewarm, and the institution was struggling to return to the latter's good graces. Any action that could be interpreted as curbing the one part of the Bank most in tune with the beliefs of the U.S. administration could have brought serious setbacks to the institution's other agendas, especially IDA, where U.S. support was essential.[53]

Matters changed rapidly in 1987. As noted in chapter 11, the research complex became the Bank's strongest activist on the debt issue, a role further strengthened by the arrival of Stanley Fischer.[54] Yet, as Fischer himself would later state, pressures by the large shareholders compromised the research effort:

> The US squelched research on this [debt] issue during the mid-80's. One of my reasons for going to the Bank was that I believed the debt issue was about to come to a head. . . . [W]e had to keep research quiet, because the institution was under political orders (not only from the US, also the Germans, and the Brits) not to raise issues of debt relief. Debt, like devaluation, is an issue where expectations can be self-fulfilling, and the reasons for creditor country skittishness are clear.[55]

Fischer's comments reflect the difficulties facing multilateral institutions. As creatures of member states, their ability to espouse a stand seriously at odds with the vital interests of their stronger governors is limited. The problem is compounded in situations where analyses are uncertain and there is fear of self-fulfilling expectations. Moreover, the Bank had a very broad array of members. There were strong possibilities that the institution would have jeopardized its effectiveness for its borrowers if it had taken a more independent and confrontational approach vis à vis its major shareholders.

52. Memorandum, Ernest Stern to Barber B. Conable, "Organizational Issues," September 2, 1986.

53. There were those who saw the acceptance of greater internal censorship as a reflection of a changing institutional culture. Thus Benjamin King, then acting vice president for economic research, remarked on the vehement defense of a point of principle made by Mark Leiserson: "On balance, he stands out as someone who will clearly not let his backbone deteriorate from atrophy, a quality by no means universal in the Bank, perhaps because it is not among the most prized." Personal communication with the authors, based on April 4, 1987, evaluation.

54. A staff member reporting on a meeting of the G-10 to discuss the Bank's role in the debt crisis recorded that "the US delegate asserted that the . . . Bank already has 'too much uncontrolled internal activism' in this regard, manifested in . . . 'papers which turn up' that go well beyond what is supported by either senior management or the Board." Memorandum, Fred Levy, July 20, 1988.

55. Letter, Stanley Fischer to Nicholas Stern, May 19, 1992.

Management in a Slower Lane

While rapid growth can complicate issues, in the World Bank as in most enter-prises, it has rendered most managerial problems more tractable. Such had been the case in the 1970s. As early as 1979 one finds Robert McNamara and Ernest Stern agreeing that the situation was changing; thanks to constraints on available resources, the growth rates of the IDA and IBRD loan portfolios were about to be sharply curtailed. The president and the senior vice president of operations were right, and this circumstance alone presented President Clausen with a challenge.

The new president had other problems. Obviously he followed a very accomplished act. His familiarity with development issues was limited. He had even less direct knowledge of politics, including Washington, D.C. He quickly felt betrayed by his fellow Republicans who had taken over the United States administration a half year before Clausen's arrival and displayed an ingrained hostility to the World Bank. In an interview with a group of former presidential office staffers it was recalled that Clausen frequently seemed ill at ease dealing with non-Americans; he talked in metaphors of American sports that befuddled people from elsewhere.[56] The president was at once buffered and (in the eyes of some) diminished by the exceptionally gifted No. 2 he inherited.

And yet, arguably, it was the slowdown in Bank funding and therefore perfor-mance that drove a new theme onto center stage, not only during the Clausen years but thereafter: how to improve the efficiency of Bank management—how to get more developmental effectiveness per loan dollar.

This is not to suggest that the quality of Bank management was a matter of indifference in earlier presidencies, but the concern was stepped up in the 1980s. One of the present authors remembers the start of a "Tidewater meeting" in October 1981 in which he remarked to some of those gathering that Mr. Clausen had come to the World Bank as the first commercial banker to occupy the presi-dency in some time. "Not as a banker," corrected Clausen, "as a manager."[57] Five years later Barber Conable arrived with incentive to give the institution an or-ganizational and managerial facelift. Ten years later Lewis Preston would come to the presidency characterizing himself as Clausen had. And in 1995 (beyond the span of this history) James Wolfensohn would take over, sounding the same mana-gerial theme. The search for improved organization and process did indeed be-come ongoing. Down to the present writing it has been studded by a series of special studies, exercises, and new departures, only a few of which can be touched on in the present account. One of the earlier ones was by a World Bank Study Team addressing the subjects of the Bank's resource-allocation and management-control

56. Author's meeting with four former executive assistants to McNamara, September 18, 1992.
57. Informal "Tidewater meetings" were annual gatherings of foreign aid chiefs and ministers, multilateral heads, and, beginning in 1979, of selected developing-country offi-cials. The first such meeting occurred at Tidewater, Maryland, in 1968. The 1981 meeting was cohosted by the president of the World Bank and the managing director of the IMF.

processes that summarized its findings in a report to President Clausen in February 1983. The study was headed by W. Bowman Cutter, who was temporarily affiliated with the World Bank.[58]

The 1983 study is memorable for the extent to which it laid out an enduring management-upgrade agenda. During the 1970s, it said, the "critical path" of Bank decisionmaking had been set by its project lending program. All of the institution's systems—its budgeting, its personnel programming, its financial intermediation, its research, its implementation and evaluation—were geared to that single (project lending) activity. Despite its advocacy of planning to its clients, the Bank lacked a single comprehensive, integrative, all-systems- encompassing, multiyear corporate plan of its own. Operations were highly centralized to serve growth; at the same time, the need for some disaggregation had yielded a set of differentiated regional vice-presidential fiefdoms. The growth focus together with personnel transfers had accentuated the preoccupation with loan *making;* implementation had lagged. Quantity had trampled quality while "a plethora of monitoring and control processes [had] evolved."[59]

To adapt to the future it foresaw, containing less of the healing balm of rapid growth, the study group recommended better strategic planning; better diagnosis of the economic, financial, and political environment in which the Bank would be operating; stronger attention to and incentives for cost-effectiveness; and, compared with Bank inputs, more focus on outputs, that is, on implementation. The group pushed for coherent decentralization and, in particular, for making the borrowing *country* program a much stronger unit of account in Bank activity.

At the time, the Cutter study appears to have made no great waves. But it began a sequence. In 1985 a Stephen Denning report that was a product of a "Future Role of the World Bank" exercise, which had been motivated by management's desire for a General Capital Increase, voiced some of the same themes more conspicuously.[60] Two years later managerial reform achieved its peak salience in the reorganization of 1987. And in a manner just a bit reminiscent of the quest for the Fountain of Youth, special pro-management initiatives and movements, importantly including the Wapenhans Report of 1992, continued in the three presidencies under review—only to experience a new surge under President James Wolfensohn.

One other facet of President Clausen's managerial style at the World Bank deserves emphasis. During at least most of the institution's history, presidents of the Bank have had regularly scheduled meetings, usually weekly, with a small group

58. Cutter, a public-systems analyst and political economist, is better known for his U.S. government positions, including the No. 2 position in President Clinton's National Economic Council.

59. Memorandum, W. Bowman Cutter to A. W. Clausen, "Executive Summary, Resource Allocation and Control Study, Phase I Report, February 16, 1983," February 16, 1983, annex 1, p. 4.

60. Memorandum, Ernest Stern to operations vice presidents, "Streamlining Bank Procedures," November 4, 1985, covering the October 25, 1985, report of the same name by Stephen Denning.

of their senior managers. If one follows the evolution in this regard from late in the McNamara years to the Clausen period, the key meeting, for one thing, became smaller. Under McNamara, the "President's Council," involving all of the institution's vice presidents and a few others, had become too large to permit a norm of much back-and-forth discussion, particularly because the president's usual mode was to do much of the talking. He announced and explained his views and decisions, invited reactions, but yielded the floor mainly only for prearranged oral reports, introductions of papers, and the like. Late in his tenure McNamara decided to add stated meetings of a very much smaller in-group (it was called the executive committee) consisting, beside himself, only of the two senior vice presidents (operations and finance), general counsel and the secretary of the Bank, who was management's link with the Executive Board. When the group of former McNamara personal assistants met with the present authors, they speculated that the motivation for the small group was to cushion the tensions that in 1979 to 1981 already were appearing between the two new senior vice presidents—and to make sure that the dynamism of neither pulled the organization off course.

The Clausen Bank gave precedence to this smaller group, albeit somewhat augmented. The President's Council was retained vestigially, but the small body was enlarged from four to about eight standing members (with other officers being called in response to the agenda); moreover, the new small group was called the Managing Committee, and its proceedings became far more formal. The label was not casual. It reflected a deliberate shift by Clausen from single (presidential) decisionmaking to collective decisionmaking. (Evidently he had followed the same practice at the Bank of America.) The committee no longer was simply advisory. The president ostensibly delegated to it his powers of decision. Accordingly, the committee needed to be run like a corporate board. Agendas and supporting papers needed to be supplied in advance; items were introduced by designated members or other staffers admitted for the purpose; decisions were arrived at, item by item (albeit by consensus rather than formal vote, yet with the option to put over an unresolved issue to a later meeting); and in the case of each item a vice president or other officer was identified to follow up the decision.

The change made for long, stilted minutes. It represented an attempt to cope with the loneliness that seems inherent in the office of the chief executive of a multilateral institution, especially one that had muted the voice of its Executive Board early on. The collective management model was rejected by Clausen's successor; under Barber Conable the weekly meetings of leaders became strictly advisory once again. But, as will be noted, Preston, with his "managing directors," would bring collective decisionmaking back after a fashion.

The Conable Paradox

Barber Conable came to office in an unusual way. Tom Clausen had been told in Seoul in October 1985 as the annual Bank-Fund meetings were about to start that the United States would not support his reelection the following year. Accordingly, in his speech the next day Clausen preempted; he announced that he would be stepping down. It was assumed that, as usual, the United States would be proposing the next president, but there was no early announcement. Secretary of the Treasury James Baker, Conable later related, had agreed the nominee had to be acceptable to, beside himself, Secretary of State George Shultz and Donald Regan, whom Baker had succeeded and who had succeeded Baker as chief of staff to the president.

In 1984 Barber Conable had retired from long-term service as a respected moderate Republican member of the U.S. House of Representatives from the environs of Rochester, New York. At the end of the winter of 1985–86 Conable, back in the Rochester area, received a call from his friend Jim Baker: the selection of a presidential nominee for the Bank was not moving well, and if the United States did not quickly produce a good nomination, the Europeans might press a candidate of their own. Could he please use Conable's name—just as an example of the kind of person the post required? Conable was reluctant; he did not know the Bank, and he had no desire to return to Washington. But Baker urged that the ruse was only tactical, and was needed to hold off the Europeans. Conable assented; two weeks later Baker called back with a sheepish report: Conable was the only one upon whom his team of three could agree. With Conable's de facto acceptance, Baker then took pains to consult with a broad array of the Bank member governments.

Conable was brought aboard as of July 1, 1986. His tenure became a study in contrasts. He perpetrated a major reorganization that was widely reputed to be a disaster. But thereafter the Bank had an upbeat quality it had lacked for several years.

In the late spring of 1986, as Conable waited in Washington to take office, he was startled to hear that, for the first time in the Bank's history, the Executive Board, with the five largest owners leading the way, had held back from endorsing the institution's administrative budget for the coming fiscal year. Conable demanded to know from his old friend, James Baker, how come, having dragged Conable into this job, Baker could deny the new president a budget to run the place. The Treasury secretary replied that there appeared to be a "lot of fat" in the institution. The major owners, objecting to the size and salaries of the staff, had resisted a request for more staff. Some of them declared that the Bank was "an organization out of control."[61] Conable decided a major reorganization was required to reestablish the institution's credentials. Soon after taking office, he retained a management consulting firm, Cresap, McCormick and Paget, recommended by David Rockefeller.[62]

61. Barber B. Conable, interview with the authors, May 8, 1991.
62. Jochen Kraske and others, *Bankers with a Mission: The Presidents of the World Bank, 1946–91* (Oxford University Press, 1969), pp. 282–85.

Given the previous rhythm of major Bank reorganizations and the changes of scale and mission that had ensued since 1972, the 1986–87 exercise was not premature. Its revisions of structure had widespread support. Most important, it furthered the 1972 move toward the conduct of operational decisionmaking within a country framework. Previously the geographically lowest levels of the Bank's loan-making structures had included both program and project units. Now their functions were joined in single country departments (for single countries or, in the most part, contiguous groups of borrowing countries). Supporting technical departments were organized for whole vice-presidential regions, in some cases, for pairs of regions. On the technical/projects side of the Bank there were complaints that the change caused an attrition of engineers and other technical specialists as the specialists lost face and clout. However, it was hard to fault the advantage of more coherent country programming.

There is little doubt that among the collateral purposes of the reorganization were desires to dampen the rivalry that had developed between the two senior vice presidents (Stern and Qureshi) and, more particularly, to check the dominance Stern had acquired during the first half of the 1980s. "Nobody would have believed I had reorganized the Bank if I left Ernie in charge of operations," Conable remarked later.[63] The scope of operations' bureaucratic terrain was somewhat narrowed. Two other senior vice presidencies, one for planning, policy, and research, the other for administration, were added, arguably to reduce the salience of the operations and finance senior vice presidencies.[64] President Conable decided that Qureshi and Stern should switch portfolios—and to the surprise of some of his adversaries, the latter accepted—for another eight years, during which his influence in the organization would be little diminished.

Leaving aside these personal dimensions, quite clearly there were good things that could be said about the 1987 reorganization. Why, then, did it induce near panic within the Bank? Because of the *process* adopted. Some of the latter was good; there was an exceptional effort, with much in-house interviewing, opinion-taking, and the use of internal advisory and steering committees, to achieve what, in other contexts, the Bank would have called staff "ownership" of the change. It is hard to avoid some backlash to such participation; it is often perceived that those who do the heaviest lifting in such an exercise find individual favor in the reassignments that result. But the 1987 affair was not badly flawed in this respect. There were three other factors that induced panic, that should have been perceived by an alert consultant or by the president, if he had known his new charge better, and that were not focused on by the youngish, cerebral task force that ran the reorganization in-house.

63. Conable, interview, May 8, 1991.
64. Thereby, noted budget director Robert Picciotto, adding to the top-heaviness that it was one purpose of the reorganization to correct. Memorandum, Robert Picciotto to David Hopper, July 8, 1987.

First, a stated purpose of the exercise—later downplayed by Conable, but widely recognized and emphasized by the owners—was to downsize the Bank's payroll. According to Edward (Kim) Jaycox, chairman of the reorganization's steering committee and staff task force, "There was no numerical objective, but there was the idea that we were going to clear out a lot of people in the process. We were going to cut a lot of costs of doing business and costs equal people."[65]

Second, compared with most other public and private employers, the Bank had an unusual staff. It was an apparently secure meritocracy. Many employees, with access to U.S. residence tied to Bank service, drew salaries far exceeding those available at home. They were encumbered with commitments (mortgages, children in elite schools and universities) whose discharge depended on keeping their jobs. For what had appeared to be very good reasons, they had acquired the mentality of a pampered elite. They were easily spooked.

Third, whether or not it had anything to do with the Bank's yen for open markets at the time, the reorganization decided to turn the institution into a wide open labor market: every job was up for reassignment. The president, with advice, picked the senior vice presidents and the vice presidents, and then these managers were licensed to bid for any and all staffers they chose. One effect was that likes tended to attract likes, so that the regional vice presidencies, somewhat more than had been the case before, tended to take on the styles of their chiefs. But another consequence, once the process was coupled with the expectation of significant downsizing, was also important. The exercise felt like a great game of musical chairs; while it was going on in the middle months of 1987, it destroyed morale and devastated the institution's work program.[66]

How much, following mid-1987, the mood of the Bank rallied was testimony to the character of Barber Conable's leadership once the reorganization trauma was past. When Conable came aboard, IDA's Eighth Replenishment, whose negotiation was due to be completed in 1987, looked problematic, especially with the United States, and the United States had been turning away from the idea of a General Capital Increase (GCI) for several years. Without overstepping the formal arm's-length relation that a multilateral head was supposed to have with a member government's legislature, Conable was active informally in reassuring one set of congressmen that, as to debt, the World Bank was not in the business of "bailing out the commercial banks" while he emphasized to others that it certainly was not promoting socialism—while favoring the private sector, it simply dealt with legitimate regimes as it found them. His political relations—also with other governments, including borrowing governments—were good-natured, surefooted, and effective.

65. Edward Jaycox, interview, World Bank Oral History Program, April 27, 1995.

66. A number of senior officers resigned at the time of the reorganization, among them David Knox, Anne Krueger, Eugene Rotberg, Enrique Lerdau, Martijn Paijmans, and Benjamin King (the last for a second time).

Programmatically, Conable was speaking from the heart when he told the present authors in late 1991 that the 1990 (Poverty) World Development Report was the most important written product of his administration. As discussed in chapter 7, it set out the institution's revived agenda in that field. Conable also gave the Bank's environment work a major lift, he was concerned about the status of women and population policy, and he was more forthcoming than his predecessors in promoting restraints on developing-country defense spending.

It was also under Conable—more particularly after Secretary Baker launched the so-called Baker Plan in October 1985—that the Bank became more engaged in the debt field. Thus once the institution got beyond the reorganization, one observed a kind of can-do programmatic exuberance in the Bank's documentation. In annual attitude surveys the staff still expressed grave self-doubts and dissatisfactions.[67] Moreover, as discussed in chapter 10, there was good substantive reason for the exuberance to be tempered. Proliferating, multitargeting use of ex ante policy conditions invited grave procedural doubts. It promised not to be sustainable. Nevertheless, the Bank's renewed head-on engagement of basic development problems refreshed the institution's morale.

One is left with the question, why did Conable retire when he did? He had developed enough support inside the Bank as well as in member governments to believe he could be reappointed if he so wanted.[68] The answer, like most such, is probably mixed. Even if he was reelectable, Conable had reached staff retirement age and had an abundance of interests and retirement options to pursue. He may also have begun to appreciate that the can-do programming he had encouraged contained some awkward contradictions. Perhaps there was another factor. Conable, as a practicing Republican with close personal ties with the Bush administration, appears to have been heartsick over the crabbed, often rancorous negativism he frequently encountered in the Bank's most powerful member government. "Here we are in the United States," he told a "Bretton Woods Committee" audience just after he had stepped down, "the nation that created the Marshall Plan, that provided key leadership in creating the Bretton Woods institutions, including the World Bank. Yet even otherwise knowledgeable Americans don't know what the World Bank is."[69]

The U.S. administration, Conable thought, displayed precious little interest in the Bank's work or in development. So, he said in an interview already cited, he had decided to leave if he thought well of the person the U.S. government would propose to succeed him, and Lewis Preston certainly qualified.

---

67. The President's Council discussed at length the portent of the 1990 survey, for example, in its minutes of the October 17 meeting, dated October 22, 1990.

68. Barber B. Conable, interview with the authors, August 19, 1991.

69. Address to the Annual Meeting of the Bretton Woods Committee, Washington, D.C., July 10, 1991.

The Preston Tour: Image Problems

Lewis Preston (1991 to early 1995) was the Bank's hard-luck president. The third commercial banker to head the institution, he was the most distinguished in that capacity. He was admired for the way he piloted J. P. Morgan through the debt crisis. Many saw him as the consummate manager: his importation of the managing-director mode of high-level organizational structuring has been noted.

But Preston was plagued by personal tragedy and bad health.[70] He was a fine tuner; he pressed ahead, for example, with Conable's renewed antipoverty and environment pushes. However, his term was most memorable for stormy public relations. The approach of the institution's fiftieth anniversary attracted public and press attention, much of it hostile. The Northern environmental NGOs came into full voice in their attacks on the Bank despite its shift to greater environmental concern. The Preston Bank got little credit for its self-critical capacities in launching either the review of the Bank's loan portfolio in 1992 or, in 1994, the critique of the large Narmada water management project in India chaired by Bradford Morse. Some of the negative publicity about the start-up excesses of the new European Bank for Reconstruction and Development in London rubbed off on the other MDBs, and the World Bank picked a poor time to be found experiencing egregious delays and cost overruns in the construction of a new main office complex in Washington. The project had, indeed, been inefficiently managed. But many in the institution regretted the way management appeared to pin the blame on a worthy, long-serving vice president, who had no involvement in the early mistakes.

The self-instigated portfolio review was a landmark, for one reason, because of its substance.[71] Its review of loan portfolio management spelled out a criticism of Bank bias that had been common since at least the early years of the McNamara regime: the Bank's lending was stronger on takeoffs than landings. Partly because of personnel incentives, rotation, and the focus on Board presentations, attention to the design and making of loans far exceeded the institution's focus on the implementation of projects and their effects. The report noted that the ratings of appraisals of projects being made by operational units and OED both were declining. The loan portfolio needed repair.

Although these ideas were not new, the candor of the reviewers was striking. So was their decision, in May of 1992, to bring in fifteen seasoned officials from borrowing countries for a two-day workshop to assess Bank operations. In the reporting the visitors remained anonymous. Their criticisms were articulate and strong. The Bank was indeed preoccupied with takeoffs. It pushed too many

70. His son died during his first summer in the job, in 1993 he had major heart surgery, and he died in May 1995, before having completed his fourth year.

71. The review was chaired by the recently retired Willi Wapenhans, who as a regional vice president had shared some of the management practices the "Wapenhans Report" now scored.

conditions simultaneously. It kept changing its mind: "The Bank," said one participant, "changes its wisdom in the passage of time." It tended to be formal and rigid in its regulations. Its paper overload—the documentation to which it subjected overworked counterparts—was overwhelming.[72]

Thus the invited borrowers also were candid. But the striking thing was that, on balance, their view of Bank operations was favorable, more so than that of the institution's staff. As OED would report in comparing Bank staff's and African clients' assessments of the same set of Bank activities at about the same time, of the two evaluating groups, the view of the in-house group was the harsher.[73]

Overall staff growth exhibited resilience onward into the Preston years after the 1987 reorganization. The organization had another behavioral characteristic that became prominent by the early 1990s: it was enmeshing itself in a mass of rules and regulations. Daniel Ritchie of the technical department serving both East and South Asia caught the problem in a memo—"OD'ing on ODs"—at the end of July 1992. A rush seemed to be under way to convert Bank policies into "Operational Directives." Ritchie reported a small study:

> The attachments offer a flavor of the Task Manager's daunting task of understanding and carrying out Bank policies. There are currently about 32 ODs published, and another 50 under preparation and 50 more planned. . . . About half of those already published refer to investment lending. In these we counted about 200 specific tasks for which the TM is responsible. . . . By crude extrapolation, I suspect that when the [further ODs planned on project appraisal, economic analysis of projects, financial analysis, project completion reports, etc.] are published TMs will have explicit responsibility for between 400 and 500 tasks for investment lending alone. . . .
>
> [A] moratorium on new ODs might not be bad idea.[74]

Three Latter-Day Questions

Certain institutional questions ran through the whole post-McNamara period. Three are of particular interest. They have to do with how the governance of the *institution* evolved (as indicated, the Bank's overt interest in the governance of its borrowing countries also changed); the institution's external relations—with the United Nations and the policy-analysis and advocacy communities around it as well as with NGOs; and the personnel side of the Bank—quality, diversity, turnover, and skills.

GOVERNANCE: FORMAL CHANGES. In the 1980s and 1990s formal changes in the governance of the Bank centered in the Executive Board. The institution's

---

72. World Bank, Borrowers' Workshop on Portfolio Management, 1992.

73. Operations Evaluatio Department, fiscal 1994 review of portfolio performance, and Africa region survey, both summarized in an OED précis, June 1996.

74. Memorandum, Daniel Ritchie to Vice Presidents Gautam Kaji and Joseph Wood, July 31, 1992.

Table 18-1. *Voting Power of World Bank Part I Members, 1947–95*

Number and power	1947	1955	1965	1975	1985	1995
Countries	44	56	102	125	149	178
Board members	12	16	20	20	21	24
Voting power						
G-7	61.7	60.0	54.9	51.3	49.7	43.3
United States	35.1	30.7	26.3	22.7	19.7	17.0
OECD	70.0	71.9	67.6	64.7	63.6	57.5

Source: World Bank.

number of Board members (see table 18-1) increased, although more slowly than the number of member countries. As the Board grew in size, with the accretion of advisers and assistants, it became more ponderous. But also, because more countries needed to be fitted in, constituencies became larger, with more of them becoming North-South mixtures.

Some executive directors regarded this last as a benign development. If the Board was a kind of parliament of country representatives meant to sort out and amalgamate the diverse interests of the owners—and this, such executive directors argued, was the better analogue for the Board than was a commercial company's panel of corporate directors—the mixed constituencies engaged individual executive directors in mediating and consolidating owner views in advance of formal Board debates.

During the 1980s and 1990s (see table 18-1) the voting power of the Bank's Part I members continued its relative decline. Votes of the G-7 fell from 51.3 percent to 43.3 percent from 1975 to 1995 and of the United States, from 22.7 percent to 17.0 percent. To preserve the U.S. veto, the constitutional majority for changing the Articles was raised from 80 to 85 percent in 1989. In 1995 the Bank's OECD members as a whole still deployed a comfortable majority (57.5 percent) of the votes.

During the recent periods blocs in the Board altered their characteristic behavior, but only marginally. The "like-minded countries" (the Dutch, Nordic members, and Canada) continued to play a more development-friendly role than the larger OECD countries, although Canada took on more of the coloration of its new colleagues once it became the last member of the G-7 in 1981. As between the Dutch and the Nordic countries, the latter moved more to the center; in Board debates the Scandinavian countries found themselves often agreeing with Germany.

Although the United States remained the strongest G-7 voice, it was quite isolated on several occasions, not least in the 1991 IFC capital increase debate over private sector development, where, among the rest of the G-7, the United States received only lukewarm support from Canada and neutrality from Japan. The

largest developing countries—China, India, Brazil—frequently made strong interventions. But the Part II countries as a whole, while by no means silent, were
circumspect; the G-24 had little influence.

The behavior of the Board changed significantly. Perhaps taking a cue from the
IDA deputies, who from the early 1970s onward had been aggressive in injecting
donors' policy views into IDA replenishment exercises, the Board from the mid-
1980s became more assertive. The first pressure point it chose was the institution's
administrative budget. After the near rejection of President Clausen's last budget,
the Board formed a Budget Procedures Committee, presaging earlier and more
systematic involvement in the budget process.[75] An accompanying change was a
drastic general overhaul of Board procedures that reacted, finally, to John McCloy's
1947 coup. The executive directors would take a more active strategic and policy
role, especially on Country Assistance Strategy and lending policy reviews, at the
same time reducing discussions of individual lending operations.[76]

World Bank Board and management shared one governance frustration in the
1980s and 1990s. Both saw the power of official actors decline relative to those
embedded in the "civil society"—the interest groups or (in the newer jargon) the
"stakeholders" surrounding them (see the discussion of NGOs a few paragraphs
hence). However, country members tended to deal with their frustrations with the
Bank qua Bank in one of two ways. They could incline toward an exit or partial exit
option, which was the choice of those Europeans who led in the building of the
EBRD and the European Union's development programs. Or, as some did increasingly in the 1980s, they could amend and, in some measure, preempt the World
Bank by supplementing its administrative budget with trust funds that operated in
support of donor-favored operations that were conducted outside the Bank's regular budget process.

Total donor Trust Fund contributions increased from $0.5 billion in fiscal 1989
to about $1.3 billion in fiscal 1995. The contributions were for lending and non-

75. Discussed in prospect by the general counsel, Ibrahim Shihata, in a memo, R66-28,
January 1986.

76. An Ad Hoc Committee on Board Procedures was formed under the Icelandic
executive director, Jonas Haralz, in 1991. Its report was finished a year later under the Venezuelan executive director, Moises Naim. World Bank, "Report of the Ad Hoc Committee on
Board Procedures," May 26, 1992. The Haralz/Naim reforms did not take effect until the
beginning of calendar year 1993. Meanwhile, in a July 1992 memorandum, Vice President/
Secretary T. Tahane and U.S. executive director E. Patrick Coady deplored the amount of time
the resident Board devoted to Board meetings. They reported that in fiscal 1992 the Board had
spent 363 hours—about nine workweeks—in Board discussions. The Haralz/Naim report,
while proposing guidelines suggesting that executive directors pursue details with staff
outside meetings, had remarked that the "need to keep statements short and to the point . . .
[is] obvious, constantly ignored, and very difficult to enforce." As of 1996, however, the sense
of the authors was "that the reforms have been quite effective in changing the work of the
board for the better." Jonas Haralz, personal communication, September 17, 1996.

lending services including cofinancing, technical assistance, ESW, and research and training. The bulk of the contributions were by fifteen bilaterals led by Japan and the Netherlands. Less than a fifth of the total came from multilaterals, with the United Nations Development Program in the lead.[77]

At the present writing, there was no clear sense in the Bank of how the "phantom economy" of trust funds, accounting in different years for something between one-sixth and one-quarter of the institution's administrative budget, was affecting that budget. The issue remained to be resolved.

EXTERNAL RELATIONS: THE UNITED NATIONS AND ITS AFFILIATES, PLUS NGOS. The World Bank, we have said, began in a standoffish mode with respect to the UN's one-flag, one-vote multilaterals based in New York, Geneva, and Rome. In George Woods's time, the Bank was friendlier to the United Nations, but then it became more self-reliant again under McNamara. As already mentioned, during the NIEO debates in the latter 1970s, the Bank cut a more conservative line than the "real" UN agencies around which the debate swirled. It is time to return to the subject.

The matter needs updating not only because of the importance of the Bank–UN relationship narrowly construed. Around the United Nations in the 1980s and 1990s was arrayed a large body of development-focused analysts, activists, and their organizations, both "North" and "South," who found themselves with a view of development issues (more to the left but non-Marxist) perceptibly different from the Bank's. The gap widened after the Bank moved into a more neoorthodox phase in 1979–81.

Representative of this contrasting view of the issues was Mahbub ul Haq, who, after leaving the Bank in 1981 and serving terms as a minister in the government of Pakistan, spent a number of years at UNDP/New York, where with the support of the agency's head, William Draper, he brought out a new annual, the *Human Development Report*. Compared with the Bank's *World Development Report*, the *Human Development Report* placed greater emphasis on social and political issues and indicators. Like James Grant, who moved from Washington's Overseas Development Council to head UNICEF in 1980, ul Haq was a ringleader of the Society for International Development's North-South Round Table, started in 1978. So was Richard Jolly, who left the directorship of the Institute of Development Studies, Sussex, to become Grant's deputy at UNICEF—and organized the "Adjustment with a Human Face" study discussed in chapters 7 and 10.

The Bank's response to the last initiative was quite positive, and, indeed, a number of people were received well in both the New York–centered and the Washington-centered pro-development camps. But it is part of the history of the World Bank that, as the 1980s and 1990s unfolded, there was in fact another activist cum intellectual (non-Marxist) pole of the development community, many of whose adherents harbored an abiding hostility to the Bank. This was reflected in a series of publications that two UN veterans—Brian Urquhart, with forty-one years

77. World Bank, "Status Report on Trust Funds." Report to the Board's Budget Procedures Committee, April 17, 1996.

of service winding up as a deputy secretary-general for many years, and the late
Erskine Childers with twenty-two years of service in various UN external relations
posts—wrote under the joint auspices of the Ford Foundation (where Urquhart
had a postretirement appointment) and the Dag Hammarskjöld Foundation. The
1994 volume in the series had been preceded by a "consultation" of nineteen
persons at Uppsala that included Adebayo Adedeji of the Economic Commission
for Africa; Chandra Hardy, former World Bank economist; Amir Jamal, member of
the Brandt Commission and former Tanzanian minister of finance; Ernst Michanek, longtime head of the Swedish International Development Agency; Frances
Stewart of Oxford University; and Charles Weiss, sometime World Bank specialist
on science and technology. To quote from the Childers-Urquhart report:

> Given [the Bank's] essential structuring . . . there was never any possibility of it complying
> with the principles, processes and intended coordinating role of the United Nations. . . .
>
> The demands of "donor" governments for "further cooperation" between the Bank
> and UN-system entities have produced initiatives like the joint World Bank-UNDP
> sponsorship of the Global Environmental Facility (GEF), creating the illusion of genuine
> coordination but the reality of Bank predominance.
>
> Such efforts at cooperation have tended to identify UN-system entities with the
> Bank's market-promotional policies. The Bank's expansion into programme lending has
> involved it in IMF-type political conditionalities on a country's national economic policies
> and programmes and loans to support the IMF's "structural adjustments.". . .
>
> It remains . . . extremely difficult to envisage the scope of reforms in the World Bank that
> would make it a compatible and appropriate specialized agency of the UN system. Beyond
> austerity air travel, not only the Bank's present lavish meeting-style, but staff remuneration
> would have to be brought into line with the UN "common system." The heavy-handedness of
> Bank loan approaches . . . is equally incompatible with the principles of respect, cooperation
> and partnership on which all United Nations development activities are based.[78]

Relations with nongovernmental organizations constitute another salient aspect
of the Bank's more recent external relations experience. NGOs, whether based
outside or inside developing countries, are engaged principally, not just in study,
research, or advocacy, but in pro-development operations. They and such official
development-promoting agencies as the World Bank coexisted, of course, from the
1950s onward. But relations with NGOs were a broadening segment of the Bank's
overall external relations during the 1980s and after. One reason was that NGOs,
both expatriate and indigenous, grew in numbers and operating scales. They
became better networked among themselves and with official development agencies, which provided part of their funding.[79]

78. Erskine Childers with Brian Urquhart, "Renewing the United Nations System,"
Development Dialogue, vol. 1 (1994), pp. 79–83.

79. See Thomas W. Dichter, "The Changing World of Northern NGOs: Problems,
Paradoxes, and Possibilities," in John P. Lewis, ed., *Strengthening the Poor: What Have We
Learned?* (New Brunswick, N.J.: Transaction Books, 1988), pp. 177–88.

But the temper of the World Bank–NGO interface also changed. The NGOs, typically, had been supporters and advocates of foreign aid, and, therefore, were pro-Bank, albeit with reservations about the elitism. In the 1980s, partly reflecting growing skepticism about the overall worth of government, but also the aggressively adversarial stance adopted by some environment-specializing NGOs (see volume 2, chapter 13), NGOs as a group posed challenges to the Bank. With their voices and silhouettes raised, moreover, they began to impinge on the multilaterals more directly. Previously NGOs wishing to convey views to the World Bank had done so via national governments, in particular, given its decibels and independence, the U.S. Congress. As the 1980s wore on, NGOs developed more direct exchanges with the Bank, which, for its part, was at greater pains to arrange regular fora for hearing them.

The institution's conduct of its external (or "public") relations during its later decades warrants a further comment. There is little argument that, in terms of public and press perceptions, the Bank's image worsened rather badly in the latter 1980s and the 1990s. It might have been assumed that, as management perceived the problem, there would have been a nearly parallel rise in the allocation of staff talent and managerial attention to external relations and public relations activity. Something like the reverse happened. The peak of external relations and public relations salience in the Bank was under McNamara when William Clark was not only external relations vice president but one of the president's closest, daily, executive-committee advisers. Thereafter, as some veteran staff members have remarked, the function experienced an intermittent slippage until, under Conable and Preston, having lost its vice presidency, it was performed by a group headed by a director rather distant from the chief executive.

PERSONNEL. The trauma about personnel downsizing that the Bank encountered in 1987 arguably had only limited effect. The number of "high level" (that is, professional) staff took a 6 percent step down in fiscal 1988, but then it resumed growth, rising at an annual rate of more than 2 percent, or more than half its growth rate during 1976–87.[80] The more striking changes in recent decades were in the composition of the staff. As indicated by the numbers on YP appointments included earlier, the diversity of the professional staff as to nationalities continued to widen. The fraction of women in the high-level staff, which had been 8.9 percent in 1975, during the 1980s grew nearly 5 percent yearly so that the figure was nearly 25 percent in 1989 and reached almost 50 percent in 1993.

80. Bank data. A member of the Board in the late 1980s and early 1990s had this impression: "Personnel size was largely contained the first years after the reorganization (1988–1991) but then took a big jump in 1992–1994 because of the increase in member countries and the proliferation of objectives (not least, environment and private sector development) as well as, perhaps, the worries about project implementation. This may be difficult to ascertain, however, [from] Bank . . . statistics." Haralz, personal communication, September 17, 1996.

Table 18-2. *World Bank Technical Specialists, Selected Years*

Technical specialist	1976		1982		1993	
	Number	Percent	Number	Percent	Number	Percent
Agriculture related[a]	139	5.6	200	6.0	135	3.4
Other	290	11.6	578	17.4	875	21.9
Total	505	20.3	778	23.5	1,010	25.2
Total, high-level staff	2,492	100.0	3,316	100.0	4,003	100.0

Source: World Bank data.

a. Agricultural credit, agriculture and agronomy, forest and tree corps, irrigation, livestock and fishery, rural development and extension.

A lively personnel concern in the 1990s was over the loss of technical staff. This was widely perceived, both by some Bank managers and some executive directors, to be an institution-wide problem. On closer inspection (see table 18-2) the losses—at least in body-count terms—were confined largely to the agricultural and rural sector, where the explanation consisted of the variety of factors reviewed in chapter 8. The fraction of other technical specialists in the total Bank staff actually increased quite sharply in the decade following the institution's peak agricultural staffing.

The general proposition that it was proving hard to sustain the institution's in-house technical expertise nevertheless prompted a good deal of internal discussion. One view was put forcefully by Percy Mistry when he was senior adviser to Senior Vice President Qureshi in the middle 1980s and then in a book after he left the Bank. It was that the institution no longer should seek to retain or reestablish in-house the degree of technical expertise it had had in the 1970s.[81] Too much had changed—indeed, the relevant technology itself was changing too rapidly—for in-house staffing (always encumbered by the generous job security and benefits the Bank provides) to keep pace. Henceforward, Mistry said, there would need to be greater reliance on consultants and consulting firms. The Bank would require on its own staff as project managers extremely knowledgeable technologists who also were adept at recruiting outside specialists. But most technical expertise would need to be hired to order.

Mistry and others made much the same point about McNamara's massive commitment to broadly based economic research. There was less need now, they said, for the Bank to sustain as large and diversified an outturn of not directly operational economic analysis as when the Chenery team was planting the institutional flag. More of what was needed could be hired from consultants and outsider research establishments, as, in fact, had been the growing tendency for some years.

The contrary school within the Bank argued that consultants were less likely than in-house staff to generate Bank ownership of new strategies and ideas; and that hired hands with renewable contracts were less apt than "tenured" staff to

81. Percy S. Mistry, *Multilateral Development Banks: An Assessment of Their Financial Structures, Policies and Practices* (The Hague: FONDAD, 1995), chap. 7.

display genuine analytical independence. In the middle 1990s the issue remained unsettled.

Conclusion

During its first fifty years the World Bank was a stalwart institution. It grew greatly, but in organizational terms its shape stayed much the same—as did the corporate culture. If one had left the Bank in 1950 and, without intervening perceptions, come back in 1990, he would have recognized his whereabouts. Despite the major turns in events in 1960 and, again, around 1980, the institution's dominant characteristic was continuity.

At the end of the half century, however, there were hints of greater, more identity-revising, changes. Among the more important of those are one set of possible administrative adjustments inside the institution, a set of substantive tensions in the Bank's operational agenda, and, finally, a pivotal question about the Bank's relations with the rest of the multilateral and nation-state scene.

Big Changes in Structure and Culture?

Internally, as noted, there had been a good deal of tinkering with the organizational architecture, especially at the top of the Bank—how many and which vice presidents, senior vice presidents, or managing directors, and what complement of either. But the basic structure was stable. The Bank was strongly hierarchical, and it was headquarters centered. Laterally, it had opened many field offices, but most of these had little operational power. Except when it traveled with the president, the organization's center of gravity never strayed outside Washington, D.C.

Bank staff was a meritocracy that, albeit without great ostentation, savored its perquisites. It was well paid. For many the Bank was their enduring employer; they were given entry-level to retirement tenure, traveling extensively but residing mainly in Washington. They stayed in first-class hotels. They still went business class and paid no income taxes. As a group they produced such a wealth of internal publications that it was hard to read past the latter and keep up with what was going on in the nonofficial professional and analytical worlds outside.

What was widely speculated about by the middle 1990s was a much more radical decentralization of decision and responsibility within the hierarchy and, geographically, more of a shift of responsibility and decision to the field. Admittedly, earlier Bank history had been full of such talk. Institutional files showed that field offices had rivaled travel policy as senior management's most frequent discussion topic for twenty years. But the middle 1990s appeared to be different. The intention seemed to have legs.

To the extent this expectation was realized, it contained a second question: How would a stronger, more empowered field staff operate? Both within the Bank and among its constituencies the answers were conflicted. Some would have staff get out much more into the villages, adopting a grassroots mode of promoting village-based (and village-bounded) projects. Some of this flavor would be generated in any event by further symbiosis with NGOs, Southern as well as Northern, committed to hands-on rural and urban development. But the dominant gait of field-centered Bank operations (it seemed in the middle 1990s) would be set by the lesson, newly learned in the 1980s, of the importance of recipient *ownership* of projects and reforms. Betting on this option, one extrapolated a Bank, operating from newly strengthened field locations, that served mainly as an informed wholesaler of resources and development doctrine, monitoring the retailing of projects being done by indigenous operators, official and otherwise.

The signals of this much of an administrative shift had become fairly evident by the mid-1990s. One had to be more intuitive to perceive the further emerging changes next listed, but arguably they would be driven by radical decentralization; and they had proponents within the Executive Board as well as in a number of activists scattered throughout the staff. The Bank, these voices intimated, might be in for a change of culture. Following the agenda of President Lewis Preston, staff would start turning over more rapidly. The Bank would have more in-and-outers, pressing the institutional agenda while they were there, but rotating out of Bank tours to a variety of other employments—with business, governments, financial institutions, and academic, research, and service organizations. During their Bank tours staff would be encouraged, putting aside their elitism, to become unreservedly service-minded. More staff would be deployed to the field. They would be less overt and abrasive in their leveraging of clients, and they would carry more weight within the Bank. In the field, more responsible assignments would be entrusted to local staff locally hired. The institution would sustain a strong, realistically grounded campaign against corruption. International staff, whether in the field or at headquarters, would work for lower wages and benefits while in service, being partly compensated by a higher accumulation of postservice benefits.

According to those thinking along these lines in the 1990s, a measure of public service austerity would enhance staff morale. But that dimension also could be strengthened, some argued, by the frequent appointment of the Bank's presidents from within the organization.

Changed Development Goals?

This final chapter on the Bank as an institution has not tried to engage the substantive programmatic issues addressed in the rest of the book. But in a discussion of institutional changes brewing in the 1990s, there must be some attention to the Bank's work agenda. Here the appearance was less of a great swing in priority goals than of a whole set of unresolved puzzles.

The dominant question was whether the Bank was becoming less committed to poverty reduction as a principal purpose. There was no evidence that the need for such interventions had disappeared. Poverty in the developing countries worldwide had been reduced. But many Bank member countries in Africa and elsewhere remained grievously poor, and even within low-income countries making robust economic progress on average, great swatches of land and people remained so poor that it was beyond the ready capacity of their national governments to cope.[82] If poverty fighting was in decline as a Bank/IDA goal, it was not because of eroded demand.

What had diminished was the institution's capacity to respond. To attack poverty, the Bank needed to promote growth. This was true even of that component or analogue of "poverty" policy preoccupied with improving equity and increasing allocations to the social sectors. It was hard to work up redistributive momentum when the overall economy was dead in the water. And the Bank's comparative advantage in growth promotion had been in arraying its cognitive contributions and interactions around a core of financial transfers—in the case of IDA, of aid-giving to needy recipients. For three decades majorities in donor governments, majorities in most developing-country governments, coalitions large enough to forestall blockages in both civil societies, and most World Bank professionals all viewed the making of such concessional transfers as appropriate and legitimate.

By the early 1990s, however, for various reasons partly reviewed in earlier chapters, development assistance had lost much of its following. Arguably the loss lacked inevitability. The need remained. Past transfers, insofar as they had been genuinely developmentally bent, had had considerable success. Lessons to increase aid effectiveness had been learned. And the economic costs to donors had been modest: with all deference to the agonies of national government budget balancing in the 1980s and 1990s, the overall scale of public concessional transfers was, in macroeconomic donor terms, next to trivial. The constraints, so solemnly observed worldwide in the mid-1990s, were essentially political.

For all that, the constraints appeared very real. The puzzle for the Bank was whether it should try to fight the alleged tide of parliamentary and public opinion in donor countries, or should the management choose graceful acquiescence? And if the latter, how weighty could the institution's pro-growth, pro-equity and other interventions be made when they had lost much of their resource ballast?

There were other major uncertainties about the Bank's substantive mission. For one thing, what about agriculture? By the mid-1980s (see chapter 8) not only had the Bank's input to agriculture declined, but many thought this appropriate. Many borrowing countries had outgrown their earlier degrees of dependence on agriculture; their priorities had shifted. There was dispute over whether the institution's loss of agricultural expertise (to age and other factors) required much repair: consultants, it was said, could fill such gaps as arose. Inside and outside the Bank

---

82. Bank studies in the 1990s were documenting that such was the case in even so dynamic a grower as China.

some agriculture and rural development specialists dissented vehemently. In terms of sectoral development strategy, they argued, agricultural growth, not to speak of improvements in rural equity, still was critical in many developing countries. The case for shrewd and perceptive external interventions was undiminished; private investors and private markets were sure to miss many of the needs. And among public sector interveners, with the contributions of bilateral donors and unofficial agencies badly eroded, the Bank, even with some of its operating knowledge and skills diminished, now had a greater *comparative* advantage in agriculture than ever before. It was essential (went this side of the case) that it pick up the challenge and rebuild. In the mid-1990s both sides of the debate pressed their contentions.

The environment—promoting a sustainable environment—was another field at issue when the Bank reexamined its substantive priorities in the 1990s. To reiterate, there was a strong case that the Bank should resist and reverse subject proliferation. By the mid-1990s the Bank had been, after a fashion, playing a pro-environment role for twenty-five years. But in two massive, type-casting cases—Polonoroeste in Brazil and Narmada in India—the Bank's handling of the environment cum settlements issue had been blasted by the environmental NGOs and the member governments the NGOs succeeded in mobilizing. Before the 1992 environment summit and even more thereafter, all kinds of other international interveners had entered the field. Prudent Bank people may have been tempted to beat a retreat and let others work the subject. But the fact was, that option was closed. By the 1990s, the Bank was too frontally and adversarially engaged in the environment to be seen fleeing the field. The institution's dominant owners were committed (via the sustainable development doctrine, the Global Environment Fund and otherwise) to a major environmental role for the Bank. That left open the question of what *kind* of pivotal environmental steward the institution would be. One danger was that it might be comparatively soft in this quadrant of its agenda while it was drawing scarce resources away from other priorities.

As the 1990s unfolded, a further mission-setting question promised to become vital for the Bank: How much, and how simplistically, would it be pushing governments to favor private ownership of industrial enterprises as compared with public, cooperative, and various mixed ownership forms? During the McNamara years, the Bank had had a fairly nuanced, nondogmatic view of this issue. Operational efficiency and the independence of enterprise managers from steering by third parties of any kind were judged more important than the pedigree (often mixed) of ownership. Views changed emphatically in the 1980s; there was a no-nonsense resumption of the institution's earlier private sector orthodoxy.

Yet as the 1990s proceeded, the same questions regained their complexity. Competition was imperfect. In such transitional economies as China, Russia, and Eastern Europe, acquisitions of ownership often were corrupt and, with few sellers, markets were suboptimal for buyers. In the nondoctrinaire precincts of the Bank there was no renewed tolerance, let alone affection, for centrally planned and controlled economies; but the institution's micropolicy preferences promised to become less absolutist, less simplistic, and more pragmatic than had been the fashion in the 1980s.

Once one starts to unroll the Bank's potential substantive agenda, there may appear to be no stopping, even when one is seeking only to illuminate the changing nature of the institution by sketching some of its business. But for present purposes the recital must stop. It is preempted by an issue: the Bank's appropriate capacity for priority subjects of any kind.

What Span of Attention for a Functional Multilateral?

By the mid-1990s it was apparent the World Bank was being crowded and crowding itself into a multilateral role for which it was poorly cast. The Bank was a multilateral, all right, but one of a particular "functional" kind meant to address only a limited array of subjects. It is a fundamental characteristic of governments, including those that own and govern the Bank, that they have a multiplicity of purposes. There is no major goal subject to willful political pursuit to which a nation-state government cannot be held accountable. Many of the stressful difficulties of national governments concern their efforts to encompass and reconcile their multiple, often conflicted, objectives.

Among multilateral agencies, the United Nations in New York—the General Assembly, Security Council, the Secretariat—and their counterparts in Geneva have been given a mandate to cover the substantive waterfront. Like their owners, they are inherently committed to pursue a great variety of objectives. The Bank, like the IMF, UNDP, FAO, UNICEF, and others, is designed to be different; it is a *functional* multilateral; it is authorized to promote and reconcile a few objectives. The number is more than one. That is one thing that differentiates the functional multilateral from the classic profit-seeking enterprise, which is modeled as if it had a single (money-making) goal. The World Bank is directed and, as it has evolved, is intended to seek more than one. According to the interpretation in this book, poverty alleviation, especially viewed in retrospect, has been the leading objective. But others also have been valued and promoted as ends in themselves: among them, recipient country growth, more equitable distributions of incomes, and country self-reliance. Nevertheless, a functional multilateral was supposed to have a short list of priorities. The institution was a specialist; it was meant to address one segment of the comprehensive agenda the multilateral system as a whole faced. Like other functional unilaterals, the Bank depended on selectivity to maintain the quality and therefore the effectiveness of its work.

The Bank's dilemma by the middle 1990s was that its span of substantive attention—its list of program priorities—had been stretched almost beyond recognition. There were all kinds of add-ons, among them, population, gender, governance, and probity, education, and commodity trade. The institution was wide open to substantive proliferation. New subjects were worthy, and the dynamism of technical and social change kept raising them. In terms of public and parliamentary relations, the Bank was running scared; it felt driven to take on new subjects as major owners and such major "stakeholders" as the NGOs so demanded. And the Bank's outreach to new subjects was animated also by an element of superciliousness about the generalist components of the United Nations. The latter (in part, it should be noted, because of poor industrialized country support) were seen to be falling short. Many in the Bank felt it was part of being the "world's leading development promotion agency" to reach into one new field after another.

More than was widely appreciated, the situation was threatening because the Bank had no clear demarcation around its appropriate zone of work. As discussed in chapter 10, in its macroeconomic work the institution had long since pushed aside the need for linking adjustment lending to a balance of payments rationale. Reasons have just been found (given the state of other interveners) for the Bank to renew its agricultural work, and a self-protective case can be made for not retreating from environmental concerns. In the 1990s, as the Bank decided to take on or not take on new subjects, the selectivity and therefore the quality of its work agenda were unlikely to be defended by a priori rules. It would have to rely on the management and the owners both joining in a *policy* of self-restraint. As already noted, there was a tendency toward the proliferation of goals and subjects back in the 1970s also. But it was better held in check. The World Bank certainly was not dysfunctionally meek at that time. But its style was to cast itself as a major player in behalf of a new purpose only if and when the institution had developed a comparative advantage in the new field. The 1990s Bank in its subject choices urgently needed to regain at least a measure of such restraint.

Some Key Events in the History of the World Bank Group, 1944–1996

1944

July 22   Articles of Agreement of the International Bank for Reconstruction and Development and the International Monetary Fund adopted at Bretton Woods, New Hampshire, in a conference of forty-five governments.

1945

June 26   The United Nations is established.

December 27   Articles of Agreement of IBRD become effective after its signature by twenty-eight governments.

1946

March 8–18   Inaugural meetings of boards of governors of the IBRD and the IMF held at Savannah, Georgia. Bylaws are adopted, executive directors are elected, and Washington, D.C., is chosen as the site for the two new institutions. The Bank's subscribed capital stands at $7.67 billion.

May 6   The first meeting of the executive directors is held. Emilio Collado, executive director for the United States, is appointed temporary chairman.

June 18   Eugene Meyer takes office as the first president of the Bank.

June 25   The World Bank formally begins operations. Bank's initial
                   authorized capital is $12 billion.

September 27   First annual meeting of the board of governors of the World
                   Bank convenes in Washington, with thirty-eight member
                   nations and a staff of seventy-two.

December 4   President Meyer resigns.

1947
March 12   Truman Doctrine proclaimed.

March 14   Eugene R. Black becomes U.S. executive director for the Bank.

March 17   John J. McCloy becomes the second president of the Bank.
                   Robert L. Garner takes office as vice president of the Bank.

May 9   Executive directors approve the Bank's first loan, to France in
                   the amount of $250 million for reconstruction purposes, one
                   of the largest loans made by the Bank in real terms in its first
                   fifty years.

June 5   U.S. secretary of state George Marshall proposes the European
                   Recovery Program (the "Marshall Plan") for the reconstruc-
                   tion of war-torn Europe.

July 15   The IBRD makes its first bond offer on the U.S. market in the
                   amount of $250 million. The offering is substantially over-
                   subscribed, and the bonds immediately sell at a premium
                   over the public offering price.

August 15   India and Pakistan become independent.

November 15   The United Nations General Assembly approves an agreement
                   formalizing its relationship with the IBRD.

1948
March 25   Executive directors approve the Bank's first loan to a developing
                   country, to Chile in the amount of $13.5 million for
                   hydroelectric development.

June 28   Yugoslavia is expelled from Soviet-led Cominform.

1949
January 1   The Council for Mutual Economic Assistance (Comecon) is
                   established to coordinate the individual economies of the
                   Soviet bloc.

May 18   John J. McCloy resigns as president of the Bank.

July 1   Eugene R. Black, executive director for the United States, be-
                 comes the third president of the Bank.

July–November   The Bank's first general survey mission (to Colombia) is headed
                 by Lauchlin Currie.

October 1   People's Republic of China is proclaimed.

1950
March 14   Poland withdraws from membership in the Bank.

June 25–27   The Korean War begins.

September 13   First loan to Africa and first development bank loan (road
                 rehabilitation in Ethiopia; new development bank in
                 Ethiopia).

1951
May 23   The IBRD's first public offering outside the United States—
                 £5 million—is placed on the London market.

September 13   First impact loan: $40 million to Belgian Congo and $30 million
                 to the Kingdom of Belgium to help carry out a ten-year
                 development plan of the Belgian Congo.

1952
August 13, 14   Japan and the Federal Republic of Germany become members
                 of the Bank, bringing the Bank's membership to fifty-three.

September   The first reorganization of the Bank is carried out. Three
                 geographical Departments of Operations (Asia and Middle
                 East; Europe, Africa, and Australasia; and Western Hemi-
                 sphere) and a Department of Technical Operations are
                 created.

1953
October 15   The first of three loans to Japan, totaling $40.2 million, is ap-
                 proved for power development.

1954
December 10   Representatives from India and Pakistan take part in discussions
                 on the Indus River system under the aegis of the Bank.

December 31   Czechoslovakia withdraws from membership in the Bank.

1955

April 15   Bank transmits charter of proposed International Finance Cor-
                poration to member governments for approval.

April 18–25   Bandung Conference marks the beginning of the "nonaligned"
                movement.

1956

January 9   The Economic Development Institute (EDI), headed by Alec
                Cairncross, is inaugurated.

July 20   The International Finance Corporation (IFC) is established as
                an affiliate of the Bank, with an authorized capital of
                $100 million.

July 24   Robert L. Garner becomes president of IFC; William Iliff,
                J. Burke Knapp, and Davidson Sommers are named vice
                presidents of the Bank.

1957

March 6   Ghana becomes independent and joins the Bank.

March 25   The European Economic Community is established when
                France, West Germany, Belgium, the Netherlands, Luxem-
                bourg, and Italy agree to the Treaty of Rome. The European
                Investment Bank is also established as a result of the treaty.

June 20   IFC makes first investment, $2 million in Siemens do Brazil.

1958

August 25–27   In the wake of a deterioration in India's balance of payments,
                the first meeting of the India aid consortium takes place in
                Washington, D.C., under the chairmanship of the Bank.

1959

April 8   Inter-American Development Bank is established.

September 16   The Bank's authorized capital is increased to $25.3 billion; the
                first and only loan for nuclear power is approved—to Italy
                through the Cassa per il Mezzogiorno.

September 28   On the occasion of the annual general meetings, the United
                States proposes establishment of the International Develop-
                ment Association (IDA) as an affiliate of the Bank.

1960

September 19   The Indus Water Treaty is signed by Pakistan, India, and the
                    World Bank in Karachi, Pakistan.

September 24   IDA is established with initial subscriptions of $912.7 million.

November 14   Cuba withdraws from membership in the Bank and IFC.

1961

May 12   IDA extends its first development credit, totaling $9 million, to
                    Honduras, for highway development and maintenance.

June 1   Martin M. Rosen becomes executive vice president of IFC.

August   The Berlin Wall is erected.

September 5   Adoption of amendment to IFC Articles of Agreement to per-
                    mit equity investment.

September 30   The Organization for Economic Cooperation and Development
                    (OECD) comes into existence in Paris, succeeding the Or-
                    ganization for European Economic Cooperation (OEEC).

October 15   With Robert L. Garner's retirement, the Bank's president as-
                    sumes presidency of IFC.

1962

February 26   IFC establishes advisory panel of investment bankers.

June   The Junior Professional Recruitment and Training Program
                    (renamed Young Professionals Program in 1966) is launched.

September 17   First education loan: a $5 million IDA credit to Tunisia for
                    school construction.

1963

January 1   George D. Woods becomes the fourth president of the Bank.

March 11–   Eighteen newly independent African countries become mem-
  September 30   bers of the Bank.

July 15   U.S. announces restrictions on American capital outflows.

August 4   African Development Bank established.

1964

March 25   Cooperative relationships with the UN Food and Agricultural
                    Organization and the UN Educational, Scientific, and Cul-
                    tural Organization are established.

June 29   The first replenishment of IDA resources becomes effective, as
                   eighteen governments agree to provide $753 million, which
                   would stretch over four years.

1965
August 17   Indonesia withdraws from membership in the Bank.

December 17   The Articles of Agreement of the IBRD are amended for the
                   first time to allow it to lend IFC up to four times IFC's un-
                   impaired subscribed capital and surplus.

1966
March 16   The Bank and representatives from nine countries meet to es-
                   tablish the Nam Ngum Development Fund for financing a
                   hydroelectric power project on the Mekong River, with the
                   Bank as administrator.

August 10   The Bank's capital is increased to $28.9 billion.

September 15   Mohamed Shoaib, former finance minister of Pakistan, be-
                   comes first Bank vice president from a developing country.

October 14   The International Centre for Settlement of Investment Dis-
                   putes (ICSID) is established.

December 8   The IFC makes its first investment in tourism.

1967
February 14   Department of Evaluation and Control is established with John
                   H. Williams as director.

April 13   Indonesia rejoins the Bank.

October 27   President Woods addresses Swedish Bankers Association in
                   Stockholm, and proposes a "grand assize" on development.

1968
April 1   Robert S. McNamara becomes the fifth president of the Bank.

May 2   The Tarbela Development Fund Agreement is signed, provid-
                   ing nearly $500 million in external financing for the Tarbela
                   Dam Project in West Pakistan, with the Bank as ad-
                   ministrator.

August 14   First public marketing of IBRD bonds in the Middle East:
                   $42 million of Kuwaiti dinar bonds.

August 19   Lester B. Pearson accepts chairmanship of the Bank-sponsored
               Commission on International Development.

October   The Bank's Area, Economics, and Projects Departments are
               restructured.

November 1   Development Finance Companies Department transfers from
               IFC to the World Bank.

November 19   Eugene H. Rotberg is appointed treasurer of the World Bank
               Group.

December 16   First savings bank issue: private placement of DM 400 million
               ($100 million) with German banks.

December 19   Asian Development Bank is established.

1969
July 23   Second replenishment of IDA resources comes into force with a
               commitment authority of $1.4 billion for the three-year fiscal
               period 1969–71.

September 15   The Pearson Commission presents its report, *Partners in
               Development.*

October 1   William S. Gaud becomes executive vice president of IFC.

1970
February 12   IBRD initiates borrowings in Japan (equivalent to $100 million)
               is announced.

May   Joint Bank-IFC Audit Committee is established. The formation
               of a Consultative Group for support of existing and new
               international agricultural research institutes is proposed.

May 7   Hollis B. Chenery is appointed economic adviser to the presi-
               dent of the Bank.

June 22   First loan for population planning ($2 million to Jamaica) is
               approved.

September 2   Operations Evaluation Unit is established to evaluate Bank
               Group operations.

October 18   Caribbean Development Bank is established.

December 31   IBRD's authorized capital is increased from $24 billion to
               $27 billion.

1971

January 1   Central economics staff is reorganized into three units, all
                 reporting to the economic adviser to the president:
                 Economics Department; Economic Program Department;
                 and Development Research Center.

February 1   Japan becomes one of the five largest subscribers to the Bank's
                 authorized capital stock (displacing India) and is thus en-
                 titled to appoint an executive director.

March 25   Capital Markets Department is established in IFC to encourage
                 the mobilization of private savings in developing countries.

April 22   Sector Program Paper on "Water Supply and Sewage" is pub-
                 lished, the first of a series.

May 18   First loan ($15 million) for pollution control (river pollution in
                 São Paulo, Brazil).

May 19   The newly founded Consultative Group on International
                 Agricultural Research (CGIAR) convenes in Washington
                 under chairmanship of the Bank, but with its Technical Ad-
                 visory Group (TAG) headquartered at FAO, Rome.

August   United States informs IMF it will no longer freely buy and sell
                 gold to settle international transactions. Par values and con-
                 vertibility of the dollar—two main features of Bretton Woods
                 system—are suspended. Sterling floated in 1972; franc
                 floated in 1973.

September 1   Bank enters agreement with WHO to establish a jointly
                 financed cooperative program in the fields of water supply,
                 waste disposal, and storm drainage.

October   Iceland, a Part II member of IDA since 1961, is the first
                 country to change to Part I status.

December 16   Bangladesh, formerly East Pakistan, comes into being.

December 18   The Smithsonian Agreement on exchange rates is concluded.
                 The dollar is devalued against major currencies.

1972

January 7   Under the guidance of a Bank steering committee, consultants
                 begin comprehensive examination of the Bank's organization
                 and structure.

February 25   World Bank Group Staff Association comes into existence.

June 30   World Bank Group reaches goal set by President McNamara to provide twice as much assistance in fiscal 1969–73 as it did in the previous five years. For the first time lending for agriculture exceeds that of any other sector.

June   McNamara addresses the United Nations Conference on the Human Environment in Stockholm.

July   Committee on Reform of the International Monetary System and Related Issues (Committee of Twenty) is established.

August 10   A major reorganization of the Bank is announced to decentralize the Bank's operations. A senior vice presidency of operations is created with five regional vice presidents and a vice president for project staff. Vice presidencies are also created for: Organization Planning and Personnel Management; Development Policy; Finance; and General Counsel.

September 22   Third replenishment of IDA resources goes into effect with commitment authority of $2.5 billion for the three-year period fiscal 1972-74.

October 31   First project audit reports: highway, power and telecommunications lending to Costa Rica.

1973

February   The first of the Bank's new (internal) country program papers is produced (for Brazil).

April 1   Robert S. McNamara begins his second term as president of the Bank.

May 1   The executive directors approve recommendations concerning the Bank's role in fighting onchocerciasis (river-blindness disease) in western Africa.

September 24   In his address to the Board of Governors at the annual general meetings in Nairobi, Kenya, President McNamara proposes a strategy for rural development with an emphasis on productivity of smallholder agriculture.

October 16   Following the Yom Kippur War, the Organization of Petroleum Exporting Countries (OPEC) raises the price of crude oil 70 percent. By December oil prices have quadrupled from their levels of early October.

1974

January 29   The United States ends capital controls.

September 1   Ladislaus von Hoffmann becomes executive vice president of
               the IFC.

October   The executive directors approve proposals to directly link the
               Operations Evaluation Unit to the executive directors, to in-
               stitute the title of director-general for the manager of the
               Operations Evaluation Unit, and to separate the Internal
               Auditing Unit from the Operations Evaluation Unit.

October   The Interim Committee (of the IMF) and the Development
               Committee (formally, the Joint Ministerial Committee of the
               Boards of Governors of the World Bank and the Inter-
               national Monetary Fund on the Transfer of Real Resources
               to Developing Countries) are established.

October 17   *Redistribution with Growth,* by Hollis Chenery and others, is
               published.

1975

January   The fourth replenishment of IDA resources becomes effective
               with a commitment authority of $4.5 billion for fiscal 1975–
               77.

June 30   During fiscal 1975, the IBRD and IDA commit nearly $1 billion
               for rural development projects.

July 29   Intermediate Financing Facility ("Third Window")—using
               OPEC contributions to provide development assistance on
               terms intermediate between those of the Bank and IDA—is
               approved.

September 1   President McNamara focuses on urban poverty in his address to
               the Board of Governors at the annual general meetings.

1976

May 4   Executive directors approve an increase in IFC's capital stock
               from $110 million to $650 million.

May 25   Disbursements to East Africa Community are suspended.

1977

February 15   Moeen Qureshi becomes executive vice president of the IFC.

May   Board of Governors approves the increase in the Bank's
               authorized capital from $27 billion to $34 billion.

August   Establishment of a Joint Committee of the World Bank and
                  IMF on Staff Compensation Issues to examine principles of
                  staff compensation.

November 29   The fifth replenishment of IDA resources goes into effect with
                  a commitment authority of $7.6 billion over the three-year
                  period, fiscal 1978–80.

1978
February 14   Agreement between the Bank and the International Fund for
                  Agricultural Development is approved.

July 1   On the retirement of J. Burke Knapp, Ernest Stern is appointed
                  vice president, Operations, and chairman of the Loan
                  Committee.

August   The first *World Development Report* is published with the
                  theme of prospects for accelerating growth and alleviating
                  poverty and identifying major policy issues affecting those
                  prospects. WDRs emerge as an annual flagship publication
                  of the World Bank.

November 7   Executive directors review environmental policies and practices
                  of the Bank and endorse a Bank policy that seeks to control
                  the environmental impact of its projects.

December 17   The Iranian revolution leads to steep hikes in oil prices that con-
                  tinue into 1979.

1979
January 16   A program to accelerate petroleum production in developing
                  countries is approved. Activities include assistance in devis-
                  ing national energy plans of oil-importing developing
                  countries, predevelopment work, and expansion of lending
                  for fuel production.

May 10   President McNamara proposes "structural adjustment" lending
                  in an address to the United Nations Conference on Trade
                  and Development in Manila, Philippines.

June 30   World Bank Group commitments for fiscal 1979 exceed $10 bil-
                  lion for the first time.

July   The Board of Governors adopts a statute establishing an inde-
                  pendent World Bank Administrative Tribunal to adjudicate
                  staff grievances.

July 24   Plans to begin lending operations in health are approved.

October   Chairman Volcker announces that the U.S. Federal Reserve
               Board will target the aggregates reporting the size of the
               supply of money instead of interest rates in controlling the
               availability of credit in the United States.

1980
January 4   The Board of Governors approves a general capital increase raising
               the Bank's authorized capital stock to $85 billion, an increase of
               approximately $44 billion. It becomes operational July 1.

March   The Independent Commission on International Development
               Issues, chaired by Willy Brandt, releases *North-South: A Pro-
               gram for Survival* calling for, among other recommenda-
               tions, a large-scale transfer of resources on both concessional
               and market terms to developing countries.

March 4   Draft statute of the Administrative Tribunal is approved by the
               Board of Directors.

March 25   The first structural adjustment loan—for $200 million to
               Turkey—is approved.

May 15   The People's Republic of China assumes representation as
               China in the World Bank Group.

July 1   A currency pooling scheme, designed to equalize exchange rate
               risks among the IBRD's borrowers, becomes operational;
               World Bank Administrative Tribunal on personnel issues
               enters into force.

1981
January 1   Hans A. Wuttke becomes executive vice president of the IFC.

July 1   A. W. Clausen, former president of Bank of America, becomes
               the sixth president of the Bank.

August 10   *Accelerated Development in Sub-Saharan Africa: An Agenda
               for Action* (known popularly as the "Berg Report"), the first
               in a series of Bank reports that focus on the development
               problems of Sub-Saharan Africa, is published.

December 8   The position of ombudsman is established.

December 15   Reorganization of economic analysis, research, and policy ac-
               tivities in the Bank is announced.

1982

January   Record deficits are projected for the U.S. budget. Interest rates
               and the dollar climb sharply.

January 5   Executive directors agree to increase IBRD lending program by
               $800 million to offset the shortfall in IDA's commitment
               authority.

May 10   Anne Krueger is appointed vice president of economics and
               research.

August   People's Republic of China joins the United Nations.

August 12   Mexico's finance minister, Jesus Silva Herzog, informs Treasury
               Secretary Regan, Chairman Volcker, and IMF Managing Direc-
               tor Jacques de Larosière that Mexico will not be able to meet
               payments on debt due on August 15. The public announce-
               ment on August 13 marks the onset of the "debt crisis."

August 24   Sixth replenishment of IDA resources for fiscal 1981-83, in the
               amount of $12 billion, becomes effective. The twenty-six
               countries that contributed to the funding of the fifth
               replenishment are joined by seven first-time donors: Argen-
               tina, Brazil, Greece, Mexico, Portugal, Romania, and
               Venezuela.

September 8   Legislative delays in approval of the United States' contributions to
               sixth IDA replenishment lead other IDA donors to agree to pro-
               vide special contributions in an amount equal to one third of
               their total contributions to IDA's sixth replenishment.

1983

January 11   A new set of cofinancing instruments ("B-loan"), linking part of
               commercial-bank flows to IBRD operations, is inaugurated.

February   A Special Assistance Program (SAP), for Bank borrowers af-
               fected by adverse external conditions, is approved by the ex-
               ecutive directors for two years. The resulting increase in
               IBRD disbursements is estimated at $2 billion.

February   The *World Debt Tables,* compiled annually for internal Bank
               use since 1972, are published and available to the general
               public for the first time.

1984

May 30   Bolivia suspends payments on its debts; Ecuador follows on June 4.

August   Bank member countries agree to a selective capital increase of
                  approximately $8 billion and propose to increase IFC's capi-
                  tal by $650 million to $1,300 million.

October 1   Sir William Ryrie becomes executive vice president of IFC.

December   Board of Directors agrees to allow the IFC to raise funds
                  directly from international capital markets. First issue
                  succeeds through private placement. Nicaragua becomes
                  the first country to go into nonaccrual status with the
                  IBRD.

1985

January   Three vice-presidencies are created at the IFC: Investment
                  Operations, Development Syndications, and Public Affairs.

March 31   Seventh replenishment of IDA resources goes into effect with a
                  commitment authority of $9 billion for the three-year period
                  fiscal 1985–87.

June 30   Lending commitments in fiscal 1985 fall by nearly $1 billion
                  from the previous year.

July 1   IDA becomes administrator of and is authorized to accept con-
                  tributions to the Special Facility for Sub-Saharan Africa,
                  which will run for three years.

September   The Plaza Accords signal a decline in the dollar.

October 8   At the World Bank and IMF annual general meetings in Seoul,
                  U.S. secretary of the treasury James A. Baker suggests a new
                  strategy for the major indebted countries, calling for in-
                  creased lending by the World Bank and commercial banks.

1986

March 27   IMF establishes structural adjustment facility (SAF) to provide
                  balance of payments assistance on concessional terms to low-
                  income developing countries.

June 27   Poland rejoins the Bank (after a thirty-six-year hiatus), bringing
                  total membership to 150.

July 1   Barber Conable becomes the seventh president of the
                  Bank.

October 8   Barber Conable announces a reorganization of the Bank.

December   A special "Poverty Task Force" comprising senior staff is estab-
              lished to review the Bank's poverty work and to propose new
              activities.

1987
May 4   The Bank is reorganized into four senior vice presidential complexes:
              Moeen A. Qureshi is named senior vice president for operations;
              Ernest Stern, senior vice president for finance; W. David Hopper,
              senior vice president for policy, planning, and research; Willi A.
              Wapenhans, senior vice president for administration.

August   Peru, Sierra Leone, and Zambia go into nonaccrual status.

September 24 Stanley Fischer is appointed chief economist and vice president
              for development economics.

December 4   Donors agree to establish the Special Program of Assistance to
              provide quick-disbursing aid to reforming low-income
              African countries.

1988
March 4   Eighth replenishment of IDA funds goes into effect with com-
              mitment authority of $12.4 billion for fiscal 1988–90.

April 12   The international convention establishing the Multilateral In-
              vestment Guarantee Agency (MIGA) as an affiliate of the
              World Bank Group takes effect.

April 28   A third general capital increase, in the amount of $74.86 billion,
              takes effect, bringing the Bank's total authorized capital to
              $171.4 billion.

July   Yoshio Terasawa is appointed the first executive vice president
              of MIGA.

Autumn   Disputes erupt between the IMF and the Bank over lending to
              Argentina.

1989
March 10   U.S. secretary of the treasury Nicholas F. Brady calls for a new
              debt strategy initiative focusing on a reduction in debt stocks
              rather than providing new money.

March 21   First freestanding NGO-implemented project is financed by the
              Bank for grassroots development initiatives in Togo.

March 30   World Bank and IMF boards reach agreement ("Concordat")
               on cooperation and collaboration.

August 1   The Debt-Reduction Facility for IDA-Only Countries, designed
               to ease the burden on those countries of external commer-
               cial debt, is established.

November 9   The Berlin Wall falls, symbolizing the end of the cold war.

1990
January 30   The largest IBRD loan (in nominal terms)—$1,260 million—to
               Mexico in support of that country's debt-reduction program,
               is approved.

March   First operation under the Debt-Reduction Facility for IDA-
               Only Countries: $9.1 million to Bolivia.

June 30   Lending for education crosses the $1 billion mark for a fiscal
               year for the first time.

October   Second phase of Special Program of Assistance (SPA II) is
               launched. Eighteen donors pledge $7.4 billion in cofinancing
               to support adjustment programs in low-income, highly in-
               debted countries of Sub-Saharan Africa.

October 3   Germany is reunited.

November 28   The Global Environment Facility, jointly administered by the
               Bank, the United Nations Development Programme, and
               the United Nations Environment Programme, is launched.

1991
January 14   Lawrence Summers takes office as vice president for develop-
               ment economics and chief economist.

January 23   The ninth replenishment of IDA resources in the amount of
               SDR 11.68 billion (approximately $15.5 billion) goes into ef-
               fect for the three-year period fiscal 1991–93. IDA governors
               limit the combined allocation of IDA funds to the two
               largest active borrowers (China and India) to 30 percent.

February   African Capacity-Building Initiative (ACBI) is launched.

Spring/Summer Yugoslavia begins to break up.

April 15   European Bank for Reconstruction and Development is
               established.

June 30   China replaces India as the largest IDA borrower.

September   *The World Bank and the Environment,* the Bank's first annual
                 report to the public on its environmental activities, is published.

September 1   Lewis T. Preston becomes the eighth president of the Bank.

September 17   President Preston announces a limited reorganization of the
                 Bank, establishing three managing directors in the office of
                 the president.

December 31   The Soviet Union officially ceases to exist.

1992
May 4   The board approves a $1 billion increase in the authorized capital
                 of the IFC, bringing total authorized capital to $2.3 billion.

May 29   Switzerland joins the Bank.

June   The Second United Nations Conference on Environment and
                 Development (UNCED II) is held in Rio de Janeiro.

June 16   The Russian Federation becomes a member of the IBRD and
                 IDA.

June 18   The report of the Independent Review of the Sardor Sarovar
                 Project, chaired by Bradford Morse, is published. Bank par-
                 ticipation in the project is canceled in 1995.

June 23–   Thirteen republics of the former Soviet Union become mem-
    September 22   bers of the IBRD.

July   Akira Iida becomes executive vice president of MIGA.

November 1   The Executive Board increases in size from twenty-two to twen-
                 ty-four executive directors with a nonelected seat created for
                 Saudi Arabia and an additional seat for Switzerland and
                 other constituents.

November 3   The report of the Task Force on Portfolio Management (the
                 "Wapenhans Report") is transmitted to the executive directors.

1993
January 1   Three additional thematic vice presidencies (dealing with environ-
                 ment, human resources, and the private sector) are established.

September 22   An independent inspection panel is established, with the man-
                 date to receive and investigate complaints if the Bank has
                 not followed its own policies and procedures with respect to

the design, appraisal, or the implementation of a development project that it supports.

December 17   The tenth replenishment of IDA resources becomes effective with a commitment authority of SDR 13 billion (equivalent to $18 billion) for the three-year period fiscal 1993–96.

1994
January 1   Jannik Lindbaek becomes executive vice president of the IFC.

January 3   The Public Information Center at the Bank's headquarters is opened.

January 6   In West Africa, the CFA franc is devalued for the first time since its creation, changing a critical parameter for Bank policy in that region.

May 3   The Bank unveils a three-year, $1.2 billion program to assist Palestinians in the West Bank and Gaza.

June   For the first time the Bank's net disbursements turn negative.

1995
March 3   With the signing of its two final loan agreements with the IBRD, the Republic of Korea becomes the first country to progress from being a purely concessional borrower to being an IDA donor and an IBRD graduate.

June 1   James D. Wolfensohn becomes the ninth president of the Bank.

1996
February 23   Trust Fund for Bosnia and Herzegovina is created.

March 19   Donors approve eleventh replenishment of IDA resources, which will allow concessional lending of $22 billion; new contributions from donor countries are expected to total approximately $11 billion, with the rest coming mainly from repayments of IDA credits and contributions from the World Bank itself.

June 25   Fiftieth anniversary of the Bank's opening for business.

Index

Page numbers for entries occurring in figures are followed by an f; those for entries in notes, by an n; and those for entries in tables, by a t.